THE OXFORD H

ANCIENT ANATOLIA

THE OXFORD HANDBOOK OF

ANCIENT ANATOLIA

10,000–323 B.C.E.

Edited by

SHARON R. STEADMAN
AND GREGORY McMAHON

OXFORD
UNIVERSITY PRESS

Oxford University Press is a department of the University of Oxford.
It furthers the University's objective of excellence in research, scholarship,
and education by publishing worldwide.

Oxford New York
Auckland Cape Town Dar es Salaam Hong Kong Karachi
Kuala Lumpur Madrid Melbourne Mexico City Nairobi
New Delhi Shanghai Taipei Toronto

With offices in
Argentina Austria Brazil Chile Czech Republic France Greece
Guatemala Hungary Italy Japan Poland Portugal Singapore
South Korea Switzerland Thailand Turkey Ukraine Vietnam

Published in the United States of America by
Oxford University Press
198 Madison Avenue, New York, NY 10016

First issued as an Oxford University Press paperback, 2016.

Library of Congress Cataloging-in-Publication Data
The Oxford handbook of ancient Anatolia (10,000–323 B.C.E.) / edited by
Sharon R. Steadman and Gregory McMahon.
p. cm.
Includes bibliographical references.
ISBN 978-0-19-537614-2 (hardcover); 978-0-19-933601-2 (paperback)
1. Turkey—Antiquities. 2. Excavations (Archaeology)—Turkey. 3. Turkey—History—To 1453.
4. Turkey—Civilization. 5. Philology—Turkey. I. Steadman, Sharon R. II. McMahon, John Gregory
III. Title: Handbook of ancient Anatolia (10,000–323 B.C.E.).
DR431.O95 2011
939'.2—dc22 2010027106

To Girish and Mindy, without whom none of this would have been possible

Contents

Part III Philological and Historical Topics

Part IV Thematic and Specific Topics

Intersecting Cultures: Migrations, Invasions, and Travelers

Acknowledgments

A volume of this size does not reach completion without help and encouragement from many quarters. The editors thank Eric Cline, who was instrumental in making our connection with the Oxford Handbook series. We also acknowledge the steady support and guidance of our editor, Stefan Vranka, throughout the long process of bringing this book to fruition. Numerous scholars gave us invaluable assistance at the many stages of the editorial process. We especially thank Jennifer Ross, Marie-Henriette Gates, Craig Melchert, Theo van den Hout, Paul Zimansky, and Scott Smith for their sage advice and recommendations. We also offer thanks to Amy Henderson-Harr, Glen Clarke, and Pam Schroeder, who have supported this and many more of our projects. We would also like to express our gratitude for the crucial financial support provided by Professor Kenneth Fuld, Dean of the College of Liberal Arts, Professor Jan Golinski, Chair of the Department of History, and Professor Burt Feintuch, Director of the UNH Center for the Humanities, all of the University of New Hampshire. Equally important to the success of this endeavor were the editors' families, who offered every kind of necessary support and aid through every stage of this project. Finally, we sincerely thank the scholars who made this volume what it is by graciously sharing their expertise in and passion for the world of ancient Anatolia.

Contributors

Guillermo Algaze is Professor of Anthropology at the University of California, San Diego.

Richard H. Beal is Senior Research Associate on the Hittite Dictionary Project of the Oriental Institute at the University of Chicago.

Gary Beckman is Professor of Near Eastern Studies at the University of Michigan.

Trevor Bryce is Honorary Research Consultant at the University of Queensland and Fellow of the Australian Academy of the Humanities.

Gabriela Castro Gessner is Research Associate in Anthropology at Binghamton University.

Altan Çilingiroğlu is Professor of Protohistory and Near Eastern Archaeology and Dean of the Faculty of Letters at Ege University.

Bleda S. Düring is Assistant Professor in Near Eastern Archaeology in the Faculty of Archaeology, Leiden University.

Asli Erim-Özdoğan is Associate Professor of Prehistory at Çanakkale Onsekiz Mart University.

Marcella Frangipane is Professor of Prehistory at the University of Rome, La Sapienza.

Marie-Henriette Gates is Associate Professor of Archaeology at Bilkent University.

Claudia Glatz is Lecturer in Mediterranean Archaeology at the University of Glasgow.

Peter Grave is Senior Lecturer in the Department of Archaeology and Palaeoanthropology at the University of New England.

Alan M. Greaves is Lecturer in Archaeology at the University of Liverpool.

Crawford H. Greenewalt Jr. is Professor of Greek and Roman Art and Archaeology at the University of California, Berkeley.

Kenneth W. Harl is Professor of Classical and Byzantine History at Tulane University.

Ömür Harmanşah is Assistant Professor of Archaeology and Ancient Western Asian Studies at the Joukowsky Institute for Archaeology and the Ancient World of Brown University.

Ian Hodder is Dunlevie Professor of Anthropology at Stanford University.

Peter Jablonka is an Archaeologist at the Institute of Prehistory and Archaeology, Eberhard Karls University Tübingen, and Co-Director of the Troy Excavations.

Lisa Kealhofer is Associate Professor of Anthropology and the Environmental Studies Institute at Santa Clara University.

Lori Khatchadourian is Assistant Professor of Archaeology in Near Eastern Studies at Cornell University.

Fikri Kulakoğlu is Professor of Archaeology at Ankara University.

Nicola Laneri is a Research Fellow at the Istituto Italiano per l'Africa e l'Oriente.

Catherine Marro is Senior Researcher at the Centre National de la Recherche Scientifique, Maison de l'Orient et de la Méditerranée, Lyon.

Timothy Matney is Associate Professor of Archaeology at the University of Akron.

Roger Matthews is Professor of Near Eastern Archaeology at the Department of Archaeology, University of Reading.

Gregory McMahon is Associate Professor of History and Humanities at the University of New Hampshire.

H. Craig Melchert is A. Richard Diebold Professor of Indo-European Studies at the University of California, Los Angeles.

Cécile Michel is Senior Researcher at the Centre National de la Recherche Scientifique, Maison de l'Archéologie et de l'Ethnologie, Nanterre.

Dirk Paul Mielke is Research Associate at the Madrid Department of the German Archaeological Institute.

James D. Muhly is Professor Emeritus of Ancient History in the Department of Near Eastern Languages and Civilizations at the University of Pennsylvania, and former Director of the American School of Classical Studies in Athens.

A. Tuba Ökse is Professor of Archaeology at Kocaeli University.

Sachihiro Omura is Director of the Japanese Institute of Anatolian Archaeology Middle East Center, Japan.

Rana Özbal is Assistant Professor in the Department of Archaeology and the History of Art at Koç University, İstanbul.

Mihriban Özbaşaran is Professor of Prehistory at İstanbul University.

Mehmet Özdoğan is Professor of Prehistory at İstanbul University.

Giulio Palumbi is Research Associate in Prehistory of the Near East at Università del Salento, Lecce.

Karen Radner is Reader in Ancient Near Eastern History at University College London.

Lynn E. Roller is Professor of Art History at the University of California, Davis.

Jacob Roodenberg is former Director of the Netherlands Institute for the Near East, Leiden, and The Netherlands Institute in Turkey (İstanbul).

Michael Rosenberg is Professor of Anthropology at the University of Delaware.

Mitchell S. Rothman is Professor of Anthropology at Widener University.

Antonio Sagona is Professor of Archaeology at the University of Melbourne.

G. Kenneth Sams is Professor of Classical Archaeology at the University of North Carolina, Chapel Hill.

Klaus Schmidt is Adjunct Professor at the Institute for Prehistory at Erlangen-Nürnberg University and Senior Research Fellow at the Orient Department of the German Archaeological Institute in Berlin.

Ulf-Dietrich Schoop is Lecturer in Archaeology at the University of Edinburgh.

Mark Schwartz is Assistant Professor of Anthropology at Grand Valley State University.

Jürgen Seeher is Senior Research Fellow at the German Archaeological Institute, İstanbul.

Sharon R. Steadman is Associate Professor of Anthropology at the State University of New York, Cortland.

Jason Ur is Associate Professor of Anthropology at Harvard University.

Theo van den Hout is Professor of Hittite and Anatolian Languages at the University of Chicago.

Mary M. Voigt is Chancellor Professor of Anthropology at the College of William and Mary.

Jak Yakar is Professor of Archaeology and Near Eastern Cultures at Tel Aviv University.

Ilya Yakubovich is Research Associate at the Institute of World Cultures at Moscow State University.

Paul Zimansky is Professor of Archaeology and Ancient History at the State University of New York, Stony Brook.

THE OXFORD HANDBOOK OF

ANCIENT ANATOLIA

CHAPTER 1

INTRODUCTION: THE OXFORD HANDBOOK OF ANCIENT ANATOLIA

GREGORY McMAHON AND SHARON R. STEADMAN

Much of the fascination that Anatolia conjures in the minds of its enthusiasts stems from the wonderful diversity, over time and place, of the people who have lived there. These early years of the twenty-first century mark roughly a century of serious scholarly study of ancient Anatolia, and this volume represents a synthesis of our current understanding at the end of this century of scholarship. It documents close to ten millennia of human occupation in Anatolia, from the earliest Neolithic to the death of Alexander the Great in 323 B.C.E. Although beyond the scope of this volume, the additional 2,300 years between Alexander and the modern day are no less rich in the procession of peoples, languages, cultures, and religions which have come to, or through, Anatolia. Romans, Parthians, Arabs, Jews, and Byzantines, as well as Türkmen, Selçuk, and Ottoman Turks have all left their impression on the memory and monuments of Anatolia. In cities like İstanbul or Ankara, one can observe many of these cultural layers literally piled on top of one another or embedded in the monuments of later people, as in the Kaiser Wilhelm Fountain in the Roman hippodrome in İstanbul, or the Roman architectural and sculptural elements incorporated into the inner citadel of the kale in Ankara. In Bursa, ancient Prusa, the (rebuilt) tombs of the first Ottoman sultans, the eponymous Osman and his successor, Orhan, are built around Roman and Byzantine columns salvaged from monuments or structures erected long before the Turks arrived in Anatolia in 1071 C.E. The forests of columns that fill the pre-Ottoman mosques in Erzurum,

Konya, and elsewhere in Anatolia include columns and capitals of Greek, Roman, and Byzantine design, mixed together and adapted to the service of a new building style and purpose.

This intermixing of culture has been operative in Anatolia for as long as we can imagine and constitutes one of the most important conditioning factors for Anatolian peoples; they have always been in constant contact with other cultural groups, current and past. This is exemplified in the dozens of ancient occupation sites, in the form of *höyüks* (mounds), which rose from the Anatolian plain over centuries or millennia as new groups moved in, or existing groups moved back, to sites that offered sufficient advantages of location and resources to justify the effort of leveling off old towns and rebuilding them. The peoples of Anatolia covered in this volume therefore lived amongst the monuments and settlements of their predecessors, thereby creating millennia-long tensions between holding on to their own cultural traditions and appropriating those of their predecessors.

In contrast to Oxford Handbooks on Hellenic or Byzantine studies, this volume is defined geographically, rather than by a culture, ethnic group, language, or polity. On its northern, western, and southwestern perimeters, Anatolia has very clear boundaries. With an exceptionally long coastline, it enjoys access to the Black Sea, Sea of Marmara, Aegean, and Mediterranean. Defining its eastern and southeastern boundary is a bit more problematic, but a number of the chapters, especially those covering the east and southeast, provide detailed arguments for what should be considered Anatolia. Modern national borders are mostly irrelevant to discussions of Anatolia in antiquity, which includes for some of our authors not only Asiatic Turkey but also parts of today's Armenia, Georgia, Syria, and Iraq.

Anatolia is one of the most diverse areas in the Middle East by topography, climate, and history. In covering as completely as possible the wealth of different lifeways and plethora of languages, ethnicities, and religions of ancient Anatolia, we have given the authors as much autonomy as possible in conceptualizing their topics. Given the difficulties of maintaining consistency in the spelling of names in a region inhabited for millennia, complicated by the changes over time in ancient place names (remarkably, often recognizable despite those changes) and the varying practices of scholars toward Latinizing of Greek names, we have followed in general the same principle of author autonomy in the spelling of names. For Turkish names we have followed its clear and fairly recently developed orthographic system, although even here there is some latitude in spelling, especially for geographical terms like Kızıl Irmak, or names of sites, like Can Hasan, or in the spelling of terms like *höyük/hüyük*.

While we recognize that there may remain topics or issues in the study of ancient Anatolia which are not addressed in this volume, we have sought the optimal balance of chapters on archaeological, historical, and philological topics, and a balance as well of chapters both very specific and broadly synthetic, each of which represents the most recent scholarship in these various fields. This volume is meant to be comprehensive, within reason, for ancient Anatolia, beginning with the Neolithic and ending with the moment when Alexander the Great swept through

Anatolia in the first stages of his conquest of the Persian Empire, unifying much of the ancient Near East politically (temporarily) and culturally, thereby permanently setting Anatolia on a path of increasing cultural homogeneity and Hellenization and altering its relationship to the rest of the ancient world.

The "Background and Definitions" section (part I) provides a starting point for approaching this enormous topic. McMahon offers an overview of some of the earliest evidence of a perspective both Anatolian and foreign on the diversity of places, people, and languages in first millennium Anatolia. Matthews provides a comprehensive synthetic history of the archaeology of preclassical Anatolia, beginning with some of the earliest explorations and excavations in the Near East, under the Ottomans, through the far more recent development of the systematic study of the many prehistoric sites of Anatolia. Yakar discusses dating techniques and the necessity of working with both material and textual evidence to develop secure chronologies for the rather daunting range of Anatolian peoples and sites. Together, these chapters provide a broad and essential introduction to the succeeding sections.

Defining Anatolia: The Key Sites

Although the section with the title "Key Sites" closes the book, explaining its structure and contents offers insight into how we, as editors, approached the composition of the entire volume. Choosing which sites to include in this section was one of the most difficult choices we faced. We settled on a set of criteria to guide our choices: long-term, established, and ongoing projects (e.g., Gordion, Çatal Höyük, Sardis, Kültepe-Kaneš); shorter term, completed, and carefully excavated sites (e.g., Titriş Höyük and Ilıpınar); and projects begun in the past decade or two that are subjects of continued research (e.g., Göbekli Tepe, Arslantepe, Ayanis, and Kaman-Kalehöyük). Snapshots of Neolithic and Chalcolithic life on the Anatolian plateau are provided by Roodenberg (Ilıpınar) and Hodder (Çatal Höyük), and Neolithic ritual at the southeastern site Göbekli is profiled by Schmidt. The Chalcolithic and Early Bronze Age southeast is represented by Arslantepe (Frangipane) and Titriş Höyük (Algaze and Matney), respectively. The important earlier second millennium on the plateau is outlined by Kulakoğlu's overview of Kültepe-Kaneš; the Hittite Empire is represented not by a single key site but by Mielke's masterful treatment of several Hittite centers; and Omura's chapter on Kaman-Kalehöyük offers a review of occupation at a site spanning the Late Bronze and Iron Ages. The breadth of Iron Age Anatolia is represented in the west (Greenewalt on Sardis), in the center (Voigt on Gordion), and finally in the east (Çilingiroğlu on Ayanis). The eleven chapters in this section offer some of the most important work that has been, and continues to be, carried out across the Anatolian peninsula and beyond.

Chronology and Geography

As noted above, the topographic and climatic diversity of Anatolia—from the Mediterranean coast, to the rolling plains of the plateau and high peaks of the mountain chains, and finally to the arid areas of the southeast—means that not only were there disparate culture areas in ancient Anatolia but also that each region and its chronological periods needed treatment in separate chapters. Also notable is the vast chronological range covered in the volume—we asked our authors to describe nearly 10,000 years of cultural lifeways to this volume's readers.

Given this regional individuality in Anatolia's prehistory and early history, we asked part II's authors to address a series of questions, including "what constitutes my period and region?" and "which sites best represent my region and period?" to guide chapter content and allow for unique approaches to the material. The results were comprehensive and up-to-date interpretive studies.

Though defining the geographical extent of a region may seem straightforward, in fact a review of numerous publications finds many authors stating that their site is "on the plateau in the Lake District" or "in the Upper Euphrates region of southeastern Anatolia." What constitutes the plateau, the southeast, the west, the east, of Anatolia? One point made clear by our authors is the dichotomy between a "region," and how we as modern archaeologists envision that region. For instance, Özbaşaran skillfully describes the topographic and climatic variability of the Anatolian plateau; however, excavated Neolithic plateau *sites* are mainly located in the northwest and southern areas. Conversely, chapters on the second and first millennia (e.g., Seeher, and Kealhofer and Grave) place *plateau life* mainly in its center at major cities such as Gordion and Ḫattuša. Certainly the editors of this volume, when envisioning "the plateau," think of the region east of Ankara and north of Cappadocia, where their research has been centered for two decades—the western and southern plateau areas are not part of our "plateau consciousness" on a daily basis. The chapter authors have provided an invaluable service in not only defining the geographical "boundaries" of their regions, slippery as they may be, but also in reminding us that while important sites may be located only in one defined area of that larger region, prehistoric and early historic inhabitants most certainly envisioned broader landscapes stretching across and beyond the few sites we know archaeologically today.

It is easier, perhaps, to understand the posing of questions such as "what constitutes my period?" in this section devoted to time and space. In their discussions of chronological stages, authors have made invaluable contributions: Rosenberg and Erim-Özdoğan ask us to recast our periodizations of the Neolithic southeast, eschewing the awkward applications of chronologies such as the "Pre-Pottery Neolithic A and B"; Schoop and Steadman are united in the struggle to define the "end" of the Chalcolithic and the "beginning" of the Early Bronze Age on the plateau, while Özbal and Ökse marshal the overwhelming amount of recently excavated data on the Chalcolithic and Early Bronze Age in the southeast into cogent discussions on what is happening where and often why. Important chapters by Marro and Palumbi on eastern Anatolia in the Chalcolithic and Early Bronze Age bring into focus the latest evidence for defining the nature of interaction between Transcaucasia and southeastern Anatolia—a decades-long topic of discussion and controversy.

Chapters featuring the early historic periods include those on the dynamic but poorly understood Iron Age on the plateau and in the east—treated in some detail by Kealhofer and Grave, and Khatchadourian, respectively. This volume represents one of the only places where a comprehensive presentation of sometimes scant and often contradictory Iron Age data from Anatolia has been undertaken. Matney's chapter profiles the Iron Age southeast—a period of empire, collapse, rebuilding, multiple cultures marching through and settling the region, and a host of other events which he lays out in a coherent and compelling form. Matney's chapter is superbly preceded by Laneri and Schwartz's treatment of the southeastern Middle Bronze Age, a period about which we formerly knew little and now can far better understand.

The authors who dealt with the Late Bronze Age, including Bryce, Seeher, and Gates, all skillfully reveal how the peoples, places, and events in each of their regions (west, central, and southeast, respectively) moved in and out of the Hittite orbit; readers understand that the Hittite Empire was always a factor, welcomed or not, in the daily undertakings of Anatolian peoples across the plateau and in the southeast. The Late Bronze Age chapters were prefaced by Michel's excellent study on the *kārum* period on the plateau, which highlights the international nature of the early second millennium plateau and the importance of the settlement at Kültepe.

The final chapter of part II treats the last of the Anatolian periods covered in this volume. Greaves offers a comprehensive exploration of the complex archaeological and historical evidence describing the intersection between Greeks and Anatolians in the western and central reaches of the peninsula, beginning with the "Greek migrations" and ending with the coming of Alexander the Great. Each chapter in this subsection on the Iron Age provides not only a complete and current overview of relevant data but also the author's own interpretations of the extant evidentiary repertoire, thereby making available to readers not only the most up-to-date study on the target place and time but also providing the benefit of an expert's evaluation of complex and often seemingly contradictory data.

Philological and Historical Topics

Before the discovery and decipherment of the textual corpora left behind by the early literate societies of the Bronze and Iron Ages in Anatolia, the only written evidence for Anatolia in this period was later Greek literary sources like Homer, Herodotus, Xenophon, and Arrian, and inscriptional evidence, mostly in Greek. Wonderful as such sources are, they can only provide the perspective of outsiders who have their own distinctive sense of identity, mostly formed before their late arrival in Anatolia. However, with the discovery and decipherment of the languages covered in this section, whose scribal traditions were developed in Anatolia, all of them preserved only in epigraphic records discovered in Anatolia (broadly defined), we can begin to appreciate an Anatolian perspective. Thus we may learn, for example, what these people called themselves and their neighbors, how they organized their politics, or how they interacted with the divine.

With the arrival of Old Assyrian traders in Anatolia in the Middle Bronze Age, writing comes to the region for the first time, dramatically altering potential approaches to the study of Anatolia. For the first time, we can put a name to the people who lived in Anatolia. The oldest of the languages preserved there, that of the Old Assyrian merchants of the Middle Bronze Age, is covered by Michel in the "Chronology and Geography" section and initiates the narrative of the development of writing technologies and their effects on the societies of ancient Anatolia. Of course, we know the Old Assyrians to have been temporary sojourners in Anatolia in the Middle Bronze Age, traveling from northern Mesopotamia to establish trading colonies on the plateau.

Picking up the thread begun in Michel's chapter, the first four chapters in part III focus on the text corpora of Anatolian cultures which discovered and developed writing and record-keeping traditions. Beckman introduces the oldest attested Indo-European language, Hittite, also one of the first lost Anatolian languages to be deciphered. Yakubovich brings to light the Luwian language, which was originally known only from scattered passages in the Hittite corpus but is now known to have survived the fall of the Hittite kingdom and the end of Hittite as a written language. Zimansky profiles the history of the discovery of the forgotten kingdom of Urartu and the deciphering of its language, yet another hitherto unknown linguistic tradition of Anatolia. Through this deciphering, the magnificent monuments of this eastern Anatolian kingdom, which extended well beyond the eastern border of present-day Turkey, come to life. The recently edited Urartian corpus described in Zimansky's chapter provides an excellent balance to Radner's chapter in part IV on the incessant conflict between Urartu and Assyria known mostly from Assyrian sources.

Although Hittite is the best-known Anatolian language of the Late Bronze Age, and Luwian spans the gap between Hittite and Neo-Hittite eras (i.e., between the Late Bronze and Iron Ages), Phrygian is the language of the most politically powerful Anatolian people of the Early Iron Age. Roller's chapter provides specific details on the alphabetic script and language of the Phrygians, which proves to be Indo-European but not part of the Anatolian family, supporting the tradition preserved by Greek authors such as Herodotus that the Phrygians were immigrants to Anatolia. Roller's comprehensive approach to the full range of available sources allows her to provide an overview of Phrygian religious practice, deities, and monuments.

Based on an exhaustive review of the relevant textual sources, Beal's chapter provides a fascinating narrative of the political history of the second millennium, focusing on the Hittite state and its capital at Ḫattuša. Not unexpectedly, we learn that the Hittites struggled (as do all empires) with issues of dynastic succession, court intrigue, and constant pressure on their borders. Beal develops the theme of the Hittites' innovative strategies to deal with such issues, including utilizing international treaties, and discusses some of the most unique texts of Anatolian antiquity, such as Ḫattušili III's sophisticated justification for deposing his nephew.

Sams provides a similar overview for the first millennium, drawing of necessity on a wider range of sources as he puts into perspective the sweeping changes of the Iron Age, with invasions by peoples of the steppe, creation and destruction of a native Anatolian empire, the arrival and settling of the Greeks on the Aegean coast, and the first large-scale and long-lived invasion and subjugation of Anatolia by outsiders, the Persians. This section concludes with an insightful overview by Harmanşah of the monuments created by the procession of Anatolian peoples described in the previous chapters. He argues that architecture and monuments are the most visible and powerful remnants of past civilizations, especially through funerary monuments, and that Anatolia, with its vast array of monuments from multitudinous peoples leaving their mark over centuries, provides a unique opportunity to study, and marvel at, what he calls the "landscape of the dead."

Thematic and Specific Topics

The thirteen chapters in part IV, "Thematic and Specific Topics," treat some of the most difficult topics in Anatolian pre- and early history. Anatolia has often been referred to as a crossroads between Europe and Asia—a description apt not just in recent history but in the ancient world as well. Most of the chapters in the "Intersecting Cultures" subsection deal with the movements of people into and across the Anatolian peninsula. Three chapters address the sharing of material culture, ideologies, and peoples between the western regions of Anatolia and Europe: Özdoğan undertakes a thorough review of evidence for interaction between Anatolia and the Balkans spanning the Neolithic through the Bronze Ages, and Harl completes the story by laying out, in fascinating detail, the early history of Greek presence along the Anatolian western coast and their progress inward. Jablonka offers readers a comprehensive review of Troy's place in the larger Aegean/Anatolian world, highlighting the continued important role this settlement played over three millennia.

To the east, Sagona tackles the bracing subject of Anatolian–Transcaucasian interactions spanning the Chalcolithic through the Bronze Age; his chapter reminds us that the national boundaries that divide these regions today do not at all reflect how ancient cultures envisioned their landscapes. Also focusing attention on the east is Radner's excellent account of the waxing and waning of Assyrian and Urartian interactions throughout the Iron Age; the battles for control of land and peoples between these two powerful entities is provided in a skillful presentation of archaeological and textual data. Also blending (very limited) archaeological data with philological studies is Melchert's comprehensive overview of the arrival and florescence of the Indo-European languages in Anatolia, the most famous of which is, of course, Hittite.

Chapters in the "Pastoralists to Empires" subsection treat the kinds of critical issues promised by the title. Castro Gessner provides the latest word on the Neolithic-Chalcolithic Halaf Tradition in southeastern Anatolia. She reviews the evolution of scholarship on the nature of Halaf social organization and lays out the difficulties in accurately defining the Halaf "cultural region" and its associated chronology. In many respects, Rothman's overview of the Uruk period provides the same service. Although the chronology of the Uruk phenomenon has become less problematic in recent decades, the exact structure of the Uruk system in southeastern Anatolia is still not fully understood; Rothman provides well-constructed arguments for how we might best comprehend not only the overall structure of the Uruk system but also its involvement with Late Chalcolithic Anatolian societies.

On the plateau Düring bravely undertakes a comprehensive overview of what he calls the "millennia in the middle," that is, the Chalcolithic period. Unlike southeastern Anatolia, where numerous sites help document a cultural prehistory, our knowledge of Chalcolithic lifeways on the plateau is spotty at best. Düring marshals the known data and offers readers an invaluable set of interpretive frameworks for understanding these three millennia in the heart of Anatolia. A marvelous chapter on the florescence of metallurgy in Anatolia is provided by Muhly. It has been far too long since a comprehensive treatment of the impact of metals and metallurgy on Anatolian societies has been attempted; Muhly addresses this admirably in a chapter reviewing this topic, from the first emergence of metal experimentation in the Neolithic to the full-blown metallurgical societies of the Bronze Age. Ur's chapter on landscape archaeology, primarily targeting recent research in the southeast, is not limited to a specific chronological period but instead provides examples of what can be learned about societies of any period or locale through landscape studies. His chapter is a blend of an overview of methodologies that can be employed, combined with fascinating revelations of what has been discovered.

The final two chapters treat the second millennium Hittite Empire from two methodological perspectives: material culture evidence and textual evidence. Glatz notes that textual sources "cannot be taken a priori as representative of the totality of Hittite imperial organization and modes of engagement" (chapter 40, p. 878) and shows how the material culture can sometimes be an even clearer lens through which scholars may view the rise and fall of this powerful empire. In many ways, van den Hout supports Glatz's assertions in his review of the Hittite texts; he describes the contradictory information that is sometimes provided by multiple texts on the same subjects. Conversely, however, he also draws out the nuanced understanding that scholars may gain regarding, for instance, royal intentions and goals, the pomp and circumstance of ritual, or the intricacy of ancient law through their close readings of the some 30,000 extant Hittite texts. The two chapters combine to offer an unparalleled examination of the Hittite Empire from its inception to its collapse.

Conclusion

Although the coverage in this volume is meant to be comprehensive, there is always more that could be said. There is fascinating ongoing work on Palaeolithic Anatolia, and naturally the history of the region does not cease with the arrival of Alexander the Great. For the period covered by this volume, we also continue to learn more. Our goal therefore has been both to provide the most complete portrait of ancient Anatolia as we understand it after a century or so of scholarly work and to allow the expertise and enthusiasm of the scholars represented herein to inspire the continuing quest to understand even more. One of Anatolia's greatest attractions is the lure of the work still to be done; scholars working in this area know that every new season of excavation or discovery of textual evidence could radically alter our understanding of the people and places we study. This volume therefore stands as a statement of our current state of understanding and an invitation to look forward to our continued exploration of the most fascinating place we know.

PART I

THE ARCHAEOLOGY OF ANATOLIA: BACKGROUND AND DEFINITIONS

CHAPTER 2

THE LAND AND PEOPLES OF ANATOLIA THROUGH ANCIENT EYES

GREGORY McMAHON

This book provides extensive coverage of a wide range of sources, archaeological and textual, for the peoples of Anatolia. The wonderfully rich archaeological evidence of prehistory is discussed in chapters on the Neolithic, Chalcolithic, and Early Bronze Ages in all regions of Anatolia. With the Middle Bronze Age and the introduction of writing to Anatolia, peoples such as the Assyrians, Hittites, Luwians, Urartians, Phrygians, and Greeks began to leave substantial written records of themselves; all of these groups have one or more chapters dedicated to them or their language. The Hittite textual corpus in particular provides a plethora of text references to names of places and peoples, allowing scholars to create the foundation of a Hittite geography and to correlate ancient and modern topoi. (See Forlanini (1998) and del Monte and Tischler (1978) for overviews of our understanding of the Late Bronze Age (LBA) geography of Anatolia.) Tarḫuntašša, temporarily the capital of the Hittite state, which remains unlocated, is the subject of especially intense interest (Alp 1995; Dinçol et al. 2000). Evidence from Luwian sources in Anatolian hieroglyphic script is increasingly being used for the geography of Neo-Hittite sites of the Iron Age (e.g., Hawkins 1998; Wäfler 1983).

I have focused my discussion on a different kind of source—the Greek texts of Homer and Herodotus—for several reasons. Neither is discussed in detail elsewhere in this volume. Both Homer's *Iliad* and Herodotus's *Historia* are composed by Greeks from Anatolia (Homer is certainly from the eastern Greek world and quite possibly from Anatolia itself). These authors, separated by three centuries, provide us with unique evidence of the Greek perspective on the geographical/linguistic/ethnic makeup of parts of Anatolia in their respective periods.

Figure 2.1 shows the "traditional" regions/ethnic groups of Anatolia in the first millennium, according to Classical sources. These sources do not necessarily factor in Neo-Hittite states or Assyrian control, but denote regions which the Greeks, and later Romans, recognized as distinct from each other. Some were well-organized states, such as Lydia and Phrygia; others are simply regions of relative ethnic homogeneity. This fairly standard "Classical" map represents the latest and fullest characterization of major Anatolian peoples and includes several peoples/regions not known to Herodotus. Galatia, for example, did not exist as a region until the arrival of the Gauls in the third century (see Sams, chapter 27 in this volume). Lycaonia does not occur in Herodotus; although Xenophon (1.2.19) describes it as "hostile territory" (to the Persians) when Cyrus the Younger marched through it in 401 B.C.E. The hegemonic nature of Hellenic culture led to the gradual but inexorable homogenizing of the Anatolian cultural landscape along Greek patterns, a process greatly accelerated by the conquest and conscious Hellenizing of Alexander the Great, the rule of the Diadochoi, and the eventual absorption of the Pergamene and Seleucid kingdoms by the Romans, who completed the process of bringing most of Anatolia into the Greco-Roman cultural orbit. Before this Hellenization of Anatolia in the later Classical and Hellenistic Ages, early encounters between Greeks and Anatolian peoples led to the Greek characterization of Anatolian peoples and places depicted in figure 2.1.

Figure 2.1. Map of sites and regions discussed in the text.

Homer, *The Iliad*

It is generally agreed that the story of the *Iliad* fits best into the end of the LBA, around 1200 B.C.E., and that Homer, if we can accept the ancient attribution of this epic poem to a poet of this name, lived in the eighth century, probably in Smyrna or Chios (see Harl, chapter 34 in this volume, for linguistic evidence on Homer's probable Anatolian origins). We do not know how Homer acquired his material, as he lived four centuries after the events he memorializes. The world he depicts seems to be a synthesis of his own Archaic Greek world and his understanding of the LBA Mycenaean world, including his rather remarkable awareness that in the time of the Trojan War there were no Greeks living in Anatolia. Ironically, it now appears probable that there were in fact Mycenaean Greeks in Anatolia in the LBA (see Bryce, chapter 15 in this volume, for Miletus VI as a Mycenaean settlement). Because most of the action of the *Iliad* takes place in Anatolia, Homer mentions a number of Anatolian peoples therein. A good place to start is with his Catalogue of Trojan Allies (*Iliad* 2.816–877), most of whom are, predictably, Anatolian.[1]

1. Trojans;
2. Dardanians, led by Aineias;
3. "They who lived in Zeleia," "Trojans," led by Pandaros;
4. "They who held Adresteia and the countryside of Apaisos, they who held Pityeia and the sheer hill of Tereia";
5. "They who dwelt in the places about Perkote and Praktion, who held Sestos and Abydos and brilliant Arisbe";
6. "Spear-fighting Pelasgians," who lived in the area of Larissa;
7. Men of Thrace;
8. "Kikonian spearmen" (Thracians, subset of 7);
9. "Paionians with their curved bows" (Probably Thracians, subset of 7);
10. Paphlagones, "from the land of the Enetoi where the wild mules are engendered";
11. The Halizones, "from Alybe far away, where silver was first begotten";
12. Mysians;
13. Phrygians;
14. Maionians, associated with the "lake Gygaian" and Mt. Tmolos;
15. Karians "of the outland speech," including Miletos, the Maiandros, and Mykale;
16. Lykians, led by Sarpedon and Glaukos "from Lykia far away."

Based on our understanding of Anatolian geography and distribution of populations, we may divide these allies into four groups. The first group, 1–5, are people of the Troad, including those living in Troy itself. Since they are presumably ethnically unified, these peoples are not identified by ethnic designations, but rather simply as the inhabitants of various geographic regions, mostly cities, in the vicinity of Troy. I should point out here that although the Trojans are clearly named for their city (i.e., place name is primary), the name of the city in turn derives from an eponymous ancestor Tros, the great-grandfather of Priam. The second group, 6–9, depending on our interpretation of Pelasgian in this context, are non-Anatolian allies from various parts of Thrace across the Hellespont. The third group, 10–11, are Black Sea peoples, one relatively poorly attested (Halizones), and one well-known group (Paphlagones) whose land is well attested in Classical sources. The fourth group, 12–16, consists of major peoples of the Aegean and Mediterranean coast, with one group from the interior (Phrygians). The allies in the final two groups are each described as a people, apparently an ethnic group, which eventually gave its name to a region of Anatolia. All but one of these regions are on the "standard" Classical map. The exception is the Maionians, discussed in more detail below.

Allies 1–5

First among the alliance defending Troy are, of course, the Trojans themselves. There are several examples of Greeks and Trojans bearing the same name, such as Agelaus (8.257, 11.302). This is presumably for literary purposes and certainly need not imply that the Trojans were Greeks. Even the ability of Trojans and Greeks to converse on the battlefield and elsewhere is probably a literary convenience. This is made clear at 2.802–806, in Iris's address to the Trojans as the Achaians approach the city:

> "Hector, on you beyond all I urge to do this, to do as I tell you:
> all about the great city of Priam are many companions,
> but multitudinous is the speech of the scattered nations:
> let each man who is their leader give orders to these men,
> and let each set his citizens in order, and lead them."

As expected, the allied army of the Trojans is multinational, with "multitudinous" languages which will require native commanders of the contingents. Thus Homer acknowledges here that even communication within the Trojan forces was complex, and we may assume that communication across battle lines was simplified by him for justifiable reasons of convenience.

The only epigraphic material discovered to date at Troy is a bronze biconvex seal, found in Level VIIB, with two personal names written in Anatolian hieroglyphic, a script typically used to write Luwian (Hawkins and Easton 1996; see Jablonka, chapter 32, and Yakubovich, chapter 23 in this volume). See Beal (chapter 26 in this volume), also for the possible treaty relations between Troy and the Hittite kingdom, and Yakubovich (chapter 23) for increasing evidence of the importance of Luwian speakers in much of Anatolia in the LBA. Troy was a very long-lived city, inhabited over centuries by a variety of peoples; the evidence of the seal may indicate that the Trojans of the LBA were Luwian speakers.

The Dardanians led by Aineias are clearly not a different ethnic group from the Trojans; Vergil certainly considered Aineias a Trojan. This group of "Trojans" presumably trace their descent to Dardanos, the grandfather of Tros, and/or they lived in the district of the Troad, which he was thought to have governed. Although the Greek tradition that Dardanos came to the Troad to found Dardania from Samothrace does not accord well with the hypothesis of a Luwian ethnicity for the Trojans, this can be explained by the general Greek tendency to look for Greek or Aegean origins for Anatolian peoples.

Allies 3–5 are various local groups identified not as peoples but by place: "those of" towns, a land, a hill, and a river, all apparently in the Troad. Their lack of ethnic designation suggests an ethnic background similar to the Trojans; the people of Zeleia are specifically called Trojans.

Allies 6–10

Ally 6, the Pelasgians, are probably not Anatolians. This word is used for a people who are non-Greeks and are described as living in several places in Greece. This term is normally construed as a common Greek term for pre-Hellenic inhabitants of Greece; Herodotus 1.57 describes a distinctly non-Greek "language of the Pelasgian peoples who settled at Placia and Scylace on the Hellespont." The Pelasgian allies of the Trojans in the *Iliad* were from Larissa, described as far from Troy; their placement in the Catalogue of Trojan Allies immediately before allies 7–9, who are "men of Thrace" (7) and two other ethnic groups also from Thrace probably indicates that they came from Thrace as well.

Allies 10–11

With ally 10, the Paphlagones, we begin the list of peoples, mostly described as groups with ethnic designations, who can be identified with "traditional" regions in Anatolia. The exception is the Halizones, who came from "Alybe far away"; their proximity to the Paphlagones suggests that they also came from the coast of the Black Sea. Strabo 12.3.20–24 discusses various theories of who these people are. Paphlagonia is well attested as a region whose northern border is the Black Sea (figure 2.1, and Xenophon *Anabasis* book 5).

Allies 12–16

Ally 12, the Mysians, are also well documented; their home is in the northwest area of Anatolia, inland from the Troad. For Homer the Gygaian Lake is in Mysia, but also apparently in Maionia (*Iliad* 2.865, 20.391), which is understandable since Mysia and Maionia (later Lydia) border one another.

As allies, the Phrygians (ally 13) are identified as a people, and the place name Phrygia seems to be secondary and derived from the name of the group. In connection with Phrygia, Homer mentions both the Hermos (20.392) and Sangarios (3.187) Rivers and the city Askania further to the northwest. Priam at 3.184f. describes a visit to "Phrygia of the vineyards," where he saw Phrygian men "with their swarming horses." Priam was an ally of the Phrygians when they were camped along the Sangarios and were attacked by the Amazons, and his wife Hecuba was Phrygian (16.718–19).

The Maionians (ally 14) are a people located in the region later known as Lydia. The home of the Maionians was "beneath Mt. Tmolos" (2.866), and their leader's father was born "of the Gygaian lake" (2.865–866). See Bryce (chapter 15 in this volume) for the possibility of linking Maionians to the Hittite place name Maša.

The Carians (ally 15) are well known from other classical writers, including Herodotus. For Homer, Caria includes Miletos, the Maiandros River, and Mt. Mykale, on the far side of the harbor from Miletos. He does not mention Halicarnassus, the other great city of Caria. Homer describes them as the Carians "of the outland speech" (*barbarophonos*). Presumably all of these allies, and the Trojans themselves, were non-Greek speakers, but Homer singles them out for their barbaric (i.e., foreign to Greek ears) language. If Homer was from Smyrna, in Ionia, he was probably in contact with Carians and knew firsthand that they spoke a non-Greek language. See Morpurgo-Davies (1982/83), Yakubovich, chapter 23 in this volume, and Melchert, chapter 31, for Carian as an Anatolian language.

Lycia and the Lycians (ally 16) are by far the best attested Anatolian people and place in the *Iliad*, other than the Troad itself. At least sixteen Lycian warriors are individually named as casualties of the war, killed by Odysseus, Patroklos, and others. Given that Lycia is easily the furthest place from Troy to provide an allied contingent of warriors, we may well ask about the connection between Troy and Lycia and why the Lycians were so prominent in the effort to defend Troy.

At *Iliad* 6.155ff., Glaukos, one of the two great heroes/leaders of the Lycians, describes his lineage, which is closely bound to that of his cousin and fellow leader Sarpedon. According to this, both were grandsons of Bellerophontes, who had been tricked into coming to Lycia to be executed, but slew the Chimaira and other potential dangers, married the king's daughter, and thus established his own dynasty there. Bellerophontes's possible Corinthian origins suggest a Greek heritage for the Lycians of the *Iliad*, but the fact that the land was called Lycia before his arrival indicates that the place name precedes the people called Lycians in the *Iliad*, who would thus seem to be Greek or at least led by Greeks. See the following discussion for a differing view from Herodotus. Certainly Glaukos has no trouble communicating with Diomedes when they discover on the battlefield that they are *xenoi*, guest friends, through their fathers. The references to the Lukka Lands in Hittite texts, to be associated with Lycia, confirm that the place, inhabited by Luwian speakers, existed before the Greek tradition about their arrival there.

By contrast, Cilicians play a small role in the *Iliad*. Two references to the Kilikes in Book 6 describe them as a people of Asian Thebe, in Troy's immediate vicinity and one of the first cities sacked by Achilleus and the Achaians. The Kilikes may have fled the Troad after the Trojan defeat and made their way to the Cilicia of the Mediterranean coast, although in Greek tradition (but not in the *Iliad*), it was Greeks, under the leadership of the seer Mopsos, who took the name of Kilikes and stayed in Anatolia, migrating to what is now thought of as Cilicia. Confirming

Mopsos's connection to Cilicia is his occurrence in the bilingual Karatepe inscription (Hawkins 2000:45–67). See Beal (chapter 26 in this volume), for Mopsos's connection to the Achaeans (i.e., Greeks).

Homer thus provides a perspective on the people, languages, and regions of Anatolia, but only as it pertains to his narrative. His focus on his story precludes more extensive discursions on interesting details of peoples and their origins.

Herodotus, *Historia*

By contrast, Herodotus of Halicarnassus exemplifies a Greek curiosity that ranges widely and provides a wealth of detail on anything he finds interesting; Herodotus never met a story he did not like. Working in the fifth century B.C.E., approximately three centuries after Homer, he lived in an Anatolia permanently changed by the Greek migrations of the post-LBA period. The vast scope of Herodotus's *Researches* includes a great deal about the geography and peoples of Anatolia; in fact he typifies the incipient Greek interest in geography. He is of course describing an Anatolia which was much better known to the Greeks of his day than it had been to Homer, partly through the forcible unification of much of Anatolia by first Lydians and then Persians.[2]

Herodotus is one of the earliest Greek authors to use the word *Asia*, along with Hecataeus and Anaximander. Not only does Herodotus utilize this geographical name, he also recognizes its origins in Anatolia. At 4.45, he acknowledges the Lydians' rejection of the Greek tradition that Asia was named after Prometheus's wife, claiming rather that Asies, the son of Cotys and grandson of Manes, is the eponym for Asia, as well as for a tribe called Asias in Sardis. The Lydian claim that the name originates in Anatolia is more in line with the probability that the name derives from the Hittite place name Aššuwa.

Two especially useful passages in Herodotus for the geography and peoples of Anatolia are his catalogue of the Persian navy, 7.89–100, and the catalogue of troops in Xerxes's army, 7.61–88. The Anatolian contingents of the navy are at 7.91–95, while the Anatolian levies for Xerxes's army are found at 7.72–77. Both of these lists describe the contributions of the provinces of the Persian Empire to the army and fleet assembled by Xerxes in 480 B.C.E. for his massive invasion of the Greek mainland.

Aiolia

The Aiolians are one of the three Greek tribes which traditionally migrated to Anatolia after the collapse of the LBA (see Greaves, chapter 21 in this volume). They are much less important than the Ionians, or even the Dorians, in Herodotus's account. Herodotus, in his general penchant for symmetry, names twelve Aiolian towns to balance out the twelve primary Ionian cities. All but one of these Aiolian cities are little known; the exception is Smyrna, which was lost by the Aiolians to the Ionians (1.150).

Armenia

Most of the references to Armenia in Herodotus are geographical; he identifies Armenia as the location of the headwaters of the Euphrates (1.180) and describes the distinctive round skin boats built by the Armenians to float goods, mostly wine, down to markets in Babylon (1.194). For him, the Euphrates is the border between Armenia and Cilicia (5.52). Armenia is part of the thirteenth Persian province according to his catalogue, along with neighbors in the Black Sea region (3.93).

Most interesting in Herodotus's treatment of Armenia is his description of them in the catalogue of troops: "The Armenians, who are Phrygian colonists, were armed in the Phrygian fashion and both contingents [i.e., Phrygian and Armenian] were commanded by Archochmes" (7.73). Since he suggests that the Phrygians themselves migrated from Macedonia to Anatolia (see later discussion), he is therefore claiming that the Armenians have come all the way from northern Greece to their home in eastern Anatolia. See Yakubovich (chapter 23 in this volume) for the Armenian self-designation, and Diakanoff (1984) for their early history. See Zimansky (chapter 24 in this volume) for the earliest occurrence of the place name Armina/Arminiya, in the Behistun inscription.

Bithynia

The only substantive reference to Bithynians occurs in the catalogue of troops: "The Thracians after their migration to Asia became known as Bithynians; previously, according to their own account, they were called Strymonians, after the River Strymon on which they lived and from which they were driven by the Teucrians and Mysians. The commander of these Asiatic Thracians was Bassaces, the son of Artabanus (7.75).

Cappadocia

For Herodotus, Cappadocia seems to comprise the north central area of Anatolia, extending all the way to the Black Sea: "the river Halys, which runs northward into the Black Sea and forms the boundary between Cappadocia and Paphlagonia" (1.7). He also considers the ethnic group to be primary and to have given their name to the region. Their origin in the south, presumably having moved into central Anatolia, is implicit in his consistency in maintaining that although the Persians refer to them as Cappadocians, the Greeks call them Syrians (1.76, 5.49). He carefully keeps these Cappadocian Syrians distinct from the Syrians who live on the Syrian coast and contributed to the Persian navy (7.89).

Caria

Herodotus, as a native of Halicarnassus, brings firsthand experience of the ethnic complexity of Caria, the region where migrating Greeks most intimately mixed with Anatolian populations. As already noted, at 1.171 Herodotus claims that the entire west coast of Anatolia (i.e., Mysia, Lydia, and Caria) was at one point inhabited by one ethnic group, which divided into three "brother races" named after the brothers Myus, Lydus, and Car. Although probably fanciful, this origins narrative indicates his perception of the closeness of these three groups/areas. Herodotus's penchant for providing alternate explanations manifests itself here as well, as he discusses the Cretan claim that the Carians were originally islanders in the time of Minos, driven thence to Anatolia by the arrival of the Greeks on Crete.

The main Carian cities, Miletos and Halicarnassus, differ in their ethnic makeup; Miletos was Carian in the *Iliad* but is considered Ionian Greek by Herodotus, whereas Halicarnassus, not mentioned in the *Iliad*, was deemed a Dorian settlement by Herodotus. The complex ethnic makeup of the Aegean coast, with speakers of three distinct Greek dialects mingling with native Anatolians, especially Lydians and Carians, can be seen in Herodotus's confusion about the ethnicity of the inhabitants of his own city. He consistently refers to Halicarnassus as a Dorian city, which it may originally have been; however Burn (1972:11) points out that two inscriptions of the fifth century from Halicarnassus are in Ionian Greek, not Dorian. This changing Greek ethnic makeup is reflected in Halicarnassus being excluded from events in the nearby Dorian cities (1.144). Carian and Greek names appear together in the inscriptions, so Halicarnassus was clearly a multiethnic community.

Other examples of the mixed Ionian/Carian nature of Caria after the Greek migrations can be seen in Themistokles's appeal to Ionian Greeks to remain neutral during Xerxes's invasion, in which he not only implores the Ionians to avoid fighting against their Greek brethren but also requests them to ask the Carians to do the same (8.22). Ionians and Carians are closely linked and live together, yet are clearly separate. They allied with the Ionians during the Ionian revolt, hoping for the autonomy that success would have brought (5.117), yet the Carians of the interior received part of the territory of Miletos when the Persians parceled it out after the destruction of Miletos at the end of the Ionian Revolt (6.20). Their contributions to the Persian navy were also kept separate by Herodotus and, apparently, by the Persians (7.93).

There are several references to Carian and Ionian mercenaries in Egypt, united by serving together in a foreign land, yet carefully kept distinct by Herodotus (2.152, 154, 163, 3.11). At 2.61–62 Herodotus provides an index of the ferocity with which expatriate Carians living in Egypt held onto their ethnic identity. During the festival at Bubastis the Carians cut themselves on the forehead to indicate that they are not Egyptian but foreigners. Distinctive traits of the Carians include a unique cult: "The Carians are the only people we know of who sacrifice to Zeus Stratius (Zeus of the Army)" (5.119). See Bryce (chapter 15 in this volume), for the possible connection of the Hittite toponym Karkiša, in western Anatolia, to Caria.

Caunians

The city of Caunus is well known today; Herodotus credits this area as home to a distinct ethnic group, living close to the Carians and Lycians. Here is a group which apparently derived its name from its place, instead of the other way around.

Although Herodotus thinks they are native to Anatolia, they claim an origin from Crete, and their language is much like Carian (or vice versa), according to Herodotus. They are probably a group of Carians who created an autonomous city-state at Caunus. Although their language has come to resemble Carian, according to Herodotus their culture is very different from that of the Carians, or indeed anyone. They apparently tried to maintain their cultural integrity by eliminating foreign cults from their territory by physically driving out intrusive gods (1.172), which may be an early response to Greek cultural influence.

Cilicia

Herodotus hints at the possibly foreign origins of the Cilicians in his description of their contribution to the Persian navy, noting that the sword they carry as part of their arms closely resembles the Egyptian long knife and, more importantly, tracing their origins to Phoenicia: "The ancient name of the Cilicians was Hypachaei; their present name they took from Cilix, the son of Agenor, a Phoenician" (7.91). The name Hypachaei (Hypachaioi) means "under-Achaeans" and reveals Herodotus's desire yet again to see Anatolians as Greek colonists/immigrants. See Oettinger (2008) on the Hypachaioi. Given Cilicia's location, the Cilicians could in fact be Phoenician colonists, or possibly took the name of Cilix the Phoenician when he came to the southern coast of Anatolia. See the foregoing discussion for Homer's different description of the origins of the Cilicians, and Hawkins (2009) for epigraphic evidence on a possible connection between the Levant and Cilicia. See Yakubovich (chapter 23 in this volume), for the Cilician royal title Syennesis, which at 1.74 and 5.118 Herodotus mistakes for the name of the king, as evidence of continued use of Luwian in Cilicia.

Cimmerians

Although the Cimmerians, like the Persians, Greeks, Romans, and Turks, clearly originated from outside Anatolia, they successfully settled there, losing their ethnic identity quite early in antiquity. Chased into Anatolia by the Scythians, they harassed Gordion (see Sams, chapter 27 in this volume) and then invaded Lydia in three waves, eventually occupying Sardis (except for the acropolis). They were expelled by Alyattes two generations later. According to Herodotus, the Cimmerian capture of Sardis took place under Ardys (1.15–16), although their invasion of Lydian territory began under Ardys's predecessor, Gyges, the first of the Mermnad kings. Herodotus claims that they settled along the southern coast of the Black Sea in the area of Sinope (4.11–12). They also raided all the way to the Aegean coast into Ionia, but did not settle there (1.6). See Harmatta (1990) for more on Herodotus's understanding of the Cimmerians and Yakubovich (chapter 23 in this volume) for their participation in the destruction of Neo-Hittite civilization.

Colchis

On the edge of Anatolia, at the eastern end of the Black Sea, Colchis is at best a frontier area of Anatolia. It was, however, incorporated into the later Anatolian kingdom of Mithridates VI in the late second and early first century B.C.E. Herodotus certainly considers it part of Asia; at 1.2 he includes a narrative about the abduction of the Colchian princess Medea as part of the feud between Europe and Asia, which helps explain the Persian invasions of Greece. His separate entry for the Colchians in the catalogue of troops indicates his conviction that they are distinct from other ethnic groups. More interestingly, he is convinced that they are of Egyptian descent, based on a fanciful tradition of an Egyptian army marching through Asia and leaving a detachment of troops in Colchis. Shared cultural traits like circumcision and a distinctive way of weaving linen are adduced as evidence for this.

Dorians

The southernmost of the three Greek tribes which were supposed to have migrated to the west coast of Anatolia were the Dorian Greeks. There were of course many Dorian cities in mainland Greece as well, the most famous of which was Sparta. The Dorian Greeks, like the Ionians, interacted most with the Carians; as noted, Herodotus, a native of Halicarnassus, considers it to be a Dorian city (2.178), despite the contemporary evidence of the Ionian inscriptions and membership in the Delian League. Knidos, on the Aegean coast, was also Dorian according to Herodotus (1.174). The "Asiatic Dorians" provided thirty ships to the Persian navy; their Peloponnesian origins meant that they were "armed in the Greek fashion" (7.93). Herodotus also mentions that Dorian (and Ionian) colonists controlled the Hellespont and Bosporus, whose towns contributed 100 ships to the Persian navy (7.95).

Ionia

The Ionians of Anatolia are the best known of the Greek immigrants to Asia (see Harl, chapter 34, and Greaves, chapter 21 in this volume). They settled mostly in Caria; see the foregoing discussion for their close relationship with the Carians. Herodotus is meticulous about keeping the three Greek tribes distinct from each other but acknowledges the complexity of ethnicity for the Greeks of Anatolia. He is convinced that the Ionians came from Achaia in the Peloponnesos, driven out by the Achaians, and debunks the claim of the Anatolian Ionians that they have the purest blood of all the Ionian tribes by describing other admixing peoples from Euboea, Orchomenos, and elsewhere. Herodotus preserved the tradition that the Ionians took refuge in Athens before their migration across the Aegean to the Anatolian coast, but points out that even those Ionians migrated without their families and took Carian wives by force after their arrival in Anatolia (1.146), creating an ethnic mix unacknowledged by the Ionians themselves. Thus for the Ionians of Herodotus's day, language and history trump lineage as the essential component of identity. Herodotus's most fundamental definition for Ionians is Greeks living in Anatolia who "originate from Athens and keep the festival of the Apaturia," an Athenian festival for the phratries. This last reminds us that Ionian identity was bound up not only in shared language (really dialect) and history but also in a common cult at the Panionion, an Anatolian shrine theoretically for all Ionians, although some were excluded for various historical reasons (1.143, 147–48, and see Harl, chapter 34 in this volume). Herodotus also records an Ionian tradition that when they arrived in Anatolia, some put themselves under native rule, accepting "kings of Lycian nationality, descended from Glaucus the son of Hippolochus," whereas others accepted rule by Greeks, "men of Caucones from Pylus, descended from Codrus the son of Melanthus" (1.147). At 9.97 Herodotus gives credit for the founding of Miletos to Neileus, son of this same Codrus, the famous and possibly last king of Athens. Taken together these passages suggest that Neileus, one of the descendants of Codrus, apparently not only led the Ionian Greeks to refuge on the Anatolian coast but remained to rule some of them. See previous discussion for Homer's understanding of Miletos as a Carian city.

Herodotus also acknowledges the diversity of dialect even within the Ionian dialect of Greek:

> There are four dialects of the Ionic language, distributed as follows: the most southerly of the Ionian towns is Miletus, with Myrus to the north of it, and then Priene, these three being in Caria and speaking the same dialect. Ephesus, Colophon, Lebedus, Teos, Clazomenae, and Phocaea are in Lydia, and share a common dialect quite distinct from what is spoken at the places previously mentioned. There are three other Ionian settlements, two being the islands of Samos and Chios and one, Erythrae, a mainland town. The two latter use the same dialect, Samos a peculiar one of its own. (1.142)

Several of the peoples noted in this passage are discussed as distinct groups elsewhere in this chapter.

Lycia

As already noted, the Lycians are prominent in the *Iliad* as allies of the Trojans, coming from the furthest away and actively aiding the Trojan cause. Herodotus's account of the origins of the Lycians has them coming from Crete, which he knows was originally inhabited by non-Greek peoples. According to him, Minos's brother Sarpedon, having lost the contest for the throne, was exiled, and sailed with his supporters to Asia, landing at Milyas, the "ancient name of the country where the Lycians live today, though it was occupied then by the Solymi" (1.173). Sarpedon's party was supposedly called Termilai in Crete and under his rule in Anatolia, but eventually when Lycus was exiled from Athens by his brother Aegeus, king of Athens, he took refuge with Sarpedon and the Termilai. They later adopted his name and were called Lycians. This does not, however, fit well with the existence of the Lukka Lands (Lycia) already in the Hittite texts of the LBA. See Bryce (chapter 15 in this volume) for a critique of Greek etymologies of the name Lycia and the epigraphically attested Lycian self-designation Trm̃mili.

Although they apparently were influenced by Carian culture, and supposedly preserved some Cretan culture as well, Herodotus considers them unusual in their matrilineal descent structure (1.173), for which there is little corroborating evidence. The "native" Solymi were presumably subsumed within the new ethnic stock of the Termilai/Lycians. In the catalogue of the navy, Herodotus is consistent in reiterating that the Lycians originated in Crete, had earlier been called Termilai, and later took their name from Lycus, an Athenian. Despite all these accounts of ethnic takeover and name change, Herodotus still lists the Milyans as a contingent in the catalogue of troops, some of whom were armed with Lycian bows (7.77). Apparently some of the Milyans maintained their ethnic identity in some part of Lycia, despite the arrival of the Cretans under Sarpedon. See Yakubovich (chapter 23 in this volume), for the Lycian B dialect as "Milyan" and Houwink ten Cate (1961) for the survival of Luwian in Lycia.

Lydia

Missing from the *Iliad*, Lydia in Herodotus's time was the empire centered at Sardis which had unified most of western Anatolia (see Sams, chapter 27, and Greenewalt, chapter 52 in this volume). Herodotus describes the Lydian Croesus as "king of all the peoples to the west of the river Halys, which runs northward into the Black Sea and forms the boundary between Cappadocia and Paphlagonia" (1.6). Croesus also was apparently the first native Anatolian dynast to come into direct contact with the Greeks of Anatolia, Ionian, Aiolian, and Dorian, by conquering and bringing them into his empire. Thus, ironically, began the extension of Greek influence beyond the western coast of Anatolia (see Harl, chapter 34 in this volume). According to Herodotus, this empire included the following peoples, many of them, except for the Greeks, known already from Homer: "In the course of time Croesus subdued all the peoples west of the river Halys, except the Cilicians and Lycians. The rest he kept in subjection—Lydians, Phrygians, Mysians, Mariandynians, Chalybians, Paphlagonians, Thracians (both Thynia and Bithynia), Carians, Ionians, Dorians, Aeolians, and Pamphylians" (1.28).

Herodotus also explains the absence of the Lydians from the *Iliad*. "Before the time of Agron, the reigning house had been of the family of Lydus, son of Atys; hence the name 'Lydians,' the people being previously known as Maeonians" (1.7). Agron was the first of the Heraklidai who supposedly ruled Lydia for twenty-two generations between the dynasty of Lydus and the Mermnadai, the dynasty that ended with Croesus. Thus the Maionians of Homer, who in the *Iliad* came from the area close to Mysia and from places associated with Lydia, became the Lydians of Herodotus.

In fact, Herodotus preserves some memory that the peoples of the entire western coast of Anatolia may "originally" have been one large group (pre-Greek migration): "In support of the claim [by the Carians] to be aboriginals, they point to an ancient temple of the Carian Zeus at Mylasa, the use of which is shared by Mysians and Lydians as brother races of the Carians—Lydus and Mysus, according to them, having been the brothers of Car" (1.171).

Herodotus's discussion of the social customs of the Lydians includes his revelation that all working-class girls in Lydia raise their own dowries through prostitution, an occupation they pursue until marriage (1.193). However, despite singling them out as "foreigners" in another passage (2.167), he acknowledges that other than the practice of prostituting their daughters, Lydian society is much like that of the Greeks (1.94). The Lydians are also one of the eight or so major people of Anatolia listed by Herodotus in his catalogue of troops in the Persian army. Here again he notes that in ancient times they were called Maeonians and only recently took their name from the eponymous Lydus (7.74)

Mysia

As noted under Lydia, the Mysians were according to Herodotus one of the three "brother races" of the west coast of Anatolia. Herodotus gives them credit for being an ancient people, which accords well with their role in the *Iliad*, in preserving a tradition that before the Trojan War an army of Mysians and Teucrians crossed the Bosporus and conquered Thrace (7.22), a tradition preserved also at 7.75, in which the Teucrians and Mysians are said to have driven the Thracians of the River Strymon out of their home and eventually to Anatolia to be called Bithynians.

In Herodotus's time, the Mysians had recently become one of the many peoples of western Anatolia to be conquered by Croesus (1.128), who later suffered the death of a son at the hands of the great boar of Mt. Olympus in Mysia, when the Mysians petitioned him for help against the savage beast (1.36). The Mysians are grouped with the Lydians in the catalogue of troops, where Herodotus claims that they are Lydian colonists known also as Olympieni after Mt. Olympus (7.74). See Beal (chapter 26 in this volume), for a suggestion that Mysia may be a survival of Hittite Maša.

Paeonians

Herodotus records the creation of a new people of Anatolia, when Paeonians, known from the *Iliad* as allies of the Trojans but living in Thrace, were forcibly moved at Darius's request from Europe to Asia. The Paeonian brothers who engineered this deportation claimed that the Paeonians were Teucrian colonists from Troy who had lived on the River Strymon close to the Hellespont. If that is true, then they were originally Anatolians, who immigrated to Europe, and then were forcibly removed/returned to Anatolia by Darius.

Pamphylia

This coastal region plays only a small part in Herodotus's narrative. In the catalogue of the navy they are listed as contributing thirty ships. Herodotus preserves the tradition that after the Trojan War some Greeks, led by the diviners

Amphilochus and Calchas, settled on the southern coast of Anatolia, and that the Pamphylians of his day were their descendants (7.91). This would make them among the earliest Greeks to colonize Anatolia. Herodotus also credits Amphilochus with founding Posideion on the border of Cilicia and Syria. See Sams (chapter 27 in this volume) for the similarity of Pamphylian Greek to the Mycenaean Greek of the Linear B tablets, which lends weight to the idea of Greek settlers in the LBA.

Paphlagonia

Also not prominent players in Herodotus's narrative, Paphlagonia is included as part of Croesus's empire (1.6) and listed in the catalogue of troops. They are grouped with even more obscure peoples like the Ligyans, Matieni, and Mariandynians, as well as the "Syrians," that is, Cappadocians (7.72). See Xenophon, *Anabasis* Book 5, for Paphlagonia's importance to his march along the Black Sea coast at the end of the fifth century B.C.E.

Phrygia

One of the most famous episodes in Herodotus is his report on the experiment conducted by the Egyptian king Psammetichus to determine the most ancient race in the world. Regardless of the validity of the experiment, we learn at 2.2 that the conclusion was reached that the Phrygian language was the most ancient language and that therefore the Phrygians were considered more ancient even than the Egyptians. We know the Phrygians primarily from their capital at Gordion (see Voigt, chapter 50 in this volume), and what we know of their language does not corroborate their great antiquity (see Roller, chapter 25 in this volume). The Midas of Herodotus's narrative is the first non-Greek to dedicate offerings at Delphi (1.14), indicating how far Greek influence had penetrated into the interior of Anatolia by the early seventh century B.C.E. Even after the destruction of the kingdom of Phrygia by the Cimmerians and the subsequent hegemony of Lydia, the Phrygians remained a recognizable ethnic group, described by Aristagoras as he tried to convince the Spartan king Cleomenes to invade the Persian empire as "richest in cattle and crops of all the nations we know" (5.49).

In the catalogue of troops, Herodotus provides his understanding of the origins of the Phrygians: "This people, according to the Macedonian account, were known as Briges during the period when they were European and lived in Macedonia" (7.73; see Roller, chapter 25 in this volume). As noted above, Herodotus also claims here that Phrygian colonists moving into eastern Anatolia became the Armenians. See Tuna, Aktüre, and Lynch (1998) for discussion of Phrygian connections to Thrace; and Roller (chapter 25) and Sams (chapter 27 in this volume), for discussion of the archaeological evidence from Gordion for a Balkan homeland for the Phrygians.

Pisidia

Pisidians do not occur in the text of Herodotus as preserved, but they are restored in the de Sélincourt translation in a lacuna that requires an ethnic name in the catalogue of troops (7.76). Their omission would be unusual, and since the missing group is described as carrying spears of Lycian workmanship, which would make sense given the proximity of Pisidia to Lycia, the restoration is quite tenable.

Pontus

Famous as a region and kingdom in the late second and first centuries B.C.E. under Mithridates VI, this area along the eastern portion of the Anatolian coast of the Black Sea is subsumed for Herodotus under the area of Cappadocia (1.7). However, he also mentions the Greeks of Pontus, acknowledging that within the land of Cappadocia are Greek colonies on the Pontus or Black Sea. Sinope is one such colony, founded by Miletos. Although he does not mention Trapezus, Xenophon's account in *Anabasis* (4.7–8) makes it clear that it was also a well-established Greek colony by the fifth century B.C.E.

Scythians

Like the Cimmerians, the Scythians, while clearly originating from outside Anatolia, do become an Anatolian people at least temporarily. The several references to the Scythians, including information gleaned from the Greeks of Pontus, make it clear that the Scythians came into Anatolia in pursuit of the Cimmerians. Herodotus claims that they took "Asia" or "Upper Asia" away from Cyaxeres king of the Medes and ruled it for twenty-eight years (1.106, 4.1). How much of Anatolia they actually controlled and for how long is unclear, but they seem to have controlled at least the area of the Araxes River and elsewhere before eventually being driven out of much of Anatolia (4.11). See Harmatta (1990) on the Scythians in Herodotus.

Teucrians

There are several brief references to a people of Anatolia called the Teucrians, descendants of Teucer (Teukros), the ancestor of the kings of Troy and the great-great-great-great-grandfather of Priam. See the previous discussion sub Mysia for a reference to the Mysians and Teucrians invading Thrace before the Trojan War (7.22, 7.75). A remnant of the ancient "Teucrians," the Gergithes, apparently lived in the Troad among Aiolian Greeks in the fifth century B.C.E., since they were crushed by the Persians in response to the Ionian Revolt (5.122). In the description of Xerxes's visit to Troy, where he visits the citadel and hears its story from local informants, we learn that the army passes the "Teucrians of Gergithos" as they march from Troy to Abydos to cross the Hellespont (7.44). Although they play essentially no role in the events of the fifth century B.C.E., other than getting caught up in Persian-Ionian conflict in Anatolia, incredibly there does seem to be a remnant of the Trojans living in the Troad in the fifth century B.C.E., with a memory of an eponymous ancestor of the LBA.

Conclusion

Anatolia in antiquity was a land rich in geographical, linguistic, and ethnic diversity. Although its geography and topography remain relatively unchanged and are still quite varied today, language and ethnic groups moved around within this landscape, being influenced by and influencing other groups. One of the most ubiquitous historical phenomena is an increase in cultural and linguistic homogeneity over time, especially with improvements in transportation and communication technologies, and the growth of larger and more closely unified polities. Despite this tendency, even two and a half centuries after Alexander, the relatively small kingdom which Mithridates VI consolidated in central Anatolia in the first century B.C.E. supposedly included twenty-two separate language groups (Pliny, *Historia Naturalis* 7.88; Quintilian, *Institutio Oratoria* 11.2.50); today perhaps four languages are spoken in that same area.

The Greeks transform our understanding of the ancient geography of Anatolia because they are as far as we know the first ancient people to seek knowledge or do research for its own sake, giving birth to disciplines such as history, ethnography, and geography. Homer's interest in the peoples of Anatolia was localized and focused on his story of the Greek attack on Troy and its allies. Herodotus, using his interest in people, languages, and geography in the service of his researches on the Persian invasion of Greece, reveals the more extensive understanding of the whole of Anatolia which the Greeks had acquired by the mid-5th century B.C.E. Neither Homer nor Herodotus knew of the Hittite, Assyrian, or Urartian sources, discussed in this volume, which describe some of the same people who occur in their narratives; they did not know of the origins of the name Lycia in the Lukka Lands of the Hittite records or the Hittite treaty with Wiluša (Wilios) long before Homer wrote about Troy. They therefore tended to favor narratives of origin that tied Anatolian peoples to Greek or Aegean origins, partly because they had none of the records we now have with which to critique such narratives.

The natural tendency toward homogeneity in Anatolia was accelerated by at least two factors after the Greeks came to Anatolia. One was the hegemonic nature of Greek civilization of the Archaic, Classical, and Hellenistic periods, which in contact with most other civilizations proved so compelling that it was influential wherever people were exposed to it. This was true even when the Greeks themselves were being conquered, by the Lydians, or by the Romans, as the poet Horace pointed out (*Epistles* Book II.1.156). This hegemonic character of Greek civilization, which would probably have spread inexorably to most of Anatolia eventually, was dramatically accelerated by Alexander's conquests of much of Anatolia and his deliberate Hellenizing efforts throughout his empire. The later Roman acquisition of the Anatolian part of his empire continued the process of homogenization through an intentional policy of Romanization. The Iron Age native and Greek cities of Anatolia, even a place like Sardis, capital of a major native Anatolian empire, now have such an overlay of Greek and Roman building and material culture that it can be difficult to perceive or remember the great ethnic differences of the people who lived in them before Alexander and the Romans brought them into the community of the Classical world. Discovering and elucidating this diversity of Anatolian cultures and languages before Alexander is thus a major focus of the scholars who work on Anatolia, and of this Handbook.

NOTES

1. All quotations are from the Richmond Lattimore translation of the *Iliad*, which preserves Greek spellings of personal and place names.
2. A good general introduction to Herodotus and his work, including his understanding of Anatolian peoples and places, is de Sélincourt (1982). See also How and Wells (1989).

REFERENCES

Primary Sources

Citations of Horace, Pliny, Quintilian, and Strabo are from standard editions.

Herodotus. *The Histories*. Trans. Aubrey de Sélincourt. Revised with introductory matter and notes by John Marincola. London: Penguin Books, 1996.

Homer. *The Iliad of Homer*. Trans. and with an introduction by Richmond Lattimore. Chicago: University of Chicago Press, 1961.

Xenophon. *The Persian Expedition (Anabasis)*. Trans. Rex Warner. London: Penguin Books, 1987.

Secondary Sources

Alp, Sedat. 1995. *Zur Lage der Stadt Tarḫuntašša*. In *Atti del II Congresso Internazionale di Hittitologia*, ed. O. Carruba, M. Giorgieri, and C. Mora, 1–11. Pavia: Gianni Iuculano Editore.

Burn, A. R. 1972. Introduction. In Herodotus, *The Histories*, 7–37. Middlesex: Penguin Books.

de Sélincourt, Aubrey. 1982. *The World of Herodotus*. San Francisco: North Point Press.

del Monte, Giuseppe F. and Johann Tischler. 1978. Die Orts-und Gewässernamen der hethitischen Texte. Répertoire Géographique des Textes Cunéiformes VI. Wiesbaden: Dr. Ludwig Reichert Verlag.

Diakonoff, Igor. 1984. *The Pre-History of the Armenian People*. Trans. L. Jennings. Delmar, N.Y.: Caravan Books.

Dinçol, Ali M., Jak Yakar, Belkıs Dinçol, and Avia Taffet. 2000. The Borders of the Appanage Kingdom of *Tarhuntašša*—A Geographical and Archaeological Assessment. *Anatolica* 26: 1–29.

Forlanini, Massimo. 1998. The Geography of Hittite Anatolia in the Light of the Recent Epigraphical Discoveries. In *Acts of the IIIrd International Congress of Hittitology*, ed. Sedat Alp and Aygül Süel, 217–22. Ankara: Nurol Matbacılık.

Harmatta, J. 1990. Herodotus, Historian of the Cimmerians and the Scythians. In *Hérodote et les peuples non Grecs: Neuf exposés suivis de discussions*, ed. Giuseppe Nenci and Olivier Reverdin, 115–30. Entretiens sur l'Antiquité Classique, tome XXV. Geneva: Fondation Hardt.

Hawkins, John David. 1998. The Land of Išuwa: The Hieroglyphic Evidence. In *Acts of the IIIrd International Congress of Hittitology*, ed. Sedat Alp and Aygül Süel, 281–95. Ankara: Nurol Matbacılık.

———. 2000. *Corpus of Hieroglyphic Luwian Inscriptions, Volume I: Inscriptions of the Iron Age*. Untersuchungen zur indogermanischen Sprach-und Kulturwissenschaft, Neue Folge 8.1. Berlin: Walter de Gruyter.

———. 2009. Cilicia, the Amuq, and Aleppo: New Light on a Dark Age. *Near Eastern Archaeology* 72.4: 164–73.

Hawkins, J. David and Donald F. Easton. 1996. A Hieroglyphic Seal from Troia. *Studia Troica* 6: 111–19.

Houwink ten Cate, Philo H. J. 1961. *The Luwian Population Groups of Lycia and Cilicia Aspera during the Hellenistic Period*. Leiden: Brill.

How, W. W. and J. Wells. 1989. *A Commentary on Herodotus in Two Volumes*. Oxford: Oxford University Press.

Morpurgo-Davies, Anna. 1982/83. Dentals, Rhotacism and Verbal Endings in the Luvian Languages. *Zeitschrift für vergleichende Sprachforschung* 96: 245–70.

Oettinger, Norbert. 2008. The Seer Mopsos (Muksas) as a Historical Figure. In *Hittites, Greeks, and Their Neighbors in Ancient Anatolia*, ed. Billie Jean Collins, Mary Bachvarova, and Ian Rutherford, 64–67. Oxford: Oxbow.

Tuna, Numan, Zeynep Aktüre, and Maggie Lynch, eds. 1998. *Thracians and Phrygians: Problems of Parallelism*. Ankara: METU, Faculty of Architecture Press.

Wäfler, Markus. 1983. Zu Status und Lage von Tabāl. In *Festschrift Annelies Kammenhuber*, ed. Gabriella Frantz-Szabó, 181–93. *Orientalia* 32.

CHAPTER 3

A HISTORY OF THE PRECLASSICAL ARCHAEOLOGY OF ANATOLIA

ROGER MATTHEWS

> In spite of its significant place in the development of local archaeological traditions Turkish archaeology, as a case study, has been largely omitted or ignored by Western scholars working on the history of archaeology.
>
> —Özdoğan (1998:121)

Introduction: A Space "In Between"?

Archaeology is the study of all aspects of the human past based on material remains, and the articulation of the scope and structure of archaeology is an achievement over the past few centuries of travelers, explorers, and academics, whose modern equivalents work within the environment of universities and state antiquities services. Although I accept that this is the definition and context of archaeology to be prioritized here, I nevertheless point to the role of nonacademic engagement as a valuable component of human approaches to the past. Within the context of the development of archaeology in Turkey, I focus on the role of explorers and academics in that story, but I stress that Turkey has another past, or multiple pasts, constructed not by travelers, university professors, and doctoral dissertations but by villagers, farmers, and families whose stories and (re)constructions of the past have a validity and a coherence that infrequently surfaces within the media of academe (Bartu Candan 2003; Dural 2007).

It is worth spending some time considering the use of various names for the landmass that today constitutes the state of Turkey or significant parts of it. Classicists generally refer to the region, particularly its western and central components, as "Asia Minor," but this term is too geographically restrictive and too historically laden to suit the context of this study. The term *Turkey*, used frequently here, allows us to include all of Turkey in Asia plus those parts of Turkey on the European side of the Bosphorus. The term *Anatolia*, also used here, is of Greek origin and thus originates from a particular sociohistorical context but today is extremely widely used by archaeologists, particularly prehistorians, including those of Turkish origin. The terms *Turkey* and *Anatolia* are used more or less interchangeably in the current chapter.

The development of archaeology in Turkey cannot be considered in isolation from the history of the discipline more broadly (Daniel 1967; Trigger 1989). The articulation of archaeology as a discipline with its own scope, aims, methods, and achievements has been a slow process. Although the archaeology of Anatolia, as a subarea of the discipline, has not been at the forefront of epistemological discussion more broadly, in recent years there has been a conscious attempt to bring Anatolian archaeology into that arena, and it is fitting that it is Turkish archaeologists who have worked most effectively at this objective (Erdur and Duru 2003; Özdoğan 1998, 2001).

Beginning with origins, the first development of archaeology in Turkey was part of a global historical process whereby post-Renaissance Western nations (particularly Germany, France, and Great Britain) engaged with other regions of the world, especially from the early nineteenth century onward. Within the context of the Middle East, this engagement took the form of a range of asymmetrical relationships, from military conquest and political absorption to mineral and labor extraction, exploitive trading, and other commercially and politically driven entanglements. The significance of Turkey in this context is that during this time much of the Middle East and beyond belonged politically to the Ottoman Empire. Thus, when we consider the early history of archaeology in regions of the Middle East outside Turkey (Yakar 1997a), such as Iraq/Mesopotamia (Lloyd 1947; Matthews 1997) or Syria (Kelly-Buccellati 1997), we must engage with the history of the Ottoman state.

Of further significance is the geophysical situation of Turkey. Frequently viewed as a land bridge between East and West or between Europe and Asia, Turkey's special status as a space "in between," physically and conceptually (Greaves 2007:2–4; Özdoğan 1998, 2007, chapter 29 in this volume; Wilhelm 2002), has significance regarding both the substantive history of society in Anatolia and as a basis for ideological constructs that have shaped the discipline itself. Thus, the sporadic Westernizing tendencies of the Ottoman state before and through the nineteenth century form the historical context within which the archaeology of Turkey as a modern discipline took its first steps.

This chapter traces the development of Anatolia's preclassical archaeology through several of its major threads, each following a chronological sequence. As with the archaeology of other regions of the Near East, discoveries have generally begun with late-period civilizations, whose remains often lie closest to the Earth's surface, followed by exploration of materials from earlier societies. In Anatolia, this sequence begins with the Hittites and other societies of historical times, before the development of knowledge of prehistoric communities of Anatolia, and I follow this historical sequence, after a consideration of the Turkish contexts for the development of preclassical archaeology.

First Steps: The Ottoman Context

The earliest stage in the history of Anatolian archaeology may be sought in the writings of travelers within the Ottoman Empire, originating from European states such as Italy, France, Germany, and Great Britain and partaking of the so-called Grand Tour (Yerasimos 1991). In concert with intellectual trends in post-Renaissance Europe, these explorations occurred within the context of Western interest in Biblical archaeology and the antiquity of the classical world. In both these arenas, Turkey had an important part to play. Such explorations are typified by those commissioned by the Dilettanti Society of London, which investigated the classical remains of southwest Turkey in the mid-eighteenth century (Slatter 1994).

Major developments in the archaeology of Turkey were begun during Ottoman times. Among them is the 1827 expedition by Friedrich Schulz to record Urartian inscriptions around Van (Lloyd 1956:27). Schulz's copies are some of the earliest records of Urartian inscriptions and were not fully understood until much later. Murdered by bandits in 1829, Schulz appears to be the first preclassical archaeologist of Turkey to lose his life in pursuit of his studies.

Initially, Turkish involvement with these developments was shaped by impact from the West (Özdoğan 1998; T. Özgüç 1982a), with the earliest Ottoman excavations taking place at classical sites, such as Sidon, Nemrut Dağı, and Alabanda. The establishment in 1846 of a collection of antiquities in İstanbul, the basis of the İstanbul Archaeology Museum, was also biased toward the Hellenistic, Roman, and Byzantine periods, in alignment with Western interests (Arık 1950, 1953).

Of major significance was the development in the later nineteenth century of a legal framework for the protection of the heritage of Turkey, an achievement of the greatest early Turkish archaeologist, Osman Hamdi Bey, curator of the Ottoman Imperial Museum. At the base of this framework were notions that all antiquities belonged to the state and excavated antiquities should stay in their home country, stipulations that clashed with the interests of Western powers, whose museums supported fieldwork to recover quantities of material to be displayed in those museums in return for their investment.

These tensions came to the fore in Heinrich Schliemann's work at Troy in the later nineteenth century when finds from the site were smuggled out of Turkey. Excavations at the mound of Hisarlık in northwest Turkey undertaken by Frank Calvert in the 1860s, Schliemann from 1871–90 (Schliemann 1875), and Wilhelm Dörpfeld from 1893–94 (Dörpfeld 1902) recovered the remains of a superimposed sequence of walled citadels spanning, as we now know, two millennia beginning in 3000 B.C.E. (Korfmann 2006), one of them identified by Schliemann as the city of Homeric Troy. The significance and authenticity of Schliemann's finds at Hisarlık persist as a subject for debate (Traill 1995).

The Turkish Republic and Archaeology

The development of archaeology in Turkey over the past eighty years is intimately connected with the country's own history. Atatürk's achievement was to formulate a national identity for Turks and Turkey that transcended both the discredited Ottoman trajectory and an emerging pan-Turkic worldview. In this exercise, archaeology was handed an important role: to explore "an ethnohistorical theory . . ., relating Sumerians and Hittites to the Turks, [that could be] integrated into the ideological framework of the new state" (Özdoğan 1998:116–17; see also Atakuman 2008; Erimtan 2008; Tanyeri-Erdemir 2006). Atatürk's impact on the development of the discipline is summarized by one of its greatest practitioners: "As a science and as a field of study and research, archaeology in Turkey owes its emergence, development and establishment to Atatürk" (T. Özgüç 1982a:xv). In a cable sent in 1931 to Prime Minister İsmet İnönü, Atatürk promotes a vision for the future of Turkey's past:

> More students should be trained in archaeology and greater care should be taken for the exploration of works and matchless treasures of ancient civilizations buried in almost all corners of our country, for their scientific preservation and classification, and for the restoration of monuments fallen into ruin due to the persistent neglect by the previous generations. (T. Özgüç 1982a:xvii)

In practical terms, this meant the despatch of Turkish students to universities in Europe, the 1931 foundation of the Turkish Historical Society, and a flourishing of fieldwork and research in archaeology and philology (T. Özgüç 1982a). Turkish academe welcomed German professors fleeing the 1930s Nazi regime, an act that contributed to the intellectual climate of Turkey through the mid-twentieth century, in archaeology and philology as in other disciplines (Darga 2001). Since the origins of the Turkish Republic, there has been a strong tradition of the involvement of women in archaeology, which continues to this day (Özdoğan 1998:119; for women throughout the Anatolian past, see Renda 1993).

Arguably the most important figure in the development of Turkish archaeology in the twentieth century, apart from Atatürk, is Hamit Koşay (1897–1984), whose career included the foundation of museums in Ankara, directorship of Turkey's museums, and in 1945 the directorship-general of the Department of Antiquities and Museums (Yakar 1997b). Among his many projects, Koşay directed excavations at Ahlatlıbel near Ankara, Kumtepe near Troy, Pazarlı in Çorum, and campaigns at Alaca Höyük, resulting in spectacular discoveries and an impressive publication output.

The structures, practices, and outputs of archaeology in Turkey are now firmly established. Turkish universities have played a major role, especially those of İstanbul (Belli 2001) and Ankara (Alparslan 2001). At the same time, the great museums of Turkey—notably the İstanbul Archaeology Museum and the Ankara Museum of Anatolian Civilizations—and many regional museums function as centers for fieldwork, research, conservation, and academic activity, recognized in the achievement of the Museum of Anatolian Civilizations in becoming European Museum of the Year in 1997.

The role of archaeologists working in Turkey has become regularized and regulated, through practice and a legal framework overseen by the Ministry of Culture and Tourism, and its Directorate-General of Monuments and Museums. Under their auspices, an annual symposium is held in Turkey, published each year in the series *Kazı Sonuçları Toplantısı*, *Araştırma Sonuçları Toplantısı*, and *Arkeometri Sonuçları Toplantısı*. Few countries can match this level of activity and output in their routine archaeological practice. Also impressive is the independent project Türkiye Arkeolojik Yerleşmeleri (TAY; Archaeological Settlements of Turkey), which since 1993 has made use of online and conventional media to produce site catalogues (Harmankaya and Erdoğu 2002; Harmankaya and Tanındı 1996; Harmankaya, Tanındı, and Özbaşaran 1997, 1998; Kozbe et al. 2008) and much related information (see http://www.tayproject.org).

Non-Turkish archaeologists continue to play their part in concert with Turkish colleagues. Much activity is channeled through major institutes resident in İstanbul and Ankara, including those from the United Kingdom (Matthews 1998), the United States (Cross 1997), Germany (Koenigs 1997), France (Yon 1997), and The Netherlands.

(Re-)Creating the Hittites and the Neo-Hittites

The reconstruction of Hittite society through archaeology is one of the greatest achievements of the study of Turkey's past (for histories of Hittite archaeology, see Collins 2007; Gorny 2002; Gurney 1952; Jean 2001; Seeher 2002a; Yakar 1997a). The 1834 explorations of Charles Texier in central Anatolia initiated investigation of this archaeological *terra incognita*. Texier encountered, without appreciating their real antiquity, the Hittite sites of Boğazköy-Ḫattuša and nearby Yazılıkaya. William Hamilton in 1836–37 (Hamilton 1842) added Alaca Höyük, Gavur Kalesi, and Eflatun Pınar to the list of known sites that came to be recognized as Hittite. These discoveries resonated with decipherment of Egyptian and Assyrian records that revealed the existence of a kingdom of Kheta or Ḫatti contemporary with Ramesses II (thirteenth century B.C.E.) and Tiglath-pileser I (twelfth–eleventh centuries B.C.E.).

The 1870s were of major importance for the rediscovery of the Hittites, a people known from Old Testament sources but whose material traces had been lost for millennia. In 1876 A. H. Sayce, at the Society for Biblical Archaeology, proposed that inscribed stone blocks found by travelers such as Burckhardt, Johnson and Jessup, and Wright at Hama and Aleppo were artifacts of the Hittite kingdom (Gurney 1952:2). Sayce linked these blocks found at Syrian sites, which we now know as Hittite hieroglyphic dating to the Neo-Hittite period of the Iron Age, with inscriptions in Anatolia at İvriz and others found by Texier and Hamilton at the central Anatolian sites of Boğazköy-Ḫattuša (see Harmanşah, chapter 28 in this volume), Yazılıkaya, and elsewhere. We now know that these central Anatolian sites are not contemporary with the Syrian Neo-Hittite sites but date to the preceding Late Bronze Age. In an 1880 paper to the Society for Biblical Archaeology, Sayce assigned all the central Anatolian inscribed monuments and those from Syria to the Hittites, a claim supported in William Wright's book, *The Empire of the Hittites* (Wright 1886; see also Collins 2007:4).

In 1876 a visit by George Smith of the British Museum to Jerablus-Carchemish on the Euphrates River, at the border between Turkey and Syria, encouraged the museum to support excavations there from 1878 to 1881 (Smith himself died in Aleppo in 1876), during which further inscribed, sculpted stone blocks were recovered for the British Museum (Lloyd 1956:20–21). Excavation techniques followed the heavy-handed method of tunneling along the stone-clad faces of monumental walls, as developed in the excavation of Assyrian palaces in northern Iraq in the 1840s (Lloyd 1947).

As the nineteenth century ended, travelers to Turkey included William Ramsay and David Hogarth in 1890 and J. G. Anderson in 1898. These tours comprised activities such as copying of inscriptions at Boğazköy-Ḫattuša and Yazılıkaya by K. Humann and O. Puchstein in 1882–83, discovery of the first Hittite clay tablets at Boğazköy-Ḫattuša, and exposure of Hittite sculptures at Alaca Höyük by Ernest Chantre in 1893–94. German excavations in 1888–92 at Zincirli (ancient Sam'al) recovered a citadel and sculpted, inscribed blocks typical of the Neo-Hittite period (Lloyd 1956:21–22). By 1900 there was sufficient material for Leopold Messerschmidt to compile a corpus of Hittite inscriptions containing ninety-six monuments with many seals and seal impressions; in 1903 he produced a monograph titled *The Hittites*, which attempted a reconstruction of Hittite history and a review of sites and monuments (Messerschmidt 1900, 1903).

Hittite studies received a further boost through the 1887 discovery of the Tell El-Amarna tablets in Egypt, which demonstrated that during the mid-fourteenth century B.C.E. the king of Ḫatti dealt on equal terms with pharaohs Akhenaton and Amenophis III. In 1902 Norwegian J. A. Knudtzon suggested that two of the tablets, one of them addressed to the king of Arzawa, were written in a language that appeared to belong to the Indo-European family, a suggestion that met with little approval (Gurney 1952:5; and see Beckman, chapter 22 in this volume).

It was clear that excavations on the Anatolian plateau would shed light on the origins of the late Hittite kingdoms attested in the sites and inscriptions of the Turco-Syrian region. The most important development was the granting of the concession for excavations at Boğazköy-Ḫattuša to the German Oriental Institute, which began work at the site in 1906 under the direction of Hugo Winckler in collaboration with Theodore Makridi, the director of the İstanbul Archaeological Museum. In 1905 Winckler had visited Boğazköy-Ḫattuša with Makridi, and apparently the intervention of Kaiser Wilhelm II swayed the Ottoman authorities in refusing a permit application made by British archaeologist John Garstang in favor of the German bid (Collins 2007:5).

The excavations at Boğazköy-Ḫattuša in 1906–12 were an astonishing success, recovering some 10,000 clay tablets, plans of state buildings, including the royal acropolis at Büyükkale, the Great Temple, and a city wall with five gates (Puchstein 1912; Winckler 1909) (figure 3.1). Destruction by fire indicated a violent end to the city's life but also served to bake the clay tablets for better preservation in the ground. The texts were largely written in the still undeciphered language attested in the two Amarna documents studied by Knudtzon, but others were in the Akkadian language well known from Assyrian and Babylonian texts (Gurney 1952:6), and they revealed that this was indeed the capital of the Land of Ḫatti. Dating of the

Figure 3.1. View of Boğazköy-Ḫattuša.

documents and the associated architecture was facilitated by the discovery of a text that recorded the Hittite version of a treaty between Ramesses II and the king of Ḫatti, dated to the twenty-first year of the pharaoh (Gurney 1952:6).

The results from Boğazköy-Ḫattuša established the existence on the Anatolian plateau of a kingdom of the mid- to late second millennium B.C.E. (today called the Late Bronze Age), which competed on equal terms with the states of Egypt, Assyria, and Babylonia. Furthermore, the kingdom of Ḫatti had clearly come to an abrupt, violent end at about 1200 B.C.E., and the material remains from the Turco-Syrian region, including Carchemish, belonged largely to a succeeding period in the earlier first millennium B.C.E. Also demonstrated was continuity in the Hittite hieroglyphic script, attested at Boğazköy-Ḫattuša in rock-cut form at Nişan Taşı and on royal seal impressions on tablets, these late second millennium B.C.E. instances being comparable to the early first millennium B.C.E. examples known from Carchemish, Zincirli, and other sites (Hawkins 2000). The building blocks of a Late Bronze Age and Iron Age chronology started to fall into place.

Hittite developments were summarized in two studies: John Garstang's *The Land of the Hittites* (1910), and Bedřich Hrozný's 1915 study of Hittite grammar, which reiterated Knudtzon's identification of the Hittite language as Indo-European (Gurney 1952:9). Philological studies on Hittite texts by scholars, including F. Sommer (1920), L. Delaporte (1929), and E. H. Sturtevant (1933), constructed a solid understanding of the languages of the Hittite texts. Knowledge of the Hittites was brilliantly synthesized in the study by A. Götze, *Kleinasien* (1933).

Excavations were resumed at Boğazköy-Ḫattuša in 1931 by Kurt Bittel (Collins 2007:12–16; Güterbock 1997) and have continued as a German project, under successive directors Peter Neve, Jürgen Seeher, and Andreas Schachner (see Mielke, chapter 48 in this volume). Excavations have investigated the citadel, the Lower and Upper Cities, and Yazılıkaya (Bittel 1970; Neve 1993; Seeher 2002b). At the same time, Hittite levels were encountered through the 1930s and '40s at Tarsus, Yümük Tepe near Mersin, and Alaca Höyük (Gurney 1952:13). Hittite discoveries at Alaca, thirty kilometers northeast of Boğazköy-Ḫattuša, began in 1861 with clearance by George Perrot of buildings adjacent to the two sphinxes that survived above ground (Lloyd 1956:36), followed by excavations conducted by Chantre in 1863, Winckler in 1906, and Makridi in 1907. A feature of this research was the input from Turkish archaeologists, stimulated by Atatürk's vision of an Anatolian integration of Hittite and Turkish identities (Özdoğan 1998:116–19; T. Özgüç 1982a, 2002a;), including the 1931 foundation of the Turkish Historical Society, which was subsequently sponsor and publisher of many studies into the Hittite and other periods of the Anatolian past.

Meanwhile, from 1907 to 1911 Garstang excavated Coba Höyük at Sakçegözü, near Gaziantep, recovering sculpted slabs from a palace in the familiar Neo-Hittite style (Garstang 1937). Similarly, in 1911–14, a second British Museum expedition to Carchemish, led by R. Campbell-Thompson, D. G. Hogarth, Leonard Woolley, and T. E. Lawrence, recovered further examples of sculpted slabs and remains of a citadel with decorated gateways (Hogarth 1914; Woolley 1921, 1952). Some of this material traveled to the British Museum, but removal of more sculpted blocks was prevented by the outbreak of war in 1914, and many pieces were damaged through exposure until their removal to the Museum of Anatolian Civilizations in Ankara.

Further hieroglyphic inscriptions from Carchemish encouraged attempts to decipher their language, hampered by the lack of substantial bilingual texts. At that time the only example was on a metal seal plate, the "Boss of Tarkondemos," comprising just ten cuneiform and six hieroglyphic signs (Gurney 1952:8). A fuller deciphering of the Hittite hieroglyphic inscriptions had to wait until the discovery in 1947 of a lengthy bilingual text inscribed on sculpted blocks at Karatepe in the Taurus foothills by the Ceyhan River (Lloyd 1956:46–47, 178). Here the text is given in Phoenician on one side of a corridor, while the other side displays the same content in Hittite hieroglyphic (Çambel 2001), thus enabling almost complete decipherment. Further discoveries of Neo-Hittite materials were made at Arslantepe near Malatya on the Euphrates from 1932 by L. Delaporte and continued by Schaeffer for the French Institute at İstanbul, where more Neo-Hittite sculptures were recovered (Delaporte 1940). Hittite hieroglyphic inscriptions are collected in the magisterial publication of Hawkins (2000).

Since World War II, the pace of development of Hittite and Neo-Hittite archaeology has quickened. Apart from ongoing work at Boğazköy-Ḫattuša, resumed in 1952, there has been investigation of other regions of the Hittite state. Excavations from 1973 to 1981 by Tahsin Özgüç at Maşat near Zile uncovered a Hittite palace and the first significant archive of Hittite texts from outside Boğazköy-Ḫattuša, illustrating life in an outpost and identifying the site as ancient Tapigga (Alp 1991a, 1991b; T. Özgüç 1978, 1982b). Excavation in 1966–67 of a Hittite temple and other structures at İnandık in Çankırı province followed the discovery of a cultic relief vessel (T. Özgüç 1988), paralleled by a more recent find of a vessel at Hüseyindede Tepesi near Çorum showing bull-leaping scenes (Sipahi 2000). To the west, Seton Lloyd's excavations in the 1950s at Beycesultan near Denizli recovered a palace and other materials of second millennium B.C.E. date (Lloyd 1972; Lloyd and Mellaart 1965).

Other major Hittite sites include Ortaköy-Šapinuwa (Süel 2002), where monumental buildings and an archive of some 3,000 texts have been retrieved, revealing a strong Hurrian component. At Kuşaklı-Šarišša, near Sivas, monumental buildings, fortifications, and archives of texts are receiving ongoing study and prompt publication (Müller-Karpe 2002), whereas at the northern limits of the Hittite state investigations of Oymaağaç-Vezirköprü in Samsun province are making strides regarding the cultic city of Nerik (Czichon and Klinger 2005; for Ortaköy and Kuşaklı, see Mielke, chapter 48 in this volume). Survey and excavation at smaller sites, such as the spring-shrine of Eflatun Pınar (Özenir 1998) (figure 3.2) and the sacred site of Gavur Kalesi (Lumsden 2002), have added further elements to the overall picture of a Late Bronze Age state devoted to cultic practice (see Harmanşah, chapter 28 in this volume). Characterizing these investigations is the employment of a range of techniques in the field and laboratory. Regional surveys of Hittite landscape and settlement across most regions of Anatolia have added to our understanding of demography, communications, and land use (Glatz and Matthews 2005; Matthews and Glatz 2009). An associated development is that of underwater archaeology, best

Figure 3.2. View of Eflatun Pınar.

illustrated in the Late Bronze Age shipwreck at Uluburun with its rich inventory of cargo and artifacts (Yalçın, Pulak, and Slotta 2005).

On the basis of these discoveries (and many others too numerous to mention), there has been a flow of synthetic publications addressing the Hittites, building on the classic 1933 work by Götze. Books by Gurney (1952), Lloyd (1956), Macqueen (1975), and Bryce (1998), and edited overview volumes such as Yener and Hoffner (2002), Hopkins (2002), and T. Özgüç (2002b; see also Beal, chapter 26, Seeher, chapter 16, Glatz, chapter 40, and van den Hout, chapter 41 in this volume), are just a few of the highlights. Melding archaeological and textual evidence has been the speciality of those who have essayed the historical geography of the Hittites, with overviews in Garstang and Gurney (1959), updated by Forlanini and Marazzi (1986). Understanding of the Hittite language has developed to the stage where reference grammars can safely be produced (Hoffner and Melchert 2008; and see Beckman, chapter 22 in this volume).

Anatolia's First Literate Society: Merchants of the Middle Bronze Age

Cuneiform texts on clay tablets, written in Akkadian, came to the attention of travelers in Turkey in the late nineteenth century (Michel 2003:v), rumored to originate from the mound of Kültepe, near Kayseri. Explorations at Kültepe by

Winckler in 1906 and by Hrozný in 1925 exposed monumental structures but failed to recover the desired texts. Eventually villagers revealed that the texts were coming from fields adjacent to the mound, not from the mound itself. Thereafter Hrozný recovered about 1,000 texts from houses that formed a commercial colony of Assyrians from the distant city of Assur on the Tigris River in Upper Mesopotamia, living in a *kārum* known as Kaneš, dated to the first three centuries of the second millennium B.C.E., or the Middle Bronze Age as we know it (Lloyd 1956:31–32, 47–48). Since 1948 there have been annual excavations at Kültepe-Kaneš, directed by Tahsin Özgüç for the Turkish Historical Society, and now by Fikri Kulakoğlu (see Kulakoğlu, chapter 47 in this volume). Much has been learned about the Anatolian kingdom whose palace and temples adorn the mound and about the Assyrian merchants living beside the mound (T. Özgüç 2003). Some 22,300 cuneiform texts have been recovered, of which only a few hundred have been published (Michel 2003:v; and see Michel, chapter 13 in this volume).

Within Anatolia, more Middle Bronze Age cuneiform texts have been found at a few sites, including Boğazköy-Ḫattuša, Alişar (possibly ancient Amkuwa/Ankuwa) (figure 3.3), and Acemhöyük (Michel 2003). At Acemhöyük (possibly ancient Burušḫattum), two heavily burned palaces of Middle Bronze Age date have been excavated in work directed by Nimet Özgüç (N. Özgüç 1966) and more recently by Aliye Öztan. Further south at Karahöyük near Konya, excavations by Sedat Alp uncovered Middle Bronze Age buildings and seals and seal impressions (Alp 1994) but no texts—they are likely to lie in the undiscovered *kārum* adjacent to the mound, as at Kültepe-Kaneš.

Figure 3.3. View of Alişar Höyük.

Investigating the Iron Age: Phrygia, Lydia, and Biainili/Urartu

During the sensational decades of the late nineteenth and early twentieth centuries, while archaeologists were encountering the remains of the Hittites and Neo-Hittites, other lost civilizations of Anatolia came to light: the Phrygians in central and west Anatolia and Urartu around Lake Van. In 1900 attention fell on Yassıhöyük in the Sakarya valley west of Ankara where German brothers Alfred and Gustav Körte explored Iron Age Phrygian remains at what was and is believed to be the Phrygian capital of Gordion (Körte and Körte 1904). They had been alerted to the site in 1893 by engineers on the nearby Berlin–Baghdad railway (Sams 2005). The Körte brothers uncovered buildings probably of sixth century B.C.E. date and investigated several of the eighty-five or so burial tumuli in the environs. From these they recovered material demonstrating connections with the Greek world of the late seventh and sixth centuries B.C.E. via the medium of the kingdom of Lydia, by then in control of territory that had earlier been Phrygia. A new series of campaigns at Gordion lasted from 1950 to 1973 under the direction of Rodney Young for the University of Pennsylvania Museum (Sams 2005), during which strides were made in establishing a chronology of Phrygian society through the Iron Age (Kealhofer 2005). The famous Midas Mound was also excavated, now known to date too early for Midas and therefore perhaps belonging to his father, Gordias (Sams 2005:20). Recent work at the site, directed by Ken Sams and Mary Voigt since 1988, has refined our understanding of Phrygian chronology as well as exploring pre- and post-Phrygian occupation (Voigt 2005, and see Voigt, chapter 50 in this volume).

Further Phrygian structures with classic tiled decoration were excavated by Koşay at Pazarlı near Ankara Koşay (1941), while in 1937–39 the French Institute excavated at Midas City in the Phrygian highlands (Berndt 2002). Excavation of Phrygian levels elsewhere, including Boğazköy-Ḫattuša, Alişar, Alaca Höyük, and Gavur Kalesi, added to the picture of Phrygian society (Lloyd 1956:192–96). In the west, investigations of the Lydian capital, Sardis, began in the nineteenth century and since 1959 have been overseen by the Archaeological Exploration of Sardis, a grouping of American academic institutions (Greenewalt 1997; and see Greenewalt, chapter 52, and Roller, chapter 25 in this volume). Like the Phrygians, the Lydians made considerable use of massive burial tumuli, as at Bin Tepe, many of which have been excavated, legally or otherwise. Some of the most spectacular discoveries have come from illicitly excavated tombs in the central-western region of Turkey (Özgen and Öztürk 1996).

Regarding Biainili/Urartu, it will be recalled that as early as 1827 Friedrich Schulz had been commissioned to examine the cuneiform inscriptions cut into the rock-face near Van (for a history of exploration of Urartu, see Zimansky 1998:286–90). The posthumous publication of Schulz's copies in the 1840 *Journal Asiatique* stimulated visits to the region by A. H. Layard and others (Lloyd 1956:28, 184). Once it had been established that the same text was repeated in three different languages, two of which could be identified as Assyrian and Old Persian, it was only a matter of time before A. H. Sayce and others succeeded in deciphering the third language by the late nineteenth century. The inscriptions revealed that Van had been the main city of a powerful state of eastern Anatolia and beyond, and they provided information on the succession of their kings and their fractious relations with neighbors to the south, Assyria, during the ninth through seventh centuries B.C.E. This state was known by the Assyrians as Urartu, from which the name Ararat is derived, but it called itself Biainili, from which the name Van is derived (see Zimansky, chapter 24, and Khatchadourian, chapter 20 in this volume).

Destructive excavations at Toprakkale near Van were undertaken by Hormuzd Rassam in 1879–80 for the British Museum (Rassam 1897:377–78). Rassam uncovered a stone temple, within which were bronze shields with cuneiform inscriptions and decorated with animals and other motifs. Some of these objects went to the British Museum, but in Rassam's frequent absence, most of them were disposed of locally, and the site suffered from illicit attention (Lloyd 1956:186). Further excavations at the site by German and Russian scholars from 1898 emphasized the significance of Toprakkale as a foundation of the king Rusa, son of Argišti, of early seventh century B.C.E. date (Sagona and Zimansky 2009:329–30).

A deeper understanding of the kingdom of Biainili/Urartu had to wait until the second half of the twentieth century. Surveys in the mid-1950s by Charles Burney (Burney 1957) led the way, followed by excavations at Urartian sites such as Altın Tepe by Tahsin Özgüç, at Çavuştepe by Afif Erzen (Erzen 1988), at Patnos by R. Temizer and Kemal Balkan, and at Adilcevaz by Emin Bilgiç (Zimansky 1998). Ongoing excavations at Ayanis by Altan Çilingiroğlu are revealing a citadel with a richly endowed temple (Çilingiroğlu and Salvini 2001; and see Çilingiroğlu, chapter 49 in this volume) and are taking innovative approaches to the study of the lower town (Stone 2005). Understanding of the Urartian language, occurring in monumental inscriptions in stone and on a few clay tablets, is now advanced (Wilhelm 2008; and see Zimansky, chapter 24 in this volume).

Making a Prehistory for the Anatolian Plateau and Beyond

The study of Anatolia's prehistory is the youngest member of Turkey's archaeological family, maturing over the past half century. Chance encounters with prehistoric remains were made during excavation of multiperiod sites, commencing with Schliemann at Troy, where architecture and treasures of what we now call the Early Bronze Age came from levels Troy I–IV (Efe 2006). From 1908 Garstang excavated at Coba Höyük near Sakçegözü, east of Gaziantep, trenching below the Neo-Hittite palace into early prehistoric levels (Garstang 1937).

Involvement of the University of Chicago Oriental Institute began in 1926 with survey and excavations directed by Hans von der Osten, including the first stratigraphic sequence from a multiperiod mound in Anatolia, at Alişar Höyük, which spans the Chalcolithic and Early Bronze Ages (von der Osten 1937) (figure 3.3). Through the 1930s, Turkish excavations at sites in the Ankara region, including Ahlatlıbel, Etiyokuşu, and Karaoğlan, increased the body of Early Bronze Age material, just as Bittel's investigations at Boğazköy-Ḫattuša reached pre-Hittite occupation beneath the palace on the citadel (Lloyd 1956:38–39). Koşay's excavations from 1935 onward at Alaca Höyük, penetrating Hittite levels, uncovered thirteen "royal" tombs of the later part of the Early Bronze Age, whose spectacular material remains form a highlight of the Museum of Anatolian Civilizations (Koşay 1953). Prehistoric connections between western Anatolia and the Aegean world were targeted by Winifred Lamb through excavations in the 1930s at Kusura near Afyon Karahisar (Gill 2000; Lamb 1936), whereas Bittel and Otto excavated prehistoric levels at Demircihöyük near Eskişehir (Bittel and Otto 1939; later excavated further by Korfmann 1983).

On the Mediterranean coast, Garstang's 1930s excavations at Yümük Tepe near Mersin recovered a prehistoric sequence from the Neolithic onward (Garstang 1953), complemented by a multiperiod sequence from nearby Gözlü Kule at Tarsus (Goldman 1950; work continues today, see Caneva and Sevin 2004). Until the late 1950s, the finds from Sakçegözü, Mersin, and Tarsus provided the only evidence for Neolithic and Chalcolithic presence in Turkey, all located at the southern and southeastern fringes of the plateau, apart from some evidence for a Chalcolithic presence at Alişar. On the plateau itself archaeologists had begun to find hints of a pre–Bronze Age presence, dated to what was called the Copper Age, now regarded as an early phase of the Early Bronze Age; work in this period was undertaken by Özgüç at Dündartepe near Samsun, Koşay and Akok at Karaz near Erzurum and at Büyük Güllücek near Alaca, Blegen at Kumtepe near Troy, Bittel at Fikirtepe on the Bosphorus, and Lloyd and Gökçe at Polatlı near Ankara (Lloyd 1956:49, 60–61, 92–96). Further investigations in the 1950s by Özgüç and Akok at Horoztepe, Koşay and Akok at Mahmatlar, Temizer at Kayapınar, and Alp at Konya-Karahöyük (Yakar 1997a:66), coupled with Burney's surveys of north Anatolia (Burney 1956), added increasing detail to the Early Bronze Age picture.

However, by the mid-1950s no convincing traces of communities on the plateau between the Palaeolithic and the Late Chalcolithic had been encountered. It appeared therefore that "the greater part of modern Turkey, and especially the region more correctly described as Anatolia, shows no sign whatever of habitation during the Neolithic period" (Lloyd 1956:53), and that during the Chalcolithic "Anatolia still remained a *terra incognita*, of whose very existence the Chalcolithic people seem only to have become aware during the very last years of their existence" (Lloyd 1956:58). As Lloyd was writing these words, this unpeopled picture of Anatolia was about to be dramatically changed by the activities of one of his colleagues, James Mellaart.

Lloyd's excavations in the 1950s at Beycesultan in Denizli province had yielded a sequence stretching back into the Late Chalcolithic (Mellaart 1998a), and it was during these campaigns that Mellaart's attention turned to the nearby site of Hacılar, where he excavated from 1957 to 1960. Mellaart's earlier surveys of southwest Anatolia had encountered much material that needed verification from excavated sequences. Hacılar appears to have been occupied in the Aceramic Neolithic Phase, the Late Neolithic, and the Chalcolithic (Mellaart 1970, 1998b), and its excavation stimulated a new interest in the prehistory of the plateau that has maintained its momentum. Further Neolithic projects got under way, as at Canhasan near Karaman, directed by David French, who can be credited with developing a modern scientific methodology to excavation in Turkey, aimed at maximum recovery of material remains, including charred plants and micro-fauna, through flotation and wet-sieving (French 1998). Other work by Solecki and Bordaz at the sites of Suberde and Erbaba in the Lake District encountered further Neolithic settlements (Duru 1999).

Far to the southeast, excavations between 1963 and 1991 at Çayönü, initially by Halet Çambel and Robert Braidwood, and more recently by Mehmet Özdoğan, revealed a sequence of occupation from the Aceramic Neolithic onwards (Çambel and Braidwood 1980). The full glory of Anatolia's Neolithic past came to light with Mellaart's excavations through the 1960s at Çatal Höyük, near Konya, where elaborate buildings of the later Neolithic were uncovered (Mellaart 1967, 1998c), followed by investigations by Ian Hodder (2006, and see Hodder, chapter 43 in this volume). Meanwhile, Ian Todd's survey of central Anatolia identified at Aşıklı near Aksaray an Aceramic Neolithic precursor to Çatal, later excavated by Ufuk Esin (Esin and Harmankaya 1999; Todd 1998; and see Özbaşaran, chapter 5 in this volume).

The pace of research into Anatolian prehistory, as with historical archaeology, has accelerated since the late 1960s, at least in part due to the multinational rescue programs of survey and excavation in advance of dam construction along the Euphrates and Tigris Rivers (Algaze et al. 1991). There is not enough space here to enumerate the archaeological discoveries and interpretations emanating from these activities and from long-term fieldwork projects at a host of sites across Turkey, conducted by both Turkish and non-Turkish archaeologists (many of whom are authors in this volume). Instead, I guide the reader to synthetic publications that bring the story up to date regarding the prehistory of Turkey. (For Anatolian prehistory generally, see Gorny 1997; Joukowsky 1996; Sagona and Zimansky 2009; Yakar 1991. For the Palaeolithic, see Kuhn 2002. For the Neolithic, see Düring 2006; Gérard and Thissen 2002; Lichter 2007; Mellaart 1975; Özdoğan and Başgelen 1999 [and see Öbaşaran, chapter 5, Rosenberg and Erim-Özdoğan, chapter 6, and Özdoğan, chapter 29 in this volume]. For the Chalcolithic and Early Bronze Age, see Schoop 2005; Yakar 1985, 1991, 1994; [and see Schoop, chapter 7, Düring, chapter 36, Özbal, chapter 8, and Palumbi, chapter 9 in this volume].)

Conclusion

In sum, the material and intellectual riches of Turkey's preclassical past have been steadily investigated through an increasing range of approaches and techniques over the past two centuries or so, with especially significant developments in the past fifty years. In 2008 no fewer than 134 excavation projects and more than 100 surface survey projects were at work in Turkey, covering all periods of the Anatolian past. By these means, long-forgotten societies and dead civilizations have had life breathed into them, and the importance of Turkey's preclassical past has come to be recognized in the global arena. At the same time, the discipline has developed into a modern, scientific, and reflexive engagement that can hold its head high among other regional archaeologies of the world.

REFERENCES

Algaze, Guillermo, Ray Breuninger, Christopher Lightfoot, and Michael Rosenberg. 1991. The Tigris-Euphrates Archaeological Reconnaissance Project: A Preliminary Report on the 1989–1990 Seasons. *Anatolica* 17: 175–240.

Alp, Sedat. 1991a. *Hethitische Briefe aus Maşat-Höyük*. Ankara: Türk Tarih Kurumu Basımevi.

———. 1991b. *Hethitische Keilschrifttafeln aus Maşat-Höyük*. Ankara: Türk Tarih Kurumu Basımevi.

———. 1994. *Zylinder-und Stempelsiegel aus Karahöyük bei Konya*. Ankara: Türk Tarih Kurumu Basımevi.

Alparslan, Meltem D. 2001. İki başkent, iki serüven: Ankara ve Hattuşa. In *Boğazköy'den Karatepe'ye. Hititbilim ve Hitit Dünyasının Keşfi*, ed. Éric Jean, 72–85. İstanbul: Yapı Kredi.

Arık, Remzi. 1950. *Les fouilles archéologiques en Turquie*. Ankara: Milli Eğitim.

———. 1953. *Türk Müzeciliğine bir Bakış*. İstanbul: Milli Eğitim.

Atakuman, Çiğdem. 2008. Cradle or Crucible: Anatolia and Archaeology in the Early Years of the Turkish Republic (1923–1938). *Journal of Social Archaeology* 8: 214–35.

Bartu Candan, Ayfer. 2003. Yerel ve Küresel Arasında Arkeoloji: Kamusal Arkeoloji ve Çatalhöyük Örneği. In *Arkeoloji: Niye? Nasıl? Ne İçin?*, ed. Oğuz Erdur and Güneş Duru, 255–58. İstanbul: Ege Yayınları.

Belli, Oktay, ed. 2001. *İstanbul University's Contributions to Archaeology in Turkey, 1932–2000*. İstanbul: İstanbul University.

Berndt, Dietrich. 2002. *Midasstadt in Phrygien*. Mainz am Rhein: Philipp von Zabern.

Bittel, Kurt. 1970. *Hattusha: The Capital of the Hittites*. New York: Oxford University Press.

Bittel, Kurt and Heinz Otto. 1939. *Demirci-Hüyük: Eine vorgeschichtliche Siedlung an der phrygisch-bithynischen Grenze*. Berlin: Deutsches Archäologische Institut İstanbul.

Bryce, Trevor. 1998. *The Kingdom of the Hittites*. Oxford: Oxford University Press.

Burney, Charles A. 1956. Northern Anatolia before Classical Times. *Anatolian Studies* 6: 179–203.

———. 1957. Urartian Fortresses and Towns in the Van Region. *Anatolian Studies* 7: 37–53.
Caneva, Isabella and Veli Sevin, eds. 2004. *Mersin-Yumuktepe. A Reappraisal.* Lecce: Congedo Editore.
Collins, Billie Jean. 2007. *The Hittites and Their World.* Atlanta: Society of Biblical Literature.
Cross, Toni M. 1997. American Research Institute in Turkey. In *The Oxford Encyclopedia of Archaeology in the Near East*, ed. Eric M. Meyers, vol. 1, 92. Oxford: Oxford University Press.
Czichon, Rainer and Jörg Klinger. 2005. Auf der Suche nach der hethitischen Kultstadt Nerik. *Alter Orient* 6: 18–19.
Çambel, Halet. 2001. *Corpus of Hieroglyphic Luwian Inscriptions. Volume II. Karatepe-Aslantaş.* Berlin: de Gruyter.
Çambel, Halet and Robert J. Braidwood, eds. 1980. *Prehistoric Research in Southeastern Anatolia.* İstanbul: İstanbul University.
Çilingiroğlu, Altan and Mirjo Salvini, eds. 2001. *Ayanis I. Ten Years' Excavations at Rusahinili Eiduru-kai 1989–1998.* Rome: Istituto per gli Studi Micenei ed Egeo-Anatolici.
Daniel, Glyn. 1967. *The Origins and Growth of Archaeology.* Harmondsworth: Penguin.
Darga, Muhibbe. 2001. İstanbul Üniversitesi'nde hititoloji'nin ilk yılları. In *Boğazköy'den Karatepe'ye. Hititbilim ve Hitit Dünyasının Keşfi*, ed. Éric Jean, 44–61. İstanbul: Yapı Kredi.
Delaporte, Louis J. 1929. *Éléments de la grammaire hittite.* Paris: Maisonneuve.
———. 1940. *Malatya. La porte des lions.* Paris: Boccard.
Dörpfeld, Wilhelm. 1902. *Troja und Ilion.* Athens: Beck and Barth.
Dural, Sadrettin. 2007. *Protecting Çatalhöyük. Memoir of an Archaeological Site Guard.* Walnut Creek: Left Coast.
Duru, Refik. 1999. The Neolithic of the Lake District. In *Neolithic in Turkey. The Cradle of Civilization*, ed. Mehmet Özdoğan and Nezih Başgelen, 165–91. İstanbul: Arkeoloji ve Sanat Yayınları.
Düring, Bleda S. 2006. *Constructing Communities. Clustered Neighbourhood Settlements of the Central Anatolian Neolithic ca. 8500–5500 Cal. BC.* Leiden: Nederlands Instituut voor Het Nabije Oosten.
Efe, Turan. 2006. Anatolische Wurzeln—Troia und die frühe Bronzezeit im westen Kleinasiens. In *Troia. Archäologie eines Siedlungshügels und seiner Landschaft*, ed. Manfred O. Korfmann, 15–28. Mainz am Rhein: Philipp von Zabern.
Erdur, Oğuz and Güneş Duru, eds. 2003. *Arkeoloji: Niye? Nasıl? Ne İçin?* İstanbul: Ege Yayınları.
Erimtan, Can. 2008. Hittites, Ottomans and Turks: Ağaoğlu Ahmed Bey and the Kemalist Construction of Turkish Nationhood in Anatolia. *Anatolian Studies* 58: 141–71.
Erzen, Afif. 1988. *Çavuştepe I.* Ankara: Türk Tarih Kurumu Basımevi.
Esin, Ufuk and Savaş Harmankaya. 1999. Aşıklı. In *Neolithic in Turkey. The Cradle of Civilization*, ed. Mehmet Özdoğan and Nezih Başgelen, 115–32. İstanbul: Arkeoloji ve Sanat Yayınları.
Forlanini, Massimo and Massimiliano Marazzi. 1986. *Atlante storico del Vicino Oriente Antico. Fascicolo 4.3. Anatolia: L'Impero Hittita.* Rome: Università degli Studi di Roma "La Sapienza."
French, David H. 1998. *Canhasan Sites 1. Canhasan I: Stratigraphy and Structures.* London: British Institute of Archaeology at Ankara.

Garstang, John. 1910. *The Land of the Hittites*. London: Constable.
———. 1937. Third Report on the Excavations at Sakje-Geuzi 1908–22. *Liverpool Annals of Archaeology and Anthropology* 24: 119–40.
———. 1953. *Prehistoric Mersin. Yümük Tepe in Southern Turkey*. Oxford: Clarendon.
Garstang, John and Oliver R. Gurney. 1959. *The Geography of the Hittite Empire*. London: British Institute of Archaeology at Ankara.
Gérard, Frédéric and Laurens Thissen, eds. 2002. *The Neolithic of Central Anatolia*. İstanbul: Ege Yayınları.
Gill, David W. J. 2000. "A Rich and Promising Site": Winifred Lamb (1894–1963), Kusura and Anatolian Archaeology. *Anatolian Studies* 50: 1–10.
Glatz, Claudia and Roger Matthews. 2005. Anthropology of a Frontier Zone: Hittite-Kaska Relations in Late Bronze Age North-Central Anatolia. *Bulletin of the American Schools of Oriental Research* 339: 47–65.
Goldman, Hetty. 1950. *Excavations at Gözlü Kule, Tarsus*. Princeton, N.J.: Princeton University Press.
Gorny, Ronald L. 1997. Anatolia: Prehistoric Anatolia. In *The Oxford Encyclopedia of Archaeology in the Near East*, ed. Eric M. Meyers, vol. 1, 122–27. Oxford: Oxford University Press.
———. 2002. Anatolian Archaeology: An Overview. In *Across the Anatolian Plateau. Readings in the Archaeology of Ancient Turkey*, ed. David C. Hopkins, 1–4. Boston: American Schools of Oriental Research.
Götze, Albrecht. 1933. *Kleinasien*. München: Beck.
Greaves, Alan M. 2007. Trans-Anatolia: Examining Turkey as a Bridge between East and West. *Anatolian Studies* 57: 1–15.
Greenewalt, Crawford H. Jr. 1997. Sardis. In *The Oxford Encyclopedia of Archaeology in the Near East*, ed. Eric M. Meyers, vol. 4, 484–88. Oxford: Oxford University Press.
Gurney, Oliver R. 1952. *The Hittites*. Harmondsworth: Penguin.
Güterbock, Hans G. 1997. Boğazköy. In *The Oxford Encyclopedia of Archaeology in the Near East*, ed. Eric M. Meyers, vol. 1, 333–35. Oxford: Oxford University Press.
Hamilton, William J. 1842. *Researches in Asia Minor, Pontus, and Armenia*. London: John Murray.
Harmankaya, Savaş and Burçin Erdoğu. 2002. *TAY—Türkiye Arkeolojik Yerleşmeleri 4: İlk Tunç*. İstanbul: Ege Yayınları.
Harmankaya, Savaş and Oğuz Tanındı, eds. 1996. *TAY—Türkiye Arkeolojik Yerleşmeleri 1: Paleolitik/Epipaleolitik*. İstanbul: Ege Yayınları.
Harmankaya, Savaş, Oğuz Tanındı, and Mihriban Özbaşaran, eds. 1997. *TAY—Türkiye Arkeolojik Yerleşmeleri 2: Neolitik*. İstanbul: Ege Yayınları.
———. eds. 1998. *TAY—Türkiye Arkeolojik Yerleşmeleri 3: Kalkolitik*. İstanbul: Ege Yayınları.
Hawkins, J. David. 2000. *Corpus of Hieroglyphic Luwian Inscriptions*. Berlin: de Gruyter.
Hodder, Ian. 2006. *Çatalhöyük. The Leopard's Tale*. London: Thames and Hudson.
Hoffner, Harry A. Jr. and H. Craig Melchert. 2008. *A Grammar of the Hittite Language*. Winona Lake, Ind.: Eisenbrauns.
Hogarth, David G. 1914. *Carchemish. Part I*. London: British Museum.
Hopkins, David C., ed. 2002. *Across the Anatolian Plateau. Readings in the Archaeology of Ancient Turkey*. Boston: American Schools of Oriental Research.
Hrozný, Bedřich. 1915. Die Lösung des hethitischen Problems. *Mitteilungen der Deutschen Orientgesellschaft* 56: 17–50.

Jean, Éric, ed. 2001. *Boğazköy'den Karatepe'ye. Hititbilim ve Hitit Dünyasının Keşfi*. İstanbul: Yapı Kredi.

Joukowsky, Martha S. 1996. *Early Turkey: Anatolian Archaeology from Prehistory through the Lydian Period*. Dubuque: Kendall/Hunt.

Kealhofer, Lisa, ed. 2005. *The Archaeology of Midas and the Phrygians*. Philadelphia: University of Pennsylvania Museum of Archaeology and Anthropology.

Kelly-Buccellati, Marilyn. 1997. History of the Field: Archaeology in Syria. In *The Oxford Encyclopedia of Archaeology in the Near East*, ed. Eric M. Meyers, vol. 3, 42–47. Oxford: Oxford University Press.

Koenigs, Wolf. 1997. Deutsches Archäologisches Institut, Abteilung Istanbul. In *The Oxford Encyclopedia of Archaeology in the Near East*, ed. Eric M. Meyers, vol. 2, 150. Oxford: Oxford University Press.

Korfmann, Manfred. 1983. *Demircihüyük I. Architektur, Stratigraphie und Befunde*. Mainz am Rhein: Philipp von Zabern.

Korfmann, Manfred O. 2006. Troia—Archäologie eines Siedlungshügels und seiner Landschaft. In *Troia. Archäologie eines Siedlungshügels und seiner Landschaft*, ed. Manfred O. Korfmann, 1–12. Mainz am Rhein: Philipp von Zabern.

Koşay, Hamit Z. 1941. *Les fouilles de Pazarlı*. Ankara: Türk Tarih Kurumu Basımevi.

———. 1953. *Alacahöyük*. Ankara: Turkish Press.

Körte, Gustav and Alfred Körte. 1904. *Gordion. Ergebnisse der Ausgrabung im Jahre 1900*. Berlin: Georg Reims.

Kozbe, Gülriz, Alpaslan Ceylan, Yasemin Polat, Taciser Sivas, Hakan Sivas, Işık Şahin, and Duygu A. Tanrıver. 2008. *TAY—Türkiye Arkeolojik Yerleşmeleri 6: Demir*. İstanbul: Ege Yayınları.

Kuhn, Steven L. 2002. Palaeolithic Archaeology in Turkey. *Evolutionary Anthropology* 11: 198–210.

Lamb, Winifred. 1936. Excavations at Kusura near Afyon Karahissar. *Archaeologia* 86: 1–64.

Lichter, Clemens, ed. 2007. *Vor 12.000 Jahren in Anatolien. Die ältesten Monumente der Menschheit*. Stuttgart: Konrad Theiss.

Lloyd, Seton. 1947. *Foundations in the Dust*. Harmondsworth: Penguin.

———. 1956. *Early Anatolia*. Harmondsworth: Penguin.

———. 1972. *Beycesultan. Vol. III Part I. Late Bronze Age Architecture*. London: British Institute of Archaeology at Ankara.

Lloyd, Seton and James Mellaart. 1965. *Beycesultan. Vol. II. Middle Bronze Age Architecture and Pottery*. London: British Institute of Archaeology at Ankara.

Lumsden, Stephen. 2002. Gavurkalesi: Investigations at a Hittite Sacred Place. In *Recent Developments in Hittite Archaeology and History*, ed. K. Aslıhan Yener and Harry A. Hoffner Jr., 111–25. Winona Lake, Ind.: Eisenbrauns.

Macqueen, James G. 1975. *The Hittites and Their Contemporaries in Asia Minor*. London: Thames and Hudson.

Matthews, Roger. 1997. History of the Field: Archaeology in Mesopotamia. In *The Oxford Encyclopedia of Archaeology in the Near East*, ed. Eric M. Meyers, vol. 3, 56–60. Oxford: Oxford University Press.

———. ed. 1998. *Ancient Anatolia. Fifty Years' Work by the British Institute of Archaeology at Ankara*. London: British Institute of Archaeology at Ankara.

Matthews, Roger and Claudia Glatz. 2009. People and Place in Paphlagonia: Trends and Patterns in Settlement through Time. In *At Empires' Edge. Project Paphlagonia Regional Survey in North-Central Turkey*, ed. Roger Matthews and Claudia Glatz, 239–49. London: British Institute at Ankara.

Mellaart, James. 1967. *Çatal Hüyük: A Neolithic Town in Anatolia.* London: Thames and Hudson.

———. 1970. *Excavations at Hacılar.* Edinburgh: Edinburgh University Press.

———. 1975. *The Neolithic of the Near East.* London: Thames and Hudson.

———. 1998a. Beycesultan. In *Ancient Anatolia. Fifty Years' Work by the British Institute of Archaeology at Ankara*, ed. Roger Matthews, 61–68. London: British Institute of Archaeology at Ankara.

———. 1998b. Hacılar: 1957–1960 Excavations. In *Ancient Anatolia. Fifty Years' Work by the British Institute of Archaeology at Ankara*, ed. Roger Matthews, 53–60. London: British Institute of Archaeology at Ankara.

———. 1998c. Çatal Hüyük: The 1960s Seasons. In *Ancient Anatolia. Fifty Years' Work by the British Institute of Archaeology at Ankara*, ed. Roger Matthews, 35–41. London: British Institute of Archaeology at Ankara.

Messerschmidt, Leopold. 1900. *Corpus Inscriptionum Hettiticarum.* Berlin: Peiser.

———. 1903. *The Hittites.* London: Nutt.

Michel, Cécile. 2003. *Old Assyrian Bibliography.* Old Assyrian Archives, Studies 1. Leiden: Nederlands Instituut voor het Nabije Oosten.

Müller-Karpe, Andreas. 2002. Kuşaklı-Sarissa. In *Die Hethiter und ihr Reich*, ed. Tahsin Özgüç, 176–89. Stuttgart: Theiss.

Neve, Peter. 1993. *Hattuša. Stadt der Götter und Tempel.* Mainz am Rhein: Philipp von Zabern.

Özdoğan, Mehmet. 1998. Ideology and Archaeology in Turkey. In *Archaeology under Fire. Nationalism, Politics and Heritage in the Eastern Mediterranean and Middle East*, ed. Lynn Meskell, 111–23. London: Routledge.

———. 2001. *Türk Arkeolojisinin Sorunları ve Koruma Politikaları.* İstanbul: Arkeoloji ve Sanat Yayınları.

———. 2007. Amidst Mesopotamia-centric and Euro-centric Approaches: The Changing Role of the Anatolian Peninsula between the East and the West. *Anatolian Studies* 57: 17–24.

Özdoğan, Mehmet and Nezih Başgelen, eds. 1999. *Neolithic in Turkey. The Cradle of Civilization.* İstanbul: Arkeoloji ve Sanat Yayınları.

Özenir, Sırrı A. 1998. Eflatunpınar Hitit anıtı 1996 Yılı Temizlik ve Kazı Çalışmaları. *Müze Kurtarma Kazıları Semineri* 8: 135–57.

Özgen, İlknur and Jean Öztürk. 1996. *The Lydian Treasure. Heritage Recovered.* Ankara: Republic of Turkey, Ministry of Culture.

Özgüç, Nimet. 1966. Excavations at Acemhöyük. *Anatolia* 10: 29–52.

Özgüç, Tahsin. 1978. *Excavations at Maşat Höyük and Investigations in its Vicinity.* Ankara: Türk Tarih Kurumu Basımevi.

———. 1982a. Atatürk ve Arkeoloji. In *Maşat Höyük II. A Hittite Center Northeast of Boğazköy*, ed. Tahsin Özgüç, ix–xiii. Ankara: Türk Tarih Kurumu Basımevi.

———. 1982b. *Maşat Höyük II. A Hittite Center Northeast of Boğazköy.* Ankara: Türk Tarih Kurumu Basımevi.

———. 1988. *İnandıktepe. An Important Cult Center in the Old Hittite Period.* Ankara: Türk Tarih Kurumu Basımevi.

———. 2002a. *Die Stellung der Hethiter im kulturellen Erbe der Türkei.* In Die Hethiter und ihr Reich, ed. Tahsin Özgüç, 14–15. Stuttgart: Theiss.

———. ed. 2002b. *Die Hethiter und ihr Reich.* Stuttgart: Theiss.

———. 2003. *Kültepe Kaniš/Neša.* İstanbul: Middle Eastern Culture Center in Japan.

Puchstein, Otto. 1912. *Boghasköi. Die Bauwerke.* Leipzig: Hinrichs.

Rassam, Hormuzd. 1897. *Asshur and the Land of Nimrod*. New York: Eaton and Mains.

Renda, Günsel, ed. 1993. *Woman in Anatolia. 9000 Years of the Anatolian Woman*. İstanbul: Ministry of Culture.

Sagona, Antonio and Paul Zimansky. 2009. *Ancient Turkey*. London: Routledge.

Sams, G. Kenneth. 2005. Gordion: Explorations over a Century. In *The Archaeology of Midas and the Phrygians*, ed. Lisa Kealhofer, 10–21. Philadelphia: University of Pennsylvania Museum of Archaeology and Anthropology.

Schliemann, Heinrich. 1875. *Troy and its Remains*. London: John Murray.

Schoop, Ulf-Dietrich. 2005. *Das anatolische Chalkolithikum*. Remshalden: Bernhard Albert Greiner.

Seeher, Jürgen. 2002a. Eine in Vergessenheit geratene Kultur gewinnt Profil. In *Die Hethiter und ihr Reich*, ed. Tahsin Özgüç, 20–25. Stuttgart: Theiss.

———. 2002b. *Hattusha Guide. A Day in the Hittite Capital*. İstanbul: Ege Yayınları.

Sipahi, Tunç. 2000. Eine althethitische Reliefvase vom Hüseyindede Tepesi. *Istanbuler Mitteilungen* 50: 63–85.

Slatter, Enid. 1994. *Xanthus. Travels of Discovery in Turkey*. London: Rubicon.

Sommer, Ferdinand. 1920. *Hethitisches*. Leipzig: Hinrichs.

Stone, Elizabeth C. 2005. The Outer Town at Ayanis, 1997–2001. In *Anatolian Iron Ages 5*, ed. Altan Çilingiroğlu and Gareth Darbyshire, 187–93. London: British Institute at Ankara.

Sturtevant, Edgar H. 1933. *A Comparative Grammar of the Hittite Language*. Philadelphia: University of Pennsylvania Press.

Süel, Aygül. 2002. Ortaköy-Šapinuwa. In *Recent Developments in Hittite Archaeology and History*, ed. K. Aslıhan Yener and Harry A. Hoffner Jr., 157–65. Winona Lake, Ind.: Eisenbrauns.

Tanyeri-Erdemir, Tuğba. 2006. Archaeology as a Source of National Pride in the Early Years of the Turkish Republic. *Journal of Field Archaeology* 31: 381–93.

Todd, Ian A. 1998. Central Anatolian survey. In *Ancient Anatolia. Fifty Years' Work by the British Institute of Archaeology at Ankara*, ed. Roger Matthews, 17–26. London: British Institute of Archaeology at Ankara.

Traill, David A. 1995. *Schliemann of Troy: Treasure and Deceit*. London: John Murray.

Trigger, Bruce. 1989. *A History of Archaeological Thought*. Cambridge: Cambridge University Press.

Voigt, Mary M. 2005. Old Problems and New Solutions. Recent Excavations at Gordion. In *The Archaeology of Midas and the Phrygians*, ed. Lisa Kealhofer, 22–35. Philadelphia: University of Pennsylvania Museum of Archaeology and Anthropology.

von der Osten, Hans H. 1937. *The Alishar Hüyük. Seasons of 1930–32*. Oriental Institute Publications 28. Chicago: University of Chicago Press.

Wilhelm, Gernot. 2002. Anatolien zwischen Ost und West. In *Die Hethiter und ihr Reich*, ed. Tahsin Özgüç, 16–17. Stuttgart: Theiss.

———. 2008. Urartian. In *The Ancient Languages of Asia Minor*, ed. Roger D. Woodard, 105–23. Cambridge: Cambridge University Press.

Winckler, Hugo. 1909. *Excavations at Boghaz-Keui in the Summer of 1907*. Washington, D.C.: Government Printing.

Woolley, C. Leonard. 1921. *Carchemish. Part II*. London: British Museum.

———. 1952. *Carchemish. Part III*. London: British Museum.

Wright, William. 1886. *The Empire of the Hittites*. London: Nisbet.

Yakar, Jak. 1985. *The Later Prehistory of Anatolia: The Chalcolithic and Early Bronze Age*. Oxford: British Archaeological Reports.

———. 1991. *Prehistoric Anatolia. The Neolithic Transformation and the Early Chalcolithic Period.* Tel Aviv: Tel Aviv University Press.
———. 1994. *Prehistoric Anatolia. Supplement 1.* Tel Aviv: Tel Aviv University Press.
———. 1997a. History of the Field: Archaeology in the Anatolian Plateau. In *The Oxford Encyclopedia of Archaeology in the Near East*, ed. Eric M. Meyers, vol. 3, 63–67. Oxford: Oxford University Press.
———. 1997b. Koşay, Hamit Zübeyr. In *The Oxford Encyclopedia of Archaeology in the Near East*, ed. Eric M. Meyers, vol. 3, 303–4. Oxford: Oxford University Press.
Yalçın, Ünsal, Cemal Pulak, and Rainer Slotta. 2005. *Das Schiff von Uluburun*. Bochum: Deutsches Bergbau-Museum.
Yener, K. Aslıhan and Harry A. Hoffner, Jr., eds. 2002. *Recent Developments in Hittite Archaeology and History*. Winona Lake, Ind.: Eisenbrauns.
Yerasimos, Stephane. 1991. *Les voyageurs dans l'empire Ottoman (XIVe–XVIe siècles)*. Ankara: Türk Tarih Kurumu Basımevi.
Yon, Marguerite. 1997. French Archaeological Missions. In *The Oxford Encyclopedia of Archaeology in the Near East*, ed. Eric M. Meyers, vol. 2, 344–46. Oxford: Oxford University Press.
Zimansky, Paul E. 1998. *Ancient Ararat: A Handbook of Urartian Studies*. Delmar: Caravan.

CHAPTER 4

ANATOLIAN CHRONOLOGY AND TERMINOLOGY

JAK YAKAR

A reliable chronological framework that encompasses the history of Anatolia from the Neolithic period to the end of the Iron Age is at the core of comparative cultural analyses as well as debates concerning historical developments and political events that involved local polities and the major powerbrokers of the ancient Near East. Even minor adjustments in the traditional chronological charts of Anatolia vacillating between higher or lower timescales could lead to the revision of resolute perceptions in debating controversial issues of a cultural and historical nature, including the origins of farming or establishing the pace and stages of material culture changes. Frequently updated chronological charts based on scientific dates provide more reliable estimates on the speed of particular cultural and technological transfers and consequently the dynamics and mechanisms that promoted them, including more precise timeframes for the socioeconomic interactions and possible population movements that took place across geocultural borders of prestate and state societies. A consensus on the current chronological infrastructures that do not incorporate problematic single-sample radiocarbon measurements or other discrepancies could help bridge the existing differences of view regarding the temporal division and subdivision of prehistoric and protohistoric cultures of Anatolia vis-à-vis the rest of the Near East.

Advances in Absolute Dating Techniques

The growing databank of high-precision self-standing ^{14}C wiggle-matched dendrochronology and calibrated radiocarbon dates from individual sites, calculated with an aggregated average, is significantly improving our understanding of the chronology of the cultural and historical periods of early Anatolia. The ongoing efforts by major laboratories to improve the accuracy of radiocarbon dates have produced universally accepted criteria in sample selection, a refined calibration curve, and a greater consensus concerning statistical modeling (Ramsey 2005; Reimer et al. 2004). In the choice of samples, short-lived grains have proven more effective for dating a destruction level than long-lived samples. These coordinated efforts aimed at isolating measurement errors due to differences in counting procedures are producing more accurate conversions of radiocarbon years into high-probability date intervals in calendar years. In multiple tested samples, the highest average result often accumulates in the center of the time range, with the plateau pointing to a range of less than ten years. Thus, it is generally surmised that the middle range reading can be closer to a true date of the sample.

It is important to stress that despite the advances made in scientific dating methods (dendrochronology in particular), there are still many instances in which the duration of an occupation level or the date of an archaeologically visible event cannot be established in a precise absolute manner. In dated samples, smearing caused by error bands accompanying the radiocarbon measurements could blur the length of gaps in occupation sequences that result from abandonment and reoccupation (Shennan 2000). Chronological inconsistencies could also occur in dating interfaces that lack culturally identifiable records. It is argued that in such cases, using the Bayesian statistical inference, which takes into consideration the relative reliability of stratigraphical observations and cultural associations, could provide approximate dates of the boundaries of a transition level (Cessford 2002:29; Wright and Rupley 2001). Although some critics of this statistical inference point out that it relies on subjective probabilities in the induction process, its supporters believe that the subjective choice of probabilities can have an objective value in the selection of the most likely probability. In other words, in the Bayesian statistical inference a hypothesis with very high support is accepted as true over the one with very low support, which is rejected as false (Box and Tiao 1992:10–24; Buck, Cavanagh, and Litton 1996; Steier and Rom 2000).

In Anatolian dendrochronology, wood samples recovered from occupation levels of archaeological sites are often construction beams cut from long-lived local trees such as *Juniperus*, *Pinus*, *Cedrus*, and *Quercus* (Newton and Kuniholm 2004; Yakar 2002a). The accuracy of dendrochronology in dating architectural levels continues to be a topic of debate by those familiar with the shortcomings of this method. Some point to differences sometimes encountered in the annual ring growth of contemporary trees in the same general area. Such variations are believed to be the outcome of differences in altitude, which can influence the rate of growth.

Moreover, dates obtained from reused timbers naturally refer to the time they were cut and not to the architectural level or context in which they are found (Keenan 2002, 2004:11).

Despite some of its shortcomings, dendrochronology remains an important scientific dating method in Anatolian archaeology. Its reliability is relative depending on the number of samples and the method used in producing fine-grained high-resolution dates, and to the extent that they do not contradict calibrated dates of short-lived organic samples from the same stratum. The combined use of scientific and traditional dating methods is providing more reliable protohistorical and historical regional chronologies (Kuniholm and Newton 1989; Manning et al. 2003; Mielke, Schoop, and Seeher 2006; Yakar 2002a, 2002b).

The Neolithic and Chalcolithic Periods

Labeling cultures using sites or regions and then dividing them into periods, phases, or stages, although inherently necessary in archaeology, has its drawbacks, since this practice tends to encapsulate cultural and technological developments within arbitrary boundaries that lack temporal and spatial flexibility. Different approaches pursued in the contextual processing and interpretation of cultural inventories from excavations contributes to terminological discords. Traditional terminologies based solely on technological aspects of cultural assemblages, with emphasis on differentiations in lithic and pottery typology (for the Late Chalcolithic see Helwing 1999, 2000), fail to provide a complete picture of prehistoric societies (Yakar 2003). Terms such as Pre-Pottery Neolithic A and B, Early and Late Neolithic, and Early-Middle-Late Chalcolithic hardly define the diverse subsistence modes, technological complexity, or social organization of Anatolian society. The ancestors of Anatolian Neolithic farmers possessed technologies that enabled them to produce copper trinkets, fine stone vessels, or white plaster wares, certainly more refined and technologically advanced than the simple pottery manufactured by their successors. The architectural and artistic sophistication encountered in some of the hunter-gatherers' villages in the central plateau or sacred sites and villages in the southeast (e.g., Schmidt, chapter 42 in this volume) give the impression that the level of Aceramic Neolithic social organization, at least in its advanced stages, could not have been significantly different from that presumed for pottery-producing Neolithic society.

The recently proposed "Early Central Anatolian" (CANeW) terminology for the central Anatolian prehistoric sequence identifies five chronologically adaptable consecutive cultural stages covering the Epipalaeolithic through the Chalcolithic periods, with emphasis on changes in the settlement pattern, material culture, burial practice, and subsistence mode (Gérard and Thissen 2002; Özbaşaran and Buitenhuis 2002).

A modified version of this CANeW system could be applied to define the chronology and nature of the socioeconomic and cultural stages in the evolution of the

Table 4.1. Recordable Stages of Socioeconomic and Technological Evolution in Anatolian Prehistory

Anatolian Stages of Cultural Evolution	Approximate Chronological Timeframes
• Villages in proximity to natural routes of communication • Possible emergence of settlement hierarchies in clan-controlled/tribal territories • Consolidation of traditional agropastoral economies by village administrations • Intensification of interregional interaction and acculturation • Abstract artistic expressions in iconography • Dominance of handmade dark burnished monochrome wares in the central plateau	3000 B.C.E. Late Chalcolithic Middle Chalcolithic
• Small kin-related communities with more developed farming economies and fenced villages and farmsteads • New farming settlements and the consolidation of those previously established • Intensification of interregional contacts beyond the south-central plateau • Clearer manifestations of ethno/geocultural group identity in material culture • Animal husbandry and herding become more important economic component	5000 B.C.E. Early Chalcolithic
• Widespread adoption of agriculture; domestication of sheep, goat, and perhaps cattle • Partial seasonal transhumance for the pursuit of herding, hunting, and gathering activities • No identifiable community buildings • Presumed family lineage, age- and gender-based social ranking; village management by council and/or chiefs; pottery production • Symbolisms relating to fecundity, life, and death in naturalistic human and animal forms • Local changes in pottery and lithic typologies and technologies reflect changes in subsistence modes	6000 B.C.E. Neolithic
• Larger permanent villages/houses and intramural burials under house floors • Special buildings for communal gatherings and rituals of socioreligious nature • First signs of social differentiation and economic diversification • Hunting and gathering–based wild resource management • Selective cultivation of wild species such as wild einkorn, emmer wheat, barley, and lentils; experimentation with sheep herding • Increasing community size could imply village management by councils and/or chiefs • Lithic industry with locally variable proportions of obsidian tools and points produced from long, regular, parallel sided blades using bipolar technology • Use of treated lime and gypsum to produce "white vessels" and plastered floors • Experimentations with the production of native copper and malachite beads	7000 B.C.E. Late Aceramic Neolithic Stage

(Continued)

Table 4.1. (*Continued*)

Anatolian Stages of Cultural Evolution	Approximate Chronological Timeframes
• Seasonal campsite occupation to village occupation resulting in socioeconomic changes • Food procurement based on more selective hunting and gathering, requiring less mobility • Intra-/intercommunal celebrations of socioreligious nature (feasting, exchange of ornaments) to strengthen communal identity and intra- and intercommunity bonds • Industrial specialization: decorated stone bowls (Hallan Çemi); deliberate firing of clay figurines and vessels (Demirköy)	8500 B.C.E. Early Aceramic Neolithic Stage

prehistoric Anatolian society, starting with hunter-gatherer bands in the process of sedentarization, to well-organized independent and interdependent farming communities (Yakar 2004). The stages of this evolution could be documented by observing the changes in the nature and scope of villages and their material inventories (tables 4.1 and 4.2).

The Neolithic and Chalcolithic Sites

This section highlights the comparative dates and phases of Neolithic and Chalcolithic sites. Specific information regarding radiocarbon data can be found in table 4.3.

The Aegean Littoral and West Central Plateau

The Troadic sites of Kumtepe Ia and Beşik-Sivritepe were occupied beginning in the early fifth millennium B.C.E. (see Gabriel 2000; Korfmann 1994; Korfmann and Kromer 1993; Korfmann et al. 1995). The early villages in the Troad are dated also on the basis of the existence or absence of "Beşik-Sivritepe/Kumtepe Ia" pattern-burnished ware, which dates to the first half of the fifth millennium B.C.E. In other words, the early villages here are contemporary with Late Vinča and Early Gumelniţa settlements in southeastern Europe, and with the "Late Neolithic" Larissa and Late Dimini in the Aegean (see also Özdoğan, chapter 29 in this volume). Additionally, the site of Ulucak was occupied from the late seventh into the early sixth millennia B.C.E. (Weninger 2007).

The west central plateau sites of Hacılar and Kuruçay have levels roughly contemporary with one another (late seventh to early sixth millennia B.C.E.); the ceramics in Kuruçay's Level 7 show strong resemblance to those found in Hacılar I–II, suggesting that Level 7 may date to ca. 5900–5700 B.C.E., or even begin slightly earlier (see Thissen 2006).

The important site of Ilıpınar offers numerous dates that testify to a seemingly unbroken occupational sequence stretching over five centuries and including seven occupational phases with up to nineteen architectural levels (Thissen 2006; and see Roodenberg, chapter 44 in this volume). Menteşe's sequence, based on nine dates, suggests that its early occupation lasted at least four centuries, from 6440 to 6000 B.C.E., with a later phase spanning approximately two centuries in the mid-sixth millennium B.C.E. (see Thissen 2006). Bademağacı's Early Neolithic I phase, found in the site's Level I, may date to as early as the late eighth to early seventh millennia B.C.E. The site's timeframe for the Early Neolithic II phase, ca. 6450–6100 B.C.E., is nearly identical to Höyücek's "shrine phase" (Thissen 2006). Finally, though only a single radiocarbon sample is available from Erbaba Level III, it suggests that this site was occupied during the middle part of the seventh millennium B.C.E.

Central Plateau and the Pontic

The Neolithic period on the plateau features a number of sites, including Kaletepe, which demonstrates occupation in the late ninth millennium B.C.E., Boncuklu whose occupation started at roughly the same time (Baird 2006), and Pınarbaşı A with occupation beginning in the mid-ninth millennium B.C.E. and lasting for approximately three centuries (Thissen 2007; Watkins 1996). Also occupied in the late ninth millennium B.C.E. is the site of Aşıklı Höyük, whose numerous dates suggest that the site was occupied between 8200 and 7500 B.C.E; following with occupational dates beginning in the mid- to late eighth millennium B.C.E. are Musular (for only a couple of centuries), and Suberde, Çatalhöyük East, and Canhasan III, all demonstrating occupation that stretches toward the mid-seventh millennium B.C.E. (Thissen 2007; and see Özbaşaran, chapter 5 in this volume). A second occupation at Pınarbaşı B, with dates obtained from a "deliberate fill within the area enclosed by a curving wall" produced an occupation range spanning the centuries 6400–5920 B.C.E. (Baird 2003; Thissen 2007; Watkins 1996). In the Chalcolithic period, the site of Köşk Höyük demonstrates occupation during the last three centuries of the sixth millennium B.C.E. (Thissen 2007), and the earliest occupation at the site of Çadır Höyük is currently dated to a range between ca. 5200 and 4900 B.C.E., placing the time of occupation at both sites in the later Middle Chalcolithic. Çadır Höyük was then continuously occupied throughout the Late Chalcolithic and into the Early Bronze periods (see Gorny et al. 2000:154; Steadman, McMahon, and Ross 2007). Contemporary to the earliest excavated levels of Çadır is the site of Güvercinkayası. Finally, Çatalhöyük West sees occupation beginning in the early sixth millennium B.C.E., and Canhasan I, though offering no radiocarbon dates from Levels 7–3, features enough dates from Levels 2A–B to place occupation at this site between 5700 and 5400 B.C.E. (Thissen 2007).

The most notable Chalcolithic site north of the plateau, in the Pontic zone, is İkiztepe. Several dates from Mound II, Level III, place the earliest occupation at the site in the fifth millennium B.C.E.

Table 4.2. **The Chronology of Regional Settlement Sequences Using Approximate Timeframes Based on *CANeW* tabulated ^{14}C and Dendro Dates in 1 Sigma Ranges that Use the OxCal v3.10 Calibration Chart (Ramsey 2005) and the IntCal04 Calibration Curve (Reimer et al. 2004)**

Period	Aegean Littoral	West-Central	Central	Cilicia	East	Southeast
3000 B.C.E.	Kumtepe Ia–b		Çadır Höyük Ic-a	XIIB		
Late	Beşiktepe	Barçın Höyük	Köşk Höyük	Yumuktepe	Arslantepe VI	Amuq E–F
Chalcolithic	Baklatepe		Güvercinkayası	XVI	Arslantepe VII	Kenan Tepe
Middle			Yarrıkkaya		Arslantepe VIII	Hacınebi A–B
			Çamlıbel Tarlası		Değirmentepe	Kazane
						Zeytinli B
5000 B.C.E.	Ulucak		Çadır Höyük Id–e	XVII		Amuq C–D
Early		Menteşe 1	Köşk Höyük			Kenan Tepe
Chalcolithic		Ilıpınar X–VB			Girikhaciyan	Kazane
		Aktopraklık	Çatalhöyük W	Yumuktepe	Domuztepe	Fistikli H
		Fikirtepe	Canhasan I 1	XXV		Gedikli IV
		Pendik	Canhasan I 2B			
		Hacılar V–I	Güvercinkayası			
		Kuruçay 10–7				
		Höyücek: sanctuary phase				

6000 B.C.E. Ceramic Neolithic	Ulucak ?	Yenikapı Menteşe 3 Barçın Höyük Erbaba 3 Hacılar IX–VI Kuruçay 13–11 Höyücek: sanctuary phase shrine phase early phase Bademağacı: EN II EN I	Köşk Höyük? Pınarbaşı B Çatalhöyük E I	XXVI Yumuktepe XXXIII		Amuq A–B Akarçay I Çayönü Kumartepe Mezraa/Teleilat
7000 B.C.E. Late Aceramic Neolithic		Aceram. Hacılar	Çatalhöyük E Pre-XII Boncuklu Canhasan III Suberde Musular Aşıklı Kaletepe Pınarbaşı A		Cafer Höyük XIII–I	Mezraa/Teleilat Hayaz Akarçay VI– Gritille Gürcütepe Göbekli–Late Nevali Çori Çayönü
8500 B.C.E. Early Aceramic Neolithic						Göbekli–Early Nevali Çori Çayönü Hallan Çemi

Table 4.3. Calibrated Radiocarbon Dates for Neolithic and Chalcolithic Sites

Region	Site	No. of Samples	Site Strata	Dates cal B.C.E.E	Source(s)
Aegean	Ulucak	4	VI–IVb2	6040–5730	Weninger (2007)
	Ilıpınar	66	X–VII	6000–5700	
			VI–VA	5700–5500	
			VB	5500–5450	
West Central Plateau	Menteşe	9	Level 3	6440–6000	Thissen (2006)
			Level 1	5730–5520	
	Hacılar	4	IX–VI	6240–6060	
			II–I	6050–5730	
	Höyücek	6	Shrine Phase	6445–6100	
	Bademağacı	1	Level 8	7030–6690	
		7	Levels 4A–1	6450–6100	
	Çadır Höyük	8	Phase Id-e	5220–4940	Gorny et al. (2000)
			Phase Ic	4520–4480	
			Phase Ib-a	3780–3360	
	Köşk Höyük	9 Dendro		5300–5000	
	Güvercinkayası	10		5200–4850	
	Canhasan I	8	2B	5700–5400	
		4 Dendro			
Central Plateau	Canhasan III	16		7600–6650	Thissen (2007)
	Çatalhöyük East	112		7460–6770	
		10 Dendro			
	Suberde	5	Level III	7460–6770	
	Pınarbaşı B	2		6400–5920	
	Pınarbaşı A	3		8540–8230	
	Kaletepe	3		8300–8000	
	Aşıklı Höyük	47		8200–7500	
	Musular	10		7570–7300	

Cilicia	Mersin-Yumuktepe	15	Neolithic levels Middle Chalcolithic levels	6700–5800 4900–4700	Thissen (2007)
Eastern Highlands	Arslantepe	ca. 36 ca. 400 Dendro	Level VIII Level VII Level VI A	4250–3900 3800–3350 3708–3389	Di Nocera (2000); Erdoğu, Tanındı, and Uygun (2003); Kuniholm (1995, 1996, 1997)
	Cafer Höyük	11	Levels XIII–I	8300–7450	
	Girikhaciyan	1		5730–5660	Bischoff (2006, 2007); Thissen and Bischoff (2006)
Southeast	Hacınebi	5	Phase B 1	4200–3700	Pearce (2000)
	Hassek Höyük	12		3294–3050	Erdoğu, Tanındı, and Uygun (2003); Willkomm (1992)
	Hayaz	2		7480–6690	Bischoff (2006, 2007)
	Akarçay Tepe	5	Levels V-I	7900–6100	Thissen and Bischoff (2006)
	Mezraa/Teleilat	8	Level IIIb Level IIb	7050–6820 6650–6530	Thissen and Bischoff (2006)
	Çayönü	6 3	"Round Bldg. Phase" "Basal Pits"	10200–8270 8570–8330	Bischoff (2006, 2007)
	Hallan Çemi	16		9800–9200	
	Göbekli Tepe	2	Layer III	9130–8620	Pustovyotov (2002); Schmidt (2001)
	Nevalı Çori	19	Levels V–I	8650–7950	
	Gritille	3		7940–6590	

Cilicia and the Eastern Highlands

In Cilicia the site of Yumuktepe (Mersin) features fifteen radiocarbon dates which provide three consecutive timeframes for the Neolithic–Middle Chalcolithic occupations, but with significant gaps in between; occupation begins ca. 6700 and stretches to 4700 B.C.E. but with breaks of several or many centuries (Thissen 2007). Two radiocarbon readings from Level XIIB indicate that the Late Chalcolithic occupation extended well into the fourth millennium B.C.E. (Erdoğu, Tanındı, and Uygun 2003).

The eastern highland site of Cafer Höyük offers a selection of radiocarbon dates for its three phases of occupation (Early Phase XIII–IX, Middle Phase VIII–V, Late Phase IV–I) that suggest the settlement's Neolithic sequence could be provisionally stretched between ca. 8300 and 7450 B.C.E.

Arslantepe, also situated in the eastern highlands, offers a long and important sequence (see Frangipane, chapter 45 in this volume). The Level VIII occupation, representing the Anatolian version of the Ubaid, is estimated somewhere within the 4250–3900 B.C.E. range, much later than the nearby Ubaid settlement at Değirmentepe (see Erdoğu, Tanındı, and Uygun 2003; Esin 2000). Arslantepe Level VII, defined as Late Chalcolithic 3–4 and culturally corresponding to the Early and Middle Uruk, provides a chronological range stretching between 3800–3350 cal B.C.E. (Di Nocera 2000). The two radiocarbon samples from Temple B and an adjacent corridor (A 796) in Level VIA provide two date ranges for this level: 3708–3543 and 3494–3389 B.C.E. (Di Nocera 2000; Frangipane 2000:446). In addition, over 400 carbonized wood fragments from Temple B provide a dendrochronological timescale within the late fourth millennium B.C.E. (Kuniholm 1995, 1996:330–31, 1997:164, fig. 4). The pre–3300 B.C.E. date of Temple B probably refers to the time the trees were cut and not its construction. Another group of dates derived from samples recovered in the gate area of Building IV, in Building III, and in Temple A, dates the VI A period to ca. 3050–2900 B.C.E. (Frangipane 2000:446).

The Early and Middle Chalcolithic is represented at Girikhaciyan, where one sample offers a date range of 5730–5660 cal B.C.E. and supports the relative date presumed for the Halaf culture in this region (see Bischoff 2006, 2007; Thissen and Bischoff 2006). Finally, the early occupation at Domuztepe can be placed at ca. 5800–5600 cal B.C.E. (Carter, Campbell, and Gauld 2003).

Southeastern Anatolia

Numerous sites in the southeastern region provide plentiful dates. The earlier Neolithic is represented at Hallan Çemi, Göbekli Tepe, and Çayönü (see Rosenberg and Erim-Özdoğan, chapter 6 in this volume). Some of the earliest dates come from Hallan Çemi and suggest that occupation began at this site between 10,100 and 9200 B.C.E. and possibly stretched for several centuries. The site of Göbekli Tepe also offers early dates and suggests that Level III enclosures started to be constructed in the late tenth or early ninth millennium B.C.E. (Kromer and Schmidt 1998:8;

Pustovoytov 2002; Schmidt 2000:48, 2001; and see Schmidt, chapter 42 in this volume). Several points of el-Khiam, Helwan, and Aswad types recovered in the fill above the enclosures further indicate that Layer III corresponds to the Pre-Pottery Neolithic A horizon of Syria. Radiocarbon readings obtained from the Layer II soil of enclosure D indicate that the Layer III sacred structures were buried during the years 8247–7780 cal B.C.E. (Peters and Schmidt 2004:182).

At Çayönü, several radiocarbon measurements of samples recovered from the "round building subphase" produced two unlinked sets of dates: ca. 10,200–9300 cal B.C.E. and ca. 8640–8270 cal B.C.E. (Bischoff 2006, 2007), pointing to the existence of a mid-ninth millennium B.C.E. village, most likely preceded by a tenth millennium campsite with round huts. The level with "basal pits," either contemporary with the "round building subphase," or slightly later, produced three dates between 8570 and 8330 cal B.C.E. The length of overlapping occupations with "round buildings," "basal pits," "grill-plan buildings," and "channeled buildings" may have covered at least four centuries (ca. 8600–8200 B.C.E.). However, because the exact provenience of some dated samples or their attribution to specific building levels are far from certain, some dates remain provisional. In particular, the last three architectural phases offer insufficient radiocarbon measurements, and the "large room sub phase," placed in the mid-seventh millennium cal B.C.E. by a single date, might have started earlier (Bischoff 2006; Erdoğu, Tanındı, and Uygun 2003).

Nevalı Çori also offers Neolithic levels, with numerous mostly reliable radiocarbon samples from Levels V–I producing a range from 8650 to 7950 B.C.E. Nine overlapping dates clustered between 8550 and 8290 cal B.C.E. indicate that the occupation was already at its peak in the third quarter of the ninth millennium B.C.E.

Dating to the mid- and later (Ceramic) Neolithic stage is the site of Akarçay Tepe, where Levels V–I present a long period of occupation, ca. 7900–6100 cal B.C.E. (Thissen and Bischoff 2006). There are no dates yet from Level VI, but it may be safe to suggest that the first village was settled in the late ninth millennium B.C.E. A similar sequence is found at Gritille, where three sets of combined dates suggest that the site was occupied, perhaps intermittently, from the early eighth to the early seventh millennium B.C.E.

Roughly overlapping in occupation are Hayaz and Kumartepe; Hayaz features two radiocarbon dates of 7480–7200 cal B.C.E. and 7180–6690 cal B.C.E., putting early occupational phases in the second half of the eighth and early seventh millennia B.C.E., whereas Kumartepe has a single date (7030–6680 cal B.C.E.), placing it in the seventh millennium B.C.E. Ceramic Neolithic period in this region (Bischoff 2006, 2007). Also spanning the early to mid-seventh millennium B.C.E. is Mezraa/Teleilat with a number of radiocarbon samples that place Level IIIb in the 7050–6820 cal B.C.E. range and date Level IIb to 6650–6530 cal B.C.E. (Thissen and Bischoff 2006).

The fifth and fourth millennia B.C.E. are represented by Hacınebi and Hassek Höyük. At Hacınebi, five samples from Phase A span between 4200 and 3700 B.C.E., four dates place Phase B1 in the second quarter of the fourth millennium B.C.E., and two dates place Phase B2 in the mid-fourth millennium B.C.E. (Pearce 2000:121, fig.19). Hassek Höyük yielded twelve dates that place the site's Uruk settlement in the second half of the fourth millennium B.C.E., probably within the 3294–3050 B.C.E. range (Erdoğu, Tanındı, and Uygun 2003; Willkomm 1992). This small Mesopotamian enclave may have been established up to two generations earlier than Habuba Kabira (3229–2921 B.C.E.) and Jebel Aruda (3259–3035 B.C.E.) on the Syrian Euphrates (Butterlin 2000; Di Nocera 2000:86).

The Early Bronze Age

The traditional tripartite division of this period (see table 4.4), although rather arbitrary, is still largely maintained to create reference points in the temporal placement of regionally differentiated cultural inventories in Anatolia. This Early Bronze Age (EBA) designation by itself hardly reflects or describes the social, economic, and political dynamics behind the gradual transformation of third millennium B.C.E. Anatolians from a prestate to an early state society. Most archaeologists would agree that the cultural and chronological line marking the division between the EBA I and

Table 4.4. Cultural, Social, and Political Stages in the Evolution of Preliterate Anatolia and the Corresponding Periods in Mesopotamia and Syria

Period	Preliterate Anatolia	Literate Mesopotamia	Preliterate and Literate Syria
2000 B.C.E. EBA IIIc	Local dynasties Territorial city states	Ur III dynasty ruling Sumer The Gutian conquest of Akkad	
2150 B.C.E. EBA IIIb	Local dynasties Territorial city states	Shu Durul of Akkad Defeated by Gutians Naram-Sin of Akkad	Kingdom of Ebla
2300 B.C.E. EBA IIIa	Emerging local seats of power	Sargonic Akkad (starting in 2334 B.C.E.) Early Dynastic III B (pre-Sargonic)	Kingdom of Ebla
2500 B.C.E. EBA IIb	Early urban	Early Dynastic III A (Fara Period)	
2600 B.C.E. EBA IIa	Early urban	Early Dynastic II (1st dynasty of Uruk)	
2700 B.C.E. EBA Ib	Proto-urban Chiefdom systems	Early Dynastic II (1st dynasty of Uruk) Early Dynastic I (1st dynasty of Kish)	
2900 B.C.E. EBA Ia 3000 B.C.E.	Proto-urban Village-based settlement hierarchies	Proto-Literate (d) (Jemdet Nasr)	

the Late Chalcolithic period could be chronologically blurred and culturally artificial for some if not most regions of Anatolia (see, for instance, Schoop, chapter 7, and Steadman, chapter 10 in this volume). Until rather recently, this line was often drawn to mark changes in the profiles and styles of local and regional pottery repertories rather than complete material inventories that could provide clues to the reasons for and nature of cultural changes.

The preplanned town-like fortified settlements with public buildings that gradually appeared in various regions of Anatolia starting in the second or third centuries of the third millennium B.C.E. were most likely the outcome of local initiatives. In other words, the socioeconomic and political seeds of the "early urban" phase in the settlement history of Anatolia were probably sown in the "proto-urban" phase of the fourth and early third millennium B.C.E. Starting in the mid-third millennium B.C.E., settlements with clearly defined administrative, residential, and industrial sectors emerged, with indications of rank, wealth, and profession related to social stratification evident among the residents. One could presume that most local rulers or ruling families would have regulated the mechanism of political succession by establishing legitimated dynasties.

The chronological division of the EBA cultural phases is not equally clear-cut in every region of Anatolia (see table 4.5). Significant progress made in the eastern highland zone in this respect compared to other regions is due to the large number of well-stratified excavations and the close cooperation of the excavators in comparing and discussing the stratigraphical reliability of their data (see Marro 2000; Mazzoni 2000).

EBA Sites

The Aegean Littoral and West Central Plateau

The relative chronology of the EBA subperiods in the coastal region continues to be based largely on intra- and interregional correlations between the cultural inventories of Troy, key west-central Anatolian sites, and Tarsus in Cilicia (Yakar 1979, 2003; and see Steadman, chapter 10 in this volume).

The Bronze Age sites in the Troad provide over 160 radiocarbon dates, including nearly a hundred from Troy and the neighboring Beşik-Yassıtepe (Troy I period). At Beşik-Yassıtepe some thirty pottery sherds from the occupation layers corresponding to early Troy I produced thermoluminescence dates of 2820 B.C.E. (Wagner and Lorenz 1992). The measurements from Troy suggest that Troy I ceased to exist by 2719 B.C.E. and that strangely enough Troy II was founded by 2793 B.C.E. (Korfmann and Kromer 1993:149–57; Yakar 2002b:448, n.15–16). Despite the stratigraphical uncertainty of the Troy I–II transition, further exacerbated by the Troy II date, the reading for the end of Troy I "final" seems to be sound.

Table 4.5. Representative Sites of the EBA Regional Settlement Sequence in Anatolia

Period	Aegean	West-Central	Central	North	Cilicia	East	Southeast
2000 B.C.E. EBA IIIc	Troy IV Limantepe	Beycesultan VII	Boğazköy Vf Alacahöyük 5 Alişar 12T Kültepe 11 Acemhöyük 8	Ikiztepe Mound I Cemetery	Tarsus	Arslantepe VID Korucutepe F Norsuntepe 8–6 Tepecik	Amuq J Gedikli IIIk Titriş Kurban III Tilbeş Kazane
2150 B.C.E. EBA IIIb	Troy III–IV	Beycesultan IX–VIII	Boğazköy Vc Alacahöyük 6 Alişar 12T 6M Kültepe 12 Acemhöyük	Ikiztepe Mound I Cemetery	Tarsus Increase in north and west contacts	Arslantepe VID Korucutepe F Norşuntepe 10–9 Tepecik	Amuq I–J Gedikli Titriş Kurban IV Tilbeş Kazane Lidar
2300 B.C.E. EBA IIIa	Troy III Troy IIg	Beycesultan XII–X Küllüoba	Alacahöyük 7 Alişar 12T 7M Kültepe 13 Acemhöyük 9	Ikiztepe Mound I Cemetery	Tarsus Cultural implant from the west	Arslantepe VID Korucutepe E Norşuntepe 12–11	Amuq I Gedikli Titriş Kurban IV Tilbeş Lidar

2500 B.C.E. EBA IIb	Limantepe	Barcın Höyük Demircihöyük Küllüoba Beycesultan XIV–XIII Karataş V	Alacahöyük 8 Alişar T13 8M Kültepe 14 Acemhöyük 10	Ikiztepe	Tarsus	Arslantepe VIC2 Korucutepe D Norşuntepe 20–13 Pulur	Amuq H Gedikli Titriş Kurban IV Tilbeş
2600 B.C.E. EBA IIa	Troy IIa Limantepe	Demircihöyük Küllüoba Beycesultan XIV Karataş III	Alacahöyük 8 Alişar T14 Kültepe 14	Ikiztepe	Tarsus From village to town	Arslantepe VIC1 Koructepe C Norşuntepe 24–21 Pulur	Amuq H Gedikli Hassek Titriş Kurban IV Tilbeş
2700 B.C.E. EBA Ib	Troy I final ca. 2719 Limantepe Baklatepe	Demircihöyük Küllüoba Beycesultan XVI Karataş I	Alacahöyük Alişar 12 M	Ikiztepe	Tarsus	Arslantepe VI B2 Koructepe C Norşuntepe 30–25 Pulur	Amuq G Gedikli Hassek Kurban V Tilbeş
2900 B.C.E. EBA Ia	Troy Ia ca. 2920 Kumtepe Ib Limantepe Baklatepe	Demircihöyük Küllüoba Beycesultan XIX–XVII	Alacahöyük Alişar 19M– Çadır Höyük	Ikiztepe	Tarsus	Arslantepe VIB1 Koructepe C Tepecik Pulur	Amuq G Gedikli IIIa Hassek Titriş KurbanV Tilbeş

In the Aegean context, Troy I is considered contemporary with the later Eutresis culture (EH I) and the advanced Grotta-Pelos culture represented by the so-called Kampos group (EC I). Therefore, radiocarbon dates from Aegean EBA sites could also be relevant to the settlement sequence in the Troad. The middle and late phases of Troy I are considered to be contemporary with the early phases of the Korakou (EH IIA) and Keros-Syros (EC IIA) cultures on the basis of imported Urfirnis and sauceboat fragments found in the corresponding levels at Troy.

Diagnostic pottery of the Late Chalcolithic–EBA I style from Limantepe has been dated with the help of oak fragments found mixed with them (Yakar 2002a:448, n.19). The calibrated time span for this pottery, 3350–3050 B.C.E., might indicate that the EBA I settlement could have been established as early as the late fourth millennium B.C.E.

Four radiocarbon dates from Phases H and E at Demircihöyük indicate that the enclosed EBA village was founded ca. 3000 B.C.E. (Korfmann and Kromer 1993; Linick 1984:101). According to a dendrochronology estimate based on an oak fragment from the third millennium strata, cross-dated with the 285-year-old oak sequence at the submerged Black Sea site of Kiten in Bulgaria, the Demircihöyük village may have lasted at least until the mid-third millennium B.C.E., perhaps longer (Korfmann and Kromer 1993:139–40; Yakar 2002a:449). The site of Küllüoba, based mainly on ceramic comparisons with key sites such as Beycesultan, Troy, and Demircihöyük, is believed to have lasted throughout the third millennium B.C.E. (Efe and Ay-Efe 2001:43–59; Yakar 2002a:449). Finally, at Karataş-Semayük, seven radiocarbon dates from the lower strata indicate that this village was established in the early third millennium B.C.E. (Stuckenrath, Coe, and Ralph 1966:352).

The Central Plateau and Northern Anatolia

The EBA III architectural remains at Boğazköy on the central plateau have been described by Neve as pertaining to "a small residence of a landlord" (1993:105). Boğazköy at this time may have been ruled by a local dynasty. Despite the legendary nature of the account involving a king of Ḫatti called Pamba who appears in a list of seventeen kings including Zipani, the king of Kaniš, there could be a small measure of historical truth in the confrontation that supposedly took place between these local rulers and the Akkadian king Naram-Sin in the later part of the third millennium B.C.E. (Bryce 1998:9, n.6–7; and see Beal, chapter 26 in this volume).

İkiztepe, on the Black Sea coast, has a Late Chalcolithic–EBA occupation, but the remains are not equally present in each of the three mounds that make up the site. The problem with the radiocarbon measurements from this site is that there is almost no chronological differentiation between the Late Chalcolithic and EBA occupations; these dates, therefore, should be considered unreliable for the time being (see Erdoğu, Tanındı, and Uygun 2003). On the other hand, a relative chronological framework can be established based on typological comparisons between the pottery and metal objects, including weapons, and the corresponding assemblages from better dated sites in neighboring regions.

Cilicia and the Eastern Highlands

Tarsus is the key site that allows the indirect use of a Near Eastern historical chronology for western and central Anatolia. The Cilician third millennium B.C.E. sequence aligns with the Amuq G–J sequence span from the Mesopotamian Protoliterate to the end of the Ur III period. Cilician correlations with the Amuq are particularly well established for Phases H, I, and J. Although the Red Gritty Ware of Tarsus EBA II could be correlated with the brittle orange ware of Amuq H (and Gedikli "EBA II"), the EBA III goblets of Tarsus also occur in the Amuq Phase I (see Ökse, chapter 11 in this volume). The ring-burnished gray bottles of the southeast Anatolian/north Syrian tradition found in the Amuq J phase appear in Tarsus EBA IIIB levels (Yakar 1979:55). As originally pointed out by Mellink (1965:110, 1992), the Amuq sequence and its correlation with Tarsus EBA I–III phases is not the only point of departure for the Cilician EBA chronology. Wheelmade ware of north Syrian tradition found at Tarsus since the EBA I levels provide good synchronizations with roughly contemporary occupation levels in southeast Anatolian/north Syrian settlements. The Tarsus EBA II "imported" wares indicate contact with the Early Dynastic IIIA and early IIIB communities in the lower Euphrates basin (Yakar 1979:57). A large number of imported north Mesopotamian ceramics, which found their way to Tarsus in the EB IIIb period, provide additional links between this period in Cilicia and the post-Akkad era in northern Syria and the Khabur region. As for the Cilician synchronism with Egypt, this is based on a reserved slip pitcher of Cilician EBA II type found in an annex to *mastaba* G 1233 at Giza, dated before the end of Cheops's life.

Sos Höyük in the eastern highlands has a pre-EBA occupation floor that dates somewhere between 3500/3300 and 3000 B.C.E. Although the four radiocarbon samples from the three EBA I floors did not produce a clear chronological pattern, some of the six samples obtained from the EBA II features produced calibrated readings within the 2800–2500 B.C.E. timeframe. The EBA III occupation at this site is dated to within a 2500–2200 B.C.E. timeframe on the strength of three calibrated radiocarbon measurements (Sagona 2000:333, 335, 352–53).

The Arslantepe VI B1–2 settlement can be placed within the time span of ca. 3100–2600 B.C.E. (Frangipane 2000:448) or ca. 2700–2900 B.C.E. based on ten radiocarbon dates (Di Nocera 2000:75). The VI C1-2 settlement, which produced Metallic and "imported" Simple wares in the local pottery assemblage, is dated to 2612–2461 B.C.E. based on seven samples taken from a single context (Di Nocera 2000:75). The VI D1 and D2 architectural phases could be roughly placed, based on sixteen radiocarbon dates, at 2451–2288 and 2140–2041 B.C.E., respectively. It is presumed that the first occupation phase of this settlement is dated to 2500 B.C.E. (Di Nocera 2000:76).

Korucutepe offers two dates from the Phase C settlement corresponding to the final VI B phase and early phase of VI C at Arslantepe (ca. 2857–2709 B.C.E.). Samples from Phase D at Korucutepe provide two overlapping timeframes: ca. 2848–2614 and 2613–2503 B.C.E., respectively. Finally two dates from Korucutepe Phase E provide an overlapping interval of 2612–2465 B.C.E. (Di Nocera 2000:76; Lawn 1973:368, 1974:223–24).

At Norşuntepe the few dates from the EBA IA–B settlement provide a 3303–2926 B.C.E. range. However, the beginning of this occupation phase is thought to begin not earlier than 3000 B.C.E. due to strong material culture similarities with Arslantepe VI B1 and Hassek Höyük (Hauptmann 2000:421–22; Abb. 1, 2). The four dates from the EBA II settlement fall within the 2881–2614 B.C.E. range (Di Nocera 2000:75–76, 83, fig. 5a); however, in Hauptmann's opinion, this occupation phase should be placed within the space of 2700–2500 B.C.E. (2000:422–23, abb. 2; Esin 2000). The five dates from the EBA IIIA occupation produce an interval of 2458–2324 B.C.E., and a multitude of other radiocarbon dates from EBA IIIB contexts cluster around 2170 B.C.E. (Di Nocera 2000: fig. 6; Hauptmann 2000:423–26, abb. 2).

Southeastern Anatolia

The important site of Titriş Höyük, in the early (ca. 2900–2600 B.C.E.), middle (ca. 2600/2500–2400 B.C.E.) and late (ca. 2400/2300–2001 B.C.E.) phases of the EBA, is estimated to have covered a total of eight centuries of occupation (see Algaze and Matney, chapter 46 in this volume). Three of the four carbonized wood samples (TH 3771, TH 8267, and TH 8274) from the late EBA outer town span the last three centuries of the third millennium B.C.E. (Algaze et al. 1996:131–32; Matney, Algaze, and Rosen 1999). The Titriş radiocarbon dates are in general agreement with the Norşuntepe, Arslantepe, and Korucutepe readings (Rupley in Algaze et al. 2001:47–50, table 11, figs. 19–20).

The Middle Bronze Age: Assyrian Colonists in Central Anatolian Principalities

The four centuries long Middle Bronze Age (MBA) of Anatolia could be politically defined as a period of principalities (table 4.6). In the central plateau this period (ca. 1935–1725/20 B.C.E.) is highlighted by the presence of the Assyrian merchants whose activities are well documented in letters and commercial documents kept in their domiciles at Kültepe, Alişar, and Boğazköy (see Michel, chapter 13 in this volume). These Old Assyrian written records indirectly shed some light on the political history of the central plateau, which was dominated by major principalities such as Kaniš, Purušḫattum, Zalpa, Ḫattuš, Waḫšaniya, and Mama, which politically subjugated smaller polities (see Bryce 2005:21–40; Veenhof and Eidem 2008:147–82). The principal source for the historical chronology of the Principalities or Old Assyrian period in Anatolia is the *limu*-eponyms provided by the Kültepe (Kaniš) documents

Table 4.6. Major Anatolian Principalities with Assyrian Merchant Colonies

Period	Historical Chronology	Kültepe (Kaneš) Kārum	Boğazköy (Ḫattuš)	Alişar (Ankuwa?)	Karahöyük	Acemhöyük (Purušḫanda?)
1600 B.C.E. MBA IV	Hittite Old Kindom Muršili I Ḫattušili I Labarna I	I a=M6	Büyükkale IVc3		I	
1700 B.C.E. MBA III	Assyrian kings Išme-Dagan Šamši-Adad	Ištar-Ebri? Zuzu Perwa Anitta Pitḫana Waršama Inar Ib = M7	Piušti Büyükkale IVd Lower City 4	10 T	II	3
1800 B.C.E. MBA II	Erišum II Naram-Sin Puzur-Aššur	Ic Ḫurmeli Ḫarpatiwa? II = M8	Büyükkale Va Lower City		III	
1900 B.C.E. MBA I 2000 B.C.E.	Šarru-kin Ikunum Erišum I	II = M8 III IV	Büyükkale Vb Lower City 5	11T 5M	IV	7

(Veenhof 2003; Veenhof and Eidem 2008:28–34). The limu-eponym lists provide rather precise timeframes for the Assyrian merchants' activities in Anatolia corresponding to the reigns of the rulers of the city of Assur. However, these historical dates do not solve the problem of fixing the regnal years of the local rulers with the same precision. For this reason, there is an increasing dependence on scientific dating methods for establishing the construction and destruction dates of local palaces at Acemhöyük and Kültepe (Yakar 2002a:561–63). The independent construction dates could give us some idea as to how long before the arrival of the Assyrian merchants the local dynasties of principalities came into existence.

The Major MBA Sites

The major site of Kültepe-Kaniš spans much of the MBA (see Kulakoğlu, chapter 47 in this volume). The lower town houses of the pre-*kārum* Levels IV–III, which were occupied by local residents, did not produce written documents. The Assyrian merchants of Level II may have arrived sometime during Erišum's reign in Assyria. The life span of Level II (1974–1836 B.C.E.) corresponds to the years of 129 Assyrian officials who served as limu (year-eponym officials) during the reigns of Erišum I (1974–1935 B.C.E.), Ikinum (1934–1921 B.C.E.), Šarru-kin (1920–1881 B.C.E.),

Puzur-Aššur II (1880–1873 B.C.E.), and Naram-Sin (1872–1829/19 B.C.E.) (Veenhof and Eidem 2008:28–32; and see Michel, chapter 13 in this volume). An additional nine eponyms (proposed by Veenhof 2003) extend the duration of this *kārum* up to 138 years (see also Newton and Kuniholm 2004:166). Level Ic represents a gap in occupation that may have lasted up to three decades, corresponding to Naram-Sin's final years on the Assyrian throne, including that of his successor, Erišum II (1829/1819–1809 B.C.E.). The rebuilt lower town of Level Ib (1798–1740 B.C.E.) was resettled by Assyrian merchants in the early years of Šamši-Adad's reign (1808–1776 B.C.E.). The *kārum* remained active until the final five years of Išme-Dagan (1775–1735 B.C.E.). After its destruction, the rebuilt Level Ia settlement was no longer inhabited by Assyrian merchants. The *kārum* of Level II can be partly dated using the 521-year floating dendrochronological scale, spanning the years 2544–2024 B.C.E. and built from the juniper door threshold timbers from some of the Old Palace rooms and a road bedding of oak logs, all recovered from the mound (Mound Level 8; Newton and Kuniholm 2004:166–67; Özgüç 2003:133–37). The *Kārum* Ib level can be dated with the help of a dendrochronological scale built with timbers recovered from the Waršama palace (Mound Level 7). This palace, probably constructed in 1835/32 B.C.E., was twice repaired, the last presumably in 1774/71 B.C.E. (Newton and Kuniholm 2004:168–69; Özgüç 2003:120–25). This palace, presumably built by Waršama, may have continued to be a royal domicile of his successors Pitḫana, Anitta, Perwa, Zuzu, and perhaps a certain Ištar-ebri (for the presumed successors of Anitta, see Beal 2003).

The palaces at Kültepe and Acemhöyük, dated using dendrochronology, provide solid ground for more precisely placing various material culture assemblages, including epigraphic material, in chronological context with other MBA sites. Furthermore, the construction date of the Sarıkaya, and a bulla from the tenth year of Šamši-Adad, suggest that this king reigned in the second and/or third quarters of the eighteenth century B.C.E. (Yakar 2002a). This evidence, as an independent timescale, favors a chronology between the Middle and Low models (Åström 1987, 1989; Gates 1987; Veenhof 2003:57–69; Weinstein 1996).

The ongoing excavations at Kaman-Kalehöyük (see Omura, chapter 51 in this volume) reveal severely burned architectural remains of a large multiroom structure, dating to the MBA, which revealed over fifty intramural burials. A nearby structure produced two clay tablets, perhaps part of a private archive of the Assyrian Colony period.

Finally, at Karahöyük-Konya numerous juniper timbers without bark were recovered from the large MBA settlement, probably cut in 1771/1768 B.C.E.; these produced a 301-year-long tree ring chronology cross-dating with that of Gordion (Kuniholm 1996:183–84; Newton and Kuniholm 2004:169). However, because of the missing bark and uncertain terminal ring, the construction date of the buildings cannot be determined accurately. This settlement is one of the candidates for historical Purušḫanda, whose king submitted to the authority of Anitta. If so, its occupation could have lasted well beyond the reign of Anitta (Yakar 2002a:563–64).

The Late Bronze Age: Hittite Old Kingdom and Empire Periods

Due to the paucity of absolute dates from stratified archaeological contexts of major Late Bronze Age (LBA) sites, archaeologists continue to correlate archaeological layers with historical dates, particularly in establishing the chronology of Hittite sites (see Genz 2006; Mielke 2006a). However, dates that are established through synchronisms of royal figures tied to events mentioned in literary sources rarely provide more than a general chronological framework. For instance, despite the synchronisms between the New Kingdom kings of Egypt, especially those of the eighteenth and nineteenth dynasties, and the Hittite Empire kings (table 4.7), any readjustment of the former up or down the chronological scale affects the latter, as does the Middle Assyrian kings list. The compiled Hittite kings list gives an idea of the royal succession and approximate regnal years that cannot be fixed within a precise timescale. The timescales provided by Hittite historical chronology could be slightly narrowed down to time segments provided by sporadic "imports" of Mycenaean and Cypriote wares or prestige objects of known provenience found in stratified Hittite contexts. As for Hittite pottery, due to its general homogeneity and slow evolution of diagnostic vessel types it is not widely considered the most precise chronological indicator in conventional typological dating (see Gates 2006:305; Schoop 2006). However, when diagnostic vessels are recovered from relatively well-dated contexts at sites such as Boğazköy (Schoop 2006:221; Schoop and Seeher 2006) or Kuşaklı (Müller-Karpe 2006), they can provide a more reliable and useful chronological scale.

Differences of opinion regarding the division of the five centuries long period of Hittite civilization (ca. 1680–1180 B.C.E.), which dominated a significant portion of Anatolia and northwest Syria, into either two or three historical phases, do not interfere with the slow progress toward establishing an unbiased chronological framework that primarily dates archaeological contexts of historical significance using scientific methods.

The three-tier division of Hittite history (table 4.8) into Old, Middle, and New or Empire periods is not unanimously accepted (see Beal, chapter 26 in this volume). Scholars such as Bryce (2005), Freu (2003), and Starke (1998) prefer a two-tier division leaving out the label of Middle Hittite, which most believe marks the period of political turmoil following the death of Telepinu (Dinçol 2006:20–21, 23). McMahon (1989), on the other hand, places Middle Hittite after the reign of Muwattalli II, suggesting that it probably lasted less than six decades. The phrase "Middle Hittite" (Archi 2003) makes more sense linguistically than archaeologically. As a linguistic label it refers to the transition period during which cumulative changes in the grammar, probably starting with Tudḫaliya I, transformed the Old Hittite language into that of the Empire period; these changes did not occur before the reign of Muršili II (Melchert 2007).

Table 4.7. **Hittite Kings and Their Contemporaries in the Ancient Near East**

	Periods	Middle Chronology	Ḫatti	Mitanni	Assyria	Egypt
	LBA IIb	Šuppiluliuma II 1207–? Arnuwanda III 1209–1207 Tudḫaliya IV 1227–1209 Kurunta 1228–1227 Tudḫaliya III 1237–1228 Ḫattušili III 1267–1237 Urhi-Teshub 1272–1267 Muwatalli II 1295–1272	Late Great Kingdom	Wasašatta Šattuara Šattiwaza	Tukulti-Ninurta 1264–1209 Šalmaneser I 1276–1246 Adad-nirari 1308–1276	Merneptah 1213–1203 Ramses II 1279–1213
1200 B.C.E.	LBA IIa	Muršili II 1321–1295 Arnuwanda II 1322–1321 Šuppiluliuma I 1344–1322 Tudḫaliya III 1360–1340 Ḫattušili II ?-1360 Arnuwanda I Tudḫaliya I/II 1400-?	Early Great Kingdom Middle Kingdom	Šuttarna III Artatama II Tušrata Artašumara Šuttarna II Artatama I Šaušatar		Horemheb 1323–1295 Tutankhamen 1334–1325 Amenhotep IV 1350–1334 Amenhotep III 1382–1344
1400 B.C.E.	LBA Ib	Muwatalli I ?–1400 Ḫuzziya? II Zidanta? II Ḫantili ? II Taḫurwaili Alluwamna 1500–?	Middle Kingdom	Parattarna Šuttarna I		
1500 B.C.E.	LBA Ia	Telepinu 1525–1500 Ḫuzziya ?–1525 Ammuna Zidanta I 1569–? Ḫantili I 1590–1560	Old Kingdom	Kirta		

Table 4.8. The Old, Middle, and Great Hittite Kingdom Occupation Sequence at the Capital and Four District Centers

Period	Boğazköy-Ḫattuša L.City	Büyükkale	Büyükkaya	U.City	Sarıkale	Ortaköy Šapinuwa	Kuşaklı Šariššа	Maşat Tappiga?	Kinet
1200 B.C.E.	1a	IIIa					Period	1	13.2
LBA IIb	1b	IIIb	lower plateau	x			IV		13.1
1300 B.C.E.		IVa		x		Buildings	III	2	14
LBA IIa	2			x		A–B			
1400 B.C.E.		IVb			x		—		15 A
LBA Ib				south ponds			II		
1500 B.C.E.	3	Vc1	nw. slope	grain silo	x		I		15C
LBA Ia									
1600 B.C.E.		Vc2							
MBA IV		Vc3	upper plateau						

The historical chronology of the Hittite kingdom can be partly established by synchronizing the reign of some of the kings with their Babylonian, Middle Assyrian, and Egyptian counterparts. The calendar dates obtained by such historical synchronisms (and therefore the number of generations of Hittite kings) change according to one's choice of chronology: high, middle, low, or ultra-low (see Åström 1989:pt. 3:64–66; tables 1–4 in Dinçol 2006:20–21, 23, 25). The middle chronology, which places Hammurabi's reign from 1792 to 1750 B.C.E., is currently less favored by historians, who prefer to work with the short chronology, which fixes the reign of Hammurabi at 1728–1686 B.C.E. and the sack of Babylon by Muršili I at 1531 B.C.E.

Despite the divergence of views concerning the middle and low chronologies, there is a majority opinion that the reign of Šuppiluliuma spanned most of the third quarter of the fourteenth century B.C.E. Estimates on the length of his reign vary from thirty-five years (Klengel 2002) to twenty-one or twenty-two years (Gorny *apud* McMahon 1989; Wilhelm 2004). Even the historical synchronizations with Egyptian rulers through the Amarna letters have failed to establish the date of Šuppiluliuma I's ascent to the Hittite throne in absolute terms. This question might be resolved if the astronomical date for the "Solar Omen of Tawannana" (in the form of an eclipse also seen at Ḫattuša) at the start of Muršili II's tenth year on the Hittite throne can be agreed on (Huber 2001; McMurray 2004:4, table 1). The likely lunar event that would have been seen at Ḫattuša is speculated to be the one that occurred on 24 June 1312 B.C.E. (McMurray 2004:5). This date places the start of Muršili II's reign in 1322 B.C.E. Allowing one or two years for Arnuwanda II's reign, the reign of Šuppiluliuma II might have ended in 1324 or 1323 B.C.E.

Now that the chronological boundaries of principal Hittite period pottery types have been roughly established for Boğazköy (see Schoop 2006), the more precise dating of individual Hittite settlements, and the length and density of their occupation levels during the historical phases corresponding to the MBA and LBA can be achieved through ceramic analogies. The chronological value of such analogies increases when pottery assemblages containing distinctive forms derive from well-stratified and radiocarbon-dated proveniences. The different final destruction dates of provincial Hittite centers indicate that disintegration of the Hittite kingdom occurred gradually, starting in the final decades of the thirteenth century B.C.E. and ending soon after the beginning of the twelfth century B.C.E. (see Seeher, chapter 16, and van den Hout, chapter 41 in this volume). The application of dendrochronologically revised dating of archaeological assemblages clarifies the significance of political and cultural changes that occurred in the LBA–Early Iron Age (EIA) transition.

The Hittite Period Sites

Boğazköy, the site of the Hittite capital of Ḫattuša, is naturally the type site for this cultural period (see Mielke, chapter 48 in this volume). A quantitative analysis of second millennium ceramic assemblages recovered from different localities led to the isolation of ten relatively consecutive groups, eight from radiocarbon-dated architectural contexts, stretching from the late *kārum* to the end of the Hittite kingdom period (Schoop 2006:figs. 2–3). Indications are that the upper plateau of Büyükkaya continued to be settled in the seventeenth century B.C.E. Recent excavations have demonstrated that Old Hittite kingdom Ḫattuša, which included central storage facilities, was significantly larger than previously assumed, and extended to the western part of the Upper City (Seeher 2006:203–11, fig. 1). The chronological realignment of the general stratigraphy may have direct implications in dating the reign of Ḫattušili I, who rebuilt and resettled Ḫattuša.

A radiocarbon series from Büyükkaya indicates that after Ḫattuša ceased to exist as the Hittite capital at the end of the thirteenth or in the first decade of twelfth century B.C.E., this neighborhood continued to be occupied or was resettled soon after by a rural community (Schoop and Seeher 2006:56–58). A site that produced a similarly long sequence of occupation is Kaman Kalehöyük, particularly Stratum IIIa–c, which spans the MBA–LBA second millennium. The chronological subdivision of this eight-centuries-long period is based on pottery typology (Katsuno 2006; see Omura, chapter 51 in this volume).

Ortaköy, ancient Šapinuwa (see Mielke, chapter 48 in this volume), offered timber from its Building A; the dendrochronological wiggle-matched reading of this sample suggests that this palace-like compound continued to function at least until the early thirteenth century B.C.E. The cuneiform texts found in the archives, and their Middle Hittite ductus and grammatical style and historical context, indicate that during the late fifteenth and fourteenth centuries B.C.E. this city could have been a second royal residence on a par with Ḫattuša. A dendrochronolgical reading of 1365 B.C.E. from a storage facility, Building B, seems to support this chronological estimate (Yakar 2002a). This city, like the distant Maşat Höyük (Tapigga?) may have ceased to exist by the mid-thirteenth century B.C.E., probably in the aftermath of attacks by the Kaška.

The Hittite Level II at the cult center of Maşat Höyük produced two seal impressions of Tudḫaliya and Šuppiluliuma I, respectively, dating this level to the fourteenth century B.C.E. (Özgüç 1978). The last Hittite level (I), which was destroyed in a serious conflagration, produced imported LH IIIB stirrup-jars (Özgüç 1978). The tree-ring date (ca. 1392 B.C.E.) for the start of this level is not very reliable because it derives from a sample with missing bark and probably a number of outer rings (Kuniholm 1993:372; Yakar 2002a:566). After applying some corrections, the beginning of this level is presumed to be prior to the reign of Ḫattušili III, in the early thirteenth century B.C.E.

Kuşaklı-Šarišša offers a large quantity of pottery recovered from the stratified occupation levels of this Hittite city, providing technological and typological details of chronological significance. Close comparisons with the Boğazköy, Ortaköy, Maşat, and İnandık stratified pottery groups contribute to the chronologically sound subdivision of the Kuşaklı material, which places the Hittite settlement within the flexible boundaries of the sixteenth–thirteenth centuries B.C.E. (Müller-Karpe 2006). The lower boundary is confirmed by more precise dates obtained through tree ring measurements of juniper and pine samples retrieved from structures in the late Old Hittite period settlement (Period I) (Mielke 2006b:266–69). It seems that Šarišša too had lost its urban character sometime during the third quarter of the thirteenth century B.C.E.

At Porsuk/Ulukışla, a large collection of juniper, pine, and cedar samples provides an LBA sequence that overlaps with the combined Kültepe and Acemhöyük MBA tree ring sequence (Kuniholm 1993:372; Kuniholm et al. 1992; Newton and Kuniholm 2004:170) and the later Gordion sequence. The Porsuk dates place the beginning of the Old Hittite kingdom dynasty somewhere in the seventeenth century B.C.E., an estimate more in agreement with middle chronology (Yakar 2002a). The problem is tying the start of LBA I construction activities with one of the Old Hittite kingdom rulers such as Ḫattušili I or his successor. Ceramic typology and technology indicate that the occupation continued into the LBA IIa–b and beyond (Yakar 1993:13).

The southerly site of Kilisetepe has a pottery assemblage from the Level III occupation that is dominated by ceramics characteristic of Hittite settlements. The following settlement (Level II) shows a departure from architectural conventions of the earlier period. The presence of LH IIIC wares in Phases IIc and d may indicate that the end of the Level III settlement could be placed sometime within the fourth quarter of the thirteenth century B.C.E. or slightly later (Postgate 2008; Yakar 2006:48).

Kinet Höyük, resting between the Mediterranean and the Amanus Mountains, offers radiocarbon dates (Gates 2006:298, n.7) and Cypriot imports from the LBA settlement indicating that Hittite material culture characteristics appeared at this site in the sixteenth century B.C.E., in other words during the course of the Old Kingdom period. Chronological classification of the Hittite period pottery, based on that from Boğazköy, facilitates the relative dating of the LBA subperiods at Kinet, specifically into subperiods 15, 14, 13.1, and 13.2 (see Gates 2006 for more details). In particular, the latest subperiod (known as Level 13.2) contains "sub-Hittite features" and could provide some indications about the timing and geocultural identity of the peoples and elements responsible for the LBA–EIA transition at this and neighboring settlements.

Finally, on the northwest coast, the site of Troy was known as Wiluša during Hittite times (see Bryce, chapter 15, and Beal, chapter 26 in this volume). Relevant strata at Troy include Levels VI–VIIa; the destruction of Troy VIIa is thought to have happened not earlier than the late LH IIIB and no later than the LH IIIB2–IIIC transition (Mountjoy 1999:300). The LH IIIC early phase pottery found in the securely dated Phase 7 settlement at Assiros in Macedonia suggests that the start of early phase pottery production in the Aegean could be placed at ca. 1250 B.C.E. This date, which is based on four radiocarbon-dated and wiggle-matched oak timbers at Assiros, could be used to readjust the date of the Troy VIIb1 settlement, which produced LH IIIC ware as well as a few handmade "Barbarian" ware examples of Thracian inspiration.

The Iron Age Chronology and Sites

The final destruction dates of Hittite, Arzawan (in post-Hittite western Anatolia), or Mycenaean centers as well as the occupation sequences of Phrygian, Lydian, Urartian, and Neo-Hittite sites are coming into better focus as the contexts of various cultural assemblages are dated independently using a combination of dendrochronological and radiocarbon systems. The latter is contributing to the more specific archaeological divisions of the Iron Age (see also Summers 2008; tables 4.9 and 4.10).

At the heart of the transition from the Hittite to the Early Iron and later Phrygian Period is the site of Gordion (see Voigt, chapter 50 in this volume). Radiocarbon determinations at this site, based on five seed samples from the Terrace Building 2A, cluster at ca. 827–803 B.C.E. (with a 95.4 percent confidence level; DeVries et al. 2003). Other dates from roofing reeds, ca. 845–800 B.C.E. (71.4 percent confidence level), indicate that this building, and therefore perhaps the citadel, was constructed in the third quarter of the ninth century B.C.E., if not earlier. The pottery and bronzes of the "Destruction Level" find good parallels in the corresponding material from the tomb sequence starting with the earliest tumulus (W) and indicate a late ninth century B.C.E. date. According to postdestruction ceramic deposits, including Corinthian Late Geometric (ca. 730–720 B.C.E.) and Early Protocorinthian (ca. 720–690), the citadel was rebuilt roughly a generation after the destruction, close to the time of Tumuli K-III and P (DeVries et al. 2003). The history of Gordion under the Phrygians requires a chronological revision due to the dendrochronological dates of burial chamber timbers in the so-called Midas tumulus (MM) (DeVries et al. 2003). With the revised 743–741 B.C.E. date, it could not have been the tomb of Midas but was probably that of

Table 4.9. Historical Synchronizations-Rulers of Anatolian States and Assyria

Approximate Calendar b.c.e.	Assyrian Empire	Kings of Carchemish and Hittite Dynastic Origins	Phrygia Based on Gordion stratigraphy	Lydia	Urartu
550 B.C.E. Iron Age III	Cyrus the Great Median Astyages Median Cyaxares Aššurbanipal Esarhaddon Sargon II Tiglath-pileser III	Pisiri	Late Phrygian Middle Phrygian Midas	Croesus Alyattes Sadyattes Ardys Gyges (Mermnad dynasty)	Rusa IV Sarduri IV Sarduri III Rusa III Erimena Rusa II Argišti II Rusa I Sarduri II
750 B.C.E. Iron Age II	Aššurdan III Šalmaneser IV Adad-nirari Šamši-Adad V Šalmaneser III Aššurnasirpal Tukulti-ninurta II	Sastura Kamani Yariri Astiruwa Sangara Katuwa Suhi II	Early Phrygian	Herodotus's Heracleid dynasty	Sarduri II Argišti I Menua Išpuini Sarduri I Aramu
900 B.C.E. Iron Age I	Adad-nirari II Aššurdan II Tiglath-pileser I	Astuwatamanza Suhi I Ura-Tarḫunza [. . .]paziti Tudḫaliya Ini-tešub Runtiya II Kuzi-tešub	Early Iron Age ca. 1100 B.C.E.	Herodotus's Atyad dynasty	
1200 B.C.E. LBA II b 1300 B.C.E.	Tukulti-ninurta Šalmaneser I	Talmi-tešub Ini-tešub Šarkuḫrunuwa	Hittite Period Town		

his ancestor. Considering the political links of the Phrygians with Anatolian polities, this minor revision of Gordion's chronology makes historical sense.

In fact, the revised destruction level date has a bearing on the chronology of early Phrygian sculptures whose styles indicate a Neo-Hittite influence. According to Roller (2008) the late-ninth-century B.C.E. Gordion sculptures correspond well with the chronology of Neo-Hittite relief sculpture. As for the rock-cut sanctuaries, monuments, and altars in the Phrygian countryside (e.g., Midas City and additional localities), they were probably commissioned during the ninth to early sixth centuries B.C.E. (see Roller, chapter 25, and Greaves, chapter 21 in this volume).

Also on the plateau, but to the south, is the site of Kilisetepe, which offers important remains dating to the Hittite/Iron Age transition. The destructions of the Phases IIc and IId settlements, which yielded LH IIIC sherds in stratified contexts, date the gradual end of Hittite political control toward the end of the thirteenth century

Table 4.10. Representative Sites of Iron Age Regional Occupation Sequence in Anatolia

Kinet	Tarsus	Kilise Tepe	Porsuk	Boğazköy "House on the Slope" area	Gordion Yassıhöyük	Troy	Approximate Calendar b.c.e.
4 5 6	Continued settlement	IIf	III	2	4 5	VIII	550 B.C.E. Iron Age III
	Section B: unit Q, R	IIe	III	3	5 6A 6B		750 B.C.E. Iron Age II
	Section B: units J, K U, P, W	IId	IV	4	7	VIIbe VIIb2	900 B.C.E. Iron Age I
13.2 13.1		IIc	V	5	8	VIIb1 VIIa VI	1200 B.C.E. LBA IIB

B.C.E., finalizing in the early twelfth century B.C.E. (Postgate 2008). Considering that significant architectural changes accompanied the Level II (e.g., Stele Building) settlement overlying the earlier one (Level III), which is characterized by central Anatolian LBA ceramics, Hittite control of this settlement may have weakened considerably in the last quarter of the thirteenth century B.C.E. The White Painted IV Cypriot type sherds among the painted and plain pottery fragments in one of the Level IIf stone-lined kilns provide a very general estimate for this occupation phase somewhere between the later eighth and early seventh centuries B.C.E. (Hansen and Postgate 1999). However, this group of ceramics is not considered an absolute chronological indicator, at least not until the contexts which produced similar wares at other sites in Cilicia and Cyprus can be dated with greater precision (Postgate 2008).

In western Anatolia the sites of Sardis and Troy offer evidence for the Lydian and Aegean-influenced Iron Age. At Sardis, the chronological markers of the archaeological records of the early Lydian Period consist mainly of painted pottery. Although the chronological ambiguity of the material inventories continues to some extent during the late Lydian and early Persian occupations, it is presumed that the smaller tumuli at Bin Tepe and their contents mostly date from the Persian Period (see Greenewalt, chapter 52 in this volume).

The LBA–EIA transition date in the Aegean littoral is open to revision due to local attempts to scientifically date the architectural contexts of certain groups of Aegean painted ceramics. The Troy VIIb2 settlement phase pottery repertory includes a few LH IIIC middle- and late-phase forms accompanied by handmade "Barbarian" and "Knobbed" wares, which can be roughly placed within the twelfth century B.C.E. (Yakar 2006:44–45).

The next Troy VIIb3 phase is culturally defined and dated by the occurrence of Protogeometric pottery, which is divided into four chronotypological groups (Lenz et al. 1998). Charred construction timbers from Assiros in Macedonia provide nearly absolute dates for the start of the Protogeometric period (EIA) in southern Greece. A century-long sequence of tree rings can be matched with the Anatolian master dendrochronological sequence. The broken Protogeometric amphora from a securely stratified and dated context in Assiros Phase 3 is similar in fabric and decoration to the example found at Troy VIIb3 (Yakar 2006:42–43). Because this vessel is considered to be a type that appeared several decades later than the earliest appearance of the Protogeometric style, the start of this cultural period in Greece can be placed within the 1100–1070 B.C.E. time segment (Newton, Wardle, and Kuniholm 2005).

The EIA archaeology and history prior to the Urartian Period in the eastern highlands requires more research and documentation (for the most comprehensive treatment of this region and period to date see Khatchadourian, chapter 20 in this volume). The question whether the earliest variants of the "grooved pottery" and cemeteries found at sites such as Dilkaya, Karagündüz, and Yoncatepe in the Van Basin could have belonged to the immediate predecessors of the Urartians is still being debated (Köroğlu and Konyar 2008). The earliest historical and archaeological records of the Urartian kingdom date to the mid-ninth century B.C.E. Following Sarduri I, most of his successors built new fortresses to strengthen the defenses of the kingdom as well as expand the state's control over the newly settled territories. These construction activities continued well into the mid-seventh century B.C.E., as demonstrated by the currently excavated fortified site of Ayanis. This fortress, which ceased to function ca. 653–650 B.C.E., offers a dendrochronological estimate for the construction of the temple of Haldi by Rusa II sometime within 677 to 666 B.C.E. (Kuniholm et al. 2005; and see Çilingiroğlu, chapter 49, Zimansky, chapter 24, and Radner, chapter 33 in this volume), which places this king between the reigns of Assyrian kings Aššurbanipal and Esarhaddon.

Conclusion

Neolithic excavations in all parts of Anatolia and the Aegean world are enriching the chronological databank with scientific dates that provide a much-needed solid basis from which we may finally understand whether the migration of Anatolian farmers was solely responsible for the development or spread of agriculture in eastern Greece and the Balkans. These dates, and the chronologically corroborated early appearance and distribution pattern of Anatolian-style artifacts (possibly carrying symbolic significance), in southeastern Europe require a review of the traditional models of colonization, demic diffusion, and population replacement in the context of the transition to farming in the Balkans (Budja 2003:esp. figs 1–6; and see Özdoğan, chapter 29 in this volume). Artifacts such as seals at key Balkan and Anatolian sites may lend support to the argument that the transformation of hunter-gatherers into farmers was largely the result of a locally selective integration of farming technologies acquired through socially active exchange networks.

The value of the historical chronology for the MBA in central Anatolia cannot be denied. The recently revised chronology constructed with eponyms retrieved mainly from *Kārum* Kaniš provides synchronizations with Old Assyrian rulers; however, it fails to date precisely the length of occupation gaps such as *Kārum* Kaniš Ic or provide clear synchronisms with other MBA centers in the central plateau and beyond that lack similar epigraphic data.

Scientific dating methods based on radiocarbon and tree-ring measurements are proving effective in estimating with ever-increasing precision the duration of Hittite cultural phases in Ḫatti proper and its peripheries. For instance, the suspicion that Hittite cultural characteristics at sites such as Kilisetepe (Level III) or Kinet Höyük (Levels 15–13.1) were replaced by new material culture traditions of provincial character some decades before the final demise of the Hittite administration in Ḫatti proper stands a better chance of being substantiated by scientific dates rather than by interregional Hittite pottery correlations based on typology and fabrics (see Gates 2006:304–5; Postgate 2008). After all, the late-thirteenth-century B.C.E. Hittite pottery forms from Boğazköy do not show remarkable changes from those of the earlier periods, only a reduction in the number of form and fabric groups (Schoop 2003:172–75).

Only when Hittite-dominated final levels at Anatolian sites can be dated in maximal absolute terms will we be better able to chart the regions and therefore the players that contributed to the slow and painful demise of Hittite administration in Anatolia (Yakar 2003).

With some exceptions, the Anatolian EIA suffers from lack of archaeological and literary documentation. So far only a few EIA sites in the central plateau have produced stratified occupational remains of some chronological significance, among them Gordion (Yassıhöyük), Boğazköy, and Kaman-Kalehöyük (Genz 2003). This roughly three-centuries-long period often defined as the Anatolian "dark age," which started with the demise of the Hittite Empire, lasted roughly until the mid-ninth century B.C.E. It is also during these three centuries that pre-Urartian cultures were referred to in the annals and inscriptions of Tiglath-Pileser I (1115–1077 B.C.E.) (Yakar 2000:432–34); however, a complete archaeological and chronological understanding of these eastern highlands during this period continues to elude us.

It is clear that even though a substantial body of textual data is available—for instance, the Hittite Empire corpus or those available from Assyrian references to Urartian or other Anatolian cultures—radiometric and dendrochronological dates are essential for understanding the historocultural transitions at individual sites. An additional plethora of absolute dates from the prehistoric sites scattered across the breadth of Anatolia are even more urgently needed to better understand, in incremental phases, the regional cultural patterns that took Anatolia from hunter-gatherer to empire over the course of the millennia covered in this volume. The data presented in this chapter have provided a current summary of how far presently available dates have allowed us to advance our understanding and how much there is yet to discover.

REFERENCES

Algaze, Guillermo, Gülay Dinçkan, Britt Hartenger, Timothy Matney, Jennifer Pournelle, Lynn Rainville, Steven Rosen, Eric Rupley, Duncan Schlee, and Regis Vallet. 2001. Research at Titriş in Southeastern Anatolia: The 1999 Season. *Anatolica* 27: 23–106.

Algaze, Guillermo, Jay Kelley, Timothy Matney, and Duncan Schlee. 1996. Late EBA Urban Structure at Titriş Höyük, SE Turkey: The 1995 Season. *Anatolica* 22: 129–43.

Archi, Alfonso. 2003. Middle Hittite–Middle Hittite Kingdom. In *Hittite Studies in Honor of Harry A. Hoffner, Jr: On the Occasion of His 65th Birthday*, ed. Gary M. Beckman, Richard H. Beal, and Gregory McMahon, 1–12. Winona Lake, Ind.: Eisenbrauns.

Åström, Paul, ed. 1987, 1989. *High, Middle or Low: Acts of an International Colloquium on Absolute Chronology*. Parts 1–2(1987) 3 (1989). Gothenburg: Åström Förlag.

Baird, Douglas. 2003. Pınarbaşı. *Anatolian Archaeology* 9: 2–4.

———. 2006. The Boncuklu Project: The Origins of Sedentism, Cultivation and Herding in Central Anatolia. *Anatolian Archaeology* 12: 13–16.

Beal, Richard E. 2003. The Predecessors of Hattusili I. In *Hittite Studies in Honor of Harry A. Hoffner, Jr: On the Occasion of his 65th Birthday*, ed. Gary M. Beckman, Richard H. Beal, and Gregory McMahon, 13–36. Winona Lake, Ind.: Eisenbrauns.

Bischoff, Damien. 2006. CANeW 14C Databases and 14C Tables. Upper Mesopotamia (SE Turkey, N Syria and N Iraq 10,000–5000 cal BC). www.canew.org

———. 2007. CANeW Material Culture Stratigraphic Tables. Upper Mesopotamia (SE Turkey, N Syria and N Iraq 10,000–5000 cal BC). www.canew.org

Box, George E. P. and George C. Tiao. 1992. *Bayesian Inference in Statistical Analysis*. New York: Wiley.

Bryce, Trevor. 1998. *The Kingdom of the Hittites*. Oxford: Calendron Press.

———. 2005. *The Kingdom of the Hittites*. 2nd ed. Oxford: Oxford University Press.

Buck, Caitlin E., William G. Cavanagh, and Clifford D. Litton. 1996. *The Bayesian Approach to Interpreting Archaeological Data*. Chichester: Wiley.

Budja, Mihael. 2003. Seals, Contracts and Tokens in the Balkans Early Neolithic: Where in the Puzzle. *Documenta Praehistorica* 30: 115–30.

Butterlin, Pascal. 2000. La vallee de l'Euphrate et l'expansion Urukeene: Problèmes stratigraphiques et chronologiques au sud du Taurus. In *Chronologies des pays du Caucase et de L'Euphrate aux IVe–IIIe Millénaires*, ed. Catherine Marro and Harald Hauptmann, 23–51. *Institut Français d'Etudes Anatoliennes d'Istanbul, Varia Anatolica XI*. Paris: De Boccard.

Carter, Elizabeth, Stuart Campbell, and Suellen Gauld. 2003. Elusive Complexity: New Data from Late Halaf Domuztepe in South Central Turkey. *Paléorient* 29.2: 117–33.

Cessford, Craig. 2002. Bayesian Statistics and the Dating of Çatalhöyük East. In *The Neolithic of Central Anatolia: Internal Developments and External Relations during the 9th–6th Millennia Cal. BC*, ed. Frédéric Gérard and Laurens Thissen, 27–31. Proceedings of the International CANeW Table Ronde, Istanbul, 23–24 November 2001. İstanbul: Ege Yayınları.

DeVries, Keith, Peter I. Kuniholm, Kenneth G. Sams, and Mary M. Voigt. 2003. New Dates for Iron Age Gordion. *Antiquity* 77.296: Project Gallery.

Dinçol, Belkıs. 2006. Über die Probleme der absoluten Datierung der Herrschaftsperioden der hethitischen Könige nach den philologischen und glyptischen Belegen. In *Strukturerung und Datierung in der hethitischen Archäeologie/Structuring and Dating in Hittite Archaeology*, ed. Dirk Paul Mielke, Ulf-Dietrich Schoop, and Jürgen Seeher, 19–32. BYZAS 4. İstanbul: Zero Prod.

Di Nocera, Gian Maria. 2000. Radiocarbon Datings from Arslantepe and Norşuntepe: The Fourth–Third Millennium Absolute Chronology in the Upper Euphrates and Transcaucasian Region. In *Chronologies des Pays du Caucase et de l'Euphrate aux IVe–IIIe Millénaires*, ed. Catherine Marro and Harald Hauptmann, 73–109. Institut Français d'Etudes Anatoliennes d'Istanbul, Varia Anatolica XI. Paris: De Boccard.

Efe, Turan and Deniz A. M. Ay-Efe. 2001. Küllüoba: Iç kuzeybatı Anadolu'da bir ilk tunç çağı kenti; 1996–2000 yılları arasında yapılan kazı çalışmalarının genel bir değerlendirilmesi. *TÜBA-AR* 4: 43–78.

Erdoğu, Burçin, Oğuz Tanındı, and Deniz Uygun. 2003. *Türkiye Arkeolojik Yerleşmeleri C14 Veri Tabanı*. İstanbul: Ege Yayınları.

Esin, Ufuk. 2000. The Main Problems in Setting Up a Chronological Framework (Caucasus, Eastern Anatolia and Northern Syria). In *Chronologies des Pays du Caucase et de l'Euphrate aux IVe–IIIe Millénaires*, ed. Catherine Marro and Harald Hauptmann, 5–9. Institut Français d'Etudes Anatoliennes d'Istanbul, Varia Anatolica XI. Paris: De Boccard.

Frangipane, Marcella. 2000. The Late Chalcolithic/EB I Sequence at Arslantepe. Chronological and Cultural Remarks from a Frontier Site. In *Chronologies des Pays du Caucase et de l'Euphrate aux IVe–IIIe Millénaires*, ed. Catherine Marro and Harald Hauptmann, 339–471. Institut Français d'Etudes Anatoliennes d'Istanbul, Varia Anatolica XI. Paris: De Boccard.

Freu, Jacques. 2003. *Histoire du Mitanni*. Paris: L'Harmattan.

Gabriel, Utta. 2000. Mitteilungen zum Stand der Neolithikumsforschung in der Umgebung von Troia (Kumtepe 1993–95; Beşik-Sivritepe 1983–84, 1987, 1998–99). *Studia Troica* 10: 233–38.

Gates, Marie-Henriette. 1987. Alalakh and Chronology Again. In *High, Middle or Low*, ed. Paul Åström, part 2, 60–86. Gothenburg: P. Åströms.

———. 2006. Dating the Hittite Levels at Kinet Höyük: A Revised Chronology. In *Strukturerung und Datierung in der hethitischen Archäeologie/Structuring and Dating in Hittite Archaeology*, ed. Dirk Paul Mielke, Ulf-Dietrich Schoop, and Jürgen Seeher, 293–309. BYZAS 4. İstanbul: Zero Prod.

Genz, Hermann. 2003. The Early Iron Age in Central Anatolia. In *Identifying Changes: The Transition from Bronze to Iron Ages in Anatolia and its Neighbouring Regions*, ed. Bettina Fischer, Hermann Genz, Éric Jean, and Kemalettin Köroğlu, 179–91. İstanbul: Eski Çağ Bilimleri Enstitüsü.

———. 2006. Imports and Their Methodological Implications for Dating Hittite Material Culture. In *Strukturerung und Datierung in der hethitischen Archäeologie/Structuring and Dating in Hittite Archaeology*, ed. Dirk Paul Mielke, Ulf-Dietrich Schoop, and Jürgen Seeher, 185–96. BYZAS 4. İstanbul: Zero Prod.

Gérard, Frédéric and Laurens Thissen, eds. 2002. The Neolithic of Central Anatolia: Internal Developments and External Relations during the 9th–6th Millennia Cal. BC. *Proceedings of the International CANeW Table Ronde*, Istanbul, 23–24 November 2001. İstanbul: Ege Yayınları.

Gorny, Ronald L., Gregory McMahon, Samuel Paley, and Sharon Steadman. 2000. The 1999 Season at Çadır Höyük. *Anatolica* 26: 153–71.

Hansen, C. K. and J. Nicholas Postgate. 1999. The Bronze and Iron Age Transition at Kilise Tepe. *Anatolian Studies* 49: 111–21.

Hauptmann, Harald. 2000. Zur Chronologie des 3. Jahrtausends v. Chr. am oberen Euphrat Aufgrund der Stratigraphie des Noruntepe. In *Chronologies des Pays du Caucase et de l'Euphrate aux IVe–IIIe Millénaires*, ed. Catherine Marro and Harald Hauptmann, 419–38. Institut Français d'Etudes Anatoliennes d'Istanbul, Varia Anatolica XI. Paris: De Boccard.

Helwing, Barbara. 1999. Cultural Interaction at Hassek Höyük, Turkey. New Evidence from Pottery Analysis. *Paléorient* 25.1: 91–99.

———. 2000. Regional Variation in the Composition of Late Chalcolithic Pottery Assemblages. In *Chronologies des Pays du Caucase et de l'Euphrate aux IVe–IIIe Millénaires*, ed. Catherine Marro and Harald Hauptmann, 45–164. Institut Français d'Etudes Anatoliennes d'Istanbul, Varia Anatolica XI. Paris: De Boccard.

Huber, Peter J. 2001. The Solar Omen of Mursili II. *Journal of the American Oriental Society* 121.4: 640–44.

Katsuno, Tadashi. 2006. Zur Keramik des 2. Jahrtausends v. Chr. von Kaman-Kalehöyük. Ein Beitrag zur Kenntnis der Keramikentwicklung von der 'Übergangsperiod' zwischen der Frühen und Mittleren Bronzezeit bis in die Spätbronzezeit. In *Strukturerung und Datierung in der hethitischen Archäeologie/Structuring and Dating in Hittite Archaeology*, ed. Dirk Paul Mielke, Ulf-Dietrich Schoop, and Jürgen Seeher, 227–92. BYZAS 4. İstanbul: Zero Prod.

Keenan, Douglas J. 2002. Why Early-Historical Carbon Dates Downwind from the Mediterranean Are too Early. *Radiocarbon* 44: 225–37.

———. 2004. Anatolian Tree-Ring Studies Are Untrustworthy. www.informath.org/ATSU04a.pdf.

Klengel, Horst. 2002. Karkamish in der hethitischen Grossreichszeit. In *Die Hethiter und ihr Reich*, ed. Kunst-und Ausstellunghalle der Bundesrepublik Deutschland, 164–67. Bonn: Theiss.

Korfmann, Manfred. 1994. Troia, ausgrabungen 1993. *Studia Troica* 4: 1–50.

Korfmann, Manfred, Çigdem Girgin, Çigdem Morçöl, and Sinan Kılıç. 1995. Kumtepe 1995: Report on the Rescue Excavation. *Studia Troica* 5: 237–89.

Korfmann, Manfred, and Bernd Kromer. 1993. Demircihüyük, Beşik-Tepe, Troia—eine Zwischenbilanz zur Chronologie dreier Orte in Westanatolien. *Studia Troica* 3: 135–71.

Köroğlu, Kemalettin and Erkan Konyar. 2008. Comments on the Early/Middle Iron Age Chronology of Lake Van Basin. *Ancient Near Eastern Studies* 45: 123–46.

Kromer, Bernd and Klaus Schmidt. 1998. Two Radiocarbon Dates from Göbekli Tepe (Southeastern Turkey). *Neo-Lithics* 3: 8–9.

Kuniholm, Peter I. 1993. A Date-List for Bronze Age and Iron Age Monuments Based on Combined Dendrochronological and Radiocarbon Evidence. In *Aspects of Art and Iconography: Anatolia and its Neighbours*, ed. Machteld J. Mellink, Edith Porada, and Tahsin Özgüç, 371–73. Ankara: Türk Tarih Kurumu Basımevi.

———. 1995. Aegean Dendrochronology Project December 1995 Progress Report. Ithaca, N.Y.: Cornell University Press.

———. 1996. The Prehistoric Aegean: Dendrochronological Progress as of 1995. *Acta Archaeologica* 67: 327–35.

———. 1997. Aegean Dendrochronology Project: 1995–1996 Results. *Arkeometri Sonuçları Toplantısı* 12: 163–75.

Kuniholm, Peter I. and Maryanne W. Newton. 1989. A 677 Tree-Ring Chronology for the Middle Bronze Age. In *Anatolia and the Ancient Near East: Studies in Honor of Tahsin*

Özgüç, ed. Kutlu Emre, Matcheld Mellink, Barthel Hrouda, and Nimet Özgüç, 279–93. Ankara: Türk Tarih Kurumu Basımevi.

Kuniholm, Peter I., Maryanne W. Newton, Carol B. Griggs, and Pamela J. Sullivan. 2005. Dendrochronological Dating in Anatolia: The Second Millennium B.C. *Der Anschnitt, Anatolian Metal III, Beiheft* 18: 41–47.

Kuniholm Peter I., Shana L. Tarter, Maryanne W. Newton, and Carol B. Griggs. 1992. Preliminary Report on Dendrochronological Investigations at Porsuk/Ulukışla, Turkey 1987–1989. *Syria* 69: 379–89.

Lawn, Barbara. 1973. University of Pennsylvania Radiocarbon Dates XIV. *Radiocarbon* 13.2: 363–77.

———. 1974. University of Pennsylvania Radiocarbon Dates. *Radiocarbon* 16.2: 219–37.

Lenz, Dirk, Florian Ruppenstein, Michael Baumann, and Richard Catling. 1998. Geometric Pottery at Troia. *Studia Troica* 8: 189–222.

Linick, Timothy W. 1984. La Jolla Natural Radiocarbon Measurements X. *Radiocarbon* 26.1: 75–110.

Manning, Sturt W., Bernd Kromer, Peter I. Kuniholm, and Maryanne W. Newton. 2003. Confirmation of Near-Absolute Dating of East Mediterranean Bronze-Iron Dendrochronology. www.antiquity.ac.uk/projGall/Manning/manning.html.

Marro, Catherine. 2000. Vers une Chronologie comparée des pays du Caucase et de I'Euphrate aux IVe–IIIe millennaires. In *Chronologies des Pays du Caucase et de l'Euphrate aux IVe–IIIe Millénaires*, ed. Catherine Marro and Harald Hauptmann, 473–94. Institut Français d'Etudes Anatoliennes d'Istanbul, Varia Anatolica XI. Paris: De Boccard.

Matney, Timothy, Guillermo Algaze, and Steven A. Rosen. 1999. Early Bronze Age Urban Structure at Titriş Höyük, Southeastern Turkey: The 1998 Season. *Anatolica* 25: 185–201.

Mazzoni, Stefania. 2000. From the Late Chalcolithic to Early Bronze I in Northwest-West Syria: Anatolian Contact and Regional Perspective. In *Chronologies des Pays du Caucase et de l'Euphrate aux IVe–IIIe Millénaires*, ed. Catherine Marro and Harald Hauptmann, 97–114. Institut Français d'Etudes Anatoliennes d'Istanbul, Varia Anatolica XI. Paris: De Boccard.

McMahon, Gregory. 1989. The History of the Hittites. *Biblical Archaeologist* 52: 62–77.

McMurray, William. 2004. Towards an Absolute Chronology for Ancient Egypt. www.egiptomania.com/EEF/ACAE1.pdf.

Melchert, H. Craig. 2007. Middle Hittite Revisited. *Studi Micenei ed Egeo-Anatolici* 49: 525–29.

Mellink, Machteld. 1965. Anatolian Chronology. In *Chronologies in Old World Archaeology*, ed. Robert W. Ehrich, 101–31. Chicago: University of Chicago Press.

———. 1992. Anatolian Chronology. In *Chronologies in Old World Archaeology*, 2nd rev. ed., ed. Robert W. Ehrich, 207–20. Chicago: University of Chicago Press.

Mielke, Dirk P. 2006a. Dendrochronologie und hethitische Archäologie-einige kritische Anmerkungen. In *Strukturerung und Datierung in der hethitischen Archäeologie/Structuring and Dating in Hittite Archaeology*, ed. Dirk Paul Mielke, Ulf-Dietrich Schoop, and Jürgen Seeher, 77–94. BYZAS 4. İstanbul: Zero Prod.

———. 2006b. İnandıktepe und Sarissa. Ein Beitrag zur Datierung althethitischer Fundcomplexe. In *Strukturerung und Datierung in der hethitischen Archäeologie/Structuring and Dating in Hittite Archaeology*, ed. Dirk Paul Mielke, Ulf-Dietrich Schoop, and Jürgen Seeher, 251–76. BYZAS 4. İstanbul: Zero Prod.

Mielke, Dirk P., Ulf-Dietrich Schoop, and Jürgen Seeher, eds. 2006. *Strukturerung und Datierung in der hethitischen Archäeologie/Structuring and Dating in Hittite Archaeology*. BYZAS 4. İstanbul: Zero Prod.

Mountjoy, Penelope A. 1999. Troy VII Reconsidered. *Studia Troica* 9: 296–340.

Müller-Karpe, Vuslat. 2006. Tempelinventar in Kuşaklı und Boğazköy im Vergleich: Ein Beitrag zur hethitischen Chronologie. In *Strukturerung und Datierung in der hethitischen Archäeologie/Structuring and Dating in Hittite Archaeology*, ed. Dirk Mielke, Ulf-Dietrich Schoop, and Jürgen Seeher, 241–50. BYZAS 4. İstanbul: Zero Prod.

Neve, Peter. 1993. Hattusha, City of the Gods and Temples: Results of the Excavations in the Upper City. *Proceedings of the British Academy* 80: 105–32.

Newton, Maryanne W. and Peter I. Kuniholm. 2004. A Dendrochronological Framework for the Assyrian Colony Period in Asia Minor. *TÜBA-AR* 7: 165–77.

Newton, Maryanne W., Kenneth A. Wardle, and Peter I. Kuniholm. 2005. Dendrochronology and Radiocarbon Determinations from Assiros and the Beginning of the Greek Iron Age. In *Conference of Archaeological Research in Macedonia and Thrace*, 173–90. Thessaloniki. www.dendro.cornell.edu/articles/newton2005.pdf.

Özbaşaran, Mihriban and Hans Buitenhuis. 2002. Proposal for a Regional Terminology for Central Anatolia. In *The Neolithic of Central Anatolia: Internal Developments and External Relations during the 9th–6th Millennia Cal. BC.*, ed. Frédéric Gérard and Laurens Thissen, 67–77. Proceedings of the International CANeW Table Ronde, Istanbul, 23–24 November 2001. İstanbul: Ege Yayınları.

Özgüç, Tahsin. 1978. *Excavations at Maşat Höyük and Investigations in its Vicinity*. Ankara: Türk Tarih Kurumu Basımevi.

———. 2003. *Kültepe. Kaniš/Neša. The Earliest International Trading Center and the Oldest Capital of the Hittites*. İstanbul: Middle Eastern Culture Center in Japan.

Pearce, Julie. 2000. The Late Chalcolithic Sequence at Hacınebi Tepe, Turkey. In *Chronologies des Pays du Caucase et de l'Euphrate aux IVe–IIIe Millénaires*, ed. Catherine Marro and Harald Hauptmann, 115–43. Institut Français d'Etudes Anatoliennes d'Istanbul, Varia Anatolica XI. Paris: De Boccard.

Peters, Joris and Klaus Schmidt. 2004. Animals in the Symbolic World of Pre-Pottery Neolithic Göbekli Tepe, South-Eastern Turkey: A Preliminary Assessment. *Anthropozoologica* 39: 179–218

Postgate, J. Nicholas. 2008. The Chronology of the Iron Age Seen from Kilise Tepe. *Ancient Near Eastern Studies* 45: 166–87.

Pustovoytov, Konstantin E. 2002. 14C-dating of Pedogenic Carbonate Coatings on Ctones at Göbekli Tepe (Southeastern Turkey). *Neo-Lithics* 2: 8–13.

Ramsey, C. Bronk. 2005. *Ox.Cal. program V3.10*. www.rlaha.ox.ac.uk/O/oxcal.php.

Reimer, Paula J., Mike G. L. Baille, Edouard Bard, Alex Bayliss, Warren J. Beck, Chanda J. H. Bertrand, Paul G. Blackwell, Caitlin E. Buck, George S. Burr, Kirsten B. Cutler, Paul E. Damon, Edwards R. Lawrence, Richard G. Fairbanks, Michael Friedrich, Thomas P. Guilderson, Alan G. Hogg, Konrad A. Hugher, Bernd Kromer, Gerry McCormac, Sturt Manning, Christopher B. Ramsey, Ron W. Reimer, Sabine Remmele, John R. Southon, Minze Stuiver, Sahra Talamo, Fred W. Taylor, Johannes van der Plicht, and Constanze E. Weyhenmeyer. 2004. IntCal04 Terrestrial Radiocarbon Age Calibration, 0–26 cal Kyr BP. *Radiocarbon* 46: 1029–58.

Roller, Lynn E. 2008. Early Phrygian Sculpture: Refining the Chronology. *Ancient Near Eastern Studies* 45: 188–201.

Sagona, Antonio. 2000. Sos Höyük and the Erzurum Region in Late Prehistory: A Provisional Chronology for Northeast Anatolia. In *Chronologies des Pays du Caucase et de l'Euphrate aux IVe–IIIe Millénaires*, ed. Catherine Marro and Harald Hauptmann, 329–73. Institut Français d'Etudes Anatoliennes d'Istanbul, Varia Anatolica XI. Paris: De Boccard.

Schmidt, Klaus. 2000. Göbekli Tepe, Southeastern Turkey. A Preliminary Report on the 1995–1999 Excavations. *Paléorient* 26.1: 45–54.

———. 2001. Göbekli Tepe and the Early Neolithic Sites of the Urfa Region: A Synopsis of New Results and Current Views. *Neo-Lithics* 1.1: 9–11.

Schoop, Ulf-Dietrich. 2003. Pottery Traditions in the Later Hittite Empire: Problems of Definition. In *Identifying Changes: The Transition from Bronze to Iron Ages in Anatolia and its Neighbouring Regions*, ed. Bettina Fischer, Hermann Genz, Éric Jean, and Kemalettin Köroğlu, 167–78. İstanbul: Eski Çağ Bilimleri Enstitüsü.

———. 2006. Dating the Hittites with Statistics: Ten Pottery Assemblages from Boğazköy-Hattuša. In *Strukturerung und Datierung in der hethitischen Archäeologie/Structuring and Dating in Hittite Archaeology*, ed. Dirk Mielke, Ulf-Dietrich Schoop, and Jürgen Seeher, 215–39. BYZAS 4. İstanbul: Zero Prod.

Schoop, Ulf-Dietrich and Jürgen Seeher. 2006. Absolute chronologie in Boğazköy-Hattuša: Das Potential der Radiokarbondaten. In *Strukturerung und Datierung in der hethitischen Archäeologie/Structuring and Dating in Hittite Archaeology*, ed. Dirk Mielke, Ulf-Dietrich Schoop, and Jürgen Seeher, 53–75. BYZAS 4. İstanbul: Zero Prod.

Seeher, Jürgen. 2006. Chronology in Hattuša: New Approaches to an Old Problem. In *Strukturerung und Datierung in der hethitischen Archäeologie/Structuring and Dating in Hittite Archaeology*, ed. Dirk Paul Mielke, Ulf-Dietrich Schoop, and Jürgen Seeher, 197–213. BYZAS 4. İstanbul: Zero Prod.

Shennan, Stephen. 2000. Population, Culture History and the Dynamics of Culture Change. *Current Anthropology* 41: 811–35.

Starke, Frank. 1998. Hattusa II. Staat und Grossreich der Hethiter. In *Der Neue Pauly*, ed. Hubert Cancik, Helmuth Schneider, and Manfred Landfester, vol. 5, 186–89. Stuttgart: Brill Academic.

Steadman, Sharon R., Gregory McMahon, and Jennifer C. Ross. 2007. The Late Chalcolithic at Çadır Höyük in Central Anatolia. *Journal of Field Archaeology* 32: 385–406.

Steier, Peter and Werner Rom. 2000. The Use of Bayesian Statistics for 14C Dates and of Chronologically Ordered Samples: A Critical Analysis. *Radiocarbon* 42.2: 183–98.

Stuckenrath, Robert Jr., William R. Coe, and Elizabeth K. Ralph. 1966. University of Pennsylavania Radiocarbon Date IX. *Radiocarbon* 8: 348–85.

Summers, Geoffrey D. 2008. Periodisation and Terminology in the Central Anatolian Iron Age: Archaeology, History and Audiences. *Ancient Near Eastern Studies* 45: 202–17.

Thissen, Laurens. 2006. CANeW SW and NW Anatolia 14C Chart. www.canew.org.

———. 2007. Central Anatolia and Cilicia 14C Databases: 9th–5th Millennia cal BC. www.canew.org.

Thissen, Laurens and Damien Bischoff. 2006. CANeW Upper Mesopotamia 14C chart. www.canew.org.

Veenhof, Klaas R. 2003. *The Old Assyrian List of Year Eponyms from Karum Kanish and Its Chronological Implications*. Ankara: Türk Tarih Kurumu Basımevi.

Veenhof, Klaas R. and Jesper Eidem. 2008. *Mesopotamia: The Old Assyrian Period. Orbis Biblicus et Orientalis 160/5*. Fribourg: Academic Press.

Wagner, A. Günther and Irmtrud B. Lorenz. 1992. Thermolumineszenz-Datierungen an Keramik vom Beşik-Yassıtepe. *Studia Troica* 2: 147–56.

Watkins, Trevor. 1996. Excavations at Pınarbaşı: The Early Stages. In *On the Surface: Çatalhöyük 1993–95*, ed. Ian Hodder, 47–57. McDonald Institute Monographs 22. Cambridge: McDonald Institute for Archaeological Research.

Weinstein, James. 1996. A Wolf in Sheep's Clothing: How the High Chronology Became the Middle Chronology. *Bulletin of the American Schools of Oriental Research* 304: 55–63.

Weninger, Bernhard. 2007. CANeW-Cologne Anatolian Radiocarbon Dating Project. www.canew.org.

Wilhelm, Gernot. 2004. Generation Count in Hittite Chronology. In *Mesopotamian Dark Age Revisited*, ed. H. Hunger and R. Pruzinszky, 71–79. The Synchronization of Civilization in the Eastern Mediterranean in the 2nd Millennium BC. Wien: Austrian Academy.

Willkomm, Horst. 1992. Radiokohlenstoffdatierungen. In *Hassek Höyük: Naturwissenschaftliche Untersuchungen und kritische Industrie*, ed. Manfred R. Behm-Blancke, 135–39. Istanbuler Forschungen 38. Tübingen: E. Wasmuth.

Wright, Henry T. and E. S. A. Rupley. 2001. Calibrated Radiocarbon Age Determinations of Uruk-Related Assemblages. In *Uruk Mesopotamia and Its Neighbors: Cross-Cultural Interactions in the Era of State Formation*, ed. Mitchell S. Rothman, 85–122. Santa Fe: School of American Research.

Yakar, Jak. 1979. Troy and Anatolian Early Bronze Age Chronology. *Anatolian Studies* 29: 51–67.

———. 1993. Anatolian Civilization Following the Disintegration of the Hittite Empire: An Archaeological Appraisal. *Journal of the Institute of Archaeology of Tel Aviv University* 20.1: 3–28.

———. 2000. *Ethnoarchaeology of Anatolia: Rural Socio-Economy in the Bronze and Iron Ages. Monograph Series no. 17*. Tel Aviv: Emery and Claire Yass Publications in Archaeology.

———. 2002a. Towards an Absolute Chronology for the Middle and Late Bronze Age Anatolia. *Anadolu Araştırmaları* 16: 557–70.

———. 2002b. Revising the Early Bronze Age Chronology of Anatolia. In *Mauerschau. Festschrift für Manfred Korfmann*, ed. Stephan Blum, Rüstem Aslan, Gabrielle Kastl, Frank Schweizer, and Diane Thumm, 445–56. Remshalden-Grunbach: Bernhard Albert Greiner.

———. 2003. Review of: Frédéric Gerard and Laurens Thissen, eds. *The Neolithic of Central Anatolia: Internal developments and External relations during the 9th–6th Millennia CAL BC: Proceedings of the International CANeW Table Ronde, Istanbul, November 23–24, 2001*. Bulletin of the American Schools of Oriental Research 331: 67–69.

———. 2004. The Socio-Economic Definition of the Neolithic and Chalcolithic Periods in the Light of New Research in Turkey. *TÜBA-AR* 7: 61–66.

———. 2006. Dating the Sequence of the Final Destruction/Abandonment of LBA Settlements: Towards a Better Understanding of Events that Led to the Collapse of the Hittite Kingdom. In *Strukturerung und Datierung in der hethitischen Archäeologie/Structuring and Dating in Hittite Archaeology*, ed. Dirk Paul Mielke, Ulf-Dietrich Schoop, and Jürgen Seeher, 33–51. BYZAS 4. İstanbul: Zero Prod.

PART II

CHRONOLOGY AND GEOGRAPHY

Anatolia in Prehistory

CHAPTER 5

THE NEOLITHIC ON THE PLATEAU

MİHRİBAN ÖZBAŞARAN

THE results of the recent research on Anatolia place the region squarely in the middle of current debates about one of the greatest thresholds in human prehistory, the Neolithic. The data in hand reveal a distinct spectrum of adaptive strategies for these prehistoric communities on the central Anatolian plateau. The neolithisation process seems to be defined basically by the distinct ecological and environmental conditions, including a rich assortment of concentrated resources and the manner in which local human relationships with the environment were incorporated into the ideology of the early sedentary communities (for discussion on contemporary sites in the Marmara and southeastern Anatolia, see Roodenberg, chapter 44, Özdoğan, chapter 29, Rosenberg and Erim-Özdoğan, chapter 6, and Schmidt, chapter 42 in this volume). Despite the small number of excavated sites, gaps in the culture chronology, and two different generations of investigation (see history of research discussion) that worked under different paradigms, the Neolithic of the plateau offers data of major importance for reassessing the process of neolithisation in the region. These findings urge us to reconsider the conventional macro-evolutionary approaches for determining the phases of the Neolithic[1] and to take greater note of local patterns rather than generalizing the data for the purpose of regional comparisons. This overview compiles data on the ninth to sixth millennium B.C.E. communities of the central Anatolian plateau, underscoring the distinctive features of each of these communities in chronological order and deliberately avoiding the traditional phase terminology of the Neolithic.

Geography

The central Anatolian plateau is bounded on the north by the flanks of the north Anatolian (Pontic) Mountains and on the south by the Taurus Mountains (for geographical descriptions, see Steadman, chapter 10, and Kealhofer and Grave, chapter 18 in this volume). The volcanic area in the east and the Lake District in the west circumscribe what is today called central Anatolia, a region classified and named by the First Geographical Congress of Turkey in 1941. The central Anatolian plateau covers an area of more than 150,000 square km and includes four main basins—the volcanic area of Cappadocia at the eastern end, the Tuz Gölü (Salt Lake) basin in the center, the Konya Plain to the south, and the Beyşehir Plain in the eastern part of the Lake District (Atalay 1995). Two major rivers, the Kızılırmak (Halys) and the Sakarya, drain the region and ultimately empty into the Black Sea. The central Anatolian plateau has a generally continental climate with cold winters and dry summers. Annual mean rainfall is 350–400 mm. Steppe-like vegetation covers the lowlands, and zonal forests occur at higher elevations.

Such a general description of the plateau conceals, however, the great diversity of the landscape on a human scale. Many microhabitats exist in the region and clearly attracted prehistoric communities. This chapter explores the relationship between the geographical and environmental characteristics of the region in relation to human cultural preferences and land use. The stories of two subareas of the plateau overlap and intensify with time; these are Cappadocia in the east and the Konya Plain in the west. The number of identified Neolithic sites in Cappadocia, both aceramic and ceramic Neolithic, exceeds twenty at present (figure 5.1), and they all are located in the volcanic area that lies north of Hasandağ (3,268 m) and the Melendiz mountain ranges (2,963 m) and around Mt. Erciyes (3,917 m). Only half as many sites are known on the Konya-Karaman Plain, and they occur along the northern flanks of the Taurus arc. The third concentration of sites, mainly known through surveys, occurs east of Beyşehir Lake and down to Suğla, along the Çarşamba River. Although a large area of the plateau has been surveyed by different teams, sites were very rare north of the Kızılırmak River and around the western part of Tuz Gölü.[2]

Although the Cappadocian landscape is generally a landscape of mountainous highlands that rise steadily from west to east with plains in between, the geomorphology of the region is quite complex. Toward the end of the Pliocene, the low basins were covered by lakes. Volcanic eruptions that probably began in the late Miocene intensified, spewing lava, ash, and sand (Esin 1998). The resulting volcano-sedimentary formations are rich sources of raw materials such as obsidian, basalt, and gypsum. The alluvial and clayey-calcareous loose sediments of the plains and basins were formed in the Quaternary. The diverse hydrology of the region has over time created a great variety of microhabitats, many of them unique. The Ihlara Valley, whose walls are very deeply cut by the Melendiz River, is one of the richest microhabitats in the area, along with the perennial or seasonal freshwater or saltwater wetlands such as Sultansazlığı and Tuzla Gölü (Kuzucuoğlu 2002). These areas provide unique habitats for a great variety of plants and animals; plant life in these microhabitats is both rich and unique in comparison to the steppic vegetation that dominates much of the plateau. Also important are the woodlands (oak) that grow above the steppe zone and below 1,500 m on the slopes of the volcanic mountains.

The Konya Plain displays a somewhat simpler and gentler topography. In the south central area lies a large depression, a former Pleistocene lake, surrounded by plateaus. The volcanic mountains of Karacadağ and Karadağ define two basins, separated from each other by the Hotamış Marsh, a remnant of a Pleistocene lake. During the early part of the Quaternary, the central Anatolian plateau had a harsh climate with strong winds and rugged steppe vegetation. The rate of evaporation was low, and the lake levels were high. The Pleistocene lake located between Konya and Ereğli was roughly 120 km long and 15–20 m deep. Tuz Gölü (which continues to exist) was also larger at the time, and its level higher (Atalay 1995:542). With the onset of the Holocene, the Pleistocene lake began to dry out, and settlements were established within the area of the former lake bed. Alluvial soils dominate much of

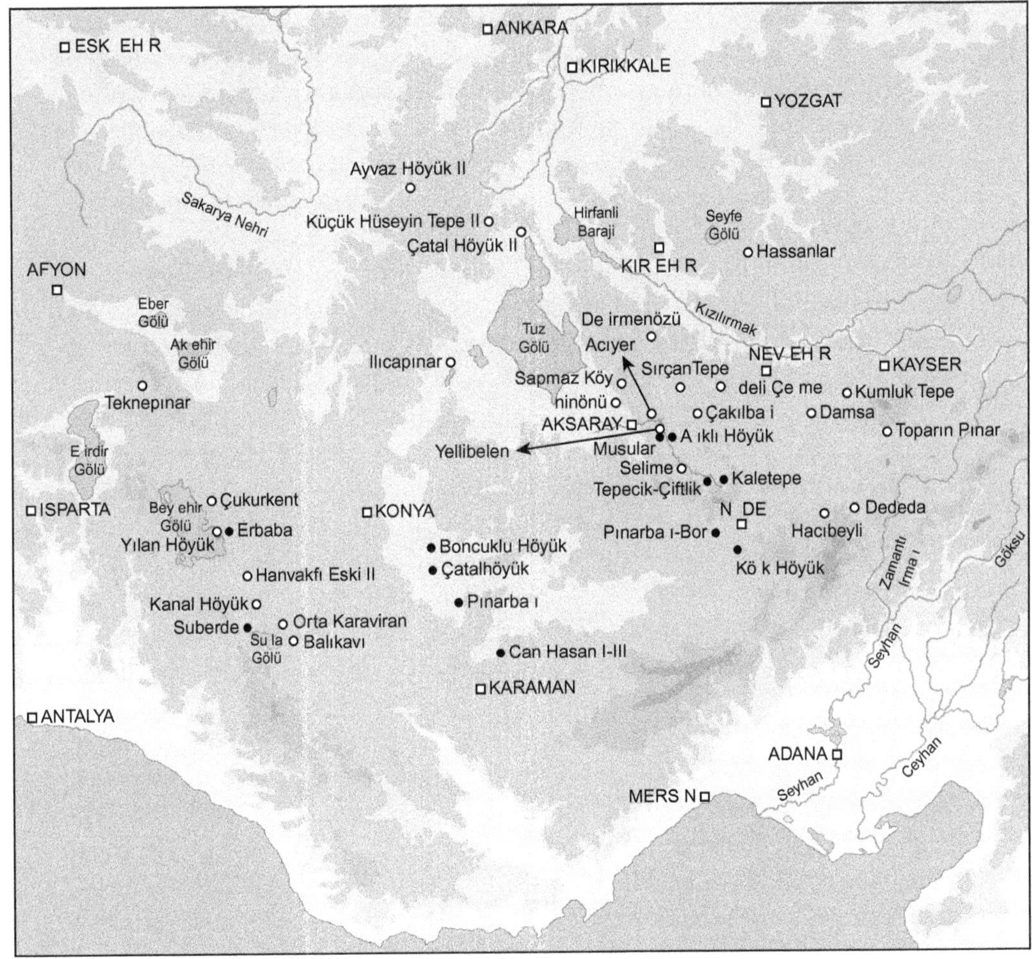

Figure 5.1. Neolithic sites of the central Anatolian plateau; dark dots indicate the excavation sites.

the Konya Plain, and the vegetation is basically steppic. An exception is the area surrounding Tuz Gölü, due to the salty, alkaline soil that accumulates on the surface as a result of evaporation; here vegetation is poorer and dominated by steppic herbs. Woodlands of oak, pine, and cedar grow above the basin steppe to an altitude of 1,400–1,500 m. On the western slopes of Karacadağ, various types of oak are widespread, with juniper scattered among them. Oak trees are also common on the southern slopes of Karadağ below 1,300 m.

History of Research

The first systematic reconnaissance survey in the region was undertaken in the 1950s by J. Mellaart. Prior to this survey, only a few prehistoric sites were known, namely, Çukurkent in the Lakes Region, Pınarbaşı-Bor in Niğde, and Ilıcapınar near Tuz Gölü (figure 5.1). The first of these sites was found by H. Ormerod in 1910, Pınarbaşı-Bor in 1938 by members of the American Prehistoric Society, and Ilıcapınar by the geologist Kleinsorge in the 1940s (Harmankaya, Tanındı, and Özbaşaran 1997). Such findspots were scarce and did not attract the attention of the researchers before Mellaart, and some believed that the region was not inhabited at all prior to the Bronze Age (Özdoğan 1996:186–87). The attempt by W. Orthmann to build a chronology for central Anatolia in the following years focused on the Early Bronze Ages (Orthmann 1963).

The recognition of the Neolithic by Mellaart's survey represents the turning point for research in the region. Mellaart excavated at Çatalhöyük between 1961 and 1965 (Mellaart 1967), which attracted worldwide attention with its exceptional finds. D. French began excavating at Can Hasan I around the same time (French 1962). He later moved to Can Hasan III, some 700 m northwest of Can Hasan I, and excavated for two seasons (French et al. 1972). In the meantime, a team from Columbia University led by R. Solecki had been surveying around the Beyşehir-Suğla basin (Solecki 1965). Their main interest was in the Palaeolithic and Mesolithic periods, but they also identified two lake shore sites, Suberde (Görüklük Tepe) on the northwestern shores of Suğla Lake and Erbaba on the eastern margin of the lake of Beyşehir. In 1964–65, J. Bordaz carried out excavations at Suberde (Bordaz 1969) and later at Erbaba (Bordaz 1970) for four seasons (1969, 1971, 1974, and 1977).

The archaeology of the eastern part of the plateau, the volcanic region called Cappadocia, was poorly known at that time. Some of the large mound sites were recognized and had been visited by a handful of researchers. Köşk Höyük was identified in 1961 by M. Ballance and revisited in 1964 by R. Harper and M. Ramsden (Summers 1993). E. Gordon, a Hittitologist from Pennsylvania University, discovered Aşıklı Höyük on the bank of the Melendiz River (Esin 1998). Pınarbaşı-Bor was visited by travelers and historians.

I. Todd compiled all these sporadic finds in his comprehensive survey of central Anatolia (Todd 1980). Over a period of two years (1964–65), he visited previously reported mounds and identified many new sites as well. His work not only highlighted the significance of the early prehistoric communities in this part of the plateau but also established the first chronology for the region. He recognized the importance of Aşıklı Höyük in the context of the survey, studied the eroded sections of the site in detail, and collected charcoal samples for absolute dating. The early dates for Aşıklı and the similarities in its architectural features to Çatalhöyük launched new discussions of the origins of the two sites. The community at Aşıklı Höyük was suggested as the possible predecessor to Çatalhöyük.

The pioneering work of Mellaart on the Konya Plain, including the spectacular finds from Çatalhöyük and Todd's extensive survey of Cappadocia initiated a brief flurry of archaeological work on the Anatolian plateau. Further research in both regions was not revived, however, for another two decades. Meanwhile, a few short-term excavations were conducted at Niğde Tepebağları (Özgüç 1973), Köşk Höyük and Pınarbaşı-Bor (Silistreli 1984), in 1973, 1981, 1982 respectively.

In 1988, the State Hydraulic Works announced the decision to raise the water level of the Mamasın Reservoir, which would partially inundate Aşıklı Höyük. The call initiated a response from U. Esin who undertook major excavations beginning in 1989; following a three-year break, excavations have continued to the present (Esin and Harmankaya 2007). The salvage excavations at Aşıklı generated new research throughout the area; excavations at Musular, the satellite site to Aşıklı, were begun in 1996 by M. Özbaşaran (2000), and E. Bıçakçı began work at Tepecik-Çiftlik in 2000 (Bıçakçı 2001). Settlement surveys were also carried out in various areas of the plateau: U. Esin and S. Gülçur surveyed in Aksaray, Nevşehir, and Niğde (Esin, Gülçur and Kurar 1998), and the Japanese expedition led by S. Omura conducted reconnaissance surveys in a wider area that included Ankara and Kırşehir (Omura 1991). Both surveys revealed sites of various ages and types, ranging from mounds to flat sites to slope settlements to artifact scatters.

Cappadocia is one of the richest sources of obsidian in southwest Asia and has been a focus of research on obsidian sourcing, trading, and raw material use since the 1960s (Renfrew, Dixon, and Cann 1966). In 1996, N. Balkan Atlı, M. C. Cauvin, and D. Binder initiated a multidisciplinary obsidian research project that combined geology, geomorphology, and geochemistry (Balkan Atlı, Binder, and Cauvin 1998). Göllüdağ and Nenezi, the two main obsidian sources, were investigated, and subsequently excavations of Neolithic obsidian workshops were undertaken at Kaletepe in 1997–2001. The project continues to the present with the aim of following obsidian from acquisition at the source areas to its use as finished tools at the settlements. Recent systematic surveys at Küçük Göllüdağ and Büyük Göllüdağ have documented the intensive exploitation of obsidian outcrops, small mobile stations, and rock-shelters used by the Neolithic communities.

The central Anatolian Salt Project, begun in 2003 and led by B. Erdoğu, aimed to define the use of salt, exploring its earliest exploitation and significance in Anatolian prehistory (Erdoğu et al. 2003). Archaeological survey and related ethnographic research were conducted around Tuz Gölü and its environs, where activity areas that likely relate to prehistoric salt exploitation and mound settlements were documented.

Ongoing surveys in Cappadocia focus on the larger human imprint on the prehistoric landscape. S. Gülçur's work focuses on the economic layouts of settlements through time in relation to topographical characteristics and the distribution of water, raw material sources, arable fields, and grazing zones. E. Bıçakçı's salvage survey project, on the east of the Melendiz Mountains, revealed the presence of Palaeolithic, Neolithic, and Chalcolithic sites, as well as late-period settlements dating from the second millennium B.C.E. to the Middle Ages.

Work at Çatalhöyük on the Konya Plain began anew in 1993 after a break of more than two decades (Hodder and Matthews 1998). Following two seasons of surface survey and scraping on the East and West mounds of Çatalhöyük, I. Hodder began excavations there using a new set of objectives, methods, and theoretical approaches (Hodder 1996; see Hodder, chapter 43 in this volume). This multidisciplinary, international Çatalhöyük Research Project includes work on the site and the surrounding area. N. Roberts began a geomorphological survey (Roberts, Boyer, and Parish 1996), and D. Baird and T. Watkins led an intensive archaeological survey of the area that included geomorphologic and geoarchaeologic studies (Baird 1996). One of the main objectives of the surveys was to identify sites predating Çatalhöyük (Baird 2002). Watkins launched excavations at Pınarbaşı in 1994 (Watkins 1996), the only Epipalaeolithic site yet known in the region. Baird continued the field survey, then joined Pınarbaşı, and most recently began excavations in 2006 on a pre-Çatalhöyük site, Boncuklu (Baird 2007a).

The Central Anatolian Plateau from the Ninth to Seventh Millennium B.C.E.

Mobile Groups Prior to the Ninth Millennium B.C.E.

The stage preceding a sedentary way of living in the plateau was unknown until recently (figure 5.2).[3] Two sites that were interpreted as open-air sites dating to the Epipalaeolithic remained uncertain in date and in context (Mellaart 1975:94). The discovery of Pınarbaşı on the Konya Plain (Watkins 1996) offers important evidence for mobile groups on the plateau prior to the ninth millennium B.C.E. The multidisciplinary work carried out at this site also provides significant insights on the origins of the Neolithic communities of the plateau (Baird 2007b:289–95). Pınarbaşı is located northeast of the Karadağ volcanic mountains, on the slope of a limestone hill. Palaeoenvironmental studies indicate the existence of a nearby marsh or lake at the time of occupation and the presence of almond and pistachio trees. Two separate areas of the Pınarbaşı locality were investigated: the rock shelter (Area B) and the small mound (areas A, C, and D). The rock shelter revealed two sequences. The upper part represented a camp site used by a mobile herding and hunting group during the seventh millennium B.C.E, contemporary with the late levels of Çatalhöyük (see later discussion). The artifacts found in the lower part of the sequence represent an Epipalaeolithic occupation, implying a date earlier than the ninth millennium B.C.E., although radiocarbon dates are not yet available. The Epipalaeolithic inhabitants used the rock shelter seasonally and hunted medium and large mammals, birds, and fish. The archaeobotanical evidence indicates that these foragers did not depend on gathered cereals or legumes, in contrast to contemporary communities in the Levant and southeast Anatolia. Phytolith analysis indicates the construction of light shelters made of reeds at the Pınarbaşı rock shelter. About 90 percent of the chipped stone tools were made of obsidian obtained from Cappadocia. Microliths dominate the chipped stone industry, especially lunates. The lack of microdebitage and related débris indicate that knapping generally did not take place at the site. The tools, mainly bladelets, small retouched flakes, and small scrapers, were brought to the site as finished tools. The presence of human burials suggests that the rock shelter served for a certain period as a dwelling. Significant is the presence of various Mediterranean shells scattered through the deposits and concentrated in the burials; for example, ninety dentalia were found inside a tortoise shell (Baird 2007b).

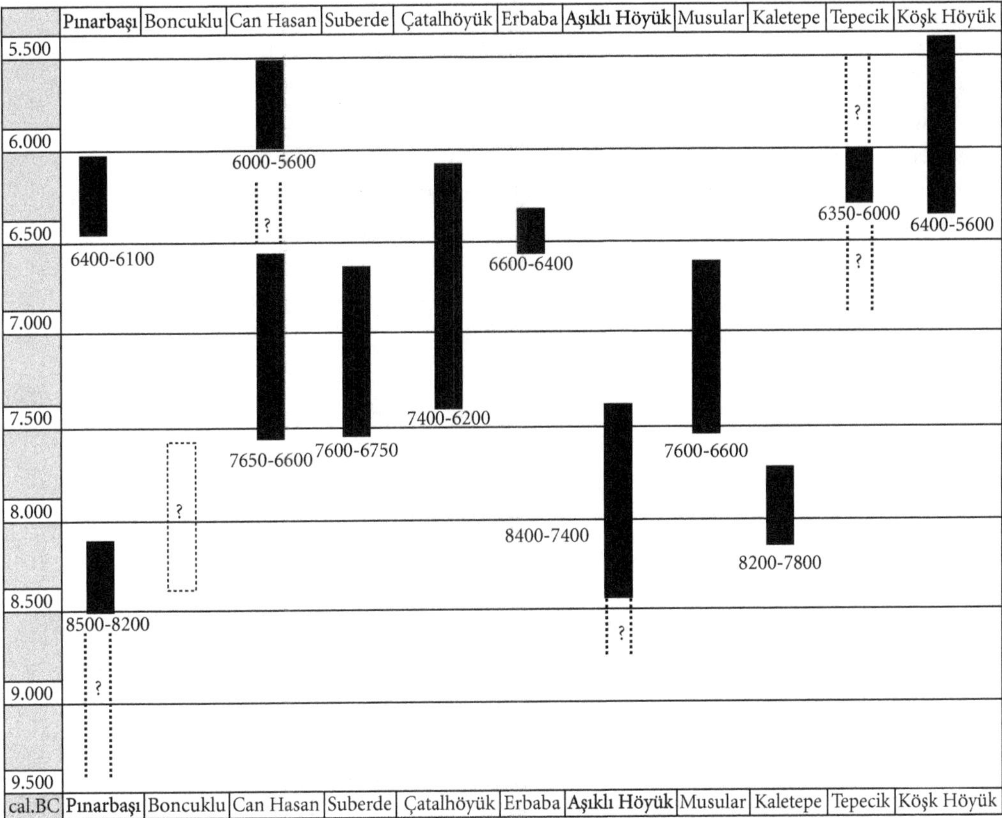

Figure 5.2. Chronological chart based on CANeW ^{14}C database (www.canew.org).

It seems clear that Pınarbaşı was a short-term settlement inhabited by mobile groups during the Epipalaeolithic. One can infer the scale of mobility or exchange ranges of these groups from the nonlocal materials at the site, specifically the sea shells and the obsidian. The raw materials indicate that the area of movement or exchange was large, with the Cappadocian obsidian sources obtained northeast of the site and the shells from the Mediterranean shore to the south. The technology and burial customs observed at Pınarbaşı display gross similarities to those of the Mediterranean and Euphrates regions, but certain other characteristics indicate some distinctly local practices as well.

Sedentary Communities: Ninth Millennium B.C.E.

Excavations of the small mound at Pınarbaşı provide information on life during the ninth millennium B.C.E. (Baird 2007b:295–302; Watkins 1996). The occupations are radiocarbon dated to 8500–8000 B.C.E. The thickness of the deposits and succession of buildings indicate an intense, long-term settlement. The structures were semi-subterranean with wattle and daub superstructures. The floors were plastered, and some were probably painted with red ochre. The structures contain features such as a hearth, a bench, and pits. The distribution of scattered stones, cooking pits, and basalt slabs in the open spaces indicates a wide range of daily outdoor activities, including animal butchery, cooking, and probably feasting. Subsistence was based mainly on hunting of aurochs and equids, fishing, and birds, and gathering wild plants and fruits such as almonds and pistachios. Burials of adults and children in the Pınarbaşı mound exhibit some differences to the Epipalaeolithic burials in the rock shelter, but they also differ from the contemporary settlement at Aşıklı Höyük where the latter present subfloor inhumations.

Obsidian was brought to Pınarbaşı as preforms, and knapping took place on site. Microliths of various forms dominate the chipped stone tool assemblages. Bipolar technology and the presence of two naviform cores suggest links to the northern Levant. Flint was also used and knapped at the site. Retouched and unretouched flint flakes and microliths indicate that different functions were performed by the obsidian and flint tools. The artifact inventory is quite diverse, including pestles, hand stones, grinding stones, small celts, shaft straighteners with incisions, bone awls, and shell and stone beads (basalt, limestone, and red marble) (Baird 2007b). The richness of the artifact inventory indicates an increase in the variety of daily activities and a heightened use of local versus distant raw material sources, probably obtained through exchange.

The site of Boncuklu is located about twenty kilometers from Pınarbaşı and nine kilometers from Çatalhöyük. It is currently the key site for understanding sedentary communities of the interval following Pınarbaşı and preceding Çatalhöyük. The site has been under excavation since 2006 (Baird 2007a). Curvilinear structures have been exposed, and one structure still preserves evidence of plastered decoration and the use of red paint, not unlike later examples found at Çatalhöyük. The characteristics of the microliths, projectile points, beads and clay objects, and so-called shaft straighteners suggest a relative age of the ninth to eighth millennium B.C.E. Obsidian from Cappadocia and shells from the Mediterranean indicate material movement patterns similar to those observed at Pınarbaşı.

By the ninth millennium B.C.E., Aşıklı Höyük is the settlement of major importance in Cappadocia. The site preserves a record of the early emergence of fully sedentary communities, radiocarbon dated to 8400–7400 B.C.E. (see Yakar, chapter 4 in this volume, for more radiocarbon data for the Neolithic). Aşıklı Höyük was founded on the bank of the Melendiz River, which originates in the Melendiz Mountains and flows northward into the steep canyons of the Ihlara Valley. The deeply incised Ihlara and Melendiz Valleys provide a rich variety of habitats for fauna and flora within a landscape of volcanic formations. Mixed groves of hackberry, wild pistachio, elm, and wild almond grow in these valleys, in contrast to the steppe vegetation of the plateau (Esin 1998:94).

Excavations at Aşıklı Höyük have revealed four levels (1–4 from top to bottom; Level 4 was recently exposed and is under excavation at present; Esin and Harmankaya 2007:256), with more than a meter of deposit at the base of the mound that has not yet been excavated. The earliest levels (3–4), explored in a deep trench, indicate a distinct form of settlement that may have been seasonal in nature; this hypothesis will be tested by future work at the site. There is continuity in the use of space in Levels 3–4, but the structures are different with respect to plan and layout from those in the later horizon (Level 2). Specifically, oval-shaped structures existed together with rectangular buildings in the early deposits, whereas rectangular structures dominate Level 2. The buildings were not tightly packed, and superimposition of buildings on old footings was not strictly practiced, in marked contrast to the succeeding Level 2. Subsistence may have been similar between the early and later occupations of the mound that have been excavated thus far, except for the slight change in the proportion of hunted animals, such as the rising importance of wild sheep relative to other hunted animals (this question currently is under investigation). The obsidian industries are similar among the excavated levels as well. Early Levels 3–4 at Aşıklı Höyük are overlain by a thick layer of silty deposits that may indicate heavy sheet wash from rain.

The more recent occupations represented by Level 2 (Aşıklı's Level 1 was almost totally destroyed by surface activities) have been extensively excavated and present a detailed picture of a fully sedentary community. The settlement displays two main sectors—the dwelling area and the area of special function buildings. Buildings on the north part of the mound (figure 5.3a) are similar to each other in plan and the methods and materials used in construction; all are constructed from mud slabs[4] and mortar without stone foundations. Stone was used only in special cases (see later discussion). Buildings were rectangular, with free-standing outer walls. They consist of one or two rooms, rarely three. Most of them had rectangular hearths lined with slabs of limestone and paved with pebbles (Özbaşaran 1998). Access between rooms within a structure was through internal doorways, but the buildings lack external doors. It is likely that the buildings had flat roofs, and that they were probably entered using wooden ladders through rooftop openings. One of the striking characteristics

Figure 5.3a. The dwelling area of the ninth and eighth millennium B.C.E. settlement of Aşıklı Höyük.

of the architecture of level 2 is the continuity, documented in ten building phases. New buildings were constructed directly on top of the old ones; débris from old walls was used to level the area, and the old wall foundations were then used for the building of the new buildings (Esin 1996). Buildings were densely packed and built in clusters with open spaces between the building groups used as middens or work areas. A number of narrow paths around the building groups lead to the commonly used open spaces. Like the buildings, midden locations did not change for hundreds of years.

Buildings in the southern area of the mound display important differences in terms of plans, overall dimensions, size of *kerpiç* blocks, and the material and treatment of the floors. This part of the settlement was separated from the dwelling area by a four-meter-wide gravel street. One of the special buildings (T) (figure 5.3b) south of the street contained lime plastered floors and walls that were painted red. Building T also contained benches, post holes in the floor, and channels of paired stone slabs leading out of the building. Its walls were thick, and the dimension of the room was large, measuring 5 × 5.6 m. Another building (HV) had a stone wall on its north side, and a row of small rooms backed by a large wall made of *kerpiç* blocks. To its west is a series of huge stone blocks that probably functioned as post bases, creating a portico-like space. The floor of Building HV was paved with large mudbricks, reaching one meter in length. A space allocated for a large, domed oven was found in the same area, close to the T and HV buildings, a unique occurrence at Aşıklı; it was probably used communally. This part of the settlement was clearly dedicated to nondomestic, special-function buildings.

Continuity through Level 2 at Aşıklı Höyük is also evidenced by the subsistence patterns and burial customs. The analyses of faunal and floral remains from Level 2

Figure 5.3b. One of the special-function buildings of Aşıklı Höyük, Building T.

indicate that the subsistence economy depended on hunting and gathering and on some cultivated plants as well. Wild sheep and goat, cattle, wild boar, fallow deer, red deer, wild horse, wolf, fox, and hare are represented among the faunal remains, with a clear dominance of ovicaprids, especially sheep. The faunal assemblage provides no clear evidence of domesticates, although the patterns of age and sex selection indicate an unusual level of control over the hunted ovicaprids that is interpreted as evidence of proto-domestication (Buitenhuis 1997). Edible green plants, wild grains, herbs, fruits, and nuts such as almond, wild pistachio, and hackberry were collected. Wild and domesticated forms of einkorn and emmer wheat, durum wheat, and domesticated and wild forms of barley were among the grains cultivated (van Zeist and de Roller 1995, 2003). Despite the presence of cultivated plants, a strong emphasis was placed on hunted game.

Daily activities in Level 2 Aşıklı Höyük included the manufacture of obsidian, bone and ground stone tools, building construction and *kerpiç* manufacture, hide and wood working, and basket making. The obsidian was obtained from Nenezi and Kayırlı, two of the main sources of Cappadocia, and brought to the settlement as big nodules or tablets (Abbes et al. 1999; Balkan Atlı 1993; Esin and Harmankaya 2007:266). Obsidian knapping was done on site in what was essentially a blade industry. Technological characterization of the unipolar and bipolar cores at Aşıklı indicates domestic use with very little specialized production. Scrapers that constitute the main category of tools are made on all kinds of blanks, thick or thin flakes, tablets, retouched or unretouched blades. Blades, with abrupt or semi-abrupt retouch, or truncated, are quite common. Arrowheads are few, whereas microliths occur throughout the whole sequence. The burials are inside structures, beneath the floors. Some of the bodies were wrapped in mats, and red ochre was included in some of the burials. Special treatment of the body was observed in rare cases, where in one example a premortem trepanation was found (Özbek 1992, 1998).

Overall, Aşıklı presents considerable evidence for the transformation into a newly settled way of life, a community bound to the past but also gradually adopting new strategies.

About 400 m west of Aşıklı, across the Melendiz River, is the site of Musular (Özbaşaran 2000). This flat site rests directly on the volcanic bedrock. Excavations revealed remains similar to those of the nondomestic, public area at Aşıklı Höyük (Özbaşaran 2003). The radiocarbon determinations place the Musular occupation between the mid-eighth and seventh millennium B.C.E. The presence of lime plastered and red-painted floors and walls in a building indicates close affinities to Aşıklı, as do the plan and the size of the building, with inner benches, post holes, and a large rectangular hearth and various types of built channels. The character of this special building, the absence of dwellings, and the contemporaneity with Aşıklı across the river all suggest that Musular was established by the Aşıklı community. Significantly, cattle remains dominate in the faunal assemblage at Musular, whereas ovicaprids outnumber other animals in the faunal assemblages from Aşıklı. Processing of cattle carcasses and consumption appear to be communal. Huge amounts of cattle bones were found in a Musular midden. The obsidian industry provides important information on the processes undertaken at Musular, thus suggesting the function of the site. The majority of the tools, almost half of the total, consist of end scrapers, followed by arrowheads (Kayacan 2003; Kayacan and Özbaşaran 2007). Use wear analysis proved that scrapers and cutting tools were used in meat and hide processing (Astruc, Kayacan, and Özbaşaran 2008). Evidence suggests that Musular was a nondomestic site, the satellite of Aşıklı,[5] with special social and ritual functions involving cattle (Duru and Özbaşaran 2005).

The Aşıklı-Musular site complex was abandoned around the middle of the seventh millennium B.C.E. The reason for abandonment is not clear, but abandonment was followed by the largest known increase in forest cover in the region (Esin 1998:75). Whether the abandonment was provoked by neoclimatic conditions or sociopolitical factors is a topic of ongoing debate and research at Aşıklı.

Contemporary with Aşıklı but functionally distinct is the obsidian knapping site at Kaletepe, also in Cappadocia (Binder and Balkan Atlı 2001; Cauvin and Balkan Atlı 1996). This Neolithic workshop site is dated to 8200–7800 B.C.E. It is situated on a flat rhyolite formation (figure 5.4a) ca. 1,600 m above sea level on the northern slopes of Göllüdağ—one of the main obsidian resources of central Anatolia. The archaeological excavations unearthed a massive quantity of obsidian artifacts and manufacturing débris (figure 5.4b) that testify to diverse knapping techniques and traditions. The great abundance of standardized cores is particularly significant, and the entire process of production is represented, from rough-outs to preforms, crested flakes to core rejuvenation tablets, exhausted cores, and lateral blades. Missing, however, are the central blades that represent the main goal of the production. Prismatic bladelets and points detached from the highly standardized

Figure 5.4a. General view of the Kaletepe Neolithic workshop (Courtesy Nur Balkan Atlı, Cappadocian Obsidian Research Project).

Figure 5.4b. Excavations at the Kaletepe Neolithic workshop (Courtesy Nur Balkan Atlı, Cappadocian Obsidian Research Project).

naviform cores indicate a high level of craftsmanship. Neither this technology nor these products are found in the Neolithic settlements of the plateau but instead occur in Pre-Pottery Neolithic B sites of the Euphrates region and on the island of Cyprus (Balkan Atlı and Binder 2007). This observation has led to the suggestion that the workshop was controlled by nonlocal craftsmen, probably of northern Levantine origin (Binder 2002:80). Ongoing research on this question focuses on the exploitation and management of the obsidian sources and strategies of distribution and exchange.

Sedentary Communities of the Eighth Millennium B.C.E.

Can Hasan III was established on the Konya Plain several hundred years after the abandonment of Pınarbaşı. The settlement is located in a flat plain, close to the dried-up river of Selereki, and is one of three mounds in the vicinity, about 750 m away from Can Hasan I and II (Payne 1972:193–94). The faunal remains and carbonized wood samples indicate a paleoenvironment of open steppe with forests along the water courses. Excavations revealed seven continuous layers (1–7) that are radiocarbon dated to the mid-eighth through mid-seventh millennium B.C.E. A large scraped area and small trench exposed quadrangular free-standing buildings made of mud walls with open spaces and narrow passages between clusters of buildings (French et al. 1972). The architectural plans and settlement pattern closely resemble that of Aşıklı Höyük (Level 2). Most were single-room structures, but a few contained two rooms. Internal doorways linked contiguous rooms, but there were no external entrances.

Subsistence at Can Hasan III was based on hunting a wide variety of animals (Martin, Russell, and Carruthers 2002:202; Payne 1972) and cultivation of wild and domestic plants. Sheep, goats, red deer, roe deer, equids, pigs, and small animals such as hares, tortoises, snakes, birds, rodents, and fish were hunted. Wild and domesticated einkorn and emmer wheat, durum wheat, hulled and naked barley, lentil, rye, and bitter vetch were gathered and/or cultivated. In addition to a variety of herbaceous plants, fruits and nuts such as walnut, hackberry, wild grape, and cherries were collected (Asouti and Fairbairn 2002:183–84). Tools were made predominantly of obsidian, and the industries contain retouched points, end scrapers, scrapers on flakes, borers, geometric microliths, lunates, and trapezoids (Ataman 1988). Some flint was used, though less frequently, and mainly for harvesting tools.

Can Hasan III displays strong similarities to Aşıklı Höyük with respect to the obsidian industry, settlement pattern, and architectural concepts. Buildings made of mud, with closely spaced free-standing walls, flat roofs, roof entrances, and tight clustering are typical architectural features; together they represent the central Anatolian model. First appearing at Aşıklı, this pattern continued into the next millennium at Çatalhöyük, Erbaba, and Can Hasan I.

Suberde is situated in a different geographical region of the plateau, on the eastern fringes of the Lake District at the western border of the Konya Plain. Suberde is radiocarbon dated to the second half of the eighth and the first half of the seventh millennium B.C.E. The site is located on a limestone ridge called Görüklük Tepe and is surrounded by the waters of Lake Suğla (Bordaz 1969). Excavations revealed four layers (I–IV from top to bottom). The second and the third layers are called the Upper Prehistoric and Lower Prehistoric Layers, respectively. Buildings made of mud walls are similar in both layers, but there are plastered walls and floors in the buildings in the Upper Layer. Stone foundations were used in some buildings of the Upper Layer. Layer IV is the sterile soil resting directly on limestone bedrock.

The site is located on the interface of the lake, forested hills, and semi-arid steppe, giving hunters access to deer, roe deer, and gazelle. Today, forests grow fifteen kilometers away from Suberde, on the slopes of the Taurus Mountains. The forest was closer to Suğla Lake at the time of settlement (Aytuğ 1967). Wild sheep, wild goat, and boar were also hunted, and the former constitutes 85 percent of the faunal assemblages. Freshwater and marine shells, fish, birds, and hares were also hunted in small numbers. There is no indication of domestic plants or animals at Suberde.

The chipped stone industry was dominated by obsidian (90 percent), and the rest was made up of flint (10 percent). The toolkit consisted of scrapers and arrowheads, sickle blades, piercing tools, and backed blades. Some points show evidence of pressure flaking. Microtools, bladelets smaller than 2.5 cm, and geometric microliths are more common in the Lower Prehistoric Layer. A few anthropomorphic and animal figurines were made out of clay, and some fragments of pottery indicate isolated experiments with clay during the Lower Prehistoric Phase (Bordaz 1969).

The ninth–eighth millennium communities seem to have had strong preferences with respect to environment and possibly to soil quality. "When Suğla Lake was at its maximum level, Suberde must have been an island" (Bordaz 1969:44); a similar situation occurs at Çatalhöyük (Roberts, Boyer, and Parish 1996:39). However, the rise of the water level was the reason for the abandonment of Suberde (Bordaz 1969).

Seventh Millennium B.C.E.: Changing Tendencies

Renewed work at Çatalhöyük (Hodder 1996:1–18) exposed early levels (pre-XII) that proved that the East Mound was first founded around 7400 B.C.E. (Cessford 2001); however, the earliest levels are known from very limited areas. Eighteen levels of occupation at Çatalhöyük document how the site retained its appealing nature for more than 1,000 years (Hodder 2005a, 2005b, 2005c).

Paleoenvironmental studies indicate that Çatalhöyük was established on the alluvial fan of the Çarşamba River, in a wetland environment. The presence of equids, deer, and cattle remains in the faunal assemblages indicate open woodlands and steppe in the surrounding area. Wetlands rich in wild plants supported intensive gathering in addition to the cultivation of cereals and pulses. Domesticated sheep and goats were the dominant meat sources, besides hunted game and a variety of birds and fish.

The settlement consisted of densely packed buildings, and the open spaces between the buildings were used as middens. Only a few streets or passages have been identified, and no public or special-function buildings have been found. The buildings were made of mud slabs, each with free-standing walls. The roofs were probably flat, with the entrances through the roofs. The plan and the inner divisions are defined similarly in each building, with a main living space, side rooms, and storage area in small separate rooms. Internal architectural features are distinctive and include hearths, ovens, platforms, benches, pillars, and bins.

Çatalhöyük differed from contemporary settlements of the plateau in many aspects. It was quite large in size—over thirteen hectares—and its population numbered several thousand people. Moreover, symbolic expressions and art are widely represented; the wall paintings, reliefs, cattle horns set into benches, figurines, and "history houses" with numerous burials underline the importance of the social and symbolic aspects of the community (see Hodder, chapter 43 in this volume). Around 6200/6000 B.C.E., the settlements at the East Mound shifted to what is known as the West Mound.

The late levels at Pınarbaşı provide evidence of seasonal camp sites on the Konya Plain in the seventh millennium B.C.E. The site revealed faunal remains of hunted aurochs, equids, birds, and domesticated sheep. Light structures, probably made of reeds and renewed many times, indicate that the camp site was used intensively by hunter and herder communities living in the vicinity of Çatalhöyük (Baird 2007b:303–8).

The Erbaba settlement was a farming community, located on a rocky protrusion of the east bank of Beyşehir Lake. The site is dated to the mid-seventh millennium B.C.E. and coincides chronologically to the second half of the Çatalhöyük sequence.

Excavations at this site revealed four layers (I–IV from top to bottom), the latest permitting relatively large exposures that reveal the layout of the settlement (Bordaz 1970). The settlement exhibits similarities to the central Anatolian model in terms of closely packed buildings, the location of the open spaces, and type of building entrance (Bordaz and Bordaz 1976). Differences exist, however, in the construction materials used and the building plans. The walls were constructed of irregular limestone blocks laid in mud mortar, and some of the buildings have internal buttresses. Benches, ovens, and painted plastered decorations occur inside the buildings (Bordaz and Bordaz 1982).

Archaeobotanical remains from Erbaba (van Zeist and Buitenhuis 1983) include cereals and pulses, with domesticated and wild forms of emmer and einkorn wheat, free threshing wheat, naked barley, peas, and lentils. The faunal remains include sheep, goat, and cattle (Bordaz and Bordaz 1982). The state of faunal domestication is debatable, especially for cattle and goats, due to limited morphometric data (Martin, Russell, and Carruthers 2002:202). Fishing and hunting of deer, boar, and birds were the major supplements of the diet. The tools were made of obsidian and flint in nearly equal proportions. Projectile points are among the rarest tools, whereas notched blades, sickle blades, and scrapers are common. Pottery was also used; the lower layer (III) yielded thin gritty monochrome ware that continued in the upper layers. The second ware group was represented by large quantities of gastropod shells tempered with clay. Gastropod ware differs in form from the former; some relief decoration also occurs on this pottery (Bordaz and 1976).

Can Hasan I lies about one kilometer southwest of Can Hasan III (French 1998:1). Seven layers were exposed in this site, of which Layers 7–4 were assigned to the Ceramic Neolithic. The exposure was limited (French 1968:71) due to the well-preserved architectural remains at the top of the sequence and a rising water table. However, "given the structural sequence from Layer 7 to Layer 4 and the form of the buildings in those layers, it can be conjectured with some probability that the structures preceding Layer 7 were similar in size and shape" (French 1998:20). The buildings were rectangular and made of *kerpiç* blocks. The walls and floors were plastered with mud, occasionally covered with white clay or red ochre. Hearths and bins were exposed, and considerable quantities of grain and seeds were found inside the bins. The botanical and zoological remains indicate a well-developed system of crop agriculture and animal husbandry at Can Hasan I. Pottery included hole mouth jars and open bowls of a dark brown and reddish color and burnished surfaces.

Two more sites in Cappadocia, Tepecik-Çiftlik and Köşk Höyük, yield interesting data on seventh millennium B.C.E. farming communities. Tepecik-Çiftlik occupies a desirable location in the center of the Melendiz Plain on alluvium that formed during the Pleistocene and early Holocene. The locality today is fed by the tributaries of the Melendiz River, which converge in the middle of the plain and flow northeast. The plain is bounded on the south by the Melendiz Mountains and by Göllüdağ on the north. Passes through these mountains give access to the plain, and the site is positioned centrally to these conduits, with links to the important obsidian resources and further south with the Taurus Mountains and distant Cilicia.

The Tepecik-Çiftlik excavations have so far revealed five levels (1–5 from top to bottom). Level 5 is assigned to the Ceramic Neolithic, and Level 4 corresponds to the transition from Neolithic to the Chalcolithic (Bıçakçı 2001; Bıçakçı et al. 2007). So far only Layer 4 is radiocarbon dated, and it dates to the end of the seventh millennium B.C.E.

Although the excavations are ongoing and the results preliminary, Tepecik-Çiftlik clearly represents the onset of changing tendencies during the second half of the seventh millennium B.C.E. The settlement is ideally located for agriculture, communication with other areas, and control over resources and the main routes of long-distance exchange. The strategic importance of its location and the artifactual material of Tepecik-Çiftlik testify to increased regional interaction.

The obsidian assemblage is of totally local obsidian except for a few imported flints (Bıçakçı et al. 2007:243). The assemblage yields bifacial retouched projectiles as the most frequent and distinctive group. Preliminary studies indicate that the projectiles are made on blanks that were probably imported. Projectiles have parallels at Çatalhöyük to the west and Köşk Höyük to the south. A large quantity and rich variety of finds present elaborately worked artifacts out of bone and various stones and indicate supraregional communication (Bıçakçı 2001). Pottery at Tepecik-Çiftlik is important for the observation of sociocultural and technological changes (Godon 2005); the early examples (Level 5) consist of local production and a few imports. The appearance of red slipped, decorated wares in Level 5 continue to appear in the later levels (3), where scenes from daily life, including hunting and husbandry, were depicted in relief (Bıçakçı et al. 2007:figs. 35–41; cf. Köşk Höyük). The site provides information on the internal evolution of a domestic settlement and its contact with neighboring areas.

Köşk Höyük displays similarities to Tepecik with regard to its strategic position. It is located in the Bor Plain (Öztan 2007), south of the Melendiz Mountains, on rocky limestone close to a perennial water source. Five levels (I–V from top to bottom) were exposed; II–V are assigned to the Ceramic Neolithic and Level I to the Early Chalcolithic. The site is radiocarbon dated between the second half of the seventh millennium and the first half of the sixth millennium B.C.E. (Öztan 2007). Domestic life at Köşk Höyük is associated with substantial, well-preserved stone architecture. Some of the buildings in III and V have walls made of mud. The buildings are rectangular and contain multiple rooms. Walls were plastered with mud; a few have white- or light orange–painted plaster. Almost all the houses have benches, hearths, and clay bins containing ground stone tools. Interesting is a wall painting in a level III house where a hunting scene was depicted (Öztan 2007:fig. 8). The houses are separated from each other by narrow passages and open spaces; some of these spaces are used as middens. Level III shows that such spaces can also be used for burials. Burials were placed in houses under the benches/platforms or walls; some late ones were buried in jars. Burial gifts consist of figurines, stamp seals made of bone, stone, and clay, bracelets, beads, and pottery in various forms. Also striking are the remodeled plastered human skulls belonging to females, males, and children. Skulls were placed on the platforms in houses either singly or in groups. Some of them were painted with red ochre (Öztan 2002:figs. 5–8; Özbek 2008).

Subsistence was based mainly on animal husbandry, hunting, and agriculture. The faunal remains were composed of domesticated and wild forms of sheep, goat, cattle, horse, deer, pig, and wolf; the first four were among the most regularly consumed. Secondary products must have had an important role in the diet of the community; for example, a milking scene of a cow was depicted on a pot in relief (Öztan 2007:fig. 16). Pottery with relief decoration also provides important and detailed information on the environment and on the community's daily practices and beliefs. A snake catching a fish, dancing women, the moon, and the sun are some of a wide variety of representations on pottery.

Köşk Höyük shares characteristics with the settlements of the previous millennium (e.g. in lithic technology) and displays intra-and interregional relations (e.g. in burial customs) with preceding and contemporary settlements (Öztan 2007).

Ilıcapınar, Sapmaz Köy, Pınarbaşı-Bor, and Çakılbaşı are some of the other settlements of the region. Except for one excavation season at Pınarbaşı-Bor (Silistreli 1984), all are known from surveys (Harmankaya, Tanındı, and Özbaşaran 1997) and therefore cannot be dated precisely. The first two sites are close to the main salt resource at Tuz Gölü, and the latter pair are situated near the obsidian sources—Çakılbaşı lies at the foot of Nenezi Mountain. Considering the distinct locations of these sites and the contents of available surface material, one can suggest a novel tendency for the establishment of sites focused on the procurement and exploitation of raw materials and exchange, and/or interfaces with other communities.

Concluding Remarks

The Anatolian plateau was first inhabited by *Homo erectus* where recent research has exposed find spots assigned to the Lower and Middle Palaeolithic periods (Slimak 2004). There is very little information available about mobile groups of the later part of the Pleistocene through Epipalaeolithic, with the important exception of the seasonal Epipalaeolithic occupation at Pınarbaşı B, which presently stands as the key site for the region. Pınarbaşı data not only evidence the existence of mobile groups in the region but also provide noteworthy information on the way of living prior to the ninth millennium B.C.E. and the emergence of sedentism.

Early sedentary settlements of the ninth millennium B.C.E. are similar to Epipalaeolithic Pınarbaşı in their adaptation to the unique environment of the region. The landscape is heterogeneous, with strong contrasts between the steppe and the rich microniches within it. These qualities of the central Anatolian region are governed in large part by the hydrology and geologic substrates of the region. Highlands with forested slopes, open steppes, wetlands, and pluvial lakes offered a suitable and biotically diverse environment for the communities that lived there. The geology of the region also presented concentrated sources of valuable raw materials. Therefore, it is perhaps not surprising that the communities on the plateau exploited their own surroundings heavily and had sufficient resources to allow them to sustain their past lifeway by establishing long-term, permanent settlements. For example the subsistence of both of the ninth millennium B.C.E. sites of Pınarbaşı and Aşıklı, in different microniches, consisted mainly of hunting and gathering. Although the Aşıklı community also possessed domesticated forms of cereals from the earliest levels on, hunting and gathering remained very important to the economy.[6]

The locations of sites close to springs, river mouths, or along the flanks of mountain ranges indicate a strong preference for and importance of diverse habitats and raw materials in the local economy. Their adaptations to local, unique conditions also made the communities different from each other. Thus the plateau displays a fine-scale pattern of social geography with respect to the exploitation of the environment, in spite of evidence for inter- and supraregional community interaction. Communities maintained contact with each other and the neighboring communities (Matthews 2002; Schoop 2005) probably via the exchange of material. The procurement of raw material, mainly obsidian, could have been one of the most important modes of interaction. The question of whether similarities between sites within the region are due to communication or to a common identity is unclear at present (Duru 2002); however, they are distinctly central Anatolian. The closely packed buildings, with communication and activity spaces on the roofs, the long legacies of superimposed construction, and building techniques founded almost entirely on mud/*kerpiç*, as well as the burial customs, are local. These practices were carried out by the communities of the ninth and eighth millenium B.C.E. and persisted for about 2,000 years. The public buildings, the lime plastering in special-function buildings, or the fully developed cereal variants might have resulted from supraregional contact with southeast Anatolia or the northern Levant.[7] External relations however, became more evident in the next millennium.

Around the middle of the seventh millennium, before 6500 B.C.E., the majority of the settlements in central Anatolia were abandoned. The abandonment coincides with changes in the Çatalhöyük chronology (Level VI), where habitation continued and the resident population may have exceeded several thousand.

The picture on the Cappadocian side at present is more fragmentary. A significant gap exists between Aşıklı Höyük and Tepecik-Çiftlik. Future excavations of the deposits below the already documented levels at Tepecik-Çiftlik promise to fill this gap. Tepecik-Çiftlik and Köşk Höyük were farming villages with fully domestic crops and animals. Both occupied privileged locations, probably for the routes of exchange, especially obsidian in the case of Tepecik-Çiftlik. Sites—identified by surveys—such as Ilıcapınar and Sapmaz Köy were strategically positioned for access to and control of salt sources, indicating possibly the establishment of resource-acquisition sites. The locations of the sites with respect to mountain passes and access to concentrated resources indicate changing economic and social agendas of plateau communities around the middle of the seventh millennium B.C.E. The hypothesis of control over the routes of long-distance exchange can be complemented by intensified contacts between regions evidenced both in material culture and the exchange of ideas. Tepecik-Çiftlik and Köşk Höyük provide noteworthy data for interregional contact. Supraregional contact or influences, on the other hand, can also be traced. The remodeled skulls and pressure flaked cores found at Köşk Höyük (although limited in number) (Öztan 2007), a few blades obtained by pressure technique at Tepecik-Çiftlik (Bıçakçı et al. 2007:244), and the presence of east Anatolian obsidian at Çatalhöyük (Carter et al. 2008) can be interpreted as the outcome of this intensifying relation between the neighboring and more distant communities.

To conclude, the data presently display local adaptations of central Anatolian Neolithic communities to their diverse habitats. In the ninth and early eighth millennia B.C.E., sedentism and a heavy reliance on naturally occurring resources constituted the way of life on the plateau. Full farming villages developed toward the second half of the eighth millennium, and settlements with specialized objectives seem to have been established in the seventh millennium. Although the picture was surely not that simplistic or linear, it provides an overall look at the neolithisation of the plateau. When it is contextualized within the "Neolithic cradle of the Near East" or compared with the Neolithic *koine*, the central Anatolian "developments" are late in chronology (Esin 2007; Thissen 2002:324, 328), which has led to long debate and diffusionist discussions on the origins of the Neolithic of the plateau. Conversely the ongoing research suggests that a local model defines the plateau Neolithic, one that stems from the preference and choice of the communities who had long lived in a privileged environment.

The present picture of the Neolithic of the central Anatolian plateau is reconstructed from only eleven excavated sites, of which six are currently under excavation. Some of the results are preliminary, and the interpretations are debatable. The ongoing studies constantly enrich the neolithisation questions not only of the plateau but also of southwest Asia.

NOTES

I am thankful to Mary Stiner of the University of Arizona, who kindly agreed to go over the text and correct the language. I am also thankful to Laurence Astruc of CNRS and Nur Balkan Atlı of Istanbul University for their help and kind contributions.

1. For such an attempt, see Özbaşaran and Buitenhuis 2002.

2. The only Neolithic site located within the arc of the Kızılırmak is Hassanlar. There are three sites north and northwest of Tuz Gölü—Ayvaz Höyük II, Küçük Hüseyin Tepesi II, and Çatal Höyük II—which were identified by S. Omura during his Central Anatolian Survey. Although Neolithic presence was inferred during the survey from sparse pot sherds or obsidian, and the sites were marked on survey maps, without detailed information the periods of occupation remain in question (Omura 1991, 1993, 1995).

3. All dates in the text are calibrated B.C.E. (see CANeW ^{14}C database at www.canew.org; Gérard and Thissen 2002; Thissen 2002).

4. There are different kinds of construction techniques at Aşıklı. The majority of mud walls were constructed by mud slabs set in mortar (Bıçakçı and Özbaşaran 1991). The thickness of the slabs and the mortar is almost identical. However, there are also examples shaped in molds with roughly standardized dimensions. To avoid confusion I call them *kerpiç* blocks. The difference between the two types—whether it is chronological or technological—is under study at present and awaits the results of the micromorphological analysis.

5. There are two more sites within one kilometer of Aşıklı, all identified through surveys. Preliminary study of the surface collection suggests that these sites—Yellibelen and Gedikbaşı—could also have been exploited by the Aşıklı community (Balkan Atlı 1998).

6. Due to the state of preservation of archaeobotanical samples, this remains a topic of debate (Asouti and Fairbairn 2002; Rene Cappers, personal communication); however, the Aşıklı excavators suggest that agriculture played a secondary role in community subsistence there (Esin and Harmankaya 1999:126).

7. This suggestion should be treated with caution because of the present state of research in the region. Excavations at Boncuklu are comparatively new, and the earliest levels of Aşıklı are not yet extensively excavated.

REFERENCES

Abbes, Frederic, Nur Balkan Atlı, Didier Binder, and Marie-Claire Cauvin. 1999. Etude téchnologique préliminaire de l'industrie lithique d'Aşıklı Höyük. *TÜBA-AR* 2: 117–37.

Asouti, Eleni and Andy Fairbairn. 2002. Subsistence Economy in Central Anatolia during the Neolithic: The Archaeobotanical Evidence In *Anatolia, 10.000–5000 cal BC, The Neolithic of Central Anatolia*, ed. Frédéric Gérard and Laurens Thissen, 181–92. İstanbul: Ege Yayınları.

Astruc, Laurence, Nurcan Kayacan, and Mihriban Özbaşaran. 2008. Technical Activities Held at Musular (VIIIth Millenium BC, Central Anatolia): A Preliminary Use-Wear Analysis of Lithic Tools. *Arkeometri Sonuçları Toplantısı* 23: 165–72.

Atalay, İbrahim. 1995. *Türkiye Bölgesel Coğrafyası*. Ankara: İnkilap Kitabevi.

Ataman, Kathryn. 1988. *The Chipped Stone Assemblage from Can Hasan III: A Study in Typology, Technology and Function*. Ph.D. dissertation, Institute of Archaeology, University College, London.

Aytuğ, Burhan. 1967. Konya Suberde dolaylarında Neolitik Çağ florasının incelenmesi. *İstanbul Üniversitesi Orman Fakültesi Dergisi* 17.2: 1–9.

Baird, Douglas. 1996. The Konya Plain Survey: Aims and Methods. In *On the Surface: Çatalhöyük 1993–95*, ed. Ian Hodder, 41–46. McDonald Institute Monographs 22. Cambridge: McDonald Institute for Archaeological Research.

———. 2002. Early Holocene Settlement in Central Anatolia: Problems and Prospects as Seen from the Konya Plain. In *Anatolia, 10.000–5000 cal BC, The Neolithic of Central Anatolia*, ed. Frédéric Gérard and Laurens Thissen, 139–59. İstanbul: Ege Yayınları.

———. 2007a. The Boncuklu Project: The Origins of Sedentism, Cultivation and Herding in Central Anatolia. *Anatolian Archaeology* 13: 14–17.

———. 2007b. Pınarbaşı: Orta Anadolu'da Epi-paleolitik Konak Yerinden Yerleşik Köy Yaşamına. In *Türkiye'de Neolitik Dönem*, ed. Mehmet Özdoğan and Nezih Başgelen, 285–311. İstanbul: Arkeoloji ve Sanat Yayınları.

Balkan Atlı, Nur. 1993. Aşıklı Höyük (Aksaray) Yontma Taş Endüstrisinin Teknolojik ve Tipolojik açıdan İncelenmesi. *Arkeometri Sonuçları Toplantısı* 8: 213–25.

———. 1998. The Aceramic Neolithic of Central Anatolia: Recent Finds in the Chipped Stone Industry. In *Light on Top of the Black Hill: Studies Presented to Halet Çambel*, ed. Güven Arsebük, Wulf Schirmer, and Machteld Mellink, 81–94. İstanbul: Ege Yayınları.

Balkan Atlı, Nur and Didier Binder. 2007. Kömürcü-Kaletepe Obsidyen İşliği. In *Türkiye'de Neolitik Dönem*, ed. Mehmet Özdoğan and Nezih Başgelen, 217–12. İstanbul: Arkeoloji ve Sanat Yayınları.

Balkan Atlı, Nur, Didier Binder, and Marie Claire Cauvin. 1998. Obsidian: Sources, Workshops and Trade in Central Anatolia. In *Neolithic in Turkey: The Cradle of Civilization*, ed. Mehmet Özdoğan and Nezih Başgelen, 133–45. İstanbul: Arkeoloji ve Sanat Yayınları.

Binder, Didier. 2002. Stones Making Sense: What Obsidian Could Tell about the Origins of the Central Anatolian Neolithic. In *Anatolia, 10.000–5000 cal BC, The Neolithic of Central Anatolia*, ed. Frédéric Gérard and Laurens Thissen, 79–90. İstanbul: Ege Yayınları.

Binder, Didier and Nur Balkan Atlı. 2001. Obsidian Exploitation and Blade Technology at Kömürcü-Kaletepe (Cappadocia, Turkey). In *Beyond Tools: Redefining the PPN Lithic Assemblages of the Levant*, ed. Isabella Caneva, 1–16. Berlin: Ex Oriente.

Bıçakçı, Erhan. 2001. Tepecik-Çiftlik Höyüğü (Niğde) Kazısı Işığında Orta Anadolu Tarihöncesi Kültürleri ile İlgili yeni bir Değerlendirme. *TÜBA-AR* 4: 25–41.

Bıçakçı, Erhan and Mihriban Özbaşaran. 1991. Aşıklı Höyük 1989, 1990: Building Activities. *Anatolica* 17: 136–45.

Bıçakçı, Erhan, Çiler Altınbilek Algül, Semra Balcı, and Martin Godon. 2007. Tepecik-Çiftlik. In *Türkiye'de Neolitik Dönem*, ed. Mehmet Özdoğan and Nezih Başgelen, 237–53. İstanbul: Arkeoloji ve Sanat Yayınları.

Bordaz, Jacques. 1969. The Suberde Excavations, Southwestern Turkey: An Interim Report. *Türk Arkeoloji Dergisi* 17: 43–71.

———. 1970. A Preliminary Report of the 1969 Excavations at Erbaba, a Neolithic Site near Beyşehir, Turkey. *Türk Arkeoloji Dergisi* 18.2: 59–64.

Bordaz, Jacques and Louise Alpers Bordaz. 1976. Erbaba Excavations, 1974. *Türk Arkeoloji Dergisi* 23.2: 39–43.

———. 1982. Erbaba: The 1977 and 1978 Seasons in Perspective. *Türk Arkeoloji Dergisi* 26.1: 85–93.

Buitenhuis, Hijlke. 1997. Aşıklı Höyük: A Protodomestication Site. *Anthropozoologica* 25–26: 655–62.

Carter, Tristan, Stéphan Dubernet, Rachel King, François-Xavier Le Bourdonnec. Marina Milic, Gérard Poupeau, and Steven M. Shackley. 2008. Eastern Anatolian Obsidians at Çatalhöyük and the Reconfiguration of Regional Interaction in the Early Ceramic Neolithic. *Antiquity* 82: 900–901.

Cauvin, Marie-Claire and Nur Balkan Atlı. 1996. Rapport sur les recherches sur l'obsidienne en Cappadoce, 1993–1995. *Anatolia Antiqua* 4: 249–71.

Cessford, Craig. 2001. A New Dating Sequence for Çatalhöyük. *Antiquity* 75: 717–25.

Duru, Güneş. 2002. Some Architectural Indications for the Origins of Central Anatolia. In *Anatolia, 10.000–5000 cal BC, The Neolithic of Central Anatolia*, ed. Frédéric Gérard and Laurens Thissen, 171–80. İstanbul: Ege Yayınları.

Duru, Güneş and Mihriban Özbaşaran. 2005. A Non-Domestic Site in Central Anatolia. *Anatolia Antiqua* 8: 15–28.

Erdoğu, Burçin, Mihriban Özbaşaran, Rabia Erdoğu, and John Chapman. 2003. Prehistoric Salt Exploitation in Tuz Gölü, Central Anatolia: Preliminary Investigations. *Anatolia Antiqua* 11: 11–19.

Esin, Ufuk. 1996. On Bin Yıl öncesinde Aşıklı: İç Anadolu'da bir Yerleşim Modeli. In *Tarihten Günümüze Anadolu'da Konut ve Yerleşme*, ed. Yıldız Şey, 31–42. İstanbul: Tarih Vakfı Yayınları.

———. 1998. Paleolitik'ten İlk Tunç Çağı'nın Sonuna: Tarihöncesi Çağların Kapadokyası. In *Kapadokya*, ed. M. Sözen, 62–123. İstanbul: Ayhan Şahenk Vakfı.

———. 2007. Anadolu Neolitiğine başka bir Bakış. In *Türkiye'de Neolitik Dönem*, ed. Mehmet Özdoğan and Nezih Başgelen, xi–xiii. İstanbul: Arkeoloji ve Sanat Yayınları.

Esin, Ufuk, Sevil Gülçur, and Hikmet Kurar. 1998. Aksaray, Nevşehir, Niğde İlleri 1996 Ortak Yüzey Araştırması. *Araştırma Sonuçları Toplantısı* 15.2: 233–46.

Esin, Ufuk and Savaş Harmankaya. 1999. Aşıklı. In *Neolithic in Turkey: The Cradle of Civilization*, ed. Mehmet Özdoğan and Nezih Başgelen, 115–32. İstanbul: Arkeoloji ve Sanat Yayınları.

———. 2007. Aşıklı Höyük. In *Türkiye'de Neolitik Dönem*, ed. Mehmet Özdoğan and Nezih Başgelen, 255–72. İstanbul: Arkeoloji ve Sanat Yayınları.

French, David H. 1962. Can Hasan, Karaman 1961. *Türk Arkeoloji Dergisi* 11.2: 36–37.

———. 1968. Can Hasan 1966. *Türk Arkeoloji Dergisi* 15.1: 69–73.

———. 1998. *Can Hasan I: Stratigraphy and Structures.* Can Hasan Sites 1, The British Institute of Archaeology at Ankara, Monograph no. 23. London: British Institute of Archaeology at Ankara.

French, David H., Gordon C. Hillman, Sebastian Payne, and Rosemary J. Payne. 1972. Excavations at Can Hasan III 1969–1970. In *Papers in Economic Prehistory*, ed. Eric S. Higgs, 181–90. Cambridge: Cambridge University Press.

Gérard, Frédéric and Laurens Thissen, eds. 2002. *Anatolia, 10.000–5000 cal BC, The Neolithic of Central Anatolia.* İstanbul: Ege Yayınları.

Godon, Martin. 2005. New Results and Remarks about Neolithic Pottery inCcentral Anatolia: A View from Tepecik-Çiftlik. *Colloquium Anatolicum* 4: 91–103.

Harmankaya, Savaş, Oğuz Tanındı, and Mihriban Özbaşaran. 1997. *Türkiye Arkeolojik Yerleşmeleri TAY 2, Neolitik.* İstanbul: Ege Yayınları.

Hodder, Ian. ed. 1996. *On the Surface: Çatalhöyük, 1993–95.* McDonald Institute Monographs 22. Cambridge: McDonald Institute for Archaeological Research.

———. ed. 2005a. *Inhabiting Çatalhöyük: Reports from the 1995–99 Seasons.* McDonald Institute Monographs 38. Cambridge: McDonald Institute for Archaeological Research.

———. ed. 2005b. *Changing Materialities at Çatalhöyük: Reports from the 1995–99 Seasons.* McDonald Institute Monographs 39. Cambridge: McDonald Institute for Archaeological Research.

———. ed. 2005c. *Çatalhöyük Perspectives: Themes from the 1995–99 Seasons.* McDonald Institute Monographs 40. Cambridge: McDonald Institute for Archaeological Research.

Hodder, Ian and Roger Matthews. 1998. Çatalhöyük: 1990s Seasons. In *Ancient Anatolia*, ed. Roger Matthews, 43–51. Ankara: British Institute of Archaeology at Ankara.

Kayacan, Nurcan. 2003. Chipped Stone Industry of the Neolithic Site of Musular (Cappadocia): Preliminary Results. *Anatolia Antiqua* 11: 1–10.

Kayacan, Nurcan and Mihriban Özbaşaran. 2007. The Choice of Obsidian and its Use at Musular—Central Anatolia. In *Les communautés du Néolithique pré-céramique d'Eurasia: de l'analyse de la diversité des systémes techniques a la caractérisation des comportements sociaux*, ed. Laurence Astruc, Didier Binder, and François Briois, 229–33. Antibes: Editions APDCA.

Kuzucuoğlu, Catherine. 2002. The Environmental Frame in Central Anatolia from the 9th to the 6th Millennia cal BC. An Introduction to the Study of Relations between Environmental Conditions and the Development of Human Societies In *Anatolia, 10.000–5000 cal BC, The Neolithic of Central Anatolia*, ed. Frédéric Gérard and Laurens Thissen, 33–58. İstanbul: Ege Yayınları.

Martin, Louise, Nerissa Russell, and Denise Carruthers. 2002. Animal Remains from the Central Anatolian Neolithic. In *Anatolia, 10.000–5000 cal BC, The Neolithic of Central Anatolia*, ed. Frédéric Gérard and Laurens Thissen, 193–216. İstanbul: Ege Yayınları.

Matthews, Roger. 2002. Homogeneity versus Diversity: Dynamics of the Central Anatolian Neolithic. In *Anatolia, 10.000–5000 cal BC, The Neolithic of Central Anatolia*, ed. Frédéric Gérard and Laurens Thissen, 91–103. İstanbul: Ege Yayınları.

Mellaart, James. 1967. *Çatalhöyük: A Neolithic Town in Anatolia.* London: Thames and Hudson.

———. 1975. *The Neolithic of the Near East.* London: Thames and Hudson.

Omura, Sachihiro. 1991. 1989 Yılı Kırşehir, Yozgat, Nevşehir, Aksaray İlleri Sınırları içinde Yürütülen Yüzey Araştırmaları. *Araştırma Sonuçları Toplantısı* 8: 69–89.

———. 1993. 1991 Yılı İç Anadolu'da Yürütülen Yüzey Araştırmaları. *Araştırma Sonuçları Toplantısı* 10: 365–86.
———. 1995. 1993 Yılında İç Anadolu'da Yürütülen Yüzey Araştırmaları. *Araştırma Sonuçları Toplantısı* 12: 215–44.
Orthmann, Winfried. 1963. *Die Keramik der Frühen Bronzezeit aus Inneranatolien*. Berlin: Gebr. Mann Verlag.
Özbaşaran, Mihriban. 1998. The Heart of a House: The Hearth—Aşıklı Höyük, a Pre-Pottery Neolithic Site in Central Anatolia. In *Light on Top of the Black Hill: Studies Presented to Halet Çambel*, ed. Güven Arsebük, Machteld J. Mellink, and Wulf Schirmer, 555–66. İstanbul: Ege Yayınları.
———. 2000. The Neolithic Site of Musular—Central Anatolia. *Anatolica* 26: 129–51.
———. 2003. Musular—Aşıklı ilişkisinde Kireç Tabanlı Yapılar. In *Ufuk Esin'e Armağan, Köyden Kente, Yakındoğu'da İlk Yerleşimler*, ed. Mehmet Özdoğan, Harald Hauptmann, and Nezih Başgelen, 361–72. İstanbul: Arkeoloji ve Sanat Yayınları.
Özbaşaran, Mihriban and Hijlke Buitenhuis. 2002. Proposal for a Regional Terminology for Central Anatolia. In *Anatolia, 10.000–5000 cal BC, The Neolithic of Central Anatolia*, ed. Frédéric Gérard and Laurens Thissen, 67–77. İstanbul: Ege Yayınları.
Özbek, Metin. 1992. Aşıklı Höyük Neolitik Insanları. *Arkeometri Sonuçları Toplantısı* 7: 145–60.
———. 1998. Skeletal Remains from Aşıklı, a Neolithic Village near Aksaray, Turkey. In *Light on Top of the Black Hill: Studies Presented to Halet Çambel*, ed. Güven Arsebük, Machteld J. Mellink, and Wulf Schirmer, 567–79. İstanbul: Ege Yayınları.
———. 2008. Remodeled Human Skulls in Köşk Höyük (Neolithic Age, Anatolia): A New Appraisal in View of Recent Discoveries. *Journal of Archaeological Science* 36: 379–86.
Özdoğan, Mehmet. 1996. Pre-Bronze Age Sequence of Central Anatolia: An Alternative Approach. In *Vom Halys zum Euphrat: Thomas Beran Festschrift*, ed. Ursula Magen and Mahmoud Rashad, 185–202. Münster: Ugarit Verlag.
Özgüç, Nimet. 1973. Haberler—Kazılar. Niğde Tepebağları Höyüğü Kazısı. *Belleten* 38: 442–43.
Öztan, Aliye. 2002. Köşk Höyük: Anadolu Arkeolojisine Yeni Katkılar. *TÜBA-AR* 5: 55–69.
———. 2007. Köşk Höyük: Niğde-Bor Ovasında bir Yerleşim. In *Türkiye'de Neolitik Dönem*, ed. Mehmet Özdoğan and Nezih Başgelen, 223–35. İstanbul: Arkeoloji ve Sanat Yayınları.
Payne, Sebastian. 1972. Can Hasan III, the Anatolian Aceramic and the Greek Neolithic. In *Papers in Economic Prehistory*, ed. Eric S. Higgs, 191–94. Cambridge: Cambridge University Press.
Renfrew, Colin, J. E. Dixon, and J. R. Cann. 1966. Obsidian and Early Culture Contact in the Near East. *Proceedings of the Prehistoric Society* 32: 30–72.
Roberts, Neil, Peter Boyer, and Romola Parish. 1996. Preliminary Results of Geoarchaeological Investigations at Çatalhöyük. In *On the Surface: Çatalhöyük 1993–95*, ed. Ian Hodder, 19–40. McDonald Institute Monographs 22. Cambridge: McDonald Institute for Archaeological Research.
Schoop, Ulf-Dietrich. 2005. The Late Escape of the Neolithic from the Central Anatolian Plain. In *How Did Farming Reach Europe? Anatolian-European Relations from the Second Half of the 7th Through the First Half of the 6th Millennium cal BC*, ed. Clemens Lichter, 41–58. BYZAS 2. İstanbul: Ege Yayınları.
Silistreli, Uğur. 1984. Pınarbaşı ve Köşk Höyükleri. *Kazı Sonuçları Toplantısı* 5: 81–85.
Slimak, Ludovic. 2004. Implantations humaines et exploitation des obsidiennes en Anatolie Centrale durant le Pléistocene. *Paléorient* 30.2: 7–20.

Solecki, Ralph S. 1965. An Archaeological Reconnaissance in the Beyşehir Suğla Area of South Western Turkey. *Türk Arkeoloji Dergisi* 13.1: 129–48.

Summers, Geoffrey D. 1993. The Chalcolithic Period in Central Anatolia, the Fourth Millenium B.C. In *Proceedings of the International Symposium Nessebur*, ed. Petya Georgieva, 29–48. Sofia: New Bulgarian University.

Thissen, Laurens. 2002. Canew 14C Databases and 14C Charts. In *Anatolia, 10.000–5000 cal BC, The Neolithic of Central Anatolia*, ed. Frédéric Gérard and Laurens Thissen, 299–337. İstanbul: Ege Yayınları.

Todd, Ian. 1980. *The Prehistory of Central Anatolia I. The Neolithic Period*. Studies in Mediterranean Archaeology 60. Göteborg: P. Aström Forlag.

van Zeist, Willem and Hijlke Buitenhuis. 1983. A Paleobotanical Study of Neolithic Erbaba, Turkey. *Anatolica* 10: 47–89.

van Zeist, Willem and Gerrit Jan de Roller. 1995. Plant Remains from Asikli Höyük, a Pre-Pottery Neolithic site in Central Anatolia. *Vegetation History and Archaeobotany* 4: 179–85.

———. 2003. Some Notes on the Plant Husbandary of Aşıklı Höyük. In *Reports on Archaeobotanical Studies in the Old World*, ed. Willem van Zeist, 115–42. Gröningen: Barkhuis.

Watkins, Trevor. 1996. Excavations at Pınarbaşı: The Early Stages. In *On the Surface: Çatalhöyük 1993–95*, ed. Ian Hodder, 47–57. McDonald Institute Monographs 22. Cambridge: McDonald Institute for Archaeological Research.

CHAPTER 6

THE NEOLITHIC IN SOUTHEASTERN ANATOLIA

MICHAEL ROSENBERG AND ASLI ERİM-ÖZDOĞAN

GEOGRAPHICALLY, southeastern Anatolia corresponds to the upper reaches of the Tigris and Euphrates drainages, north of the ~400 mm isohyet, which constitutes the southern limit of reliable dry farming. The Neolithic sites in this area (figure 6.1) display a degree of internal cultural similarity that distinguishes them from those farther south and allows them to be discussed as a group.

The matter of chronological terminology is more complex. A half century ago, when confronted with the need to subdivide chronologically the surprisingly deep Aceramic Neolithic deposits at Jericho, Kenyon (1957) seized on the obvious transition from curvilinear to rectilinear architecture to differentiate the two main aceramic periods at that site, designating them Pre-Pottery Neolithic A (PPNA) and Pre-Pottery Neolithic B (PPNB), respectively. This eventually led to the almost casual application of the terms "PPNA" and "PPNB" to sites in other areas as well. This was typically done to invoke the relatively convenient chronological connotations of Kenyon's designations, but they were sometimes also used to imply a more general and problematic cultural tie of one sort or another (e.g., Cauvin 1988).

Leaving aside the highly debatable issue of cultural associations (see Rosenberg 2004 for a more detailed discussion), even the conservative, strictly chronological usage is problematic. For example, referring to Anatolian sites as PPNA or PPNB implies that the full *local* period into which these Anatolian sites fall corresponds in both its beginning as well as its end to the concomitant Levantine period, not to mention implying a similar level of development.

The most commonly offered rationale for the continued usage of these terms is that "everyone understands what they mean." We would argue that this is not exactly true. Yes, everyone *recognizes* the terms, but *knowing* what they mean is a different matter entirely, because they mean different things for different scholars when used outside the Levant. In fact, when used outside of the Levant, all the terms "PPNA" and "PPNB" do consistently is convey the rough chronological meaning of "early" and "late" Aceramic Neolithic (for PPNA and PPNB, respectively) and do even that poorly because they further vaguely imply that the early and late aceramic were both similar and spanned the same length of time in both areas.

For that reason, this chapter will simply refer to the local round house horizon in southeastern Anatolia as the Early Aceramic Neolithic (EA) and the local rectilinear house horizon as the Mature Aceramic Neolithic (MA). This leaves them free to be discussed on their own terms and avoids the necessity of trying to jam rectilinear pegs into curvilinear holes or otherwise having to reconcile discrepancies here between absolute age and cultural features in southeastern Anatolia as compared to the Levant.

The Early Aceramic I (EA I)

The earliest firmly dated settled village sites thus far known from southeastern Anatolia are a set of three sequential sites situated along the Batman River, a tributary of the Tigris, that together straddle the terminus of the proto-Neolithic and the first several hundred years of the EA and exemplify the transition from the

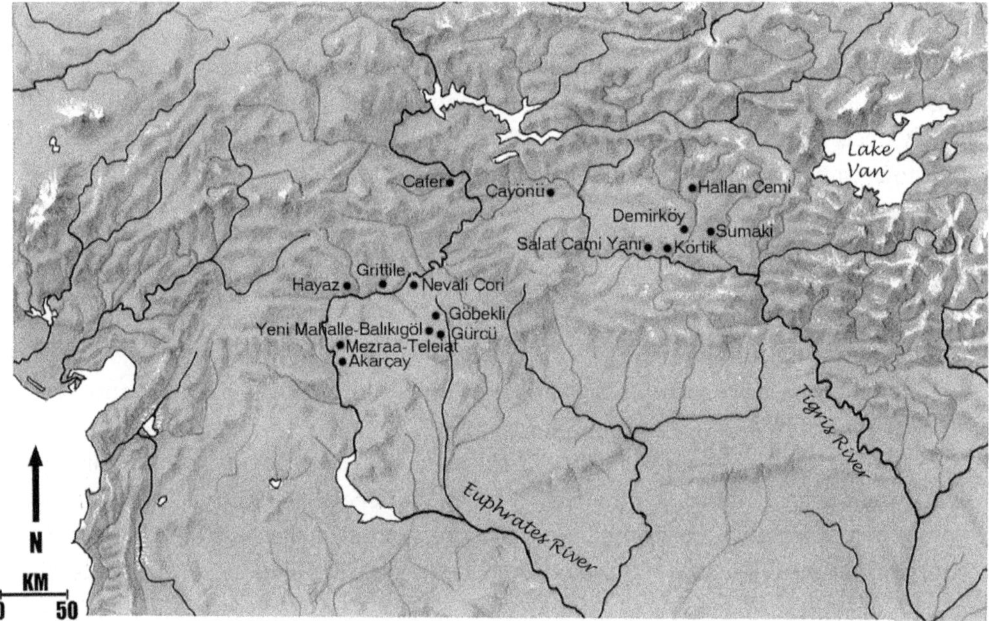

Figure 6.1. Map of southeastern Anatolia with sites mentioned in the text indicated.

former to the latter in the upper Tigris area. The oldest of these sites is Hallan Çemi. A set of sixteen accelerator dates (OxA 12298–99, 12328–41) tightly dates the last three building levels of this site to approximately the last few hundred years of the eleventh millennium B.P. in ^{14}C years. The occupation at Hallan Çemi is followed immediately by one at the site of Demirköy, a site situated about forty kilometers downriver from Hallan Çemi. According to two accelerator dates (OxA 12488–89), Demirköy dates to the first century of the tenth millennium B.P. The occupation of Demirköy, in turn, is followed closely by an occupation at the site of Körtik (Beta 178241–42),[1] a site situated another twenty kilometers downriver from Demirköy, near the confluence of the Batman and Tigris Rivers. These three sites likely represent the sequential relocation of a single community within the Batman drainage over time.

In the Euphrates drainage, the beginning of this period is perhaps represented by the sites of Biris Mezarlığı and Söğüt Tarlası (see Hauptmann 1999, 2007), located northwest of Urfa, near Bozova, and excavated by B. Howe in 1964. Neither test excavation yielded any recognizable traces of architecture, and the lithic assemblages from both remain to be analyzed in detail. Thus, for the moment, nothing more can be said about these sites other than that they appear to be early and that the lithic assemblages do not resemble the ones found at the Batman River sites (M. Özdoğan and B. Peasnall, personal communications).

Culturally, Hallan Çemi is clearly derived from the Zarzian, a culture that spans the Epipalaeolithic through proto-Neolithic and is thus far known only from the Zagros flanks of Iraq and Iran (presumably for lack of excavated Epipalaeolithic sites in southeastern Anatolia). The Hallan Çemi assemblage shares significant chipped stone (e.g., scalene geometrics) and worked bone (e.g., bone "buttons") artifact types with Zarzian sites, most notably the proto-Neolithic site of Zawi Chemi in the Mosul region of northern Iraq (e.g., see Rosenberg 1994; Rosenberg and Davis 1992). The cultural association of Anatolian and Iraqi sites continues into the Aceramic Neolithic, with all three Anatolian sites sharing significant types (e.g., sculpted stone pestles, Nemrik points) with approximately contemporary Aceramic Neolithic sites (e.g., Nemrik) in the Mosul region. Though the Iraqi sites (e.g., Nemrik, Qermez Dere) do show indications of contact with contemporary Levantine cultures, primarily through the presence of Levantine Khiam type points (in addition to the typically local Nemrik points), such Levantine points do not appear in the Batman River sites, indicating that the Levantine points are simply a localized foreign overlay on an otherwise indigenous culture at the Iraqi sites. There are, however, also significant points of difference between the Batman River sites and those in the Mosul region, as in the important social role of stone bowls at the former (see later discussion) and their absence at the latter. Thus Hallan Çemi, Demirköy, and Körtik can reasonably be considered a diverging regional offshoot of a more widespread proto-Neolithic culture that existed along the upper reaches of the Tigris at least as far south as northern Iraq, and which had its roots in the indigenous Epipalaeolithic culture of this wider region, the Zarzian.

Although no architecture was encountered in the relatively small soundings at Demirköy, both Hallan Çemi and Körtik are characterized by curvilinear structures (as are the northern Iraqi Neolithic sites) made of stone, as well as of wattle and daub at least in the case of Hallan Çemi. Also, at least in the case of Hallan Çemi, public structures are evident in the form of two exceptionally large (relative to other structures at that site) stone-lined semi-subterranean buildings in the uppermost preserved building level, one of which once had a complete aurochs skull attached to the wall facing the entrance (e.g., see Rosenberg 1999). Both had been carefully resurfaced multiple times over cleaned floors. Whatever other matters were being conducted in these public buildings, they included the use of exotic materials brought in by long-distance trade. A total of four small pieces of copper ore were recovered during the excavation; all were found in association with the two public buildings. Obsidian was also imported from both the Van and Bingöl Areas and used extensively in all parts of the site, but the only two non-exhausted obsidian cores found during the excavation were recovered, along with associated debitage, from the uppermost floor of the "aurochs skull" building, indicating that it was being worked there.

Another aspect of public life at Hallan Çemi seems to have revolved around public feasting. The structures there were arranged around an open central activity area whose deposits consisted almost entirely of densely packed fire-cracked stones, interspersed with very large quantities of carbon and animal bone, the latter often in the form of still articulated body parts. Although similar public areas have not yet been identified at the other two Batman River sites, all three sites yielded elaborately carved stone "pestles" and numerous stone bowls (figure 6.2), the former often carved into stylized animal heads and the latter often elaborately incised with both

Figure 6.2. Stone bowls and stone pestle in the form of a goat head from Hallan Çemi.

geometric and naturalistic motifs (e.g., see Rosenberg 1999, 2007a). In the case of the stone bowls, the intensity and elaborateness of such decorations seem to reach an apogee with the examples from Körtik (see Özkaya and San 2007). The most common geometric motifs are nested serpentine meanders, circular "targets," and triangular areas filled in with cross-hatching. The most common naturalistic motifs are snakes and scorpions (e.g., figure 6.3), but other forms also occur. Both the bowls and pestles are typically made of a chloritic stone and to approximately the same scale, suggesting they were used together in the formal preparation and consumption of food or drink, presumably in association with said feasting. Another artifact type presumably related to this behavioral complex and found at both Hallan Çemi and Körtik are large, hemispherical, solid stone "platters," also made of the same chloritic stone.

A last type of object, thus far found only at Körtik, deserves special mention. These are a series of small stone plaques that all depict the same kind of creature in raised relief (figure 6.4). To begin with, these representations are not decorative, since these highly worked objects themselves have no other apparent function than to represent this creature (i.e., they are not bowl fragments, pendants, etc.). They are thus fetishes of some kind. On first impression, these fetishes seem to depict either a sheep or goat; a closer inspection points to the depiction more likely being that of a bee (e.g., drooping antennae, folded wing along back, limbs only coming off the thorax, curled abdomen, etc.). Second, the depiction is not completely realistic, with only two limbs, instead of four (if it were an ovicaprid) or six (if it were a realistic depiction of a bee), despite their makers' obvious capability of

Figure 6.3. Stone bowl fragment from Körtik decorated with snakes, scorpions, targets, and anthropomorphic figures (courtesy V. Özkaya).

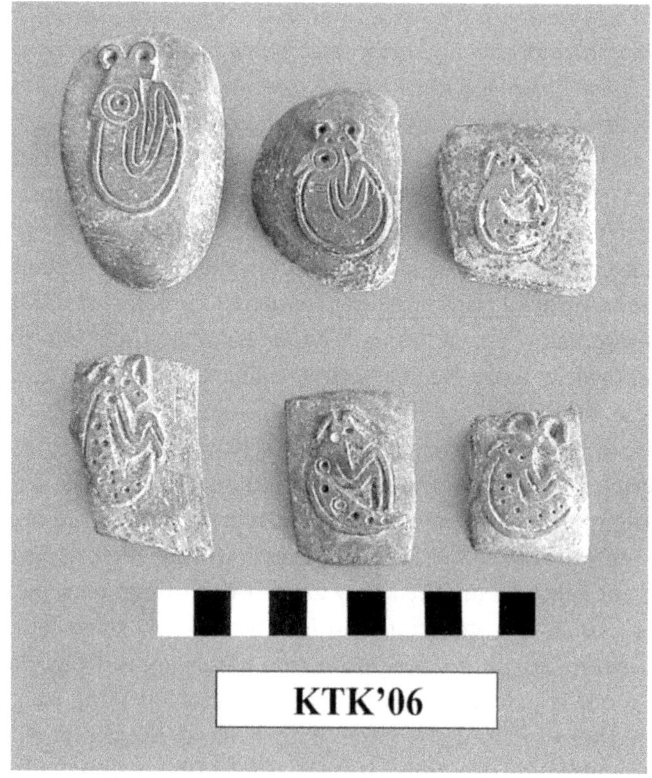

Figure 6.4. Examples of the bee fetishes from Körtik (courtesy V. Özkaya).

depicting other multilegged creatures accurately (e.g., see scorpions in figure 6.3). This, along with the general consistency of the representations, suggests that for these fetishes, either the aesthetics of the composition (only room for two limbs without cluttering it) was paramount and/or what is being depicted was widely and clearly understood in its cultural context even in the absence of strict representational accuracy. In other words, what these fetishes arguably represent is a specific mythic individual, as opposed to a general category of animal. Last, the "target" motif, which occurs elsewhere in isolation as a decorative motif (e.g., figure 6.3), is directly associated only with this creature in superposition (see figure 6.4 representations). Whether this target represents the abdominal segment rings of a bee, the circular patch visible on the back of a bee's thorax, or some other feature is unclear. However, it seems highly likely that when this motif appears in isolation, which it does as early as at Hallan Çemi, it is the symbolic representation of this (mythic) creature.

One noteworthy social trend visible at the Batman River sites involves changing mortuary practices, which go from off-site to on-site burials, as expected of sites bridging the proto-Neolithic and Neolithic. At Hallan Çemi it can be said with some certainty that interment of the dead was off-site, perhaps at some as yet undiscovered nearby cave cemetery, as was the case at Zawi Chemi and at contemporary

Levantine Natufian sites. In contrast, at Demirköy, burials are present at the site, but other than an occasional artifact, no grave goods were interred with the dead. At Körtik, the pattern of on-site primary interment continues, but now valuable grave goods, often including numerous elaborately decorated stone bowls and multiple strands of stone beads, were interred with the dead (see Özkaya and San 2007). In a potentially related vein, it should be noted that there were two small canid burials also found at Demirköy (see Rosenberg 2007b; Rosenberg and Peasnall 1998).

Other noteworthy trends include the appearance of baked clay objects at Demirköy (absent at Hallan Çemi) and a decline in obsidian usage at Demirköy (as compared to the heavier usage at Hallan Çemi). The pattern of obsidian usage at Demirköy indicates that obsidian continued to be a highly valued raw material for the manufacture of stone tools (see Peasnall and Rosenberg 2001). Thus, the decreased quantities of obsidian at Demirköy suggest that the relocation from Hallan Çemi to Demirköy (or other changes occurring at the same time), at least initially, had a detrimental impact on the long-distance trade in this valuable commodity.

Although economic data are not yet available for Körtik, the faunal and botanical data for the earlier sites of Hallan Çemi and Demirköy indicate that the economies of both those communities revolved around the exploitation of a wide variety of wild animals and plants, presumably through hunting and gathering. However, at Hallan Çemi, at least, there is evidence of rudimentary experimentation with animal husbandry involving pigs (Redding and Rosenberg 1998; Rosenberg et al. 1998), presumably to mitigate the risk of local animal resource depletion attendant on the new sedentary lifeway.

There is as yet no evidence that such rudimentary pig husbandry continued into the occupation at Demirköy, suggesting that the practice may have been abandoned by the later community for some as yet undetermined reason, though the replacement of pigs by ovicaprids as the focus of experimentation is a possible reason weakly hinted at by the Demirköy faunal data (R.W. Redding, personal communication). It is also worth noting that there is no evidence from either Hallan Çemi or Demirköy for the significant exploitation of large-seeded grasses (i.e., "cereals"), in either wild or domesticated forms. Rather, nuts, pulses, and sea club rush seeds seem to be the staples of the plant food economy at both sites (see Savard, Nesbitt, and Jones 2006). Thus, the faunal and botanical data from these early sites point to an interesting conclusion: the process of domestication was not, as it is so often conceived of, a simple linear progression of ever more intensive exploitation of some important resource (e.g., cereals, ovicaprids), culminating eventually in its domestication. Instead, it would seem that the beginnings of settled village life in southeastern Anatolia was an economically fluid period involving experimentation designed to meet the new economic exigencies of settled village life by individual local communities. In this context, practices were adopted and abandoned as circumstances warranted, with the lessons learned from each such experiment being carried forward to possible new applications as needed, ultimately resulting in full-scale domestication of those resources that best served the specific needs of specific local communities at the time that such domestication took place.

The Early Aceramic II (EA II)

Çayönü Tepesi, located in the Ergani Plain, about 125 km further up the Tigris from the Batman River sites, is the only other aceramic site in the Tigris drainage that is known from significant excavation. That it belongs to the same general "cultural tradition" as the Batman River sites seems clear. It also seems clear that Çayönü temporally follows those sites, but how closely remains an open question.

The lowest building levels at Çayönü, usually referred to as the round plan subphase, are characterized by curvilinear architecture and clearly date to the EA "round-house horizon." The subsequent building levels at Çayönü are characterized by the rectilinear architecture that characterizes the MA cultures of southwestern Asia, making the round-house phase at Çayönü the final expression of the round-house horizon along the upper Tigris. The cultural connection of Çayönü to (and derivation from EA communities similar to) the EA Batman River sites is evident in the continuity of several artifact types, notably including the presence at Çayönü of the same type of stone bowls and sculpted pestles as are present at the Batman region sites.

Three carbon dates are available for the round house levels at Çayönü (see A. Özdoğan 1999; Erim-Özdoğan 2007): two from the lowest level (10,020 ± 240 and 10,230 ± 200), and one from a structure (RB) higher up in that subphase (9050 ± 140). Three dates (9320 ± 55, 9250 ± 60, and 9175 ± 55) are available from the transitional so-called basal pits, and two more from the initial (grill plan) phase of the MA levels (9040 ± 70 and 9090 ± 50). As a group they suggest that the transition from EA to MA at Çayönü took place ca. 9200 B.P., a bit later than the similar transition in the Levant (see Yakar, chapter 4 in this volume, for further discussion of chronological issues). The two dates from the lowest level seemingly make the inception of the round plan subphase at Çayönü contemporary with the occupation of Hallan Çemi, but accepting them at face value would require one also to accept that the round plan subphase at Çayönü persisted for a full millennium, a questionably long duration for the apparent depth of the corresponding deposits. More importantly, certain cultural elements (e.g., on-site interment at Çayönü) are inconsistent with such an ascribed contemporaneity with Hallan Çemi. The absence of geometrics and presence of hollow base and fish tail (i.e., Nevalı Çori) points in the Çayönü chipped stone assemblage also suggest a somewhat later date. It is therefore noteworthy that the two early dates for the round plan subphase both have very large standard deviations in both absolute terms and as compared to the other available carbon dates from Çayönü. Thus, a beginning date for the round plan phase at Çayönü that is closer to the middle of the tenth millennium B.P. (i.e.,~ca. 9500) and closer to the dates for Körtik seems a reasonable reading of the dates as a whole.

Since a comparable transition from EA to MA is not visible at the Batman River sites, we cannot say how much later the EA persisted there beyond the abandonment of Körtik. However, the importance of stone bowls at Körtik and their relative insignificance at Çayönü, as suggested by their relative paucity at that site, as well as further changes in mortuary practices are points of inconsistency that argue for Çayönü following Körtik in time. However, by how much cannot be determined.

In the Euphrates drainage, the oldest site for which we have detailed information is Göbekli Tepe. The dates for Layer III (9452 ± 73 and 9559 ± 53) at Göbekli (see Kromer and Schmidt 1998) put this oldest level approximately contemporary with the round plan subphase at Çayönü, a conclusion corroborated by the presence of curvilinear public buildings, as well as Nemrik and Helwan points at Göbekli (though the few crude Byblos type points also present are somewhat anomalous[2]). The derivation of the culture represented by Göbekli is unclear. One possible source is the local earlier cultures, as represented by Biris Mezarlığı and Söğüt Tarlası but, as already noted, we still know little of substance about those sites. Another possible source, based on the presence of similar type stone bowls and projectile points at Göbekli, as are present at the various Tigris sites, are the same proto-Neolithic cultures that gave rise to Hallan Çemi in the Tigris drainage. A third possible source is the actual spread of EA communities out of the Tigris drainage west into the Euphrates drainage. Of the three, either of the last two best accounts for the available data, but it is unclear which of them is the more likely possibility.

Göbekli is best known for its relatively numerous, massive, public "cult" buildings (see Schmidt, chapter 42 in this volume). Like the round plan subphase at Çayönü, Layer III at Göbekli constitutes the lowest level of a site that is initially occupied at the end of the EA and continues well into the MA. More importantly, in both cases what we see in the lowest levels of these two sites is the initial development of cultural institutions and certain socially significant practices that depart from the EA I mode, but which characterize the MA in their respective areas. Thus, just as Hallan Çemi can most profitably be considered transitional from proto-Neolithic to EA, the lowest levels at Çayönü and Göbekli can best be understood if considered transitional from EA to MA.

As noted, EA-type stone bowls and sculpted pestles are evident at Çayönü (see Erim-Özdoğan 2007:89; Özdoğan 1999:59). However they are a relatively rare type at that site. Stone bowls of similar type are also relatively rare at Göbekli. This suggests that during the transition to the MA, the importance of the public feasting that presumably underlay the usage of these stone bowls and pestles seems to have waned significantly or come to rely on a different set of accoutrements. Moreover, it suggests that whatever function these types had come to be appropriated for, it did not require the same quantities as had been necessary earlier, it was not as individualistically oriented, and that such artifacts were apparently not needed by individuals in the afterlife (since they were no longer included as grave goods, as they had been at Körtik). On the other hand, public buildings and public spaces apparently play a much more prominent and formal role in communal life at MA sites, judging from their size, variety, and elaboration as compared to EA sites. More significantly, these collectively employed aspects of culture (as opposed to individually employed stone bowls/pestles) became the primary focus of elaborate artistic expression. To the degree that artistic effort reliably expresses the relative importance of the thing being decorated and the actions associated with it, then during the EA II a more collective community identity arguably comes to supersede a more individualized community identity (that is, a community that is merely the sum of its individuals).

In the earliest, round plan subphase at Çayönü the pattern of public spaces is one of structures arranged around open central areas in a pattern similar to the one at Hallan Çemi, but differing from the latter in that there were apparently multiple such clusters at Çayönü. This difference is likely nothing more than an artifact of Çayönü's larger size. However, a substantial building is also present, and it differs from the seemingly more general purpose "public" buildings at Hallan Çemi in having a special "cultic" purpose (see A. Özdoğan 1999).

This earliest public building at Çayönü is curvilinear in form and built on virgin soil. Although it is difficult to say with absolute certainty that its initial construction dates to the beginning of the round plan subphase, it is apparently in existence by the end of that subphase. This curvilinear building is the initial expression of what is commonly called the "skull building," which was rebuilt in rectilinear form in subsequent periods. In essence it is a charnel house, at which various steps in the multistage preparation and interment of corpses were carried out (see Yilmaz 2010 for a detailed discussion). Two large standing stones, perhaps cruder ritually functional parallels to the central pillars in Göbekli's public buildings (see later discussion), were apparently a feature of this structure.

The earliest (Layer III) public buildings at Göbekli are also curvilinear (as is the domestic architecture through IIB), but they are more massive, and considerably more elaborate than the skull building at Çayönü (see Schmidt 2000, 2007, and chapter 42 in this volume). As at Çayönü, they appear to be special-purpose "cultic" buildings, and we again find expressions of the same type of building in later periods at both the same and other sites (i.e., Nevalı Çori), again indicating that such cultic structures are just an early expression of cultural institutions that characterize the MA and not the EA (see Harmanşah, chapter 28 in this volume, for a discussion of the role of built monuments in Anatolian prehistory and history).

The most distinctive feature of the Göbekli buildings are the T-shaped stone columns that stood in their interior and were decorated with carved reliefs of various types of animals, as well as stylized anthropomorphic figures. The animals depicted include both carnivorous and herbivorous mammals, reptiles, and birds, including several of the animal motifs depicted at EA sites (e.g., bulls, snakes, and carnivores). The specific function of these buildings remains unclear, but speculation centers on their use at least in part relating to ancestor/mortuary cults (see Schmidt, chapter 42 in this volume), even though there is no evidence that the Göbekli public buildings were actually used to inter the dead, as was the Çayönü "skull building." On the other hand, neither is there extensive evidence for a general practice of scattered individual interments at Göbekli, leaving open the question of what the modal mortuary practices were at this site.

There is as yet no direct evidence (other than the implications of their very size) for food production at either Göbekli or Çayönü during this period, and, as at EA I sites, a wide variety of plants and animals were exploited. However, there are differences by drainage reinforcing the picture of local economic variability during the

EA. At Çayönü, as at the earlier Tigris sites, pulses figure prominently in the plant assemblage, and large seeded grasses (i.e., wild "cereals") do not, whereas at Göbekli, wild "cereals" were apparently exploited. At Çayönü also, pig exploitation is again an important element of the community's economy (Hongo et al. 2009).

In essence, what we see in the earliest levels of both Çayönü and Göbekli are communities that still retained the EA mode of economic and domestic organization, as reflected in curvilinear architecture, with its implications for the organization of production and consumption at the community level, the dominance of generalized reciprocal exchanges, and by extension at least nominal if not true egalitarianism (see Flannery 1972). However, the organization of public life has already developed into the more formal, MA mode. This new mode was characterized by specialized ceremonial buildings and communal mortuary/ancestor cults involving secondary interments.

The Mature Aceramic Neolithic I–III (MA I–III)

The MA was first known from the sequence at Çayönü, where the full span is represented by five sequential subphases, each characterized by a distinctive architectural pattern. It remains the archetypal sequence. From earliest to latest they are referred to as the grill plan,[3] channel plan, cobble-paved floor, cell plan, and large room subphases. Reliable carbon dates for the MA levels at Çayönü are only available for the beginning of the grill plan subphase (see foregoing discussion), which put it at ca. 9300–9200 B.P. Çayönü remains the only MA site thus far excavated to any significant degree in the Tigris drainage. However, a significant number of MA sites are known from the Euphrates drainage—Cafer, Nevalı Çori, Göbekli, Hayaz, Gritille, Gürcütepe, Akarçay, and Mezraa-Teleilat in the Urfa-Malatya region, and Yeni Mahalle-Balıklıgöl inside the city of Şanlıurfa proper.

Of these, Cafer represents an equally long sequence as Çayönü, with its "early phase" (XIII–IX) architecturally corresponding to the grill through cobble-paved subphases at Çayönü, "middle phase" (VIII–V) corresponding to the cell plan subphase at Çayönü, and "late phase" (IV–I) corresponding to the large room subphase (see Cauvin et al. 1999, 2007). The dates for the early phase at Cafer are spread between 9560 ± 190 and 8950 ± 80, but as a whole suggest that the early phase spans the last few hundred years of the tenth millennium B.P., a date consistent with the grill plan subphase dates from Çayönü. Excluding an outlier derived from a doubtful sample, the middle phase dates (8920 ± 160 and 8480 ± 140) indicate that it spanned approximately the first half of the ninth millennium B.P., and those from the late phase (8980 ± 150, 8450 ± 160, and 8150 ± 210) that it spanned the remainder of the ninth millennium B.P. Thus, based on the two longest sequences, the MA in southeastern Anatolia seems to span slightly more than a millennium from ca. 9300/9200 B.P.

to ca. 8000 B.P. in carbon years and can be divided into three phases: here designated MA I, II, and III (corresponding to Cafer's early, middle, and late phases), with the MA I further subdivided into three subphases Ia, Ib, and Ic (corresponding to the grill, channel, and cobble subphases).

Last, although Cauvin et al.'s (1999) consolidation of the five Çayönü subphases into a three-phase sequence is reasonable given significant elements of continuity in the grill through cobble subphases, their correlation of their three phases to the Levantine early, middle, and late PPNB is questionable. That is, although their late phase approximately corresponds with the Levantine late PPNB temporally, what is happening at sites such as Çayönü during the large plan subphase (i.e., late phase) is arguably more consistent with what happens at Levantine sites during the Pre-Pottery Neolithic C. This is just one concrete example of why Levantine terms should be avoided altogether when dealing with southeastern Anatolia.

Of the other Euphrates sites, the occupation of Nevalı Çori spans the grill through cobble-paved subphases (i.e., MA I) on the basis of architecture (Hauptmann 1999, 2007). Göbekli IIA, with its now rectilinear public buildings (see Schmidt 2007), likely dates to the beginning of this interval as well, on the assumption of occupational continuity with the preceding IIB.

At Mezraa-Teleilat, the lowest Aceramic level with architectural remains (IV) is characterized by cell plan-type structures, and the lowest excavated level (V) is attributable to the same interval on artifactual grounds (see M. Özdoğan 2007). The single date of 9324 ± 59 for Level IV seems more consistent with those from the Çayönü grill plan subphase and Cafer early phase, and the date should probably be viewed with caution in view of both its inconsistency with the architectural remains and the large gap between it and the four dates for Level III (transitional early Pottery Neolithic), which cluster tightly at ~ ca. 8000 B.P.

Akarçay Tepe presents an even more complicated case (see Özbaşaran and Molist 2007). Levels 11–9 are characterized by grill plans, and the initial occupation of the site thus apparently dates to the beginning of the MA Ia. However, channel buildings seem to be absent in the subsequent levels, and instead MA II type cell plans are the modal type from Level 8 all the way through Level 3. Moreover, to further complicate matters, MA III-type large room structures seem to be present in early MA II Levels 8 and 7. The absence of channel buildings is puzzling given the apparent continuity of occupation at Akarçay through at least the cell building subphase. However, given the close evolutionary relationship of grill to channel buildings in structural terms, and the basic similarity in their associated material culture, the absence of channel buildings can be glossed over on grounds that at least the direction of change is consistent with what we know from contemporary sites. Unfortunately, the same cannot be done with the presence of large room structures in Levels 8 and 7, the earliest cell building levels. Thankfully, Çayönü offers a possible parallel that would explain this anomaly. At Çayönü, at least one large room structure (Building EA) was terraced into the underlying cell building levels and placed in the open area between two of the cell buildings (Buildings DS and CT), so that its absolute elevation was the same as that of the two cell-plan buildings between which it was inserted. Assuming a similar situation here would resolve the anomaly of MA III-type large room structures being present in the earliest MA II plan levels and further extend the occupation of this site through the end of the MA.

Yeni Mahalle-Balıklıgöl is only known from very limited excavation (see Çelik 2000, 2007). Based on the chipped stone tool types present (see following discussion), it would appear to be approximately contemporary with Nevalı Çori, a temporal attribution that is also consistent with the style of stone sculptures present at that site.

The four mounds at Gürcütepe (i.e., I–IV), Hayaz, and the Neolithic levels of Gritille are also only known from limited excavations. All three appear to postdate at least the MA I on artifactual grounds—primarily chipped stone types, and for Gritille also architecture. Gürcütepe apparently dates to the MA III (Hauptmann 1999; Schmidt 1997, 1999), Hayaz Höyük (see Roodenberg 1989) can be firmly dated to the MA III by carbon dates (8300 ± 60 and 8040 ± 170), and Gritille (see Ellis and Voigt 1982; Voigt 1985) to the end of the MA III (7770 ± 150, 7860 ± 80, 7950 ± 120) (see Yakar, chapter 4 in this volume, for chronological discussions of these and other sites). While Building 2 at Gritille is vaguely reminiscent of cell plan construction, it arguably resembles the late-phase architecture at nearby Cafer more, which would make the architecture consistent with the dates.

The MA saw the participation of southeastern Anatolian Neolithic communities in what is often referred to as the "PPNB interaction sphere" (Bar-Yosef and Belfer-Cohen 1989), characterized by the diffusion of distinctive chipped stone types throughout much of Anatolia and the Levant in the context of obsidian trade. Specifically, we get the appearance over the entire region of naviform core technology for the production of large relatively straight blades as well as large, stemmed Levantine type points (e.g., Byblos points), typically as an overlay on local point types (e.g., Nevalı Çori points).

At Çayönü, Byblos points make an initial appearance at the end of the grill plan subphase (i.e., MA Ia) as an overlay on the local hollow base/fishtail points (i.e., Nevalı Çori points), which disappear by the end of the MA I (see A. Özdoğan 1999; see also Caneva et al. 1994). Naviform cores are also substantially present in the chipped stone assemblage by the cobble-paved (i.e., MA Ic) subphase, but disappear by the MA III Phase. At Cafer (see Cauvin et al. 1999), the occasional appearance of Byblos points is somewhat earlier, occurring at the very beginning of the MA I Phase sequence (XIII) as an overlay on the local point tradition there (Cafer points). However, naviform core technology is in evidence only by the MA II Phase. In that vein, it is worth noting that Çayönü tools, a local tool type which is present at the type site from late in the MA Ia Phase onward, also do not appear at Cafer until the MA II Phase (Level VI). All these various types continue to be present through Cafer's MA III Phase (see Binder 2007).

At Nevalı Çori (see Schmidt 1994), hollow base/fishtail points are again restricted to the lower levels of that site, as is another, relatively early Levantine, type (Helwan points). Byblos points appear to replace both types by the upper levels of that site. However, naviform cores here precede the appearance of Byblos points, being present at Nevalı Çori throughout the entire sequence. Preliminary indications are that the chipped stone assemblage from Göbekli is basically similar. That is, Helwan and Byblos points, along with naviform cores, are present through the entire sequence, though Nevalı Çori points seem to be rare (Schmidt 2000). The small chipped stone assemblage from Yeni Mahalle-Balıklıgöl also appears to be quite similar to that from Nevalı Çori. That is, the majority of the points appear to be variations of the Byblos type, with hollow base and Helwan types also present (see Çelik 2007).

Byblos and what may be a few relatively late Amuq points are represented in the Hayaz assemblage, along with naviform cores (see Roodenberg 1989). This is consistent with Hayaz's late date. Byblos points, in at least some cases made on blades that appear struck from naviform cores, appear to be the only point type present at Gritille (see Voigt 1985), also consistent with its post-MA I date.

The only clear pattern visible in the timing of the diffused elements is the relative early appearance of both naviform cores and Byblos points in the Euphrates drainage as compared to Çayönü on the Tigris. However, even there, the timing of their appearance is not uniform. Moreover, their apparent very early presence in Göbekli III and the rarity of the expected (early local type) Nevalı Çori points at that site is an anomaly that remains to be resolved (but see note 2).

Public spaces and elaborated public buildings are important features of public life during the MA. They are clearly evident at Çayönü, Göbekli, and Nevalı Çori, the three MA sites with substantial horizontal exposures. What may be a public building is also present at Gürcü II.

At Çayönü (see Erim-Özdoğan 2007; A. Özdoğan 1999; Özdoğan and Özdoğan 1989), a rectilinear rebuilding of the "skull building" occurs, apparently during the later stages of the channeled plan (MA Ib) subphase, and with three renewals continues in use through the cobble-paved (MA Ic) subphase. No stone stelai/pillars (as in its earlier curvilinear form) were a feature of this later, rectilinear rebuilding, but a slab stone "altar" was. In a practice reminiscent of Hallan Çemi, and not surprising given the aforementioned cultural connection between Çayönü and the Batman River sites, an aurochs skull once hung from one of the walls of this later construction. By the MA Ia a second public building is also in existence. Commonly called the "flagstone building," it was paved with large limestone slabs and contained three large standing stones. The incarnation of the skull building that is (partially) contemporary with this flagstone building also had a slab-paved floor. By the end of the cobble paved (MA Ic) subphase a third public building had been constructed. Commonly called the "bench building," it is a relatively small single-room building with benches running along three of its walls. Although this building was clearly built later than the flagstone building, it remains unclear whether the latter had gone completely out of use by the time of its construction. By the MA II all three of the above buildings were out of use, and a large terrazzo-floored building had been constructed. It sits atop the remains of two earlier (partially excavated) buildings that were likely both also public buildings and perhaps contemporary with one or more of the above-mentioned MA I ones, but about which no specifics are known. What may be three public buildings were also noted in the large room MA III Phase. The most noteworthy aspect of these buildings is that they are no longer spatially separated from the domestic structures, but were rather interdigitated with them.

By the cobble paved (MA Ic) subphase a large pebble-paved "plaza" was also in existence. It featured two rows of standing stones and two large horizontal grooved stone slabs. This earlier plaza is replaced in the MA II by an unpaved "earth plaza" with a prepared surface that was renewed several times. This unpaved plaza continues in use through the end of the MA III Phase, but its upkeep was neglected during the MA III, suggesting that it no longer functioned for the same formal public purpose. In that vein, it should be noted that the several possible public buildings associated with this last phase no longer display the distinctive attributes that earlier public buildings did.

Göbekli IIA (see Schmidt 2007, and chapter 42 in this volume) and Nevalı Çori (see Hauptmann 1993, 1999, 2007) both contained essentially the same type of public buildings—rectilinear derivations of the curvilinear ones found in Göbekli III (surface finds at Hamzan and Karahan suggest that these two sites were also home to similar public structures). At Nevalı Çori, there appears to have been only one that was rebuilt several times. At Gobekli, there appear to be several smaller ones clustered in the same general areas as the Layer III structures. As in the case of the early variant of this type, the rectilinear variant at both sites is characterized by massive T-shaped stone columns, typically sporting relief carvings of humans and/or animals. At Nevalı Çori, a stone bench was also set against the walls. A variety of other stone sculptures of humans and animals are also present at both sites and may very well have been associated with these public structures. Collectively, the animals represented include felines, birds, bovids, snakes, pigs, insects (bees?), and others too problematic to identify.

The MA economies for which we have data are all characterized by some degree of food production and the appearance of domesticates from sometime in the MA I onward. At Cafer, einkorn, emmer, and lentils were cultivated from the beginning of the MA I (i.e., early phase), though animal husbandry never seems to have become an established practice at all, and the hunting of various game animals (including ovicaprids) continues unabated (Cauvin et al. 1999, 2007). Nevalı Çori exhibits a similar pattern of plant food production (einkorn, emmer, lentils), modified by the additional presence of peas and broad beans. However, at Nevalı Çori, while hunting again continued to make an important contribution to the site's economy, animal husbandry involving sheep and goats was also practiced (Hauptmann 1999, 2007). At Çayönü morphologically wild wheat was probably being cultivated by the MA Ib Phase (van Zeist and de Roller 1994, 2003). As early as the MA Ia Phase, the inhabitants of Çayönü may have renewed experimentation with rudimentary pig husbandry, and by the MA Ib Phase with the rudimentary husbandry of sheep, goats, and perhaps even cattle as well (Hongo et al. 2004, 2009). By the MA II the husbandry of domesticated sheep and goats was being practiced at Çayönü, and by the MA III, the extensive exploitation of domesticated ovicaprids is well documented at both Gritille and Çayönü (Hongo et al. 2004; Stein 1989), making the anomaly of their absence at Cafer all the more puzzling.

Mortuary practices vary somewhat between the Çayonü and Euphrates sites and, in the case of Çayönü, change over the course of the Mature Aceramic's phases (see A. Özdoğan 1999, M. Özdoğan 2007). During the MA I, at least one of the public buildings at Çayönü, the "skull building," is clearly associated with mortuary practices (though scattered interments also occur throughout the site), whereas no such direct association is evident for the public buildings at the Euphrates MA I sites. Decapitated burials are present at sites in both areas. Scattered interments apparently continue to be the norm at the Euphrates sites through the MA III (Cafer). Scattered interments also become the norm at Çayönü by the MA II, but disappear during the MA III in apparent favor of extramural interment.

In general terms, the MA I saw the initial development of the MA way of life, based on food production, the surpluses that tend to be attendant on such economic practices, and the development of formal ceremonial systems revolving around public structures and constructed spaces. The MA I also saw the piecemeal incorporation of southeast Anatolia into the wider southwestern Asian regional trade network. The MA II saw the full flowering of that way of life, with a rich and elaborate public domain, and evidence for social differentiation (based on variances in house size and associated finds) in at least the case of Çayonü (see Özdoğan and Özdoğan 1989). At least in the case of Çayönü we then see a decrease in the formality of public ceremonial life during the MA III. Also, the interdigitation of public and domestic structures at Çayönü during the MA III hints at a break-up of the collective community identity (construed from the spatial separation of public buildings during the EA II through MA II), in favor of a more fragmentary sum-of-residential/kinship units identity, which perhaps foreshadows the shift to generally smaller sites during the Pottery Neolithic.

The Pottery Neolithic

As the name implies, the Pottery Neolithic is defined by the widespread, large-scale manufacture and usage of ceramic vessels. However, this technological innovation is just the most obvious expression of a wider set of changes that, unfortunately, remain poorly understood.

Though presumably unrefined, the basic principles of baked-clay technology, its basic limitations and benefits, were already known in the EA I, as evidenced by the presence of baked clay figurines at Demirköy (Rosenberg and Peasnall 1998), not to mention later aceramic sites such as Çayönü (Özdoğan and Özdoğan 1993). Moreover, at Demirköy, it is quite clear that the inhabitants were also occasionally *purposefully* making crude ceramic copies of stone bowls (see Rosenberg and Peasnall 1998:199, 206, fig. 6), which incidentally raises the obvious question of just how many ceramic vessels from other aceramic sites—by default, implicitly considered "accidentally fired" in the absence of clear evidence to the contrary—were also purposefully fired (compare Özdoğan and Özdoğan 1993 and A. Özdoğan 1999; Erim-Özdoğan and Yalman 2004).

The point is that the widespread adoption of ceramic technology at the beginning of the Pottery Neolithic period was not the product of a technological discovery. Rather, it was a widespread, choice-based behavioral change from one technology, for the production of stone vessels, to a competing technology for the production of ceramic vessels, both of which were long known. Unfortunately, at the immediate level, whether this choice reflects a shift from "quality" (very labor-intensive but highly durable stone bowls) to "quantity" (less labor-intensive and less durable ceramic vessels), some gender-related change (i.e., who was making what and for what purpose), and/or other possible factors[4] remains unclear. Moreover, any proposed immediate basis for such a choice to innovate raises a potential set of higher level questions (e.g., why change from an emphasis on quality to quantity; why do male-produced or female-produced vessels become more widely used at the expense of those produced by the opposite sex; etc.) that cannot be addressed at all because we do not know which ones to ask.

In southeastern Anatolia, the Pottery Neolithic period is well represented at five excavated sites—Çayönü, Sumaki, and Salat Cami Yanı on the Tigris and Akarçay and Mezraa-Teleilat on the Euphrates. On the Tigris, the only site with a clear continuity of occupation from the MA III into the Pottery Neolithic is Çayönü. Three pottery-bearing building levels were originally distinguished (see Özdoğan and Özdoğan 1993:91ff.) and designated 1 to 3 from youngest to oldest. A reanalysis (see Erim-Özdoğan and Yalman 2004) reduced these to two major building levels on the basis of the building materials used. The older level, designated PNK, is characterized by wattle and daub architecture and the upper level, designated PNS, is characterized by stone architecture.

The earliest pottery, coming from the bottom of the PNK level, is a coarse, brittle, poorly fired ware, tempered with a variety of materials, and fashioned into a limited variety of thick-sided, simple bowls and jars with flat bases. It is soon replaced (still in PNK) by a burnished, red slipped or painted ware, typically mineral tempered and occasionally having added incised/impressed decorations, which remains the dominant type for the rest of PNK. Much less common, but also found in the same contexts as the red slipped/painted ware, is a white or cream slipped ware and a kind of Dark Face Burnished Ware (DFBW), in the broadest sense of its common usage.

The PNS level is dominated by a somewhat more typical DFBW in the form of short- and long-necked jars and deep bowls and often (atypically) decorated with small button-like knobs that point to a Transcaucasian connection. Also present is a pale burnished ware with vertical lug-like handles and some relief, finger-impressed dimples, and incised/scraped decorations. Red slipped/painted ware, white/cream slipped ware, and "husking trays" are also present, but rare. In the case of the DFBW the ware becomes finer, and the quality of the burnishing improves over time, such that the frequency of "typical" DFBW becomes more common toward the end of the sequence. In the case of the pale burnished ware, the lug-like handles decrease in frequency over time, as does the frequency of both impressed dimple and relief decorations.

Sumaki, currently under excavation by one of us (see Erim-Özdoğan 2010), is located in the Garzan River drainage, the next significant tributary of the Tigris east (i.e., downriver) of the Batman River. The site contains two major strata,[5] separated from each other by an occupational hiatus of unknown duration that is manifest in the form of an alluvial accumulation that preserved the lower phase walls to a height of 1.2 m. The lower phase is dominated by a DFBW and a mineral tempered ware that are generally well burnished and well fired; it may correspond to the lower (PNK) level of the Çayönü sequence.

The upper phase at Sumaki contains almost no DFBW and the mineral tempered ware is more rare. Rather, it is dominated by a chaff tempered plain or red-washed ware. Present, but rare, are sherds with painted decorations that are similar to Hassuna Archaic painted ware. The red-washed ware found at Sumaki is not found at Çayönü and is distinguishable from the red-painted ware of the Çayönü PNK levels by the relative thinness of the red paint wash, the lack of burnishing and decoration, the presence of distinct forms (e.g., carinated bowls, oval shallow bowls with thick bases), being better fired, and by association with rare "husking trays." Preliminary indications are that this upper phase also predates the Çayönü PNS levels.

Salat Cami Yanı (see Miyake 2007) is located along the Tigris about fifteen kilometers west of its confluence with the Batman River. There are three major stratigraphic levels (Phases 1–3) at this site that appear more or less to parallel the sequence at Sumaki. That is, differences in type frequencies (notably Red-Washed Ware) aside, the lowest level at Salat Cami Yanı (Phase 1) seems to correspond to the lower level at Sumaki and the next two levels with the upper level at Sumaki. There are, however, some elements of the Phase 3 Salat Cami Yanı ceramic assemblage that are either not found at Sumaki (e.g., deep vessels with knob decorations) or are very rare at Sumaki (e.g., husking trays and painted decorations). Two dates of 7425 ± 35 and 7325 ± 20 B.P. are available for Phase 1 and two dates of 7690 ± 25 and 7355 ± 25 B.P. are available for Phase 2 (Miyake 2007).

At Mezraa-Teleilat, on the Euphrates (like Cayönü on the Tigris), there is continuity of occupation between the aceramic and pottery Neolithic, with Level III being transitional and a DFBW first appearing toward the end of that level (IIIA). The most distinctive aspect of the preceding Level IIIB assemblage is the limestone human figurines (M. Özdoğan 2003:519–23; 2007:figs. 17–30), many of which appear to be in a semi-reclining pose. A red-slipped/painted ware and husking trays appear in IIC along with a buff, chaff tempered ware. Both are sometimes decorated with raised knobs or crescents. The only available date from Mezraa-Teleilat IIC is 8360 ± 80 B.P., but it is considered unreliable by the excavator (see M. Özdoğan 2007). In IIB we get the appearance of an impressed/incised ware of uncertain relationship to the very limited number of incised shards found at the Tigris sites.

Decorative incised motifs on this type include rows of elongated "dots," "rockers," wavy lines, and so on (see M. Özdoğan 2007:figs. 52–57). Three dates from IIB cluster well at ~ 7800 B.P.

At Akarçay Tepe the earliest pottery, referred to at that site as the "black series," first appears in the final levels of the aceramic sequence (Level 3). But given the complexity of the stratigraphy at that site (e.g., the above-mentioned large room buildings seemingly associated with Levels 8 and 7, but probably later), the chronological implications of that association must be left open. It is a calcite-tempered, well-burnished fine ware, with a brown to gray or buff surface color. The typical form is a small, round based, hole-mouth vessel, sometimes having flat handles with holes (Özbaşaran and Molist 2007). In general terms, it is comparable to early phase DFBW from Sumaki and DFBW from Mezraa Teleilat IIIA (compare M. Özdoğan 2007). This ware continued to be used into the following levels with minor changes in the density of temper and in the production techniques. The latest wares of Akarçay include both a fine ware and a rough ware. The fine ware dominates the assemblage and comes in painted, slipped, slipped + burnished, painted on a light slipped surface, wet-smoothed, and plain burnished variants. The rough ware is vegetal or vegetal and mineral tempered and only sometimes burnished. Both come in a rich variety of forms. Husking trays with various "designs" are common in the upper levels (as they are at Mezraa-Teleilat).

Generalizations concerning the above-mentioned pottery types are difficult to make due to their intersite variability and the fact that a systematic comparative study of these ceramic assemblages still remains to be done. Even the few types that have something approaching a region-wide distribution (e.g., red-washed/painted ware, DFBW, chaff tempered ware) are variable and often hint at localized outside influences. For example, the button-like knob decorations on the DFBW from Çayönü are atypical for DFBW and hint at connections to the northeast (see Özdoğan and Özdoğan 1993:100), and the Mezraa-Teleilat impressed ware hints at connections to the west. It is worth noting, however, that such variability is consistent with one interesting implication of Pottery Neolithic architecture.

At Çayönü, the only level with preserved architectural remains is PNS. The structures here represent a clear departure from the architectural norms of the aceramic levels, consisting of large compounds of rooms and courtyards, as opposed to self-contained rectilinear structures, that furthermore lack the conformity to a plan type that characterizes the earlier aceramic levels. Such nonstandardized and seemingly additive/agglutinative structures can also be seen developing at Mezraa-Teleilat by IIB.[6] The same process may also be unfolding at Sumaki and Salat Cami Yanı, though self-contained structures still appear to be the modal form in the lower phase of Sumaki (the upper phase seems to be a product of seasonal occupations without distinct architectural remains). Though the architectural remains at Salat Cami Yanı are too limited to permit generalizations, it is safe to say that the Phase 1 architecture appears similar to that from the lower phase at Sumaki.

Although the known Pottery Neolithic sites are not necessarily smaller than any and all known MA sites, they are generally smaller than such sites and much smaller than the MA "mega" sites such as Çayönü. Thus it is safe to say that the Pottery Neolithic is characterized by generally smaller communities than was the MA. Why this might have happened is an interesting but tangential problem. Suffice it to say here that the trend is not confined to southeastern Anatolia (see Gopher and Gophna 1993; Mellaart 1975; Rollefson and Köhler-Rollefson 1989).

As noted in the earlier discussion of the MA, there is an apparent decrease in the formality of public ceremonial life during the MA III, which, along with the newly instituted interdigitation of public and domestic structures, hints at a break-up of the collective community identity that we have suggested characterized the earlier phases of the MA. To date, no clearly identifiable public structures have been discerned at Pottery Neolithic sites, suggesting that this trend toward a greatly reduced public domain and fragmented community identity is not reversed in the Pottery Neolithic. To that end, it can be argued that the smaller size of Pottery Neolithic sites and the additive/agglutinative nature of the architecture at such sites represent the culmination of that trend.

The size of self-contained structures is fixed at the time of construction and thus is not amenable to expansion. Whatever the type of family group such structures can be said to have housed, the numerical size of that group was ultimately limited by the dimensions of the structure that housed them. When that group size exceeded the structure's capacity, an additional structure would need to have been built, and some kind of fissioning process would need to have taken place to physically divide such an excessively large group between the two structures. With additive structures, such fissioning is unnecessary, as more space can be created as needed by expanding the original structure through the contiguous construction of additional spaces.

The point is that self-contained structures, as are the norm through the Mature Aceramic (and into the early Pottery Neolithic at Mezraa-Teleilat, Sumaki, and Salat Cami Yanı), suggest that the dispersal of kin groups within the community (or perhaps even beyond) was not something to be avoided, because (as suggested) residential-group identity was more communally based than it was kin-based through at least the MA II. The shift to additive architecture suggests that the opposite has become the case later in the Pottery Neolithic and that the physical proximity of close kin within a single expandable residence has become a prime consideration. Since there are no significantly greater logistical drawbacks to economic cooperation between neighbors as compared to co-residents, the implication is that by the Pottery Neolithic group identity, and by extension the organization of production and consumption within communities, has shifted to one based on some kind of extended family structure. That coupled with the smaller size of Pottery Neolithic communities suggests that such communities have ceased to be socially integrated villages and have instead become kin-based and more self-contained homesteads, a pattern that continues into the later Halaf period, at which time we again begin to see the emergence of larger communities as an overlay on the substrate of homesteads and a decrease in intersite ceramic variability.

Conclusion

In southeastern Anatolia, as elsewhere in southwestern Asia, the changes attendant on the Neolithic, while revolutionary in their consequences for the evolution of human cultural and social systems, are gradual. In the EA we see the development of sedentary communities based on important economic changes, but ones that still retain major elements of the earlier hunter-gatherer, egalitarian social system. However, those elements are now buttressed with institutions (e.g., general-purpose public buildings, feasting) that permit the now somewhat larger communities to remain intact on a long-term basis and to act as a whole. In the MA, we see some of those same institutions (public buildings and spaces) evolving to (of necessity) more strongly promote group identity at the community level in the still larger communities that characterize the MA.

Beginning in the MA III and continuing through the early part of the Pottery Neolithic, we see the gradual disintegration of the Aceramic Neolithic lifeway and its replacement by one that is quite different, wherein kinship appears to play a larger, more formal role. These social changes are intertwined with important economic changes (the development of the full southwestern Asia domesticate complex) and technological changes (the widespread adoption of ceramic technology), but the specifics of how they are related remains an open question.

NOTES

We are deeply grateful to K. Schmidt for generously sharing with us thus far unpublished information concerning the finds at Göbekli and V. Özkaya for graciously providing us with the illustrations of the Körtik material used in this chapter.

1. Both dates were run on bone collagen from human burials relatively close to the surface of the site because there was some question as to whether all the burials were of the same age. Beta 178242 yielded a date of 9870 ± 40, in the expected range suggested by other aspects of the site. The other (Beta 178241) yielded a date of 8370 ± 40 and can best be considered unreliable.

2. Their anomalousness is mitigated somewhat by their small size, which potentially allows them to be considered tanged variants of Nemrik points (Schmidt 2000:52), a subtype known also from Demirköy (see Peasnall and Rosenberg 2001).

3. The early grill buildings are considered by the excavators to date to the EA II, primarily on the basis of affinities within the lithic assemblages, and the later grill buildings are considered by them to date to the MA I on the same grounds. On the other hand, it could be argued that the association of the early grill buildings with *specialized* public buildings (see later discussion) creates a potentially strong case for considering them MA I. This chapter is not the proper forum for a discussion concerning the relative primacy of technological versus social considerations in making such a temporal assignment, or for a discussion of other lines of evidence supporting one or the other temporal assignment. we

skirt the issue at this time and variably deal with the grill plan levels (i.e., collectively or distinguishing between early/late) depending on the specific subject at hand.

4. For example, both stone bowls and ceramic vessels were being produced at Mezraa-Teleilat and relative prestige appears to be a factor there (see M. Özdogan 2007:195, figs. 37–38).

5. And, a possible third, very short-term occupation about which little can be said for the moment.

6. The structures of IIC, though quite variable, are still self-contained.

REFERENCES

Bar-Yosef, Ofer and Anna Belfer-Cohen. 1989. The Levantine "PPNB" Interaction Sphere. In *People and Culture in Change: Proceedings of the Second Symposium on Upper Palaeolithic, Mesolithic, and Neolithic Populations of Europe and the Mediterranean Basin*, ed. Israel Hershkovitz, 59–72. BAR International Series 508(1). Oxford: Bar International.

Binder, Didier. 2007. PPN Pressure Technology: Views from Anatolia. In *La diversité des systèmes techniques des communautés du Néolithique pré-céramique: vers la caractérisation des comportements sociaux 5e colloque international sur les industries lithiques du Néolithique pré-céramique*, ed. Laurence Astruc, Didier Binder, and François Briois, 239–46. Antibes: Éditions APDCA.

Caneva, Isabella, Anna Maria Conti, Cristina Lemorini, and Daniela Zampetti. 1994. The Lithic Production at Çayönü: A Preliminary Overview of the Aceramic Sequence. In *Neolithic Chipped Stone Industries of the Fertile Crescent: Proceedings of the First Workshop on PPN Chipped Stone Industries, Berlin 1993*, ed. Hans G. Gebel and Stefan K. Kozlowski, 253–66. Studies in Early Near Eastern Production, Subsistence, and Environment 1. Berlin: Freie Universität.

Cauvin, Jacques. 1988. La néolithisation de la Turquie du sud-est dans son contexte Proche-Oriental. *Anatolica* 15: 69–80.

Cauvin, Jacques, Olivier Aurenche, Marie-Claire Cauvin, and Nur Balkan-Atlı. 1999. The Pre-Pottery Site of Cafer Höyük. In *The Neolithic in Turkey: The Cradle of Civilization, New Discoveries*, ed. Mehmet Özdoğan and Nezih Başgelen, 87–103. İstanbul: Arkeoloji ve Sanat Yayınları.

———. 2007. Cafer Höyük. In Türkiye'de Neolitik Dönem: Yeni Kazılar, Yeni Bulgular, ed. Mehmet Özdoğan and Nezih Başgelen, 99–114. İstanbul: Arkeoloji ve Sanat Yayınları.

Çelik, Bahattin. 2000. An Early Neolithic Settlement in the Center of Şanlıurfa, Turkey. *Neo-Lithics* 2–3: 4–6.

———. 2007. Yeni Mahalle-Balıklıgöl. In *Türkiye'de Neolitik Dönem: Yeni Kazılar, Yeni Bulgular*, ed. Mehmet Özdoğan and Nezih Başgelen, 165–78. İstanbul: Arkeoloji ve Sanat Yayınları.

Ellis, Richard S. and Mary M. Voigt. 1982. 1981 Excavations at Gritille, Turkey. *American Journal of Archaeology* 86: 319–32.

Erim-Özdoğan, Aslı. 2007. Çayönü. In *Türkiye'de Neolitik Dönem: Yeni Kazılar, Yeni Bulgular*, ed. Mehmet Özdoğan and Nezih Başgelen, 57–97. İstanbul: Arkeoloji ve Sanat Yayınları.

———. 2010. Sumaki Höyük, Ilısu Dam Area/Turkey-Batman-Beşiri. In *Interpreting the Late Neolithic of Upper Mesopotamia*, ed. Olivier Nieuwenhuyse, Peter M. M. G. Akkermans, and Reinhard Bernbeck. Turnhout: Brepols Publishers.

Erim-Özdoğan, Aslı and Nurcan Yalman. 2004. Katkılı Kil Kaplar ve Çanak Çömlek: Çayönü Çanak Çömleksiz ve Çanak Çömlekli Neolitik Buluntuları: Üzerinden bir Yorum. In Complex Societies in Prehistory: Studies in Memoriam of the Braidwoods. *TÜBA-AR* 7: 67–92.

Flannery, Kent V. 1972. The Origin of the Village as a Settlement Type in Mesoamerica and the Near East. In *Man, Settlement and Urbanism*, ed. Peter J. Ucko, Ruth Tringham, and George W. Dimbleby, 23–53. London: Duckworth.

Gopher, Avi and Ram Gophna. 1993. Cultures of the Eighth and Seventh Millennia BP in the Southern Levant: A Review for the 1990's. *Journal of World Prehistory* 7: 297–353.

Hauptmann, Harald. 1993. Ein kultgebäude in Nevalı Çori. In *Between the Rivers and Over the Mountains: Archaeologica Anatolica et Mesopotamica Alba Palmieri Dedicata*, ed. Marcella Frangipane, Harald Hauptmann, Mario Liverani, Paolo Matthiae, and Machteld Mellink, 37–69. Roma: Dipartimento di Scienze Storiche Archeologiche ed. Antropologiche dell'Antichità, Università di Roma "La Sapienza."

———. 1999. The Urfa Region. In *The Neolithic in Turkey: The Cradle of Civilization, New Discoveries*, ed. Mehmet Özdoğan and Nezih Başgelen, 65–86. İstanbul: Arkeoloji ve Sanat Yayınları.

———. 2007. Nevali Çori ve Urfa Bölgesinde Neolitik Dönem. In *Türkiye'de Neolitik Dönem: Yeni Kazılar, Yeni Bulgular*, ed. Mehmet Özdoğan and Nezih Başgelen, 131–64. İstanbul: Arkeoloji ve Sanat Yayınları.

Hongo, Hitomi, Richard H. Meadow, Banu Öksüz, and Gülçin İlgezdi. 2004. Animal Exploitation at Çayönü Tepesi, Southeastern Anatolia. In Complex Societies in Prehistory: Studies in Memoriam of the Braidwoods. *TÜBA-AR* 7: 107–19.

Hongo, Hitomi, Jessica Pearson, Banu Öksüz, and Gülçin İlgezdi. 2009. The Process of Ungulate Domestication at Çayönü, Southeastern Turkey: A Multidisciplinary Approach Focusing on *Bos* sp. and *Cervus elaphus*. *Anthropozoologica* 44: 63–78.

Kenyon, Kathleen M. 1957. *Digging Up Jericho*. New York: Praeger.

Kromer, Bernd and Klaus Schmidt. 1998. Two Radiocarbon Dates from Göbekli Tepe, Southeastern Turkey. *Neo-Lithics* 3.98: 8–9.

Mellaart, James. 1975. *The Neolithic of the Near East*. London: Thames and Hudson.

Miyake, Yutaka. 2007. Salat Cami Yanı. In *Türkiye'de Neolitik Dönem: Yeni Kazılar, Yeni Bulgular*, ed. Mehmet Özdoğan and Nezih Başgelen, 37–46. İstanbul: Arkeoloji ve Sanat Yayınları.

Özbaşaran, Mihriban and Miguel Molist. 2007. Akarçay Tepe. In *Türkiye'de Neolitik Dönem: Yeni Kazılar, Yeni Bulgular*, ed. Mehmet Özdoğan and Nezih Başgelen, 179–87. İstanbul: Arkeoloji ve Sanat Yayınları.

Özdoğan, Aslı. 1999. Çayönü. In *The Neolithic in Turkey: The Cradle of Civilization, New Discoveries*, ed. Mehmet Özdoğan and Nezih Başgelen, 35–63. İstanbul: Arkeoloji ve Sanat Yayınları.

Özdoğan, Mehmet. 2003. A Group of Neolithic Stone Figurines from Mezraa Teleilat. In *From Villages to Cities, Early Villages in the Near East, Studies Presented to Ufuk Esin*, eds. Mehmet Özdoğan, Harald Hauptmann, and Nezih Başgelen 511–23. İstanbul: Arkeoloji ve Sanat Yayınları.

———. 2007. Mezraa-Teleilat. In *Türkiye'de Neolitik Dönem: Yeni Kazılar, Yeni Bulgular*, ed. Mehmet Özdoğan and Nezih Başgelen, 189–201. İstanbul: Arkeoloji ve Sanat Yayınları.

Özdoğan, Mehmet and Aslı Özdoğan. 1989. Çayönü: A Conspectus of Recent Work. *Paléorient* 15: 65–74.

———. 1993. Pre-Halafian Pottery of Southeastern Anatolia: With Special Reference to the Çayönü Sequence. In *Between the Rivers and Over the Mountains: Archaeologica Anatolica et Mesopotamica Alba Palmieri Dedicata*, ed. Marcella Frangipane, Harald Hauptmann, Mario Liverani, Paolo Matthiae, and Machteld Mellink, 87–103. Roma: Dipartimento di Scienze Storiche Archeologiche ed. Antropologiche dell'Antichità, Università di Roma "La Sapienza."

Özkaya, Vecihi and Oya San. 2007. Körtik Tepe. In *Türkiye'de Neolitik Dönem: Yeni Kazılar, Yeni Bulgular*, ed. Mehmet Özdoğan and Nezih Başgelen, 21–36. İstanbul: Arkeoloji ve Sanat Yayınları.

Peasnall, Brian and Michael Rosenberg. 2001. A Preliminary Description of the Lithic Industry from Demirköy Höyük. In *Beyond Tools: Redefining the PPN Lithic Assemblages of the Levant. Proceedings of the Third Workshop on PPN Chipped Stone Industries, Venice 1998*, ed. Isabella Caneva, Cristina Lemorini, Daniela Zampetti, and Paolo Biagi, 363–87. Studies in Early Near Eastern Production, Subsistence, and Environment 9. Berlin: Freie Universität.

Redding, Richard W. and Michael Rosenberg. 1998. Ancestral Pigs: A New (Guinea) Model for Pig Domestication in the Near East. In *Ancestors for the Pigs: Pigs in Prehistory*, ed. Sarah M. Nelson, 65–76. MASCA Research Papers in Science and Archaeology vol. 15. Philadelphia: University of Pennsylvania Press.

Rollefson, Gary O. and Ilse Köhler-Rollefson. 1989. The Collapse of Early Neolithic Settlements in the Southern Levant. In *People and Culture in Change: Proceedings of the Second Symposium on Upper Palaeolithic, Mesolithic, and Neolithic Populations of Europe and the Mediterranean Basin*, ed. Israel Hershkovitz, 73–90. BAR International Series 508(1). Oxford: BAR International.

Roodenberg, Jacob. 1989. Hayaz Höyük and the Final PPNB in the Taurus Foothills. *Paléorient* 15:9 1–101.

Rosenberg, Michael. 1994. A Preliminary Description of the Lithic Industry from Hallan Çemi. In *Neolithic Chipped Stone Industries of the Fertile Crescent: Proceedings of the First Workshop on PPN Chipped Stone Industries, Berlin 1993*, ed. Hans G. Gebel and Stefan K. Kozlowski, 223–38. Studies in Early Near Eastern Production, Subsistence, and Environment 1. Berlin: Freie Universität.

———. 1999. Hallan Çemi. In *The Neolithic in Turkey: The Cradle of Civilization, New Discoveries*, ed. Mehmet Özdoğan and Nezih Başgelen, 25–33. İstanbul: Arkeoloji ve Sanat Yayınları.

———. 2004. Braidwood's Axiom and Kenyon's Chronology: Complexities and the Neolithic of Southwestern Asia. In Complex Societies in Prehistory: Studies in Memoriam of the Braidwoods. *TÜBA-AR* 7: 53–60.

———. 2007a. Hallan Çemi. In *Türkiye'de Neolitik Dönem: Yeni Kazılar, Yeni Bulgular*, ed. Mehmet Özdoğan and Nezih Başgelen, 1–9. İstanbul: Arkeoloji ve Sanat Yayınları.

———. 2007b. Demirköy. In *Türkiye'de Neolitik Dönem: Yeni Kazılar, Yeni Bulgular*, ed. Mehmet Özdoğan and Nezih Başgelen, 13–19. İstanbul: Arkeoloji ve Sanat Yayınları.

Rosenberg, Michael and Michael Davis. 1992. Hallan Çemi Tepesi, an Early Aceramic Neolithic Site in Eastern Anatolia: Some Preliminary Observations Concerning Material Culture. *Anatolica* 18: 1–18.

Rosenberg, Michael and Brian Peasnall. 1998. A Report on Soundings at Demirköy Höyük, an Aceramic Neolithic Site in Eastern Anatolia. *Anatolica* 24: 195–207.

Rosenberg, Michael, Richard W. Redding, Mark Nesbitt, and Brian Peasnall. 1998. Hallan Çemi Tepesi and Post-Pleistocene Adaptations along the Taurus-Zagros Arc. *Paleorient* 24.1: 25–41.

Savard, Manon, Mark Nesbitt, and Martin K. Jones. 2006. The Role of Wild Grasses in Subsistence and Sedentism: New Evidence from the Northern Fertile Crescent. *World Archaeology* 38: 179–96.

Schmidt, Klaus. 1994. The Nevalli Çori Industry: Status of Research. In *Neolithic Chipped Stone Industries of the Fertile Crescent: Proceedings of the First Workshop on PPN Chipped Stone Industries, Berlin 1993*, ed. Hans G. Gebel and Stefan K. Kozlowski, 239–51. Studies in Early Near Eastern Production, Subsistence, and Environment 1. Berlin: Freie Universität.

———. 1997. Snakes, Lions and Other Animals: The Urfa-Project 1997. *Neo-Lithics* 3.97: 8–9.

———. 1999. Boars, Ducks, and Foxes—The Urfa Project 99. *Neo-Lithics* 3.99: 12–15.

———. 2000. Göbekli Tepe, Southeastern Turkey. A Preliminary Report on the 1995–1999 Excavations. *Paléorient* 26: 45–54.

———. 2007. Göbekli Tepe. In *Türkiye'de Neolitik Dönem: Yeni Kazılar, Yeni Bulgular*, ed. Mehmet Özdoğan and Nezih Başgelen, 115–29. İstanbul: Arkeoloji ve Sanat Yayınları.

Stein, Gil. 1989. Strategies of Risk Reduction in Herding and Hunting Systems of Neolithic Southeast Anatolia. In *Early Animal Domestication and its Cultural Context*, ed. Pam Crabtree, Kathleen Ryan, and Douglas Campana, 87–97. Philadelphia: University of Pennsylvania Press.

van Zeist, Willem G. and Gerrit J. de Roller. 1994. The Plant Husbandry of Aceramic Çayönü, SE Turkey. *Palaeohistoria* 33–34: 65–96.

———. 2003. The Çayönü Archaebotanical Record. In *Reports on Archaeobotanical Studies in the Old World*, ed. Willem van Zeist, 143–66. Groningen.

Voigt, Mary M. 1985. Village on the Euphrates: Excavations at Neolithic Gritille in Turkey. *Expedition* 27: 10–24.

Yılmaz, Yasemin. 2010. Les Pratiques Funéraires des Populations Néolithiques d'Anatolie: le Cas de Çayönü. École doctorale des Sciences et Environnements, Thèse de doctorat, Université Bordeaux 1, Inédit. *Neolitik Dönem'de Anadolu'da Ölü Gömme Uygulamaları*: Çayönü Örneği, İstanbul Üniversitesi, Sosyal Bilimler Enstitüsü, Prehistorya Bilim Dalı.

CHAPTER 7

THE CHALCOLITHIC ON THE PLATEAU

ULF-DIETRICH SCHOOP

THE recognition of a separate "Chalcolithic" phase within the Anatolian prehistoric sequence is relatively recent in Turkey's history of archaeological exploration (figure 7.1). This is true despite the fact that several sites now attributed to this period were investigated at quite an early stage. Among these early examples are Beşik-Sivritepe in the Troad (1879), the caves of Ayio Gala (on the Greek island of Chios) (1887), and Pendik near the Sea of Marmara (1922). It has been suspected that the initial reluctance to attribute pre–Bronze Age dates to prehistoric sites was due to diffusionist attitudes which aimed to deny the cultures of the Anatolian plateau any great antiquity (Özdoğan 1996, 1997). Because the combination of diffusionist inclinations with other dubious motives appeared quite convincing, this argument has since been repeated in numerous publications by different authors. A closer inspection of the circumstances surrounding Anatolian archaeology in the first half of the twentieth century reveals a different picture, however. Contradicting Özdoğan's suggestion, in the scenarios painted by *diffusionist* authors Anatolia has always been populated with Neolithic and Chalcolithic cultures (even at times when no corresponding archaeology was available yet). The background for these hypotheses was the need to integrate the painted-pottery traditions of the Neolithic Balkans with the known sequences in Mesopotamia and Syria into a logically coherent picture (e.g., Milojčić 1950/1951; Schachermayr 1949/1950; von der Osten 1937; see Özdoğan, chapter 29 in this volume, for more extensive discussion on this topic). This desire led to the creation of extremely broad chronological schemes in which the placement of the constituent units was often based on rather weak arguments. Deductions of the latter kind were increasingly opposed by more methodologically minded scholars. Archaeologists like the decidedly nondiffusionist Kurt Bittel (1934, 1939; and later Orthmann 1963) stressed the importance of regional sequences and demanded that positive local evidence must be provided for each claim of great antiquity. As such was initially difficult to supply for many early Anatolian assemblages, they opted for the late dating which now (after the introduction of radiocarbon dating and new evidence) proves to be erroneous in part. The eventual discovery of very early sites by James Mellaart and David French in the 1950s, therefore, did not lead to a paradigmatic shift—it was, rather, the unexpected character of these settlements that caused excitement.

The current chronological framework used in Anatolian archaeology is mainly based on a local variant of the Three Age System whose transitional dates are mostly imported from outside the region. The start of the Early Bronze Age is defined by the sequences of Troy and Tarsus-Gözlükule, whose dating was derived from Aegean terminology (Karg 1999). Any assemblage of demonstrably pre-Trojan date which contained metal artifacts therefore implied a "Chalcolithic" attribution. This is the reason for early ascriptions of this chronological label to sites like Kumtepe, Alişar, or Beycesultan. The beginning of the Chalcolithic, in turn, has been defined by the sequence of Mersin-Yumuktepe. Here, the chronological terminology was modeled on Mesopotamian conventions by John Garstang (1953), who had already been responsible for the introduction of the Three Age System to the southern Levant (see Weippert 1991). Accordingly,

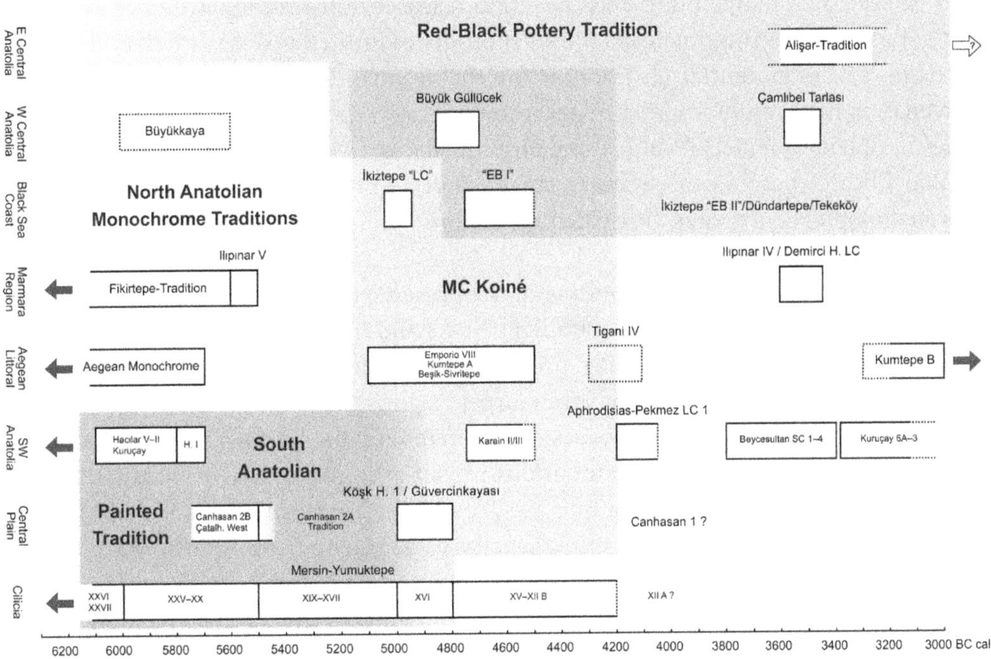

Figure 7.1. Simplified chronological scheme showing cultural development on the Anatolian Plateau.

the Early Chalcolithic was defined by the introduction of painting on beige-slipped pottery in Mersin-Yumuktepe XXV. James Mellaart, who excavated Hacılar and Çatalhöyük West, and David French, excavator of Canhasan, later imported the scheme onto the Anatolian plateau. The underlying assumption, of course, was that the transition to painted pottery should be typical for the whole of Anatolia. It has since been shown, however, that such a practice was followed in the southern plateau only. This is the background of the awkward situation in which assemblages with monochrome pottery along the Aegean coast or in the Marmara region are often classified as Neolithic, although they are in part contemporary with the Early Chalcolithic in the south.

At both the start and the end of the Anatolian "Chalcolithic" there is no perceptible break in cultural continuity (see Özbaşaran, chapter 5, and Steadman, chapter 10 in this volume). The present terminological choice is between the use of either a unified classification system with an illogical foundation or of conflicting Three Age Systems within one strongly interconnected geographical area. A possible way out of this dilemma would be the establishment of local sequences that are still too fragmentary to be individually viable. Partly responsible for this latter situation is the traditional concentration on the stratigraphies of single sites at the expense of the definition of larger multisite typo-chronological units. As a result, we mostly lack robust information about the spatial and chronological extent of archaeological phenomena and of their internal variation. Current archaeological fashion does not promise a change in this situation anytime soon. Although the study of the distribution of radiocarbon dates sometimes appears to be seen as a magic bullet to relieve the researcher from the burden of "soft" typological reasoning, such an approach produces limited insight as well because of the lack of potential abstraction for the results. The only possible way to overcome the present impasse appears to be an approach that embraces both the development of material culture and absolute dates. In the study of the Anatolian Chalcolithic, much work remains to be invested at a relatively low level of archaeological inference (see Düring, chapter 36 in this volume, for current research directions).

In this chapter, I offer an outline of the present state of knowledge about the Chalcolithic sequence on the Anatolian plateau and in western Anatolia. Because archaeological knowledge is not represented continuously over the whole area, it will be treated in the context of seven larger regions: the central Anatolian Plain (including Cappadocia with occasional references to Cilicia), the southwest Anatolian Lake District (a mountainous region around the city of Burdur), the Aegean coast (extending north into the Troad), the area around the Sea of Marmara, the Porsuk region (around the city of Eskişehir), the Black Sea coast (between the cities of Sinop and Trabzon), and north-central Anatolia within the bend of the Kızıl Irmak River. The discussion identifies the main archaeological traditions and their chronological relationships. I also offer an overview of the chronological arguments and contentious issues. All dates are given in calibrated radiocarbon values.

"Early Chalcolithic" (ca. 6100–5500 B.C.E.)

Southwestern Lake District

As mentioned earlier, the sequence of the Hacılar mound in the southwest Anatolian Lake District was instrumental for Mellaart's definition of the Early Chalcolithic (Mellaart 1970). Here (figure 7.2), as elsewhere, the transition from the Late Neolithic to the Early Chalcolithic in Layer V does not constitute a major cultural break at the site. Red-Slipped and Red-on-Cream Painted pottery represents at first a minor addition to a monochrome assemblage of the Late Neolithic tradition. The proportion of painted pottery grows steadily over time. The best architectural remains come from Layer II, where we see two rows of laterally abutting houses facing each other across a large courtyard. Hacılar II and Hacılar I are divided by a stratigraphical and typological discontinuity representing either—as initially proposed by Mellaart—the appearance of an invading population, or—more likely—an interruption of settlement at this site. No "pure" Hacılar V–II assemblage has yet been found at any other site. Based on his own excavations in the Lake District, Refik Duru challenged Mellaart's sequence and stated that Red-on-Cream Painted pottery from Kuruçay 12–7, Höyücek, and Bademağacı reached far into the Neolithic period (Duru 1989, 2008). Duru's reconstruction is not supported by the radiocarbon dates, however. The pottery from the latter sites displays mixed traits of

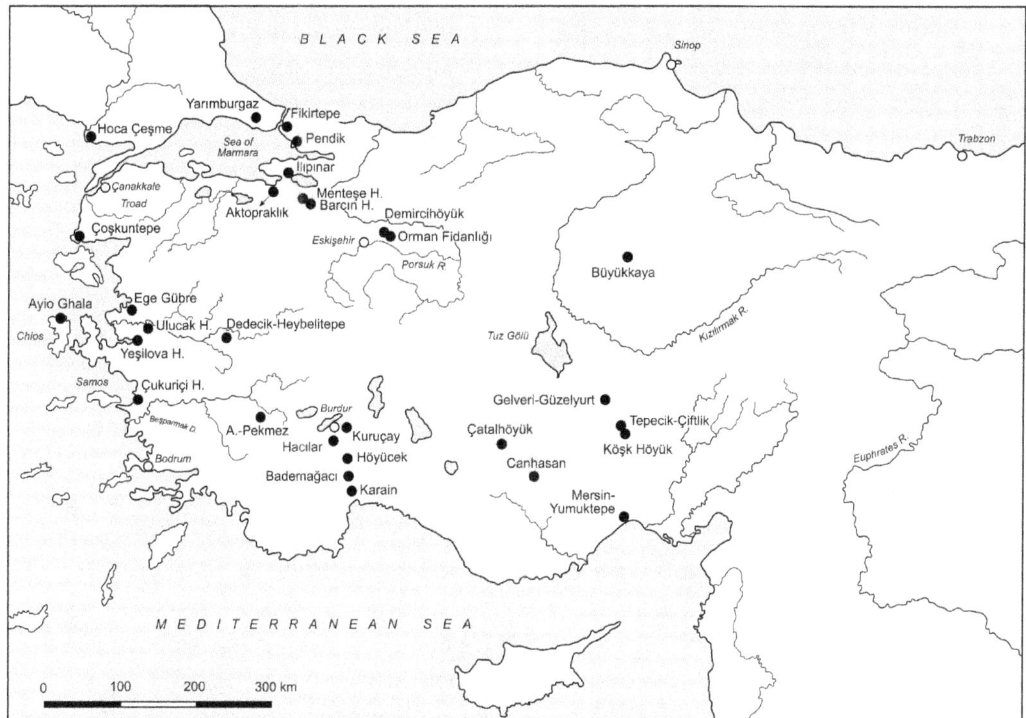

Figure 7.2. Map of Turkey showing Early Chalcolithic sites mentioned in the text.

Hacılar II and I and appears to fill the gap between these layers at Hacılar (Schoop 2002). If this reconstruction is correct, Hacılar V–II appear to represent only a short segment of time, most probably in the range of ca. 6100–6000 cal B.C.E. The sequence breaks off with the last dates from Hacılar I around 5700 B.C.E., followed by a lengthy gap in the Lake District. This situation obviously does not imply a termination of the Hacılar I *tradition* of material culture, whose further development remains hidden for the time being.

A remarkable find are hundreds of anthropomorphic images painted on the walls of rock shelters in the coastal Beşparmak (Latmos) Mountains north of the city of Bodrum. These paintings have been linked typologically with Early Chalcolithic traditions of pottery decoration in the Lake District (Peschlow-Bindokat 2003). Little is known as yet about the creators and the function of these rather isolated works of parietal art.

Central Anatolian Plain

Evidence for the early part of the Chalcolithic sequence in the central Anatolian plain comes mainly from the mounds of Çatalhöyük West in the more westerly part of the plain and Can Hasan at its southern border. Clearly, both excavations have captured an already developed stage of the painted tradition. The two Early Chalcolithic phases from Çatalhöyük West appear to be roughly contemporaneous to Can Hasan 3/2B (Mellaart 1965). A deep sounding at the latter site has revealed older layers with monochrome pottery. The radiocarbon dates for Can Hasan 2B cover more than the first half of the sixth millennium B.C.E. (Thissen 2002:303; see Schoop 2005a:144; and see Yakar, chapter 4 in this volume), clearly not a realistic result. The reason is that they have been obtained from charcoal and large wooden building elements, such as are typically used for long spans of time in settlements of the steppe. Fortunately, some additional information is provided by the sequence at Mersin-Yumuktepe, immediately south of the Taurus Mountains (Caneva and Sevin 2004; Garstang 1953). Pottery shapes and painted motifs comparable to Çatalhöyük and Canhasan are present in the Mersin Layers XXVI–XX, radiocarbon dated to the second quarter of the sixth millennium B.C.E. If this connection is correct, a gap of about 400–500 years opens between the known occupation layers of Çatalhöyük East and West, during which cultural development in the plain is poorly understood. The new excavations at Çatalhöyük will probably produce evidence to resolve this question (Biehl and Rosenstock 2009; see Hodder, chapter 43 in this volume).

In Can Hasan 2A (which—strictly speaking—already belongs to the following "Middle Chalcolithic"), we see a transformation in the structure of pottery decoration. A striking introduction is the use of polychrome painting. Settlement continuity is well documented, as many of the 2A houses are "slotted" into older 2B foundations (French 1998). Again, we see a parallel typological development at Mersin XIX–XVII, which covers the second half of the sixth millennium B.C.E. These layers at Mersin display strong Halafian influence; except for a handful of imported Halaf sherds immediately north of the Taurus passes, no substantial traces of this Near Eastern tradition have been documented on the plateau so far. The settlement at Can Hasan 2A probably did not exist for this long time span, but sherds of the Can Hasan 2A *style* have been found in settlements of the early fifth millennium B.C.E. (such as at Köşk Höyük and Güvercinkayası), indicating a continuation of this tradition over roughly half a millennium.

The Cappadocian margin of the plain appears to have been in the possession of groups using monochrome pottery decorated with different techniques but with somewhat similar motifs. One of these sites is Gelveri-Güzelyurt, with pottery whose swirling designs, executed in a stab-and-drag technique, has often been taken to represent Balkan influences of the fourth millennium B.C.E. (Esin 1993; Makkay 1993; Özdoğan 1996; Steadman 1995). Pottery of this type has now appeared at Tepecik-Çiftlik, seemingly in contexts of the 6th millennium B.C.E. (Bıçakcı et al. 2007; Godon 2005). It is preceded there by layers containing pottery with striking figurative relief decoration, especially known from the site of Köşk Höyük (Öztan 2007).

Aegean Coast and Sea of Marmara

The excavations over the past decades have made it clear that once we leave the southern margin of the Taurus Mountains, we enter a very different cultural area in which (among other features) monochrome dark-faced wares predominate (Seeher 1987a, 1990). Along the Aegean coast a string of settlements extending from the modern cities of Aydın in the south to Çanakkale in the north display roughly similar characteristics. The mound of Ulucak near İzmir is one of the most impressive examples (Abay 2005; A. Çilingiroğlu et al. 2004; Çilingiroğlu and Çilingiroğlu 2007; Ç. Çilingiroğlu 2009). Their material culture evolves without a break from the seventh millennium B.C.E. Typical in the pottery inventories are red slips and shapes that partly reflect contemporaneous trends in the Lake District. Painted pottery, however, appears in small numbers only. A characteristic feature in the early sixth millennium B.C.E. is the use of vessels whose outsides are densely covered by fingernail impressions ("*impresso* technique"). Similar to the situation further to the south, the development cannot be traced later than the first third of the sixth millennium B.C.E., after which there is a gap. The chronological position of these assemblages has only been established recently. A number of ongoing excavations (such as those at Yeşilova Höyük, Dedecik-Heybelitepe, Çukuriçi Höyük, and Ege Gübre) will certainly change our knowledge of Aegean development in the sixth millennium B.C.E. (Derin 2007; Herling et al. 2008; Horejs 2008; Lichter 2005; Sağlamtimur 2007).

Toward the north, around the Sea of Marmara, a group of sites with similar material culture is known as the "Fikirtepe Culture." This group is probably the best-researched cultural tradition in Chalcolithic Anatolia so far and has been investigated at a number of sites, among them the eponymous Fikirtepe itself. The longest sequence so far has been documented at the mound of Ilıpınar, while the earliest stages are represented at Menteşe Höyük (Roodenberg 1995; Roodenberg and Thissen 2001;

Roodenberg and Alpaslan Roodenberg 2008; and see Roodenberg, chapter 44 in this volume). New excavations at Barcın Höyük will certainly enlarge our current understanding of this cultural group (Roodenberg, van As, and Alpaslan Roodenberg 2008). Fikirtepe pottery displays dark burnished surfaces, which sometimes boast incised decoration. A typical element is small decorated clay "tables" which are often found in graves (Schwarzberg 2005, 2006). Among the nonpottery elements, an elaborate polished-bone industry is worth mentioning. Most Fikirtepe settlements are mounds, but there are also large agglomerations of round huts on river and lakeside locations that practiced a fishing economy. These are mostly seen as a separate chronological stage in the Fikirtepe development (Özdoğan 1999) but, alternatively, might have served a specialized functionality (Schoop 2005a:211–12). The Fikirtepe sequence begins in the Late Neolithic, that is, the second half of the seventh millennium B.C.E. It has been subdivided into an archaic, a classic, and a developed stage (Özdoğan 1997; and see Özdoğan, chapter 29 in this volume, for further discussion). Most Fikirtepe sites are found east of the Bosporus (the cave of Yarımburgaz representing one of the few "European" exceptions), often on the shorelines of the large lakes characteristic of the region. Shortly before 5500 B.C.E., a number of changes can be seen both in architecture and the pottery assemblages (Thissen 2008). Some of the new pottery features (including the technique of channeling on black-polished pottery) have been taken to establish a connection to the Vinča culture in the Southern Balkan region (Efe 1990; 1996). The new site of Aktopraklık has produced a long cultural sequence that extends into this poorly understood segment of time (Karul 2007).

Eskişehir/Porsuk Region and North Central Turkey

On the northwestern plateau, the region around the city of Eskişehir has been well explored by surface survey but has seen little excavation. Early stages with a clear affinity to the Fikirtepe tradition are represented at Demircihöyük, where a substantial body of pottery was found, contained in the mudbricks of the site's Early Bronze Age architecture (Seeher 1987a). A remarkable feature of this material is that it contains a small amount of (possibly imported) Red-on-Cream Painted Ware, which reflects Early Chalcolithic traditions of the Lake District. The important site of Orman Fidanlığı, which terminates in Layer V with the appearance of "vinčoid" elements in the pottery assemblage, may slightly postdate the Fikirtepe tradition (Efe 1990, 2001). We do not have radiocarbon dates from this area.

In the northern parts of central Turkey, little is known so far archaeologically from these early periods. A small settlement excavated at Boğazköy-Büyükkaya probably dates into the first half of the sixth millennium B.C.E. (Schoop 2005b). The pottery from this site firmly belongs to the dark-faced monochrome group and betrays some general similarity with material from the Porsuk area. There is some decoration with motifs in the stab-and-drag technique. A small number of cream-slipped painted sherds appear imported. A number of sites with similar surface material show that this tradition had a wider distribution in the general area (Kuzucuoğlu et al. 1997; Matthews 2009). No such early evidence comes directly from the Black Sea littoral as yet. The absence of remains older than the sixth millennium B.C.E. from this area is generally ascribed to a lacuna in research (Düring 2008; Marro 2000; Özdogan 1996; Parzinger 1993a). It may, however, be that the situation reflects the demanding nature of this mountainous and formerly heavily forested region, which would not have been attractive to early farmers (Schoop 2005c). If so, this would render this region the only area in Anatolia where new land was taken in possession by settled human communities at such a late point in time.

In general, it seems safe to say that in most Anatolian regions the Early Chalcolithic emerges without a break from the preceding traditions; the subdivision is a convention and essentially arbitrary in nature. The production and consumption of cream-slipped pottery with elaborately painted motifs is a phenomenon belonging to a narrow strip of communities along the northern flank of the Taurus Mountains. All the areas to the north of this region continue to use pottery with dark surfaces and a generally much more restricted repertoire of shapes. However, in much smaller numbers, decoration in other techniques (incision and impresso) also appears in these traditions. The motifs reflect a shared iconographic repertoire with the south. The reasons behind this development remain unexplained so far. They demonstrate, however, the existence of communication systems transcending the cultural boundaries within this large area. Additionally, small amounts of painted pottery appear to have been traded into the "monochrome" northern areas, indicating some degree of physical contact. Conversely, polished marble bracelets were manufactured and used mainly in the northern half of Anatolia (Ünlüsoy 2002). These bracelets were imported into the central Anatolian plain (which does not have marble deposits of its own) but were not in demand in the Lake District.

A disturbance of the general cultural development is visible in the material culture wherever the sequences extend into the second half of the sixth millennium B.C.E. Because information about this latter period is missing almost everywhere, it is hard to arrive at a clear assessment of this situation.

"Middle Chalcolithic" (ca. 5500–4250 B.C.E.)

The middle part of the Anatolian Chalcolithic has only recently come into its own as a time period of some extension (figure 7.3). In earlier scholarship, typified by a general lack of calibrated radiocarbon dates, the early part of the sequence was mostly stretched and the later part compressed, leaving no room for a Middle Chalcolithic. The substantial change in character between Early and Late Chalcolithic assemblages was often seen as the result of population replacement. Until the

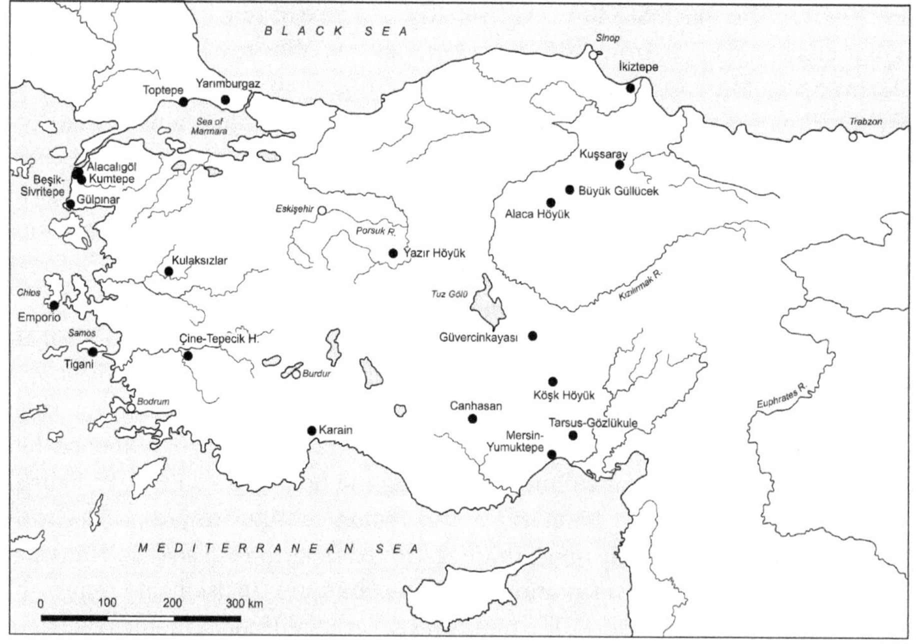

Figure 7.3. Map of Turkey showing Middle Chalcolithic sites mentioned in the text.

1980s, authors using the term "Middle Chalcolithic" did so to express doubts over this reconstruction of abrupt change (e.g., Eslick 1980; Seeher 1987a). This picture has changed considerably, and especially the fifth millennium B.C.E. emerges as a period of significant cultural development. It is worthwhile to keep in mind, however, that the obvious typological differences between Middle Chalcolithic and Early Chalcolithic assemblages may well appear exaggerated by our ignorance of development in the second half of the sixth millennium B.C.E. As of today, the validity of the concept of a separate Middle Chalcolithic phase with consistent character has never been systematically demonstrated or defined.

Aegean Coast and Southern Anatolia

One of the most crucial discoveries was made at Kumtepe, a small settlement mound situated in the Troad (Sperling 1976). Since its initial excavation in the 1930s, this site was considered one of the type sites for the Late Chalcolithic. The two main layers were thought to represent the development immediately predating the Early Bronze Age. Not until the early 1990s was doubt cast on the correct dating of the older part of the Kumtepe sequence (Özdoğan 1991). A long hiatus between Layers A and B finally emerged from renewed excavations at the site. A series of radiocarbon dates established the dimension of this gap in absolute chronology (Gabriel 2000; Korfmann et al. 1995). Kumtepe A clearly dates to the first quarter of the fifth millennium B.C.E. A number of other sites in the Troad, such as Beşik-Sivritepe,

Gülpınar, and Alacalıgöl, produced similar material with more developed features (Gabriel, Aslan, and Blum 2004; Seeher 1985, 1987b; Takaoğlu 2006). Radiocarbon dates from Beşik-Sivritepe fall into the second quarter of the fifth millennium B.C.E. (Korfmann and Kromer 1993).

The chronological shift in the Troad has serious consequences for the dating of a number of sites much further south. Emporio on Chios and Tigani on Samos are situated on islands that were part of the mainland in prehistory. At Emporio (Layers X–VI), a prehistoric sequence around a local water source has been investigated (Hood 1981). At Tigani, the remains of truncated prehistoric layers were analyzed in one of the most rigorous treatments of the prehistoric chronology in this area (Felsch 1988). Felsch subdivided this sequence into four Phases (I–IV), of which Tigani IV is the most recent. The sequences from these two sites were originally seen as overlapping and connecting the Early Chalcolithic (as at Hacılar) and Late Chalcolithic (as at Beycesultan and Kumtepe) in the neighboring regions. Because no radiocarbon dates are available from these excavations, their chronology is dependent on cross-dating with the Troad. As such, Emporio VIII can be paralleled with Kumtepe A and represents together with the later Tigani Phases II–III the first half of the fifth millennium B.C.E., after which the sequences appear to be interrupted. Emporio X–IX and Tigani I belong to the few assemblages within the general Anatolian sphere that fall into the second half of the sixth millennium B.C.E. (Schoop 2005a:229–72). The tradition—defined by a distinctive pattern burnish and a repertoire of characteristic vessel shapes including conical-necked jars, horned handles, and incised decoration—therefore appears to have a distinctive coastal affiliation. The only inland site with a contemporary assemblage identified so far is Çine-Tepecik Höyük (Aydın) (Günel 2006, 2008). Similar assemblages can also be traced along the southern Mediterranean coast, as shown by finds from Karain and Tarsus-Gözlükule (Goldman 1956; Seeher 1989).

Close to the latter site, at Mersin-Yumuktepe, we find a rather special situation (Caneva and Sevin 2004; Garstang 1953). Layer XVI of this site is architecturally typified by a fortification wall with a gate structure. Behind the fortification lies a building whose tripartite plan betrays strong Ubaid influences. The pottery consists of types typical for the Halaf/Ubaid transitional period. A small percentage, however, belongs to the above-noted Anatolian tradition of the beginning of the fifth millennium B.C.E.

Very similar pottery has been found at Güvercinkayası, Köşk Höyük, and other settlements at the Cappadocian fringe of the central Anatolian plain (Gülçur 2004; Öztan and Özkan 2003; Summers 1991). The layout of these settlements still reflects older traditions of the plain. A small portion of the pottery is painted with motifs that show that the tradition typical for earlier Can Hasan 2A must still be active during this time. Pattern burnish, however, as part of this package is not in evidence in either Mersin-Yumuktepe or central Anatolia. A number of radiocarbon dates from Güvercinkayası cluster around the turn of the sixth to the fifth millennium B.C.E.

Northern Anatolia

Further to the north, within the bend of the Kızıl Irmak River, the sites of Büyük Güllücek, Alaca Höyük IV, and Kuşsaray (see Parzinger 1993a; Schoop 2005a; Summers 1993; Thissen 1993) display the same general ceramic attributes in combination with shapes that still recall features known from the preceding period.

One of the most controversial sites is İkiztepe at the Black Sea littoral. This multiperiod site, consisting of a group of four mounds, has been continuously excavated since 1974. In between the mounds is a burial ground whose graves contained some of the site's most spectacular finds. The larger part of İkiztepe's prehistory, including the cemetery, is dated by the excavators to the Early Bronze Age (EBA), that is, into the third millennium B.C.E. (Alkım, Alkım, and Bilgi 1988, 2003; Bilgi 2001). This is preceded by a "Late Chalcolithic," which is thought to belong to the second half of the fourth millennium B.C.E. The early material (attributed to the Late Chalcolithic and the EB I periods) belongs to the İkiztepe II mound, whereas the more recent "EB II" and "EB III" material has mostly been found on İkiztepe I. The dating of the latest EBA material at İkiztepe, which has good parallels from the end of the third millennium B.C.E. elsewhere in Anatolia, is relatively secure. The dating of the EB I layers of İkiztepe II, on the other hand, rests entirely on the strong typological connections this material displays with Büyük Güllücek further inland (the now obsolete EB I dating for Büyük Güllücek used to be the lynchpin for the early part of a regional chronological system expounded by Winfried Orthmann [1963], which has been authoritative for several decades and is still valid in parts). The İkiztepe layers that predate the EB III have remained contentious. In contrast to the assessments made by the excavators, a number of scholars have pointed to the strong stylistic parallels which metalwork from the İkiztepe cemetery shares with finds from southeast Europe, which would imply a date in the first half of the fourth millennium B.C.E. (Lichter 2006; Maran 2000; Parzinger 1993a, 1993b; Zimmermann 2007; but contra: Yakar 2006). The İkiztepe EB I pottery displays parallels with early to middle fifth millennium B.C.E. assemblages from the southern Balkans (Thissen 1993) and, increasingly, other regions in Turkey. The layers designated Late Chalcolithic, separated by a stratigraphic gap from the overlaying strata, may even extend into the late sixth millennium B.C.E. (Schoop 2005a:324–31).

In general, it can be said that by the early fifth millennium B.C.E., the whole of Anatolia has seen a change of character. One of the most notable innovations is a shared set of features in the pottery repertoire (both shapes and decoration), which establish a *koiné* that encompasses most of Anatolia but reaches far into the northern Aegean and the southern Balkans. At the same time, however, pottery traits (or, as in Güvercinkayası, settlement layout and other artifact groups) testify to the continuity of older traditions.

Most of the sites belonging to the early fifth millennium B.C.E. display evidence of the production and consumption of metals, either in the shape of simple metal artifacts (flat axes, pins, and awls) or as crucibles or slag. At a number of sites, pressure-flaked arrowheads made from flint appear. Naturalistic clay figurines, typical in preceding periods, have disappeared. Along the Aegean coast, schematic marble figurines of the Kiliya style represent a new type, although its roots may well extend back into the sixth millennium (Seeher 1992). At Kulaksızlar near Manisa, a workshop for the manufacture of such figurines has been identified (Takaoğlu 2005). The use of marble beakers in the same area is a feature that extends further into the Aegean.

"Late Chalcolithic" (ca. 4250–3000 B.C.E.)

There is little evidence that the cultural koiné just mentioned as a characteristic of the preceding period extends further than the second third of the fifth millennium B.C.E. In many areas, there is a lack of evidence for the later fifth and early fourth millennia B.C.E. The only area where the outlines of a continuous sequence appear to become more visible is in southwest Anatolia and along the southern and middle Aegean coast (figure 7.4). The pottery complex from Tigani IV appears to contain both pattern burnished pottery of the familiar shapes and new shapes, including a distinctive style of painting in white color (Felsch 1988). Noteworthy are bowls boasting a band of white-painted motifs around the inner rim. A very similar assemblage is represented in Aphrodiasias-Pekmez VIII; it has produced

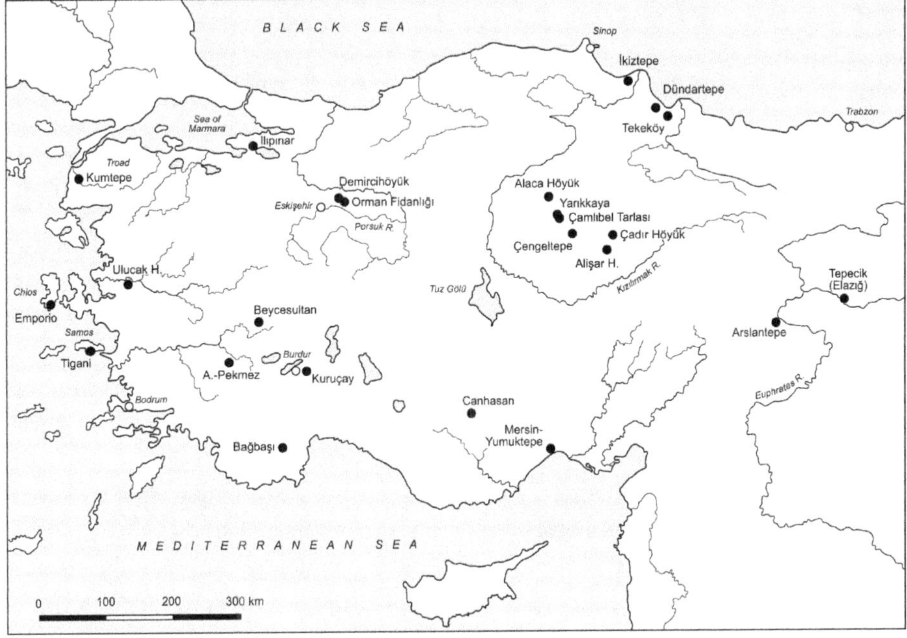

Figure 7.4. Map of Turkey showing Late Chalcolithic sites mentioned in the text.

two radiocarbon dates that fall into the second half of the fifth millennium B.C.E. (Sharp Joukowsky 1986).

Fourth millennium chronology in general is dominated by evidence from the large mound of Beycesultan (Lloyd and Mellaart 1962). Here, a long sequence of twenty-one settlement layers was encountered at the base of the mound. They were grouped together by Mellaart into four stages, the Beycesultan Late Chalcolithic 1–4. At its upper end, the sequence leads—as far as the excavators were concerned—without a break into the EBA. Indeed, since its discovery the Beycesultan Late Chalcolithic has served as a chronological reference point for other assemblages of similar date. This Beycesultan paradigm has been so strong that it was never challenged, although researchers dealing with related assemblages have had difficulties integrating their material into this alleged path of development. Such assemblages were either summarily matched with Beycesultan (such as in Bağbaşı [Eslick 1992], Pekmez [Sharp Joukowsky 1986], Tigani [Felsch 1988]) or, if the differences were too pronounced, as was the case at Late Chalcolithic Kuruçay, dated to an earlier time period (Duru 1996).

How robust is the Beycesultan sequence (see Schoop 2005a:149–96 for a more detailed discussion)? A closer inspection reveals that there is indeed a stratigraphical discontinuity after the Late Chalcolithic: the whole mound appears to have been leveled when the EBA fortification wall was built. Pottery typology as well does not support the hypothesis of continuity. Two radiocarbon dates from Beycesultan fall into the first half of the fourth millennium B.C.E. and not toward its end. A series of dates from Kuruçay, on the other hand, are situated shortly after 3500 B.C.E., that is, later than Beycesultan. If we accept this modified sequence (which would also solve several problems of pottery development), it can be shown that pattern burnish at first continues along with white painting but falls out of use at the beginning of the fourth millennium B.C.E. White painting appears to see a climax in Beycesultan's LC 1 and 2 but declines in quantity afterward. At Kuruçay, in the later part of the fourth millennium B.C.E., the pottery assemblage is essentially monochrome.

Aegean Coast, Sea of Marmara, and Eskişehir/Porsuk Region

Further toward the north, the Late Chalcolithic is defined by Kumtepe B. This material is clearly a forerunner of Troy I. Surface finds have revealed a wide distribution along the northern and central Aegean coast. The southernmost finds so far have been made on Chios (Emporio) and in the İzmir area, but their relationship to other Anatolian cultural provinces is difficult to define. A number of radiocarbon dates from Kumtepe itself cover the second half of the fourth millennium B.C.E. (Gabriel 2000), but the chronological depth of this tradition remains unclear.

The Late Chalcolithic cemetery of Ilıpınar in the Burdur region revealed an interesting inventory of metal finds but belongs to a different tradition of material culture (Roodenberg 2001, and see Roodenberg, chapter 44, and Muhly, chapter 39 in this volume). Some pottery shapes from the Ilıpınar graves find counterparts on the plateau, particularly in the Eskişehir region. Parallels can be seen in the Demircihöyük fabric types D and F, part of which originate from stratified layers at the base of the mound. More substantial remains must be present at Demircihöyük, but excavation was impeded by the groundwater level. Probably older than Demircihöyük are Orman Fidanlığı VI and VII. Although Jürgen Seeher (1987a) and Turan Efe (2001) saw these assemblages as reflecting the development immediately preceding the EBA (as present in stratified layers at Demircihöyük), I have argued for a much more fragmentary picture in which Orman Fidanlığı VI/VII still belongs to the (late) fifth millennium B.C.E. (Schoop 2005a). Very clear, however, is that the ties between this area and the development in southwest Anatolia are much stronger than in the Troad or around the Sea of Marmara.

Northern and Southern Central Anatolia

Somewhat different is the situation further to the east. Here, we appear to be confronted with a cultural development along a different trajectory whose outlines began to emerge only recently. Situated in the center of this development is the settlement mound of Alişar, a multiperiod site with a long stratigraphy spanning from the Chalcolithic to the Iron Age. The investigations at Alişar, executed by Hans Henning von der Osten on behalf of the Oriental Institute (1927–32), were the first to produce pre–Bronze Age material on the Anatolian plateau. The prehistoric material from Alişar originates almost entirely from an impressive twenty-nine-meter-deep sounding cut into the flank of the mound. The "Chalcolithic" Layers 19–12M at Alişar underlie another set of strata that have been given the misleading name "Copper Age" by von der Osten but clearly belong to the middle part of the Early Bronze Age (see Steadman, chapter 10 in this volume, for further discussion). There has been considerable controversy in the interpretation of the Alişar Chalcolithic, and some of the problems remain unsolved. Three crucial issues have been under debate: (1) the antiquity of the sequence, (2) its continuity or discontinuity, and (3) the nature of the transition to the Copper Age EBA. The Chalcolithic assemblage at Alişar is dominated by ceramic wares with a differential coloring of the inner and outer surfaces. Closed vessels display a black or dark gray color on the outer surface; their insides generally boast a reddish hue. Bowls, on the other hand, show black polished insides while the outsides display yellow or orange colors. Within a range of different vessel shapes, we also find cups and trumpet-shaped jugs. Besides this "Red-Black Ware," high "fruit stands" with a slender base and shallow bowls with incurving rims, and bell-shaped jars with a line of fingernail impressions around the shoulder are typical components of the assemblage. Similar pottery has been found at Alaca Höyük, Çengeltepe, Yarıkkaya South Slope, and, most recently, at Çadır Höyük.

It is very difficult to come up with a line of diachronic development that would convincingly integrate the characteristic shapes of this assemblage with earlier and later assemblages of the region. This typological difficulty has sometimes been circumvented by ingenious yet necessarily speculative reconstructions in which the deepest layers at the base of the Alişar mound (from which von der Osten only published a very small amount of material) play a crucial role. Many different and otherwise poorly dated traditions have been suspected to be represented here, such as those known from Büyük Güllücek, Yarıkkaya-Plateau, and Gelveri-Güzelyurt, or even unknown traditions with affinities to Early Chalcolithic Hacılar (see Özdoğan 1996; Parzinger 1993a; Thissen 1993). None of these claims have been substantiated yet.

No less difficult to explain is the transition into the EBA of the Copper Age type (see Steadman, chapter 10 in this volume) although an immediate chronological transition is mostly assumed. Typologically, such a hypothesis is almost impossible to substantiate, a point already made by von der Osten (1937:408 n.18, 419). All later explanations have so far failed to engage with this observation.

As at least parts of the Copper Age tradition are undeniably fixed in the middle of the third millennium B.C.E., three competing possibilities arise that have all found their followers: (1) the Copper Age extends much deeper into the past than commonly thought, encompassing additionally the beginning of the third millennium B.C.E. (Thissen 1993; von der Osten 1937); (2) the typological characteristics of the "Alişar Chalcolithic" extend far into the third millennium B.C.E. until they merge with the Copper Age (Bittel 1950; Orthmann 1963; Steadman, McMahon, and Ross 2007; Steadman et al. 2008); and (3) there is still a gap in the sequence in which the beginning of the third millennium is hidden (Dittmann 2009; Schoop 2005a).

It is clear that parts of the Alişar Chalcolithic are rooted in the middle of the fourth millennium B.C.E., as demonstrated by the first radiocarbon dates from Çadır Höyük (Gorny et al. 2002). This conclusion had already been reached by the recognition of typical central Anatolian shapes in association with Late Uruk pottery east of the Taurus, in the Malatya area, such as at Arslantepe and Tepecik (Esin 1982; Frangipane and Palmieri 1983; Özdoğan 1991; Thissen 1993; see now, with more detail, Dittmann 2009). These central Anatolian influences coincide in this area with others coming from the Transcaucasian region (see Sagona, chapter 30 in this volume). Red-black pottery appears to be a central Anatolian contribution to this new "package" (Palumbi 2003, 2008; and see Palumbi, chapter 9 in this volume).

It is quite possible that the Alişar complex is situated on another—eastern—regional trajectory rather than the earlier and more westerly oriented traditions found at Büyükkaya, Büyük Güllücek, and İkiztepe (Schoop 2005a:349–51). New discoveries, however, indicate still stronger regional fragmentation in north central Anatolia: the small site of Çamlıbel Tarlası close to Boğazköy has produced radiocarbon dates in the middle of the fourth millennium (Schoop 2008, 2009). Although it also belongs to the general family of red-black pottery, the shapes and decoration differ from the tradition represented within the Alişar sphere. At the Black Sea coast, no strictly Alişar type pottery has been discovered yet, although red-black pottery is well represented at İkiztepe, Dündartepe, and Tekkeköy (Thissen 1993). It is possible that the Black Sea area followed yet another trajectory beneath the broad umbrella of the red-black "eastern" tradition.

Despite this general eastern affiliation, there exists a distinctive type of figurine which connects the area to the southern Balkans. The so-called ring-shaped figurines are flat metal objects of stylized female shape, mostly made from silver, lead, or gold. A concentration of such figurines in northern Anatolia has been seen as evidence of contact—possibly seaborne—with the west coast of the Black Sea, namely, Bulgaria (see Lichter 2006; Zimmermann 2007). An open clay casting mold from Çamlıbel

Tarlası now testifies to the production of such objects here at the easternmost margin of their distribution area (Schoop 2009:65).

Although Mellaart (1963) found a large number of sites with white-painted pottery in the central Anatolian plain, Can Hasan Layer 1 has remained the only excavated site from this period so far (French 1998). It is difficult to date in the absence of sites with related material, and there are no radiocarbon dates. In Cilicia, Mersin-Yumuktepe has a long Ubaid sequence which does not show much contact with the north. The exception is in Layer XIIA, where an intrusion of white-painted pottery types appears to display connections to similar traditions on the plateau. The important role that the appearance of white-painted pottery in Cilician contexts played in the systems of comparative chronology of the preradiocarbon era is almost forgotten today (Eggert and Lüth 1987; Korfmann 2004).

Relatively little can be said on the topic of Late Chalcolithic architecture, mostly because of the limited extent of excavated area at the major sites. Several of the mounds established in the fourth millennium B.C.E. developed later to enormous dimensions (such as Alişar or Beycesultan). They must have represented impressive settlements already in the Late Chalcolithic. Other settlements are of considerably smaller size. Whether we are already dealing with relationships of dependence is an open question. Frequently, the architecture appears to consist of densely packed multiroom buildings, often with relatively thin mudbrick walls. Strongly contrasting with this schema are sites with a few large free-standing one-room buildings surrounded by ample space (e.g., in Can Hasan 1, Camlıbel Tarlası, earlier also in İkiztepe). The social, economic, or ecological factors producing these contrasting architectural models are not clear at present (on Late Chalcolithic architecture in Anatolia, see Schachner 1999; Steadman 2000).

The fourth millennium B.C.E. saw the introduction of new metals, silver, lead, and gold, albeit in small quantities. New artifact types were produced; especially striking is the widespread appearance of triangular daggers (Zimmermann 2004–2005). There is some evidence for substantial subterranean copper ore mining (e.g., at Kozlu in central Anatolia). The use of arsenical copper appears to be a hallmark of the time (Begemann, Pernicka, and Schmitt-Strecker 1994; Yener 2000). Although there are many indications of increasing social and economic complexity during this time, which seem to lead gradually into the EBA, there is nothing to suggest the emergence of proto-urban structures as are typical for the Upper Euphrates region or in northern Syria (see Çevik 2007).

Conclusions

Covering more than three millennia, the Chalcolithic period in Anatolia extends over an extremely broad span of time (figure 7.1). The period is not well defined, nor does the region display unified cultural development during this time. The limits of the period have been defined by reference to chronological systems outside Anatolia and have not proven to be particularly well suited to describe cultural development within the region. Thus, the "Early Chalcolithic" cultures dating from the end of the seventh to the middle of the sixth millennium B.C.E. clearly represent a continuation of the Neolithic tradition. During this time, the south of Anatolia is characterized by beige-slipped wares with elaborate painting and a large spectrum of shapes, whereas the north (covering the greater part of the country) uses dark-faced monochrome wares with a much more restricted shape repertoire. The situation changes during the poorly understood second half of the sixth millennium B.C.E. By the beginning of the fifth millennium B.C.E., a number of shared features with a distribution reaching far into the Balkan Peninsula unify the whole region. At the same time, older local traditions inherited from earlier periods persist in the assemblages. This aspect of unity is lost during the last third of the fifth millennium B.C.E., another segment of time that is not yet well documented by excavation. The fourth millennium B.C.E. (the "Late Chalcolithic") is characterized by traditions with a strongly pronounced regional character, which tends to obscure cross-cultural comparisons. The limited evidence at hand suggests that the transition into the EBA was gradual, although this circumstance is strictly proven only in the Troad so far. Again, the criteria for the Late Chalcolithic–EBA transition are essentially arbitrary in nature.

One of the main obstacles to reach interpretations of a higher level in Anatolia is the general lack of defined cultural units with specified spatial and chronological extension. Most regions are represented only by a few sites or even a single excavation during any particular period, making it very difficult to arrive at generalizing statements. It will be an important task for the future to overcome this type-site perspective and multiply the available evidence by the investigation of contemporary sites of similar cultural affiliation. Although much new evidence has enlarged and diversified our view of the segment of Anatolian prehistory designated the Chalcolithic, the sequences and the whole picture are still fundamentally incomplete. In this sense, we are still struggling with problems not entirely unlike those of von der Osten, Bittel, and others nearly eight decades ago.

REFERENCES

Abay, Eşref. 2005. Neolithic Settlement at Ulucak and its Cultural Relations with Neighbour Regions in Western Anatolia. In *How Did Farming Reach Europe? Anatolian-European Relations from the Second Half of the 7th through to the First Half of the 6th Millennium Cal BC*, ed. Clemens Lichter, 75–84. BYZAS 2. İstanbul: Ege Yayınları.

Alkım, U. Bahadır, Handan Alkım, and Önder Bilgi. 1988. *İkiztepe I. Birinci ve İkinci Dönem Kazıları. The First and Second Season's Excavations (1974–1975)*. Ankara: Türk Tarih Kurumu Basımevi.

———. 2003. *İkiztepe II: Üçüncü, Dördüncü, Beşinci, Altıncı, Yedinci Dönem Kazılar (1976–1980)*. Ankara: Türk Tarih Kurumu Basımevi.

Begemann, Friedrich, Ernst Pernicka, and Sigrid Schmitt-Strecker. 1994. Metal Finds from Ilıpınar and the Advent of Arsenic Copper. *Anatolica* 20: 203–19.

Biehl, Peter F. and Eva Rosenstock. 2009. Von Çatalhöyük Ost nach Çatalhöyük West. Kulturelle Umbrüche an der Schwelle vom 7. zum 6. Jt. v. Chr. in Zentralanatolien. In *Zurück zum Gegenstand. Festschrift für Andreas E. Furtwängler*, ed. Ralph Einicke, Stephan Lehmann, Henryk Löhr, Gundula Mehnert, Andreas Mehnert, and Anja Slawisch, 471–82. Langenweißbach: Beier and Beran.

Bilgi, Önder. 2001. *Protohistorik Çağ'da Orta Karadeniz Bölgesi Madencileri. Hind-Avrupalıların Anavatanı Sorununa Yeni bir Yaklaşım. Metallurgists of the Central Black Sea Region. A New Perspective on the Question of the Indo-Europeans' Original Homeland*. İstanbul: TASK Vakfı.

Bittel, Kurt. 1934. *Prähistorische Forschung in Kleinasien*. İstanbul: Deutsches Archäologisches Institut.

———. 1939. Archäologische Funde aus der Türkei 1934–1938. *Archäologischer Anzeiger* 1939: 94–207.

———. 1950. Zur Chronologie der anatolischen Frühkulturen. In *Reinecke Festschrift: zum 75. Geburtstag von Paul Reinecke am 25. September 1947*, ed. Gustav Behrens and Joachim Werner, 13–25. Mainz: E. Schneider.

Bıçakçı, Erhan, Çiler Altınbilek Algül, Semra Balcı, and Martin Godon. 2007. Tepecik-Çiftlik. In *Türkiye'de Neolitik Dönem. Anadolu'da Uyarlığın Doğuşu ve Avrupa'ya Yayılımı. Yeni Kazılar–Yeni Bulgular*, ed. Mehmet Özdoğan and Nezih Başgelen, 237–53. İstanbul: Arkeoloji ve Sanat Yayınları.

Caneva, Isabella and Veli Sevin, eds. 2004. *Mersin-Yumuktepe. A Reappraisal*. Lecce: Congedo Editore.

Çevik, Özlem. 2007. The Emergence of Different Social Systems in Early Bronze Age Anatolia: Urbanization versus Centralization. *Anatolian Studies* 57: 131–40.

Çilingiroğlu, Altan and Çiler Çilingiroğlu. 2007. Ulucak. In *Türkiye'de Neolitik Dönem. Anadolu'da Uyarlığın Doğuşu ve Avrupa'ya Yayılımı. Yeni Kazılar–Yeni Bulgular*, ed. Mehmet Özdoğan and Nezih Başgelen, 361–72. İstanbul: Arkeoloji ve Sanat Yayınları.

Çilingiroğlu, Altan, Zafer Derin, Eşref Abay, Haluk Sağlamtimur, and İlhan Kayan. 2004. *Ulucak Höyük. Excavations Conducted between 1995 and 2002*. Louvain: Peeters.

Çilingiroğlu, Çiler. 2009. Central-West Anatolia at the End of 7th and Beginning of 6th Millennium B.C.E. in the Light of Pottery from Ulucak (İzmir). Ph.D. dissertation. University of Tübingen. tobias-lib.uni-tuebingen.de/volltexte/2009/4278.

Derin, Zafer. 2007. Yeşilova Höyüğü. In *Türkiye'de Neolitik Dönem. Anadolu'da Uyarlığın Doğuşu ve Avrupa'ya Yayılımı. Yeni Kazılar–Yeni Bulgular*, ed. Mehmet Özdoğan and Nezih Başgelen, 377–84. İstanbul: Arkeoloji ve Sanat Yayınları.

Dittmann, Reinhard. 2009. Randnotizen zu den frühen Beziehungen Anatoliens. *Altorientalische Forschungen* 36: 3–15.

Duru, Refik. 1989. Were the Earliest Cultures at Hacılar Really Aceramic? In *Anatolia and the Ancient Near East. Studies in Honour of Tahsin Özgüç*, ed. Kutlu Emre, Barthel Hrouda, Machteld Mellink, and Nimet Özgüç, 99–106. Ankara: Türk Tarih Kurumu Basımevi.

———. 1996. *Kuruçay Höyük II: The Late Chalcolithic and Early Bronze Age Settlements*. Ankara: Türk Tarih Kurumu Basımevi.

———. 2008. *From 8000 BC to 2000 BC: Six Thousand Years of the Burdur-Antalya Region*. İstanbul: Suna-İnan Kıraç Akdeniz Medeniyetleri Araştırma Enstitüsü.

Düring, Bleda S. 2008. The Early Holocene Occupation of North-Central Anatolia between 10,000 and 6,000 BC cal: Investigating an Archaeological Terra Incognita. *Anatolian Studies* 58: 15–46.

Efe, Turan. 1990. An Inland Anatolian Site with Pre-Vinča Elements, Orman Fidanlığı, Eskişehir. A Reexamination of Balkan-Anatolian Connections in the Fifth Millennium B.C. *Germania* 68: 67–113.

———. 1996. The Excavations at Orman Fidanlığı, an Inland Anatolian Site with Pre-Vinča Elements. In *The Vinča Culture, its Role and Cultural Connections. International Symposium on the Vinča Culture, Timişoara, Romania, October 1995*, ed. Florin Draşovean, 41–58. Timişoara: Museum of Banat.

———. 2001. *The Salvage Excavations at Orman Fidanlığı: A Chalcolithic Site in Inland Northwestern Anatolia*. İstanbul: TASK.

Eggert, Manfred and Friedrich Lüth. 1987. Mersin und die absolute Chronologie des europäischen Neolithikums. *Germania* 65: 17–28.

Esin, Ufuk. 1982. Die kulturellen Beziehungen zwischen Ostanatolien und Mesopotamien sowie Syrien anhand einiger Grabungs-und Oberflächenfunde aus dem oberen Euphrattal im 4. Jt. v.Chr. In *Mesopotamien und seine Nachbarn. Politische und kulturelle Wechselbeziehungen im Alten Vorderasien vom 4. bis 1. Jahrtausend v.Chr. XXV*, ed. Hans-Jörg Nissen and Johannes Renger, 13–21. Rencontre Assyriologique Internationale Berlin 3. bis 7. Juli 1978. Berlin: Reimer.

———. 1993. Gelveri–ein Beispiel für die kulturellen Beziehungen zwischen Zentralanatolien und Südosteuropa während des Chalkolithikums. *Anatolica* 19: 47–56.

Eslick, Christine. 1980. Middle Chalcolithic Pottery from Southwest Anatolia. *American Journal of Archaeology* 84: 5–14.

———. 1992. *Elmalı-Karataş I: The Neolithic and Chalcolithic Periods, Bağbaşı and Other Sites*. Bryn Mawr, Pa.: Bryn Mawr Archaeological Monographs.

Felsch, Rainer C. S. 1988. *Das Kastro Tigani. Die spätneolithische und chalkolithische Siedlung*. Samos II. Bonn: Rudolf Habelt.

Frangipane, Marcella and Alba Palmieri. 1983. A Protourban Centre of the Late Uruk Period. In *Perspectives on Protourbanization in Eastern Anatolia: Arslantepe (Malatya). An Interim Report on the 1975–1983 Campaigns*, ed. Marcella Frangipane and Alba Palmieri. *Origini* 12: 287–454.

French, David H. 1998. *Canhasan Sites I, Stratigraphy and Structures*. London: British Institute of Archaeology at Ankara.

Gabriel, Utta. 2000. Mitteilungen zum Stand der Neolithikumsforschung in der Umgebung von Troia (Kumtepe 1993–1995; Beşik-Sivritepe 1983–1984, 1987, 1998–1999). *Studia Troica* 10: 233–38.

Gabriel, Utta, Rüstem Aslan, and Stephan W. E. Blum. 2004. Alacalıgöl: Eine neuentdeckte Siedlung des 5. Jahrtausends v. Chr. in der Troas. *Studia Troica* 14: 121–33.

Garstang, John. 1953. *Prehistoric Mersin, Yumuk Tepe in Southern Turkey*. Oxford: Clarendon Press.

Godon, Martin. 2005. New Results and Remarks about Neolithic Pottery in Central Anatolia: A View from Tepecik-Çiftlik. *Colloquium Anatolicum* 4: 91–103.

Goldman, Hetty. 1956. *Excavations at Gözlü Kule, Tarsus II. From the Neolithic through the Bronze Age*. Princeton, N.J.: Princeton University Press.

Gorny, Ronald L., Gregory McMahon, Samuel Paley, Sharon Steadman, and Bruce Verhaaren. 2002. The 2000 and 2001 Seasons at Çadır Höyük in Central Turkey: A Preliminary Report. *Anatolica* 28: 109–36.

Gülçur, Sevil. 2004. Güvercinkayası: The Black/Dark Burnished Pottery. A General Overview. *TÜBA-AR* 7: 141–64.

Günel, Sevinç. 2006. New Contributions to Western Anatolian Cultural History: Aydın Region Survey Project. *Praehistorische Zeitschrift* 81.2: 153–74.

——. 2008. Çine-Tepecik Kazıları ve Bölge Arkeolojisine Katkılar: In *Batı Anadolu ve Doğu Akdeniz Geç Tunç Çağı Kültürleri Üzerine Yeni Araştırmalar*, ed. Armağan Erkanal-Öktü, Sevinç Günel, and Ulaş Deniz, 129–39. Ankara: Hacettepe Üniversitesi Yayınları.

Herling, Lothar, Kirstin Kasper, Clemens Lichter, and Recep Meriç. 2008. Im Westen nichts Neues? Ergebnisse der Grabungen 2003 und 2004 in Dedecik-Heybelitepe. *Istanbuler Mitteilungen* 58: 13–65.

Hood, Sinclair. 1981. *Excavations in Chios 1938–1955. Prehistoric Emporio and Ayio Gala.* Athens: Thames and Hudson.

Horejs, Barbara. 2008. Erster Grabungsbericht zu den Kampagnen 2006 und 2007 am Çukuriçi Höyük bei Ephesos. *Jahreshefte des Österreichischen Archäologischen Instituts in Wien* 77: 91–106.

Karg, Norbert. 1999. Tarsus and Anatolian Chronology in Retrospect. *Olba* 2: 283–301.

Karul, Necmi. 2007. Aktopraklık. Kuzeybatı Anadolu'da Gelişkin Bir Köy. In *Türkiye'de Neolitik Dönem. Anadolu'da Uyarlığın Doğuşu ve Avrupa'ya Yayılımı. Yeni Kazılar-Yeni Bulgular*, ed. Mehmet Özdoğan and Nezih Başgelen, 387–92. İstanbul: Arkeoloji ve Sanat Yayınları.

Korfmann, Manfred. 2004. Zum Stand der Chronologiediskussion ca. 1980 oder "Zum absoluten Zeitansatz beim komparativen Stratigraphiesystem von V. Milojčić." Eine Rückschau. In *Zwischen Karpaten und Ägäis: Neolithikum und ältere Bronzezeit. Gedenkschrift für Viera Němejcová-Pavúková. Studia Honoraria 21*, ed. Bernhard Hänsel and Etela Studeníková, 109–19. Rahden/Westf.: Marie Leidorf.

Korfmann, Manfred, Çiğdem Girgin, Çiğdem Morçöl, and Sinan Kılıç. 1995. Kumtepe 1993. Bericht über die Rettungsgrabung. *Studia Troica* 5: 237–89.

Korfmann, Manfred and Bernd Kromer. 1993. Demircihüyük, Beşik-Tepe, Troia–Eine Zwischenbilanz zur Chronologie dreier Orte in Westanatolien. *Studia Troica* 3: 135–71.

Kuzucuoğlu, Catherine, Catherine Marro, Aslı Özdoğan, and Aksel Tibet. 1997. Prospection archéologique franco-turque dans la région de Kastamonu (Mer Noire). Deuxième rapport préliminaire. *Anatolia Antiqua* 5: 275–306.

Lichter, Clemens. 2005. Western Anatolia in the Late Neolithic and Early Chalcolithic: The Actual State of Research. In *How Did Farming Reach Europe? Anatolian-European Relations from the Second Half of the 7th through to the First Half of the 6th Millennium Cal BC*, ed. Clemens Lichter, 59–74. BYZAS 2. İstanbul: Ege Yayınları.

——. 2006. Varna und İkiztepe: Überlegungen zu transpontischen Kulturbeziehungen im 5. und 4. Jahrtausend. In *Hayat Erkanal'a Armağan: Kültürlerin Yansıması. Studies in Honor of Hayat Erkanal: Cultural Reflections*, ed. Armağan Erkanal-Öktü, Engin Özgen, Sevinç Günel, A. Tuba Ökse, Halime Hüryılmaz, Halil Tekin, Nazlı Çınardalı-Karaaslan, Bora Uysal, F. Ayşe Karaduman, Atilla Engin, Reinhild Spieß, Ayşegül Aykurt, Rıza Tuncel, Ulaş Deniz, and Ash Rennie, 526–34. İstanbul: Homer Kitabevi.

Lloyd, Seton and James Mellaart. 1962. *Beycesultan I: The Chalcolithic and Early Bronze Age Levels.* London: British Institute of Archaeology at Ankara.

Makkay, János. 1993. Pottery Links between Late Neolithic Cultures of the NW Pontic and Anatolia, and the Origins of the Hittites. *Anatolica* 19: 117–28.

Maran, Joseph. 2000. Das ägäische Chalkolithikum und das erste Silber in Europa. In *Studien zur Religion und Kultur Kleinasiens und des ägäischen Bereiches. Festschrift für Baki Öğün zum 75. Geburtstag* (Asia Minor Studien 39), ed. Cengiz Işık, 179–93. Bonn: Habelt.

Marro, Catherine. 2000. Archaeological Survey in the Kastamonu Region, Turkey: Remarks on the Preclassical Cultural Geography of the Southern Black Sea. In *Proceedings of the First International Congress on the Archaeology of the Ancient Near East. Rome, May 18th–23rd, 1998*, ed. Paolo Matthiae, Alessandra Enea, Luca Peyronel and Frances Pinnock, 945–65. Rome: Dipartimento di Scienze Storiche Archeologiche e Antropologiche dell'Antichità, Università di Roma "La Sapienza."

Matthews, Roger. 2009. Silent Centuries: Paphlagonia from the Palaeolithic to the Early Bronze Age, 200.000–200 BC. In *At Empires' Edge: Project Paphlagonia. Regional Survey in North-Central Turkey*, ed. Roger Matthews and Claudia Glatz, 75–105. London: British Institute at Ankara.

Mellaart, James. 1963. Early Cultures of the South Anatolian Plateau, II. The Late Chalcolithic and Early Bronze Ages in the Konya Plain. *Anatolian Studies* 13: 199–236.

———. 1965. Çatal Hüyük West. *Anatolian Studies* 15: 135–56.

———. 1970. *Excavations at Hacılar.* Edinburgh: Edinburgh University Press.

Milojčić, Vladimir. 1950/1951. Zur Chronologie der jüngeren Steinzeit Griechenlands. *Jahrbuch des Deutschen Archäologischen Institutes* 65/66: 1–90.

Orthmann, Winfried. 1963. *Die Keramik der frühen Bronzezeit aus Inneranatolien.* Istanbuler Forschungen 14. Berlin: Gebrüder Mann.

Özdoğan, Mehmet. 1991. Eastern Thrace before the Beginning of Troy I. An Archaeological Dilemma. In *Die Kupferzeit als historische Epoche. Symposion Saarbrücken und Otzenhausen 6.–13.11.1988*, ed. Jan Lichardus, 217–25. Bonn: Habelt.

———. 1996. Pre–Bronze Age Sequence of Central Anatolia: An Alternative Approach. In *Vom Halys zum Euphrat. Thomas Beran zu Ehren*, ed. Ursula Magen and Mahmoud Rashad, 185–202. Münster: Ugarit-Verlag.

———. 1997. The Beginning of Neolithic Economies in Southeastern Europe: An Anatolian Perspective. *Journal of European Archaeology* 5.2: 1–33.

———. 1999. Northwestern Turkey: Neolithic Cultures in between the Balkans and Anatolia. In *Neolithic in Turkey. The Cradle of Civilization*, ed. Mehmet Özdoğan and Nezih Başgelen, 201–24. İstanbul: Arkeoloji ve Sanat Yayınları.

Öztan, Aliye. 2007. Niğde-Bor Ovası'nda Bir Neolitik Yerleşim. In *Türkiye'de Neolitik Dönem. Anadolu'da Uyarlığın Doğuşu ve Avrupa'ya Yayılımı. Yeni Kazılar–Yeni Bulgular*, ed. Mehmet Özdoğan and Nezih Başgelen, 223–35. İstanbul: Arkeoloji ve Sanat Yayınları.

Öztan, Aliye and Süleyman Özkan. 2003. Çizi ve Nokta Bezeli Köşk Höyük Seramikleri. In *Köyden Kente. Yakındogu'da Ilk Yerleşimler. Ufuk Esin'e Armağan. From Village to Cities. Early Villages in the Near East. Studies Presented to Ufuk Esin*, ed. Mehmet Özdoğan, Harald Hauptmann, and Nezih Başgelen, 447–58. İstanbul: Arkeoloji ve Sanat Yayınları.

Palumbi, Giulio. 2003. Red-Black Pottery: Eastern Anatolia and Transcaucasian Relationships around the Mid-Fourth Millennium BC. *Ancient Near Eastern Studies* 40: 80–134.

———. 2008. Mid-Fourth Millennium Red-Black Burnished Wares from Anatolia: A Cross-Comparison. In *Ceramics in Transition: Chalcolithic through Iron Age in the Highlands of Caucasus and Anatolia*, ed. Karen S. Rubinson and Antonio Sagona, 39–58. Louvain: Peeters.

Parzinger, Hermann. 1993a. Zur Zeitstellung der Büyükkaya-Ware: Bemerkungen zur vorbronzezeitlichen Kulturfolge Zentralanatoliens. *Anatolica* 19: 211–29.

———. 1993b. *Studien zur Chronologie und Kulturgeschichte der Jungstein-, Kupfer-und Frühbronzezeit zwischen Karpaten und mittlerem Taurus.* Mainz: von Zabern.

Peschlow-Bindokat, Anneliese. 2003. *Frühe Menschenbilder. Die prähistorischen Felsmalereien des Latmos-Gebirges (Westtürkei).* Mainz: von Zabern.

Roodenberg, Jacob J., ed. 1995. *The Ilıpınar Excavations I*. Leiden: Nederlands Institut voor het Nabije Oosten.

Roodenberg, Jacob. 2001. A Late Chalcolithic Cemetery at Ilıpınar in Northwestern Anatolia. In *Lux Orientis. Archäologie zwischen Asien und Europa. Festschrift für Harald Hauptmann zum 65. Geburtstag*, ed. Rainer Michael Boehmer and Joseph Maran, 351–55. Rahden: Marie Leidorf.

Roodenberg, Jacob J. and Songül Alpaslan Roodenberg, eds. 2008. *Life and Death in a Prehistoric Settlement in Northwest Anatolia. The Ilıpınar Excavations III. With Contributions on Hacılartepe and Menteşe*. Leiden: Nederlands Institut voor het Nabije Oosten.

Roodenberg, Jacob J. and Laurens C. Thissen, eds. 2001. *The Ilıpınar Excavations II*. Leiden: Nederlands Institut voor het Nabije Oosten.

Roodenberg, Jacob J., Abram van As, and Songül Alpaslan Roodenberg. 2008. Barcın Hüyük in the Plain of Yenişehir (2005–2006). A Preliminary Note on the Fieldwork, Pottery and Human Remains of the Prehistoric Levels. *Anatolica* 34: 53–66.

Sağlamtimur, Haluk. 2007. Ege Gübre Neolitik Yerleşimi. In *Türkiye'de Neolitik Dönem. Anadolu'da Uyarlığın Doğuşu ve Avrupa'ya Yayılımı. Yeni Kazılar–Yeni Bulgular*, ed. Mehmet Özdoğan and Nezih Başgelen, 373–76. İstanbul: Arkeoloji ve Sanat Yayınları.

Schachermayr, Fritz. 1949/1950. Die orientalisch-mittelmeerischen Grundlagen der vorgeschichtlichen Chronologie. *Praehistorische Zeitschrift* 34/35.I: 17–48.

Schachner, Andreas. 1999. *Von der Rundhütte zum Kaufmannshaus. Kulturhistorische Untersuchungen zur Entwicklung prähistorischer Wohnhäuser in Zentral-, Ost-und Südostanatolien*. Oxford: Archaeopress.

Schoop, Ulf-Dietrich. 2002. Frühneolithikum im südwestanatolischen Seengebiet? Eine kritische Betrachtung. In *Mauerschau. Festschrift für Manfred Korfmann*, ed. Rüstem Aslan, Stephan Blum, Gabriele Kastl, Frank Schweizer, and Diane Thumm, 421–36. Remshalden-Grunbach: BA Greiner.

———. 2005a. *Das anatolische Chalkolithikum. Eine chronologische Untersuchung zur vorbronzezeitlichen Kultursequenz im nördlichen Zentralanatolien und den angrenzenden Gebieten*. Remshalden-Grunbach: BA Greiner.

———. 2005b. Early Chalcolithic in North-Central Anatolia: The Evidence from Boğazköy-Büyükkaya. *TÜBA-AR* 8: 15–37.

———. 2005c. The Late Escape of the Neolithic from the Central Anatolian Plain. In *How Did Farming Reach Europe? Anatolian-European Relations from the Second Half of the 7th through to the First Half of the 6th Millennium cal BC. Proceedings of the International Workshop Istanbul, May 20–22, 2004*. BYZAS 2, ed. Clemens Lichter, 41–58. İstanbul: Ege Yayınları.

———. 2008. Ausgrabungen in Çamlıbel Tarlası 2007. In *Die Ausgrabungen in Boğazköy-Ḫattuša 2007. Archäologischer Anzeiger* 2008: 148–57.

———. 2009. Ausgrabungen in Çamlıbel Tarlası 2008. In *Die Ausgrabungen in Boğazköy-Ḫattuša 2008. Archäologischer Anzeiger* 2009: 56–67.

Schwarzberg, Heiner. 2005. Prismatic Polypod Vessels and Their Way to Europe. In *How Did Farming Reach Europe? Anatolian-European Relations from the Second Half of the Seventh through the First Half of the Sixth Millennium cal BC*, ed. Clemens Lichter, 255–73. *BYZAS* 2. İstanbul: Ege Yayınları.

———. 2006. Figurale Ständer–Sozialkeramik des frühen Neolithikums aus Kırklareli-Aşağı Pınar, Türkisch-Thrakien. *TÜBA-AR* 9: 97–123.

Seeher, Jürgen. 1985. Vorläufiger Bericht über die Keramik des Beşik-Sivritepe. *Archäologischer Anzeiger* 1985: 172–82.

———. 1987a. *Demircihüyük III.1: Die Keramik 1. A: Die Neolithische und chalkolithische Keramik. B: Die frühbronzezeitliche Keramik der älteren Phasen (bis Phase G)*. Mainz: von Zabern.

———. 1987b. Prähistorische Funde aus Gülpınar-Chryse. Neue Belege für einen vortrojanischen Horizont an der Nordwestküste Kleinasiens. *Archäologischer Anzeiger* 1987: 533–56.

———. 1989. Antalya yakınlarında Karain mağarasındaki kalkolitik buluntuları. *Araştırma Sonuçları Toplantısı* 5: 221–38.

———. 1990. Der Übergang vom Neolithikum zum Chalkolithikum in Nordwestanatolien. Türk Tarih Kongresi X, Ankara 22–26 Eylül 1986. Kongreye sunulan bildiriler, 57–64. Ankara: Türk Tarih Kurumu Basımevi.

———. 1992. Die kleinasiatischen Marmorstatuetten vom Typ Kiliya. *Archäologischer Anzeiger* 1992: 153–70.

Sharp Joukowsky, Martha. 1986. *Prehistoric Aphrodisias. An Account of the Excavations and Artifact Studies*. Providence, R.I.: Brown University, Center for Old World Archaeology and Art.

Sperling, Jerome. 1976. Kumtepe in the Troad: Trial Excavations 1934. *Hesperia* 45: 305–64.

Steadman, Sharon R. 1995. Prehistoric Interregional Interaction in Anatolia and the Balkans: An Overview. *Bulletin of the American Schools of Oriental Research* 299/300: 13–32.

———. 2000. Spatial Patterning and Social Complexity on Anatolian Tell Sites: Models for Mounds. *Journal of Anthropological Archaeology* 19.2: 164–99.

Steadman, Sharon R., Gregory McMahon, and Jennifer C. Ross. 2007. The Late Chalcolithic at Çadır Höyük in Central Anatolia. *Journal of Field Archaeology* 32: 385–406.

Steadman, Sharon R., Jennifer C. Ross, Gregory McMahon, and Ronald L. Gorny. 2008. Excavations on the North-Central Plateau: The Chalcolithic and Early Bronze Age Occupation at Çadır Höyük. *Anatolian Studies* 58: 47–86.

Summers, Geoffrey D. 1991. Chalcolithic Pottery from Kabakulak (Niğde) Collected by Ian Todd. *Anatolian Studies* 41: 125–31.

———. 1993. The Chalcolithic Period in Central Anatolia. In *The Fourth Millennium. Proceedings of the International Symposium Nessebuhr*, ed. Petya Georgieva, 29–33. Sofia: Nov Bŭlgarski Universitet.

Takaoğlu, Turan. 2005. *A Chalcolithic Marble Workshop at Kulaksızlar in Western Anatolia. An Analysis of Production and Craft Specialization*. Oxford: Archaeopress.

———. 2006. The Late Neolithic in the Eastern Aegean: Excavations at Gülpınar in the Troad. *Hesperia* 75: 289–315.

Thissen, Laurens. 1993. New Insights in Balkan-Anatolian Connections in the Late Chalcolithic: Old Evidence from the Turkish Black Sea Littoral. *Anatolian Studies* 43: 207–37.

———. 2002. Appendix I: CANeW 14C databases and 14C charts, Anatolia, 10,000–5000 cal BC. In *The Neolithic of Central Anatolia. Internal Developments and External Relations during the 9th–6th Millennia cal BC. Proceedings of the International CANeW Table Ronde Istanbul, November 23–24, 2001*, ed. Frédéric Gérard and Laurens Thissen, 299–337. İstanbul: Ege Yayınları.

———. 2008. The Pottery of Phase Vb. In *Life and Death in a Prehistoric Settlement in Northwest Anatolia. The Ilıpınar Excavations III. With Contributions on Hacılartepe and Menteşe, ed. Jacob J. Roodenberg and Songül Alpaslan Roodenberg, 91–115*. Leiden: Nederlands Institut voor het Nabije Oosten.

Ünlüsoy, Sinan. 2002. Neolithische und chalkolithische Steinarmringe: Untersuchungen zur Chronologie und Verbreitung von Steinarmringen im Nahen Osten und in der

Ägäis. In *Mauerschau. Festschrift für Manfred Korfmann*, ed. Rüstem Aslan, Stephan Blum, Gabriele Kastl, Frank Schweizer, and Diane Thumm, 541–66. Remshalden-Grunbach: BA Greiner.

von der Osten, Hans Henning. 1937. *The Alishar Hüyük. Seasons of 1930–32*. Part III. OIP XXX. Researches in Anatolia vol. IX. Chicago: University of Chicago Press.

Weippert, Helga. 1991. Metallzeitalter und Kulturepochen. *Zeitschrift des deutschen Palästina-Vereins* 107: 1–23.

Yakar, Jak. 2006. The Ethno-Cultural Affiliation of the North-Anatolian Early Bronze Age. In *Hayat Erkanal'a Armağan: Kültürlerin Yansıması. Studies in Honor of Hayat Erkanal: Cultural Reflections*, ed. Armağan Erkanal-Öktü, Engin Özgen, Sevinç Günel, A. Tuba Ökse, Halime Hüryılmaz, Halil Tekin, Nazlı Çınardalı-Karaaslan, Bora Uysal, F. Ayşe Karaduman, Atilla Engin, Reinhild Spieß, Ayşegül Aykurt, Rıza Tuncel, Ulaş Deniz, and Ash Rennie, 809–14. İstanbul: Homer Kitabevi.

Yener, K. Aslıhan. 2000. *The Domestication of Metals. The Rise of Complex Metal Industries in Anatolia*. Leiden: Brill.

Zimmermann, Thomas. 2004–2005. Early Daggers in Anatolia—A Necessary Reappraisal. *Anodos* 4–5: 251–62.

———. 2007. Anatolia and the Balkans, Once Again—Ring-Shaped Idols from Western Asia and a Critical Reassessment of Some "Early Bronze Age" Items from İkiztepe, Turkey. *Oxford Journal of Archaeology* 26: 25–33.

CHAPTER 8

THE CHALCOLITHIC OF SOUTHEAST ANATOLIA

RANA ÖZBAL

THE Chalcolithic period in southwest Asia covers over 3,000 years, from the beginning of the sixth to the end of the fourth millennium cal B.C.E. In comparison with the well-researched Neolithic and the Urban Revolutions between which it is sandwiched, the Chalcolithic has received considerably less attention. Because it is geographically part of the Fertile Crescent, the archaeological styles, cultural elements, and developments in southeast Anatolia were closely connected to those in northern Mesopotamia. Trade and economic relations continuing over the millennia and analogous social and political trajectories have contributed to a high degree of regional interdependence. Moreover, the lack of well-defined local southeast Anatolian ceramic sequences (excluding perhaps the Amuq region), has resulted in a threefold division of the cultural chronology based on the better defined northern Mesopotamian Halaf, Ubaid, and Uruk or Late Chalcolithic phases. The easily distinguishable painted wares of the Halaf and Ubaid periods and the distinctive shapes of the Uruk phase are such hallmarks that they tend to override local ceramic assemblages. Moreover, local ware groups seem to show variability within southeast Anatolia, and identifying dominant supraregional styles has proved difficult. One of our aims should be to construct local typochronological markers and to see how they vary from subregion to subregion.

Although the cultural similarity between these supraregional areas during the Chalcolithic is undeniable, one could argue, especially for the Halaf and Ubaid phases, that some of the stylistic overlap may be a result of Mesopotamia-centric research traditions and related biases in publications. Distinct local and regional differences between southeast Anatolia and the north Mesopotamian steppe cannot be ignored. This chapter attempts to provide a balanced overview of both local and Mesopotamian-influenced styles and traditions in the Chalcolithic of this region. Rather than supply the reader with a compendium of every excavated Chalcolithic site, I outline general characteristics and present a few key settlements. The discussion of the Chalcolithic is chronologically divided into millennia, based on calibrated dates. The sixth, fifth, and fourth millennia B.C.E., respectively, roughly refer to the Early, Middle, and Late Chalcolithic in which Halaf-, Ubaid-, and Uruk-type materials are correspondingly prevalent.

Overall, the Chalcolithic of Anatolia has come a long way from the "dark age" that it was labeled three decades ago (Burney 1977:118, 120). In particular, the Upper Euphrates Valley in southeast Anatolia has been intensively researched since the late 1970s as surveys and excavations have focused in regions affected by dam lakes, and as many Mesopotamian archaeologists have set up research projects in Turkey following the Gulf Wars.

Geography

Archaeologically speaking, the most important geographical features characterizing this region are the Euphrates and Tigris River valleys, since most known Chalcolithic sites are located along the rivers and their tributaries (figures 8.1, 8.2). These riverine environments have been the most intensively surveyed and investigated, especially, as mentioned, prior to the many dam-building projects.

Southeast Anatolia is bounded to the north by the 2,000–3,000 m high Taurus and Anti-Taurus mountain chains. Earlier assumptions that the mountain range marked the limit of north Mesopotamian influence (e.g., Dönmez and Brice 1949) have been challenged by the discovery of "Esh-Sheikh-type" Ubaid wares in the Elbistan Plain (Brown 1967) as well as Halaf, Ubaid, and Uruk-related pottery in the Keban Dam area of the Upper Euphrates region (Aksoy and Diamant 1973; Esin and Arsebük 1974; Gülçur 2000; Hauptmann 1976, 1982; van Loon 1978; Wright and Whallon 1998). North Mesopotamian–influenced occupation during the Chalcolithic also occurs on the highland plateaus and the undulating piedmont zones of Maraş, Adıyaman, Malatya, Muş, Diyarkabır, Batman, and Van, which form the Taurus foothills (Blaylock 1998; Blaylock, French, and Summers 1990; Carter et al. 1997; Carter, Campbell, and Snead 1999; Gürdil 2002; Korfmann 1982; Ozan forthcoming; Parker and Creekmore 2002; Reilly 1940; Rothman and Kozbe 1997; Yakar and Gürsan-Salzmann 1978). To the south of the foothills lie the lowland plains of the Amuq, İslahiye, Kilis, Birecik, Suruç, Harran, Mardin, Cizre, and Silopi, west to east, respectively.

The Euphrates and Tigris Rivers cut through these landforms, forming steep gorges in some places and broad alluvial plains in others, further shaping the geography. The two river valleys are geologically divided by the Karacadağ volcanic

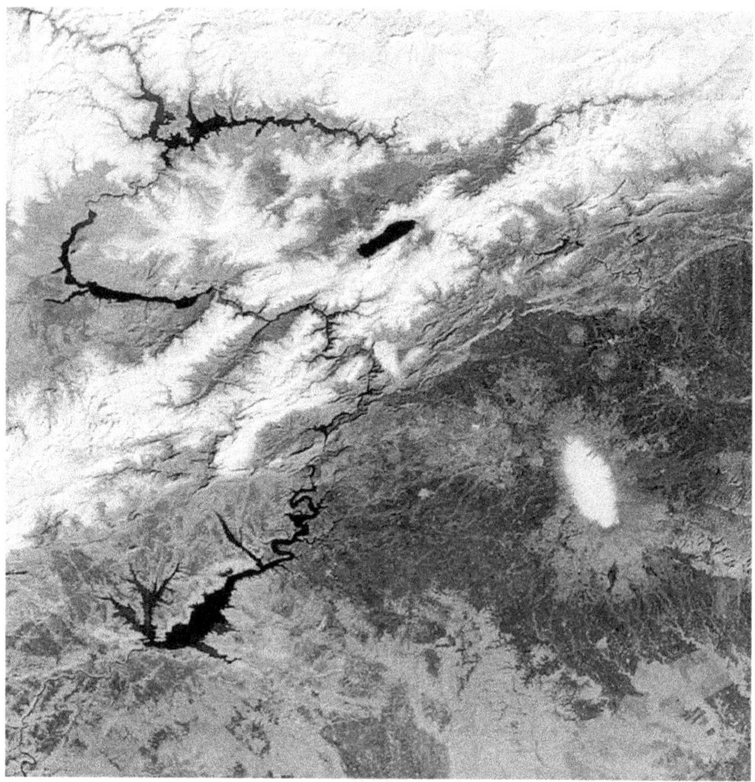

Figure 8.1. Satellite image by "Earth Snapshot Chelys," which shows the snowcapped Taurus Mountain chain in the north from which both the Tigris and Euprates Rivers originate. Notable also are the Keban, Karakaya, and Atatürk (or Karababa) Dam lakes on the Euphrates from north to south, respectively. The highland lake surrounded by snow is the seismically active Hazar Lake, which is known to be one of the sources of the Tigris. The nearly 2,000 m high Karacadağ Mountain stands out in the center right of the image.

basalt-rich massif near Diyarbakır, which rises to a height of 1,938 m (see figure 8.1; Erinç 1980). The region to the west of Karacadağ is characterized by the low-lying limestone plateaus of Urfa and Gaziantep. In contrast to gently rolling hills and plateaus found to the west, to the east of the Karacadağ Massif one finds a characteristically rugged terrain. The Diyarbakır Basin, cut diagonally—northwest to southeast—by the Tigris River, is bordered to the north by the Taurus Mountains and to the south by the Tur Abdin outcrop or the so-called Mardin-Midyat threshold, which rises to a height of 1,200–1,300 m.

Much of the mountain ranges remains unsurveyed, so it is difficult to assess highland habitation during the Chalcolithic period, yet research by Casana and Wilkinson in the Amanos Mountain Range yielded Middle and Late Chalcolithic sites such as AS 238 (Serinyol Kale) and AS 246 (Çakallı Karakol) strategically located within the Belen Pass, the route between the Mediterranean and the Amuq Plain (Casana 2003:214–15; Casana and Wilkinson 2005). Clearly, other geographically notable mountain passes in southeast Anatolia and beyond must have been occupied in prehistory, and future research will no doubt bring them to light.

The Sixth Millennium (Cal B.C.E.)

The beginning of the Chalcolithic in southeast Anatolia traditionally corresponds with the origin and proliferation of Halaf-type painted pottery[1] in northern Mesopotamia around 6000 or 5900 cal B.C.E. (Campbell 2007; Cruells and Nieuwenhuyse 2004; Nieuwenhuyse 2007; and see Rosenberg and Erim-Özdoğan, chapter 6, and Castro Gessner, chapter 35 in this volume). This is not to say that painted pottery was absent prior to the sixth millennium B.C.E., but it was less common than other wares. Dark-Faced Burnished Wares were the most dominant ware group in Syro-Cilicia during the Neolitihic or the Amuq A and B Phases (Balossi 2004; Braidwood and Braidwood 1960), whereas light-colored, unburnished, and often chaff tempered wares seem to characterize the pottery traditions further to the east (Campbell 1992; Cruells and Nieuwenhuyse 2004; Miyake 2007; Nieuwenhuyse 2007; Özdoğan and Özdoğan 1993; Tekin 2003, 2007; but see Nieuwenhuyse, Akkermans and van der Plicht 2010). More than a chronological shift, the widespread appearance of painted wares marks a notable change in pottery production technologies and suggests salient changes in social organization (Campbell 2007:128).

The styles, motifs, and shapes of painted Halafian pottery across all the sites in the region are easily distinguishable and identifiable. Besides obvious advantages

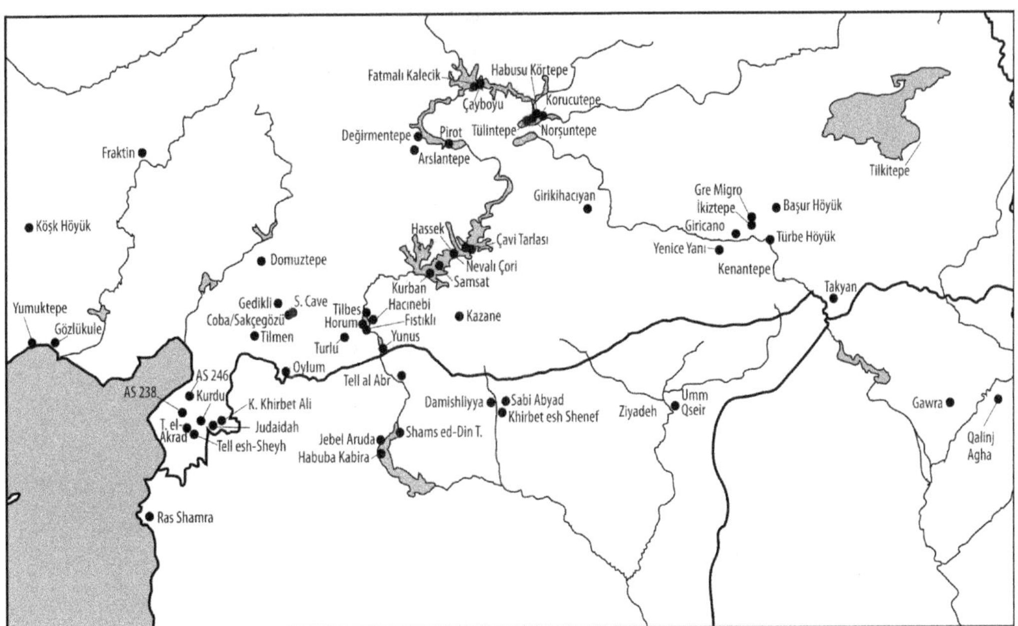

Figure 8.2. Map of sites mentioned in the text.

for archaeologists, this pottery type bears the drawback of becoming pigeonholed into a culture group that has been described as being remarkably homogenous (Redman 1978; see Castro Gessner, chapter 35 in this volume, for additional discussion on this topic). In addition to distinctively painted pottery, Halafian cultural elements typically (although not exclusively) include geometric stamp seals and circular buildings often with rectangular antechambers referred to as *tholoi* (Matthews 2003; Redman 1978; Watson 1983). Although some level of cultural overlap is indisputable, at times sites with a minor percentage of Halafian-type painted sherds among a large corpus of local wares and other local elements become engulfed in this umbrella term.

Virtually all Early Chalcolithic sites in southeast Anatolia and beyond—into the Keban area, the Lake Van region, as well as the Cilician coast—have yielded Halaf painted pottery, although ceramic percentages in many cases are drastically lower than at sites in northern Syria and Iraq. Instead, chaff/vegetal or grit tempered plain wares dominate assemblages in most sites (e.g., Algaze 1989:224ff; Bernbeck and Pollock 2003; Blaylock, French, and Summers 1990:93; Rosenberg and Toğul 1991:244; von Wickede and Herbordt 1988:20; Watson and LeBlanc 1990; Woolley 1934:151). Unfortunately, the disproportional focus on decorated ceramics has led to an underrepresentation of unpainted wares in publications. A basic assessment of formal, functional, stylistic, or technological characteristics of local assemblages across southeast Anatolia, however, suggests considerable regional variability and little in terms of supraregional connections. Hence Halafian type wares are among the few that "unify" the diverse range of ceramic traditions in the sixth millennium B.C.E., perhaps justifying why these painted ceramics have gained so much attention (Akdeniz 2004).

Traditionally, the Halafians of northern Mesopotamia have been characterized as sedentary farmers (Watson 1983:238). However, new evidence (and the reassessment of old evidence, e.g., Pollock forthcoming) from Syrian sites like Khirbet esh-Shenef, Damishliyya, Umm Qseir, and possibly Shams ed-Din Tannira suggest that pastoral herding may also have been practiced and that some sixth millennium B.C.E. inhabitants followed semi-nomadic or seasonally based pastoral lifestyles centered around animal husbandry (Akkermans 1993; Akkermans and Schwartz 2003:117–21; Akkermans and Wittmann 1993; Pollock forthcoming; Seeden and Kaddour 1983; Uerpmann 1982). The idea that semi-nomadic populations were on the move and in constant contact and communication with sedentary sites and their residents provides a mechanism through which Halafian material elements and ideas became distributed across distant regions.

Recently, researchers have proposed that a nomadic or transhumant lifestyle may also be the case for contemporaneous sites in southeast Anatolia as well. This has been argued for Fıstıklı Höyük (Bernbeck and Pollock 2003) and more recently for Çavi Tarlası (Pollock forthcoming). At Yunus (Carchemish) the "superimposed . . . temporary kilns" (Woolley 1934:149) excavated by Woolley are quite clearly tholoi, probably also representing seasonal occupation. In fact, Woolley recognizes their short-term nature and suggests that they "may well be separated by months rather than years" (1934:149). One wonders, moreover, whether the frequent incidences of abandonment and reoccupation at Girikihacıyan could similarly be considered evidence for short seasonal occupation (Watson and LeBlanc 1990). Tholoi of comparable construction and proportions were found at Kurban Höyük (Marfoe and Ingraham 1990:25–28), Tell Turlu (Breniquet 1987, 1991), and at Nevalı Çori (Mellink 1991:127–28), although more detailed analysis of the architecture and stratigraphy as well as faunal/seasonality studies must be done for all the above-mentioned sites to assess whether some of their inhabitants were indeed (semi-)nomadic (see Castro Gessner, chapter 35 in this volume).

In addition to small seasonal campsites arguably for transhumant groups, the Early Chalcolithic in southeast Anatolia has yielded new evidence for settlements that clearly do not conform to this model. The region harbors a few sites with Halaf affiliation of previously unheard-of sizes, ranging between ten and twenty hectares, including Takyan Höyük (twelve hectares), Kazane Höyük (twenty hectares), Domuztepe (twenty hectares), Tell Kurdu (twelve to fifteen hectares), and possibly Samsat (Algaze 1989:229; Algaze et al. 1991; Bernbeck, Pollock, and Coursey 1999; Blaylock, French, and Summers 1990:89; Campbell et al. 1999; Carter, Campbell, and Gauld 2003; Özbal, Gerritsen, and Yener 2003; Özbal et al. 2004; Yener et al. 2000a, 2000b). At Domuztepe, the excavators have demonstrated occupation across the whole twenty-hectare site (Campbell et al. 1999), but for the other settlements it must still be established what proportion was occupied simultaneously.

Nonetheless, these settlements stand out as being substantially larger than most other contemporaneous sites in northern Mesopotamia and beyond; they may, in fact, represent regional centers in a two- or three-tiered settlement hierarchy. While Takyan Höyük awaits excavation (Algaze et al. 1991:195; Kozbe 2006, 2007), Kazane, Domuztepe, and Tell Kurdu, investigated in recent years, have yielded evidence that is bringing new perspectives to how this period and the Halafian connections can be interpreted. Much information comes from Domuztepe, where excavations have been continuing for more than a decade. Research has yielded a "Death Pit" in which disarticulated and butchered bones of at least thirty-eight individuals mixed in with faunal remains were found (Kansa and Campbell 2002; Kansa et al. 2009). The disproportionally high percentage of cattle bones in the Death Pit indicates that this species may have carried special importance. Bucranium-adorned ceramics have long been viewed as a signature characteristic of the Halaf period, but the discovery of cattle in ritual contexts as at Domuztepe brings their probable ceremonial attributes to the fore. Cattle also appear to have special significance at other large excavated sixth millennium B.C.E. sites such as Kazane Höyük and Tell Kurdu. At the former site, a cache of over fifty-six cattle astragali (McCarty 2009) and at the latter, the discovery of a minimum number of five cows in what appears to be a refuse concentration (R. Özbal 2006) as well as caches of bovid horn-cores in liminal locales (Özbal et al. 2004) may indicate that cattle were connected to ritual practices and/or feasts. Though few of the large sixth millennium B.C.E. sites have been extensively excavated, this evidence suggests that different worldviews or subsistence strategies may have prevailed at these settlements than were at the smaller seasonally occupied sites. One interesting question worth researching is whether such concentrations of cattle bones are present also in smaller sites and to assess whether this species carried comparable significance. It is well known that in southwest Asia transhumant populations today are often sheep and goat herders (Tapper 1979:53–56; e.g., Barth 1953, 1965; Ehmann 1975:59–64; Irons 1972, 1974, 1975; also see Arbuckle 2006). In the Late Neolithic levels at the small site of Sabi Abyad, which yielded convincing evidence for (semi-)nomadism, for example, sheep/goat comprises 70 percent of the faunal remains (Cavallo 1996:477).

The broad exposures yielded by the excavations at Domuztepe also bring insights to aspects of community organization. The excavators propose that the settlement may have been divided into different quarters or wards by intentionally laid and maintained ditches, requiring us to reconceptualize how we envision intrasite dynamics at this time (Carter and Campbell 2008:124). Perhaps most surprising has been a vessel with an image of gabled-roofed buildings (Carter and Campbell 2008:125). Carter and Campbell have identified a roughly contemporaneous structural parallel on a seal from Arpachiyah (Mallowan and Rose 1935:fig. 51:4) suggesting that this architectural tradition may extend far beyond the Maraş Plain. Architecture considered unusual for the Halaf period was also encountered at the Amuq C levels of Tell Kurdu where rectangular buildings were discovered aligned along streets built in an agglutinative style typical of Anatolian settlements (figure 8.3; Özbal et al. 2004; R. Özbal 2006).

Overall, these sites located in modern-day Turkey, far from what has traditionally been viewed as the Halafian "heartland," are interesting because they add depth and variability to the Halaf period, which until recently has been viewed as a static cultural whole. Moreover, the fusion and amalgamation of local and Halaf cultural styles has brought many insights toward understanding the intricate dynamics of the sixth millennium B.C.E. in northern Mesopotamia and southeastern Anatolia.

Toward the end of the sixth millennium B.C.E., Ubaid type pottery begins to appear across sites in northern Mesopotamia (Evin 1995:15). Often referred to as the Halaf-Ubaid Transitional (HUT) Phase (Breniquet 1996; Campbell 2007; Copeland 1979:261; Davidson 1977; Davidson and Watkins 1981; Mallowan 1946), this rather short period is usually included either within Halaf or Ubaid chronologies and is poorly defined. However, when we look at the available data *beyond* northern Iraq, where Halafian or Ubaid painted ceramics tend to capture most interest, we are able to identify pottery traditions that exemplify this phase of transition.

For the northern Levant and beyond, but best known at sites like Tell Kurdu (Amuq D) and Ras Shamra (Phase IV B-A), the HUT is typified by characteristic types of surface treatments like red-wash ware (Leenders 1989) and shapes like bow rim vessels (Davidson 1977; Davidson and Watkins 1981:fig. 3). A similar instance where the assemblage is not overwhelmed by the more alluring Halafian pottery and other local ceramic traditions gain importance can be found in the Keban area. This is a unique region that amalgamates both traditions that swept east–west across central and eastern Anatolia as well as north Mesopotamian traditions from the south. Here sites spanning this phase such as Korucutepe, Habusu Körtepe,

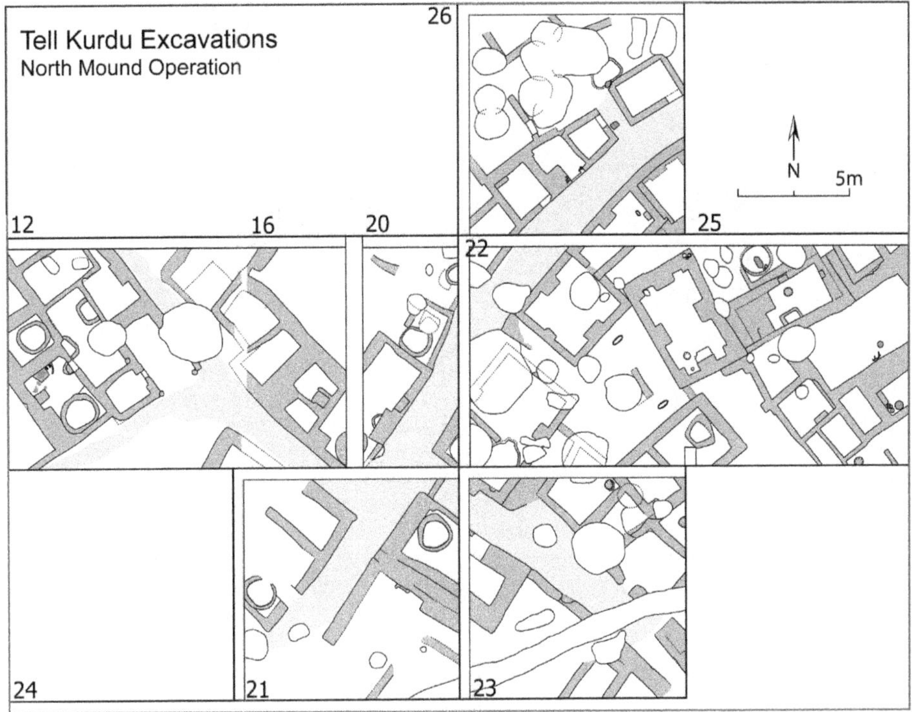

Figure 8.3. Settlement plan of the Amuq C levels at Tell Kurdu (after Özbal 2006:fig. 1.3).

Norşuntepe, and Tülintepe yielded examples of Graphite or Mica-Slipped Ware (MSW) (Arsebük 1979; Esin 1993; Gülçur 2000; Hauptmann 1976; van Loon 1978; Whallon 1979). Esin classifies MSW, often decorated in relief, as a "local fabric in the Keban region which did not reach south of the Plain of Malatya" (1993:106). The tradition of plastic decoration found in the Keban region at this time appears to be akin to the Chalcolithic sites in central Anatolia.

By far the best known and most thoroughly excavated site that spans this period is Tülintepe, in the Altınova Plain, where excavations were able to expose over 2,000 m^2 of deposits (figure 8.4). Large proportions of a village, which at its maximum extent would have been comprised of approximately thirty-five houses, were uncovered (Arsebük 1983). Rectangular mudbrick buildings, each with a large living space surrounded by depots, entry rooms, or oven spaces, were identified (Özbaşaran 1992). Although the houses are free-standing, the need for streets, as evident in Phase 2, suggests that in a more mature and circumscribed phase, the architectural set-up could eventually have developed into the agglutinative plan typical of Anatolian settlements (Steadman 2000). Halafian-like and Ubaid type painted ceramics are rare at Tülintepe, but they exceed the percentages from other contemporaneous sites in the Altınova Plain (Özbaşaran 1992).

Based on Garstang's excavations at Mersin Yumuktepe, Level XVI has typically been assigned to the transition from the Halaf to the Ubaid period (Caneva 2004;

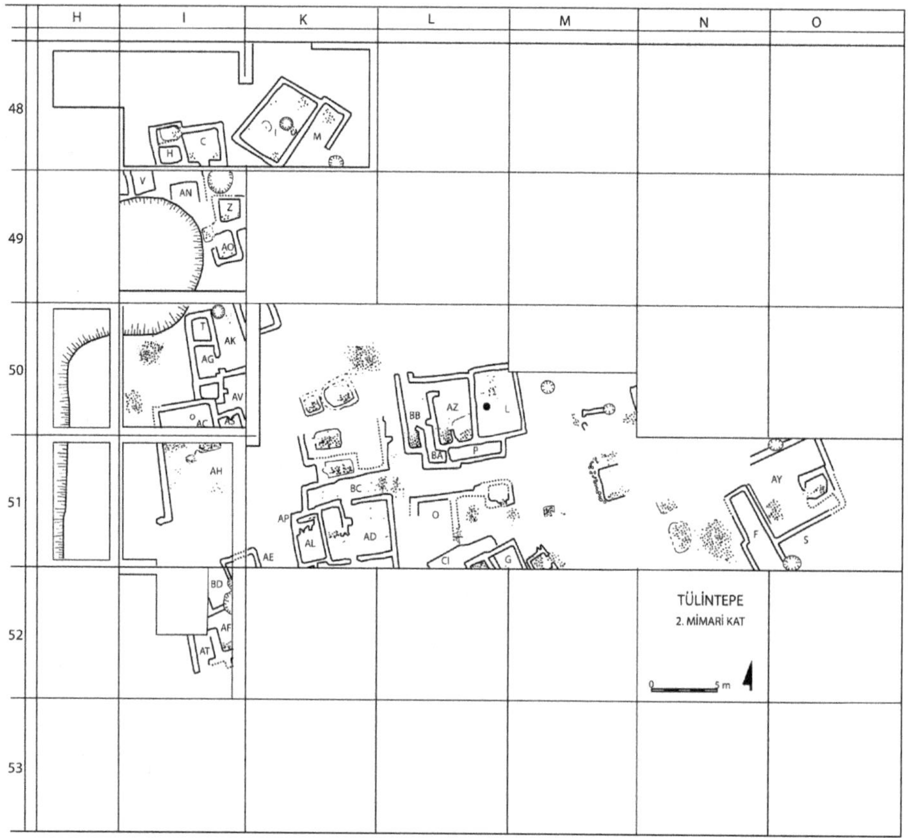

Figure 8.4. Settlement plan of Tülintepe Level 2 (after Özbaşaran 1992:fig. 22).

Garstang 1953:141–42). However, given that one finds Ubaid-like motifs already in Levels XIX–XVII (Braidwood and Braidwood 1960:509) it may prove useful to reanalyze a larger corpus of both the plain and painted wares of Chalcolithic Yumuktepe.[2] In terms of architecture, renewed excavations of Mersin Level XVI and the discovery of complex terracing activities have shown that the exposed structures of this phase show considerable variability (Caneva 2004; see also Garstang 1953:fig. 79; Garstang and Goldman 1947:379). Nonetheless, the overall plan of arrangement around an open courtyard is also found at the contemporaneous levels of not too distant Köşk Höyük Level 1, located near the Niğde Pass (Arbuckle 2006:fig. 2.13; and see Schoop, chapter 7 in this volume). Ceramics found at Mersin that have been interpreted as imitation Halafian wares (Davidson 1977) are missing from Koşk Höyük, but relief decoration (like that described for Tülintepe) is a common form of vessel adornment (Öztan 2002).

Few other sites spanning the HUT have been excavated in southeastern Turkey. Although represented at Tell Kurdu during the Amuq D phase, perhaps in Level A at Korucutepe, and Level XIV at Pirot Höyük, too little is known about the period in question at these sites. Sites like Domuztepe end just at this critical period and cannot be used to further define this amorphous transitional phase (Campbell 2007; Campbell and Fletcher 2010). However, precisely because this period straddles a transient and short-lived window in which neither Halaf nor Ubaid influences were particularly strong, further research could prove promising for highlighting local chronologies, wares, and styles. This may ultimately shift the emphasis to the local, rather than to one of the two dominant cultures, which dictate the Chalcolithic of eastern and southeastern Anatolia and Syro-Cilicia.

The Fifth Millennium (Cal b.c.e.)

North Mesopotamian Ubaid influences in southeast Anatolia intensify in the fifth millennium B.C.E. However, our information on social, political, and economic issues and daily life as well as the significant question of how Ubaid influences change these aspects is limited because this is the most poorly investigated phase of the Chalcolithic period in this region. Painted Ubaid wares are known to have reached far beyond the north Mesopotamian steppe and foothills and have been discovered as far north as Kayseri and the Elbistan-Afşin Plain (Brown 1967; T. Özgüç 1956), as far west as Mersin (Akkermans 1988:110; Garstang 1943:8), and as far east as the area now explored in the Upper Tigris (Algaze 1989; Algaze et al. 1991; Bernbeck, Costello, and Ünal 2004; Kozbe 2006, 2007; Ozan 2009; Parker et al. 2008, 2009; Sağlamtimur and Ozan 2007).

Compared with the previous Halaf phase, in the Ubaid period pottery production becomes significantly more efficiency-oriented. Vessels are painted with less care and produced on a slow wheel, but the ceramics remain as distinctive and easy to identify as before (Perkins 1949; Redman 1978). Much of our knowledge of the Ubaid period in Turkey is based on this recognizable pottery style, as we have little evidence on architecture and associated finds. Ubaid pottery was found, for example, near İslahiye in the Plain of Sakçegözü at Coba Höyük and the nearby cave site, at Gedikli as well as at Tilmen Höyük (U. B. Alkım 1962; H. Alkım 1979; Alkım and Alkım 1966; du Plat Taylor, Williams, and Waechter 1950; Waechter, Göğüs, and Williams 1951). Yet the related architectural fragments detected in the plain, such as the wattle and daub wall remnants found in Coba Level IV and Gedikli IVa, were too piecemeal to make sense of (du Plat Taylor, Williams, and Waechter 1950; U. B. Alkım 1968:21–22). In the north, sites in the Altınova Plain like Korucutepe, Fatmalı-Kalecik, Norşuntepe, and Tülintepe yielded small percentages of Ubaid-like ceramics but no associated architecture (Esin and Arsebük 1974, 1982; Gülçur 2000; Hauptmann 1982; Özbaşaran 1992; van Loon 1978; Wright and Whallon 1998:780). Similarly, Ubaid wares were discovered in excavations and surveys in the Kilis, Adıyaman, Birecik, and Harran Plains (Blaylock 1998; Blaylock, French, and Summers 1990; Fuensanta et al. 2007; Özgen, Helwing, and Engin 2002; Özgen et al. 2003; Summers and French 1992; Yardımcı 1993, 2001:46–47), but the only site yielding any substantial architecture was a single-phase mound excavated by the Tilbes Project (Fuensanta et al. 2006).

Most recently, with the upcoming Tigris dams, intensified research in Diyarbakır, Batman, Siirt, and Şırnak have determined a rich Ubaid presence along the Upper Tigris and its tributaries (Algaze 1989; Algaze et al. 1991; Bernbeck, Costello, and Ünal 2004; Kozbe 2007, 2008; Ozan 2009; Parker et al. 2008, 2009; Sağlamtimur and Ozan 2007), yet Kenan Tepe remains the sole site to have yielded extensive architecture (Parker et al. 2008, 2009). Further west, excavations or detailed ceramic analyses have been conducted at many Cilician Syro-Anatolian sites like Mersin, Tarsus Gözlükule, and a number of Amuq settlements including Tell Kurdu, Judaidah, Tell esh-Sheikh, Tabara el-Akrad, and Karaca Khirbet Ali (Braidwood and Braidwood 1960; French 1985; Garstang 1953; Goldman 1956; Hood 1951; R. Özbal 2006; Özbal et al. 2004; Woolley 1959:5–6; Yener et al. 2000a, 2000b). However, because the results of the Tell esh-Sheikh excavations still await publication (French 1985; Woolley 1959), the only architecture to speak of in this northwestern sector of the "Ubaid expansion" comes from Tell Kurdu and Mersin XV. Değirmentepe on the Malatya Plain is perhaps an exception with its large corpus of Ubaid tripartite structures (Esin 1983, 1985, 1989, 1993, 1994, 1996; Esin and Harmankaya 1986, 1987, 1988), but excavation of the fifth millennium levels at not-too-distant Pirot Höyük yielded hardly any discernible architecture (Akdeniz 2004; Karaca 1985). Overall, in other words, in southeast and eastern Anatolia our knowledge of Middle Chalcolithic occupation, beyond ceramics, is based on a mere handful of sites.

By the first half of the fifth millennium B.C.E., Ubaid ceramics comprised a notable part of pottery assemblages in northern Mesopotamia across a broad east–west arc (Campbell 2007; Hammade and Yamazaki 1995, 2006:431; Parker et al. 2008; Yener et al. 2000a). This phase is sometimes referred to as the Ubaid 3 phase based on the southern Mesopotamian chronology. Sites west of the Euphrates like Tell Kurdu (Diebold 2000; Edens and Yener 2000), Mersin (Garstang 1953), and possibly the Sakçegözü Cave Site (French and Summers 1988) have yielded ceramics that could be identified as early northern Ubaid. Research in Turkey east of the Euphrates has been much less intensive, but radiocarbon dates from Kenantepe indicate that the earliest levels of Ubaid occupation here predate 4700 cal B.C.E. (Campbell 2007; Parker et al. 2008). During the early northern Ubaid painted ceramic percentages tended to be relatively high. The Ubaid-related levels at Tell Kurdu, for example, show an "overwhelmingly Ubaid complexion" (Braidwood and Braidwood 1960:511) in the Amuq E Phase, when 45 percent of the pottery is painted in the northern Ubaid style (Diebold 2000; R. Özbal 2010).

Architecture shows considerable variability in this region at this time. At Mersin, small rectangular rooms with peculiar rounded corners were identified in Level XV (Garstang 1953:156). Further east, in the Amuq, the architecture shows more parallels with northern Ubaid sites. Particularly notable is a grill-like structure, for example, discovered at Tell Kurdu (R. Özbal 2010:298), resembling ones from Tell Ziyadeh Level 1 (Arzt 2001:fig. 2.1); Tepe Gawra Levels XV, XVA, and XVI (Tobler

1950:XV–XVII); and Tell al-'Abr Level 7 (Hammade and Koike 1992:fig. 12; Hammade and Yamazaki 2006). Such structures are assumed to have been used as granaries or storage structures (Akkermans and Schwartz 2003:166). Although not grill-planned, excavations of roughly contemporaneous levels at Kenan Tepe near Bismil also yielded many cell-planned structures most probably used for storage (Parker et al. 2008:107).

Radiocarbon dates for the following phase, often labeled the Ubaid 4, indicate that it begins around the mid-fifth millennium B.C.E. and ends roughly around 4300 cal B.C.E. (Akkermans and Schwartz 2003; Balossi Restelli 2008; Rothman 2001a; Wright and Rupley 2001; Yakar, chapter 4 in this volume). The far northern reaches of the Euphrates around Malatya and Elazığ also contribute to our knowledge of occupation at this time. Flint-scraped Coba bowls, considered the hallmark of the Terminal Ubaid, are widespread throughout northern Mesopotamia and are found as far east as Muş (Russell 1980) and as far west as the Elbistan Plain (Brown 1967).

Northern Mesopotamia has few examples of tripartite structures. They are best known from Tepe Gawra in northern Iraq and Değirmentepe near Malatya. At Kenan Tepe's later Ubaid levels, a residential complex called "Ubaid Structure 4" was uncovered (Parker et al. 2009). There appears to be a central courtyard flanked by rows of side rooms to the north and east. Although it cannot currently be ascertained, Parker and colleagues (2009:90) mention the high likelihood of a parallel flank along the western wall making the structure tripartite. Finally, Fuensanta et al. (2006:446) report that prior to flooding by Birecik Lake, the presence of an Ubaid tripartite building as well as two bipartite ones were exposed in a 1,300 m^2 area, as part of the Tilbes Project. The structure has been assigned to the Terminal Ubaid phase, however the analysis of the ceramics currently awaits publication (Fuensanta et al. 2006).

Referred to as the Ubaid "type-site" in Turkey, Değirmentepe in Malatya combines typically Ubaid tripartite architectural structures with a characteristically Anatolian agglutinative plan (Gürdil 2010; Stein and Özbal 2007). Excavations yielded traces of wall painting and evidence for various craft activities like metal production and lithic knapping (Esin and Harmankaya 1988). Each residential structure appears to have encapsulated ritual aspects as indicated by offering podia, altars, and burials as well as nearby pits containing ash and sacrificial offerings, uniquely mixing northern and southern cultural styles (Esin and Harmankaya 1988:92–93, 104–5; Gürdil 2010; Helwing 2003:68; Stein and Özbal 2007).

Recently, an under-researched post–Ubaid phase dating to the last three centuries of the fifth millennium B.C.E., assigned to the LC 1 and LC 2 (based on the SAR chronology by Rothman 2001a) has been the topic of investigation at a number of southeast and eastern Anatolian sites (Balossi Restelli 2008). Perhaps the most complete information on this period comes from Arslantepe VIII, where excavations yielded at least two occupational phases of architecture (Balossi Restelli 2008; Balossi Restelli and Guarino 2010). Other sites that yielded similar types of ceramics include Oylum Höyük Stratum 6–2 (Özgen et al. 1999), Coba Höyük IVC (du Plat Taylor, Williams, and Waechter 1950), Norşuntepe Phases II–III (Gülçur 2000),

Hayaz Höyük 5–4 (Thissen 1985), Korucutepe XII–XXX (van Loon 1978); Yenice Yanı Level 4 (Kennedy 2008), and much of the prehistoric pottery from Horum Höyük (Fletcher 2007). More research is necessary to assess the exact chronological relationships between the above-mentioned settlements and how the phase differs or relates to the traditional Late Ubaid.

The ceramics in this phase show variability from site to site, yet there appears to be a close relationship between the wares from Oylum Höyük (Özgen et al. 1999), Arslantepe VIII (Balossi Restelli 2008), and Hammam et-Turkman VA-B (Akkermans 1988). This includes high percentages of flint-scraped pottery and occasionally other forms of decoration, like incised appliqué. Some shapes resemble Amuq F wares even though the phase would be more accurately placed in a hiatus between Amuq E and F. Mass-produced Coba bowls continue to be dominant, in some cases comprising as much as half the assemblage (Trufelli 1994). Many regional variants of this distinctive mass-produced bowl exist (Akkermans 1988; Gülçur 2000:377; Özgen et al. 1999:41–42; Trufelli 1997). Painted Ubaid sherds are still present, though in declining numbers in most assemblages (Akkermans 1988; Gülçur 2000; Özgen et al. 1999; van Loon 1978).

Excavations at Arslantepe VIII and at Oylum Höyük Stratum 5 have yielded architecture associated with this Post-Ubaid Phase. At both sites the exposed areas include large courtyards in which craft activities took place (Balossi Restelli 2008; Özgen et al. 1999:41). The courtyard at Arslantepe was probably used for food preparation and cooking because a number of ovens, hearths, and other food processing implements were recovered. Small domestic rooms were exposed around the large open courtyard, two of which yielded in situ door sockets and thresholds (Balossi Restelli 2008).

Although the "Ubaid Expansion" and "Uruk Expansion" appear to be propelled by completely different mechanisms of transmission and dispersal (Stein and Özbal 2007), there is still much debate about how, for the former period, material cultural aspects found their way across southeast Anatolia and even beyond into the Taurus Mountains. Trade (Oates 1993; Oates and Oates 2004), colonial expansion (Esin and Harmankaya 1988; Gürdil 2005), spread of an ideology (Breniquet 1996), and the peaceful appropriation of Ubaid elements within local assemblages (Stein and Özbal 2007) are among the proposals that have been made. Further research into the understudied LC 1 or LC 2 Phases may provide insights into the local reactions to the changing foreign influences.

The Fourth Millennium (Cal b.c.e.)

The radiocarbon dates for the Post-Ubaid phase, as compiled by Balossi Restelli (2008), and for the Uruk period as researched by Wright and Rupley (2001), demonstrate that the beginnings of incipient state formation, evidence for social reorganization, and the formation of new political connections date to the beginning of the fourth millennium B.C.E. (Adams 1966, 1981; Frangipane 2007; Nissen 2000; Pollock 1992; Wright 2001). Although it was originally presumed that early state systems were restricted either to the southern Mesopotamian alluvium or to Uruk-influenced sites/colonies in the north, over the past few decades excavations of the precontact levels at sites like Arslantepe (Frangipane 1993, 1997a, 1997b), Hacınebi (Stein 1999, 2001, 2002), Hamoukar (Gibson et al. 2002) and Tell Brak (Oates et al. 2007) have made it clear that the indigenous societies with whom the Urukians interacted had already independently evolved into complex administrative centers (for Anatolia specifically, see Sagona and Zimansky 2009).

This section outlines some of the developments that characterize southeastern Anatolia in the fourth millennium B.C.E. Compared with the sixth and fifth millennia already described, the fourth millennium has been researched quite extensively. Because the Uruk presence in southeastern Anatolia is covered in detail elsewhere in this volume (see, e.g., chapter 37 by Rothman), and Arslantepe is one of the key sites discussed (see chapter 45 by Frangipane), this section largely confines itself to the local Late Chalcolithic and the notable changes in social, political, and economic spheres (see Foster 2009; Pearce 2008:24–32; Sagona and Zimansky 2009:144–62). All evidence for the Euphrates region points toward incipient complexity that is indigenous to the regions and settlements in question. Evidence for monumental architecture is consistently present prior to Uruk contact (Frangipane 1997b; N. Özgüç 1992; Stein 2002; Stein et al. 1998). This marks the first appearance of urban spaces and town planning at the settlement level (Frangipane 1993; Gibson et al. 1997a; 2002; Oates and Oates 1997; Oates et al. 2007; Stein et al. 1998; Ur, Karsgaard, and Oates 2007). At Hacınebi already in Level A evidence for a massive stone buttressed wall, nearly four meters in height, and monumental mudbrick platforms, were discovered (Stein et al. 1998). At Arslantepe, too, excavations yielded a large tripartite structure, clearly of public importance, with wall paintings and mudbrick column bases in Level VII, prior to any Uruk impact (Frangipane 1993, 1997a; Frangipane and Balossi 2004). Although excavations were limited, part of a fortification wall was uncovered at Samsat Level XXIV (Algaze 1993:34; Mellink 1989; N. Özgüç 1992).

Having said this, evidence suggests considerable interregional differentiation. Although the Upper Euphrates region clearly illustrates indigenous social complexity, this may not be the case for the sites in the Upper Tigris Valley, perhaps due to their relative isolation (Creekmore 2007; Foster 2009). Although further excavations may prove otherwise, public or monumental structures, town planning, and specialized production found at precontact sites in the Euphrates Valley appear to be absent from at least the site of Kenantepe in the Upper Tigris. This situation is coupled by a seeming resistance to foreign influence. Even when Uruk presence in the region is confirmed by the presence of beveled rim bowls (Algaze 1989: 244; Algaze et al. 1991; Schachner 2004; Şenyurt 2002; Velibeyoğlu, Schachner, and Schachner 2002), other evidence for Uruk influence is meager (Foster 2009). Further excavations especially at Giricano near Bismil and Başur Höyük in the

Botan—both with comparatively more compelling evidence for Uruk connections—could prove otherwise (Sağlamtimur 2009; Schachner 2004).

In addition to regional differences in how Uruk presence was internalized, evidence also points to variability across sites in the same region (but see Lupton 1996:20). Regional surveys suggest a two- or three-tiered settlement hierarchy, with larger towns surrounded by agricultural sites in the countryside (Algaze 1989, 1993:92–95; Algaze et al. 1991; Algaze, Breuninger, and Knudstad 1994; Lupton 1996:22–26; Özdoğan 1977; Ur 2002; Whallon 1979). Samsat in the Karababa Dam area and Arslantepe in the Malatya Plain may be considered examples of focal sites at the head of three-tiered settlement hierarchies (Frangipane 1993; Lupton 1996:53). Similarly for the Late Chalcolithic period in the Batman region, Algaze (1989:244) identifies a few large sites that must have dominated the fourth millennium landscape B.C.E., notably İkiztepe and Gre Migro.

This variability can be extended even to the intrasite level as noted by Pearce (2008:29; see also Gibson et al. 2002; Oates et al. 2007). At Norşuntepe on the Euphrates, for example, we find larger and smaller residences within the same settlement. The architecture from Level 10 shows a road or alleyway flanked by smaller structures to the west and a larger complex to the east (Hauptmann 1976, 1982). As at Arslantepe some buildings had red and black painted walls (Hauptmann 1976). Unfortunately the exposures at Norşuntepe are too small to extrapolate too much about town planning and the details of the intrasite variability, but the density of structures suggests similarities with contemporary north Mesopotamian sites like Tepe Gawra (Rothman 2001b:397) and Qalinj Agha (Abu al-Soof 1967; Lupton 1996). Small portions of regular planned buildings were exposed in excavations in the Upper Tigris, most notably at Giricano (Schachner et al. 2002:557–58) and Kenan Tepe (Foster 2009; Parker et al. 2009).

Record-keeping artifacts such as stamp seals and seal impressions are clear indications for complex and hierarchical administrative practices (Ferioli and Fiandra 1983; Pittman 2001; Reichel 2002; Wright and Johnson 1975). Used as ways to monitor individual or family property and ownership, stamp seals and sealings are found in increasingly larger numbers in southeast Anatolia by the fourth millennium B.C.E. and demonstrate that status differences were becoming more pronounced (Frangipane 1993, 1994; Hauptmann 1976; Pittman 1996, 1999, 2001; Schachner 2004; Stein 2001:274–75; see also Pearce 2008:28). Other administrative artifacts like bullae with seal impressions make their first appearance in this region during the Late Chalcolithic (Hauptmann 1976; Pittman 2001:416; Stein et al. 1998:148; Wright 2001:141–42).

Evidence exhibits specialization in crafts and the apparent need for efficiency in ceramic manufacture. This is a development that began in the fifth millennium B.C.E., as already described. Ceramics in the Late Chalcolithic gradually show increasing signs of low-cost production (Pearce 2000:122, 2008:26; Trufelli 1994). Elaborate painting and decoration of previous horizons is conspicuously missing. Chaff tempering, standardization, and low temperature firings may be characterized as strategies to cut costs (Akkermans 1988; Pearce 2008; Trufelli 1994). The discovery of potters' marks extensively across northern Mesopotamia and beyond at this time indicates a preference for mass firings (Lupton 1996:20; Pearce 2008:26; Stein et al. 1998). The fact that these characteristics are consistently found at all sites indicates supraregional transformations in the social and technological realms of ceramic production processes. However, only a few ceramic shapes show cross-regional similarities. As Lupton (1996:20) puts it, "the pre-contact period in north Mesopotamia and southeast Anatolia comprised a number of distinct regional entities, which were interconnected, at one level, in a basic technological sense, and at another level through a limited range of characteristic types." Yet a great majority of the ceramics in each region is "idiosyncratic to that region alone" (Lupton 1996:20; Pearce 2000:121–22). Similarly, evidence points to the increased production of other crafts in the fourth millennium B.C.E. like the manufacture of metal tools (de Jesus 1980; Esin 1976; Hauptmann 1976; H. Özbal 1996, 1997; H. Özbal, Adriens, and Earl 1999; Palmieri, Sertok, and Chernykh 1993; Stein 2001:277; Yener 2000; and see Muhly, chapter 39 in this volume) and textiles (Keith 1998).

Metal artifacts in graves have been used to signify a growing élite class at some sites (Yener 2000). At Hacınebi, for example, excavations yielded jar burials of infants and small children, one of which was buried with a copper ring, two silver earrings, and a miniature ceramic vessel (Stein 2001:273; Stein et al. 1996:96). Silver is extremely rare in this period, and its discovery associated with the infant may indicate ascribed status (Stein 2001:274). Child burials with precious gifts were also discovered in northern Mesopotamia at Tepe Gawra and Qalinj Agha (Abu al-Soof 1967:71–72; Rothman 2001b:393). Other sites like Kenan Tepe lack evidence for an élite presence (Foster 2009).

The second half of the fourth millennium B.C.E. was a time of intense change and adjustment for the inhabitants of southeast Anatolia and northern Mesopotamia as southern Mesopotamians settled across or interacted with settlements in the Upper Euphrates, Upper Tigris, and beyond in their quest to obtain raw materials. A fascinating aspect of this interaction between the local and the Uruk is the varied manner in which relations played out at different sites. Whereas some sites appear to have functioned as stations or outposts for Urukians, others were places in which Uruk inhabitants set up residence and created foreign neighborhoods within or near a preexisting local settlement (Algaze 1993). At the same time, however, there are also Late Chalcolithic sites where little Uruk presence is seen (Foster 2009; Steadman 1996).

Hassek Höyük in the Karababa Dam area, has been interpreted as an Uruk "station" established to control the access of goods (Behm-Blancke et al. 1984:40). This has been based on the fact that excavations yielded southern Mesopotamian type courtyard buildings built directly on virgin soil, not unlike those from Jebel Aruda and Habuba Kabira Süd (Behm-Blancke et al. 1984; Sürenhagen 1986). Other architectural features like wallcones similar to those used to adorn and protect walls of public structures in the southern alluvium (see Lloyd and Safar 1943), and the discovery of bones of swordfish native to the Persian Gulf (Lupton 1996:60–61), leave little doubt of a strong Uruk presence in the area. Yet research by Helwing has aptly demonstrated that many Uruk style artifacts and ceramics from Hassek Höyük may in fact have local undertones (Helwing 1999, 2002).

Recently Sağlamtimur (2009) conducted excavations at Başur Höyük, which he describes as a "station" along the Botan tributary of the Upper Tigris, near Siirt. A series of depot rooms, some with walls as wide as 150 cm, containing stores of lentils, barley, and wheat as well as large quantities of beveled-rim bowls were discovered. Sağlamtimur believes that these structures may have been part of a public administrative complex, but it is still too early to make a conclusive assessment of the settlement's function in the greater Uruk Expansion.

Our best knowledge of an Uruk "enclave" comes from Hacınebi Tepe located on the Euphrates in Birecik (Stein 1999, see also Young 1986 for a description of Godin Tepe, another "enclave"). The Late Chalcolithic residents living in Hacınebi Phase A began sharing the site with southerners by Phase B2, dating to around 3400 cal B.C.E. Located at the northeast side of the settlement in their own quarter, the Urukians showed different preferences in their diet (Stein 1999:145–46; Stein and Nicola 1996), the ways in which they butchered meat (Stein 1999), and their lithic tool manufacturing technologies (Edens 1996, 1997, 1999). In Phase B2, wheel-made and mineral tempered Uruk-type ceramics and typical Uruk vessel shapes like beveled-rim bowls and spouted jars inundate the ceramic assemblage (Pearce 2000, 2008).

Contrasting starkly with sites in which southern Mesopotamian presence is strong, one also finds, as mentioned above, local Late Chalcolithic settlements dating to the second half of the fourth millennium B.C.E., which surprisingly appear *not* to have been influenced by Uruk colonists. One such site is Kenan Tepe located in the Upper Tigris region (Parker et al. 2008). Another area lacking Uruk influences is Cilicia. This may be a result of the distance involved and the region's "isolationist" policy (Steadman 1996). For Kenan Tepe, it is possible that the inhabitants of this village settlement may not have reached the type of emergent complexity that other settlements had (Foster 2009). If so, this would have been an obstacle in adopting the urban Uruk ways of life. Indeed, research by Foster (2009) shows that the excavated portions of the settlement lack the types of craft facilities discovered at other Late Chalcolithic sites. Although excavations yielded a great number of cooking ovens, no kilns or smelting furnaces were discovered. The areas exposed are naturally limited, but the current data indicate a lack of burials with ascribed status, and intrasite variability among households (Foster 2009).

Kenan Tepe offers the potential to explore diachronic change in the Late Chalcolithic. Perhaps most remarkable is an increasing reliance on pig husbandry in the Late Chalcolithic 5 Period when an Uruk presence would most strongly have been felt in southeast Anatolia. Foster (2009) argues that a reliance on pigs is a "risk-abatement strategy" at times of economic instability or influx and further implies that the Kenan Tepe residents may have been asserting "independence" during this period when the political and economic repercussions of Uruk presence in the area—like at nearby Giricano (see Schachner 2003, 2004; Schachner et al. 2002)—were undoubtedly felt. Her argument stems from the idea that pig rearing is relatively efficient and may have been preferred by small detached households at times of economic uncertainty, given the abundant offspring pigs yield and the limited time it takes them to reach maturity. Overall, the intensified excavations along the Tigris, in advance of the planned dams, are bound to continue to add to the varied mosaic of the local Late Chalcolithic in this region and add depth to our expanding understanding of the varied Uruk presence in Turkey.

Conclusion

Overall, the developments taking place in southeast Anatolia during the three millennia covered in this chapter closely parallel those in northern Mesopotamia. Yet the perspectives provided by the research conducted in modern-day Turkey significantly enrich the picture. For example, the discovery that southeast Anatolia houses exceptionally large sixth millennium B.C.E. sites with Halafian-like affinities is relatively recent but has the potential to stir and reshape static ideas about the Halaf period. Detailed, long-term excavations like those at Domuztepe broaden our understanding of how such large sixth millennium B.C.E. settlements may have functioned and provide new insights into intrasettlement dynamics.

Our knowledge of the fifth millennium B.C.E. in southeast Anatolia, especially in aspects of architecture and settlement organization, is less comprehensive. Değirmentepe has often been labeled as the Ubaid type-site in Anatolia. There is little doubt that this is a truly exceptional settlement, but the focus on its Ubaidness has meant that many of its local aspects, like a great majority of its ceramics, have consequently been understudied. Our aim for this period should be to analyze sites, characterize local elements, gain insights into lifestyles, understand settlement dynamics, and define what constitutes a local community for the specific region studied. Only then can further research not only discover how local Anatolian aspects combined with Ubaid characteristics but also clarify questions on the expansionary dynamics of Ubaidians or Ubaid elements to the region in question. Perhaps another way to investigate the fifth millennium B.C.E. would be to focus on the transitional phases that precede and follow the Ubaid period (such as the HUT or the Post-Ubaid) because less well-defined intervening stages may in fact carry less archaeological and scholarly baggage.

Research over the past few decades in southeastern Anatolia, especially the Upper Euphrates and environs at sites like Hacınebi and Arslantepe, has transformed our understanding of the fourth millennium B.C.E. significantly. There is now little doubt that local settlements in the Taurus piedmont zone of southeast Anatolia had ample evidence for a high level of social complexity even *before* contact with Uruk polities. Yet now the salvage excavations along the Tigris have set the scene for investigations of the fourth millennium B.C.E. in a new region. Although the idea that each site was affected differently by the Uruk phenomenon is not new, the discovery of Late Chalcolithic levels at Kenan Tepe in the Upper Tigris Valley, a site devoid of Uruk elements all together, triggers new questions and possibilities toward further understanding Mesopotamian colonization at this time.

NOTES

This chapter was completed at the Prehistory Section of the Department of Archaeology at Istanbul University through post-doctoral funding provided by The Turkish Academy of Sciences (TÜBA). Many thanks go to the editors of this volume as well as Andy Creekmore and Fokke Gerritsen for their insightful comments on this text. I am grateful to Francesca Balossi Restelli, Ali Ozan, and Stuart Campbell, who kindly shared their unpublished articles with me. I would also like to thank Güven Arsebük and Mihriban Özbaşaran for allowing me to include a plan of Tülintepe in figure 8.4.

1. Recently, as new absolute dates have come to light and researchers have recognized that Halafian-type pottery and architecture have roots going back well into the Neolithic, many have begun to categorize the Halaf period as "Late Neolithic," rather than "Early Chalcolithic" (Akkermans and Schwartz 2003; Campbell 2007; Cruells and Nieuwenhuyse 2004).
2. Another site with levels spanning this period where the ceramics deserve thorough reanalysis is Tell esh-Sheikh (Woolley 1959). The published ceramics do show some overlap with Yumuktepe XIX–XIII but too little is known to further extrapolate.

REFERENCES

Abu al-Soof, Behnam. 1967. More Soundings at Qalinj Agha (Erbil). *Sumer* 23: 69–74.
Adams, Robert M. 1966. *The Evolution of Urban Society*. Chicago: Aldine.
———. 1981. *Heartland of Cities*. Chicago: University of Chicago Press.
Akdeniz, Engin. 2004. Halaf ve Obeyd Kültürleri Üzerine Bazı Gözlemler ve Pirot Höyüğün Halaf ve Obeyd Boyalı Çanak Çömleği. *Anadolu Araştırmaları* 17.2: 1–48.
Akkermans, Peter M. M. G. 1988. An Updated Chronology for the Northern Ubaid and Late Chalcolithic Periods in Syria: New Evidence from Tell Hamman et-Turkman. *Iraq* 50: 109–45.
———. 1993. *Villages in the Steppe: Later Neolithic Settlement and Subsistence in the Balikh Valley, Northern Syria*. Archaeological Series 5. Ann Arbor, Mich.: International Monographs in Prehistory.
Aksoy, Behin and Steven Diamant. 1973. Çayboyu 1970–71. *Anatolian Studies* 23: 97–108.
Algaze, Guillermo. 1989. A New Frontier: First Results of the Tigris-Euphrates Archaeological Reconnaissance Project, 1988. *Journal of Near Eastern Studies* 48.4: 241–81.
———. 1993. *The Uruk World System. The Dynamics of Expansion of Early Mesopotamian Civilization*. Chicago: University of Chicago Press.

Algaze, Guillermo, Ray Breuninger, and James Knudstad. 1994. The Tigris-Euphrates Archaeological Reconnaissance Project: Final Report of the Birecik and Carchemish Dam Survey Areas. *Anatolica* 20: 1–71.

Algaze, Guillermo, Ray Brueninger, Chris Lightfoot, and Michael Rosenberg. 1991. The Tigris-Euphrates Archaeological Reconnaissance Project: A Preliminary Report of the 1989–1990 Seasons. *Anatolica* 17: 175–240.

Alkım, Handan. 1979. Gedikli (Karahüyük) Çanak Çömleğine Toplu Bir Bakış. *Türk Tarih Kongresi, Kongreye Sunulan Bildiriler* 8: 135–42.

Alkım, U. Bahadır. 1962. Dördüncü Dönem Tilmen Höyük Kazısı. *Türk Arkeoloji Dergisi* 12.1: 5–7.

———. 1968. Recent Archaeological Research in Turkey. *Anatolian Studies* 18: 21–43.

Alkım, U. Bahadır and Handan Alkım. 1966. Excavations at Gedikli, First Preliminary report. *Belleten* 30: 27–57.

Arbuckle, Benjamin. 2006. The Evolution of Sheep and Goat Pastoralism and Social Complexity in Central Anatolia (Turkey). Ph.D. dissertation. Harvard University.

Arsebük, Güven. 1979. Altınova'da (Elazığ), Koyu Yüzlü Açkılı ve Karaz Türü Çanak Çömlek Arasındaki İlişkiler. *Türk Tarih Kongresi: Kongreye Sunulan Bildiriler* 8: 81–92.

———. 1983. Tülintepe: Some Aspects of a Prehistoric Village. In *Beiträge zur Altertumskunde Kleinasiens, Festschrift für Kurt Bittel*, ed. Rainer M. Boehmer and Harald Hauptmann, 51–57. Mainz am Rhein: Philipp von Zabern.

Arzt, Jennifer M. 2001. Excavations at Tell Ziyadeh, Syria: The Northern Ubaid Reconsidered. Ph.D. dissertation. Yale University.

Balossi, Francesca. 2004. New Data for the Definition of the DFBW Horizon and its Internal Developments. *Anatolica* 30: 109–49.

Balossi Restelli, Francesca. 2008. Post-Ubaid Occupation on the Upper Euphrates: Late Chalcolithic 1–2 at Arslantepe (Malatya, Turkey). In *Proceedings of the 4th International Congress of the Archaeology of the Ancient Near East: The Reconstruction of Environment: Natural Resources and Human Interrelations through Time; Art History: Visual Communication*, ed. Hartmut von Kühne, Rainer M. Czichon, and Florian Janoscha Kreppner, vol. 2, 21–32. Wiesbaden: Harrassowitz Verlag.

Balossi Restelli, Francesca and Paulo Guarino. 2010. Domestic Behaviour and Cultural Milieu North and South of the Taurus in the Mid IV Millennium BC, as Inferred from the Pottery Production and Use at the Sites of Arslantepe and Zeytinli Bahçe. In *Proceedings of the Sixth International Congress on the Archaeology of the Ancient Near East*, ed. Paolo Matthiae, 641–652. Roma: Università di Roma "La Sapienza."

Barth, Frederic. 1953. *Principles of Social Organization in Southern Kurdistan*. Oslo: Jørgensen.

———. 1965. *Nomads of South Persia, the Baseri Tribe of the Khamseh Confederacy*. New York: Humanities Press.

Behm-Blancke, Manfred R., Manfred Hoh, Norbert Karg, Ludwig Masch, Franz Parsche, Karl Ludwig Weiner, Alwo von Wickede, and Gerfried Ziegelmayer. 1984. Hassek Höyük. Vorläufiger Bericht über die Grabungen in den Jahre 1981–1983. *Istanbuler Mitteilungen* 34: 31–150.

Bernbeck, Reinhard, Sarah Costello, and Necdet Ünal. 2004. Excavations at Yenice Yanı 2002. *Kazı Sonuçları Toplantısı* 25: 117–26.

Bernbeck, Reinhard and Susan Pollock. 2003. The Biography of an Early Halaf Village: Fıstıklı Höyük 1999–2000. *Istanbuler Mitteilungen* 53: 9–77.

Bernbeck, Reinhard, Sarah Pollock, and Cheryl Coursey. 1999. The Halaf Settlement at Kazane Höyük: Preliminary Report on the 1996 and 1997 Seasons. *Anatolica* 25: 109–44.

Blaylock, Stuart. 1998. Adıyaman Survey 1985–1991. *In Ancient Anatolia: Fifty Years' Work by the British Institute of Archaeology at Ankara*, ed. Roger Matthews, 101–10. London: British Institute of Archaeology at Ankara.

Blaylock, Stuart R., David H. French, and Geoffrey D. Summers. 1990. The Adıyaman Survey: An Interim Report. *Anatolian Studies* 40: 81–135.

Braidwood, Robert J. and Linda S. Braidwood. 1960. *Excavations in the Plain of Antioch. Vol. 1. The Earlier Assemblages, Phases A–J.* Oriental Institute Publications 61. Chicago: University of Chicago Press.

Breniquet, Catherine. 1987. Nouvelle hypothèse sur la disparition de la culture de Halaf. In *Préhistoire de la Mesopotamie*, ed. Jean-Louis Huot, 231–41. Paris: Éditions du CNRS.

———. 1991. Un site halafien en Turquie méridionale: Tell Turlu. Rapport sur la campagne de fouilles de 1962. *Akkadica* 71: 1–35.

———. 1996. *La disparition de la culture de Halaf: les origines de la culture d'Obeid dans le nord de la Mésopotamie. Bibliothèque de la délégation archéologique française en Iraq no 9*. Paris: Editions Recherche sur les civilizations.

Brown, Gavin H. 1967. Prehistoric Pottery from the Antitaurus. *Anatolian Studies* 17: 123–64.

Burney, Charles. 1977. *From Village to Empire: An Introduction to Near Eastern Archaeology.* Oxford: Phaidon Press.

Campbell, Stuart. 1992. *Culture, Chronology and Change in the Later Neolithic of North Mesopotamia*. Ph.D. dissertation. University of Edinburgh.

———. 2007. Rethinking Halaf Chronologies. *Paléorient* 33.1: 103–36.

Campbell, Stuart, Elizabeth Carter, Elizabeth Healey, Seona Anderson, Amanda Kennedy, and Sarah Whitcher. 1999. Emerging Complexity on the Kahramanmaraş Plain: The Domuztepe Project 1995–1997. *American Journal of Archaeology* 103: 395–418.

Campbell, Stuart and Alexandra Fletcher.2010. Questioning the Halaf-Ubaid Transition. The Emergence of Ubaid styles at Tell Kurdu: A Local Perspective. In *Beyond the Ubaid: Transformation and Integration in the Late Prehistoric Societies of the Middle East*, ed. Robert A. Carter and Graham Philip, 69–83. Chicago: Oriental Institute of the University of Chicago.

Caneva, Isabella. 2004. Of Terraces, Silos and Ramparts (6000–5800). In *Mersin-Yumuktepe: A Reappraisal*, ed. Isabella Caneva and Veli Sevin, 45–56. Lecce: Congedo Editore.

Carter, Elizabeth, Hadi Bozkurt, Stuart Campbell, James Snead, and Lynn Swartz. 1997. Report on the Archaeological Work in Domuztepe and its Environs in 1995. *Kazı Sonuçları Toplantısı* 18: 173–88.

Carter, Elizabeth and Stuart Campbell. 2008. The Domuztepe Project. *Kazı Sonuçları Toplantısı* 29.3: 123–36.

Carter, Elizabeth, Stuart Campbell, and Suellen Gauld. 2003. Elusive Complexity: New Data from Late Halaf Domuztepe in Southcentral Turkey. *Paléorient* 29.2: 117–34.

Carter, Elizabeth, Stuart Campbell, and James Snead. 1999. Excavations and Surveys at Domuztepe 1996. *Anatolia Antiqua* 7: 1–17.

Casana, Jesse. 2003. From Alalakh to Antioch: Settlement, Land Use, and Environmental Change in the Amuq Valley of Southern Turkey. Ph.D. dissertation. University of Chicago.

Casana, Jesse J. and Tony J. Wilkinson. 2005. Archaeology and Landscapes of the Amuq Region. In *The Amuq Valley Regional Projects, Volume 1—Surveys in the Plain of Antioch and Orontes Delta, Turkey, 1995–2002*, ed. K. Aslıhan Yener, 25–66. Oriental Institute Publications 131. Chicago: Oriental Institute Press.

Cavallo, Chiara. 1996. The Animal Remains—A Preliminary Account. In *Tell Sabi Abyad: The Late Neolithic Settlement*, ed. Peter M. M. G. Akkermans, vol. 2, 475–520. İstanbul: Nederlands Historisch-Archaeologisch Instituut.

Copeland, Lorraine. 1979. Observations on the Prehistory of the Balikh Valley Syria, during the 7th to 4th Millennia BC. *Paléorient* 7: 251–75.

Creekmore, Andrew. 2007. The Upper Tigris Archaeological Research Project (UTARP): A Summary and Synthesis of the Late Chalcolithic and Early Bronze Age Remains from the First Three Seasons at Kenan Tepe. *Anatolica* 33: 75–128.

Cruells, Walter and Olivier Nieuwenhuyse. 2004. The Proto-Halaf Period in Syria: New Sites, New Data. *Paléorient* 30.1: 47–68.

Davidson, Thomas E. 1977. *Regional Variation within the Halaf Ceramic Tradition*. Ph.D. dissertation. University of Edinburgh.

Davidson, Thomas E. and Trevor Watkins. 1981. Two Seasons of Excavation at Tell Aqab in the Jezirah, N.E. Syria. *Iraq* 43: 1–18.

de Jesus, Prentiss S. 1980. *The Development of Prehistoric Mining and Metallurgy in Anatolia*. Oxford: British Archaeological Reports.

Diebold, Benjamin. 2000. Preliminary Report on the Ceramic assemblage at Tell Kurdu. In *Tell Kurdu Excavations 1999*, ed. K. Aslıhan Yener, Christopher Edens, Jesse Casana, Benjamin Diebold, Heidi Ekstom, Michelle Loyet, and Rana Özbal. *Anatolica* 26: 58–65.

Dönmez, Ahmet and William Charles Brice. 1949. The Distribution of Some Varieties of Early Pottery in Southeast Turkey. *Iraq* 11: 44–58.

du Plat Taylor, Joan, Marjory Veronica Seton Williams, and John Waechter. 1950. The Excavations at Sakçe Gözü. *Iraq* 12: 53–138.

Edens, Christopher. 1996. Hacınebi Chipped Stone—1995. In *Hacınebi, Turkey: Preliminary Report on the 1995 Excavations. Anatolica* 22: 100–104.

———. 1997. Chipped Stone. In *Excavations at Hacınebi Turkey—1996: Preliminary Report. Anatolica* 23: 124–27.

———. 1999. The Chipped Stone Industry at Hacınebi: Technological Styles and Social Identity. *Paléorient* 25.1: 23–34.

Edens, Christopher and K. Aslıhan Yener. 2000. Excavations at Tell Kurdu, 1996 and 1998. *American Journal of Archaeology* 104: 198–215.

Ehmann, Dieter. 1975. *Bahtiyaren—Persische Bergnomaden im Wandel der Zeit B 15*. Wiesbaden: Beihefte zum Tübinger Atlas des Vorderen Orients.

Erinç, Sırrı. 1980. Kültürel Çevrebilim Açısından Güneydoğu Anadolu. In *İstanbul ve Chicago Üniversiteleri Karma Projesi Güneydoğu Anadolu Tarihöncesi Araştırmaları*, ed. Halet Çambel and Robert Braidwood, 65–82. İstanbul: İstanbul Edebiyat Fakültesi Yayınları.

Esin, Ufuk. 1976. Tepecik Excavations, 1972. In *Keban Project 1972 Activities*, 97–117. Ankara: Middle East Technical University Press.

———. 1983. Zur Datierung der vorgeschichtlichen Schichten von Değirmentepe bei Malatya in der östlichen Türkei. In *Beiträge zur Altertumskunde Kleinasiens. Festschrift Kurt Bittel*, ed. Rainer M. Boehmer and Harald Hauptmann, 175–90. Mainz: Philipp von Zabern.

———. 1985. Some Small Finds from the Chalcolithic Occuption at Değirmentepe (Malatya) in Eastern Turkey. In *Studi di paletnologia in onore di Salvatore M. Puglisi*, ed. Mario Liverani, Alba Palmieri, and Renato Peroni, 253–64. Roma: Università di Roma "La Sapienza."

———. 1989. An Early Trading Center in Eastern Anatolia. In *Anatolia and the Ancient Near East, Studies in Honor of Tahsin Özgüç*, ed. Kutlu Emre, Barthel

Hrouda, Machteld Mellink, and Nimet Özgüç, 135–41. Ankara: Türk Tarih Kurumu Basımevi.

———. 1993. The Relief Decorations on the Prehistoric Pottery of Tülintepe in Eastern Anatolia. In *Between the Rivers and over the Mountains: Archaeologica Anatolica et Mesopotamica Alba Palmieri Dedicata*, ed. Marcella Frangipane, Harald Hauptmann, Mario Liverani, Paolo Matthiae, and Machteld Mellink, 105–19. Roma: Università di Roma "La Sapienza."

———. 1994. The Functional Evidence of Seals and Sealings of Değirmentepe. In *Archives before Writing*, ed. Piera Ferioli, Enrica Fiandra, Gian Giacomo Fissore, and Marcella Frangipane, 59–81. Roma: Università di Roma "La Sapienza."

———. 1996. Doğu Anadolu'da Bulunan Obeyd Tipi Çanak Çömlek ve Değirmentepe (Malatya) Kazısı. In *Türk Tarih Kongresi 9. Kongreye Sunulan Bildiriler*, vol. 1, 81–92. Ankara: Türk Tarih Kurumu.

Esin, Ufuk and Güven Arsebük. 1974. Tülintepe Kazısı 1971. *Türk Arkeoloji Dergisi* 20.2: 63–78.

———. 1982. *Tülintepe Kazısı. Keban Projesi 1974–1975 Çalışmaları*, 119–34. Ankara: Middle East Technical University Series.

Esin, Ufuk and Savaş Harmankaya. 1986. 1984 Değirmentepe (Malatya) Kurtarma Kazısı. *Kazı Sonuçları Toplantısı* 7: 53–85.

———. 1987. 1985 Değirmentepe (Malatya-İmamlı Köyü) Kurtarma Kazısı. *Kazı Sonuçları Toplantısı* 8: 95–137.

———. 1988. Değirmentepe (Malatya) Kurtarma Kazısı 1986. *Kazı Sonuçları Toplantısı* 9: 79–125.

Evin, Jacques. 1995. Possibilité et nécessité de la calibration des datations C-14 de l'archéologie du Proche-Orient. *Paléorient* 21: 5–16.

Ferioli, Piera and Enrica Fiandra. 1983. Clay Sealings from Arslantepe VI: Administration and Bureaucracy. *Origini* 12.2: 455–509.

Fletcher, Alexandra. 2007. The Prehistoric Ceramic Assemblage from Horum Höyük. *Anatolian Studies* 57: 191–202.

Foster, Catherine P. 2009. *Household Archaeology and the Uruk Phenomenon: A Case Study from Kenan Tepe, Turkey*. Ph.D. dissertation. University of California.

Frangipane, Marcella. 1993. Local Components in the Development of Centralized Societies in Syro-Anatolian Regions. In *Between the Rivers and over the Mountains: Archaeologica Anatolica et Mesopotamica Alba Palmieri Dedicata*, ed. Marcella Frangipane, Harald Hauptmann, Mario Liverani, Paolo Matthiae, and Machteld Mellink, 133–61. Roma: Università di Roma "La Sapienza."

———. 1994. The Record Function of Clay Sealings in Early Administrative Systems as Seen from Arslantepe-Malatya. In *Archives before Writing. Piera Ferioli, Enrica Fiandra, Gian Giacomo Fissore, and Marcella Frangipane*, 125–37. Roma: Università di Roma "La Sapienza."

———. 1997a. Arslantepe-Malatya: External Factors and Local Components in the Development of Early State Society. In *Emergence and Change in Early Urban Societies*, ed. Linda Manzanilla, 43–58. New York: Plenum Press.

———. 1997b. A Fourth Millennium Temple/Palace Complex at Arslantepe-Malatya. North South Relations and the Formation of Early State Societies in the Northern Regions of Southern Mesopotamia. *Paléorient* 23: 45–73.

———. 2007. Different Types of Egalitarian Societies and the Development of Inequality in early Mesopotamia. *World Archaeology* 39.2: 151–76.

Frangipane, Marcella and Francesca Balossi. 2004. The 2002 Exploration Campaign at Arslantepe-Malatya. *Kazı Sonuçları Toplantısı* 25.1: 397–404.

French, David. 1985. Mersin and Tell esh-Sheikh. In *Studi di paletnologia in onore di Salvatore M. Puglisi*, ed. Mario Liverani, Alba Palmieri, and Renato Peroni, 265–71. Roma: Università di Roma "La Sapienza."

French, David and Geoffrey Summers. 1988. Sakçagözü Material in the Gaziantep Museum. *Anatolian Studies* 38: 71–84.

Fuensanta, Jesus Gil, Eyüp Bucak, Eduardo Crivelli, Petr Charvat, and Rafael Moya. 2006. The Research of the Tilbes Project, 2004. *Kazı Sonuçları Toplantısı* 27.2: 445–52.

Fuensanta, Jesus Gil, Eyüp Bucak, Eduardo Crivelli, Hasan Karabulut, Herbert Sauren, Petr Charvat, and Rafael Moya. 2007. The Tilbes Project Research in 2005: Surtepe Höyük Excavations. *Kazı Sonuçları Toplantısı* 28.2: 457–70.

Garstang, John. 1943. The Discoveries at Mersin and Their Significance. *American Journal of Archaeology* 47.1: 1–14.

———. 1953. *Prehistoric Mersin*. Oxford: Clarendon Press.

Garstang, John and Hetty Goldman. 1947. A Conspectus of Early Cilician Pottery. *American Journal of Archaeology* 51.4: 370–88.

Gibson, McGuire, Arm Al-Azm, Clemens Reichel, Salam Quntar, Judith Franke, Lamya Khalidi, Carrie Hritz, Mark Altaweel, Colleen Coyle, and Carlo Colantoni. 2002. Hamoukar: A Summary of Three Seasons of Excavation. *Akkadica* 123.1: 11–34.

Goldman, Hetty. 1956. *Excavations at Gözlü Kule, Tarsus: From the Neolithic through the Bronze Age*. Princeton, N.J.: Princeton University Press.

Gülçur, Sevil. 2000. Norşuntepe: Die Chalkolithische Keramik (Elazığ/Ostanatolien). In *Chronologies des pays du Caucase et de L'Euphrate aux IVe–IIIe Millénaires*, ed. Catherine Marro and Harald Hauptmann, 375–418. Institut Français d'Etudes Anatoliennes d'Istanbul, Varia Anatolica XI. Paris: De Boccard.

Gürdil, Bekir. 2002. A Late Halaf Site in the Kahramanmaraş Valley. *Anatolica* 28: 137–58.

———. 2005. *Architecture and Social Complexity in the Late Ubaid Period: A Study of the Built Environment of Değirmentepe in East Anatolia*. Ph.D. dissertation. University of California, Los Angeles.

———. 2010. Exploring Social Organizational Aspects of the Ubaid Communities: A Case Study of Değirmentepe in Eastern Turkey. In *Beyond the Ubaid: Transformation and Integration in the Late Prehistoric Societies of the Middle East*, ed. Robert A. Carter and Graham Philip, 361–375. Chicago: Oriental Institute of the University of Chicago.

Hammade, Hamido and Yayoi Koike. 1992. Syrian Archaeological Expedition in the Tishreen Dam Basin: Excavations at Tell al Abr 1990 and 1991. *Damascener Mitteilungen* 6: 107–75.

Hammade, Hamido and Yayoi Yamazaki. 1995. A Preliminary Report on the Excavation at Tell al-'Abr on the Upper Euphrates, 1992. *Akkadica* 93: 4–10.

———. 2006. *Tell al-'Abr (Syria). Ubaid and Uruk Periods*. Publications de la Mission archéologique de l'Université de Liège en Syrie. Leuven: Peeters.

Hauptmann, Harald. 1976. Die Grabungen auf dem Norşun Tepe. *Keban Activities*. Ankara: Middle East Technical University Series.

———. 1982. Die Grabungen auf dem Norşun Tepe. *Keban Activities*. Ankara: Middle East Technical University.

Helwing, Barbara. 1999. Cultural Interaction at Hassek Höyük, Turkey: New Evidence from Pottery analysis. *Paléorient* 25:95–101.

———. 2002. Hassek Höyük II: Die spätchalkolithische Keramik. *Istanbuler Forschungen Band* 45. Tübingen: Ernst Wasmuth.

———. 2003. Feasts as a Social Dynamic in Prehistoric Western Asia—Three Case Studies from Syria and Anatolia. *Paléorient* 29.2: 63–85.

Hood, Sinclair. 1951. Excavations at Tabara el Akrad, 1948–49. *Anatolian Studies* 1: 113–47.

Irons, William. 1972. Variation in Economic Organization: A Comparison of the Pastoral Yomut and the Basseri. In *Perspectives on Nomadism*, ed. William Irons and Neville Dyson-Hudson, 88–104. Leiden: Brill.

———. 1974. Nomadism as a Political Adaptation: The Case of the Yomut Turkmen. *American Ethnologist* 1: 635–58.

———. 1975. *The Yomut Turkmen: A Study of Social Organization among a Central Asian Turkic-Speaking Population*. Anthropological Papers 58. Ann Arbor, Mich.: Museum of Anthropology Publications.

Kansa, Sarah Whitcher and Stuart Campbell. 2002. Feasting with the Dead? A Ritual Bone Deposit at Domuztepe, Southeastern Turkey (c. 5550 cal BC). In *Behaviour Behind Bones: The Zooarchaeology of Ritual, Religion, Status and Identity*, ed. Sharyn Jones O'Day, Wim Van Neer, and Anton Ervynck, 2–13. International Council of Archaeozoology. Durham: Oxbow.

Kansa, Sarah Whitcher, Suellen C. Gauld, Stuart Campbell, and Elizabeth Carter. 2009. Whose Bones Are Those? Preliminary Comparative Analysis of Fragmented Human and Animal Bones in the "Death Pit" at Domuztepe, a Late Neolithic Settlement in Southeastern Turkey. *Anthropozoologia* 44.1: 159–72.

Karaca, Özgen. 1985. Pirot Höyük 1983 Kazıları. *Kazı Sonuçları Toplantısı* 6.1: 37–48.

Keith, Kathryn. 1998. Spindle Whorls, Gender, and Ethnicity at Late Chalcolithic Hacınebi Tepe. *Journal of Field Archaeology* 25.4: 497–515.

Kennedy, Jason R. 2008. *Terminal Ubaid Ceramics at Yenice Yani: Implications for Terminal Ubaid Organization of Labor and Commensality*. M.A. thesis. State University of New York, Binghamton.

Korfmann, Manfred. 1982. *Tilkitepe: Die ersten Ansätze prähistorischer Forschung in der östlichen Türkei*. Tübingen: Ernst Wasmuth.

Kozbe, Gülriz. 2006. Şırnak İli, Cizre-Silopi Ovası 2004 Yılı Yüzey Araştırması. *Araştırma Sonuçları Toplantısı* 23.1: 293–308.

———. 2007. Şırnak İli Cizre-Silopi Ovası Yüzey Araştırması, 2005. *Araştırma Sonuçları Toplantısı* 24.1: 307–26.

———. 2008. Şırnak İli Yüzey Araştırmaları, 2006. *Araştırma Sonuçları Toplantısı* 25.1: 175–86.

Leenders, Roger. 1989. The Red Wash Ware Ceramic Assemblage in Syria: A Review. In *To the Euphrates and Beyond: Archaeological Studies in Honor of Maurits van Loon*, ed. Odette M.C. Haex, Hans H. Curvers, and Peter M. M. G. Akkermans, 89–102. Rotterdam: Balkema.

Lloyd, Seton and Fuad Safar. 1943. Tell Uqair: Excavations by the Iraq Government Directorate of Antiquities in 1940–41. *Journal of Near Eastern Studies* 2: 131–58.

Lupton, Alan. 1996. *Stability and Change: Socio-Political Development in North Mesopotamia and South-East Anatolia 4000–2700 BC*. BAR International Series 627. Oxford: Tempus Reparatum.

Mallowan, Max E. L. 1946. Excavations in the Balikh Valley (1938). *Iraq* 8: 111–56.

Mallowan, Max E. L. and John C. Rose. 1935. Excavations at Tell Arpachiyah, 1933. *Iraq* 2: 1–178.

Marfoe, Leon and Michael L. Ingraham. 1990. Area A. In *Town and Country in Southeastern Anatolia. Vol. II. The Stratigraphic Sequence at Kurban Höyük*, ed. Guillermo Algaze, 23–63. Oriental Institute Publications 110. Chicago: Oriental Institute Press.

Matthews, Roger D. 2003. *The Archaeology of Mesopotamia: Theories and Approaches*. New York: Routledge.

McCarty, Sue Ann. 2009. Telling the Future or Hoarding the Past?: A Halaf Cattle Astragalus Cache from Kazane Höyük, Southeastern Turkey. Poster presented at the *Interpreting the Late Neolithic Conference*, organized by P. Akkermans, R. Bernbeck, and O. Nieuwenhuyse. Leiden, 26–28 March 2009.

Mellink, Machteld. 1989. Archaeology in Asia Minor. *American Journal of Archaeology* 93: 105–33.

———. 1991. Archaeology in Anatolia. *American Journal of Archaeology* 95: 123–53.

Miyake, Yutaka. 2007. Salat Cami Yanı: Dicle Havzası'nda Çanak Çömlekli Neolitik Döneme Ait Yeni Bir Yerleşme. In *Türkiye'de Neolitik Dönem* ed. Mehmet Özdoğan and Nezih Başgelen. İstanbul: Arkeoloji ve Sanat Yayınları.

Nieuwenhuyse, Olivier. 2007. *Plain and Painted Pottery: The Rise of Late Neolithic Ceramic Styles on the Syrian and Northern Mesopotamian Plains*. Turnhout: Brepols.

Nieuwenhuyse, Olivier, Peter M. M. G. Akkermans and Johannes van der Plicht. 2010. Not So Coarse, Nor Always Plain – The Earliest Pottery of Syria. *Antiquity* 84: 71–85.

Nissen, Hans. 2000. Mesopotamian Hierarchy in Action in Ancient Uruk. In *Hierarchies in Action. Cui Bono?*, ed. Michael Diehl, 210–17. Carbondale: Center for Archaeological Investigations, Southern Illinois University.

Oates, Joan. 1993. Trade and Power in the Fifth and Fourth Millennia BC: New Evidence from Northern Mesopotamia. *World Archaeology* 24.3: 403–22.

Oates, Joan and David Oates. 1997. An Open Gate: Cities of the Fourth Millennium BC (Tell Brak 1997). *Cambridge Archaeological Journal* 7: 287–97.

———. 2004. The Role of Exchange Relations in the Origins of Mesopotamian Civilization. In *Explaining Social Change: Studies in Honour of Colin Renfrew*, ed. John Cherry, Chris Scarre, and Stephen Shennan, 177–92. Cambridge: McDonald Institute Monographs.

Oates, Joan, Augusta McMahon, Philip Karsgaard, Salam Al Quntar, and Jason Ur. 2007. Early Mesopotamian Urbanism: A New View from the North. *Antiquity* 81: 585–600.

Ozan, Ali. 2009. Siirt-Botan vadisinde Ubaid Dönemi. In *Altan Çilingiroğlu'na Armağan: Yukarı Denizin Kıyısında Urartu Krallıgı'na Adanmış Bir Hayat (Studies in Honour of Altan Çilingiroğlu: A Life Dedicated to Urartu on the Shores of the Upper Sea)*, ed. Haluk Sağlamtimur, Eşref Abay, Zafer Derin, Aylin Ü. Erdem, Atilla Batmaz, Fulya Dedeoğlu, Mücella Erdalkıran, Mahmut B. Baştürk, and Erim Konakçı, 407–25. İstanbul: Arkeoloji ve Sanat Yayınları.

———. Forthcoming. *Halaf döneminde Botan, Garzan ve Batman vadilerinin Siirt-Türbe Höyük kazıları ışığında değerlendirilmesi*. Paper presented at the 1. Uluslararası Batman ve Çevresi Tarih ve Kültür Sempozyumu, Batman.

Özbal, Hadi. 1996. Chemical Analysis of a Copper Chisel from Hacınebi Tepe. *Anatolica* 22: 109–10.

———. 1997. Early Metal Technology at Hacınebi Tepe. In "Excavations at Hacınebi Turkey—1996: Preliminary Report." *Anatolica* 23: 139–43.

Özbal, Hadi, Mieke Adriaens, and Brian Earl. 1999. Hacınebi Metal Production and Exchange. *Paléorient* 25.1: 57–66.

Özbal, Rana. 2006. *Households, Daily Practice and Cultural Appropriation at Sixth Millennium Tell Kurdu*. Ph.D. dissertation. Northwestern University.

———. 2010. The Emergence of Ubaid Styles at Tell Kurdu: A Local Perspective. In *Beyond the Ubaid: Transformation and Integration in the Late Prehistoric Societies of the Middle East*, ed. Robert A. Carter and Graham Philip, 293–310. Chicago: Oriental Institute of the University of Chicago.

Özbal, Rana, Fokke Gerritsen, Benjamin Diebold, Elizabeth Healey, Nihal Aydın, Michelle Loyet, Frank Nardulli, David Reese, Heidi Ekstrom, Sabrina Sholts, Nitzan Mekel-Bobrov, and Bruce Lahn. 2004. Tell Kurdu Excavations 2001. *Anatolica* 30: 37–108.

Özbal, Rana, Fokke Gerritsen, and K. Aslıhan Yener. 2003. 2001 Tell Kurdu Kazıları. *Kazı Sonuçları Toplantısı* 24.1: 501–12.

Özbaşaran, Mihriban. 1992. *Doğu ve Güneydoğu Anadolu Kalkolitik Mimarisinde Tülintepe Yerleşmesinin Yeri*. Ph.D. dissertation. İstanbul Üniversitesi.

Özdoğan, Mehmet. 1977. *Lower Euphrates Basin: 1977 Survey*. Middle East Technical University. Lower Euphrates Project Publications, series 1, no. 2. Ankara: Orta Doğu Teknik Üniversitesi.

Özdoğan, Mehmet and Aslı Özdoğan. 1993. Pre-Halafian Pottery of Southeastern Anatolia with Special Reference to the Çayönü Sequence. In *Between the Rivers and over the Mountains: Archaeologica Anatolica et Mesopotamica Alba Palmieri Dedicata*, ed. Marcella Frangipane, Harald Hauptmann, Mario Liverani, Paolo Matthiae, and Machteld Mellink, 87–103. Roma: Università di Roma "La Sapienza."

Özgen, Engin, Barbara Helwing, and Atilla Engin. 2002. The Oylum Regional Project: Archaeological Prospection 2000. *Araştırma Sonuçları Toplantısı* 19.2: 217–28.

Özgen, Engin, Barbara Helwing, Atilla Engin, Olivier Nieuwenhuyse, and Richard Spoor. 1999. Oylum Höyük 1997–1998. Die spätchalkolithische Siedlung auf der Westterrasse. *Anatolia Antiqua* 7: 19–67.

Özgen, Engin, Barbara Helwing, Lothar Herling, and Atilla Engin. 2003. The Oylum Höyük Regional Project: Results of the 2001 Prospection Season. *Araştırma Sonuçları Toplantısı* 20.2: 151–58.

Özgüç, Nimet. 1992. The Uruk Culture at Samsat. In *Von Uruk nach Tuttul. Eine Festschrift für Eva Strommenger: Studien und Aufsätze von Kollegen und Freunden*, ed. Barthel Hrouda, Stephan Kroll, and Peter Z. Spanos, 151–65. München: Profil.

Özgüç, Tahsin. 1956. Fraktin Kabartması Yanındaki Prehistorik Ev. *Anadolu* 1.1: 59–64.

Öztan, Aliye. 2002. Köşk Höyük: Anadolu Arkeolojisine Yeni Katkılar. *Tüba-Ar* 5: 55–69.

Palmieri, Alberto M., Kemal Sertok, and Evgenij Chernykh. 1993. From Arslantepe Metalwork to Arsenical Copper Technology in Eastern Anatolia. In *Between the Rivers and over the Mountains: Archaeologica Anatolica et Mesopotamica Alba Palmieri Dedicata*, ed. Marcella Frangipane, Harald Hauptmann, Mario Liverani, Paolo Matthiae, and Machteld Mellink, 563–99. Roma: Università di Roma "La Sapienza."

Parker, Bradley and Andrew Creekmore. 2002. The Upper Tigris Archaeological Research Project: A Final Report from the 1999 Field Season. *Anatolian Studies* 52: 19–74.

Parker, Bradley, Catherine P. Foster, Jennifer Henecke, Marie Hopwood, David Hopwood, Andrew Creekmore, Arzu Demirergi, and Melissa Eppihimer. 2008. Preliminary Report from the 2005–2006 Field Seasons at Kenan Tepe. *Anatolica* 34: 103–76.

Parker, Bradley J., Catherine P. Foster, Kathleen Nicoll, Jason R. Kennedy, Philip Graham, Alexia Smith, David E. Hopwood, Marie Hopwood, Kristin Butler, Elizabeth Healey, M. Barış Uzel, and Reilly Jensen. 2009. The Upper Tigris Archaeological Research Project (UTARP): A Preliminary Report from the 2007 and 2008 Field Seasons at Kenan Tepe. *Anatolica* 35.1: 85–152.

Pearce, Julie. 2000. The Late Chalcolithic Sequence at Hacınebi Tepe, Turkey. In *Chronologies des Pays du Caucause et de l'Euphrate aux IVe–IIIe Millénaires*, ed. Catherine Marro and Harald Hauptmann, 115–44. Institut Français d'Etudes Anatoliennes d'Istanbul, Varia Anatolica XI. Paris: De Boccard.

———. 2008. *Hacınebi Tepe and the Uruk Expansion: A Ceramic Perspective on Culture Contact*. Ph.D. dissertation. University of Pennsylvania.

Perkins, Ann L. 1949. *The Comparative Archaeology of Early Mesopotamia*. Chicago: University of Chicago Press.

Pittman, Holly. 1996. Preliminary Report on Glyptic Art: Hacınebi 1993. In *Uruk Colonies and Mesopotamian Communities: An Interim Report on the 1992–1993 Excavations at Hacınebi, Turkey. American Journal of Archaeology* 100.2: 230–33.

———. 1999. Administrative Evidence from Hacınebi Tepe: An Essay on the Local and the Colonial. *Paléorient* 25.1: 43–50.

———. 2001. Mesopotamian Intra-Regional Relations Reflected through Glyptic Evidence in the Late Chalcolithic. In *Uruk Mesopotamia and its Neighbors: Cross-Cultural Interactions in the Era of State Formation*, ed. Mitchell S. Rothman, 403–44. Santa Fe, N.M.: School of American Research Press.

Pollock, Susan. 1992. Bureaucrats and Managers, Peasants and Pastoralists, Imperialists and Traders: Research on the Uruk and Jemdet Nasr Periods in Mesopotamia. *Journal of World Prehistory* 6: 297–336.

———. Forthcoming. Subjects and Objects: Defining a Halaf Tradition. In *Interpreting the Late Neolithic of Upper Mesopotamia*, ed. Anna Russell, Olivier P. Nieuwenhuyse, Peter M. M. G. Akkermans, and Reinhard Bernbeck. Turnhout: Brepols.

Redman, Charles L. 1978. *The Rise of Civilization: From Early Farmers to Urban Society in the Ancient Near East.* San Francisco: Freeman.

Reichel, Clemens. 2002. Administrative Complexity in Syria during the Fourth Millennium BC: The Seals and Sealings from Tell Hamoukar. *Akkadica* 123: 35–56.

Reilly, Edward Bowen. 1940. Test Excavations at Tilkitepe (1937). *Türk Tarih, Arkeologya ve Etnografya Dergisi* 4: 145–65.

Rosenberg, Michael and Hakan Togul. 1991. The Batman River Archaeological Site Survey, 1990. *Anatolica* 17: 241–54.

Rothman, Mitchell S. 2001a. The Local and the Regional: An Introduction. In *Uruk Mesopotamia and its Neighbors: Cross-Cultural Interactions in the Era of State Formation*, ed. Mitchell S. Rothman, 3–26. Santa Fe, N.M.: School of American Research Press.

———. 2001b. The Tigris Piedmont, Eastern Jazira, and Highland Western Iran in the Fourth Millennium BC. In *Uruk Mesopotamia and its Neighbors: Cross-Cultural Interactions in the Era of State Formation*, ed. Mitchell S. Rothman, 349–403. Santa Fe, N.M.: School of American Research Press.

Rothman, Mitchell and Gülriz Kozbe. 1997. Muş in the Early Bronze Age. *Anatolian Studies* 47: 105–26.

Russell, Henry F. 1980. *Pre-Classical Pottery of Eastern Anatolia: Based on a Survey by Charles Burney of Sites along the Euphrates and around Lake Van*. BAR International Series 85. Oxford: British Archaeological Reports.

Sagona, Antonio and Paul Zimansky. 2009. *Ancient Turkey*. London: Routledge.

Sağlamtimur, Haluk. 2009. Ilısuya Yeni Kurban: Botan'da 9 Bin Yıl. *Atlas 119 (Şubat)*: 36–37.

Sağlamtimur, Haluk and Ali Ozan. 2007. Siirt—Türbe Höyük Kazısı—Ön Rapor (Siirt—Türbe Höyük Excavation—Preliminary Report). *Arkeoloji Dergisi (Ege Üniversitesi Edebiyat Fakültesi Yayınları)* 10.2: 1–32.

Schachner, Andreas. 2003. 2000–01 Yılı Giricano Kazıları. *Kazı Sonuçları Toplantısı* 24.2: 447–60.

———. 2004. Vorbericht über die Ausgrabungen in Giricano, 2001. In *TAÇDAM: Activities in 2001*, ed. Numan Tuna, Jean Özturk, and Jale Velibeyoğlu, 505–46. Ankara: Middle East Technical University Press.

Schachner, Andreas, Michael Roaf, Karen Radner, and Rainer Pasternak. 2002. Vorläufiger Bericht über die Ausgrabungen in Giricano. In *TAÇDAM: Activities in 2000*, ed. Numan Tuna and Jale Velibeyoğlu, 587–630. Ankara: Middle East Technical University Press.

Seeden, H. and M. Kaddour. 1983. Space, Structures and Land in Shams ed-Din Tannira on the Euphrates: An Ethnoarchaeological Perspective. In *Land Tenure and Social Transformation in the Near East*, ed. Tarif al-Khalidi, 495–526. Beirut: American University of Beirut Press.

Steadman, Sharon R. 1996. Isolation or Interaction: Prehistoric Cilicia and the Fourth Millennium Uruk Expansion. *Journal of Mediterranean Archaeology* 9.2: 131–65.

———. 2000. Spatial Patterning and Social Complexity on Prehistoric Anatolian Tell Sites, Models for Mounds. *Journal of Anthropological Archaeology* 19: 164–99.

Stein, Gil. 1999. *Rethinking World-Systems: Diasporas, Colonies, and Interaction in Uruk Mesopotamia.* Tucson: University of Arizona Press.

———. 2001. Indigenous Social Complexity at Hacınebi (Turkey) and the Organization of Uruk Colonial Contact. In *Uruk Mesopotamia and its Neighbors: Cross-Cultural Interactions in the Era of State Formation*, ed. Mitchell S. Rothman, 265–306. Santa Fe, N.M.: School of American Research Press.

———. 2002. From Passive Periphery to Active Agents: Emerging Perspectives in the Archaeology of Interregional Interaction. *American Anthropologist* 104: 903–16.

Stein, Gil J., Reinhard Bernbeck, Cheryl Coursey, Augusta McMahon, Naomi F. Miller, Adnan Mısır, Jeffrey Nicola, Holly Pittman, Susan Pollock, and Henry Wright. 1996. Uruk Colonies and Anatolian Communities: An Interim Report on the 1992–1993 Excavations at Hacınebi, Turkey. *American Journal of Archaeology* 100.2: 205–60.

Stein, Gil J., Christopher Edens, Julie P. Edens, Kenneth Boden, Nicola Laneri, Hadi Özbal, Brian Earl, Mieke Adriaens, and Holly Pittman. 1998. Southeastern Anatolia before the Uruk Expansion: Preliminary Report on the 1997 Excavations at Hacınebi, Turkey. *Anatolica* 24: 143–93.

Stein, Gil and Jeffrey Nicola. 1996. Late Chalcolithic Faunal Remains from Hacınebi. In *Uruk Colonies and Mesopotamian Communities: An Interim Report on the 1992–3 Excavations at Hacınebi, Turkey. American Journal of Archaeology* 100: 205–60.

Stein, Gil and Rana Özbal. 2007. A Tale of Two Oikumenai: Variation in the Expansionary Dynamics of Ubaid and Uruk Mesopotamia. In *Settlement and Society: Ecology, Urbanism, Trade and Technology in Mesopotamia and Beyond (Robert McC. Adams Festschrift)*, ed. Elizabeth C. Stone, 356–70. Los Angeles: Cotsen Institute of Archaeology Press.

Summers, Geoffrey D. and David H. French. 1992. 1990 Adıyaman Yüzey Araştırması. *Araştırma Sonuçları Toplantısı* 9.1: 505–22.

Sürenhagen, Dietrich. 1986. The Dry-Farming Belt: The Uruk Period and Subsequent Developments. In *The Origins of Cities in Dry-Farming Syria and Mesopotamia in the Third Millennium B.C.*, ed. Harvey Weiss, 7–43. Guilford: Four Quarters.

Şenyurt, S. Y. 2002. 2000 Excavations at Aşağı Salat. In *TAÇDAM: Activities in 2000*, ed. Numan Tuna, Jean Öztürk, and Jale Velibeyoğlu, pp. 688–722. Ankara: Middle East Technical University Press.

Tapper, Richard. 1979. The Organization of Nomadic Communities in Pastoral Societies of the Middle East. In *Pastoral Production and Society*, 43–65. Cambridge: Cambridge University Press.

Tekin, Halil. 2003. Hakemi Use 2001 Kazısı. *Kazı Sonuçları Toplantısı* 24: 59–70.

———. 2007. Hakemi Use: Güneydoğu Anadolu'da Son Neolitik Döneme ait yeni bir merkez. In *Türkiye'de Neolitik Dönem*, ed. Mehmet Özdoğan and Nezih Başgelen, 47–56. İstanbul: Arkeoloji ve Sanat Yayınları.

Thissen, Laurens. 1985. The Late Chalcolithic and Early Bronze Age Pottery from Hayaz Höyük. *Anatolica* 12: 75–130.

Tobler, Artur. 1950. *Excavations at Tepe Gawra*, vol. 2. Philadephia: University of Pennsylvania Press.

Trufelli, Franca. 1994. Standardisation, Mass Production and Potters' Marks in the Late Chalcolithic Pottery of Arslantepe (Malatya). *Origini* 18: 248–89.

———. 1997. Ceramic Correlations and Cultural Relations in IVth Millennium Eastern Anatolia and Syro-Mesopotamia. *Studi Micenei ed. Egeo-Anatolici* 39.1: 5.

Uerpmann, Hans-Peter. 1982. Faunal Remains from Shams ed-Din Tannira, a Halafian Site in Northern Syria. *Berytus* 30: 3–52.

Ur, Jason. 2002. Settlement and Landscape in Northern Mesopotamia: The Tell Hamoukar Survey 2000–2001. *Akkadica* 123: 57–88.

Ur, Jason, Philip Karsgaard, and Joan Oates. 2007. Early Urban Development in the Near East. *Science* 317: 1188.

van Loon, Maurits. 1978. Architecture and Stratigraphy. In *Korucutepe. Final Report on the Excavations of the Universities of Chicago, California (Los Angeles) and Amsterdam in the Keban Reservoir, Eastern Anatolia 1968–1970*, ed. Maurits van Loon, 3–11. *Amsterdam: North-Holland.*

Velibeyoğlu, Jale A., Andreas Schachner, and Şenay Schachner. 2002. Botan Vadisi ve Çattepe (Tilli) Yüzey Araştırmalarının İlk Sonuçları. In *Salvage Project of the Archaeological Heritage of the Ilısu and Carchemish Dam Reservoirs, Activities in 2000*, ed. Numan Tuna and Jale Velibeyoğlu, 783–835. Ankara: Middle East Technical University.

von Wickede, Alwo and Suzanne Herbordt. 1988. Çavi Tarlası. Bericht über die Ausgrabungskampagnen 1983–1984. *Istanbuler Mitteilungen* 38: 5–36.

Waechter, John, Sabahat Göğüs, and Marjory Veronica Seton Williams. 1951. The Sakçe Gözü Cave Site 1949. *Belleten* 15: 193–201.

Watson, Patty Jo. 1983. The Halafian Culture: A Review and Synthesis. In *The Hilly Flanks and Beyond: Essays on the Prehistory of Southwestern Asia Presented to Robert J. Braidwood*, ed. T. Cuyler Young, Philip E. L. Smith, and Peder Mortensen, 231–49. Studies in Ancient Oriental Civilization 36. Chicago: Oriental Institute.

Watson, Patty Jo and Stephen LeBlanc. 1990. *Girikihaciyan: A Halafian Site in Southeastern Turkey.* Institute of Archaeology Monographs 33. Los Angeles: University of California Institute of Archaeology.

Whallon, Robert. 1979. *An Archaeological Survey of the Keban Reservoir Area of East-Central Turkey.* Ann Arbor: University of Michigan, Museum of Anthropology.

Woolley, C. Leonard. 1934. The Prehistoric Pottery from Carchemish. *Iraq* 1: 146–62.

———. 1959. *A Forgotten Kingdom: Being a Record of the Results Obtained from the Excavations of Two Mounds, Atchana and Al Mina in the Turkish Hatay*, rev. ed. London: Parrish.

Wright, Henry. 2001. Cultural Action in the Uruk World. In *Uruk Mesopotamia and its Neighbors: Cross-Cultural Interactions in the Era of State Formation*, ed. Mitchell S. Rothman, 123–49. Santa Fe, N.M.: School of American Research Press.

Wright, Henry and Gregory Johnson. 1975. Population, Exchange, and Early State Formation in Southwestern Iran. *American Anthropologist* 77.2: 267–89.

Wright, Henry and Eric Rupley. 2001. Calibrated Radiocarbon Age Determinations of Uruk-Related Assemblages. In *Uruk Mesopotamia and its Neighbors: Cross-Cultural*

Interactions in the Era of State Formation, ed. Mitchell S. Rothman, 85–122. Santa Fe, N.M.: School of American Research Press.

Wright, Henry T. and Robert Whallon. 1998. Investigations at Fatmalı Kalecik: A Chalcolithic Hamlet in the Upper Euphrates Valley. In *Light at the Top of the Black Hill: Studies Presented to Halet Çambel*, ed. Güven M. Arsebük, Machteld J. Mellink, and Wulf Schirmer, 775–810. İstanbul: Ege Yayınları.

Yakar, Jak and Ayşe Gürsan-Salzmann. 1978. The Provinces of Malatya and Sivas. *Expedition* 20: 59–62.

Yardımcı, Nurettin. 1993. Excavations, Surveys and Restoration Works at Harran. In *Between the Rivers and over the Mountains: Archaeologica Anatolica et Mesopotamica Alba Palmieri Dedicata*, ed. Marcella Frangipane, Harald Hauptmann, Mario Liverani, Paolo Matthiae, and Machteld Mellink, 437–52. Roma: Università di Roma "La Sapienza."

———. 2001. 1999 Yılı Harran Yüzey Araştırması Çalışmaları. *Araştırma Sonuçları Toplantısı* 18.2: 45–56.

Yener, K. Aslıhan. 2000. *The Domestication of Metals: The Rise of Complex Metal Industries in Anatolia.* Leiden: Brill.

Yener, K. Aslıhan, Christopher Edens, Jesse Casana, Benjamin Diebold, Heidi Ekstrom, Michelle Loyet, and Rana Özbal. 2000a. Tell Kurdu Excavations 1999. *Anatolica* 26: 32–117.

Yener, K. Aslıhan, Christopher Edens, Timothy P. Harrison, Jan Verstraete, and Tony J. Wilkinson. 2000b. The Amuq Valley Regional Project, 1995–1998. *American Journal of Archaeology* 104: 163–220.

Young, T. Cuyler. 1986. Godin Tepe Period VI/V and Central Western Iran at the End of the Fourth Millennium. In *Gamdat Nasr: Period or Regional Style?*, ed. Uwe Finkbeiner and Wolfgang Röllig, 212–28. Wiesbaden: Ludwig Reichert.

CHAPTER 9

THE CHALCOLITHIC OF EASTERN ANATOLIA

GIULIO PALUMBI

Geography

Eastern Anatolia, which can be defined as the part of eastern Turkey located south of the Pontic Range, bordered to the west by the upper stretches of the Euphrates River and, to the south, by the Taurus Mountains, is mainly a region of mountains and highlands. The Taurus Range, which runs west to east from the Mediterranean almost as far as the Zagros Mountains, forms the region's southern backbone and acts as a clear-cut geographic and ecological border that separates the eastern Anatolian highlands from the lowlands of southeastern Anatolia and northern Syria. Much more difficult to identify are its geographical eastern borders, because of the strong geographic and ecological continuity with the Lesser Caucasus.

The climate of eastern Anatolia is a typical continental climate (long and harsh winters and very hot summers, with a temperature range varying between −30°C and +40°C and an annual rainfall of between 400 and 1,500 mm). The region belongs to the Irano-Turanic phytogeographic area, with alpine rangelands reaching to above 2,500 m above sea level (asl), oak, ash, and juniper woodlands lying below 2,500 m asl, and more steppic vegetation in the plains (Dewdney 1971; Erol 1983:145; Güldalı 1979:20; Newton 2004:104; van Zeist and Bottema 1991:20–22; Willcox 1974:122–23). Some 70 percent of the eastern Anatolian territory could potentially be forested, but at the moment only 14 percent is actually under tree cover; the lunar landscapes that characterize the region at present are the product of its human history and economics, so we should think of eastern Anatolia in antiquity as having been much greener and more densely forested than it is today

(Kuzucuoğlu and Roberts 1997:20–21; Miller 1997:205; Newton 2004:108–10; van Zeist and Bottema 1991:23).

Many features of eastern Anatolia's landscape, such as the tufa and basalt plateaus, the most imposing and highest massifs (like the Ararat, the Nemrut, and the Supan Dağ), Lake Van (the largest lake in Turkey), and the abundant obsidian deposits of the Bingöl, Van, Kars, and Sarıkamış districts remind us that the region has a volcanic formation.

The Araxes, Çoruh, Kara Su, Murat, and Euphrates are the largest rivers in the region. The first three drain the northernmost watersheds, and the Murat drains the southernmost hydrographic basins. Except for the Çoruh, which crosses the Pontic Mountains to run into the Black Sea, the direction taken by the Kara Su, Araxes, and Murat is determined by the orography of the mountain chains, which basically run east–west. However, unlike the Kara Su and the Murat, the Araxes, which springs from the easternmost edges of the Erzurum region, runs from west to east, in the direction of the Ararat Plain and, together with its valley, constitutes one of the main natural links to the westernmost areas of the southern Caucasus.

The Erzurum Plain, at an elevation of 2,000 m, drains off the waters that converge and feed the Kara Su, which, after crossing the Erzincan Plain (elevation 1,200 m), loops southwest, bordering the slopes of the Munzur Dağları, and runs down toward the confluence with the Murat. The Murat, which flows in a northeast–southwest direction, runs close to Lake Van and, after crossing the deep gorges of the Bingöl Mountains (which still belong to the Taurus mountain system), enters a series of wide valleys (the Altınova Plain and the Aşvan region) before flowing into the Kara Su near the modern Keban Dam.

Officially, the Euphrates is formed by the confluence of the Kara Su and the Murat, and after crossing the westernmost edges of the Malatya Plain its course cuts across the Taurus Mountains, running through narrow, deep gorges for about ninety kilometers before entering the lower hills of the Urfa and Gaziantep regions. The area comprising the lower reaches of the Murat (starting from the Altınova Plain), the final stretch of the Kara Su, and the upper course of the Euphrates River as far as the northern slopes of the Taurus, defines what is known as the Upper Euphrates Valley. The Euphrates, Kara Su, Murat, and Araxes therefore form part of a complex natural communication system connecting eastern Anatolia both to the southern Caucasus and the Upper Euphrates Valley and, more indirectly, to the lowlands of southeastern Anatolia and northern Syria.

A Brief History of Studies: Terminologies and Chronologies

Prehistoric investigations in eastern Anatolia began in the early twentieth century. Tilkitepe, on Lake Van (figure 9.1), was the first site excavated (Belck 1899; Korfmann and Schiele 1977; Reilly 1937); it was not until the 1950s that Koşay focused his

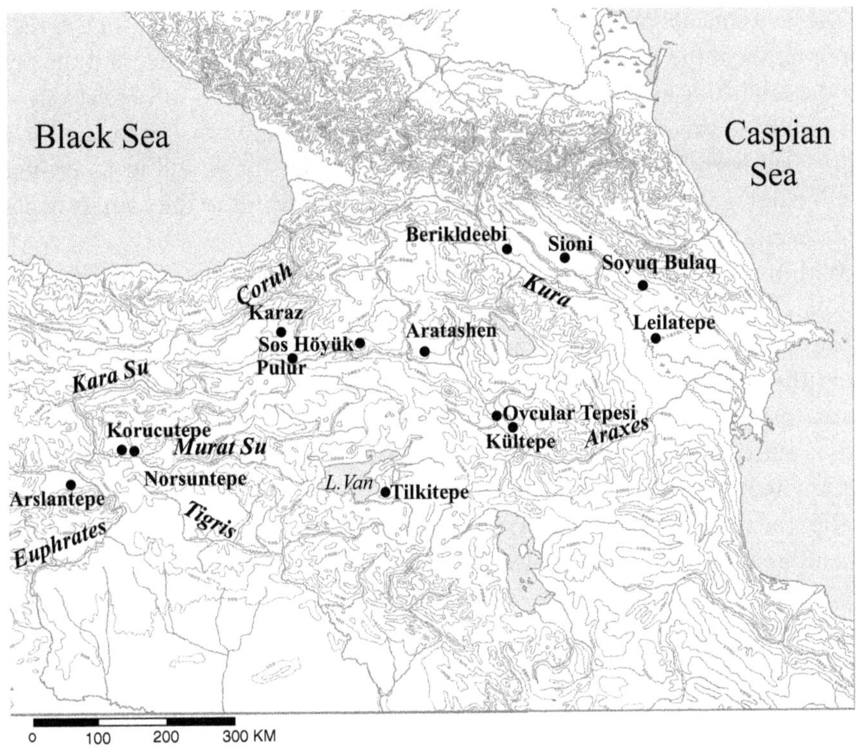

Figure 9.1. Eastern Anatolia, southern Caucasus, and the main sites mentioned in the text.

research in northeastern Anatolia, on the Erzurum Plain, where he excavated the *höyüks* of Karaz, Pulur, and Güzelova (Koşay and Turfan 1959; Koşay and Vary 1964, 1967; Sagona 2000). Over the same period, a number of pioneering surveys were conducted by Burney in several parts of the region, from the Upper Euphrates to the slopes of Mt. Ararat (Burney 1958; Russell 1980).

However, after these explorations, eastern Anatolia was neglected by archaeological research for quite some time (excluding the investigations of Urartu). From the 1990s onward, however, studies of the region's prehistory acquired a new impetus. This occurred both in connection with the excavation of new sites (Sos Höyük, Büyüktepe, Karagündüz, and Dilkaya) and a series of more recent surveys systematically conducted in the region of Lake Van and in the districts of Doğubeyazit, Ağrı, Iğdır, Bayburt, and Muş. At the same time, the new and increasingly intense flow of scientific information from the southern Caucasus, following the collapse of the Soviet Union and the formation of the new independent states of Armenia, Azerbaijan, and Georgia, has conferred a new centrality to eastern Anatolia in relation to the cultural, political, and historical role played by this region in the dynamics and processes of cultural development of south Caucasian prehistory. Despite all this new information, however, eastern Anatolia is still a frontier area as far as research is concerned, with dramatic information gaps; Neolithic developments are little known in this region, and the Chalcolithic is more enigmatic still.

The very concept of the Chalcolithic is still very difficult to define for this region both in terms of the sociocultural structures relevant in this period and the problems of establishing an absolute chronology. *Chalcolithic* itself is still a relatively new term applied to this region, as the old (and now obsolete) term—in Russian scholarship—had been *Eneolithic*. In any event, the scholarship is still in its early and provisional stages, marked by a great deal of uncertainty due to the scarcity of absolute dates and stratified contexts.

Within the framework of a relative chronology, the Chalcolithic in eastern Anatolia should be dated to between the end of the neolithisation process and the emergence of a new sociocultural model, known as "Kura-Araks" (following the tradition of Russian and south Caucasian studies, and named after the two most important rivers in the southern Caucasus) (Kuftin 1941:114) or "Early Transcaucasian Culture" (in Western scholarship) (Burney 1958; Burney and Lang 1971).

Kiguradze and Sagona (2003) have suggested subdividing the south Caucasian and eastern Anatolian Chalcolithic into an Early Phase (between 4800 and 4000 B.C.E.) and a Middle-Late Phase (between 4000 and 3100/3000 B.C.E.); a similar dating scheme has been reiterated by Lyonnet for the southern Caucasus (Early Chalcolithic 4900–4000 and Late Chalcolithic 3900–3000 B.C.E.) (Lyonnet 2007). However, for the moment, there is very little evidence that can be used to construct an absolute chronological framework for this period or to see whether the data suggesting an internal periodization can actually be associated with any transformations or changes in the social or cultural patterns of the Chalcolithic communities of the region. In both these hypotheses, the periodization is similar to what Kiguradze (2000) first proposed, subdividing the south Caucasian Chalcolithic developments into an early phase, known as *Early Sioni*, and a more recent phase called *Late Sioni* (see Sagona, chapter 31 in this volume).

This terminology, which essentially refers to the ceramic traditions, is named after the eponymous site Sioni in eastern Georgia (Menabde and Kiguradze 1981), the remains of which are mainly represented by a large circular structure built on stone foundations and characterized by a dark-colored and grit (or obsidian) tempered pottery with typical decorations incised on the rims of the vessels (parallel oblique lines or spirals and circular impressions, often filled with a whitish paste) (figure 9.2; Kiguradze 2000; Marro 2007:90; Sagona and Zimansky 2009:164). The Late Sioni phase, conversely, which does not refer to the site of the same name at all, is characterized by the emergence of a new chaff tempered ceramic tradition and rectangular architectural plans.

Since Kiguradze's publication, the term *Sioni* has often been used somewhat misleadingly, ignoring the original distinction between an earlier phase, more specifically linked to the site of Sioni, and a later phase belonging to the first half of the fourth millennium B.C.E., to refer generically to the Chalcolithic cultural developments of the eastern Anatolian and south Caucasian communities in the fifth and fourth millennia B.C.E. We shall see whether the data currently available provide any justification for making this distinction between Early Chalcolithic and

Figure 9.2. Grit tempered ceramics from Sioni (eastern Georgia), Early–Middle Chalcolithic (with kind permission of the curator M. Menadbe, Georgian National Museum).

(pre-Kura-Araks) Late Chalcolithic, and whether it really corresponds to different periods in the cultural history of the region.

The Neolithic Background

The earliest evidence discovered so far in eastern Anatolia is at Tilkitepe, on the southeastern shores of Lake Van. Even though the excavations of this small mound have a long history, little certain data exist, and there are many doubts and uncertainties regarding its cultural sequence. In an attempt to combine the documentation from the excavations conducted in different periods, Korfmann (1982) has proposed a sequence of three phases, distinguishable on the basis of the presence (and absence) of painted ceramics belonging to chronologically and culturally differing horizons.

Level III, the earliest, is characterized by the presence of Halaf painted ware (Watson 1982) which in terms of the quantities found would suggest that Tilkitepe formed part of a system of interactions oriented toward the upper Mesopotamian, Syrian, and southeastern Anatolian areas. Together with Tülintepe and Korucutepe (Brandt 1978; Esin 1976:160, 1979, 1982a:130–33), in the Upper Euphrates Valley, Tilkitepe is one of the northernmost sites providing evidence of the Halaf culture, which certainly differs from the occasional findings of Halaf ceramics in the southern Caucasus (at Aratashen and Verin Khatunarkh in the Ararat Plain and at Kültepe-Nakhichevan in the Araxes Valley), which were more likely to have been the result of occasional and mediated interactions with the Halaf world (Abibullaev 1982; Badalyan et al. 2004, 2007; Palumbi 2007). The presence of Halaf pottery at

Tilkitepe (resulting from a local community engaged in close relations with the south, or seasonal visits by southern groups?) must clearly be seen in relation to the obsidian deposits at Lake Van (Nemrut and Süphan Dağ), which attracted people to settle in this region to form part of a system of exchange relations with the neighboring areas.

Though the dating of the Halaf phenomenon to as early as the beginning of the sixth millennium B.C.E. has recently been confirmed (Campbell 2007; and see Castro-Gessner, chapter 35 in this volume, for further discussion of Halaf topics), the data that emerge from Tilkitepe and the surveys conducted on the Muş Plain (Rothman and Kozbe 1997) show the existence of a rather extensive interaction with the southern lowlands which occurred in the later Neolithic. Probably dating no later than to the last quarter of the sixth millennium B.C.E., the southernmost areas of eastern Anatolia were directly involved in a system of interactions linking them (perhaps also through the Upper Euphrates Valley) to the southeastern Anatolian, Syrian, and northern Mesopotamian regions.

The Chalcolithic Period

After the end of the sixth millennium B.C.E., and throughout the whole of the fifth—the period that should represent the earliest phases of the eastern Anatolian Chalcolithic—the cultural developments in the region, at least from our present knowledge, are decidedly more difficult to establish because of a very serious dearth of information. The only site that might possibly document an occupation that could better clarify this phase is, once again, Tilkitepe. Korfmann's Level II witnesses an undecorated chaff pottery production, but the typological repertoire seems to be rather heterogeneous, combining "archaic" shapes (deep bowls with square bases and hole-mouth jars) very closely resembling the Neolithic ceramics from the Ararat Plain (Harutunyan 2008; Palumbi 2007) with decidedly different and more articulated profiles. These latter shapes, such as truncated conical bowls with a flat base, short-necked jars, and jars with outflaring neck, are very similar in typological and technological terms both to those of the next Level I, and to those found at the south Caucasian Chalcolithic sites (such as Aratashen Phase 0), which can be dated to the second half of the fifth millennium B.C.E. (figure 9.3) (Palumbi 2007).

Despite the paucity of currently available data, it appears likely that Tilkitepe Level II does not exist as such, but is rather a mixture of materials from lower and upper levels. With regard to the latter, however, Level I—the most recent—offers interesting material for the study of what might have been the cultural developments in this part of Anatolia in the fifth millennium B.C.E. The pottery production from Level I belongs to the chaff tempered tradition and comprises hemispherical bowls and different typologies of jars (such as short-necked jars or jars with long outflaring necks), in addition to painted pottery (also chaff tempered) with black,

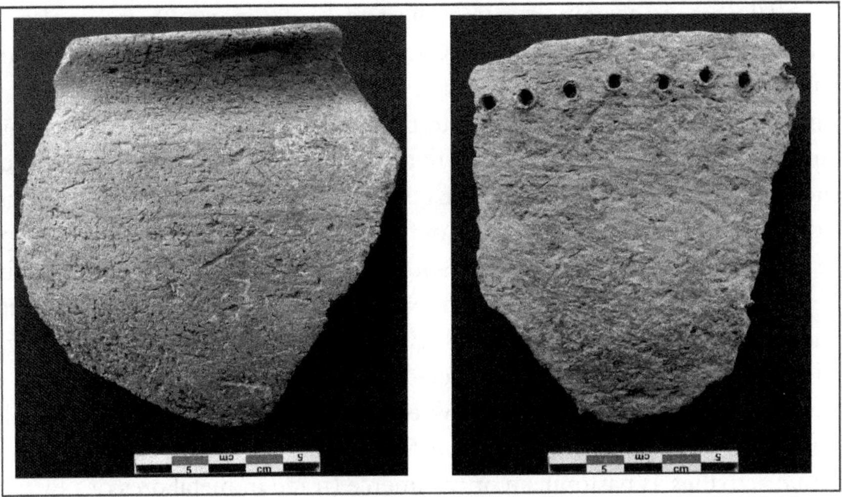

Figure 9.3. Chaff tempered ceramics from Aratashen (Ararat Plain, Armenia), Middle Chalcolithic.

reddish, or brown vertical wavy lines on a whitish or buff slipped background (Korfmann 1982:fig. 5).

The trend toward standardization in the Tilkitepe Level I ceramic repertoire (both open and closed shapes) and the rarity and simplification of the painted decorative motifs, is a process that finds parallels in other Chalcolithic sites of the southern Caucasus, such as the recently excavated Ovcular Tepesi in Nakhichevan (Marro, Bakhshaliyev, and Ashurov 2009:49) and follows the same process of development (and impoverishment) of the repertoires and decorations characteristic of the pottery production in the final phases of the Ubaid period in the whole of the northern Mesopotamian, Syrian, and southeast Anatolian areas (Akkermans 1988:291–92; Akkermans and Schwartz 2003:169–70; Helwing 2000; Schwartz 2001:237–38; Trufelli 1997:8–9). From this point of view, then, it might be feasible to suggest a date around the final quarter of the fifth millennium B.C.E. for both Tilkitepe Level I and the other sites in the Van region (such as Yılantaş) that are characterized by painted ware similar to that found at Tilkitepe I (Marro 2007, 2008; Marro and Özfırat 2004).

The broadening of the technological horizon of the chaff tempered ceramics, which some authors correlate to the Amuq E–F phases, is a widespread phenomenon that can certainly also be seen in the Upper Euphrates Valley from the latter half of the fifth millennium B.C.E. onward, in, for instance the Chalcolithic Schichten 1–7 at Norşuntepe (Gülçür 2000:376–80; Hauptmann 1973:96, 1976:86, 1979:74, 1982:60), at Değirmentepe (Esin 1983), at Arslantepe VIII (Trufelli 1997), and in the upper Tigris region, at Kenan Tepe (Parker et al. 2006, 2008). The widespread nature of this chaff tempered ceramic horizon is further corroborated by surveys conducted in the regions of Van (Marro and Özfırat 2003, 2004, 2005; Özfırat 2006) and Muş (Rothman 1994:283–84; Rothman and Kozbe 1997:108), and is also evidenced further east in the southern Caucasus (Chataigner 1995:101–2; Marro, Bakhshaliyev, and Ashurov 2009; Palumbi 2007).

This process appears to be related to the transformation of the role, function, and meaning of the ceramics, reflected in an extreme simplification of the decorative motifs and the increasing standardization of the formal repertoires. It seems to be both the cause and the consequence of the introduction of new production processes, tending toward greater specialization, and is consistent with what one finds in the pottery production of the adjacent Near Eastern regions in the same period.

In spite of this interregional technological trend, some authors have specifically linked the diffusion of the chaff tempered ceramics in eastern Anatolia and the southern Caucasus to the presence (between the end of the fifth and the first half of the fourth millennia B.C.E.) of northern Mesopotamian groups involved in such economic activities as pastoralism or commerce (trade in metal ores or raw materials) (Akhundov 2007; Lyonnet 2007, 2009; Marro 2005, 2007, 2008). However, the data gathered in the surveys carried out in the Van region, beyond these "northern Mesopotamian-oriented" communities, also point to the existence of other "indigenous" sites, distinguishable in terms of the presence of painted ceramics similar to Tilkitepe I (so-called Tilkitepe culture settlements) and/or grit tempered ware with incised rim decorations reminiscent of those found at Sioni (so-called Late Sioni culture settlements) (Marro 2007, 2008). According to this interpretation, the highlands of eastern Anatolia may well have hosted a complex system of complementary interactions between groups of differing origins and with different cultures (Mesopotamian and Transcaucasian) that occupied ecologically differentiated areas depending on the different economic activities in which they engaged (Marro 2007:92–93, and Marro, chapter 12 in this volume).

The problem with this interpretation, at least as far as eastern Anatolia is concerned, is that it is based solely on ceramic data, which cannot be properly compared with reliable stratigraphic sequences, and the presumed synchronic relationship between the different ceramic traditions (and/or cultural communities) may, conversely, be a "horizontal" distortion of the information gathered from the surveys. It is not unlikely that the pottery belonging to the grit tempered "Sioni" tradition, the painted Tilkitepe I pottery and the chaff ware, may have been a diachronic development in the ceramic cultures of eastern Anatolia during the fifth and into the first half of the fourth millennia B.C.E. However, the latest stratified data from Ovçular Tepesi in Nakhicevan show the coexistence, in the latter quarter of the fifth millennium B.C.E., of local chaff ware and nonlocal grit tempered Sioni sherds, thus underscoring a synchronicity between these two ceramic traditions (Marro, Bakhshaliyev, and Ashurov 2009). Indeed, the suggestion of a "northern Mesopotamian" expansion into eastern Anatolia from the end of the fifth to the first half of the fourth millennium B.C.E. is a hypothesis that is not based on the availability of regional stratified data and seems to be built in relation to the discovery of a series of fourth millennium sites in the southern Caucasus and to the processes that eventually took place in this latter region.

The remains of a fortification wall and a large mudbrick rectangular building (interpreted as a temple) belonging to Level V at Berikldeebi in Georgia (Djavakhishvili 1998; Kiguradze and Sagona 2003) and dated to the first half of the fourth millennium (3955–3778 cal B.C.E. and 3820–3640 cal B.C.E.) (Badalyan et al. 1992:48; Kiguradze and Sagona 2003:n. 1), constitute a significant novelty in this region. The Level II rectangular buildings at Leilatepe—which have been interpreted on the basis of their size and the type of internal infrastructure as dwellings, stores, or areas used for craft activities (copper slags have been found) (Akhundov 2007; Aliev and Narimanov 2001:10–17)—are also quite unusual (if compared to the earlier building traditions). The pottery from these sites belongs to the chaff tempered horizon, which in many respects resembles the Syrian, upper Mesopotamian, and middle Euphrates technological, typological (flat beaded bowls, "casseroles," short-necked jars with everted rims), and productive traditions (potter's marks) (Narimanov, Akhundov, and Aliev 2007).

Last, the adoption of new funerary customs, such as élite tombs built using mudbricks resembling those found at Tepe Gawra XI–IX and Korucutepe (Rothman 2001:390–91; Tobler 1950:70–75; van Loon 1978:10–12) built underneath earthen funerary tumuli (the north Caucasian tradition of the *kurgans*) (Lyonnet 2009; Makharadze 2007), are further elements that help strengthen the impression of increased Syro-Mesopotamian influences overlapping the cultural substratum of the Late Chalcolithic communities in the Caucasus (both northern and southern). As things stand at present, it is difficult to identify the factors and vehicles driving the introduction of these new traditions into the region, and although one cannot a priori exclude the physical presence of northern Mesopotamian communities, it may also be the case that this phenomenon could have been the outcome of a more complex process that was decidedly more extensive in scope.

In the Syrian and northern Mesopotamian regions, in southeastern Anatolia, and in the Upper Euphrates, the first half of the fourth millennium B.C.E. was characterized by the formation of large and important regional centers, a general reorganization of the craft production (with a growing specialization), and the final emergence of stratified societies and élite groups (Frangipane 1993, 1996:147–65, 2001; Palmieri 1985:196; Schwartz 2001:246–47; Stein 2001). With regard to the élite groups, the increasing demand for metal ores, precious stones, and exotic goods, used to fuel an economic system based on wealth finance (Frangipane 1996:158–62; Rothman 2001:391), may have encouraged these élite groups to step up trading relations between the main centers in upper Mesopotamia, the Upper Euphrates and northern Syria, and the eastern Anatolian and south Caucasian regions, which are particularly well endowed with raw materials (for additional discussion see Muhly, chapter 39 in this volume).

At the same time, a series of structural and organizational changes may have occurred in the south Caucasian—and the eastern Anatolian—communities in this period (territorial mobility, pastoral specialization, and the capacity to exploit ecologically differentiated resources) (Chataigner et al. 2010; Kiguradze 2000; Marro 2007:91–93;). These could have been symptomatic of an increased internal social and productive heterogeneity, which may have offered a better organized response to fuel the growing interactions with the south and meet the demands of the southern élites.

Perhaps the first evidence of Chalcolithic funerary tumuli in the southern Caucasus, which in some cases preserve luxury grave goods (such as the kurgan from Soyuq Bulaq, in Azerbaijan: Akhundov and Makhmudova 2008:31–43; Lyonnet 2009), may be indicative of the formation of small local élites that came into being as a result of the interregional interactions and the new social and economic value that interactions between the highlands and the lowlands may have acquired at that particular moment in history. This process of cultural rapprochement between the southern Caucasus, possibly eastern Anatolia, and the areas toward the south, which takes place in the first half of the fourth millennium B.C.E., may therefore have been the result of synergies between different factors, each of which may have had, in different ways, the effect of encouraging the establishment of "Syro-Mesopotamian" cultural traits in the highlands.

If, on one hand, it is possible to suggest that in this period, called the Late Chalcolithic, the southern Caucasus and the southernmost areas of eastern Anatolia may have interacted more intensively with the Upper Euphrates, upper Mesopotamia, and northern Syria, then on the other hand, the developments in the northernmost areas of eastern Anatolia could have been quite different and are decidedly more enigmatic to decipher at the moment. The first point one notices is that the comparatively more numerous (or more easily recognizable) settlements in the southernmost areas contrast with the very small number of rarified Neolithic or Chalcolithic (pre-Kura-Araks) settlements in the northern areas. Indeed, the surveys conducted in the Bayburt region have only identified two settlements (Gundulak and Pulur-Gökçedere), which may be dated to the period between the Neolithic and the (pre-Kura-Araks) Chalcolithic (Kiguradze and Sagona 2003:figs. 3.42–3.43; Sagona and Sagona 2004:460–61, 516–17). Levels dating from the very end of the fifth millennium B.C.E. have recently been excavated at Pulur (the only Chalcolithic site discovered so far in the Erzurum Plain), where the pottery from these levels is defined as a grit tempered "Black Burnished" ware, bearing similarities to the ceramics from the second half of the fourth millennium B.C.E. found at the relatively nearby site of Sos Höyük (Işıklı 2008:272). These data offer material for reflecting on a number of different aspects.

The first aspect might be the absence in the northernmost regions (as the surveys in the Bayburt region have confirmed) of the chaff tempered pottery horizon that was so common in the southernmost areas, thereby not only establishing a basic difference between the Chalcolithic ceramic traditions from the northern and southern areas of eastern Anatolia but also perhaps pointing to the existence of different cultural developments and separated networks of interaction that may have involved these areas in the same period. The second aspect has to do with the possible continuity between, or the cultural contribution of, the northeastern Anatolian Chalcolithic pottery traditions—such as the grit tempered Black or Dark Burnished Wares—in the formation of the mid-fourth millennium B.C.E.

Kura-Araks cultural phenomenon, suggesting (as is discussed in the next section) that some of its cultural origins (such as the Red-Black Burnished Ware) may have first developed in these areas (Palumbi 2003, 2008a, 2008b; Sagona and Sagona 2004:166; see also Sagona, chapter 30 in this volume).

Eastern Anatolia and the Kura-Araks Culture in the Fourth Millennium B.C.E.

It was around the mid-fourth millennium B.C.E. that radical changes occurred simultaneously in the southern Caucasus and in eastern Anatolia, marking the end of the previous Late Chalcolithic cultures and transforming these regions into drivers of a new and disrupting cultural model which, for almost a whole millennium, was a powerful identity-based benchmark of the highland communities of northern Iran, the southern Caucasus, and eastern Anatolia. It is still very difficult to understand where the Kura-Araks phenomenon might have begun, and even more difficult to identify the factors and dynamics that gave rise to it (see Sagona, chapter 30 in this volume). One can, however, say with certainty that there was little continuity, and rather sharp fractures, between the Kura-Araks culture and the earlier Late Chalcolithic traditions in terms of settlement patterns and material culture.

At the moment, there are only two sites that constitute a valid benchmark for establishing the initial phases of this phenomenon both in cultural and chronological terms: Sos Höyük in eastern Anatolia and Level IV at Berikldeebi (also see Sagona, chapter 30 in this volume, for discussion of these sites). Sos Höyük, which lies on the easternmost border of the Erzurum region, not far from the Araxes valley, documents a long sequence of uninterrupted occupation beginning in the latter half of the fourth millennium B.C.E.

Phase VA (Late Chalcolithic in the internal periodization of the site), dating from between 3500 and 3000 B.C.E., is the earliest, and reveals a close succession of occupations by domestic structures (always with internal circular hearths), followed by the construction of a large circular building on stone foundations, which might have marked an internal symbolic, functional, or social division within the site, since it stands on the highest part of the mound (Sagona et al. 1997, 1998; Sagona and Sagona 2000:59; Sagona and Zimansky 2009:164). The first phase of the circular wall ended when it collapsed around 3100 B.C.E., perhaps as a result of an earthquake. This event did not however interrupt the continuity of the occupation of the surrounding area. New superimposed levels were built on top of the débris of the wall, the first of which is represented by a careful preparation of flooring furnished with a circular hearth (known as the Ceramic Floor), followed by a circular dwelling (known as the Round House), also with a hearth, cut by a pit dating to

3345–2915 cal B.C.E. (2σ) (Kiguradze and Sagona 2003; Sagona and Sagona 2000:61; Sagona and Zimansky 2009:164). Around 3000 B.C.E., the circular wall was rebuilt, but this was a shorter phase, because shortly afterward the whole structure was completely destroyed. This point is considered to be the final break, marking the end of Phase VA (and the Late Chalcolithic at Sos) and the beginning of Phase VB (and Early Bronze I) (Sagona and Sagona 2000). Phase VA ceramics have been subdivided into different groups based on the features of the pastes (mixed or grit tempered), the coloring, and surface treatments (burnished or unburnished) (Kiguradze and Sagona 2003:48–49; Palumbi 2003:91–92; Sagona and Sagona 2004:163–68; Sagona and Zimansky 2009:164–66).

There are, in my opinion, two particularly significant aspects of the pottery production from Sos VA. The first is the presence of Red-Black Burnished Ware (RBBW), characterized by the typical fixed pattern with contrasting colors between the outer surfaces (always black) and the inner surfaces (red, brown, orange) of the same container. The fact that this ware has been found in the earliest levels at Sos emphasizes that RBBW in northeastern Anatolia must date back to at least the mid-fourth millennium B.C.E. Considering that in this same period it was absent from the southern Caucasus, where it became very common at the end of the fourth millennium B.C.E., it has been suggested that this pottery tradition may have originated in Anatolia (Palumbi 2003, 2008a, 2008b; for an alternative view see Marro, chapter 12 in this volume). Even though it varied from one Anatolian region to another in terms both of the chromatic patterns (fixed or alternate) and from the point of view of the typological repertoires used, it nevertheless demonstrates the existence of a technological substrate and an aesthetic taste (perhaps linked to chromatic symbolisms) that were shared among the communities of central Anatolia at Çadır Höyük and Alişar (Gorny et al. 2002:113; Orthmann 1963:35, 17; Schoop 2008), the Upper Euphrates in Arslantepe Phases VII final and VIA, at Tepecik (Esin 1982b:114–15; Frangipane 2001; Frangipane and Palmieri 1983:354–61; Frangipane and Palumbi 2007; Palumbi 2003), and in northeastern Anatolia at Sos Höyük. Furthermore, its almost simultaneous emergence in these areas just before or around the middle of the fourth millennium B.C.E., with a possible chronological primacy of central Anatolia (Steadman, McMahon, and Ross 2007:396, 400), suggests that around that time specific networks of central and eastern Anatolian interactions existed, based in large part on the geographical contiguity, which linked these regions through flows of information, commonly shared material culture traditions, and possibly economic relations.

The second aspect to be emphasized regarding the pottery production in Sos Phase VA is that it already shows (RBBW included) typological repertoires (large shallow bowls with S-shaped profile, cylindrical or truncated-conical necked jars, flat lids and trays), functional features (such as handles and knobs), and decorative motifs and techniques (grooved and relief decorations, postfiring incisions, ladder patterns, and double spirals), which represent some of the most typical traits of the Kura-Araks ceramic tradition and which are shared, in this same period, with the communities of the southern Caucasus. There are also very strong similarities in relation to other material spheres, such as those connected with the shape, function, and the symbolic centrality of circular hearths, portable hearths, and andirons, which stress further analogies with the southern Caucasian domestic model (Kiguradze and Sagona 2003:fig. 3.41; Sagona and Zimansky 2009:164). As early as the fourth millennium B.C.E., then, the material culture of Sos seems to have combined elements that clearly belong to the Kura-Araks tradition with others more closely linked to the traditions of Central Anatolia and the Anatolian Upper Euphrates (Red-Black and Black Burnished Wares).

The entrenched all-pervasiveness of "Kura-Araks" features in such an early phase suggests that the cultural developments at Sos, and perhaps more generally in the northeastern Anatolian communities, were already in close correspondence with the profound changes that were taking place in the southern Caucasus beginning in the middle of the fourth millennium B.C.E. With regard to the latter region, Level IV at Berikldeebi, dating back to 3682 ± 269 cal B.C.E. (2σ) (Kiguradze 2000:327), which overlaps with Phase V, provides some of the earliest evidence of the Kura-Araks culture in the southern Caucasus and documents the remains of a circular hut with a central hearth (Djavakhishvili 1998). The Level IV pottery differs radically from the chaff tempered ware of the previous Phase V and is represented by burnished monochrome and grit tempered ceramics (brown, buff, gray, but not RBBW) characterized by a repertoire of cylindrical necked jars, trays, bowls, and lids (invariably with handles and pierced lugs) in the typical Kura-Araks tradition (figure 9.4; Djavakhishvili 1998; Palumbi 2008a).

Despite a lack of specific information on the southernmost areas of eastern Anatolia and the Armenian highlands, the data on Sos Höyük and Berikldeebi provide fairly reliable evidence that beginning in the middle of the fourth millennium B.C.E., there was a new cultural phenomenon in eastern Anatolia and in the southern Caucasus. This was the Kura-Araks culture, which, in both these regions, exhibited both local aspects as well as the widespread presence of uniformly distributed elements that were broadly shared in geographically distant areas with different cultural backgrounds.

Figure 9.4. Monochrome Kura-Araks ceramics from Berikldeebi IV (inner Georgia) (with kind permission of the curator M. Menadbe, Georgian National Museum).

In relation to this point, Kohl (2007) has suggested that the Kura-Araks cultural phenomenon, generally considered to be primarily (or originally) a "south Caucasian" development (Kushnareva 1997:49; Sagona 1984:97–98) might in reality have been the result of interactions and synergies originating in different areas of the Anatolian, Iranian, and Caucasian highlands (Kohl 2007:88–89, 96; Palumbi 2008a; Sagona and Zimansky 2009:166, 168; Smith 2005:258). In this regard, northeastern Anatolia, with its own specific traditions, might have contributed to the formation of the Kura-Araks culture by transmitting, in a south Caucasian and northern Iranian direction, a set of elements (including RBBW) that became some of the most widespread and characteristic hallmarks of the Kura-Araks culture toward the end of the fourth millennium B.C.E. (Palumbi 2003).

The second half of the fourth millennium B.C.E. was therefore the period in which a new cultural model was being formed, whose more specific Caucasian/eastern Anatolian character and nature was probably a symptom of a change in the dynamics and the directions of the interaction between the communities of these regions. This is manifested in an increased intensity in the internal relations and communications between eastern Anatolia, the Caucasus, and northern Iran, and, at the same time, a drastic reduction in the external interactions that had previously been directed toward the more southern regions (such as Upper Mesopotamia). In the mid-fourth millennium B.C.E., there was a shift in the pace and direction of the social and cultural development of the region, from the Late Chalcolithic communities that seem to have hinged more around the Syro-Mesopotamian processes and models, to the Kura-Araks communities, which became centers of elaboration and transmission of an absolutely original and autonomous culture of the highlands which wielded far-reaching influences lasting for almost a millennium. These constituted an alternative political and cultural pole to the Syro-Mesopotamian lowlands societies.

Cultures and Chronologies: A Discussion

In light of these data, where should we place the cultural and chronological division between the end of the Chalcolithic and the beginning of the Early Bronze in eastern Anatolia? How far should this periodization be aligned to the periodizations in the adjacent Anatolian regions?

In the Upper Euphrates, the periodization proposed for the final phases of the Chalcolithic at the Santa Fe seminar now appears to be firmly established, dividing Late Chalcolithic into five different periods (LC1–LC5) between the end of the fifth and the end of the fourth millennia B.C.E. (figure 9.5) (Rothman 2001; and see Rothman, chapter 37, and Özbal, chapter 8 in this volume). In the case of eastern

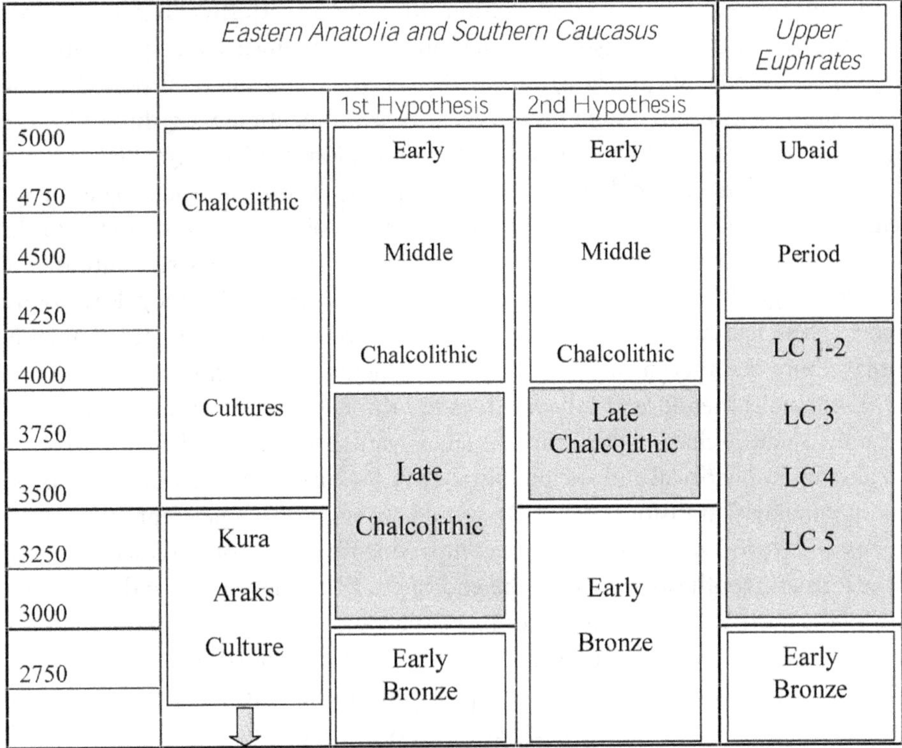

Eastern Anatolia and Southern Caucasus
Upper Euphrates
1st Hypothesis
2nd Hypothesis
5000
4750
4500
4250
4000
3750
3500
3250
3000
2750
Chalcolithic
Cultures
Kura
Araks
Culture
Early
Middle
Chalcolithic
Late
Chalcolithic
Early
Bronze
Early
Middle
Chalcolithic
Late
Chalcolithic
Early
Bronze
Ubaid
Period
LC 1-2
LC 3
LC 4
LC 5
Early
Bronze

Figure 9.5. Cultural and chronological periodization of the fifth and fourth millennium B.C.E. in eastern Anatolia and southern Caucasus.

Anatolia there are not enough data available to be able to propose such a detailed periodization, but, as we saw, Phase VA at Sos Höyük (3500–3000 B.C.E.) already testifies to the presence of the Kura-Araks culture, and thus Sagona incorporates it into the Late Chalcolithic (Sagona 2000). Although this proposal makes it possible to link the eastern Anatolian periodization to that of the Upper Euphrates, and indirectly to the Syro-Mesopotamian areas, I believe it is necessary to reflect on the sense and the significance of the Chalcolithic periodization and chronology in this region.

It has already been shown that the developments in eastern Anatolia in this period are still hard to define both culturally and chronologically. This certainly applies to the earliest phases of the Chalcolithic, where there is a total lack of any absolute dates and very little data. These earliest phases might tentatively be attributed to the beginning of the fifth millennium B.C.E., whereas the more recent phases (to be placed in the first half of the fourth millennium) are better characterized than the earlier ones because of the "peak" of the southern influences recorded in the region. These are also the phases in which, around 3500 B.C.E., the Kura-Araks culture appeared.

The centrality that this cultural phenomenon acquired in eastern Anatolia and the southern Caucasus since its beginnings has often encouraged scholars to adopt a "culture-oriented" regional periodization (Kura-Araks I, II, III, and in some cases IV) (Burney and Lang 1971:55–85; Glumac and Anthony 1992:203–204; Kushnareva 1997:53–54; Sagona 1984:table 2) rather than a more conventional periodization (Chalcolithic and Early Bronze Age) that is more compatible with those of other regions (Kushnareva and Chubinishvili 1970:61–62; Kavtaradze 1983:table 2).

Metallurgy, in terms of both quantity and quality, is not a sufficient criterion for clearly defining the transition between the Late Chalcolithic cultures and the initial moments of the Kura-Araks culture in this region because of the basic continuity of the technological traditions between these two periods (Courcier 2007; Kavtaradze 1999:73). The fact remains, however, that the latter marked a powerful change in terms of both the internal and external developments in the region.

The issue is therefore as follows: does the Kura-Araks phenomenon represent not only a new archaeological horizon (Badalyan, Avetisyan, and Smith 2009:35) but also a new historical and sociocultural cycle for eastern Anatolia, and hence an "epoque-making" transformation? Or should we use a more conventional terminology and periodization that is more comparable with those of the adjacent areas? If the former hypothesis is correct, the end of the Late Chalcolithic and the beginning of the Early Bronze Age in eastern Anatolia (and therefore also in the southern Caucasus) should be dated to around the middle of the fourth millennium B.C.E. (Badalyan, Avetisyan, and Smith 2009:42–51; Marro 2008:10), and if this is compared with the periodizations of the adjacent Anatolian regions (central Anatolia, the Upper Euphrates, and southeastern Anatolia) it would give a very early date for the beginning of the Early Bronze throughout the whole of the Near East.

If the second hypothesis proves correct, the eastern Anatolian Late Chalcolithic would continue, as Sagona (2000) proposed, until the end of the fourth millennium, and would therefore include widely differing development phases, namely, the late Chalcolithic pre-Kura-Araks cultures (first half of the fourth millennium B.C.E.) and the first phase of the development of the Kura-Araks culture (Kura-Araks I) in the second half of the fourth millennium B.C.E. How far is this latter periodization appropriate for the specific eastern Anatolian context and for the nature of the changes taking place in the region in the fourth millennium B.C.E.? Considering that the Kura-Araks phenomenon continued for almost a millennium (from approximately 3500 to 2500 B.C.E.), the second of these two solutions would entail a terminological separation and a different periodization between the developments of the Kura-Araks culture in the fourth millennium B.C.E. (and hence the Chalcolithic Kura-Araks) and those of the third millennium B.C.E. (and hence the Early Bronze Kura-Araks) (Kavtaradze 1999:fig. 3). However, this phenomenon typically demonstrated a fundamental unity of development, whose most distinctive elements emerged as early as the middle of the fourth millennium B.C.E., and continued basically without interruption into the first half of the third millennium B.C.E.

The internal periodization of the eastern Anatolian Chalcolithic and its positioning within an absolute chronological framework are therefore still in the process of being defined and continue to be subjects of open debate. Constructing and motivating a regional chronological periodization is not simply a matter of ordering absolute dates and describing the past on the basis of predetermined time periods; rather, as is always the case in archaeological practice, it is a process of historical interpretation.

REFERENCES

Abibullaev, Osman. 1982. *Eneolit i Bronza na Territorii Nakhičevanskoj ASSR*. Baku: Elm.

Akhundov, Tufan. 2007. Sites de Migrants Venus du Proche-Orient en Transcaucasie. In *Les Cultures du Caucase (VIe–IIIe millénaires avant notre ère). Leurs Relations avec le Proche-Orient*, ed. Bertille Lyonnet, 95–122. Paris: CNRS Editions.

Akhundov, Tufan and Bafa Makhmudova. 2008. *Južnij Kavkaz v Kavkazko-Peredneazitiskikh Etnokul'turnykh Prozessakh IV tys. do n.e.* Baku.

Akkermans, Peter M. 1988. The Period V Pottery. In *Hammam et-Turkman*, ed. Maurits N. van Loon, vol. 1, 287–350. İstanbul: Nederlands Historisch-Archaeologisch Instituut te Istanbul.

Akkermans, Peter M. and Glenn M. Schwartz. 2003. *The Archaeology of Syria*. Cambridge: Cambridge University Press.

Aliev, Namik G. and Ideal G. Narimanov. 2001. *Kultura Severnovo Azerbajžana v Epokhu Poznevo Eneolita*. Baku: Nacional'naja Akademija Nauk Azerbjdžana Institut Arkheologii i Etnografii.

Badalyan, Ruben, Pavel Avetisyan, and Adam T. Smith. 2009. Periodization and Chronology of Southern Caucasia: From the Early Bronze Age to the Iron III Period. In *The Archaeology and Geography of Ancient Transcaucasian Societies*, ed. Adam T. Smith, Ruben Badalyan, and Pavel Avetisyan, vol. 1, 33–93. Oriental Institute Publications 134. Chicago: Oriental Institute.

Badalyan, Ruben, Christopher Edens, Philip L. Kohl, and Armen Tonikyan. 1992. Archaeological Investigations at Horom in the Shirak Plain of Northwestern Armenia, 1990. *Iran* 30: 31–48.

Badalyan, Ruben, Pierre Lombard, Pavel Avetisyan, Christine Chataigner, Jacques Chabot, Emmanuelle Vila, Roman Hovsepyan, George Willcox, and Hugues Pessin. 2007. New Data on the Late Prehistory of the Southern Caucasus. The Excavations at Aratashen (Armenia): Preliminary Report. In *Les Cultures du Caucase (VIe–IIIe millénaires avant notre ère). Leurs Relations avec le Proche-Orient*, ed. Bertille Lyonnet, 37–61. Paris: CNRS Editions.

Badalyan, Ruben, Pierre Lombard, Christine Chataigner, and Pavel Avetisyan. 2004. The Neolithic and Chalcolithic Phases in the Ararat Plain (Armenia): The View from Aratashen. In *A View from the Highlands. Archaeological Studies in Honour of Charles Burney*, ed. Antonio Sagona, 399–420. Ancient Near Eastern Studies, Supplement 12. Herent: Peeters.

Belck, Waldemar. 1899. Brief aus Van vom 4 Juli 1899. *Zeitschrift für Ethnologie* 31: 580.

Brandt, Roelof W. 1978. The Chalcolithic Pottery. In *Korucutepe*, ed. Maurits van Loon, 57–60. Amsterdam: North-Holland.

Burney, Charles. 1958. Eastern Anatolia in the Chalcolithic and Early Bronze Age. *Anatolian Studies* 8: 157–209.

Burney, Charles and David M. Lang. 1971. *The Peoples of the Hills*. London: Weidenfeld and Nicolson.

Campbell, Stuart. 2007. Rethinking Halaf Chronologies. *Paléorient*, 33.1: 103–36.

Chataigner, Christine. 1995. *La Transcaucasie au Néolithique et au Chalcolithique*. BAR International Series 624. Oxford: Tempus Reparatum.

Chataigner, Christine, Pavel Avetisyan, Giulio Palumbi, and Hans Uerpmann. 2010. Godedzor, a Late-Ubaid-Related Settlement in Southern Caucasus. In *Beyond the Ubaid. Transformation and Integration in the Late Prehistoric Societies of the Middle East*, ed. Robert Carter and Graham Philip, 377–394. Chicago: Oriental Institute Publications.

Courcier, Antoine. 2007. La Métallurgie dans les Pays du Caucase au Chalcolithique et au Début de l'Age du Bronze: Bilan des Etudes et Perspectives Nouvelles. In *Les Cultures du Caucase (VIe–IIIe millénaires avant notre ère). Leurs Relations avec le Proche-Orient*, ed. Bertille Lyonnet, 199–232. Paris: CNRS Editions.

Dewdney, John C. 1971. *Turkey*. London: Chatto and Windus.

Djavakhishvili, Aleksandre. 1998. Ausgrabungen in Berikldeebi (Šida Kartli). *Georgica* 21: 7–20.

Erol, Oğuz. 1983. *Die Natürraumliche Gliederung der Türkei*. Beihefte zum Tübinger Atlas der Vorderen Orients, Reihe A no. 13. Wiesbaden: Ludwig Reichert Verlag.

Esin, Ufuk. 1976. Tülintepe Excavations, 1972. In *Keban Project 1972 Activities*, ed. Sevim Pekman, 147–63. Keban Project Publications, Series 1, no. 5. Ankara: Middle East Technical University.

———. 1979. Tülintepe Excavations, 1973. In *Keban Project 1970 Activities*, ed. Sevim Pekman, 121–25. Keban Project Publications, Series 1, no. 4. Ankara: Middle East Technical University.

———. 1982a. Tülintepe Excavations, 1974. In *Keban Project 1974–75 Activities*, ed. Sevim Pekman, 127–33. Keban Project Publications, Series 1, no. 7. Ankara: Middle East Technical University.

———. 1982b. Tepecik Excavations, 1974. In *Keban Project 1974–75 Activities*, ed. Sevim Pekman, 95–118. Keban Project Publications, Series 1, no. 7. Ankara: Middle East Technical University.

———. 1983. Zur Datierung der Vorgeschichtlichen Schichten von Değirmentepe bei Malatya in der Östliche Türkei. In *Beiträge zur Altertumskunde Kleinsasiens, Festchrift für Kurt Bittel*, ed. Rainer M. Boehmer and Harald Hauptmann, 175–90. Mainz: Philipp von Zabern.

Frangipane, Marcella. 1993. Local Components in the Development of Centralized Societies in Syro-Anatolian Regions. In *Between the Rivers and over the Mountains*, ed. Marcella Frangipane, Harald Hauptmann, Mario Liverani, Paolo Matthiae, and Machteld J. Mellink, 133–62. Roma: Università di Roma "La Sapienza."

———. 1996. *La Nascita dello Stato nel Vicino Oriente*. Bari: Laterza.

———. 2001. Centralization Processes in Greater Mesopotamia. Uruk "Expansion" as the Climax of Systemic Interactions among Areas of the Greater Mesopotamian Region. In *Uruk Mesopotamia and its Neighbors*, ed. Mitchell S. Rothman, 307–48. Santa Fe, N.M.: School of American Research Press.

Frangipane, Marcella and Alba Palmieri. 1983. A Protourban Centre of the Late Uruk Period. *Origini* 12: 287–454.

Frangipane, Marcella and Giulio Palumbi. 2007. Red-Black Ware, Pastoralism, Trade, and Anatolian-Transcaucasian Interactions in the 4th–3rd Millennium BC. In *Les Cultures du Caucase (VIe-IIIe millénaires avant notre ère). Leurs Relations avec le Proche-Orient*, ed. Bertille Lyonnet, 233–56. Paris: CNRS Editions.

Glumac, Peter and David W. Anthony. 1992. Culture and Environment in the Prehistoric Caucasus: The Neolithic through the Early Bronze Age. In *Chronologies in*

Old World Archaeology, ed. Robert W. Ehrich, 196–206. Chicago: University of Chicago Press.

Gorny, Ronald L., Gregory McMahon, Samuel Paley, Sharon Steadman, and Bruce Verhaaren. 2002. The 2000 and 2001 Seasons at Çadır Höyük in Central Turkey: A Preliminary Report. *Anatolica* 28: 109–36.

Gülçür, Sevil. 2000. Norşuntepe: Die Chalkolitische Keramik. In *Chronologies des Pays du Caucase et de l'Euphrate aux IVe–IIIe Millénaires*, ed. Catherine Marro and Harald Hauptmann, 375–418. Paris: Institut Français d'Etudes Anatoliennes d'Istanbul.

Güldalı, Nuri. 1979. *Geomorphologie der Türkei*. Beihefte zum Tübinger Atlas des Vorderen Orients, Reihe A no. 4. Wiesbaden: Ludwig Reichert Verlag.

Harutunyan, Armine. 2008. Keramika Poselenija Aknashen. *Kultura Drevnej Armenii* 14: 37–43.

Hauptmann, Harald. 1973. Die Grabungen auf dem Norşuntepe, 1971. In *Keban Project 1970 Activities*, ed. Sevim Pekman, 87–99. Keban Project Publications, Series 1, no. 4. Ankara: Middle East Technical University.

———. 1976. Die Grabungen auf dem Norşuntepe, 1972. In *Keban Project 1972 Activities*, ed. Sevim Pekman, 71–90. Keban Project Publications, Series 1, no. 5. Ankara: Middle East Technical University.

———. 1979. Die Grabungen auf dem Norşuntepe, 1973. In *Keban Project 1973 Activities*, ed. Sevim Pekman, 61–78. Keban Project Publications, Series 1, no. 6. Ankara: Middle East Technical University.

———. 1982. Die Grabungen auf dem Norşuntepe, 1974. In *Keban Project 1974–75 Activities*, ed. Sevim Pekman, 41–70. Keban Project Publications, Series 1, no. 7. Ankara: Middle East Technical University.

Helwing, Barbara. 2000. Regional Variation in the Composition of Late Chalcolithic Pottery Assemblages. In *Chronologies des Pays du Caucase et de L'Euphrate aux IVe-IIIe Millenaires*, ed. Catherine Marro and Harald Hauptmann, 145–64. Institut Français d'Etudes Anatoliennes d'Istanbul, Varia Anatolica vol. 11. Paris: De Boccard.

Işıklı, Mehmet. 2008. Recent Investigations at Pulur (Erzurum): Observations on Northeast Anatolian Ceramics. In *Ceramics in Transitions*, ed. Karen S. Rubinson and Antonio Sagona, 267–90. Ancient Near Eastern Studies, Supplement 27. Leuven: Peeters.

Kavtaradze, Giorgi L. 1983. *K Khronologii Epokhi Eneolita i Bronzy Gruzii*. Tbilisi: Metsniereba.

———. 1999. The Importance of Metallurgical Data for the Formation of a Central Transcaucasian Chronology. In *The Beginnings of Metallurgy*, ed. Harald Hauptmann, Ernst Pernicka, Rehren Thilo, and Yalçın Ünsal, 67–101. Der Anschnitt, Beiheft 9. Bochum: Deutsches Bergbau-Museum.

Kiguradze, Tamaz. 2000. The Chalcolithic-Early Bronze Age Transition in the Eastern Caucasus. In *Chronologies des Pays du Caucase et de L'Euphrate aux IVe–IIIe Millénaires*, ed. Catherine Marro and Harald Hauptmann, 321–28. Institut Français d'Etudes Anatoliennes d'Istanbul, Varia Anatolica, vol. 11. Paris: De Boccard.

Kiguradze, Tamaz and Antonio Sagona. 2003. On the Origins of the Kura-Araks Cultural Complex. In *Archaeology in the Borderlands: Investigations in Caucasia and Beyond*, ed. Adam Smith and Karen S. Rubinson, 38–94. Los Angeles: Cotsen Institute of Archaeology.

Kohl, Philip L. 2007. *The Making of Bronze Age Eurasia*. Cambridge: Cambridge University Press.

Korfmann, Manfred. 1982. *Tilkitepe*. Tübingen: Verlag Ernst Wasmuth.

Korfmann, Manfred and Wolfgang Schiele. 1977. Die Ausgrabungen von Kirsoop und Silvia Lake in den Jahren 1938 und 1939 am Burgfelsen von Van (Tuşpa) un in Kalecik. *Berytus* 25: 173–200.

Koşay, Hamit Z. and Kemal Turfan. 1959. Erzurum-Karaz Kazısı Raporu. *Belleten* 23: 349–413.

Koşay, Hamit Z. and Hermann Vary. 1964. *Die Ausgrabungen von Pulur. Bericht über die Kampagne von 1960*. Fen-Edebiyat Fakültesi-Arkeoloji Serisi no. 9. Ankara: Atatürk Üniversitesi Yayınları.

———. 1967: *Ausgrabungen von Güzelova*. Fen-Edebiyat Fakültesi-Arkeoloji Serisi no. 20. Ankara: Atatürk Üniversitesi Yayınları.

Kuftin, Boris. 1941. *Arkheologičeskie Raskopki v Trialeti*. Tbilisi: Akademii Nauk Gruzinskoj SSR.

Kushnareva, Kariné K. 1997. *The Southern Caucasus in Prehistory*. Philadelphia: University Museum, University of Pennsylvania.

Kushnareva, Kariné K. and Tariel Chubinishvili. 1970. *Drevnie Kultury Južnogo Kavkaza*. Leningrad: Izdatel'stvo Nauka.

Kuzucuoğlu, Catherine and Neil Roberts. 1997. Evolution de l'Environnement en Anatolie de 20000 à 6000. *Paléorient* 23.2: 7–24.

Lyonnet, Bertille. 2007. Introduction. In *Les Cultures du Caucase (VIe–IIIe millénaires avant notre ère). Leurs Relations avec le Proche-Orient*, ed. Bertille Lyonnet, 11–20. Paris: CNRS Editions.

———. 2009. Péripherie de la Mésopotamie à la Periode d'Uruk (IVe Millénaire): Le Cas des Régions du Caucase. In *Centre et Périphérie: Approches Nouvelles des Orientalistes*, ed. Jean-Marie Durand and Antoine Jacquet, 1–28. Paris: Librairie d'Amérique et d'Orient Jean Maissoneuve.

Makharadze, Zurab. 2007. Nouvelles Données sur le Chalcolithique en Géorgie Orientale. In *Les Cultures du Caucase (VIe–IIIe millénaires avant notre ère). Leurs Relations avec le Proche-Orient*, ed. Bertille Lyonnet, 123–31. Paris: CNRS Editions.

Marro, Catherine. 2005. Cultural Duality in Eastern Anatolia and Transcaucasia in Late Prehistory (c. 4200–2800 B.C.). In *Mountains and Valleys. A Symposium on Highland-Lowland Interaction in the Bronze Age Settlement Systems of Eastern Anatolia, Transcaucasia and Northwestern Iran*, ed. Barabara Helwing and Aynur Özfırat, 27–34. *Archäologisches Mitteilungen aus Iran und Turan* 37.

———. 2007. Upper-Mesopotamia and Transcaucasia in the Late Chalcolithic Period (4000–3500 BC). In *Les Cultures du Caucase (VIe–IIIe millénaires avant notre ère). Leurs Relations avec le Proche-Orient*, ed. Bertille Lyonnet, 77–94. Paris: CNRS Editions.

———. 2008. Late Chalcolithic Ceramic Cultures in the Anatolian Highlands. In *Ceramics in Transitions*, ed. Karen S. Rubinson and Antonio Sagona, 9–38. Ancient Near Eastern Studies, Supplement 27. Leuven: Peeters.

Marro Catherine, Vali Bakhshaliyev, and Safar Ashurov. 2009. Excavations at Ovcular Tepesi (Nakhchivan, Azerbaijan). First Preliminary Report: The 2006–2008 Seasons. *Anatolia Antiqua* 17: 31–87.

Marro, Catherine and Aynur Özfırat. 2003. Pre-Classical Survey in Eastern Turkey. First Preliminary Report: The Ağrı Dağ (Mount Ararat) Region. *Anatolia Antiqua* 11: 385–422.

———. 2004. Pre-Classical Survey in Eastern Turkey. Second Preliminary Report: the Erciş Region. *Anatolia Antiqua* 12: 227–65.

———. 2005. Pre-Classical Survey in Eastern Turkey. Third Preliminary Report: Doğubeyazit and the Eastern Shore of Lake Van. *Anatolia Antiqua* 13: 319–56.

Menabde, Medea and Tamaz Kiguradze. 1981. *Arkheologicheskie Pamiatniki s.Sioni*. Tbilisi: Metsniereba.

Miller, Naomi F. 1997. The Macrobotanical Evidence for Vegetation in the Near East, c. 18000/16000 BC to 4000 BC. *Paléorient* 23.2: 197–207.

Narimanov, Ideal, Tufan Akhundov, and Namik G. Aliev. 2007. *Leilatepe*. Baku: Nacional'naja Akademija Nauk Azerbajdžana, Institut arkheologii i etnografii.

Newton, Jennifer C. 2004. The Environmental Setting. In *Archaeology at the North-East Anatolian Frontier I*, ed. Antonio Sagona and Claudia Sagona, 99–110. Ancient Near Eastern Studies, Supplement 14. Louvain: Peeters.

Orthmann, Winfried. 1963. *Die Keramik der Frühen Bronzezeit aus Inneranatolien*. Berlin: Verlag Gebr. Mann.

Özfırat, Aynur. 2006. Pre-Classical Survey in Eastern Turkey. Fifth Preliminary Report. Van Lake Basin and Mt. Ağrı Region. *Studi Micenei ed Egeo Anatolici* 48: 177–207.

Palmieri, Alba. 1985. Eastern Anatolia and Early Mesopotamia Urbanization: Remarks on Changing Relations. In *Studi di Paletnologia in Onore di S.M. Puglisi*, ed. Mario Liverani, Alba Palmieri, and Renato Peroni, 191–213. Roma: Università "La Sapienza."

Palumbi, Giulio. 2003. Red-Black Pottery: Eastern Anatolian and Transcaucasian Relationships around the Mid-Fourth Millennium BC. *Ancient Near Eastern Studies* 40: 80–134.

———. 2007. A Preliminary Analysis on the Prehistoric Pottery from Aratashen (Armenia). In *Les Cultures du Caucase (VIe–IIIe millénaires avant notre ère). Leurs Relations avec le Proche-Orient*, ed. Bertille Lyonnet, 63–72. Paris: CNRS Editions.

———. 2008a. *The Red and Black*. Roma: "La Sapienza" Università di Roma.

———. 2008b. Mid-Fourth Millennium Red-Black Burnished Wares from Anatolia: A Cross-Comparison. In *Ceramics in Transitions*, ed. Karen S. Rubinson and Antonio Sagona, 39–58. Ancient Near Eastern Studies, Supplement 27. Leuven: Peeters.

Parker, Bradley J., Lynn Dodd, Andrew Creekmore, Elizabeth Healey, and Catherine Painter. 2006. The Upper Tigris Archaeological Research Project (UTARP): A Preliminary Report from the 2003 and 2004 Field Seasons at Kenan Tepe. *Anatolica* 32: 72–151.

Parker, Bradley J., Catherine P. Foster, Jennifer Henecke, Dave Hopwood, Andrew Creekmore, Arzu Demirergi, and Melissa Eppihimer. 2008. Preliminary Report from the 2005–2006 Field Seasons at Kenan Tepe. *Anatolica* 34: 103–76.

Reilly, Edward B. 1937. Test Excavations at Tilki Tepe. *Türk Tarih Arkeologya ve Etnografya Dergisi* 4: 156–65.

Rothman, Mitchell S. 1994. The Pottery of the Muş Plain and the Evolving Place of a High Border Land. *Araştırma Sonuçları Toplantısı* 12: 281–99.

———. 2001. The Local and the Regional: An Introduction. In *Uruk Mesopotamia and its Neighbors*, ed. Mitchell S. Rothman, 3–26. Santa Fe, N.M.: School of American Research Press.

Rothman, Mitchell S. and Gülriz Kozbe. 1997. Muş in the Early Bronze Age. *Anatolian Studies* 47: 105–26.

Russell, Harry. 1980. *Pre-Classical Pottery of Eastern Anatolia*. British Institute of Archaeology at Ankara. BAR International Series 85. Oxford: BAR International.

Sagona, Antonio. 1984. *The Transcaucasian Region in the Early Bronze Age*. BAR International Series 214. Oxford: BAR International.

———. 2000. Sos Höyük and the Erzurum Region in Late Prehistory: A Provisional Chronology for Northeast Anatolia. In *Chronologies des Pays du Caucase et de l'Euphrate aux IVe–IIIe Millénaires*, ed. Catherine Marro and Harald Hauptmann,

329–74. Institut Français d'Etudes Anatoliennes d'Istanbul, Varia Anatolica, vol. 11. Paris: De Boccard.
Sagona, Antonio, Mustafa Erkmen, Claudia Sagona, and Sarah Howells. 1997. Excavations at Sos Höyük 1996. Third Preliminary Report. *Anatolica* 23: 181–226.
Sagona, Antonio, Mustafa Erkmen, Claudia Sagona, Ian McNiven, and Sarah Howells. 1998. Excavations at Sos Höyük, 1997: Fourth Preliminary Report. *Anatolica* 24: 31–64.
Sagona, Antonio and Claudia Sagona. 2000. Excavations at Sos Höyük, 1998 to 2000: Fifth Preliminary Report. *Ancient Near Eastern Studies* 37: 56–127.
———. 2004. *Archaeology at the North-East Anatolian Frontier I*. Ancient Near Eastern Studies, Supplement 14. Louvain: Peeters.
Sagona, Antonio and Paul Zimansky. 2009. *Ancient Turkey*. London: Routledge.
Schoop, Ulf-Dietrich. 2008. Ausgrabungen in Çamlıbel Tarlası 2007. In *Die Ausgrabungen in Boğazköy-Hattuša 2007*, ed. Andreas Schachner, 148–61. *Archäologischer Anzeiger* 2008/1.
Schwartz, Glenn. 2001. Syria and the Uruk Expansion. In *Uruk Mesopotamia and its Neighbors*, ed. Mitchell S. Rothman, 233–64. Santa Fe, N.M.: School of American Research Press.
Smith, Adam. 2005. Prometheus Unbound: Southern Caucasia in Prehistory. *Journal of World Prehistory* 19: 229–79.
Steadman, Sharon R., Gregory McMahon, and Jennifer C. Ross. 2007. The Late Chalcolithic at Çadır Höyük in Central Anatolia. *Journal of Field Archaeology* 32: 385–406.
Stein, Gil J. 2001. Indigenous Social Complexity at Hacınebi (Turkey) and the Organization of Uruk Colonial Contact. In *Uruk Mesopotamia and its Neighbors*, ed. Mitchell S. Rothman, 265–305. Santa Fe, N.M.: School of American Research Press.
Tobler, Arthur. 1950. *Excavations at Tepe Gawra, Volume 2*. Philadelphia: University of Pensylvania Press.
Trufelli, Franca. 1997. Ceramic Correlations and Cultural Relations in IVth Millennium Eastern Anatolia and Syro-Mesopotamia. *Studi Micenei ed Egeo Anatolici* 39.1: 5–33.
van Loon, Maurits. 1978. Architecture and Stratigraphy. In *Korucutepe*, ed. Maurits van Loon, 3–44. Amsterdam: North-Holland.
van Zeist, Willem and Sytze Bottema. 1991. *Late Quaternary Vegetation of the Near East*. Beihefte zum Tübinger Atlas des Vorderen Orients, Reihe A no. 18. Wiesbaden: Ludwig Reichert Verlag.
Watson, Patty J. 1982. The Halafian Pottery of Tilkitepe, Seen in the Hittite Museum, Ankara (Citadel), 1955. In *Tilkitepe*, ed. Manfred Korfmann, 203–12. Tübingen: Verlag Ernst Wasmuth.
Willcox, George. 1974. A History of Deforestation as Indicated by Charcoal Analysis of Four Sites in Eastern Anatolia. *Anatolian Studies* 24: 117–33.

The Early Bronze Age

CHAPTER 10

THE EARLY BRONZE AGE ON THE PLATEAU

SHARON R. STEADMAN

DEFINING the boundaries of the Anatolian "plateau," ably addressed by other authors in this volume (Özbaşaran, chapter 5; Schoop, chapter 7; and Kealhofer and Grave, chapter 18), is far easier than outlining the chronology of the Early Bronze Age in this same region (table 10.1). This period begins with controversy, because the transition between the end of the Late Chalcolithic and the beginning of the Early Bronze I period is far from clear (see Schoop, chapter 7, and Özdoğan, chapter 29 in this volume). The Early Bronze II is far from well understood, and the final Early Bronze III period sees extensive changes that pave the way for Anatolia's first empire. The recent appearance of excellent books on Anatolia (e.g., Düring 2011; Sagona and Zimansky 2009) and, it is hoped, the contributions in the present volume, serve to better our understanding of this intersecting period between Anatolian prehistory and its first imperial phase.

THE GEOGRAPHY OF THE PLATEAU

The boundaries of the plateau are dictated not only by climate and topography but also by the location of sites (figure 10.1). Therefore, while the Pontic Mountains describe the northern limit of the plateau, the important Black Sea site of İkiztepe is often included in discussions of plateau cultural developments. Similarly in the south, the Taurus Mountains would seemingly form the southern boundary to the

Table 10.1. Early Bronze Age Chronology (after Düring 2011; Yakar 2002)

Period	Dates	Type Site Phasing
Early Bronze III	2300—2000 B.C.E.	Troy III; Beycesultan XII–VIII Alişar 7–5M, 13T; Tarsus III
Early Bronze II	2700/2600—2300 B.C.E.	Troy II; Beycesultan XVI–XIII; Alişar 9–8M; Tarsus II
Early Bronze I	3000—2700/2600 B.C.E.	Troy I; Beycesultan XIX–XVII Alişar 13–10M; Tarsus Ib

plateau except for the key Early Bronze (EB) site of Tarsus resting on the Mediterranean coast.

To the west the division between the plateau climate and topography and the "Mediterranean" coastal region and its differing vegetation lies near the headwater regions of the major western rivers, the Büyük Menderes (ancient Maeander) and Gediz (ancient Hermos). The headwaters for these rivers are found several hundred kilometers east of the coast, in the Lake District and Porsuk Valley (near Kütahya); the "formal" western edge of the plateau can then be placed at the intersection of these climatological and topographical zones. However, crucial sites that inform us on plateau life in the EB rest to the west of this "boundary."

The eastern boundary may be the easiest to define: once one travels eastward from the Kızıl Irmak (Halys River), excavated Early Bronze Age sites become very

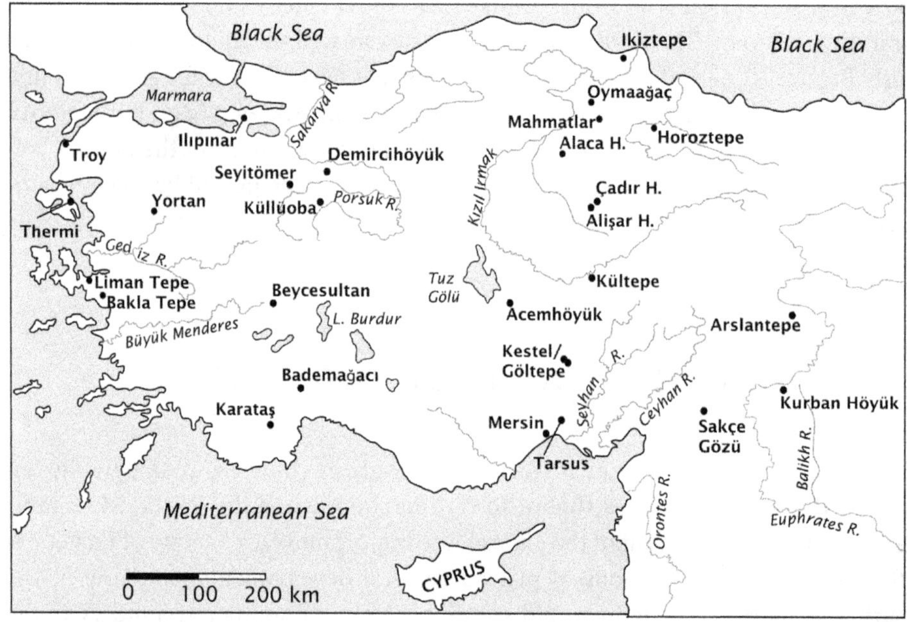

Figure 10.1. Early Bronze II plan of Demircihöyük settlement (after Korfman 1983:190).

thin on the ground (discussion of the Keban Dam sites can be found in chapters devoted to eastern Anatolia, e.g., Marro, chapter 12, and Palumbi, chapter 9 in this volume); and one runs up against the Anti-Taurus, which forms both a geographical and a cultural boundary between central and eastern/southeastern Anatolia. Drawing a line more or less straight up from modern Malatya to Trabzon offers a fairly accurate eastern boundary to the plateau.

The Early Bronze Age in Context: Urbanization and Migration

The Early Bronze Age (EBA) on the central plateau has been identified as a period of "urbanization," or at least the age in which complex society emerged, including the rise of an extensive trade network, established by the second half of the third millennium B.C.E. Although seemingly a "late" development in relation to southeastern sites such as Arslantepe (e.g., Frangipane 1993, 1996, 1997, 2002, and see Frangipane, chapter 45 in this volume), it is hardly productive to compare differing regional urbanization stages. Far more interesting is an inquiry into why plateau residents made the transition, willingly or otherwise, from "the quiet life" of the rural farm to the "hustle and bustle" of the city.

Urbanization and Trade in the Anatolian EBA

When discussing the "rise to complex society" in the Near East, many envision the Uruk system and its rapid urbanization process, though the pathways to urban status are of course varied (e.g., Oates et al. 2007). As a recent article establishes (Çevik 2007), a "typical" urbanization process is not what occurred on the plateau in the latter half of the third millennium B.C.E. It is more accurate, Çevik (2007:137) asserts, to describe the EBA as a period in which regional polities or centers, that is, medium-sized settlements (approximately eight to nine hectares), featured a developing élite/leadership class that held sway over residents not only within the settlement but in the regional hinterland as well. However, the level of control a larger settlement, perhaps called a town (but Çevik notes that this term is beset by interpretive problems), had over nearby villages was far less structured than in a more urban-based system such as that of Uruk, although the exact nature of the relationships between central towns and their hinterlands is still unclear.

The question of when this regional centralization process began is important. It may be that its origins lie not in the EBA but in the preceding Late Chalcolithic at sites that exhibit sufficient size, evidence of élite occupation, and defensive or other public (religious or secular) architecture. In the northwest the Troy I occupation and in the southwest the Beycesultan, Karataş, and Küllüoba settlements all suggest possible transition from heterarchical to slightly or even substantially hierarchical social structures; the western coastal site of Liman Tepe also offers significant evidence of an urbanization process by the EB II period (Erkanal 1996; Özdoğan 2007; Şahoğlu 2005, 2008). In the north central plateau the Çadır Höyük settlement offers similar trends, as do Tarsus and Mersin in Cilicia. There are doubtless a number of other sites that might have functioned as quasi-regional centers in the late fourth and early third millennia B.C.E., but the exact timing of nascent centralization and urbanization awaits further research. What is clear is that by the mid- to late third millennium B.C.E. the centralization process is demonstrated clearly on the landscape of the plateau. The number of EBA III sites increases, as does the corresponding population density (Matthews 2007; Sagona and Zimansky 2009:175–76; Şahoğlu 2005). The interaction between settlements and regions becomes far more active, and new developments such as metallurgy and wheelmade pottery make a dramatic appearance.

Another aspect of the process of regional centralization is the appearance of extramural cemeteries, particularly in western Anatolia, beginning in the EB II period. A large cemetery at Demircihöyük-Sarıket, twenty-five kilometers west of Eskişehir, featured some 500 burials (Seeher 2000), including many multi-individual tombs (perhaps representing kin groups); the variety of burial goods at Demircihöyük-Sarıket and at other cemeteries such as Karataş-Semayük (near the modern town of Elmalı [Wheeler 1974]) and Yortan (near the Aegean coast [Kâmil 1982]) suggest socioeconomic differentiation among the residents of these developing centers. By the EB III period, cemeteries featuring architecture and rich burial goods can be found in the north central area of the plateau (see later discussion). The burial patterns on the plateau are reflective of the movement toward socioeconomic differentiation and increasingly complex society in the latter half of the third millennium B.C.E.

Perhaps the most difficult question regarding the EBA centralization process is *why* it occurred (when and how are easier to address archaeologically). One cause seems quite obvious: metallurgy and metals trade (see Muhly, chapter 39 in this volume). Beginning late in the EB II, metal goods began to appear across the plateau; by the EB III ceramic forms such as two-handled tankards, the Trojan *depas* vessel, and wheelmade plain plates and bowls, are found at sites stretching from Liman Tepe on the Aegean coast to Tarsus on the southern Anatolian coast, and beyond. Such discoveries have led a number of scholars to propose the existence of a pan-Anatolian EB trade route that included the Black Sea area and southeastern Anatolia (Efe and Ay-Efe 2001; Mellink 1986, 1989, 1998; Ökse 2007; Özdoğan 2007; Özgüç 1986; Zimmerman 2005, 2007a), recently termed the international "Anatolian Trade Network" (Şahoğlu 2005, 2008) or the "Great Caravan Route" (Efe 2003, 2007a).

The EB II–III metal goods (some of which were tin bronze) include, for instance, toggle-headed pins—strongly reminiscent of forms and styles found in Cilicia and northern Syria (Efe 2003, 2007b). These metal artifacts have been found at southwestern settlements such as Karataş (Efe and Fidan 2006; Mellink 1994), on the

Aegean coast at Liman Tepe and Bakla Tepe (Erkanal and Özkan 1999, 2000; Şahoğlu 2004, 2005, 2008), and in the Eskişehir and northwestern regions at Küllüoba and Demircihöyük (Efe 2002; Seeher 2000). The EB utilization of a tin source in the Taurus Mountains (see following discussion) and the commencing of tin mining operations may have spurred metal production in this area, followed by metal exports to the plateau and western Anatolia (or perhaps the ore and metallurgical technology were the actual exports).

The trade network appears to have been a two-way street, as western Anatolian goods also began to appear in Cilicia. As already noted, early in the EB III vessels of west Anatolian origin can be found at Tarsus (Mellink 1989) and at Mersin (Garstang 1953); they are attested at southeastern Anatolian sites as well. That central Anatolia played a role in this link is demonstrated by the presence of Cilician and west Anatolian ceramic styles at sites such as Acemhöyük and at other sites near Niğde and in the Konya Plain (Mellink 1989; Özgüç 1986; Öztan 1989). The EB III layers at Kültepe form an important intersection between Cilicia, southeastern Anatolia, and the west. Besides west Anatolian styles, Kültepe's EB III ceramic assemblage features wares and forms typical of middle Euphrates sites (Ökse 2007; Özgüç 1986; Şahoğlu 2005; Zimmermann 2005). These links, also demonstrated by metal items, ceramics, and other forms of material culture (e.g., seals, architectural patterns) and a growing number of translated texts describing trade routes (Ökse 2007) testify to the major developments taking place on the Anatolian plateau in the second half of the third millennium B.C.E.

Indo-European Languages and People and the Anatolian Plateau

A topic perhaps intimately related to the subject of urbanization and trade (or alternatively, completely divorced from it) is the timing and nature of the arrival of the Indo-European language and people on the Anatolian plateau. By the time of the Old Assyrian Colony period in the early second millennium B.C.E. (see Michel, chapter 13 in this volume) the languages spoken on the plateau included Hattian, an indigenous Anatolian language, Hurrian (spoken in northern Syria), and Indo-European languages known as Luwian, Hittite, and Palaic (Özgüç 2003; and see Beckman, chapter 22 in this volume). Later in the millennium, the Hittite Empire established their Indo-European language as the "state" language, although it is certain that a significant portion of the indigenous population continued to speak their own native languages (McMahon 2010). The question, then, is when did the Indo-European language and its associated people enter the Anatolian plateau? Another chapter in this volume (Melchert, chapter 31) addresses the linguistic aspect of this question in fine detail. Archaeologically it is fair to say that there are essentially two main "camps" with a minor third contingent regarding this argument. One set of scholars suggests that populations speaking the proto-languages of what would later be Hittite/Luwian/Palaic entered and settled in Anatolia during the Neolithic period (Bellwood 2005; Makkay 1992; Renfrew 1987; Thomas 1992). The second main argument has carriers of the Indo-European languages arriving in Anatolia sometime during the Chalcolithic to EBA periods (Anthony 1991, 2007; Burney and Lang 1971; Mallory 1989; Yakar 1981, 1989). The final contingent suggests that Anatolia was actually part of the original Proto-Indo-European-speaking homeland and thus no "migration" was necessary since both indigenous and Indo-European-based languages existed side by side on the plateau from earliest times (Gamkrelidze and Ivanov 1985; Merpert 1987; Sherratt 1997; Zvelebil and Zvelebil 1988).

The reason for three such divergent theories among scholars is that archaeology has offered little help to document an Indo-European "entry" into Anatolia at any particular stage. The negative evidence of migration is used to support the assertion that Anatolia is *part* of the Proto-Indo-European homeland, but linguistic evidence suggests otherwise. A recent compelling discussion of this subject was offered by David Anthony (2007), who combined archaeological and linguistic evidence to document the movements of these language carriers to Asia and Europe. Linguistically, according to Anthony, the speakers of what would become Hittite, Luwian, and Palaic most likely arrived in Anatolia sometime in the fifth or possibly fourth millennium B.C.E., thereby moving the date of entry onto the plateau well before the EBA. If this is indeed the case, the sites discussed in this chapter may have hosted a mixture of indigenous Anatolians and the "new" (from a millennium before) arrivals speaking different languages. Alternatively some settlements may have been populated by indigenous Anatolians, and others by descendants of the migrants; a final scenario (though there are many others beyond those presented here) is an EB Anatolian landscape consisting of communities of indigenous Anatolians surrounded by, perhaps in a symbiotic relationship, pastoralist groups of Indo-European speakers. Clearly, significantly more archaeology is needed to sort out the ethnic makeup of the Anatolian plateau in the third millennium B.C.E.

EBA Chronology and the Western Plateau

As already noted, incipient urbanization or elements of increasing social complexity are found in western sites including Troy, Küllüoba, Karataş, and possibly Beycesultan. Some material culture hallmarks appearing in the first stages of the EB in this region include the megaron (the "hall and porch") architectural type, the fast wheel, and the so-called distinctive depas vessel and two-handled tankards. Metallurgy and extramural cemeteries become a normal phenomenon by the EB II, and a pan-plateau trade network criss-crosses Anatolia, extending perhaps from southeastern Anatolia to the Aegean, in the EB III.

The Early Bronze I

In the northwest one of the main type sites for the entire EBA is Troy. Corresponding generally with the EB I phase on the plateau, Troy I begins ca. 3000 B.C.E. and ends at or near 2700, possibly as late as 2500 B.C.E. (Korfmann and Kromer 1993; Kuniholm 2001; Manning 1997; Yakar 2002, and Yakar, chapter 4 in this volume; see Jablonka, chapter 32 in this volume, for an end date of 2550 B.C.E.). Troy's lengthy excavation history (for an excellent summary of Troy excavations see Sazcı 2007), has offered a plethora of often conflicting data. Most problematic are Schliemann's decidedly unscientific 19th century excavations of the Troy I–III periods. Starting in the 1930s, Blegen attempted to clarify Schliemann's work by concentrating on the first five strata of the settlement, dividing Stratum I into Phases a–j, which reflected several rebuildings of this earliest occupation (Blegen 1963; Blegen et al. 1950; Sazcı 2007:75–77).

Troy I begins what is called the "Trojan Maritime Culture," referring to the strong material cultural ties Troy seems to have had with offshore sites such as Thermi and Poliochni (Efe 2006; Sazcı 2005). Troy I ceramic forms are handmade, sand tempered, and include conical bowls, most with thickened inverted rims and an occasional pedestaled foot. One-handled cups and larger pots with rounded bases and three legs, the latter perhaps for cooking, and globular jars with straight necks and flared rims, some with handles on the shoulder, comprise the main assemblage (Blegen et al. 1950; Çaliş-Sazcı 2006). Except for a very light burnish, decoration is only occasional and in the form of punctate or incised design in rectilinear patterns often infilled with white paste.

The Troy I settlement in the north-northwestern area of the mound rests on the natural bedrock. Heavy Troy II period rebuilding obscured much of the small Troy I settlement. What remains are remnants of a small village on a low rise that offered a good view of the sea and Aegean islands. A substantial, sloped stone wall, 2.5 m thick and featuring three gates, may have served as protection, perhaps from a growing maritime trade culture in the Dardanelles and beyond. One of the earliest Troy I buildings (corresponding to Blegen's Troy Ia phase) was an apsidal structure (Room 103), possibly built in a megaron form. In Blegen's Phase Ib, additional domestic structures were built in a "row house" fashion (Ünlüsoy 2006), with four megaron-style rectilinear rooms set side by side, all with mudbrick walls supporting flat roofs. To the north, where Room 103 once stood, a new rectangular structure (Room 102) was constructed in formal megaron style with anteroom and an inner hall 7.0 × 18.5 m in size (Blegen et al. 1950).

A second, more inland region is best represented by the site of Demircihöyuk; it features seventeen stratigraphic levels dating to the EB I–II periods (Korfmann 1983:191). The EB I levels include E–H (Korfmann and Kromer 1993; see Yakar, chapter 4 in this volume); excavations revealed the entire village plan. The ceramic assemblage at Demircihöyük contains vessels that are black burnished or that have a red wash and burnish, with a final group of coarse wares. Forms include handmade bowls, some with vertical handles, and small cups, spouted globular pitchers, and pithoi; some vessels bear incised decoration (Efe 1987; Seeher 1987). Several hundred figurines in both human and animal form were also discovered at the site.

The architecture at EB I Demirci is remarkable in its preservation and layout (figure 10.2). The village, built mainly of mudbrick with occasional wattle and daub construction, was circular with a diameter of about seventy meters and was enclosed by a wall (Korfmann 1983:242); though the excavator suggests the wall was defensive, it may have functioned as a flood barrier between the settlement and the swampy surrounding area (Düring 2011). Houses were generally two-roomed, though a few had three, and were based on the megaron style; structures were trapezoidal with the back of the house wider than the entrance (Korfmann 1983:190, 243). The village was laid out in a radial plan, with all entrances facing an internal common area. Demirci is not the only settlement plan that features domestic structures arrayed around a central open area (a settlement pattern called the *Anatolisches Siedlungsschema*—Anatolian Settlement Plan—by Korfmann [1983]). Similar plans, though not circular, can be found at the nearby site of Küllüoba, discussed below, and in the earlier Chalcolithic levels at Ilıpınar (Roodenberg 2008, and see Roodenberg, chapter 44 in this volume).

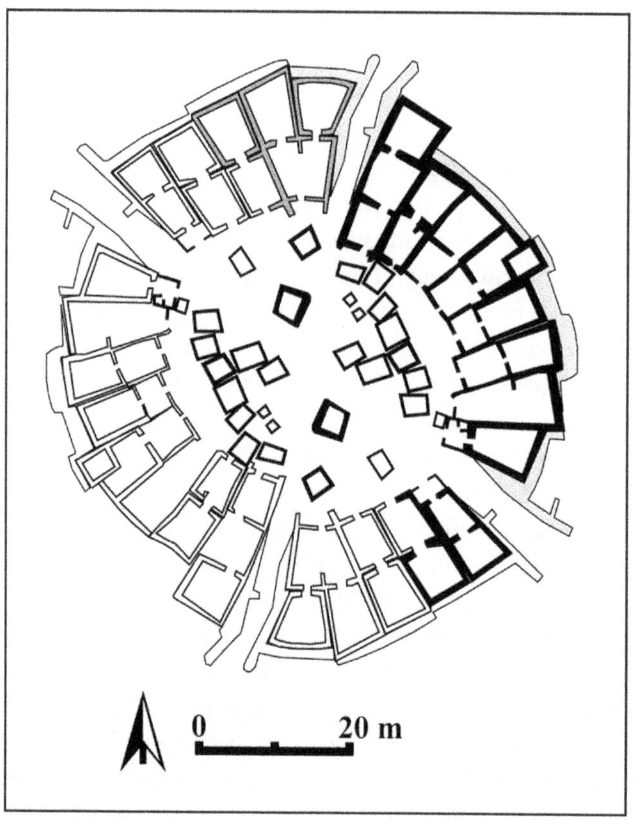

Figure 10.2. Typical western Anatolian depas forms.

In the southwestern region, along the old course of the Maeander River, lies the site of Beycesultan (Lloyd and Mellaart 1962; Mellaart 1998), one of the largest prehistoric sites in western Anatolia. Levels XIX–XVII at the site correspond to the EB I period. Although there are some parallels in architectural styles, there is little similarity between the Trojan and Beycesultan ceramic assemblages. The ceramics from EB I Beycesultan are all handmade but are of quite fine quality. The excavators assert that the ceramic assemblage is the most "aesthetically pleasing" of the southwestern Bronze Age (Lloyd and Mellaart 1962:116); they note that some elements in the EB I assemblage have roots in the later Late Chalcolithic forms and styles (1962:117). Thus, in spite of new styles appearing in the EB I, the overall ceramic assemblage suggests a continuity of settlement. EB I coarse wares are generally identical to those from earlier phases and include reddish or brownish two-handled jars and cooking pots, flat baking platters, and three-legged cooking pots. The finer quality ceramics, ranging in color from pale red or orange to blackish-gray are generally slipped and burnished. Some feature vertical or horizontal fluting on the body of larger jars and jugs; the white-filled incision found at Troy is "exceedingly rare" (Lloyd and Mellaart 1962:116). The excavators note one "weird" decoration in the form of a fish-scale pattern on two-handled jugs (Lloyd and Mellaart 1962:116–17). A few rising lips and cutaway beak spouts appear in the EB I assemblage, but not in the ubiquitous numbers and dramatic forms found in the next period. In general the EB I Beycesultan assemblage, at least regarding the fine wares, can be called gracefully formed and well made.

Architectural remains from Beycesultan Levels XIX–XIII are scant and offer little understanding of village layout. The single trench reaching EB I levels (trench SX) uncovered part of a single structure in Level XVII, which the excavators call a "shrine" (Lloyd and Mellaart 1962:29–33) mainly because later phase buildings in this spot were designated as such (see later discussion). Besides the architecture, several hearths and clay storage bins were excavated.

Material culture recovered from the Level XVII structure included infant jar burials; marble figurines; copper needles and knives/daggers; clay, stone, and bead necklaces; and grinding stones. Figurines were generally made of white marble and are fiddle-shaped (Lloyd and Mellaart 1962:269). Thirteen of the fifteen flat marble fiddle-shaped figurines were found in the back room of the megaron structure. The presence of these figurines and the copper daggers suggest to the excavators that the EB I structure was for specialized usage.

Küllüoba offers occupation spanning the Late Chalcolithic through the Early Bronze III periods (Efe 2000, 2001, 2003, 2005). The site is interesting for its material culture that reflects elements of both the Troy I and the Beycesultan XIX–XVII assemblages, and its radial settlement plan that is roughly similar to Demircihöyük's. Late Chalcolithic to EB I remains are found in the western area of the mound; levels 5–3 are transitional into EB I, and Levels 2–1 correspond to EB I. On the lower eastern slope EB II and III levels have been excavated (Efe and Ay 2000; Efe and Ay-Efe 2001).

The EB I western slope architecture features a mudbrick wall, built on roughly a "zigzag" plan, which appears to encircle the settlement; built up against the wall are residences, many based on a modified megaron plan. Although the entire Level 3–2 village has not been excavated, the exposed layout suggests that the doorways of residences faced an internal open space in similar fashion to the settlement plan at Demircihöyük. The EB II settlement layout has been more extensively excavated on the eastern slope, where a radial plan is indeed evident (see later discussion). The EB I ceramic assemblage at Küllüoba offers the fluting and barbotine decoration found in Beycesultan XIX–XVII levels; surfaces are slipped and burnished and range in color from red and gray/brown to black (Efe and Ay 2000).

Early Bronze II

Depending on the chronology employed, Troy I ends somewhere between 2700–2500 B.C.E. (Kuniholm 2001; Yakar 2002, and see Yakar, chapter 4 in this volume). The Troy II occupation, comprising twelve phases (a–g with several subphases), is built partially atop the Troy I settlement and is much larger; Troy II also has an outer wall that appears defensive in nature. Early in the occupation at least five substantial megara were constructed, the largest of which, Megaron IIA, is at the center of the settlement. These megara were probably not for domestic use, but their actual function has not been securely determined. Arrayed around these larger buildings were smaller hall-and-porch–style structures that were probably houses; most buildings were built of mudbrick and timber, and Megaron IIA rested on a stone platform.

In the earliest Troy II phases the ceramics do not differ much from those of Troy I, perhaps due to the overlap in occupation. By the later Troy II phases, however, new forms develop, perhaps resulting from the introduction of the fast wheel (probably in Troy IIb). Most notable are the Troy II tankards and the depas *amphikypellon* (figure 10.3). The tankards have flat bottoms, globular bodies, and flaring necks; two vertical rounded handles attach body to neck. External surfaces are slipped and burnished and often reddish, but they also occur in gray and black. The depas amphikypellon looks something like a straightened and elongated tankard. A flat-bottomed tubular body with a slightly flaring rim is flanked by two vertical handles that tend toward oblong rather than round; Blegen et al. (1950:230) describes these depas as a "heart-shaped ensemble," which is quite appropriate. Decoration of vessels differs little from that found in Troy I; new Troy II additions include plastic/appliqué decoration in the form of loops on the sides of jars (often in the shape of an elaborate mustache), and the images of faces found on lids and a few jars. Blegen et al. (1950:242) note that this practice had its origins in the Troy I assemblage, where far more vague representations of human faces were found on some bowls. Handleless flaring bowls become common in Troy II as well, particularly in IIb, and result from the fast wheel (Blegen et al. 1950:225–26). Although this ceramic repertoire has been considered "Trojan," recent work at inland sites including at Küllüoba (see later discussion), offer the possibility that the origin of "Trojan" forms may have been further inland (Efe and İlaslı 1997).

Figure 10.3. Typical western Anatolian depas forms.

Finally, it was in the Troy IIg phase that the so-called treasure was located (note that this was the largest of several metal hoards found in the EB Trojan levels). This phase was heavily burned, and one scenario is that the treasure was dropped or left behind in the haste to escape the flames. An excellent overview of the treasure, its context, and its contents can be found in Göksel Sazcı's recent study (2007; and see Jablonka, chapter 32, and Muhly, chapter 39 in this volume).

EB II levels at Beycesultan include XVI–XIII (note that Yakar, chapter 4 in this volume, places XVI in the late EB I period). The small trench revealed only two structures which the excavators identify as shrines built side by side and in megaron style (Lloyd and Mellaart 1962:36–46). Building interiors were filled with vessels, and each structure contained a built plaster and clay feature designated an "altar"; storage bins, some for grain, hearths, benches, and platforms comprise the other built furniture. Whether domestic or religious, it does seem clear that some unusual, extradomestic activities may have occurred in these structures.

Although EB II Beycesultan architecture is modeled on EB I patterns, there is a decided change in the nature of the ceramic assemblage. The fast wheel forms found in the later Troy II assemblage are absent here, as are tankards and depas. The Becesultan handmade pottery sees some changes in color; black and red predominate in Level XVI, whereas vessels become progressively lighter in later levels where buff, light gray, and orange-yellow predominate in Level XIII. Surfaces are still slipped and burnished but with less care. Grooved and ribbed decoration, incised designs that are sometimes white-filled, and the plastic adornment of bars and lugs comprise the most common surface treatments. The most notable deviation from previous levels is the vessels themselves, which are thick, heavy, and large, in "strong contrast to the refined E.B. 1 pottery" (Lloyd and Mellaart 1962:135). Level XIV sees the rise of bowls with conical feet or pedestals, jugs, juglets, and pitchers with cut-away beak spouts and sometimes three conical feet, and loop or strap handle cups. Beginning in Level XV a few new shapes make their appearance, including pedestaled bowls with two, three, or four horns projecting from the rim and pedestaled bowls with high twisted handles (resembling a bread basket handle) (Lloyd and Mellaart 1962:148–52). The ceramics from levels XV–XIV are not a close fit with Troy I or II, but there are more similarities with the Karataş assemblage in the southwest (see later discussion). Level XIII ended in conflagration, and with the rebuilding in the next level came a change in both architecture and ceramics.

At Küllüoba, Level IV in the eastern area of the mound and Level 1 in the west (Efe 2005, 2007a, 2007b; Efe and Ay-Efe 2001) offer an extensive architectural plan and ceramic assemblage. On the upper mound, the radial plan hinted at in the EB I period is fully realized in the EB II phases. The upper settlement is surrounded by a wall, and at least three gates offer access first to courtyards then to the interior buildings, many of which appear nondomestic in function. Two complexes (I and II) form the heart of the upper town and were, according to the excavator, most likely administrative buildings (Efe 2007a:49). A large megaron, not dissimilar from Megaron IIA at Troy II, rests on the western acropolis next to complex II; it is accompanied by at least two other large megara, all of nondomestic function and possibly religious in nature. Besides a radial plan there is at least one trapezoidal house (see EB I–II Demircihöyük), located on the western side of the upper town. In the lower town, houses were also built on the hall-and-porch plan, some free-standing and some built in complexes (Efe 2007a, 2007b).

The ceramic assemblage at Küllüoba is very similar to that at Troy II (Efe 2005, 2007a) including the heavy red-slipped tankards and depas (note that excavations at the site of Seyitömer Höyük near Kütahya offer a similar ceramic assemblage [Efe 2007a]). Forms also include jugs and pitchers with cut-away beak spouts such as are found in Beycesultan EB II levels, and decorative techniques such as fluting and ribbing are common as well. Küllüoba's assemblage appears to offer the full range of western Anatolian forms. This impressive settlement was clearly an important node on what appears to be a regional interaction sphere (or beyond just the region, see later discussion) at least as early as the EB II period.

The southwestern site of Karataş offers architectural and ceramic ties to the more northern settlements. In the EB I phase, Karataş I–III, there was a large and palisaded rectangular "central structure" on the high mound; in Karataş I–II small circular huts dotted the surrounding lower mound, but in Karataş III the megaron structure emerged, occasionally apsidal in form (Warner 1994). In the EB II period (Karataş IV–V), erosion had damaged the central structure. However, the lower town featured megaron-style free-standing domestic architecture, with the occasional back storage room (Warner 1994:137–38). The ceramic repertoire has strong parallels to the Beycesultan assemblage, including cut-away spouts and white-filled incised decoration; a significant portion of the Karataş assemblage is of red or darker color, slipped, and burnished (Eslick 2009:101–58). In addition to parallels with Beycesultan, the Karataş assemblage also displays similarities to ceramics from sites in the Lake District, including Kuruçay (Eslick 2009:217).

Early Bronze III

The Early Bronze III period in the western plateau features fewer large settlements (at least excavated and published ones) than in the previous periods. This situation in part led some to believe there was a break in occupation between the EB II and EB III periods in the region. However, a continuity of occupation is found in Aegean settlements such as Poliochni and Thermi, at inland sites such as Seyitömer and Küllüoba, at Bakla Tepe and Liman Tepe on the coast, and at Troy III and Beycesultan.

Troy III is the last of the "Maritime Culture" levels; beginning with Troy IV, the settlement's focus turns landward and is called "Anatolian" in nature. The Troy IV occupation dates to the very end of the third millennium B.C.E., and thus while technically falling within the EB III, it can be considered a transitional phase to the second millennium Middle Bronze Age (although see Jablonka, chapter 32 in this volume).

Blegen and others postulated that there was a break in occupation after the Troy IIg conflagration (Blegen et al. 1950; Joukowsky 1996). However, more recent work suggests that although the citadel may have been left unoccupied for some time after the fire, lower city occupation continued essentially uninterrupted (Korfmann and Kromer 1993).[1] Troy III architecture is not markedly different from that found in the Troy II lower town. In general, structures were built in complexes rather than in free-standing format (Blegen, Caskey, and Rowson 1951). One notable change is a far greater reliance on stone rather than mud or *pisé*—reflecting, perhaps, a desire for nonflammable building materials in the wake of the Troy IIg fire. There is also continuity in form and style in the ceramic assemblage found in the Troy II–III lower settlement (Blegen 1963; Düring 2011; Sazcı 2005; Ünlüsoy 2006).

Levels XII–VIII at Beycesultan correspond to the EB III period. Although the excavators include VII–VI in the EBA (Lloyd and Mellaart 1962:58 ff.), these levels date to the early second millennium B.C.E. and have marked changes in material culture—they are not considered here. After the Level XIII fire, construction was minimal and there are few architectural remains in Levels XII–XI. In Levels X–VIII a complex consisting of at least four megara, built side by side, was recovered, demonstrating that the hall-and-porch architectural style persists into the late third millennium B.C.E. The ceramic assemblage does not change significantly from the EB II levels; the potter's wheel arrived at Beycesultan in this phase, which led to the production of mass-produced plain wares bearing a red, buff, or brown wash (Lloyd and Mellaart 1962:199). The finer wares of earlier phases are still present but in far fewer numbers, and the incised decoration, fluting, ribbing, and heavy slip and burnish are missing from the assemblage. In these levels far more correlates with the Troy II–III assemblage are recognized, including the handleless bowls, loop-handled cups and bowls, beak-spouted jugs, and pitchers with handles connecting an elongated neck to the body. A few forms can be labeled "tankard" style in the Beycesultan EB III assemblage, and a few examples of depas vessels appear as well.

EBA Chronology and the North Central Plateau

The north central plateau presents a significant challenge to the researcher who wishes to build a later prehistoric sequence. A recent survey in the Paphlagonia region, carried out by Roger Matthews and Claudia Glatz (Glatz and Matthews 2005; Matthews 2007; Matthews and Glatz 2009), has done much to identify important prehistoric and second millennium B.C.E. sites and settlement patterns, but excavated sites are few in number. In addition to the Alaca Höyük EBA III "Royal Tombs," Alişar Höyük has long been used as a type site but presents as many problems as it solves. A recently excavated site near Alişar, Çadır Höyük, not only offers a check and balance for the Late Chalcolithic to EBA I transition but also exhibits EBA III occupation as well.

Early Bronze I

The best-known northern plateau site with Chalcolithic and EB levels is Alişar Höyük, excavated in the 1920s and 1930s; recent excavations at the nearby site of Çadır Höyük (Gorny et al. 1995, 1999, 2000, 2002; Steadman et al. 2008) have begun to help clarify the ceramic sequences in these periods. The prehistoric sequence at Alişar is problematic on several levels. Von der Osten excavated the center of the mound down to a depth of 30 m, but with very minimal clearance (less than 10 × 10 m). The lowest level, 19M, probably dates to the mid/late-fourth millennium B.C.E. (see Schoop 2005 and chapter 7 in this volume); according to von der Osten's final publication (1937) Levels 18–12M date to Late Chalcolithic and thus to the later fourth millennium B.C.E. Von der Osten's "Copper Age" levels, 11–7M, present the greatest difficulties for interpretation; of import here is that an earlier publication (von der Osten, Martin, and Morrison 1933) reported that Levels 13–12M were originally ascribed to the Copper Age. The "Copper Age" was meant to describe a post-Chalcolithic metal-using phase with an associated change in the ceramic assemblage (von der Osten 1937:110).

Some serious problems arise from von der Osten's labeling of levels, that is, "Chalcolithic," "Copper Age," and "Early Bronze Age" with no clearly defined ceramic sequences or absolute dates accompanying these designations. Schoop (chapter 7 in this volume) notes that there are several solutions to terminology/ceramic problems (especially as there is a noticeable change in ceramic styles from von der Osten's Chalcolithic to Copper Age), one being an acknowledgment of an occupational break between the Chalcolithic and Copper Age levels, and another being the recognition that Chalcolithic-style ceramics extend into the early third millennium B.C.E., that is, into the EBA. Regarding the occupational levels at Alişar, it is here suggested that 13–12M should be assigned to the very end of the fourth millennium or beginning of the third millennium B.C.E. in what might be considered a "transitional" phase between Chalcolithic and EBA (perhaps, to use von der Osten's terminology, these would be the Copper Age levels). The ceramic break between Levels 12M and 11M (see later discussion) could well represent a gap in occupation. Von der Osten's Copper Age 11–7M (generally referred to as Alişar Ib [Yakar 1985]) might fit far more comfortably into the late EB I and EB II periods of the north central plateau. Using this scheme, the following discussion describes the minimal evidence for architectural styles and slightly better evidence for ceramic styles in these transitional and EB I periods in the north central plateau.

Architectural remains from Alişar Level 13M (here dating to the very beginning of the third millennium B.C.E.) were minimal and were nonexistent in 12M. Level 13M demonstrated several walls built, according to von der Osten (1937:31), by "piling up handfuls of mud tempered with reeds, straw, or grass and afterward smoothing the surfaces by hand." This is perhaps a modified pisé style of building. Two partial rectilinear rooms (perhaps *spaces* is the better term) were revealed; contents included loom weights, ceramics, a hearth, and ten burials, eight of which were child burials. There were three burial styles: simple inhumation, burial in pots, and several stone or wooden box burials (von der Osten 1937:42–44). Von der Osten's Copper Age Levels 11–10M may also date to the EB I period, though very late in the phase. The architecture in these levels is still minimal, but it is clear that by this stage residents had begun placing stones at the foundations of their walls (perhaps set in mud as they were at Çadır Höyük, see next paragraph).

At EB I Çadır Höyük (Level IIc.1) mud was laid as a foundation for walls, and in some cases stones were placed within the mud, presumably to act as a stabilizer for the wall's superstructure (note the rough similarity to Alişar architecture). Wall superstructure was a mix of pisé and mudbricks. The EB I occupation at Çadır consists of small one-roomed structures (portions of at least five have been recovered thus far) measuring roughly 2 × 3 m in size. The open areas between these rooms had numerous fire pits and some hearths; several child burials in jars were recovered from this level as well. There are, therefore, some correlations in architectural styles between the Alişar 13M level and the EB I phases at Çadır Höyük.

Those correlations extend to the ceramic assemblage as well. At Çadır Höyük the EB I ceramic assemblage, all handmade and chaff/grit tempered, includes the black or red/orange-slipped and burnished surface treatments so common in the Late Chalcolithic, though the frequency of this surface treatment is far lower than in earlier times; forms include small carinated bowls (outward carination usually within two centimeters below the rim), small cups, and fruitstands. At Çadır the fruitstand, a bowl with a long funneled neck on a flaring pedestaled foot, begins to appear in the later Chalcolithic; whether fruitstands were still being made in the EB I period or are simply present as heirlooms is not yet apparent from the Çadır assemblage. Fruitstands also appear in the Alişar 13–12M levels, as do the slipped and burnished styles and forms. Beginning in Level 14M at Alişar and becoming increasingly common in Levels 13–12M (von der Osten 1937:53–54) were plain wares, ranging in color from gray to buff; these were wet-smoothed but not slipped and burnished. These same styles appear at EB I Çadır as well, and are as common (if not more so) than the EB I slipped and burnished styles. Forms include handleless and one-handled cups (figure 10.4), hole-mouth pots, one-handled jugs, and simple bowls (Steadman et al. 2008). Decoration, generally on the plain wares, includes incised geometric design (squares, lozenges), and on larger pots finger-pinching occurs (more for functionality perhaps than for decorative reasons); these surface treatments were also found in Alişar 17–12M levels (von der Osten 1937:57). The Copper Age levels at Alişar (11–7M) contain some of these plain wares and a few incised pieces, but the majority of the ceramics bear a red slip and burnish (sometimes patterned) and are of coarser quality than in previous periods. It is possible that Level 11M, and possibly 10M, belong in the EB I period, but it would seem that most of von der Osten's Copper Age levels fit more comfortably, stylistically at least, in the EB II period.

Early Bronze II

Data become even more scarce for the north central plateau in the EB II period. The only EB II materials at Çadır Höyük (Phase IIb) are sherds recovered from pits—no

Figure 10.4. Early Bronze I plain ware cups from Çadır Höyük.

architecture has yet been excavated. At Alişar the remains from Levels 9–7M (on the mound) and Level 13T (on the terrace) bear consideration here, though it is quite possible, even likely, that 7M and 13T should be assigned to the EB III period or at the juncture between EB II–III. Walls with stone foundations continue to be the norm in Levels 9–7M on the mound (von der Osten 1937:112–14); wall superstructures were built entirely of mudbricks, though the function of the rooms is unclear—they may have been domestic structures. A small area of a "fortification" wall was excavated in the northwestern area of the mound (von der Osten 1937:116–18); this substantial wall had a stone foundation over a meter in width and a probable mudbrick superstructure.

The ceramic assemblage includes a surfeit of bowls, along with round-bottomed one-handled cups, and pitchers with globular bodies and short necks with flared rims. Surfaces generally have a thick red slip with a thorough burnish, sometimes with haphazard patterning; decoration is almost nonexistent. Vessels are thicker and coarser on average than those from earlier periods. The EB II period in this area of the plateau remains something of a mystery.

Early Bronze III

In the EB III period significant changes such as urbanization and pan-Anatolian trade, already discussed, become well ensconced on the plateau. The best evidence for interregional connections is found in the EB III tombs at sites such as Alaca Höyük, Mahmatlar, and Horoztepe. Hints of a centralization process can be found at both Çadır and Alişar.

The EB III remains at Çadır Höyük are limited, but they provide an interesting contrast to the near lack of data for the EB II. Extant EB III (Phase IIa) occupation has been exposed on the eastern side of the mound where the substantial step trench (ca. 30 × 4 m) stretches from the mound's base to its summit and demonstrates a settlement history that spans the EB III to the Byzantine with almost no gaps. The EB III architecture consists of a one-meter-wide perimeter wall with a foundation of fist- and head-sized stones; its curved nature suggests that it ran around the EB III settlement. This wall may have served as the basis of a defensive structure or as a secure footing on which to build other structures (it was, in fact, used for this purpose in the Middle Bronze). A sounding further up the mound exposed significant EB III stone walls that may have belonged to domestic or public architecture. A ^{14}C sample yielded a date for these walls of ca. 2670–2300 B.C.E. (Beta #180275). The size of these features and the effort that went into constructing them suggest that the EB III occupation at Çadır was not insignificant.

The EB III period at Alişar (generally called Alişar III) is represented by Levels 6–5M, possibly including the preceding 7M on the mound, and 13T on the terrace. Excavated remains, though relatively minimal, do demonstrate the presence of a substantial settlement in the EB III period. A city wall, located on the terrace, may have been constructed in the 13T level. A second wall, likely defensive in nature, was constructed on the mound in Level 6M, rebuilt in 5M after a severe destruction (von der Osten 1937:208–14). The reconstructed 5M wall, approximately three meters wide, featured a paved gateway flanked by two towers; the external opening was accessed by following a pathway lined by two stone and mudbrick walls at oblique angles to the gate—seemingly to prevent a headlong rush at the gate. The construction of substantial EB III walls at both Çadır and Alişar suggests that significant economic and sociopolitical developments may have taken place on the northern plateau at this time.

The EB III pottery recovered from both sites is generally handmade with carinated bowls dominating (von der Osten 1937:230–47). The assemblages include examples of "Intermediate Ware," so named (Gorny et al. 1995:78) because of its position marking the transition between the end of the EB and beginning of the Middle Bronze. Intermediate Ware vessels range in color from buff to orange with purple to reddish slips applied (on the upper portion of vessels). Painted designs are usually rendered as geometric figures and include chevrons, zigzags, bands, and wavy lines. Von der Osten (1937:236–40) notes that Intermediate Ware appears in the last "Copper Age" layers (e.g., 7M and 13T) and continues throughout levels 6–5M; it is better levigated and vessels are better fired and finer than "typical" EB wares. Both standard EB III wares and Intermediate examples feature the same forms and decorative patterns—EB III vessels have either reddish-buff or yellow-buff slip with minimal burnishing; painted decoration is either in brown, black, or red. One category of "polychrome" ware features a reddish slip on which cream-colored panels are applied; red-painted designs are applied to the panels, the latter often outlined with brown or black lines (von der Osten 1937:240). A few "Cappadocian"-style examples (often included in the category of Intermediate Ware) were also recovered (see later discussion). Rough parallels to this assemblage can be found at Mercimektepe near Yozgat (Zoroğlu 1977:200). Some rare examples of ceramics that might be related to the north Syrian "bottles" (Schmidt 1932:147, 176; von der Osten 1937:43) found at Alişar, Kültepe, and Tarsus (see later discussion) may indicate that Alişar was at least tangentially involved in the EB III Anatolian trade network criss-crossing the plateau.

One of the most remarkable north central plateau discoveries are the burials at Alaca Höyük (Arık 1937; Koşay and Akok 1944). The date of the Alaca tombs has been in some flux since their excavation in the 1930s, but their attribution to the EB III period (Gürsan-Salzmann 1992) has been accepted by most. The nineteen Alaca tombs, fourteen of which were termed "royal" by the excavator, consisted of wood- and stone-lined cist tombs, each usually containing one individual, although some had two or three. The stone-lined tombs (dug into the earth at varying levels, thus complicating the stratigraphy [see Özyar 1999 for discussion]) were then covered with wood, on which animal remains were deposited (perhaps as offerings or the result of feasting). Grave goods include metal standards and weapons, animal and human figurines, metal and ceramic vessels, and jewelry; the metal items were made of gold, silver, and electrum, and some were copper. A number of the standards feature animal motifs, often bull or antelope/deer; these may have decorated animal-drawn carts or wagons (Mellaart 1966; see also Anthony 2007 and Düring 2011 for extensive discussion on wagons and standards). Although not as spectacular, burials at other north central sites including Horoztepe (Özgüç and Akok 1958), Oymaağaç (Özgüç 1980), Resuloğlu (Yıldırım 2006; Yıldırım and Ediz 2006, 2008), Salur North (Matthews 2004), and Kalınkaya (Zimmermann 2007a), attest to the practice of creating extramural cemeteries with burials containing items presumably representing significant wealth.

It is clear that the tombs at sites such as Alaca, Resuloğlu, and others indicate that some social phenomenon was occurring on the EB III north central plateau. The metal goods from these sites, some of which were made of tin bronze, indicate that residents were engaged in the trade network that stretched across the plateau and may have included circumpontic settlements (Zimmermann 2007a, 2007b).

EBA Chronology and the South Central Plateau

In many ways, the south central plateau is an even more difficult terrain for sketching out EB settlement because of the relatively few excavated and published sites. Tarsus, not technically on the plateau, offers some guidance, and the pre-*kārum* occupation at Kültepe also shines some light on EB III settlement in this area. Available data for the EB I–II periods are very scant.

An extremely important development in the latter centuries of the EB II and into the EB III, as already noted, is metallurgy (see Muhly, chapter 39 in this volume) and with it the beginnings of the search for important ores such as tin. In the late 1980s, Aslıhan Yener and colleagues undertook an archaeometallurgical survey in the Bolkardağ region of the Taurus Mountains (Yener et al. 1989a, 1989b). There they discovered Kestel Mine, which contained low-grade tin ore; the excavator speculates that an EBA settlement two kilometers away, known as Göltepe, was where the Kestel miners lived and processed the ore (Yener 1994, 1995; Yener and Özbal 1987). The announcement of an EBA tin mine in Anatolia set off an avalanche of scholarly debate that mainly revolved around whether ancient miners would consider such low-grade tin worth the effort, whereas some suggested that other ores (such as gold or iron) might have been mined there (e.g., Hall and Steadman 1991; Muhly 1993; Muhly et al. 1991; Muhly, chapter 39 in in this volume; Pernicka et al. 1992); such publications elicited replies from the excavators (e.g., Yener and Goodway 1992; Yener and Vandiver 1993).

Yener's continued work at Göltepe and Kestel demonstrated that Göltepe was, without doubt, a processing site—the presence of furnaces, crucibles, powdered ore, refuse pits with metallurgical débris, and storage jars containing ore nodules littered the site (Yener 1994, 1995, 2000:102–4, 112–13). Evidence that the Göltepe miners were specifically processing tin is found in the presence of tin residue on crucibles and powdery ore (with tin content) in measuring cups (Yener 2000:104–5). The modern presence of low-grade tin in the enormous Kestel mine may be explained, according to the excavators, by the ancient removal of higher grade ores (Yener 2000:73–75, 2008); essentially Kestel was "mined out," after which it may have been abandoned. The evidence from the site and mine has convinced a number of scholars that tin mining was taking place in this region in the EBA (Düring 2011; Laughlina and Todd 2000; Sagona and Zimansky 2009). The existence of a tin source in the Taurus Mountains would certainly have played a significant role in centralization processes and the development of trade networks already discussed.

Early Bronze I

The anchor site for this region and much of the plateau, Tarsus, was excavated in the 1930s–1940s under the direction of Hetty Goldman (1956); renewed work began again in 2000 (Özyar 2005). Mellink (1992) divides the Tarsus EB I levels into two phases, a and b, the earlier Ia phase dating to the later fourth millennium B.C.E. (and thus the Late Chalcolithic in present terminology) and the Ib to the first three centuries of the third millennium B.C.E. The EB I settlement features a street, or open area, flanked on one side by a substantial wall that may have stood at the settlement's boundary. Two circular stone structures, about 2.5 m in diameter, may have been towers or guard rooms at a gated entrance (Goldman 1956:9). Other architecture includes living and storage rooms, hearths, clay bins, pits, and platforms, some of which may have been for ritual purposes (Goldman 1956:10).

In the Late Chalcolithic and into the very beginning of the EB I period, the ceramic assemblage at Tarsus features forms and styles also found in the Amuq (primarily Phase F) and at other sites east of Tarsus such as Sakçe Gözü and as far away as Kurban Höyük (Algaze 1990:243–52; du Plat Taylor, Seton-Williams, and Waechter 1950; Mellink 1992; Steadman 1994a, 1994b). Typical wares from this period include the Chaff-Faced and Reserve Slip Wares, the latter often with horizontal patterning (see Ökse, chapter 11 in this volume, for further discussion); some locally painted styles appear at Tarsus as well. In the later Tarsus EB I phase Red Burnished and Red Gritty Plain and Burnished Wares displace their Late Chalcolithic counterparts (Steadman 1994a, 1996). Red Gritty Ware, brick red in color, is often painted a white or purplish-red; forms such as the beaked pitcher make an appearance in this period, similar in form to those found at southern plateau sites (French 1965; Mellink 1989). Small wheelmade bowls, some with incised/scraped decoration, also appear in the assemblage. The rather sudden adjustment to a reliance on Red Gritty Ware, especially in Tarsus EB Ib, reflects an alteration in the settlement's interaction sphere from the north Syrian/Mesopotamian regions in the Late Chalcolithic to the Anatolian plateau in the earliest third millennium B.C.E. Explanations for this change range from a reorientation of the trade network, perhaps due to the new exploitation of the Taurus area tin mines, to the conscious rejection of an expanding/collapsing Uruk system that may have appeared to engulf southeastern Anatolia and the Amuq (Steadman 1994a, 1996). By the close of the Tarsus EB I occupation, the settlement appears to be interacting comfortably with the Anatolian plateau. EB I period data for the southern plateau north of the Taurus mountains are extremely thin. Excavations at Acemhöyük (Öztan 2007) may offer more substantial data in the near future.

Early Bronze II

In the Tarsus EB II phase the EB I street/open area was leveled and then covered with a layer of clay to create a proper building surface on which residents then constructed possibly two-storey rectangular structures (not megara) with two or even three rooms, most containing a hearth and storage bins (Goldman 1956:12–13, 15). The area suffered a conflagration, after which a substantial (nearly three meters wide) fortification wall was erected over some of the previous houses. This wall was rebuilt slightly later and featured a gated entry into the settlement complete with tower and gate room (Goldman 1956:20–24). Inside the fortification wall was a narrow street or alley, on the other side of which were mudbrick structures similar to those from the earliest EB II phase. The EB II occupation at Tarsus remained fortified for the rest of the period, suggesting some perceived need for protection.

The EB II ceramic assemblage contains the Red Gritty and Chaff-Faced Wares so common in the EB I. Red Gritty Ware often has some incised decoration in the form of chevrons, "cross-stitch," or simple lines (Goldman 1956:108–10); this most common EB II ware includes the pitchers with rising spout seen at numerous other EB II sites. New in the EB II and apparently a local innovation is "Light Clay Ware," which includes wheel-turned hemispherical bowls with smoothed and occasionally scraped surfaces; fabrics are yellow-buff to pink and orange, and are finely made (Goldman 1956:105–6). Also in the Light Clay collection are corrugated jars and goblets, Reserve Slip bowls (a variation on this type from the EB I), and jars that receive some burnish and an occasional purplish-red slip or paint. Black burnished bowls and cups with white-filled incision demonstrate ties with the southern and western plateau, and parallels with ceramic styles in southeastern Turkey and northern Syria (including the Khabur) indicate that any earlier disruption in interaction had been overcome by the EB II period (Mellink 1989; Steadman 1994a). Tarsus had become a nexus in a trade network that stretched from the southeast to the southern plateau; this network reached its zenith in the following EB III period.

The settlement at Bademağacı, north of Antalya (Duru and Umurtak 2007, 2008, 2009), is quite far west and might fit just as comfortably in the foregoing discussion of the "western plateau." It certainly offers affinities to settlement types found in the west, but is also a good type site for the southern plateau as it rests in reasonable proximity to the Lake District, a region rich in prehistoric sites (especially Neolithic and Chalcolithic; see Özbaşaran, chapter 5, Schoop, chapter 7, and Düring, chapter 36 in this volume).

There are at least three EB II occupational levels at Bademağacı, and these are preceded by several Neolithic layers (Duru 2004; Duru and Umurtak 2004:297). EB II

Bademağacı demonstrates the type of "radial plan" settlement seen at Demircihöyük. At Bademağacı houses were arrayed so that their backs ran along an elliptically shaped downward slope covered with stones (probably a protection against flooding [Duru 2008]); the entrances of the houses faced the interior of the settlement. The buildings were built in the "megaron style" (Duru 2004:554) with stone foundations and mudbrick superstructures; residences share a wall in most (but not all) cases. Although the entire EB II settlement has not been excavated, it is clear that it is at least twice if not three times the size of Demircihöyük (about twenty-five to twenty-six houses); Bademağacı may have had somewhere between sixty and ninety structures, or more, suggesting a rather substantial population in the EB II period. The ceramic assemblage from this site does not deviate substantially from the styles generally found in the southwest, including reddish jugs and bowls with substantial burnishing, pitchers with cut-away spouts, and three-footed jars (similar to those found at EB II Beycesultan). One interesting category of finds from this site is the clay stamp seals with incised lines (Duru 2004; Duru and Umurtak 2008, 2009), perhaps demonstrating the rudiments of an administrative system at EB II Bademağacı.

Early Bronze III

Metal ore mining in the Taurus Mountains, beginning as early as the EB II, may have been one of the main catalysts for the expansion of trade networks in the EB III period (but see Muhly, chapter 39 in this volume). However, as has consistently been the case in this region, evidence for the EB III period is scant. At Tarsus a fire destroyed the latest EB II occupation, and Goldman's excavations of the EB III phases turned up very few recoverable remains (in part due to terracing activities by later farmers). The settlement seems to have experienced several building phases in the last centuries of the third millennium B.C.E.; Goldman divides the EB III into four phases (EB IIIA–D) with one, EB IIIC, divided into four subphases. Such steady rebuilding of the excavated portion of the settlement may reflect dynamic changes taking place at EB III Tarsus. In general the area remained residential; the earliest EB III architecture retained the EB II street-lined row house plan. After the conflagration at the end of the EB II, some of the surviving houses were fixed up and reinhabited and other new ones were built (Goldman 1956:32–33).

The Tarsus EB III ceramic assemblage offers some insights into the settlement's external interactions. As already noted, west Anatolian vessels known as tankards and depas appear in the Tarsus EB III assemblage, as do west Anatolian–style bowls (Goldman 1956:131; Mellink 1989). Red Gritty Ware continues, but the shapes and decorative techniques of earlier periods are gone and new forms such as bowls and pithoid jars become common; the Light Clay tradition also continues into the EB III, perhaps demonstrating a continuity of occupation. Besides western Anatolian styles, the Tarsus EB III assemblage also provides evidence of contact with southeastern Anatolia/northern Syria through the presence of Syrian bottles (a flask with pointed base and elongated neck) and goblets (Goldman 1956:135; Mellink 1986,

1998; Ökse 2007). Some examples of Cappadocian Ware at Tarsus demonstrate ties with the plateau.

Kültepe-Kaneš near Kayseri also offers some EB III data. The Kültepe settlement is far better known for its second millennium B.C.E. *kārum* and trading center (see Kulakoğlu, chapter 47, and Michel, chapter 13 in this volume), but the EB III occupational levels on the mound (Levels 13–11) suggest that Kültepe was, at this time, already an important center on the plateau (Özgüç 1986, 1999). The main excavated structure is a large square building with stone foundations and mudbrick walls, measuring about 22 × 20 m in size. Inside the structure are a number of rooms, including one interior hall measuring 10.5 × 17 m (Özgüç 1986:31). Thick internal walls and wooden beams supported a roof that may have been substantial enough for rooftop activities or a second storey. This was certainly a building of monumental size, suggesting that the EB III settlement at Kültepe was one of significant importance on the southern plateau.

Material culture recovered from the EB III levels at Kültepe testify to its regional and international connections. The presence of Cappadocian Ware (or "Intermediate Ware") attests to connections with the northern plateau and sites such as Alişar and Çadır. Tankards and depas reminiscent of (imported from?) those at sites in the west appear, as do the shorter and more truncated versions found at Tarsus (Mellink 1989; Özgüç 1986); north Syrian bottles also find their way to Kültepe. The excavator notes that examples of "Metallic Ware," associated with the Khabur, are present in the EB III levels at Kültepe (Özgüç 1986:37–38). A lapis lazuli Mesopotamian-style cylinder seal (unfortunately a surface find), and gold, silver, and electrum jewelry from tombs round out the items that indicate strong contacts with northern and perhaps even southern Mesopotamia in the EB III (Özgüç 1986). Kültepe's importance in the later centuries of the third millennium B.C.E. goes far in demonstrating why it was chosen as the main plateau trading center during the Old Assyrian Colony period of the succeeding millennium.

Conclusion

The third millennium B.C.E. on the plateau is one that can be described as a time of transition; Late Chalcolithic trends toward urbanization saw their florescence in the EBA. Chalcolithic period interregional trade with regions as far afield as Transcaucasia and possibly southeastern Europe (Özdoğan 1993, and chapter 29 in this volume; Palumbi 2003, 2008, and chapter 9 in this volume; Sagona 2004; Steadman 1995; Steadman, McMahon, and Ross 2007; Steadman et al. 2008; Thissen 1993) were strengthened by connections ranging across the plateau, stretching into the Aegean and southeastward to northern Mesopotamia and beyond. Monumental architecture appears, and metallurgy not only serves to change the utilitarian household assemblage but also becomes an important indicator of wealth and social position. The third millennium B.C.E., obviously important in its own right, also creates the platform on which the first major international centers and empires emerge in the second millennium. Continued work on the plateau will no doubt fill many gaps with invaluable data detailing the lifeways of Anatolians and their resident neighbors during the millennium that brings the plateau from "prehistory" to "imperial center."

NOTES

I am indebted to Antonio Sagona and Paul Zimansky who generously allowed me to read an early version of their book (2009) to help me begin to frame the present chapter. I also offer sincere thanks to Gregory McMahon for his encouragement and support during the writing of this chapter, and for being such an outstanding co-editor for this entire volume.

1. It should be noted that there is not universal agreement on Troy phasing. Some place the Troy II occupation in the EB III period and push Troy III into the late EB or early Middle Bronze periods (Efe 2006, 2007a; Mellink 1986). A detailed discussion of phasing issues can be found in Düring (2011).

REFERENCES

Algaze, Guillermo. 1990. *Town and Country in Southeastern Anatolia II: The Stratigraphic Sequence at Kurban Höyük*. Oriental Institute Publications 110. Chicago: Oriental Institute.

Anthony, David W. 1991. The Archaeology of Indo-European Origins. *Journal of Indo-European Studies* 19:193–222.

———. 2007. *The Horse, the Wheel, and Language: How Bronze-Age Riders from the Eurasian Steppes Shaped the Modern World*. Princeton, N.J.: Princeton University Press.

Arık, Remzi O. 1937. *Les fouilles d'Alaca Höyük: Entreprises par la Socieċteċ d'histoire turque: Rapport preċliminaire sur les travaux en 1935*. Ankara: Türk Tarih Kurumu Basımevi.

Bellwood, Peter. 2005. *First Farmers: The Origins of Agricultural Societies*. Oxford: Blackwell.

Blegen, Carl W. 1963. *Troy and the Trojans. Ancient Peoples and Places*. London: Thames and Hudson.

Blegen, Carl W., John L. Caskey, and Marion Rawson. 1951. *Troy. The Third, Fourth and Fifth Settlements*, vol. 2. Princeton, N.J.: Princeton University Press.

Blegen, Carl W., John L. Caskey, Marion Rawson, and Jerome Sperling. 1950. *Troy: General Introduction: The First and the Second Settlements*, vol. 1. Princeton, N.J.: Princeton University Press.

Burney, Charles and David M. Lang. 1971. *The Peoples of the Hills*. London: Weidenfeld and Nicolson.

Çalış-Sazcı, Devrim. 2006. Die Troianer und das Meer—keramik und handelsbeziehungen der sog. Maritimen Troyia-Kultur. In *Troia. Archäologie eines Siedlungshügels und seiner Landschaft*, ed. Manfred O. Korfmann, 201–8. Mainz am Rhein: Philipp von Zabern.

Çevik, Özlem. 2007. The Emergence of Different Social Systems in Early Bronze Age Anatolia: Urbanisation versus Centralisation. *Anatolian Studies* 57: 131–40.

du Plat Taylor, J., M. V. Seton-Williams, and J. Waechter. 1950. The Excavations at Sakçe Gözü. *Iraq* 12: 53–138.

Duru, Refik. 2004. Bademağacı Kazıları 2002 ve 2003 Yılları Çalışma Raporu. *Belleten* 68: 519–60.

———. 2008. *From 8000 BC to 2000 BC. Six Thousand Years of the Burdur—Antalya Region.* İstanbul: Suna-İnan Kıraç Akdeniz Medeniyetleri Araştırma Enstitüsü.

Duru, Refik and Gülsün Umurtak. 2004. Bademağacı kazıları-2002. *Kazı Sonuçları Toplantısı* 25.1: 297–302.

———. 2007. Bademağacı Kazıları, 2005. *Kazı Sonuçları Toplantısı* 28.1: 639–46.

———. 2008. Bademağacı Kazıları, 2006. *Kazı Sonuçları Toplantısı* 29.2: 187–96.

———. 2009. Bademağacı Kazıları, 2007 Yılı Çalışmaları. *Kazı Sonuçları Toplantısı* 30.1: 255–68.

Düring, Bleda S. 2011. *The Prehistory of Asia Minor: From Complex Hunter-Gatherers to Early Urban Societies, 20.000–2.000 BC.* Cambridge: Cambridge University Press.

Efe, Turan. 1987. *Demircihöyük: die Ergebnisse der Ausgrabungen, 1975–1978, Die frühbronzezeitliche Keramik der jüngeren Phasen (ab Phase H).* Mainz am Rhein: Philipp von Zabern.

———. 2000. Küllüoba 1999 Yılı Kazısı. *Kazı Sonuçları Toplantısı* 22.1: 105–18.

———. 2001. Küllüoba 2000 Yılı Kazısı. *Kazı Sonuçları Toplantısı* 23.2: 315–26.

———. 2002. The Interaction between Cultural/Political Entities and Metalworking in Western Anatolia during the Chalcolithic and Early Bronze Ages. In *Anatolian Metal II*, ed. Ünsal Yalçın, 49–65. Bochum: Deutsches Bergbau-Museum.

———. 2003. Küllüoba and the Initial Stages of Urbanism in Western Anatolia. In *From Village to Cities. Early Villages in the Near East. Studies Presented to Ufuk Esin*, ed. Mehmet Özdoğan, Harald Hauptmann, and Nezih Başgelen, 265–82. İstanbul: Arkeoloji ve Sanat Yayınları.

———. 2005. Küllüoba 2003 Yılı Kazı Çalışmaları. *Kazı Sonuçları Toplantısı* 26.1: 29–44.

———. 2006. Anatolische wurzeln—roia und die frühe Bronzezeit im westen Kleinasiens. In *Troia. Archäologie eines Siedlungshügels und seiner Landschaft*, ed. Manfred O. Korfmann, 15–28. Mainz am Rhein: Philipp von Zabern.

———. 2007a. The Theories of the "Great Caravan Route" between Cilicia and Troy: The Early Bronze Age III Period in Inland Western Anatolia. *Anatolian Studies* 57: 47–64.

———. 2007b. Küllüoba 2005 Yılı Kazı Çalışmaları. *Kazı Sonuçları Toplantısı* 28.1: 71–90.

Efe, Turan and Deniz Ş. M. Ay. 2000. Early Bronze Age I Pottery from Küllüoba Near Seyitgazi, Eskişehir. *Anatolia Antiqua* 8: 1–87.

Efe, Turan, and Deniz Ş. M. Ay-Efe. 2001. Küllüoba: İç Kuzeybatı Anadolu'da bir İlk Tunç Çağı Kenti, 1996–2000 Yılları Arasında Yapılan Kazı Çalışmalarının Genel Değerlendirmesi. *TUBA-AR* 4: 43–78.

Efe, Turan and Erkan Fidan. 2006. Pre-Middle Bronze Metal Objects from Inland Western Anatolia: A Typological and Chronological Evaluation. *Anatolia Antiqua* 14: 15–43.

Efe, Turan and Ahmet İlaslı. 1997. Pottery Links between the Troad and Inland Northwestern Anatolia during the Trojan Second Settlement. In *Poliochni e L'Antica Etá del Bronzo Nell'egeo Settentrionale*, ed. C. G. Doumas and V. La Rosa, 595–609. Athens: Scuola Archeologica Italiana de Atene.

Erkanal, Hayat. 1996. Early Bronze Age Urbanization in the Coastal Region of Western Anatolia. In *Housing and Settlement in Anatolia. A Historical Perspective*, ed. Yıldız Sey, 70–82. İstanbul: Türkiye Ekonomik ve Toplumsal Tarih Vakfı.

Erkanal, Hayat and Turhan Özkan. 1999. Balka Tepe kazıları. In *Tahtalı Dam Area Salvage Project*, ed. Turhan Özkan and Hayat Erkanal, 12–41, 108–37. İzmir: T. C. Kültür Bakanlığı, Anıtlar ve Müzeler Genel Müdürlüğü, İzmir Arkeoloji Müzesi Müdürlüğü.

———. 2000. 1998 Bakla Tepe kazıları. *Kazı Sonuçları Toplantısı* 21: 263–78.

Eslick, Christine. 2009. *Elmalı-Karataş: The Early Bronze Age Pottery of Karataş: Habitation Deposits.* Oxford: Archaeopress.

Frangipane, Marcella. 1993. Local Components in the Development of Centralized Societies in Syro-Anatolian Regions. In *Between the Rivers and over the Mountains. Archaeologica Anatolica et Mesopotamica Alba Palmieri Dedicata*, ed. Marcella Frangipane, Harald Hauptmann, Mario Liverani, Paolo Matthiae, and Machteld Mellink, 133–61. Roma: Università di Roma "La Sapienza."

———. 1996. Models of Urbanization in Eastern Anatolia. In *Housing and Settlement in Anatolia. A Historical Perspective*, ed. Yıldız Sey, 60–69. İstanbul: Türkiye Ekonomik ve Toplumsal Tarih Vakfı.

———. 1997. Arslantepe-Malatya: External Factors and Local Components in the Development of an Early State Society. In *Emergence and Change in Early Urban Societies*, ed. Linda Manzanilla, 43–58. New York: Plenum Press.

———. 2002. "Non-Uruk" Developments and Uruk-Linked Features on the Northern Borders of Greater Mesopotamia. In *Artefacts of Complexity. Tracking the Uruk in the Near East*, ed. Stuart Campbell and Nicholas Postgate, 123–48. Warminster: Aris and Phillips.

French, David H. 1965. Prehistoric Sites in the Göksu Valley. *Anatolian Studies* 15: 177–201.

Gamkrelidze, Thomas V. and Vjacheslav V. Ivanov. 1985. The Migrations of Tribes Speaking the Indo-European Dialects from the Original Homeland in the Near East to Their Historical Habitations in Eurasia. *Journal of Indo-European Studies* 13: 49–91.

Garstang, John. 1953. *Prehistoric Mersin. Yümük Tepe in Southern Turkey.* Oxford: Clarendon Press.

Glatz, Claudia and Roger Matthews. 2005. Anthropology of a Frontier Zone: Hittite-Kaška Relations in Late Bronze Age North-Central Anatolia. *Bulletin of the American Schools of Oriental Research* 339: 47–65.

Goldman, Hetty. 1956. *Excavations at Gözlü Kule, Tarsus. From the Neolithic through the Bronze Age*, vol. 2. Princeton, N.J.: Princeton University Press.

Gorny, Ronald L., Gregory McMahon, Samuel Paley, and Lisa Kealhofer. 1995. The Alişar Regional Project: 1994. *Anatolica* 21: 68–100.

Gorny, Ronald L., Gregory McMahon, Samuel Paley, and Sharon Steadman. 2000. The 1999 Alişar Regional Project Season. *Anatolica* 26: 153–71.

———. 2002. The 2000 and 2001 Seasons at Çadır Höyük in Central Turkey. *Anatolica* 28: 109–36.

Gorny, Ronald L., Gregory McMahon, Samuel Paley, Sharon Steadman, and Bruce Verhaaren. 1999. The 1998 Alişar Regional Project Season. *Anatolica* 25: 149–83.

Gürsan-Salzmann, Ayşe. 1992. *Alaca Hoyuk: A Reassessment of the Excavation and Sequence of the Early Bronze Age Settlement.* Ph.D. dissertation. University of Pennsylvania.

Hall, Mark E. and Sharon R. Steadman. 1991. Tin and Anatolia: Another Look. *Journal of Mediterranean Archaeology* 4.2: 217–34.

Joukowsky, Martha Sharp. 1996. *Early Turkey: Anatolian Archaeology from Prehistory through the Lydian Period*. Dubuque, Iowa: Kendall/Hunt Publishing.

Kâmil, Turhan. 1982. *Yortan Cemetery in the Early Bronze Age of Western Anatolia*. BAR International Series 145. Oxford: BAR International.

Korfmann, Manfred. 1983. *Demircihüyük. Die Ergebnisse Der Ausgrabungen 1975–1978*, vol. 1. Mainz am Rhein: Philipp von Zabern.

Korfmann, Manfred and Bernd Kromer. 1993. Demircihüyük, Beşiktepe, Troia: Eine Zwischenbilanz zur Chronologie dreier Orte in Westanatolien. *Studia Troica* 3: 135–46.

Koşay, Hamit Z. and Mahmut Akok. 1944. *Ausgrabungen von Alaca Höyük: ein Vorbericht über die im Auftrage der Türkischen Geschichtskommission im Sommer 1936 durchgeführten Forschungen und Entdeckungen*. Ankara: Türk Tarih Kurumu Basımevi.

Kuniholm, Peter I. 2001. Aegean Dendrochronology Project 1999–2000 Results. *Arkeometri Sonuçları Toplantısı* 16.1: 79–84.

Laughlina, Gary J. and Judith A. Todd. 2000. Evidence for Early Bronze Age Tin Ore Processing. *Materials Characterization* 45.4–5: 269–73.

Lloyd, Seton and James Mellaart. 1962. *Beycesultan*, vol. 1. London: British Institute of Archaeology at Ankara.

Makkay, J. 1992. A Neolithic Model of Indo-European Prehistory. *Journal of Indo-European Studies* 20: 193–228.

Mallory, J. P. 1989. *In Search of the Indo-Europeans: Language, Archaeology and Myth*. London: Thames and Hudson.

Manning, Sturt. 1997. Troy, Radiocarbon, and the Chronology of the Northeast Aegean in the Early Bronze Age. In *Poliochni e L'Antica Etá del Bronzo Nell'egeo Settentrionale*, ed. C. G. Doumas and V. La Rosa, 498–521. Athens: Scuola Archeologica Italiana de Atene.

Matthews, Roger. 2004. Salur North: An Early Bronze Age Cemetery in North-Central Anatolia. In *A View from the Highlands, Archaeological Studies in Honour of Charles Burney*, ed. Antonio Sagona, 55–66. Herent: Peeters.

———. 2007. An Arena for Cultural Contact: Paphlagonia (North-Central Turkey) through Prehistory. *Anatolian Studies* 57: 25–34.

Matthews, Roger and Claudia Glatz, eds. 2009. *At Empires' Edge. Project Paphlagonia Regional Survey in North-Central Turkey*. London: British Institute at Ankara.

McMahon, Gregory. 2010. Agency, Identity, and the Hittite State. In *Agency and Identity in the Ancient Near East: New Paths Forward*, ed. Sharon R. Steadman and Jennifer C. Ross, 181–89. London: Equinox.

Mellaart, James. 1966. *The Chalcolithic and Early Bronze Ages in the Near East and Anatolia*. Beirut: Khayats.

———. 1998. Beycesultan. In *Ancient Anatolia. Fifty Years' Work by the British Institute of Archaeology at Ankara*, ed. Roger Matthews, 61–68. London: British Institute of Archaeology at Ankara.

Mellink, Machteld J. 1986. The Early Bronze Age in West Anatolia: Aegean and Asiatic Correlations. In *End of the Early Bronze Age in the Aegean*, ed. Gerald Cadogan and John L. Caskey, 139–52. Leiden: Brill.

———. 1989. Anatolian and Foreign Relations of Tarsus in the Early Bronze Age. In *Anatolia and the Ancient Near East: Studies in Honour of Tahsin Özgüç*, ed. Kutlu Emre, Barthel Hrouda, Machteld Mellink, and Nimet Özgüç, 319–31. Ankara: Türk Tarih Kurumu Basımevi.

———. 1992. Anatolian Chronology. In *Chronologies in Old World Archaeology*, ed. Robert W. Ehrich, 207–20. Chicago: University of Chicago Press.

———. 1994. The EB II-III Transition at Karataş—Mayük: Village Center and Cemetery. *Kazı Sonuçları Toplantısı* 15: 457–59.

———. 1998. Anatolia and the Bridge from East to West in the Early Bronze Age. *TÜBA-AR* 1: 1–8.

Merpert, Nicolai J. 1987. Ethnocultural Change in the Balkans on the Border between the Eneolithic and the Early Bronze Age. In *Proto-Indo-European: The Archaeology of a Linguistic Problem. Studies in Honor of Marija Gimbutas*, ed. Susan N. Skomal and Edgar C. Polomé, 122–35. Washington, D.C.: Institute for the Study of Man.

Muhly, James D. 1993. Early Bronze Age Tin and the Taurus. *American Journal of Archaeology* 97.2: 239–53.

Muhly, J. D., F. Begemann, Ö. Öztunalı, E. Pernicka, S. Schmitt-Strecker, and G. A. Wagner. 1991. The Bronze Metallurgy of Anatolia and the Question of Local Tin sources. *Archaeometry* 90: 209–20.

Oates, Joan, Augusta McMahon, Philip Karsgaard, Salam Al Quntar, and Jason Ur. 2007. Early Mesopotamian Urbanism: A New View from the North. *Antiquity* 81: 585–600.

Ökse, A. Tuba. 2007. Ancient Mountain Routes Connecting Central Anatolia to the Upper Euphrates Region. *Anatolian Studies* 57: 35–45.

Özdoğan, Mehmet. 1993. Vinča and Anatolia: A New Look at a Very Old Problem. *Anatolica* 19: 173–93.

———. 2007. Amidst Mesopotamia-Centric and Euro-Centric Approaches: The Changing Role of the Anatolian Peninsula between the East and the West. *Anatolian Studies* 57: 17–24.

Özgüç, Tahsin. 1980. Some Early Bronze Age Objects from the District of Çorum. *Belleten* 44: 80–134.

———. 1986. New Observations on the Relationship of Kültepe with Southeast Anatola and North Syria during the Third Millennium B.C. In *Ancient Anatolia. Aspects of Change and Cultural Development, Essays in Honor of Machteld J. Mellink*, ed. Jeanny V. Canby, Edith Porada, Brunilde S. Ridgeway, and Tamara Stech, 31–47. Madison: University of Wisconsin Press.

———. 1999. *Kültepe-Kaniš/Neša Sarayları ve Mabedleri/The Palaces and Temples of Kültepe Kaniš/Neša. Türk Tarih Kurumu Yayınlarından 46*. Ankara: Türk Tarih Kurumu Basımevi.

———. 2003. *Kültepe Kanis/Nesa, The Earliest International Trade Center and the Oldest Capital City of the Hittites*. İstanbul: Middle Eastern Culture Center in Japan.

Özgüç, Tahsin and Mahmut Akok. 1958. *Horoztepe. An Early Bronze Age Settlement and Cemetery*. Ankara: Türk Tarih Kurumu Basımevi.

Öztan, Aliye. 1989. A Group of Early Bronze Age Pottery from the Konya and Niğde region. In *Anatolia and the Ancient Near East: Studies in Honour of Tahsin Özgüç*, ed. Kutlu Emre, Barthel Hrouda, Machteld Mellink, and Nimet Özgüç, 407–18. Ankara: Türk Tarih Kurumu Basımevi.

———. 2007. 2005 Yılı Acemhöyük Kazıları. *Kazı Sonuçları Toplantısı* 28.2: 549–60.

Özyar, Aslı. 1999. Reconsidering the "Royal" Tombs of Alacahöyük: Problems of Stratigraphy According to the Topographical Location of the Tombs. *TÜBA-AR* 2: 79–85.

———. 2005. *Field Seasons 2001–2003 of the Tarsus-Gözlükule Interdisciplinary Research Project*. İstanbul: Ege Yayınları.

Palumbi, Giulio. 2003. Red-Black Pottery: Eastern Anatolian and Transcaucasian Relationships around the Mid-Fourth Millennium BC. *Ancient Near Eastern Studies* 40: 80–134.

———. 2008. Mid-Fourth Millennium Red-Black Burnished Wares from Anatolia: A Cross-Comparison. In *Ceramics in Transitions*, ed. Karen S. Rubinson and Antonio Sagona, 39–58. Ancient Near Eastern Studies, Supplement 27. Leuven: Peeters.

Pernicka, E., G. A. Wagner, J. D. Muhly, and Ö. Öztunalı. 1992. Comment on the Discussion of Ancient Tin Sources in Anatolia. *Journal of Mediterranean Archaeology* 5.1: 90–98.

Renfrew, Colin. 1987. *Archaeology and Language*. New York: Cambridge University Press.

Roodenberg, Jacob. 2008. The Inhabitants. In *Life and Death in a Prehistoric Settlement in Northwest Anatolia. The Ilıpınar Excavations*, vol. 3, ed. Jacob Roodenberg and Songül Alpaslan-Roodenberg, 69–90. Leiden: Nederlands Instituut voor het Nabije Oosten.

Sagona, Antonio. 2004. Social Boundaries and Ritual Landscapes in Late Prehistoric Trans-Caucasus and Highland Anatolia. In *A View from the Highlands, Archaeological Studies in Honour of Charles Burney*, ed. Antonio Sagona, 475–538. Herent: Peeters.

Sagona, Antonio and Paul Zimansky. 2009. *Ancient Turkey*. London: Routledge.

Sazcı, Göksel. 2005. Troia I–III, die Maritime und Troia IV–V, die Anatolische Troia-Kultur: eine Untersuchung der Funde und Befunde im mittleren Schliemanngraben (D07, D08). *Studia Troica* 15: 33–98.

———. 2007. *The Treasures of Troia*. İstanbul: Aygaz.

Schmidt, Erich. 1932. *The Alishar Hüyük, Seasons of 1928 and 1929*. Oriental Institute Publications 19. Chicago: University of Chicago Press.

Schoop, Ulf-Dietrich. 2005. *Das anatolische Chalkolithikum. Eine chronologische Untersuchung zur vorbronzezeitlichen Kultursequenz im nördlichen Zentralanatolien und den angrenzenden Gebieten*. Remshalden-Grunbach: Greiner.

Seeher, Jürgen. 1987. *Demiricihüyük, Die Ergebnisse der Ausgrabungen 1975–1978 III/1; Die Keramik 1; A, Die neolithische und chalcolithische Keramik; B, Die frühbronzezeitliche Keramik der älteren Phasen (bis phase G)*. Mainz am Rhein: Philipp von Zabern.

———. 2000. *Die Bronzezeitliche Nekropole von Demircihüyük-Sarıket*. Istanbuler Forchungen 44. Tübingen: E. Wasmuth.

Sherratt, Andrew. 1997. *Economy and Society in Prehistoric Europe*. Princeton, N.J.: Princeton University Press.

Steadman, Sharon R. 1994a. *Isolation vs. Interaction: Prehistoric Cilicia and its Role in the Near Eastern World System*. Ph.D. dissertation. University of California, Berkeley. Ann Arbor: UMI.

———. 1994b. Prehistoric Sites in the Cilician Plain: Analysis of the Prehistoric Pottery from the 1991 Bilkent University Survey. *Anatolian Studies* 44: 85–103.

———. 1995. Prehistoric Interregional Interaction in Anatolia and the Balkans: An Overview. *Bulletin of the American Schools of Oriental Research* 299/300: 13–32.

———. 1996. Isolation or Interaction: Prehistoric Cilicia and the Fourth Millennium Uruk Expansion. *Journal of Mediterranean Archaeology* 9.2: 131–65.

Steadman, Sharon R., Gregory McMahon, and Jennifer C. Ross. 2007. The Late Chalcolithic at Çadır Höyük in Central Anatolia. *Journal of Field Archaeology* 32.4: 385–406.

Steadman, Sharon R., Jennifer C. Ross, Gregory McMahon, and Ronald L. Gorny. 2008. Excavations on the North-Central Plateau: The Chalcolithic and Early Bronze Age Occupation at Çadır Höyük. *Anatolian Studies* 58: 47–86.

Şahoğlu, Vasif. 2004. Interregional Contacts around the Aegean during the Early Bronze Age: New Evidence from the İzmir Region. *Anatolia* 27: 97–120.

———. 2005. The Anatolian Trade Network and the Izmir Region during the Early Bronze Age. *Oxford Journal of Archaeology* 24.4: 339–61.

———. 2008. Crossing Borders, The Izmir Region as a Bridge between the East and the West during the Early Bronze Age. In *Crossing Borders. Proceedings of the 7th, 8th, and 9th International Workshops, Athens 1997–1999*, ed. Carole Gillis and Birgitta Sjöberg, 153–73. Sävedalen: Paul Aström Förlag.

Thissen, Laurens. 1993. New Insights in Balkan-Anatolian Connections in the Late Chalcolithic: Old Evidence from the Turkish Black Sea Littoral. *Anatolian Studies* 43: 207–37.

Thomas, Homer L. 1992. The Indo-European Problem: Complexities of the Archaeological Evidence. *Journal of Indo-European Studies* 20: 1–29.

Ünlüsoy, Sinan. 2006. Vom reihenhaus zum megaron—roia I bis Troia III. In *Troia. Archäologie eines Siedlungshügels und seiner Landschaft*, ed. Manfred O. Korfmann, 133–44. Mainz am Rhein: Philipp von Zabern.

von der Osten, Hans H. 1937. *The Alishar Hüyük, Seasons of 1930–32*. Oriental Institute Publications 28. Chicago: University of Chicago Press.

von der Osten, Hans H., Richard A. Martin, and John A. Morrison. 1933. *Discoveries in Anatolia, 1930–31*. Oriental Institute Communications no. 14. Chicago: University of Chicago Press.

Warner, Jayne L. 1994. *Elmalı-Karataş II. The Early Bronze Age Village of Karataş*. Bryn Mawr, Penn.: Bryn Mawr College.

Wheeler, Tamara S. 1974. Early Bronze Age Burial Customs in Western Anatolia. *American Journal of Archaeology* 78: 415–25.

Yakar, Jak. 1981. The Indo-Europeans and Their Impact on Anatolian Cultural Development. *Journal of Indo-European Studies* 9: 94–111.

———. 1985. *The Later Prehistory of Anatolia*. BAR International Series 268. Oxford: BAR International.

———. 1989. The So-Called Anatolian Elements in the Late Chalcolithic and Early Bronze Age Cultures of Palestine: A Question of Ethocultural Origins. In *L'urbanisation de la Palestine à l'age du Bronze ancien*, ed. by Pierre de Miroschedji, 341–54. BAR International Series 527. Oxford: BAR International.

———. 2002. Revising Early Bronze Age Chronology of Anatolia. In *Mauershau: Festschrift für Manfred Korfmann Volume I*, ed. Rüstem Aslan, Stephan Blum, Gabriele Kastl, Frank Schweizer, and Diane Thumm, 445–56. Remshalden-Brunbach: Bernhard Albert Greiner.

Yener, K. Aslıhan. 1994. Göltepe/Kestel 1992. *Kazı Sonuçları Toplantısı* 15: 201–9.

———. 1995. Göltepe 1993 Kazı Sonuçları. *Kazı Sonuçları Toplantısı* 16: 177–88.

———. 2000. *The Domestication of Metals: The Rise of Complex Metal Industries in Anatolia*. Leiden: Brill.

———. 2008. Revisiting Kestel Mine and the Dynamics of Local Provisioning of Tin during the Early Bronze Age. In *Ancient Mining in Turkey and the Eastern Mediterranean*, ed. Ünsal Yalçın, Hadi Özbal, and A. Gürhan Paşamehmetoğlu, 57–64. Ankara: Atılım University of Turkey Historical Research Center.

Yener, K. Aslıhan and M. Goodway. 1992. Response to Mark E. Hall and Sharon R. Steadman, "Tin and Anatolia: Another Look." *Journal of Mediterranean Archaeology* 5.1: 77–90.

Yener, K. Aslıhan and Hadi Özbal. 1987. Tin in the Turkish Taurus Mountains: The Bolkardağ Mining District. *Antiquity* 61: 64–71.

Yener, K. Aslıhan, Hadi Özbal, Ergun Kaptan, A. Necip Pehlivan, and Martha Goodway. 1989a. Kestel: An Early Bronze Age Source of Tin Ore in the Taurus Mountains, Turkey. *Science* 244: 200–203.

Yener, K.A., H. Özbal, A. Minzoni-Deroche, and B. Kasoy. 1989b. Bolkardağ: Archaeometallurgy Surveys in the Taurus Mountains, Turkey. *National Geographic Research* 5.3:477–94.

Yener, K. Aslıhan and Pamela B. Vandiver. 1993. Reply to J.D. Muhly, "Early Bronze Age Tin and the Taurus." *American Journal of Archaeology* 97: 255–64.

Yıldırım, Tayfun. 2006. An Early Bronze Age Cemetery at Resuloğlu, Near Uğurludağ, Çorum. A Preliminary Report of the Archaeological Work Carried Out between the Years 2003–2005. *Anatolia Antiqua* 14: 1–14.

Yıldırım, Tayfun and İsmet Ediz. 2006. 2004 Yılı Resuloğlu Mezarlık Kazısı. *Kazı Sonuçları Toplantısı* 27.2: 57–64.

———. 2008. 2006 Yılı Resuloğlu Eski Tunç Çağı Mezarlık Kazısı. *Kazı Sonuçları Toplantısı* 29.2: 443–54.

Zimmerman, Thomas. 2005. Perfumes and Policies: A "Syrian Bottle" from Kinet Höyük and Anatolian Trade Patterns in the Advanced Third Millennium BC. *Anatolica* 31: 161–69.

———. 2007a. Anatolia as a Bridge from North to South? Recent Research in the Hatti Heartland. *Anatolian Studies* 57: 65–75.

———. 2007b. Anatolia and the Balkans, Once Again—Ing-Shaped Idols from Western Asia and a Critical Reassessment of Some "Early Bronze Age" Items from İkiztepe, Turkey. *Oxford Journal of Archaeology* 26.1: 25–33.

Zoroğlu, Levent. 1977. Yozgat—Mercimektepe sondajı. *Türk Arkeoloji Dergisi* 24: 195–212.

Zvelebil, Marek and Kamil V. Zvelebil. 1988. Agricultural Transition and Indo-European Dispersals. *Antiquity* 62: 574–83.

CHAPTER 11

THE EARLY BRONZE AGE IN SOUTHEASTERN ANATOLIA

A. TUBA ÖKSE

Geographical Zones

The region between the Amanus Mountains, the eastern Taurus Mountains and the Turkish-Syrian border is characterized by undulating plateaus and wide flood plains formed by the Euphrates and Tigris rivers (figure 11.1). The region is divided into two main zones by the Karacadağ Massif, with sections reflecting individual cultural properties, correlating with cultural systems in northern Syria and northern Mesopotamia.

The western zone covers the Amuq-İslahiye-Maraş depression, the high plateau of Gaziantep, the Queiq River valley, and the Middle Euphrates region enclosing the Sajur Valley in the west and the Balikh Valley in the east. The western section of this zone is defined by the Amuq sequence (Braidwood and Braidwood 1960) related to the sequence of Tarsus (Goldman 1956) in Cilicia and Tell Mardikh (Porter 2007) in northwestern Syria. The chronology of the İslahiye Plain is set according to the sequences found at Tilmen Höyük and Gedikli Karahöyük (H. Alkım 1979; Alkım and Alkım 1966).

The Middle Euphrates region is defined by a series of dams built on the Euphrates River. The Atatürk Dam (formerly named the Karababa Dam) at the alluvial plains of Adıyaman and Şanlıurfa forms the northern section, and the alluvial plain widening toward the Syrian border where the Birecik and Carchemish dams are located defines the southern section. The cultural structure and chronological sequence on both sides of the Euphrates River is similar (Abay 1997; Carter and Parker 1995:98, fig. 14.1; Curvers 1988:359, 381; Engin 2007:277, fig. 18:9–10; Kühne 1976:516–23, map 4; Mazzoni 1985:10; Thissen 1989:206).

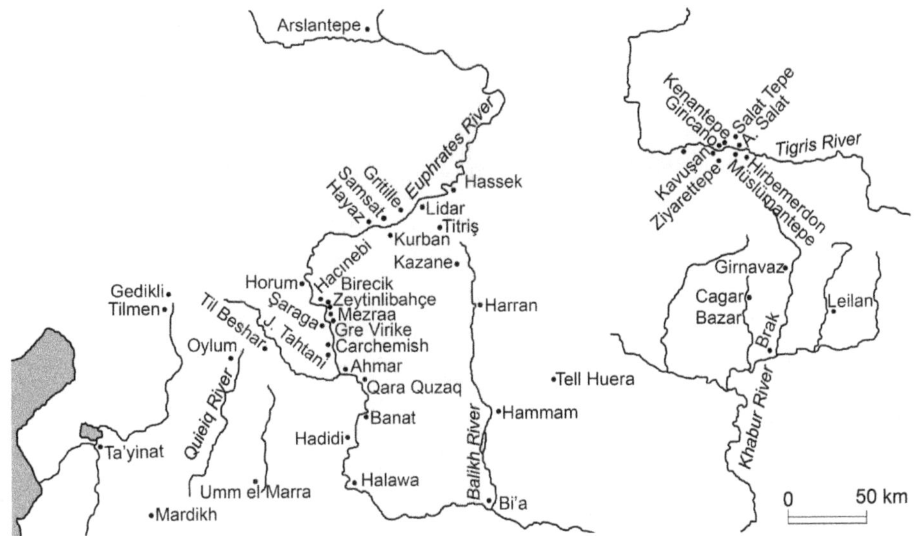

Figure 11.1. Map of sites mentioned in the text.

The northern section has strong connections to the Upper Euphrates region (Malatya Plain and the Keban and Karakaya dams); therefore the sequences of Samsat Höyük (Abay 1997), Kurban Höyük (Algaze 1990), Titriş Höyük (Algaze, Mısır, and Wilkinson 1992), and Hassek Höyük (Behm-Blancke 2003) define this section, correlated with the Arslantepe sequence in the Upper Euphrates region (Frangipane 2000).

The chronology of the southern region is based on the sequence at Horum Höyük (Marro 2007), Tilbes and Tilvez (Fuensanta 2007), the Birecik EBA cemetery (Sertok 2007), Zeytinlibahçe (Frangipane 2007:124, fig. 8.1 map) and Gre Virike (Engin 2007) on the Euphrates, and Tilbeshar (Kepinski 2007) on the Sajur River, as well as Oylum Höyük on the Kilis Plain (Özgen 1990). This area has a relatively homogenous cultural structure with the Tishrin Dam, defined by the sequences of Jerablus Tahtani (Peltenburg 2007:7) and Tell Ahmar (Jamieson 1993), and finally Tell Hammam et-Turkman (Curvers 1988) on the Balikh River.

The eastern zone is divided into two regions. The northern area includes the Upper Tigris region, forming a wide flood plain including strong tributaries of the Tigris River, namely the Batman, Garzan, and Bothan Rivers. The southern section is the Upper Khabur region formed by several streams cutting across the Mardin Massif and joining the Khabur River.

The material culture of both areas is parallel to northeastern Syrian (Khabur region, the Syrian Jezirah) and northern Mesopotamian (Middle Tigris region) cultures (Abay 1997; Frangipane 2007:124, fig. 8.1). The Upper Tigris region seems to have developed a local character in the Early Bronze Age (EBA), newly defined by recent excavations at Üçtepe (Özfırat 2006), Kenantepe (Creekmore 2007), Ziyaret Tepe (Matney and Rainville 2005), and Kavuşan Höyük within the flooding zone of the Ilısu Dam. The EBA of the Upper Khabur region is recovered at Girnavaz (Uysal 2007); unfortunately, the material from this site is not published yet, and thus the EBA chronology for this section is defined mainly by the sequences at Tell Brak (Oates, Oates, and McDonald 2001) and Tell Leilan (Schwartz 1988), located south of the Turkish-Syrian border.

Chronologies

The EBA chronology of southeastern Anatolia is parallel to northern Syrian chronologies. The traditional EBA I–III chronology of Anatolia is based on the Tarsus sequence (Mellink 1992) and the EBA I–IV chronology of northwestern Syria on the Amuq and Tell Mardikh sequences (Akkermans and Schwartz 2003; Schwartz and Weiss 1992), as represented in table 11.1.

For the Middle Euphrates region both EB I–III, found in Hauptmann (2000) and Frangipane (2000), and EB I–IV in Frangipane and Marro (2000) and Abay (1997) is used; however, the chronological studies on Arslantepe (Conti and Persiani 1993:table 2; Frangipane 2000), the Keban Basin (Marro and Helwing 1995:fig. 5), and the Karababa Basin (Abay 1997:fig. 47; Gerber 2000) show local differences, and the periodization of Kurban Höyük (Algaze 1990) continues to be discussed.

In northeastern Syria the Mesopotamian cultural periods (Kühne 1976) and the Early Jezirah periodization (EJ 0–V) is used (Lebeau 2000; Marro 2000; Pfälzner 1998; Pruss 2000); however, this chronology is not well adapted to the eastern zone of southeastern Anatolia. The division of the EBA is not clearly attested in this region yet, so this period is generally divided into a first half and a second half of the EBA for the Upper Tigris region.

The earlier half of the third millennium B.C.E. correlates to the EBA I–II. Mellink's EBA IA defines the Late Chalcolithic–EBA transition, parallel to Abay's Period I, and to the EJ 0 Level, which dates to the last centuries of the fourth and to the beginning of the third millennium B.C.E. This subperiod is contemporary to the Jamdat Nasr Period of Mesopotamia. Mellink's EBA IB (3000–2700 B.C.E.) is parallel to Abay's Period II, and EJ 0–I dates to 3100/3000–2800/2650 B.C.E., differing in several studies. This period is contemporary to Mesopotamian Early Dynastic I. EBA II is dated to 2700–2400 B.C.E. by Mellink and to 2800–2500 B.C.E. by Hauptmann (2000) and Frangipane (2000), parallel to Abay's Period III (2600–2500 B.C.E.) and EJ II, which dates to 2800/2700–2600/2500 B.C.E. in several studies. This period is contemporary to Mesopotamian Early Dynastic II.

The latter half of the third millennium B.C.E. is generally defined as EBA III or III–IV, depending on the chronological sequence used. Mellink's EBA IIIA (2400–2200 B.C.E.) is parallel to Abay's Period IV A (2350–2100 B.C.E.) and to EJ III dating to 2600/2500–2350/2275 B.C.E. in several studies. In Anatolia and the Upper Euphrates region, this period is divided into two phases (EBA IIIA–B).

Table 11.1. Table of Synchronized Periodizations

	Mellink (1992)	Hauptmann (2000)	Abay (1997)	Jamieson (1993)	Marro (2000)		Lebeau (2000) Pruss (2000)	Akkermans and Schwartz (2003)
3300 —	EBA IA							
3200 —			Period I					
3100 —								
3000 —	EBA IB	EBA IA-B	Period II	Horizon IA		HME I	EJ 0	EBA I
2900 —					EJ 0			
2800 —				Horizon IB	EJ I			
2700 —	EBA II	EBA IIA-B	Period III		EJ II	HME II	EJ I	EBA II
2600 —							EJ II	EBA III
2500 —		EBA IIIA-B	Period IVA	Horizon IIA	EJ IIIA	HME III	EJ IIIA	
2400 —	EBA IIIA				EJ IIIB		EJ IIIB	EBA IVA
2300 —				Horizon IIB	EJ IV			
2200 —	EBA IIIB	EBA IIIC			EJ V	HME IV	EJ IVA-B	EBA IVB
2100 —			Period IVB				EJ V	
2000 —								

The EBA IIB–IIIA of Marro and Helwing (1995) and the EBA IIIb of Gerber (2000), the EBA IIIB of Mellink (1992), the Period 2 of Conti and Persiani (1993), and Period III of Abay (1997) are parallel to west Syrian EBA III/IVA, consistent with EJ III and Early Dynastic III. The EBA IIIB–IIIC of Marro and Helwing, EBA IIIb of Gerber and EBA IIIB of Mellink (2200–2000 B.C.E.) all correlate with one another; the Period 3 of Conti and Persiani and Period IVB of Abay (2100–2000 B.C.E.) are all parallel to west Syrian EBA IV/IVB and contemporary with EJ IV–V and the Akkad and Ur III periods in Mesopotamia.

The distribution of ceramic groups and special vessel types reflects geographical and chronological differences throughout the third millennium B.C.E. The relative chronologies of geographical zones and individual periods are based mainly on ceramic distributions; absolute dates obtained from radiocarbon analyses are rare.

The Western Zone

Early Bronze Age I

The EBA in the western region (table 11.2) includes ceramic assemblages that are particular to the sites and region, whereas others can be tied into the Late Uruk assemblages common to the east and southeast.

The Chronological Sequence

Mellink (1992:table 2–3) suggested that the EBA IA period dates to 3400–3000 B.C.E., which is defined based on the presence of Chaff-Faced Ware at relevant sites, including the early Amuq G phase, Tarsus EB I–early, and Arslantepe VI A. An adjustment to this is made by Abay (1997:figs. 46–48), who dates the EBA IA (which he terms Period 1) to 3300–3100 B.C.E., using the ceramic assemblages of Samsat e, Kurban Höyük VIA, and Hassek Höyük 5; he asserts that these are contemporary with Tell Leilan IV and Tell Brak TW 12.

A similar periodization differentiation between Mellink's and Abay's models arises regarding the EBA IB. Mellink's model dates the EBA IB to 3000–2700 B.C.E. and includes the late Amuk G phase, Tarsus EB I–late, and Arslantepe VI B, based on relevant ceramic assemblages (see following discussion). Abay, however, divides the period into two phases, known as Period II early and late, based on the Atatürk Dam sites and their ceramic sequences. The early Period II phase includes Samsat c, Kurban Höyük VB, Hassek Höyük 4–3, and Arslantepe VI B 1–2; dating to the later Period II are Samsat c, Hassek Höyük 2–1 with grave 12, Arslantepe VI B–terminal, and Kurban Höyük VA (Abay 1997:figs. 46–48). Abay's scheme also includes Tell Mardikh I, Tell Leilan IIIa–b, and Tell Brak TW 10–9, and 8–2.

Table 11.2. Synchronization of the Sites in the Western Zone

Tarsus Gözlükule	Tell Mardikh	Amuq Sequence	Gedikli Karahöyük	Samsat Höyük	Kurban Höyük	Hassek Höyük	Arslantepe	Hammam et-Turkman	Gre Virike	Birecik EBA Cemetery	Zeytinlibahçe	Tilbes	Tilbeshar	Ceramic Groups									
														Flaring Rim Bowls	Early Wheelmade HGoblets Early Pedestaled Bowls Cyma Recta Bowls	Brittle Orange Ware Brick-Red Incised Ware	Euphrates Banded Ware	Reserved Slip Ware	Metallic Ware Spiral Burnished Ware Conical Cups	Caliciform Assemblage Grooved Hama Goblets	Karababa Painted Ware	Smeared Wash Ware	Depa
EB IA		G	III k–h M1	e	VB	5	VIA			Birecik Cemetery	EB IA	X	IIIA 1–2					horizontal					
EB IB	I			c	VA	4 3	VIB 1–2	VI east	I		EB IB												
	II A	H				2 1	VIB term.					IX	IIIB					Diagonal-vertical					
EB II				XX	IVC		VIC1	Town wall															
	II B1	I	Cre-mation Burials	XIX	IV B-A		VIC2	Burned levels 1–2	IIA	Oylum graves			III C-D										
EB IIIA				XVIII	IIIB		VID1					VIII											
EB IIIB	II B2	J		XVII a-b			VID 2–3	VI west															
EB-MB				XVI	IIB				IIB														

Also dating to the EBA IB/Period II phase are Hacınebi, Horum Höyük III-2, Mezraa Höyük V, Zeytinlibahçe B8:4, Tilbeshar IIIA2, and earlier Gre Virike I (2900–2500/2400 B.C.E.), although Engin (2007:267–68) dates Gre Virike I to the EBA II. Dating to the later Period II in Abay's scheme are Zeytinlibahçe C6–7:9, Mezraa Höyük IV–III, and Jerablus Tahtani 2A, and in a refinement Kepinski dates Tilbeshar IIIA2 to 2900–2700 B.C.E. (Abay 2007:152–53). These levels are contemporary to the Birecik EBA cemetery (3100–2600 B.C.E.) (Sertok and Ergeç 1999) and the Şaraga cemetery (Sertok and Kulakoğlu 2001).

Ceramic Assemblages

Chaff-Faced Ware is found at the sites dating to Mellink's EBA IA and Abay's Period I. In addition to this ware Reserved Slip Ware with horizontal patterning also defines the earliest EBA period. However, both these wares continue to be used in the later EBA phases (the Reserved Slip Ware with diagonal-vertical patterning). Flaring Rim Bowls, however, are limited to the EBA IA, thereby defining the Late Chalcolithic to EBA transition. Flaring Rim Bowls occur at sites already noted as possessing EBA IA levels, including the early Amuq G phase (Judaidah JK3/Floor 20–18), Arslantepe VI A, Samsat e, Kurban Höyük VIA, and Hassek Höyük 5, as well as at Tilbeshar IIIA1, which dates to 3100–2900 B.C.E. (Kepinski 2007:152–53; Peltenburg 2007:4, table 1.1), Tilbes X, with radiocarbon dates placing it within the 3100–2900 B.C.E. range (Fuensanta 2007:tab 9.1), and Zeytinlibahçe B8 (Frangipane 2007:131–36).

The Chaff-Faced and Reserved Slip Wares, as well as Red-Black Burnished Wares, are found in the later EBA phase (IB or Period II), but the Flaring Rim Bowls do not extend into this phase. Also present in the IB phase are carinated bowls with band rims, occurring frequently at Kurban Höyük V (Algaze 1986:fig. 4.FF, GG, 11.Y), Samsat Höyük II, Horum Höyük III1–2 (Marro 2007:fig. 15.1), Birecik EBA cemetery (Sertok and Ergeç 1999:pl. 7A–I, 8.A–F), Zeytinlibahçe B8, Gre Virike I (Engin 2007:268–70), and the "champagne period" of Carchemish (Woolley and Barnett 1952:pl. 57–59).

Reserved Slip Ware with diagonal and vertical stripes is common at Late Uruk sites; however, this decoration appears also during the EBA I at Tarsus (Goldman 1956:fig. 236), as well as Amuq G–H (Braidwood and Braidwood 1960:fig. 218–20) and in other sites together with Flaring Rim Bowls, as already mentioned. Late diagonal Reserved Slip Ware appears in EBA I–II contexts at Arslantepe (Frangipane and Palmieri 1983:545), Kurban Höyük V (Algaze 1990:pl. 49–50), Samsat Höyük Period II, Horum Höyük III3–4 (Marro 2007:223–25), Gre Virike I (Engin 2007:272), and Tell Ahmar Horizon IA (Jamieson 1993:41). The Late Uruk red slipped ware shows a similar distribution, suggesting a possible common ceramic distribution sphere throughout the region in the Late Uruk period (see Özbal, chapter 8 in this volume).

In the Middle Euphrates region, Plain Simple Ware, a mass-produced pottery throughout the EBA, is represented by diagnostic shapes such as short funnel-necked pots, which occur at Gre Virike I. Other EBA I types such as fruitstands with rounded body and inverted rim are found at the Birecik EBA cemetery (Sertok

2007:241–42), and band-rim ledge-rim bowls occur at Zeytinlibahçe EBA I (Frangipane 2007:131–36), Tilbes X–VIII (Fuensanta 2007:143–45), Tilbeshar III A1 (Kepinski 2007:152–53), and Arslantepe VI B2 (Frangipane 2000). Wavy incised decoration is typical of vessels in the Amuq G phase (Braidwood and Braidwood 1960:fig. 220:23–25) and in Zeytinlibahçe B8 EBA IA contexts.

Cyma recta cups—sinuous-sided cups and bowls with small ring bases (Akkermans and Schwartz 2003:226)—appear in EBA IB and continue into EBA II and early EBA III. Abay (1997:fig. 46–48) points to the frequency of these vessels within the earlier half of the EBA IB and their infrequent appearance during the late half of the phase. These vessels are found in the late phases of Tarsus EB I and Amuq G and in the early phase of Amuq H, Samsat Höyük Levels c and XX, Kurban Höyük VB-A-IVC, Hassek Höyük 4–2, Arslantepe VIB-C1, at Tell Mardikh I–IIA, and Hammam et-Turkman VI East. Cyma recta cups are present in Zeytinlibahçe EBA IB (Frangipane 2007:129–36), Tilbeshar IIIA1–2 (Kepinski 2007:152–53), Tilbes X, Tilvez EBA I (Fuensanta 2007:table 9.1), and Gre Virike I contexts (Engin 2007:268–70) together with Reserved Slip Ware.

Architecture and Other Material Culture

The Late Chalcolithic settlement hierarchy seems to have disappeared in the beginning of the third millennium B.C.E.; the settlements are generally dispersed, small scale, and mostly newly founded in the region. In the northern part of the Middle Euphrates Valley, Arslantepe, Kurban Höyük, and Hassek Höyük continue to be occupied (Wilkinson 1990; Wilkinson in Algaze, Mısır, and Wilkinson 1992). Lidar Höyük, Hassek Höyük 5 (Behm-Blancke et al. 1981, 1984:104), and Titriş Höyük—occupying about six hectares—are surrounded by thick defensive walls (Algaze 1990:547–48; Algaze and Matney, chapter 46 in this volume). In the southern part of the region, the number and size of the sites decrease; small settlements are founded in Horum Höyük, Zeytinlibahçe, Yarım Tepe (Rothman et al. 1998), and Carchemish (Algaze, Breuninger, and Knudstad 1994; Peltenburg 2007:13). Horum Höyük is a multiphase site (Marro 2007); similarly, in all four levels at Zeytinlibahçe (Frangipane 2007:129–32) the buildings have similar plans and locations throughout thirteen sublevels, similar to the Late Chalcolithic and EBA I levels in Tilbes Höyük (Fuensanta 2007:143, table 9.1). In the EBA IA Zeytinlibahçe is a village-like settlement, and in the EBA IB it develops into a planned settlement with streets and large buildings; in contrast, Tilbeshar III A1 is a small fortified settlement of about six hectares in extent, becoming a nonfortified site with primitive domestic architecture used by Early Transcaucasian metal smiths in the upper level (III A2) (Kepinski 2007:152–54). These alterations in settlements can be correlated with settlement developments in neighboring regions.

High terraces are established on the Middle Euphrates Valley. Late Uruk–EBA I platforms at Surtepe and Tilbes Höyük (Fuensanta 2007:146, 143, table 9.1), and a rectangular terrace with irregular contours, covering a 1,750 m^2 area and dating to the late EBA I, at Gre Virike (Ökse 2007a) point to the presence of high terraces with ritual facilities and monumental tombs. A similar distribution of monumental tombs is also present in the Syrian Middle Euphrates (Akkermans and Schwartz 2003:246–53).

Extramural cemeteries are found near Hassek Höyük (Behm-Blancke et al. 1984), Lidar Höyük, Titriş Höyük, the Birecik cemetery (Sertok and Ergeç 1999), Tilbeshar, and Carchemish (Woolley and Barnett 1952). In Zeytinlibahçe EBA IB (Frangipane 2007:136) and Birecik cemetery (Sertok and Ergeç 1999), rich metal finds are found in cist graves, contemporary to Hassek Höyük and the Arslantepe VI B tomb (Frangipane 2000). The metal objects consist of several types of pins, pendants, figurines, flat axes, tripartite spearheads, and daggers (Squadrone 2007:205–8) showing similar typological characteristics to objects in EBA I–II contexts. The glyptic styles in the northern part of the Middle Euphrates region belong to the ED I–II tradition (Algaze 1999:544).

Early Bronze Age II

Although the earliest stage of the EBA presents some level of differential phasing as offered by various scholars, as is discussed next, the EBA II period (2700–2400 B.C.E.) is in considerably greater flux.

The Chronological Sequence

The EBA II period includes the Amuq H phase, which is contemporary to Tarsus EB IB–late/EB II–early. Mellink, however, dates Tarsus II and Amuq H exclusively to the EBA II (1992:table 2–3); she also dates Arslantepe VI C to this period. On the other hand, Schwartz (2007:table 1) dates Amuq H to EBA III, contemporary to Tell Banat IV and Tell Mardikh IIA (2900–2400 B.C.E.; see also Schwartz and Weiss 1992:236–40).

Abay's Period II is broken into early and late phases. The earlier phase corresponds to Tarsus EB II, the latter half of the Amuq G phase, Samsat Höyük XX, Kurban Höyük IVC, and Arslantepe VI C1 (Abay 1997:figs. 46–48). On the contrary, Mellink dates Arslantepe VI C to the end of Tarsus EB II and Kurban Höyük IV to Tarsus EB II and Amuq H. Contemporary with these levels in Abay's scheme are Tell Mardikh IIA, the Tell Hammam et-Turkman town wall, Tell Brak TW 8–2, Tell Leilan IIIc, Ninevite V, Chagar Bazaar 5–2, and the Tell Chuera Kleiner Antentempel. The latter half of Abay's Period II includes the Amuq I phase, Samsat Höyük XIX–XVIII, Kurban Höyük IVB–A, and Arslantepe VI C2–D1. This correlation fits Conti and Persiani's (1993) dating of Arslantepe VI D1 and the later phases of Kurban Höyük IV to the end of Tarsus EB II. On the other hand Marro and Helwing (1995) suggest a later date for these levels; they date Arslantepe VI D1 and the later phases of Kurban Höyük IV to Tarsus EB III and to Amuq J, and the earlier phases of Kurban Höyük IV to Tarsus EB II and to the later phase of Amuq I.

Peltenburg (2007:4, table 1:1) dates Gre Virike IIA, Horum Höyük III3–4, Tilbeshar IIIB–C, Mezraa Höyük II, and Jerablus Tahtani 2B to ca. 2500–2200 B.C.E., and

Kepinski (2007:154) dates Tilbeshar IIIB to 2700–2500 B.C.E. This suggests that these sites span the EBA II, with Tilbeshar IIIC perhaps falling more comfortably into the EBA III phase.

Ceramic Assemblages

Abay's early Period III is based on the presence of cyma recta cups, and the earliest examples of Metallic Ware at the sites as dating to the early Period III phase. By the latter half of this phase, the cyma recta cups disappear and Metallic Ware, the earliest examples of corrugated cups, horizontal Reserved Slip Ware, and Smeared Wash Ware appear (keyed to the Amuq I phase and contemporary levels at sites already noted). This sub-period is correlated with Tell Mardikh IIB1 and the burned Levels 1–2 in Hammam et-Turkman according to the presence of horizontal Reserved Slip Ware, as well as with Tell Brak CH, ER, Phase III, Tell Leilan IIIc, and the Tell Chuera Kleiner Antentempel according to the presence of Metallic Ware.

The early wheelmade goblets, early pedestal bowls with grooved decoration on their high stems, and cyma recta dominate the vessel repertoire of the Plain Simple Ware. These types are known from Tarsus EB II (Goldman 1956:figs. 248:240), Amuq H (Braidwood and Braidwood 1960:368), and Gedikli IIIk–h (H. Alkım 1979:pl. 89:17–18) in the western region. These vessels are found in the Middle Euphrates in the EBA I levels at Kurban Höyük V (Marro 1997:82), the Birecik EBA cemetery (Sertok 2007:239–41), Hacınebi (Stein et al. 1997:131), Zeytinlibahçe EBA I, Gre Virike I, in the "champagne-cup" horizon of Carchemish (represented by burials on the acropolis: Falstone and Sconzo 2007:77; Woolley and Barnett 1952:56–59) and at Tilbeshar IIIA1–2 (Kepinski 2007:152–53). The "corrugated cups" appear toward the end of the EBA II in the Amuq I phase, as well as at Samsat Höyük XIX–XVIII and Kurban Höyük IV (Abay 1997:fig. 46–48), and conical cups are found in northern Syria in EBA II contexts (Lebeau 2000:173).

Reserved Slip Ware appears with horizontal stripes in EBA II and also continues into the late EBA. This ware is found in Amuq I–J phases, at Samsat Höyük XIX–XVIII (Period III–IV), Kurban IV B–A, Horum Höyük III 3 (Marro 2007:223–25), Birecik EBA cemetery (Sertok and Ergeç 1999:pl. 7.A–I, 8.A–F), and Zeytinlibahçe (Frangipane et al. 2002:fig. 11). Parallel findings also come from Tell Mardikh IIB1 and Tell Hammam et-Turkman burned Levels 1–2. Further examples are found in the late EBA at Gre Virike II (Engin 2007:fig. 18.4.5–6) and Kurban Höyük III.

In the EBA II new wheelmade ware groups appear in the western zone and continue through the EBA III. The Brittle Orange Ware of the İslahiye region is well known from Tilmen Höyük (H. Alkım 1979:139) and Gedikli IIIk-h (Alkım and Alkım 1966:40–42). An incised version of this ware group—the brick-red incised ware—is found at Tarsus (Goldman 1956:figs. 278–83) and in the Amuq and at Gedikli.

The "Pseudo Metallic Ware"—known as "Red Metallic Ware" at Harran (Prag 1970:78)—appears during this period in the Samsat Höyük XX–XVIII levels,

Kurban Höyük IVC–A, Gre Virike I (Engin 2007:273, fig. 18.5), and at Arslantepe VI C2–D1 (Abay 1997:figs. 46–48). This ware is thought to be contemporary to the Metallic Ware of Tell Brak CH, ER, Phase III, and Tell Leilan IIIc. The Euphrates Banded Ware (Kelly-Buccellati and Shelby 1977:12; Porter 1995:9, 16)—also known as *Metallische ware mit Streifenbemalung* (Kühne 1976:taf. 8)—appears in the EBA II and is similar to the red banded ware of Tarsus EB II (Goldman 1956:fig. 245, 263); this ware continues until the end of the EBA. The earliest EBA II examples are found in the Birecik EBA cemetery (Sertok 2007:242). The Karababa Painted Ware is found during this period in Hayaz Höyük 3–2 (Thissen 1985), in Samsat Höyük XX–XVIII levels (Abay 1997:figs. 46–48) and at Kurban Höyük IVC–A, and is also represented at Arslantepe VIC2–D1. This ware continues to be used also into the late EBA.

Architecture and Other Material Culture

Most of the sites are continuously settled during EBA I–II. The urbanization process is established in Hassek Höyük, Kurban Höyük, and Titriş Höyük; the latter covers an area of about thirty-five hectares (Algaze 1999:548). The settlement in Tilbeshar III B is enlarged to about thirty hectares by a lower town with facilities for producing olive oil and wine (Kepinski 2007:154), and on the upper town a high terrace is built (Kepinski-Lecomte and Ergeç 1999).

On the terrace at Gre Virike (Period I) several cultic installations were built (Ökse 2006c), which are composed of two pools and a channel combined with stone-built offering pits resembling those at Gedikli (U. B. Alkım 1967:7–8, fig. 8–9; Alkım and Alkım 1966:21, 498) and a spring grotto with a stairway similar to those in Tilmen Höyük and Kırışkal Höyük (U. B. Alkım 1967:8, 1970:41–42, fig. 15; Alkım and Alkım 1966:42). Near extramural cemeteries, such as the cist graveyard near Lidar Höyük and the Birecik cemetery, intramural graves are also used in Şaraga Höyük (Sertok and Kulakoğlu 2002:355–57) and Hacınebi (Stein et al. 1997:183).

Early Bronze III

The EBA III, sometimes combined with the EBA IV, dates to ca. 2400–2100 B.C.E. It has generally been divided into early (A) and later (B) phases. There is a significant amount of differentiation among scholars in their correlation of phases of EBA III sites.

The Chronological Sequences

It is asserted here that the Amuq I phase is contemporary to the Tarsus EB II–late/EB IIIA phases. Mellink, however, suggests that Tarsus EB IIIA is contemporary with the Amuq J phase as well as with Arslantepe VI D (1992:table 2–3). This is due to the dates she and Schwartz and Weiss (1992) assign the Amuq I and J phases (2400–2250 B.C.E. for I, and 2250–2000 B.C.E. for J). The boundary date between

Amuq I and J vary by a century according to various scholars; Marro and Helwing (1995) consider the transition to have occurred quite early, ca. 2550 B.C.E., whereas Abay (1997) suggests a date closer to 2425 B.C.E. In similar fashion, Abay dates the boundary between Kurban Höyük IV and III to 2420 B.C.E., and Marro and Helwing to 2250 B.C.E. Carter and Parker (1995:101, table 14.1) join the fray by dating the EBA IV sequence of Tell Hadidi and Kurban Höyük IVA to Ebla IIB2, Arslantepe VI D2–3, and Amuq J.

Unlike Mellink, who dates the Gedikli tomb M-1 to EBA II, Carter and Parker (1995:111) date this tomb to 2400–2200 B.C.E. and therefore to the EBA III period (this is based primarily on the appearance of conical bowls). The dates given to Tell Mardikh IIB1 (2400–2250 B.C.E.) by Schwartz and Weiss (1992:236–40) fit Carter and Parker's dating; however, Schwartz later refined the dates of Tell Mardikh IIB1 to fit into the EBA IVA period together with Ebla's Palace G, the Amuq I phase, and several monumental tomb complexes on the Middle Euphrates River (2007:48–49, 61, table 1). Porter (2007:82, 93, chart 1, 2) assigns Tell Banat IV–III to the EBA IVA and makes it contemporary with Tell Chuera IC–D and Tell Brak L–M in the Upper Khabur region.

Conti and Persiani date Arslantepe VI D 2–3 and Kurban Höyük III to Tarsus EB III and Amuq J. Likewise, Abay (1997:figs. 46–48) dates his Period IVA to Tarsus EB IIIA–B, Amuq J, and Tell Mardikh IIB1 and early IIB2 in the west, Tell Hammam et-Turkman VI West on the Balikh and Arslantepe VI D2–3 in the north, and Tell Brak II–early I, Tell Leilan II, and Tell Chuera Palast F2a and Ib–a in the east. He dates Samsat Höyük XVII a–b, and Kurban Höyük III to this period, according to the presence of Metallic Ware, horizontal Reserved Slip Ware, Karababa Painted Ware, and grooved Hama cups (Abay 1997:370).

Peltenburg (2007:4, table 1:1) dates Gre Virike IIA (Engin 2007:267–68; Ökse 2006b), Horum III3–4, Tilbeshar IIIC, Mezraa Höyük II, and Jerablus Tahtani 2B to ca. 2400/2500–2200 B.C.E. The chamber tomb at Gre Virike, Tell Hadidi (Dornemann 1985:52), Tomb 302 in Jerablus Tahtani 2B (Peltenburg et al. 1995:19), and the *hypogée* at Tell Ahmar Horizon IIA (Bunnens 1992:2) are contemporary; radiocarbon analyses date Tell Banat Tomb 1 (Porter 1995:21) to 2890–2490 B.C.E. All these sites are contemporary to the Amuq I phase, Kurban Höyük IV, and Tell Mardikh IIB1. Kepinski (2007:155–57) dates Tilbeshar IIIC to 2500–2300 B.C.E., contemporary to Ebla Palace G, Tell Hadidi (Dornemann 1979), Tilmen Höyük (Duru 2003), and Umm el-Marra (Schwartz et al. 2003).

Ceramic Assemblages

The EBA III period is characterized by the disappearance of early wheelmade goblets, early pedestal bowls, and the cyma recta and the appearance of the caliciform assemblage of mass-produced conical cups, corrugated/grooved Hama cups (in several publications called goblets), high pedestal bowls with vertical burnished and undecorated stems (Engin 2007:269–70), and the spiral burnished ware derived from buff and gray slipped versions of the Plain Simple Ware.

Conical cups appear in the late EB II and extend into the EBA III contexts of Tarsus (Goldman 1956:115), at Gedikli tomb M-1 (Alkım and Alkım 1966:fig. 41), and in the Middle Euphrates region at Kurban Höyük (Algaze 1990:pl. 77J). They are also found at Samsat Höyük (Abay 1997:154, Type I–III), Tilbeshar IIIB (2700–2500 B.C.E.; Kepinski 2007:152–53), Gre Virike II A (Engin 2007:fig. 18.5.4–32), and in the hypogée at Tell Ahmar (Thureau-Dangin and Dunand 1936:pl. XX). Similar vessels are found in the Upper Khabur region at Girnavaz (Erkanal 1991:284, 288) and at Tell Chuera (Kühne 1976:fig. 10–18). The caliciform and corrugated cups are frequently represented at Tarsus, Tell Ta'yinat (Braidwood and Braidwood 1960:fig. 337–38), and Gre Virike II (Engin 2007:fig. 18.3.1–8). Tripod bowls at Horum Höyük III3 (Marro 2007:223–25), Zeytinlibahçe Mound C5–6, and Gre Virike IIA are typical for the southern region of the Middle Euphrates during the EBA III–IV.

The Gray Matt-Slipped Pseudo Metallic Ware is represented at Tilbeshar IIIB, with a few vessels appearing in IIIC (Kepinski 2007:152–53), at Zeytinlibahçe C 5–6 (EBA III–IV) (Frangipane 2007:136–38), and Gre Virike II (Engin 2007:273). Spiral Burnished Ware is frequently represented in Tarsus EB IIIA levels (Goldman 1956:154) and in the EBA III sites of the Middle Euphrates region but is found even more frequently in the EBA IV period (Lebeau 2000:172).

Brittle Orange Ware in the Amuq I phase (Braidwood and Braidwood 1960:264) is parallel to the "Red Gritty Ware" at Tarsus EB IIIA (Goldman 1956:109). This ware is also represented in the northern section of the Middle Euphrates region (Samsat Höyük XVI, Kurban Höyük IIB). The brick-red incised ware is found in EB IIIA contexts at Tarsus (Goldman 1956:figs. 278–83), and in the cremation burials of Gedikli (H. Alkım 1979). The Euphrates Banded Ware from Tilbeshar IIIC is dated to 2500–2300 B.C.E. (Kepinski 2007:152–53) and is sporadically found in the Upper Khabur region such as the examples from Tell Brak (Fielden 1977:249).

Cooking pots with triangular lugs are frequent in EBA III contexts at Kurban Höyük III–IV (Algaze 1990:pl. 93:I, 135:E), Samsat Höyük III–IV, Horum Höyük III3–4 (Marro 2007:223–25), and Gre Virike II (Engin 2007:277), as well as in Upper Khabur sites (Kühne 1976:pl. 38).

Architecture and Other Material Culture

In 2600–2200 B.C.E. a settlement hierarchy composed of urban centers, smaller towns, and villages appears. The four-tiered settlement system defines a complex social stratification in the northern part of the Middle Euphrates (Wilkinson 1990, 1994) around urban centers at Titriş Höyük, Kurban Höyük, Samsat Höyük, and Lidar Höyük with upper and lower towns. Titriş Höyük (Algaze 1999:548–49) is a well-planned fortified settlement covering an area of approximately 43 ha, with farmsteads of about 1.5 ha in an area of an approximately 4–5 km radius around the settlement (see Algaze and Matney, chapter 46 in this volume). In Lidar Höyük a pottery workshop is established near the town, pointing to the development of an artisan district (Hauptmann 1999:71). A similar development is also determined in the southern regions. Tilbeshar III C has the characteristics of an urban center covering an area of about fifty-six hectares, carrying out olive oil and wine production (Kepinski 2007:155–57), as was also practiced at Titriş Höyük. Tilmen Höyük is also an urban center in this period (Duru 2003), and an outer town appears at Carchemish (Woolley and Barnett 1952). The burned building at Tilbes Höyük resembles a temple (Fuensanta 2007:148).

A great variety of grave types occur in this period. The earthen grave is the most frequent type, and chamber tombs with rich finds are the second most frequent group (Carter and Parker 1995; Ökse 2007b). Chamber tombs are found in Hayaz Höyük (Roodenberg 1979/80:7, fig. 7–8), Titriş Höyük (Algaze et al. 1992:38–39, fig. 8; Laneri 1999:229, 239, fig. 5), Lidar Höyük (Hauptmann 1982:96–97, 1984:227–28, 1987:204–5), Oylum Höyük (Özgen, Helwing, and Tekin 1997:59–62, fig. 10), Gedikli Karahöyük (Alkım and Alkım 1966:14–18), and Tilmen Höyük IIId (U. B. Alkım 1964:505). At Gre Virike (Period IIA) three chamber tomb complexes with rich grave goods were constructed, each composed of a subterranean chamber tomb and attached offering chambers (Ökse 2006b). Such monumental tombs point to the existence of social stratification and powerful élites, probably local administrators.

The other groups, according to their frequency, are respectively jar graves, cist graves, and shaft graves. Most of these graves were used during the EBA III–IVA. Cist and jar graves are known from Titriş Höyük (Algaze et al. 1992:38–39; Laneri 1999:229–31), Samsat Höyük (Özgüç 1986:221), Gritille (Ellis 1983:245), Hayaz Höyük (Roodenberg 1979/80:7–8; 1982:29–30), Oylum Höyük (Özgen, Helwing, and Tekin 1997:59–62), Tilbeshar (Kepinski-Lecomte and Ergeç 2001:134), Birecik cemetery (Sertok and Ergeç 1999:88), Şaraga Höyük (Sertok and Kulakoğlu 2001:456), and Carchemish (Woolley 1914:88–90, 1921:133; Woolley and Barnett 1952:215–24). The cremation burials at Gedikli Karahöyük point to the beginning of a new tradition in the region.

Metal objects found in several burials show a rich typology compared with the earlier phases (Squadrone 2007:208–9). Torques, bracelets, toggle-pins, leaf- and crescent-shaped pendants, and bi- and tripartite spearheads with bent tangs appear in this period; in later graves spiral-head pins and spiral rings are found in several contexts, and toggle-pins and bracelets increase. The seal impressions from Gre Virike IIA, deriving their design from a peripheral Jamdat Nasr style resembling the Northwest Syrian local glyptic style (Ökse 2006d), suggest the existence of a local workshop in the region.

Early Bronze Age IV

As noted in the previous section, the division between the EBA III and IV phases is disputed by a number of scholars, with entire levels of a wide variety of sites falling into one period or another depending on the dating scheme employed. Beyond the divide between these two phases, the correlation between various sites and their stratigraphic levels continues to be an area of discussion among archaeologists.

The Chronological Sequences

The Amuq J phase is contemporary to Tarsus EB IIIB and the Early Bronze–Middle Bronze (MBA) transition. Mellink (1992:table 2–3) dates Tarsus EB IIIB, Amuq J, and the Arslantepe VI D town wall to 2200–2000 B.C.E., similar to Schwartz and Weiss's (1992:236–40) dates for Tell Mardikh IIB2. On the other hand Porter (2007:table 1–2) and Schwartz, in a recent refinement (2007:table 1), date Tell Mardikh IIB2 and the Archaic Palace, Tell Bi'a Palace A, and Tell Banat III to the EBA IVB period (2400–2250 B.C.E.), contemporary to Tell Chuera 1D and Tell Brak M in the Upper Khabur region. Yet another dating scheme is offered by Mazzoni (1985), who dates Tell Mardikh IIB2 to the EBA IVA period. Porter dates the Late Archaic Palace to 2250–2100 B.C.E., unlike Mazzoni's later date to EBA IVC (2100–2000 B.C.E.; Mazzoni 1985). Abay (1997:figs. 46–48) dates his Period IVB to the EBA–MBA transition at Tarsus, contemporary with the Amuq J phase and Tell Mardikh IIIA (Porter 2007:82, 93). He assigns these sites to his Period IVB according to the presence of Smeared Wash Ware, Metallic Ware, Brittle Orange Ware, caliciform and conical cups, and the grooved Hama cups. Horum Höyük III5 (2100–1900 B.C.E.) is also contemporary to Abay's EBA–MBA transition Period IVB (Marro 2007:223–25). Peltenburg (2007:4, table 1:1) dates Gre Virike IIB to the EBA IVB Period, and Engin (2007:267–68) also dates Horum Höyük III5, Tilbeshar IIID, Zeytinlibahçe C5–6 levels, and Mezraa's SE slope to the same period, ca. 2200–2000 B.C.E.

Ceramic Assemblages

The EBA III wares such as the horizontal Reserved Slip Ware, the "Syrian bottles" of the Spiral Burnished Ware, and distinctive shapes of the Plain Simple Ware, such as conical cups, grooved Hama goblets and bottles, as well as the caliciform assemblage, continue into the EBA IV period (Mellink 1992:214–15). These types are found at Tarsus EB IIIB (Goldman 1956:154), Tell Ta'yinat (Braidwood and Braidwood 1960:451), and Tilmen IIId (U. B. Alkım 1964:505) in the western area, and at Kurban Höyük IV–III, Samsat Höyük III–IV (Abay 1997:97, 184), and Titriş Höyük in the northern region of the Middle Euphrates. Similar assemblages in the southern Middle Euphrates region are also found at the following sites: Harran (Prag 1970:fig. 8.39–40), Oylum Höyük (Özgen 1990:fig. 1:1), Tilbeshar IIID (2300–2100 B.C.E.) (Kepinski 2007:152–53), Horum Höyük III3–5 (Marro 2007:fig. 15.3), Tilbes VIII (Fuensanta 2007:table 9.1), Zeytinlibahçe Mound C5–6 (Frangipane 2007:131–36), Gre Virike II, Carchemish (Woolley and Barnett 1952:pl. 58 b5), and Jerablus Tahtani (Peltenburg et al. 1995:21). On the Balikh, these wares are found at Hammam et-Turkman VI West (Curvers 1988:pls. 118.17–20).

Deep bowls with conical bodies, hemispherical bowls with thickened rims, and band rim bowls are typical for EBA IV contexts in Gre Virike IIA (Engin 2007:fig. 18.5.10–23) and the hypogée at Tell Ahmar (Jamieson 1993:52; Thureau-Dangin and Dunand 1936:fig. 30). Imported vessels such as the depa and tankards of western and central Anatolia are found at Tell Ta'yinat (Braidwood and Braidwood 1960:450–51) and in the Gedikli cremations (H. Alkım 1979:140–41), dating these contexts to 2200–2100 B.C.E. (Carter and Parker 1995:111).

Plain Simple Ware vessels, decorated with incised, impressed, and relief patterns, are found at Horum Höyük (Marro, Tibet, and Bulgan 2000:pl. 6.12–13) and Gre Virike II (Engin 2007:272) in the southern Middle Euphrates region. The latest examples of the Euphrates Banded Ware are represented in the İslahiye region (H. Alkım 1979:pl. 89) and at Gre Virike IIB (Engin 2007:276–77). In EBA IVB the horizontal Reserved Slip Ware and the Karababa Painted Ware disappear, and a "painted simple ware with incision" and Smeared Wash Ware appear in the late Amuq J levels of Tell Ta'yinat (Mellink 1992:214–15), in Samsat Höyük XVI, and in Kurban Höyük IIB.

Architecture and Other Material Culture

The urban character of the centers continues in this period. At Titriş Höyük large houses covering areas of about 200 m^2 are composed of ten to fifteen rooms arranged around open courts with standard areas, determining the existence of extended family households (Algaze 1999:549, and see Algaze and Matney, chapter 46 in this volume); in some of these houses, intramural tombs are found. In Tilbes Höyük the multiroomed "big building" at the center of the mound, which contained a pithos sherd with its capacity inscribed thereon, suggests an economic center surrounded by a series of small domestic buildings (Fuensanta 2007:148–49) containing sickle blades, granaries, awls, and spindle whorls.

Toward the end of this period, the balance of power seems to have changed. After Naram-sin's destruction of Ebla (2100 B.C.E.), a change in settlement patterns is recognizable (Algaze 1999:552; Peltenburg 2007:16). Tilbeshar III D and Kurban III are abandoned (Kepinski 2007:157–58), and small dispersed sites increase, pointing to the collapse of the urban centers and a migration toward rural sites in the southern part of the Middle Euphrates region. Monumental tombs disappear toward the end of the third millennium B.C.E.; mostly cist graves, jar, and earth burials are found, such as those at Horum Höyük and Tell Ta'yinat (Braidwood and Braidwood 1960:395; Marro, Tibet, and Ergeç 1998:289–91), whereas at Gre Virike (Period IIB) infant and child graves of various types (stone shaft grave, an oval chamber tomb, earthen and jar graves, a mudbrick cist grave, and a stone cist grave) are encountered (Ökse 2006a). Also the diversity and quality of the metal work decrease in this period (Squadrone 2007:209–10); toggle-pins, bracelets, torques, and spiral rings show a rather coarse fabric.

Towards the end of the third millennium B.C.E. the settlements in the northern part of the Middle Euphrates (Atatürk Dam region) and the Balikh region (Kazane Höyük) are reduced in size; however, the stratigraphical sequences show continuity within the Middle Euphrates region and its environment in the cultural sphere from the latest EBA to early MBA (Marro and Kuzucuoğlu 2007:map 1–4). Only some major sites like Titriş Höyük are abandoned in the northern part of the region; a large-scale abandonment is observed mostly in the Syrian Middle Euphrates. The proportions of grave types (Ökse 2007b) and the quality of pottery and small finds point to a change in the sociocultural structure of the Middle Euphrates region and its environment.

The Eastern Zone

The relatively fewer excavated sites in the eastern zone can, in part, be dated according to the presence of Mesopotamian (Uruk, Ninevite V, and Akkadian) material culture (table 11.3).

Late Uruk–Early Bronze Age I Transition

Schwartz and Weiss (1992:fig. 3) date Tell Leilan IV and Tell Brak CH 9–12 to the Late Uruk Period, contemporary with the Amuq G early phase. After the Late Uruk settlements are abandoned, small sites with Ninevite V assemblages appear in the region; however, the earliest vessels of the Ninevite V develop from Late Uruk wares (Numoto 1991:88–92, 1998; Roaf and Killick 2003:74–75; Rova 1988:141–47; Schwartz 1985:6).

At Aşağı Salat 7 (Şenyurt 2004:659) sherds of the proto-Ninevite vessels dating to the beginning of the third millennium B.C.E. (Lebeau 2000:table IX) and Late Uruk Flaring Rim Bowls are found together, placing this level in the Late Uruk–EBA transitional period. A Flaring Rim Bowl is found together with pedestal bowls and pattern burnished sherds at Ziyaret Tepe Area IA and in the lowest step of Operation E at this same site (Matney and Rainville 2005:23).

At Kenantepe the Late Uruk–EBA transitional period and the early EBA are established in four levels in the Lower Town. According to radiocarbon analyses Area F Level 4 is dated to 3360–3020 B.C.E. (Creekmore 2007:83–84); the ^{14}C sample from a context in the step trench on the northern slope offers a date of ca. 3000 B.C.E. (Parker and Dodd 2005:75–78). In Kenantepe Levels 2–4 Plain Simple Ware is represented by pedestaled, ring, and flat based bowls with simple straight and incurving rims, band-rim bowls, pedestal jars, and incurved rim bowls (Creekmore 2007:fig. 5–6). Similar forms are also found at Aşağı Salat (Şenyurt 2002:687, fig. 14). These forms are quite widespread in the western zone at sites such as the Amuq G phase (Braidwood and Braidwood 1960:279), Kurban V (Algaze 1990:pl. 51L), in Late Uruk/EB I levels at Zeytinlibahçe (Frangipane and Bucak 2001:fig. 5:8), and in the early EBA graves of the Birecik Cemetery (Sertok and Ergeç 1999:fig. 8K).

In Kenantepe contemporary levels, a wet smoothed fine ware with ridged grooved shouldered vessels, conical, flat, or pedestaled bases, and straight or ledged rims is present (Creekmore 2007:fig. 4), which correlates with Ninevite V ware. Handmade cooking pots found at Kenantepe (Creekmore 2007:fig. 8) resemble

Table 11.3. Synchronization of the Sites in the Eastern Zone

Tell Brak	Tell Leilan	Cagar Bazar	Tell Chuera	Girnavaz	Üçtepe	Ziyarettepe	Kenantepe	Aşağı Salat	Hirbemerdon	Kavuşan Höyük	Ceramic Periods: Ninevite-V Periods	Ceramic Periods: Metallic Ware	Ceramic Periods: Drob
H	IV					Op. E lowest step	Area F	7					
J	III a-b		Steinbau	Burials				6-4 graves			Painted Incised		
	IIIc-d	5-2									Painted Incised Excised		
K			1B		12-13	Op. E/6 Op. D			Sub-phase B				
L	II a-b		IC-E							IX	Late Excised		
M													

those from Kurban Höyük V (Algaze 1990:pl. 52) and Hassek Höyük (Hoh 1981:abb. 17.3). A few diagonal Reserved Slip and Red-Black Burnished sherds (Creekmore 2007:87:fig. 7A) are parallel to Arslantepe ceramics (Frangipane 2000:fig. 16:4) dating to 3100–2600 B.C.E.

Early Bronze Age I–II

According to most scholars, dating of sites is defined by the presence of various types of Ninevite V wares. For this reason, the chronological sequences and ceramic assemblages' discussion are combined in this section.

Chronological Sequences and Ceramic Assemblages

The Ninevite V culture is defined in five periods based on the stylistic evolution of Ninevite V over the period ca. 3100–2550/2500 B.C.E. (Lebeau 2000:172–73; Rova 1988, 2003:1–10). The "Transitional Period" is represented by the earliest painted ware and Plain Ninevite V ware (Rova 2000:231) contemporary to EJ 0 in northern Syria (Lebeau 2000:table II–IV).

Plain Ninevite V ware is represented in the Upper Tigris region in Trench 06 at Giricano, which is dated to the end of the fourth/beginning of the third millennia B.C.E. (Schachner 2002:48–49). At Aşağı Salat 6–4, Plain Ninevite V assemblages are also established (Şenyurt 2004:659–60). The Interval Period (ca. 2900–2750 B.C.E.) is represented by the painted and the earliest incised Ninevite V groups found at Girnavaz (Uysal 2007:table 1).

The following period (early and middle phases of Ninevite V) features the painted, early incised, and ribbed wares represented at Girnavaz, Tell Leilan IIIa, which is also dated to the Amuq G late phase (Schwartz and Weiss 1992:234), at Tell Brak J TW1 (Oates, Oates, and McDonald 2001:1739–40), and Chagar Bazaar 5 (Mallowan 1964). The Incised–Excised Ninevite V period is represented at Girnavaz and Tell Leilan IIIb–c contemporary to Amuq H (Schwartz and Weiss 1992:fig. 3) and Chagar Bazaar 5–4 mainly in the form of cups with slightly inverted simple or bead rims and pointed bases, chalices with pedestal bases, and cyma recta bowls. The painted group decreases during this subperiod, which is consistent with EJ I–II (Akkermans and Schwartz 2003:213–15; Lebeau 2000:168). Hammam et-Turkman VI-East (Akkermans and Schwartz 2003:214–15) and the Amuq G phase (Schwartz 2007:table 1) are correlated with EJ I.

Tell Leilan IIId and Tell Chuera IB, ending ca. 2600–2550 B.C.E., are contemporary with EJ II and Amuq H; they are characterized by the appearance of the earliest Metallic Ware vessels together with incised and excised Ninevite V wares (Akkermans and Schwartz 2003:246; Schwartz 2007:48–49, 61, table 1), the Late Reserved Slip Ware, and cyma recta bowls (Rova 2000:234–37).

In the Upper Tigris region the latest level (Level 1) of Kenantepe Area F is characterized by ring-based and pedestal bowls with vertical burnishing (Creekmore 2007:78–80). Similar vessels are found at Zeytinlibahçe (Frangipane et al. 2002:63), Gre Virike I, and Tell Banat (Porter 1995:fig. 17–18). In Area 1A/Operation E at Ziyaret Tepe (Matney and Rainville 2005:23), pedestal bowls and a few examples of the Reserved Slip Ware, pattern burnished ware, and the excised Ninevite V Ware have been recovered.

Architecture and Other Material Culture

After the Late Uruk settlements are abandoned, small sites with Ninevite V assemblages appear in the region; Tell Leilan and Tell Brak flourish in the Upper Khabur region. A similar decline in settlement density and sizes is observed during field surveys in the Upper Tigris region (Algaze 1999:555). This feature is frequently interpreted as the result of an increasing pastoralism or that major trade routes moved to the south (Creekmore 2007:98–99).

The Late Chalcolithic–EBA I period in Kenantepe is represented by two large retaining walls supporting a mudbrick platform in trenches A2 and A8 (Parker and Dodd 2005:76) under a later occupation level. In Area F multiphase mudbrick structures, ovens, and pebble stone-plastered open courtyards, demonstrating a domestic character, show a continuity in architectural planning throughout the Late Chalcolithic and early EBA sequences (Creekmore 2007:77, 81–85). In Giricano only a small area belonging to the early EBA is unearthed in *Schnitt* 06. The lower level is represented by collapsed mudbrick walls overlain by a room related to several pits dug into the débris (Schachner 2002:20, 48–49, fig. 10; 2004:541, fig. 22). Giricano, Aşağı Salat, and Kenantepe seem to have been abandoned in the middle of the third millennium B.C.E.

The EBA cemetery to the southwest of Aşağı Salat consists of stone cist graves (Şenyurt 2002:695, fig. 6, 12–14; 2004:662–67). In Müslümantepe several stone cist graves (Ay 2004:384, fig. 6–7), in Kenantepe Area G pot burials dating to Late Chalcolithic and EBA I (Creekmore 2007:78–81; Parker et al. 2008:123), and in Girnavaz (Erkanal 1991) earth, cist, and pot burials with rich pottery are found. In the domestic quarter and burials at Kenantepe numerous perforated sherds, beads, figurines, cylinder seals, andirons, and metal pins have been collected (Creekmore 2007:96). A cylinder seal of the "Burnt Steatite Style" engraved in the "piedmont style" found in Ziyaret Tepe Operation E step 6 is dated to the Jamdat Nasr–Early Dynastic II period (Matney et al. 2003:181–83, 212, fig. 4). The intramural burials at Girnavaz contain several pots and cups, toggle-pins, bronze spear heads, and beads, reflecting a similar tradition of grave goods within the eastern zone.

Early Bronze Age III–IV

As in the previous section, periodizations are intimately tied to the presence or absence of ceramic types. Therefore, chronology and ceramic assemblages are offered in tandem.

Chronological Sequences and Ceramic Assemblages

The Late Excised Ninevite V is found in Girnavaz and Tell Leilan IIa, which are considered contemporary to the Amuq I phase (Schwartz and Weiss 1992:235), Tell Chuera IC, and Tell Brak Late ED III levels; these correlate to the EJ IIIa phase

(Akkermans and Schwartz 2003:214–15). In these contexts, band painted ware, polychrome painted stands with incrustations (Erkanal 1991:283), cooking pots with triangular lugs, round based cups, and collared rim jars are present. The Metallic Ware, Jezireh Gray Ware, and the Red-Black Euphrates Ware (Pruss 2000:table 2–3) appears within the contexts of the EJ IIIb in the Upper Khabur region (Lebeau 2000:table IX), which is contemporary to the EBA IV of the western zone. Schwartz and Weiss (1992:fig. 3) date Tell Leilan IIb to Tell Brak and the Amuq J–early phase.

The post-Ninevite V Sargonic period at Tell Leilan IIb, Tell Chuera ID, and Tell Brak Late ED III levels (Akkermans and Schwartz 2003:214–15; Schwartz 2007:table 1) correlate with EJ IIIb (EJ IVa in Lebeau 2000:table II–IV). This period is contemporary with Tell Banat IV and III (ca. 2450–2300 B.C.E. and ca. 2600–2450 B.C.E., respectively) on the lower Middle Euphrates and to the early Amuq I (EBA IVA) (contemporary with Tell Leilan IIb, Tell Chuera IE, and the Naram-sin Palace in Tell Brak), which is dated to EJ IVa (EJ IVb in Lebeau 2000:table II–IV). In these levels Metallic Ware, Jezireh Gray Ware, and the Black Euphrates Ware are represented (Pruss 2000:table 2–3). The post-Akkadian Tell Brak N (CH 2–1), Tell Hammam et-Turkman VId-West on the Balikh river, and Amuq J are dated to EBA IVB and EJ IVb (EJ V in Lebeau 2000:table II–IV).

In Levels 12–13 of Üçtepe, Plain Simple Ware, which is produced throughout the third millennium B.C.E. (Özfırat 2006:12), shows typological differences in each subperiod, similar to these variations at Samsat XVI–XX, Kurban III–IV, Hayaz EBA III–IV, Horum EBA IV, Amuq I–J, Zeytinlibahçe EBA III, Gre Virike Period II, Tell Hadidi Area D EBA III–IV, Harran II, Hammam VI EBA III, and Tell Chuera *Kleiner Antentempel* and *Steinbau* 1 and 2. Tell Brak Palace Level 6 is dated by Spiral Burnished Ware; Plain Simple Ware with incised, impressed, and relief decoration; Smeared Wash Ware, cooking pots with triangular lugs, and conical cups.

The Metallic Ware with conical cups, and short necked jars with spherical bodies, are found at Ziyaret Tepe (Matney et al. 2002:536); these wares also appear at Üçtepe 13–12 (Özfırat 2006:13) and in the subphase B at Hirbemerdon (Laneri et al. 2006:157–58). The ceramic assemblage in Ziyaret Tepe's Operation D (Matney et al. 2002:61, 63) is similar to Samsat XVI–XX, Kurban III, Amuq I–J, Zeytinlibahçe EBA III, Gre Virike Period II, Qara Quzaq IV, Tell Brak 2, CH, and B73.

Dark Rimmed Orange Bowls dating to the Early Jezirah IIIb–V are found in the Upper Khabur region, specifically at Tell Brak F52b (Oates, Oates, and McDonald 2001:627–29), within Akkadian and Post-Akkadian contexts (Oates, Oates, and McDonald 2001:161–62; Lebeau 2000:table V). This ware is established in the Upper Tigris region at Üçtepe 13–12 (Özfirat 2006:15), Ziyaret Tepe Operation E in Step 6, and in the Operation D monumental mudbrick structure (Matney and Rainville 2005:22; Matney et al. 2002:61–63, 2003:178–79). It is also found in subphase B at Hirbemerdon, and similar vessels are found in Ebla IIB and Halawa A3.

A Red-Brown Slipped and Burnished Ware represented by low pedestal bowls with slightly inverted rims, frequently with one horizontal groove on the exterior, and thickened rims, was found at Üçtepe 12–13 (Özfırat 2006:14, pl. XIV–XV). Some of these forms resemble the Plain Simple Ware of Amuq J (Braidwood and

Braidwood 1960:440), Kurban Höyük V, and Tell Brak SS, FS, ST 2–4 and CH, ER 6 (Oates, Oates, and McDonald 2001:fig. 441). However, this ware also appears in Kavuşan Höyük level VIII, which has been dated to the EBA–MBA transition period; in addition, coarse examples of the Red-Brown Wash Ware (Laneri 2008:179), which is usually dated to the MBA (Ökse and Görmüş 2006:186–87; Özfırat 2006:14, 21; Parker and Dodd 2005:78–79), appears along with Metallic Ware, Dark Rimmed Orange Bowls, and the cooking pots with triangular lugs in Level IX of Kavuşan Höyük, which falls in the EBA IV period (Kozbe 2010, personal communication).

Architecture and Other Material Culture

The dimensions of sites are not exactly measured in the Upper Tigris region; however, the site at Pir Hüseyin reflects an urban character, since it extends up to about nineteen hectares (Algaze 1999:555), and new settlements are founded at Hirbemerdon and Üçtepe. Although these sites occupy large areas, only very small parts dating to the late EBA have been uncovered. Mudbrick buildings are excavated in Üçtepe 12–13 (Özfırat 2006:11–12); the settlement in the lower town of Kenantepe (Parker and Dodd 2005:77) is composed of domestic habitations, with several open places and pathways pointing to the existence of outdoor activities.

In the twenty-third-century B.C.E. Akkadian period, Naram-Sin's interest in the region is demonstrated by his palace at Tell Brak, control of the Khabur trade route, the Tell Leilan II settlement in the Upper Khabur region, and the Naram-sin stele at Pir Hüseyin in the Upper Tigris region. After 2200 B.C.E. a demographic decline occurs in the Khabur region; Tell Leilan is abandoned, and Tell Brak becomes a small scale settlement (Peltenburg 2007:16). The excavations in the Upper Tigris region are ongoing; however, preliminary observations point to a continuity of settlements in the MBA. Ceramic traditions and architectural features show continuity in the cultural sphere, so, contrary to the Upper Khabur region, the sociopolitical system of the northern part of southeastern Anatolia seems to have survived. Some of the sites in the Upper Khabur region are abandoned, and others are reduced in size (Marro and Kuzucuoğlu 2007:map 1–4), demonstrating a change in the social structure of this subregion.

Conclusion

The EBA chronologies of the Near East differ in each geographical zone. These regional periodizations have been discussed in several workshops, resulting in the detailed analysis provided herein. Salvage excavations undertaken within the dam projects on the Middle Euphrates Valley are completed. The EBA sequences of most of these sites and those to the west of this region are synchronized with the western Syrian Chronology, as discussed. The EBA chronology of the eastern zone is still problematic, since none of the sites with EBA contexts are sufficiently published. Salvage excavations in the Upper Tigris region within the scope of the Ilısu Dam project are ongoing, so the chronological sequences as well as the cultural and sociopolitical character of this subregion will be better understood in the near future.

A further study of the periodization of the third millennium B.C.E. of the Near East, including several subregions from the Mediterranean coast to the Zagros zone is in progress within the ARCANE project (www.arcane.uni-tuebingen.de) covering additional subphases (varying from six to nine). In the scope of this project, southeastern Anatolia is divided into four subregions; the region to the west of the Middle Euphrates Valley is included in the northern Levant, the Middle Euphrates region includes both the Turkish and Syrian Euphrates Valley and its environs, the Balikh and Khabur regions are included in the Jezirah region, and the Upper Tigris region forms the northern part of the Tigridian region. The synchronization of these new regional chronologies is expected to bring homogeneity to the EBA chronology of the Near East and Eastern Mediterranean.

REFERENCES

Abay, Eşref. 1997. *Die Keramik der Frühbronzezeit in Anatolien mit "syrischen Affinitäten."* Münster: Ugarit Verlag.

Akkermans, Peter M. M. G. and Glenn M. Schwartz. 2003. *The Archaeology of Syria from Complex Hunter-Gatherers to Early Urban Societies (ca. 16,000–300 BC)*. Cambridge: Cambridge University Press.

Algaze, Guillermo. 1986. Kurban Höyük and the Late Chalcolithic Period in the Northwest Mesopotamian Periphery: A Preliminary Assessment. In *Gamdat Nasr: Period or Regional Style?*, ed. Uwe Finkbeiner and Wolfgang Röllig, 274–315. Tübinger Atlas des Vorderen Orients Series B. Wiesbaden: Reichert.

———. ed. 1990. *Town and Country in Southeastern Anatolia Vol. II: The Stratigraphic Sequence at Kurban Höyük*. Oriental Institute Publications 110. Chicago: Oriental Institute of the University of Chicago.

———. 1999. Trends in the Archaeological Development of the Upper Euphrates Basin of South-Eastern Anatolia during the Late Chalcolithic and Early Bronze Ages. In *Archaeology of the Upper Syrian Euphrates. The Tishrin Dam Area. Proceedings of the International Symposium Held at Barcelona, January 28th–38th, 1998*, ed. Gregorio del Olmo Lete and Juan Luis Montero Fenollós, 535–72. Barcelona: Editorial Ausa.

Algaze, Guillermo, Ray Breuninger, and James Knudstad. 1994. The Tigris-Euphrates Archaeological Reconnaissance Project: Final Report of the Birecik and Carchemish Dam Survey Areas. *Anatolica* 20: 1–96.

Algaze, Guillermo, Adnan Mısır, and Tony Wilkinson. 1992. Şanlıurfa Museum/University of California Excavations and Surveys at Titriş Höyük, 1991: A Preliminary Report. *Anatolica* 18: 33–60.

Alkım, Handan. 1979. Gedikli (Karahöyük) Çanak-Çömleğine Toplu Bir Bakış. *VIII. Türk Tarih Kongresi* 1: 135–42.

Alkım, Uluğ Bahadır. 1964. Archaeological Activities in Turkey (1962). *Orientalia* 33: 500–512.

———. 1967. İslahiye Bölgesi Araştırmaları. Gedikli ve Kırışkal Höyük Kazıları. *Türk Arkeoloji Dergisi* 16.2: 5–13.

———. 1970. Tilmen ve Kırışkal Höyük Kazıları; (1970). *Türk Arkeoloji Dergisi* 19.2: 39–50.

Alkım, Uluğ Bahadır and Handan Alkım. 1966. Gedikli (Karahöyük) Kazısı Birinci Ön-Rapor. *Belleten* 30/117: 1–57.

Ay, Eyyüp. 2004. Müslümantepe Excavations 2001. In *Salvage Project of the Archaeological Heritage of the Ilısu and Carchemish Dam Reservoirs Activities in 2001*, ed. Numan Tuna, Jean Öztürk, and Jâle Velibeyoğlu, 375–86. Ankara: Middle East Technical University.

Behm-Blancke, Manfred Robert. 2003. Northern Frontiers: Early Ninevite 5 Contacts with Southeastern Anatolia. In *The Origins of North Mesopotamian Civilization: Ninevite 5 Chronology, Economy, Society*, ed. Harvey Weiss and Elena Rova, 481–92. Subartu 9. Turnhout: Brepols.

Behm-Blancke, Manfred Robert, Joachim Boesneck, Angela von den Driesch, Manfred Roman Hoh, and G. Wiegand. 1981. Hassek Höyük. Vorläufiger Bericht über die Ausgrabungen in den Jahren 1978–1980. *Istanbuler Mitteilungen* 31: 11–94.

Behm-Blancke, Manfred Robert, Manfred Roman Hoh, Norbert Karg, L. Masch, Franz Parsche, K. L. Weiner, Alwo von Wickede, and G. Ziegelmayer. 1984. Hassek Höyük. Vorläufiger Bericht über die Grabungen in den Jahren 1981–1983. *Istanbuler Mitteilungen* 34: 31–150.

Braidwood, Robert John and Linda Schreiber Braidwood. 1960. *Excavations in the Plain of Antioch I: The Earlier Assemblages. Phases A–J.* Oriental Institute Publications 61. Chicago: University of Chicago Press.

Bunnens, Guy. 1992. Melbourne University Excavations at Tell Ahmar on the Euphrates. Short Report on the 1989–1992 Seasons. *Akkadica* 79–80: 1–13.

Carter, Elizabeth and Andrea Parker. 1995. People and the Archaeology of Death in Northern Syria and Southern Anatolia in the Latter Half of the Third Millennium BC. In *The Archaeology of Death in the Ancient Near East*, ed. Stuart Campbell and Anthony Green, 96–116. Oxbow Monograph 51. Oxford: Oxbow Books.

Conti, Anna Maria and Carlo Persiani. 1993. When Worlds Collide: Cultural Developments in Eastern Anatolia in the Early Bronze Age. In *Between the Rivers and over the Mountains: Archaeologica Anatolica et Mesopotamica. Alba Palmieri Dedicata*, ed. Marcella Frangipane, Harald Hauptmann, Mario Liverani, and Machteld J. Mellink, 361–413. Roma: Università di Roma "La Sapienza."

Creekmore, Andrew. 2007. The Upper Tigris Archaeological Research Project (UTARP): A Summary and Synthesis of the Late Chalcolithic and Early Bronze Age Remains from the First Three Seasons at Kenan Tepe. *Anatolica* 33: 75–128.

Curvers, Hans H. 1988. The Period VII Pottery. In *Hammam et-Turkman I: Report on the University of Amsterdam's 1981–84 Excavations in Syria I*, ed. Maurits van Loon, 396–485. Leiden: Brill.

Dornemann, Rudolph H. 1979. Tell Hadidi: An Important Center of the Mitannian Period and Earlier. In *Le Moyen Euphrate: Zone de contacts et d'échanges. Actes du Colloque de Strasbourg, 10–12 Mars 1977*, ed. Jean Claude Margueron, 217–34. Travaux du centre de recherche sur le Proche-Orient et la Grèce antique 5. Leiden: Brill.

———. 1985. Salvage Excavations at Tell Hadidi in the Euphrates River Valley. *Biblical Archaeologist* 48.1: 49–59.

Duru, Refik. 2003. *A Forgotten Capital City Tilmen. The Story of a 5400 Year Old Settlement in the İslahiye Region—Southeast Anatolia.* İstanbul: Türsab Cultural Publications.

Ellis, Richard. 1983. Gritille, 1982. *Anatolian Studies* 33: 244–46.

Engin, Atilla. 2007. The Carchemish Region as a Ceramic Province in the Early Bronze Age: Analysis of the Ceramics from the Carchemish Dam Focusing on the Material of Gre Virike. In *Euphrates Valley Settlement. The Carchemish Sector in the Third Millennium BC*, ed. Edgar Peltenburg, 267–85. Levant Supplementary Series 5. Oxford: Oxbow Books.

Erkanal, Hayat. 1991. 1989 Girnavaz Kazıları. *Kazı Sonuçları Toplantısı* 12.1: 277–92.

Falstone, Gioacchino and Paola Sconzo. 2007. The "Champagne-Cup" Period at Carchemish. A Review of the Early Bronze Age Levels on the Acropolis Mound and the Problem of the Inner Town. In *Euphrates Valley Settlement. The Carchemish Sector in the Third Millennium BC*, ed. Edgar Peltenburg, 73–93. Levant Supplementary Series 5. Oxford: Oxbow Books.

Fielden, Kate. 1977. Tell Brak 1976: The Pottery. *Iraq* 39: 245–55.

Frangipane, Marcella. 2000. The Late Chalcolithic/EB I Sequence at Arslantepe: Chronological and Cultural Remarks from a Frontier Site. In *Chronologies des Pays du Caucase et de L'Euphrate aux IVe–IIIe Millénaires*, ed. Catherine Marro and Harald Hauptmann, 439–71. Institut Français d'Etudes Anatoliennes d'Istanbul, Varia Anatolica XI. Paris: De Boccard.

———. 2007. Establishment of a Middle/Upper Euphrates Early Bronze I Culture from the Fragmentation of the Uruk World. New Data from Zeytinli Bahçe Höyük (Urfa, Turkey). In *Euphrates Valley Settlement. The Carchemish Sector in The Third Millennium BC*, ed. Edgar Peltenburg, 122–41. Levant Supplementary Series 5. Oxford: Oxbow Books.

Frangipane, Marcella, Corrado Alvaro, Francesca Balossi, and Giovanni Siracusano. 2002. Zeytinlibahçe Höyük 2000 Yılı Kazı Çalışmaları. In *Salvage Project of the Archaeological Heritage of the Ilısu and Carchemish Dam Reservoirs Activities in 2000*, ed. Numan Tuna and Jâle Velibeyoğlu, 41–100. Ankara: Middle East Technical University.

Frangipane, Marcella and Eyüp Bucak. 2001. 1999 Yılı Zeytinlibahçe Höyük Kazı ve Araştırmaları. In *Salvage Project of the Archaeological Heritage of the Ilısu and Carchemish Dam Reservoirs Activities in 1999*, ed. Numan Tuna, Jean Öztürk and Jâle Velibeyoğlu, 65–132. Ankara: Middle East Technical University.

Frangipane, Marcella and Catherine Marro. 2000. Concluding Remarks. In *Chronologies des Pays du Caucase et de L'Euphrate aux IVe–IIIe Millénaires*, ed. Catherine Marro and Harald Hauptmann, 503–8. Institut Français d'Etudes Anatoliennes d'Istanbul, Varia Anatolica XI. Paris: De Boccard.

Frangipane, Marcella and Alba Palmieri. 1983. Cultural Development at Arslantepe at the Beginning of the Third Millennium. *Origini* 12.2: 523–74.

Fuensanta, Jesús Gil. 2007. The Tilbes Project (Birecik Dam, Turkish Euphrates): The Early Bronze Evidence. In *Euphrates Valley Settlement. The Carchemish Sector in the Third Millennium BC*, ed. Edgar Peltenburg, 142–51. Levant Supplementary Series 5. Oxford: Oxbow Books.

Gerber, Christoph. 2000. Die Keramik der frühen Bronzezeit im Karababa-Becken. In *Chronologies des Pays du Caucase et de l'Euphrate aux IVe–IIIe Millénaires*, ed. Catherine Marro and Harald Hauptmann, 213–30. Institut Français d'Etudes Anatoliennes d'Istanbul, Varia Anatolica XI. Paris: De Boccard.

Goldman, Hetty. 1956. *Excavations at Gözlü Kule, Tarsus: From the Neolithic through the Bronze Age I–II.* Princeton, N.J.: Princeton University Press.

Hauptmann, Harald. 1982. Lidar Höyük 1981. *Türk Arkeoloji Dergisi* 26.1: 93–110.

———. 1984 Lidar Höyük 1983. *Anatolian Studies* 34: 226–28.

——. 1987. Lidar Höyük and Nevila Çori, 1986. *Anatolian Studies* 37: 203–6.

——. 1999. Fırat Bölgesi Kazıları: Norşun Tepe ve Lidar Höyük. In *Kayıp Zamanların Peşinde: Alman Arkeoloji Enstitüsü Anadolu Kazıları*, 65–80. İstanbul: Yapı Kredi Kültür Sanat Yayınları.

——. 2000. Zur Chronologie des 3. Jahrtausends v. Chr. am oberen Euphrat aufgrund der Stratigraphie des Norşuntepe. In *Chronologies des Pays du Caucase et de l' Euphrate aux IVe–IIIe millénaires*, ed. Catherine Marro and Harald Hauptmann, 419–38. Institut Français d'Etudes Anatoliennes d'Istanbul, Varia Anatolica XI. Paris: De Boccard.

Hoh, Manfred Roman. 1981. Die Keramik von Hassek Höyük. *Istanbuler Mitteilungen* 31: 31–82.

Jamieson, Andrew. 1993. The Euphrates Valley and Early Bronze Age Ceramic Traditions. *Abr-Nahrain* 31: 36–92.

Kelly-Buccellati, Marilyn and William R. Shelby. 1977. Terqa Preliminary Report no. 4: A Typology of Ceramic Vessels of the Third and Second Millennia from the First Two Seasons. *Syro-Mesopotamian Studies* 1.6: 1–56.

Kepinski, Christine. 2007. Dynamics, Diagnostic Criteria and Settlement Patterns in the Carchemish Area during the Early Bronze Age Period. In *Euphrates Valley Settlement. The Carchemish Sector in the Third Millennium BC*, ed. Edgar Peltenburg, 152–63. Levant Supplementary Series 5. Oxford: Oxbow Books.

Kepinski-Lecomte, Christine and Rifat Ergeç. 1999. Til Beshar 1998. *Anatolia Antiqua* 7: 245–51.

——. 2001. Researches at Tilbeshar. *Kazı Sonuçları Toplantısı* 22.1: 133–36.

Kozbe, Gülriz. 2010. Kavuşan Höyük 2008 Yılı Kazıları. *Kazı Sonuçları Toplantısı* 31.4: 173–197

Kühne, Hartmut. 1976. *Die Keramik vom Tell Chuera und Ihre Beziehungen zu Funden aus Syrien-Palaestina, der Türkei umd dem Iraq*. Vorderasiatische Forschungen der Max Freiherr von Oppenheim-Stiftung 1. Berlin: Gebrüder Mann.

Laneri, Nicola. 1999. Intramural Tombs. A Funerary Tradition of the Middle Euphrates Valley during the IIIrd Millennium BC. *Anatolica* 25: 221–41.

——. 2008. The Hirbemerdon Tepe Archaeological Project 2006–2007. A Preliminary Report on the Middle Bronze Age "Architectural Complex" and the Survey of the Site Catchment Area. *Anatolica* 34: 177–241.

Laneri, Nicola, Anacleto D'Agostino, Mark Schwartz, Stefano Valentini, and Giuseppe Pappalardo. 2006. A Preliminary Report of the Archaeological Excavations at Hirbemerdon Tepe, Southeastern Turkey, 2005. *Anatolica* 32: 153–88.

Lebeau, Marc. 2000. Stratified Archaeological Evidence and Compared Periodizations in the Syrian Jezirah during the Third Millennium B.C. In *Chronologies des Pays du Caucase et de l'Euphrate aux IVe–IIIe millénaires*, ed. Catherine Marro and Harald Hauptmann, 167–92. Institut Français d'Etudes Anatoliennes d'Istanbul. Varia Anatolica XI. Paris: De Boccard.

Mallowan, Max Edgar Lucien. 1964. Ninevite 5. In *Vorderasiatische Archäologie, Studien und Aufsätze. Festschrift A. Moortgat*, ed. Kurt Bittel, Ernst Heinrich, Barthel Hrouda, and Wolfram Nagel, 142–54. Berlin: Verlag Gebrüder Mann.

Marro, Catherine. 1997. *La Culture du Haut-Euphrate au Bronze Ancien: essai d'interprétation à partir de la céramique peinte de Keban (Turquie)*. Varia Anatolica VIII. Paris: De Boccard.

——. 2000. Vers une chronologie comparée des pays du Caucase et de l'Euphrate aux IVe–IIIe millénaires. In *Chronologies des Pays du Caucase et de l'Euphrate aux IVe–IIIe millénaires*, ed. Catherine Marro and Harald Hauptmann, 473–96. Institut Français d'Etudes Anatoliennes d'Istanbul. Varia Anatolica XI. Paris: De Boccard.

———. 2007. The Carchemish Region in the Early Bronze Age. In *Euphrates Valley Settlement. The Carchemish Sector in the Third Millennium BC*, ed. Edgar Peltenburg, 222–37. Levant Supplementary Series 5. Oxford: Oxbow Books.

Marro, Catherine and Barbara Helwing. 1995. Vers une Chronologie des Cultures du Haut-Euphrate au troisième millénaire—Untersuchungen zur bemalten Keramik des 3. Jt. am Oberen und Mittleren Euphrat. In *Beiträge zur Kulturgeschichte Vorderasiens. Festschrift für Rainer Michael Boehmer*, ed. Uwe Finkbeiner, Reinhard Dittmann, and Harald Hauptmann, 341–84. Mainz: Philipp von Zabern.

Marro, Catherine and Catherine Kuzucuoğlu. 2007. Northern Syria and Upper Mesopotamia at the End of the 3rd Millennium BC: Did a Crisis Take Place? In *Sociétés humaines et changement climatique à la fin du troisième millénaire: une crise a-t-elle eu lieu en Haute-Mésopotamie?*, ed. Catherine Kuzucuoğlu and Catherine Marro, 584–90. Varia Anatolica XIX. Paris: De Boccard.

Marro, Catherine, Aksel Tibet, and Fatma Bulgan. 2000. Fouilles de Sauvetage de Horum Höyük (Province de Gaziantep). Quatrième Rapport Préliminaire. *Anatolia Antiqua* 8: 257–78.

Marro, Catherine, Aksel Tibet, and Rifat Ergeç. 1998. Fouilles de Sauvetage de Horum Höyük (Province de Gaziantep). Troisième Rapport Preliminaire. *Anatolia Antiqua* 7: 285–307.

Matney, Timothy, John MacGinnis, Helen McDonald, Kathleen Nicoll, Lynn Rainville, Michael Roaf, Monica L. Smith, and Diana Stein. 2003. Archaeological Investigations at Ziyaret Tepe 2002. *Anatolica* 29: 175–221.

Matney, Timothy and Lynn Rainville, eds. 2005. Archaeological Investigations at Ziyarettepe 2003–2004. *Anatolica* 31: 153–88.

Matney, Timothy, Michael Roaf, John MacGinnis, and Helen McDonald. 2002. Archaeological Excavations at Ziyaret Tepe, 2000 and 2001. *Anatolica* 28: 47–89.

Mazzoni, Stefania. 1985. Elements of Ceramic Cultures of Early Syrian Ebla in Comparison with Syro-Palestinian EB IV. *Bulletin of the American Schools of Oriental Research* 257: 1–18.

Mellink, Machteld J. 1992. Anatolia. In *Chronologies in Old World Archaeology*, ed. Robert W. Ehrich, 171–220. Chicago: University of Chicago Press.

Numoto, Hirotoshi. 1991. Painted Designs of the Ninevite 5 Pottery. *al-Rafīdan* 12: 85–155.

———. 1998. Late Uruk and the Transitional Ninevite 5 Pottery from Tall Thalathat no. 5. *al-Rafīdan* 19: 53–73.

Oates, David, Joan Oates, and Helen McDonald. 2001. *Excavations at Tell Brak 2: Nagar in the Third Millennium BC*. Cambridge: McDonald Institute of Archaeological Research.

Ökse, A. Tuba. 2006a. Early Bronze Age Graves at Gre Virike (Period II B): An extraordinary Cemetery on the Middle Euphrates River. *Journal of Near Eastern Studies* 65.1: 1–37.

———. 2006b. Early Bronze Age Chamber Tomb Complexes at Gre Virike (Period II A) on the Middle Euphrates. *Bulletin of the American Schools of Oriental Research* 339: 21–46.

———. 2006c. Gre Virike (Period I): Early Bronze Age Ritual Facilities on the Middle Euphrates. *Anatolica* 32: 1–29.

———. 2006d. Gre Virike'de Bulunan Silindir Mühür ve Kaplar Üzerindeki Silindir Mühür Baskıları. *Studies in Honor of Hayat Erkanal. Cultural Reflections*, ed. Armağan Erkanal-Öktü, Engin Özgen, Sevinç Günel, A. Tuba Ökse, Halime Hüryılmaz, Halil Tekin, Nazlı Çınardalı-Karaaslan, Bora Uysal, F. Ayşe Karaduman, Atilla Engin,

Reinhild Spieß, Ayşegül Aykurt, Riza Tuncel, Ulaş Deniz, and Ash Rennie, 546–51. Ankara: Homer Kitabevi.

———. 2007a. A "High" Terrace at Gre Virike to the North of Carchemish: Power of Local Rulers as Founders? In *Euphrates River Valley Settlement. The Carchemish Sector in the Third Millennium BC*, ed. Edgar Peltenburg, 94–104. Levant Supplementary Series 5. Oxford: Oxbow Books.

———. 2007b. Continuity and Change in Mortuary Practices of the Early and Middle Bronze Ages in the Middle Euphrates Region. In *Sociétés humaines et changement climatique à la fin du troisième millénaire: une crise a-t-elle eu lieu en Haute-Mésopotamie? Actes du Colloque de Lyon, 5–8 décembre 2005*, ed. Catherine Kuzucuoğlu and Catherine Marro, 139–56. Varia Anatolica XIX. Paris: De Boccard.

Ökse, A. Tuba and Ahmet Görmüş. 2006. Excavations at Salat Tepe in the Upper Tigris Region: Stratigraphical Sequence and Preliminary Results of the 2005–2006 Seasons. *Akkadica* 127: 119–49.

Özfırat, Aynur. 2006. *Üçtepe II. Tunç Çağları (Kazı ve Diyarbakır-Bismil Yüzey Araştırması Işığında)*. İstanbul: Ege Yayınları.

Özgen, Engin. 1990. Oylum Höyük: A Brief Account of Investigations Conducted in 1987 and 1989. *Anatolica* 16: 21–29.

Özgen, Engin, Barbara Helwing, and Halil Tekin. 1997. Vorläufiger Bericht über die Ausgrabungen auf dem Oylum Höyük. *Istanbuler Mitteilungen* 47: 39–90.

Özgüç, Nimet. 1986. Samsat 1984 Yılı Kazıları. *Kazı Sonuçları Toplantısı* 7:221–27.

Parker, Bradley J. and Lynn Swartz Dodd. 2005. The Upper Tigris Archaeological Research Project. A Preliminary Report from the 2002 Field Season. *Anatolica* 31: 69–110.

Parker, Bradley, J., Catherine P. Foster, Jennifer Henecke, Marie Hopwood, Dave Hopwood, Andrew Creekmore, Arzu Demirergi, and Melissa Eppihimer. 2008. Preliminary Report from the 2005–2006 Field Seasons at Kenan Tepe. *Anatolica* 34: 103–76.

Peltenburg, Edgar. 2007. New Perspectives on the Carchemish Sector of the Middle Euphrates River Valley in the 3rd millennium BC. In *Euphrates Valley Settlement. The Carchemish Sector in the Third Millennium BC*, ed. Edgar Peltenburg, 3–24. Levant Supplementary Series 5. Oxford: Oxbow Books.

Peltenburg, Edgar, Stuart Campbell, Paul Croft, Dorothy Lunt, Mary Anne Murray, and Marie E. Watt. 1995. Jerablus-Tahtani, Syria, 1992–4: Preliminary Report. *Levant* 27: 1–28.

Pfälzner, Peter. 1998. Eine Modification der Periodizierung Nordmesopotamiens im 3. Jtsd. v. Chr. *Mitteilungen der Deutschen Orientgesellschaft* 130: 69–71.

Porter, Anne. 1995. Tell Banat-Tomb 1. *Damaszener Mitteilungen* 8: 1–50.

———. 2007. You Say Potato, I Say . . . Typology, Chronology and the Origins of the Amorites. In *Sociétés humaines et changement climatique à la fin du troisième millénaire: Une crise a-t-elle eu lieu en Haute Mésopotamie? Actes du Colloque de Lyon, 5–8 décembre 2005*, ed. Catherine Marro and Catherine Kuzucuoğlu, 69–115. Varia Anatolica XIX. Paris: De Boccard.

Prag, Kay. 1970. The 1959 Deep Sounding at Harran in Turkey. *Levant* 2: 63–94.

Pruss, Alexander. 2000. The Metallic Ware of Upper Mesopotamia: Definition, Chronology and Distribution. In *Chronologies des Pays du Caucase et de l'Euphrate aux IVe–IIIe millénaires*, ed. Catherine Marro and Harald Hauptmann, 193–204. Institut Français d'Etudes Anatoliennes d'Istanbul, Varia Anatolica XI. Paris: De Boccard.

Roaf, Michael and Robert Killick. 2003. The Relative Chronology of Ninevite 5 Sites in the Tigris Region and Beyond. In *The Origins of North Mesopotamian Civilization: Ninevite 5 Chronology, Economy, Society*, ed. Harvey Weiss and Elena Rova, 73–82. Subartu 9. Turnhout: Brepols.

Roodenberg, Jacob J. 1979/80. Premiers Resultats des recherches archéologiques à Hayaz Höyük. *Anatolica* 7: 3–19.

———. 1982. Note sur la troisième campagne de Fouilles a Hayaz Höyük. *Anatolica* 9: 27–32.

Rothman, Mitchell, Rifat Ergeç, Naomi Miller, Jill Weber, and Gülriz Kozbe. 1998. Yarım Höyük and the Uruk Expansion. Part I. *Anatolica* 24: 65–99.

Rova, Elena. 1988. *Distribution and Chronology of the Nineveh 5 Pottery and Its Culture.* Contributi e Materiali di Archeologia Orientale 2. Roma: Università Degli Studi di Roma, "La Sapienza."

———. 2000. Early Third Millennium B.C. Painted Pottery Traditions in the Jezirah. In *Chronologies des Pays du Caucase et de l'Euphrate aux IVe–IIIe millénaires*, ed. Catherine Marro and Harald Hauptmann, 231–53. Institut Français d'Etudes Anatoliennes d'Istanbul, Varia Anatolica XI. Paris: De Boccard.

———. 2003. Ninevite 5 Relative Chronology, Periodization and Distribution: An Introduction. In *The Origins of North Mesopotamian Civilization. Ninevite 5 Chronology, Economy, Society*, ed. Harvey Weiss and Elena Rova, 1–10. Subartu 9. Turnhout: Brepols.

Schachner, Andreas. 2002. Ausgrabungen in Giricano (2000–2001). Neue Forschungen an der Nordgrenze des Mesopotamischen Kulturraums. *Istanbuler Mitteilungen* 52: 9–57.

———. 2004. Vorbericht über die Ausgrabungen in Giricano, 2001. In *Salvage Project of the Archaeological Heritage of the Ilısu and Carchemish Dam Reservoirs Activities in 2001*, ed. Numan Tuna, Jean Öztürk, and Jâle Velibeyoğlu, 505–46. Ankara: Middle East Technical University.

Schwartz, Glenn M. 1985. The Ninevite Period and Current Research. *Paléorient* 11.1: 53–69.

———. 1988. *A Ceramic Chronology from Tell Leilan: Operation I.* New Haven, Conn.: Yale University Press.

———. 2007. Taking the Long View of Collapse: A Syrian Perspective. In *Sociétés humaines et changement climatique à la fin du troisième millénaire: Une crise a-t-elle eu lieu en Haute Mésopotamie? Actes du Colloque de Lyon, 5–8 décembre 2005*, ed. Catherine Marro and Catherine Kuzucuoğlu, 45–67. Varia Anatolica XIX. Paris: De Boccard.

Schwartz, Glenn M., Hans H. Curvers, Sally Dunham, and Barbara Stuart. 2003. A Third Millennium B.C. Elite Tomb and Other New Evidence from Tell Umm el-Marra, Syria. *American Journal of Archaeology* 107: 325–61.

Schwartz, Glenn M. and Harvey Weiss. 1992. Syria, ca. 10.000–2000 BC. In *Chronologies in Old World Archaeology I*, ed. Robert W. Ehrich, 221–43. Chicago: University of Chicago Press.

Sertok, Kemal. 2007. Fruit Stands and the Definition of a Cultural Area around Carchemish. In *Euphrates Valley Settlement. The Carchemish Sector in the Third Millennium BC*, ed. Edgar Peltenburg, 238–49. Levant Supplementary Series 5. Oxford: Oxbow Books.

Sertok, Kemal and Rifat Ergeç. 1999. A New Early Bronze Age Cemetery: Excavations near the Birecik Dam, Southeastern Turkey: Preliminary Report (1997–98). *Anatolica* 25: 87–107.

Sertok, Kemal and Fikri Kulakoğlu. 2001. Results of the 1999 Season Excavations at Şaraga Höyük. In *Salvage Project of the Archaeological Heritage of the Ilısu and Carchemish Dam Reservoirs Activities in 1999*, ed. Numan Tuna and Jean Öztürk, 453–86. Ankara: Middle East Technical University.

———. 2002. Şaraga Höyük 2000. In *Salvage Project of the Archaeological Heritage of the Ilısu and Carchemish Dam Reservoirs Activities in 2000*, ed. Numan Tuna and Jâle Velibeyoğlu, 351–81. Ankara: Middle East Technical University.

Squadrone, Filomena Fausta. 2007. Regional Culture and Metal Objects in the Area of Carchemish during the Early Bronze Age. In *Euphrates River Valley Settlement. The*

Carchemish Sector in the Third Millennium BC, ed. Edgar Peltenburg, 198–213. Levant Supplementary Series 5. Oxford: Oxbow Books.

Stein, Gil J., Kenneth Boden, Christopher Edens, Julie P. Edens, Kathryn Keith, Augusta McMahon, and Hadi Özbal. 1997. Excavations at Hacınebi, Turkey—1996: Preliminary Report. *Anatolica* 23: 111–71.

Şenyurt, Süleyman Yücel. 2002. Aşağı Salat 2000 Yılı Kazısı, 2000 Excavations at Aşağı Salat. In *Salvage Project of the Archaeological Heritage of the Ilısu and Carchemish Dam Reservoirs Activities in 2000*, ed. Numan Tuna and Jâle Velibeyoğlu, 671–97. Ankara: Middle Eastern Technical University.

———. 2004. Aşağı Salat 2001 Yılı Kazısı, 2001 Excavations at Aşağı Salat. In *Salvage Project of the Archaeological Heritage of the Ilısu and Carchemish Dam Reservoirs Activities in 2001*, ed. Numan Tuna, Jean Öztürk, and Jále Velibeyoğlu, 641–68. Ankara: Middle Eastern Technical University.

Thissen, Laurens C. 1985. The Late Chalcolithic and Early Bronze Age Pottery from Hayaz Höyük. *Anatolica* 12: 75–130.

———. 1989. An Early Bronze III Pottery Region between the Middle Euphrates and Habur: New Evidence from Tell Hammam et-Turkman. In *To the Euphrates and Beyond: Archaeological Studies in Honour of Maurits N. van Loon*, ed. O. M. C. Haex, H. H. Curvers, and P. M. M. G. Akkermans, 195–211. Rotterdam: Balkema.

Thureau-Dangin, François and Maurice Dunand. 1936. *Til-Barsib*. Haute-Commission Française Syrie et Liban no. 23. Paris: Geuthner.

Uysal, Bora. 2007. Ninive 5 Kültürü'nün Güneydoğu Anadolu Bölgesi'ndeki Yayılımı. *Elektronik Sosyal Bilimler Dergisi* 19:48–62.

Wilkinson, Tony J. 1990. *Town and Country in Southeastern Anatolia. Vol. I. Settlement and Land use at Kurban Höyük and Other Sites in the Lower Karababa Basin*. Oriental Institute Publications 109. Chicago: Oriental Institute.

———. 1994. The Structure and Dynamics of Dry-Farming States in Upper Mesopotamia. *Current Anthropology* 35: 483–520.

Woolley, Charles Leonard. 1914. Hittite Burial Customs. *Liverpool Annals of Archaeology and Anthropology* 6: 87–98.

———. 1921. *Carchemish—Report on the Excavations at Jerablus on Behalf of the British Museum: The Town Defences*. London: British Museum Press.

Woolley, Charles Leonard and Richard David Barnett. 1952. *Report on the Excavations at Jerablus on Behalf of the British Museum. The Excavations in the Inner Town*. Carchemish III. London: Trustees of the British Museum.

CHAPTER 12

EASTERN ANATOLIA IN THE EARLY BRONZE AGE

CATHERINE MARRO

The Early Bronze Age in eastern Anatolia is in many ways an enigma. To apprehend it fully, it would seem necessary to venture beyond the strictly chronological and geographical limits suggested by the title of this chapter. In short, one has to take into consideration the material assemblages coming from the south Caucasus, western Iran, the northern Levant, and central Anatolia, as well as to extend our analysis back into the Chalcolithic period.

This situation partly results from methodological issues—the earlier stage of the Kura-Araxes culture, to which east Anatolian Early Bronze Age cultures are linked—being considered part of the "Chalcolithic" period by several Russian and Caucasian colleagues. But this situation also reflects the cultural complexity that characterizes the whole region at the dawn of urban civilization in the Syro-Mesopotamian lowlands. To make a long story short, east Anatolian Bronze Age cultures are involved in long-term, interregional developments, which reveal complex relationships between lowland-focused (the Ubaid and later the Uruk phenomenon [see Rothman, chapter 37, Özbal, chapter 8, and Ur, chapter 38 in this volume]) and highland-focused cultural entities (the Chaff-Faced Ware horizon [e.g., Ökse, chapter 11 in this volume] and the Kura-Araxes world).

At the other end of this timespan, it would also be short-sighted to assess the Early Bronze cultures of eastern Anatolia without considering their legacy in the Middle Bronze Age, so close are some links with the assemblages in the first half of the second millennium B.C.E. (e.g., see Laneri and Schwartz, chapter 14 in this volume).

The resulting picture is that of a long and complex evolution spanning more than 2,000 years; the study of the whole region would in fact encompass the Late

Chalcolithic, the Early Bronze, and the Middle Bronze Ages. However, because this study focuses on eastern Anatolia, it is mostly the Early Bronze Age that will be dealt with here.

During the period that for most scholars is recognized as the Early Bronze Age (ca. 3100–2100 B.C.E.), eastern Anatolia was occupied by an intriguing cultural complex related to the Kura-Araxes culture as it has been described by Kuftin after his excavations in Transcaucasia (Kuftin 1941). This complex has alternatively been called "Karaz," "Red Black Burnished," or "Early Transcaucasian" depending on the viewpoint adopted by successive scholars. Of all the labels used for describing the Early Bronze Age *faciès* of eastern Anatolia, the term Early Transcaucasian Culture (ETC), originally coined by Charles Burney, seems to be the most appropriate, as it implies an organic relationship between East Anatolian cultural assemblages and Transcaucasia (see Sagona, chapter 30 in this volume, for additional discussion). Indeed, even if this issue is still a matter of debate, today most of the evidence points to a Transcaucasian origin for the east Anatolian Early Bronze Age.

EASTERN ANATOLIA AND THE ORIGINS OF THE ETC CULTURE

The question of the origins of the ETC culture (figure 12.1) is central for understanding many issues relating to the pace and significance of its development throughout the fourth and third millennia B.C.E. Arguing that the hallmark of the ETC culture, the contrasting color scheme that characterizes its ceramic production,[1] is absent from the Armeno-Georgian plateau until the end of the fourth millennium B.C.E., a recent study has concluded that the Transcaucasian Red-Black Burnished Ware (RBBW) must derive from Anatolian prototypes; RBBW vessels are indeed attested at Arslantepe VII, Sos Höyük VA, and Çadır Höyük from ca. 3500 B.C.E. onward (Frangipane and Palumbi 2007; Palumbi 2003:100–105; and see Palumbi, chapter 9 in this volume). According to this hypothesis, the RBBW trend of eastern Anatolia is deemed to originate from the Anatolian plateau and not Transcaucasia.

This scenario, however, appears somewhat counterintuitive, as most other traits characterizing the early RBBW culture, such as metal artifacts or portable hearths, do have strong links with Transcaucasia. More important, it has been recently contradicted by the find in Nakhchivan of a typical RBBW pottery assemblage that dates back to the end of the fifth millennium B.C.E. This assemblage was found at Ovçular Tepesi, scattered over the floor of a house dated to the Late Chalcolithic,[2] next to some Chaff-Faced Ware (Marro, Bakhshaliyev, and Ashurov in press); among Black-Burnished jar and bowl fragments, the upper part of an RBBW pithos was found that bears a characteristic rail-rim and traces of a Nakhchivan lug. In line with several observations pointing to the antiquity of the RBBW in the Middle Araxes basin (Burney and Lang 1971:52–54; Marro and Özfırat 2003:391), it now seems clear that the most ancient ETC pottery (including RBBW) known to this day comes from the south Caucasus, not eastern or central Anatolia.

Thus, the whole pattern of the ETC development in eastern Anatolia is inflected accordingly. The ETC culture, which marks a sharp break in almost every field in its material sequence with the previous Late Chalcolithic culture, most probably followed an east to west trajectory, from the Caucasus to eastern Anatolia, and further into the northern Levant.

One of the main characteristics of the ETC phenomenon lies in its modes of development: by the middle of the third millennium B.C.E. the geographical span covered by ETC sites had become amazingly wide, stretching from the north Caucasus down to Palestine. But it must be stressed that not all regions were settled by ETC communities at the same time.

Taking into account the last discoveries made in Nakhchivan, the earliest traces of an ETC *component* in the Middle Araxes basin date back to the end of the fifth millennium. But the first ETC *settlements*, as evidenced at Kültepe I and II, are only attested around the middle of the fourth millennium B.C.E. (Seyidov 2003). It is possible, however, that a settlement like Maxta I, whose lower occupation levels cannot be excavated because of the height of the water table, dates to the very beginning of

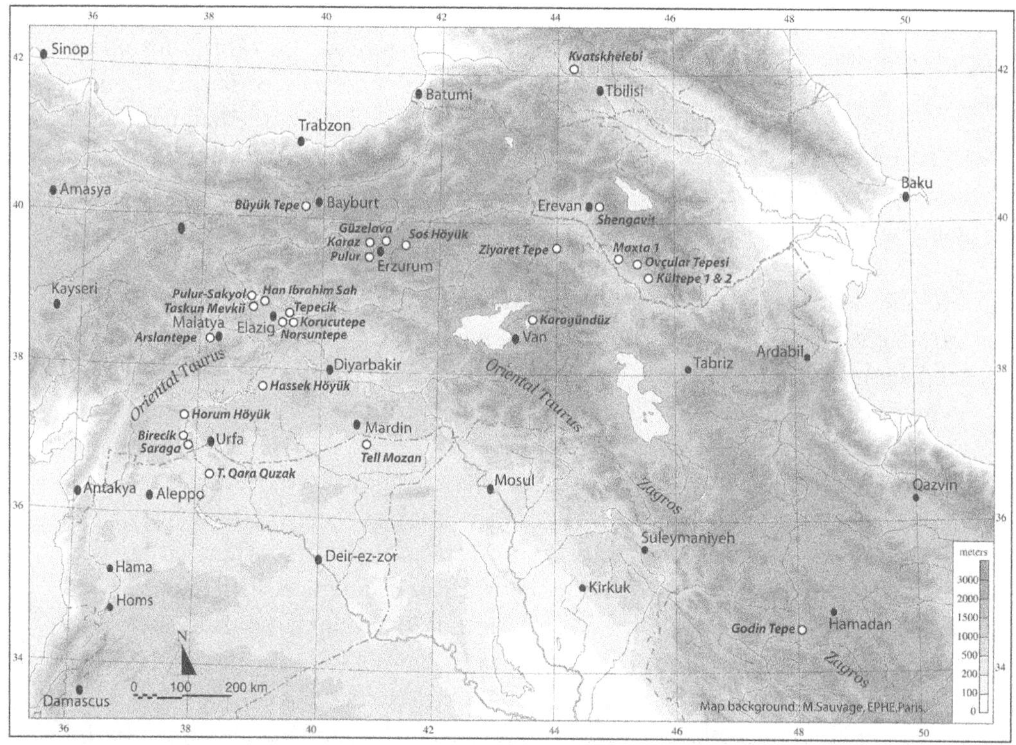

Figure 12.1. Sites mentioned in the text.

the fourth millennium B.C.E.; a number of EBA pot sherds showing close technological affinities with the local Late Chalcolithic Chaff-Faced Ware were indeed retrieved from this site, such as Black-Burnished jar fragments with an inside comb-scraped surface (Ashurov 2005:fig. 7). Apart from these features, which suggest some kind of hybridization, the whole stratigraphic sequence at Maxta I has a typical ETC character.

If we start mapping ETC artifacts chronologically throughout the area, a slow progression of ETC communities from the east to the west and southwest (but also to the southeast, as shown by the example of Godin Tepe in Iran) is without doubt perceptible.[3]

In northeastern Anatolia, the earliest ETC settlements evidenced so far are located in the Erzurum Plain and Bayburt area: the sites of Sos Höyük and Büyüktepe, excavated in the 1990s by a team from the University of Melbourne. The first occupation phase at Sos Höyük, termed Phase VA, was dated by ^{14}C analyses to the second half of the fourth millennium B.C.E. (Sagona 2000:351), whereas the EBA settlement at Büyüktepe, which is deemed to be a camp site, is dated within the 3300–2600 B.C.E. timespan (Sagona 1994:229). The site of Karaz, also located in the vicinity of Erzurum, unfortunately gives very little information relating to its earliest occupation level, as only brief reports of the excavations are available (Koşay and Turfan 1959).

In the Upper Euphrates Valley, only traces of an ETC culture are perceptible in the second half of the fourth millennium B.C.E. at Arslantepe (end of Period VII and Period VI A); a small part of the pottery assemblage (2 percent), which is otherwise composed of typical Amuq F Chaff-Faced Ware, is represented in Period VII by small to medium RBBW jars (Palumbi 2008:42–44). As in the case of Ovçular Tepesi, the ETC pottery from Arslantepe VII and later, Period VI A, is in fact associated with a local Late Chalcolithic context (see Frangipane, chapter 45 in this volume).

Only later, at the beginning of the third millennium B.C.E., do ETC settlements appear in the Upper Euphrates; this includes Arslantepe (Period VI B1), Han İbrahim Şah, Pulur-Sakyol, and Taşkun Mevkii. Interestingly, even when they are located in the same region, all the existing sites were not systematically settled by ETC groups at the same time; at the beginning of the third millennium (ca. 3000 B.C.E.), Norşuntepe was indeed occupied by a typical Syro-Mesopotamian, not an ETC, population. It is only in the second quarter of the third millennium (ca. 2800–2600 B.C.E.) that Norşuntepe was settled by an ETC community (Marro 1997, 2005). Clearly, ETC groups, as they expanded toward the west and southwest, colonized existing settlements only progressively, as if arriving in successive waves (Marro 1997:170–74; Rothman 2003).

Last, RBBW traces are attested in Palestine in the second quarter of the third millennium B.C.E., when another branch of the ETC complex, there labeled "Khirbet Kerak," develops around 2800–2700 B.C.E. In comparison with a situation already attested on the Upper Euphrates, ETC cultural remains from several Palestinian sites, such as Khirbet Kerak itself (also called Bet Yerah), are found next to but often separate from a purely local pottery assemblage (Greenberg 2007:259–61).

Contrary to a hypothesis put forward by P. de Miroschedji, who suggested that mostly ETC pots—but few people—had in fact reached the southern Levant (de Miroschedji 2000:264), Greenberg insists that the presence of Khirbet Kerak Ware (KKW) at many settlements in the Jordan valley does correspond to some kind of migration. His argument is based on the evolution and spatial distribution of the KKW. Interestingly, he notes that if the distribution of KKW appears to be restricted to a few houses in the earlier occupation levels at Bet Yerah, the segregation between KKW and local pottery groups later becomes "blurred," as KKW grows more evenly distributed throughout the settlement. In the meantime however, the technological specificity of the KKW remains unchanged, showing that if KKW components appear to mingle with local artifacts by the end of EB III, some kind of "separateness" is still perceptible. The "maintaining of technological separateness," as Greenberg puts it, is interpreted as a form of "social boundary-marking" expressing the identity of a human group coexisting with other communities (Greenberg 2007:266). In this interpretation, the KKW from Bet Yerah would thus result from the presence of Transcaucasian communities at the site itself.

If we now summarize the evidence from the Caucasus to the Levant, the spread of the ETC phenomenon covers a wide territory, but it has to be stressed that this territory is fairly homogenous. As Kelly-Buccellati rightly pointed out, this expansion was generally contained within the mountainous zone arcing from the Levant to the Zagros, which she calls the "Outer Fertile Crescent" (Kelly-Buccellati 1978:73–75). No ETC settlement has ever been found in the lowland regions of Upper Mesopotamia, such as the plain of Diyarbakır, nor in the lowest and wettest part of the region of Antioch, namely, the area of Samandağ (Pamir 2005:67–98). Only a few pot sherds of RBBW type are attested here and there in the Khabur triangle, for example at Tell Mozan, testifying to the existence of some exchange between the ETC and Syro-Mesopotamian sites. The ETC is clearly a highland culture.

An exception may be made for the KKW occupation of the Levantine lowlands, which Greenberg describes as "a semi-arid landscape dominated by tell-based settlement in fortified towns and villages" (Greenberg 2007:258). Strangely enough, ETC groups in Palestine settled in an environment that is fairly alien to their ecological habits. It is thus probably no coincidence that ETC communities remained in the southern Levant only for about 300 years, as if they had overreached their adaptive abilities; eventually, they just ebbed back or disappeared into the local substratum.

The incredible expansion of the ETC phenomenon over the Caucasian and Anatolian highlands certainly corresponds to a major feature in the history of the ancient Near East. Unfortunately, the reasons lying behind such a wide-ranging phenomenon are still a matter of guesswork: is the ETC expansion linked to migration waves and changing economic strategies (Rothman 2003)? Or are we faced with the result of an acculturation process following the establishment of intensive trade networks (Palumbi 2009)? The analysis of this phenomenon is in fact extremely complex and requires a good understanding of the social and economic processes at work at an interregional level. Before tackling these issues, I describe some of the behavioral habits that characterize ETC communities throughout the area, again taking examples from eastern Anatolia, Transcaucasia, and Palestine to bring out what I consider to be meaningful trends.

The ETC and its Neighbors: On Multiculturalism and Acculturation

As is evident from the foregoing discussion, another major characteristic of the ETC phenomenon, particularly conspicuous in the Elazığ-Malatya Area, lies in its propensity to coexist with other cultures. The recent discovery at Ovçular Tepesi of Kura-Araxes pottery in an otherwise Chaff-Faced Ware context suggests that this tendency dates back to the earliest times.

The analysis of south Caucasian assemblages, compared with the evidence from eastern Anatolia and Palestine, suggests that the appearance of the ETC followed a similar pattern everywhere; in the three cases considered, the array of ETC artifacts appears in full bloom, with hardly any trace of a genesis. Indeed, this is even true of the RBBW pottery found in a Late Chalcolithic context at Ovçular Tepesi, which quite surprisingly corresponds to a mature phase of the pottery sequence that includes black and red chromatic contrast, rail-rim, and Nakhchivan lug. Some of the black burnished pottery associated with the RBBW *pithos* also bears traces of graphite.

It is not clear yet whether the early ETC vessels from Ovçular Tepesi were locally produced in the Middle Araxes or should be considered imports. This question of course brings us back to the perplexing issue of the origins of the ETC cultural complex: does the ETC result from some local evolution, or should these communities be considered as newcomers? The presence of Kura-Araxes pottery next to Chaff-Faced Ware on the same floor makes at least one point clear: in the Middle Araxes basin, the ETC phenomenon is *not* a development from the local Late Chalcolithic culture, as their pottery assemblages are clearly contemporary while the vessels are designed and crafted along contrasting conceptual lines.

The same question arises for the ETC artifacts found in the Late Chalcolithic (Phase VII) or Late Uruk-related (Phase VI A) occupation levels of Arslantepe—should they be considered imports? According to Palumbi, these vessels were in fact probably locally produced (Palumbi 2008: 44). Even then, the interpretation of such artifacts is not straightforward; RBBW pots and jars from Period VII and VI A may have been produced by semi-nomadic ETC groups living in the vicinity of Arslantepe, only occasionally interacting with the Late Chalcolithic villagers. It is noteworthy that just as at Ovçular Tepesi, where the presence of ETC pottery constitutes an odd find within an otherwise Late Chalcolithic settlement, Red-Black Burnished jars and fruitstands represent a minority at Arslantepe, even if the proportion of RBBW within the whole pottery assemblage has risen from 2 percent to 12 percent (in some contexts) by the end of the fourth millennium B.C.E. (Palumbi 2008:45).

Interactions between Early Transcaucasian and Late Chalcolithic communities are thus attested during most of the fourth millennium B.C.E. In the Upper Euphrates region, these interactions have evolved into a clear case of cultural duality by the beginning of the third millennium B.C.E., whereas a similar phenomenon is attested in Palestine during the second quarter of the third millennium B.C.E.

In the Upper Euphrates Valley, the cultural evolution of Arslantepe between 3300 and 2800 B.C.E. represents an emblematic case; Syro-Mesopotamian and Transcaucasian-related occupation levels alternate over more than 500 years. After a Late Chalcolithic occupation strongly influenced by Late Uruk components (Period VI A), the following VI B1 period has a typical ETC character, whether it be for its architectural traits (wattle and daub rectangular houses with rounded corners) or its pottery repertoire (Black-Burnished Ware and RBBW). Period VI B2 again may clearly be likened to Syro-Mesopotamian cultural models at home in the Middle Euphrates Valley (multicellular mudbrick houses on stone foundations, Plain Simple Ware with Late Reserved-Slip Ware). Last, Periods VI B3 (also called "Terminal VI B"), VI C, and D occupation levels are linked to the ETC horizon (Black-Burnished Ware), even if many traits in the architecture of Period VI D (multicellular mudbrick houses on stone foundations) recall Syro-Mesopotamian more than Transcaucasian traditions (Palmieri 1985; Palumbi 2009). However, it has to be stressed that circular buildings are also attested here, especially in Period VI C (Conti and Persiani 1993).

As already noted, there are also clear instances of ETC settlements coexisting with Syro-Mesopotamian sites; this is the case with Pulur-Sakyol and Norşuntepe for instance, as Pulur-Sakyol was characterized by an ETC settlement during the first quarter of the third millennium, whereas Norşuntepe, and probably Tepecik, clearly had Syro-Mesopotamian overtones (Marro 2005:fig. 1). The Upper Euphrates region, which Frangipane rightly calls a "frontier" area (Frangipane 2000) represents one of the best examples of cultural duality in the protohistory of the ancient Near East. It is in this region that the demarcation line between southern-focused and northern-focused cultural entities continually ebbs back and forth through time.

A Paradigm of Cultural Duality: The "Royal Tomb" of Arslantepe

The cultural duality that characterized the Upper Euphrates during the 3100–2800 B.C.E. timespan is best illustrated by the so-called Royal Tomb brought to light in 1996 on the western slope of the tell at Arslantepe (see Frangipane, chapter 45 in this volume, for additional details on this tomb). This funerary complex is composed of two graves located on top of each other: T1, which is a cist grave containing the burial of a single individual (male) together with a large collection of metal goods (sixty-five pieces), and S150, an earth grave containing four individuals (two males and two females), lying over the large slabs covering T1, together with metal artifacts (ten pieces). Both T1 and S150 contained a series of earthenware vessels, mostly jars (S150) or jars and bowls (T1). Most interestingly, this pottery repertoire is almost equally divided between typical ETC pots bearing clear Transcaucasian affinities and Syro-Mesopotamian pottery (figure 12.2), among which Plain Simple and Reserved-Slip Ware take an important place (Frangipane 2001; Frangipane et al. 2001).

The parallelism between the two series is such that it is impossible from the pottery repertoire alone to decide whether this tomb should be attributed to a Syro-Mesopotamian or a Transcaucasian occupation level. Unfortunately, the stratigraphic sequence is not of much help here, as the Royal Tomb stands in a rather isolated context next to a disturbed area. The tomb itself cuts the southwest corner of the public building (XXIX) belonging to Period VII, as well as one wattle and daub house belonging to Period VI B1. The tomb either belongs to a phase postdating VI B1 or to VI B1 itself, as this period possibly corresponds to a series of overlapping short, seasonal occupations (Palumbi 2009:223); the tomb may have been dug in between two VI B1 architectural phases.

Thus the Royal Tomb stands almost as a riddle. Judging by the funerary paraphernalia, the individual buried in T1 certainly had an outstanding status and may

Figure 12.2. Syro-Mesopotamian and ETC jars from the Royal Tomb of Arslantepe (burial S150). © Archives of the Italian Archaeological Mission in Eastern Anatolia (photo by R. Ceccacci) (Frangipane et al. 2001:fig. 16).

as such be considered some kind of leader. But for which community? Syro-Mesopotamian or Transcaucasian? As he addresses this question, Palumbi makes interesting parallels between the funerary architecture of the tomb itself, located as it is within a prominent tell in the Malatya Plain, and the kurgans of Transcaucasia; in the eyes of the ETC people, the tell of Arslantepe could represent what he calls "a ready-made" tomb, comparable to the labor-intensive kurgans built for funerary purposes in the Caucasus during the Early Bronze Age (Palumbi 2009:151).

In my opinion, a major element that argues in favor of a Transcaucasion attribution for this tomb lies in the assemblage of metal objects. From a stylistic point of view, most of the objects have clear Transcaucasion affinities, even if some of them, such as the spearheads, have also been found in Syro-Mesopotamian contexts at Hassek Höyük, Birecik, or Tell Qara Quzak. Stylistic references to Transcaucasian aesthetics in the metal assemblage of the Arslantepe tomb are evident in the double or quadruple spiral-headed pins; spirals and concentric circles are indeed among the most frequent motifs encountered on ETC ceramics not only in Transcaucasia but also in northeast Anatolia and the Upper Euphrates itself (figure 12.3).

All the pins but one that were found in T1 or S150 belong to the double/quadruple spiral-headed type. This contrasts with the metal assemblage from the contemporary cemetery of Birecik, for instance, where almost all the pins belong to the conical-headed type (Squadrone 2007:198–99)—spiral-headed pins are rare in the Birecik cemetery as they are in general south of the Güney Doğu Toroslar (southeastern Taurus).

An even more striking element lies in the three diadems found associated with two individuals from S150 and the leader from T1: these jewels, which no doubt must be considered outstanding objects invested with strong symbolic value, have close parallels with a diadem from Kvatskhelebi in Georgia. If the diadems from Arslantepe are decorated with rather simple geometric patterns, the Georgian one bears unmistakable ETC motifs such as birds and caprids.

The significance of the Royal Tomb of Arslantepe of course changes greatly whether it is considered Syro-Mesopotamian or Transcaucasian. If this tomb was built for a Syro-Mesopotamian leader, it would be in keeping with the evidence of social and economic complexity brought to light in the public buildings of Period VII and the palace/temples of VI A. But if the tomb belongs to a Transcaucasian leader, the social and political implications would be more far-reaching; this tomb would be proof that social hierarchy and complexity existed within ETC communities. Furthermore, this tomb would embody a different form of power, possibly built on kinship, as opposed to the centralized, administrative power structure of the Syro-Mesopotamian polities (Frangipane 2001).

Whether this tomb belongs to a Syro-Mesopotamian or a Transcaucasian chief, its pottery repertoire certainly testifies to the existence of a dual culture in the Upper Euphrates during the first quarter of the third millennium B.C.E. Cultural duality or multiculturality probably characterized this region at least from the middle of the fourth millennium B.C.E. onward, as suggested by the regular presence of RBBW and the later intrusion of Late Uruk features in the ceramic and architectural fields.

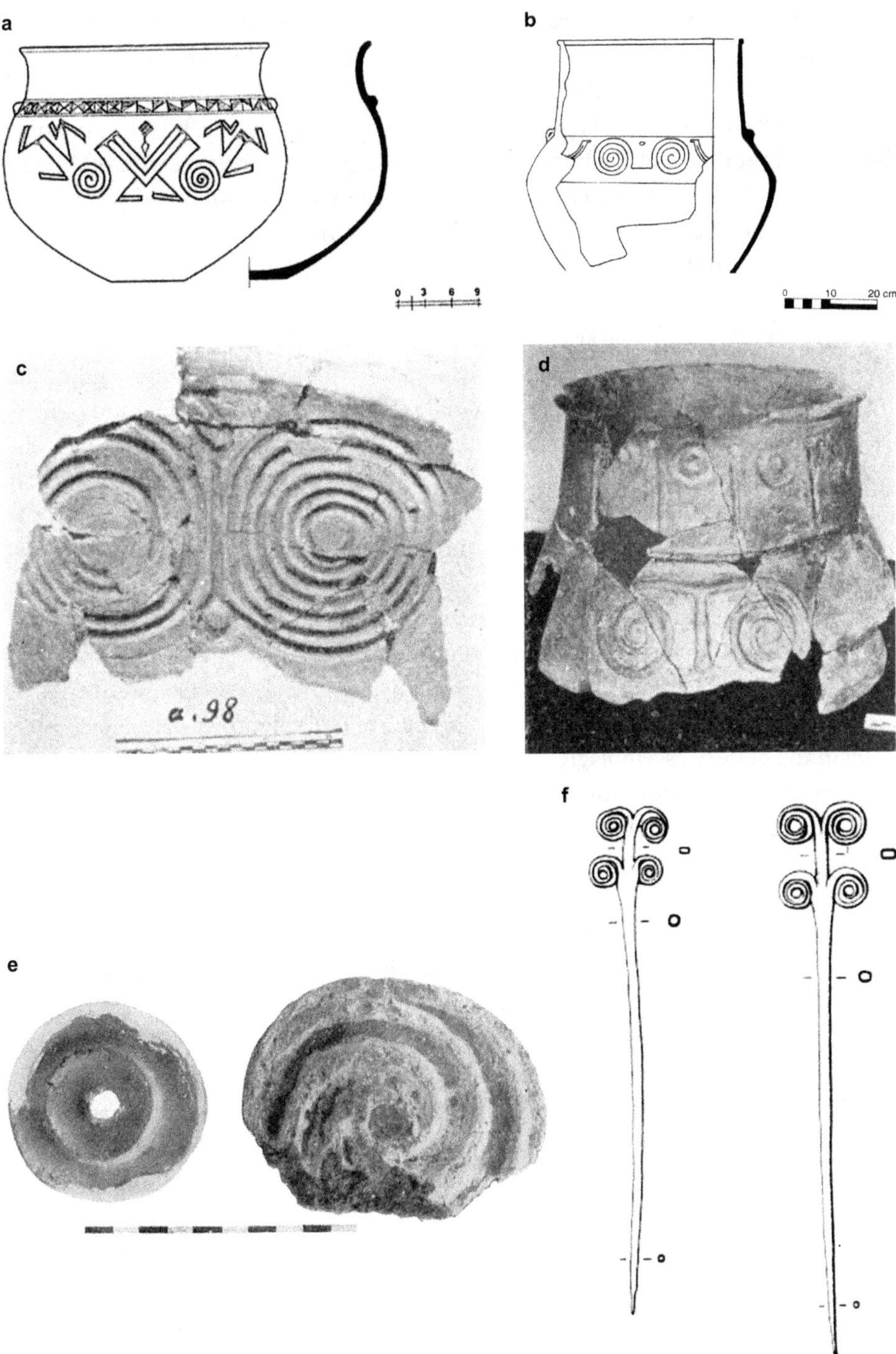

Figure 12.3. Examples of the spiral motif in the iconography of the Early Transcaucasian culture: (a) Gegharot, Armenia (Hayrapetyan 2008:fig. 2:14); (b) Kiketi, Georgia (Kiguradze and Sagona 2003:fig. 3.28:5); (c) Karaz, Turkey (Koşay and Turfan 1959:403) (a98); (d) Karaz, Turkey (Koşay and Turfan 1959:391); (e) Pulur-Sakyol (Turkey), terra cotta stamp-seals (Koşay 1976:pl. 69:353, 360); (f) Arslantepe (Turkey), spiral-headed pins from the Royal Tomb (Frangipane et al. 2001:fig. 19:19–20).

It is noteworthy that no clear case of cultural duality has been documented in northeastern Anatolia so far, as if its settlement pattern was more homogenous. It must be stressed, however, that this region is still little known in spite of the pioneering work conducted by H. Koşay and A. Sagona, respectively. It is thus possible that in the Erzurum and Bayburt Plains, too, ETC groups coexisted with other cultures such as the Late Sioni communities, whose exact definition and geographic extension are in fact virtually unknown (Marro 2008).

Whether or not cases of multiculturality are attested in northeastern Anatolia, it is clear that the evolution of northeast Anatolia through the Late Chalcolithic to the Early Bronze Age is markedly different from that of the Upper Euphrates Area. Whereas the Upper Euphrates experiences a cultural breakdown at the end of the fourth millennium B.C.E., resulting in a major shift from southern-focused polities (as embodied by Late Uruk–related settlements) to northern-focused cultural entities, northeast Anatolia develops at a slower pace from a previous local Late Chalcolithic substratum. As Palumbi puts it, "change took place in continuity with the older local traditions and consistently in harmony with contemporary developments in the South Caucasus" (Palumbi 2009:303).

If multiculturality is attested in many of the regions occupied by the ETC complex over the fourth and third millennia B.C.E., it should be noted that in several cases, the coexistence between neighboring communities also led to some degree of acculturation. This is particularly visible in the Upper Euphrates Valley again, especially in the pottery assemblage.

Evidence of acculturation is at times striking, as in the case of a high-stemmed fruitstand from Tepecik, whose shape and decoration type (cut-out triangles in the stem) recall late fourth millennium B.C.E. examples more at home in the Middle Euphrates basin, especially in the region of Carchemish (Şaraga and Horum Höyük, unpublished material). Interestingly, the fruitstand from Tepecik is hand-made and burnished dark gray (Esin 1979:pl. 57, no. 6), which is strongly reminiscent of ETC technology, whereas the vessels from the Middle Euphrates, whether from the Carchemish or Karababa Areas, are wheelthrown with a plain, cream, or beige-colored surface (Helwing 2002:54, pl. 94:364).

The presence of painted pottery within an otherwise Transcaucasian assemblage has also been analyzed as the result of an acculturation process between Upper Euphrates and Middle Euphrates communities. This painted repertoire progressively develops from the beginning of the EB II (ca. 2750 B.C.E.) mainly in the regions of Keban and Karakaya; technologically and stylistically speaking, this pottery appears as an oddity within the RBBW or Black-Burnished assemblage of the Malatya-Elazığ regions (Marro 1997:102–11). Furthermore, comparative studies (focused on stylistic motifs and patterns) between the Keban-Karakaya repertoire and the painted pottery from the region of Karababa have shown that the painted pottery of the north (Upper Euphrates) probably started as some imitation of the painted repertoires of the south (Middle Euphrates and Khabur Area).

Further east and at an earlier date, traces of hybridization between the local Chaff-Faced tradition and the ETC pottery have often been pointed out, whether it be in the Doğubeyazıt Plain (Ziyaret Tepe) or the Middle Araxes region (Ovçular Tepesi, Maxta I). These cases had so far been interpreted as some kind of "Proto-Kura-Araxes ware" (Marro, Bakhshaliyev, and Ashurov 2009:54; Marro and Özfırat 2003:391), but the recent find of early RBBW at Ovçular Tepesi has radically altered this perspective; pottery mixing technological or morphological traditions should now be analyzed as "hybrid" ware, not Proto-Kura-Araxes pottery.

Clearly, ETC communities throughout the highlands have a tendency to appropriate for themselves some of the cultural traditions of their neighbors. The many examples testifying to the existence of "local" (i.e., non-ETC) traits in the material culture of ETC settlements should, in my opinion, be analyzed in terms of acculturation between coexisting communities, not as evidence of "local roots" precluding the existence of migrations (*contra* Palumbi 2009:*passim* and 325); ETC communities may have migrated into eastern Anatolia and adopted some of the local traditions, or even renewed their own traditions in the aftermath of migration, as is strongly suggested by the distinct character of the Levantine RBBW.

Such behavioral patterns probably reflect the fluid nature of ETC social and/or political structures. An example of this fluidity is given by R. Greenberg in an interesting analysis based on the evolution of the settlement pattern at Khirbet Kerak. He shows how the arrival of ETC people at Khirbet Kerak was followed by the repair of some of the buildings within the former settlement area, while other buildings were left unoccupied and used for garbage disposal, and still others were razed and used as open-air areas (Greenberg 2007:259). This settlement pattern strongly recalls the behavior of squatters, who adapt to existing infrastructures instead of imposing their own system.

The time has come to proceed to the analysis of the social, economic, and political structures of East Anatolian Bronze Age cultures to give meaning to these parallels.

Sociopolitical Structures and Subsistence Strategies in Eastern Anatolia During the Early Bronze Age

Surprisingly little is known of the economy and social structures of ETC communities in eastern Anatolia; this is partly due to the scarcity of ecofactual data, which, when published, tend to be heterogenous. Information on the palaeobotanical record, for instance, is virtually absent. Most clues testifying to the socioeconomic bases of the Transcaucasian culture are thus indirect; they are inferred from settlement patterns and artifact distribution.

An exception concerns the faunal assemblages, for which consistent data from Arslantepe and Sos Höyük have been published (Bartosiewicz 1998; Bökönyi 1983,

1993; Frangipane and Siracusano 1998; Howell-Meurs 2001). Data on the wild fauna from Korucutepe are also available (Boessneck and von den Driesch 1975) and were later compared (Boessneck and von den Driesch 1976, 1979) with the information retrieved from three other sites of the Keban Area (Norşuntepe, Tepecik, and Tülintepe). This information is difficult to use, however, as quantitative data as well as chronological indications are usually lacking, which is of course a major problem with multiperiod sites.

The available information on wild fauna, which reveals a predominance of red deer and the presence of bear, suggests that the Upper Euphrates during the Early Bronze Age was covered with dense forests, as was the case during the fourth millennium B.C.E.

In spite of a stable vegetation cover, subsistence strategies at Arslantepe (Period VI A), seemingly undergo a sharp change in the last quarter of the fourth millennium B.C.E.; herding practices, which tend to be balanced between cattle and ovicaprids during Period VII, evolve at the expense of both cattle and pig with the development of a sudden predominance of ovines and caprines (Frangipane and Siracusano 1998:239, fig. 2). Thus, a specialized form of herding develops at Arslantepe from Period VI A onward, favoring sheep and goat; this trend lasts well into the third millenium B.C.E. (however, data on the second half of the third millennium are not available). This evolution is interpreted as resulting more from cultural than environmental changes, as it is both radical and abrupt, whereas environmental conditions remained basically the same (Frangipane and Siracusano 1998:241).

Considering the evidence belonging to the first EB I occupation level at Arslantepe (VI B1), the development of a specialized form of herding, focused on ovicaprids, could be correlated with the rise of a strong nomadic component in the social structure of Upper Euphrates communities. Indeed, this hypothesis would be in keeping with the development of wattle and daub architecture, which suggests some form of seasonal occupation, in sharp contrast with the previous large mudbrick buildings from Period VI A (Frangipane 2000:compare figs. 1, 9). It has to be remembered however, that change in herding practices seemingly occurs in Period VI A, precisely at the time when Arslantepe appears as a major sedentary polity, characterized by a sturdy administration and a centralized economy. According to Palumbi, the evolution of herding practices would thus be correlated to a change of economic rather than subsistence strategies; it would be a response to "the growing demand for secondary products as important resources [for] internal distribution or . . . commercial exchanges" (2009:76). For economic reasons, the VI A communities would thus have favored dairy- and wool-producing strategies at the expense of meat-producing practices.

It is in fact possible that the causes behind the development of specialized herding differ in Period VI A and Period VI B; the analysis of the settlement pattern in the region of Malatya reveals the existence of a sharp break between the Late Chalcolithic and Early Bronze I, which mirrors the change in architectural traditions. If most of the population appears to have been concentrated in Arslantepe or its immediate surroundings during Period VI A, this pattern evolves into a series of small sites scattered throughout the Malatya Plain during EB I and II (Di Nocera 2005:66–68). Whatever the causes of the development of specialized herding during Period VI A, the predominance of ovicaprids in Period VI B could indeed reflect the development of semi-nomadic groups in relationship with the settlement of Transcaucasian communities.

It is interesting to note that the focus on ovicaprids in the herding strategies of the ETC communities in the Upper Euphrates is not paralleled by similar trends in the Erzurum region, where the balance between cattle and ovicaprids seems to be the norm. At Sos Höyük, the rearing strategies were not specialized, with the percentage of ovicaprids reaching 56 percent against 42 percent for cattle. Pig, on the other hand, is very marginal (0.3 percent). According to Palumbi, this type of herding is "very similar to those in use in Transcaucasia where a fundamental balance between sheep/goat and cattle is often recorded" (Palumbi 2009:221).

It would be of particular interest to compare the herding strategies of Arslantepe and Sos Höyük with those of another major ETC site, Karagündüz, which is located up in the highlands, at an altitude of 1,890 m on the shore of Lake Erçek near Van. This site was excavated between 1994 and 1999 by a team from the University of İstanbul, but unfortunately, no information on the faunal remains has been published so far.

It seems all the more difficult to grasp the nature of ETC socioeconomic structures in eastern Anatolia because there seems to be no uniform settlement system, even between the sites from the same region. Turning back to the Upper Euphrates again, not only is the settlement pattern in EB I divided between Syro-Mesopotamian and Transcaucasian sites, but ETC sites themselves do not offer a homogenous picture. If the ETC settlement at Arslantepe is composed of wattle and daub houses, also attested at Norşuntepe (in EB II) and Taşkun Mevkii (Hauptmann 1979:pl. 40, 1982:pl. 29, 30; Sagona 1994:fig. 10), the neighboring site of Pulur-Sakyol, located in the Asvan Valley, is characterized by adjoining houses organized in a circular pattern, testifying to some form of village planning. Houses are built in mudbrick or with pisé and pebbles; in both cases the walls rest on a single row of stone foundations (Koşay 1976:132). No such plan is attested elsewhere in the Upper Euphrates Valley, but it should be noted that a very similar settlement pattern has been found at Karagündüz (Kozbe 2004:fig. 1.1). In both cases, houses are built with party walls and organized along a longitudinal axis. Unfortunately, no indication is given as to the exact date of the Karagündüz settlement.

Wattle and daub houses are themselves reminiscent of the architecture attested on the contemporary site of Khvatskhelebi (Level C) in Georgia, where a village of twenty-five rectangular free-standing houses with rounded corners has been brought to light (Sagona 1993:fig. 6). Excavations at neither Karaz, Pulur, nor Güzelova produced complete house plans, much less a village plan, but it appears from the publications that the houses are rectangular and built with stone foundations (Koşay and Turfan 1959; Koşay and Vary 1964:plan 9, 1967:pl. III). It should be mentioned that contemporary settlements in the south Caucasus (dated to the beginning of the third millennium B.C.E. but there considered EB II) are often characterized by free-standing circular houses as in Shengavit or Ovçular Tepesi (Marro, Bakhshaliyev, and Ashurov 2009:fig. 7); according to Sagona, this type of house, whose diameter may reach six to eight meters in the earlier period, characterizes ETC architecture during the third millennium B.C.E. (Sagona 1993:469). Circular buildings are so far attested in eastern Anatolia only at Arslantepe VI C, around 2750–2500 B.C.E.

In the Upper Euphrates, the ETC architecture attested in the first half of the third millennium B.C.E., which suggests fairly egalitarian communities with no visible hierarchy at the settlement level, follows an interesting evolution that is well illustrated by a succession of large (official?) buildings attested at Norşuntepe during EB III. I have demonstrated elsewhere that the development of settlement hierarchy at Norşuntepe is concurrent with the uniformization of regional painted pottery trends in EB III, whereas in EB II, the multiplicity of pottery groups clearly reflects the political fragmentation of ETC communities in the Keban and Karakaya regions (Marro 1997:123–60). The combined analysis of the painted pottery and the architecture shows that at least in the Upper Euphrates, ETC communities evolve in the second half of the third millennium B.C.E. into a fairly large polity that has no equivalent elsewhere in eastern Anatolia.

This singular evolution is probably linked to the specific location of the Upper Euphrates, at the frontier between the Syro-Mesopotamian and the Transcaucasian worlds, although no clear traces of acculturation under the influence of southern models are perceptible so far apart from the painted pottery (Marro 1997:174–75).

Thus, if we are to summarize the socioeconomic dynamics of ETC communities in eastern Anatolia, it is clear that no single model emerges. The main characteristic of the Transcaucasian culture, in Anatolia and elsewhere, is summed up by its fluidity, an extraordinary power of adaptation, which alone may account for the multiplicity of its regional variations.

The ETC is probably best described by Sagona (after Rowton) as a "dimorphic state," which he defines as "a tribe . . . organised into nomadic and sedentary groups which share territorial rights and co-operate on a political level" (Sagona 1993:454). Dimorphism or even polymorphism is certainly a characteristic ascribable to the Transcaucasian communities of Anatolia, which evolve into strikingly different lines throughout the third millennium B.C.E.

The End of the Early Bronze Age in Eastern Anatolia

As is to be expected, the fate of the Early Bronze Age (EBA) cultures of eastern Anatolia differs greatly from one region to the next. Again, most of the information comes from the Erzurum Plain and the Upper Euphrates Valley, but some indirect data are also available for the highlands around Lake Van, following the recent work conducted on Middle Bronze Age (MBA) cultures by A. Özfırat (2001).

The work conducted at Sos Höyük by the Melbourne team has shown that around the middle of the third millenium B.C.E., new influences arrived from the East and mingled with the existing ETC culture. A "proto-Trialeti" jar was found in a shaft grave next to a simple Kura-Araxes pit burial in EB III (Period VD), whereas Trialeti and Martkopi vessels have been found, together with late Kura-Araxes pottery ("Kura-Araxes Late Gritty") during the two phases of the Middle Bronze Age (Period IV A and IV B, ca. 2200–2000 and 2000–1500 B.C.E.). This unexpected combination of pottery traditions, once thought to follow each other in time, is a clear indication that the "EBA traditions" of northeast Anatolia lingered on after the putative end of the Early Bronze Age (Sagona 2000:338–40). The passage from EBA to MBA in the Erzurum region is marked by undisputable continuity (but see Sagona, chapter 30 in this volume).

It is interesting to compare this situation with the passage from EBA to MBA in the Upper Euphrates region, where several sites with important MBA remains have been excavated (Di Nocera 1998:67–69). On a site such as Norşuntepe in particular, the end of EB III is marked by the severe destruction of the last "palatial" building (Horizon VIII C) and its replacement by simple domestic houses. Similarly, the pottery repertoire that develops after the Black-Burnished Ware of Transcaucasian tradition is crafted on fairly different technological and morphological lines. There is, however, a major exception to this picture: in line with the repertoire of the EBA, a corpus of MBA painted pottery is attested next to other types of pottery, namely brown-burnished and red-slipped ware. The chemical and petrographic analysis undertaken on MBA painted pottery, together with EBA painted vessels, has shown that there are absolutely no differences, as far as clay groups are concerned, between Early Bronze III (2600–2150 B.C.E.) and Middle Bronze I (2150–2000 B.C.E.) productions (Marro and Schneider 2003:247). There again, the passage from the EBA to the MBA is not as abrupt as once thought, so much so that it has been suggested that the last centuries of the third millennium B.C.E. should be attributed to the EBA IV instead of the MBA I (Marro 2000).

In the highlands around Lake Van, on the other hand, a strong break between the EBA and MBA is perceptible in the evolution of the settlement pattern, as well as in the development of a new type of pottery, mostly painted with black motifs on a brown or red-orange paste, the Van-Urmiah Ware (Özfırat 2001). Although most of the evidence from this area is derived from surveys and should thus be considered with care, it seems clear that most forms of sedentary life had disappeared in the highlands by the end of the third millennium B.C.E.; the only evidence of human occupation are tombs and cemeteries, as if MBA communities had adopted an entirely nomadic lifestyle.

Pretty much as they started to expand across the "outer fertile crescent" at different rates, so did ETCs disappear from eastern Anatolia in different modes, slowly absorbed, or by contrast, swiftly swept away by incoming trends.

NOTES

1. With contrasting red and black surfaces, hence the label coined by the Braidwoods "Red-Black-Burnished Ware" (Braidwood and Braidwood 1960).

2. This house may be dated through two radiocarbon dates to the 4200-4000 B.C.E. timespan: LTL5311A - 4230-3940 B.C.E. cal. (on seed); LTL5312A - 4230-3950 B.C.E. cal. (on charcoal). These dates, which come from occupation levels located immediately on top of the house, provide a *terminus ante quem* for the house itself.

3. The expansion of the ETC culture toward the northern Caucasus is not considered here, as it is beyond the scope of this chapter.

REFERENCES

Ashurov, Safar. 2005. An Introduction to Bronze Age Sites in the Sarur Plain. *Archäologische Mitteilungen aus Iran und Turan* 37: 89–99.

Bartosiewicz, László. 1998. Interim Report on the Bronze Age Animal Bones from Arslantepe (Malatya, Anatolia). In *Archaeozoology of the Near East III*, ed. Hijlke Buitenhuis, László Bartosiewicz, and Alice Choyke, 221–32. Gröningen: ARC Publications.

Boessneck, Joachim A. and Angela von den Driesch. 1975. Tierknochenfunde vom Korucutepe bei Elazığ in Ostanatolien. In *Korucutepe: Final Report on the Excavations of the University of Chicago, California (Los Angeles) and Amsterdam in the Keban Reservoir, Eastern Anatolia 1968–1970*, vol. 1, ed. Maurits van Loon, 1–191. Amsterdam: North Holland.

———. 1976. Die Wildfauna der Altınova in vorgeschichtlicher Zeit, wie sie die Knochenfunde vom Norşuntepe und anderen Siedlungshügeln erschliessen. In *Keban Project 1972 Activities*, 91–100. Keban Project Publications, series I, no. 5. Ankara: Middle Eastern Technical University.

———. 1979. Die Tierknochen aus den Ausgrabungen 1970 bis 1973 auf dem Tepecik. In *Keban Project 1973 Activities*, 113–14. Keban Project Publications, series I, no. 6. Ankara: Middle Eastern Technical University.

Bökönyi, Sandor. 1983. Late Chalcolithic and Early Bronze Age I Animal Remains from Arslantepe (Malatya), Turkey: A Preliminary Report. *Origini* 12: 581–98.

———. 1993. Hunting in Arslantepe, Anatolia. In *Between the Rivers and over the Mountains. Archaeologica Anatolica et Mesopotamica Alba Palmieri Dedicata*, ed. Marcella Frangipane, Harald Hauptmann, Mario Liverani, Paolo Matthiae, and Machteld Mellink, 341–59. Roma: Università of Rome "La Sapienza."

Braidwood, Robert and Linda Braidwood. 1960. *Excavations in the Plain of Antioch I. The Earlier Assemblages, Phases A–J*. Oriental Institute Publications 61. Chicago: University of Chicago Press.

Burney, Charles and David Lang. 1971 (2001). *The Peoples of the Hills. Ancient Ararat and the Caucasus*. London: Phoenix Press.

Conti, Anna Maria and Carlo Persiani. 1993. When Worlds Collide. Cultural Developments in Eastern Anatolia in the Early Bronze Age. In *Between the Rivers and over the Mountains. Archaeologica Anatolica et Mesopotamica Alba Palmieri Dedicata*, ed. Marcella Frangipane, Harald Hauptmann, Mario Liverani, Paolo Matthiae, and Machteld Mellink, 361–413. Roma: Università di Roma "La Sapienza."

de Miroschedji, Pierre. 2000. La céramique de Khirbet Kerak en Syro-Palestine: état de la question. In *Chronologie des Pays du Caucase et de l'Euphrate aux IVème–IIIème Millénaires. Actes du Colloque d'Istanbul, 16–19 décembre 1998*, ed. Catherine Marro and Harald Hauptmann, 255–78. Varia Anatolica XI. Paris: De Boccard.

Di Nocera, Gian Maria. 1998. Die Siedlung der Mittelbronzezeit von Arslantepe. *Arslantepe*, vol. 8. Roma: Università di Roma "La Sapienza."

———. 2005. Mobility and Stability: Preliminary Observations on the Early Bronze Age Settlement Organisation in the Malatya Plain. *Archäologische Mitteilungen aus Iran und Turan* 37: 3–69.

Esin, Ufuk. 1979. Tepecik Excavations, 1973. In *Keban Project 1973 Activities*, 97–112. Keban Project Publications, series I, no. 5. Ankara: Middle Eastern Technical University.

Frangipane, Marcella. 2000. The Late Chalcolithic/EB I Sequence at Arslantepe. Chronological and Cultural Remarks from a Frontier Site. In *Chronologie des Pays du Caucase et de l'Euphrate aux IVème–IIIème Millénaires. Actes du Colloque d'Istanbul, 16–19 décembre 1998*, ed. Catherine Marro and Harald Hauptmann, 439–71. Varia Anatolica XI. Paris: De Boccard.

———. 2001. The Transition between Two Opposing Forms of Power at Arslantepe (Malatya) at the Beginning of the 3rd Millennium. *TÜBA-AR* 4: 1–24.

Frangipane, Marcella, Gian Maria Di Nocera, Andreas Hauptmann, Paola Morbidelli, Alberto Palmieri, Laura Sadori, Michael Schultz, and Tyede Schmidt-Schultz. 2001. New Symbols of a New Power in a "Royal" Tomb from 3000 BC Arslantepe, Malatya (Turkey). *Paléorient* 2.2: 105–39.

Frangipane, Marcella and Giulio Palumbi. 2007. Red-Black Ware, Pastoralism, Trade, and Anatolian-Transcaucasian Interactions in the 4th–3rd Millennium BC. In *Les Cultures du Caucase (VIème–IIIème millénaires avant notre ère). Leurs relations avec le Proche-Orient*, ed. Bertille Lyonnet, 233–55. Paris: CNRS Editions.

Frangipane, M. and Giovanni Siracusano. 1998. Changes in Subsistence Strategies in East Anatolia during the 4th and 3rd Millennium BC. In *Man and the Animal World: Studies in Archaeozoology, Archaeology, Anthropology and Palaeolinguistics in Memoriam Sándor Bökönyi*, ed. Sándor Bökönyi, Peter Anreiter, László Bartosiewicz, Erzsébet Jerem, and Wolfgang Meid, 237–46. Budapest: Archaeolingua Alaptivány.

Greenberg, Raphael. 2007. Transcaucasian Colors: Khirbet Kerak Ware at Khirbet Kerak (Tel Bet Yerah). In *Les cultures du Caucase (VIème–IIIème millénaires avant notre ère).Leurs relations avec le Proche-Orient*, ed. Bertille Lyonnet, 257–68. Paris: CNRS Editions.

Hauptmann, Harald. 1979. Die Grabungen auf dem Norşuntepe, 1973. *Keban Project 1973 Activities*, 61–78. Keban Project Publication, series I, no. 6. Ankara: Middle East Technical University.

———. 1982. Die Grabungen aus dem Norşuntepe, 1974–75. In *Keban Project 1974–75 Activities, 40–70*. METU Series I, no. 7. Ankara: Middle Eastern Technical University.

Hayrapetyan, Armine. 2008. Some Technical Aspects of the Pottery of the Early Bronze Age Site of Gegharot (Armenia). In *Ceramics in Transitions*, ed. Karen S. Rubinson and Antonio Sagona, 71–86. Ancient Near Eastern Studies, Supplement 27. Leuven: Peeters.

Helwing, Barbara. 2002. Hassek *Höyük II. Die spätchalkolitische Keramik*. Istanbuler Forschungen Band 45. Tübingen: Ernst Wasmuth Verlag.

Howell-Meurs, Sarah. 2001. *Early Bronze and Iron Age Animal Exploitation in Northeastern Anatolia. The Faunal Remains from Sos Höyük and Büyüktepe Höyük*. BAR International Series 945. Hadrian: British Archaeological Reports.

Kelly-Buccellati, Marilyn. 1978. The Early Bronze Age Pottery. Descriptive and Comparative Analysis. In *Korucutepe 2*, ed. Maurits van Loon, 67–88. Amsterdam: North-Holland.

Kiguradze, Tamaz and Antonio Sagona. 2003. On the Origins of the Kura-Araxes Cultural Complex. In *Archaeology in the Borderlands: Investigations in Caucasia and Beyond*, ed. Adam T. Smith and Karen S. Rubinson, 38–94. Los Angeles: Cotsen Institute Press.

Koşay, Hamit Z. 1976. *Keban Project—Pulur Excavations 1968–1970*. Keban Project Publications, series 3, no. 1. Ankara: Middle Eastern Technical University.

Koşay, Hamit Z. and Kemal Turfan. 1959. Erzurum-Karaz Kazısı Raporu. *Belleten* 23: 349–413.

Koşay, Hamit Z. and Hermann Vary. 1964. *Die Ausgrabungen von Pulur. Bericht über die Kampagne von 1960*. Atatürk Üniversitesi Yayınları 24, Fen Edebiyat Fakültesi Arkeoloji Serisi no. 9. Ankara: Türk Tarih Kurumu Basımevi.

———. 1967. *Ausgrabungen von Güzelova*. Atatürk Üniversitesi Yayınları 46. Fen Edebiyat Fakültesi Arkeoloji Series no. 20. Ankara: Türk Tarih Kurumu Basımevi.

Kozbe, Gülriz. 2004. Activity Areas and Social Organisation within Early Trans-Caucasian Houses at Karagündüz Höyük, Van. In *A View from the Highlands. Archaeological Studies in Honour of Charles Burney*, ed. Antonio Sagona, 35–53. Ancient Near Eastern Studies, Supplement 12. Louvain: Peeters.

Kuftin, Boris. 1941. *Arkheologischeskie Raskopki v Trialeti*. Tbilisi: Akademii Nauk Gruzinkoj SSR.

Marro, Catherine. 1997. *La culture du Haut-Euphrate au Bronze Ancien: essai d'interprétation à partir de la céramique peinte de Keban (Turquie)*. Varia Anatolica VIII. Paris: De Boccard.

———. 2000. Vers une chronologie comparée des Pays du Caucase et de l'Euphrate aux IVème–IIIème millénaires. In *Chronologie des Pays du Caucase et de l'Euphrate aux IVème–IIIème Millénaires. Actes du Colloque d'Istanbul, 16–19 décembre 1998*, ed. Catherine Marro and Harald Hauptmann, 473–94. Varia Anatolica XI. Paris: De Boccard.

———. 2005. Cultural Duality in Eastern Anatolia and Transcaucasia in Late Prehistory (c. 4200–2800 B.C.). In *Mountains and Valleys. A Symposium on Highland-Lowland Interaction in the Bronze Age Settlement Systems of Eastern Anatolia, Transcaucasia and Northwestern Iran*, ed. Barbara Helwing and Aynur Özfırat. *Archäologisches Mitteilungen aus Iran und Turan* 37: 27–34.

———. 2008. Late Chalcolithic Cultures in the Anatolian Highlands. In *Ceramics in Transitions: Chalcolithic through Iron Ages in the Highlands of the Southern Caucasus and Anatolia*, ed. Karen S. Rubinson and Antonio Sagona, 9–27. Ancient Near Eastern Studies, Supplement 27. Leuven: Peeters.

Marro, Catherine, Veli Bakhshaliyev, and Safar Ashurov. 2009. Excavations at Ovçular Tepesi (Nakhchivan, Azerbaijan). First Preliminary Report: The 2006–2008 Seasons. *Anatolia Antiqua* 17: 31–87.

———. In press. Excavations at Ovçular Tepesi (Nakhchivan, Azerbaijan). Second Preliminary Report: The 2009–2010 Seasons. *Anatolia Antiqua* 19.

Marro, Catherine and Aynur Özfırat. 2003. Pre-Classical Survey in Eastern Turkey. First Preliminary Report: The Ağrı Dağ (Mount Ararat) Region. *Anatolia Antiqua* 11: 385–422.

Marro, Catherine and Gerwulf Schneider. 2003. The Upper Euphrates in the Early Bronze Age: Comparative Archaeometric Analysis of Keban and Karakaya Painted Potteries (Turkey). In *From Village to Cities—Studies presented to Ufuk Esin*, ed. Mehmet

Özdoğan, Harald Hauptmann, and Nezih Başgelen, 233–64. İstanbul: Arkeoloji ve Sanat Yayınları.

Özfirat, Aynur. 2001. *Yayla Kültürleri*. İstanbul: Arkeoloji ve Sanat Yayınları.

Palmieri, Alba. 1985. Eastern Anatolia and Early Mesopotamian Urbanisation: Remarks on Changing Relations. In *Studi di Paletnologia in Onore di S.M. Puglisi*, ed. Mario Liverani, Alba Palmieri, and Renato Peroni, 191–213. Roma: Università "La Sapienza."

Palumbi, Giulio. 2003. Red-Black Pottery: Eastern Anatolian and Transcaucasian Relationships around the Mid-Fourth Millennium BC. *Ancient Near Eastern Studies* 40: 80–134.

———. 2008. Mid-Fourth Millennium Red-Black Burnished Wares from Anatolia: A Cross-Comparison. In *Ceramics in Transitions: Chalcolithic through Iron Ages in the Highlands of the Southern Caucasus and Anatolia*, ed. Karen Rubinson and Antonio Sagona, 39–58. Ancient Near Eastern Studies, Supplement 27. Leuven: Peeters.

———. 2009. *The Red and Black. Social and Cultural Interaction between the Upper Euphrates and Southern Caucasus Communities in the Fourth and Third Millennium BC*. Studi di Preistoria Orientale no. 2. Roma: Università di Roma "La Sapienza."

Pamir, Hatice. 2005. The Orontes Delta Survey. In *The Amuq Valley Regional Projects, vol. 1. Surveys in the Plain of Antioch and Orontes Delta, Turkey, 1995–2002*. ed. Kutlu Aslıhan Yener, 67–98. Oriental Institute Publications 131. Chicago: Oriental Institute.

Rothman, Mitchell. 2003. Ripples in the Stream: Transcaucasia-Anatolian Interaction in the Murat/Euphrates Basin at the Beginning of the Third Millennium B.C. In *Archaeology in the Borderlands: Investigations in Caucasia and Beyond*, ed. Adam Smith and Karen Rubinson, 95–110. Los Angeles: Cotsen Institute of Archaeology, UCLA.

Sagona, Antonio. 1993. Settlement and Society in Late Prehistoric Trans-Caucasus. In *Between the Rivers and over the Mountains. Archaeologica Anatolica et Mesopotamica Alba Palmieri Dedicata*, ed. Marcella Frangipane, Harald Hauptmann, Mario Liverani, Paolo Matthiae, and Machteld Mellink, 453–74. Roma: Università di Roma "La Sapienza."

———. 1994. *The Aşvan Sites 3: Keban Rescue Excavations, Eastern Anatolia. The Early Bronze Age*. BIAA monograph no. 18. London: British Institute of Archaeology.

———. 2000. Sos Höyük and the Erzurum Region in Late Prehistory: A Provisional Chronology for Northeast Anatolia. In *Chronologie des Pays du Caucase et de l'Euphrate aux IVème–IIIème Millénaires. Actes du Colloque d'Istanbul, 16–19 décembre 1998*, ed. Catherine Marro and Harald Hauptmann, 329–73. Varia Anatolica XI. Paris: De Boccard.

Seyidov, Abbas. 2003. *Nahçıvan VII–II minillikde*. Baku: Elm.

Squadrone, Filomena. 2007. Regional Culture and Metal Objects in the Area of Carchemish during the Early Bronze Age. In *Euphrates River Valley Settlement. The Carchemish Sector in the Third Millennium BC*, ed. Edgar Peltenburg, 198–213. Levant Supplementary Series 5. Oxford: Oxbow Books.

The Middle Bronze Age

CHAPTER 13

THE *KĀRUM* PERIOD ON THE PLATEAU

CÉCILE MICHEL

DURING the first centuries of the second millennium B.C.E., Assyrian merchants originating from Assur, on the Upper Tigris, organized large-scale commercial exchanges with central Anatolia. They settled in several localities, called *kārums*. This Akkadian word, which usually designates the quay or port in Mesopotamian cities, refers in Anatolia to the Assyrian merchant district and its administrative building. Thus, the *kārum* period—which comprises the Old Assyrian period—covers the time during which the Assyrians traded in Anatolia, from the middle of the twentieth to the end of the eighteenth century B.C.E.; it corresponds, more or less, to the Middle Bronze Age. In Anatolia, this period is characterized by an important phase of urbanization, with a flourishing material culture mixing native and foreign styles.

The center of the Assyrian commercial network in Anatolia was located at Kaniš, later Neša (modern Kültepe), northeast of Kayseri. The site has been excavated without interruption for sixty years, first by T. Özgüç and K. Emre (1948–2005), and then by F. Kulakoğlu (since 2006; see Kulakoğlu, chapter 47 in this volume). Its stratigraphy serves as the chronological scale of reference for the Anatolian plateau during the first half of the second millennium B.C.E. The site is divided into two major sectors: the citadel and the *kārum* (T. Özgüç 2003). Among the eighteen occupational levels distinguished in the citadel, ranging from the Early Bronze Age to the Roman Empire, Levels 10–6 date to the Middle Bronze Age. The *kārum*, north and east of the citadel, has its own stratigraphy.

The phase called *Kārum* II represents the main period of activity of the Assyrian merchants in Anatolia. They were still living and working there during *Kārum* Ib; Level Ia corresponds to the period following their departure. Written documents

Citadel Levels	*Kārum* Levels	Date
10	IV	End of the third mill. B.C.E.
9	III	End of the third mill. B.C.E.
8	II (Assyrian archives)	Mid-twentieth–nineteenth cent. B.C.E.
7	Ib (Assyrian archives)	Eighteenth cent. B.C.E.
6	Ia	Beginning of the seventeenth cent. B.C.E.

have been uncovered only in Levels II and Ib. The *kārum* period lasted about three and a half centuries.

The Assyrian trade network covered the major part of central Anatolia, where many of the sites that include Middle Bronze Age levels are located. East of the plateau, the Assyrian caravans coming from the Mesopotamian Plain had to cross the Taurus Range through a limited number of passes. Southeast of the Taurus, the Euphrates was another natural border (Barjamovic 2011; Veenhof 2008b; see Laneri and Schwartz, chapter 14 in this volume; figure 13.1). To the west, located on the border of the plateau, the most important excavated site, Beycesultan, five kilometers southwest of Çivril, did not produce any seals or seal impressions that might attest to a potential involvement in the Assyrian trade. Its ceramics show local developments and are quite different from those found in the central Anatolian sites (Joukowsky 1996). By contrast, at Karahöyük Konya, one of the very few known Middle Bronze settlements located in the area southwest of the Tuz Gölü, the excavations unearthed a large number of seal impressions (Alp 1968). The *kārum* period on the Anatolian plateau is documented by more than 24,000 cuneiform documents, written mainly by Assyrian merchants who settled in Kaniš and other localities. These archives give some data about the institutions, economy, and society of the Anatolian kingdoms, as well as elements of their political and economic history.

Archaeological Data

Two different sets of data are available to study the *kārum* period in central Anatolia: the archaeological exploration of many sites as well as large areas of the plateau, and the cuneiform documents mainly found at Kültepe. I explore the archaeological information first.

At the beginning of the second millennium B.C.E., much of the Anatolian plateau was covered with woods. In addition to agricultural and pasture lands, the region also had numerous mineral resources. Many archaeological sites located by surveys and unearthed by excavations were occupied during the *kārum* period, but very few of them have been identified by their ancient names, apart from Kültepe, which is the ancient city of Kaniš, Boğazköy, the ancient Ḫattuš, and Alişar Höyük, whose ancient name was Amkuwa, later Ankuwa.

General Presentation

The Anatolian plateau may be divided into several different areas, each having its own resources (Yakar 2000). The primary and most densely inhabited area is the central part of this plateau. The Kızıl Irmak, which cuts through the plateau, works as a natural border. The area located inside the bend of the river is a rich and fertile land, with metal ores on the north. This is where the biggest settlements of the Middle Bronze Age lie (Barjamovic 2011; Sagona and Zimansky 2009:225–52). West of the river, the density of sites decreases; the land is drier, although the Tuz Gölü provides an important mineral resource. The southwestern part of the plateau, the Konya Plain, is well watered but counts only a small number of settlements, whose population lives mainly on agriculture and animal husbandry. Southeast of the river lies the Kayseri Plain; Kültepe is one of the few Middle Bronze Age sites in this area. The other sites, of much smaller size, are concentrated further east, in the Göksun, Elazığ, and Elbistan Plains. In the north, the Pontic region is well known for its natural resources in copper, silver, and wood. Thus, between the Yeşil Irmak and the Kızıl Irmak, there are several important urban centers dated from this period (Dönmez and Beyazit 2008).

The *kārum* period saw the development of several fortified towns on the main roads showing an organization similar to that of Kültepe: a huge palace as well as

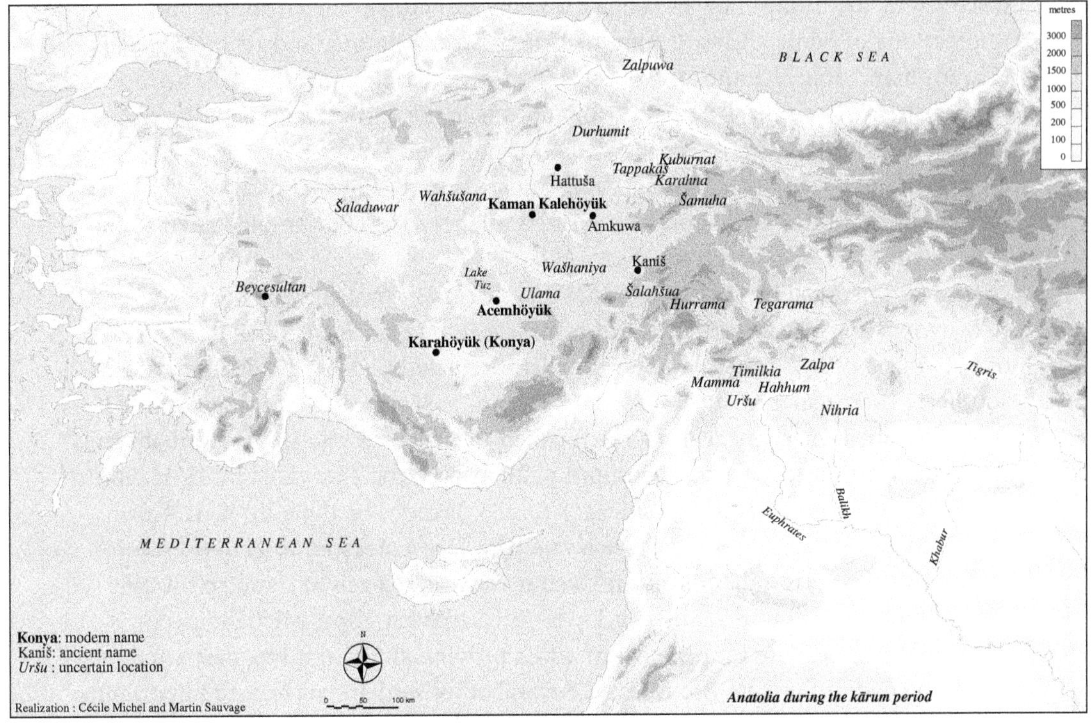

Figure 13.1. Map of Anatolia and Upper Mesopotamia during the *kārum* period.

several temples built on the top of the mound, with a lower terrace, where the occupation area is made up of two-storey houses constructed with wood and mudbricks over stone foundations (T. Özgüç 2003). Kültepe provided a rich *Kārum* II level, whereas other cities like Acemhöyük, Alişar, and Boğazköy present an important *Kārum* Ib level (figure 13.1).

Important Middle Bronze Sites

In addition to Kültepe, which is the key site for this period, and Boğazköy, the later capital of the Hittites, a small number of excavated sites that include important Middle Bronze Age levels deserve a short discussion.

Acemhöyük, one of the biggest mounds (800 × 700 m) dated to the *kārum* period, is located 18 km northwest of Aksaray, south of the Tuz Gölü. This large oval mound, occupied since the Early Bronze Age, was excavated in the 1960s by Nimet Özgüç and later Aliye Öztan (Ankara University). Its stratigraphy includes twelve levels; Levels 3 and 4 belong to the Middle Bronze Age. The main excavated buildings are two palaces dated from *Kārum* Ib, Sarıkaya in the southeast, and Hatipler in the northwest, along with the West/Service Building. Dendrochronological analyses of the Sarıkaya palace wood beams suggest a date around 1777/1774 B.C.E. (Kuniholm et al. 2005; Michel and Rocher 2000). The site was destroyed by fire at the end of the *Kārum* Ib period. No commercial district has been found, and the site did not produce cuneiform tablets. However, many objects were discovered, including clay bullae with short cuneiform inscriptions and seal impressions of Šamšī-Adad I, king of Upper Mesopotamia, and of his servants (Karaduman 2008; Veenhof 1993), seals, various ceramics and rhyta, bone tools, stone axes, faience animal figurines, and objects made of rock crystal, ivory, silver, and bronze (Joukowsky 1996:224–25; N. Özgüç 1966; Öztan 2007). The site has long been identified with Burušḫattum (most recently Kawakami 2006), but we know now that this town should be located further west (Barjamovic 2011, 2008; Hecker 2006).

Alişar, the ancient town of Amkuwa, written Ankuwa in the Hittite sources (Gorny 1995), is a large settlement of central Anatolia (520 × 350 m); it lies north of the village of the same name, in the plain irrigated by the Kanak Suyu, in the southeast of Yozgat province. The main mound is surrounded, on the southeast side, by a crescent-shaped lower town called the Terrace; the site was inhabited from the fourth to the first millennium B.C.E. It was first excavated by H. H. von der Osten (Oriental Institute, Chicago, 1927–32); then, in 1993, by R. L. Gorny, who focused on the Late Bronze Age levels. The layer corresponding to the *kārum* period was formerly called Stratum II, later renamed Levels 11T and 10T. Cuneiform tablets were found mainly in Level 10 (Dercksen 2001; Michel 2003a:126–27). During the Hittite Empire, Alişar was a provincial town; it was destroyed by fire at the end of the Late Bronze Age. Several other settlements feature important Middle Bronze occupational levels, including Boğazköy/Ḫattuš(a), Kaman Kalehöyük, and Kültepe/Kaniš. All of these sites can be found in part V, "Key Sites," in this volume.

Material Culture

At the beginning of the second millennium B.C.E., some sites on the plateau became very large, like Acemhöyük (fifty-six hectares), Karahöyük Konya (fifty hectares), Kültepe (fifty hectares), and Alişar (twenty-eight hectares). For reasons still being discussed by scholars, they attracted the interest of Assyrian merchants during this period (Lumsden 2008). The creation of *kārums* and *wabartums* (smaller trading posts) brought important sociopolitical and economic changes that influenced local Anatolian material culture. New ceramic traditions and miniature art on cylinder seals flourished; at the same time, production became standardized. Besides the Early Bronze (EB) III Cappadocian ware, characterized by open vessels with colored geometric decorations, there was a significant production of large wheelmade vessels, with red or brownish slips and fine decorated rectangles, and pitchers with curved spouts and high pedestals. Some ceramics were decorated with animal figures on the rim or handles; this tradition continues into Hittite wares of the Late Bronze Age (Sagona and Zimansky 2009:225–52). Some ceramics were imported from Mesopotamia (Emre 1995, 1999; Joukowsky 1996; Kulakoğlu 1996). There was an important tradition of figurative art with zoomorphological rhyta, and lead and ivory figurines, many unearthed in graves. The buried bodies under the floors of the houses together with the artifacts found in the graves attest to Assyrian burial customs (Emre 2008). The impact of trade is also visible in the standardization of weights and of molds for casting metal bars (Dercksen 1996).

The seal industry is the best example of these transformations; seals are good witnesses of the many influences existing between local styles and imports. Mesopotamian cylinder seals were widely used in Anatolia in the Old Assyrian period, although Anatolian stamp seals also remained in use (see Kulakoğlu, chapter 47 in this volume). Four main stylistic groups of cylinder seals may be distinguished, among which three were imported: the Old Babylonian group typically shows presentation scenes of a human being to a seated divinity, the Old Assyrian group includes many procession scenes, the Old Syrian group started with small representations whose size and precision grew during the *kārum* period, and the Old Anatolian iconography combined several elements and filled the empty spaces with animal figures (Blocher 2003; N. Özgüç 1965, 2006; Tessier 1994). The seals of this last group were used both by Assyrians and Anatolians (figure 13.2). At the same time, some Ur III cylinder seals were still in use. During the *Kārum* Ib period, the importance of stamp seals with geometric, floral, and animal representations grew and took over the cylinder seals in the local administrations (Lumsden 2008). The evidence of the material culture shows that during the *kārum* period, Anatolia saw a permanent evolution, partly because of the Assyrian presence.

Figure 13.2. Envelope of a loan contract bearing Old Assyrian and Old Anatolian seal imprints (Kt 93/k 941a, Kültepe, *Kārum* II, photo C. Michel).

Textual Data

The cuneiform texts discovered in central Anatolia, produced by merchants of Assur, are written in an Old Assyrian dialect of Akkadian. Even if their main purpose was to keep records of long-distance trade, they documented several aspects of the sociopolitical and economic history of ancient Anatolia.

Epigraphic Discoveries

The *kārum* period is well documented by 22,660 cuneiform tablets, discovered mostly at Kültepe (Michel 2003a, 2006a). The huge *Kārum* Ib palace, built on the top of the citadel, was empty at the time of its destruction by fire, so almost no tablets were found in it. Only forty cuneiform tablets were found in the citadel, mainly in the ruins of houses dated both from Level II and Ib. A vast majority, 22,000 texts, were discovered in private houses of the *kārum* dated from Level II. Only 420 tablets come from the later Ib level (eighteenth century B.C.E.). The tablets were lying in warehouses, originally stored in groups of twenty to thirty units in baskets, boxes, or clay jars with sealed clay labels. Most of the archaeological material found in the houses was of a purely Anatolian style. The Assyrians used local products, and thus the tablets are the main artifacts allowing an identification of their owner's ethnic origin. Some Anatolians living in the *kārum* were involved in the trade but did not play a role in the administration of the trading post.

Besides Kültepe, other sites have produced few documents. Seventy-two documents were unearthed in a layer dated from *Kārum* Ib, in the lower town at Boğazköy, ancient Ḫattuš(a), capital of the later Hittite Empire (Dercksen 2001:49–60). Alişar, the old city of Amkuwa, has produced sixty-three tablets, also predominantly belonging to *Kārum* Ib (Dercksen 2001:39–49). One text was found at Kaman Kalehöyük in 2001 (Yoshida 2002) and another one at Kayalıpınar in 2005 (Sommerfeld 2006).

These tablets constitute the private archives of Assyrian merchants settled at Kaniš, and few of them belonged to Anatolian traders. Archives are made up of private letters protected during their transport by clay envelopes, legal documents including various contracts involving many Anatolians, and various lists, private notices, and memoranda. The local population is often referred to in these business relationships. The letters provide us with some data about the organization of the trade, the relations with the local population, and insights into the geopolitical and economical situation of central Anatolia.

Historical Documents and Chronology

The Old Assyrian tablets are mainly commercial, but several documents deal with other topics: family contracts, school tablets, and incantations (Michel 2003a:135–41). A few historical texts were discovered at Kültepe: two copies of the Assyrian king Erišum I's inscriptions and an Old Assyrian Sargon legend. Several copies of the Kültepe eponym list have been published recently: six copies date from *Kārum* II and one from *Kārum* Ib (Günbattı 2008a, 2008b; Veenhof 2003a). Among the first group, the most complete copy reveals the succession of 129 eponym names (*līmum*), each corresponding to a year, and the reign of the Assyrian kings to which they belong, from Erišum I (1974–1935 B.C.E.) to Narām-Sîn (1872–1829/19 B.C.E.). Most of the archives discovered in Kültepe contexts are dated from the first half of the nineteenth century B.C.E.; this period ended at some point during the last decades of the century. According to Kültepe eponym list manuscript G, *Kārum* Ib covered the whole eighteenth century B.C.E. These tablets help us reconstruct the Assyrian and Anatolian chronologies (Barjamovic, Hertel, and Larsen forthcoming). The treaties concluded between Assyrian institutions and local Anatolian rulers to support the long-distance trade, as well as many of the letters, give an insight into Anatolian history as well. Four treaties were found, three of them dating from *Kārum* Ib (Çeçen and Hecker 1995; Günbattı 2004; Veenhof 2008a:183–218; figure 13.3); one was found at Tell Leilan (Eidem 1991).

The political and administrative structure of the Anatolian kingdoms is only visible through their contacts with the Assyrian merchants. For the most part, the documents are not dated and are usually rather short and laconic; for example we do not know the main city-states' rulers' names. The citadel produced a unique letter, dated from *Kārum* Ib, sent by Anum-Ḫirbi, king of Mamma, to Waršama, king of Kaniš (Balkan 1957; Michel 2001:no. 62).

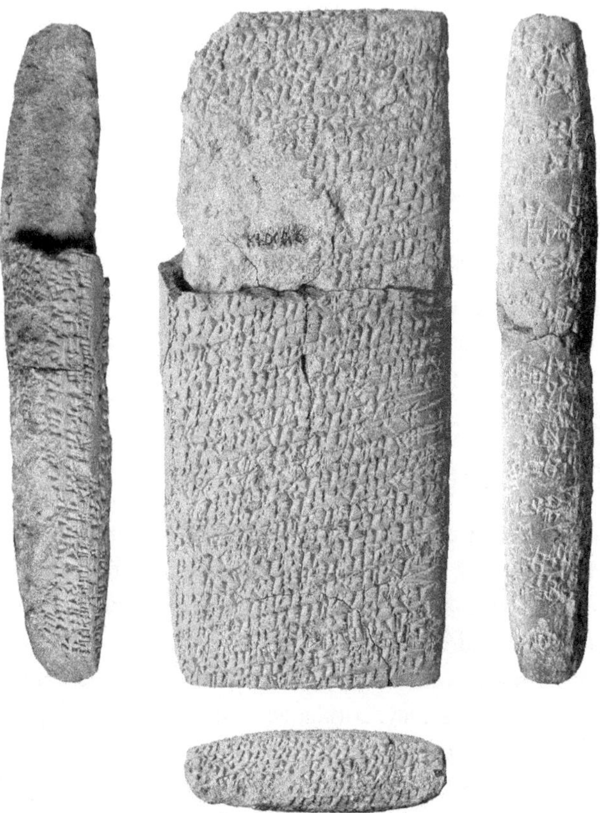

Figure 13.3. Reverse of the treaty between Kaniš and the Assyrians (Kt 00/6, Kültepe, *Kārum* Ib, photo C. Michel).

Political History of the Plateau During the *Kārum* Period

At the beginning of the second millennium B.C.E., the Anatolian plateau appears to be politically fragmented. There were numerous centers, some of them small fortified city-states, others real territorial states, with a capital and several villages. We have almost no information about their hierarchy, but one can imagine that the Assyrians settled in the biggest and economically strongest ones. The data provided by the archives concern predominantly the Anatolian élite, that is, kings and palace officials with whom the Assyrian traders dealt; they also document each event that affected trade. The few extant Anatolian archives also deal with the trade and consist mostly of loans and sale contracts (Albayrak 2005; Donbaz 1988; Veenhof 1978).

Political Powers

Countries and Cities

The Assyrian vocabulary referring to Anatolian political powers is quite vague. The word for land, *mātum*, refers to the territory of a city-state but corresponds as well to the countryside. During *Kārum* II, the texts mention the lands of Burušḫattum, Kaniš, Luḫusaddia (east of Kaniš), Waḫšušana (north of the Tuz Gölü), and Zalpa, to the north. The toponym Ḫattum does not correspond to a town but to the land inside the Kızıl Irmak bend; it contained several cities, among which are Amkuwa, Ḫattuš, Tawinia, and Tuḫpia (figure 13.1). During the *Kārum* Ib period, the land of Mamma became more important, and both Kaniš and Mamma had vassal states. The archives mention hundreds of toponyms corresponding either to small villages or to bigger towns which might be centers of independent states (Michel 2008c). Twenty cities housed a *kārum* during the Level II period[1] and fifteen a *wabartum*.[2] During the Level Ib period, the data give a list of fewer than ten *kārums*[3] and five *wabartums*;[4] important centers like Burušḫattum had disappeared from the Assyrian trade network, perhaps being too far west (Dercksen 2001:60–61; it could be located at Karahöyük Konya).

Kaniš might have been the first town settled by the Assyrians; it certainly remained their administrative center during the whole period. Anatolian archives as well as tablets from the citadel, with a list of the palace personnel, give names of villages belonging to the Kaniš state. During *Kārum* II, the city was surrounded by ten or so villages; during *Kārum* Ib, the kingdom was apparently even bigger, with almost twenty villages (Dercksen 2004; Forlanini 1992; Günbattı 1987).

Anatolian Rulers and Political History

Each city-state, whatever its size, had its local dynasties. The Anatolian rulers were called *rubā'um* ("prince") and *rubātum* ("princess") or designated with a *nisbe* (nisbes derive from a place-name and are used to indicate the geographical origin of people and objects), for example, Wahšušanaium, "the Man of Wahšušana."[5] A prince is attested during *Kārum* II in more than fifteen towns;[6] in Burušhattum, the local ruler is occasionally designated as the "great prince" (*rubā'um rabium*). The Assyrian archives never give the name of the local king, except for Labarša, whose accession to the throne of an unknown city-state is used to date a transaction. At the end of *Kārum* II, a text mentions the death of Luhusaddia's prince, Asu (Kryszat 2008b:156–59). Letters refer to hostilities, rebellions, the death of a local ruler, and so on, but no names or dates are given.

During *Kārum* II, there are several mentions of coalitions between Anatolian kingdoms, for example, between Wahšušana and Kaniš, and between the rulers of Šinahutum, Amkuwa, and Kapitra, who made an alliance against Hattuš at the end of *Kārum* II or the beginning of *Kārum* Ib (Larsen 1972; Michel 2001:no. 63). Similarly, wars and hostilities between two cities are discussed in some letters because they could slow down or stop the trade. Thus, a conflict between Tawiniya and perhaps Wašhania involved an Assyrian accused by the second of acting as a spy for the first city (Günbattı 2001; Michel 2008c; Michel and Garelli 1996). The western cities of Burušhattum and Wahšušana were often fighting against each other, sometimes involving Šaladuwar; the Assyrian community had to leave Wahšušana at the end of *Kārum* II, while Burušhattum became more influential (Barjamovic, Hertel, and Larsen forthcoming; Veenhof forthcoming). Several kingdoms experienced local revolts, for example in Hahhum, Kunanamit, Burušhattum, Wahšušana, or in Ulama where turmoil started after the death of the king (Michel 2008c; figure 13.1). Travels of kings are also mentioned because they disrupted the caravan traffic. These movements indicate the existence of diplomatic and political contacts among the Anatolian rulers.

The situation is quite different during *Kārum* Ib. Thanks to Anatolian legal documents that were written under the supervision of the local ruler and/or the "chief of the stairway" (Donbaz 1989, 1993, 2004), it is possible to reconstruct the sequence of Kaniš kings during this later period: Hurmeli (or ruler of Mamma?), Harpatiwa, Inar and his son and successor Waršama, Pithana and his son and successor Anitta (Great King), and Zuzu (Great King) (Barjamovic, Hertel, and Larsen forthcoming; Dercksen 2004; Forlanini 1995, 2004, 2008; Kryszat 2008b:161–65, 2008c; Michel 2001:117–23; Veenhof 2008a:167–73;).[7] According to the letter sent by king Anum-Hirbi of Mamma to Waršama of Kaniš and discovered in the Kültepe palace, the king of Taišama (a vassal kingdom of Kaniš), taking advantage of a defeat of Anum-Hirbi, invaded his territory and looted some of his villages (Balkan 1957; Miller 2001). Anum-Hirbi, protesting, mentioned the long siege of Harsamna by Inar. A recently excavated Old Assyrian letter sent to *kārum* Kaniš by Assur's assembly refers to the war between Harsamna and Zalpa, just after Išme-Dagan ascended the throne (Günbattı 2005). A Hittite document, Anitta's *res gestae*, also gives some elements of Anatolian political history (Carruba 2003). Anitta's father, Pithana, ruler of Kuššara, conquered Neša (Kaniš) during a night raid and captured its king, Waršama. Anitta, who became king of Kaniš and Amkuwa, achieved also several military conquests and took the title

Great King. A bronze dagger bearing Anitta's name was found in a building southeast of the citadel of Kaniš. Zuzu, king of Alaḫzina, also conquered Kaniš and took the title of Great King for himself; he ruled at the end of the eighteenth century B.C.E. The end of *Kārum* Ib might in fact be the result of Anatolian rivalries between several powerful kingdoms.

During *Kārum* Ia, there were still foreign travelers in Kaniš according to the archaeological remains, such as "Syrian bottles" or a Mesopotamian cylinder seal (Emre 1995, 1999; Kulakoğlu 2008), but no epigraphic material is extant from this period.

The Anatolian Palace and its Administration

The prince or royal couple lived in the palace, a huge building that represented the center of the Anatolian administration and could host hundreds of people; the enclosure wall of the Kültepe Ib palace is 110 × 120 m (T. Özgüç 2003:187–92, and see Kulakoğlu, chapter 47 in this volume). During *Kārum* II, the palaces, which are the local authorities with whom the Assyrians had to deal, are attested for several towns,[8] but for *Kārum* Ib, only the palace of Šalaḫšuwa is mentioned. The palace administration, headed by the royal couple, comprised many officials in charge of different services, workers, and craftsmen. The archives quote fifty different Anatolian titles; this high number indicates that the Anatolian administration was highly structured. The titles referred to in the Old Assyrian texts are translations into Assyrian of Anatolian realities. Among the highest officials, the "chief of the stairway" could correspond to the crown prince, whereas the *rabi sikkitim* ("chief of the . . .") had military and trade duties. The "chief scepter bearer," the "chief cupbearer," and the "chief of tables" were directly attached to the service of the king. The craftsmen were under the supervision of the "chief of the workers," distributed among various services, each of them with a chief ("chief of the fullers," "chief of the blacksmiths," etc.). The duties of some others are not clear to us, for example the *šinaḫilum*, "man in second" or the steward (*alaḫḫinnum*). It was possible to bear two different titles, and some of these could be given by the prince in exchange for a gift (Veenhof 2008a:219–45).

Economy and Trade

The Anatolian palaces were also economic centers that dealt with the Assyrian merchants: their wealth came from the production of their fields and their metallurgical resources. But they were also in need of tin, textiles, and other raw material brought by the Assyrians.

Agriculture, Animal Husbandry, and Food Production

The economy of the Anatolian cities was mainly based on agriculture and animal husbandry, depending on villages and domains. The land was owned by farmers and palace officials, although some fields belonged to the palace itself. The rest of the population—town inhabitants and foreign merchants in the *kārum*—had no land and depended on the surplus food sold on the market (Dercksen 2008a). Along the roads, some inns were able to feed huge quantities of people and animals forming the Assyrian caravans. Some lands were linked to a service obligation (*tuzinnum*); domains (*ubādinnum*) were offered by the king to its high officials (Dercksen 2004 and later discussion herein). Some private properties (*bētum*) also existed. The landowners had to give part of their harvest to the palace in taxes. The owners of whole villages could provide enormous amounts of grain in loans, whereas poor farmers could only produce for their own subsistence and were obliged to borrow grain from local dignitaries, palace officials, and priests to make it to the next harvest, sometimes giving their own fields as security. Joint land ownership was quite common. Anatolian loan contracts are dated according to the agricultural calendar.

Archaeobotanical studies at Kaman Kalehöyük counted half a dozen cereal varieties, but according to the texts, the biggest part of the nonirrigated land was planted with barley and wheat (Dercksen 2008b). The grain might be put in large bags to be sold on the market or in huge jars to be stored in palace storerooms under the responsibility of a "chief of the storehouses." Cereals were ground into flour to make bread or prepared into different kinds of bulgur and porridges, and fermented barley and malt were used to prepare beer (Michel 1997, 2009). Sesame oil was used for food but also for lamps and perfumes; a "chief of oil" was in charge of the collection of oil and its distribution inside the palace. Ḫaḫḫum and Kaniš are well known for their oil production. Irrigated parcels were used as orchards whose owners had to pay a tax to the chief of the irrigated fields. In the gardens, people grew vegetables, fruit trees, and animal fodder (Michel 1997; Sturm 2008). They also cultivated aromatic plants and spices. The palace had its own orchards, with gardeners. Grapes were cultivated north of Kaniš and made into wine.

The steppe and fallow fields were used as pasture for herds of sheep and goats. These animals were bred for their meat and fat, their milk, and their wool, which was sold by the palace. Wool from Mamma and Luḫusaddia could be found in marketplaces. The "chief of the herdsmen" could be very wealthy. According to the *Kārum* Ib letter of the king of Mamma, the palace owned horses, mules, dogs, and oxen (Dercksen 2008a). Archaeozoological studies in Kaman Kalehöyük and Acemhöyük show that Anatolians ate mainly sheep and goats, as well as some cattle and pigs. In private gardens, people could keep a few animals, but the consumption of meat was a privilege of wealthy people (Michel 1997, 2006c).

Metal Resources

Mining and metallurgy were the other main resource of the Anatolian plateau (Dercksen 2005; see Muhly, chapter 39 in this volume). Metal production was a primary attraction for the Assyrians, who wanted to bring gold and silver back to their homeland. There were galena and argentiferous lead deposits in the area of Bolkardağ, south of Niğde, in the Taurus Mountains (Yener 1986). Silver was also found further west, in the area of Burušḫattum, a main silver market according to the texts. The metal was melted, refined, and circulated in the form of ingots, bracelets, rings, and scraps. Silver was the main means of payment in Anatolia besides copper and grain. Part of the silver was exchanged for gold by the Assyrians. There were sources of gold in the west and southwest of Anatolia (Jesus 1980) and in the Ḫaḫḫum Mountains, northeast of Malatya (Gudea, Statue B, vi 33–35; Edzard 1997:34). The Assyrians could buy gold in Burušḫattum, Waḫšušana, Durḫumit, and Kaniš. The metal circulated in the form of nuggets, rings, beads, and various objects; one shekel (about 8.3 g) of gold amounted to six to eight shekels of silver.

Many Anatolian copper mines were exploited during the *kārum* period; this very cheap metal was used as a means of payment for daily products or small purchases, to make objects, or alloyed with tin to produce bronze. The main copper exploitations were located along the Black Sea coast in the area of the Kızıl Irmak or near Ergani (Dercksen 1996). Thus, Durḫumit appears to have been the location of the principal copper market, besides Taritar or Tišmurna, which produced poor-quality copper (Michel 1991:fig. 13.1). From there, the Assyrian merchants brought the metal in huge quantities to the western and southern cities of Burušḫattum and Waḫšušana, or to Kaniš, to exchange it, after treatment, for silver. The metal was sold in the form of ingots, small blocks, scraps, or even old sickles. To prepare the bronze needed in daily activities, Anatolians depended on the Assyrian caravans bringing the tin from the northwest of Iran and Uzbekistan. Three circular tin ingots, weighing between twenty-five and fifty grams, have been found in a *Kārum* Ib house at Kaniš. The bronze was produced locally, by Anatolian metalworkers (Sturm 2001), to make tools, weapons, and household objects, many of which have been found in the houses and graves of the *kārum*: spearheads, axes, daggers, forks, needles, nails, and chains (T. Özgüç 1986, 2003). The textual documentation mentions a variety of pots, cauldrons, knifes, spoons, hoes, axes, sickles, and so on (Dercksen 1996:76–80). Metal workshops have been found at Kültepe; they contained numerous molds for bronze tools, weapons, and ingots (Müller-Karpe 1994:49–66; T. Özgüç 1986:39–51). Other metals circulated in small quantities, such as the expensive native iron imported from Assur or found on the plateau in small deposits; two iron blocks have been unearthed in Peruwa's house in the *kārum* of Kaniš.

Trade and Commercial Treaties

The inhabitants of Kaniš could buy grain, slaves, animals, and various commodities on the local market. For tin and textiles, the palace and the élite dealt with the Assyrian merchants; the exchanges were ruled by commercial treaties concluded with each Anatolian ruler. According to these texts, in exchange for several taxes levied on the Assyrian caravans in both directions, the Anatolian ruler promised to protect individuals and goods. In case of murder, he had to deliver the murderer. If goods were lost, he had to replace them. If caravan traffic was stopped because of war, he was sure to be supplied with tin. The Assyrians were settled in *kārums* and *wabartums* that were legally independent from the local authorities. They were protected in the *kārums* as well as on the roads. Anatolian rulers were eager to sign the treaties that guaranteed these relationships to get some profit out of the trade, which was mutually beneficial to both parties.

Kārum Ib treaties found in Kaniš and concluded with the ruler of Kaniš, during the reign of Anitta or Zuzu, and with Ḫaḫḫum dignitaries (Günbattı 2004) show a slightly different situation than during *Kārum* II. Some Assyrians, settled in Kaniš and not involved any more in the international trade, were less rich, being strongly indebted and even detained by Anatolians as debt slaves, whereas during the former period, Anatolian rulers had to "wash the debts" of the local population, who were often deeply indebted to Assyrians. In Ḫaḫḫum, three dignitaries were allowed to levy taxes and receive gifts: the "export ministry," the "second in command," and the "son-in-law" (Veenhof 2008a:147–82).

The Society of Kaniš

Social Classes of Anatolian Society

Anatolian society showed an important difference between the palace and its high officials on one hand, and the rest of the population, predominantly famers and shepherds, on the other. These latter were free but poor people who belonged to the lower class (*ḫupšum*); they were cultivating just enough land for their family subsistence and often had to borrow grain to survive. The land belonged predominantly to the urban élite and to the palace. The high palace officials received some domains and even whole villages from the king, either as a gift that could be sold or as compensation for a service obligation (Dercksen 2004). There were different kinds of service obligation. The *arḫālum*, originally an agricultural tool, encompassed several forms of service, among which was the *unuššum corvée*, attested during *Kārum* Ib (Dercksen 2004:140–47).

Slaves were in charge of different tasks in the households; many of them were debt slaves, sold into slavery by themselves or by a parent. They could be redeemed if double (or more) of the original price was paid within a restricted time limit. Anatolian slave sales were supervised by the local ruler or his representative; the seller was liable to heavy penalties in the case of a claim against the buyer.

Ethnic Origins of the Kaniš Population

In the *kārum*, Assyrians lived near local merchants. They owned a house in the *kārum*, and bought slaves, food, oil, and wood from the local population. They apparently did not wish to own land, but some Assyrians had a field gained as security for a loan. The Assyrians referred to local inhabitants as *nuwa'um* (Anatolian) without any distinction, but onomastic studies provide us with some clues about their ethnic origin. The anthroponyms quoted in the tablets belong to several different languages, as indicated by some loanwords: Hattic, Luwian, Hittite, and Hurrian (Dercksen 2002; Garelli 1963:127–68; Goedegebuure 2008; Michel 2001:40–41; Wilhelm 2008). The Hattian people spoke an agglutinative language that does not belong to any known linguistic family; they were already settled in the bend of the Kızıl Irmak in the third millennium B.C.E. The Indo-European Luwians arrived in central Anatolia during the last centuries of the third millennium B.C.E. The Hittites came into this area perhaps at the very beginning of the second millennium B.C.E., and they adopted many cultural features of the Hattians. The Indo-European Hittite language was later called *nešili*, "from the city of Neša" (Kaniš). Hurrians arrived from the mountains of Upper Mesopotamia and were well established in the eastern part of Anatolia during the *Kārum* Ib period; the best-known king bearing a Hurrian name was Anum-Ḫirbi, king of Mamma (Wilhelm 2008).

Communication between Assyrians and Anatolians

Assyrians and Anatolians apparently had no communication problems, so bilingualism must have been fairly common. The very few translators mentioned in the documents were employed by the palace administrations (Michel 2008a, 2010; Ulshöfer 2000; Veenhof 1982). The Assyrians introduced writing to Anatolia, and there is no evidence of an attempt by the Anatolians to adapt the cuneiform script to their language during the *kārum* period. Old Assyrian was used in the commercial treaties drawn between Assyrians and local rulers; it even served as the diplomatic written language between the Anatolian kings. Treaties and royal letters were certainly written by official scribes employed by the palaces. Some Anatolians, such as Peruwa, whose archives were discovered in the *kārum*, adopted the cuneiform script and Old Assyrian dialect. In fact, the Assyrians themselves used a simplified cuneiform script with fewer than 200 signs. Many Assyrians were able to read and write, and this might have encouraged the local people to learn to read and write as well (Kryszat 2008a; Michel 2008a).

The Old Assyrian dialect shows several loanwords borrowed from the Hattic language spoken in the city at least since the beginning of the nineteenth century B.C.E. (Dercksen 2007). Moreover, some Anatolian officials bore titles that did not exist in the Assyrian administration and were thus translated from Hittite or built on Hurrian words; this makes the work of the historians who try to understand the function and activities behind them more complicated.

Family

Marriage and divorce contracts give information on local family law. Husband and wife enjoyed equal status, and they owned house and goods in common. Both could divorce, and contracts were established under the supervision of the local ruler and his second-in-command. In case of divorce, they shared their house, or the wife could take everything out of the house, including the slaves, and give up her rights on the domain and the linked service obligation (*tuzinnum*). Once the divorce was settled, if the husband or wife made a claim, he or she was subject to a heavy fine and there could even be a death penalty (Veenhof 2003b). After the divorce, children were brought up by either the wife or the husband. When an Anatolian was indebted, he could give his wife and children as a guarantee to his creditor; if he could not pay his debt, then his wife and children became the property of the creditor and they lost their liberty (Michel 2003b).

Adoption is also attested; the adopted child lived with his or her new family. Adults were adopted for economic reasons. One tablet describes a couple who adopted a young man, who then had to sustain his new parents and became their unique heir (Michel 1998; Veenhof 2003b). Several Anatolian contracts dated from *Kārum* Ib show joint ownership among two to four young men presented as brothers (*athū*); they had to share the household with their old parents, even if some of them were already married, to maintain an economically strong household. They thus shared the service duties linked to the property. They could divide the property between them only after the death of their parents (Veenhof 1997).

The Mixed Community

The relationships between Anatolians and Assyrians were primarily commercial. The first generation of Assyrians who came to Anatolia was made up from men who left their families in Assur; their involvement in the Anatolian society was a purely economical one. They stayed for a while in Anatolia and came back to Assur because they had to take over their family affairs. As more and more Assyrians settled in Kaniš and in other *kārums* and *wabartums*, the relations between the two populations changed (Michel 2010; Veenhof 1982). During their long stay in Anatolia, the Assyrians often contracted a second marriage, most of the time with an Anatolian woman. This was done with respect to two rules: they could not have two wives with the same status (*aššatum*, "main wife," *amtum*, "secondary wife"), and they could not have both wives in the same place (Kienast 2008; Michel 2006b; Veenhof 2003b). The Anatolian wives of the Assyrian merchants stayed at home in Kaniš, bringing up their children, taking care of the household, and doing agricultural tasks, while their husbands were traveling and trading inside Anatolia and sometimes as far as to Assur where their Assyrian wives were waiting for them. When some of the Assyrians went to retire in Assur, they left their Anatolian wives and drew up a divorce contract; the women typically could keep the house in which they lived, the furniture, and some divorce money (Michel 2008b). They usually kept their younger children, the father paying for their upbringing, but he could decide to take some of his Anatolian children to Assur.

Many Anatolians living in the *kārum* could improve their position in society through the business they conducted with the Assyrians. Some even acted as creditors toward Assyrians and integrated with the Assyrian family firms by choosing their spouses from among the Assyrian community. With the increase of mixed marriages, the *kārum* became a "social colony"—so much so that in several families, brothers and sisters bore Assyrian as well as Anatolian names.

Conclusion

The Old Assyrian presence in Anatolia, known best through its archives excavated at Kültepe, gives an important insight into local culture and history. During the *kārum* period, the Anatolian plateau was divided into city-states and small territorial states, which, through coalitions and wars, became more or less influential. Each state had its own dynasty, with a prince or royal couple who lived in the palace, which represented the state administrative center. Anatolian states developed a very highly organized administration, according to the fifty official titles mentioned in the Old Assyrian archives, without having their own writing system.

The Assyrian presence in central Anatolia during the nineteenth and eighteenth centuries B.C.E. did not have a political character but was purely economic. The Assyrians represented the most numerous foreign people in Anatolia and the best structured community in the *kārum* of Kaniš, where they lived together with local inhabitants and other foreigners. The relationships between Assyrians and Anatolians were first commercial and then evolved with an increasing number of mixed marriages between the two communities into a "social colony."

The nineteenth century B.C.E. is very well documented, but there are many fewer tablets for the eighteenth century B.C.E., and we do not know how the Old Assyrian trade in Anatolia came to an end. A general impoverishment of the Assyrians not involved anymore in the international trade can be observed. Their departure seems to be the consequence of a deteriorated political situation among the Anatolian states. With the departure of the Assyrians, writing disappeared from Anatolia within a century, to be reintroduced later in a different form by the Hittites.

NOTES

1. Burušḫattum, Durḫumit, Ḫaḫḫum, Ḫattuš, Kaniš, Niḫria, Nenašša, Šaladuwar, Šalaḫšuwa, Šamuḫa, Šimala, Šinaḫutum, Tawinia, Tegarama, Timilkia, Tišmurna, Tuḫpiya, Uršu, Waḫšušana, southern Zalpa.

2. Amkuwa, Ḫanaknak, Ḫurrama, Karaḫna, Kuburnat, Kuššara, Mamma, Šamuḫa, Šuppilulia, Ulama, Upē, Ušša, Wašḫania, northern Zalpa, Zimisḫuna.

3. Durḫumit, Kaniš, Kuburnat, Šamuḫa, Šaladuwar, Šuppilulia, Tawinia, Tegarama, Waḫšušana?, Wašḫania.

4. Amkuwa, Ḫurrama?, Mamma, Šamuḫa, Tegarama, Timilkia?.

5. Some rulers are mentioned by a nisbe in Hattuš, Nenašša, Waḫšušana, and Timilkia.

6. Amkuwa, Burušḫattum, Durḫumit, Ḫattuš, Ḫurrama, Kaniš, Kuburnat, Luḫusaddia, Mamma, Nenašša, Šinaḫutum, Tawinia, Timilkia, Tuḫpia, Waḫšušana, Wašḫania.

7. During this period, rulers are also attested in Amkuwa, Kaniš, Luḫusaddia, Mamma, Šalaḫšuwa, and Tawinia.

8. Burušḫattum (Garelli 1989), Durḫumit (Michel 1991), Ḫurrama, Kaniš, Luḫusaddia, Niḫria, Nenašša, Šamuḫa, Tegarama, Tišmurna, Waḫšušana, Wašḫania, and both Zalpas.

REFERENCES

Albayrak, İrfan. 2005. Fünf Urkunden aus dem Archiv von Peruwa, Sohn von Šuppibra. *Jaarbericht van het Vooraziatisch—Egyptisch Genootschap Ex Oriente Lux* 39: 95–105.

Alp, Sedat. 1968. *Zylinder und Stempelsiegel aus Karahöyük bei Konya*. Türk Tarih Kurumu Yayınlarından V/26. Ankara: Türk Tarih Kurumu Basımevi.

Balkan, Kemal. 1957. *Letter of King Anum-Hirbi of Mama to King Warshama of Kanish*. Türk Tarih Kurumu Yayınlarından VII/31a. Ankara: Türk Tarih Kurumu Basımevi.

Barjamovic, Gojko. 2008. The Geography of Trade. Assyrian Colonies in Anatolia c. 1975–1725 BC and the Study of Early Interregional Networks of Exchange. In *Anatolia and the Jazira during the Old Assyrian Period*, ed. Jan Gerrit Dercksen, 87–100. Old Assyrian Archives Studies 3. Publications de l'Institut historique-archéologique néerlandais de Stambul CXI. Leiden: Nederlands Instituut voor het Nabije Oosten.

———. 2011. *A Historical Geography of Anatolia in the Old Assyrian Colony Period*. Carsten Niebuhr Institute Publications 38. Copenhagen: Copenhagen University.

Barjamovic, Gojko, Thomas Hertel, and Mogens T. Larsen. Forthcoming. *Ups and Downs at Kanesh—Observations on Chronology, History and Society in the Old Assyrian Period*. Old Assyrian Archives Studies 5. Publications de l'Institut historique-archéologique néerlandais de Stambul. Leiden: Nederlands Instituut voor het Nabije Oosten.

Blocher, Felix. 2003. Chronological Aspects of the Karum Period (Middle Bronze Age). In *The Synchronisation of Civilisation in the Eastern Mediterranean in the Second Millennium B.C.*, vol. 2, ed. Manfred Bietak, 379–80. Wien: Verlag der Österreichischen Akademie der Wissenschaften.

Carruba, Onofrio. 2003. *Anitta res gestae. Anitta, King of the Hittites*. Studia Mediterranea 13, Series Hethaea 1. Pavia: Italian University Press.

Çeçen, Salih and Karl Hecker. 1995. *Ina mātīka eblum*, Zu einem neuen Text zum Wegerecht. In *Festschrift für Wolfram Freiherrn von Soden zum 85. Geburtstag am 19. Juni 1993*, ed. Manfred Dietrich and Oswald Loretz, 31–41. Alter Orient und Altes Testament 240. Münster: Ugarit-Verlag.

Dercksen, Jan Gerrit. 1996. *The Old Assyrian Copper Trade in Anatolia*. Publications de l'Institut historique-archéologique néerlandais de Stambul 75. Leiden: Nederlands Instituut voor het Nabije Oosten.

———. 2001. "When We Met in Hattuš." Trade According to Old Assyrian Texts from Alishar and Boğazköy. In *K.R. Veenhof Anniversary Volume*, ed. Wilfred H. van Soldt, J. G. Dercksen, N. J. C. Kouwenberg, and T. J. H. Krispijn, 39–66. Publications de l'Institut historique-archéologique néerlandais de Stambul 89. Leiden: Nederlands Instituut voor het Nabije Oosten.

———. 2002. Kultureller und wirtschaftlicher Austausch zwischen Assyrern und Anatoliern (Anfang des zweiten Jahrtausends v. Chr.). In *Brückenland Anatolien? Ursachen, Extensität und Modi des Kulturaustausches zwischen Anatolien und seinen Nachbarn*, ed. Hartmut Blum, Betina Faist, Peter Pfälzner, and Anne M. Wittke, 35–43. Tübingen: Attempto Verlag.

———. 2004. Some Elements of Old Anatolian Society in Kanis. In *Assyria and Beyond. Studies Presented to Mogens Trolle Larsen*, ed. Jan Gerrit Dercksen, 137–78. Publications de l'Institut historique-archéologique néerlandais de Stambul C. Leiden: Nederlands Instituut voor het Nabije Oosten.

———. 2005. Metals According to Documents from Kültepe-Kanish Dating to the Old Assyrian Colony Period. In *Anatolian Metal III*, ed. Ü. Yalcun, 17–34. Der Anschnitt, Beiheft 18. Bochum: Deutsches Bergbau-Museum.

———. 2007. On Anatolian Loanwords in Akkadian Texts from Kültepe. *Zeitschrift für Assyriologie* 97: 26–46.

———. 2008a. Subsistence, Surplus and the Market for Grain and Meat at Ancient Kanesh. *Altorientalische Forschungen* 35: 86–102.

———. 2008b. Observations on Land Use and Agriculture in Kaneš. In *Old Assyrian Studies in Memory of Paul Garelli*, ed. Cécile Michel, 139–57. Leiden Old Assyrian Archives Studies 4. Publications de l'Institut historique-archéologique néerlandais de Stambul 112. Leiden: Nederlands Instituut voor het Nabije Oosten.

Donbaz, Veysel. 1988. The Business of Ašēd, an Anatolian Merchant. *Archiv für Orientforschung* 35: 48–63.

———. 1989. Some Remarkable Contracts of 1-B Period Kültepe Tablets. In *Anatolia and the Ancient Near East. Studies in Honor of Tahsin Özgüç*, ed. Kutlu Emre, Barthel Hrouda, Machteld Mellink, and Nimet Özgüç, 75–98. Ankara: Türk Tarih Kurumu Basımevi.

———. 1993. Some Remarkable Contracts of 1-B Period Kültepe Tablets II. In *Aspects of Art and Iconography: Anatolia and its Neighbors. Studies in Honor of Nimet Özgüç*, ed. Machteld J. Mellink, Edith Porada, and Tahsin Özgüç, 131–54. Ankara: Türk Tarih Kurumu Basımevi.

———. 2004. Some Remarkable Contracts of 1-B Period Kültepe Tablets III. In *Šarnikzel. Hethitologische Studien zum Gedenken an Emil Orgetorix Forrer*, ed. Detlev Groddek and Şevket Rößle, 271–84. Dresdner Beiträge zur Hethitologie 10. Dresden: Harrassowitz Verlag.

Dönmez, Şevket and Aslıhan Y. Beyazit. 2008. A General Look at the Central Black Sea Region during the Middle Bronze Age and a New Approach to the Zalpa Problem in the Light of New Evidence. In *Anatolia and the Jazira during the Old Assyrian Period*, ed. Jan Gerrit Dercksen, 101–35. Old Assyrian Archives Studies 3. Publications de l'Institut historique-archéologique néerlandais de Stambul 111. Leiden: Nederlands Instituut voor het Nabije Oosten.

Edzard, Dietz Otto. 1997. *Gudea and His Dynasty*. The Royal Inscriptions of Mesopotamia, Early Periods 3/1. Toronto: University of Toronto Press.

Eidem, Jesper. 1991. An Old Assyrian Treaty from Tell Leilan. In *Marchands, diplomates et empereurs. Études sur la civilisation mésopotamienne offertes à Paul Garelli*, ed. Dominique Charpin and Francis Joannès, 185–207. Paris: Éditions Recherche sur les Civilisations.

Emre, Kutlu. 1995. Pilgrim-Flasks from Level I of the *Kārum* of Kaniş. *Bulletin of the Middle Eastern Culture Center in Japan* 8: 173–200.

———. 1999. Syrian Bottles from the *Kārum* of Kaniş. *Bulletin of the Middle Eastern Culture Center in Japan* 11: 39–50.

———. 2008. A Group of Metal Vessels from *Kārum* Kültepe/Kaneš. In *Old Assyrian Studies in Memory of Paul Garelli*, ed. Cécile Michel, 3–12. Leiden Old Assyrian Archives Studies 4. Publications de l'Institut historique-archéologique néerlandais de Stambul 112. Leiden: Nederlands Instituut voor het Nabije Oosten.

Forlanini, Massimo. 1992. Am Mittleren Kızılırmak. In *Hittite and Other Anatolian and Near Eastern Studies in Honour of Sedat Alp*, ed. Heinrich Otten, Ekrem Akurgal, Hayri Ertem, and Aygül Süel, 171–79. Ankara: Türk Tarih Kurumu Basımevi.

———. 1995. The Kings of Kaniš. In *Atti del II Congresso Internazionale di Hittitologia*, ed. Onofrio Carruba, Mauro Giorgieri, and Clelia Mora, 123–32. Studia Mediterranea 9. Pavia: Centro ricerche egeo-anatoliche dell'Università di Pavia.

———. 2004. La nascita di un impero. Considerazioni sulla prima fase della storia hittita: da Kaniš a Hattuša. *Orientalia* 73: 363–89.

———. 2008. The Historical Geography of Anatolia and the Transition from the *Kārum*-Period to the Early Hittite Empire. In *Anatolia and the Jazira during the Old Assyrian Period*, ed. Jan Gerrit Dercksen, 57–86. Old Assyrian Archives Studies 3. Publications de l'Institut historique-archéologique néerlandais de Stambul 111. Leiden: Nederlands Instituut voor het Nabije Oosten.

Garelli, Paul. 1963. *Les Assyriens en Cappadoce.* Bibliothèque archéologique et historique de l'Institut français d'archéologie d'Istanbul 19. Paris: Institut français d'archéologie d'Istanbul.

———. 1989. Le marché de Burušhattum. In *Anatolia and the Ancient Near East. Studies in Honor of Tahsin Özgüç*, ed. Kutlu Emre, Barthel Hrouda, Machteld Mellink, and Nimet Özgüç, 149–52. Ankara: Türk Tarih Kurumu Basımevi.

Goedegebuure, Petra M. 2008. Central Anatolian Languages and Language Communities in the Colony Period: A Luwian-Hattian Symbiosis and the Independent Hittites. In *Anatolia and the Jazira during the Old Assyrian Period*, ed. Jan Gerrit Dercksen, 137–80. Old Assyrian Archives Studies 3. Publications de l'Institut historique-archéologique néerlandais de Stambul 111. Leiden: Nederlands Instituut voor het Nabije Oosten.

Gorny, Ronald L. 1995. Hittite Imperialism and Anti-Imperial Resistance as Viewed from Alişar Höyük. *Bulletin of the American Schools of Oriental Research* 299/300: 65–89.

Günbattı, Cahit. 1987. Yeniden İşlenen Bir Kültepe Tableti (Kt g/t 42+z/t 11). *Belleten* 51: 1–10.

———. 2001. The River Ordeal in Ancient Anatolia. In *K. R. Veenhof Anniversary Volume*, ed. Wilfred H. van Soldt, J. G. Dercksen, N. J. C. Kouwenberg, and T. J. H. Krispijn, 151–60. Publications de l'Institut historique-archéologique néerlandais de Stambul 89. Leiden: Nederlands Instituut voor het Nabije Oosten.

———. 2004. Two Treaty Texts Found at Kültepe. In *Assyria and Beyond. Studies Presented to Mogens Trolle Larsen*, ed. Jan Gerrit Dercksen, 249–68. Publications de l'Institut historique-archéologique néerlandais de Stambul C. Leiden: Nederlands Instituut voor het Nabije Oosten.

———. 2005. 2000 ve 2001 Yılı Kültepe Kazılarında Ele Geçen Bazı I-b Tabletleri. In *V. Uluslararası Hititoloji Kongresi Bildirileri, Çorum 02–08 Eylül 2002*, ed. Aygül Süel, 445–51. Ankara: Balkan Cilt Evi.

———. 2008a. An Eponym Kist (KEL G) from Kültepe. *Altorientalische Forschungen* 35: 103–32.

———. 2008b. A List of Eponyms (KEL D) from Kültepe. In *Old Assyrian Studies in Memory of Paul Garelli*, ed. Cécile Michel, 125–35. Leiden Old Assyrian Archives Studies 4. Publications de l'Institut historique-archéologique néerlandais de Stambul 112. Leiden: Nederlands Instituut voor het Nabije Oosten.

Hecker, Karl. 2006. Purušhattum. *Reallexikon der Assyriologie und Vorderasiatischen Archäologie*, vol. XI–1/2, ed. Michael Streck, 119–20. Berlin: Walter de Gruyter.

Jesus, Prentiss S. de. 1980. *The Development of Prehistoric Mining and Metallurgy in Anatolia*. BAR International Series 74. Oxford: British Archaeological Reports.

Joukowsky, Martha Sharp. 1996. *Early Turkey. Anatolian Archaeology from Prehistory through the Lydian Period*. Dubuque, Iowa: Kendall/Hunt.

Karaduman, Ayşe. 2008. Acemhöyük Sarıkaya Sarayı'nda Bulunmuş olan Etiketlerden bir Grup. In *Muhibbe Darga Armağanı*, ed. Taner Tarhan, Aksel Tibet, and Erkan Konyar, 283–90. İstanbul: Sadberk Hanım Müzesi.

Kawakami, Naohiko. 2006. The Location of Purušhanta. *al-Rāfidān* 27: 59–99.

Kienast, Burkhart. 2008. Altassyrisch amtum = "Zweitfrau." *Altorientalische Forschungen* 35: 35–52.

Kryszat, Guido. 2008a. The Use of Writing among the Anatolians. In *Anatolia and the Jazira during the Old Assyrian Period*, ed. Jan Gerrit Dercksen, 231–38. Old Assyrian Archives Studies 3. Publications de l'Institut historique-archéologique néerlandais de Stambul 111. Leiden: Nederlands Instituut voor het Nabije Oosten.

———. 2008b. Herrscher, Kult und Kulttradition in Anatolien nach den Quellen aus den altassyrischen Handelskolonien. Teil 3/1: Grundlagen für eine neue Rekonstruktion der Geschichte Anatoliens und der assyrischen Handelskolonien in spätaltassyrischer Zeit. *Altorientalische Forschungen* 35: 156–89.

———. 2008c. Herrscher, Kult und Kulttradition in Anatolien nach den Quellen aus den altassyrischen Handelskolonien. Teil 3/2: Grundlagen für eine neue Rekonstruktion der Geschichte Anatoliens und der assyrischen Handelskolonien in spätaltassyrischer Zeit II. *Altorientalische Forschungen* 35: 195–219.

Kulakoğlu, Fikri. 1996. Ferzant-Type Bowls from Kültepe. *Bulletin of the Middle Eastern Culture Center in Japan* 11: 69–86.

———. 2008. A Hittite God from Kültepe. In *Old Assyrian Studies in Memory of Paul Garelli*, ed. Cécile Michel, 13–19. Leiden Old Assyrian Archives Studies 4. Publications de l'Institut historique-archéologique néerlandais de Stambul 112. Leiden: Nederlands Instituut voor het Nabije Oosten.

Kuniholm, Peter I., Maryanne W. Newton, Carol B. Griggs, and Pamela J. Sullivan. 2005. Dendrochronological Dating in Anatolia: The Second Millennium B.C.: Significance for Early Metallurgy. *Deutsches Bergbau-Museum, Der Anschnitt* 18: 41–47.

Larsen, Mogens T. 1972. A Revolt against Hattuša. *Journal of Cuneiform Studies* 24: 100–101.

Lumsden, S. 2008. Material Culture and the Middle Ground in the Old Assyrian Colony Period. In *Old Assyrian Studies in Memory of Paul Garelli*, ed. Cécile Michel, 21–43. Leiden Old Assyrian Archives Studies 4. Publications de l'Institut historique-archéologique néerlandais de Stambul 112. Leiden: Nederlands Instituut voor het Nabije Oosten.

Michel, Cécile. 1991. Durhumid, son commerce et ses marchands. In *Marchands, diplomates et empereurs. Études sur la civilisation mésopotamienne offertes à Paul Garelli*, ed.

Dominique Charpin and Francis Joannès, 253–73. Paris: Éditions Recherche sur les Civilisations.

———. 1997. A table avec les marchands paléo-assyriens. In *Assyrien im Wandel der Zeiten. XXXIXe Rencontre Assyriologique Internationale, Heidelberg*, 6–10 Juli 1992, ed. Hartmut Waetzoldt and Harald Hauptmann, 95–113. Heidelberger Studien zum Alten Orient 6. Heidelberg: Heidelberger Orientverlag.

———. 1998. Les enfants des marchands de Kaniš. In *Enfance et éducation au Proche-Orient ancien, Actes de la table ronde, Nanterre, Décembre 1997*, ed. Brigitte Lion, Cécile Michel, and Pierre Villard. *Ktèma* 22: 91–108.

———. 2001. *Correspondance des marchands de Kaniš au début du IIe millénaire av. J.-C.* Littératures du Proche-Orient ancien 19. Paris: Éditions du Cerf.

———. 2003a. *Old Assyrian Bibliography of Cuneiform Texts, Bullae, Seals and the Results of the Excavations at Aššur, Kültepe/Kaniš, Acemhöyük, Alişar and Boğazköy*. Old Assyrian Archives Studies 1. Publications de l'Institut historique-archéologique néerlandais de Stambul 97. Leiden: Nederlands Instituut voor het Nabije Oosten.

———. 2003b. Les femmes et les dettes: problèmes de responsabilité dans la Mésopotamie du début du IIe millénaire avant J.-C. *Méditerranées* 34–35: 13–36.

———. 2006a. Old Assyrian Bibliography 1 (February 2003–July 2006). *Archiv für Orientforschung* 51: 436–49.

———. 2006b. Bigamie chez les Assyriens du début du IIe millénaire. *Revue Historique de Droit Français et Etranger* 84: 155–76.

———. 2006c. Les suidés dans la documentation de Kaniš au début du IIe millénaire avant J.-C. In *De la domestication au tabou: le cas des suidés au Proche-Orient ancien, Actes du colloque international, Nanterre, 1–3 décembre 2005*, ed. Brigitte Lion and Cécile Michel, 169–80. Travaux de la Maison René-Ginouvès 1. Paris: De Boccard.

———. 2008a. Écrire et compter chez les marchands assyriens du début du IIe millénaire av. J.-C. In *Muhibbe Darga Armağanı*, ed. Taner Tarhan, Aksel Tibet, and Erkan Konyar, 345–64. İstanbul: Sadberk Hanım Müzesi.

———. 2008b. Les Assyriens et leurs femmes anatoliennes. In *Anatolia and the Jazira during the Old Assyrian Period*, ed. Jan Gerrit Dercksen, 209–29. Old Assyrian Archives Studies 3. Publications de l'Institut historique-archéologique néerlandais de Stambul 111. Leiden: Nederlands Instituut voor het Nabije Oosten.

———. 2008c. New Anatolian Geographical Data According to Recent Kültepe Archives. In *New Perspectives on the Historical Geography of Anatolia in the II and I Millennium B.C.*, ed. Karl Strobel. *Eothen* 16: 235–52.

———. 2009. "Dis-moi ce que tu bois . . ." Boissons et buveurs en haute Mésopotamie et Anatolie au début du IIe millénaire av. J.-C. In *Et il y eut un esprit dans l'Homme. Jean Bottéro et la Mésopotamie*, ed. Xavier Faivre, Brigitte Lion, and Cécile Michel, 197–220. Travaux de la Maison René-Ginouvès 6. Paris: De Boccard.

———. 2010. Les comptoirs de commerce assyriens en Anatolie: emprunts réciproques et acculturation. In *Portrait de migrants, portraits de colons*, vol. 2, ed. Pierre Rouillard, 1–12. Colloques de la Maison René-Ginouvès 6. Paris: De Boccard.

Michel, Cécile and Paul Garelli. 1996. Heurts avec une principauté anatolienne. In *Festschrift für Hans Hirsch zum 65. Geburtstag gewidmet von seinen Freunden, Kollegen und Schülern*, ed. Arne A. Ambros and Markus Köhbach, 277–90. Wiener Zeitschrift für die Kunde des Morgenlandes 86. Wien: Institut für Orientalistik.

Michel, Cécile and Patrick Rocher. 2000. La chronologie du début du IIe millénaire revue à l'ombre d'une éclipse de soleil. *Jaarbericht van het Vooraziatisch-Egyptisch Genootschap Ex Oriente Lux* 35–36: 111–26.

Miller, Jared. 2001. Anum-Hirbi and His Kingdom. *Altorientalische Forschungen* 28: 65–101.

Müller-Karpe, Andreas. 1994 *Altanatolisches Metallhandwerk*. Neumünster: Wachholtz.

Özgüç, Nimet. 1965. *Kültepe Mühür Baskılarında Anadolu Grubu/The Anatolian Group of Cylinder Seal Impressions from Kültepe*. Türk Tarih Kurumu Yayınları V/22. Ankara: Türk Tarih Kurumu Basımevi.

———. 1966. Acemhöyük kazıları/Excavations at Acemhöyük. *Anatolia* 10: 1–52.

———. 2006. *Kültepe-Kaniš/Neša. Yerli Peruwa ve Aššur-imittī'nin oğlu Assur'lu Tüccar Uşur-ša-Ištar'ın Arşivlerine ait Kil Zarfların Mühür Baskıları/Seal Impressions on the Clay Envelopes from the Archives of the Native Peruwa and Assyrian Trader Uşur-ša-Ištar son of Aššur-imittī*. Türk Tarih Kurumu Yayınları V/50. Ankara: Türk Tarih Kurumu Basımevi.

Özgüç, Tahsin. 1986. *Kültepe-Kaniş II. Eski Yakındoğu'nun Ticaret Merkezinde Yeni Araştırmalar. New Researches at the Trading Center of the Ancient Near East*. Türk Tarih Kurumu Yayınları V/41. Ankara: Türk Tarih Kurumu Basımevi.

———. 2003. *Kültepe Kaniš/Neša. The Earliest International Trade Center and the Oldest Capital City of the Hittites*. İstanbul: Middle Eastern Culture Center in Japan.

Öztan, Aliye. 2007. Acemhöyük'den Assur Ticaret Kolonileri çağına ait iki Ender Buluntu. In *Belkıs Dinçol ve Ali Dinçol'a Armağan VITA. Festschrift in Honor of Belkıs Dinçol and Ali Dinçol*, ed. Metin Alparslan, Melten Doğan-Alparslan, and Hasan Peker, 609–21. İstanbul: Ege Yayınları.

Sagona, Antonio and Paul Zimansky. 2009. *Ancient Turkey*. London: Routledge World Archaeology.

Sommerfeld, Walter. 2006. Ein altassyrisches Tafelfragment aus Kayalıpınar (Untersuchungen in Kayalıpınar 2005). *Mitteilungen der Deutschen Orientgesellschaft* 138: 231–33.

Sturm, Thomas. 2001. Puzur-Annā—Ein Schmied des *Kārum* Kaniš. In *K.R. Veenhof Anniversary Volume*, ed. Wilfred H. van Soldt, J. G. Dercksen, N. J. C. Kouwenberg, and T. J. H. Krispijn, 475–501. Publications de l'Institut historique-archéologique néerlandais de Stambul 89. Leiden: Nederlands Instituut voor het Nabije Oosten.

———. 2008. Allanu—Haselnüsse als Delikatesse im karum-zeitlichen Handel von Anatolien nach Nordmesopotamien (ca. 1930–1730 v. Chr). *Altorientalische Forschungen* 35: 296–311.

Tessier, Béatrice. 1994. *Sealing and Seals on Texts from Kültepe Kārum Level* 2. Publications de l'Institut historique-archéologique néerlandais de Stambul 70. Leiden: Nederlands Instituut voor het Nabije Oosten.

Ulshöfer, Andrea. 2000. Sprachbarrieren und ihre überwindung: Translatorisches Handeln im alten Orient, In *Landscapes, Territories, Frontiers and Horizons in the Ancient Near East. Papers Presented to the XLIV Rencontre Assyriologique Internationale Venezia, July 7–11, 1997*, ed. Lucio Milano, Stefano de Martino, Federico M. Fales, and Giovanni B. Lanfranchi, 163–69. History of the Ancient Near East/Monographs-III/1–3. Padova: S.a.r.g.o.n. Editrice e Librería.

Veenhof, Klaas R. 1978. An Ancient Anatolian Money-Lender. His Loans, Securities and Debt-Slaves. In *Festschrift Lubor Matouš*, vol. 2, ed. Blahoslav Hruška and Géza Komoróczy, 279–311. Budapest: Eötvös Loránd Tudományegyetem, Ókori Történeti tanszék.

———. 1982. The Old Assyrian Merchants and Their Relations with the Native Population of Anatolia. In *Mesopotamien und seine Nachbarn. Politische und kulturelle Wechselbeziehungen im Alten Vorderasien vom 4. bis 1. Jahrtausend v. Chr.*, ed. Hartmut Kühne, Hans Jörg Nissen, and Johannes Renger, 147–55. Berliner Beiträge zum Vorderen Orient 1. Berlin: Dietrich Reimer Verlag.

———. 1993. On the Identification and Implications of Some Bullae from Acemhöyük and Kültepe. In *Aspects of Art and Iconography: Anatolia and its Neigbors. Studies in Honor of Nimet Özgüç*, ed. Machteld J. Mellink, Edith Porada, and Tahsin Özgüç, 645–57. Ankara: Türk Tarih Kurumu Basımevi.

———. 1997. Old Assyrian and Ancient Anatolian Evidence for the Care of the Elderly. In *The Care of the Elderly in the Ancient Near East*, ed. Marten Stol and Sven P. Vlemings, 119–60. Leiden Studies in the History and Culture of the Ancient Near East 14. Leiden: Brill-Verlag.

———. 2003a. *The Old Assyrian List of Year Eponyms from Karum Kanish and its Chronological Implications*. Türk Tarih Kurumu Yayınları VI/64. Ankara: Türk Tarih Kurumu Basımevi.

———. 2003b. The Old Assyrian Period. In *A History of Ancient Near Eastern Law*, ed. Raymond Westbrook, 431–84. Handbuch der Orientalistik 72. Leiden: Brill-Verlag.

———. 2008a. The Old Assyrian Period. In *Annäherungen* 5, ed. Markus Wäfler, 13–264. Orbis Biblicus et Orientalis 160/5, part I. Fribourg: Academic Press Fribourg.

———. 2008b. Across the Euphrates. In *Anatolia and the Jazira during the Old Assyrian Period*, ed. Jan Gerrit Dercksen, 3–29. Old Assyrian Archives Studies 3. Publications de l'Institut historique-archéologique néerlandais de Stambul 111. Leiden: Nederlands Instituut voor het Nabije Oosten.

———. Forthcoming. War and Peace. In *Krieg und Frieden im Alten Vorderasien. LIIe Rencontre Assyriologique Internationale, Münster, 17–21 Juli 2006*, ed. Hans Neumann.

Wilhelm, G. 2008. Hurrians in the Kültepe Texts. In *Anatolia and the Jazira during the Old Assyrian Period*, ed. Jan Gerrit Dercksen, 181–94. Old Assyrian Archives Studies 3. Publications de l'Institut historique-archéologique néerlandais de Stambul 111. Leiden: Nederlands Instituut voor het Nabije Oosten.

Yakar, Jak. 2000. *Ethnoarchaeology of Anatolia. Rural Economy in the Bronze and Iron Ages.* Tel Aviv University Monograph Series 17. Tel Aviv: Tel Aviv University, Institute of Archaeology.

Yener, K. Aslıhan. 1986. The Archaeometry of Silver in Anatolia: The Bolkardağ Mining District. *American Journal of Archaeology* 90: 469–72.

Yoshida, Daisuke. 2002. Ein altassyrische Text aus Kaman-Kalehöyük. Kaman-Kale-höyük 11. *Anatolian Archaeological Studies* 11: 133–37.

CHAPTER 14

SOUTHEASTERN AND EASTERN ANATOLIA IN THE MIDDLE BRONZE AGE

NICOLA LANERI AND
MARK SCHWARTZ

THE numerous rescue archaeology projects undertaken over the past forty years in eastern Anatolia have furnished archaeologists with a great amount of data that can be used to develop important interpretive and reconstructive frameworks for an area that has been *terra incognita* until recent times. This is particularly the case for the Middle Bronze Age period (MBA; ca. 2000–1600 B.C.E.), during which an increase in long-distance commercial exchanges between Mesopotamian (i.e., Syria and Iraq), Iranian, Transcaucasian, and Anatolian communities transformed the settlement patterns of the involved regions both in terms of density and size.

Geography

The area here considered (figure 14.1) is a wide region that is morphologically very diverse and divisible by geographical limitations into numerous ecological niches, such as the Euphrates Valley, the uplands of northeastern Anatolia, the Upper Tigris

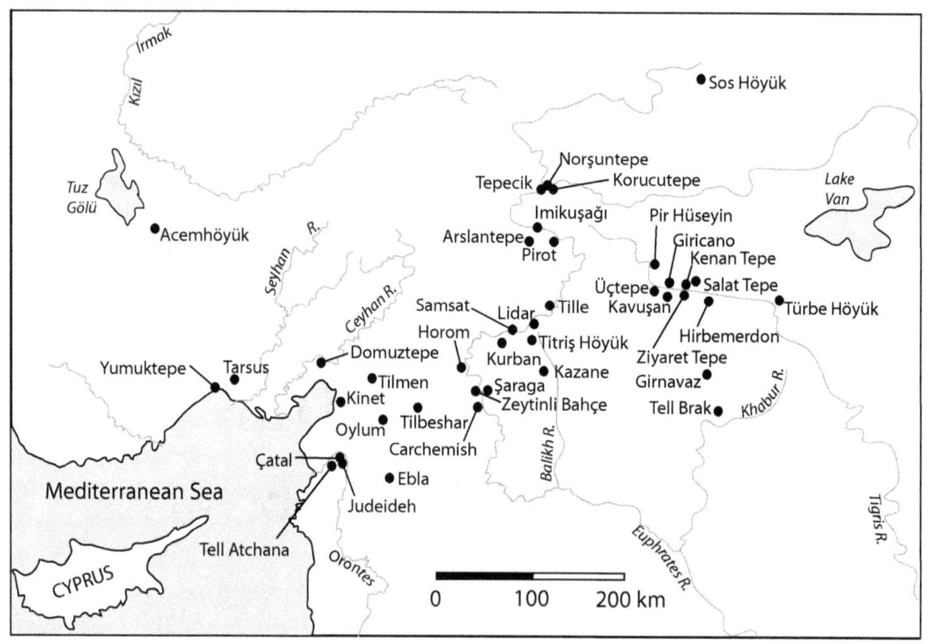

Figure 14.1. Map of sites discussed in the text.

River Valley, the Muş Plain, the Van Lake area, and the high plains bordering modern Iran. These ecological niches conditioned the development of diverse cultural groups, which shared common elements but also express diversity in their archaeological records. In addition, climatic conditions have proven to be very effective in determining the forms of economic subsistence adopted by both ancient and modern societies, for example, an agriculturally based economy with a predominance of Mediterranean polyculture along the major rivers in southeastern Anatolia and a pastoral economy in the uplands and high plains of eastern Anatolia.

Within this geoclimatic landscape, different groups in the MBA developed interactions based both on internal and external forces and elements. The groups located along the Euphrates River basin were heavily involved in intense cultural and economic exchanges with neighboring societies located to the south (i.e., the city-states of Syria) and the north (i.e., the commercial ports of central Anatolia), whereas most of the other eastern Anatolian regions show strictly local material culture, continuity with previous periods, and few examples of imported prestige objects. Within this perspective and as available from both textual and archaeological data, the availability of raw materials, such as copper and other metals, and commodities, such as wine and ivory, requested by Mesopotamian élites from this area, created a form of asymmetrical exchange between local and exogenous groups from which private merchants and entrepreneurs profited significantly (Yener 2007).

However, clear local differences emerge from the archaeological data available from the MBA of eastern Anatolia, and as a consequence, to have a better picture of this area during the first half of the second millennium B.C.E., we have chosen to divide it into three major regional environs that group together some of the previously mentioned ecological niches into the following: the Euphrates River Valley, northeastern Anatolia, and, finally, the Upper Tigris River Valley and the neighboring regions. The important MBA city-state of Girnavaz (Erkanal 1991), located in the Nusaybin province near the northeastern Syrian border, is not included in this contribution due to its limited archaeological investigation, an almost total lack of published reconnaissance surveys in this region and, most particularly, because of its geographic and cultural similarities with the city-states of the Syrian Jezirah that make it a unique case in the Anatolian side of this wide plain.

Chronological and Cultural Frameworks by Region

In terms of chronology, the whole MBA can be subdivided into two major sequences: the MBA I, ca. 2000–1800 B.C.E., and the MBA II, ca. 1800–1600 B.C.E. according to the Syrian chronology (Akkermans and Schwartz 2003:fig. 9.2). The first phase corresponds to the involvement of the area in the Old Assyrian Trade Colony system, whereas the second phase appears to be marked by local cultural phenomena and contacts with the Old Hittite Kingdom.

The Euphrates Valley

By the end of the third millennium B.C.E., the phenomenon of urbanization that characterized the Euphrates Valley experienced a dramatic decrease in both the quality and quantity of settlement patterns and urban fabric, thus reducing the density and size of most of the settlements (Cooper 2006). However, the Euphrates alluvial plain guaranteed the ecological circumstances necessary to develop a combined agropastoral subsistence economy, a crucial component for the socially transformed groups inhabiting this region. This allowed them to survive the dramatic climatic changes that affected the whole region during this period (Dalfes, Kukla, and Weiss 1997). Archaeological evidence suggests continuity in numerous sites between the Early Bronze and Middle Bronze Age (Marro 2007), although written records inform us about an increasing ethnic fragmentation of societies resulting from the presence of groups with a variegated cultural background, for example, the Amorites and the Hurrians (Nichols and Weber 2006).

The beginning of the second millennium B.C.E. (i.e., MBA I) is marked by a "regenerative" process of urbanization featuring either settlements that were previously occupied or the constitution of new ones, all of which increased in importance (Cooper 2006:275–77). Along these lines, the Euphrates Valley became a central passage area used by the Old Assyrian merchants on their usual routes to reach the major commercial ports (*kārums* in Akkadian) located in central Anatolia (especially at the ancient site of Kaneš [modern Kültepe], see Michel, chapter 13, and Kulakoğlu, chapter 47 in this volume). For example, the site of Ḫaḫḫum appears to be of great importance and was most probably located along the western bank of the Euphrates north of Şanlıurfa and across from Niḫriya (Barjamovic 2008; Forlanini 2006). Through an exchange of information between archaeologists and philologists, an attempt has been made to hypothesize the location of some intermediate stations (*wabartum* in Akkadian) or main ports. For example, the ancient site of Niḫriya has been associated with the ancient site of Lidar Höyük, and Šubat-Šamaš with Kazane Höyük (Forlanini 2006). This is, however, still in the realm of speculation, and only a few texts have been discovered during the archaeological excavation of these sites. However, the enactment of this commercial exchange was definitely a driving force in the development of settlement patterns along the Euphrates Valley, as is demonstrated by the architectural features discovered at numerous sites in which small areas featuring private dwellings were brought to light by archaeologists. Thus, the archaeological data of this period testify to an increasing presence of large centers (e.g., Carchemish, Samsat), medium-size sites (e.g., Lidar Höyük) and small fortified centers (e.g., Zeytinlibahçe Höyük, Şaraga Höyük, Horum Höyük) that probably served as fortified outposts along the river, based on the consistent presence of thick fortification walls at these sites (Abay 2007; Alvaro, Balossi, and Bloom 2004; Balossi, Di Nocera, and Frangipane 2007; Marro 2007; Sertok, Kulakoğlu, and Squadrone 2004). Of great importance for these smaller sites is the presence of areas dedicated to craft production such as potter's workshops (Balossi, Di Nocera, and Frangipane 2007:374–75).

The creation of city-states in southeastern Anatolia during the MBA II was further increased after the collapse of the Old Assyrian Trading Colony system (ca. 1730 B.C.E.). This circumstance may have developed, as understood from letters of Old Assyrian merchants found at the *kārum* in Kaneš (Michel 2001:118–70), by the turmoil that emerged among the rulers of local Anatolian city-states, such as Anum-ḫirbi, king of Mama and Ḫaššum, or by new restrictions and controls emanating from more centralized authorities, such as the Old Assyrian king Šamši-Adad I. The importance of these local rulers during and after the Old Assyrian Trading Colony system is also clearly rendered in the written texts from the royal archives of the most important northern Mesopotamian city-states, for example, the archive of King Zimri-lim at Mari/Tell Hariri and the archive of Šamši-Adad I at Šubat-Enlil/Tell Leilan. These texts testify to a continuous exchange of commodities, such as ivory and copper, as well as of skilled artisans, between the major city-states and peripheral units (Yener 2007). In particular, the cellars of the famous palace of Zimri-lim of Mari were constantly refilled with the famous wine produced and imported from the ancient city of Carchemish (Durand 1997:353). This extraordinary socioeconomic landscape of dynamic exchange was brought to a halt during the second half of the seventeenth century B.C.E. when we witness the military campaigns of the first rulers of the Old Hittite Kingdom, Ḫattušili I and Muršili I, in Syria and Mesopotamia (Akkermans and Schwartz 2003:325–26; and see Beal, chapter 26 in this volume).

With this historical perspective in mind, the written data also provide information about the different degrees of importance and the nature of relationships that the major political powers of Syria, for example, Mari/Tell Hariri, Ebla/Tell Mardikh, and Yamḫad/Alep, had with the Anatolian rulers. According to these texts, we can determine that the most prominent city-state of the MBA in the Euphrates region and surroundings was Carchemish, whereas Alalakh (modern Tell Atchana) and Ḫaššum were of secondary importance, while still functioning as the seats of important royal families which were vassals of the royal kingdom of Yamḫad (Marchetti 2006).

The increasing power of these southeastern Anatolian city-states is also demonstrated by the valuable archaeological data recovered in the excavations at these sites. Obviously, we are missing fundamental information available from the most important city-state (i.e., Carchemish), but other sites inform us about this period.

Thanks to the Turkish and, later, Turkish-Italian projects, the modern site of Tilmen Höyük, located in the valley of the İslahiye River in the modern province of Gaziantep, enhances our knowledge of the complex urban fabric that characterized these MBA city-states (Alkım 1969; Duru 2003; Marchetti 2006). During the MBA II (ca. 1750–1550 B.C.E.), the city was divided into a lower town and a citadel (figure 14.2). The lower town was marked by the presence of a temple, areas dedicated to craft production (e.g., metalworking), fortresses, a fortification wall planned with the creation of a casemate and two posterns, a monumental entrance with a two-sided statue of lions, and a staircase that led toward the main fortified citadel. In the fortified citadel, archaeologists discovered a royal palace (building A), a ceremonial building (temple E), a fortress (H), and another possible palace (C). The impressive architecture found at this site shows a continuous use of basalt blocks to construct both the monumental walls and the buildings found inside, as well as for the decoration of some of the rooms' walls with orthostats.

Another important city-state of the MBA in southeastern Anatolia is represented by the twenty-hectare site of Tell Atchana (ancient Alalakh), located in the plain of Antioch near the Orontes River valley; it was excavated initially by Leonard Woolley (1955) in the late 1930s and 1940s and currently by a team from the Oriental Institute of Chicago (Yener 2007). The site has multiple phases, and its chronological sequence has origins in the Neolithic periods. However, the most important phase of occupation, Levels VIII–VII, pertains to the MBA II period (Heinz 1992; McClellan 1989). During this period the site was the seat of the king of Mukiš, who was also a vassal of the kingdom of Yamḫad. The layout of the city is similar to other Syro-Anatolian city-states of this period. As in the case of Tilmen Höyük, it was divided into a fortified citadel and a lower town. Moreover, the fortification wall was similar to those of other northern Syrian cities, such as Ebla (Matthiae 1981), and was constructed with a very wide (about 15 meters) earthen rampart on top of which a thick mudbrick wall (about four to five meters wide) was built. The gateways were

Figure 14.2. Aerial photograph of the southeastern sector of the ancient city of Tilmen Höyük (phases MBA II and Late Bronze Age I) in which are visible (from left): Temple E; Royal Palace A; Fortress H and Gate K-6 with Building K-1; Area G; Building C and K5; and the monumental Staircase K-5 (courtesy Nicolò Marchetti, director of the Turkish-Italian Joint Archaeological Expedition at Tilmen Höyük by the Universities of Bologna and İstanbul).

also built using the traditional MBA chained chambers system sided by two rectangular towers. The famous palace of King Yarim-lim I (ca. 1790–1770 B.C.E.) was discovered by the archaeologists within the limits of the fortified citadel (figure 14.3). The royal palace was constructed next to the inner fortification wall using a terrace system; it was monumental in plan and had basalt orthostats decorating the lower part of the walls, wooden columns to sustain roofs and decorate doors, and, in some rooms, frescoes with naturalistic motifs that were reminiscent of the Minoan palaces (Woolley 1955). However, the most extraordinary element of the palace is the presence of a royal archive in the northern (official) wing, featuring cuneiform tablets written using a local Akkadian idiom. This important discovery allows us to determine the ancient name of the city as well as understand the socio-economic and political landscape of this period. Next to the palace, the archaeologists brought to light an *in antis* temple with very thick walls that recalls classic Old Syrian typologies; it was built using a fenced outdoor area and possessed a small antechamber that led to the main temple's cella.

Due to its size, the site of Tilbeshar (approximately fifty-six hectares), located in the Sanjur River valley about twenty kilometers southeast of Gaziantep, might also be considered among the MBA city-states (Kepinski 2005). The site, recently excavated by a French archaeological expedition, is a multiphase settlement. The initial archaeological data illustrate an MBA settlement in which the lower town (about

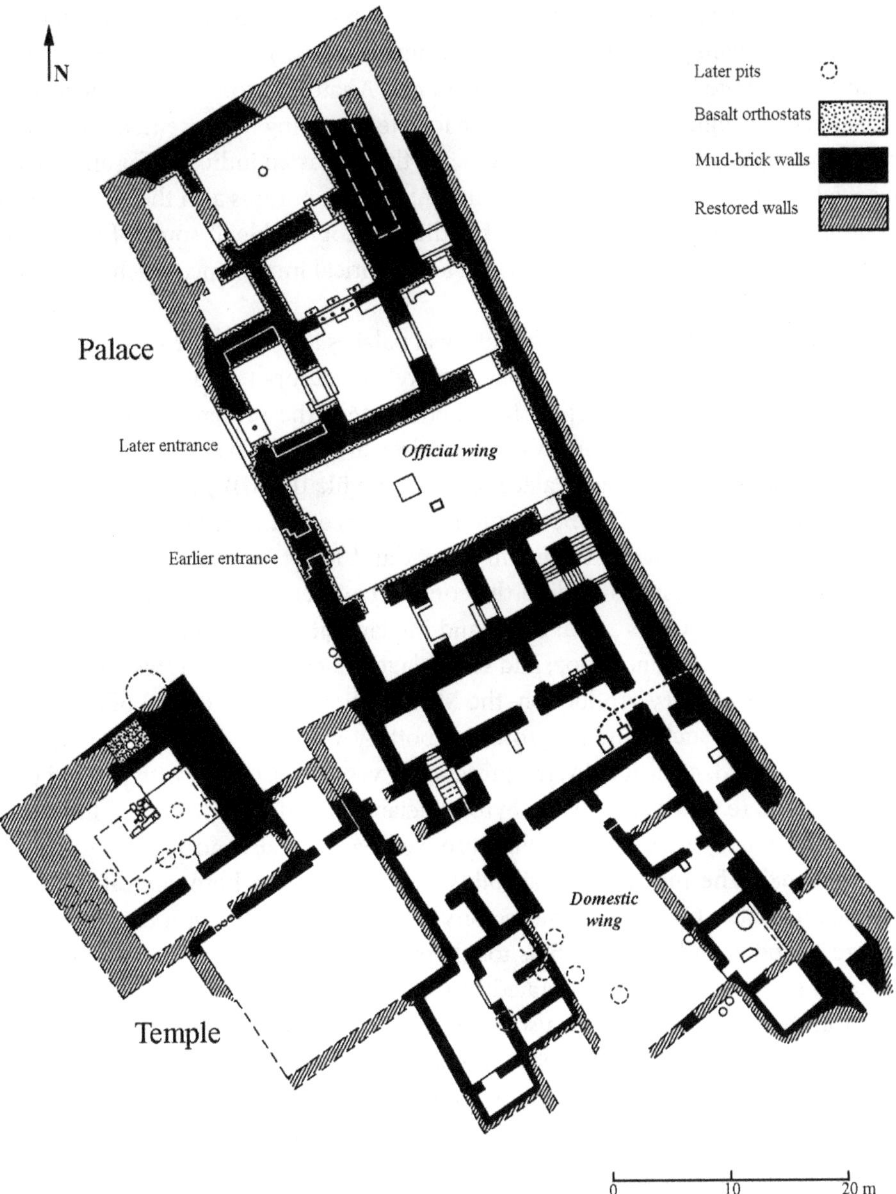

Figure 14.3. Plan of Palace and Temple from the MBA citadel of Tell Atchana/Alalakh (level VII) (redrawn from Woolley 1955:fig. 12).

fifty hectares of extension) revealed private dwellings separated by thoroughly planned streets, drainage systems, and outdoor areas in which graves were found. Signs of craft production areas were also found in the lower town, where it has been possible to define a clear cultural continuity between the Early and Middle Bronze Age phases (for additional discussion on the Early Bronze Age, see Ökse, chapter 11 in this volume).

The MBA period is thus a period of increasing visibility of local city-states in the Euphrates Valley as well as the surrounding regions. The enhancement in long-distance exchange between Mesopotamian and Anatolian communities during the MBA I period might have been the cause for the blooming of the settlements. However, it is not only the size of the settlements that act as an indicator for an increase in social complexity in this region during this phase, but it is also the monumental architecture of religious and palatial buildings recognizable at some of these sites that gives us a clue of the socioeconomic and political importance reached by these city-states.

In fact, the continuous presence of royal palaces and associated temples stands as a marker of the Syrian and Anatolian, as well as Mesopotamian, city-states especially during the MBA II period (Marchetti 2006). The presence of such palatial structures in Anatolia (i.e., the Waršama Palace at Kaneš Level VII corresponding to the *kārum* Ib, the "Sarıkaya Palace" at Acemhöyük, the MBA II Palace at Tilmen Höyük, the "Burnt Palace" at Beycesultan, the Palace of Yarim Lim at Alalakh VII, and, possibly, other palaces at Oylum Höyük and Kinet Höyük) witness the presence of important families leading the commercial network with exogenous merchants (Akar 2009; Gates 2000; Lloyd and Mellart 1965; Marchetti 2006; N. Özguç 1965; T. Özguç 2003; Yener 2007; and see Kulakoğlu, chapter 47 in this volume).

In terms of pottery production, the MBA embraces types typical of the Syrian cultural horizon, such as mass-produced pottery with coarser tempers and carinated shapes, and, occasionally, the presence of vessels decorated with painted geometric motifs (e.g., Khabur Ware, Syro-Cilician Painted Ware), incised lines (i.e., "comb-decorated" ware), and applied grooved bands (Kaschau 1999; Nigro 1998; Oguchi 1998). The increasing availability of copper (from both central Anatolia, Cilicia, and, later, Cyprus) in the region's market brought about a broader use of bronze weapons and tools, such as toggle pins with spherical and grooved heads, socketed spearheads, and fenestrated "duckbills" and shaft-hole axes, not only by the royal and religious élites but also by families of emergent entrepreneurs involved in long-distance trade (Yener 2007). Metal figurines made using portable trinket molds are also a late third millennium B.C.E. tradition that continues into the MBA period (Marchetti 2003). Handmade and molded human figurines are also typical of this cultural horizon. In addition, the cylinder seal impressions recognizable on the tablets found in the royal archive of the palace of Yarim-lim I at Alalakh/Tell Atchana helped art historians delineate the predominant type of iconography of this period, which consists of the famous scene of the king or the owner of the seal standing in front of a deity with a more diminutive goddess introducing them (Collon 1975).

In terms of iconography, the extraordinary discovery of the head of a male statue in basalt, considered by Woolley (1955) to be the head of the ruler Yarim-lim I, found in the palace of Alalakh, and the stele recently found at Tilmen Höyük (Marchetti 2006), on which a high dignitary is depicted standing before a deity, are fundamental elements in allowing the study of cultural connections between this region and Syria. However, the shift in the commercial routes for copper during the mid-eighteenth century B.C.E. from central Anatolia to Cyprus determined the stronger influences of Cypriot and Egyptian styles on the local material culture (Barjamovic 2008), as demonstrated by the frescoes and the head of an Egyptian male statue in basalt discovered at Alalakh Level VII (Woolley 1955). The cultural connection between these areas is also evident in the production of ivory objects found at numerous Syrian and Anatolian sites (e.g., Ebla, Acemhöyük, Kaneš, and Alalakh); moreover, the discovery of whole elephant tusks in the MBA II levels of Alalakh suggests that the ivory might originate from this region, indicative of the long-distance commercial exchange typical of this period (Yener 2007:fig. 1). Recent surveys in the Amuq region and near the site of Kinet Höyük (Yener 2005:197–200) demonstrate the possible location of ancient harbors in the area (e.g., the site of Sabuniye) and, consequently, the establishment of maritime commerce starting from this period (Akar 2009).

Given these data, we subscribe to Maurits van Loon's view (1985:36) that "second millennium Anatolia, due to its Syro-Mesopotamian contacts, underwent an amalgamation of three traditions [local, Syrian, and Mesopotamian] in religion and iconography." To this statement we would like to add that the artistic environment of the MBA expresses an "international style" that became typical during the Late Bronze Age, showing influences from both the Egyptian and the Minoan worlds (Molfese 2007).

The northern section of the Euphrates, including the Malatya and Elazığ provinces, is geographically quite secluded and during the MBA is marked by a local cultural horizon that is recognizable in the archaeological record from the sites of Arslantepe, İmikuşağı, İmamoğlu Höyük, Şemsiye Tepe, Pirot Höyük, Tepecik, Norşuntepe, and Korucutepe (Şerifoğlu 2007). At these sites, the recovered archaeological data give us a clear impression of a cultural continuity between the Early and Middle Bronze Age (Di Nocera forthcoming). Moreover, at Arslantepe, İmikuşağı, İmamoğlu Höyük, Norşuntepe, and Korucutepe fortification walls are found in the MBA II assemblage (Di Nocera 1998; Hauptmann 1982; Şerifoğlu 2007; Uzunoğlu 1985; van Loon 1980). In terms of other architectural features, most of the sites show rectangular private dwellings with stone foundations and mudbrick superstructure, as is the case at Imikuşağı (Sevin 1984). Arslantepe (level VI) features a private dwelling with a double horseshoe-shaped hearth in the main courtyard and a series of small rectangular houses placed next to circular and subcircular buildings in a pattern reminiscent of the Early Bronze Age period architectural layout. At Norşuntepe (Hauptmann 1982), the beginning of the second millennium B.C.E. is instead characterized by the abandonment of the Early Bronze Age palace and by the presence of several rectangular houses with rounded hearths. The importance of specialized craft production areas at the MBA sites of this region is demonstrated not only by the numerous architectural features associated with metalworking but also by the presence of features associated with pottery production, such as the example of the kiln found at the site of Tepecik (Esin 1982).

In terms of pottery, Black Polished Ware, Gray Ware, and Brown Burnished Ware are the most common categories of the Upper Euphrates region (Di Nocera

1998). Among pottery types, the jars with "rail rims" are very common. Even though the whole region seems to be marked by locally produced ware (e.g., both Plain Simple Burnished and unburnished wares), some imported examples are recognizable in the archaeological record, such as the Red Slipped Ware that can link the region with central Anatolia and especially the *kārum* (level II) at Kültepe (Di Nocera forthcoming) or the Orange/Red Burnished Ware that shows clear Hittite influences (Şerifoğlu 2007:table 1). A category of pottery that can allow us to indicate links with more eastern regions is represented by the painted ware decorated with geometric motifs (Çilingiroğlu 1984) (figure 14.4).

According to Şerifoğlu (2007:111–12, fig. 5) the whole area can be subdivided into three subregions, in which zone 1 (i.e., the region west of the Upper Euphrates Valley) has stronger links with central Anatolia (especially during the MBA II) and northern Syria, zone 2 (i.e., the region east of the Upper Euphrates Valley) is a buffer zone, whereas zone 3 (i.e., the Altınova region) has more connections with eastern Anatolia. This model for Zone 1 sites is further confirmed by iconographic *comparanda* between the few human figurines, such as a possible divine female figurine found at İmikuşağı (Sevin 1984), and stamp and cylinder seals found at İmikuşağı, Arslantepe, and Korucetepe, and those typical of central Anatolia and northern Syria (Şerifoğlu 2007:105).

Northeastern Anatolia

Moving further east toward the modern border with Georgia and Armenia, we encounter a more diverse geographical landscape characterized by the presence of mountains and uplands. In this environment, transhumance and nomadism have developed in conjunction with pastoralism as the primary form of subsistence for the groups inhabiting this region from prehistoric times until today. In this difficult geographical terrain, it has been almost impossible for archaeologists to undertake excavations or surveys, and only a few projects, most along the Baku-Tiblisi-Ceyhan pipeline project, have revealed data for the creation of a coherent chronological framework for this area (Laneri et al. 2003; Sagona 2004, and Sagona, chapter 30 in this volume). This is particularly the case for the MBA, which, compared to the previous period, appears to be typified by a dramatic transformation in settlement patterns (Edens 1995). In fact, we witness a decrease in the density of permanent settlements that are very small in size and feature buildings with small rectangular rooms built using a combined system of cobble and stone foundations and mud-brick superstructure with rounded hearths in the middle, for example, at Sos Höyük Level IV in the Erzurum province (Sagona and Sagona 2000:figs. 3–4), and an increase in cemeteries, for example the necropolis of Ani (Özfırat 2001:68–70), that appear to be linked to temporary encampments similar to modern summer encampments, or *yayla* in Turkish. Although some of these cemeteries include simple cist graves, most common in this period are artificial funerary mounds of different sizes, known as *kurgans*, which consist of single or multiple cist graves covered with small to medium stones; kurgans are most often located along the

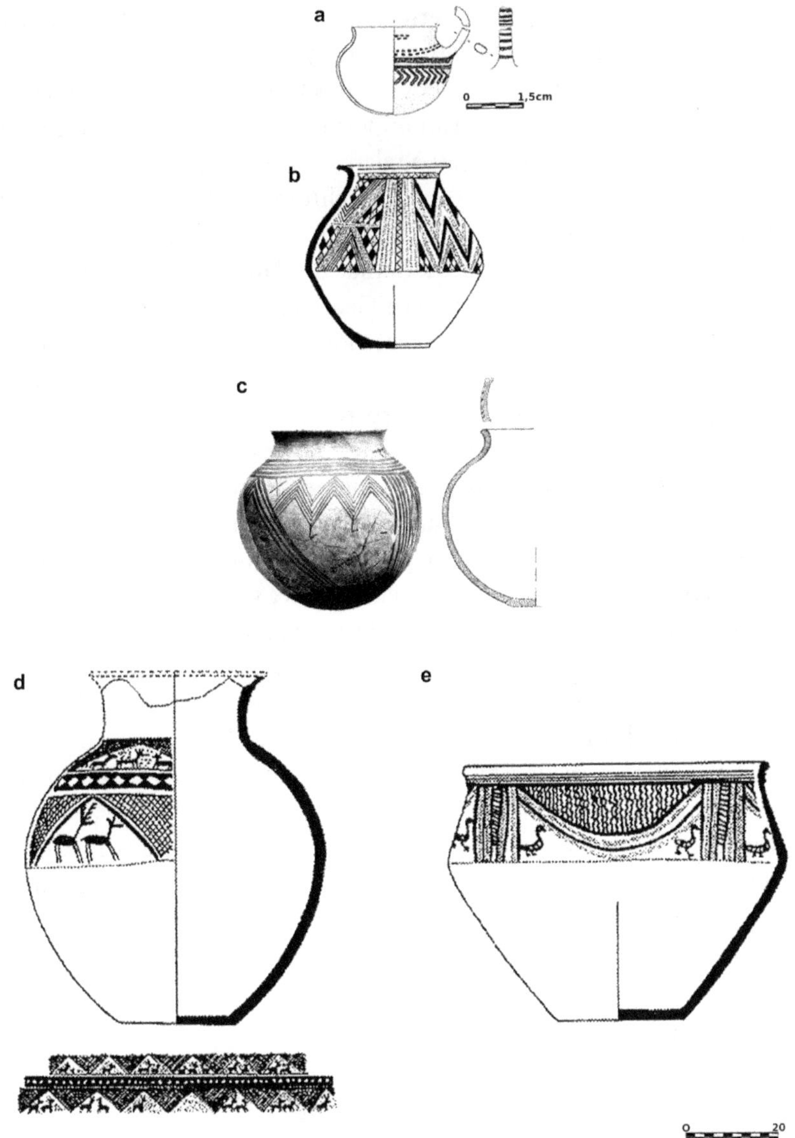

Figure 14.4. Drawings of MBA painted ware from (A) Arslantepe; (B) Van region; (C) Tepecik; (D and E) Erzurum region (redrawn from Di Nocera 1998:tafel 6.23; Esin 1972:table103.2; Özfırat 2001:lehva 38.1,4 and 103.4).

edges of hills (e.g., Suluçem IV [Özfırat 2001:71–75, photo 28–31] and Sos Höyük IVA [Sagona 2004]). This type of funerary deposition is typical of a particular chronological horizon, the Martkopi cultural horizon, that begins at the end of the third millennium B.C.E. and continues well into the Middle/Late Bronze Age transitional phase, for example, the Trialeti/Bedeni cultural horizon (Edens 1995). Moreover, these mounded funerary features mark a wide area of the upland landscape of

Transcaucasia that includes northeastern Anatolia, Georgia, Armenia, Azerbaijan, Nahçivan, and northwestern Iran (Puturidze 2003).

We have only a few remains of MBA architecture, and thus the pottery found within the tombs allows us to create an important typology to determine the cultural framework (and, consequently, the relative chronology) of this period. Black Burnished Ware, Brown Burnished Ware, Polychrome, and Monochrome Ware are the most represented ceramic categories found in funerary contexts of the MBA in northeastern Anatolia (e.g., Ani, Küçük Çatma, Sos Höyük IV) as well as in northwestern Iran, Nahçivan, Armenia, eastern Georgia, and Azerbaijan (Çilingiroğlu 1984; Özfırat 2001:23–26; 2008). In terms of morphological properties, the painted ware assemblage (figure 14.4) consists both of closed (e.g., short-necked jars with everted rims) and open shapes (e.g., deep bowls with inverted and externally thickened rim) with an overall brown slip and red, black, and white painted decoration that consists of geometric triangles and wavy lines, and animal (e.g., wild goats, deer, ducks, and snakes) decorative motifs (Özfırat 2001:pl. 114). Together with this assemblage, the presence of pottery resembling wares widely known from eastern regions, for example the Trialeti Ware, suggests a strong social and cultural interconnection between northeastern Anatolia and the Transcaucasian area (Puturidze 2003:5.3–5.6; Sagona 2004). Additionally, Black Burnished Ware, which is also decorated with incised decorative patterns (Laneri et al. 2003), can also be used to synchronize interregional chronological sequences in the Upper Euphrates Valley with areas located further east, such as Georgia and the eastern Black Sea coast.

As already noted, another important element of this period is the increasing quality and quantity of metal objects made of bronze, gold, and silver found in the MBA funerary contexts in the whole region south of the Caucasus (Burney and Lang 1971:86–126; Puturidze 2003:5.7; Sagona 2004).

The Upper Tigris River Valley

Many of the major sites along the Upper Tigris River Valley were originally identified by Algaze in his surveys (Algaze et al. 1991; Algaze, Breuninger, and Knudstad 1994), but only recent excavations, as part of the Ilısu Dam Rescue Project, have fully illuminated the social and political landscape of the MBA in this region (Laneri et al. 2009). In addition, due to similarity in pottery assemblages, it is still difficult to chronologically distinguish an early (MBA I) from a later (MBA II) phase of the MBA and, thus, in this section the MBA will be discussed as part of broader chronological horizon. Moreover, this area lies at a crucial intersection between the developing states of central Anatolia and the reconfigured city-states of northern Mesopotamia. During the late third and beginning of the second millennia B.C.E., the Upper Tigris River Valley was marked by the emergence of numerous small to mid-sized settlements (e.g., Üçtepe, Kavuşan Tepe, Kenan Tepe, Salat Tepe, Ziyaret Tepe, Hirbemerdon Tepe, Müslüman Tepe, Ahmetli Tepe, and Türbe Höyük) that show forms of cultural continuity between the Early and Middle Bronze Age.

However, it is during the MBA I that we witness an increase in terms of quantity and quality of archaeological data from this region.

Many of these sites were located on the Tigris's lower terraces, surrounded by the floodplain and cultivable terraces (Doğan 2005; Kuzucuoğlu 2002), and may have been situated in such a strategic position as to control arable land (Ökse 2006). The majority of these sites had important similarities, which include architectural features containing storage facilities at Kavuşan Tepe and Ziyaret Tepe (Kozbe, Köroğlu, and Sağlamtemir 2004; Matney and Rainville 2005), evidence of relative monumentality and centralized planning at sites such as Üçtepe Building Level 11, Salat Tepe Monumental Building, and the Hirbemerdon Tepe architectural complex (Laneri et al. 2006,2008,2009; Ökse and Görmüş 2006:fig. 7; Özfırat 2005), and signs of specialized craft production activities such as textile production at Salat Tepe (Ökse and Görmüş 2006), metallurgy at Kenan Tepe Operation C and at Kavuşan Tepe (Kozbe, Köroğlu, and Sağlamtemir 2004; Parker and Dodd 2003:36), and wine making at Hirbemerdon Tepe (Laneri et al. 2008, 2009).

Hirbemerdon Tepe provides us with the greatest amount of detail concerning the social organization of communities inhabiting this region during the MBA period. During this long chronological period (2010–1464 cal B.C.E.), the site's northern side of the high mound was characterized by the construction of a large architectural complex. Since the beginning of the archaeological work at the site in 2003, the Italian-American team has uncovered more than 1,000 m^2 of the architectural complex (Laneri 2005; Laneri et al. 2008:181). Spatial distribution and functional analyses of Hirbemerdon Tepe's different districts within the well-preserved architectural complex reveal that no building has any domestic features, such as central hearths or courtyards. The whole complex was differentiated into two main sectors: one central sector dedicated to ceremonial activities, and another area, separated from the central one by a long alley and a large outdoor space (the piazza) that is marked by long, narrow buildings built in an agglutinated manner with clear signs of working activities, such as mortars, pestles, grinding stones, and hydraulic facilities (Laneri et al. 2008:182).

In addition, this former sector dedicated to craft production was composed of narrow partitioned buildings, each with an entrance from the main alley. The architectural layout consisted of rooms for working activities and smaller rooms for temporary storage. The central room, paved with flagstones, may have functioned as an open area providing light for the other rooms (Laneri et al. 2008:185–86). As mentioned, all of the rooms in these buildings lacked hearths and were too small to have served as domestic spaces; the numerous ground stones found within these structures point to their use as food processing areas. Only one large room in this sector was probably dedicated to cooking activities as confirmed by the presence of a large circular burned feature and numerous cooking pots found in situ (Laneri et al. 2006).

Faunal remains from the architectural complex suggest that in general the animal economy was focused on domestic animals, with cattle supplying a significant proportion of meat. Deer hunting played a more important role than expected at this site during the MBA as is exemplified by the high percentage (approximately 35 percent) of deer bones encountered during preliminary analyses; this is quite high compared to other sites in the region (Laneri et al. 2008:195–200). In addition, the great abundance of deer antlers suggests that the hunting was focused not on subsistence but rather on craft production and ceremonial activities (Berthon in Laneri et al. 2009; Berthon forthcoming).

The botanical assemblage from Hirbemerdon Tepe is typical for the MBA in this region, in comparison to contemporary sites such as Tell Brak in northeast Syria (Charles and Bogaard 1997; Colledge 2004) and consists of cereal grains, barley, emmer wheat and wheat chaff, pulses such as lentils, and a single example of oat (Laneri et al. 2008:195). Similar assemblages were found at Kenan Tepe (Parker and Dodd 2003). Besides grain, wild or domesticated grape (*Vitis* sp.) seeds were also identified in these deposits (Parker, Creekmore, and Dodd 2004) as well as at Kavuşan Tepe (Kozbe, Köroğlu, and Sağlamtemir 2004) and Salat Tepe (Ökse and Görmüş 2006). A high density of seeds and the whole fruit of *Vitis vinifera* (grape) were recovered in a specific room of the production sector at Hirbemerdon Tepe (Laneri et al. 2008:194). The Upper Tigris lies within the natural range of wild grapes (Zohary and Hopf 2000). Because the grapes of Turkey have smaller and fewer seeds, a low acidity, and are moderately sweet, they are ideal for wine production (McGovern 2003:20). Moreover, agricultural statistics in the Diyarbakır province from 1933 to 1950 demonstrate the high yield potential of grapes in this region (Gorny 1996:144). Wine is mentioned in the Old Assyrian texts (Oppenheim, Reiner, and Biggs 1971:203), and viticulture is well established in southeastern Anatolia in the MBA (Powell 1995).

Some of the built-in basins and drainage installations found in the northern sector of the MBA architectural complex at Hirbemerdon Tepe could also be associated with wine processing. In fact, the high density of seeds and the presence of a whole fruit of *V. vinifera* found in a room with drainage installations, in context with a curved stone bench, suggests that this space was part of a productive unit dedicated to processing wine. These and other stone benches and basins adjacent to the main alley bear similarities to plaster basins used for grape pressing at the late third millennium B.C.E. site of Titriş Höyük (Algaze et al. 2001; Algaze and Matney, chapter 46 in this volume; Laneri 2007; Laneri et al. 2008:186).

How wine functioned within the political economy of the region is of crucial interest. Wine may have served to bolster élite power in the contexts of feasting (Joffe 1998), and the control of its production could have provided economic strength to emerging élite households (Laneri 2007). Contemporaneous evidence from the Sinjar in Iraq points to the importance of wine in the palace economy of second millennium B.C.E. urban sites such as Tell al Rimah (Oates 1970). More than likely it was exchanged across the Tur ʿAbdin Mountains to cities in northern Mesopotamia, possibly by merchants, as ancient texts seem to imply (Forlanini 2006). In addition, texts from MBA contexts in northern Mesopotamia state clearly that wine imported from southeastern Turkey (e.g., the Carchemish area) was exported to important Mesopotamian city-states, such as Mari (Chambon 2009). The important role played by exporting wine from southeastern Turkey to northern Syria is an element that should be taken into consideration when dealing with the region's economy during the MBA.

The control of productive activities in the settlements of the Upper Tigris region was probably enacted by local élites, who were also controlling the ceremonial activities within these complexes. This is clearly demonstrated by the case of Hirbemerdon Tepe, in which the central sector of the architectural complex consists of a large outdoor space (the piazza) and a series of buildings that might have had public purposes. This is especially the case for a building that lies east of the piazza that had one entrance from the main street and consisted of two vestibules and two long rooms with traces of altars built within them. In addition, the piazza itself likely had ceremonial purposes as demonstrated by the presence of a large stone basin and the deliberate disposal of numerous ritual objects (highly decorated ceramic vessels, human and animal clay figurines, and clay votive plaques) found next to the basin; such items have been found almost exclusively in this context (Laneri et al. 2008).

In terms of pottery categories, the area is marked by distinctive local wares that continue the tradition of the late third millennium B.C.E. Dark-Rimmed Orange Bowls (DROBs). The DROB has a distinctive dark red dusky-colored band along the exterior rim and chronologically belongs to a post-Akkadian, late third millennium B.C.E. horizon. DROBs have been found in excavations at numerous sites on the Upper Tigris region: at Üçtepe Level 13 to Level 11 (Özfırat 2005), at Kavuşan Höyük Level III (Kozbe, Köroğlu, and Sağlamtemir 2004), at Ziyaret Tepe (Matney and Rainville 2005), and at Türbe Höyük (Sağlamtemir and Ozan 2007), as well as on the surface of numerous sites in the area such as Tepeköy, Çubuklu, Gökçetevek, Karacalı, Eliaçık, Yukarı Bağpınar, Beşiktepe, Kayapınar, and Körtepe to the north of the Tigris and at Kazıktepe, Tavşantepe, İncirtepe, Türkmenhacı, Ziyaret Tepe, Kazancı, and Aktepe along the Upper Tigris (Özfırat 2005). Material culture belonging to this phase has been radiocarbon dated at Hirbemerdon Tepe to the late third millennium B.C.E. (2297–2198 cal B.C.E.). Advanced petrographic, geochemical, and mineralogical analyses of DROBs suggest that they were manufactured in the Bismil area of the Upper Tigris River basin and then imported into northern Mesopotamia (Kibaroğlu 2008).

As mentioned before, DROB have strong similarities with a pottery category that first appears during the late third millennium B.C.E. and then marks the repertoire of the MBA settlements in the region. This pottery has been defined by Algaze as Red Brown Wash Ware (RBWW) (Algaze et al. 1991:184) and represents a distinct local pottery tradition found at all the MBA sites in the Upper Tigris region (Laneri et al. 2008; Parker and Dodd 2003). Because of its likely iron-rich composition, the slip coating covering either the entire exterior vessel body or only its upper rim-shoulder section can assume a color ranging from red to reddish brown to black based on its firing conditions (Laneri et al. 2008:187; Özfırat 2005).

The RBWW typology demonstrates MBA characteristics, including carinated shapes, straight walls, and slightly everted rims (Laneri et al. 2008:189; Nigro 1998). Examples include open shallow bowls with a carination near the rim at Hirbemerdon

Tepe (Laneri et al. 2008:189, fig. 9), Giricano (Schachner 2002:fig. 35a), Üçtepe Level 11 (Özfırat 2005:pl. 34:13–18, 35–45; Sevin 1993:fig. 5:1–2), the Ziyaret Tepe brightly burned building (Matney et al. 2003:fig. 6:9–10), and deep carinated bowls at Hirbemerdon Tepe (Laneri et al. 2008:fig. 10), Üçtepe (Sevin 1993:fig. 4:2.4), and Ziyaret Tepe (Matney et al. 2003:fig. 5:5–6). Among the forms are numerous storage containers with a short neck and everted and externally thickened rims, as well as holemouth jars (Laneri et al. 2008:178). Moreover, decorative elements consisting of grooves and waves are usually applied below the rim or on the upper body of the vessel (Özfırat 2005).

Cooking jars with triangular lugs along the rim and decorated lids are also part of the pottery assemblages of the MBA in the Upper Tigris River Valley (Laneri et al. 2008:figs. 12–13). Moreover, the cooking jars were a standard part of the ceramic assemblage in this area as well as in other Anatolian regions since the mid-third millennium B.C.E. (Ökse and Görmüş 2006:187–88).

Cultural contacts with northern Mesopotamia are exemplified by the presence of Grey Ware at sites such as Hirbemerdon Tepe and Kavuşan Höyük in this region (Kozbe, Köroğlu, and Sağlamtemir 2004; Laneri et al. 2008), in addition to the presence of the characteristic painted ware from the northern Jezirah of Syria, known as Khabur Ware. This ware gives its name to the initial phase of the Khabur Ware period (ca. 1815–1550 B.C.E., Khabur Ware period 2–3 [Oguchi 1997:196–99, fig. 1]), and it has been found in small quantities associated with RBWW at Üçtepe (Sevin 1992:12–14, figs. 2–3, 1993:177, fig. 7), Kenan Tepe (Parker and Dodd 2003:66), Salat Tepe (Ökse and Görmüş 2006), Kavuşan Höyük (Kozbe, Köroğlu, and Sağlamtemir 2004), and Hirbemerdon Tepe (Laneri et al. 2006, 2008). At the site of Hirbemerdon Tepe all but three Khabur Ware sherds contained certain banded forms and were decorated using the same techniques as the RBWW rather than paint. These appear to be local imitations of this style from northern Syria, hence the application of the term pseudo-Khabur ware (Laneri et al. 2006:163, 2008:fig 13); the presence of pseudo-Khabur ware demonstrates a cultural influence from northern Syria rather than a large-scale material importation.

Cultural contacts and interregional exchanges with Anatolian as well as northern Mesopotamian regions are demonstrated by the presence of decorated andirons and portable hearths at numerous sites such as Hirbemerdon Tepe (Laneri et al. 2006:fig. 9), Salat Tepe (Ökse and Görmüş 2006:fig. 46), Müslüman Tepe (Eyyüp Ay, personal communication), and Üçtepe (Özfırat 2005:pl. 94:7, 95:13). Another distinctive cultural element of the Upper Tigris region is represented by the presence of decorated votive clay plaques (figure 14.5). These plaques were characterized by a central anthropomorphic or "stick" figure framed by a series of geometric elements. Some of these plaques were found at Hirbemerdon Tepe (Laneri et al. 2008) and Salat Tepe (Ökse and Görmüş 2006:176, fig. 21), whereas at Üçtepe tools used for decorating these plaques were found (Özfırat 2005:pl. 78:4, 79:4, 94:5–6). The plaques found at the MBA sites of the Upper Tigris are distinct from the contemporary ones discovered in southern Mesopotamia, and thus they appear to be unique examples.

Although societies in the Upper Tigris exhibit clear signs of complexity in the form of specialized production, ritual complexes, and settlement hierarchy, these

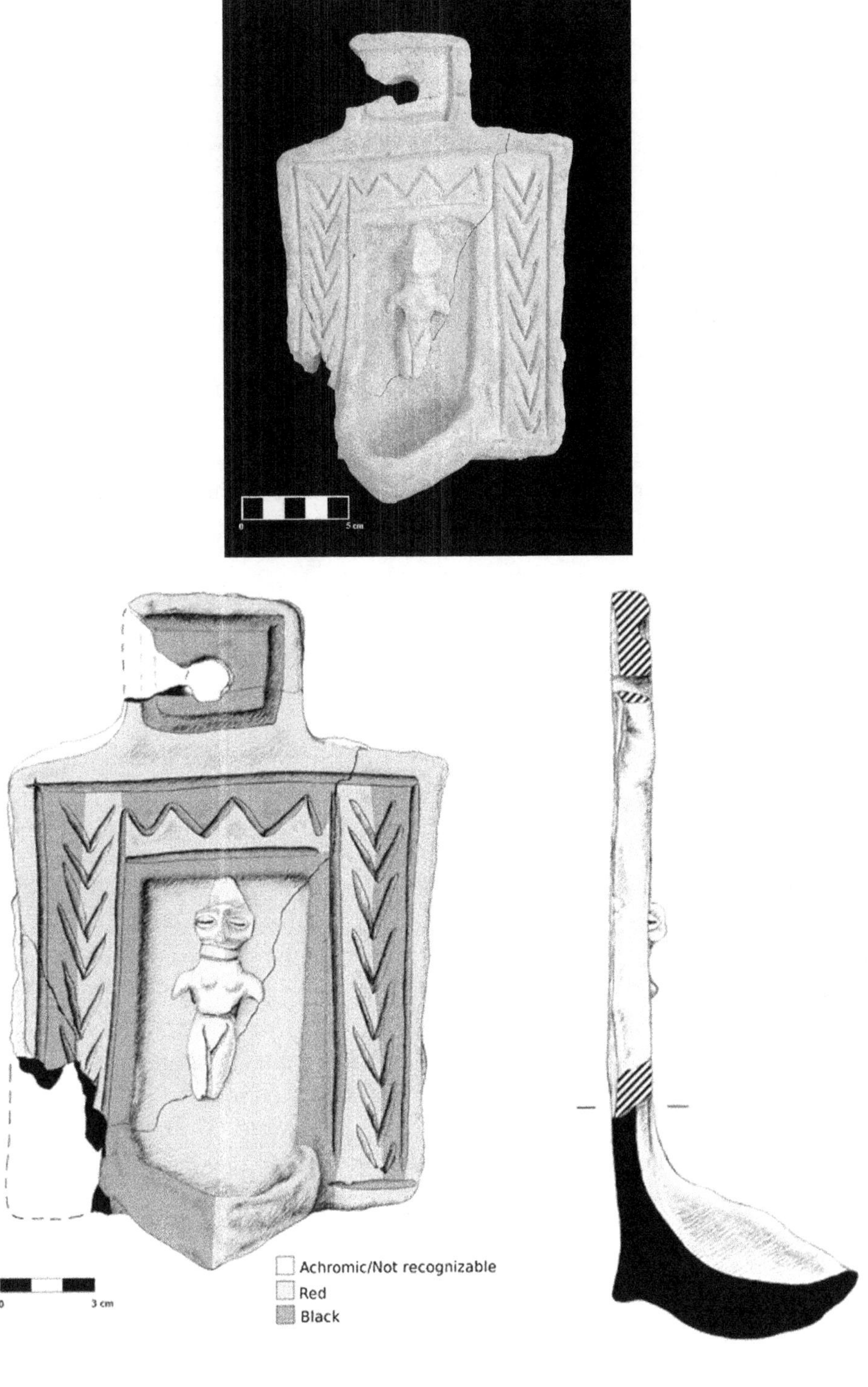

Figure 14.5. Photo and drawings (section and frontal) of a clay votive plaque found within the MBA level at Hirbemerdon Tepe (courtesy Hirbemerdon Tepe Archaeological Project).

communities do not seem to fit into classic hierarchical models of complex organization. For instance, elements of administrative control such as an impressed pottery fragment found at Hirbemerdon Tepe (Laneri et al. 2008:224) are rare and suggest the existence of an organization different from the standard Mesopotamian system of administration. In fact, apart from Pir Hüseyin, which has an area of about fifteen hectares but has never been properly excavated (Peasnall and Algaze 2010), none of the centers in the Upper Tigris exceed five hectares in size in the MBA, and there is no evidence that a hierarchical superstructure existed integrating these mid-range sites together.

It seems that a true heterarchical system of polities was operating in the Upper Tigris region (Crumley 1995), in which each mid-sized site served not as a population center but as a specialized production settlement, most likely serving a powerful kin group that legitimated its position through a ritual system that was publicly visible. The majority of the population most likely resided in small villages or pastoral communities (Ur and Hammer 2009) and contributed surplus staples and labor to sites such as Hirbemerdon Tepe.

Conclusion

It is clear from these data that southeastern and eastern Anatolia were more resilient than northern Mesopotamia and never endured the collapse suffered in northern Mesopotamia at the end of the third millennium B.C.E. On the contrary, the mixed subsistence economy and the relatively lower levels of urbanism and reliance on intensive dry-farming made these Anatolian societies more resilient and less prone to ecological disaster. Thus, the climatic catastrophe that devastated numerous urban centers of northern Mesopotamia did not affect the Anatolian regions, which instead show clear signs of continuity between the Early and the Middle Bronze Age periods. In addition, interregional exchange between these regions and northern Mesopotamia played an important part in the further development of these communities during the MBA and in creating the framework for the creation of important city-states, especially along the Upper Euphrates River Valley, and for strengthening local networks of chiefly estates, primarily in the Upper Tigris region.

NOTE

We would like to thank the Ministry of Culture and Tourism of Turkey and the Archaeological Museum of Diyarbakır for their support during our archaeological research in Turkey. To Nicolò Marchetti (University of Bologna) goes our warmest acknowledgment for providing us with aerial photos of the site of Tilmen Höyük.

REFERENCES

Abay, Eşref. 2007. Southeastern Anatolia after the Early Bronze Age: Collapse or Continuity? A Case Study from the Karababa Dam Area. In *Sociétés humaines et changement climatique à la fin du troisième millénaire: Une crise a-t-elle eu lieu en Haute Mésopotamia? Actes du Colloque de Lyon, 5–8 décembre 2005*, ed. Catherine Kuzucuoğlu and Catherine Marro, 403–14. Varia Anatolica 19. Paris: De Boccard.

Akar, Murat. 2009. The Role of Harbour Towns in the Re-Urbanization of the Levant in Middle Bronze Age II (1800–1600 BC). Perspectives from Cilicia and the Amuq Plain of Hatay. *ArchAtlas*, February, Edition 4. www.archatlas.org/workshop09/works09-akar.php.

Akkermans, Peter M. M. G. and Glenn M. Schwartz. 2003. *The Archaeology of Syria: From Complex Hunter-Gatherers to Early Urban Societies (ca. 16,000–300 BC)*. Cambridge: Cambridge University Press.

Algaze, Guillermo, Ray Breuninger, and James Knudstad. 1994. The Tigris-Euphrates Archaeological Reconnaissance Project: Final Report of the Birecik and Carchemish Dam Survey Areas. *Anatolica* 20: 1–96.

Algaze, Guillermo, Ray Breuninger, Chris Lightfoot, and Michael Rosenberg. 1991. The Tigris-Euphrates Archaeological Reconnaissance Project: A Preliminary Report of the 1989–1990 Seasons. *Anatolica* 17: 175–240.

Algaze, Guillermo, Gülay Dinckan, Britt Hartenberger, Timothy Matney, Jennifer Pournelle, Lynn Rainville, Steve Rosen, Eric Rupley, Duncan Schlee, and Regis Vallet. 2001. Research at Titriş Höyük in Southeastern Turkey: The 1999 Season. *Anatolica* 27: 23–106.

Alkım, U. Bahadır. 1969. The Amanus Region in Turkey. *Archaeology* 22: 280–89.

Alvaro, Corrado, Francesca Balossi, and Joanita Bloom. 2004. Zeytinli Bahçe, a Medieval Fortified Settlement. *Anatolia Antiqua* 12: 191–213.

Balossi, Francesca, Gian Maria Di Nocera, and Marcella Frangipane. 2007. The Contribution of a Small Site to the Study of Settlement Changes on the Turkish Middle Euphrates between the Third and Second Millennium BC: Preliminary Stratigraphic Data from Zeytinli Bahçe Höyük (Urfa). In *Sociétés humaines et changement climatique à la fin du troisième millénaire: Une crise a-t-elle eu lieu en Haute Mésopotamie? Actes du Colloque de Lyon, 5–8 décembre 2005*, ed. Catherine Kuzucuoğlu and Catherine Marro, 355–82. Varia Anatolica 19. Paris: De Boccard.

Barjamovic, Gojko. 2008. The Geography of Trade. Assyrian Colonies in Anatolia c. 1975–1725 BC and the Study of Early Interregional Networks of Exchange. In *Anatolia and the Jazira during the Old Assyrian Period*, ed. J. G. Dercksen, 87–100. Old Assyrian Archive Studies 3. Istanbul: Nederlands Instituut voor het Nabije Oosten.

Berthon, Remi. Forthcoming. Animal Exploitation in the Upper Tigris Valley: A First Regional View from Middle Bronze Age Hirbemerdon Tepe and Kenan Tepe. In *Güney Doğu Anadolu Araştırmaları Sempozyum Bildirileri 30 Nisan–1 Mayıs 2009, Ankara*, ed. Burcu Erciyas. İstanbul: Ege Yayınları.

Burney, Charles and David M. Lang. 1971. *The Peoples of the Hills. Ancient Ararat and the Caucasus*. History of Civilization series. London: Phoenix Press.

Chambon, Gregory. 2009. *Florilegium Marianum XI. Les Archives du vin à Mari*. Mémoires de NABU 12. Paris: SEPOA.

Charles, Mike and Amy Bogaard. 1997. Palaeobotany. In *Excavations at Tell Brak, vol. 1: The Mitanni and Old Babylonian Periods*, ed. David Oates, Joan Oates, and Helen McDonald, 128–30. London: British School of Archaeology in Iraq.

Çilingiroğlu, Altan. 1984. The Second Millennium Painted Pottery Tradition of the Van Lake Basin. *Anatolian Studies* 34: 129–40.

Colledge, Sue. 2004. Plants and People. In *Excavations at Tell Brak vol. 4: Exploring an Upper Mesopotamian Regional Centre, 1994–1996*, ed. Roger Matthews, 389–416. London: British School of Archaeology in Iraq.

Collon, Dominique. 1975. *The Seal Impressions from Tell Atchana/Alalakh*. Kevelaer: Butzon and Bercker.

Cooper, Lisa. 2006. The Demise and Regeneration of Bronze Age Urban Centers in the Euphrates Valley of Syria. In *After Collapse. The Regeneration of Complex Societies*, ed. Glenn M. Schwartz and John J. Nichols, 18–37. Tucson: University of Arizona Press.

Crumley, Carole L. 1995. Heterarchy and the Analysis of Complex Societies. In *Heterarchy and the Analysis of Complex Societies*, ed. Robert M. Ehrenreich, Carole L. Crumley, and Janet E. Levy, 1–5. Archaeological Papers of the American Anthropological Association, no. 6. Washington, D.C.: American Anthropological Association.

Dalfes, H. Nüzhet, George Kukla, and Harvey Weiss, eds. 1997. *Third Millennium Abrupt Climate Change and Old World Social Collapse*. Heidelberg: Springer Verlag.

Di Nocera, Gian Maria. 1998. Die Siedlung der Mittelbronzezeit von Arslantepe: eine Zentralsiedlung von Beginn des zweiten Jahrtausends v. Chr. in der Ebene von Malatya (Türkei). Arslantepe, vol. 8. Roma: Visceglia.

———. Forthcoming. The Beginning of the Second Millennium BC in the Upper Euphrates: Isolation or Strong Regional Identity? In *Looking North. The Socio-Economic Dynamics of the Northern Mesopotamian and Anatolian Regions during the Late Third and Early Second Millennium BC*, ed. Nicola Laneri, Peter Pfälzner, and Stefano Valentini. Tübingen: Studien zur Urbanisierung Nordmesopotamiens.

Doğan, Uğur. 2005. Holocene Fluvial Development of the Upper Tigris Valley (Southeastern Turkey) as Documented by Archaeological Data. *Quaternary International* 129: 75–86.

Durand, Jean-Marie. 1997. *Les documents épistolaires du palais de Mari 1*. Paris: Les Éditions du Cerf.

Duru, Refik. 2003. *A Forgotten Capital City: Tilmen, The Story of a 5400 Year Old Settlement in the İslahiye Region-Southeast Anatolia*. İstanbul: Türsab Cultural Publications.

Edens, Christopher. 1995. Transcaucasia of the Early Bronze Age. *Bulletin of the American Schools of Oriental Research* 299/300: 53–64.

Erkanal, Hayat. 1991. 1989 Girnavaz Kazıları, *Kazı Sonuçları Toplantısı* 12.1: 261–273.

Esin, Ufuk. 1972. Tepecik Excavations, 1970. In *Keban Project 1970 Activities*, ed. Sevim Pekman, 149–58. Keban Project Publications, Series 1, no. 3. Ankara: Middle East Technical University.

———. 1982. Tepecik Excavations, 1974. In *Keban Project 1974–75 Activities*, ed. Sevim Pekman, 95–118. Keban Project Publications, Series 1, no. 7. Ankara: Middle East Technical University.

Forlanini, Massimo. 2006. Étapes et itinéraires entre Assur et l'Anatolie des marchands paléo-assyriens: nouveaux documents et nouveaux problèmes. *Kaskal* 3: 147–76.

Gates, Marie-Henriette 2000. Kinet Höyük (Hatay, Turkey) and MB Levantine Chronology. *Akkadika* 119–120: 77–103.

Gorny, Ronald L. 1996. Viticulture and Ancient Anatolia. In *The Origins and Ancient History of Wine*, ed. Patrick E. McGovern, Stuart J. Fleming, and Solomon H. Katz, 133–74. Australia: Gordon and Breach.

Hauptmann, Harald. 1982. Die Grabungen auf dem Norşuntepe, 1974. In *Keban Project 1974–75 Activities*, ed. Sevim Pekman, 41–70. Keban Project Publications, Series 1, no. 7. Ankara: Middle East Technical University.

Heinz, Marlies. 1992. *Tell Atchana/Alalakh. Die Schichten VII–XVII.* Kevelaer: Butzon and Bercker.

Joffe, Alexander H. 1998. Alcohol and Social Complexity in Ancient Western Asia. *Current Anthropology* 39.3: 297–322.

Kaschau, Gundela. 1999. *Lidar Höyük: Die Keramik der Mittleren Bronzezeit. Archaeologica Euphratica, Bd. 3.* Mainz: Philipp von Zabern.

Kepinski, Christine. 2005. Tilbeshar—A Bronze Age City in the Sajur Valley (Southeast Anatolia). *Anatolica* 31: 145–60.

Kibaroğlu, Mustafa. 2008. *Petrographische und geochemische Untersuchungen an archäologischer Keramik aus Nordost-Syrien, Südost-Anatolien, Ost-Anatolien und Ost-Georgien.* Ph.D. dissertation. Institute for Geosciences, University of Tübingen.

Kozbe, Gülriz, Kemalettin Köroğlu, and Haluk Sağlamtemir. 2004. 2001 Excavations at Kavuşan Höyük. In *Salvage Project of the Archaeological Heritage of the Ilısu and Carchemish Dam Reservoirs Activities in 2001*, ed. Numan Tuna, Jean Greenhalgh, and Jale Velibeyoğlu, 463–504. Ankara: Middle East Technical University.

Kuzucuoğlu, Catherine. 2002. Preliminary Observation on the Tigris Valley Terraces between Bismil and Batman. In *Salvage Project of the Archaeological Heritage of the Ilısu and Carchemish Dam Reservoirs Activities in 2000*, ed. Numan Tuna and Jale Velibeyoğlu, 766–71. Ankara: Middle East Technical University.

Laneri, Nicola. 2005. Hirbemerdon Tepe 2003: A Preliminary Report. *Kazı Sonuçları Toplantısı* 26: 63–72.

———. 2007. Burial Practices at Titriş Höyük, Turkey: An Interpretation. *Journal of Near Eastern Studies* 66.4: 241–66.

Laneri, Nicola, Anacleto D'Agostino, Mark Schwartz, Stefano Valentini, and Giuseppe Pappalardo. 2006. A Preliminary Report of the Archaeological Cxcavations at Hirbemerdon Tepe, Southeastern Turkey. *Anatolica* 32: 153–88.

Laneri, Nicola, Özgür Gökdemir, Rosario Valentini, and Giulio Palumbi. 2003. A Note for the Preliminary Report of the Ardahan-Horasan Archaeological Survey in North-Eastern Turkey, 2001. *Annali dell'Istituto Universitario Orientale di Napoli* 63: 111–19.

Laneri, Nicola, Mark Schwartz, Jason Ur, Stefano Valentini, Anacleto D'Agostino, Remi Berthon, and Mette Marie Hald. 2008. The Hirbemerdon Tepe Archaeological Project 2006–2007: A Preliminary Report on the Middle Bronze Age "Architectural Complex" and the Survey of the Site Catchment Area. *Anatolica* 34: 177–240.

Laneri, Nicola, Mark Schwartz, Stefano Valentini, Anacleto D'Agostino, and Simone Nannucci. 2009. The Hirbemerdon Tepe Archaeological Project: The First Four Seasons of Archaeological Work at a site in the Upper Tigres River Valley, SE Turkey. *Ancient Near Eastern Studies* 46: 212–76.

Lloyd, Seton, and James Mellaart. 1965. *Beycesultan vol. II. Middle Bronze Age Architecture and Pottery.* Occasional Publications of the British Institute of Archaeology at Ankara no. 8. London: British Institute of Archaeology at Ankara.

Marchetti, Nicolò. 2003. Workshops, Trading Routes and Divine Figures: On the Early Middle Bronze II Syro-Anatolian Lead Figurines. *Orientalia* 72: 390–420.

———. 2006. Middle Bronze Age Public Architecture at Tilmen Höyük and the Architectural Tradition of Old Syrian Palaces. In *Ina Kibrat Erbetti. Studi di Archeologia Orientale Dedicati a Paolo Matthiae*, ed. Francesca Baffi, Rita Dolce,

Stefania Mazzoni, and Frances Pinnock, 275–308. Roma: Università di Roma "La Sapienza."

Marro, Catherine. 2007. Continuity and Change in the Birecik Valley at the End of the Third Millennium: The Archaeological Evidence from Horum Höyük. In *Sociétés humaines et changement climatique à la fin du troisième millénaire: Une crise a-t-elle eu lieu en Haute Mésopotamie? Actes du Colloque de Lyon, 5–8 décembre 2005*, ed. Catherine Kuzucuoğlu and Catherine Marro, 341–54. Varia Anatolica 19. Paris: De Boccard.

Matney, Timothy, John MacGinnis, Helen McDonald, Kathleen Nicoll, Lynn Rainville, Michael Roaf, Monica L. Smith, and Diana Stein. 2003. Archaeological Investigations at Ziyarettepe—2002. *Anatolica* 29: 175–221.

Matney, Timothy and Lynn Rainville, eds. 2005. Archaeological Investigations at Ziyarettepe 2003–2004. *Anatolica* 31: 153–88.

Matthiae, Paolo. 1981. *Ebla: An Empire Rediscovered.* Garden City, N.Y.: Doubleday.

McClellan, Thomas L. 1989. The Chronology and Ceramic Assemblages of Alalakh. *In Essays in Ancient Civilization Presented to Helene J. Kantor*, ed. Albert Leonard Jr. and Bruce B. Williams, 181–212. Studies in Ancient Oriental Civilizations 47. Chicago: Oriental Institute Publications.

McGovern, Patrick E. 2003. *Ancient Wine.* Princeton, N.J.: Princeton University Press.

Michel, Cécile. 2001. *Correspondance des Marchands de Kaniš au Début du IIe Millénaire avant J.-C.* Paris: Les Éditions du Cerf.

Molfese, Cristiana. 2007. Prime manifestazioni dello "stile internazionale" nel Medio Bronzo? Il caso dei sigilli e degli avori. *Kaskal* 4: 83–115.

Nichols, John J. and Jill A. Weber. 2006. Amorites, Onagers, and Social Reproduction in Middle Bronze Age Syria. In *After Collapse. The Regeneration of Complex Societies*, ed. Glenn M. Schwartz and John J. Nichols, 38–58. Tucson: University of Arizona Press.

Nigro, Lorenzo. 1998. Ebla and the Ceramic Provinces of Northern Syria in the Middle Bronze Age: Relationships and Interconnections with the Pottery Horizon of Upper Mesopotamia. In *About Subartu: Studies Devoted to Upper Mesopotamia vol. 1. Landscape, Archaeology, Settlement*, 271–304. Subartu IV.1. Turnhout: Brepols.

Oates, David. 1970. The Excavations at Tell Al Rimah, 1968. *Iraq* 32: 1–26.

Oguchi, Hiromichi. 1997. A Reassessment of the Distribution of Khabur Ware: An Approach from an Aspect of its Main Phase. *Al Rafidan* 18: 195–224.

———. 1998. Notes on Khabur Ware from Sites outside its Main Distribution Zone. *Al-Rafidan* 19: 119–33.

Oppenheim, A. Leo, Erica Reiner, and Robert D. Biggs, eds. 1971. *The Assyrian Dictionary of the Oriental Institute of the University of Chicago*, vol. 8. Chicago: Oriental Institute Press.

Ökse, A. Tuba. 2006. A Monumental Middle Bronze Age Building at Salat Tepe on the Upper Tigris (SE Turkey). *Antiquity* 80.309. (London) project galleries, antiquity.ac.uk/projgall/okse1/index.html.

Ökse, A. Tuba and Ahmet Görmüş. 2006. Excavations at Salat Tepe in the Upper Tigris Region: Stratigraphical Sequence and Preliminary Results of the 2005–2006 Seasons. *Akkadica* 127.2: 167–98.

Özfırat, Aynur. 2001. *Doğu Anadolu Yayla Kültürleri: M.Ö. II. binyıl.* Eski Anadolu Uygarlıkları Dizisi, 5. İstanbul: Arkeoloji ve Sanat Yayınları.

———. 2005. *Üçtepe II. Tunç Çağları (Kazı ve Diyarbakır-Bismil Yüzey Araştırması Işığında).* İstanbul: Ege Yayınları.

———. 2008. The Highland Plateau of Eastern Anatolia in the Second Millennium B.C.E.: Middle/Late Bronze Ages. In *Ceramics in Transition. Chalcolithic through Iron Age in the Highlands of the Southern Caucasus and Anatolia*, ed. Karen S. Rubinson and Antonio Sagona, 101–23. Ancient Near Eastern Studies Supplement 27. Leuven: Peeters.

Özgüç, Nimet. 1965. Excavations at Acemhöyük. *Anadolu* 10: 29–52.

Özgüç, Tahsin. 2003. *Kültepe-Kanis/Nesa. The Earliest International Trade Center and the Oldest Capital City of the Hittites*. İstanbul: Middle Eastern Culture Center in Japan.

Parker, Bradley J., Andrew Creekmore, and Lynn Swartz Dodd. 2004. The Upper Tigris Archaeological Research Project (UTARP): A Preliminary Synthesis of the Cultural History of Kenan Tepe. In *Salvage Project of the Archaeological Heritage of the Ilısu and Carchemish Dam Reservoirs Activities in 2001*, ed. Numan Tuna, Jean Greenhalgh, and Jale Velibeyoğlu, 547–602. Ankara: Middle East Technical University.

Parker, Bradley J. and Lynn Swartz Dodd. 2003. The Early Second Millennium Ceramic Assemblage from Kenan Tepe, Southeastern Turkey. A Preliminary Assessment. *Anatolian Studies* 53: 33–70.

Peasnall, Brian L. and Guillermo Algaze. 2010. The Survey of Pir Hüseyin, 2004. *Anatolica* 36: 165–195.

Powell, Marvin A. 1995. Wine and the Vine in Ancient Mesopotamia: The Cuneiform Evidence. In *The Origins and Ancient History of Wine*, ed. Patrick E. McGovern, Stuart Fleming, and Solomon Katz, 97–122. Cooper Station, N.Y.: Gordon and Breach.

Puturidze, Marina. 2003. Social and Economic Shifts in the South Caucasian Middle Bronze Age. In *Archaeology in the Borderlands. Investigations in Caucasia and Beyond*, ed. Adam T. Smith and Karen S. Rubinson, 111–28. Monograph 47. Los Angeles: Cotsen Institute of Archaeology.

Sağlamtemir, Haluk and Ali Ozan. 2007. Siirt—Türbe Höyük Excavation. Preliminary Report. *Arkeoloji Dergisi* 10.2: 1–32.

Sagona, Antonio G. 2004. Social Boundaries and Ritual Landscapes in Late Prehistoric Trans-Caucasus and Highland Anatolia. In *A View from the Highlands: Archaeological Studies in Honour of Charles Burney*, ed. Antonio G. Sagona, 475–538. Ancient Near Eastern Studies Series 12. Louvain: Peeters.

Sagona, Antonio G. and Claudia Sagona. 2000. Excavations at Sos Höyük, 1998–2000: Fifth Preliminary Report. *Ancient Near Eastern Studies* 37: 56–127.

Schachner, Andreas. 2002. Ausgrabungen in Giricano (2000–2001). Neue Forschungen an der Nordgrenze des Mesopotamischen Kulturraums. Mit Beiträgen von Peter V. Bartl und Josef Heigermoser. *Istanbuler Mitteilungen* 52: 9–57.

Sertok, Kemal, Fikri Kulakoğlu, and Filomena Squadrone. 2004. Şaraga Höyük 2001. In *Salvage Project of the Archaeological Heritage of the Ilısu and Carchemish Dam Resevoirs Activities in 2001*, ed. Numan Tuna, Jean Greenhalgh, and Jale Velibeyoğlu, 293–305. Ankara: Middle East Technical University.

Sevin, Veli. 1984. Imikuşağı. *Anatolian Studies* 34: 221–22.

———. 1992. Diyarbakır/Üçtepe Höyüğü Orta Tunç Çağı Seramiği. *Orient Express* 2: 12–14.

———. 1993. 1992 yılı Diyarbakır/Üçtepe höyüğü kazıları. *Kazı Sonuçları Toplantısı* 15.1: 399–416.

Şerifoğlu, Tevfik Emre. 2007. The Malatya-Elazığ Region during the Middle Bronze Age: A Re-Evaluation of the Archaeological Evidence. *Anatolian Studies* 57: 101–14.

Ur, Jason A. and Emily L. Hammer. 2009. Pastoral Nomads of the Second and Third Millennia AD on the Upper Tigris River, Turkey: Archaeological Evidence from the Hirbemerdon Tepe Survey. *Journal of Field Archaeology* 34: 37–56.

Uzunoğlu, Esin. 1985. İmamoğlu Kazıları 1984 Yılı Çalışmaları. *Kazı Sonuçları Toplantısı* 7: 181–200.

van Loon, Maurits, ed. 1980. *Korucutepe 3. Final Report on the Excavations of the Universities of Chicago, California (Los Angeles), and Amsterdam in the Keban Reservoir, Eastern Anatolia 1968–1970*. Volume 3. Amsterdam: North Holland.

———. 1985. *Anatolia in the Second Millennium BC.* Iconography of Religions 15.12. Leiden: Brill.

Woolley, C. Leonard. 1955. *Alalakh. An Account of the Excavations at Tell Atchana in the Hatay, 1937–1949*. London: Society of Antiquarians.

Yener, K. Aslıhan, ed. 2005. *The Amuq Valley Regional Projects Volume 1. Surveys in the Plain of Antioch and Orontes Delta, Turkey, 1995–2001*. Oriental Institute Publications 131. Chicago: Oriental Institute.

———. 2007. The Anatolian Middle Bronze Age Kingdoms and Alalakh: Mukish, Kanesh and Trade. *Anatolian Studies* 57: 151–61.

Zohary, David and Maria Hopf. 2000. *Domestication of Plants in the Old World*, 3rd ed. Oxford: Oxford University Press.

The Late Bronze Age

CHAPTER 15

THE LATE BRONZE AGE IN THE WEST AND THE AEGEAN

TREVOR BRYCE

In this chapter, the phrase "western Anatolia" encompasses the regions extending along Anatolia's western and southwestern coasts, from the Troad in the north to Lukka in the south, and inland to the regions stretching north and south of the (Classical) Hermus and Maeander Rivers. During the Late Bronze Age, these regions were occupied by an array of states and population groups known to us from numerous references to them in the tablet archives of the Hittite capital Ḫattuša.

Arzawa: The Historical Background

Prominent among the western Anatolian territories was a land called Arzawa (variant Arzawiya). This land appears a number of times in the Ḫattuša texts, often in conflict with the kingdom of Ḫatti. It is first attested in the reign of the Hittite king Ḫattušili I (r. 1650–1620 B.C.E.),[1] who conducted a brief raid into Arzawan territory (§3 of Annals of Ḫattušili I, trans. Gary Beckman in Chavalas 2006:220), perhaps in the context of disputes over the frontier areas that lay between Arzawa and Ḫatti. In the following century, Arzawiya was listed among the cities and countries that rose against the Hittites during the reign of the Hittite king Ammuna (Beckman in Chavalas 2006:231). In addition, around 1400 B.C.E., Arzawa appeared among the western countries that fought against and were conquered by the Hittite king Tudḫaliya I/II[2] (Garstang and Gurney 1959:121). Despite the apparent decisiveness of Tudḫaliya's western campaigns, hostilities between Arzawa and Ḫatti continued through the following decades, culminating in the invasion by Arzawan forces of Hittite subject territory in the reign of Tudḫaliya III (early to mid-fourteenth century B.C.E.), and their occupation of this territory up to the southwestern boundaries of the so-called Hittite homeland in north-central Anatolia (Bryce 2005:146–47). The success of their military operations, at the same time that other enemy forces were launching massive incursions into the homeland from other directions, prompted Amenhotep III, pharaoh of Egypt, to make diplomatic overtures to the Arzawan king Tarḫundaradu, offering him a marriage alliance, no doubt in the expectation that Arzawa was about to replace Ḫatti as the superpower of the Anatolian region (Moran 1992:31; see Beal, chapter 26 in this volume).

However, his approach to Tarḫundaradu was premature. The Hittites regained their lost territories in a series of retaliatory military campaigns of which the Hittite prince Šuppiluliuma, son of Tudḫaliya, appears to have been the principal architect (for more on the Hittite Empire, see Beal, chapter 26 in this volume). One of Šuppiluliuma's major tasks was to drive the Arzawans from the occupied territories in the southwest, in the region called the Lower Land. He apparently succeeded in doing so after a series of hard-fought contests. Nevertheless, Arzawa continued to threaten Ḫatti's western and southwestern frontier territories. An abortive Hittite campaign against the Arzawan leader Anzapaḫḫadu served to emphasize that the Arzawans remained a formidable military opponent. When Anzapaḫḫadu refused a demand from Šuppiluliuma to return refugees from Hittite authority, Šuppiluliuma dispatched to the region an army led by his commander Ḫimuili to enforce his demand. The Hittite army was ambushed and destroyed, and Šuppiluliuma was obliged to take the field at the head of another expeditionary force to complete the mission (from the "Deeds of Šuppiluliuma," trans. Harry A. Hoffner Jr. in Hallo and Younger 2003:vol. 1, 188). After his accession to the Hittite throne, he installed one of his ablest military commanders, Ḫannutti, as governor of the Lower Land, clearly intending this region to serve as a base for further military operations against Arzawan territories (Bryce 2005:151).

The Geographical Extent and Political and Ethnic Composition of the Arzawa Lands

From these scattered pieces of information, it is clear that Arzawa constituted a major threat to the security of the kingdom of Ḫatti from the kingdom's early days, and at one point in the fourteenth century B.C.E. may have come close to achieving political and military supremacy over much of the Anatolian region, even including the land of Ḫatti. That at least seems to be the implication of Amenhotep III's approach to Tarḫundaradu. But what do we actually know of Arzawa, its geographical extent, and political composition? In a broad sense, the territories comprising this land stretched from the Aegean coast through much of western Anatolia, from the Troad region in the northwest probably to the western edges of the Plain of Konya. Most scholars believe that these territories had been settled by large numbers of Luwian-speaking peoples during the early centuries of the second millennium B.C.E. This belief is based to some extent on the fact that the name "Luwiya" in early versions of the Hittite laws (§§5, 19–21, 23a, trans. Harry A. Hoffner Jr. in Hallo and Younger 2003:vol. 2, 107, 108) is replaced by "Arzawa" in later versions. It is generally assumed that the regions to which the two names refer were virtually one and the same. This leads to the further assumption that the Arzawa lands were occupied by Luwian-speaking population groups. But the explanation for the name replacement remains a matter for debate. Recently, Yakubovich has argued that the Arzawa regions were settled predominantly by ancestors of the Carian population groups, who occupied a large part of southwestern Anatolia from the late second millennium B.C.E. onward, as attested in Classical texts (see later discussion). He argues that what Luwian presence there was in the west may have been due (in part at least) to population deportation from south-central Anatolia, a major area of Luwian settlement, in the aftermath of Arzawan attacks on the Lower Land (Yakubovich 2009; and see Yakubovich, chapter 23 in this volume, for additional discussion of Luwian). For the more traditional view, that substantial numbers of Luwian speakers had spread into western Anatolia by the Late Bronze Age and were responsible for the formation of the Arzawa states, see Bryce in Melchert (2003:27–38). In any case, there seems no doubt that the Arzawan regions, and western Anatolia in general, had a substantial Indo-European population in the Late Bronze Age (Luwian and Carian are both Indo-European languages), although these regions almost certainly contained a large non-Indo-European population as well, whose ancestral roots may have extended back many generations—indeed many centuries—before the arrival of the first Indo-Europeans.

As a geopolitical term, *Arzawa* is used in Hittite texts sometimes in a purely generic sense, sometimes more specifically to refer to up to five states or kingdoms constituting the Arzawa Lands. The clearest references to individual Arzawan kingdoms are to be found in the texts of the Hittite king Muršili II, son and (second) successor of Šuppiluliuma, and Muwattalli II, Muršili's own son and successor (see Beal, chapter 26 in this volume). What was apparently the most important of these kingdoms became a prime target of Muršili's early military campaigns. On his accession, Muršili was confronted with aggression by many neighboring enemy countries and widespread rebellions among his own subject territories. In the west, Arzawa played a leading role in the uprisings. Here, a king of Arzawa called Uḫḫaziti sought to win or force Hittite subject states in the region away from their allegiance and provided asylum for refugees from Hittite authority. Muršili invaded and conquered Uḫḫaziti's kingdom in a campaign he conducted against Arzawa in the third and fourth years of his reign, though Uhhaziti himself avoided capture by fleeing to an offshore island (trans. Beal in Hallo and Younger 2003:vol. 2, 85–86). Many scholars believe that Uhhaziti's kingdom served as a political and military nucleus of the Arzawa lands. For this reason, it is commonly referred to as Arzawa Minor (or Arzawa Proper). Uhhaziti's royal seat was located at Apaša, almost certainly to be identified with the site at Ayasuluk, near Classical Ephesus (Büyükkolancı 2000). Here, perhaps, the invasion of Hittite territory in the reign of the Hittite king Tudhaliya III was organized under the leadership of the above-mentioned Tarhundaradu, who was conceivably one of Uhhaziti's predecessors on the throne at Apaša. After his victories in Arzawan territory, Muršili may have decided to end all further threats posed to his kingdom by Arzawa Minor by evacuating its population and allocating its territory to neighboring states. He claims to have deported 65,000 (or 66,000) of its inhabitants to the Hittite homeland. According to a proposal first put forward by S. Heinhold-Krahmer (1977:136–47), Arzawa Minor now ceased to exist.

Very likely the greatest (if not the sole) beneficiary of its dismantling was the kingdom called Mira. This was one of four western Anatolian kingdoms commonly designated as Arzawa lands. The others were Šeha River Land, Wiluša, and Hapalla. Hapalla was the easternmost of these lands and is probably to be located in central-western Anatolia to the northwest of the Hittite Lower Land. As a follow-up to his Arzawan campaigns, Muršili sought to consolidate his authority in the west by imposing vassal status on the kingdoms of the region. Treaties that he drew up with the rulers of three of them—Targašnalli of Hapalla, Kupanta-Kurunta of Mira-Kuwaliya, and Manapa-Tarhunda of Šeha River Land—are still partially extant (Beckman 1999:74–82, 82–86, 69–73 respectively). Also extant is a treaty which Muršili's son and successor Muwattalli II drew up with Alakšandu, king of Wiluša (Beckman 1999:87–93). This treaty partly confirms the identity of the above-mentioned lands as members of the Arzawa complex: "You are the four kings of the Arzawa lands: you Alakšandu, Manapa-Tarhunda [modern correction from Manapa-Kurunta in the original], Kupanta-Kurunta, and Ura-Hattuša" (assumed to have been king of Hapalla at the time) (Alakšandu treaty §14, after Beckman 1999:90). Could the Arzawa lands have once formed part of a single united kingdom of Arzawa, before their division into separate independent states? None of the surviving Arzawa texts give any indication of this. In fact, in one of the earliest of these texts, Arzawa (Minor?), Šeha River Land, and Hapalla are listed quite separately among the countries against which Tudhaliya I/II campaigned on his first of four campaigns in the west (Garstang and Gurney 1959:121). Wiluša (in the form Wilušiya) is the only "Arzawa land" to appear in a list of twenty-two countries forming what is commonly known as the Aššuwan Confederacy (Aššuwa was the name of the region in which they lay), which Tudhaliya defeated on his second campaign (Garstang and Gurney 1959:121–22). The Arzawan countries may sometimes have combined their forces for large-scale military operations, particularly against powerful enemies like the Hittites. But the confederacies they formed included states and peoples who were not part of the Arzawa complex, and on some occasions confederacies with an

Arzawan component did not extend to all the Arzawa lands. There is no indication that any sense of kinship ties or a common ethnic background had anything to do with the formation of these confederacies.

Nonetheless, Arzawa played a leading role in many of the western military alliances. The Arzawa lands are the only known western states with whose rulers Hittite kings, at least from Muršili II onward, drew up treaties. They are thus accorded a status that clearly differentiated them from other western Anatolian peoples and communities, with whom Hittite relations were apparently less formal and more irregular. The largest and most powerful of the Arzawa states, at least from the late fourteenth century B.C.E. onward, was the kingdom of Mira. I have referred to the likelihood that Muršili II incorporated much if not all of what we have called Arzawa Minor into its territory. It was further increased by the addition of a land called Kuwaliya. The latter has been plausibly located by Hawkins (1998:22–24) near the headwaters of the Maeander River, its chief city perhaps to be identified with the site of Beycesultan. The kingdom's northern boundary may have been marked in part by an inscribed monument located twenty-eight kilometers east of İzmir, in a pass through the Tmolus Mountain Range. The relief of an armed human figure is accompanied by a weathered inscription in Luwian hieroglyphs. The inscription, recently deciphered by Hawkins (1998:4–10), identifies the figure as a king of Mira called Tarkašnawa. This man occupied Mira's throne in the final decades of the thirteenth century B.C.E., during the reign of the Hittite king Tudḫaliya IV, and may well have been accorded by Tudḫaliya the status of a regional overlord, with extensive authority over much of the western Anatolian coastal region (see Bryce 2005:306–8).

To the north of Mira lay the country called Šeḫa River Land. Around 1318 B.C.E., the kingdom's ruler Manapa-Tarḫunda rebelled against Muršili II but resubmitted to Hittite authority to save his capital from destruction when Muršili's army prepared to lay siege to it (trans. Beal in Hallo and Younger 2003:vol. 2, 86; Beckman 1999:83 §4; see Beal, chapter 26 in this volume). Muršili accepted his submission, allegedly after Manapa-Tarḫunda had sent to him a deputation consisting of his mother and other elderly citizens to plead for mercy. Its territory was expanded to include a land called Appawiya (otherwise unknown), and the island Lazpa (Greek Lesbos) was also a dependency of it (see Houwink ten Cate 1985–86:44–46). A northwestern location for the kingdom thus seems assured, and the Šeḫa River itself is probably to be identified with the Classical Caicus (modern Bakır) or the Hermus (modern Gediz) River.

The other western Anatolian state included by the Hittite king Muwattalli II among the Arzawa lands is the kingdom of Wiluša. From a letter written by Manapa-Tarḫunda to his Hittite overlord Muwattalli II (Houwink ten Cate 1985–86:34–64), we learn that a Hittite army dispatched to Wiluša to restore order in the country proceeded into it by way of Šeḫa River Land. We may conclude from this that Wiluša lay north of Šeḫa River Land (because Mira was almost certainly the latter's immediate neighbor to the south), and if so, the only space left for it in coastal Anatolia is the northwest corner, that is, the region the Classical Greeks called the Troad.

We thus appear to have geographical support for the identification of Wiluša with Troy/(W)ilios, as first suggested by the Swiss scholar Emil Forrer in the 1920s and much debated since then. Most scholars now accept the identification—prompting fresh scrutiny of the Hittite texts that refer to Wiluša (see Jablonka, chapter 32 in this volume).

As already noted, the name first appears in Hittite texts, in the form Wilušiya, in the list of western countries forming the anti-Hittite Aššuwan Confederacy, ca. 1400 B.C.E. It is the penultimate name on the list. Taruiša, the last name, has been equated with Homeric Troia. In the *Iliad*, (W)ilios and Troia are used interchangeably for the city of Priam. A possible explanation for this is that their Hittite equivalents, Wilušiya and Taruiša, were originally separate but adjoining countries that subsequently merged, with local tradition preserving the latter's name until it resurfaced in the form Troia as an alternative to Ilios in Homeric tradition. Some time after the destruction of the Aššuwan Confederacy, Wiluša became one of Ḫatti's vassal states, and in the early decades of the thirteenth century B.C.E., its king Alakšandu concluded a treaty with Muwattalli II, as noted. Wiluša may have been occupied by enemy forces on at least one occasion during the thirteenth century B.C.E., and/or destabilized by uprisings among its own population (Bryce 2006:184). Toward the end of the century, its last known ruler, Walmu, appears to have been driven from his throne but was restored to it by the Hittite king Tudḫaliya IV (Beckman 1999:145).

A number of attempts have been made to link the snippets of information provided about Wiluša in Hittite texts with the Greek tradition of a Trojan War (e.g., Latacz 2004). In my view, none have been convincing (see Bryce 2006:182–86). Although the Late Bronze Age Level at Troy (Troy VI) does have a few (very superficial) similarities to the city of Priam described in Homer's *Iliad*, the destruction of this level, probably in the early decades of the thirteenth century B.C.E. (see Mountjoy 1999), almost certainly predates any of the thirteenth-century references to Wiluša. Also, none of the passages referring to Wiluša associate it with Late Bronze Age Greeks, with the probable exception of the so-called Tawagalawa letter, referred to below.

Aḫḫiyawa and its Role in Western Anatolia

Among the tablets found in Ḫattuša, there are twenty-six (mostly edited by Sommer in 1932), the majority of them very fragmentary, which refer to a land called Aḫḫiyawa, and sometimes to a king of Aḫḫiyawa. All are written in Hittite cuneiform. The now widely accepted identification of Aḫḫiyawa with the Late Bronze Age Greek world dates back to the 1920s when Forrer (1924) argued that Aḫḫiyawa was the Hittite form of the Greek name *Achaiwia*, an archaic form of *Achaia*. He noted that "Achaian" is one of the three names by which the Greeks are known in the *Iliad*. Late Bronze Age Greeks are now commonly referred to as Mycenaeans, a name coined in the late nineteenth century by Heinrich Schliemann from Mycenae, the archetypal Late Bronze Greek site, and in Greek legendary tradition the seat of Agamemnon, leader of the Greek forces in the Trojan War. On the basis of its Mycenaean identification, the term Aḫḫiyawa appears to be used in Hittite texts (1) as a general ethnogeographical designation encompassing all areas of Mycenaean settlement, both in mainland Greece and overseas; (2) to designate a specific Mycenaean kingdom, at least one of whose rulers corresponded with his counterpart in Ḫatti; and (3) to designate this kingdom in a broader sense, including the territories attached to it as political and military dependencies. Mycenae is generally assumed to have been the seat of the kingdom called Aḫḫiyawa in Hittite texts, but Thebes in Boeotia has also been suggested (see, e.g., Latacz 2004:242–44). What is of particular importance in the identification of the Mycenaean world with Aḫḫiyawa is that the Aḫḫiyawa texts provide our very first written sources of information on the contacts, relationships, and interactions between the Greek and Near Eastern worlds.

This information provides a valuable complement to the relevant archaeological data—which on their own have told us little about the nature of Aegean–Near Eastern contacts in the Late Bronze Age. Mycenaean products have come to light at a large number of sites along Anatolia's Aegean coast as well as in Rhodes, Cyprus, Egypt, and the Levant. But the evidence for an actual Mycenaean presence in these regions is extremely sparse. Mycenaean settlements on Rhodes and other islands of the Dodecanese may have been no more than merchant enclaves within a native population, and we have no evidence that Mycenaeans ever established settlements in Cyprus or on the Levantine coast. Indeed, it is questionable whether the presence of Mycenaean artifacts at the great majority of sites where they were found indicate that Mycenaean merchants themselves were directly involved in trading activities at these sites. Much of the trade in Mycenaean products may have been in the hands of intermediaries, like the merchant-operators of the ill-fated vessels that foundered off the coast of southwestern Anatolia (the Uluburun and Cape Gelidonya wrecks). The only clear evidence we have for significant Mycenaean settlement anywhere in the Near Eastern region is at Miletus on the southwestern Anatolian coast, at the mouth of the Maeander River, and at the site now called Müsgebi, further to the south, where a large number of Late Helladic IIIA–C chamber tombs have come to light (Mee 1978:137–42).

The earliest archaeologically attested Aegean settlers at Miletus were immigrants from Minoan Crete. Two periods of Minoan settlement have been identified. The first dates to the Middle Bronze Age (c. 2000–1650 B.C.E.; Miletus Level III), extending from the Middle Minoan IA to the Middle Minoan IIB Period. The second postdates the destruction of the city ca. 1650 B.C.E., and belongs to the first of the city's three Late Bronze Age phases (Level IV). Evidence of the earlier period of Minoan settlement is provided, according to the site's excavator W.-D. Niemeier, by a substantial quantity of Minoan domestic ware and a couple of Minoan-type seals and a seal impression that may be indicative of a Minoan administration (Niemeier 2005:3). Evidence of the later period is provided by Minoan-type kitchenware (including tripod cooking pots and large quantities of domestic pottery) and fragments of frescoes, Minoan in both technique and content, from the wall of a building that may have been used for cultic purposes.

The destruction of the second Minoan settlement in the first half of the fifteenth century B.C.E. may have been due to Mycenaean conquerors. A Mycenaean settlement was perhaps established on the site at this time, if we can so judge from the substantial quantity of Mycenaean pottery and a number of Mycenaean-type tombs found at Miletus and dating to this period (Miletus V). But the clearest evidence for Mycenaean settlement belongs to Level VI, in the city's third and final Late Bronze Age phase beginning ca. 1400 B.C.E. The city's fortifications, Mycenaean-type pottery, domestic architecture, and burial practices all seem to indicate that the city in this phase of its existence was predominantly a Mycenaean settlement, though still with a significant admixture of Anatolian elements. (For comprehensive treatments of both the Minoan and the Mycenaean presence in western Anatolia, see Niemeier 1998, 2005.)

In this context we can begin correlating archaeological data about western Anatolia with information provided by Hittite texts. In these texts, Miletus is called Milawata, or Millawanda. The Hittite king Muršili II reports that in his third regnal year, ca. 1318 B.C.E., he dispatched a Hittite army to destroy Milawata for joining an alliance with a king of Aḫḫiyawa (Goetze 1933:36–37). The implication is that Milawata was considered a Hittite subject territory at that time and had broken its allegiance to Ḫatti. In the same year, the Arzawan king Uḫḫaziti was forced to flee Hittite authority, as we have noted, taking refuge on one of the offshore islands that were under the control of the Aḫḫiyawan king (see Beal, chapter 26 in this volume). In a letter that a Hittite king, almost certainly Ḫattušili III, grandson and second successor of Muršili, wrote to his Aḫḫiyawan counterpart (the first part of the letter that must have contained both author's and recipient's names is now lost), Aḫḫiyawa again appears to have been a disruptive force in the western Anatolian region (Garstang and Gurney 1959:111–14; Sommer 1932:2–194). On this occasion, its king was accused of supporting the activities of a man called Piyamaradu, leader of anti-Hittite resistance movements in the west. (Piyamaradu is in fact the principal subject of the letter that is commonly but inappropriately referred to as the Tawagalawa letter.) The Hittite king sought Aḫḫiyawan cooperation in putting an end to his operations in Hittite subject territory. In this letter also, the author indicates that Wiluša had once been the subject of a dispute, perhaps even a military conflict, in which he had engaged with his Aḫḫiyawan counterpart (see Güterbock 1986:37).

Hittite texts thus provide an important additional dimension to the study of Late Bronze Age Greek contacts with western Anatolia. On the basis of archaeological evidence alone, we might conclude that these contacts were confined to trading activities (which were perhaps conducted in many cases by intermediaries), of which the Mycenaean settlement established ca. 1400 B.C.E. at Miletus may have provided the focal point, in the wake of earlier Minoan trading colonies on the site. But written evidence makes clear that Aḫḫiyawans were politically and militarily involved in the region as well. Already around the end of the fifteenth century B.C.E., an Aḫḫiyawan leader called Attaršiya (Attarišiya) had established a base in western Anatolia and had at his disposal a small army of infantry and 100 chariots (Beckman 1999:156). He appears not to have had the status of a king (LUGAL) (see Bryce 2006:102). But his military enterprises may have paved the way for later Aḫḫiyawan kings to attempt to establish control over parts of the Anatolian coastlands, perhaps using disaffected Hittite subjects as the agents for the expansion of their interests in this region. Inevitably, this constituted a serious challenge to Hittite sovereignty in the western Anatolian states. Disaffection with Hittite rule in a number of these states may well have encouraged Aḫḫiyawan enterprise. In the face of this challenge, and in the light of the Hittites' general reluctance to commit their military resources to repeated campaigns in the west, Hittite kings may have sought to resolve the crises in the region by diplomacy wherever possible rather than by force. Thus it is likely that Miletus, though subject to Ḫatti in the early years of Muršili II's reign, was ceded by the end of the century to a king of Aḫḫiyawa, and henceforth became subject territory of this king, as acknowledged by Ḫattušili in the Tawagalawa letter. This is consistent with the archaeological data, which indicate that Miletus was a substantially Mycenaean settlement at this time (extracts in Garstang and Gurney 1959:111–15; Sommer 1932:2–196).

In the course of his letter, Ḫattušili refers to his addressee as "My Brother," and "Great King," thus ranking him as one of the Great Kings of the Near Eastern world. (Other members of this exclusive group were the rulers of Assyria, Babylon, and Egypt.) But it is very likely that the use of these honorifics in the Hittite letter may simply be a piece of ad hoc political expediency, used by Ḫattušili to win the goodwill and cooperation of his addressee, rather than a genuine acknowledgment of the Aḫḫiyawan's actual status in the Near Eastern world. None of the other Great Kings make even a passing reference to a king of Aḫḫiyawa (or for that matter to a country called Aḫḫiyawa), let alone accord such a king a status equal to their own. But if Ḫattušili did seek by diplomatic means to win Aḫḫiyawan cooperation in restoring stability to the Hittites' western states, his efforts appear to have failed. Aḫḫiyawa continued to threaten the Hittites' hold over their western territories. In the reign of Ḫattušili's son and successor, Tudḫaliya IV, an Aḫḫiyawan king (perhaps the successor of Ḫattušili's addressee) was accused of aiding and abetting another anti-Hittite rebellion in the west. In this case, the uprising was led by a man called Tarḫunaradu who had seized the throne of Šeḫa River Land from its legitimate Hittite-endorsed occupant (Bryce 2005:304–5).

Quite possibly, the Aḫḫiyawan king's support of the rebel was one of the factors that prompted Tudḫaliya to set about removing the Aḫḫiyawan presence once and for all from western Anatolia—if we may so conjecture from a document dated to Tudḫaliya's reign and commonly known as the Milawata letter (Beckman 1999:144–46). The letter is very fragmentary, and its interpretation is problematic.

But one of the conclusions to be drawn from it is that Tudḫaliya eventually succeeded in restoring Milawata/Miletus to Hittite overlordship. If so, he would thus have deprived the Aḫḫiyawan king of his only known base of operations in Anatolia. It is just possible that the end of the Aḫḫiyawan power in Anatolia is reflected in the draft of a treaty that Tudḫaliya drew up with his Syrian vassal Šaušgamuwa, ruler of the kingdom called Amurru. Originally, the king of Aḫḫiyawa was among the Great Kings listed on the tablet. But his name was removed by having a line drawn through it while the clay was still soft (Beckman 1999:106 §11). There are of course a number of possible explanations for the erasure.

Other Western Anatolian Peoples

In addition to the Arzawan kingdoms, the western Anatolian geopolitical complex consisted of a number of peoples, countries, and communities over which Hittite influence was less direct. The country called Maša was one of these. It probably lay in the northwestern sector of Anatolia. The name has been linked, very conjecturally, with the Maeonians of Classical legendary tradition, whose homeland lay at the base of Mt. Tmolus (modern Boz Dağı) in the region of Lydia. Apparently governed by a council of elders rather than a king, Maša was not part of the Hittite vassal system—though the Hittites took military action against it when it provided asylum for a rebel Hittite vassal who sought refuge there (Bryce 2005:212–14). A contingent from Maša fought on the Hittite side in the battle of Qadesh, probably in a mercenary capacity (Gardiner 1960:8). In a recently discovered inscription in Ḫattuša, the so-called Südburg inscription, Maša is listed among the western lands conquered and annexed by the last Hittite king Šuppiluliuma II (1207–B.C.E.) (Hawkins 1995:22–23). It thus appears to have been incorporated into Hittite subject territory as the kingdom of Ḫatti was entering its final years.

Also in the west lay the country Karkiša, which like Maša was governed by a council of elders. It, too, remained independent of Hittite authority, sometimes collaborating with the Hittites, sometimes in conflict with them. The name Karkiša may be etymologically linked with that of Caria, a country occupying a large part of southwestern Anatolia during the Classical Period. Herodotus (1.171) states that the Carians came there as immigrants from the Aegean islands, after being displaced from their original homelands by Ionian and Dorian Greeks. But he notes that the Carians themselves claimed that they were native Anatolians, and had always been called Carians. Homer's reference to them in the *Iliad* (2.867) as "speakers of a barbarian language" clearly distinguishes them from immigrant Greeks. Though we cannot draw any firm conclusions from these literary sources, it remains a distinct possibility that the Carians of the Classical Period had ancestral roots in Late Bronze Age Anatolia—consistent with Yakubovich's theory that the occupants of the Arzawa lands were at least in part of proto-Carian stock.

A further, and perhaps more clear-cut, example of population continuity between the Late Bronze and Iron Ages is provided by the inhabitants of Lukka, or the Lukka lands. Lukka-people, who were among the Luwian-speaking population groups, are referred to relatively frequently in Hittite texts, with an occasional reference to them in Egyptian records as well (see Bryce in Melchert 2003:40–45). We can conclude from the Hittite sources that the term *Lukka* was used not in reference to a state with a clearly defined political organization but to a conglomerate of independent communities, with close ethnic affinities and lying within a roughly definable region in southwestern Anatolia, extending from the western end of Pamphylia through Lycaonia, Pisidia, and Lycia (the later Classical names). Furthermore, although it seems clear that there was a central Lukka region, a "Lukka homeland," various elements of the Lukka population may have been widely scattered through southern and western Anatolia, and may in some cases have settled temporarily or permanently in states with formal political organizations. The first millennium B.C.E. country called Lycia (Lykia) in Classical texts was almost certainly part of the region occupied by the Late Bronze Age Lukka people. Indeed the name *Lycia* appears to have been derived from Lukka—though unwittingly, since Classical tradition assigned various Greek etymologies (all false) to the name. In their own language, the Lycians called their country Trm̃misa and themselves Trm̃mili. The Lycian language, attested in ca. 200 inscriptions carved in stone (mainly on rock-cut tombs), has a number of affinities with the Bronze Age Luwian language (see Melchert, chapter 31, and Yakubovich, chapter 23 in this volume). Some of the major Lycian deities are of Bronze Age origin. In addition, Luwian onomastic elements are found in the inscriptions of Lycia, Pisidia, Pamphylia, Isauria, Lycaonia, and Cilicia, with a particular concentration of Luwian names in Lycia and Cilicia Tracheia/Aspera (Rough Cilicia) (Houwink ten Cate 1965). These areas almost certainly continued to be inhabited by peoples of Luwian ethnic origin until at least the early first millennium C.E. They provide the most enduring link we have between Anatolia's Late Bronze Age civilizations and their successors in the Iron Age and Classical Periods.

Conclusion

During the Late Bronze Age, western Anatolia was the homeland of a wide range of states and population groups. The most important and most powerful of these was a group of kingdoms that are attested in Hittite texts as the Arzawa Lands. Most scholars associate the development of these kingdoms with Luwian-speaking populations who had occupied large parts of Anatolia from (at least) the early second millennium B.C.E. Though their rulers became vassals of the Great King of Ḫatti, they frequently took up arms against their overlord and were prone to forming military confederacies, which ultimately threatened the security of Hittite core territory. Interference in western Anatolian affairs by rulers from a land called Aḫḫiyawa in Hittite texts further increased the region's volatility. Almost all scholars now agree that Aḫḫiyawa refers to the Mycenaean Greek world. Miletus, called Milawata (Millawanda) in Hittite texts, became for a time subject territory of a king of Aḫḫiyawa, and the base for Aḫḫiyawan enterprises in the region. The city had previously been settled, in the Middle and early Late Bronze Ages, by immigrants from Minoan Crete. Maša and Karkiša were among the western Anatolian lands that remained independent of Hittite control. Karkiša's population may have had ethnic links with the later Carians. But the most enduring link between Anatolia's Late Bronze Age civilizations and their first millennium B.C.E. successors is provided by the Lukka people, one of the Luwian-speaking population groups of southwestern Anatolia. They were almost certainly among the most important agents for the continuity and spread of Luwian culture in southern Anatolia throughout the first millennium B.C.E.

NOTES

1. All regnal dates are approximate, and are based on the so-called Middle Chronology.
2. It is uncertain whether there were one or two Hittite kings of this name in the late fourteenth to early thirteenth century B.C.E.

REFERENCES

Primary Sources

Herodotus. *The Histories*. Trans. Robin Waterfield. Oxford: Oxford University Press, 1998.
Homer. *Iliad*. Trans. Richmond Lattimore, *The* Iliad *of Homer*. Chicago: University of Chicago Press, 1961.

Secondary Sources

Beckman, Gary. 1999. *Hittite Diplomatic Texts*, 2nd ed. Atlanta: Scholars Press.
Bryce, Trevor R. 2005. *The Kingdom of the Hittites*, new ed. Oxford: Oxford University Press.
———. 2006. *The Trojans and Their Neighbours*. London: Routledge.
Büyükkolancı, Mustafa. 2000. Excavations on Ayasuluk Hill in Selçuk/Turkey. A Contribution to the Early History of Ephesus. In *Die Ägäis und das Westliche Mittelmeer. Beziehungen und Wechselwirkungen 8. bis 5. Jh. v. Chr. (Archäologischen Forschungen Bd 4), Akten des Symposions, Vienna, March 24–27, 1999*, ed. Friedrich Krinzinger, 39–43. Vienna: Österreichische Akademie der Wissenschaften.
Chavalas, Mark W., ed. 2006. *The Ancient Near East. Historical Sources in Translation*. Oxford: Blackwell.

Forrer, Emil. 1924. Die Griechen in den Boghazköi-Texten. *Orientalische Literaturzeitung* 27: 113–18.

Gardiner, Alan. 1960. *The Kadesh Inscriptions of Ramesses II*. Oxford: Ashmolean Museum.

Garstang, John and Oliver R. Gurney. 1959. *The Geography of the Hittite Empire*. London: British Institute of Archaeology at Ankara.

Goetze, Albrecht. 1933. *Die Annalen des Muršilis*. Leipzig: Mitteilungen der vorderasiatisch-ägyptischen Gesellschaft 38 (rept. Darmstadt, 1967).

Güterbock, Hans G. 1986. Troy in Hittite Texts? Wilusa, Ahhiyawa, and Hittite History. In *Troy and the Trojan War. A Symposium Held at Bryn Mawr College, October 1984*, ed. Machteld J. Mellink 33–44. Bryn Mawr, Penn.: Bryn Mawr College.

Hallo, William W. and K. Lawson Younger. 2003. *The Context of Scripture. Canonical Compositions from the Biblical World*, vols. 1, 2. Leiden: Brill.

Hawkins, J. David. 1995. *The Hieroglyphic Inscription of the Sacred Pool Complex at Hattuša (SÜDBURG)*. Wiesbaden: Harrassowitz.

———. 1998. Tarkasnawa King of Mira. "Tarkondemos," Boğazköy Sealings and Karabel. *Anatolian Studies* 48: 1–31.

Heinhold-Krahmer, Susanne. 1977. *Arzawa, Untersuchungen zu seiner Geschichte nach den hethitischen Quellen*. Heidelberg: Carl Winter.

Houwink ten Cate, Philo H. J. 1965. *The Luwian Population Groups of Lycia and Cilicia Aspera during the Hellenistic Period*. Leiden: Brill.

———. 1985–86. Sidelights on the Ahhiyawa Question from Hittite Vassal and Royal Correspondence. *Jaarbericht ex Oriente Lux* 28: 33–79.

Latacz, Joachim. 2004. *Troy and Homer*. Oxford: Oxford University Press.

Mee, Christopher. 1978. Aegean Trade and Aegean Settlement in Anatolia. *Anatolian Studies* 28: 121–56.

Melchert, H. Craig. 2003. *The Luwians*. Leiden: Brill.

Moran, William L. 1992. *The Amarna Letters*. Baltimore, Md.: Johns Hopkins University Press.

Mountjoy, Penelope. 1999. The Destruction of Troy VIh. *Studia Troica* 9: 253–93.

Niemeier, Wolfgang-Dietrich. 1998. The Mycenaeans in Western Anatolia and the Problem of the Origins of the Sea Peoples. In *Mediterranean Peoples in Transition: Thirteenth to Early Tenth Cenuries B.C.E.: In Honor of Professor Trude Dothan*, ed. Seymour Gitin, Amihai Mazar, and Ephraim Stern, 17–65. Jerusalem: Israel Exploration Society.

———. 2005. Minoans, Mycenaeans, Hittites, and Ionians in Western Asia Minor. New Excavations in Bronze Age Miletus-Milawata. In *The Greeks in the East*, ed. Alexandra Villing, 1–36. London: British Museum.

Sommer, Ferdinand. 1932. *Die Ahhijavā-Urkunden*. Munich: Bayerischen Akademie der Wissenschaften (rept. Hildesheim, 1975).

Yakubovich, Ilya. 2009. *Sociolinguistics of the Luvian Language*. Brill's Studies in Indo-European Languages and Linguistics, vol. 2. Leiden: Brill.

CHAPTER 16

THE PLATEAU: THE HITTITES

JÜRGEN SEEHER

Geographical Remarks

During the second millennium B.C.E., the Hittites established the first empire in what was later called Anatolia and then Asia Minor. This large peninsula is surrounded by seas on three sides, but the Hittites were largely inland-oriented. This is due to the structure of the terrain, which accounted for environmental and political conditions. The folded ranges of the Pontic Mountains in the north and the Taurus Mountains to the south create the limits of the semi-arid highlands, which formed the homeland of the Hittites and the stage for the development of this Bronze Age superpower. Also called the Anatolian plateau, this vast stretch of land is not flat, but is hilly in most parts and often formed by small plains separated by more or less wide mountainous ridges. The largest of these plains is the Konya Plain, an area which comprises much of what was called the Lower Land by the Hittites. The Upper Land, on the other hand, was the mountainous region around the upper Kızıl Irmak, the river called Maraššantiya by the Hittites (and Halys in antiquity). In between the two, that is, in and around the large bend of the Kızıl Irmak River in the center of Anatolia south of the Pontus Mountains, lay the Hittite heartland, or perhaps one might better say the nucleus, of the kingdom (concise summary in Bryce 1998:44–63).

The reconstruction of Hittite geography derives only in small part from excavations at archaeological sites (see Glatz, chapter 40 in this volume). In general, it relies on cuneiform textual evidence. Most informative concerning geographical matters are the itineraries of the cult travels of the king, as well as the reports of military campaigns (see Beal, chapter 26 in this volume). The narrations include hundreds of names of towns visited, rivers crossed, and mountains passed, not to mention countries and territories visited, invaded, and/or subjugated. But these texts contain neither cardinal directions nor measurements of distances. In rare instances the number of days traveled serves as a hint for distance, but not knowing in which direction the journey headed and where and how often the direction changed leaves a broad margin of error for possible geographical reconstructions. As a result, the scholarly debate is lively, and the location of only a very few of the Hittite towns mentioned in the texts is generally agreed upon (see Mielke, chapter 48 in this volume).

Chronological Remarks

The contributions of Beal and van den Hout as well as Bryce in this volume give a synopsis of Hittite history as it can be reconstructed from the evidence of ancient written sources. Unfortunately, field archaeology has not kept pace with the historical studies. In view of this ready-to-use model, which has constantly been refined for more than a century by scores of philologists and historians, archaeologists working at Hittite sites have always tried to adjust and have too long refrained from developing an independent scheme in reconstructing the "archaeological history" of the second millennium B.C.E. (Schoop 2008:35). Of course, the correlation of documented historical events and archaeological evidence is a problem. Only a few instances of building, destruction, conquest, or the like mentioned in the ancient texts can be identified in an excavation. This is all the more true because Hittite field archaeologists have worked—and still are working—to a large extent almost exclusively with relative dating. Only in recent years have absolute dating methods like radiocarbon dating and dendrochronology been employed at some excavations, yielding eye-opening results (Mielke, Schoop, and Seeher 2006, and esp. Mielke 2006; Schoop and Seeher 2006; Yakar 2002, and Yakar, chapter 4 in this volume). The best example is the redating of much of the history of development of the capital Ḫattuša (Seeher 2006).

In the meantime, Hittite archaeology struggles with a confusing terminology and chronology. In the early years, it was a common practice at archaeological projects to distinguish between Old Kingdom and New Kingdom or Empire period layers, thus following the philological distinction between Old Hittite and an Empire period script. Later, however, a Middle Hittite script was identified and became a tool for the understanding of historical events of the fifteenth and fourteenth centuries B.C.E. Similarly, the progress of research on archaeological sites shows the need for a further distinction—Middle Hittite has been postulated, although it is still ill-defined (A. Müller-Karpe 2003). Nowadays, some scholars do use this as a basis for the separation of the Old Kingdom–Middle Kingdom–Empire periods, but others stick to the two-stage scheme (overview: Dinçol 2006). The Empire period is understood by some to begin with the accession to the throne of Tudḫaliya I, whereas others prefer to apply this designation with the accession of Šuppiluliuma I half a century later. Additional confusion is brought about by the fact that the two-stage supporters and the three-stage supporters do not all use the same divisions, and even a general consensus on the sequence of Hittite kings is not in sight—for example, the authenticity of a second Ḫattušili and a third Tudḫaliya is debated. Finally, the existence of long, middle, and short chronologies adds further fuel to scholarly debate and confusion (Yakar 2002; see Beal, chapter 26 in this volume).

The beginning of the Hittite kingdom follows the collapse of the *kārum* period network of Assyrian trade colonies. Conflagrations have been observed at various sites, but their contemporaneity is a supposition based on the knowledge of historical events, rather than archaeological evidence. Generally speaking, they mirror a difficult period known to us from the cuneiform texts that saw the struggle of various groups and eventually the emergence of the Ḫatti kingdom based at Ḫattuša and the area within the bend of the Marašsantiya/Kızıl Irmak River (for the political history of this kingdom, see Beal, chapter 26 in this volume).

The rise of Ḫattuša as the capital of the kingdom is conventionally dated to the second half of the seventeenth century B.C.E. To consolidate their rule, Hittite kings followed an active settlement policy that meant not only the maintenance of existing settlements but also the foundation of new provincial centers. The best example is the site of Kuşaklı, located 210 km southeast of the capital Ḫattuša in what was then called the Upper Land. Founded in the sixteenth century B.C.E., this city has been identified as Šarišša, the seat of a local king. Temple, official buildings, fortifications and city gates, as well as the material culture in general are almost identical with examples from the capital and provide evidence of a powerful system already in place at this early stage (A. Müller-Karpe 2002; see Mielke, chapter 48 in this volume).

The ups and downs of Hittite history, as well as the oscillation of Hittite state territory in the course of time reflected in the cuneiform texts, cannot yet be traced in the archaeological record—too little is the amount of substantial excavations at Hittite sites in various parts of the country. Even the most threatening event to the survival of the Hittite state still lacks archaeological confirmation at most known sites, including Ḫattuša: the concentric invasion during the reign of Tudḫaliya III around the middle of the fourteenth century B.C.E., when enemy attacks from almost everywhere led to heavy losses of territory and power and the conflagration of the capital. In addition, the recovery of the state and the massive development of Hittite rule during the Empire period is, at least for the time being, reflected in details rather than in evidence of such phenomena as widespread city growth or monumental architecture; one example is the creation of rock reliefs, furnished with the names of Hittite kings and princes, in the thirteenth century B.C.E. (see Harmanşah, chapter 28 in this volume). The distribution of these kinds of monuments, together with other reliefs on stone stelai and architectural monuments, from Akpınar in the hinterland of İzmir on the western coast of Turkey to Karakuyu and Kayalıpınar in the eastern part of the plateau and to Sirkeli and Hemite in Cilicia, south of the Taurus range, reflects the size of the empire as it is also known from the texts (figure 16.1). The variation of the material culture in this vast territory, however, is as yet little known and far from being an instrument to define cultural developments, provinces, or the like. Finally, our knowledge about the collapse of the empire and the end of the Late Bronze Age around 1200/1180 B.C.E. is based almost totally on textual evidence as well. This means we know almost nothing about the reasons and the course of events that led to the disappearance of the Hittites from the central plateau. Some Empire period sites have yielded evidence of fiery destruction, which may or may not represent extensive conflagrations and which may or may not have to be assigned to a single period and a single reason. Although the few Early Iron Age sites identified so far have yielded a pronounced non-Hittite material culture (Kealhofer and Grave, chapter 18 in this volume), it seems likely that these newcomers were not conquerors but simply settlers who took advantage of deserted landscapes. A sound archaeological basis for the reconstruction of the fate of Hittite cities and settlements on the plateau is still missing.

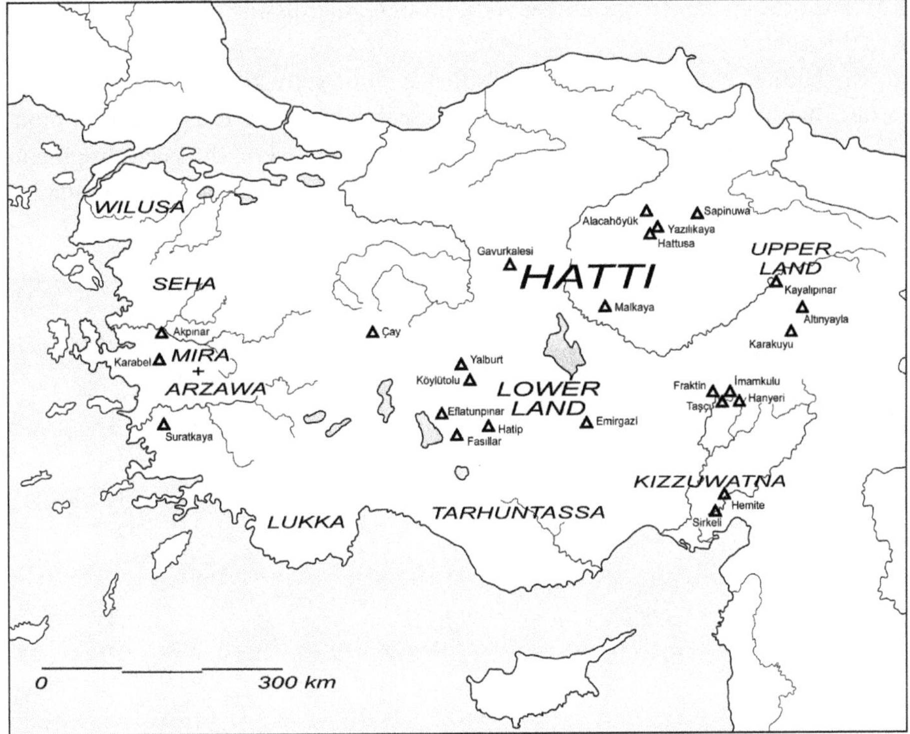

Figure 16.1. Distribution of Hittite Empire period stone reliefs.

Sites of Interest

What is the archaeological basis for our knowledge of the Hittites? Due to its extent and long duration, the excavations in the capital (Mielke, chapter 48 in this volume) have provided the main pillar in almost every respect for the reconstruction of Hittite culture: from cuneiform texts to architectural monuments and to finds of all categories. Besides this, excavations and surveys of settlement mounds on the Anatolian plateau have almost inevitably yielded layers and finds of the Hittite period, thus witnessing the wide extent of Hittite material culture.

To give an idea of archaeological investigations at Hittite sites it is still appropriate to separate Old Hittite from the Empire period. Further breakdown in chronological periods is desirable, but not feasible due to the disparate character of the evidence presently available. To facilitate geographical orientation, the following description of sites comprises distances from the capital Ḫattuša as the crow flies.

Very close to the capital, Eskiyapar and Alaca Höyük (respectively twenty and twenty-five kilometers northeast of Ḫattuša) are two mounds with long settlement traditions, which also yielded substantial remains of the Hittite period. In the Empire period, Alaca Höyük was furnished with some of the finest examples of Hittite rock art—the Sphinx Gate with rows of orthostats (figure 16.2), which adorned the entrance to a central district furnished with official buildings, the so-called temple palace. Alaca Höyük is a candidate for the location of the Hittite cult cities of Arinna or Zippalanda, but unequivocal proof is still missing (see Mielke, chapter 48 in this volume).

The Hittite settlement at Ortaköy, situated some sixty kilometers northeast of Ḫattuša, has been identified with Šapinuwa (Süel 2008). Here the remains of monumental buildings have been unearthed, together with several thousand fragments of cuneiform tablets—the largest collection outside of the capital. The foundation

Figure 16.2. Sphinx Gate at Alaca Höyük.

date of this town close to the northern border of the kingdom, as well as its settlement history, remain in the dark, but it seems to have been inhabited until the end of the Empire period (see Mielke, chapter 48 in this volume).

The Hittite state did not have close relations with the Black Sea littoral during most of its existence. Initially, the whole of the Pontic region seems to have been under Old Hittite rule (V. Müller-Karpe 2001). Later however, various groups moved in, and local tribes gained strength, which made the Hittites retreat as far as the southern limits of the Pontic Mountains. The new inhabitants of these regions were the Kaška, a collective term for a loose conglomerate of tribes always ready to harry or even deeply invade the border zones of the empire in moments of weakness; during the time of Tudḫaliya III, Kaškans were even able to invade the Hittite homeland as far as the southern bend of the Maraššantiya River (Bryce 1998:158–65; see Beal, chapter 26 in this volume). Important Old Hittite cult centers in this Pontic region, like Zalpa and Nerik, were lost after Kaška attacks, only to be regained and restored during the Empire period when the north came once again under Hittite control through vassal treaties. Various ideas have been put forward on the localization of these two towns, but proof is still missing. Recently a new project in search of Nerik has been launched at the large mound of Oymaağaçtepe, some 150 km northeast of Ḫattuša and 50 km south of the Black Sea shoreline (Czichon and Klinger 2006). Nevertheless, Hittite archaeological remains of the Empire period in the north are rare—although not as rare as they once seemed (Glatz and Matthews 2005)—which certainly points to the fact that the north was not the focus of Hittite attention. Unappealing environmental conditions for living and economy on the one hand and the lack of promising destinations beyond the mountains on the other are likely to be the reason.

Looking in a more easterly direction, a major site is Maşat Höyük, lying at a distance of 100 km from the capital (Özgüç 1978, 1982). Already inhabited in the *kārum* and Old Hittite period, this settlement was Hittite Tapigga, which gained special importance later when it became the seat of a governor of the border province of the empire—an important outpost in the fight against the Kaška people. Excavated remains comprise a palace-like building in Level III with a substantial collection of Middle Hittite cuneiform tablets, which have added much to our knowledge of the organization of Hittite rule in this part of the country (see Beal, chapter 26, and Mielke, chapter 48 in this volume).

Seventy kilometers to the southeast of the capital, still within the Hittite core area, lies the mound of Alişar Höyük (Gorny 1995). Excavated already in the 1920s and 1930s, this huge prehistoric tell is one of the main reference sites for the Late Chalcolithic/Early Bronze Age (EBA) in central Anatolia. A long fortification wall with casemates and gates surrounding the terrace below the mound is the hallmark of the Old Hittite period on this site. As far as can be ascertained, this is the earliest Hittite city wall detected so far and typologically a precursor of the oldest fortification at Ḫattuša. After a destruction level, the settlement seems to have lingered, on a much smaller scale, possibly without fortification, during the Empire period. This site possibly is to be identified as Hittite Ankuwa, but as with most Hittite cities, other identifications have been put forward, and Ankuwa has also been sought elsewhere. The same is true for the neighboring settlement mound of Çadır Höyük, thirteen kilometers northwest of Alişar Höyük, which is considered by its excavators to be a candidate for the Hittite city of Zippalanda (Gorny 1997).

The site of Kültepe, just south of the Kızıl Irmak/Maraššantiya River and about 155 km to the southeast of Ḫattuša, had been the powerful hub of central Anatolia during the *kārum* period and thus an early center of Hittite culture (see Kulakoğlu, chapter 47, and Michel, chapter 13 in this volume). However, its rulers lost the competition for dominance during the formation of the Hittite state, and Kültepe was deserted. Instead, other centers arose in the east, in the area called the Upper Land by the Hittites (Gurney 2003). Excavated in recent years with modern methods, the above-mentioned Kuşaklı/Šariššа has become an important site in Hittite archaeology. This provincial center and cult site did not escape destruction during the years of turmoil in the fourteenth century B.C.E., but it was soon revived and continued to serve right down to the end of the Empire period. Only about fifty kilometers northwest of this site, another Hittite town is currently being excavated at Kayalıpınar (A. Müller-Karpe 2006). The remains of monumental buildings, together with cuneiform tablets, prove the importance of this place, which is a possible candidate for the Hittite town of Šamuḫa—a stronghold for the Hittite king in the Upper Land during the time when much of the core area of the kingdom was besieged and destroyed by enemy attacks during the fourteenth century B.C.E.

The eastern limits of the Hittite kingdom are difficult to establish. The region east of the Upper Land, that is, east of Sivas and the upper Kızıl Irmak, is a rugged terrain formed by the merging ranges of the Pontic and the Taurus Mountains. A harsh climate restricts effective agricultural activities to a few plains, and the Hittites did not spend much effort to expand into these parts of the country. However, sites in the Malatya-Elazığ region like Arslantepe (Frangipane, chapter 45 in this volume), Korucutepe (van Loon 1980), İmikuşağı (Konyar 2006), or Norşuntepe (Korbel 1985), that is, 370–450 km southeast of Ḫattuša, display Hittite features both in architecture and material culture. Seal impressions and textual evidence, however, make it clear that this is basically the territory of Iššuwa, a neighboring country that only later became part of the empire, but which had adopted Hittite cultural elements from very early times onward.

If we now turn westward from the capital Ḫattuša, the site of İnandık must be mentioned (Özgüç 1988). Situated about 100 km northwest of Ḫattuša, this settlement mound was occupied from the EBA to the Iron Age and yielded substantial layers from the Old Hittite period. A few hundred meters to the west of the site proper, a large multiroomed building complex was found sitting on a ridge. Destroyed in a violent conflagration, a unique Old Hittite cult inventory was preserved in its ruins. It consisted of many vessels of superb make, among them the famous İnandık vase with relief depiction of cult scenes. A rather similar situation was encountered at Yörüklü/Hüseyindede some forty-five kilometers northwest of the capital Ḫattuša. Here, too, burned Old Hittite building remains yielded cult vessels, two of them with relief decoration (Sipahi 2000; Yıldırım 2000, 2006). As at İnandık, this building also stood separate from the settlement. This is a typical feature of Hittite cult practice, which is also reflected in the cuneiform texts; in addition to temples situated within the cities, sanctuaries were also erected in the countryside.

A perfect counterpart for the relief vases from İnandık and Yörüklü/Hüseyindede comes also from the site of Bitik, a huge settlement mound 170 km west of Ḫattuša (Özgüç 1957). This is the westernmost appearance of this kind of Old Hittite cult vessel. The excavations at the site have been very limited, but they seem to have yielded substantial Old Hittite period layers. Further to the west, sites like Gordion (Mellink 1956), Ilıca (Orthmann 1967), Yanarlar (Emre 1978), Çavlum (Bilgen 2005), and Demircihöyük (Seeher 2000) have yielded cemeteries (the latter also a settlement) that can be dated at least partially to the Old Hittite period; at the present state of investigation it is not clear how much this western part of the plateau was under the influence of Hittite rule. According to the textual evidence, this area lay outside of its realm at that time, but parallels in the material culture are obvious and prove close connections. Excavated sites with Empire period material, however, are rare—Gordion is one example, and sherds and a seal impression from Şarhöyük/Dorylaion constitute another (Darga 2004). Apparently, this northern part of western inner Anatolia was a backwater during most of the Late Bronze Age.

Politically much more important was its southern counterpart. According to their texts, many of the Hittite kings initiated military actions in the western ranges of the highlands and beyond, sometimes even toward the Aegean shoreline. Especially during the time of the Empire, raids in the west seem to have been routine. The lack of excavations, however, deprives us of the possibility of better understanding the basis of Hittite expansion in this direction. Surveys in the dry steppe region around and south of the Tuz Gölü (Salt Lake) have yielded extremely few sites, which is to be expected due to the unfavorable conditions for agriculturally based settlements. Further south in the fertile Konya Plain various surveys have yielded an abundance of sites with occupation in the Middle and Late Bronze Age, but the only site of this period which has been excavated to a certain extent is Karahöyük near Konya. This large mound was the site of a fortified *kārum* period settlement, but after this it seems to have been deserted.

From the economic point of view, the region beyond the western part of the plateau was not of much interest to the Hittites. From the political point of view, however, this part of Anatolia was another buffer zone that was under constant threat from countries occupying the valleys and coastal areas, above all Arzawa—an enemy which had been able to overrun large parts of western Anatolia reaching as far as southeastern Cappadocia in the fourteenth century B.C.E. To protect this western flank of the Hittite mainland it was mandatory to fight, create alliances, and sign vassal treaties. Furthermore, this was also a way to ward off another potential enemy: the Ahhiyawans, who ruled the Aegean Sea and were keen on extending their influence onto the Anatolian mainland (see Bryce, chapter 15, and Beal, chapter 26 in this volume). They would not have had the means to invade the highlands, but certainly they had enough potential to create unrest in the western provinces of the empire.

Finally, the extension and orientation of the Hittite realm toward the south was clearly dominated by a pronounced economic—and thus also political—interest, very similar to the preceding *kārum* period, which saw the establishment of the Assyrian trade colony network (see Michel, chapter 13 in this volume). Beyond the Taurus Range lay Kizzuwatna with access to the land routes to the northern Levant and Mesopotamia but also to the seaborne trade along the shores of the eastern Mediterranean. These resources fostered the Hittite will to expand in this direction to guarantee open trade routes and thus the economic welfare of the country (see Gates, chapter 17 in this volume).

Two main access routes led from the Lower Land on the plateau into these southern realms. One led via the valley of the Göksu River through the territory of Tarḫuntašša, which covered the western part of the Taurus range. Perhaps due to this geopolitical situation, Tarḫuntašša was so important that King Muwatalli II temporarily moved the capital from Ḫattuša to this city, and a few decades later it even became, after Karkamiš, the second viceroyalty of the Hittite Empire. For the time being, a major excavation yielding Hittite levels has been conducted only at Kilisetepe near Mut (Postgate and Thomas 2007).

The second route went further east, passing the Taurus via a pass called the Cilician Gates (north of modern Tarsus in the plain of Adana). Close by, on the southern fringe of the Lower Land and 280 km south of Ḫattuša, sits the large mound of Porsuk-Ulukışla. This site is not only near to the main access route between the highlands and the harbors in the eastern Mediterranean but is also close to the silver mines of Bulgarmaden; already in the Old Hittite period there are traces of metalworking at the site. The fortified Hittite Empire period Level V was destroyed in a conflagration around the beginning of the twelfth century B.C.E.

Selected Topics of Material Culture

The classification of Hittite pottery has been based primarily on the material unearthed in the capital (Fischer 1963; A. Müller-Karpe 1988; Parzinger and Sanz 1992). However, in recent years, new studies from other sites (e.g., Mielke 2006) and a reevaluation of the pottery sequence at Ḫattuša currently under way (Schoop 2006) have led to a more diversified picture. Generally speaking, Hittite pottery is a local Anatolian development that reflects clearly the tradition of the central Anatolian EBA/MBA (Middle Bronze Age) of the third/early second millennium B.C.E. Regarding quality, the best items of this wheelmade pottery occur during the MBA/Old Hittite period; extremely well-made vessels with polished surfaces and perfect proportions are abundant, but even everyday ware shows a will to create a variety of elegant shapes, adorned with colored shiny slips and plastic decorative elements.

The hallmark of this period is the beak spouted jug (figure 16.3), which occurs in various shapes as fine tableware or a cult vessel, as well as a simple water jug or as a large provision container.

After the sixteenth century B.C.E., a decline in the quality of the pottery toward simpler shapes, poorer manufacturing, and less decoration becomes obvious, and the Empire period pottery is characterized by a mass production of rather coarse fabric and is almost completely without decoration. The beak spouted jug almost disappears from the archaeological record, although it still plays a prominent role in the depiction of cultic scenes on seals and rock reliefs.

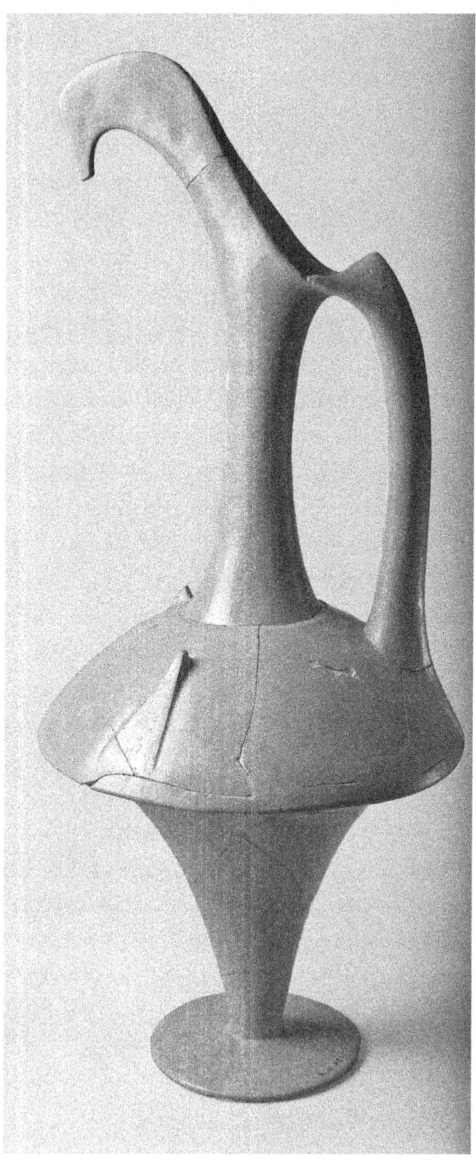

Figure 16.3. Beak spouted jug from the Old Hittite period.

Perhaps here metal vessels are shown, a category of finds almost completely absent from the archaeological record.

The distribution of Hittite-type pottery indicates a powerful regime which already in the early period was able to create a kind of common material culture over large stretches of central Anatolia. In the Empire period, an extremely consistent pottery production from Cilicia in the south to the Pontic Mountains in the north is discernible: a clear trace of a state organization with centralized control of the production and distribution of goods.

The development of international relations by the Hittites also led to the importation of certain categories of pottery into the highlands. The most obvious examples are spindle bottles, high slender jugs with a disc-shaped base, long neck, and delicate handle. Thought to be containers for perfumed oil or the like, they can be found at every Hittite site dating to the fifteenth to twelfth century B.C.E., but their center of production is sought in Cyprus (Knappett et al. 2005). Another example is the rare occurrence of Mycenaean pottery of the fourteenth/thirteenth century B.C.E. in the highlands, for example, at Ḫattuša, Maşat Höyük/Tapigga, and Kuşaklı/Šarišša, likely to be imported through the harbors in the Cilician Plain or the northern Levant (Genz 2004; see Bryce, chapter 15 in this volume).

Among the small finds from Hittite settlements, lumps of clay with the impressions of the seals of Hittite officials and kings, the so-called bullae, form a prominent part. Found by the thousands, they were once attached to letters, contracts, consignments of goods, and even to the locking bolts of city gates. The typical Hittite seal is the stamp seal, made of metal, stone, or ivory (figures 16.4a, 16.4b). It was either furnished with a handle or was disc- or button-shaped. Seal rings are rare, and cylinder seals, so common in the preceding *kārum* period, are almost nonexistent. Usually a Hittite seal displays the name and function of its bearer in Luwian hieroglyphics, but especially on the royal seals the name and genealogy of the king are given in cuneiform as well. This makes seal impressions a powerful tool for chronological issues in Hittite archaeology. But there is also a formal development: early seals have a handle and a flat seal surface, which often displays a ring of ornamental bands around the center, where the name of the bearer is written (figure 16.4c). In the course of time, patterns change and two-faced seals come into fashion—flat, disc-shaped seals, plano-convex seals with one flat and one convex surface, and eventually knob-shaped biconvex seals (figure 16.4d).

Especially during the last two centuries, the seals of the Hittite kings saw a vivid development. In some cases idealized representations of the seal holder or of a god—and sometimes both—were incorporated in the seal design (figure 16.4e). At the same time, monumental versions of such depictions of kings, princes, and gods were picked into rock façades in various parts of the country, thus forming a new genre of art (see Harmanşah, chapter 28 in this volume).

In contrast, most other small finds have not been found in sufficient numbers to outweigh the shortcomings of insufficient stratigraphic observations in the excavations—many items seem to be startlingly long-lived, even those with nonfunctional decorative elements that are elsewhere easily subject to fashion and change

Figure 16.4. Hittite seals (a–b) and seal impressions on clay bullae from Ḫattuša. (a) Disk-shaped ivory seal; (b) plano-convex bronze seal; (c) Old Hittite period seal impression of a scribe; (d) Empire period seal impression of a scribe; (e) seal impression of Great King Tudḫaliya IV. Not to scale.

over time. Here the lack of burials (see later discussion) is painfully felt and leaves us with little means to change this situation quickly. Chance finds and better excavation techniques will eventually lead to a more differentiated picture.

Objects of metal are extremely underrepresented in the archaeological record because they were mostly recycled. However, the descriptions of objects in Hittite texts and a few chance finds like the decorated ax from Şarkışla or the silver and bronze rhyta provide us with a glimpse of the excellence of Hittite smiths (Aruz, Benzel, and Evans 2008:179–84). Hittite metallurgy was state of the art, and although excavations in Hittite settlements have yielded almost no object of iron, their texts show that this metal was in use from the beginning of Hittite rule; during the Old Kingdom, precious iron was exclusively used for symbols of power, that is, throne, scepter, and cult objects. In the Empire period weapons of iron are mentioned for the first time, but they too must have been rather rare and by far outnumbered by weapons of bronze (Siegelová 2005).

An intriguing example of change can be seen with objects used for weaving; whereas spindle whorls and crescent-shaped loom weights are well known from Old Hittite contexts (and can be traced back to EBA origins), they seem to disappear more or less completely during the Empire period. It is tempting to interpret this as proof for a change in economy, that is, cloth was no longer produced but rather brought in from somewhere else. More probable, though, is a change in technology—the same work was accomplished in a different way with a different set of tools which left no trace in the archaeological record.

Burials

The number of Hittite burials discovered thus far is very limited, and as far as can be ascertained almost all of them belong to the Old Hittite period. This lack of evidence is a serious problem for the reconstruction of Hittite spiritual and religious beliefs and customs; at the same time, the lack of graves also means the absence of grave goods, that is, accumulations of objects that were laid down at the same time and thus can help establish reliable chronological schemes for the development of a variety of objects. This is a serious drawback which distinguishes Hittite archaeology from that of the preceding and the following eras, not to mention other cultural contexts.

The present evidence shows that the Hittites used to bury their dead extramurally; only occasionally have burials been encountered within settled areas, often children who may have been considered unfit to be buried far away from home.

The Old Hittite burials show a clear continuation of EBA customs; the dead are usually buried in a flexed "Hocker" position in large vessels (*pithoi*), simple stone cists, or pits with or without stone lining, sometimes covered with parts of pottery vessels. Grave offerings, such as one or several vessels (mostly jugs), and an occasional object of metal, clay, or bone, are the rule. The interment of the bodies lying on their backs, as it was observed in Kazankaya (Özgüç 1978:69–88) and Alişar Höyük (von der Osten 1937:84–108), seems to be a local deviation from the rule.

Whereas some cemeteries yielded only inhumations, there are others where inhumations are by far outnumbered by cremations. At Boğazköy/Osmankayası a minimum of seventy-one cremations put into vessels and at least twenty-two complete and partial inhumations were found in a large grotto-like niche in a rock outside of the capital (Bittel et al. 1958). At Ilıca only 4 out of 131 burials consisted of inhumations; the rest were cremations buried in vessels (Orthmann 1967). Also the top (latest) MBA level of Konya-Karahöyük yielded, in addition to inhumations in pithoi, cremations covered with pithos sherds (Alp 1961). The cremation of the deceased is attested during this period for the first time on the Anatolian plateau. Whether this is due to an influence from across the Taurus Mountains, where cremations dating to the second half of the third/beginning of the second millennium B.C.E. have been excavated at Gedikli (Duru 2006:162–73), is open to discussion.

The combined occurrence of these two different burial customs in the same cemetery has led to speculations about different groups of different belief systems burying their dead together. However, ethnographic studies in different regions of the world have yielded a vast number of examples where both customs are practiced by the same group of people—the difference in burial is meant to perpetuate the different status the dead person had during his or her life. A good proof for this observation comes from the MBA cemetery of Demircihöyük-Sarıket, where several cremations were discovered to have been put into previously buried pithoi with normal inhumations (Seeher 1993).

A big riddle in Hittite archaeology is the lack of cemeteries from the Empire period. As far as can be ascertained, only the latest burials of the cemetery at Osmankayası can be dated to the fourteenth century B.C.E.; other than that, from Ferzant (Özgüç 1986) and Kazankaya east of Ḫattuša to Demircihöyük-Sarıket and Ağızören (Türktüzün 2002) at the northwestern rim of the highlands, all ten or so known cemeteries belong to the MBA/Old Hittite period. It is hard to imagine that Hittite rule had the means to abolish this custom all over the state within a rather short span of time, because the way people lay their dead to rest is an emotionally loaded ritual and certainly not easily liable to change. At the moment, no answer is available, and as is so often the case, the Hittite texts remain silent in this matter.

Conclusion

The investigation of Hittite rule in Anatolia is dominated by the overwhelming amount of data supplied by the philological sources. Until now, archaeological field research is limited to a small amount of sites, often only "tested" rather than excavated. However, we know that from the beginning, the Hittite kings followed an active settlement policy on the Anatolian plateau. Sites in disparate areas show a remarkable uniformity in architecture and material culture and thus document a strong system with well-organized structures of production and distribution. Basically inland oriented, the Hittite state maintained close connections to the coast only in southern Asia Minor, which meant access to the trade routes in the eastern Mediterranean and the northern Levant. The loss of these trade routes, together with various other factors, seems to have led to the collapse of the empire around or shortly after 1200 B.C.E. and the abandonment of many (if not all) Hittite settlements on the central Anatolian plateau.

Chronological developments during the more than four centuries of Hittite rule can be established for some kinds of artifacts, whereas others remain undifferentiated due to the scarcity of evidence. Generally speaking, Hittite archaeology is desperately in need of modern excavations, scientific dating, in-depth studies of artifact categories, and eventually solving the riddle of the missing graves. This will supply us with a second basis for the reconstruction of Hittite chronology and geography, independent of the shortcomings of contemporary textual evidence, for example, the chance preservation of cuneiform tablets as well as biased recording dependent on the perspective of individual rulers.

REFERENCES

Alp, Sedat. 1961. Konya, Kara Höyük Kazısı. *Türk Arkeoloji Dergisi* 11.2: 8–9.

Aruz, Joan, Kim Benzel, and Jean M. Evans. 2008. *Beyond Babylon. Art, Trade, and Diplomacy in the Second Millenium B.C.* Metropolitan Museum of Art, New York. New Haven, Conn.: Yale University Press.

Bilgen, A. Nejat. 2005. *Çavlum. Eskişehir Alpu Ovası'nda bir Orta Tunç Çağı Mezarlığı.* Eskişehir: Anadolu Üniversitesi Yayınları.

Bittel, Kurt, Wolf Herre, Heinrich Otten, Manfred Röhrs, and Johann Schaeuble. 1958. *Die hethitischen Grabfunde von Osmankayası.* Boğazköy-Hattuša 2. Berlin: Verlag Gebr. Mann.

Bryce, Trevor. 1998. *The Kingdom of the Hittites.* Oxford: Clarendon Press.

Czichon, Rainer-Maria and Jörg Klinger. 2006. Interdisziplinäre Geländebegehung im Gebiet von Oymaağaç-Vezirköprü /Provinz Samsun. *Mitteilungen der Deutschen Orient-Gesellschaft* 138: 157–97.

Darga, Muhibbe. 2004. Şarhöyük—Dorylaion (Eskişehir) Kazılarında Hitit Buluntuları (1989–2003). In *Anadolu'da Doğdu. Festschrift für Fahri Işık zum 60. Geburtstag*, ed. Taner Korkut, 269–83. İstanbul: Ege Yayınları.

Dinçol, Belkıs. 2006. Über die Probleme der absoluten Datierung der Herrschaftsperioden der hethitischen Könige nach den philologischen und glyptischen Belegen. In *Structuring and Dating in Hittite Archaeology*, ed. Dirk P. Mielke, Ulf-Dietrich Schoop, and Jürgen Seeher, 19–32. İstanbul: Zero Prod. Ltd.

Duru, Refik. 2006. *Gedikli Karahöyük I.* Ankara: Türk Tarih Kurumu.

Emre, Kutlu. 1978. *Yanarlar. A Hittite Cemetery near Afyon.* Ankara: Türk Tarih Kurumu.

Fischer, Franz. 1963. *Die hethitische Keramik von Boğazköy.* Boğazköy-Ḫattuša 4. Berlin: Verlag Gebr. Mann.

Genz, Hermann. 2004. Eine mykenische Scherbe aus Boğazköy. *Archäologischer Anzeiger*: 77–84.

Glatz, Claudia and Roger Matthews. 2005. Anthropology of a Frontier Zone: Hittite-Kaska Relations in Late Bronze Age North-Central Anatolia. *Bulletin of the American Schools of Oriental Research* 339: 47–65.

Gorny, Ronald L. 1995. Hittite Imperialism and Anti-Imperial Resistance as Viewed from Alişar Höyük. *Bulletin of the American Schools of Oriental Research* 299/300: 65–89.

———. 1997. Zippalanda and Ankuwa: The Geography of Central Anatolia in the Second Millennium B.C. *Journal of the American Oriental Society* 117: 549–57.

Gurney, Oliver R. 2003. The Upper Land, mātum elītum. In *Hittite Studies in Honor of Harry A. Hoffner Jr. on the Occasion of His Birthday*, ed. Gary Beckman, Richard Beal, and Gregory McMahon, 119–26. Winona Lake, Ind.: Eisenbrauns.

Knappett, Carl, Vassilis Kilikoglou, Val Steele, and Ben Stern. 2005. The Circulation and Consumption of Red Lustrous Wheelmade Ware: Petrographic, Chemical and Residue Analysis. *Anatolian Studies* 55: 25–59.

Konyar, Erkan. 2006. Old Hittite Presence in the East of the Euphrates in the Light of the Stratigraphical Data from İmikuşağı (Elazığ). In *Structuring and Dating in Hittite Archaeology*, ed. Dirk P. Mielke, Ulf-Dietrich Schoop, and Jürgen Seeher, 333–48. İstanbul: Zero Prod.

Korbel, Günther. 1985. *Die Spätbronzezeitliche Keramik von Norşuntepe.* Mitteilungen no. 4. Hannover: Institut für Bauen und Planen in Entwicklungsländern.

Mellink, Machteld J. 1956. *A Hittite Cemetery at Gordion*. Philadelphia: University Museum Press.
Mielke, Dirk Paul. 2006. *Die Keramik vom Westhang*. Kuşaklı-Sarissa 2. Rahden/Westf.: Verlag Marie Leidorf.
Mielke, Dirk Paul, Ulf-Dietrich Schoop, and Jürgen Seeher, eds. 2006. *Structuring and Dating in Hittite Archaeology*. Byzas 4. İstanbul: Zero Prod.
Müller-Karpe, Andreas. 1988. *Hethitische Töpferei der Oberstadt von Hattuša*. Marburger Studien 10. Marburg—Lahn: Hitzeroth Verlag.
———. 2002. Kuşaklı-Sarissa. In *Die Hethiter und ihr Reich. Volk der tausend Götter, Exhibition Catalogue*, 176–89. Bonn: Kunst- und Ausstellungshalle der Bundesrepublik Deutschland.
———. 2003. Remarks on Central Anatolian Chronology of the Middle Hittite Period. In *The Synchronisation of Civilizations in the Eastern Mediterranean in the Second Millennium B.C.*, ed. Manfred Bietak, 385–94. Contributions to the Chronology of the Eastern Mediterranean 4. Wien: Österreichische Akademie der Wissenschaften.
———. 2006. Untersuchungen in Kayalıpınar. *Mitteilungen der Deutschen Orient-Gesellschaft* 138: 41–74.
Müller-Karpe, Vuslat. 2001. Zur frühhethitischen Kultur im Mündungsgebiet des Maraššantija. In *Akten des IV. Internationalen Kongresses für Hethitologie Würzburg, 4–8 Oktober 1999*, ed. G. Wilhelm, 430–42. Studien zu den Boğazköy-Texten 45. Wiesbaden: Harrassowitz.
Orthmann, Winfried. 1967. *Das Gräberfeld bei Ilıca*. Wiesbaden: Franz Steiner Verlag.
Özgüç, Tahsin. 1957. The Bitik Vase. *Anatolia* 2: 57–78.
———. 1978. *Excavations at Maşat Höyük and Investigations in its Vicinity*. Ankara: Türk Tarih Kurumu.
———. 1982. *Maşat Höyük 2. A Hittite Center Northeast of Boğazköy*. Ankara: Türk Tarih Kurumu.
———. 1986. The Hittite Cemetery at Ferzant: New Observations on the Finds. *Belleten* 50: 393–402.
———. 1988. *İnandıktepe. An Important Cult Center in the Old Hittite Period*. Ankara: Türk Tarih Kurumu.
Parzinger, Hermann and Rosa Sanz. 1992. *Die Oberstadt von Hattuša: Hethitische Keramik aus dem Zentralen Tempelviertel: Funde aus den Grabungen 1982–1987*. Boğazköy-Hattuša 15. Berlin: Verlag Gebr. Mann.
Postgate, Nicholas, and David Thomas, eds. 2007. *Excavations at Kilise Tepe, 1994–98: From Bronze Age to Byzantine in Western Cilicia*. Cambridge: McDonald Institute for Archaeological Research.
Schoop, Ulf-Dietrich. 2006. Dating the Hittites with Statistics: Ten Pottery Assemblages from Boğazköy-Hattusa. In *Structuring and Dating in Hittite Archaeology*, ed. Dirk P. Mielke, Ulf-Dietrich Schoop, and Jürgen Seeher, 215–40. İstanbul: Zero Prod.
———. 2008. Wo steht die Archäologie in der Erforschung der hethitischen Kultur? Schritte zu einem Paradigmenwechsel. In *Hattuša—Boğazköy. Das Hethiterreich im Spannungsfeld des Alten Orients*, ed. Gernot Wilhelm, 35–60. Wiesbaden: Harrassowitz Verlag.
Schoop, Ulf-Dietrich and Jürgen Seeher. 2006. Absolute Chronologie in Boğazköy-Hattuša: Das Potential der Radiokarbondaten. In *Structuring and Dating in Hittite Archaeology*, ed. Dirk P. Mielke, Ulf-Dietrich Schoop, and Jürgen Seeher, 53–75. İstanbul: Zero Prod.
Seeher, Jürgen. 1993. Körperbestattung und Kremation-ein Gegensatz? *Istanbuler Mitteilungen* 43: 219–26.

———. 2000. *Die bronzezeitliche Nekropole von Demircihüyük-Sarıket.* Istanbuler Forschungen 44. Tübingen: Ernst Wasmuth.
———. 2006. Chronology in Hattuša: New Approaches to an Old Problem. In *Structuring and Dating in Hittite Archaeology*, ed. Dirk P. Mielke, Ulf-Dietrich Schoop, and Jürgen Seeher, 197–213. İstanbul: Zero Prod.
Siegelová, Jana. 2005. Metalle in hethitischen Texten. In *Anatolian Metals III*, ed. Ünsal Yalçın, 35–39. Bochum: Deutsches Bergbaumuseum.
Sipahi, Tunç. 2000. Eine althethitische Reliefvase vom Hüseyindede Tepesi. *Istanbuler Mitteilungen* 20: 63–86.
Süel, Mustafa. 2008. *Bir Hitit Başkenti Ortaköy Şapinuva.* Ankara: Uyum Ajans.
Türktüzün, Metin. 2002. Kütahya ili, Merkez, Ağızören Köyü'ndeki Hitit Nekropolü Kurtarma Kazısı. 12. *Müze Çalışmaları ve Kurtarma Kazıları Sempozyumu*: 241–50.
van Loon, Maurits N., ed. 1980. *Korucutepe 3: Final Report on the Excavations of the Universities of Chicago, California and Amsterdam in the Keban Reservoir, Eastern Anatolia, 1968–70.* Amsterdam: North Holland.
von der Osten, Hans Henning. 1937. *The Alishar Hüyük. Seasons of 1930–32 Part II.* Chicago: University of Chicago Press.
Yakar, Jak. 2002. Towards an Absolute Chronology for Middle and Late Bronze Age Anatolia. *Anadolu Araştırmaları* 16: 557–70.
Yıldırım, Tayfun. 2000. Yörüklü/Hüseyindede: Eine neue hethitische Siedlung im Südwesten von Çorum. *Istanbuler Mitteilungen* 20: 43–62.
———. 2006. Eski Hitit Çağı'na Ait Yeni Bir Kült Vazosu. *Anadolu Medeniyetleri Müzesi 2005 Yıllığı*: 339–70. Ankara: Museum of Anatolian Civilizations.

CHAPTER 17

SOUTHERN AND SOUTHEASTERN ANATOLIA IN THE LATE BRONZE AGE

MARIE-HENRIETTE GATES

The Late Bronze cultures of southern and southeastern Anatolia remain ill-defined because of factors both stemming from past research directives and innate to their material cultures. For southern Anatolia, these constraints are being redressed by intensive fieldwork and tighter typological control. An immediate result has been the realization that most archaeological criteria in use since the major excavations of the 1930s, such as Tarsus, were misguided, and that the region's second millennium B.C.E. sequence must be reworked from its very foundations. Efforts have begun on several fronts, but corrections will emerge slowly. This chapter will thus need adjustments, not least to assimilate the changes reshaping Late Bronze archaeology in central Anatolia. Research on southeastern Anatolia has been led by other issues, also prejudicial. The two regions form an awkward partnership, both in this summary, and during the Late Bronze Age.

History of Research

Southern Anatolia's Late Bronze profile was created, in the 1930s–1940s, by excavations at large mounds: in Cilicia at Mersin-Yumuktepe (Garstang 1953) and Tarsus (Goldman 1956), in the Amuq at Tell Atchana (Woolley 1955), and at Judeideh and Çatal Höyük for the Oriental Institute of Chicago's survey project (Haines 1971; McEwan 1937) (see figure 17.1). Among that era's other regional surveys, Seton-Williams's work in Cilicia and the Bay of İskenderun gave a comprehensive overview (Seton-Williams 1954). Their aims and findings produced a synthesis charting historical events, migrations, invasions, and trade as primary cultural agents (e.g., Hanfmann 1948). This consensus remained fixed until the 1990s, when new fieldwork started at previously untested sites (Kilise Tepe, Kinet Höyük, Sirkeli, Soloi Höyük [recently also referred to as Soli Höyük], Tatarlı Höyük), and older sites were reopened. To these were added excavations on the peripheries (Porsuk, Tilmen), and new surveys in the Amuq (Yener 2005) and eastern Cilicia (Killebrew, Lehmann, and Gates 2009; Salmeri and D'Agata 2009). These have stimulated a review of the region's Late Bronze components, among other issues.

In contrast, most fieldwork in the southeast has been carried out by salvage projects, in anticipation of hydroelectric dams on the Euphrates, the Tigris, and tributary rivers, from the 1960s until the present. Their pressured agendas maximize returns by focusing on accessible and instructive periods. Late Bronze occupation is sparsely documented, mainly at fortified sites, whose circuit walls are encountered in step-soundings down high mounds (e.g., İmikuşağı, Korucutepe). Late Bronze pottery also proved difficult to recognize on survey (Dodd 2007; Wilkinson 1990:110–13). Progress in both regions can be gauged from summaries in Yildirim and Gates (2007).

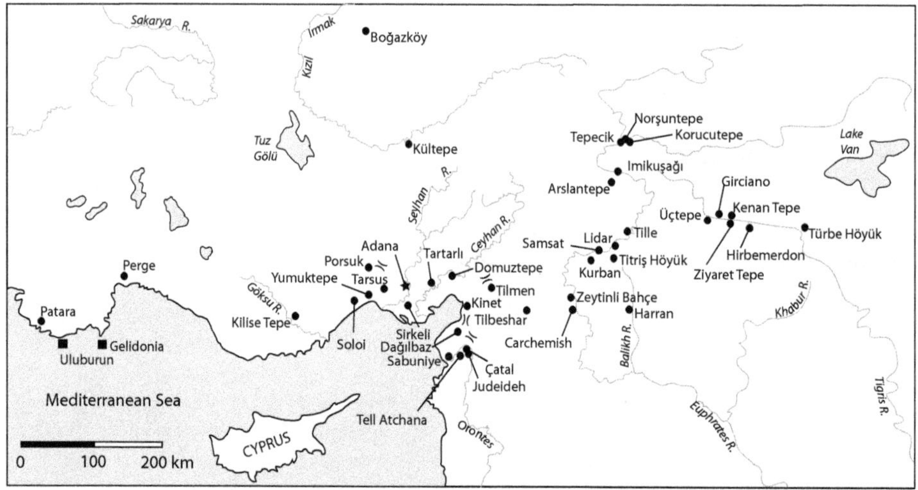

Figure 17.1. Map of sites discussed in the text.

Cultural Parameters

Chronology

Since the early twentieth century's first systematic research, Late Bronze southern Anatolia was conceived as a historical framework into which archaeological findings were inserted. Typologies and changes in material culture were described and explained according to a political schema drawn from textual evidence. This restrictive format survived without challenge until recently, in part because the fifty-year hiatus in regional fieldwork offered little incentive to reexamine these premises, and especially because sequences to which they could compare, in Anatolia and northern Syria, followed similar principles.

Late Bronze levels at Tarsus provided the primary reference for the immediate region and beyond. The excavation's prompt and assertive report proposed a complete record of archaeological expectations for the second half of the second millennium B.C.E. (Goldman 1956), in contrast to the insufficient data, or site-specific narratives, of the other major projects: Mersin-Yumuktepe (Levels VII–V: Garstang 1953; Jean 2006), the original Amuq survey (Phase M: Haines 1971; Swift 1958), and Tell Atchana (Levels VI/V–I: Woolley 1955). Late Bronze Tarsus was seen to comprise two historical periods, supported by epigraphic finds: the first under the local dynasty of Kizzuwatna, in fluctuating alliance with the Mittanni kingdom, followed by annexation into the Hittite Empire under Šuppiluliuma I, or thereabouts (Goldman 1956:62–63). Occupational levels at Tarsus were then grouped into two main phases: Late Bronze (LB) I and LB II. They corresponded to the two historical periods and coincided with dating conventions in Palestine. LB II was further divided into LB IIa, an impressive architectural level in Hittite style, later destroyed by fire, and LB IIb, a squatters' occupation whose Aegeanizing pottery (LH IIIC "Granary Style") was linked to Sea Peoples' raids in the eastern Mediterranean, and to the historical end of the Late Bronze Age (Goldman 1956:44–59). Reanalysis of the second millennium B.C.E. stratigraphic and ceramic sequence at Tarsus modified some aspects but preserved the overall rationale (Slane 1987). Finally, absolute dates were calculated from these historical criteria, and confirmed by ceramic cross-dating: LB I = ca. 1650–1450 B.C.E., LB IIa = ca. 1450–1225 B.C.E., and LB IIb = ca. 1225–1100 B.C.E. (Goldman 1956). Current views would lower the beginning of LB I by one century, and of LB IIa by four decades, to the mid-sixteenth and late fifteenth centuries B.C.E., respectively (Bietak and Höflmayer 2007).

The Tarsus chronology's strength lies in conforming to an eastern Mediterranean template that supercedes regional boundaries and facilitates comparative assessments, whereas the longer, better articulated sequence at Tell Atchana was formulated to track the site's internal historical trajectory (Woolley 1955) and cannot be widely applied. However, Tarsus's excavated Late Bronze occupation is incomplete, as newly confirmed by results from Kilise Tepe and Kinet Höyük, to its west and east. Pottery from Tarsus's latest stratum assigned to LB I, "The Pottery Storage Room Unit" (Goldman 1956:46–48, the 5.00 M. Phase in Section A; Slane 1987:467–68, Level A.VI) is precisely matched by the Middle Bronze II/III assemblage at Kinet (Gates 2000; for earlier doubts, see Fischer 1963; Mellink 1965; Symington 1987). Thus Late Bronze Tarsus is, at present, limited to a single coherent architectural level: the "Hittite Temple" in Section A and housing in Section B (Goldman 1956:49–50; Slane 1987:12, Levels A.IX–B.IX). The Late Bronze stratigraphy at Kilise Tepe (Phases III–IIa–c/d) and Kinet (Phase IV, Periods 15–13.2) can now substitute for Tarsus to represent the entire period. Like LB IIb Tarsus (A.X–B.X), these two sites also document the decline of their Late Bronze culture, and its eventual Iron Age replacement (Gates 2006; Postgate and Thomas 2007:111–58).

In southeastern Anatolia, the Late Bronze's stratigraphic definition is meager and treated as a single horizon encompassing two historical phases: the Mittanni kingdom (ca. 1500–1350 B.C.E.), followed by the Middle Assyrian one, contemporary with and outlasting the Hittite Empire (ca. 1350–1050 B.C.E.; see Matney, chapter 19, and Radner, chapter 33 in this volume, for additional discussion of Assyrian topics). With some exceptions, site levels refer to these periods rather than to Late Bronze phases (e.g., Schachner 2003). This system is also favored for Late Bronze Syria (Akkermans and Schwartz 2003:327–33) and northern Mesopotamia, southeastern Anatolia's closest archaeological references. In the Upper Euphrates, a cultural and political frontier zone in this period as in others, excavations have applied labels that are either culture-historical, or archaeological: for example, İmikuşağı's Habur (= MB II) and Hittite Old Kingdom phases (= late MB II/LB I) (Konyar 2006), in contrast to Korucutepe's LB I Phase I (= Hittite Old Kingdom) and LB II Phase J (= Hittite Empire) (van Loon 1978:28–34). In the absence of an agreed-upon chronology, and because few key sites are published, the Upper Euphrates and southeastern Anatolia assume a marginal place in Late Bronze archaeological discussions. In fact, this discretion accurately reflects a time when permanent settlement became sporadic and dispersed.

Diagnostic Material Culture

The Late Bronze ceramic assemblage in both regions was professionally manufactured in plain, light-colored fabrics and featured a narrow range of tablewares: plates, shallow bowls, craters, and flasks or pitchers. Their banality matched, even in shape and appearance, the uniform output of potmakers throughout Syria and northern Mesopotamia during the second millennium B.C.E. (Akkermans and Schwartz 2003:331; Mazzoni 2002; Pfälzner 1997; Postgate 2007). Local traditions were superceded by a common set of kitchen and dining utensils, pointing to a broad trend in the substance and serving of meals.

In the south, the source for the local ceramic industry was central Anatolia under Hittite administration (not Syria). Indicators are white- or yellow-slipped bottles with tall necks and pointed bases; three-handled pilgrim flasks; coarseware baking platters, plain or with a red-burnished band at the rim; red- or brown-burnished zoomorphic vessels such as bulls and birds of prey, or with zoomorphic protomes; miniature saucers; and potmarks incised before firing (e.g., Gates 2001, 2006). Excluding potmarks, these types, together with plates, bowls, and containers making up the majority of the assemblage, appeared on the Anatolian plateau with the Middle Bronze "*kārum* period," and evolved there over the following centuries (Mielke 2006; Mielke in Müller-Karpe 1998:123–29; Schoop 2006; and see Michel, chapter 13, and Kulakoğlu, chapter 47 in this volume, for the *kārum* period). But their introduction to Cilicia was abrupt, replacing the Middle Bronze serving set (the Cilician Painted trefoil-mouthed pitcher and cup) and cooking pot (a deep casserole with loop handles and a short spout) (Gates 2000). Whether the process behind this new pottery's implantation was a regulatory economic system (Gates 2001) or on-site administrative presence (Postgate 2007), it heralded close Hittite involvement (Postgate 2007).

Less evident is when this change occurred. The narrow and repetitive repertoire, called "Drab Ware" at Tarsus, was attributed there and at Mersin to the Hittite Empire, when Šuppiluliuma I annexed Kizzuwatna (Garstang 1953:237–38; Goldman 1956:203–5). Hittite mass-produced ceramics were thus made to characterize LB II (LB IIa at Tarsus), and assigned to the fourteenth and thirteenth centuries B.C.E., in accordance with Boğazköy. The revision of Boğazköy's ceramic sequence to span the entire Hittite period, from the sixteenth century B.C.E. onward (Schoop 2003, 2006), makes these chronological assumptions invalid. Nor can they be redressed by applying Glatz's criterion of a "north-central Anatolian (NCA) style" based on seven diagnostic types (Glatz 2009, and see Glatz, chapter 40 in this volume), because it is their subtle modulations that calibrate the four-century evolution (Schoop 2003, 2006). Kilise Tepe (Level IIIa–e) and Kinet Höyük (Phase IV:2, Period 15C–A) show the Hittite assemblage in place in LB I, by the sixteenth or early fifteenth century B.C.E. (Gates 2006; Postgate 2007). In the Amuq, it probably arrived later (Atchana Level III), to be clarified by the new excavations. Both Amuq surveys found this period ceramically indistinct and elusive (Casana 2009; Casana and Wilkinson 2005; Swift 1958:23–30).

For the Euphrates frontier, texts relating a Hittite military presence in Išuwa are supported by archaeological findings and a central Anatolian ceramic assemblage. It was introduced to the northern Elazığ-Malatya region, at İmikuşağı, Korucutepe, and elsewhere, including Arslantepe, at the start of the Old Kingdom; painted and burnished decorations, relief impressions, and flaring-necked storage jars precede the onset of mass production (Konyar 2006). These distinctive types, close to their "*kārum* period" forebears, soon yielded to the faster, efficient production already discussed, including the potmarks (Murray 1987; Umurtak 1996). It is best documented at Norşuntepe and Korucutepe Phases I and J (the latter a mixed sample, however: Griffin 1980; Murray 1987). Further south, the pertinent phases from Tille have been redated from the Late Bronze to its transition into the Early Iron Age (Griggs and Manning 2009; Summers 2010; compare Summers 1993); and other Late Bronze sites in the region remain unpublished (Lidar, Samsat) or inadequately sampled (Carchemish).

In the face of this conservative assemblage, high-visibility imports play the noble role for dating, especially Cypriot Bichrome (MB II/III–early LB I, ca. 1560–1460 B.C.E.), and White Slip and Base-Ring Wares (LB I–II), despite internal chronological disputes (Bietak and Höflmayer 2007; Crewe 2007:14–15; Merrillees 1992; e.g., Kozal 2005). Their replacement by Aegeanizing, Late Helladic/Late Cypriot IIIC pottery announces the close of the Late Bronze Age in the twelfth century (Cadogan 1998). True Mycenaean ceramics are rare, restricted to the late fourteenth and thirteenth centuries B.C.E. (LH IIIA/B = LB II), and from fills, except at Kilise and Atchana (E. French 2007; Mühlenbruch 2009:25–32). The few pieces that made their way east (e.g., to Tille, Summers 1993:45) are chronologically insignificant.

For southeast Anatolia, the fine, light-on-dark Nuzi Ware has served a fundamental purpose, singling out as diagnostic a class of "coarse chaff-tempered jars and bowls" that otherwise defied identification, for example, on the high mound at Titriş, and at Giricano (Algaze, Mısır, and Wilkinson 1992:43; Schachner 2002). Üçtepe's Phase 10, from a small sounding, produced comparable bowls and plates, for which parallels were proposed from central Anatolia and the Upper Euphrates, to northern Syria, but only the few associated Nuzi Ware sherds assured this pottery's Late Bronze attribution (Özfırat 2005:34–35). Because reliance on the presence or absence of imports and fine wares to recognize Late Bronze assemblages is problematic on many levels (e.g., Casana 2009:12), the ceramic typology here remains uncertain.

Epigraphic finds have thus proven valuable, overriding problematic contexts. Hittite writing, in Hieroglyphic Luwian (HL; see Yakubovich, chapter 23, and Melchert, chapter 31 in this volume), is widely distributed in an instructive pattern, from provincial centers to smaller sites. Tarsus produced the largest number (about sixty), and longest span: seal-impressed clay tags (conical bullae) for documents written on perished materials, one HL seal-impressed cuneiform tablet, one seal-impressed jar handle, and biconvex seals with personal names. They recorded transactions by, among others, the early Kizzuwatnan king Išputaḫšu (fifteenth century B.C.E.), Ḫattušili III's queen Puduḫepa (early thirteenth century B.C.E.), and resident royal Hittite administrators (Gelb 1956). Other Hittite princes were based in Atchana/Alalakh III–II/I (LB II), according to tablets, seals, and an exceptional orthostat depicting "Tudḫaliya, the king's son" (Fink 2007; Wiseman 1953:117–18; Woolley 1955:266–67). Biconvex seals from Mersin-Yumuktepe and Kilise Tepe, bullae from Tatarlı and Soloi Höyük, and two stamped jar handles from Kinet tied into the same bureaucratic system of the Hittite Empire (Gates 2008; Sevin and Köroğlu 2004; Symington 2007b; Ünal and Girginer 2010; Yağcı 2003). So also did bullae and biconvex seals in the Euphrates Valley, from Korucutepe (Güterbock 1973, 1980) to Tille (Collon 1993) and Lidar, where two bullae of Kuzi-Tešub, king of Carchemish in the early twelfth century B.C.E., connect that capital's Late Bronze and Iron Age dynasties (Hauptmann 1987; Hawkins 1988; Sürenhagen 1986).

The nonroyal biconvex seals, hieroglyphic script, and Luwian language became popular in the thirteenth century B.C.E. in semi-official and private sectors, which maintained them after the demise of the Hittite state and its cuneiform archival tradition (Yakubovich 2008, and see Yakubovich, chapter 23 in this volume). For the regions discussed here, the only examples from secure contexts were the four in Kilise Tepe's Level IIb/c Stele Building, an administrative complex destroyed ca. 1180 B.C.E. (Postgate and Thomas 2007:137; Symington 2007b); other "stratified" finds were typically found in pits dug into final LB II levels (Tarsus, Korucutepe) and in transitional LB/EIA destruction débris (Tille, Lidar). As a group, these HL finds reflect the state's close oversight of provincial centers (Tarsus, Alalakh, Lidar) during the late Empire (Yakar 2000:259–69), its practice in secondary townships (Kilise Tepe), and a degree of regional literacy pervasive enough to survive the collapse of a centralized system.

Akkadian cuneiform archives from Tell Atchana's Niqmepa Palace and Level IV report the historical, economic, and social life of this LB I (fifteenth century B.C.E.) Hurrian kingdom before its Hittite annexation (von Dassow 2005). In the lightly populated Upper Tigris, a single tablet provides an LB I (fifteenth/fourteenth century B.C.E.) date to a fortress at Türbe Höyük (Yildirim and Gates 2007: 300), and a cache of fifteen tablets identifies at Giricano an enclave that housed Middle Assyrian tax collectors over several generations (twelfth–mid-eleventh century B.C.E.) (Schachner 2002).

Other types of portable material culture and technologies, such as metalwork, cylinder and scarab seals, and the minor plastic arts, adhered to an eastern Mediterranean Late Bronze standard. They are best illustrated in the Uluburun shipwreck (e.g., Pulak 1998) and the civic, religious, and funerary contexts at Atchana (Woolley 1955). A limestone statue of Idrimi, ruling at Alalakh for his Mittanni overlord Barattarna (LB I, fifteenth century B.C.E.), is remarkable for its style and autobiographical text; it was discovered in the site's late LB II temple precinct in a secondary setting, like the Hittite orthostat of Tudḫaliya (see Fink 2007, with references). Finds at the other sites come from habitation deposits, with incomplete, damaged, and recycled inventories.

Geography, Environment, and the Human Landscape

Southern and southeastern Anatolia present three contrasting zones, differentiated by topography, elevation, climate, soils, and connectivity to neighboring regions. In the Late Bronze Age as at other times, they offered varied options for human exploitation and settlement and reflected different cultural and political inclinations. Historical geography provides little assistance, since few of their archaeological sites can be associated with ancient toponyms.

Cilicia

The Çukurova Plain—Cilicia Campestris of classical antiquity—is a low-lying alluvial fan of exceptional size (approximately 140 km wide). It was formed by three rivers and their many tributaries, flowing from the steep Taurus Mountains that enclose the plain on three sides, down into the Mediterranean. Rich and perennially renewed soil, high rainfall, and a temperate climate ensured predictable agricultural yields. These provided, close at hand, the food to support large populations in closely spaced nucleated settlements over the long term, an essential requirement for stable urban life (Jongman 1988). The multiperiod mounds that extend, at twenty- to thirty-kilometer intervals, in an arc from the plain's western to eastern borders, are located beside or within the plain's modern towns and cities. Together they attest to conditions favorable for continuous settlement from Neolithic times onward, on scales appropriate to respective periods. Beyond them, to the north, a second looser tier of large centers, such as Tatarlı, extended into the interior valleys, although this piedmont stayed populated only through Early Byzantine times (Seton-Williams 1954). Cilicia's urban sites on mounds were all occupied during the Late Bronze Age.

South of this arc, formed by a gravelly alluvial fan underlying the earliest occupation at Tarsus (Öner, Hocaoğlu, and Uncu 2005), stretched the delta's marshlands and lagoons. The modern coastline was in place by Roman times and maintained a string of seaside harbors (Seton-Williams 1954). But preclassical ports were situated inside estuaries and were vulnerable to silting and abandonment, on terrain unsuitable for sustained habitation (Yakar 2000:345, citing Strabo). Harbors and fishing villages can be hypothesized from the many small sites with discontinuous or short occupations that were identified by surveys in the delta proper, along its southern banks (Taffet 2001). Long-lived exceptions are Bronze Age ports on Cilicia's western and eastern borders, where the mountains draw near the sea: at Soloi, Mersin-Yumuktepe, Kinet, and on the coastal strip around İskenderun Bay. Cilicia's maritime connections, invariably emphasized by classical historians because of its visible Roman ports (Hellenkemper and Hild 1986; Rosenbaum, Huber, and Onurkan 1967), developed early in the second millennium B.C.E., when an autonomous eastern Mediterranean economy based on seafaring first emerged. Cilicia also fostered ancillary maritime industries like shipbuilding, its forested mountains providing ready timber (Yakar 2000:352, citing Strabo). Cargoes from the LB II wrecks at Uluburun and Cape Gelidonya document the commerce in metals, raw materials, and finished goods that such boats transported (Bass 1967; Pulak 1998).

In contrast, the few land routes into this plain were difficult and seasonal, in precipitous valleys cutting through the mountain barriers. The shortest route from the Anatolian interior crossed, above Tarsus, an elevated pass known since classical times as the Cilician Gates, near modern Pozantı. A second route to the northeast, the highland road from Gaziantep eastward, followed the narrow gorge of the upper Ceyhan through the Hasanbeyli Pass above modern Bahçe, before taking a long descent into the plain. Tributary valleys also gave access from the north (from Kayseri and, eventually, Sivas), through rough terrain marked by Late Bronze and Iron Age rock reliefs and inscriptions (Darga 1992:174–82; Ehringhaus 2005; Seeher 2009). Entry into Late Bronze Cilicia was protected by fortresses at Porsuk/Zeyve Höyük and Domuztepe (Alkım 1952; Beyer et al. 2008).

A third, strenuous passage from the central plateau bisects the wide mountainous buffer, known as Rough Cilicia or Cilicia Tracheia, that protects the delta's western flank. This isolated route, down the deeply encased Göksu Valley from the Konya Plain to a coastal outlet at Silifke, was sparsely settled, since the region is more suited to a rural economy and transhumant lifestyle (D. French 1965; Yakar 2000:353–55). The site at Kilise Tepe was an exception, situated to oversee the last descent to the coast (Postgate and Thomas 2007:11–13, 18). The valley acted as a channel for Mediterranean products into central Anatolia in the Late Bronze Age (Symington 2001). It perhaps found favor by skirting intermediaries in the urbanized delta, and its nomadic population offered predictable transport for goods during cyclical migrations (Klengel 1977; Yakar 2000). Second millennium B.C.E. ports would be expected at frequent intervals along Rough Cilicia's rocky coastline west of Silifke, but no predecessors for its many Hellenistic and Roman ones are attested archaeologically (Dinçol et al. 2001; Symington 2007a). Further west, on the Pamphylian and Lycian shores, LB II coastal habitation has been probed by recent soundings only at Perge, preclassical Parḫa, and Patara, preclassical Patar (Yildirim and Gates 2007:308).

Despite the topographical contrast between the eastern plain and western mountains, the two formed a single cultural zone recognized since antiquity by classical geographers and confirmed by archaeological research since the early twentieth century (D. French 1965; Postgate and Thomas 2007:5–7; Symington 2007a). They represented two Late Bronze historical entities: Kizzuwatna in the plain and Tarḫuntašša in the mountains, although the latter's territorial domain was realized by a diplomatic maneuver of the late Hittite Empire (Jasink 2001). Together, they stood geographically apart from inland neighbors, whose incursions could be monitored closely, and instead turned to the eastern Mediterranean, which in the Late Bronze Age offered direct entry to an international market. Cilicia's economic advantages led Hittite rulers to draft treaties with generations of Kizzuwatnan kings, from ca. 1500 B.C.E. onward, more than with any other dynastic region (Trémouille 2001; and see Beal, chapter 26 in this volume, for a history of such treaties), although military interest in the route to western Syria is often cited for these diplomatic efforts (Symington 2007a; Trémouille 2001). The appeal and benefits of a Mediterranean outlet underlie textual references to the port of Ura, whose location in western Cilicia remains contested (Symington 2007a); recent excavations at Soloi make it an attractive candidate (Yağcı 2003).

At best, the only accepted Late Bronze (Hittite) toponyms for archaeological sites in Cilicia are Tarsus (Tarša) at Gözlü Kule, and Adana (Adaniya) at Tepebağ Höyüğü, thanks to the persistence of their place names. Periodic efforts to label others (e.g., Forlanini 2001; Trémouille 2001) have yet to be confirmed by epigraphic proof from the sites themselves.

The Amuq Plain

The Amuq Plain was also low-lying, and fed by three rivers, but it constituted a self-contained inland entity. Like Cilicia, climate and alluvial soil provided reliable agricultural resources, supplied by villages to one second millennium B.C.E. urban center, at Tell Atchana (Casana 2007, 2009; Casana and Wilkinson 2005). Farming contended with poor drainage and swamps, but the plain's small size (30 × 40 km) is more likely to have been the factor that limited settlement density to a single large site (Casana 2009). It connected with the Mediterranean, about thirty-five kilometers distant, via the narrow valley of the Orontes, whose estuary sheltered at least one Late Bronze port, that of Sabuniye (Pamir and Nishiyama 2002). The Amuq especially looked inland; straightforward roads led east into Syria and northward up the İslahiye valley, guarded by Bronze Age Tilmen Höyük. From there they turned east into the highlands of Gaziantep and on to the Upper Euphrates and the Tigris. The Amuq's only neighbor with difficult access was Cilicia, screened off by the Amanus Range, and reached through the steep pass at Belen, overlooking İskenderun's coastline. The route was watched by a second millennium B.C.E. site identified through survey at Dağılbaz, in the western foothills below Belen (Killebrew, Lehmann, and Gates 2009).

This topographic barrier gave different affiliations to the two regions. Unlike Cilicia, the Amuq's cultural and socioeconomic dynamics stemmed from overland ties; proximity to the Mediterranean merely provided a conduit for commerce and income. The dominant Late Bronze populations also spoke different languages: Luwian in Cilicia, Hurrian and West Semitic in the Amuq (Melchert 2003:12; von Dassow 2008; and see Yakubovich, chapter 23 in this volume). When geographers placed the Pylae Syriae (the gateway from Asia Minor and Cilicia into Syria) at İskenderun, they evoked a cultural separation already imprinted in the Bronze Age.

The historical and demographic framework of the Late Bronze Amuq is also in sharper focus. Tell Atchana's tablets identify it as ancient Alalakh, seat of the minor but well-connected second millennium B.C.E. kingdom of Mukiš, more tightly integrated than Tarsus into the Mittanni kingdom (Alalakh VI/V–IV, LB I). Detailed entries from its Level IV archives about towns, villages, and households present an exceptional and newly tapped source for reconstructing one Late Bronze society in depth (von Dassow 2008). Like Tarsus, Alalakh was governed by Hittite administrators during the fourteenth and thirteenth centuries B.C.E. (Alalakh III–II, LB II).

The archival inventories of LB I Alalakh's dependent settlements and their sizes coincide poorly with survey data, which record fewer Late Bronze sites than the texts imply. The kingdom's human and landed properties evidently included holdings outside its territorial limits, making efforts to reconcile toponyms with local sites a futile exercise (Casana 2009). The archaeological pattern, in contrast, reflects a reasonable balance between urban center and village network, the agricultural hinterland that underpinned the city's other economic activities.

The Southeast

Southeastern Turkey's highlands are discussed elsewhere in this volume (see Sagona, chapter 30, Marro, chapter 12, and Laneri and Schwartz, chapter 14). The Late Bronze landscape differed from its configuration in the mid-third to mid-second millennium B.C.E., however. Various factors conspired to precipitate this change: irregular rainfall and increased aridity (Freydank 2009; Konyar 2006; Riehl 2009), the creation of the Hittite state's eastern border at the Euphrates, and the dissolution of large-scale commerce between the Anatolian plateau and northern Mesopotamia. These factors resulted in the abandonment of most Middle Bronze centers, intermittent occupation at the few that endured, and the founding of fortified outposts to administer Hittite, Mittanni, and Middle Assyrian bureaucracy and control the circulation of people and goods.

Southeast Anatolia subsisted on ovicaprid husbandry and on rainfed agriculture under less favored conditions than in the west, because of poorer soil, higher rates of erosion, and a climate with seasonal extremes. To sustain a population on an urban or ostentatious scale required extensive farmlands and extraterritorial enterprise. Most settlements were therefore rural, and the few hubs they supplied were widely dispersed (Archi, Pecorella, and Salvini 1971:9–15; Wilkinson 1990:11–60). Prosperity and survival depended on a delicate balance of natural and external advantages that was apparently disrupted throughout the Late Bronze Age. A review of recent excavations underlines the extent of this post–MB II hiatus. In the Tigris/Ilısu Valley, Hirbemerdon and Kenan Tepe were abandoned, and Late Bronze occupation is found only on Ziyaret Tepe's high mound and the fortress at Türbe Höyük. A similar break occurred in the Urfa and Gaziantep areas at Zeytinli Bahçe and Tilbeshar, whose countryside was also depleted (Kepinski-Lecomte et al. 1996; Matney et al. 2002; Yildirim and Gates 2007:300–3). Survey in the vicinity of Arslantepe confirmed a gap in settlements of any size after MB II; so did previous evidence to the south from Titriş Höyük, Kurban Höyük, and Harran, where habitation was thin, if at all present, throughout the second millennium B.C.E. (Prag 1970; Wilkinson 1990:129–33). Unstable and discontinuous occupation is also indicated at the few attested Late Bronze sites. Architectural remains are slight at Giricano (Schachner 2002, 2003), interspaced with erosional phases even at Hittite outposts like İmikuşağı and Korucutepe (Konyar 2006; van Loon 1978:28–39), or temporary, with pits and fireplaces but little else, as is the case at Tille (Summers 1993).

Official installations were located in strategic passes and at river crossings: the Hittite ones on the Sakçagözü-Maraş passage from Cilicia toward the Euphrates and Carchemish (Dodd 2007), and in the Euphrates Valley from Elazığ to Carchemish and Emar; to their east, the Mittanni-Middle Assyrian ones were similarly situated. The countryside they invested was populated by subsistence farmers and transient pastoralists whose archaeological existence is invisible. It is also largely anonymous, apart from equating Malatya with Maldiya/Malitija and Djerablus with Carchemish (Jasink 1994); the lack of provenience for Ḫattušili I's letter to a vassal in Tikunani, with references to Ḫaḫḫum (Lidar?) and other towns, is indeed regrettable (Salvini 1994, 1998). When the Hittite state reoriented central Anatolia's supply network to the south's maritime markets (Seeher 2005), the southeast lost its lucrative overland connections and reverted to a rural economy and precarious village life.

Settlement Layout and Architecture

Late Bronze settlement layout in these regions is gauged from mounds of formal, "urban" type and from specialized sites such as forts, one provincial town (Kilise), and one port (Kinet). Village life must be inferred from the declining stages of LB II. Largely missing are cemeteries, represented only in the Carchemish area (Woolley 1914), by incidental tombs on the mound at Tell Atchana (Woolley 1955) and perhaps by a funerary monument above Muwatalli II's rock relief at Sirkeli (Ahrens et al. 2008; Ehringhaus 1999). Extramural cemeteries, for inhumation and cremation, are assumed from this evidence.

In keeping with Bronze Age practice, civic buildings and residences were situated on high mounds, perhaps in isolation there. In the southeast, lower towns disappeared with the Late Bronze Age, when inhabitants chose the security of an elevated site. Such may have been the case too in Cilicia and the Amuq, but this is unexplored except at Kinet, where buildings on the shoreline, admittedly essential to the harbor's business, were overseen by those on its mound (Gates 2006). Official structures are attested by the broad exposures at Tell Atchana and Tarsus, and, to some extent, reflect historical affiliations. The Level IV ("Niqmepa") palace at Tell Atchana (LB I), with entrance portico, two-chambered audience suites, and orthostats lining the formal rooms, was built in western Syrian style (Woolley 1955:110–31), as was the small, contemporary temple, whose porch, anteroom, and cella are aligned and of equal width. Temple rebuildings during the LB II preserved its Syrian features, although the incomplete Level III version is obscure (for a reworked temple sequence, see Fink 2007). In contrast, the monumental temple at Tarsus, dominating the mound's highest point and east side, was unquestionably Hittite in plan and construction, circumstances dating it, perhaps wrongly, to LB IIa (see foregoing discussion; Goldman 1956:49–50). A second Hittite temple, recognized by its cyclopean masonry and compartmented foundations, is under excavation at Tatarlı, where it likewise occupied the site's eastern lookout (Girginer 2008). Hittite builders were claimed for the massive casemate platform ("citadel") at Atchana III–II (LB II) (Woolley 1955:166–70); in the absence of any superstructure, however, neither its plan nor its type can be evaluated (Fink 2007). The large-scale structures at Kinet, overlooking its harbors, are also difficult to assess from their incomplete plans (Period 15, LB I; Period 14, early LB II: Gates 2006, compare with 2009). Finally, Kilise Tepe's unpretentious "Stele Building," combining administrative and cultic functions, suited official life in a provincial town; three wings, for storage and other activities, enclosed a room with an altar-like feature and a painted slab (the stele) (Phase II a–c, late LB II: Postgate and Thomas 2007). No public structures are published for the southeastern sites but could be expected at Lidar. Private housing on these mounds ranged from sturdy, multiroomed residences with internal courts at Tarsus and Atchana, to rural accommodations by the close of LB II (Gates 2006; Goldman 1956:50–59; Summers 1993).

Military architecture followed standards common to the Late Bronze eastern Mediterranean, including Hittite central Anatolia. With the (possible) exception of

Mersin, the known sites were all castles for a military and official presence, not residential places protected by a walled enclosure. Mudbrick fortification walls, for example, at Mersin VII–V, were set on stone casemates with rectangular projecting towers, fronted by a screen wall (Garstang 1953:237–41; Jean 2006). They are exceptionally illustrated by the burnt fortress at Zeyve Höyük/Porsuk (Phase V: LB II); its casemates stored grain and other supplies, and its western gate was guarded by two inner towers with internal staircases, whose brick and timber superstructures stand two stories high (four meters) (Beyer et al. 2008). The Euphrates examples show that few buildings were inside: warehouses and a square tower-like structure at İmikuşağı (LB I); small, sporadic domestic structures at Korucutepe and Tepecik (Konyar 2006; van Loon 1978); and at Lidar (LB II), a central open area with a brick-lined cistern (Hauptmann 1987). The LB I stronghold at Tilmen, at the crossroads south into the Amuq and west into Cilicia, consisted of a reused tower (Fortress H, like the one at İmikuşağı) beside an official residency (Building C), situated at the highest point of the destroyed MB II city (Colantoni 2010; Marocchi et al. 2010). East of Hittite territory, the fortress at Türbe Höyük was designed on a similar scale (70 × 30 m) to monitor the confluence of the Tigris and Botan Rivers (Yildirim and Gates 2007:300).

End of the Late Bronze Age

The Late Bronze cities, towns, and forts in southern and southeastern Anatolia endured various fortunes in the twelfth century B.C.E., but all experienced the eventual termination of this cultural, political, and economic phase (Gates 2010). Most were destroyed, and lay deserted for centuries (e.g., Lidar), or their ruins were reoccupied by squatters and migrants, then abandoned (Porsuk, Tarsus). Some deteriorated into villages, attracted new settlers, then ceased altogether (Kilise Tepe, Kinet). Others were abandoned outright (Atchana) and replaced by a new settlement nearby (Tayinat). Prosperity did not revive them fully until the Middle Iron Age, ca. 1000 B.C.E., at the earliest.

References

Ahrens, Alexander, Ekin Kozal, Christoph Kümmel, Ingrid Laube, and Mirko Novák. 2008. Sirkeli Höyük—Kulturkontakte in Kilikien. Vorbericht über die Kampagnen 2006 und 2007 der deutsch-türkischen Mission. *Istanbuler Mitteilungen* 58: 67–107.

Akkermans, Peter M. M. G. and Glenn Schwartz. 2003. *The Archaeology of Syria from Complex Hunter-Gatherers to Early Urban Societies (ca. 16,000–300 BC)*. Cambridge: Cambridge University Press.

Algaze, Guillermo, Adnan Mısır, and Tony Wilkinson. 1992. Şanlıurfa Museum/University of California Excavations and surveys at Titriş Höyük, 1991: A Preliminary Report. *Anatolica* 18: 33–60.

Alkım, U. Bahadır. 1952. Sixth Season's Work at Karatepe. *Belleten* 16: 134–36.

Archi, Alfonso, Paulo Emilio Pecorella, and Mirjo Salvini. 1971. *Gaziantep e la sua Regione*. Incunabula Graeca 48. Roma: Edizioni dell'Ateneo.

Bass, George. 1967. *Cape Gelidonya: A Bronze Age Shipwreck*. Transactions of the American Philosophical Society 57.8. Philadelphia: American Philosophical Society.

Beyer, Dominique, Isabelle Chalier, Françoise Laroche-Traunecker, Julie Patrier, and Aksel Tibet. 2008. Zeyve Höyük (Porsuk): Rapport sommaire sur la campagne de 2007. *Anatolia Antiqua* 16: 313–44.

Bietak, Manfred and Felix Höflmayer. 2007. Introduction: High and Low Chronology. In *The Synchronisation of Civilisations in the Eastern Mediterranean in the Second Millennium B.C. 3. Proceedings of the SCIEM 2000—2nd EuroConference. Vienna, 28th of May–1st of June 2003*, ed. Manfred Bietak and Ernst Czerny, 13–23. Wien: Österreichischen Akademie der Wissenschaften.

Cadogan, Gerald. 1998. The Thirteenth Century in Cyprus. In *Mediterranean Peoples in Transition. Thirteenth to Early Tenth Centuries B.C.E., in Honor of Professor T. Dothan*, ed. Seymour Gitin, Amihai Mazar, and Ephraim Stern, 6–16. Jerusalem: Israel Exploration Society.

Casana, Jesse. 2007. Structural Transformations in Settlement Systems of the Northern Levant. *American Journal of Archaeology* 112: 195–221.

———. 2009. Alalakh and the Archaeological Landscape of Mukish: The Political Geography and Population of a Late Bronze Age Kingdom. *Bulletin of the American Schools of Oriental Research* 353: 7–37.

Casana, Jesse and Tony Wilkinson. 2005. Settlement and Landscapes in the Amuq Region. In *The Amuq Valley Regional Project 1: Surveys in the Plain of Antioch and Orontes Delta, Turkey, 1995–2002*, ed. K. Aslıhan Yener, 25–65, 203–280. Oriental Institute Publications 131. Chicago: Oriental Institute of the University of Chicago.

Colantoni, Alessandro. 2010. Some Observations on the Late Bronze Age Pottery Assemblages of Tilmen Höyük. In *Societies in Transition. Evolutionary Processes in the Northern Levant between Late Bronze Age II and Early Iron Age. Papers Presented on the Occasion of the 20th Anniversary of the New Excavations in Tell Afis, Bologna, 15th November 2007*, ed. Fabrizio Venturi, 103–10. Studi e testi orientali 9, Serie Archeologica 2. Bologna: Clueb.

Collon, Dominique. 1993. The Seals. In *Tille Höyük 4. The Late Bronze Age and the Iron Age Transition*, ed. Geoffrey Summers, 171–77. British Institute of Archaeology at Ankara Monograph 15. Ankara: British Institute of Archaeology at Ankara.

Crewe, Lindy. 2007. *Early Enkomi. Regionalism, Trade and Society at the Beginning of the Late Bronze Age on Cyprus*. BAR International Series 1706. Oxford: Archaeopress.

Darga, A. Muhibbe. 1992. *Hitit Sanatı*. İstanbul: Anadolu Sanat Yayınları.

Dinçol, Ali, Jak Yakar, Belkıs Dinçol, and Avia Taffet. 2001. Die Grenzen von Tarhuntašša im Lichte geographischer Beobachtungen. In *La Cilicie: Espaces et pouvoirs locaux (2e millénaire av. J.-C.–4e siècle ap. J.-C.). Actes de la table ronde internationale, Istanbul, 2–5 novembre 1999*, ed. Éric Jean, Ali Dinçol, and Serra Durugönül, 79–86. Varia Anatolica 13. İstanbul: De Boccard.

Dodd, Lynn Swartz. 2007. Strategies for Future Success: Remembering the Hittites during the Iron Age. *Anatolian Studies* 57: 203–16.

Ehringhaus, Horst. 1999. Vorläufiger Bericht über die Ausgrabung auf dem Sirkeli Höyük, Provinz Adana/Türkei im Jahre 1997. *Istanbuler Mitteilungen* 49: 83–140.

———. 2005. *Götter, Herrscher, Inschriften. Die Felsreliefs der hethitischen Großreichszeit in der Türkei*. Mainz: von Zabern.

Fink, Amir S. 2007. Where Was the Statue of Idrimi Actually Found? The Later Temples of Tell Atchana (Alalakh) Revisited. *Ugarit-Forschungen* 39: 161–207.

Fischer, Franz. 1963. *Die hethitische Keramik von Boğazköy. Boğazköy-Ḫattuša 4*. Berlin: Mann.

Forlanini, Massimo. 2001. Quelques notes sur la géographie historique de la Cilicie. In *La Cilicie: Espaces et pouvoirs locaux (2e millénaire av. J.-C.–4e siècle ap. J.-C.). Actes de la table ronde internationale, Istanbul, 2–5 novembre 1999*, ed. Éric Jean, Ali Dinçol, and Serra Durugönül, 553–63. Varia Anatolica 13. İstanbul: De Boccard.

Freydank, Helmut. 2009. Kār-Tukultī-Ninurta als Agrarprovinz. *Altorientalische Forschungen* 36.1: 16–84.

French, David. 1965. Prehistoric Sites in the Göksu Valley. *Anatolian Studies* 15: 177–201.

French, Elisabeth. 2007. The Mycenaean Pottery. In *Excavations at Kilise Tepe, 1994–1998. From Bronze Age to Byzantine in Western Cilicia*, ed. J. Nicholas Postgate and David Thomas, 373–76. British Institute of Archaeology at Ankara Monograph 30. Cambridge: McDonald Institute for Archaeological Research and British Institute at Ankara.

Garstang, John. 1953. *Prehistoric Mersin. Yümük Tepe in Southern Turkey*. Oxford: Clarendon Press.

Gates, Marie-Henriette. 2000. Kinet Höyük (Hatay, Turkey) and MB Levantine Chronology. *Akkadica* 119–20: 77–101.

———. 2001. Potmarks at Kinet Höyük and the Hittite Ceramic Industry. In *La Cilicie: Espaces et pouvoirs locaux (2e millénaire av. J.-C.-4e siècle ap. J.-C.). Actes de la table ronde internationale, Istanbul, 2–5 novembre 1999*, ed. Éric Jean, Ali Dinçol, Serra Durugönül, 137–57. Varia Anatolica 13. İstanbul: De Boccard.

———. 2006. Dating the Hittite levels at Kinet Höyük: A Revised Chronology. In *Strukturierung und Datierung in der hethitischen Archäologie. Structuring and Dating in Hittite Archaeology*, ed. Dirk Paul Mielke, Ulf-Dietrich Schoop, and Jürgen Seeher, 293–309. Byzas 4. İstanbul: Ege Yayınları.

———. 2008. 2006 Season at Kinet Höyük (Yeşil-Dörtyol, Hatay). *Kazı Sonuçları Toplantısı* 29.2: 281–98.

———. 2009. 2007 Season at Kinet Höyük (Yeşil-Dörtyol, Hatay). *Kazı Sonuçları Toplantısı* 30.2: 351–68.

———. 2010. Potters and Consumers in Cilicia and the Amuq during the "Age of Transformations" (13th–10th centuries BC). In *Societies in Transition. Evolutionary Processes in the Northern Levant between Late Bronze Age II and Early Iron Age. Papers Presented on the Occasion of the 20th Anniversary of the New Excavations in Tell Afis, Bologna, 15th November 2007*, ed. Fabrizio Venturi, 65–81. Studi e testi orientali 9, Serie Archeologica 2. Bologna: Clueb.

Gelb, Ignace. 1956. Hittite Hieroglyphic Seals and Seal Impressions. In *Excavations at Gözlü Kule, Tarsus 2: From the Neolithic through the Bronze Age*, ed. Hetty Goldman, 242–54. Princeton, N.J.: Princeton University Press.

Girginer, K. Serdar. 2008. Ceyhan/Tatarlı Höyük Kazı Çalışmaları 2007. *Türk Eskiçağ Bilimleri Enstitüsü Haberler* 26: 15–17.

Glatz, Claudia. 2009. Empire as Network: Spheres of Material Interaction in Late Bronze Age Anatolia. *Journal of Anthropological Archaeology* 28.2: 127–41.

Goldman, Hetty. 1956. *Excavations at Gözlü Kule, Tarsus 2: From the Neolithic through the Bronze Age*. Princeton, N.J.: Princeton University Press.

Griffin, Elizabeth. 1980. The Middle and Late Bronze Age Pottery. In *Korucutepe 3*, ed. Maurits van Loon, 3–109. Amsterdam: North-Holland.

Griggs, Carol and Sturt Manning. 2009. A Reappraisal of the Dendrochronology and Dating of Tille Höyük. *Radiocarbon* 51.2: 711–20.

Güterbock, Hans G. 1973. Hittite Hieroglyphic Seal Impressions from Korucutepe. *Journal of Near Eastern Studies* 32.1/2: 135–47.

———. 1980. Hittite Hieroglyphic Seal Impressions. In *Korucutepe 3*, ed. Maurits van Loon, 127–32. Amsterdam: North-Holland.

Haines, Richard. 1971. *Excavations on the Plain of Antioch 2: The Structural Remains of the Later Phases. Chatal Hüyük, Tell al-Judaidah, and Tell Ta'yinat*. Oriental Institute Publications 95. Chicago: Oriental Institute of the University of Chicago.

Hanfmann, George. 1948. Archaeology in Homeric Asia Minor. *American Journal of Archaeology* 52: 135–55.

Hauptmann, Harald. 1987. Lidar Höyük and Nevalı Çori, 1986. *Anatolian Studies* 37: 203–7.

Hawkins, J. David. 1988. Kuzi-Tešub and the "Great Kings" of Karkamiš. *Anatolian Studies* 38: 99–108.

Hellenkemper, Hansgerd and Friedrich Hild. 1986. *Neue Forschungen in Kilikien*. Veröffentlichungen der Kommission für die Tabula Imperii Byzantini 4. Wien: Verlag der Österreichischen Akademie der Wissenschaften.

Jasink, Anna Margherita. 1994. Il medio Eufrate: Continuità e innovazioni tra il secondo et il primo millennio A.C. *Mesopotamia* 29:7 3–88.

———. 2001. Kizzuwatna and Tarhuntašša: Their Historical Evolution and Interactions with Hatti. In *La Cilicie: Espaces et pouvoirs locaux (2e millénaire av. J.-C.-4e siècle ap. J.-C.). Actes de la table ronde internationale, Istanbul, 2–5 novembre 1999*, ed. Éric Jean, Ali Dinçol, Serra Durugönül, 47–56. Varia Anatolica 13. İstanbul: De Boccard.

Jean, Éric. 2006. The Hittites at Mersin-Yumuktepe: Old Problems and New Directions. In *Strukturierung und Datierung in der hethitischen Archäologie. Structuring and Dating in Hittite Archaeology*, ed. Dirk Paul Mielke, Ulf-Dietrich Schoop, and Jürgen Seeher, 311–32. Byzas 4. İstanbul: Ege Yayınları.

Jongman, Willem. 1988. *The Economy and Society of Pompeii*. Dutch Monographs on Ancient History and Archaeology 4. Amsterdam: Gieben.

Kepinski-Lecomte, Christine, Frédéric Gerard, Éric Jean, and Aksel Tibet. 1996. Tilbeshar 1994, 1995. *Anatolia Antiqua* 4: 291–301.

Killebrew, Ann, Gunnar Lehmann, and Marie-Henriette Gates. 2009. Summary of the 2007 Cilicia Survey (İskenderun Bay Region). *Araştırma Sonuçları Toplantısı* 26.3: 227–38.

Klengel, Horst. 1977. Nomaden und Handel. *Iraq* 39.2: 163–69.

Konyar, Erkan. 2006. Old Hittite Presence in the East of the Euphrates in the Light of Stratigraphical Data from İmikuşağı (Elazığ). In *Strukturierung und Datierung in der hethitischen Archäologie. Structuring and Dating in Hittite Archaeology*, ed. Dirk Paul Mielke, Ulf-Dietrich Schoop, and Jürgen Seeher, 333–48. Byzas 4. İstanbul: Ege Yayınları.

Kozal, Ekin. 2005. Unpublished Middle and Late Cypriot Pottery from Tarsus-Gözlükule. In *Field Seasons 2001–2003 of the Tarsus-Gözlükule Interdisciplinary Research Project*, ed. Aslı Özyar, 135–44. İstanbul: Ege Yayınları.

Marrochi, Marta, Giuseppe Bargossi, Giorgio Gasparotto, and Michele Dondi. 2010. Vitrification of Basalt Orthostats and Mud Building Components from Tilmen Höyük

(South-Eastern Turkey): An Experimental and Geoarchaeological Approach. *Journal of Archaeological Science* 37: 488–98.

Matney, Timothy, Michael Roaf, John Macginnis, and Helen McDonald. 2002. Archaeological Excavations at Ziyaret Tepe, 2000 and 2001. *Anatolica* 28: 47–89.

Mazzoni, Stefania. 2002. Late Bronze Age pottery Production in Northwestern Central Syria. In *Céramique de l'âge du Bronze en Syrie, 1. La Syrie du sud et la vallée de l'Oronte*, ed. Michel al-Maqdissi, Valérie Matoïan, and Christophe Nicolle, 129–42. Bibliothèque archéologique et historique 161. Beirut: Institut français d'archéologie du Proche-orient.

McEwan, Calvin. 1937. The Syrian Expedition of the Oriental Institute. *American Journal of Archaeology* 41: 8–16.

Melchert, H. Craig, ed. 2003. *The Luwians*. Handbuch der Orientalistik 1, The Near and Middle East 68. Leiden: Brill.

Mellink, Machteld. 1965. Anatolian Chronology. In *Chronologies in Old World Archaeology*, ed. Robert H. Ehrich, 101–31. Chicago: University of Chicago Press.

Merrillees, Robert. 1992. The Absolute Chronology of the Bronze Age in Cyprus: A Revision. *Bulletin of the American Schools of Oriental Research* 288: 47–52.

Mielke, Dirk Paul. 2006. İnandıktepe und Sarissa. Ein Beitrag zur Datierung althethitischer Fundcomplexe. In *Strukturierung und Datierung in der hethitischen Archäologie. Structuring and Dating in Hittite Archaeology*, ed. Dirk Paul Mielke, Ulf-Dietrich Schoop, and Jürgen Seeher, 251–76. Byzas 4. İstanbul: Ege Yayınları.

Murray, Ann. 1987. Work in Elazığ and Pamukkale Museum. *Araştırma Sonuçları Toplantısı* 3: 273–78.

Mühlenbruch, Tobias. 2009. *Die Synchronisierung der nördlichen Levante und Kilikiens mit der ägäischen Spätbronzezeit*. Contributions to the Chronology of the Eastern Mediterranean 19. Wien: Österreichischen Akademie der Wissenschaften.

Müller-Karpe, Andreas. 1998. Untersuchungen in Kuşaklı 1997. *Mitteilungen der Deutschen Orient-Gesellschaft* 130: 93–174.

Öner, Ertuğ, Beycan Hocaoğlu, and Levent Uncu. 2005. Palaeogeographical Surveys around the Mound of Gözlükule (Tarsus). In *Field Seasons 2001–2003 of the Tarsus-Gözlükule Interdisciplinary Research Project*, ed. Aslı Özyar, 69–82. İstanbul: Ege Yayınları.

Özfırat, Aynur. 2005. Üçtepe 2. *Tunc Çağları Kazı ve Yüzey Araştırmaları Işığında*. İstanbul: Ege Yayınları.

Pamir, Hatice and Shinichi Nishiyama. 2002. The Orontes Valley Delta Survey: Archaeological Investigation of Ancient Trade Stations/Settlements. *Ancient West and East* 1.2: 294–314.

Pfälzner, Peter. 1997. Keramikproduktion und Provinzverwaltung im mittelassyrischen Reich. In *Assyrien im Wandel der Zeiten*, ed. Hartmut Waetzoldt and Harald Hauptmann, 337–45. Heidelberg: Heidelberger Orientverlag.

Postgate, J. Nicholas. 2007. The Ceramics of Centralisation and Dissolution: A Case Study from Rough Cilicia. *Anatolian Studies* 57: 141–50.

Postgate, Nicholas and David Thomas, eds. 2007. *Excavations at Kilise Tepe, 1994–1998. From Bronze Age to Byzantine in Western Cilicia*. British Institute of Archaeology at Ankara Monograph 30. Cambridge: McDonald Institute for Archaeological Research and British Institute at Ankara.

Prag, Kay. 1970. The Deep Sounding at Harran in Turkey. *Levant* 2: 63–94.

Pulak, Cemal. 1998. The Uluburun Shipwreck: An Overview. *International Journal of Nautical Archaeology* 27.3: 188–224.

Riehl, Simone. 2009. Archaeobotanical Evidence for the Interrelationship of Agricultural Decision-Making and Climate Change in the Ancient Near East. *Quaternary International* 197: 93–114.

Rosenbaum, Elisabeth, Gerhard Huber, and Somay Onurkan. 1967. *A Survey of Coastal Cities in Western Cilicia. Preliminary Report*. Türk Tarih Kurumu Yayınlarından 6. Seri no. 8. Ankara: Türk Tarih Kurumu.

Salmeri, Giovanni and Anna Lucia D'Agata. 2009. Cilicia Survey 2007. *Araştırma Sonuçları Toplantısı* 26.2: 119–23.

Salvini, Mirjo. 1994. Una lettera di Ḫattušili I relativa alla spedizione contro Ḫaḫḫum. *Studi Micenei ed Egeo-Anatolici* 34: 61–80.

———. 1998. Un royaume hourrite en Mésopotamie du Nord à l'époque de Ḫattušili I. *Subartu* 4.1: 305–11.

Schachner, Andreas. 2002. Ausgrabungen in Giricano (2000–2001). Neue Forschungen an der Nordgrenze des Mesopotamischen Kulturraums. *Istanbuler Mitteilungen* 52: 9–57.

———. 2003. From the Bronze to the Iron Age. Identifying Changes in the Upper Tigris Region. The Case of Giricano. In *Identifying Changes: The Transition from Bronze to Iron Ages in Anatolia and its Neighbouring Regions*, ed. Bettina Fischer, Hermann Genz, Éric Jean, and Kemalettin Köroğlu, 151–63. İstanbul: Ege Yayınları.

Schoop, Ulf-Dietrich. 2003. Pottery Traditions of the Later Hittite Empire: Problems of Definition. In *Identifying Changes: The Transition from Bronze to Iron Ages in Anatolia and its Neighbouring Regions*, ed. Bettina Fischer, Hermann Genz, Éric Jean, and Kemalettin Köroğlu, 167–78. İstanbul: Ege Yayınları.

———. 2006. Dating the Hittites with Statistics: Ten Pottery Assemblages from Boğazköy-Ḫattuša. In *Strukturierung und Datierung in der hethitischen Archäologie. Structuring and Dating in Hittite Archaeology*, ed. Dirk Paul Mielke, Ulf-Dietrich Schoop, and Jürgen Seeher, 215–39. Byzas 4. İstanbul: Ege Yayınları.

Seeher, Jürgen. 2005. Überlegungen zur Beziehung zwischen dem hethitischen Kernreich und der Westküste Anatoliens im 2. Jahrtausend v. Chr. In *Interpretationsraum Bronzezeit, Bernhard Hänsel von seinen Schülern gewidmet*, ed. Barbara Horejs, Reinhard Jung, Elke Kaiser, and Biba Teržan, 33–44. Bonn: Dr. Rudolf Habelt GmbH.

———. 2009. Der Landschaft sein Siegel aufdrücken-hethitische Felsbilder und Hieroglyphen-inschriften als Ausdruck der herrscherlichen Macht-und Territorialanspruchs. *Altorientalische Forschungen* 36: 119–39.

Seton-Williams, M. Veronica. 1954. Cilician Survey. *Anatolian Studies* 4: 121–74.

Sevin, Veli and Kemalettin Köroğlu. 2004. Late Bronze at Yumuktepe: New Evidence from Step-Trench South. In *Mersin-Yumuktepe. A Reappraisal*, ed. Isabella Caneva and Veli Sevin, 73–83. Lecce: Congedo Editore.

Slane, Dorothy. 1987. *Middle and Late Bronze Age Architecture and Pottery in Gözlü Kule, Tarsus: A New Analysis*. Ann Arbor, Mich.: University Microfilms International.

Summers, Geoffrey. 1993. *Tille Höyük 4. The Late Bronze Age and the Iron Age Transition*. British Institute of Archaeology at Ankara Monograph 15. Ankara: British Institute of Archaeology at Ankara.

———. 2010. Revisiting the End of the Late Bronze Age and the Transition to the Early Iron Age at Tille Höyük. *Iraq* 77: 193–200.

Sürenhagen, Dietrich. 1986. Ein Königssiegel aus Kargamish. *Mitteilungen der Deutschen Orient-Gesellschaft* 118: 183–90.

Swift, Gustavus F. 1958. *The Pottery of the 'Amuq Phases K to O, and its Historical Relationships*. Ann Arbor, Mich.: University Microfilms.

Symington, Dorit. 1987. Remarks on the Tarsus Late Bronze Age I Pottery in the Adana Museum. *Araştırma Sonuçları Toplantısı* 3: 279–85.

———. 2001. Hittites at Kilise Tepe. In *La Cilicie: Espaces et pouvoirs locaux (2e millénaire av. J.-C.-4e siècle ap. J.-C.). Actes de la table ronde internationale, Istanbul, 2–5 novembre 1999*, ed. Éric Jean, Ali Dinçol, and Serra Durugönül, 167–84. Varia Anatolica 13. İstanbul: De Boccard.

———. 2007a. Que. B. Archäologie. *Reallexikon der Assyriologie und Vorderasiatischen Archäologie* 11.3/4: 195–201.

———. 2007b. Seals with Hieroglyphic Inscriptions. In *Excavations at Kilise Tepe, 1994–1998. From Bronze Age to Byzantine in Western Cilicia*, ed. J. Nicholas Postgate and David Thomas, 441–43. British Institute of Archaeology at Ankara Monograph 30. Cambridge: McDonald Institute for Archaeological Research and British Institute at Ankara.

Taffet, Avia. 2001. The Likely Locations of Middle and Late Bronze Harbors in Cilicia. An Assessment Based on Levantine Models. In *La Cilicie: Espaces et pouvoirs locaux (2e millénaire av. J.-C.-4e siècle ap. J.-C.). Actes de la table ronde internationale, Istanbul, 2–5 novembre 1999*, ed. Éric Jean, Ali Dinçol, and Serra Durugönül, 127–35. Varia Anatolica 13. İstanbul: De Boccard.

Trémouille, Marie-Claude. 2001. Kizzuwatna, terre de frontière. In *La Cilicie: Espaces et pouvoirs locaux (2e millénaire av. J.-C.-4e siècle ap. J.-C.). Actes de la table ronde internationale, Istanbul, 2–5 novembre 1999*, ed. Éric Jean, Ali Dinçol, and Serra Durugönül, 57–78. Varia Anatolica 13. İstanbul: De Boccard.

Umurtak, Gülsun. 1996. *Korucutepe 2. 1973–1975 Dönemi Kazılarında Bulunmuş Olan Hitit Çağı Çanak Çömleği*. Ankara: Türk Tarih Kurumu.

Ünal, Ahmet and K. Serdar Girginer. 2010. Tatarlı Höyük Kazılarında Bulunan "Anadolu Hiyeroglifli" Damga Mühür Baskısı. In *Veysel Donbaz'a Sunulan Yazılar DUB.SAR É. DUB.BA.A Studies Presented in Honour of Veysel Donbaz*, ed. Ş. Dönmez, 275–281. İstanbul: Ege Yayınları.van Loon, Maurits N., ed. 1978. *Korucutepe 2*. Amsterdamd: North-Holland.

von Dassow, Eva. 2005. Archives of Alalaḫ IV in Archaeological Context. *Bulletin of the American Schools of Oriental Research* 338: 1–69.

———. 2008. *State and Society in the Late Bronze Age: Alalaḫ under the Mittani Empire*. Bethesda, Md.: CDL Press.

Wilkinson, Tony. 1990. *Town and Country in Southeastern Anatolia 1. Settlement and Land Use at Kurban Höyük and Other Sites in the Lower Karababa Basin*. Oriental Institute Publications 109. Chicago: Oriental Institute of the University of Chicago.

Wiseman, Donald. 1953. *The Alalakh Tablets*. London: British Institute of Archaeology at Ankara.

Woolley, C. Leonard. 1914. Hittite Burial Customs. *Annals of Archaeology and Anthropology, Liverpool* 6: 87–98.

———. 1955. *Alalakh: An Account of the Excavations at Tell Atchana in the Hatay, 1937–1949*. Oxford: Oxford University Press.

Yağcı, Remzi. 2003. The Stratigraphy of Cyprus WS II and Mycenaean Cups in Soli Höyük Excavations. In *Identifying Changes: The Transition from Bronze to Iron Ages in Anatolia and its Neighbouring Regions*, ed. Bettina Fischer, Hermann Genz, Éric Jean, and Kemalettin Köroğlu, 93–106. İstanbul: Ege Yayınları.

Yakar, Jak. 2000. *Ethnoarchaeology of Anatolia. Rural Socio-Economy in the Bronze and Iron Ages*. Tel Aviv University, Sonia and Marco Nadler Institute of Archaeology Monograph Series 17. Jerusalem: Institute of Archaeology, Tel Aviv University.

Yakubovich, Ilya. 2008. Hittite-Luvian Bilingualism and the Development of Anatolian Hieroglyphs. In *Colloquia Classica et Indogermanica 4*. Acta Linguistica Petropolitana 4.1, ed. Nikolai Kazansky, 9–36. St. Petersburg: Russian Academy of Sciences/Nanka.
Yener, K. Aslıhan, ed. 2005. *Surveys in the Plain of Antioch and Orontes Delta, Turkey, 1995–2002. The Amuq Valley Regional Projects, 1*. Oriental Institute Publications 131. Chicago: Oriental Institute of the University of Chicago.
Yildirim, Bahadir and Marie-Henriette Gates. 2007. Archaeology in Turkey, 2004–2005. *American Journal of Archaeology* 111: 275–356.

The Iron Age

CHAPTER 18

THE IRON AGE ON THE CENTRAL ANATOLIAN PLATEAU

LISA KEALHOFER AND PETER GRAVE

ARCHAEOLOGICAL views of the Iron Age in inland Anatolia have been dominated by the two main polities that developed during the first millennium B.C.E.: Urartu in the east and Phrygia in the west. Our understanding of how these and other Iron Age societies developed in the aftermath of the Late Bronze Age Hittite collapse, how new polities emerged and forged new political and economic relations, however, is limited by the rarity of excavated Early Iron Age sites in the region (Genz 2003; Grave et al. 2009; Kealhofer et al. 2009, 2010).

One of the keys for understanding Iron Age dynamics is the development of a regional chronological framework. Since 2000, each of the sites discussed here has produced new Iron Age dates, often substantially altering our interpretation of the relationships between sites, the rate of change within Iron Age societies, and the timing and scale of interaction (figure 18.1). Results from these excavations are beginning to define an exceptionally dynamic and volatile period of society building. However, constraints in the development of a high-resolution regional chronology (radiocarbon calibration plateaus, sampling issues) continue to challenge our ability to adequately map the dynamics of Iron Age societies.

After describing the geographical context of the Anatolian plateau, we outline advances and constraints in the development of a regional chronological framework. Our current understanding of the Iron Age is then explored based on recent excavations of Iron Age levels at four sites: Gordion, Boğazköy, Kaman-Kalehöyük, and Çadır Höyük. Recent work at Kerkenes Dağ and Dorylaion/Eskişehir, as well as regional surveys, provide some additional shape to this still fragmentary picture (e.g., Durbin 1971).

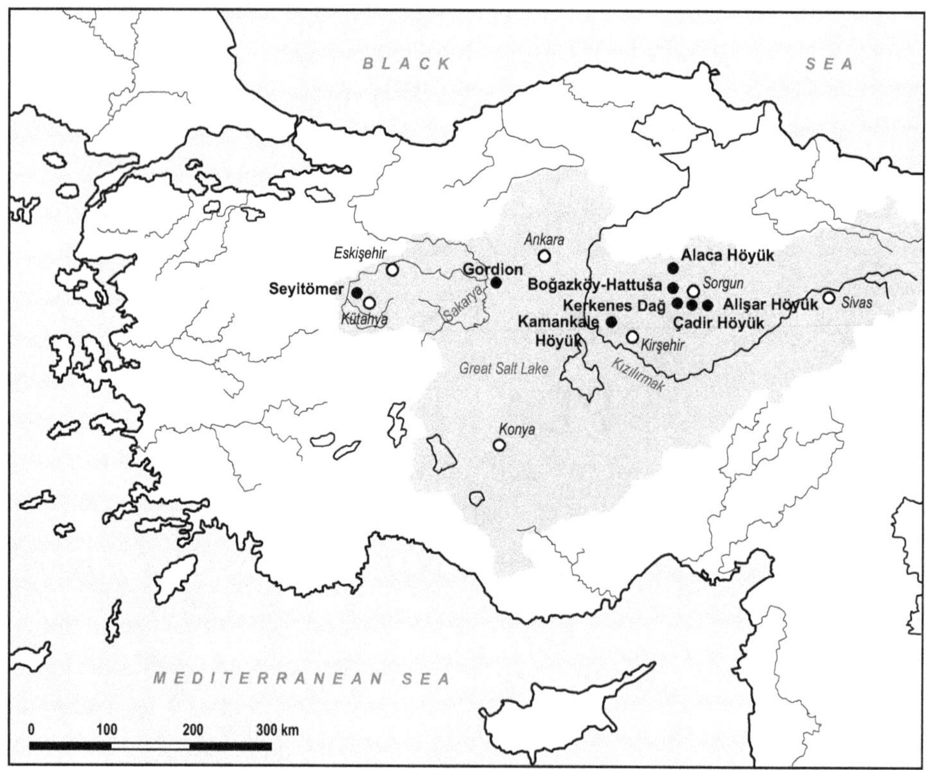

Figure 18.1. Map of Anatolia showing central Anatolian plateau and topography, geographic features, and sites mentioned in the text: Gordion, Boğazköy, Kaman-Kalehöyük, Çadır Höyük, Kerkenes Dağ, Alişar, Seyitömer, Dorylaion/Eskişehir, Tilkigediği; Konya, Kütahya, Ankara, Sivas, Kırşehir, Sorgun (modern towns). Also shown are major features including Tuz Gölü (Great Salt Lake), the Konya basin (internal drainages), Kızıl Irmak, Sakarya (rivers).

Geography

The plateau of central Anatolia is geographically defined by a series of mountain ranges and includes flat to rolling terrain with several lakes and rivers (figure 18.1). Topographically, the region ranges between 600 and 1,200 m, with elevations higher in the east than the west. Modern towns around its perimeter include Kütahya in the west, Ankara in the central north, Sivas in the east, and Konya in the south. The Salt Lake, or Tuz Gölü, and the Konya basin, both internal drainage basins, are centrally located in the plateau; major rivers include the Kızıl Irmak in the north and the Sakarya in the west.

The plateau, in part, is a zone of several active plate collisions: the North Anatolian fault zone in the north and the East Anatolian fault zone to the southeast, where the Arabian and Eurasian plates collide (Fisher 1978). The plateau itself is comprised of a series of uplifted blocks as well as troughs or basins, making its interior quite hilly. A complex tectonic history is reflected in an even more complex lithology, with volcanic, ophiolitic, sedimentary (marls, limestones, etc.), and metamorphic formations. Agro-pastoralism and overgrazing have led to slope erosion and commensurate alluviation of valley floors (e.g., Marsh 2005).

In terms of climate, the region is semi-arid, with dry summers and wet winters; average precipitation is about 400 mm, although annual variation is high. Drought can be a significant factor for local farming communities. Average monthly temperatures in Ankara range from 0°C in January to 22°C in August.

Politically, this region has been integrated several times, first in the Bronze Age, and subsequently under the political hegemony of multiple empires, from the Achaemenids to the Ottomans. The extent of Iron Age cultural and/or political integration on the plateau remains an open question in Anatolian archaeology. The Urartian polity in the east does not seem to have extended as far west as the plateau; however, historical evidence indicates some interaction (Hawkins 1982). However, the Phrygian polity certainly influenced, if it did not directly control, much of the western plateau (DeVries 2000).

Chronology

The Iron Age is conventionally divided into three periods: Early (sometimes referred to as the Dark Age), Middle, and Late. Several different chronological frameworks are currently in use for the Iron Age: historical, ceramic, and absolute (both radiocarbon and dendrochronology). The concordance between these is often problematic (DeVries et al. 2003; Summers 2008).

Historical Frameworks

Sams (chapter 27 in this volume) provides a detailed discussion of the historical context of the first millennium B.C.E. The historical framework initially framed our understanding of major events during the Iron Age (Assyrian incursions, Cimmerian invasions, Lydian battles, Persian battles, etc.), particularly at the site of Gordion. Although no historical records exist for the Iron Age from central Anatolia, contemporary late eighth-century B.C.E. Assyrian (Sargon II) texts and later Greek and Roman texts (Herodotus, Strabo) make note of the Phrygians and King Midas (King Mita of the Muški) in particular (e.g., Herodotus 7.73). Assyrian texts also record the Cimmerian (Scythian?) invasion of Anatolia in the late eighth century B.C.E., an event that until recently was tied to the main destruction level at Gordion (Hawkins 1982). While the historical texts provide interesting insights into the political structures of the eighth century B.C.E., they have often proven to be misleading when used to date and interpret archaeological sites (e.g., DeVries 2005; Summers 2008).

Absolute Chronologies

Absolute chronologies for the Iron Age have been slow to develop in central Anatolia and are still contentious (e.g., Muscarella 2004). As early as 1961 radiocarbon dating was used on samples from the site of Gordion, but the dates were at odds with the historical frameworks prevalent at the time (DeVries et al. 2003; Rose and Darbyshire forthcoming; Manning and Kromer forthcoming). Absolute dating has been difficult for several reasons. First, each of the sites discussed has had its own dating issues. At Gordion, radiocarbon dating focused on the Destruction Level and the tumuli rather than the stratigraphic sequence. In addition, early dates were most often on tree charcoal, which necessarily predated their depositional context (old wood, outer rings removed, or reuse of beams). In addition, over the course of the 1960s and early 1970s, these dates were calibrated according to several different systems, giving almost a 200-year variation in age range (Rose and Darbyshire forthcoming; Ralph, Henry, and Han 1973). When excavations resumed under the direction of Mary Voigt in 1988, additional samples were taken for radiocarbon dating; however, the general understanding was that the most expansive periods of Phrygian development fell inside the four-century radiocarbon calibration plateau of the first millennium (750–350 B.C.E.). Where multiple wood samples are available, dendrochronology can provide the best dates for the Middle and Late Iron Age. DeVries's reassessment of Greek ceramics from the South Cellar and other post–Destruction Level contexts on the Citadel Mound, suggesting a pre–700 B.C.E. date, led to the radiocarbon dating of more (appropriate short-lived) samples, redefinition of the date of the Destruction Level (ca. 800 B.C.E.), and a lengthening of the Middle Phrygian Period by 100 years (DeVries et al. 2003). The remainder of the Middle Phrygian Period falls within the calibration plateau, rendering the radiocarbon dating of Middle and Late Iron Age contexts of limited utility (hence the temptation to rely on historical texts for this period).

At Kaman Kalehöyük, although many samples have been dated, only recently have the contexts and the nature of the samples been carefully reexamined and refined (Matsumura 2000, 2005, forthcoming; Omori and Nakamura 2006, 2007; for an architectural discussion of this site, see Omura, chapter 51 in this volume). These recent reevaluations have focused on the North Sector Iron Age remains (Matsumura forthcoming). Dates selected from hearth (seeds) and burial contexts (bone) were subjected to a Bayesian analysis constrained by Harris matrix relationships (stratigraphic) between the samples. Without Bayesian analysis, the 2 σ dates for the Iron Age strongly overlap with the radiocarbon plateau. Based on their analyses, the boundary between Phase IId1–3 and IIc2–3 ranges between 900 and 850 B.C.E. (seven samples; Matsumura forthcoming; Omori and Nakamura 2007). This can be matched with the single dendrochronology (cutting) date of ca. 884 B.C.E. from a IId1 Level timber beam (Newton and Kuniholm 2001). The next boundary, between IIc2–3 and IIa6–IIc1, falls between 825–800 B.C.E. Subsequent phases fall within the radiocarbon plateau and are not yet well defined. The Iron Age strata end after 375 B.C.E. The two major anomalies in this sequence appear to be the dating of the end of the Late Bronze Age (LBA) and the beginning of the Iron Age levels (an apparent gap of a couple hundred years) and the very short phases for the Middle Iron Age (two phases in the ninth century B.C.E.). Radiocarbon ages do not provide a clear terminus for the Iron Age.

Systematic excavations of Iron Age levels on Büyükkaya at Boğazköy occurred from 1994 to 1998 under the direction of Jürgen Seeher (Genz 2000, 2004). Genz (2004) published the entire sequence of fourteen radiocarbon dates from Büyükkaya, covering a range from the end of the thirteenth century B.C.E. into the ninth century B.C.E. (EIA and MIA in the Boğazköy sequence). A series of radiocarbon dates for the "Dark Age"—or Early Iron Age (EIA)—was published by Schoop and Seeher (2006). The EIA, based on a building sequence, was divided into three short phases (1 σ [68.2 percent] calibrated range) of 1180–1125 (Early), 1125–1065 (Middle), and 1070–990 (Late) B.C.E. (Schoop and Seeher 2006:68). From the age difference between radiocarbon estimates of the last LBA construction (silo) prior to the EIA occupation, they estimate the interval between the LBA and the EIA as less than sixty years (68.2 percent probability; Schoop and Seeher 2006:70).

Subsequent work on the Northwest Slope of Büyükkaya revealed a sequence of Late Iron Age (LIA) deposits. The discovery of the EIA remains, as well as those of later Middle and Late Iron Age provided the first evidence for the continued occupation of the site after the collapse of the Hittite Empire (Genz 2000; Seeher 1997, 1998). The EIA ceramics suggest some continuation of LBA Hittite manufacturing traditions, and continuity between these phases of occupation. No material for radiocarbon dating was found in the LIA Northwest Slope sequence, but based on ceramic parallels, Genz (2004) suggests that the LIA ranges from the seventh–sixth centuries, possibly extending into the fifth century B.C.E. Note that this range includes Gordion's late Middle Phrygian and early Late Phrygian phases.

Excavations at Çadır Höyük have focused mainly on the Hittite, Chalcolithic, and Byzantine periods, with less attention paid to the Iron Age until recently. Two radiocarbon determinations have been reported for the EIA, ranging from 1270–910 B.C.E. to 1190–840 B.C.E. from an oven and a pit in grid unit 780.890 (2σ: 1270–910 B.C.E. cal Beta 146703 and 1190–840 B.C.E. cal Beta 146704) (F5) (Gorny et al. 2002). This context is interpreted as representing the LBA–EIA transition (Gorny et al. 2002:120; Ross 2010).

In the 1970s, Peter Kuniholm began a long-term project to create a tree ring sequence for the Mediterranean, including western and central Anatolia. Kuniholm's 1977 University of Pennsylvania doctoral thesis, the "Dendrochronology at Gordion and on the Anatolian Plateau," was the first part of this project. The timbers (*Pinus negra* and two *Juniperus* species) from Tumulus MM at Gordion have formed the core of the Iron Age sequence, eventually providing a more than 1,000-year floating ring sequence, which has subsequently been extended (Kuniholm et al. 1996). The youngest timber (juniper) from Tumulus MM provided a date of 740 B.C.E. Only two buildings on the City Mound provided enough samples for confident dating (TB2A and CC3). These buildings seem to have been constructed very close to 850 B.C.E. and 900 B.C.E., respectively (note a contemporary building phase at Kaman, also based on tree ring data). Thus the sequence of tree ring dates for the Phrygian period runs from 1071 B.C.E. (Meg 9) to 740 B.C.E. (MMT). The tree ring data also reveal evidence about the climate, and Manning and Kromer (forthcoming) suggest that the late Early Phrygian/early Middle Phrygian (Yassıhöyük Stratigraphic Sequence [YHSS] 6–5) period appears to have been one of moister, cooler climate with more reliable rainfall, perhaps making it a more stable period for agricultural production.

A Gordion monograph on chronology, currently in preparation (Rose and Darbyshire forthcoming), presents a history of the changing understanding of the chronology at the site as well as current interpretations. The combination of new radiocarbon and tree ring work has focused on redating the Destruction Level (ca. 800 B.C.E.), its relationship to the MM tumulus (ca. 740 B.C.E.), and to a lesser extent the foundation (ca. 900 B.C.E.) and remodeling of the Early Phrygian citadel. Other portions of the site's chronology are not as well defined, including the date of the LBA/EIA and the MIA/LIA transitions.

Ceramic Frameworks

Ceramic parallels are by far the most common means for assessing Iron Age chronology and comparing Anatolian sites. Ceramic dating in Anatolia has been based on the presence/absence of particular styles and manufacturing techniques (figure 18.2). Because few sites actually have ceramic assemblages with the full range of Iron Age (IA) forms and styles, it has not been possible to undertake systematic statistical or seriational analysis (however see Schoop 2006 for LBA ceramics). Ceramic dating, by nature, is linked to cultural regions. Central Anatolia, arguably, had several cultural regions during the Iron Age (Summers 2008), making direct comparisons across the entire region difficult. A handful of regional trade wares, when present, is often used to provide chronological markers between regions (e.g., Lustrous Black Fine Ware or Silhouette Ware/Alişar IV).

The various phases of the Iron Age display a degree of coherence in ceramic production and style, despite local variations. For the Early Iron Age (ca. 1100–900 B.C.E.), most assemblages contain a large proportion of handmade vessels, sharply contrasting with the relatively standardized wheelmade Drab Wares of the Late Bronze Age (e.g., the Hittite period). Decoration includes burnishing, incising, and/or impressions. Typical forms include a limited range of bowls, jars, and cooking pots. However, at most sites there is also a mix of material that retains characteristics of LBA ceramics. At different sites this is argued either to reflect continued production of Hittite forms (Boğazköy) or to be upcast from lower levels in the process of digging semi-subterranean houses or pits (Gordion), a common feature of the Early Iron Age. A local variant of red decorated wares occurs in the northeast (Genz 2001).

By the Middle Iron Age (ca. 900–550 B.C.E.), wheelmade forms are once again dominant. In the west, Gray Ware is most common, with matte painted Brown on Buff wares not common. In the east, Gray Wares are relatively rare, and Brown on

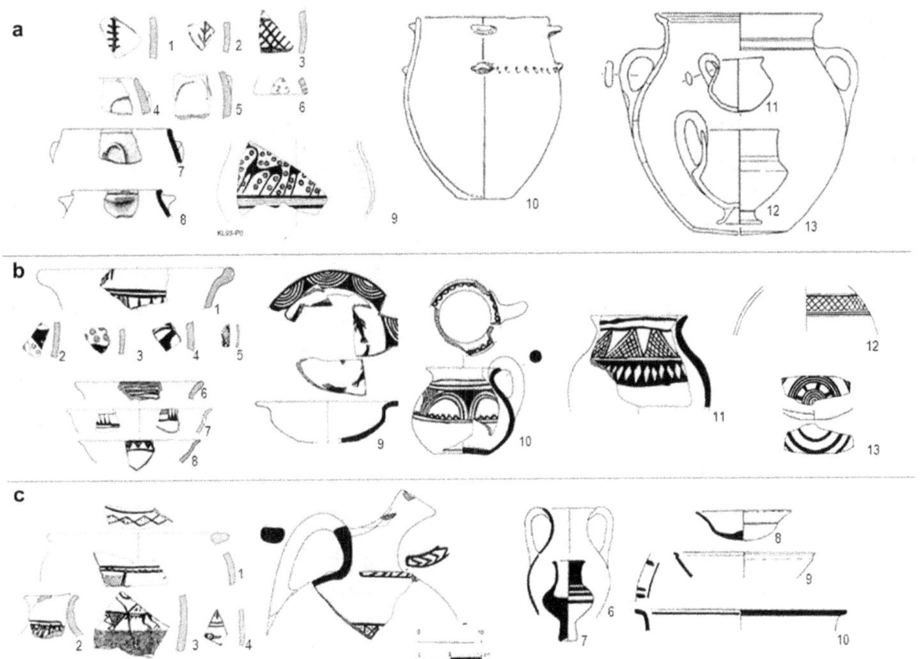

Figure 18.2. (a) Early Iron Age, a1–a6 EIA pottery, Çadır Höyük (Genz 2001:fig. 1); a7–a8 EIA pottery, Büyükkaya, Boğazköy (Kealhofer et al. 2009:fig. 3); a9 EIA pottery Kaman Kalehoyuk fig IId1–3; a10 EIA handmade ware; a11–a13 EIA wheelmade ware, Gordion (Voigt and Hendrickson 2000:figs. 3, 4). (b) Middle Iron Age, b1–b8 MIA decorated ware Çadır Höyük (Genz 2001:figs. 2,3); b9–11 MIA pottery from Büyükkaya (Kealhofer et al. 2009:fig. 3), MIA decorated ware from Gordion; b12 black polished ware, b13 Southwest Anatolian Black on Red ware (Henrickson 1993a: fig. 16). (c) Late Iron Age, c1–c4 LIA pottery, Çadır Höyük (Genz 2001:fig. 4); c5 LIA pottery, Northwest Slope, Boğazköy; c6–c10 LIA pottery, Gordion (Voigt et al. 1997:fig. 30).

Buff decorated wares are much more common. Decorative elements are mainly geometric, but include some naturalistic elements as well: stylized deer, wild goat, Silhouette Ware/Alişar IV, and so on. A larger range of forms are found in the MIA, notably a range of jugs and juglets, but also table wares and storage jars. By the eighth century B.C.E., Greek and East Greek styles, if not actual imports, are introduced and become more common over time.

The Late Iron Age (ca. 550–330 B.C.E.) reveals significant influences from the west, in terms of both form and decoration. Polychrome decoration, or decoration painted on white panels, occurs across the region. In addition, red banded wares, or red decoration in general, becomes more common. Forms now include a much expanded range of tablewares, as well as specialty small jar/pot forms that reveal Greek and East Greek influences, particularly on the western plateau.

The limitations of radiocarbon dating for much of the first millennium B.C.E., as well as the limited number of quite variable excavated sequences from the Middle and Late Iron Age, have resulted in broad categories for ceramic dating. In most instances, Greek ceramic imports, or other types of diagnostic imports, provide a much firmer chronological sequence for many sites beginning in the eighth century B.C.E. (Gordion in particular; e.g., DeVries et al. 2003; DeVries 2005).

Another interpretive challenge for the Iron Age in central Anatolia is the lack of coherence in phasing across the region (see figure 18.3). Dates for the beginning and the end of early, middle, and late Iron Age vary site by site (see also Summers 2008:table 1–3). This is partly based on presumed historical attributions (like the Cimmerian invasions) and partly on changes in regional ceramic decorative styles. The rate of movement in ceramic styles across the region has a major effect on the interpretation of interaction and trade. For example, the presence or absence of Gray Wares in the east can either be seen as related to Phrygian hegemony (Summers 1994) or as a slow local acquisition of stylistic elements (Genz 2006c in reference to Boğazköy). Establishing a regional stylistic chronology for different areas of central Anatolia remains critical to understanding patterns of regional dynamics.

Iron Age phases are commonly site-specific and based on architectural building phases or destruction events. At Gordion YHSS 7–4 phases are considered to be Iron Age but are not directly correlated with more conventional Iron Age phases, as is true of the Kaman II sequence. While Boğazköy's chronology has been defined in terms of Early, Middle, and Late Iron Age, these phases do not dovetail with YHSS phases (e.g., Boğazköy's 'short' MIA vs. Gordion's 'long' MP; see MIA/LIA in figure 18.3). Even

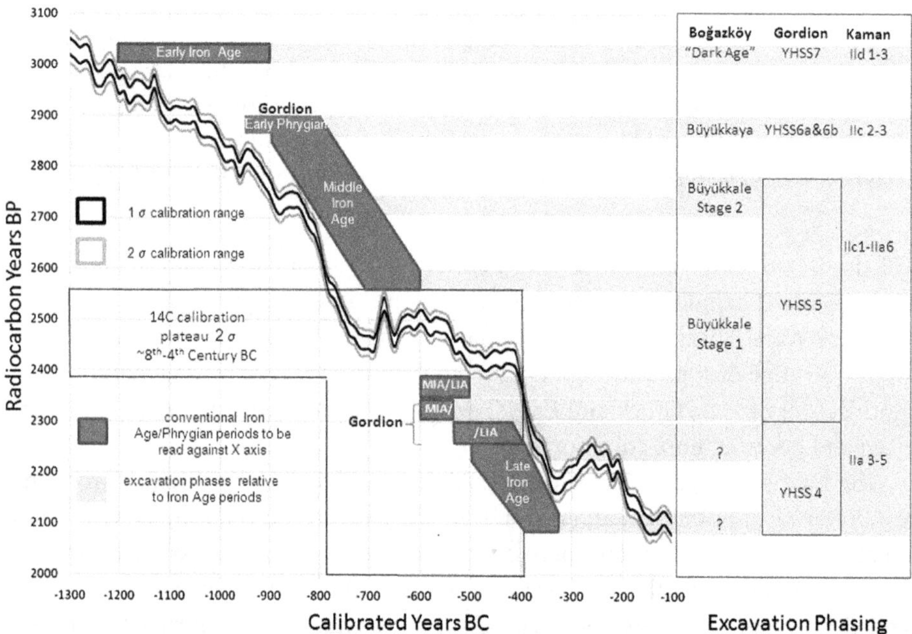

Figure 18.3. Comparative chronological framework for principal sites discussed in the chapter showing relative excavation phases, Iron Age periodization, and absolute radiocarbon calibration curve (based on IntCal09; Reimer et al. 2009). Note extended region of the radiocarbon calibration plateau from the Middle to Late Iron Ages.

within these phases, there are often significant ambiguities. For example, the Gordion Destruction Level, traditionally seen as defining the end of the Early Phrygian Period, when interpreted in light of the "Unfinished Project" (ongoing reconstruction of the élite quarter), is no longer a defining architectural event (Voigt forthcoming). As yet there is a lack of agreement about region-wide boundaries between Early/Middle/Late Iron Age phases, or what they should be based on (figure 18.3; see also Summers 2008).

Sites

Although it is clear that Iron Age central Anatolia was a rapidly changing milieu, as yet there are only a handful of published, excavated sites that span (most of) this period: Boğazköy, Çadır Höyük, Gordion, and Kaman Kalehöyük. Ongoing work at Şar Höyük, Seyitömer, and other sites will undoubtedly broaden our understanding as these sites are published. Kerkenes Dağ, despite a relatively short Iron Age occupation, as well as limited excavation, provides a unique view on the (late) Middle–Late Iron Age. Discussion here focuses mainly on the results from the four sites already noted. Three of these sites (all but Çadır Höyük) are also discussed in the Key Sites section (part V of this volume) in detail.

The Late Bronze ends with the collapse of the Hittite Empire in central Anatolia ca. 1200 B.C.E., or shortly thereafter. The Sea Peoples and the overall dramatic changes in the eastern Mediterranean are often seen to play a significant role in Hittite collapse (e.g., Sherratt 1998; Yakar 2006). However, over the past decade or so, what had been assumed to be a fast and catastrophic dissolution of the Hittite Empire has been shown to be a more complex process, both in time and space (Yakar 2006). Arguments for the Hittite collapse are varied and speculative and range from military invasions, western alliances, in-migration of populations from the east (and/or west), agricultural stress, to various combinations of internal and external mechanisms (Bryce 2005; Singer 2000).

Compared to our understanding of the end of the Bronze Age, the subsequent Early Iron Age is even more poorly known and less problematized (Genz 2003). The earliest part of the Iron Age is historically seen as a period of substantial population movement, with major shifts in material cultural assemblages often attributed to these new populations (e.g., Voigt and Henrickson 2000). All of the sites discussed here have domestic EIA architecture; however, the degree and/or nature of cultural continuity from the LBA into the EIA remains an open question (see later discussion). Major cultural changes occur, as housing shifts to semi-subterranean houses (Gordion, Kaman, Boğazköy, and possibly Çadır). Technological traditions change dramatically as handmade pottery is reintroduced, and herding strategies also shift (e.g., Hongo 2003; Zeder and Arter 1994). In general, the Early Iron Age in central Anatolia features smaller and more insular ceramic zones than in the LBA (Genz 2003).

By the end of the EIA, Phrygia, the most significant polity in the region during the Middle Iron Age, emerged with a capital at Gordion (Sams 1995, and see Sams, chapter 27 in this volume; Voigt and Henrickson 2000). Even after sixty years of work at Gordion, our understanding of Phrygian influence across central Anatolia remains largely ephemeral. Historical narratives indicate that Phrygia lost its political hegemony as Lydian influence (and armies) expanded eastward in the early sixth century B.C.E. and was further disrupted by the Persians later in the same century (see Harl, chapter 34 in this volume). The Middle Phrygian period at Gordion ends ca. 540 B.C.E. (YHSS 5–4) with the Persian attack on the town, but this transition is less well dated at other sites, with dates for the end of the MIA quite variable (Summers 2008). Despite this dramatically changing political landscape, Late Iron Age economies appear to have flourished across the region with an expansion of trade and interaction. The LIA ended in the late fourth century B.C.E. with Alexander the Great conquering much of Anatolia, and the subsequent overlay of a very different Hellenistic economy and political structure.

Boğazköy

The walled city of Boğazköy (approximately 180 ha), just over 200 km east of Ankara, is best known as the capital of the Hittite Empire (Seeher 2006). The area immediately in and around the site, however, contains evidence of occupation extending from the Chalcolithic to the historical period. A discussion of the archaeology at Boğazköy is presented in the "Key Sites" section (part V in this volume, see especially Mielke, chapter 48). Excavations at Büyükkaya (within the precinct of the Hittite city) in the 1990s provide one of the few well-dated Early Iron Age sequences in central Anatolia (see figure 18.3). Genz (2004) has summarized the 1990s excavations. The discovery of the Early Iron Age occupation on Büyükkaya provided the first clear evidence of continuous occupation from the LBA into the EIA (Genz 2004:710). Furthermore, excavations undertaken on the Büyükkale Northwest Slope have provided new evidence from Late Iron Age contexts, adding to the occupational history and defining the ceramic inventory for the later parts of the Iron Age (Genz 2006b:98–107). As a result, Iron Age occupation at Boğazköy now appears both longer and more extensive than previously thought.

Multiple locations on the site (Büyükkaya, Büyükkale, and the Upper City) have yielded domestic and other structural deposits dated to the Iron Age (Genz 2006a, 2006b). The EIA settlement appears to have been a small village located on the hill of Büyükkaya (Genz 2004:7–10) with evidence elsewhere on site for reuse of abandoned Hittite buildings. Subsequently, a larger regional political center developed in the Middle and Late Iron Age. During the MIA and LIA there is evidence of both public buildings and fortified occupation areas, both on hilltops (Südburg) and on the Northwest Slope (Genz 2007), as well as a cemetery with evidence of burials of varied economic status (Genz forthcoming). A monumental, multiroom, multiple-courtyard LIA building has been identified (at least 30 m × 40 m), although its function remains uncertain (Genz 2007). Occupation seems to have ended during the LIA (end of sixth century B.C.E./beginning of fifth century B.C.E.), as there is apparently a hiatus before the Hellenistic period, although it is currently undated.

Ceramics

Genz has analyzed the Iron Age ceramics from the various excavations at Boğazköy (e.g., Genz 2000, 2004, 2006a, and 2006b). His descriptions of the assemblages of each phase of the Iron Age are summarized here (see also Kealhofer et al. 2009).

The Early Iron Age pottery (twelfth to tenth centuries B.C.E.) is generally handmade (Genz 2003:179, 2004:24–26), although about 30 percent of the earliest EIA phase pottery is wheelmade. Forms are utilitarian bowls, jugs, jars, and hole-mouth cooking pots. Some have labor-intensive finishes such as burnishing, and there is a low frequency of red-painted generally geometric decoration (dot-filled triangles), not identified to the west. Incised decoration is rare. Fabrics include only a "common" fabric and a coarser cooking pot fabric. Production looks to be at the household scale (Genz 2003:179–81, 2004:24–28). Genz suggests that the technological style shows strong continuity with Hittite traditions in the earliest phase of the EIA (Genz 2006c). He also notes the strong parallels between the Early and Middle Bronze Age, and EIA forms from adjacent regions—making an argument for some type of underlying cultural continuity in the larger region (Genz 2006c:82).

In the Middle Iron Age (late tenth or early ninth centuries B.C.E. to the late eighth century B.C.E.), wheelmade wares reappear (corresponding to Early Phrygian). When pottery is decorated, dark matte paint predominates, with both geometric (cross-hatched bands and triangles) and naturalistic animal and "tree" motifs (see figure 18.2:4-6; Bossert 2000; Genz 2004:29–35).

In the Late Iron Age (early eighth to the sixth? century B.C.E.), marked changes occur in the local pottery (Genz 2006b:107–22). Matte-painted decoration disappears and is replaced by lustrous paint (often polychrome) decoration. In general, painted decoration becomes less common, but still includes geometric and figurative motifs, while gray or black burnished pottery (10 percent of the pottery assemblages at Boğazköy), and red burnished pottery (< 5 percent of the assemblage) increase (Bossert 2000:27–28; Genz 2006b:122). Forms include hemispherical or carinated bowls, beaked or trefoil-mouth jugs, large two-handled crater-like vessels, globular jugs, and faceted jars. A few finds of West Anatolian, Greek, and Cypriot imports at Boğazköy provide firm evidence of long distance interaction (Bossert 2000:145–51; Genz 2006b:119).

Recent Neutron Activation Analysis (NAA) of Iron Age ceramics from Boğazköy provides additional evidence for Iron Age developments (Kealhofer et al. 2009). All of the EIA samples were of local provenience; in the MIA one nonlocal ceramic (fine ware) was introduced, but the use of local ceramic sources/technologies shifted significantly. In Boğazköy's LIA, nonlocal fabrics represented approximately 20 percent of the sampled assemblage, suggesting a substantial increase in nonlocal interaction and an expansion of Boğazköy's role in the larger region. Most of the styles that appeared exotic to Boğazköy proved to be local emulations. Even for the imports, like Black Polished ware, local emulations were also present. Nonlocal ceramics were all tablewares, revealing interaction in a larger social sphere, with less evidence for the import of bulk goods in ceramic vessels (Kealhofer et al. 2009).

Çadır Höyük

Several important Iron Age sites or occupations have been identified in the Yozgat province, to the south and east of Sorgun. Çadır Höyük is one of the more archaeologically prominent of these (see Gorny et al. 2002; Gorny 2006; Steadman et al. 2008). Excavations at Çadır are ongoing, with a focus on Chalcolithic, Hittite, and Byzantine occupation levels. As yet little of the Iron Age ceramic assemblage from Çadır has been published, but as one of the few sites providing evidence for the transition from the Late Bronze Age into the Iron Age, it is of considerable interest (Genz 2001; and see Ross 2010).

Areas on the mound with stratified evidence of the Iron Age include the North Trenches and the Upper South Slope. Units in the Upper South Slope were originally opened in 2001, yielding LIA pottery in 2003, and a MIA city wall and part of a gate in 2004; more recent excavations have provided EIA remains and ceramics. In 2000, two stratigraphically contemporary samples from an oven and a pit provided radiocarbon ranges in the Early Iron and Middle Age. In 2005, EIA deposits were excavated, producing ceramics that included what looked like "transitional" LBA/EIA (Gorny 2006). The 2005 EIA ceramics included what looked like "transitional" LBA/EIA. An unusual set of several round plaster surfaces were also uncovered, which the excavators suggest might be related to wool or other materials processing (loom weights, spindle whorls, an iron hook, and other tools were found in association). Hittite remains occurred immediately below the earliest Iron Age deposits, with no break in occupational sequence, suggesting continuity between LBA and EIA occupation. The North Slope excavations revealed an LBA (Hittite) stone gated entry into the second millennium B.C.E. settlement. Iron Age ceramics, mixed into the upper fill, suggest a first millennium B.C.E. usage of this area. A trench located stratigraphically above the second millennium B.C.E. remains provided Late, and possibly Middle, Iron Age architecture, including a LIA wall with possible associated gate. Although limited, these contexts indicate a substantial fortified settlement with some economic specialization, occupied throughout the Iron Age.

The nearby (late) Middle–Late Iron Age site of Kerkenes Dağ, and the regional surveys undertaken in relation to both the Kerkenes Project and the Alişar project (Gorny 1994; Gorny et al. 1995, 1999; Summers and Summers 1995; Summers et al. 1996), provide additional information about the Iron Age in this area of central Anatolia. The nearby site of Alişar, excavated in the 1920s and 1930s by von der Osten (1930, 1937), provides the main ceramic sequence for the region. Alişar IV and Alişar V ware formed the original Iron Age ceramic "types" across central

Anatolia. Unfortunately, the lack of absolute dating, as well as the character of the 1930s excavation and recording strategies, make any detailed interpretation of Alişar's Iron Age sequence extremely difficult.

Located 10.5 km north of Çadır Höyük, the hilltop site of Kerkenes is one of the largest fortified cities in Anatolia (walled area of 2.5 km^2). The site has been intensively mapped using a variety of remote sensing techniques, allowing a detailed reconstruction of its original layout (Summers 2006). Excavations began in 2003, focusing on the Palace Complex and the Cappadocia Gate (Branting 2005). Several unusual finds include an Old Phrygian inscription (Brixhe and Summers 2006) and a cult statue (Brixhe and Summers 2006; Draycott and Summers 2008). The site has been linked to the historical site of Pteria (Herodotus); however radiocarbon dating has proved to be problematic because it falls within the extended 400-year radiocarbon plateau of the mid–first millennium B.C.E. Summers (2006) suggests that it is a short-lived Late Iron Age site (ca. end of seventh to mid-sixth century B.C.E.) (note this falls within Gordion's Middle Phrygian Period). Remote sensing imagery supports a relatively short occupation period, with only one main building phase evident. Occupation seems to have ended when the main buildings at the site were burned and the seven-kilometer defensive wall was razed, apparently as a single event sometime in the mid-sixth century B.C.E. The cultural inventory of the site shows links to western Anatolia, but beyond the use of Phrygian inscriptions and graffiti, there is little at the site that is definitively Phrygian, Lydian, or Median (Summers 2006). Summers (2006) provides a discussion of the historical framework of Kerkenes (see also www.kerkenes.metu.edu.tr). The ceramics have not been described in any detail as the ceramic corpus has been small.

Ceramics

Genz (2001) provided the first summary of Iron Age ceramics from Çadır, based on survey-collected unstratified ceramics found at various locations on the mound, most from an area of slump on the south slope. One incised bowl rim is typical EIA, and he describes other red decorated wares as being comparable to the later phases of the EIA at Büyükkaya (red triangles, dots, tree motif).[1] Other EIA types include cooking pots with horseshoe shaped handles and strainers (for jugs?). The dates at Büyükkaya for these forms are middle to late EIA, or eleventh—tenth centuries (Seeher 2000). Sherds of the "Silhouette" style (Alişar IV), typically from large craters, were also found, generally dated to the early MIA (ninth century B.C.E.). Finds of Alişar IV style ceramics in the Early Phrygian V levels at Gordion suggest that it likely dates there to the ninth century B.C.E. The LIA ceramics for the region are not well defined, based on Alişar V ceramics, but Genz includes red banded wares (bowls) and polychrome panel decoration, including a polychrome goose, in Çadır's LIA assemblage. Ross (2010) has recently provided a detailed analysis of Iron Age ceramics and architecture at Çadır Höyük.

More recently, Iron Age ceramic samples from stratified contexts were analyzed with NAA (Kealhofer et al. 2010). This assemblage is apparently quite different from that analyzed by Genz (2001). The range of forms was dominated by jar/jug sherds, with a smaller proportion of (open) bowl forms. Decoration, when present, was predominantly Brown on Buff, with a smaller percentage of burnished, Red on Brown, Brown on Cream, and only a few polychrome examples (no red on buff or red banded wares). This excavated assemblage appears, therefore, to represent an earlier range of late EIA and MIA wares. Two particularly interesting patterns emerge from the NAA data. During this period there are a large number of regionally local groups present on site, suggesting that Çadır was actively involved in regional networks and likely a central place. About 10 percent of the Iron Age assemblage is imported (mainly MIA styles of bowls, jugs, and jars), often with Silhouette/Alişar IV type decoration (pendant lines, concentric circles, etc.). Given the preeminence that Alişar Höyük is usually seen to have in the local region, it is somewhat surprising that these imports are not actually from Alişar (based on regional sediment sampling). Either Silhouette Ware/Alişar IV ware was not produced at Alişar, or there was more than one production center (which might not be too surprising).

In sum, the two current analyses of Iron Age ceramics from Çadır provide strong indications that this site was an important regional center in the EIA and MIA. Given the presence of transitional LBA/EIA levels and ceramics (mix of burnished and painted and handmade forms), Çadır provides another important example of cultural continuity through the period of Hittite collapse. The nature of Çadır's occupation in the LIA is less clear, although occupation clearly continued through this period, and there is evidence of a town wall. The massive fortified MIA/LIA hilltop city at Kerkenes must have had a strong, albeit shortlived, influence on the neighboring population at Çadır. The presence of other fortified hilltop towns nearby, such as Tilkigediği (Summers and Summers 1995), also suggests a period of considerable regional conflict.

At Kerkenes, preliminary analysis of the ceramics from the Palace and the Cappadocia Gate, surprisingly, present a very different picture from those from Çadır (Kealhofer et al. 2010). The forms are more strongly dominated by jugs and/or jars and include a much larger proportion of what appear to be nonlocal wares (approximately 50 percent). Many of the sherds are either undecorated or have lost their surfaces due to poor preservation. The high proportion of jugs or jars suggests quite a different set of functions in these élite buildings, possibly related to the import of goods. In terms of those that are decorated, the assemblage is dominated by mainly Late Iron Age styles (polychrome and panel decoration, red bands, etc.), with a few possibly Middle Iron Age (or MP e.g., Black Polished Ware with incised decoration) (Kealhofer et al. 2010).

Gordion

The Citadel Mound of Gordion is approximately 100 km southwest of Ankara on the Sakarya River and was occupied from at least the MBA to the Medieval period. Several chapters in this volume discuss Gordion and Phrygia in some detail: Voigt presents a detailed discussion of Gordion in part V, Roller discusses Phrygia and the Phrygians, and Sams covers the historical context of the first millennium B.C.E. in Anatolia, making it possible to focus on the Iron Age here. The long history of excavations at Gordion under the direction of Rodney Young (1950–73) and Mary Voigt (1988–2005), with Ken Sams as Project Director (1989-present), provide one of the most complete Iron Age sequences in central Anatolia (Voigt 2005). The Early Phrygian Destruction Level (ca. 800 B.C.E.) and the tumuli (mid-ninth–first century B.C.E.) were major foci for Young's excavations, along with the city wall and various exploratory trenches (see Voigt, chapter 50 in this volume). Voigt's more recent work has served to provide a more complete sequence for the site, with a revised dating of the Destruction Level, adding substantial information on the western, non-élite portion of the mound as well as the Lower and Outer Towns. Kuniholm's dendrochronological studies of beams from both the tumuli (MMT in particular) and the major Phrygian buildings (CC[3] and TB[2A]) have served as the basis for defining the master tree ring sequence for the region and dating Early Phrygian building construction (beginning in the tenth century B.C.E.; Kuniholm et al. 1996; Manning et al. 2001).

The Iron Age sequence at Gordion begins with domestic EIA (YHSS 7B and 7A) contexts that reveal a mix of handmade and wheelmade (mainly) buff wares associated with semi-subterranean houses (e.g., the Burnt Reed House [BRH]; Voigt and Henrickson 2000). Although there is no evidence of destruction or clear disruption, EIA material culture, foodways, and architecture are substantially different from those of the final phase of LBA settlement. These distinctive cultural shifts have been interpreted as representing the influx of a new population in the Iron Age, generally thought to have come from the west (or Thrace) (Sams 1995; Voigt and Henrickson 2000). Another cultural shift occurs during the EIA, perhaps linked to ongoing population movements.

The domestic deposits of the EIA are followed by what appears to be the rapid development of a Phrygian polity. The Early Phrygian (Early Phrygian YHSS 6A and 6B) town (ca. 950–800 B.C.E.) includes a substantial walled settlement with élite architecture around a paved courtyard. As yet, the nature and timing of this political and economic transformation is not well understood. The Early Phrygian Citadel Mound is best known from Rodney Young's excavations, which reveal phases of élite building (tenth century B.C.E.?) and rebuilding (early ninth century B.C.E.) subsequently destroyed by a conflagration of ca. 800 B.C.E. (referred to as the "Destruction Level"). Detailed analysis of these earlier Phrygian levels has revealed that the élite zone was undergoing major architectural renovation at the time of the fire, which was resumed promptly on top of a deep (up to five meter) fill level after the ca. 800 B.C.E. destruction (DeVries and Voigt forthcoming; Voigt forthcoming). In fact, Voigt (forthcoming) suggests that the Early Phrygian citadel may have been in a constant state of remodeling. The Early Phrygian élite complex included a monumental gate complex, an inner and outer courtyard both with large megara, and an elevated terrace with an "industrial complex" (service buildings) for food and textile production as well as storage

(DeVries 1980; Sams 1995). The immediate burial of the Destruction Level by meters of fill as part of renovations preserved the largest contemporary corpus of evidence yet recovered for Phrygian Gordion. The earliest tumuli date to the end of the Early Phrygian Period.

Much of the subsequent Middle Phrygian city (YHSS 5 800-540 B.C.E.), although larger and grander than the Early Phrygian city, was robbed out in the course of later construction phases (Voigt forthcoming). As a consequence, solid evidence for the Middle Phrygian is known only from a few excavation areas (e.g., the Mosaic Building, and Op. 17: Voigt forthcoming). An inner wall and glacis protected the Citadel Mound, and the Lower Town was also walled with several fortresses incorporated in the wall (Kuş Tepe and Küçük Höyük). The Middle Phrygian élite are best known from the excavated burial tumuli that mainly date to this period and later, of which the MM tumulus (ca. 740 B.C.E.) is the largest and best known (see Roller, chapter 25 in this volume). As part of the process of defining the Yassıhöyük Stratigraphic Sequence (YHSS) at the site, Miller and Zeder (2009) analyzed the botanical and faunal material, respectively. These data reveal a major shift in agricultural strategies during the Middle Phrygian Period, when agriculture became more important than agro-pastoralism (increase in cattle, pig, and domesticated crops). Manning and Kromer (forthcoming) suggest that this was in some part influenced by climate; nevertheless, the agricultural strategies of the Phrygian polity appear to have significantly intensified.

The Late Phrygian Period (YHSS 4) is clearly defined in Mellink's excavations at Küçük Höyük, part of an outer fortified wall complex enclosing the Lower Town (see Voigt, chapter 50 in this volume). These excavations reveal a destruction event, with weaponry, argued to correspond with the attack by the Persians in 540 B.C.E. Buildings such as the Mosaic Building and the Painted House on the Citadel Mound date to the first half of this period (540–400 B.C.E.). The limited evidence suggests that Gordion, although not politically important, remained an important economic hub for the region until ca. 400 B.C.E. Tumuli of this period (e.g., Tumulus A ca. 540–530 B.C.E.) are some of the few that contain gold. The Late Phrygian ceramic assemblage includes a wide range of nonlocal styles and imports (DeVries 1997; Henrickson 1993b). Late Iron Age Gordion ends with Alexander the Great's campaign across western Anatolia and marks the beginning of a substantial Hellenistic occupation at the site (YHSS 3B and 3A).

Ceramics

The Gordion Iron Age ceramic corpus has been studied by multiple scholars. The major works include that of G. K. Sams (1994), who undertook the study of the Early Phrygian ceramics; K. DeVries (1997, 2005, 2007, 2008), who studied the imported Attic and East Greek ceramics; and R. Henrickson (1993a, 1993b, 1994, 1995, 2005; Henrickson and Blackman 1996; Henrickson, Vandiver, and Blackman 2002), who analyzed ceramic production techniques from the LBA to the Hellenistic period. In addition, there are several more narrowly focused studies (e.g., Grave et al. 2009; Schaus 1992; Winter 1973).

Henrickson (1993a, 1993b) analyzed both LBA and Iron Age ceramic production at Gordion. Local (workshop?) production in the LBA reproduced the typical limited range of Hittite Drab Ware forms (shallow bowls, plates, pots, and jars). With the major political and economic transition to the EIA (YHSS 7: 1100–950 B.C.E.), ceramic technology shifted to an even more limited range of highly variable handmade forms, with burnished and incised decoration, suggesting household production. Early Phrygian (YHSS 6: ca. 950–800 B.C.E.) potters resumed the use of the wheel for small vessels, with slab and coil, and tournette techniques used for larger storage jars, likely indicating workshop production. Middle (ca. 800–540 B.C.E.) and Late Phrygian (540–330 B.C.E.) forms were generally very conservative, following in the same tradition as the Early Phrygian forms, although some were elaborated and decorative styles shifted. Reduction fired wares became increasingly important by the end of the Early Phrygian and throughout the Middle Phrygian and Late Phrygian (particularly Gray Ware) and dominate the assemblage (75–95 percent). In the Late Phrygian, buff wares began to increase again, and external stylistic influences in both form and decoration became more significant (Henrickson 1993b:table 4; Voigt et al. 1997). Geometric decoration on plain or slipped buff wares, however, is found in all Phrygian periods and particularly in élite contexts (Sams 1994).

Obviously imported vessels, based on style and form, are rare in the Early Phrygian (however see discussion of NAA below). Recent redating of the Destruction Level to the end of the ninth century B.C.E. (DeVries et al. 2003) links the initiation of trade and interaction with Greeks (and East Greeks) to the Middle Phrygian Period (eighth century B.C.E.). Even more dominant in the assemblage by the end of the Middle Phrygian is a strong Lydian influence, again both in forms (lydions, fruitstands) and decoration (bands, marbleizing, red decoration) (Schaus 1992). Greek transport amphoras begin to arrive from the Hellespont with Persian occupation (after 525 B.C.E.) and their control of Greek trade within Anatolia, although trade networks varied considerably during the Hellenistic period (Voigt et al. 1997). Other Anatolian imports are somewhat less identifiable, but the well-known Silhouette Ware/Alişar IV style is found at Gordion in levels just below the Destruction Level (late ninth century B.C.E.), and still occurs at least a century later as dated by the South Cellar deposit (ca. 700 B.C.E. to early seventh century: DeVries 2008; Sams 1994).

Decorative styles have different chronological envelopes during the Iron Age (Sams 1994). Based on the subset of ceramics studied by Grave and colleagues (2009), a sequence of styles from the Early Phrygian to the Late Phrygian can be suggested tentatively for this region of central Anatolia. Mica sheen, incised decoration (EIA Handmade), hatched decoration (in brown or red), and a distinctive wavy line decoration are unique to the Early Phrygian. A few styles are both Early Phrygian and Middle Phrygian: checkerboard patterns, Complex Brown on Buff Ware, red/orange burnished ware, and Black/brown on Red painted wares. The Middle Phrygian includes an additional range of styles, many of which continue into the Late Phrygian: line and/or band decoration, Lydianizing or streaky slip decoration, polychromes, and to a lesser extent Brown on White and other bichrome decoration. Red wash or slip is the only decorative style that is found throughout the Phrygian periods. Black lustrous wares are most common in the Middle Phrygian but continue into Late Phrygian contexts with a pattern burnished variant by the fourth century B.C.E. Brown slipped wares are not common and are found only in the Late Phrygian. Black glazed wares are first imported in the Middle Phrygian but seem only to be locally produced in the late Late Phrygian and heavily dominate the Hellenistic period. Although black glazed decoration is the most common, brown glazed samples also occur in both the Late Phrygian and Hellenistic period, and red glazed samples are common in the Late Phrygian. Waveline Ware and a Red Dots and Triangles style are also present in the Late Phrygian. In terms of overall decorative style diversity, all the Phrygian Periods are more diverse than later Classical periods; however, the Late Phrygian has the widest range of styles. This diversity is primarily based on the addition of emulative glazed decorative styles.

Sams's work (1994) focused on defining Early Phrygian ceramics in terms of their formal and stylistic characteristics. Henrickson's work (e.g., 1993, 1994, 2005) focused on understanding the nature of ceramic production at Gordion and how it has changed over time. This means that the assemblage of local versus nonlocal styles in ceramics has not yet been well described for the Middle or Late Phrygian Periods. DeVries's (1980, 1988, 1997, 2005) work on the Greek ceramics at Gordion is a significant exception. The extent to which the styles of these periods, particularly the Middle Phrygian, represent local developments or emulations of other styles in the larger region has yet to be established. Certainly, Late Phrygian styles include emulations of western Anatolian, East Greek, and Greek styles in addition to more local central Anatolian styles.

Distinctive imported ceramics have been used extensively both to date archaeological contexts at Gordion (DeVries 1988, 1997, 2007; DeVries et al. 2003; Sams 1994; Schaus 1992; Voigt et al. 1997; Winter 1973, 1988) and to highlight links with other groups/polities. However, little systematic investigation of exchange patterns has been possible without the use of both style and characterization techniques. This is currently under way (Grave et al. 2009; Kealhofer et al. 2010).

At least three sets of characterization data exist for Gordion ceramics. Williams and colleagues (1987) published an overview of PIXE (Proton Induced X-ray Emission) data for more than forty Hellenistic sherds, noting the presence of ten identifiable groups (local and nonlocal) and suggest that the Black Glazed Wares were not locally produced. Henrickson and Blackman (1996) subsequently undertook a much larger study of production patterns over time at Gordion and included a sample of local clays from both the mound and nearby clay beds. Most recently, we have revised and added to the Henrickson and Blackman study (Grave et al. 2009). Surprisingly, this study revealed an abundance of imported ceramics in Early Phrygian and Destruction Level contexts.

Kaman Kalehöyük

Kaman Kalehöyük is a large mound approximately 100 km southeast of Ankara (see Omura, chapter 51 in this volume). The sequence at this site extends at least from the Bronze Age into the Medieval period. Stratum II on the mound is (mostly) Iron Age and is divided into four substrata, IIa (latest) to IId (earliest), with multiple subphases. The Iron Age, based on ceramics and other material evidence, has subsequently been divided into five Phases: IIa1–2, IIa3–5, IIa6-IIc1, IIc2–3, IId1–3 (Matsumura 2009). The Iron Age deposits are dominated by domestic remains, with some evidence of larger buildings in the LIA (Omura 2005). As already noted, the dating of the Iron Age sequence has been difficult to define. Radiocarbon estimates, using 2 σ ranges, overlap for the Early and Middle Iron Age levels (ninth century B.C.E.), and are again problematic for the 800–400 cal B.C.E. period (Omori and Nakamura 2006).

Kaman IIa is further broken into two sets of subphases that extend into IIc. The latest subphase IIa1–IIc2 is dated to 370–205 B.C.E., whereas the phases from IIa6–IIc1/IIa3–IIa5 range from 820 to 655 B.C.E. The ceramics seem to fall within a late seventh to fourth century B.C.E. envelope (Matsumura 2000; Omori and Nakamura 2006). The Iron Age deposits are complicated by a sequence of heavily disturbed domestic occupations. Finds are quite diverse, however, from a broad range of ceramics to fibulae, cylinder seals, and other small finds. A large building with traces of fourteen pillars and stone pillar foundations was interpreted as part of a sequence of remodeled megaron-like structures. Another massive IIa building was cleared in 2005, with potentially an earlier large building below it.

Although initially a IIb phase was defined, this now appears to be contemporary with IIa6–IIc1. Phase IIc included half basement structures, with a stone foundation and mudbrick walls. Mixed in with semi-subterranean houses were ground-level stone houses. Pits associated with these included bronze fibulae as well as beads, jewelry molds[?], and other small finds. Houses of this period were somewhat more substantial than earlier houses, with thicker stone walls.

The earliest Levels IId1–3 and IIc2–3 include single room semi-subterranean dwellings and date from the end of the tenth century to the first quarter of the ninth century B.C.E. (Matsumura 2001; Newton and Kuniholm 2001) with considerable continuity between phases. The IId structures were composed of narrow stone walls, only slightly recessed (twenty centimeters) into the ground and exhibit substantial evidence of burning (Omura 2000). During this phase there is evidence for a sequence of three (burned) fortification walls (Matsumura 2008). Matsumura suggests that the construction techniques show strong similarities to those used at Zincirli (to the south).

Ceramics

Matsumura (2005) summarizes much of the technological work on ceramics that has been done at the site over the past twenty years as well as much of what is known about Iron Age Kaman. Both Gray Wares and Buff wares are found at Kaman, as well as variants of these including Black Polished and Black Burnished, shiny micaceous ware, and a range of slipped and unslipped Cream Ware (Matsumura 2000). Phase IIc2–3 and IId1–3 ceramics are both wheelmade with bichrome (dark brown and red) decoration (Matsumura 2008, forthcoming). Geometric motifs are most common; parallel lines and parallel wavy line decoration is also common. Phase IId1–3 forms include the crater, big mouth round jug, narrow-necked jar, and carinated bowls. Matsumura (2000) does not identify direct connections between LBA and IId forms, though he recognizes some continuity in production techniques ("upside down wheel technique"). Phase IId1–3 fabrics, however, are very different (micaceous and "straw tempered") and usually buff in color. Some nonlocal ceramics include pendant circle decoration (Protogeometric in style but Anatolian in origin?). Matsumura (2008) argues that the IId1–3 decoration most closely parallels Porsuk IV, suggesting strong links to the southeast, rather than with other EIA centers in central Anatolia.

Silhouette Ware/Alişar IV decoration first appears in Phase IIc2–3. This phase includes very little Gray Ware (Matsumura 2001). Apart from minor differences in size and rim projection, IIc forms repeat IId forms, although in more "elegant" shapes (Matsumura 2000, 2001). Fabrics are very similar for IId and IIc. Matsumura (2000) notes that Cream Ware are typical of IIc as well. The late ninth–eighth century B.C.E. dates for this phase are comparable to the dating of Silhouette Ware at Gordion (see previous discussion).

Only in Phase IIa does the amount of Gray Ware in the assemblage increase (total > 20 percent), although reduction fired wares in general increased earlier (e.g., Plumbeous Ware, Matsumura 2001). Phase IIa decorative styles include a range of polychrome painted wares, some with panel decoration (bichrome on white panel). The IIa forms seem to develop from IIc forms. Glossy micaceous, gray and glossy gold surfaced vessels also appear in this period (Plumbeous Gray and Gold Wash in Matsumura 2000).

Recent NAA studies reveal that local ceramics at Kaman came from a surprisingly large number of local regional sources, suggesting a very dense pattern of local ceramic production and exchange (Grave and Kealhofer 2006; Kealhofer et al. forthcoming). At least eight different nonlocal sources are represented in the assemblage, mostly in the form of jars rather than table wares, suggesting that many of the imports to Kaman may have been traded as containers for goods rather than for the jars themselves. Black Wares, known best from Gordion, are also found at Kaman, and NAA data suggest that many local villages were supplying Kaman with Black Ware. The relative abundance of Black Wares, and their local production, suggests a regional tradition of this vessel style and decoration, which was mainly expressed through emulation rather than exchange. Though Gray Ware is found at Kaman, the limited number of forms and their relatively low frequency suggests that they had a very different significance from the Gray Ware traditions further west, centered on Gordion and Eskişehir. The lack of standardization in any of the wares suggests that Gray Ware was also locally or regionally produced.

Concluding Remarks

Understanding Iron Age dynamics in central Anatolia poses several challenges, beginning most fundamentally with chronology. One of the most critical of these relates to the Early Iron Age, specifically the nature of social and political reformulation after the collapse of the Hittite Empire (see also Fischer et al. 2003). The evidence from the sites discussed here suggests occupational continuity across this significant political threshold at major sites, despite indications of significant socioeconomic and political changes. In EIA Gordion there is substantial evidence for the influx of new peoples, seen in major changes in the form of houses, the nature of ceramic technology, foodways, and settlement organization (Voigt and Henrickson 2000). Change at other sites is also substantial, including many of these same variables, although at Kaman and Boğazköy changes are interpreted as simply a shift in their economic strategies rather than population influx. Although house forms and foodways change at Boğazköy, Genz (2003) argues that Hittite ceramic traditions only slowly shift (from wheelmade to handmade) during the EIA, suggesting in situ cultural change. The EIA at Kaman is quite different, with continuing production of wheelmade ware (Matsumura 2000). However, if the IId4–6 levels are EIA rather than LBA (contra Matsumura 2008), this would suggest a much stronger continuity between LBA and EIA communities at Kaman. Even at Gordion, Voigt and Henrickson (2000) suggest that local populations remain in the area, living side by side with incoming groups, so the nature of the interaction and transition at this time is critical if difficult to define. Genz (2006c:76) emphasizes the development of clear regionalization during the EIA. Because of the significant differences at these sites, the EIA is seen as a period of cultural and political fragmentation (e.g., Genz 2003; Summers 2008).

In contrast, the subsequent Middle Iron Age is a period of political consolidation, albeit with considerable regional variation. Although a focus on Gordion has provided relatively high-resolution data from the core area of Phrygia, the great distance between excavated Iron Age sites—as well as differences in excavation strategies—challenges any attempt to produce a coherent understanding of the dynamics of the Phrygian polity, the development of other polities (such as Pteria), or the extent and nature of their interactions. These can only be indirectly inferred through Assyrian and later Greek texts. Recent work on exchange at central Anatolian sites seems to suggest that the vessels that were being moved around the landscape were typically table wares, associated with food consumption rather than the transport of goods, although Kerkenes provides an important exception.

The recent Iron Age excavations at Boğazköy, as well as preliminary indications in LIA levels at Kaman, suggest that urban centers were expanding both economically and politically. In the region around Kerkenes, there is evidence that conflict or at least tensions increase, as the investment in fortifications and fortified sites seems to increase. Kerkenes also provides some evidence of provisioning based on the relatively high percentage of exotic jars identified. That (eastern) central Anatolia becomes a military target for the Lydians, the Persians, and subsequently the Greeks suggests not only its strategic resource-rich location but also recognition of its emergent role as a regional political power.

As yet we can only sketch these dynamics, with much of central Anatolian archaeology focused on the Hittite and earlier Chalcolithic periods. Notwithstanding the substantial challenges posed by the first millennium B.C.E., the developments in this period clearly laid the foundations for the importance of central Anatolia in the expansion of subsequent empires across the region and deserve renewed archaeological attention.

NOTES

We thank H. Genz, K. Matsumura, G. K. Sams, S. R. Steadman, G. Summers, and M. M. Voigt for their comments on earlier versions of this chapter.

1. Very similar decoration occurs in LIA contexts at Gordion.

REFERENCES

Primary Sources

Herodotus. *Histories*. Trans. A. D. Godfrey. London: Heinemann Young Books, 1920–1925.

Secondary Sources

Bossert, Eva-Marie. 2000. *Die Keramik Phrygischer Zeit von Boğazköy*. Mainz am Rhein: Verlag Philipp von Zabern.

Branting, Scott. 2005. Kerkenes Dağ project. *Oriental Institute Annual Report '04–'05*, 69–73. Chicago: Oriental Institute.

Brixhe, Claude and Geoffrey D. Summers. 2006. Les Inscriptions Phrygiennes de Kerkenes Dağ (Anatolie Centrale). *Kadmos* 45: 93–135.

Bryce, Trevor. 2005. *The Kingdom of the Hittites*. Oxford: Oxford University Press.

DeVries, Keith, ed. 1980. *From Athens to Gordion. The Papers of a Memorial Symposium for Rodney S. Young, held at the University Museum, May 3rd, 1975*. Philadelphia: University of Pennsylvania Museum.

———. 1988. Gordion and Phrygia in the Sixth Century BC. In *Phrygian Art and Archaeology, Special Issue*, ed. Oscar White Muscarella. *Source: Notes in the History of Art* 7.3/4: 51–59.

———. 1997. The Attic Pottery from Gordion. In *Athenian Potters and Painters*, ed. John H. Oakley, William D. E. Coulson and Olga Palagia, 447–55. Oxford: Oxbow Books.

———. 2000. Gordion. *Expedition* 42.1: 17–19.

———. 2005. Greek Pottery and Gordion Chronology. In *The Archaeology of Midas and the Phrygians*, ed. Lisa Kealhofer, 35–55. Philadelphia: University of Pennsylvania Museum Press.

———. 2007. The Date of the Destruction Level at Gordion: Imports and the Local Sequence. In *Anatolian Iron Ages 6, Proceedings of the Sixth Anatolian Iron Ages Symposium, Eskişehir*, ed. Altan Çilingiroğlu and Antonio Sagona, 79–101. Ancient Near Eastern Studies, Supplement 20. Leuven: Peeters.

———. 2008. The Age of Midas at Gordion and Beyond. *Ancient Near Eastern Studies* 45: 30–64.

———. Forthcoming. The Creation of the Old Chronology. In *The Chronology of Iron Age Gordion* ed. Brian Rose and Gareth Darbyshire, 6–16. Philadelphia: University of Pennsylvania Museum.

Rose, Brian and Gareth Darbyshire, eds. Forthcoming. *The Chronology of Iron Age Gordion*. Philadelphia: University of Pennsylvania Museum.

DeVries, Keith, Peter Kuniholm, G. Kenneth Sams, and Mary Voigt. 2003. New Dates for Iron Age Gordion. *Antiquity* 77.296: Project Gallery. antiquity.ac.uk/ProjGall/devries/devries.html.

DeVries, Keith and Mary M. Voigt. forthcoming. Emerging Problems and Doubts. In *The Chronology of Early Iron Age Gordion*, ed. Brian Rose and Gareth Darbyshire. Philadelphia: University of Pennsylvania Press.

Draycott, Catherine M., Geoffrey D. Summers, contribution by Claude Brixhe, Turkish summary by G. Bike Yazıcıoğlu. 2008. *Kerkenes Special Studies 1: Sculpture and Inscriptions from the Monumental Entrance to the Palatial Complex at Kerkenes Dağ, Turkey*. Chicago: Oriental Institute of the University of Chicago.

Durbin, Gail E. S. 1971. Iron Age Pottery from the Provinces of Tokat and Sivas. *Anatolian Studies* 21: 99–124.

Fischer, Bettina, Hermann Genz, Éric Jean, and Kemalettin Köroğlu, eds. 2003. *Identifying Changes: The Transition from Bronze to Iron Ages in Anatolia and its Neighboring Regions. Proceedings of the International Workshop Istanbul, 8–9 November 2002*. İstanbul: Türk Eskiçağ Bilimleri Enstitüsü.

Fisher, William B. 1978. *The Middle East, A Physical, Social and Regional Geography*, 7th ed. London: Routledge.

Genz, Hermann. 2000. The Early Iron Age in Central Anatolia in Light of Recent Research. *Near Eastern Archaeology* 63: 111.

———. 2001. Iron Age Pottery from Çadır Höyük. *Anatolica* 27: 159–70.

———. 2003. The Early Iron Age in Central Anatolia. In *Identifying Changes: The Transition from Bronze to Iron Ages in Anatolia and its Neighboring Regions. Proceedings of the International Workshop Istanbul, 8–9 November 2002*, ed. Bettina Fischer, Hermann Genz, Éric Jean, and Kemalettin Köroğlu, 179–92. İstanbul: Türk Eskiçağ Bilimleri Enstitüsü.

———. 2004. *Büyükkaya I: Die Keramike der Eisenzeit*. Mainz am Rhein: Philipp von Zabern.

———. 2006a. Die eisenzeitliche Besiedlung im Bereich der Grabungen an den Ostteichen 1996–1998. In *Ergebnisse der Grabungen an den Ostteichen und am mittleren Büyükkale-Nordwesthang in den Jahren 1996–2000*, ed. Jürgen Seeher, 26–38. Boğazköy-Berichte 8. Mainz: Philipp von Zabern.

———. 2006b. Die eisenzeitliche Besiedlung im Bereich der Grabungen am mittleren Büyükkale-Nordwesthang 1998–2000. *Ergebnisse der Grabungen an den Ostteichen und am mittleren Büyükkale-Nordwesthang in den Jahren 1996–2000*, ed. Jürgen Seeher, 98–158. Boğazköy-Berichte 8. Mainz: Philipp von Zabern.

———. 2006c. Thoughts on the Origin of the Iron Age Pottery Traditions in Central Anatolia. *Anatolian Iron Ages V Proceedings*, ed. A. Çilingiroğlu and G. Darbyshire, 75–84. Ankara: British Institute of Archaeology in Ankara.

———. 2007. Late Iron Age Occupation on the Northwest Slope at Boğazköy. In *Anatolian Iron Ages 6: The Proceedings of the Sixth Anatolian Iron Ages Colloquium, August 16–20, 2004, Eskişehir*, ed. Altan Çilingiroğlu and Antonio Sagona, 125–52. Leuven: Peeters.

———. Forthcoming. Eisenzeitliche Gräber aus Boğazköy.

Gorny, Ronald L. 1994. The 1993 Season at Alişar in Central Turkey. *Anatolica* 20: 191–202.

———. 2006. The 2002–2005 Excavation Seasons at Çadır Höyük. *Anatolica* 32: 29–54.

Gorny, Ronald L., Gregory McMahon, Samuel Paley, and Lisa Kealhofer. 1995. The Alişar Regional Project: 1994. *Anatolica* 21: 68–100.

Gorny, Ronald L., Gregory McMahon, Samuel Paley, Sharon Steadman, and Bruce Verhaaren. 1999. The 1998 Alişar Regional Project Season. *Anatolica* 25: 149–83.

———. 2002. The 2000–2001 Seasons at Çadır Höyük in Central Turkey: A Preliminary Report. *Anatolica* 28: 109–36.

Grave, Peter and Lisa Kealhofer. 2006. Investigating Iron Age Trade Ceramics at Kaman-Kalehöyük. *Anatolian Archaeological Studies, Kaman-Kalehöyük* 15: 140–50.

Grave, Peter, Lisa Kealhofer, G. Kenneth Sams, Mary M. Voigt, and Keith DeVries. 2009. Production and Provenience at Gordion, Central Anatolia. *Journal of Archaeological Science* (doi: 10.1016/j.jas.2009.05.029).

Hawkins, J.D. 1982. The Neo-Hittite States in Syria and Anatolia. In *The Cambridge Ancient History*, vol. 3, part 1, ed. John Boardman, I. E. S. Edwards, N. G. L. Hammond and E. Sollberger, 372–441. Cambridge: Cambridge University Press.

Henrickson, Robert C. 1993a. Politics, Economics and Ceramic Continuity at Gordion in the Late Second and First Millennia B.C. In *Social and Cultural Contexts of New Ceramic Technologies, Ceramics and Civilization VI*, ed. W. D. Kingery, 86–176. Westerville, Ohio: American Ceramic Society.

———. 1993b. Pottery, Politics, and Ethnicity at Gordion in the Middle Phrygian through Hellenistic periods (700–150 B.C.). *American Journal of Archaeology* 97: 303.

———. 1994. Continuity and Discontinuity in the Ceramic Tradition of Gordion during the Iron Age. In *Proceedings of the Third International Anatolian Iron Age Symposium*, ed. David French and Altan Çilingiroğlu, 95–129. London: British Institute of Archaeology.

———. 1995. Hittite Pottery and Potters: The View from Late Bronze Age Gordion. *Biblical Archaeologist* 58.2: 82–90.

———. 2005. The Local Potter's Craft at Phrygian Gordion. In *The Archaeology of Midas and the Phrygians*, ed. Lisa Kealhofer, 124–35. Philadelphia: University of Pennsylvania Museum.

Henrickson, Robert C. and M. James Blackman. 1996. Large-Scale Production of Pottery at Gordion: A Comparison of the Late Bronze and Early Phrygian Industries. *Paléorient* 22: 67–87.

Henrickson, Robert C., Pamela B. Vandiver, and James Blackman. 2002. Lustrous Black Fine Ware at Gordion, Turkey: A Distinctive Sintered Slip Technology. In *Materials Issues in Art and Archaeology VI, Materials Research Society Symposium Proceedings*, ed. P. B. Vandiver, M. Goodway and J. L. Mass, vol. 7:12: 391–400. Pittsburgh: Materials Research Society.

Hongo, Hitomi. 2003. Continuity or Changes: Faunal Remains from Stratum IId at Kaman-Kalehöyük. In *Identifying Changes: The Transition from Bronze to Iron Ages in Anatolia and its Neighboring Regions. Proceedings of the International Workshop*

Istanbul, 8–9 November 2002, ed. Bettina Fischer, Hermann Genz, Éric Jean, and Kemalettin Köroğlu, 257–69. İstanbul: Türk Eskiçağ Bilimleri Enstitüsü.

Kealhofer, Lisa, Peter Grave, Hermann Genz, and Ben Marsh. 2009. Post-Collapse: The Re-Emergence of Polity in Iron Age Boğazköy. *Oxford Journal of Archaeology* 28.3: 275–300.

Kealhofer, Lisa, Peter Grave, Benjamin Marsh, and Kimiyoshi Matsumura. Forthcoming. Analysis of Specialized Iron Age Wares at Kaman-Kalehöyük. Anatolian Archaeological Studies XVII. *Anatolian Archaeological Studies, Kaman-Kalehöyük* 17.

Kealhofer, Lisa, Peter Grave, Ben Marsh, Sharon Steadman, Ronald Gorny, and Geoffrey D. Summers. 2010. Characterizing Iron Age Ceramics from Çadır, Kerkenes, and Tilkigediği. *Anatolian Studies* 60: 71–92.

Kuniholm, Peter. 1977. Dendrochronology at Gordion and on the Anatolian Plateau. Ph.D. dissertation. University of Pennsylvania.

Kuniholm, Peter I., Bernd Kromer, Sturt W. Manning, Maryanne Newton, Christine E. Latini, and Mary Jaye Bruce. 1996. Anatolian Tree Rings and the Absolute Chronology of the Eastern Mediterranean. *Nature* 381 (June 27): 780–83.

Manning, Sturt W. and Bernd Kromer. Forthcoming. Radiocarbon Dating Iron Age Gordion and the Early Phrygian Destruction in Particular. In *The Chronology of Iron Age Gordion*, ed. Brian Rose and Gareth Darbyshire, 69–150. Philadelphia: University of Pennsylvania Museum Press.

Manning, Sturt W., Bernd Kromer, Peter I. Kuniholm, and Maryanne Newton. 2001. Anatolian Tree-Rings and a New Chronology for the East Mediterranean Bronze-Iron Ages. *Science* 294: 2532–35.

Marsh, Ben. 2005. Physical Geography, Land Use, and Human Impact at Gordion. In *The Archaeology of Midas and the Phrygians*, ed. Lisa Kealhofer, 161–71. Philadelphia: University of Pennsylvania Museum Press.

Matsumura, Kimiyoshi. 2000. On the Manufacturing Techniques of Iron Age Ceramics from Kaman-Kalehöyük. *Anatolian Archaeological Studies, Kaman-Kalehöyük* 9: 119–35.

———. 2001. On the Manufacturing Techniques of Iron Age Ceramics from Kaman-Kalehöyük (II); The Cultural Influence of Phrygia at Kaman-Kalehöyük. *Anatolian Archaeological Studies, Kaman-Kalehöyük* 10: 101–10.

———. 2005. Die Eisenzeitliche Keramik in Zentral Anatolien, aufgrund der Grundlage der Ausgrabung von Kaman-Kalehöyük. Fachbereich Geschichts- und Kulturwissenschaften. Ph.D. dissertation. Freie Universität.

———. 2008. The Early Iron Age in Kaman-Kalehöyük: The Search for its Roots. In *Fundstellen Gesammelte Schriften zur Archäologie und Geschichte Altvorderasiens ad honorem Hartmut Kühne*, ed. Dominik Bonatz, Rainer M. Czichon and F. Janoscha Kreppner, 42–51. Wiesbaden: Harrassowitz Verlag.

———. 2009. The Iron Age Chronology in Anatolia Reconsidered: The Results of the Excavations at Kaman-Kalehöyük. *Proceedings of the 6th International Congress on the Archaeology of the Ancient Near East (May 2008)*, ed. Paolo Matthiae. Rome: Harrassowitz Verlag.

Miller, Naomi and Melinda Zeder. 2009. From Food and Fuel to Farms and Flocks: The Integration of Plant and Animal Remains in the Study of the Agropastoral Economy at Gordion, Turkey. *Current Anthropology* 50.6: 915–24.

Muscarella, Oscar W. 2004. The Date of the Destruction of the Early Phrygian Period at Gordion. *Ancient West and East* 2.2: 225–52.

Newton, Maryanne W. and Peter I. Kuniholm. 2001. Dendrochronological Investigations at Kaman-Kalehoyuk: Dating Early Iron Age Level IId. *Anatolian Archaeological Studies, Kaman-Kalehöyük* 10: 125–28.

Omori, Takayuki and Toshio Nakamura. 2006. Radiocarbon Dating of Archaeological Materials Excavated at Kaman-Kalehöyük: Initial Report. *Anatolian Archaeological Studies, Kaman-Kalehöyük* 15: 263–68.

———. 2007. Radiocarbon Dating of Archaeological Materials Excavated at Kaman Kalehöyük: Second Report. *Anatolian Archaeological Studies, Kaman-Kalehöyük* 16: 111–23.

Omura, Sachihiro. 2000. Preliminary Report on the 15th Excavation Season at Kaman-Kalehöyük. *Anatolian Archaeological Studies, Kaman-Kalehöyük* 10: 1–36.

———. 2005. Preliminary Report on the 19th Excavation Season at Kaman-Kalehöyük. *Anatolian Archaeological Studies, Kaman Kalehoyuk* 14: 1–54.

Ralph, Elizabeth K., Henry N. Michael, and M. C. Han. 1973. Radiocarbon Dates and Reality. *MASCA Newsletter* 9.1 (August): 1–20.

Reimer, Paula J., Mike G. L. Baillie, Edouard Bard, Alex Bayliss, J. Warren Beck, Chanda J. H. Bertrand, Paul G. Blackwell, Caitlin E. Buck, George S. Burr, Kirsten B. Cutler, Paul E. Damon, R. Lawrence Edwards, Richard G. Fairbanks, Michael Friedrich, Thomas P. Guilderson, Alan G. Hogg, Konrad A. Hughen, Bernd Kromer, Gerry McCormac, Sturt Manning, Christopher Bronk Ramsey, Ron W. Reimer, Sabine Remmele, John R. Southon, Minze Stuiver, Sahra Talamo, F. W. Taylor, Johannes van der Plicht, and Constanze E. Weyhenmeyer. 2009. IntCal09 and Marine09 Radiocarbon Age Calibration Curves, 0–50,000 Years cal BP. *Radiocarbon* 51.4: 1111–50.

Ross, Jennifer C. 2010. The Iron Age at Çadır Höyük. *Anatolica* 36: 67–87.

Sams, G. Kenneth. 1994. *The Early Phrygian Pottery, Volume IV. The Gordion Excavations 1950–1973: Final Reports.* Philadelphia: University of Pennsylvania Museum.

———. 1995. Midas of Gordion and the Anatolian Kingdom of Phrygia. In *Civilizations of the Ancient Near East*, ed. Jack Sasson, 1147–59. New York: Scribner.

Schaus, Gerald P. 1992. Imported West Anatolian Pottery at Gordion. *Anatolian Studies* 42: 151–77.

Schoop, Ulf-Dietrich. 2006. Dating the Hittites with Statistics: Ten Pottery Assemblages from Boğazköy-Hattusa. In *Structuring and Dating in Hittite Archaeology*, ed. Dirk Mielke, Ulf-Dietrich Schoop, and Jürgen Seeher, 215–40. Byzas 4. İstanbul: Zero Prod.

Schoop, Ulf-Dietrich and Jürgen Seeher. 2006. Absolute chronologie in Boğazköy-Hattuša: Das Potential der Radiokarbondaten. In *Structuring and Dating in Hittite Archaeology*, ed. Dirk Mielke, Ulf-Dietrich Schoop, and Jürgen Seeher, 53–75. Byzas 4. İstanbul: Zero Prod.

Seeher, Jürgen. 1997. Die Ausgrabungen in Boğazköy-Hattuša 1996. *Archäologischer Anzeiger*: 317–41.

———. 1998. The Early Iron Age Settlement on Büyükkaya, Boğazköy: First Impressions. In *Thracians and Phrygians: Problems of Parallelism, Proceedings of an International Symposium on the Archaeology, History, and Ancient Languages of Thrace and Phrygia, Ankara, June 3–4, 1985, Middle East Technical University*, ed. Numan Tuna, Zeynep Aktüre, and Maggie Lynch, 71–78. Ankara: Middle East Technical University.

———. 2000. Die Ausgrabungen in Boğazköy-Hattuša 1999. *Archäologischer Anzeiger*: 355–76.

———. 2006. Chronology in Hattuša: New Approaches to an Old Problem. *Byzas* 4: 197–213.

Sherratt, Stephen. 1998. "Sea Peoples" and the Economic Structure of the Late Second Millennium BC in the Eastern Mediterranean. In *Mediterranean Peoples in Transition*, ed. Seymour Gitin, Amihai Mazar, and Ephraim Stern, 292–313. Jerusalem: Israel Exploration Society.

Singer, Itamar. 2000. New Evidence of the End of the Hittite Empire. In *The Sea Peoples and Their World: A Reassessment*, ed. Eliezer D. Oren, 21–35. University of Pennsylvania Monographs 108. Philadelpia: University of Pennsylvania Press.

Steadman, Sharon R., Jennifer C. Ross, Gregory McMahon, and Ronald L. Gorny. 2008. Excavations on the North-Central Plateau: The Chalcolithic and Early Bronze Age Occupation at Çadır Höyük. *Anatolian Studies* 58: 47–86.

Summers, Geoffrey D. 1994. Grey Ware and the Eastern Limits of Phrygia. In *Anatolian Iron Ages* 3, ed. A. Çilingiroğlu and D. French, 241–52. London: British Institute of Archaeology at Ankara.

———. 2006. Aspects of Material Culture at the Iron Age Capital on the Kerkenes Dağ in Central Anatolia. *Ancient Near Eastern Studies* 43: 164–202.

———. 2008. Periodisation and Technology in the Central Anatolian Iron Age. Archaeology, History and Audiences. *Ancient Near Eastern Studies* 45: 202–17.

Summers, Geoffrey D. and Françoise Summers. 1995. The Regional Survey at Kerkenes Dağ: An Interim Report on the Seasons 1993 and 1994. *Anatolian Studies* 45: 43–68.

Summers, Geoffrey D., Françoise Summers, Nilüfer Baturayoğlu, Ömür Harmanşah, and Elspeth R. McIntosh. 1996. The Regional Survey at Kerkenes Dağ: An Interim Report on the Seasons 1993 and 1994. *Anatolian Studies* 46: 201–34.

Voigt, Mary M. 2005. Old Problems New Solutions: Recent Excavations at Gordion. In *The Archaeology of Midas and the Phrygians*, ed. Lisa Kealhofer, 22–35. Philadelphia: University of Pennsylvania Museum Press.

———. 2009. The Chronology of Phrygian Gordion. In *Tree-Rings, Kings, and Old World Archaeology and Environment: Papers Presented in Honor of Peter Ian Kuniholm*, ed. Sturt W. Manning and Mary Jaye Bruce, 3–26. Oxford: Oxbow.

Voigt, Mary M., Keith DeVries, Robert C. Henrickson, Mark Lawall, Ben Marsh, Ayşe Gursan-Salzmann, and T. Cuyler Young Jr. 1997. Fieldwork at Gordion 1993–1995. *Anatolica* 23: 1–59.

Voigt, Mary M. and Robert C. Henrickson. 2000. The Early Iron Age at Gordion: The Evidence from the Yassihöyük Stratigraphic Sequence. In *The Sea Peoples and their World: A Reassessment*, ed. Eliezer D. Oren. 327–60. University Museum Monograph 108. Philadelphia: University of Pennsylvania Press.

von der Osten, Hans H. 1930. *The Alishar Hüyük*. Oriental Institute Publication 6. Chicago: University of Chicago Press.

———. 1937. *The Alishar Hüyük, Seasons of 1930–1932*. Oriental Institute Publications 28, parts 1–3. Chicago: University of Chicago Press.

Williams, Evan T., Gardy Cadet, Noel A. Guardala, Eric Huang, and Frederick A. Winter. 1987. Analysis of Pottery by PIXE: Late Classical and Hellenistic Imports to Gordion. Nuclear Instruments and Methods. *Physics Research* B22: 430–32.

Winter, Frederick A. 1973. Late Classical and Hellenistic Pottery from Gordion. *American Journal of Archaeology* 77: 232–33.

———. 1988. Phrygian Gordion in the Hellenistic Period. *Source: Notes in the History of Art* 8.3&4: 60–71.

Yakar, Jak. 2006. Dating the Sequence of the Final Destruction/Abandonment of LBA Settlements: Toward a Better Understanding of Events that Led to the Collapse of the Hittite Kingdom. In *Structuring and Dating in Hittite Archaeology*, ed. Dirk Mielke, Ulf-Dietrich Schoop, and Jürgen Seeher, 33–51. Byzas 4. İstanbul: Zero Prod.

Zeder, Melinda and Suzanne Arter. 1994. Changing Patterns of Animal Utilization at Ancient Gordion. *Paléorient* 20.2: 105–18.

CHAPTER 19

THE IRON AGE OF SOUTHEASTERN ANATOLIA

TIMOTHY MATNEY

ARCHAEOLOGICAL fieldwork conducted over the past two decades has led to significant refinements in our understanding of Iron Age chronology in southeastern Anatolia. Much of this work is a direct result of the excavation of dozens of archaeological sites with Iron Age components undertaken as salvage initiatives in advance of the construction of the Karkamiş, Biricik, Atatürk, Karakaya, and Keban Dams on the Euphrates River, and the proposed Ilısu Dam on the Tigris River. Although most of the sites excavated in these regions have been published only in preliminary reports, they nonetheless form the basis for a reworking of the Iron Age chronology of southeastern Anatolia.

Geography and Setting

For purposes of this reassessment, I define southeastern Anatolia as the lowland area bordered by the Taurus Mountains on the north and the Tur Abdin Mountains to the south, the latter a low limestone mountain range with elevations between 900 m and 1,400 m (Radner 2006). The hinterlands of the Upper Euphrates River and its various tributaries form the natural western border of the area considered here, while the hinterlands of the Tigris River and its various tributaries in turn mark its eastern extent. The southern limit of the study area presents some difficulties.

Both geographically and culturally, the high rolling plains of southeastern Turkey blend imperceptibly with the upper Mesopotamian plains of northern Syria and northern Iraq, and the historical trajectory of the upper Mesopotamian plains—now encompassed by the modern nations of Turkey, Syria, and Iraq—constitutes a single coherent unit of study in antiquity. At no time is this clearer than in the Iron Age, when developments in large portions of southeastern Turkey are closely tied to the ebb and flow of the political fortunes of the Assyrian Empire based to the south in what is today northern Iraq.

This region is characterized by well-watered, narrow valleys cut by the Euphrates and Tigris Rivers as they emerge from the Taurus Mountains and are fed by a number of major tributaries and smaller wadi systems. Between the rivers are fertile rolling plains with sufficient rainfall to support dry farming in all but the driest years (Weiss 1983; Wilkinson 1994). The same conditions allow pastoral exploitation even in its most marginal areas (Ur and Hammer 2009). However, the density of settlement within the plains was not homogeneous in antiquity. Rainfall, while sufficient for reliable cereal agriculture, is highly seasonal, so that sustained human occupation in this region could only take place immediately near the rivers or their perennial tributaries that provided year-round sources of potable water or, if away from the rivers, in lower lying portions of the plains where wells could tap into the water table.

Crafting an outline of the historical trajectories of Iron Age societies within as large and diverse an area of study as outlined is inherently difficult and is further compounded by two factors. First, large portions of areas within modern southeastern Turkey remain largely unexplored through systematic archaeological reconnaissance. Second, where surveys exist, they are of varying intensity, reliability, and coverage, making regional comparisons difficult. One of the challenges of this chapter, then, is to bring into a single coherent framework the Iron Age chronologies from a large area which, as will be shown, was differentially affected by cultural and political influences during the late second and first millennia B.C.E.

Accordingly, much of the historical trajectory of the Upper Euphrates and Upper Tigris regions of Turkey in the Iron Age is defined by political events happening elsewhere in the ancient Near East, for example, the rise and fall of the Hittite, Middle and Late Assyrian, Urartian, and Achaemenid states (see Beal, chapter 26, Radner, chapter 33, and Harl, chapter 34 in this volume). Constructing a chronology for these areas of southeastern Turkey in the Iron Age therefore requires that we correlate the larger historical trends that affected much of the ancient Near East with the material culture derived from archaeological excavations outside the limited area of specific concern here. This can be achieved via careful periodizations based on changing ceramic types and their associations with absolute dates, when available. The problem with such an approach, as outlined recently by Çevik (2008), and by many others before, is that changes in pottery sequences often do not neatly correspond with shifts in social systems (see also Summers 2009:658), and this problem is accentuated in areas marginal to newly emergent centers of power elsewhere. Mindful of these caveats, I do not attempt to introduce either an entirely new strategy for discussing Iron Age chronology in southeastern Anatolia or to radically alter existing schemes. Rather, what I propose to do is to update the criteria currently in place for discussing the Iron Age chronology of southeastern Turkey to allow for cross-cultural comparisons with contemporary regions across the ancient Near East.

Chronological Sequences

Iron Age chronology is traditionally divided into three periods: Early, Middle, and Late; this convention is followed in this chapter as well. In addition to the description of source material used to describe these periods, brief descriptions of relevant ceramics, their find spots, and their appearance or disappearance help to shape the parameters of each period.

Source Material

Two primary sources form the basis for this reassessment of the Iron Age chronology of southeastern Turkey: published data from excavated sites and contemporary textual sources (see Radner, chapter 33, and Zimansky, chapter 24 in this volume). Additionally, however, there is also some pertinent survey data as well, and these data are noted when relevant. Although existing survey data are key to properly understanding broad social and demographic trends within southeastern Turkey in the Iron Age, readers should note that what surveys we do have were mostly done before significant excavation had taken place in southeastern Turkey, and their results are generally marred by the lack of accurate ceramic typologies. This affects all periods, to be sure, but is particularly acute for the Iron Age because early surveyors were often able to recognize the previously well-documented foreign assemblages and wares of intrusive imperial powers centered elsewhere (i.e., Assyrian, Achaemenid, etc.) but were generally not able to recognize the material culture of indigenous populations that existed in southeastern Turkey before and after those intrusions, which are only now being defined through site-specific excavation. Because of this bias, we must rely foremost on excavated data for our reconstruction.

In the Upper Euphrates region, archaeological work was undertaken in large part as salvage work in advance of a series of hydroelectric dams which were built as part of the Güneydoğu Anadolu Projesi (GAP). A number of dams were completed along the Euphrates River, creating a series of lakes and flooding hundreds of archaeological sites. These dam projects include Keban Dam (1975), Karakaya Dam (1987), Atatürk Dam (1992), Karkamiş Dam (1999), and Birecik Dam (2000). In terms of the chronology of the Iron Age, a number of key sites were excavated as part of this decades-long salvage operation. The sites of Norşun Tepe, Lidar Höyük, and Tille Höyük (figure 19.1) are of primary importance to our understanding of Iron Age chronology, as they have long Iron Age stratigraphic sequences (Müller 2004). In the upper Tigris region, salvage excavation started two decades after that in the Euphrates region, as the proposed construction of the Ilısu Dam led first to broad reconnaissance work in the late 1980s (Algaze et al. 1991) and finally to new site-based excavation projects starting in the mid-1990s. In the past decade, over two dozen sites have been excavated in the Ilısu project area; most remain published only in preliminary fashion. Similarly, excavations along the main Tigris tributaries—the Batman, Garzan, and Bohtan Rivers—are now under way. Preliminary results of these projects are published in the journal *Kazı Sonuçları Toplantısı* by the Turkish Ministry of Culture and Tourism, and fieldwork done from 1998 to 2001 can be found in a bilingual series of edited monographs published by the Middle East Technical University (Tuna, Greenhalgh, and Velibeyoğlu 2004; Tuna and Öztürk 1999; Tuna, Öztürk, and Velibeyoğlu 2001, 2002).

An important secondary source for the chronology of the Iron Age are the proceedings from a series of six conferences specifically focused on the Iron Age chronology of Anatolia organized by Altan Çilingiroğlu (Çilingiroğlu 1987; Çilingiroğlu and Darbyshire 2004; Çilingiroğlu and French 1991, 1994; Çilingiroğlu and Matthews 1999; Çilingiroğlu and Sagona 2007; for a history of the conferences see Roller 2009). Finally, a volume of *Ancient Near Eastern Studies* titled "A Re-Assessment of Iron Ages Chronology in Anatolia and Neighboring Regions" represents an important secondary source for Iron Age chronology (SFACSA 2008). None of these secondary sources, it must be noted, are devoted exclusively to southeastern Anatolia.

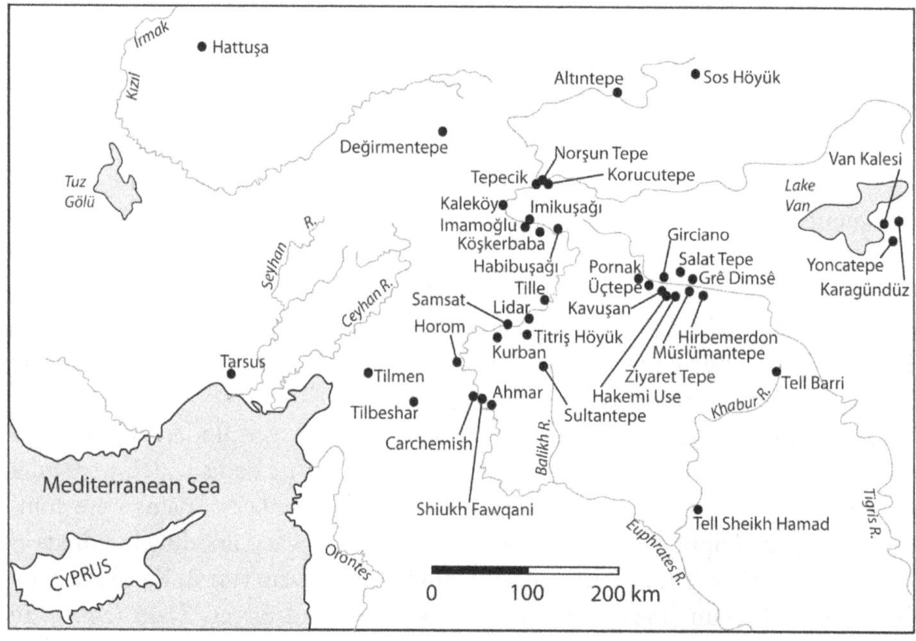

Figure 19.1. Map of sites discussed in the text.

Early Iron Age

Unlike the coastal regions of the Levantine littoral, southeastern Anatolia was not directly affected by the invasions that took place around 1200 B.C.E. traditionally associated with the so-called Sea Peoples (Bartl 1995). However, southeastern Turkey was certainly touched by the related historical dislocations that also affected much of the ancient Near East at the end of the Late Bronze Age. Two such events are particularly pertinent to this discussion: the collapse of the Hittite Empire centered in the Anatolian plateau that had occupied large portions of the Upper Euphrates basin all the way down to Carchemish in the first half of the twelfth century B.C.E. and the collapse of the Middle Assyrian Empire centered along the Tigris in northern Iraq, which had extended minimally up to the southern bank of the east–west-running Tigris River south of Diyarbakır in the first half of the eleventh century B.C.E. In a sense, the sequential disappearance of these foreign occupying powers from both the Upper Euphrates and Upper Tigris basins represents the start of the Early Iron Age in southeastern Anatolia, a period that is largely documented only through material culture.

Archaeologically, the last centuries of the second and the first century of the first millennia B.C.E. in southeastern Anatolia are marked in part by the arrival and widespread distribution of a new type of pottery known as Groovy Pottery (figure 19.2). With some variations, Groovy Pottery is recognized widely across the Upper Euphrates and Tigris region, east to Lake Van and northwestern Iran (Roaf and Schachner 2004:fig. 4). Groovy Pottery in southeastern Anatolia is predominantly handmade, with hemispherical and deep bowl forms, occasionally with spouts or handles, and decorated with horizontal grooved lines around the rim (see Bartl 2001 for a general description; also Roaf and Schachner 2004:116; see also Khatchadourian, chapter 20 in this volume).

As already noted, the start of the Early Iron Age in the Euphrates region has traditionally been correlated with political events surrounding the collapse of the Hittite Empire and the abandonment of the Hittite capital of Ḫattuša around 1180 B.C.E., although the effect that this event had on different settlements of the Euphrates region is far from uniform. Müller (2004; see Seeher, chapter 16 in this volume) has argued that the transition in material culture from the Late Bronze Age to the Early Iron Age is a gradual one without significant social disruptions and that the shift to Early Iron Age material culture took place earlier in the north than in the south of the Upper Euphrates region. The appearance of Groovy Pottery at Norşun Tepe in the early twelfth century and at Lidar Höyük in the late twelfth century B.C.E. (Müller 2004:111–13) is taken by him to mark the beginning of the Early Iron Age. Similar pottery is well known from other Keban and Karababa Dam sites at Korucutepe, Tepecik, Değirmentepe, Habibuşağı, İmikuşağı, Değirmentepe, Köşkerbaba, and Tille Höyük (Bartl 1995:208).

Groovy Pottery is also found in the Upper Tigris region, but it appears to have been introduced there later than was the case along the Euphrates, possibly because the Upper Tigris area continued to be occupied by the Middle Assyrians

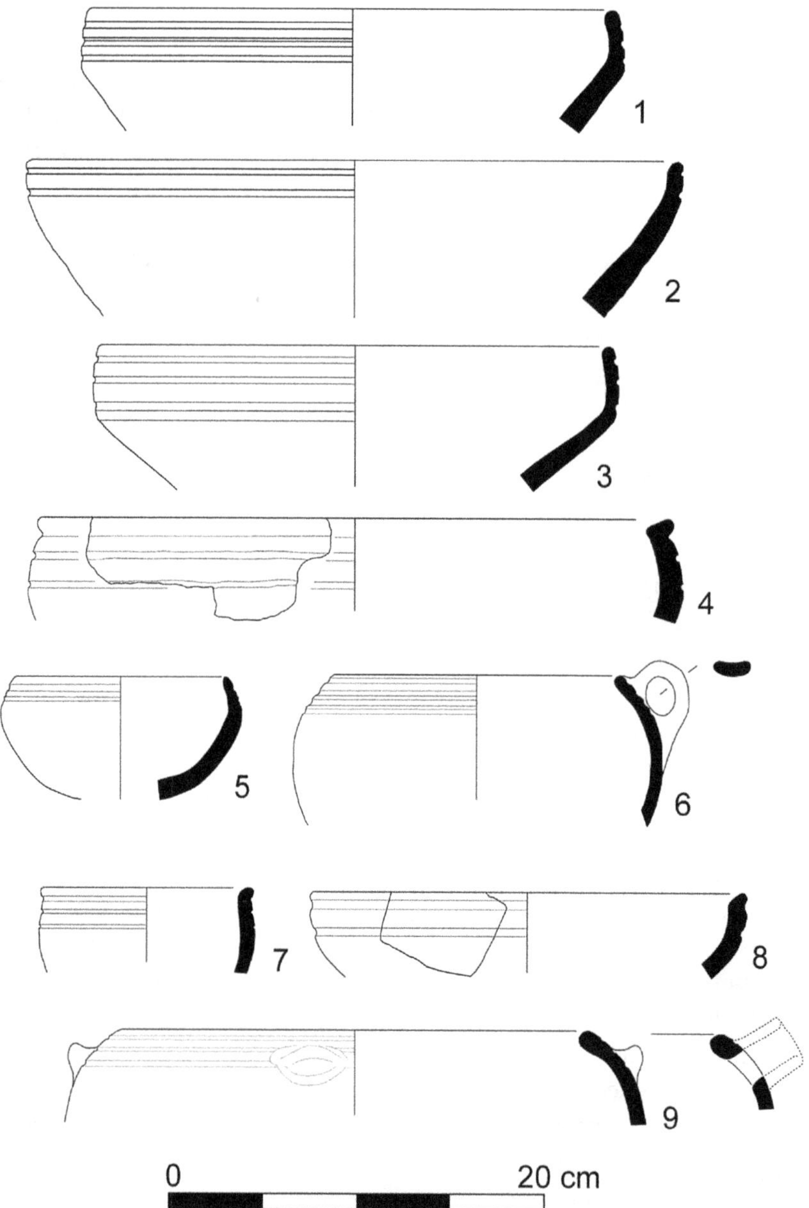

Figure 19.2. Groovy Pottery typical of the Early Iron Age in southeastern Turkey. Ziyaret Tepe, 1–9.

for a century or so after the Hittite collapse in the west. This is suggested by recent excavations at Giricano Tepe and Ziyaret Tepe, which have confirmed the claims made in Assyrian Royal Annals that the upper Tigris region was under the control of the Middle Assyrian kings starting with the reign of Šalmaneser I (1273–1244 B.C.E.). An important discovery of cuneiform tablets at Giricano Tepe, written between 1068 and 1056 B.C.E., shows that this part of the Upper Tigris River remained in Assyrian hands at least through the middle of the eleventh century B.C.E. (Radner 2004; Roaf and Schachner 2004:119), after which time the Upper Tigris region presumably came under the control of nascent Aramaean polities, which filled the vacuum left behind by the Assyrian collapse. As Roaf points out, there is no evidence of building activity by an Assyrian king between 1030 and 935 B.C.E., although continuity from the Middle to Late Assyrian periods is seen, for example, in the location of royal tombs and stelai at Assur from the fourteenth to the ninth centuries B.C.E. (Roaf 2001). This continuity is seen in the Assyrian heartland of northern Iraq, but not in the peripheral regions of the empire, where significant discontinuities are seen archaeologically. At this point, the Late Bronze Age ceramic tradition of wheelmade Middle Assyrian pottery in the Tigris region is replaced by handmade Groovy Pottery, now widely recognized as typical of the Early Iron Age across southeastern Turkey (Roaf and Schachner 2004; see also Köroğlu and Konyar 2008). As summarized by Szuchman: "Whenever Groovy Pottery appears in Turkey, it seems to coincide with the end of Hittite or Middle Assyrian political authority. The Upper Tigris Valley, however, was unaffected by the events that brought the Bronze Age to an end in Syria and western Anatolia. Correspondingly, EIA pottery appears later in the Upper Tigris than it does elsewhere" (Szuchman 2009:59–60).

Although the dates of the transition away from imperial (Hittite or Middle Assyrian) control or influence differ by as much as a century and a half on the Upper Euphrates and Upper Tigris Rivers, respectively, what is clear is that the onset of the Early Iron Age in both areas is characterized by significant changes in social organization. The principal exception to this is Carchemish, which, perhaps owing to its privileged position at the head of a historical Euphrates ford, became the center of an indigenous Iron Age city-state claiming to be a successor to the Hittite Empire (Thuesen 2002). Samsat, now flooded, may have been the capital of the lesser Neo-Hittite city-state of Kummuḫ, which also survived the Hittite collapse (Thuesen 2002:49). However, such exceptions aside, what is most striking about southeastern Anatolia at the onset of the Iron Age is its nonurban nature.

Bartl is correct when she argues that "the Early Iron Age . . . is characterised by a less developed settlement structure, seemingly a conglomerate of non-centrally organised villages" which "seem to echo the former presence of a rural culture void of any higher form of centrality, be it of cultic or administrative nature" (Bartl 1995:209). Such Early Iron Age villages have been uncovered at Korucutepe and Norşun Tepe, both in the Keban area, and others are common in the Elazığ-Malatya, Middle Euphrates, and Upper Tigris regions area as well (Köroğlu and Konyar 2008:128–29). Further down on the Euphrates, in the environs of Samsat, the Iron Age occupation at Lidar Höyük was characterized by houses clustered on the site's acropolis (Müller 2004:112), and a similar case obtains at the larger regional center of Titriş Höyük, where surveys show that Iron Age remains are limited only to the acropolis and a small portion of the site's terrace (Algaze and Matney, chapter 46 in this volume). A comparable case existed in the Upper Tigris, where surveys and excavations indicate that Iron Age occupations were restricted in extent and amounted to nothing more than small agricultural villages or hamlets (Algaze, Breuninger, and Knudstad 1994; Parker 2001). The collapse of urbanism in the Tigris region at the onset of the Iron Age is best seen at what had been the major Middle Assyrian urban centers of Üçtepe/Tidu (Köroğlu 2003) and Ziyaret Tepe/Tušḫan (Matney et al. 2002). Both were dramatically reduced in size, and although Early Iron Age ceramics at these centers are widely attested, they appear largely associated with pits or small isolated houses.

Szuchman has attempted to explain the ruralization of southeastern Anatolia in the Early Iron Age in the context of tribe-state encounters, arguing that the widespread adoption of Groovy Pottery after the collapse of Middle Assyrian interests along the Upper Tigris River may have been an explicit rejection of "Assyrian forms of cultural and political domination" by a largely Aramaean population (Szuchman 2008:62). This is not to say that Groovy Pottery is strictly an Aramaean marker; such an inflexible identification of specific ceramic types with individual linguistic or ethnic groups has already been widely, and correctly, rejected (Matney 2010; Roaf and Schachner 2004; Szuchman 2009), but rather to note that the spatial and temporal extent of Groovy Pottery and available historical evidence for an Aramaean presence in southeastern Anatolia are at least partly coterminous. Basing his argument largely on available Assyrian historical documentation, Postgate argues that by 900 B.C.E., Aramaean groups had coalesced into minor dynasties across much of northern Mesopotamia (Postgate 1992:249). This may be so, but there is little evidence in the archaeological record of southeastern Anatolia for such petty regional polities, unless of course the polities in question were hierarchically organized agropastoral groups with dual fluid, sedentary and nomadic components such as the tribal confederacies in southwestern Iran in the late nineteenth and early twentieth centuries (Barth 1961; Beck 1986). If so, the Iron Age pattern we observe over much of southeastern Anatolia may be but the visible half of polities that also had a substantial pastoral nomadic component of the sort that often escapes easy archaeological recognition.

The end of the Early Iron Age in southeastern Turkey is best defined by reference to the historical trajectory of two imperial polities with cores outside of the region, namely, the rise of the Late Assyrian state in northern Iraq and the spread of their influence up the Tigris River Valley, and the Urartian state in eastern Turkey and its subsequent expansion in the Euphrates region (see Radner, chapter 33, and Zimansky, chapter 24 in this volume). As will be discussed, these events occur across nearly the entire ninth century B.C.E., leaving us without a single unifying event or date to mark the end of the Early Iron Age.

Middle Iron Age

The relative homogeneity in the rural nature of Early Iron Age occupations across southeastern Anatolia away from the historical fords of the Euphrates came to an end during the transition from the Early Iron Age to the Middle Iron Age in the early ninth century B.C.E., when a disjuncture between the developmental trajectories of the Euphrates and Tigris regions becomes apparent. In the Upper Euphrates region, the Middle Iron Age is marked by the rise of the Urartian state and the arrival of Urartian pottery, seen in the Keban-Malatya area of the Euphrates starting in the mid-ninth century B.C.E. (Bartl 1995:208; Köroğlu and Konyar 2008). Some scholars have suggested that there may have been a hiatus of occupation between the Early and Middle Iron Ages in the uppermost reaches of the Euphrates in Turkey, spanning as much as a century or two (Bartl 1995:207–208), whereas others argue for a continuous occupational sequence, as seen at sites such as Norşun Tepe (Müller 2004:108).

In the Tigris region, the transition to the Middle Iron Age is usually marked in political terms by the reestablishment of an Assyrian occupational presence under Aššurnaṣirpal in 882 B.C.E. and the introduction of a standard, wheelmade Assyrian ceramic tradition (figure 19.3). In both cases, however, it is clear that the

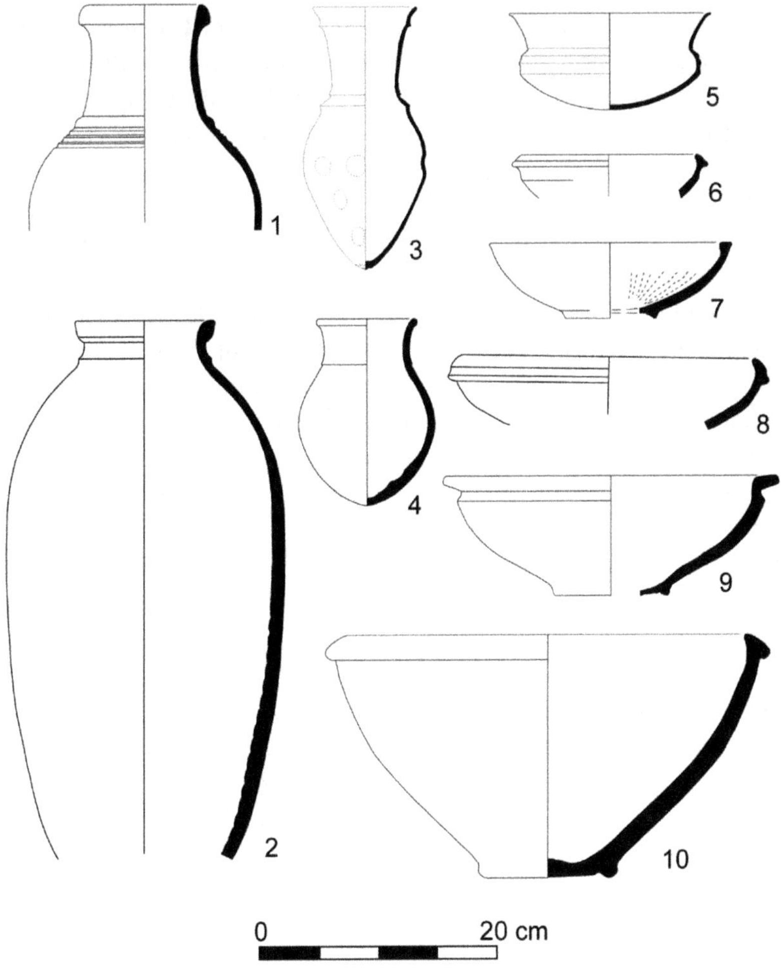

Figure 19.3. Late Assyrian wheelmade pottery typical of the Middle Iron Age in southeastern Turkey. Ziyaret Tepe, 1–10.

Early Iron Age ceramic tradition of Groovy Pottery continued into the Middle Iron Age. This is seen, for example, in the presence of indigenous pottery found together with Late Assyrian pottery on floor deposits at Ziyaret Tepe (Matney et al. 2009) and in eastern Anatolian Urartian graves at Yoncatepe and Karagündüz, both in the Lake Van Basin (Köroğlu and Konyar 2008:129–130; see also Roaf and Schachner 2004:121). It is now certain that this "hallmark" of the Early Iron Age continues in use until the seventh century B.C.E. in parts of southeastern and eastern Turkey.

As had been the case for the Middle Assyrian period at the end of the Late Bronze Age, the Tigris River formed the northernmost frontier of the aggressively expanding Late Assyrian Empire in the Middle Iron Age. Accordingly, the Middle Iron Age in the Tigris basin of southeastern Turkey saw the imposition of a string of fortified urban settlements along the southern bank of the Upper Tigris River by the Assyrian state at Ziyaret Tepe/Tušḫan, near the modern town of Tepe, Üctepe/Tidu, just west of modern Bismil, and Pornak/Sinabu, some thirty kilometers west of Bismil, as well as smaller satellite military outposts situated at periodic intervals between the larger urban settlements along the southern bank of the river (Kessler 1980). Assyrian military control was secure, and the land along the Tigris was clearly part of the "Land of Assur" as the province of Tušḫan (Matney et al. 2002:50–51; Postgate 1992).

The Assyrian presence along the Upper Tigris, however, also appears to have included a significant demographic component away from the larger administrative and military centers, and it is quite possible that deportees from elsewhere may have been forcibly resettled along the Upper Tigris (Oded 1979). In fact, the southern bank of the Tigris is dotted with small agricultural communities with a strong Late Assyrian material culture. Excavated examples of such communities include Kavuşan Tepe (Kozbe, Köroğlu, and Sağlamtemir 2004), Hakemi Üse (Tekin 2004), and Müslümantepe (Ay 2004) (see Matney 2010 for a model of this system). Small rural sites with a predominantly Late Assyrian material culture also exist toward the highlands north of the Tigris River at sites like Grê Dimsê (Karg 2002). Finally, small non-Assyrian or indigenous communities still populated the uplands away from the river itself; these are attested largely on the basis of survey (Parker 2001).

In the Upper Euphrates region, it appears that Urartian fortresses do not come further west than Altıntepe in the vicinity of modern Erzincan, near the very source of the river's headwaters (Summers 2009:661). Accordingly, we have no evidence that the bulk of the Euphrates region to the south ever came under Urartian control, although some interaction did take place between the Urartian Empire and southeastern Anatolian Iron Age polities, because scattered Urartian pottery and other artifacts have been recovered at the sites of Kaleköy and Habibuşağı, both in the Elazığ region (Köroğlu 2003:233). In contrast, Assyrian interest in the Upper Euphrates region was long-standing and left very clear and much more permanent archaeological traces. Assyrian activities in the area started with military campaigns under Aššur-dan II in the late tenth century B.C.E. and culminated in the campaigns of Aššurnaṣirpal II (reigned ca. 883–859 B.C.E.), who campaigned in the area in his eighteenth regnal year, receiving tribute from the Neo-Hittite indigenous kingdoms of the Upper Euphrates while camped at the site of Sultantepe, near Harran. Much of the area, today corresponding to the Şanlıurfa province, was annexed to Assyria in 856 B.C.E., early in the reign of Šalmaneser III after he defeated a coalition of petty kings. Arslantaş, forty-five kilometers southwest of the modern city of Şanlıurfa, was selected as the site of a royal palace and military stronghold (Kuhrt 1995:483–87; Kulakoğlu 2006:517). Harran and its immediately surrounding plain, in fact, remained firmly in Assyrian hands throughout the Middle Iron Age, until the collapse of the Assyrian Empire, but those developments are well known and need no elaboration here (e.g., see Kuhrt 1995). To the south, Til Barsip (now located within modern Syria) helped anchor the Late Assyrian presence on the Euphrates and served as an advance point for further expansion westward toward the Levantine coast (Bunnens 1997).

In general terms, then, the Upper Euphrates and Tigris regions in the Middle Iron Age were firmly under Assyrian control, and we see the emergence of urban centers connected directly with the Assyrian imperial policy of expansion and military control, for example, Ziyaret Tepe, Üçtepe, Pornak, and Diyarbakır/Amedi along the Tigris and Harran-Sultantepe along the Euphrates. A network of smaller Late Assyrian settlements also existed leading to and from these larger settlements. Again, this is best documented along the Tigris on the basis of textual documentation discussed by Kessler (1980) and more recent archaeological research on the upper Tigris (see Matney 2010). No doubt comparable connecting sites also existed in the Euphrates basin, although details are less clear.

Nonetheless, as strong as the Assyrian grip on southeastern Anatolia may have been in the Middle Iron Age, the earlier occupants of the area were generally not displaced as part of the otherwise widespread deportation policies of the empire, and indeed there is a continuing presence of earlier groups in the material record. For example, Groovy Pottery was found in Middle Iron Age levels at Köşkerbaba, İmamoğlu, and Habibuşağı in the Lake Van region, the latter dated in part by an inscription of the Urartian king Sarduri II in the mid-eighth century B.C.E. (Köroğlu and Konyar 2008:129–30). Groovy Pottery is also found in secure Late Assyrian contexts at Ziyaret Tepe/Tušḫan (Matney et al. 2009:54). Likewise, Neo-Hittite and Aramaean artistic influences are clearly seen in the Middle Iron sculptures of Carchemish and other sites in the Şanlıurfa region (Kulakoğlu 2006:517).

Late Iron Age

The transition to the Late Iron Age is marked politically by the collapse of the Urartian kingdom in the late seventh century B.C.E. at the hands of Assyria and the subsequent collapse of the Late Assyrian Empire, in turn, after the sack of Nineveh in 612 B.C.E. by the Babylonians and the Medes. It would seem logical that either the Babylonian or Median kings, having destroyed the Assyrian heartland, would take control of the Upper Tigris and Upper Euphrates regions, filling the void left by the loss of Assyrian control. The Babylonian king Nabopolassar spent the years 609 to 607 B.C.E. securing the northern Babylonian mountain boundary, but thereafter Babylonian interests largely focused on the struggle with Egypt for control of northern Syria (Kuhrt 1995:590). Although there is little evidence for Neo-Babylonian influence in the Upper Tigris region following Nabopolassar's reign, the justly famous Stela of Nabonidus, which was found reused as a paving stone in the medieval mosque at Harran, leaves no doubt of the renewal of Babylonian cultural interest in parts of southeastern Anatolia by the end of the Neo-Babylonian period (Gadd 1958). That interest must have been accompanied by some sort of presence on the ground, as it included the rebuilding the temple of the moon god Sin at Harran (Kuhrt 1995:598–601), but we know little about the scope of Babylonian activities in southeastern Turkey away from Harran itself.

The nature of Median control of the Upper Tigris region is even less clear, in part due to their lack of a written tradition (Van der Mieroop 2007:270). Herodotus tells us that under a series of strong kings, starting with Deioces, the Medes emerged as a unified state in the Zagros Mountains that for a time was able both to subjugate the Persians and, under Cyaxares, to capture Nineveh (Herodotus, *Histories* I:96–107; see Brown 1986). The zenith of Median influence was, however, short-lived as the Persian king Cyrus led a revolt against the Medes, culminating in a decisive victory of Cyrus II over Astyages in 550 B.C.E. (Herodotus, *Histories* I:123–30). Summers has noted that there is no Median pottery identified in eastern Turkey, except at the site of Tille Höyük on the Euphrates, where pottery of the Median occupation is "almost indistinguishable from those of the preceding two levels (post-Neo-Assyrian and Neo-Assyrian respectively)" (Summers 1993:88). In short, we have no convincing evidence that either the Babylonians or the Medes rushed in to take political control of the Assyrian interests in southeastern Turkey.

Since we have no recognizable ceramic horizon markers that can definitively be attributed to that time period, some scholars have suggested that the Upper Tigris and Upper Euphrates were largely unoccupied for most of the sixth and fifth centuries B.C.E., or were only inhabited by nomadic or semi-sedentary peoples. Be that as it may, when occupation across these regions is again recognized archaeologically, the predominant ceramic form is a type of pottery that Dyson has dubbed "Western Triangle Ware" (Dyson 1999b:127) and that he has dated using comparative materials and radiocarbon dates between 400 and 250 B.C.E. in the area of northwestern Iran; this is equivalent to the Hasanlu IIIA phase (Dyson 1999a); see later discussion. The initial survey of the Upper Tigris region by Algaze failed to find any evidence for occupation between their Iron Age/Late Assyrian and Hellenistic periods (Algaze et al. 1991), but again it is unclear whether this represents an actual pattern on the ground or simply our lack of familiarity with the ceramic indicators spanning that chronological range. If we presume the former, it follows that it is not until a century and a half after the foundation of the Achaemenid Empire by Cyrus in 559 B.C.E. that recognizable Achaemenid ceramics become commonly distributed in southeastern Turkey in the early fourth century B.C.E.

Archaeologically, it seems highly likely that Late Assyrian forms continued to be in use in southeastern Turkey well after the end of the empire. In the Upper Tigris region of Iraq, just south of the current border with Turkey, British excavations at Qasrij Cliff and Khirbet Qasrij also found a substantial amount of ceramic continuity between the Late Assyrian and immediately following periods (Curtis 1989). A similar but better documented situation also obtains in the Khabur region of northeastern Syria, for instance at Tall Sheikh Hamad, where an extensive study of the ceramics from the Red House excavated by Hartmut Kühne has shown convincingly that Late Assyrian ceramic forms continue in use through the sixth and into the early fifth centuries B.C.E. (Kreppner 2008). The dating of this structure comes from four inscriptions mentioning the reign of Nebuchadnezzar; a later squatter occupation dated via three inscribed Aramaic ostraca appears firm and extends the use of Late Assyrian ceramic forms, at least in the Khabur region, 100 to 150 years after the fall of the empire (Kreppner 2008:151). Kreppner also cites a similar pattern for other sites in northeastern Syria, notably at Tell Shiukh Fawqani, Tell Barri, and Tell Ahmar (Kreppner 2008:149). Additional data are needed to confirm that the same conditions held in the Upper Tigris and Euphrates regions of southeastern Turkey, but it appears likely that further research will show that the current "dark age" between the Assyrian Empire and the arrival of Achaemenid interests in southeastern Anatolia should not be interpreted as a wholesale abandonment of these rich river valleys, and that future excavations may eventually reveal a continued use of Late Assyrian ceramic forms.

There is circumstantial evidence supporting this hypothesis in the textual sources, especially Xenophon and Herodotus, as well as Strabo writing several centuries later, who suggest that southeastern Anatolia was inhabited during the sixth and fifth centuries B.C.E. (Xenophon, *Anabasis* IV:1–4; Strabo, *Geography*, XI:12:3–4, XVI:21–25; Herodotus, *Histories* V:52–54). Sagona has argued that up until a treaty between Darius and the kingdom of Carduchia on the Aras River in 552 B.C.E., the area around the Batman River was possibly inhabited by a tribal remnant of the Median state, known alternatively as the Mardii by Ptolemy and the Mardi or Amardi by Strabo (Sagona 2004:86–87). Herodotus describes the Mardians as "tribes of nomads" among the Persian tribes (Herodotus, *Histories* I:25; Briant 2002:729). The Achaemenid system of rule has been described as a patrimonial kingdom, following the concepts of Weber and Eisenstadt (Root 1991:4). In this system, local élites were allowed to continue administering their territories in peripheral areas that were incorporated within the Achaemenid Empire, as long as tribute was paid to the Achaemenid king. Root notes that edicts were written and promulgated in local languages, an important symbolic procedure typical of this approach, for example, the Behistun inscription. The implication of this for archaeologists is that we are less likely to see a sudden appearance of Achaemenid material culture into the Upper Tigris region than was true in the Assyrian period when a strong military presence was imposed and then forcibly maintained along the fortified Assyrian centers: Ziyaret Tepe/Tušḫan, Üçtepe/Tidu, and Pornak/Sinabu (Kessler 1980).

Complicating the issue of the archaeological visibility of the Achaemenids in the Upper Tigris region during the Late Iron Age is the fact that much of the area along the river within southeastern Turkey was situated between the established satrapies of the Achaemenid rulers. These include the satrapies of Cappadocia to the northwest and western Armenia to the northeast, which form a northern border for the Upper Tigris region. Summers (1993) suggested that the sites of Altıntepe and nearby Cimin Tepe II, near Erzincan, were the seat of the latter, being built on an earlier fortified Urartian settlement. Briant (2002:742–43) has questioned the degree to which these satrapies were in control of the region, noting that evidence of Achaemenid material culture is largely limited to the Van region through excavations at Altın Tepe, Arin-Berd, and Armavir-blur. Xenophon describes the area immediately east of the Upper Tigris while leading the remains of Greek mercenary forces away from Babylon after Cyrus the Younger's unsuccessful coup attempt. He notes numerous villages from which provisions are obtained by the fleeing Greek forces, showing that the region was occupied by indigenous groups, although villages were often located away from the rivers (i.e., where archaeological surveys have been conducted) due to warfare, for example, with the Carduchians (Xenophon, *Anabasis* IV:4). Similarly, Sagona notes that Achaemenid influence "was felt most strongly in maintaining routes of communication and the troops that policed them" (Sagona 2004:89) hence their control of the rivers in the Upper Tigris region but not the areas away from the river.

As already noted, toward the end of the fifth, and certainly by the early fourth century B.C.E., we see the arrival and spread of a new painted ceramic type called Western Triangle Ware in the upper Tigris and Euphrates regions (figure 19.4:1–6). Dating of Western Triangle Ware at Hasanlu IIIA to the beginning of the fourth century B.C.E. accords with the dating in the Van region (Sevin 2002:476–77). It has long been recognized that this painted ware tradition enters into the archaeological record of western Iran during the Hasanlu III period at a point of a "marked cultural shift" (Young 1965:59). This has been confirmed at a variety of other sites in Iran, and Stronach, arguing that the painted pottery traditions of western Iran were part of a single coherent tradition of the late first millennium B.C.E., links Triangle Ware with Festoon Ware. The latter dates to no earlier than 400 B.C.E. based on excavated materials from Pasargadae and Susa (Stronach 1974:244–45). A detailed restudy of Triangle Ware by Dyson led him to define three variations: Classic Triangle Ware, a Western Triangle Ware variant, and an Eastern Triangle Ware variant (Dyson 1999b:127). Only the western variation is present in eastern Turkey where it is widely distributed at, for example, Köskerbaba Höyük, Altın Tepe, and Van Kalesi (Dyson 1999b), and more specifically in the Upper Tigris region in a variety of contexts on the citadel at Ziyaret Tepe (Matney et al. 2009:53), at Üçtepe, where it is found on a floor with other Hellenistic materials (Köroğlu 1998), and at Kavuşan Höyük and Salat Tepe (Köroğlu 2008).

Dyson described the Western Triangle Ware as wheelmade and hard-fired; common forms tend toward deep or shallow carinated bowls. The fabric is usually grit or sand tempered (Dyson 1999a:102). Designs frequently comprised groups of radial lines, zigzags, or rows of solid triangles. Vessels tended to be heavier, thicker, and larger than the Classic Triangle Ware, generally smoothed or slightly burnished

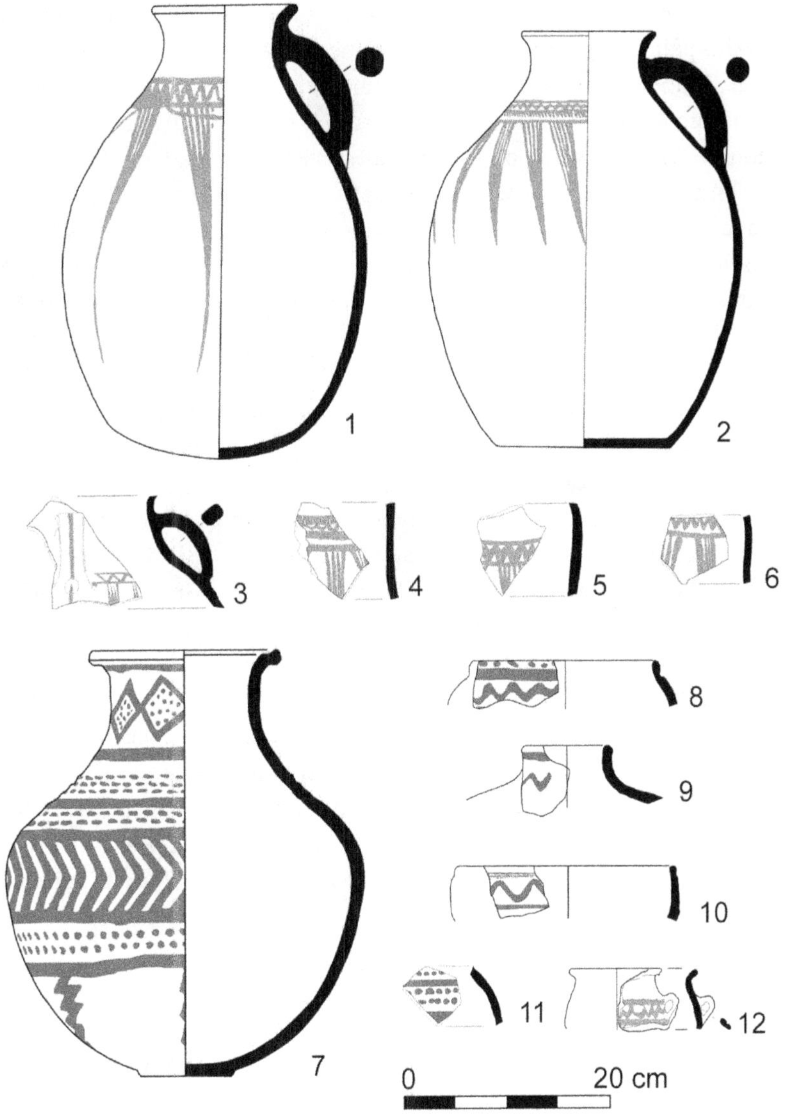

Figure 19.4. Painted Iron Age pottery from southeastern Turkey. Triangle and Festoon Ware (1–6): 1–2. Giricano Tepe (redrawn after Schachner 2004:fig. 5); 3–6 Ziyaret Tepe. Plum Painted Ware (7–12): 7 Grê Dimsê (redrawn after Karg 2001: fig. 9, not to scale, no original scale provided); 8–10 Norşuntepe (redrawn after Bartl 2001:figs. 3:12–14); 11–12 Ziyaret Tepe.

with pinkish-buff cores, often with a yellowish or pinkish cream slip which overfires to a greenish hue. Paint is usually dark brown or red (Dyson 1999b:125). Importantly, Dyson also notes that the clays used to make the Western Triangle Ware vessels at Hasanlu were local, based on neutron activation analysis (Dyson 1999b:125). We would expect, therefore, that sherds of similar style found in the Upper Tigris would show local variation, if only in clay source.

The origin of the Western Triangle Ware in western Iran is not clear. Dyson notes that this painted pottery assemblage "appears after a long hiatus in the Hasanlu occupation. It appears fully developed from elsewhere, although generally made locally. It has no obvious connections with earlier pottery at Hasanlu, but has clear connections with other areas of Azerbaijan, eastern Turkey, Georgia, and eastern Iran" (Dyson 1999a:105). Recently, excavations at Ziyaret Tepe in the Upper Tigris region have recovered what appears to be a possible early variant of the Triangle and Festoon Wares. This pottery type has been provisionally called Plum Painted Ware because the paint is a plum or purple-red color, which contrasts with the later Triangle and Festoon Wares which are redder in color in the Upper Tigris region (figure 19.4:7–12). The painted designs feature dots and curvy lines organized into bands, with occasional wavy lines and triangles, and the forms are small bowls, usually handmade with thick walls. The paint is found on the exterior surfaces and the rim (Matney et al. 2009:56, fig. 17).

The Plum Painted Ware at Ziyaret Tepe comes from good Early Iron Age contexts, including a well-stratified pit (Matney et al. 2002:66–68) and a layer of leveling fill sealed by the construction of a two-meter-thick Late Assyrian mudbrick platform on the citadel at Ziyaret Tepe. Likewise, Plum Painted Ware is also found in the so-called Warrior's Tomb at Grê Dimsê (figure 19.4:7; Karg 2001:fig. 9). This tomb had a Plum Painted Ware jar with an upturned Groovy Pottery bowl serving as a lid, suggesting an Early Iron Age date to Karg (2001). Its occurrence at Ziyaret Tepe and Grê Dimsê in the Early Iron Age layers, that is, before Aššurnaṣirpal II's arrival in 882 B.C.E., would suggest a long developmental sequence in which the Triangle and Festoon Wares of the Achaemenid period that appear in western Iran around 400 B.C.E. developed in fact out of the Plum Painted Ware that had its origins some five centuries earlier.

Conclusion: The End of the Iron Age

Providing a terminal date for the end of the Iron Age in southeastern Turkey is a somewhat arbitrary exercise. As noted, the region under consideration is not of particular political interest to the conquering Babylonians, nor to their successors, the Achaemenid Persians. The material culture of southeastern Turkey during the sixth, fifth, and fourth centuries B.C.E. is poorly documented, although a few painted ceramic horizon markers are now known. Neither the terms "post-Assyrian" nor "Achaemenid" appears to accurately describe the last centuries of the Late Iron Age in the region culturally. The Late Iron Age ends with the conquests by Alexander of Macedon and the beginning of the Hellenistic period in the latter third of the fourth century B.C.E.

In summary, the periodization of the Iron Age of southeastern Anatolia has traditionally been defined by reference to events occurring outside of the region.

Recent salvage archaeological fieldwork stimulated by the ambitious GAP economic development project has produced a wealth of new information on the Iron Age chronology of the region, and although much of these data are still only preliminarily published, we now have a skeletal internal chronology. The material culture recovered via surface survey and excavation has started to fill in the gaps present in the historical records, especially in areas peripheral to the great imperial centers. There are still important elements to flesh out. For example, a more precise developmental sequence of Groovy Pottery would add substantially to our understanding of Early and Middle Iron Age chronology. Likewise, the painted pottery traditions of the Late Iron Age are still only rudimentarily documented in southeastern Anatolia and require more fieldwork and systematic study. Consequently, much of what is presented here will need to be revised considerably within the next decade as the final reports, specialist analyses, and broader syntheses of these salvage projects are brought to publication.

REFERENCES

Primary Sources

Herodotus. *The Histories*. Trans. Aubrey de Sélincourt. Rev. introduction and notes by John Marincola. Further rev. edition. Harmondsworth: Penguin Books, 2003.

Strabo. *The Geography of Strabo*. Trans. Horace Leonard Jones. Loeb Classical Library. Cambridge, Mass.: Harvard University Press, 1930.

Xenophon. *The Anabasis of Cyrus*. Trans. Wayne Ambler. Ithaca, N.Y.: Cornell University Press, 2008.

Secondary Sources

Algaze, Guillermo, Ray Breuninger, and J. Knudstad. 1994. The Tigris-Euphrates Archaeological Reconnaissance Project: Final Report of the Birecik and Carchemish Dam Survey Areas. *Anatolica* 20: 1–96.

Algaze, Guillermo, Ray Breuninger, Chris Lightfoot, and Michael Rosenberg. 1991. The Tigris-Euphrates Archaeological Reconnaissance Project: A Preliminary Report of the 1989–1990 Seasons. *Anatolica* 17: 175–240.

Ay, Eyyüp. 2004. Müslümantepe Excavations 2001. In *Salvage Project of the Archaeological Heritage of the Ilısu and Carchemish Dam Reservoirs: Activities in 2001*, ed. Numan Tuna, Jean Greenhalgh, and Jean Velibeyoğlu, 383–407. Ankara: Middle East Technical University.

Barth, Fredrik. 1961. *Nomads of South Persia: The Basseri Tribe of the Khamseh Confederacy*. Boston: Little, Brown.

Bartl, Karin. 1995. Some Remarks on Early Iron Age in Eastern Anatolia. *Anatolica* 21: 205–12.

———. 2001. Eastern Anatolia in the Early Iron Age. In *Migration und Kulturtransfer: Der Wandel vorder-und zentralasiatischer Kulturen im Umbruch vom 2. zum 1. vorchristlichen Jahrtausend*. Bonn: Dr. Rudolf Habelt GmbH.

Beck, Lois. 1986. *The Qashqa'i of Iran*. New Haven, Conn.: Yale University Press.

Briant, Pierre. 2002. *From Cyrus to Alexander: A History of the Persian Empire*. Winona Lake, Ind.: Eisenbrauns.

Brown, Stuart C. 1986. Media and Secondary State Formation in the Neo-Assyrian Zagros: An Anthropological Approach to an Assyriological Problem. *Journal of Cuneiform Studies* 38: 107–19.

Bunnens, Guy. 1997. Til Barsib under Assyrian Domination. In *Assyria 1995: Proceedings of the Neo-Assyrian Text Corpus Project, Helsinki, September 7–11, 1995*, ed. Simo Parpola and R. M. Whiting, 17–28. The Neo-Assyrian Text Corpus Project. Helsinki: University of Helsinki Press.

Çevik, Özlem. 2008. Periodisation Criteria for Iron Age Chronology. *Ancient Near Eastern Studies* 45: 1–20.

Çilingiroğlu, Altan, ed. 1987. *Anadolu Demir Çağları. Anatolian Iron Ages. 24–27 Nisan 1984 Tarihleri Arasında İzmir'de Yapılan I. Anadolu Demir Çağları Sempozyumuna Sunulan Bildiriler. Papers presented to the I. Anatolian Iron Ages Symposium, Izmir during April 24th –27th, 1984*. İzmir: Ege Üniversitesi Edebiyat Fakültesi Yayınları.

Çilingiroğlu, Altan and Gareth Darbyshire, eds. 2004. *Anatolian Iron Ages 5: Proceedings of the Fifth Anatolian Iron Ages Colloquium held at Van, August 10, 2001*. London: British Institute of Archaeology at Ankara.

Çilingiroğlu, Altan and David French, eds. 1991. *Anatolian Iron Ages. The Proceedings of the Second Anatolian Iron Ages Colloquium held at İzmir, May 4–8, 1987*. Oxford: British Institute of Archaeology at Ankara.

———. 1994. *Anatolian Iron Age* 3. Oxford: British Institute of Archaeology at Ankara.

Curtis, John. 1989. *Excavations at Qasrij Cliff and Khirbet Qasrij*. British Museum Western Asiatic Excavations I. London: British Museum Publications.

Çilingiroğlu, Altan and Roger Matthews, eds. 1999. *Anatolian Iron Ages 4*. Anatolian Studies 49. London: British Institute of Archaeology at Ankara.

Çilingiroğlu, Altan and Antonio Sagona, eds. 2007. *Anatolian Iron Ages 6: Proceedings of the Sixth Anatolian Iron Ages Colloquium held at Eskişehir, August 16–20, 2004*. Leuven: Peeters.

Dyson, Robert H. Jr. 1999a. The Achaemenid Painted Pottery of Hasanlu IIIA. *Anatolian Studies* 49:1 01–10.

———. 1999b. Triangle-Festoon Ware Reconsidered. *Iranica Antiqua* 34: 115–44.

Gadd, Cyril J. 1958. The Harran Inscriptions of Nabonidus. *Anatolian Studies* 8: 35–92.

Karg, Norbert. 2001. First Soundings at Grê Dimsê 1999. In *Salvage Project of the Archaeological Heritage of the Ilısu and Carchemish Dam Reservoirs: Activities in 1999*, ed. Numan Tuna, Jean Öztürk, Jâle Velibeyoğlu, 671–93. Ankara: Middle East Technical University.

———. 2002. Sounding at Gre Dimse 2000. In *Salvage Project of the Archaeological Heritage of the Ilısu and Carchemish Dam Reservoirs: Activities in 2000*, ed. Numan Tuna and Jâle Velibeyoğlu, 699–738. Ankara: Middle East Technical University.

Kessler, Karlheinz. 1980. *Untersuchen zur historischen Topographie Nordmesopotamiens nach keilschriftlichen Quellen des 1.* Jahrtausends v. Chr. Beihefte zum Tübiger Atlas des Vorderen Orients B 26. Wiesbaden: Ludwig Reichert Verlag.

Kozbe, Gülriz, Kemalettin Köroğlu, and Haluk Sağlamtemir. 2004. 2001 Excavations at Kavuşan Tepe. In *Salvage Project of the Archaeological Heritage of the Ilısu and Carchemish Dam Reservoirs: Activities in 2001*, ed. Numan Tuna, Jean Greenhalgh, and Jâle Velibeyoğlu, 494–503. Ankara: Middle East Technical University.

Köroğlu, Kemalettin. 1998. *Üçtepe I*. Ankara: Türk Tarih Kurumu Basımevi.

———. 2003. The Transition from Bronze Age to Iron Age in Eastern Anatolia. In *Identifying Changes: The Transition from Bronze to Iron Ages in Anatolia and its Neighboring Regions: Proceedings of the International Workshop Istanbul, November 8–9, 2002*, ed. Bettina Fischer, Hermann Genz, Éric Jean, and Kemalettin Köroğlu, 231–44. İstanbul: Türk Eskiçağ Bilimleri Enstitüsü.

———. 2008. Yukarı Dicle Bölgesinde Yeni Asur Krallığı Sonrasına Ilişkin Kültürel Değişimin Tanımlanması: Geç Demir Çağı ve Hellenistik Dönem'in Izleri. In *Muhibbe Darga Armağani*, ed. Taner Tarhan, Aksel Tibet, and Erkan Konyar, 335–43. İstanbul: Sadberk Hanım Museum Publications.

Köroğlu, Kemalettin and Ethan Konyar. 2008. Comments on the Early/Middle Iron Age Chronology of Lake Van Basin. *Ancient Near Eastern Studies* 45: 123–46.

Kreppner, Florian J. 2008. The Collapse of the Assyrian Empire and the Continuity of Ceramic Culture: The Case of the Red House at Tall Sheikh Hamad. *Ancient Near Eastern Studies* 45: 147–65.

Kuhrt, Amélie. 1995. *The Ancient Near East, c. 3000–330 BC*, vol. 2. London: Routledge.

Kulakoğlu, Fikri. 2006. Some Neo-Assyrian Sculptures from Şanlıurfa Province (Upper Balikh). In *Studies in Honor of Hayat Erkanal: Cultural Reflections*, ed. Armağan Erkanal-Öktü, Engin Özgen, Sevinç Günel, A. Tuba Ökse, Halime Hüryılmaz, Halil Tekin, Nazlı Çınardalı-Karaaslan, Bora Uysal, F. Ayşe Karaduman, Atilla Engin, Reinhild Spieβ, Ayşegül Aykurt, Riza Tuncel, Ulaş Deniz, and Ash Rennie, 515–22. İstanbul: Homer Kitabevi.

Matney, Timothy. 2010. Material Culture and Identity: Assyrians, Aramaeans, and the Indigenous Peoples of Iron Age Southeastern Anatolia. In *Agency and Identity: New Paths Forward*, ed. Sharon R. Steadman and Jennifer C. Ross, 129–47. London: Equinox.

Matney, Timothy, Tina Greenfield, Britt Hartenberger, Azer Keskin, Kemalettin Köroğlu, John MacGinnis, Willis Monroe, Lynn Rainville, Mary Shepperson, Tasha Vorderstrasse, and Dirk Wicke. 2009. Excavations at Ziyaret Tepe 2007–2008. *Anatolica* 35: 37–84.

Matney, Timothy, Michael Roaf, John MacGinnis, and Helen McDonald. 2002. Archaeological Excavations at Ziyaret Tepe, 2000 and 2001. *Anatolica* 28: 47–89.

Müller, Uwe. 2004. Norşun Tepe and Lidar Höyük: Two Examples for Cultural Change during the Early Iron Age. In *Anatolian Iron Ages 5: Proceedings of the Fifth Anatolian Iron Ages Colloquium Held at Van, August 6–10, 2001*, ed. Altan Çilingiroğlu and Gareth Darbyshire, 107–14. London: British Institute of Archaeology at Ankara.

Oded, Bustenay. 1979. *Mass Deportations in the Neo-Assyrian Empire*. Wiesbaden: Ludwig Reichert Verlag.

Parker, Bradley. 2001. *The Mechanics of Empire: The Northern Frontier of Assyria as a Case Study in Imperial Dynamics*. Helsinki: University of Helsinki Press.

Postgate, J. Nicholas. 1992. The Land of Assur and the Yoke of Assur. *World Archaeology* 23.3: 247–63.

Radner, Karen. 2004. *Das Mittelassyrische Tontafelarchiv von Giricano/Dunnu-ša-Uzibi*. Ausgrabungen in Giricano 1. Subartu 14. Turnhout: Brepols.

———. 2006. How to Reach the Upper Tigris: The Route through the Tūr Abdīn. *State Archives of Assyria Bulletin* 15: 273–305.

Roaf, Michael. 2001. Continuity and Change from the Middle to the Late Assyrian Period. In *Migration und Kulturtransfer: Der Wandel vorder-und zentralasiatischer Kulturen im Umbruch vom 2. zum 1. vorchristlichen Jahrtausend*, ed. Ricardo Eichmann and Hermann Parzinger, 357–69. Bonn: Dr. Rudolf Habelt GmbH.

Roaf, Michael and Andreas Schachner. 2004. The Bronze Age to Iron Age Transition in the Upper Tigris Region: New Information from Ziyaret Tepe and Giricano. In *Anatolian Iron Ages 5: Proceedings of the Fifth Anatolian Iron Ages Colloquium held at Van, August 6–10, 2001*, ed. Altan Çilingiroğlu and Gareth Darbyshire, 115–23. London: British Institute of Archaeology at Ankara.

Roller, Lynn. 2009. The Anatolian Iron Ages Conferences. A Tribute to Altan Çilingiroğlu. In *Studies in Honour of Altan Çilingiroğlu: A Life Dedicated to Urartu on the Shores of the Upper Sea*, ed. Haluk Sağlamtimur, Eşref Abay, Aylin Ü. Erdem, Atilla Batmaz, Fulya Dedeoğlu, Mücella Erdakıran, Mahmut Bilge Baştürk and Erim Konakçı, 61–64. İstanbul: Arkeoloji ve Sanat Yayınları.

Root, Margaret Cool. 1991. From the Heart: Powerful Persianisms in the Art of the Western Empire. In *Achaemenid History VI: Asia Minor and Egypt: Old Cultures in a New Empire*, eds. H. Sancisi-Weerdenburg and A. Kuhrt, 1–25. Leiden: Nederlands Instituut voor Het Nabije Oosten.

Sagona, Claudia. 2004. Literary Tradition and Topographic Commentary. In *Archaeology at the North-East Anatolian Frontier, I: An Historical Geography and a Field Survey of the Bayburt Province*, ed. A. Sagona and C. Sagona, 25–96. Ancient Near Eastern Studies Supplement 14. Louvain: Peeters.

Schachner, Andreas. 2004. Vorbericht über die Ausgrabungen in Giricano, 2001. In *Salvage Project of the Archaeological Heritage of the Ilısu and Carchemish Dam Reservoirs: Activities in 2001*, ed. Numan Tuna, Jean Greenhalgh, and Jâle Velibeyoğlu, 534–80. Ankara: Middle East Technical University.

School of Fine Arts, Classical Studies and Archaeology, University of Melbourne. 2008. A Re-Assessment of Iron Ages Chronology in Anatolia and Neighboring Regions. Ancient Near Eastern Studies 45. Louvain: Peeters.

Sevin, Veli. 2002. Late Iron Age Pottery of the Van Region. Eastern Anatolia in the Light of the Karagündüz Excavations. In *Mauerschau. Festschrift für Manfred Korfmann, vol. 1*, ed. Rüstem Aslan, Stephen Blum, Gabriele Kastl, Frank Schweizer, and Diane Thumm, 475–82. Remshalden: Bernhard Albert Greiner.

Stronach, David. 1974. Achaemenid Village I at Susa and the Persian Migration to Fars. *Iraq* 36.1/2: 239–48.

Summers, Geoffrey. 1993. Archaeological Evidence for the Achaemenid Period in Eastern Turkey. *Anatolian Studies* 43: 85–108.

———. 2009. Between Urartu and Phrygia: The North-Central Anatolian Plateau in the Iron Age. In *Studies in Honour of Altan Çilingiroğlu: A Life Dedicated to Urartu on the Shores of the Upper Sea*, ed. Haluk Sağlamtimur, Eşref Abay, Aylin Ü. Erdem, Atilla Batmaz, Fulya Dedeoğlu, Mücella Erdakıran, Mahmut Bilge Baştürk and Erim Konakçı, 657–72. İstanbul: Arkeoloji ve Sanat Yayınları.

Szuchman, Jeffrey. 2008. Mobility and Sedentarization in Late Bronze Age Syria. In *The Archaeology of Mobility: Old World and New World Nomadism*, ed. Hans Barnard and Willeke Wendrich, 397–412. Cotsen Advanced Seminars 4. Los Angeles: Cotsen Institute of Archaeology.

———. 2009. Bit Zamani and Assyria. *Syria* 86: 53–64.

Tekin, Halil. 2004. Preliminary Results of the 2001 Excavations at Hakemi Use. In *Salvage Project of the Archaeological Heritage of the Ilısu and Carchemish Dam Reservoirs: Activities in 2001*, ed. Numan Tuna, Jean Greenhalgh, and Jâle Velibeyoğlu, 450–94. Ankara: Middle East Technical University.

Thuesen, Ingolf. 2002. The Neo-Hittite City-States. In *A Comparative Study of Thirty City-State Cultures*, ed. Mogens Herman Hansen, 43–55. Copenhagen: Danish Academy of Sciences and Letters.

Tuna, Numan, Jean Greenhalgh, and Jâle Velibeyoğlu, eds. 2004. *Salvage Project of the Archaeological Heritage of the Ilisu and Carchemish Dam Reservoir: Activities in 2001*. Ankara: Middle Eastern Technical University.

Tuna, Numan and Jean Öztürk, eds. 1999. *Salvage Project of the Archaeological Heritage of the Ilısu and Carchemish Dam Reservoirs: Activities in 1998*. Ankara: Middle Eastern Technical University.

Tuna, Numan, Jean Öztürk, and Jâle Velibeyoğlu, eds. 2001. *Salvage Project of the Archaeological Heritage of the Ilısu and Carchemish Dam Reservoir: Activities in 1999*. Ankara: Middle Eastern Technical University.

———. 2002. *Salvage Project of the Archaeological Heritage of the Ilısu and Carchemish Dam Reservoir: Activities in 2000*. Ankara: Middle Eastern Technical University.

Ur, Jason and Emily Hammer. 2009. Pastoral Nomads of the 2nd and 3rd Millennia A.D. on the Upper Tigris River, Turkey: The Hirbemerdon Tepe Survey. *Journal of Field Archaeology* 34.1: 37–56.

Van der Mieroop, Marc. 2007. *History of the Ancient Near East, ca. 3000–323 B.C.*, 2nd ed. Maldon, Mass.: Blackwell.

Weiss, Harvey. 1983. Excavations at Tell Leilan and the Origins of North Mesopotamian Cities in the Third Millennium B.C. *Paléorient* 9: 39–52.

Wilkinson, Tony. 1994. The Structure and Dynamics of Dry-Farming States in Upper Mesopotamia. *Current Anthropology* 35: 483–520.

Young, T. Cuyler. 1965. A Comparative Ceramic Chronology for Western Iran, 1500–500 B.C. *Iran* 3: 53–86.

CHAPTER 20

THE IRON AGE IN EASTERN ANATOLIA

LORI KHATCHADOURIAN

> For the poet, it is gold and silver; but for the philosopher, it is iron and wheat that have civilized man and ruined the human race. . . . It is very difficult to guess how men came to know and use iron, for it is incredible that . . . they thought of drawing the ore from the mine and performing the necessary preparations on it for smelting it before they knew what would result. . . . [W]e must suppose them to have had a great deal of courage and foresight to undertake such a difficult task and to have envisaged so far in advance the advantages they could derive from it.
>
> —Rousseau (1987 [1755]:65–66)

Decades before C. J. Thomsen (1836) advanced his Three Age system of stone, bronze, and iron in the 1830s to supplant prevailing historical chronologies, Rousseau attributed to iron—the final marker in Thomsen's eventual dating scheme—a far more revolutionary significance. Rousseau's political theory shackled the working of iron inextricably to the origins of inequality and the numerous resulting vices of civil society. He held that the advent of iron technology indeed marked a new phase in human history, prefiguring (as did Lucretius before him) a tradition of archaeological periodization that has predominated from Thomsen's day to the present. To Rousseau, however, this technological innovation was salient not for its utility as the culminating stage in a relative chronology of prehistory. Rather, it was the radical social repercussions of this novel technology (e.g., the division of labor required for the specialized skills of mining and smelting) that placed iron metallurgy at the watershed of a new age.

Across much of southwest Asia, including parts of eastern Anatolia (Badalyan, Smith, and Avetisyan 2003), the dubious distinction of first institutionalizing inequality belongs to those primary complex political communities that harnessed the technologies of bronze, not iron. We may thus balk at certain details in Rousseau's account. But then how are we to understand the contours of social life after the adoption of iron, and what can eastern Anatolia contribute to this wider conversation? Rousseau's ahistorical schematization of the constitution of society consequent to the emergence of iron technology poses a challenge to the archaeology of the Iron Age in eastern Anatolia. Here, archaeology has been more committed to matters of chronology and the description of empirical findings than to the analysis of social life. Perhaps partly as a result of the latent evolutionary implications of the Three Age system (Lucas 2005), by the time the terminal stage is reached—when concerns over such primordial questions as the emergence of food production, incipient social differentiation, and originary political complexity no longer pertain—social life appears to fall away from the archaeological gaze. In large measure, this chapter also engages most directly with crucial problems of chronology in Iron Age eastern Anatolia (see Matney, chapter 19 in this volume). But chasing the ever-receding mirage of a putatively definitive linear chronology only serves to forestall archaeological interpretation indefinitely. Chronology is thus reviewed here not as an end in itself but in the service of broader concerns relating to the practices of collective life among Iron Age communities of eastern Anatolia.

An approach to Iron Age chronology that remains mindful of the social worlds on which we graft this temporal scheme inevitably confronts one of the shortcomings of the Three Age system: the anachronistic basis for demarcating its ultimate terminus. What marks the end of the Iron Age, when steel (an alloy of iron) is the most widely used material of modern industry and infrastructure? In keeping with the paradigms of Thomsen's day, archaeological convention holds that the appearance of written history provides a turning point that separates an entirely new epoch from that which came before (prehistory). At this juncture, the imperfect timepieces of archaeological chronology are shelved, replaced by texts that supply dates drawn from dynastic genealogies, royal annals, and narrative histories. In much of the Old World, however, including Iron Age eastern Anatolia, textually derived chronologies coexist alongside the Three Age system, sometimes even influencing its internal periodization. The boundary between prehistory and history thus oftentimes proves rather porous. As a result, difficulties beset the transition from an archaeological to a historical system for measuring time. The logic of the Three Age system established the limits of its ambition on the assumption of a radical break between history and prehistory. However, today archaeology has productively intruded into the study of even the very recent past (e.g., Buchli 1999; Buchli and Lucas 2001; Leone and Potter 1999), undermining efforts to arrange archaeological and historical chronologies into a neat order of succession. This destabilizes the entire armature of reasoning that continues to delimit the Iron Age and ultimately occasions considerable ambivalence about this last phase of the Three Age system, as currently conceived.

With these concerns in mind, this chapter takes up the problems surrounding the periodization of the Iron Age in eastern Anatolia and the relation between archaeological and historical ways of reckoning time. There is no ready solution to the dilemma over whether to retain the Iron Age as traditionally deployed, notwithstanding its inherent anachronism, or to deconstruct it in favor of an alternative system of periodization that accords archaeology an independence from the very specific mode of temporality measured by history. But in an effort at least to begin to transcend the prehistory/history divide in this region, I extend the Iron Age well into historical periods to the upper time limit embraced by this volume.

Geography

The complexities of chronology and periodization that this chapter confronts are only slightly more intricate than those of geography. Where is "eastern Anatolia?" A standard definition identifies Anatolia as "the peninsula of land that today constitutes the Asian portion of Turkey,"[1] or the part of Turkey that lies east of the Aegean and the Bosporus. Indeed, with some exceptions (e.g., Köroğlu 2003), most archaeological accounts delimit eastern Anatolia as the upland plateau that extends from the northern Euphrates eastward to the Turkish border (e.g., Bartl 2001; Çilingiroğlu 2001; Yakar 2000). But the borders of modern nation-states have no relevance for an inquiry into the Iron Age and can serve, quite detrimentally, only to conjure artificial ancient frontiers.

Topography offers one means for delimiting regions that is independent of historical contingencies and thus provides a workable alternative to today's political borders. Yet it is an alternative not without a certain arbitrariness of its own. The region in question lies in a continental collision zone. The suturing of the Eurasian and Arabian tectonic plates gave rise to a dense conglomeration of high-altitude mountains and plains averaging 2,000 m above sea level that stretches from the Taurus Mountains in the west to the furthest limits of the Elbruz and Zagros Ranges in the east. Confusingly, geographers have assigned three terms to this single geological zone to designate regions that partially or largely overlap: the eastern Anatolian plateau, the Armenian plateau, and the Iranian plateau. The first two of these designations overlap substantially, such that the terminological differences, which also exist in archaeological parlance, primarily result from the shifting political fortunes and cultural trajectories of the region since the nineteenth century.[2] To accommodate the contrasting orientations and perspectives that lurk beneath these equally entrenched terms, I use the terms *eastern Anatolian* and *Armenian plateau* interchangeably.

The eastern Anatolian plateau rises up from central Anatolia at the Taurus Mountains, which sweep northeastward from the Mediterranean to converge with the Pontic Range (figure 20.1). The Pontic Range marks the plateau's northern border—a nearly impenetrable wall of mountains that roughly shadows the coast of the Black Sea, separating low-lying coastal areas from the inland highlands. East of the Black Sea the mountains of the lesser Caucasus mark the northeastern border, which arc from the northwest to southeast to form the eastern limit of the plateau. The southern boundary of the eastern Anatolian highland coincides with the southern reaches of the Antitaurus Mountains, particularly the Malatya, Muş, Van, and Kurdish (or Hakkari) Ranges. A boundary is most difficult to discern in the southeast, however, because the northern Zagros Mountains merge seamlessly with the mountain ranges south and east of Lake Van, thus linking the Armenian plateau with the Iranian highland to the southeast—a region largely beyond the scope of this study. Within these various fixed and fluid topographical boundaries of the plateau, several smaller mountain chains either collide with or roughly parallel one another, forming a cluttered and intricate web of mountains interrupted by plains. These are generally rich in volcanic soil and watered by a complex hydrological system that includes the northern Euphrates and its major arteries (Murat and Kara), as well as the Çoruh, Kura, and Araks Rivers and their tributaries. As a whole, the Armenian plateau boasts the highest elevations and densest

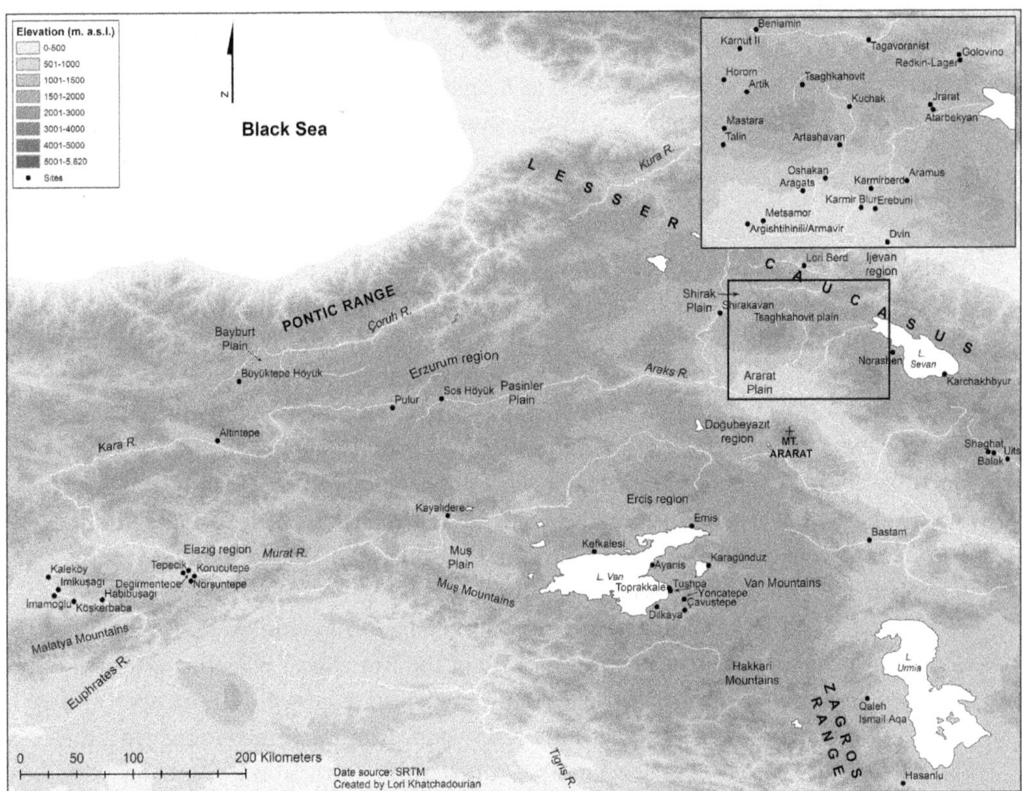

Figure 20.1. Map showing sites mentioned in text.

concentration of mountains in southwest Asia. Highland pastures far exceed agricultural land.

In the discussion that follows, geographical concerns reemerge in relation to the spatial distribution of archaeological horizons and historical phenomena during various phases of the Iron Age within the fuzzy boundaries of the eastern Anatolian plateau. However, mapping the geographic scope of a given archaeological horizon with any confidence requires robust datasets so as to permit the reasonable interpolation of phenomena from individual sites to broader regions. Such datasets are not yet available for the Iron Age across much of the region.

The phenomenon of Urartu presents an important exception (see Zimansky, chapter 24, and Radner, chapter 33 in this volume). Since the nineteenth century, antiquarian and archaeological research in eastern Turkey and Armenia has attended closely to the distinctive fortress ruins of this empire, such that the extent of the Urartian polity is broadly discernible on archaeological grounds. In contrast, earlier phases of the Iron Age are known to us at present only in disparate pockets of the highlands and only in the broadest outlines. Salvage excavations and surveys conducted during the 1960s and 1970s in the area of the Keban, Karakaya, and Atatürk Dams of eastern Turkey opened up the Euphrates region as one such zone. Recently revitalized investigations into pre-Urartian periods in the Van and Erzurum regions to the east are building on the isolated excavations and surveys of earlier decades in those areas. Archaeologists in Armenia have maintained a steady interest in the earliest phases of the Iron Age at least since the 1960s, with the publication of Martirosyan's (1964) pioneering prehistory that defined the Iron Age as a discrete phase. Concerns over chronology and periodization have, however, overshadowed efforts to discern the spatial distribution of shared material practices. The archaeological geography of later phases of the Iron Age, particularly the period of Achaemenid Persian hegemony, remains especially obscure due to the nearly complete neglect of this period in the archaeology of the Armenian plateau.

Distinct intellectual traditions in Turkey and Armenia have given rise to different terminological frameworks for the internal periodization of the Iron Age. In Turkey, the tripartite division used for the Bronze Age extends to the Iron Age, but for the awkward fact that a "Late" Iron Age is conspicuously undefined (pace Köroğlu and Konyar 2008; McConchie 2004; Sagona and Sagona 2004b). Following Martirosyan, in Armenia the Iron Age was once divided into the "Early Iron Age" and "the age of the broad dissemination of Iron" (coterminous with Turkey's Middle Iron Age). Recent research in Armenia has advanced a terminological modification, in accordance with the more salutary numerical system used in Iran: Iron 1, Iron 2, Iron 3, and so on (Khatchadourian 2008; Smith, Badalyan, and Avetisyan 2009). Given the challenges that surround the close of the Iron Age, I prefer to avoid terminology that implies a firm terminal stage and instead employ this more open and flexible numerical scheme. Thus, in this discussion, Iron 1 is coterminous with the Early Iron Age (sometimes called the pre-Urartian Period), Iron 2 coincides with what others have termed the Middle Iron Age (or in historical terms, the Urartian era), and Iron 3 can be equated with the period of the poorly understood Median polity and the Achaemenid Empire (i.e., the post–Urartian Period).

Iron 1

In the closing centuries of the second millennium B.C.E., communities across the eastern Anatolian highlands adopted a metallurgical technology that was implicated in the long-term transformation of the contours of social life, although how, at what pace, and to what extent remain obscure. The exploitation of readily available iron ores may have alleviated what had once been a pressing concern for Bronze Age societies: access to the limited and scattered sources of copper and tin. With the aid of iron tools forged from locally available ores, communities could revitalize their productive subsistence activities without the requirement to enter into long-distance obligations of trade and travel. The accessibility of iron might have upset the reciprocal dependencies that had concentrated wealth in the hands of the privileged few who commanded access to coveted sources of raw materials for the making of bronze. Given what is known about trade, wealth, and power in the Anatolian Bronze Age (see Laneri and Schwartz, chapter 14 in this volume), we might expect the wide-scale adoption of iron to have ushered in significant transformations in the fabric of communities living on the Armenian plateau and occasioned new forms of social control.

Yet the start of the Iron Age is not marked by a sudden and exclusive appearance of iron artifacts, conveniently stratified atop lower deposits containing bronze. Available evidence suggests that the shift from bronze to iron was more gradual than abrupt. In some parts of the region, bronze and iron metallurgy coexisted well into the Iron 3 period. Unlike bronze, however, iron does not survive well in the aerated and moist soils of the eastern Anatolian plateau (McConchie 2004:13), making it difficult to assess the pace of the technological transformation. Archaeologists of the region have thus constructed a rationale for the first phase of the Iron Age for which the occurrence of iron is ironically deemphasized.

Within the large expanse of the Armenian highlands, different historical trajectories and variations in the pace and form of material culture change during the late second and early first millennia B.C.E. preclude a single unified account of the Iron 1 period, even as there are certain broad, regional commonalities. For instance, the cataclysmic disruptions once attributed to the so-called Sea Peoples, which brought the Bronze Age to an end in much of the eastern Mediterranean, do not pertain in this region. In certain regions of the plateau, there appears to have been considerable continuity from the Late Bronze Age to the Iron 1 period, such that the two phases are not easily distinguished; in other regions, a Late Bronze Age is itself difficult to isolate at present. What follows is a consideration of the key sites, ceramic assemblages, and radiocarbon dates that inform the chronology and periodization of the

Iron 1 period in the four regions of the plateau that have received the most attention: the Elazığ region, the Van region, the Erzurum region, and southern Caucasia.

The Elazığ Region

Situated near the western limit of the eastern Anatolian plateau, the Elazığ region fell broadly within the ambit of the Late Bronze Age Hittite Empire (Sevin 1991; Seeher, chapter 16, and Beal, chapter 26 in this volume). The collapse of this polity in ca. 1200 B.C.E. thus provides a historical marker for the start of the Iron Age, which accords with the appearance of new ceramic and architectural traditions in the region. These new traditions are known to us principally from the well-stratified and thoroughly investigated mound sites of Norşuntepe and Korucutepe, as well as a number of nearby sites (Tepecik, Değirmentepe/Elazığ, and İmikuşağı) that survey and rescue excavations in the vicinity of the Keban and Karakaya Dams have revealed (see Bartl 2001). Norşuntepe and Korucutepe hosted occupations during the Late Bronze and Iron 1 periods. After a possible brief hiatus following a series of burning events that destroyed the Late Bronze phase, the sites underwent partial rebuilding. A more modest masonry characterizes the reoccupations, suggestive of unplanned village architecture that bears no resemblance to the earlier structures (Bartl 1988, 1995, 2001; Hauptmann 1969/70; Köroğlu 2003; Müller 2005; van Loon 1978).

In addition to a smattering of iron artifacts (McConchie 2004:tables 11, 12), these humble Iron 1 buildings introduce a new ceramic repertoire, the most predominant component of which has come to be called grooved ware (see Matney, chapter 19 in this volume). The name of this ware derives from the series of parallel horizontal furrows that appear between the rim and shoulder of bowls and pots (figure 20.2) (Bartl 2001:figs. 2, 4, 5; Konyar 2005:fig. 2; Müller 2005; Sevin 1991:figs. 2–6; Winn 1980). This distinctive monochrome pottery, which appears in a variety of surface treatments and colors, has come to be emblematic of the Iron 1 period, particularly in this region of the eastern Anatolian plateau (Bartl 2001). It has no parallels in the pottery traditions of the Hittites, not least because grooved ware appears to have been handmade rather than thrown on a fast wheel.[3] Two radiocarbon samples from reoccupation deposits at Korucutepe, long taken as a type-site for the period (van Loon 1978:42), in large measure account for the assignment of grooved ware to the Iron 1 period. With calibrated date ranges of 1371–925 B.C.E. and 1050–845 B.C.E. (2 σ) (table 20.1), these dates fall substantially within the established date range of the Iron 1 period. This dating from Korucutepe has been extended to other sites in the region on the basis of stylistic similarities with the Korucutepe assemblages.

Despite these oft-cited absolute dates, considerable imprecision besets the dating of grooved ware, making it a rather undependable marker of the Iron 1 era. Although a number of sites in the Elazığ region are assigned to the Iron 1 period in large measure on the basis of the existence of grooved pottery (Sevin 1991:95), in the wider Euphrates basin this style of pottery has also appeared in excavated contexts

Table 20.1. Iron Age Radiocarbon Dates from the Anatolian/Armenian Plateau

Site/ID	Conventional Date B.P.	Calibrated Date (IntCal 04)	Context	Material	Publication
Iron 1					
Korucutepe	2921 ± 71	1371–925 (95.4%) 1316–925 (93.6%)			van Loon (1978:42)
Korucutepe	2805 ± 35	1050–845 (95.4%) 1050–891 (90.5%)			van Loon (1978)
Pulur OZG 068		1376–1267	Sector A1: lime-plaster floor or pit	Charcoal	Işıklı (2008):271; Işıklı and Can (2007:9)
Pulur OZG 889	3030 ± 40	1408–1132 (95.4%) 1408–1192 (91.5%)		Bone	Courtesy of A. Sagona
Karagündüz OZG 597	2960 ± 40	1368–1042 (95.4%) 1314–1042 (94.9%)	K6 (chamber tomb)	Charcoal	Sevin (2004:187). Uncalibrated date courtesy V. Sevin
Karagündüz OZG 600	2860 ± 40	1191–914 (95.4%) 1131–914 (92.2%)		Charcoal	
Sos Höyük Beta-74450	2960 ± 60	1380–1009 (95.4%) 1323–1009 (89.9%)	J14: eroded scarp, below plaster floor	Charcoal	Sagona et al. (1995:198. 1996:table 1)
Sos Höyük Beta-74451	2810 ± 90	1256–806 (95.4%) 1215–806 (94.0%)	J14: exposed scarp, above plaster floor	Charcoal	Sagona et al. (1995:198) Sagona et al. (1996:table 1)
Sos Höyük Beta-74455	2840 ± 60	1208–843 (95.4%) 1135–843 (88.8%)	M16C	Charcoal	Sagona et al. (1996:table 1)
Sos Höyük Beta-84370	2900 ± 70	1310–907 (95.4%)	M16AB	Charcoal	Sagona et al. (1996:table 1)
Sos Höyük Beta-95214	2860 ± 60	1258–896 (95.4%) 1217–896 (93.3%)	L16D: from burned fill atop thick plaster floor	Charcoal	Sagona et al. (1996:table 1) Sagona et al. (1997:183)
Sos Höyük OZD-712	2790 ± 60	1114–817 (95.4%)		Charcoal	Courtesy A. Sagona
Metsamor GIN-9340	2750 ± 40	997–816 (95.4%)		Charcoal	Courtesy R. Badalyan
Metsamor GIN-9341	2750 ± 110	1266–595 (95.4%) 1266–751 (93.9%)		Charcoal	Courtesy R. Badalyan
Dvin LE–?	2670 ± 70	1009–594 (95.4%) 1009–751 (92.2%)		Charcoal	Courtesy R. Badalyan
Artik LE-818	2850 ± 50	1208–898 (95.4%)	Tomb no. 223	Wood	Badalyan and Avetisyan (2007:77). Uncalibrated date courtesy R. Badalyan

(Continued)

Table 20.1. (*Continued*)

Site/ID	Conventional Date B.P.	Calibrated Date (IntCal 04)	Context	Material	Publication
Horom AA-12860	2850 ± 55	1211–856 (95.4%)	B2.4, loc. 10	Charcoal	Badaljan et al. (1994:29)
Horom AA-11129	2770 ± 55	1049–810 (95.4%)	B2, TT4, level 4	Charcoal	Badaljan et al. (1994:9)
Horom AA-10193	2975 ± 55	1386–1027 (95.4%) 1326–1027 (87.3%)	Surface-C3a, area G, locus 31		Badaljan et al. (1994:10)
Horom LE-3598	2890 ± 70	1302–902 (95.4%)	Burial 116	Bone	Courtesy R. Badalyan
Gekhakar AA 66902	2962 ± 56	1377–1013 (95.4%) 1321–1013 (90.5%)	PT1a	Bone	Courtesy R. Badalyan
Lchashen LE-689	2840 ± 60	1208–843 (95.4%) 1135–843 (88.8%)	Quarters 24	Charcoal	Courtesy R. Badalyan
Kanagekh GIN-11662	2690 ± 40	914–789 (95.4%)	Burial 4	Bone	Courtesy R. Badalyan
Iron 2					
Metsamor LE-4484	2455 ± 75	773–403 (95.5%)		Charcoal	Courtesy R. Badalyan
Horom AA-10194	2520 ± 55	800–417 (95.4%) 800–501 (90.5%)	B1 a–c, gateway		Badaljan et al. (1994:9)
Horom AA-10189	2465 ± 55	766–411 (95.4%)	B2, locus 4		Badaljan et al. (1994:9)
Horom AA-12861	2485 ± 50	776–415 (95.4%) 776–481 (86.1%)	B-2/4, locus 16	Charcoal	Badalyan et al. (1994:29)
Horom AA-12862	2480 ± 55	773–414 (95.4%)	B-2/4	Charcoal	Badalyan et al. (1994:29)
Horom AA-12863	2540 ± 55	810–418 (95.4%) 810–507 (93.2%)	B-2/4	Charcoal	Badalyan et al. (1994:29)
Horom AA-12866	2570 ± 55	831–520 (95.4%)	B-2/3, locus 6	Charcoal	Badalyan et al. (1994:29)
Horom AA-12867	2490 ± 60	786–415 (95.4%) 786–481 (85.6%)	B-2/5, locus 4		Badalyan et al. (1994:29)
Horom AA-12868	2520 ± 55	800–417 (95.4%) 800–501 (90.5%)	D-1, quarter 3	Charcoal	Badalyan et al. (1994:29)
Horom AA-12869	2485 ± 55	778–414 (95.4%) 778–479 (85.1%)	D-1, quarter 2	Charcoal	Badalyan et al. (1994:29)
Tagavoranist UCIAMS-48411	2485 ± 15	763–538 (95.4%) 673–538 (67.5%)	T-5, 35	Charcoal	Courtesy R. Badalyan
Büyüktepe Beta-55335	2610 ± 70	917–521 (95.4%)	S35B/T35B	Bone	A. Sagona personal communication
Shaghat OxA-15773	2498 ± 29	781–516 (95.4%)	NBD-10 Locus 13	Charcoal	Cherry et al. (2007:68)
Shaghat OxA-15774	2490 ± 29	776–421 (95.4%) 776–509 (94.2%)	NBD-10 Locus 19	Charcoal	Cherry et al. (2007:68)
Shaghat OxA-15777	2475 ± 29	766–416 (95.4%) 766–486 (89.7%)	NS1 Locus 6	Charcoal	Cherry et al. (2007:68)

Table 20.1. (*Continued*)

Site/ID	Conventional Date B.P.	Calibrated Date (IntCal 04)	Context	Material	Publication
Shaghat OxA-15822	2534 ± 29	796–544 (95.4%) 651–544 (42.3%) 796–732 (35.2%)	NSI Locus 6	Charcoal	Cherry et al. (2007:68)
Shaghat OxA-15875	2714 ± 33	921–807 (95.4)	ST1/1 Locus 4	Charcoal	Cherry et al. (2007:68)
Shaghat Hd-25296	2548 ± 17	797–593 (95.4%) 797–590 (67.6%)	NS1 Locus 9	Charcoal	Cherry et al. (2007:68)
Shaghat Hd-25294	2531 ± 22	792–551 (95.4%) 646–551 (40.1%) 792–745 (34.7%)	NS1 Locus 9	Charcoal	Cherry et al. (2007:68)
Uits OxA-17127	2517 ± 30	792–539 (95.4%) 695–539 (68.1%)	DT2 Locus 4	Charcoal	Cherry et al. (2007:68)
Uits OxA-17205	2496 ± 28	778–517 (95.4%)	DT2 Locus 5	Charcoal	Cherry et al. (2007:68)
Iron 3					
Tsaghkahovit AA-66875	2483 ± 42	773–416 (95.4%) 773–484 (87.8%)	SLT6 Locus 5	Charcoal	Khatchadourian (2008:270)
Tsaghkahovit AA-66880	2494 ± 40	787–417 (95.4%) 787–502 (90.5%)	WSC2 Locus 10	Charcoal	Khatchadourian (2008:270)
Tsaghkahovit AA-66882	2491 ± 56	786–415 (95.4%) 786–483 (86.5%)	WSE Locus 3	Charcoal	Khatchadourian (2008:270)
Tsaghkahovit AA-72366	2460 ± 34	756–413 (95.4%)	WSG Locus 12	Charcoal	Khatchadourian (2008:270)
Tsaghkahovit AA-72367	2438 ± 34	752–406 (95.4%) 596–406 (64.5%)	WSG Locus 12	Charcoal	Khatchadourian (2008:270)
Tsaghkahovit AA-72368	2517 ± 34	793–538 (95.4%)	WSH Locus 18	Charcoal	Khatchadourian (2008:270)
Tsaghkahovit AA-72370	2455 ± 34	756–411 (95.4%) 601–411 (54.4%)	WSH Locus 18	Charcoal	Khatchadourian (2008:270)
Tsaghkahovit AA-72369	2442 ± 34	753–407 (95.4%) 597–407 (61.9%)	WSH Locus 30	Charcoal	Khatchadourian (2008:270)
Tsaghkahovit AA-72371	2542 ± 42	804–538 (95.4%)	WSH Locus 40	Charcoal	Khatchadourian (2008:270)
Tsaghkahovit AA-72372	2522 ± 34	795–538 (95.4%)	WSI Locus 20	Charcoal	Khatchadourian (2008:270)
Tsaghakhovit AA-52904	2499 ± 38	790–418 (95.4%) 790–506 (92.5%)	C3 Locus A7	Charcoal	Khatchadourian (2008:270)
Balak OxA-15823	2221 ± 30	382–203 (95.4%)	BTT1 Locus 3	Charcoal	Cherry et al. (2007:68)
Horom AA-12865	2410 ± 55	754–395 (95.4%) 599–395 (67.2%)	B2.4, loc 6, fea. 4		Badaljan et al. (1994:29)
Tagavoranist UCIAMS-48412	2440 ± 15	737–410 (95.4%) 848–410 (68.6%)	T5, 40	Charcoal	Courtesy R. Badalyan

alongside better known wares of the Neo-Assyrian or Urartian horizons that date no earlier than the eighth century B.C.E.—well into the Iron 2 period (Konyar 2005; Köroğlu 2003; Ökse 1988; Sevin 1991). Sites such as Köşkerbaba (Bilgi 1991), İmamoğlu (Ökse 1992), Kaleköy (Bakır and Çilingiroğlu 1987), and Habibuşağı (Işık 1987) fall into this group. Given the limited distribution of grooved ware elsewhere in the Upper Euphrates region and its occurrence in Iron 2 contexts (e.g., Tille Höyük) (Bartl 2001:392), it would appear that this pottery tradition has been associated with the Iron 1 period to a degree disproportionate to its salience. Indeed, as we shall see, in other regions of the Armenian plateau, grooved ware is conspicuous either for its scarcity or its association with assemblages of later date. This contested style of pottery has nevertheless long dominated discussion on the chronology of the Iron 1 period.

The Van Region

Debate over the dating of grooved ware has intensified in recent years in relation to the areas surrounding Lake Van, where the absence of stratified Iron 1 levels severely impedes our understanding of the era. The very existence of a detectable Iron 1 occupation in this region hinges on the dating of burials from four cemeteries: Karagündüz (Sevin 1999; Sevin and Kavaklı 1996; Sevin and Özfırat 2001), Dilkaya (Çilingiroğlu 1991), Yoncatepe (Belli and Konyar 2001b, 2001c), and Ernis-Evditepe (Belli 2001; Belli and Konyar 2003b). Setting aside details of burial practices, tomb architecture, and inventories (many rich in iron ornaments and ceremonial weapons), grooved pottery predominated in all of these burials. In light of the findings from the Elazığ region, excavators assigned the cemeteries to the Iron 1 period. The grooved pottery from the Van region burials ranged in form and differed in color from the Elazığ corpus. Vessels appear to have been wheel-made, in notable contrast to most grooved pottery from the Euphrates region. A single radiocarbon sample from one of the burials at Karagündüz yielded a calibrated date of 1250–1120 B.C.E. (2 σ) (Sevin 2004). Veli Sevin has discerned two phases of Iron 1 activity at Karagündüz based on differences in tomb construction, burial practices, and pottery.

However, the presence of another kind of pottery in the burials—a red or red-brown burnished ware distinctive of Urartian assemblages from fortress centers of the empire—complicates the dating of the cemeteries. This so-called palace ware is thought not to appear before the eighth century B.C.E., and thus proponents of an Iron 1 dating of the Van necropoleis interpret the occurrence of burnished red ware (in characteristically Urartian forms, yet somewhat poorer quality) as evidence for a pre-Urartian antecedent to the later state assemblage (Sevin and Özfırat 2001). Although plausible in principle, it is difficult to substantiate such an interpretation given the absence of stratified Iron 1 deposits. The Van cemeteries may thus instead date to the Iron 2 period (Konyar 2005; Köroğlu 2003; Köroğlu and Konyar 2008). Nevertheless, excavations at Urartian fortresses revealed quite limited quantities of grooved ware,[4] such that this style may indeed represent a pre–Iron 2 ceramic tradition that later trickled into fortress settings (Çevik 2008). We have already seen in the Upper Euphrates region that the production of grooved ware persisted into the Iron 2 period. Moreover, several of the burials in the cemeteries contained familiar artifacts of the Urartian era, such as fibulae (at Yoncatepe) and a stamp (at Karagündüz), thus making an Iron 1 dating of these cemeteries more difficult to sustain.

Limited information from the settlements associated with the cemeteries further undermines the case for assigning the latter to the Iron 1 period. At the mound sites of Karagündüz and Dilkaya, Iron 2 (Urartian) levels lay immediately atop Early Bronze Age levels, without any intervening cultural deposits (Konyar 2005; Köroğlu and Konyar 2008).[5] At the excavated building complex of Yoncatepe, Iron 1 levels were likewise absent from the stratigraphic column, and grooved pottery occurred not only alongside the characteristic red-polished vessels of Urartu but also with highly diagnostic Urartian metal ornaments (fibulae, pins, and earrings) (Konyar 2005). A single radiocarbon determination of 1092–956 B.C.E. run on a sample collected from a pit at Karagündüz does not necessarily constitute a sufficient basis for asserting an Iron 1 occupation at this site. Solitary radiocarbon dates that contravene relative archaeological chronologies can be called into question on grounds of sample corruption or highly insignificant burning episodes. Nevertheless, such absolute dates cannot be lightly dismissed.

Efforts to justify the apparent hiatus in settlement activity during the Iron 1 period in this region rest on an argument for predominantly nomadic lifeways (Sevin 1999, 2004). But even mobile societies leave traces on the landscape, especially if communities make pilgrimages for centuries to the places of their ancestors to bury the dead (a situation now relatively well known from the Middle Bronze Age of the South Caucasus). This argument from silence is particularly unpersuasive since the weight of the positive evidence at present appears to favor an Iron 2 dating of the Van cemeteries. A single radiocarbon date from a single Karagündüz burial constitutes the only affirmative evidence for Iron 1 activity in this one necropolis. The ^{14}C date resists easy explanation, given that multiple individuals were buried in the chamber tombs at Karagündüz (and the other cemeteries). One possible interpretation of the data would suggest that the earliest uses of the cemetery occurred in the closing centuries of the second millennium B.C.E., even as later interments introduced more recent material culture to the assemblage. But as Konyar (2005:110) notes, in order to accommodate both the radiocarbon date and the Red-Burnished Ware (eighth century B.C.E. or later), the burials must have remained in use for at least 400 years, a highly improbable occurrence. Köroğlu and Konyar (2008) recently advanced a compelling resolution to the problem of the Van burials, suggesting that the fortress-centered traditions of research into Urartu have led investigators to misconstrue synchronic social difference as diachronic variability. The burials may belong to those rural segments of Urartian society whose material practices (i.e., extensive production of grooved ware, unique tomb constructions) deviate somewhat from familiar Urartian élite culture.

There is thus a lacuna in the archaeological record of the Lake Van region during the centuries preceding the Urartian Empire. Given the current state of knowledge, several recent unsystematic regional surveys conducted north and west of Lake Van understandably refrained from distinguishing the Iron 1 period (Marro and Özfırat 2003, 2004, 2005; Rothman 2004) from the Late Bronze Age, which is also poorly understood in this region (Çilingiroğlu 2001; French and Summers 1994). In other reconnaissance efforts around Lake Van and to the north, investigators have identified Iron 1 fortresses (as many as twenty, some with associated necropoleis) on the basis of the presence of grooved ware, fortress planning, wall masonry, and tomb construction. Sevin (2004) regards these fortresses as strongholds belonging to a settled élite who ruled a nomadic or semi-nomadic populace. But given the absence of stratified Iron 1 levels in the Van region and the ambiguities surrounding grooved ware, the dating of these sites is still uncertain (Belli 2005; Belli and Konyar 2001a, 2003a). A persistent question, for instance, is whether these fortresses and associated cemeteries could instead (or also) belong to the Late Bronze Age, when fortress-based polities (surrounded by cemeteries of similarly constructed tombs) emerged in other parts of the Armenian plateau (Smith et al. 2009).

At stake in the archaeological recognition of an Iron 1 occupation in the Lake Van region, as yet unaccomplished, is more than the mere filling in of regional chronology. Reconstructing Iron 1 activity out of the scanty evidence currently available also brings archaeological data into conformity with the textual record, specifically the cuneiform annals of the thirteenth century B.C.E. Assyrian kings Šalmaneser I and Tukulti-Ninurta. These kings refer to cities and fortresses controlled by highland principalities of lands known as Uruatri and Nairi, thus testifying to rudimentary political organizations that could constitute the primordial and autochthonous origins of Urartu in the Lake Van region (Belli 2005; Belli and Konyar 2001a; Çilingiroğlu 2001; Sevin 1999). The identification of Iron 1 fortresses thus dovetails nicely with these accounts, even if other aspects of the texts are so unlikely—for instance, the existence of cities and of sixty kings—that they should alert us to the hazards of reading literally the ideological productions of distant hegemonic powers. The forebears of Urartian cultural and political traditions in the Van region thus remains an open question (see Smith in press).

The Erzurum Region

In the central zone of the eastern Anatolian plateau, recent research in the Erzurum region offers the prospect of a breakthrough in Iron 1 chronology. The neighboring Erzurum and Pasinler Plains, bounded on the north and south by east–west mountain chains, occupy a narrow swath of the central highlands, where the headwaters of two prominent rivers, the Karasu and Araks, arise. Long a neglected area in the archaeology of Anatolia, the region has attracted increased attention since Australian and Turkish teams began excavations at Sos Höyük, located on the western Pasinler Plain, in 1994. Other regional and site-based investigations followed.

Boasting stratified deposits and a long history of occupation, the Sos Höyük mound is a key site for the emerging chronology and periodization of this region, not least for the light it sheds on the little understood transition from the Late Bronze to the Iron 1 periods (A. Sagona 1999).

The relevant soundings (J14, M16, L16) revealed clearly stratified Iron 1 cultural levels whose dating was verified by multiple radiocarbon readings that fall in the approximate range of the thirteenth through ninth centuries B.C.E. (table 20.1). Iron 1 deposits consisted of a series of rooms with thick lime plaster floors that were covered with a burnt layer (Sagona et al. 1997). Two particularly critical radiocarbon dates capture the period immediately before the construction of this thick plaster floor and that of the destruction level just above it (Sagona et al. 1996). The Iron 1 floors sealed the Late Bronze Age contexts below and contained a ceramic corpus quite distinct from the earlier levels. Judging by radiocarbon samples taken from above and below the level of the plaster floor, it would appear that Iron 1 occupation began at Sos Höyük sometime between the thirteenth and eleventh centuries (A. Sagona, personal communication). Notably, grooved ware occurs rarely here, just as in several regions of the Armenian plateau (Sagona and Sagona 2004b:186). Vessels with gray or black cores and brownish or black burnished surfaces in the form of jars, spouted jars, open bowls, and carinated bowls predominate at Sos (Parker 1999; Sagona et al. 1996), alongside occasional white-painted or gadrooned vessels (figure 20.2) (Sagona et al. 1997).

Sos Höyük provides important new assemblages, but the challenge nevertheless exists to isolate an Iron 1 phase in the archaeology of the central Armenian highland. Recently revived excavations at the mound site of Pulur in the neighboring Erzurum Plain unearthed deep deposits in sector A1, which Mehmet Işıklı assigns to the transition between the Late Bronze and Iron 1 periods based on a radiocarbon reading that falls at the very earliest end of the spectrum of Iron 1 dates from Sos Höyük (Işıklı 2008; Işıklı and Can 2007) (table 20.1). But the cultural features at Pulur, including lime-plastered floors and pits, as well as the main ceramic wares, most closely resemble Late Bronze Age Sos. The Iron Age 1 thus remains murky in this region. In surveys and reconnaissance of the Erzurum and Pasinler Plains (as well as the Bayburt and Erzincan Plains to the west), distinguishing subphases within the long Iron Age based on surface ceramics has proven difficult despite the sound comparanda now available from Sos (Ceylan 2005; Işıklı and Can 2007; Sagona and Sagona 2004b; C. Sagona 1999).

Southern Caucasia

We turn now to the highlands of the middle Araks River and its drainages, a geographic province of the wider South Caucasus defined as southern Caucasia (Smith 2009). In these northeasterly reaches of the eastern Anatolian plateau, Martirosyan (1964) first established a periodization and chronology of the Iron 1 era (within his pioneering scheme for regional prehistory) that, in its broad outlines, has largely

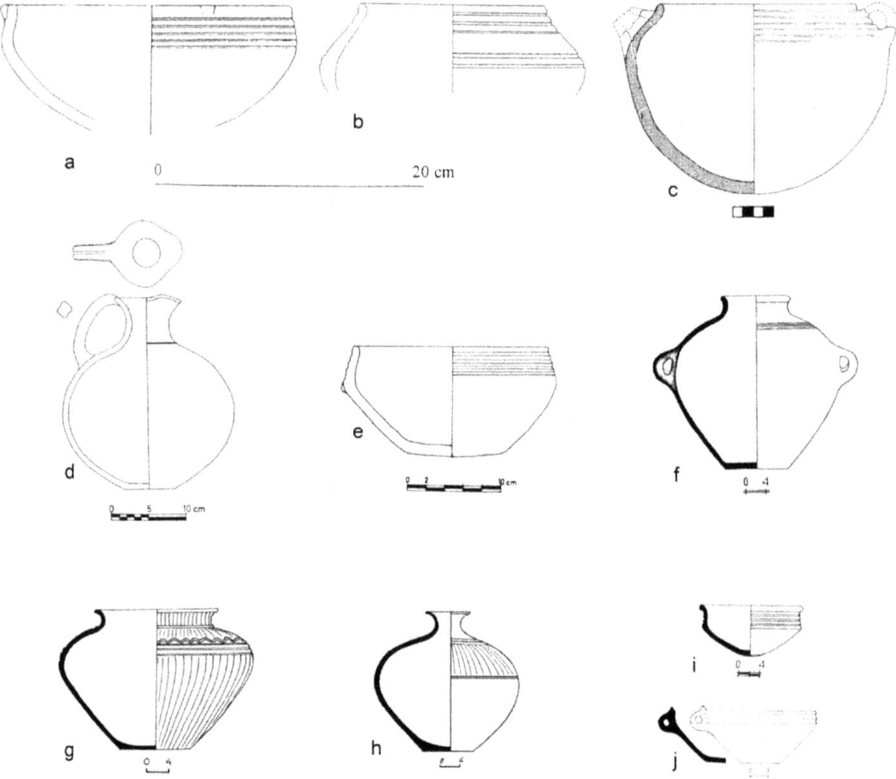

Figure 20.2. Iron 1 pottery of the Anatolian/Armenian Plateau.

endured the proliferation of systematic investigations since the 1960s (Avetisyan et al. 1996). The parameters of the Iron 1 period in southern Caucasia are today relatively well established. They are derived from stratified deposits at key settlements, the contextual seriation of mortuary assemblages, and a growing corpus of radiocarbon dates.

Iron 1 material traditions continue uninterrupted in this region from those of the preceding Late Bronze Age. A single archaeological horizon termed the Lchashen-Metsamor culture (so named after two type sites) embraces both of these eras on account of the appreciable material continuities that extend from the fifteenth through ninth centuries B.C.E. Despite consistencies within this long-lasting Lchashen-Metsamor horizon, however, palpable transformations in metallurgical and ceramic production allow for the parsing of a distinct Iron 1 assemblage. The appearance of new ceramic forms alongside those of earlier Lchashen-Metsamor phases characterizes this era, coupled with the notable increase in iron tools and weapons relative to artifacts of bronze. Although vessels with incised grooves on their shoulders exist in the Iron 1 assemblage, grooves are also common on Late Bronze Age ceramics and thus fall outside the diagnostic features exclusive of the Iron 1. The features that constitute Iron 1 pottery are more intricate than a single surface ornament and also include other typical decorative elements (e.g., waves, *canelures*, triangles) and a wide range of vessel forms and surface treatments (some only subtly different from Late Bronze forms). The Iron 1 era in southern Caucasia is itself partitioned into what have come to be called Lchashen-Metsamor 4 (Iron 1A) and Lchashen-Metsamor 5 (Iron 1B) (Badalyan, Avetisyan, and Smith 2009). The variable ceramic assemblages of each have received systematic treatment by Badalyan, Avetisyan, and Smith (2009) and are thus not detailed here (figure 20.2).

The settlement of Metsamor on the Ararat Plain provides a key linchpin around which archaeologists have constructed the chronology and periodization of the Iron 1. The level of Urartian occupation at this site rests atop burned levels of an earlier settlement whose destruction is attributed to the Urartian incursions of the eighth century B.C.E. (Khanzadyan, Mkrtchian, and Parsamian 1973). The materials associated with this burned level belong to the Lchashen-Metsamor 5 phase, and radiocarbon dates from this same context contribute to the dating of Lchashen-Metsamor 5 from the late eleventh to the early eighth century B.C.E. (table 20.1). Although lacking an Urartian occupation, a similar situation exists at Dvin, where a burned layer dated by a single radiocarbon sample seals a deposit marked by Lchashen-Metsamor 5 materials (table 20.1) (Kushnareva 1977). These securely dated contexts from Dvin and Metsamor in turn date the Iron 1 occupation at Karmir-Blur that precedes the Urartian constructions (Avetisyan and Avetisyan 2006:50). Beyond the Ararat Plain, the Artik, Horom, Karnut II, and Kuchak cemeteries and the settlements of Horom, Shirakavan, Karmirberd, Talin, and Oshakan further contribute to the absolute and relative dating of Lchashen-Metsamor 5 (table 20.1) (Avetisyan and Avetisyan 2006; Badalyan and Avetisyan 2007; Badaljan et al. 1992, 1993, 1994; Badaljan, Kohl, and Kroll 1997; Esayan 1967; Esayan and Kalantarian 1988; T. Khachatryan 1975, 1979; Torosyan, Khnkikyan, and Petrosyan 2002).

The preceding Lchashen-Metsamor 4 phase of the Iron 1 period designates the interval between the relatively securely dated Lchashen-Metsamor 5 and the Lchashen-Metsamor 3 assemblages of the terminal Late Bronze Age (Badalyan, Avetisyan, and Smith 2009). One of the key sites in the determination of Lchashen-Metsamor 4 is the cemetery of Talin in west-central Armenia (for a complete bibliography see Badalyan and Avetisyan 2007:242), where researchers uncovered several burials containing a transitional assemblage of both Lchashen-Metsamor 3 and ceramics that anticipate but are distinct from Lchashen-Metsamor 5 (Avetisyan and Avetisyan 2006:53). The notable increase in iron artifacts within such burials exhibiting mixed ceramic assemblages, in which replicas of Late Bronze Age vessels nevertheless predominate, further distinguishes the Lchashen-Metsamor 4 contexts of the Iron 1 period (Badalyan, Avetisyan, and Smith 2009). In addition to Talin, other cemetery sites that exhibit burials of the Lchashen-Metsamor 4 phase include Mastara, Redkin-Lager, Karnut II, and Oshakan (Badalyan and Avetisyan 2007; Esayan and Kalantarian 1988; Esayan and Oganesyan 1969). In the absence of radiocarbon dates from Lchashen-Metsamor 4 contexts, convention ascribes this phase of the Iron 1 period to the mid-twelfth through late eleventh century B.C.E. Thus, although the end date of the Iron 1 period in southern Caucasia rests on secure foundations, its start date is rather more conjectural.

Iron 2

During the centuries following the Iron 1 period, iron production proliferated on the eastern Anatolian plateau, enabling new technologies of construction, warfare, subsistence, and perhaps even social control. Urartu's craftsmen used iron picks and hammers to forge horizontal planes out of bedrock on which to erect the empire's numerous and imposing stone fortresses. Knives, daggers, swords, arrowheads, spearheads, armor scales, and helmets discovered in these fortresses were produced on a mass scale and speak to an impressive military apparatus, unprecedented for this region. Three-pronged forks, axes, hoes, adzes, spades, and sickles are only some of the iron tools existing in large quantities that would have facilitated large-scale agricultural work and the activities of daily life. As the preferred metal for the production of tools, weapons, and other instruments, iron was widely disseminated (Wartke 1991).[6] It advanced the efforts of Urartu's authorities to formalize and centralize power behind hilltop fortresses, extract labor, and create subjects out of the conquered. Postulating the relation between metallurgy and empire, Zimansky (1985:97) once cautiously opined that "Urartu could only have come into existence in the Iron Age."

Ironically, the conventions of the Three Age system would require that the curtain be drawn on the Iron Age at just the point when iron acquired broad ubiquity on the Armenian plateau, for the chronology and periodization of Iron 2 hinge almost exclusively on written sources. Indeed, the historically derived concept of an "Urartian Period" largely displaces the terminology of the archaeological timescale. A dynastic genealogy constructed through the interdigitation of Assyrian documents and native Urartian texts provides the scaffolding for the chronology and periodization of the period (Arutyunian 2001; Salvini 2009). Although some ambiguity surrounds the sequence of the dynasty's later kings (Sagona and Zimansky 2009:327), the monarchy's reign appears to have endured from approximately the 830s through 630s B.C.E. Urartu's kings carved cuneiform inscriptions out of rock at most of the major fortresses they built, thus leaving a chronicle of their campaigns and building activities (Zimansky, chapter 24 in this volume). Though the last attested reference to an Urartian king in 639 B.C.E. is increasingly taken as the approximate endpoint for the empire's existence, older traditions of scholarship draw on Herodotus's account of the Median conquest of this region to place the empire's collapse at around 590 B.C.E. The agents and timing of Urartu's demise remain unresolved (Kroll 1984; Steele 2008).

On the basis of the content and distribution of Urartu's inscriptions, the rule of the kingdom can be subdivided into an expansionary phase and a period of renovation. During the former, King Sarduri, the first known Urartian dynast, built the fortress of Tušpa east of Lake Van as his capital. His son and successor, Išpuini, further secured the imperial homeland, after which Išpuini and his son Minua expanded their domain northward and built several fortresses in their wake. Minua continued the expansions, campaigning further northward, westward, and toward the southeast from the imperial heartland. Successors Argišti I and then Sarduri II extended the reach of the empire further still during the second half of the eighth and the first part of the seventh centuries, consolidating these conquests with new fortresses on the Ararat Plain (Erebuni and Argištihnili) and in the heartland (Çavuştepe). Following military setbacks at the hands of the Assyrians during the last decades of the eighth century B.C.E. (see Radner, chapter 33 in this volume), this initial phase of frequent campaigning gave way to a period of renovation or even renaissance, as the powerful King Rusa devoted his energies less to territorial expansion than to an ambitious and innovative building program (at Karmir Blur, Bastam, Ayanis, Toprakkale, and Kefkalesi) (Zimansky 2005).

The archaeology of the Iron 2 period on the eastern Anatolian plateau in large measure centers on Urartu's fortresses—and not only those whose founding dates are fixed by royal inscriptions (other investigated fortresses include Altıntepe, Aragats, Aramus, Hasanlu, Horom, Kayalıdere, and Qaleh Ismail Aqa).[7] Iron 2 chronology is thus largely an inquiry into a governmental apparatus at the highest echelons (Zimansky 1995). The dating of archaeological remains derives from dynastic history insofar as the architecture and material assemblages of fortresses known by inscriptions to date to the reign of a particular king provide a comparative corpus for the dating of fortresses and ceramics with no associated absolute dates (Kafadaryan 1984; Kleiss 1994; Kroll 1976). To be sure, Urartu's material assemblage does signal a radical break from the past—one that archaeologists can discern quite apart from the information for a historical rupture provided in the textual record. Architectural innovations such as the leveling of bedrock, the working of ashlar or semi-ashlar masonry, and the incorporation into fortifications of towers and buttresses at regular intervals depart from earlier fortress traditions in the region. Urartu's ceramic repertoire, marked especially by massive storage vessels (*pithoi*; see Radner, chapter 33 in this volume) and a distinctive red ware rendered in the form of bowls and trefoil jugs that often bear highly burnished surfaces, presents an equally new element in the archaeology of the region (although the latter do not become prevalent until the seventh century) (figure 20.3).

Archaeology's ongoing contribution to the study of Urartu—its political, economic, cultural, and religious institutions—has been significant. But its contribution to the chronology and periodization of the Iron 2 era is rather more equivocal. The recent use of dendrochronological and radiocarbon dating at the fortress of Ayanis holds the promise for an archaeologically derived chronology to complement the established historical framework (Kuniholm and Newton 2001; Newton and Kuniholm 2007) and resolve questions concerning the sequence of Rusa's seventh-century B.C.E. constructions (Erdem and Batmaz 2008; for a discussion of Ayanis see Çilingiroğlu, chapter 49 in this volume).

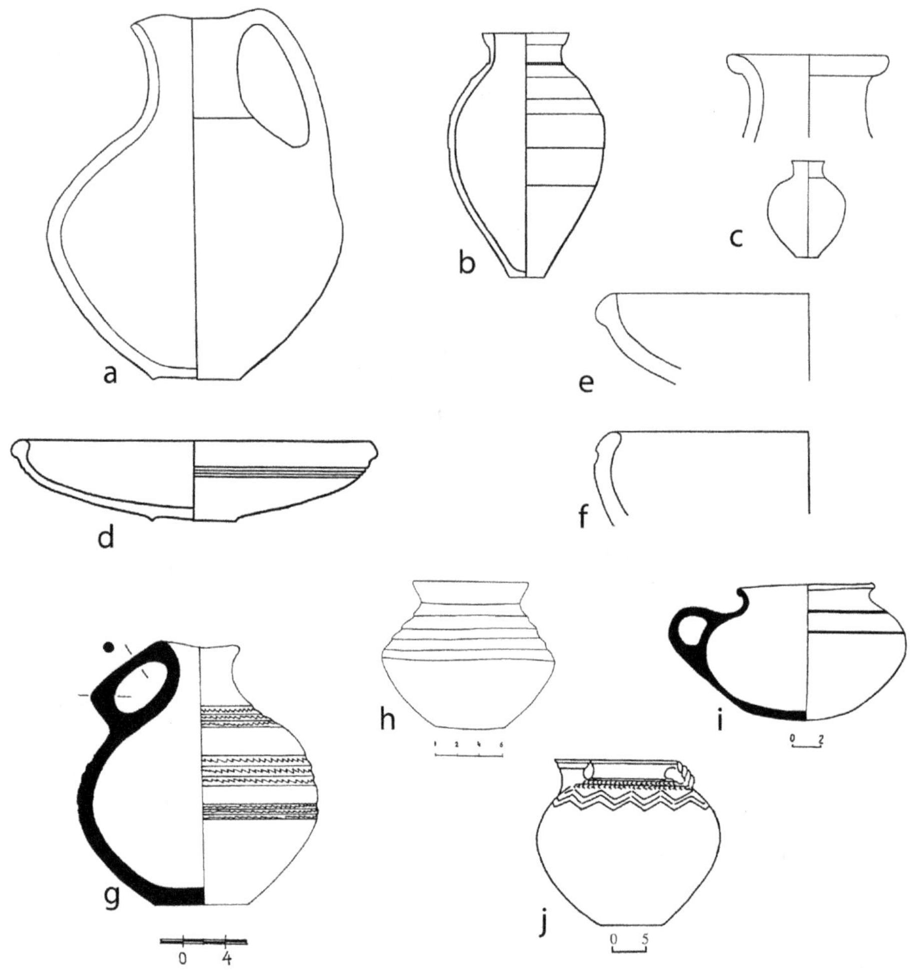

Figure 20.3. Iron 2 pottery of the Anatolian/Armenian Plateau.

If archaeology were committed solely to the study of the most privileged segments of past societies, an Iron 2 chronology derived from the inscriptions of Urartu's kings would suffice. Difficulties arise, however, when the archaeological gaze moves beyond the rarified confines of the empire's fortresses. In such contexts, not only do the material forms so characteristic of Urartu occur sporadically or not at all, but the rhythms of material change often disregard those of political history. For example, in southern Caucasia, alongside Urartian ceramic wares and their local imitations (H. Avetisyan 1992), Lchashen-Metsamor traditions continued into the centuries of Urartian rule, constituting what has come to be called the Lchashen-Metsamor 6 phase or the "local" ceramic productions of the Urartian era (figure 20.3) (Avetisyan and Avetisyan 2006:55–81; Badalyan, Avetisyan, and Smith 2009). A similar pattern prevails in eastern Turkey, where sites with predominantly Iron 1 pottery are dated to the Iron 2 period due to the presence of distinctive Urartian ceramics (Bilgi 2001).

Nevertheless, particularly in Armenia, an archaeological chronology of the Iron 2 period is evolving that hinges on the changing relationship between Urartian wares and "local" Lchashen-Metsamor wares within both settlement and burial contexts. Avetisyan and Avetisyan (2006) identify two phases, the first in which Urartian and local wares remain isolated from one another (Iron 2a, dating to the early eighth through early seventh century B.C.E.) and the second (Iron 2b, from the early seventh century to the last quarter of the sixth century B.C.E.) in which the two repertoires co-occur, in some cases becoming somewhat hybridized, such that a given assemblage is not easily assigned to one or the other archaeological culture. Central to these analyses are select burials within the cemeteries of Oshakan, Karmir Blur, Metsamor, Lori Berd, Artashavan, Golovino, and Karchakhbyur (Avetisyan, Yengibaryan, and Sargsyan 1998; Devedzhyan 1981; Esayan and Kalantarian 1988; Khanzadyan, Mkrtchian, and Parsamian 1973; Martirosyan 1954, 1961; Yengibaryan 2002). These contexts in which Urartian and "local" wares co-occur in turn provide greater clarity on the distinctive features of the Lchashen-Metsamor 6 corpus, enabling the dating of collections that lack the diagnostic Urartian wares. Stratified deposits from Metsamor and Horom that contain both Urartian and Lchashen-Metsamor 6 wares further support the relative chronology (Kohl and Kroll 1999), to some degree corroborated by radiocarbon dates that frustratingly fall on the so-called Hallstatt plateau on the calibration curve (table 20.1).

Dates and stratified deposits are also accumulating from settlements further from the Ararat Plain that are not, strictly speaking, Urartian fortresses, such as Tagavoranist, Shaghat, Uits, Sos Höyük, and Büyüktepe Höyük, where local ceramic traditions predominate (Cherry et al. 2007; Palanjyan 2008; Sagona, Pemberton, and McPhee 1993). Over the long term, such investigations hold great promise to expand our understanding of the contours of social life in the Iron 2 period beyond Urartu's privileged locales. Furthermore, they provide a foundation for ceramic typologies of non-Urartian Iron 2 wares from the Armenian plateau that could enable the dating of surface collections. In some regional surveys, Red-Burnished Ware and its local imitations are often taken as the prime marker of Urartian occupation (Rothman 2004). In others, sites are assigned to the Urartian era not only due to the presence of such classic Urartian wares (rarely encountered beyond the fortresses), but also on the basis of local productions of the Iron 2 period whose dating is often left unexplained, despite the acknowledged absence of excavated stratified Iron 2 levels in a region (Marro and Özfırat 2003, 2004, 2005). As others have noted (Hmayakyan 2002; Sagona and Sagona 2004a:188), Urartian-type red-slipped ware continued to be manufactured into the Iron 3 period (Karapetyan 2003; Khachatryan 1970; Khatchadourian 2008), such that only the highly glossy, so-called Toprakkale ware, is specifically diagnostic of Urartian-era occupation. We are relatively ill-equipped to date surface collections of local and course wares to the era of Urartian hegemony.

This has consequences for our understanding of the geographical scope of the empire. Adam T. Smith (1996:22) has described Urartu as an "'imperial archipelago'—a spatial organization of political authority which, though confined to small 'islands' in physical space, forwarded the appearance of coherence and legitimacy." How is imperial coherence beyond the islands of authority to be gauged? Maps of the empire often embrace large swaths of the eastern Anatolian plateau, including the spaces that lie between the empire's archipelagic fortress nodes. To a large extent, such borders of Urartu derive from the wide distribution of cuneiform royal inscriptions that describe lands subdued by military campaigns, building activities, and cultic practices. In contrast to such historical geographies (Köroğlu 2005), a strictly archaeological cartography would constrict the empire to the lands surrounding fortified centers. This would certainly include the area around Lake Van and the Ararat plain, atop whose hilltop peaks Urartu's main fortresses were perched, as well as areas west and south of Lake Sevan (Biscione, Hmayakyan, and Parmegiani 2002) and west and north of Lake Urmia, where a plethora of fortresses stood, in the orbit of Rusa's citadel at Bastam (Kleiss 1973, 1974, 1975, 1979a, 1979b, 1980, 1988; Kleiss and Kroll 1979; Pecorella and Salvini 1984). The Elazığ region east of the Euphrates also fell within the empire's embrace. The Erzincan, Erzurum, and Shirak Plains occupy a more ambiguous place within the map of the empire, despite the Urartian-type fortresses at Horom and Altıntepe.[8] An archaeological mapping of Urartu thus provides a less contiguous and coherent picture of an empire than one based generously on the kings' attestations of conquest recorded in cuneiform inscriptions.

Iron 3

The Iron 3 period is the least understood phase in the archaeology of the Armenian plateau. Variously called the "Late Iron Age," the "Early Armenian period," the "post-Urartian period," and the "Achaemenid period," a shroud hangs over the centuries following the collapse of Urartu in the region's archaeological imagination. If the study of the Iron 2 period straddles the conventional divide between prehistory and history, then Iron 3 falls squarely within the domain of inquiry in which historical narrative holds a firm privilege. Despite some exceptions and some recent breakthroughs that augur new directions in research, archaeology in the Anatolian highlands has largely forsaken the study of the mid-first millennium B.C.E.

Historical sources thus provide the chronological and geographical parameters of the era and therefore warrant brief review here. The circumstances and timing of the region's initial capitulation to Achaemenid Persian rule is uncertain; however, the combined weight of Greek, Babylonian, and Persian textual sources offer grounds for suspecting that the plateau was one of the many lands conquered by Cyrus in his sweep across parts of southwest Asia in the mid-sixth century B.C.E. By 525 B.C.E. the region must have been folded into the Achaemenid sphere of control as a satrapy, or province, for in the years following the Persian king Darius's rise to power, a place called Urartu/Armenia joined other regions of the empire in mounting a series of rebellions that Darius reported in the Bisitun inscriptions to have quashed. On this trilingual monument, the word Urartu appears in the Babylonian version in the same position as Armenia in the Old Persian and Elamite versions (see Zimansky, chapter 24 in this volume). Toponyms can endure longer than empires, and considerable evidence points to the fact that by the mid-first millennium B.C.E., Urartu and Armenia were roughly homologous geographic referents. The satrapy of Armenia remained a constituent part of the Persian Empire right up until its collapse in 330 B.C.E. What little archaeological research has been done on the Iron 3 period focuses on the two-century timespan from the middle of the sixth century B.C.E. to the third quarter of the fourth century B.C.E.

There is a great deal of extrapolation entailed in any enterprise in historical geography, and the case of the Achaemenid Empire's northern highlands is no exception. Drawing on passing references in a number of classical texts (in some cases oblique and contradictory), including the so-called *nomoi* lists and chaotic geographic insights offered by Herodotus, historians have proposed divergent reconstructions of the geography of the satrapy (or satrapies) and tribes that occupied the eastern Anatolian plateau (Hewsen 1983; C. Sagona 2004; Tiratsyan 1980, 1981). Favoring the Persian sources over those of distant Greek writers in modeling the administrative system of the empire, Jacobs (1994, 2006) has made a strong case for envisioning the satrapy known to the Persians as Armenia as one of the core provinces of the empire (a great many of the satrapies mentioned in Herodotus's confused ethnocartography are not known from Persian texts and may well be inventions). This satrapy's jurisdiction may have spanned much of the highlands. Such an administrative cartography is cobbled together from an array of citations in the works of Xenophon and Herodotus, along with inferences about modern equivalents to ancient toponyms (Jacobs 1994, 2006). These and other sources also imply that the satrapy of Armenia was partitioned into an eastern and a western administrative division.

Close engagement with the primary written sources—both classical and Persian—provides only the most disjointed political history and schematic chronology and geography of the Armenian plateau during the centuries of Achaemenid rule. Historical accounts shed little light on the routines and transformations of social life. Their utility is further constrained by the twin biases of the sources, whether written by foreigners (Greeks) or conquerors (Persians). The total absence of "native" texts in the Armenian highlands in some sense renders the period more akin to prehistory than to the preceding Iron 2 phase, insofar as a regional archaeological chronology cannot be tethered to local records of local events with discrete material consequences, such as the fortress building activities of kings (see Yakar, chapter 4 in this volume, for similar views). Any refinement of the internal periodization of the mid-first millennium B.C.E. and any substantive understanding of the distribution of shared cultural and social practices across space can only emerge from archaeology.

The foundations for such inquiries are at present quite weak due to the scarcity of Iron 3 deposits in stratified contexts. The former Urartian fortresses at Altıntepe and Erebuni, both excavated in the 1950s, anchor what little archaeological research has been done on the Iron 3 period in both the eastern and western divisions of the satrapy. At both sites, the preserved foundations of colonnaded halls, dated on the basis of stratigraphic relationships and through formal comparisons with monumental hypostyle halls in the Achaemenid capitals, stand atop or beside earlier Urartian constructions (Khatchadourian forthcoming; Summers 1993; Ter-Martirosov 2001; Tiratsyan 1960). The careful reanalysis of the ceramics at Altıntepe has made it a key site for the relative dating of both stratified and surface collections (Summers 1993). The Altıntepe excavations unearthed sherds belonging to a pottery tradition that has come to be known as "Classic" and "Western" Triangle Ware (figure 20.4) (Dyson 1999a; Kroll 2000; see Matney, chapter 19 in this volume). Though some early studies ascribed this ware to the Iron 2 period (von der Osten 1952, 1953), others advanced a later dating to the Iron 3 (Kroll 1975, 1976; Stronach 1974). Since the 1990s, thanks to the reanalysis of the stratigraphy of Hasanlu II/IIIA (Dyson 1999a, 1999b) and the restudy of the pottery from the Van region (Tarhan 1989; Tarhan and Sevin 1990, 1991), opinion has converged in favor of the later dating. The so-called Triangle Wares simply do not occur in Urartian cultural levels (Kroll 2000).

This determination has contributed to the recent identification of Iron 3 occupations not only in the vicinity of Altıntepe (M. Işıklı personal communication; Summers 1993), but elsewhere on the eastern Anatolian plateau, such as the Karagündüz mound (Sevin 2002). The presence of a Black Burnished Ware that is known to exist in the Van region alongside Triangle Ware assists in the identification of Iron 3 activity at Büyüktepe and many other surveyed sites on the Bayburt Plain (Sagona and Sagona 2004a:198). At the outer town of Ayanis, however, the scanty presence of Triangle Ware appears not to be associated with an Iron 3 occupation (P. Zimansky personal communication; see Erdem and Batmaz 2008). The number of excavated sites in eastern Turkey with clear Iron 3 levels whose materials have been published is quite limited.

At least one sherd of Triangle Ware was found at the site of Armavir on the Ararat Plain, where it is otherwise rarely encountered (Tiratsyan 2003 [1965]:pl. 11:3). But the archaeology of the Iron 3 period in southern Caucasia rests on somewhat more robust foundations than the presence of a single ware type. The recognition of a distinct archaeological horizon belonging to the Iron 3 era can be traced to the 1950s and 1960s, with Mnatsakanyan, Martirosyan, and Esayan's excavations of burials at Jrarat, Atarbekyan, Karmir Blur, and Karmir Berd (see Karapetyan 2003:6–7). By identifying among these mortuary assemblages formal lines of departure from previous Urartian material culture repertoires, along with morphological similarities to materials from Achaemenid Iran and Asia Minor, these researchers began to define the broad contours of a discrete Iron 3 material horizon. As the study of the later centuries of the first millennium B.C.E. intensified with the excavations at Garni, Armavir, and Artashat, scholars further refined the earlier conventions for the Iron 3 period. It became feasible to trace not only formal deviations from Iron 2 material repertoires but also possible antecedents to later forms. In the near absence of thoroughly investigated stratified settlement deposits, material similarities with Achaemenid Iran, coupled with nuanced differences from the material culture of the preceding Urartian and succeeding Hellenistic/Roman phases, form the basis for defining an Iron 3 archaeological horizon.

One of the most typical ceramic forms of the Iron 3 assemblage is the carinated bowl (so-called *phiale*), often occurring in red, red-brown, and black, with highly polished surfaces (figure 20.4). Although also common among Urartian and Hellenistic ceramics of the region (Khachatryan 1970; Kroll 1976), the Iron 3 carinated bowl is distinguishable from its earlier and later peers (Dusinberre 1999; Karapetyan 1971) and has appeared in cemeteries and settlements across southern Caucasia, including Erebuni, Armavir, Jrarat, Atarbekyan, and Norashen (Karapetyan 2003:40). Such distinctive bowls also make up the largest share of all diagnostic vessels at the site of Tsaghkahovit, located in modern central Armenia, one of the few sites of the Armenian plateau where ongoing intensive investigations specifically target the study of the Iron 3 period (Khatchadourian 2008). Short-lived excavations at Karchakhbyur and the ongoing but largely unpublished excavations at Beniamin likewise have focused expressly on the Iron 3 era (Karapetyan 1978, 1979; Ter-Martirosov and Deschamps 2007).

The significance of Tsaghkahovit for the study of the Iron 3 period derives from the fact that radiocarbon determinations and associated small finds place the dating of the ceramic assemblage on solid footing, thus holding the promise for reexamination of earlier ceramic conventions. Tsaghkahovit exhibits the full suite of ceramic forms conventionally assigned to the Iron 3 period in the archaeology of the eastern Anatolian highlands (with the exception of Triangle Ware), including not only carinated bowls (and a great diversity of other red- and black-polished bowls) but gadrooned and cannelure vessels as well as vessels with zoomorphic adornments that imitate Achaemenid metal prototypes and are known from other sites in the highlands (Karapetyan 2003:40–1; Khatchadourian 2008:492, 511; Sagona et al. 1996:fig. 5:4, 6). By way of relative dating, distinctive small finds such as an ibex- (or gazelle-) shaped vessel and a footless serpentine plate have their closest parallels in the archaeology of the Achaemenid heartland (figure 20.4). Hundreds of morphologically identical chert and serpentine plates filled select rooms of the treasury at Persepolis and allow the secure dating of the Tsaghkahovit plate to the reign of the Persian king Xerxes (486–465 B.C.E.), thus providing a firm *terminus post quem* for the occupation of the settlement. Preliminary Bayesian analysis of eleven radiocarbon dates suggests, however, that the site's occupation began earlier, in the second quarter of the sixth century B.C.E., and extended until the last quarter of the fifth century B.C.E. (Khatchadourian 2008:226–32) (table 20.1).

Radiocarbon dates for the Iron 3 period are also emerging from the excavations of sites scattered throughout southern Caucasia. Several dates are available from Shaghat and Balak, in the Vorotan valley of southern Armenia (Cherry et al. 2007). A single date from Tagavoranist in northern Armenia complements the ceramic data from that site to suggest a possible Iron 3 occupation (Palanjyan 2008). Inhabitants resettled the fortress of Horom in western Armenia during the Iron 3 period,

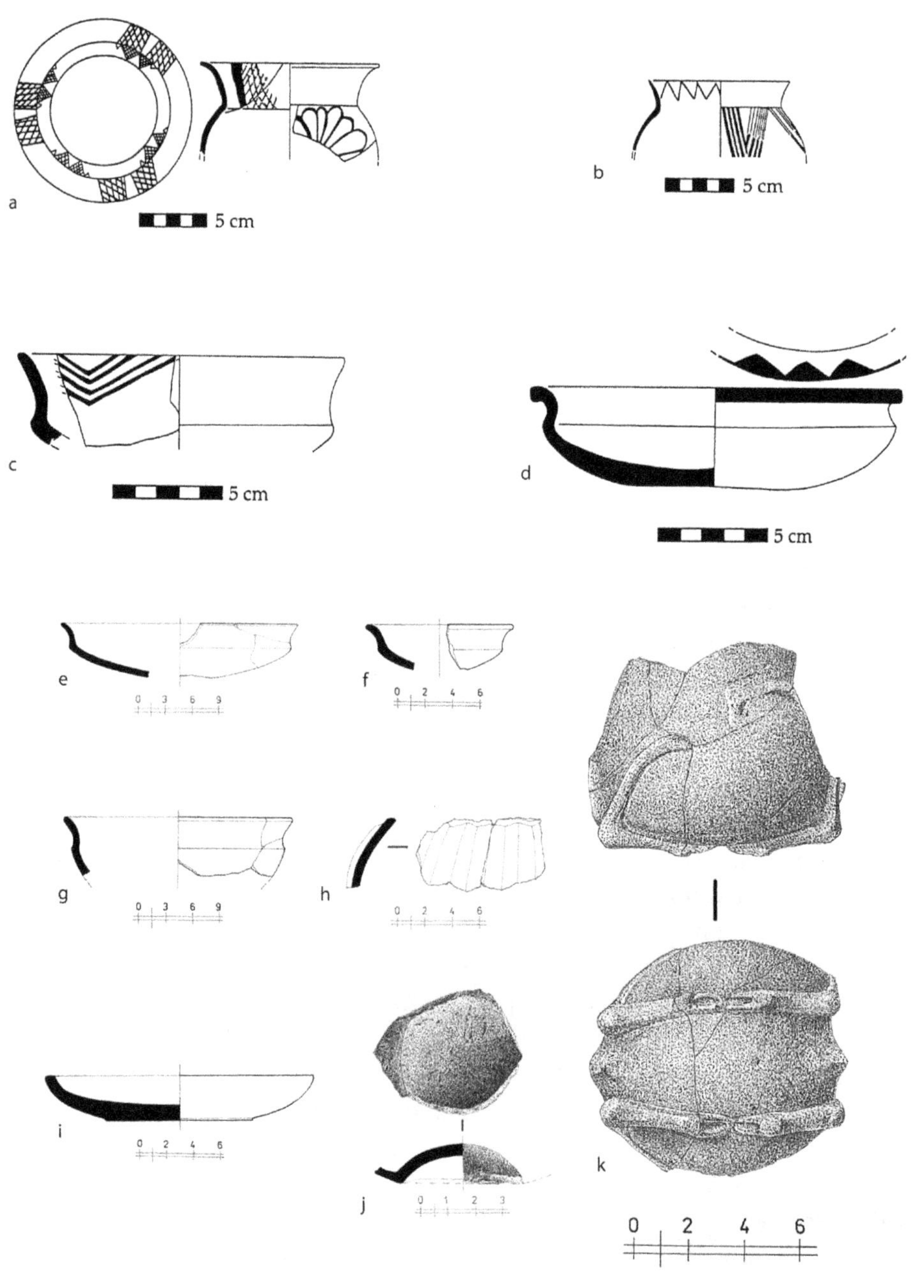

Figure 20.4. Iron 3 pottery of the Anatolian/Armenian Plateau.

although the relevant radiocarbon date comes from a different sector of the site than the area of reoccupation (Kohl and Kroll 1999) (table 20.1).

Recent attention to this long neglected phase in the archaeology of the Armenian plateau opens the possibility for a mapping of the satrapy that recasts the vacant geographic expanse defined by historical reconstruction into a peopled landscape. The challenges to the study of settlement patterns during the mid-first millennium

B.C.E. on the highlands are formidable, because truly systematic surveys are few and ceramic chronologies are nascent. Nevertheless, preliminary comparative analysis of surveys conducted in the Ijevan region (Esayan 1976), the Doğubeyazit and Erciş regions (Marro and Özfırat 2003, 2004, 2005), the Tsaghkahovit Plain (Smith, Badalyan, and Avetisyan 2009), the southern Lake Sevan basin (Biscione, Hmayakyan, and Parmegiani 2002), Lake Urmia (Kleiss 1973, 1974, 1975, 1979a; Kleiss and Kroll 1976; Pecorella and Salvini 1984), and the Muş Plain (Rothman 2004) suggests that several regions that were either in the heartland of the Urartian Empire and inscribed with numerous fortress constructions (such as Doğubeyazit and Erciş), or those regions that hosted major Urartian fortresses (such as the Lake Urmia region, with Bastam) were substantially vacated by the Iron 3 period. Bearing all caveats of undeveloped ceramic chronologies in mind, it is as though there was an exodus away from regions that were dense with Iron 2 fortresses and particularly near to the major fortresses of the Urartian governmental apparatus. Even as regions that were near to Urartu's political establishment witnessed a severe out-migration, locales that had, as it seems, remained largely beyond the sphere of Urartian rule (Ijevan and Tsaghkahovit) came to be settled in the subsequent centuries. It is possible that, on a very general scale, people were moving northward in the Iron 3 period, perhaps following the removal of Urartian controls that had concentrated labor and resources near royal fortresses (Khatchadourian 2008:342–89).

Conclusion

Stepping back from the morass of details provided by an ever-expanding corpus of sites, ceramics, and radiocarbon dates, it is worth pausing to consider how the temporal framework now under diligent construction can advance our understanding of the Iron Age past in the mountainous expanse stretching from the Euphrates River to the lesser Caucasus. What key concerns need to be raised in order to forward investigations into the contours of social life after the adoption of iron, and what can the archaeology of eastern Anatolia contribute to this discussion? Chronology and periodization constitute essential building blocks of archaeological research, yet they are easily misunderstood as problems that require resolution in advance of any effort at archaeological interpretation. To be sure, basic time/space systematics for certain phases of the Iron Age remain inchoate. By turning attention to some of the broader questions at stake in the archaeology of the eastern Anatolian plateau during the Iron Age, however, the imperative to establish a workable chronology comes into clearer focus.

The roughly 900 years embraced by the Iron Age marked a period of radical political transformations shaped first and foremost by the rise and fall of empires. How Urartu emerged in the ninth century B.C.E. is a question whose answer lies most immediately in the opening centuries of the Iron Age. Currently, the very roughest outlines of two different scenarios exist. In the western Armenian plateau, relatively flat settlement hierarchies (compared to the preceding Late Bronze Age) and undifferentiated built spaces in what appear to be village-like constructions at key sites in the Euphrates basin provide few clues for precursors to the kinds of consolidated political institutions that came to reproduce Urartian hegemony. At the other end of the highlands, however, especially in southern Caucasia but perhaps also further west, a political tradition characterized by imposing fortresses continued from the Late Bronze Age, potentially signaling the earliest foundations of Urartu's archipelagic fortress polity (Smith in press). These scenarios invite a two-pronged inquiry into the Iron 1 period focused both on the production of power and authority by an emergent political élite, perched within the stone citadels of the highland mountains, and on the constitution of social difference through routine practices among the region's subject communities. Surveys conducted in several regions of the highlands suggest that settlement densities either remained stable or increased during the Iron Age, in some cases far exceeding all previous periods. Bound up in the existence of stone-built fortresses, therefore, were new dispositions toward mobility and subsistence strategies that were possibly altered by the twin forces of new forms of social control and a new technology of metal production.

Out of this murky prehistory of empire arose not only the first relatively unified regime of the highlands but, indeed, the last highland polity for centuries to govern the region unbeholden to outside powers. Urartu was a remarkable experiment in local political consolidation. Yet in fixing scholarly attention understandably on sensational fortresses, inscriptions, associated artistic assemblages, and even ceramic chronologies, little concern has been directed toward the ways in which processes of Urartian imperialism were insinuated into the routines of daily life (pace Stone and Zimansky 2003). As a result we remain at a loss to explain how the empire was reproduced. Thanks to regional survey and reconnaissance efforts across the highlands, a plethora of nonroyal and nonfortress sites—in the Muş, Urmia, Sevan, Bayburt, Vorotan, Euphrates, Van, and Ararat Plain regions—await sustained investigations that might inform the ways in which everyday practices contributed to the making and remaking of the region's first homegrown empire.

The Iron 3 period is such uncharted territory in the archaeology of the eastern Anatolian plateau that it demands less an evaluation of current priorities than, at a more rudimentary level, creative engagement on what constitutes a meaningful starting point. Two broad lines of inquiry might productively launch earnest efforts to fill this gaping void in the region's archaeological traditions. The communities of the highlands in the mid-first millennium B.C.E. stood in place and time betwixt and between two powerful historical phenomena—one, the local Urartian past, the other, the "global" Achaemenid present. This Janus-faced positioning requires that studies of this imperial province chart a careful interpretive path: on the one hand probing the hegemonic conventions that pulled highland communities into the orbit of the Persian Empire through their material and spatial practices and, on the other, examining the ways in which local highland political and social traditions of the Urartian past were recuperated, modified, or repudiated in the construction of new community identities.

The relationship between sociopolitical complexity and iron metallurgy connects these potential directions of research across the long span of the Iron Age. We return, in other words, to Rousseau's provocative meditation on the impact of iron technology on human communities. Does the advent of iron technology usher in a meaningful transformation in the social history of this region, such that it merits the determinative position it now occupies in the archaeological ordering of time? The challenge for future archaeological research into the Iron Age on the Armenian plateau is to open such questions concerning the social life during the age of iron even while continuing to refine still nascent frameworks of chronology and geography.

NOTES

This chapter benefited from the insights and data provided by Ruben Badalyan and Tony Sagona, and I am thankful to them both. Thanks are also due to Adam T. Smith for his close reading of the draft manuscript. I am especially grateful to Sharon Steadman and Gregory McMahon for inviting me to contribute to this volume and for their editorial input.

1. "Anatolia," in *Encyclopaedia Britannica* (2009), online. Accessed April 24, 2009.
2. Archaeologists who favor the term "eastern Anatolia" tend to set the limits of their inquiry at the eastern border of modern Turkey, whereas those who use "Armenian plateau" or "Armenian highland" have in mind an area that reaches further east, into the lesser Caucasus.
3. Scholars have identified grooved ware in the Elazığ region that was supposedly made on a slow wheel (Bartl 2001; Winn 1980). But as Courty and Roux (1995) show, it can be difficult to differentiate between wheelformed and wheelfinished pottery on the basis of surface features alone.
4. Ayanis and Van are among the only settlements in which grooved and red-burnished pottery co-occur (Kozbe, Çevik, and Sağlamtimur 2001; Sevin 1994; Tarhan 1994).
5. For a different reading of the stratigraphy see Sevin and Özfırat (2001).
6. Museum collections and publications would suggest that bronze predominates within the Urartian material assemblage. Iron, however, is more common for the kinds of utilitarian objects that have traditionally received less attention due to their mundane quality and their relatively poor state of preservation (Wartke 1991).
7. For a complete bibliography of the investigations at these and other Urartian fortresses as of 1998, see Zimansky (1998). See also Avetisyan and Avetisyan (2006).
8. For further discussions on the geography of Urartu and a comprehensive map, see Zimansky (1985:9) and Kleiss and Hauptmann (1976).

REFERENCES

Arutyunian, Nikolai V. 2001. *Korpus urartskikh klinoo'braznykh nadpisei*. Yerevan: Izdatel'stvo Gitutyun.

Avetisyan, Haik G. 1992. *Biainskaia keramika iz pamiatnikov Araratskoi doliny*. Yerevan: Izdatel'stvo Erevanskogo Universiteta.

Avetisyan, Haik G. and Pavel S. Avetisyan. 2006. *Araratyan dashti mshakuyte m.t.a. XI–VI tarerum*. Yerevan: Erevani hamalsarani hratarakjutyun.

Avetisyan, Pavel, Ruben Badalyan, Simon Hmayakyan, and Ashot Piliposyan. 1996. Hayastani bronz-erkati darashrchanneri parerayman ev zhamanakagrutyan hartseri shurj (H. Martirosyani sandghakn ardi hnagitutyan himnakhndirneri hamatekstum). In *Hayastani hanrapetutunum 1993–1995tt. hnagitakan hetazotutyunneri ardyunknner-in nvirvats 10-rd kitakan nstashrjan*, ed. Aram Kalantaryan, 8–10. Yerevan: HH GAA hnakitutyan ev azgagrutyan institut.

Avetisyan, Pavel, Nora Yengibaryan, and Gagik Sargsyan. 1998. Hayastani norahayt hnagitakan hushardzanner (Artashavani dambaranadasht). *Handes Amsorya* 1.12: 193–247.

Badaljan, Ruben S., Christopher Edens, Ronald Gorny, Philip L. Kohl, David Stronach, Armen V. Tonikjan, Simon Hamayakjan, Sergei Mandrikjan, and Mkrdich Zardarjan. 1993. Preliminary Report on the 1992 Excavations at Horom, Armenia. *Iran* 31: 1–24.

Badaljan, Ruben S., Christopher Edens, Philip L. Kohl, and Armen V. Tonikjan. 1992. Archaeological Investigations at Horom in the Shirak Plain of Northwestern Armenia, 1990. *Iran* 30: 31–48.

Badaljan, Ruben S., Philip L. Kohl, and Stephan Kroll. 1997. Bericht über die amerikanisch-armenisch-deutsche archäologische Expedition in Armenien. *Archäologische Mitteilungen aus Iran und Turan* 29: 191–228.

Badaljan, Ruben S., Philip L. Kohl, David Stronach, and Armen V. Tonikjan. 1994. Preliminary Report on the 1993 Excavations at Horom, Armenia. *Iran* 32: 1–29.

Badalyan, Ruben S. and Pavel S. Avetisyan. 2007. *Bronze and Early Iron Age Archaeological Sites in Armenia*. BAR International Series 1697. Oxford: Archaeopress.

Badalyan, Ruben S., Pavel Avetisyan, and Adam T. Smith. 2009. Periodization and Chronology of Southern Caucasia: From the Early Bronze Age through the Iron II Period. In *The Archaeology and Geography of Ancient Transcaucasian Societies: Vol. I Regional Survey in the Tsaghkahovit Plain, Armenia*, ed. Adam T. Smith, Ruben S. Badalyan, and Pavel Avetisyan, 33–93. Chicago: Oriental Institute Press.

Badalyan, Ruben, Adam T. Smith, and Pavel Avetisyan. 2003. The Emergence of Socio-Political Complexity in Southern Caucasia. In *Archaeology in the Borderlands: Investigations in Caucasia and Beyond*, ed. Adam T. Smith and Karen S. Rubinson, 144–66. Los Angeles: Cotsen Institute of Archaeology.

Bakır, Güven and Altan Çilingiroğlu. 1987. Kaleköy (Baskil) Excavations, 1979. In *Aşağı Fırat Projesi 1978–1979 Çalışmaları*, 169–75. Ankara: Orta Doğu Teknik Üniversitesi Aşağı Fırat Projesi Yayınları.

Bartl, Karin. 1988. *Norşun-Tepe: Die frühe Eisenzeit*. Berlin: Freie Universität Berlin.

———. 1995. Some Remarks on Early Iron Age in Eastern Anatolia. *Anatolica* 21: 207–12.

———. 2001. Eastern Anatolia in the Early Iron Age. In *Migration und Kulturtransfer: der Wandel vorder- und zentralasiatischer Kulturen im Umbruch vom 2. zum 1. vorchristlichen Jahrtausend: Akten des Internationalen Kolloquiums, Berlin, 23. bis 26. November 1999*, ed. Ricardo Eichmann and Hermann Parzinger, 383–410. Bonn: Habelt.

Belli, Oktay. 2001. An Early Iron Age Cemetery in the Van Region: Ernis-Evditepe. In *Istanbul University's Contributions to Archaeology in Turkey (1932–2000)*, ed. Oktay Belli, 145–49. İstanbul: Istanbul University Rectorate.

———. 2005. Research on Early Iron Age Fortresses and Necropoleis in Eastern Anatolia. In *Anatolian Iron Ages 5: Proceedings of the Fifth Anatolian Iron Ages Colloquium Held at Van, August 6–10, 2001*, ed. Altan Çilingiroğlu and Gareth Darbyshire, 1–13. Ankara: British Insitute at Ankara.

Belli, Oktay and Ethan Konyar. 2001a. Archaeological Survey on Early Iron Age Fortresses and Necropoleis in northeast Anatolia. In *Istanbul University's Contributions to Archaeology in Turkey (1932–2000)*, ed. Oktay Belli, 331–35. İstanbul: Istanbul University Rectorate.

———. 2001b. Excavations at Van-Yoncatepe Fortress and Necropolis. *Tel Aviv* 28.2: 169–212.

———. 2001c. Excavations of Van-Yoncatepe Fortress and Necropolis (1997–1999). In *Istanbul University's Contributions to Archaeology in Turkey (1932–2000)*, ed. Oktay Belli, 150–56. İstanbul: Istanbul University Rectorate.

———. 2003a. *Doğu Anadolu Bölgesi'nde Erken Demir Çağı Kale ve Nekropolleri/Early Iron Age Fortresses and Necropoleis in East Anatolia*. İstanbul: Arkeoloji ve Sanat Yayınları.

———. 2003b. Ernis-Evditepe: The Largest Early Iron Age Necropolis in Eastern Anatolia. *Tel Aviv* 30.2: 167–203.

Bilgi, Önder. 1991. Iron Age Pottery from Köşkerbaba Höyük. In *Anatolian Iron Ages: The Proceedings of the Second Anatolian Iron Ages Colloquium held at Izmir, May 4–8, 1987*, ed. Altan Çilingiroğlu and David H. French, 11–28. Oxford: Oxbow Books.

———. 2001. Köşkerbaba Excavations. In *Istanbul University's Contributions to Archaeology in Turkey (1932–2000)*, ed. Oktay Belli, 110–14. İstanbul: Istanbul University Rectorate.

Biscione, Raffaele, Simon Hmayakyan, and Neda Parmegiani. 2002. *The North-Eastern Frontier: Urartians and Non-Urartians in the Sevan Lake Basin*. Rome: Istituto di studi sulle Civiltà dell'Egeo e del Vicino Oriente.

Buchli, Victor. 1999. *An Archaeology of Socialism*. Oxford: Berg.

Buchli, Victor and Gavin Lucas. 2001. *Archaeologies of the Contemporary Past*. London: Routledge.

Ceylan, Alparslan. 2005. The Erzincan, Erzurum and Kars Region in the Iron Age. In *Anatolian Iron Ages 5: Proceedings of the fifth Anatolian Iron Ages Colloquium held at Van, August 6–10, 2001*, ed. Altan Çilingiroğlu and Gareth Darbyshire, 21–29. London: British Institute at Ankara.

Cherry, John F., Sturt W. Manning, Susan E. Alcock, Armen V. Tonikyan, and Mkrdich H. Zardaryan. 2007. Radiocarbon Dates for the Second and First Millennia B.C. from Southern Armenia: Preliminary Results from the Vorotan Project 2005–2006. *Aramazd: Armenian Journal of Near Eastern Studies* 2: 52–71.

Courty, Marie-Agnès and Valentine Roux. 1995. Identification of Wheel Throwing on the Basis of Ceramic Surface Features and Micro-Fabrics. *Journal of Archaeological Science* 22.1: 1–29.

Çevik, Özlem. 2008. Periodization Criteria for Iron Age Chronology in Eastern Anatolia and Neighboring Regions. *Ancient Near Eastern Studies* 45: 1–20.

Çilingiroğlu, Altan. 1991. The Early Iron Age at Dilkaya. In *Anatolian Iron Ages: The Proceedings of the Second Anatolian Iron Ages Colloquium held at İzmir, May 4–8, 1987*, ed. Altan Çilingiroğlu and David H. French, 29–38. Oxford: Oxbow Books.

———. 2001. Migration in the Lake Van Basin: East Anatolia in the Late 2nd Millennium B.C. and the Foundation of a Kingdom. In *Migration und Kulturtransfer: Der Wandel vorder- und zentralasiatischer Kulturen im Umbruch vom 2. zum 1. vorchristlichen Jahrtausend. Akten des Internationalen Kolloquiums Berlin, 23. bis 26. November 1999*, ed. Ricardo Eichmann and Hermann Parzinger, 371–81. Bonn: Habelt.

Devedzhyan, Seda G. 1981. *Lori berd I*. Yerevan: H.H.G.A.A. Gitutyun Hratarakchutyun.

Dusinberre, Elspeth R.M. 1999. Satrapal Sardis: Achaemenid Bowls in an Achaemenid Capital. *American Journal of Archaeology* 103.1: 73–102.

Dyson, Robert H. 1999a. The Achaemenid Painted Pottery of Hasanlu IIIA. *Anatolian Studies* 49: 101–10.

———. 1999b. Triangle-Festoon Ware Reconsidered. *Iranica Antiqua* 34: 115–44.

Erdem, Aylin Ü. and Atilla Batmaz. 2008. Contributions of the Ayanis Fortress to Iron Age Chronology. *Ancient Near Eastern Studies* 45: 65–84.

Esayan, Sergei A. 1967. *Katalog arkheologicheskikh predmetov Museia Istorii Goroda Erevana* 2. Yerevan: Sostavitel'.

———. 1976. *Drevnaia kul'tura plemen severo-vostochnoi Armenii (III–I tyc. do n.e.) (The Ancient Culture of the Tribes of Northeastern Armenia [3rd–1st millennium BC]).* Yerevan: Izdatel'stvo Akademii Nauk Armianskoi SSR.

Esayan, Sergei A. and Aram Kalantarian. 1988. *Oshakan*. Yerevan: Izdatel'svto Akademii Nauk Armianskoi SSR.

Esayan, Sergei A. and G. A. Oganesyan. 1969. *Katalog arkheologicheskikh predmetov Dilizhansckogo Muzeya*. Yerevan: Akademiia Nauk Armianskoe SSR.

French, David H. and Geoffrey D. Summers. 1994. Pre-Urartian and Urartian Pottery from the Muş Region. *Anatolian Studies* 44: 77–84.

Hauptmann, Harald. 1969/70. Norşuntepe: Historische Geographie und Ergebnisse der Grabungen 1968/69. *Istanbuler Mitteilungen* 19–20: 21–78.

Hewsen, Robert H. 1983. Introduction to Armenian Historical Geography II: the boundaries of Achaemenid "Armina." *Revue des Études Arméniennes* 17: 123–43.

Hmayakyan, Simon. 2002. The Urartians on the Southern Coast of the Lake Sevan. In *The North-Eastern Frontier: Urartians and Non-Urartians in the Sevan Lake Basin*, ed. Raffaele Biscione, Simon Hmayakyan, and Neda Parmegiani, 277–300. Rome: Istituto di studi sulle Civiltà dell'Egeo e del Vicino Oriente.

Işık, Cengiz. 1987. Habibuşağı Nekropolü. *Belleten* 51.200: 85–89.

Işıklı, Mehmet. 2008. Recent Investigations at Pulur (Erzurum): Observations on North-east Anatolian Ceramics. In *Ceramics in Transitions: Chalcolithic through Iron Age in the Highlands of the Southern Caucasus and Anatolia*, ed. Karen S. Rubinson and Antonio Sagona, 267–89. Leuven: Peeters.

Işıklı, Mehmet and Birol Can. 2007. The Erzurum Region in the Early Iron Age: New Observations. In *Anatolian Iron Ages 6: The Proceedings of the Sixth Anatolian Iron Ages Colloquium Held at Eskişehir, August 16–20, 2004*, ed. Altan Çilingiroğlu and Antonio Sagona, 153–66. Leuven: Peeters.

Jacobs, Bruno. 1994. *Die Satrapienverwaltung im Perserreich zur Zeit Darius' III. Beihefte zum Tübinger Atlas des Vorderen Orients*. Reihe B, Geisteswissenschaften no. 87. Wiesbaden: L. Reichert.

———. 2006. Achaemenid Satrapies. Online at Iranica.com.

Kafadaryan, Koryun. 1984. *Argishtihinili kaghaki chartarapetutyune*. Yerevan: Hakakan SSH GA Hratarakchutyun.

Karapetyan, Inesa A. 1971. M.t.a. VI–III dareri vagh haykakan taseri mi khumb. *Patma-banasirakan handes* 3.54: 276–80.

———. 1978. Raskopki karchakhpiura. *Arkheologicheskie otkrytiia* 1977g: 523.

———. 1979. Raskopki karchakhpiura. *Arkheologicheskie otkrytiia* 1978g: 268–77.

———. 2003. *Hayastani nyutakan mshakuyte m.t.a. VI–IV dd.* Yerevan: H.H.G.A.A. Gitutyun Hratarakchutyun.

Khachatryan, Telemak S. 1975. *Drevniaia kul'tura Shiraka*. Yerevan: Yerevan State University.

———. 1979. *Artikskii nekropol': katalog*. Yerevan: Yerevan State University.

Khachatryan, Zhores D. 1970. Hayastani m.t.a. VII–I dareri khetsegheni bnorosh mi dzev. *Patma-banasirakan handes* 1: 269–78.

Khanzadyan, Emma V., Koryun H. Mkrtchian, and Elma S. Parsamian. 1973. *Metsamor: Usumnasirut'yun 1965–1966 t't' peghumneri tvyalnerov*. Yerevan: Akademiia Nauk Armianskoe SSR.

Khatchadourian, Lori. 2008. *Social Logics under Empire: The Armenian "Highland Satrapy" and Achaemenid Rule, ca. 600–300 BC*. Ph.D. dissertation. University of Michigan, Ann Arbor.

———. Forthcoming. An Archaeology of Hegemony: The Achaemenid Empire and the Remaking of the Fortress in the Armenian Highlands. In *Empires and Complexity: On the Crossroads of Archaeology, History, and Anthropology*, ed. Gregory Areshian. Los Angeles: Cotsen Institute of Archaeology.

Kleiss, Wolfram. 1973. Planaufnahmen Urartäischer Burgen in Iranisch-Azerbaidjan im Jahre 1972. *Archaeologische Mitteilungen aus Iran* 6: 81–89.

———. 1974. Planaufnahmen Urartäischer Burgen. *Archaeologische Mitteilungen aus Iran* 7: 79–106.

———. 1975. Planaufnahmen Urartäisher Burgen und Urartäische Neufunde in Iranisch-Azerbaidjan im Jahre 1974. *Archaeologische Mitteilungen aus Iran* 8: 51–70.

———. 1979a. Zum Stand der Urartu-Forschung in Iran. *Archäologischer Anzeiger* 145–57.

———. ed. 1979b. *Bastam I: Ausgrabungen in den Urartäischen Anlagen 1972–1975*. Berlin: Mann.

———. 1980. Bastam: An Urartian Citadel Complex of the Seventh Century B.C. *American Journal of Archaeology* 84.3: 299–304.

———, ed. 1988. *Bastam II: Ausgrabungen in den Urartäischen Anlagen 1976–1978, Teheraner Forschungen V.* Berlin: Mann.

———. 1994. Notes on the Chronology of Urartian Defensive Architecture. In *Anatolian Iron Ages 3: The Proceedings of the Third Anatolian Iron Ages Colloquium Held at Van, August 6–12, 1990*, ed. Altan Çilingiroğlu and David H. French, 131–37. Ankara: British Institute of Archaeology at Ankara.

Kleiss, Wolfram and Harald Hauptmann. 1976. *Topographische Karte von Urartu: Verzeichnis der Fundorte und Bibliographie*. Berlin: Reimer.

Kleiss, Wolfram and Stephan Kroll. 1976. Zwei Plätze des 6. Jahrhunderts v. Chr. in iranisch Azerbaidjan. *Archaeologische Mitteilungen aus Iran* 9: 107–24.

———. 1979. Vermessene Urartäische Plätze in Iran (West Azerbaidjan) und Neufunde (Stand der Forschung 1978). *Archaeologische Mitteilungen aus Iran* 12: 183–243.

Kohl, Philip L. and Stephan Kroll. 1999. Notes on the Fall of Horom. *Iranica Antiqua* 34: 243–59.

Konyar, Ethan. 2005. Grooved Pottery of the Lake Van Basin: A Stratigraphical and Chronological Assessment. *Colloquium Anatolicum* 4: 105–27.

Kozbe, Gülriz, Özlem Çevik, and Haluk Sağlamtimur. 2001. Pottery. In *Ayanis I: Ten Years' Excavations at Rusahinili Eiduru-kai 1989–1998*, ed. Altan Çilingiroğlu and Mario Salvini, 85–153. Roma: Istituto per gli Studi Micenei ed Egeo-Anatolici.

Köroğlu, Kemaletin. 2003. The Transition from Bronze Age to Iron Age in Eastern Anatolia. In *Identifying Changes: The Transition from Bronze to Iron Ages in Anatolia and its Neighbouring Regions: Proceedings of the International Workshop, Istanbul, November 8–9, 2002*, ed. Bettina Fischer, Hermann Genz, Éric Jean, and Kemaletin Köroğlu, 231–44. İstanbul: Türk Eskiçağ Bilimleri Enstitüsü.

———. 2005. The Northern Border of the Urartian kingdom. In *Anatolian Iron Ages 5: Proceedings of the Fifth Anatolian Iron Ages Colloquium Held at Van, August 6–10, 2001*, ed. Altan Çilingiroğlu and Gareth Darbyshire, 99–106. Ankara: British Institute at Ankara.

Köroğlu, Kemaletin and Ethan Konyar. 2008. Comments on the Early/Middle Iron Age Chronology of Lake Van Basin. *Ancient Near Eastern Studies* 45: 123–46.

Kroll, Stephan. 1975. Ein Schüssel der Triangle Ware aus Azerbaidschan. *Archaeologische Mitteilungen aus Iran* 8: 71–74.

———. 1976. *Keramik Urartäischer Festungen in Iran. Vol. Ergänzungsband 2, Archaeologische Mitteilungen aus Iran*. Berlin: Reimer.

———. 1984. Urartus Untergang in anderer Sicht. *Istanbuler Mitteilungen* 34: 151–70.

———. 2000. Nordwest-Iran in Achaimenidischer Zeit: Zur Verbreitung der Classic Triangle Ware. *Archäologische Mitteilungen aus Iran und Turan* 32: 131–37.

Kuniholm, Peter I. and Maryanne W. Newton. 2001. Dendrochronological Investigations at Ayanis: Dating the Fortress of Rusa II: Rusahinili Eiduru-Kai. In *Ayanis I: Ten Years' Excavations at Rusahinili Eiduru-kai*, ed. Altan Çilingiroğlu and Mario Salvini, 377–79. Rome: Istituto per gli Studi Micenei ed Egeo-Anatolici.

Kushnareva, Karine K. 1977. *Drevneishie pamiatniki Dvina*. Yerevan: Academiia Nauk.

Leone, Mark P. and Parker B. Potter. 1999. *Historical Archaeologies of Capitalism*. New York: Kluwer Academic/Plenum Publishers.

Lucas, Gavin. 2005. *The Archaeology of Time*. London: Routledge.

Marro, Catherine and Aynur Özfırat. 2003. Pre-Classical Survey in Eastern Turkey, First Preliminary Report: The Agri Dag (Mount Ararat) Region. *Anatolia Antiqua* 11: 385–422.

———. 2004. Pre-Classical Survey in Eastern Turkey, Second Preliminary Report: The Ercis Region. *Anatolia Antiqua* 12: 227–66.

———. 2005. Pre-Classical Survey in Eastern Turkey, Third Preliminary Report: Doğubeyazit and the Eastern Shore of Lake Van. *Anatolia Antiqua* 13: 319–56.

Martirosyan, Harutyun. 1954. *Raskopki v Golovino: rezul'taty rabot 1929 i 1950gg*. Yerevan: Izdatel'stvo Akademiia Nauk Armyanskoi SSR.

———. 1961. *Gorod Teishebaini: po raskopkam 1947–1958gg*. Yerevan: Akademiya Nauk Armyanskoi SSR.

———. 1964. *Armenia v epochu bronzi i rannego zheleza*. Yerevan: Akademiia Nauk Arianskoi SSR.

McConchie, Matasha. 2004. *Archaeology at the North-East Anatolian Frontier, V: Iron Technology and Iron-Making Communities of the First Millennium BC*. Leuven: Peeters.

Müller, Uwe. 2005. Norşun Tepe and Lidar Höyük: Two Examples for Cultural Change during the Early Iron Age. In *Anatolian Iron Ages 5: Proceedings of the Fifth Anatolian Iron Ages Colloquium Held at Van, August 6–10, 2001*, ed. Altan Çilingiroğlu and Gareth Darbyshire, 107–14. Ankara: British Institute at Ankara.

Newton, Maryanne W. and Peter I. Kuniholm. 2007. A Revised Dendrochronological Date for the Fortress of Rusa II at Ayanis: Rusahinili Eiduru-Kai. In *Anatolian Iron Ages 6: The Proceedings of the Sixth Anatolian Iron Age Colloquium Held at Eskişehir, August 16–20, 2004*, ed. Altan Çilingiroğlu and Antonio Sagona, 195–206. Leuven: Peeters.

Ökse, Tuba A. 1988. *Mitteleisenzeitliche Keramik Zentral-Ostanatoliens mit dem Schwerpunkt Karakaya-Stauseegebiet am Euphrat*. Berlin: D. Reimer.

———. 1992. İmamoğlu in der Eisenzeit: Keramik. *Istanbuler Mitteilungen* 42: 31–66.

Palanjyan, Ruzanna. 2008. Tagavoranisti m.t.a. VII–V khetsegheni shurj. *Hin haiastani mshakuyte* 14: 175–80.

Parker, Anna. 1999. Northeastern Anatolia: On the Periphery of Empires. *Anatolian Iron Ages 4. Proceedings of the Fourth Anatolian Iron Ages Colloquium Held at Mersin, May 19–23, 1997. Anatolian Studies* 49: 133–41.

Pecorella, Paolo E. and Mirjo Salvini. 1984. *Tra lo Zagros e l'Urmia: Ricerche storiche ed archeologiche nell'Azerbaigian iraniano*. Roma: Edizioni dell'Ateneo.

Rothman, Mitchell. 2004. Beyond the Frontiers: Muş in the Late Bronze to Roman Periods. In *A View from the Highlands: Archaeological Studies in Honour of Charles Burney*, ed. Antonio Sagona, 121–78. Dudley, Mass.: Peeters.

Rousseau, Jean Jacques. 1987 [1755]. Discourse on the Origin of Inequality. In *Jean-Jacques Rousseau: The Basic Political Writings*, 25–109. Indianapolis, Ind.: Hackett.

Sagona, Antonio. 1999. The Bronze Age–Iron Age Transition in Northeast Anatolia: A View from Sos Höyük. *Anatolian Iron Ages 4: Proceedings of the Fourth Anatolian Iron Ages Colloquium held at Mersin, May 19–23, 1997. Anatolian Studies* 49: 153–57.

Sagona, Antonio, Mustafa Erkmen, Claudia Sagona, and Sarah Howells. 1997. Excavations at Sos Höyük, 1996: Third Preliminary Report. *Anatolica* 23: 181–226.

Sagona, Antonio, Mustafa Erkmen, Claudia Sagona, and Ian Thomas. 1996. Excavations at Sos Höyük, 1995: Second Preliminary Report. *Anatolian Studies* 46: 27–52.

Sagona, Antonio, Elizabeth Pemberton, and Ian McPhee. 1993. Excavations at Büyüktepe Höyük, 1992: Third Preliminary Report. *Anatolian Studies* 43: 69–83.

Sagona, Antonio, Claudia Sagona, and Hilmi Özkorucuklu. 1995. Excavations at Sos Höyük, 1994: First Preliminary Report. *Anatolian Studies* 45: 193–218.

Sagona, Antonio and Claudia Sagona. 2004a. An Archaeological Survey of the Bayburt Province. In *Archaeology at the North-East Anatolian Frontier, I: An Historical Geography and a Field Survey of the Bayburt Province*, ed. Antonio Sagona and Claudia Sagona, 111–233. Leuven: Peeters.

———. eds. 2004b. *Archaeology at the North-East Anatolian Frontier, I: An Historical Geography and Field Survey of the Bayburt Province*. Leuven: Peeters.

Sagona, Antonio G. and Paul Zimansky. 2009. *Ancient Turkey*. London: Routledge.

Sagona, Claudia. 1999. A Survey of the Erzurum Province, 1999: The Region of Pasinler. *Ancient Near Eastern Studies* 36: 108–31.

———. 2004. Literary Tradition and Topographic Commentary. In *Archaeology at the North-east Anatolian Frontier, I: An Historical Geography and Field Survey of the Bayburt Province*, ed. Antonio Sagona and Claudia Sagona, 25–71. Leuven: Peeters.

Salvini, Mirjo. 2009. *Corpus dei testi urartei: Le iscrizioni su pietra e roccia*. Rome: Istituto di studi sulle Civiltà dell'Egeo e del Vicino Oriente.

Sevin, Veli. 1991. The Early Iron Age in the Elazığ Region and the Problem of the Mushkians. *Anatolian Studies* 41: 87–97.

———. 1994. The Excavations at the Van Castle Mound. In *Anatolian Iron Ages 3: The Proceedings of the Third Anatolian Iron Ages Colloquium Held at Van, August 6–12, 1990*, ed. Altan Çilingiroğlu, 221–28. Ankara: British Institute of Archaeology.

———. 1999. The Origins of the Urartians in the Light of the Van/Karagündüz Excavations. *Anatolian Studies (Anatolian Iron Ages 4)* 49: 159–64.

———. 2002. Late Iron Age Pottery of the Van Region Eastern Anatolia: In the Light of the Karagündüz Excavations. In *Mauerschau: Festschrift für Manfred Korfmann*, ed. Rüstem Aslan, Stephan Blum, Gabriele Kastl, Frank Schweizer, and Diane Thumm, 474–82. Remshalden-Grunbach: Greiner.

———. 2004. Pastoral Tribes and Early Settlements of the Van Region, Eastern Anatolia. In *A View from the Highlands: Archaeological Studies in Honour of Charles Burney*, ed. Antonio Sagona, 179–203. Dudley, Mass.: Peeters.

Sevin, Veli and Ersin Kavaklı. 1996. *Bir Erken Demir Çağı Nekropolü Van/Karagündüz. An Early Iron Age Cemetery*. İstanbul: Arkeoloji ve Sanat Yayınları.

Sevin, Veli and Aynur Özfırat. 2001. Van-Karagündüz Excavations. In *Istanbul University's Contributions to Archaeology in Turkey (1932–2000)*, ed. Oktay Belli, 140–44. İstanbul: Istanbul University Rectorate.

Smith, Adam T. 1996. *Imperial Archipelago: The Making of the Urartian Landscape in Southern Transcaucasia*. Tucson: Department of Anthropology, University of Arizona.

———. 2009. Archaeology in Armenia: An Introduction to Project ArAGATS. In *The Archaeology and Geography of Ancient Transcaucasian Societies, vol. 1: The Foundations of Research and Regional Survey in the Tsaghkahovit Plain, Armenia*, ed. Adam T. Smith, Ruben S. Badalyan, and Pavel Avetisyan. Oriental Institute Publications 134. Chicago: Oriental Institute.

———. Forthcoming. The Prehistory of the Urartian Landscape. In *Biainili-Urartu*, ed. Stephan Kroll, Paul Zimansky, Ursula Hellwag, Claudia Gruber, and Michael Roaf. Leuven: Peeters.

Smith, Adam T., Ruben Badalyan, and Pavel Avetisyan. 2009. *The Archaeology and Geography of Ancient Transcaucasian Societies, vol. 1: The Foundations of Research and Regional Survey in the Tsaghkahovit Plain, Armenia*. Oriental Institute Publications 134. Chicago: Oriental Institute.

Steele, Laura. 2008. Urartu and the *Medikos Logos* of Herodotus. *American Journal of Ancient History* 2.2: 5–16.

Stone, Elizabeth C. and Paul Zimansky. 2003. The Urartian Transformation in the Outer Town of Ayanis. In *Archaeology in the Borderlands: Investigations in Southern Caucasia and Beyond*, ed. Adam T. Smith and Karen S. Rubinson, 213–28. Los Angeles: Cotsen Institute of Archaeology.

Stronach, David. 1974. Achaemenid Village I at Susa and the Persian Migration to Fars. *Iraq* 26: 239–48.

Summers, Geoffrey D. 1993. Archaeological Evidence for the Achaemenid Period in Eastern Turkey. *Anatolian Studies* 43: 85–105.

Tarhan, Taner. 1989. Van Kalesi ve Eski Van Şehri Kazıları, 1987. *Kazı Sonuçları Toplantısı* 10.1: 369–428.

———. 1994. Recent Research at the Urartian Capital Tushpa. *Tel Aviv* 21.1: 22–57.

Tarhan, Taner and Veli Sevin. 1990. Van Kalesi ve Eski Van Şehri Kazıları, 1988. *Kazı Sonuçları Toplantısı* 11.1: 355–75.

———. 1991. Van Kalesi ve Eski Van Şehri Kazıları;, 1989. *Kazı Sonuçları Toplantısı* 12.1: 429–56.

Ter-Martirosov, Felix I. 2001. The Typology of the Columnar Structures of Armenia in the Achaemenid Period. In *The Royal Palace Institution in the First Millennium BC*, ed. Inge Nielsen, 155–63. Aarhus: Aarhus University Press.

Ter-Martirosov, Felix I. and Stéphane Deschamps. 2007. Données récentes sur l'Arménie et l'empire perse achéménide. *Les dossiers d'archéologie* mai-juin 2007: 68–72.

Thomsen, Christian J. 1836. Kortfattet udsigt over mindesmærker og oldsager fra Nordens oldtid. In *Ledetraad til Nordisk Oldkyndighed*, ed. C. C. Rafn, 27–90. Copenhagen: Kgl. Nordisk Oldskriftselskab.

Tiratsyan, Gevork A. 1960. Arin-berdi syunazard dahlije ev satrapakan kentronneri hartse Haykakan lernashkharhum. *Teghekagir hasarakakan kitutyunneri* 7–8: 99–114.

———. 1980. Yervandyan Hayastani taratske (m.t.a. 6-rd dar). *Patma-banasirakan handes* 4: 84–95.

———. 1981. Yervandyan Hayastani taratske (m.t.a. 6-rd dari verch-3-rt dari verch). *Patma-banasirakan handes* 2: 68–84.

———. 2003 [1965]. On Painted Pottery in Ancient Armenia. In *From Urartu to Armenia: Florilegium Gevork A. Tirats'yan*, ed. R. Vardanyan, 104–14. Neuchatêl: Recherches et Publications.

Torosyan, Rafik M., Onnik S. Khnkikyan, and Levon A. Petrosyan. 2002. *Hin Shirakavan (1977–1981 tt. peghumneri ardyunknere)*. Yerevan: Haiastani Hanrapetutyun Gitutyunneri Azgayin Akademia "Gitutyun."

van Loon, Maurits N. 1978. *Korucutepe: Final Report on the Excavations of the Universities of Chicago, California (Los Angeles) and Amsterdam in the Keban Reservoir, Eastern Anatolia 1968–1970*, vol. 2. Amsterdam: North-Holland.

von der Osten, Hans H. 1952. Die Urartäische Töpferei aus Van und die Möglichkeiten ihrer Einordnung in die anatolische Keramik 1. *Orientalia* 21: 307–28.

———. 1953. Die Urartäische Töpferei aus Van und die Möglichkeiten ihrer Einordnung in die anatolische Keramik 2. *Orientalia* 22: 329–54.

Wartke, Ralf-Bernhard. 1991. Production of Iron Artifacts. In *Urartu: A Metalworking Center in the First Millennium B.C.E.*, ed. Rivka Merhav, 322–31. Tel Aviv: Sabinsky Press.

Winn, Milton W. 1980. The Early Iron Age Pottery. In *Korucutepe: Final Report on the Excavations of the Universities of Chicago, California (Los Angeles) and Amsterdam in the Keban Reservoir, Eastern Anatolia*, ed. Maurits N. van Loon, 155–75. Amsterdam: North-Holland.

Yakar, Jak. 2000. *Ethnoarchaeology of Anatolia: Rural Socio-Economy in the Bronze and Iron Ages*. Tel Aviv: Emery and Claire Yass Publications in Archaeology.

Yengibaryan, Nora. 2002. The Graves of the Urartian Period of Karchaghbyur. In *The North-Eastern Frontier: Urartians and Non-Urartians in the Sevan Lake Basin*, ed. Raffaele Biscione, Simon Hmayakyan, and Neda Parmegiani, 417–54. Rome: Istituto di studi sulle Civiltà dell'Egeo e del Vicino Oriente.

Zimansky, Paul E. 1985. *Ecology and Empire: The Structure of the Urartian State*. Chicago: Oriental Institute.

———. 1995. Urartian Material Culture as State Assemblage: An Anomaly in the Archaeology of Empires. *Bulletin of the American School of Oriental Research* 299/300: 103–15.

———. 1998. *Ancient Ararat: A Handbook of Urartian Studies*. Delmar, N.Y.: Caravan Books.

———. 2005. The Cities of Rusa II and the End of Urartu. In *Anatolian Iron Ages 5: Proceedings of the Fifth Anatolian Iron Ages Colloquium Held at Van, August 6–10, 2001*, ed. Altan Çilingiroğlu and Gareth Darbyshire, 235–40. London: British Institute at Ankara.

CHAPTER 21

THE GREEKS IN WESTERN ANATOLIA

ALAN M. GREAVES

PRIOR to the coming of Alexander, the west coast of Anatolia was home to numerous settlements that can be considered, at least by the end of the Greek Archaic Period (494 B.C.E.), to be predominantly "Greek." These coastal Anatolian states interacted as peers with the Greek states of the Aegean, becoming increasingly closely engaged in military and political matters in that region as a result of the Persian and Peloponnesian Wars. They also entered into alliances with Aegean islands to form regional groupings, including the Ionian League (with Chios and Samos) and the Dorian Hexapolis (with Kos and the Rhodian *poleis*).

Aegean cultural influence penetrated progressively further inland over time (Cook 1973; Marchese 1986). However, during the early Iron Age, Greek communities in Anatolia were largely (although not exclusively) limited to the western coastal region. Their cultural influence in the interior was relatively limited, only becoming dominant after Alexander (see Harl, chapter 34 in this volume). Nevertheless, evidence of Greek inspiration can be detected in certain aspects of Phrygian culture and along the south coast into Caria and Lycia from the later archaic period (sixth century B.C.E.) onward (see Roller, chapter 25 in this volume). However, the precise dating and direction of flow of cultural exchanges between the coastal Greeks and their Anatolian neighbors needs careful consideration; other than at a few key sites, there is a dearth of secure evidence from stratified locations inland to illustrate this process at work.

This chapter begins with an overview of the geographical context within which these Greek settlements existed and a discussion of the region's chronology. There follows a brief examination of the key sites of Old Smyrna, Phokaia, Miletos, and Knidos. Finally, three key themes in the archaeology of this region are examined:

the mythical and archaeological evidence for the coming of the Greeks to Anatolia, the nature of the relationship between Greeks and non-Greeks in the region, and the local identities of the settlements here.

Geography

The west coast of Anatolia is dominated by a series of long east-west-oriented peninsulae, extending out into the Aegean Sea and separated by wide bays and broad, flat valleys extending deep into the Anatolian interior. These valleys are drained by large river systems, which rapidly filled the flat shallow bays at their mouths with deposited alluvium. In geological terms this was a rapid process—rapid enough to be palpable to the ancient Greeks themselves (Pausanias 8.24.11). Greek settlements affected in this way included Ephesos, Miletos, Myous, and probably Priene, the archaic phase of which has yet to be located as it is presumably lost beneath the silt of the Maeander River. As a result of this process the modern landscapes of these former bays have been transformed into vast open plains ringed by redundant ancient harbor towns, long since separated from the sea, which makes it difficult to imagine what past landscapes originally looked like.

In their original configuration, these bays and peninsulae would have created a long coastal zone of liminal contact between the Greek cultural sphere of the Aegean and the periphery of the Anatolian mainland. In this region, the two were destined always to be closely associated, making the question of "when" Greek culture first came into contact with these Anatolian coastal regions a spurious one. Whenever there were "Greek" peoples in the islands of the Aegean, they would have been aware of and almost certainly actively engaged with the lands and peoples of the adjacent regions of Anatolia and vice versa. It is also necessary to consider the close cultural, political, and military ties that existed between these coastal Greeks and the major island states of Lesbos, Chios, Samos, and Rhodes. For the purposes of this general review, however, discussion will be limited to consideration of the coastal settlements of western Anatolia because they are well understood, even if precise details of their Anatolian contemporaries are not.

The question of how the Greek Aegean and Anatolian mainland cultures came into contact with one another is a more complex matter, one where geographical considerations are again important. Given the topographic features of the region outlined above, the sea was obviously always going to be a central feature of the Greek settlement in the region, as the mountainous ridges effectively prevented easy north–south communications. Control of good harbors, which are rare on the rocky, steep-sided peninsulae, was therefore important. Consequently, where good natural harborage existed, settlements sprang up early and flourished, in some cases for millennia, with the result that their earliest occupation levels are overlain by multiple settlement deposits, making extensive archaeological investigation of early levels difficult (Greaves 2007).

The valleys which these mountain ridges separate are broad, flat-bottomed, and steep-sided, and proximity to these played an important role in the historical development of the coastal Greeks; their value as trade routes and the role of harbors as nexuses of interaction between the Near East and the West should not be underestimated. In particular, Ephesos and Miletos appear to have particularly benefited from such positioning. The river systems that drained these three valleys were, from north to south: the Hermos (modern Gediz), the Caystor (modern Küçük Menderes), and the Maeander (modern Büyük Menderes). The Maeander River is the best known of these three river systems, with its big winding loops and unpassable upper reaches, although it was navigable in its lower courses (Herodotus 2.29, 7.26; Thonemann forthcoming).

Ultimately, these valleys and bays also marked the end of the large Greek city-states of the west coast as the progressive alluviation of the rivers that emptied out into the bays eventually led to the silting up of those crucial harbors and the abandonment of many cities. Over a period of centuries, population relocated to sites further along the coast that were not subject to alluviation (e.g., Ephesos to Kuşadası) or further inland away from the malarial lagoons of the advancing deltas (e.g., Miletos to Söke).

Chronology

The regions of the west coast of Anatolia and the Aegean islands have had cultural interactions and associations that predate the emergence of recognizable "Greek" culture in the region. Cycladic style figurines which date back as far as the Early Bronze Age have been found on the west coast of Anatolia, and influences of the Middle and Late Bronze Age Minoan and Mycenaean cultures of the Aegean and Greek mainland were present at certain locations on the western Anatolian coast (see Bryce, chapter 15 in this volume). However, understanding the chronology of the coastal region is complicated by the fact that this is the dividing line between two regional chronologies—that of the Aegean and that of Anatolia. This is not only a matter of the specifics of the terminology used (e.g., the Anatolian "Chalcolithic" versus the Aegean "Final Neolithic") but also one of chronological methodology. That is, whereas in the Aegean very precise pottery typologies have been developed and a great deal of work has been done on establishing an absolute chronology for the region, the corresponding Hittite chronology is a relative chronology derived from king lists and pottery typologies more limited than in the Aegean (Greaves 2007). Such chronological issues persist into the Iron Age, where it is difficult to relate the precise chronology of the painted pottery styles of mainland Greek centers such as Corinth and Athens to those of Anatolia (Greaves 2010:7–9).

It has only recently been possible to properly trace the chronological development of the local pottery typologies of the region, the so-called East Greek styles, because of new stratigraphic excavations at the major production center of Miletos. These excavations have shown that two of the region's most important pottery styles, Wild Goat (or "Animal Frieze"; see figure 21.1) and Fikellura, developed out of one another (Schlotzhauer 2007). Their chronology can now be related to the better understood mainland figured styles such as Corinthian, Black Figure, and Red Figure, creating a better chronological scheme for the region as a whole (Kerschner and Schlotzhauer 2005). Analysis of fabrics has also shown that there are numerous local production centers in the Greek cities of the west coast and in Caria (M. Akurgal et al. 2002; Kerschner et al. 2002). These new understandings make the painted pottery of the region one of the most useful dating tools for the Iron Age in Anatolia. Stylistically, the non-Greek pottery styles of western Anatolia were greatly inspired by those of the coastal Greeks, but this should not be read to imply any "artistic" or cultural superiority over these derivative local traditions, which were created within, and reflect, localized aesthetic and cultural traditions (Greaves 2010:210).

The dating of major horizons (usually destructions) in the Greek cities of western Anatolia has often relied on the interpretation of literary references. However, this is a fallible methodology in a region and a period that existed on the periphery of Greek history and therefore has only a restricted historical framework on which to hang such dates—as the Gordion redating proves (Voigt and Henrickson 2000). Whereas the Archaic Period on the Greek mainland starts in the eighth century B.C.E. and ends with the Persian invasion of Greece in 480 B.C.E., culminating in the sack of Athens, for western Anatolia a more appropriate end date for that era would be the Battle of Lade and resulting sack of Miletos in 494 B.C.E., an event that marked

Figure 21.1. Middle Wild Goat II (SiA Id) style stemmed dish decorated with ducks (© Garstang Museum of Archaeology at the University of Liverpool).

the end of the Ionian Revolt and resulted in destruction levels across several major sites and sanctuaries (Greaves 2010:xii). In the classical period, from Lade to the coming of Alexander, historical and epigraphic sources become more abundant (see Harl, chapter 34 in this volume).

Key Sites

It is clear on the basis of archaeological evidence that the major sites of the region were all well established by the eighth century B.C.E., but when and how they originated is much less certain. Discussion of these questions has often relied more heavily on the literary traditions of later Greek history and myth than it has on sound archaeological evidence (see discussion below). Whatever their origins, these sites provide us with an apparent wealth of archaeological evidence from over a century of excavations (figure 21.2). However, on closer examination this material is often late in date and published in piecemeal fashion.

Figure 21.2. The fountain near the theatre at Ephesus (photograph by Gertrude Bell 1899. © Gertrude Bell Photographic Archive at the University of Newcastle upon Tyne).

There were three groupings within the Greek settlements of the region: Aeolis, which extended south from the Troad to Smyrna and included the island of Lesbos; Ionia, which included the coastal settlements from Phokaia to Miletos and the islands of Samos and Chios; and, in the very southwest corner of Anatolia, the Dorian Hexapolis, which included Knidos, Rhodes, and Kos (see also Harl, chapter 34 in this volume). The following selection of key sites provides an indication of the nature of the evidence available.

Old Smyrna was originally part of Aeolis, but at some point in its history it evidently changed allegiance to become part of the Ionian bloc of states, an event that should lead us to question the rigidity of these regional constructs in the historical sources. Although extensively excavated over a long period of time, detailed final publications from Old Smyrna are few, and the site is not as well known and understood as it deserves to be. It is an early find spot for pottery from the Greek mainland, including Proto-Geometric, Geometric, Proto- and Early Corinthian, and Black Figure pottery (E. Akurgal 1983; Tuna-Nörling 1995). Extensive excavations, combined with the fact that the city was refounded elsewhere in the fourth century B.C.E. (the site known just as Smyrna) have resulted in a detailed understanding of the settlement plan. This appears to have included both rectangular and oval houses, a pattern that is also seen elsewhere in the region, including Aeolian Lesbos and Ionian Miletos (E. Akurgal 1983; Heilmeyer 1986; Lamb 1931/2:45; Spencer 1995). The site's temple of Athena has also been very important in understanding the chronology of temple building on a grand scale and regional architectural styles, for both of which the region is famous. In particular the column capitals from this building have been important in fixing the development of the Aeolian architectural style. Begun in the sub-Geometric Period, the temple had four phases and stood on a large raised podium approached by a polygonal masonry ramp (M. Akurgal 2007). Deposits from the temple include weapons and images of a winged Athena on pottery (Cook and Nicholls 1998; Villing 1998).

Phokaia is the most northerly city in the Ionian regional grouping, although it does not form a contiguous land bloc with its fellow Ionians, indicating the importance of the role of the sea as a means for connecting these groups. Although it was long suspected that Phokaia may have been a more important place than Herodotus's account of the Battle of Lade indicates, to which the city sent only three ships, it is only recently that excavations have pieced together an impression of the true extent of the city from excavations across the modern town of Eski Foça (Özyiğit 2006; Roebuck 1959:23). Remarkable features of the site are its defenses, sanctuaries, and burials (Özyiğit 2003). Although described by Herodotus (1.161–4), the city walls of Phokaia proved elusive until a nearly complete standing section of the walls was found incorporated into the Maltepe tumulus (figure 21.3). Here the wall is faced with finely carved stone blocks and equipped with a sloping forward glacis that is somewhat reminiscent of the defenses of Sardis and Kerkenes Dağ. Elsewhere the settings of the wall can be traced, cut into the bedrock, and it is calculated to have measured five kilometers in length in the early sixth century B.C.E. (Özyiğit 1994). The sanctuaries and burials of Phokaia displayed both Anatolian and Greek

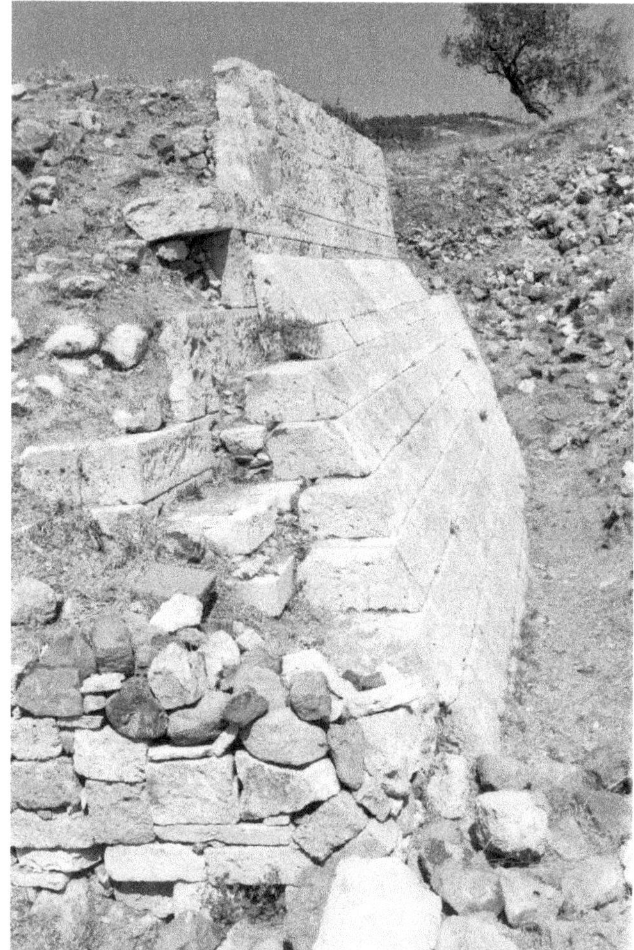

Figure 21.3. A standing section of the city walls of Phokaia, at Maltepe.

traditions. In addition to the temple of Athena, which overlooked the city's harbor, there are known to have been four sanctuaries to Cybele, one of which is directly beneath the temple of Athena and one on an island opposite the harbor entrance. In terms of burial practices, there are burials in terracotta sarcophagi, similar to the practice at the other Ionian city of Klazomenai, as well as non-Greek traditions. These reflect Lydian influence, in the burial tumulus at Maltepe and the rock-cut chambered tomb at Şeytan Hamamı, and Persian connections at the Taş Kule tomb (figure 21.4). This tower-like structure is carved from the standing bedrock and is dated to the mid-sixth century B.C.E.; it is related in its architecture to the Tomb of Cyrus in Iran (Cahill 1988). These monumental burials reflect the shifting allegiances, and possibly composition, of the ruling élite of Phokaia throughout the archaic and classical periods.

Miletos, the southernmost Ionian state, is crucial to understanding the history of the western Anatolian Greeks because of its long history of excavation (since 1899),

Figure 21.4. Taş Kule, near Phokaia.

numerous publications, pottery production (see foregoing discussion), and central role in major historical events (Cobet et al. 2007; Gorman 2001; Greaves 2002; and see Harl, chapter 34 in this volume). Milesian citizens were responsible for instigating and leading the Ionian Revolt of 499–494 B.C.E., a defining moment in the region's history, and through its numerous colonies the region's pottery and culture were spread widely in the Black Sea, Aegean, and eastern Mediterranean. Excavations at the domestic and artisans' quarter of Kalabaktepe have provided a stratigraphic sequence for occupation here (Senff 2007). In addition to establishing a pottery sequence for the region, these excavations have shown that the settlement here was originally undefended, only being walled in the third quarter of the seventh century B.C.E., and that it had a long settlement history, including at least one earthquake, prior to its destruction at the hands of the Persians. The site also has a number of important temples, such as that to Athena inside the city (Held 2000; von Gerkan 1925), Aphrodite just outside the city walls (Senff 2003), and Branchidai-Didyma deep in Milesian territory, fourteen kilometers to the south (Tuchelt 1991).

Knidos, during the archaic and classical periods, was located on the south side of a long peninsula that juts out into the Aegean between Kos and Rhodes at the site known today as Burgaz/Datça. Excavations at Burgaz/Datça have uncovered evidence of domestic dwellings and a street plan, whereas across the bay, within sight, stood a temple to Apollo Kerneios, at Emecik (Berges 2006). According to Herodotus (1.174), when the Persians threatened the city in 540 B.C.E., the defending Knidians attempted to cut through the narrow isthmus in an attempt to cut it off from the mainland. Although this effort was eventually abandoned, the episode does demonstrate the unique geography of this peninsula and the relative importance of the sea, that explains the close relationships that it developed with the adjacent island states. It was also the location of important sea battles during the classical period.

Key Themes

Migration Myths

One of the most abiding questions in the discussion of the archaeology of the Greeks in western Anatolia is how and when Greek communities first came to be in the region. In answer to this question, the ancient Greeks themselves had evidently created a set of migration myths and foundation stories that explained the origins of the major Greek communities of the west coast, the so-called Ionian Migration cycle of stories (Sakellariou 1958; Vanschoonwinkel 2006; and see Harl, chapter 34 in this volume). Although only committed to writing centuries, or possibly even a millennium or more, after the events that they purport to record, these myths were uncritically accepted as fact by earlier generations of scholars in their interpretations of the archaeology of the region (e.g., Kleiner 1966:14, on domestic structures at Miletos). Although modern scholarship has generally adopted more critical approaches, precisely how these myths should be accommodated into new readings of the archaeology of the region remains a bone of contention.

On one side are those scholars who freely accept the essential historicity of the Ionian Migration and work elements of it into their interpretations of the archaeology of the region (e.g., Kerschner, Kowalleck, and Steskal 2008 on the identification of Koressos in Ephesos). On the other are those who, although accepting the validity of the myths as an indicator of social and political attitudes at the time they were written down, argue that they have little or no relevance to the discussion of the earlier periods of history (e.g., Cobet 2007) and challenge traditional classical archaeological approaches that "fetishize" texts (Greaves 2010:224).

Midway between these two countervailing positions is the argument that certain kernels of historical truth about the arrival of the Greeks in Anatolia exist within the cycle of migration myths that can be proven by detailed reference to the extant archaeological evidence. However, the evidence needed to prove or disprove the historicity of this complex set of foundation stories has been slow to come to light, with the crucial periods in question—the transition from the Late Bronze Age to the early Iron Age, the Mycenaean LH III, the Sub-Mycenaean, and Proto-Geometric Periods—proving to be elusive at many sites. Excavations in recent decades have greatly increased our understanding of these periods, and it is now possible to make a more critical assessment of the relationship between myth and archaeology. Irene Lemos (2002, 2007) has used such a critical archaeological approach to argue that core elements of the foundation myths, such as the mixed composition of the Greek settlers (Herodotus 1.146) and the initial cause of the outward migration from mainland Greece, might reasonably be accepted as historical facts. Another core "fact" of the migrations is that a number of the foundation stories record that there was a pre-Greek population at these sites and that the Ionian Migration was not a virgin soil foundation (Miletos [Herodotus 1.146]; Ephesos [Athenaios 8.62.361 ap. Kreophylos]). This is apparently confirmed by archaeological evidence that is suggestive of continuity of settlement and cult practice from the Bronze Age through to the early Iron Age, at sites such as Miletos (Niemeier 2005) and Ephesos (Bammer 1990), and by enduring elements of pre-Greek Anatolian cultural practice (Greaves 2010).

The single factor that most limits the resolution of this long-running debate is the lack of extensive stratigraphic excavations of the earliest levels of the region's key sites. This is a situation that has multiple causes and is not easily remedied (Greaves 2007). Until such time as definitive archaeological evidence is available, individual scholars' acceptance, accommodation, or outright rejection of elements of later textual source materials into their interpretive frameworks is likely to remain more an article of faith than agreed methodology.

Greeks and Non-Greeks in Western Anatolia

If taken as a template for Greek–Anatolian interactions in the region, foundation myths such as the Ionian Migration would appear to suggest that a rapid influx of militarily and culturally superior Greeks swept aside pre-existing populations in the region. However, on closer analysis of the archaeological evidence this initial picture breaks down. Whereas in the historical traditions there are repeated references to struggle with the indigenous Anatolian populations of the major sites of the migration period, such references can be reframed as a motif of "suffering" within the template of foundation stories of the Athenian literary tradition of the fifth century B.C.E. (Greaves 2010:222–23).

When viewed over a longer historical timeframe and through archaeological and not just historical means, the interaction between Greek and non-Greek populations in the region can be cast not as a conflict between two diametrically opposed cultural and ethnic groups but as a complex, centuries-long process of adaptation in which the Greeks were only one element (Greaves 2010 passim, esp. 225–27). The late adoption of extensive field survey as a means to supplement and contextualize the understanding of key sites achieved by a century of excavations has succeeded in identifying a number of important "Phrygian"-style rock-cut cult installations in the near territories and urban peripheries of the key sites of Ephesos, Priene, Erythrai, Miletos, Phokaia, and elsewhere (Greaves 2010:193–97).

The net result of this new analysis is an image of the local "Greek" cultures of western Anatolia as dynamic and adaptive communities that could accommodate into themselves the presence of new ruling élites from within Anatolia (see Harl, chapter 34 in this volume). This can be seen in the adoption of Lydian-style tumulus burials at Phokaia, Klazomenai, and Ephesos during the period of Lydian rule over the region (Özyiğit 2003; Ersoy 2007; Bammer 2007, respectively) and the Persian style tomb at Taş Kule, near Phokaia (see previous discussion). However, it was not only the culture of the predominant powers that was in evidence in the material record of the region. During the period of Persian rule, Attic Greek influence can be seen to appear in the pottery and possibly even burial traditions of these western Anatolian communities (Berlin and Lynch 2002; von Graeve 1989, respectively).

Teasing out the complex interactions of cultures in Iron Age western Anatolia and the position of the Greek culture within that mix is, therefore, a complex matter, and rigid adherence to Greek historical texts as the starting point of any analysis can only serve to provide a single perspective on the region's complex cultural history.

Regional and Local Identities of the Western Anatolian Greeks

The Greek states of western Anatolia are sometimes collectively referred to as the "East Greeks." However, such terminology not only relegates them to being a regional subdivision of the core Greek world of the Aegean and the Greek peninsula, it can also give the reader the spurious impression that they had a single, recognizable, and common identity. As the foregoing discussions illustrate, to conceive of the Greek communities of western Anatolia as monoculturally "Greek" would not only ignore the significant differences that existed between them in key aspects of their material culture, such as their pottery, but would also misrepresent our current understanding of the situation in contemporary mainland Greece, where the importance of distinctive local characteristics during the Archaic Period is now widely recognized (Hall 1997). The only meaningful way to understand these communities is therefore as a series of fiercely independent political entities, each with its own identity and traditions.

The three main divisions within the Greeks of western Anatolia, that is, into Aeolian, Ionian, and Dorian, were first known to have been defined in the fifth century B.C.E., several centuries after these groups allegedly first arrived, and were defined on the basis of dialectal differences that could be perceived between them (Herodotus 1.142). Even within these three dialect groups, local dialectal variations existed, with Herodotus differentiating four local Ionian dialects: the "Carian," "Lydian," "North Island," and "Samian." However, on closer analysis, these regional dialects can be shown to have had complex origins that defy simplistic explanations as a single migration movement (Parker 2008; Rose 2008).

In addition to their dialect, these regional groupings are often associated with distinctive schools of architecture (Koenigs 2007; and see Harl, chapter 34 in this volume). Although the Doric architectural style appears to have been established by the sixth century B.C.E., the Ionian school did not become clearly established until the fifth century B.C.E. The distinctive fluted columns and "frontality" that were to become such a feature of this "Ionic" school of architecture were not in evidence during the Archaic Period, and the major archaic temples of Artemis at Ephesos and Apollo at Branchidai-Didyma had unfluted columns decorated with human figural reliefs. There may also have been Anatolian influence on the design of some of the temples of the coastal Greeks, such as the hypaethral (open-air) formation of the temple of Apollo at Branchidai-Didyma, which shares similarities with the design of the Urartian temples of eastern Anatolia (Greaves 2002:111–14). Neither were all religious structures in the region built temple structures, as in recent years a number of relief decorated niches have been identified on the west coast, which if found in central Anatolia might be described as "Phrygian" in style (Greaves 2010:195–97). The formulation of an Ionic school of architecture and indeed an Ionian regional identity itself can therefore be argued to be a relatively late development (Greaves 2010:175–76).

Another feature of the region's temples that sets it apart from those elsewhere in the Greek world is their sheer scale. The Ionian temples of Ephesos, Didyma, and Samos (an Ionian island state) were the biggest in the Greek world. There are a number of explanations that may account for this fact, such as the wealth of these states and the availability of the raw materials for temple construction. Anthony Snodgrass (1986) has suggested that the size of Greek temples was a product of the way contemporary states engaged in competitive emulation with one another by means of peer-polity interaction, whereby each polis was motivated to build larger and more splendid temples than its neighbors. This reasoning can also be extended to include the way in which the Greek states of western Anatolia defended their cities with large, finely constructed city walls. An example of this process at work are the five-kilometer-long city walls of Phokaia, which were built of neatly fitting stone blocks and fronted in an Anatolian style (see previous discussion). In this instance it can be seen that the inspiration to build large defenses came not just from their fellow Greek communities in the coastal region but also from the power centers of inland Anatolia, with whom they may have considered themselves to be in competitive emulation, or by whom they may have felt threatened (Greaves 2010:156–63).

Conclusions

The fundamental problem that has dogged many serious studies of this region is that the traditional methodologies of classical archaeology that can be applied in mainland Greece break down in the regions of the east Aegean and western Anatolia. Whereas in Athens and other regions of the Greek mainland it is possible to work within the cultural frameworks established by extant Greek literature, in western Anatolia it is harder to demonstrate a definitive link between the material culture record and the written testimonies of writers who were not just writing in Athens and whose works were produced within the literary genres and sociopolitical milieu of that city. Through the continuing excavation and publication of new data from the region, better connections to the chronology and cultures of Anatolia are now becoming established, and these will ultimately lead to new understandings of the region that address the imbalance toward the written sources of Greek history that is evident in many studies of the region. When viewed in such a way, there can be seen to be a long, complex, and changing relationship between these Greek settlements on the west coast and their contemporaries elsewhere in Anatolia.

REFERENCES

References to Athenaios, Herodotus, and Pausanias are to standard editions.

Akurgal, Ekrem. 1983. *Alt-Smyrna 1: Wohnschichten und Athenatempel.* Ankara: Türk Tarih Kurumu Basımevi.

Akurgal, Meral. 2007. Hellenic Architecture in Smyrna 650–546 B.C. In *Frühes Ionien: eine Bestandsaufnahme*, ed. Justus Cobet, Volkmar von Graeve, Wolf-Dietrich Niemeier, and Konrad Zimmermann, 125–36. Mainz am Rhein: Philipp von Zabern.

Akurgal, Meral, Michael Kerschner, Hans Mommsen, and Wolf-Dietrich Niemeier. 2002. *Töpferzentren der Ostägäis: Archäometrische und archälogische Untersuchungen zur mykenischen, geometrischen und archaischen Keramik aus Fundorten in Westkleinasien.* Vienna: Österreichisches Archäologisches Instituts Wien.

Bammer, Anton. 1990. A "Periteros" of the Geometric Period in the Artemision of Ephesus. *Anatolian Studies* 40: 137–60.

———. 2007. Archäologische Überreste auf dem Bademliktepe bei Ayasoluk-Selçuk. *Anatolia Antiqua* 15: 103–11.

Berges, Dietrich. 2006. *Knidos: Beiträge zur Geschichte der archaischen Stadt.* Mainz: Philipp von Zabern.

Berlin, Andrea M. and Kathleen Lynch. 2002. Going Greek: Atticizing Pottery in the Achaemenid World. *Studia Troica* 12: 168–78.

Cahill, Nicholas. 1988. Taş Kule: A Persian-Period Tomb Near Phokaia. *American Journal of Archaeology* 92.4: 499–501.

Cobet, Justus. 2007. Das alte Ionien in der Geschichtsschreibung. In *Frühes Ionien: Eine Bestandsaufnahme*, ed. Justus Cobet, Volkmar von Graeve, Wolf-Dietrich Niemeier, and Konrad Zimmermann, 729–43. Mainz am Rhein: Philipp von Zabern.

Cobet, Justus, Volkmar von Graeve, Wolf-Dietrich Niemeier, and Konrad Zimmermann, eds. 2007. *Frühes Ionien: Eine Bestandsaufnahme.* Mainz am Rhein: Philipp von Zabern.

Cook, John M. 1973. *The Troad: An Archaeological and Topographical Study.* Oxford: Clarendon.

Cook, John M. and Richard V. Nicholls. 1998. *Old Smyrna Excavations: The Temples of Athena.* London: British School at Athens.

Ersoy, Yaşar. 2007. Notes on the History and Archaeology of Early Clazomenae, In *Frühes Ionien: Eine Bestandsaufnahme*, ed. Justus Cobet, Volkmar von Graeve, Wolf-Dietrich Niemeier, and Konrad Zimmermann, 148–78. Mainz am Rhein: Philipp von Zabern.

Gorman, Vanessa B. 2001. *Miletos: The Ornament of Ionia.* Ann Arbor: University of Michigan Press.

Greaves, Alan M. 2002. *Miletos: A History.* London: Routledge.

———. 2007. Trans-Anatolia: Examining Turkey as a Bridge between East and West. *Anatolian Studies* 57: 1–15.

———. 2010. *The Land of Ionia: Society and Economy in the Archaic Period.* Malden, Mass.: Wiley-Blackwell.

Hall, Jonathan M. 1997. *Ethnic Identity in Greek Antiquity.* Cambridge: Cambridge University Press.

Heilmeyer, Wolf-Dieter. 1986. Die Einordung Milets in die Siedlungszonen der griechischen Frühzeit. In *Milet 1899–1980*, ed. Wolfgang Müller-Wiener, 105–12. Istanbuler Mitteilungen, Beiheft 31. Tübingen: Ernst Wasmuth.

Held, Winfried. 2000. *Das Heiligtum der Athena in Milet.* Mainz am Rhein: Philipp von Zabern.

Kerschner, Michael, Ireen Kowalleck, and Martin Steskal. 2008. *Archäologische Forschungen zur Siedlungsgeschichte von Ephesos in geometrischer, archaischer und klassischer Zeit: Grabungsbefunde und Keramikfunde aus dem Bereich von Koressos*. Vienna: Österreichisches Archäologisches Instituts Wien.

Kerschner, Michael, Hans Mommsen, Christine Rogl, and Alexander Schwedt. 2002. Die Keramikproduktion von Ephesos in griechischer Zeit. Zum Stand der archäometrischen Forschungen. *Jahreshefte des Österreichischen Archäologischen Instituts in Wien* 71: 189–206.

Kerschner, Michael and Udo Schlotzhauer. 2005. A New Classification System for East Greek Pottery. *Ancient West and East* 4.1: 1–56.

Kleiner, Gerhard. 1966. *Alt-Milet*. Wiesbaden: Franz Steiner.

Koenigs, Wolf. 2007. Archaische Bauglieder aus Stein in Ionien. In *Frühes Ionien: Eine Bestandsaufnahme*, ed. Justus Cobet, Volkmar von Graeve, Wolf-Dietrich Niemeier, and Konrad Zimmermann, 669–80. Mainz am Rhein: Philipp von Zabern.

Lamb, Winifred. 1931/2. Antissa 1931–2. *Annual of the British School at Athens* 32: 41–67.

Lemos, Irene S. 2002. *The Protogeometric Aegean: The Archaeology of the Late Eleventh and Tenth Centuries BC*. Oxford: Oxford University Press.

———. 2007. The Migrations to the West Coast of Asia Minor: Tradition and Archaeology. In *Frühes Ionien: Eine Bestandsaufnahme*, ed. Justus Cobet, Volkmar von Graeve, Wolf-Dietrich Niemeier, and Konrad Zimmermann, 713–27. Mainz am Rhein: Philipp von Zabern.

Marchese, Ronald T. 1986. *The Lower Maeander Flood Plain: A Regional Settlement Study*. British Archaeological Reports International Series no. 292. Oxford: British Archaeological Reports.

Niemeier, Wolf-Dietrich. 2005. Minoans, Mycenaeans, Hittites and Ionians in Western Asia Minor: New Excavations in Bronze Age Miletus-Millawanda. In *The Greeks in the East*, ed. Alexandra Villing, 1–36. London: British Museum Press.

Özyiğit, Ö. 1994. The City Walls of Phokaia. *Révue des Études Anciennes* 96: 77–109.

———. 2003. Recent Work at Phokaia in the Light of Akurgal's Excavations. *Anadolu/Anatolia* 25: 109–27.

———. 2006. Phokaia. In *Stadtgrabungen und Stadtforschung in westlichen Kleinasien: Geplantes und Erreichtes. Internationales Sympioson 6./7. August 2004 in Bergama (Türkei)*, ed. W. Radt, 303–14. BYZAS 3. İstanbul: Ege Yayınları.

Parker, Holt N. 2008. The Linguistic Case for the Aiolian Migration Reconsidered. *Hesperia* 77.2: 431–64.

Roebuck, Carl. 1959. *Ionian Trade and Colonization*. New York: Archaeological Institute of America.

Rose, Brian C. 2008. Separating Fact from Fiction in the Aiolian Migration. *Hesperia* 77.2: 399–430.

Sakellariou, Michel B. 1958. *La Migration Grecque en Ionia*. Athens: Institut Français d'Athènes.

Schlotzhauer, Udo. 2007. Zum Verhältnis zwischen sog. Tierfries-und Fikellurastil (SiA I und II) in Milet. In *Frühes Ionien. Eine Bestandsaufnahme*, ed. Justus Cobet, Volkmar von Graeve, Wolf-Dietrich Niemeier, and Konrad Zimmermann, 263–93. Mainz am Rhein: Philipp von Zabern.

Senff, R. 2003. Das Aphroditeheiligtum von Milet. *Asia Minor Studien* 49: 11–25.

Senff, Reinhard. 2007. Die Ergebnisse der neuen Grabungen im archaischen Milet—Stratigraphie und Chronologie. In *Frühes Ionien. Eine Bestandsaufnahme*, ed. Justus Cobet, Volkmar von Graeve, Wolf-Dietrich Niemeier, and Konrad Zimmermann, 319–26. Mainz am Rhein: Philipp von Zabern.

Snodgrass, Anthony M. 1986. Interaction by Design: The Greek City-State. In *Peer Polity Interaction and Socio-Political Change*, ed. Colin Renfrew and John F. Cherry, 47–58. Cambridge: Cambridge University Press.

Spencer, Nigel. 1995. Early Lesbos between East and West: A "Grey Area" of Aegean Archaeology. *Annual of the British School at Athens* 90: 269–306.

Thonemann, Peter. In press. *The Maeander.* Cambridge: Cambridge University Press.

Tuchelt, Klaus. 1991. *Branchidai-Didyma.* Zaberns Bildbände zur Archäologie 3. Mainz am Rhein: Philipp von Zabern.

Tuna-Nörling, Yasemin. 1995. *Die Ausgrabungen von Alt-Smyrna und Pitane: Die Attisch-Schwartzfigurige Keramik und der attische Keramikexport nach Kleinasien.* Istanbuler Forschungen Band 41. Tübingen: Ernst Wasmuth.

Vanschoonwinkel, Jacques. 2006. Greek Migrations to Aegean Anatolia in the Dark Age. In *Greek Colonisation: An Account of Greek Colonies and Other Settlements Overseas, vol. 1*, ed. Gocha R. Tsetskhaldze, 115–42. Leiden: Brill.

Villing, Alexandra. 1998. Athena as Ergane and Promachos. In *Archaic Greece: New Approaches and New Evidence*, ed. Nick Fisher and Hans van Wees, 147–68. London: Classical Press of Wales.

Voigt, Mary M. and Robert C. Henrickson. 2000. Formation of the Phrygian State: The Early Iron Age at Gordion. *Anatolian Studies* 50: 37–54.

von Gerkan, Armin. 1925. *Milet 1.4: Der Poseidonaltar bei Kap Monodendri.* Berlin: Georg Reimer.

von Graeve, Volkmar. 1989. Eine spätarchaische Anthemienstele aus Milet. *Istanbuler Mitteilungen* 36: 143–51.

PART III

PHILOLOGICAL AND HISTORICAL TOPICS

CHAPTER 22

THE HITTITE LANGUAGE: RECOVERY AND GRAMMATICAL SKETCH

GARY BECKMAN

DESPITE the fact well illustrated by Beal (chapter 26 in this volume) that the Hittite state of the mid- to late second millennium B.C.E. was one of the most important political entities of its day in western Asia, interacting peacefully and holding its own in war with such powerful countries as Assyria, Babylonia, and pharaonic Egypt, all memory of Ḫatti (as the Hittites referred to their realm) and its language had apparently been lost by the time of the great Classical poets and historians. Although a few of Homer's Trojans and their allies bear personal names that may be distortions of those of Luwian rulers of the western fringes of Anatolia during the Hittite Empire period (see Bryce, chapter 15 in this volume), the Greek bard displays no knowledge of the kings of Ḫatti or of their capitals, Ḫattuša and Tarḫuntašša. Herodotus, himself a native of Anatolian Halicarnassus, is largely ignorant of Asia Minor east of Lydia, populating the former Hittite homeland with Amazons (Book 4:110) and attributing a surviving Hittite monument in his own neighborhood to a mythical Egyptian ruler (Book 2:106, Strassler ed.:161–62; see Ehringhaus 2005:87–91).

Although the Hebrew Bible mentions "Hittites" interacting with the patriarchs and governing parts of Syria, the pertinent scriptural passages in fact refer to later inhabitants of a region once subject to Hittite dominion and therefore still called "(Great) Ḫatti" by its neighbors in the Iron Age. Their ruling groups preserved aspects of imperial Hittite culture (royal names, architectural traditions, the Anatolian hieroglyphs) well into the first millennium B.C.E. and may to a certain extent have been genetically descended from the northern invaders of the Late Bronze

Age, but they were hardly Anatolians (see Hoffner 2004; Singer 2006; and McMahon, chapter 2, and Yakubovich, chapter 23 in this volume).

Rediscovery of the Hittites

The emergence of Ḫatti from three millennia of historical oblivion began in the late nineteenth century of our era, when Hittites appeared in the newly deciphered Egyptian historical records as dangerous adversaries of the New Kingdom pharaohs.[1] A connection was soon drawn between these northern rivals of the Egyptians and the Hieroglyphic Luwian monuments that European travelers had encountered in Syria and Turkey. Since the greatest concentration of these inscriptions was in Syria, and since the Hebrew Bible located its Hittites in Syro-Palestine, early researchers (e.g., Wright 1884) concluded that the Hittite state had been centered in Syria and had only secondarily expanded to the north. Although this is precisely the reverse of the actual historical development, a more accurate picture of the history of Ḫatti and her people could be drawn only after her own written records had been recovered, deciphered, and interpreted.

"Decipherment"

The first successful modern reading of a Hittite cuneiform document was not really a decipherment in the strict sense, given that the script employed by the Hittites did not differ significantly from that used in contemporary Babylonia (Hawkins 1986), and that this writing system had long since yielded most of its secrets to students of Akkadian texts. Accordingly, the first modern scholars undertaking to read Hittite were immediately able to assign more or less correct phonetic values to the syllabic signs and thus discern the approximate phonological repertoire of the language. Thus, from the start they could search for familiar vocabulary, as well as for patterns in word formation and grammatical usage.

The Norwegian scholar J. A. Knudtzon was the first to make a significant attempt to translate a Hittite text, in connection with his edition of all pieces of the cuneiform archive uncovered at Tell el-Amarna in Egypt in the late 1880s (see Moran 1992). Most of this corpus of some 400 tablets consisted of the diplomatic correspondence of pharaohs Amenhotep III and Amenhotep IV-Akhenaten with their Palestinian and Syrian vassals, as well as with their equals (Great Kings) on the international political stage. Almost all of these letters were written in Akkadian, the diplomatic language of the day, and thus posed no insuperable problems for Knudtzon. However, three of them had been composed in other idioms, unintelligible to him as well as to other researchers of the late nineteenth century.

Nonetheless, it was possible to identify the senders and recipients of these three missives, since they had been provided with the usual stereotyped Akkadian-language heading: "Say to so-and-so, ruler of such-and-such a place: Thus says so-and-so, ruler of (some other) place." Therefore it was immediately clear that the longest of these mystery letters had been sent by the king of the Syrian state of Mittanni to the pharaoh. The language of this record was later recognized as Hurrian and does not concern us further here. The longer of the remaining letters (EA 31) was addressed by Amenhotep III to Tarḫuntaradu, king of Arzawa, a country situated in south-western Anatolia (see Bryce, chapter 15 in this volume). The final piece (EA 32) was a reply by the Arzawan ruler to this letter. Although Knudtzon and his contemporaries naturally concluded that these documents had been composed in the "Arzawan" tongue, they were in fact written in what we call Hittite.

Knudtzon dutifully undertook the study of the "Arzawan" documents as part of his larger project, and early in the twentieth century he published his startling conclusions (Knudtzon 1902). In addition to his comprehension of the formulaic headings of the letters, he was able to discern the gist of the initial portion of the body of the larger piece, since many of the words in this section had been rendered not in Hittite but in Sumerographic or Akkadographic form.[2] He also benefited from a comparison of this letter with other pieces of royal correspondence in the Amarna corpus written entirely in Akkadian. Following the heading, these letters often continued with a report by the sender on the prosperous state of his land and of all of his goods and subjects, followed by the wish that the recipient's land and belongings should likewise flourish.

The larger Arzawa letter (EA 31) begins:

> THUS SAYS NIMUTRIYA (Amenhotep III), GREAT KING, KING OF EGYPT:
> SAY TO TARḪUNTARADU, KING OF THE LAND OF ARZAWA:
> *<ḫu-u-ma-an> kat-ti=**mi*** WELL-*in* HOUSES=***mi*** WIVES=***mi***
> CHILDREN=***mi*** NOBLEMEN-*aš* SOLDIERS=***mi*** HORSES=***mi***
> *pí-ip-pí-it=**mi*** LANDS=***mi***=*kan an-da ḫu-u-ma-an* WELL-*in*
> *du-uq-qa kat-ta ḫu-u-ma-an* WELL-*in e-eš-tu* HOUSES=***ti*** WIVES=***ti***
> CHILDREN=***ti*** NOBLEMEN-*aš* SOLDIERS=***ti*** HORSES=***ti***
> *pí-ip-pí-it=**ti*** LANDS=***ti*** *ḫu-u-ma-an* WELL-*in* ***e-eš-tu.***[3]

Those elements which Knudzon could read with certainty are rendered here in capitalized English. Hittite words are presented sign by sign in italics. According to the considerations just outlined, Knudtzon surmised that the first paragraph ought to contain pronouns referring to the writer, and the second section pronouns appropriate to his correspondent. That is, first "my" and then "your" possessions are called for. Such pronouns are indeed found here and have been rendered in boldface: we now know that *-mi* means "to me," and *-ti* "to you" in Hittite. The similarity of these small words to the personal pronouns of the Indo-European language family was obvious to Knudtzon. (To *-mi* compare English ***me*** and French ***moi***; to *-ti* compare English ***thou*** and French ***toi***.)

Second, Knudtzon expected to find a verb of wish or command—an imperative—in the second section. Indeed, the cuneiform *eštu* (also indicated in boldface) is extremely close to the Classical Greek form for "let it be!" (*ἔστω*). It was primarily these features of the "Arzawan" language that convinced the Norwegian that it belonged to the Indo-European family. In this conclusion he was enthusiastically supported by the Indo-European linguists—and his Oslo colleagues—Sophus Bugge and Alf Torp, who each contributed lengthy remarks to Knudtzon's book.

Sadly, the arguments of Knudtzon and his associates were not well received, seemingly due to both historical preconceptions and to scholarly caution. A century ago no one expected to find an Indo-European language at home in ancient western Asia, and linguists consequently demanded overwhelming proof before accepting such a notion. Also, in reaction to the excesses of unsystematic speculation that had marred the early study of the languages of this region, most of Knudtzon's contemporaries were wary of drawing conclusions with far-reaching historical and linguistic consequences on the basis of what might very well prove to be no more than coincidental similarities in sound (*Kling-Klang-Philologie*). It certainly did not help that the textual basis for the first attempted decipherment of Hittite was flawed: the larger Arzawa letter had been composed in Egypt by a scribe whose knowledge of Hittite was defective (Starke 1982), and both missives—consisting in any case of a total of just sixty-three lines of text—were available to Knudtzon and his critics only in relatively poor copies.

More material was called for, and it was soon forthcoming. It had already been observed that fragmentary tablets recovered by a French mission of 1893–94 to Boğazköy in north-central Turkey were written in the same language as the Arzawa letters. The prospect that additional texts were to be found in the extensive ruins at the site led to the dispatch of a German expedition under Hugo Winckler, which excavated there from 1906 through 1912 (Haas 1998; Winckler 1914). The site was soon revealed as ancient Ḫattuša, capital of the Hittite kings. Winckler's workmen brought to light around 10,000 tablets and fragments from the royal archives, many of which were taken to Berlin for study, while others were deposited in İstanbul.

Since the Hittites, like the contemporary Egyptians, had made use of Akkadian in composing diplomatic records such as treaties and international correspondence, many important texts could be read immediately upon their excavation. On the basis of these Akkadian-language documents, scholars (e.g., Meyer 1914) quickly reconstructed the broad outlines of Hittite history—several years before the native language of the bulk of the texts could be understood.

The interpretation of the Hittite-language texts and their language was initially undertaken by their excavator himself, and Winckler had reportedly made significant advances in this project before his untimely death in 1913. The task of studying the native-language texts from Boğazköy fell to others. Among them was a Czech professor at the University of Vienna, Friedrich (Bedřich) Hrozný, who even in the dark years of World War I traveled to İstanbul to study and copy tablets in the Royal Ottoman Museum (Hrozný 1931). He announced the successful results of his work in a lecture delivered in Berlin in October 1915 (Hrozný 1915).

The scholar from Vienna reported that his study of the newly recovered tablets vindicated the opinion of the derided pioneer Knudtzon: the language of the Hittite Empire indeed belonged to the Indo-European group. The centerpiece of Hrozný's decipherment was a single sentence drawn, as we now know, from a collection of regulations for temple employees (Ehelolf 1925:no. 4, col. ii, line 70): *nu* NINDA-*an e-ez-za-at-te-ni wa-a-tar-ma e-ku-ut-te-ni*. The second word in this sentence is written with a Sumerian ideogram accompanied by a Hittite phonetic indicator. When he considered this word, as an Assyriologist Hrozný immediately recognized that it must mean "bread." Then, further along in the line, he found the sequence of signs *wa-a-tar*, which is strikingly similar to English *water* and German *Wasser*. Noting that each of these nouns was followed by a word ending in the same pair of signs (*-te-ni*), a suffix which other passages suggested must mark the second person plural in verbs, it occurred to the scholar that these words ought to indicate the consumption of a foodstuff and of a liquid, respectively. The first word (*ezzateni*) called to mind Latin *edo*, German *essen*, and English *eat*. The second (*ekutteni*), which Hrozný now fully expected to mean "drink," was reminiscent of Latin *aqua*, "water." Soon he was able to translate this sentence as "Then you will eat bread and drink water," and to point to Indo-European etymologies for most of its elements (some now to be corrected; see Kloekhorst 2008).

Although early in his studies Hrozný had discounted the Indo-European affiliation of Hittite, the vocabulary of this sentence dispelled his skepticism. Poring over the hundreds of tablets at his disposal, he collected material for the first thorough analysis of Hittite grammar and vocabulary, presenting them in a book published two years later (Hrozný 1917). Within less than a decade, most authorities had come to accept Hrozný's views concerning the linguistic affiliation of the language, and a few linguists even began to brave the "treacherous difficulties" of the cuneiform writing system (Sommer 1947:39) to participate directly in Hittitological research. Ever more evidence studied by a growing number of scholars soon resulted in a clearer picture of Hittite grammar and of the place of the language within the Indo-European family.

Today we have achieved a fairly sophisticated understanding of the Hittite language, as illustrated by an exhaustive recent grammar (Hoffner and Melchert 2008), a number of linguistic sketches (Rieken 2007; Watkins 2004), and several ongoing dictionary projects (Friedrich, Kammenhuber, and Hoffman 1975–; Güterbock, Hoffner, and van den Hout 1980–; Puhvel, 1984–). In what follows, I present a bare-bones outline of this most ancient Indo-European tongue, referring the reader to these resources for greater detail.

The Hittite Language

The Ḫattuša Archive

Although in recent years significant numbers of Hittite cuneiform records have been found at several provincial sites in central Anatolia (Maşat Höyük/Tapikka, Alp 1991; Kuşaklı/Šariššа, Wilhelm 1997; Ortaköy/Šapinuwa, Süel 2002; and see

Mielke, chapter 48 in this volume), by far the bulk of the relevant material comes from the central archives at the capital Boğazköy/Ḫattuša (see van den Hout, chapter 41 in this volume). These Hittite texts include exclusively documents and compositions inscribed to facilitate the duties of the king and his bureaucracy in fulfillment of the royal duties as chief priest, highest administrator and judge, and commander in chief of the armies of Ḫatti (Beckman 1995). That is, there are no Hittite private records on clay; such documents were apparently set down on tablets of wood, none of which have survived the ravages of time (Marazzi 1994).

Several languages are represented in the Boğazköy cuneiform collections (Forrer 1919): first of all, of course Hittite, the idiom of state administration, but also Palaic, Luwian, and the non-Indo-European Hattic and Hurrian, primarily in the form of incantations embedded within a Hittite-language matrix in religious texts. Semitic Akkadian (a peripheral form of Babylonian) was, as we have seen, employed in diplomatic letters and international treaties, as well as in some early internal compositions, whereas the ancient cultural tongue Sumerian, a linguistic isolate, played a limited role in advanced scribal education.

The Anatolian Family

The cohort of Indo-European languages at home in Anatolia may be divided into two groups: on one hand those written in cuneiform during the second millennium B.C.E. (Hittite, Palaic, and Luwian), plus the dialect of Luwian represented in the Anatolian Hieroglyphs (whose use extended into the Iron Age), and on the other those inscribed in epichoric Greek alphabets during the first millennium B.C.E. (Lycian, Lydian, Carian, Pisidian, and Sidetic). Although it is of course attested in inscriptions recovered in central Turkey, Phrygian is not a member of the Anatolian subfamily but is more closely related to Greek (see Roller, chapter 25 in this volume). Finally, despite ancient traditions that the Etruscans had migrated to Italy from Anatolia (Herodotus, Book 1:94, Strassler ed.: 55–56), it is still debated whether Etruscan is an Indo-European language; it certainly does not belong to the Anatolian family. (For more detail on Indo-European, see Melchert, chapter 31 in this volume.)

Hittite

The earliest researchers to concern themselves with the language of Ḫatti naturally called it "Hittite," but strictly speaking this designation is appropriate only in the sense that it served as the administrative language of the realm. In fact, further acquaintance with the sources revealed that the ancients themselves referred to their tongue as *nišili* or *nešumnili*, "[the language] of (the city of) Kaneš/Neša," an early center of the population that established the Hittite state. However, by the time this was recognized, the inexact term had become firmly entrenched and could not be displaced (Güterbock 1959).

The writing of Hittite texts spanned nearly half a millennium, from the mid-seventeenth century into the early twelfth century B.C.E., and naturally the language changed over the course of that period. Recognizing that certain characteristics of the local cuneiform script also developed over time (Neu and Rüster 1989), scholars are now able to assign individual tablets an approximate date of inscription and discriminate between records surviving from the era of their composition and those available only in later copies. In current dictionaries and linguistic studies, writers are careful to specify both the date of original composition of a text or grammatical form and that of the tablet on which it has been preserved. The major hiatus—between Old Hittite and New Hittite—occurred early in the empire period, around 1350 B.C.E., but many scholars also recognize a transitional Middle Hittite stage to be assigned to the first half of the fourteenth century B.C.E.

In considering the discussion that follows, keep in mind that the scribes of Ḫatti have left us no grammatical treatises on their language, and that all terminology employed in the description of Hittite has been assigned by modern scholars.

The Writing System

Although writing was practiced in Anatolia before the establishment of the Hittite state—namely, by the merchants working in the trading settlements of the twentieth and nineteenth centuries B.C.E. (see Kulakoğlu, chapter 47, and Michel, chapter 13 in this volume)—the variety of cuneiform they employed was not ancestral to the script later adopted by the Hittites. Rather, to judge from the sign values and shapes of the characters, the kings of Ḫatti imported their writing system, along with other booty, from northern Syria in the course of their early campaigns there. Indeed, it is likely that the reintroduction of literacy to Anatolia was effected by Syrian scribes carried off to the Hittite capital (Beckman 1983; see van den Hout, chapter 41 in this volume).

The Boğazköy script largely follows Old Babylonian usage in regard to the shape and values of signs, but it ignores the distinction made in Syro-Mesopotamia among the voiced, voiceless, and emphatic series of consonants. Thus, for example, Hittite scribes employed the signs KA, GA, and QA promiscuously. Instead, they represented consonants with a voiced (lax?) pronunciation with a single sign (e.g., *a-pa-a-aš* = /*abas*/, "that one"), while geminating voiceless (tense?) consonants (e.g., *at-ta-aš* = /*atas*/, "father"). Obviously, this orthographic distinction could not be made at the beginning or end of words.

Phonology

In general, as a syllabary, the cuneiform script is not an ideal vehicle for expressing Hittite or any other Indo-European language, since the members of this family are well provided with consonant clusters, which the system cannot render in word-initial or word-final position. In addition, it is unlikely that cuneiform's repertoire of vowels (a, e, i, u) is sufficient for an accurate representation of Hittite. Our reconstruction of the phonology of the language therefore remains most uncertain.

Nominal Forms

The Hittite noun and adjective are characterized by gender (common gender and neuter), number (singular and plural), and case. Cases in general function like those of the other early Indo-European languages: nominative (nom.) for the subject of a transitive or intransitive verb; accusative (acc.) for the object of a transitive verb; vocative (voc.) for direct address; genitive (gen.) for possession or appurtenance; dative (dat.) for indirect object; locative (loc.) for position; allative (all.) for goal of movement; ablative (abl.) for point of departure; and instrumental (inst.) for means. The ergative (erg.), found only in Hittite, is used when it is necessary for a neuter noun to serve as the subject of a transitive verb.

The following chart presents an idealized schema of the nominal endings, ignoring some rare forms and the significant collapsing of distinctions found in later texts.

	Singular	**Plural**
com. nom.	*-š, -ø*	*-eš*
acc.	*-n, -an*	*-uš*
neut., nom.-acc.	*-ø, -n*	*-ø, -a, -i*
voc.	*-e, -i, -ø*	—
erg.	*-anza (-/ants/)*	*-anteš*
gen.	*-aš*	*-an, -aš*
dat.-loc.	*-i, -ya, -ø*	*-aš*
all.	*-a*	—
	Numerically Indifferent	
	abl. *–az, -za (-/ts/)*	
	inst. *-it, -da*	

Pronouns

Personal Pronouns

Inherited independent pronouns are found only for the first and second persons, singular and plural.

	Singular		**Plural**	
	First	**Second**	**First**	**Second**
nom.	*ūk*	*zīk*	*wēš*	*šumeš*
acc.	*ammuk*	*tuk*	*anzaš*	*šumaš*
gen.	*ammel*	*tuēl*	*anzel*	*šumenzan*
dat.-loc.	*ammuk*	*tuk*	*anzāš*	*šumāš*
abl.	*ammēdaz*	*tuēdaz*	*anzēdaz*	*šumēdaz*

For the third person, see the section on Demonstrative Pronouns.

Enclitic Personal Pronouns

For the first and second persons, personal pronouns occurring in the enclitic chain at the beginning of a sentence (see table) are restricted to a single form functioning as both accusative and dative.

	Singular		Plural	
	First	**Second**	**First**	**Second**
acc.-dat.	*-mu*	*-ta, -du*	*-naš*	*-šmaš*

The system for the third person is fuller (in each instance the second form is that found in later texts).

	Singular	**Plural**
com. nom.	*-aš*	*-e, -at*
acc.	*-an*	*-uš, -aš*
neut., nom.-acc.	*-at*	*-e, -at*
dat.	*-še, -ši*	*-šmaš*

Possessive Pronouns

In older texts, the possessive relationship is expressed through enclitic pronouns (e.g., *išḫaš=miš*, "my lord"), which are replaced in later compositions by the genitive of the independent pronoun (e.g., *ammel išḫaš*, "id."). The declensional paradigm for attachment to singular nouns as in the example just given is as follows.[4]

	Singular			Plural		
	First	**Second**	**Third**	**First**	**Second**	**Third**
com. nom.	*-miš*	*-tiš*	*-šiš*	*-šummiš*	*-šmiš*	*-šmiš*
acc.	*-man, -min*	*-tan, -tin*	*-šan, -šin*	*-šumman, -šummin*	*-šman, -šmin*	*-šman, -šmin*
neut., nom.-acc.	*-met*	*-tet*	*-šet*	*-šummet*	*-šmet*	*-šmet*
gen.	*-maš*	*-taš*	*-šaš*	*-šummaš*	**-šmaš*	**-šmaš*
dat.-loc.	*-mi*	*-ti*	*-ši*	*-šummi*	*-šmi*	*-šmi*
all.	*-ma*	*-ta*	*-ša*	**-šumma*	**-šma*	**-šma*
abl.-inst.	*-mit*	*-tit*	*-šit*	**-šummit*	*-šmit*	*-šmit*

The schema in use with plural nouns (e.g., *išḫeš=miš*, "my lords").

	Singular			Plural		
	First	Second	Third	First	Second	Third
com. nom.	*-miš*	*-teš,*	*-šeš,*	*-šummeš,*	*-šmeš,*	*-šmeš,*
		-tiš	*-šiš*	*-šummiš*	*-šmiš*	*-šmiš*
acc.	*-muš*	*-tuš*	*-šuš*	*-šummuš*	*-šmuš*	*-šmuš*
neut., nom.-acc.	*-met,*	**-tet,*	*-šet,*	*-šummet*	**-šmet*	*-šmet,*
	-mit	**-tit*	*-šit*			*-šmit*
gen.	*-man,*	**-tan,*	**-šan,*	**-šumman,*	**-šman,*	**-šman,*
	**-maš*	**-taš*	**-šaš*	**-šummaš*	**-šmaš*	**-šmaš*
dat.-loc.	**-maš*	*-taš*	*-šaš*	**-šummaš*	**-šmaš*	**-šmaš*

Demonstrative Pronouns

Hittite originally displayed triptotic deixis (Goedegebuure 2002/3): proximal ("this") *kā-*, medial ("that") *apā-*, and distal ("that yonder") *aši*, but the third term dropped out early and appears only sporadically as an archaism, often employed and/or declined incorrectly. The living system distinguished only between the demonstratives *kā-*, "this," and *apā-*, "that." The latter also substitutes for the missing personal pronoun of the third person. The basic pattern of these words combines inherited nominal and pronominal elements.

	Singular		Plural	
com. nom.	*kāš*	*apāš*	*kē*	*apē*
acc.	*kūn*	*apūn*	*kūš*	*apūš*
neut., nom.-acc.	*kī*	*apāt*	*kē*	*apē*
gen.	*kēl*	*apēl*	*kenzan*	*apenzan*
dat.-loc.	*kēdani*	*apēdani*	*kēdaš*	*apēdaš*
		Numerically Indifferent		
		Abl. *kez, apēz*		
		Inst. *kedanda, apedanda*		

Relative Pronouns

The relative pronouns, which also function as indefinites ("which[ever]"), are as follows.

	Singular	Plural
com. nom.	*kuiški*	*kuiēška*
acc.	*kuinki*	*kuiuška*
neut., nom.-acc.	*kuitki*	*kuekka*
gen.	*kuēlka*	**kuenzanka*
dat.-loc.	*kuedanikki*	*kuedaška*
	Numerically Indifferent	
	Abl. *kuēzka*	

Numbers

Because of the almost exclusive use of numerals in the texts, the phonetic realization of most numbers is uncertain or even unknown, but it is clear that Hittite had cardinal, ordinal, multiple, and fractional numbers. Bases of which we can be relatively certain are: *šia*-, "one" (Goedegebuure 2006); **duya*-, "two"; *teri*-, "three"; *meyu*-, "four"; and **šiptam*-, "seven." Large numbers are invariably expressed through ideograms (Hoffner 2007).

The Verb

The Hittite verb is characterized by person (first, second, third), number (singular and plural), voice (active and medio-passive), tense/aspect (present and preterite = imperfective and perfective), and mood (indicative and imperative). There are two conjugational patterns, customarily called after the ending found in the first person singular of the active present, -*mi*- verbs and -*ḫi*- verbs. The patterns differ only in the singular in the active present, preterite, and imperative, and solely in the third person singular throughout the medio-passive.

The ideal schema of the verbal desinences follows. Considerable mutual contamination may be observed between the -*mi*- and -*ḫi*- conjugations in later texts.

	Active Present		
	Singular		**Plural**
	-*mi*- verb	-*ḫi*- verb	
First	-*mi*	-*ḫi*	-*weni*, -*meni*
Second	-*ši*	-*ti*	-*teni*
Third	-*zi* (-/*tsi*/)	-*i*	-*anzi*

	Active Preterite		
	Singular		**Plural**
	-*mi*- verb	-*ḫi*- verb	
First	-*un*, -*nun*	-*ḫun*	-*wen*, -*men*
Second	-*š*	-*ta*, -*t*	-*ten*
Third	-*t*	-*š*	-*ir*

	Medio-Passive Present	
	Singular	**Plural**
First	-(*ḫ*)*ḫa*(*ri*)	-*wašta*(*ti*)
Second	-*ta*(*ri*)	-*tuma*(*ri*)
Third	-*mi*- verb -*ta*(*ri*) -*ḫi*- verb -*a*(*ri*)	-*anta*(*ri*)

Medio-Passive Preterite		
	Singular	**Plural**
First	*-(ḫa)ḫat(i)*	*-waštati*
Second	*-tat(i)*	*-tumat(i)*
Third	*-mi-* verb *-tat(i)*	*-antat(i)*
	-ḫi- verb *-a(ti)*	

Active Imperative			
	Singular		**Plural**
	-mi- verb	*-ḫi-* verb	
First	*-(a)llu*	*-(a)llu*	*-weni*
Second	*-ø, -i, -t*	*-ø, -i*	*-ten*
Third	*-tu*	*-u*	*-antu*

Medio-Passive Imperative		
	Singular	**Plural**
First	*-(ḫa)ḫaru*	*-waštati*
Second	*-ḫut(i)*	*-tumat(i)*
Third	*-mi-* verb *-taru*	*-antaru*
	-ḫi- verb *-aru*	

Notice that there are no specially marked optative or subjunctive forms. Potentiality, desires, and contrary-to-fact conditions are expressed through the use of particles (*man* for possibilities, wishes, or irrealis; *numān* for negative wishes). The adverb *kāša/kāšma* indicates imperfective aspect or immediacy, for example, *ḫaššuš kāša uizzi*, "The king is just now coming." The suffixes *-ške-* and *-anna/i-* also render a verbal stem imperfective.

Deverbal Nouns

Although not necessarily attested for every lexeme, four types of nouns may in principle be formed for each verb. The participle in *-ant-* expresses a state, normally passive to a transitive verb (e.g., *appant-*, "captured; prisoner" < *ēp-*, "to seize") and resultative to an intransitive (e.g., *pant-*, "gone" < *pai-*, "to go"). The verbal substantive in *-war/-mar* (*-ātar* for a small group of *-mi-* verbs) indicates an action, as does the English gerund (e.g., *pauwar*, "going"; *appātar*, "seizing"); in general, it is inflected only in the nominative and genitive. The indeclinable infinitive in *-anzi/-manzi* (*-anna* for a small group of *-mi-* verbs; e.g., *walḫuwanzi*, "to strike; be struck" < *walḫ-*; *appanna*, "to seize; be seized") is unmarked for voice and is employed in a number of special constructions (e.g., *walḫuwanzi zinnai*, "he finishes striking" < *zinne-*, "to bring to conclusion"). Finally, the supine in *-(u)wan*, also indeclinable, appears only in association with auxiliary *dai-*, "to put," or *tiya-*, "to step," indicating the commencement of an action (e.g., *memiškiuwan dāiš*, "began to speak" < *mema/i-*, "to speak").

Adverbs

The meaning of a verb, explicit or implied, may be modified through the use of an adverb. These may be temporal: for example, *kāru*, "previously"; *kinun*, "now"; *lukkatta*, "in the morning"; local: for example, *kā*, "here"; *šarā*, "upward"; *šer*, "above"; or indicate manner: for example, *kiššan*, "thus"; *kuwatka*, "however"; *ḫudak*, "suddenly, immediately." The negations *natta* and *lē* (used only with prohibitions) also belong here. Furthermore, many adverbs may be employed as postpositions (e.g., *parni anda*, "in the house") or preverbs (e.g., *šarā paizzi*, "[s]he goes up"). On occasion it may be impossible to distinguish between these usages, as in: *nu=kan ḫaššuš ḫappiri anda ēšta*, "And the king was in the city."

Conjunctions

Coordination of sentences and clauses is effected with the independent conjunctions *šu*, *ta* (both in use only in early sources), and *nu*, "and," or by means of enclitic *-a/-ya*, "and," or *-a/-ma*, "but." There are also many subordinating conjunctions, such as *mān*, "like, as"; *maḫḫan*, "when, if"; *kuitman*, "while"; and so on.

Particles

Several small enclitic lexemes that appear in the sentence-initial chain (see following discussion) are extremely important for the expression of meaning. These include the reflexive particle *=az/=za* (/ts/), the quotative *=wa(r)*, the emphatic marker *=pat* (which may also be affixed to words elsewhere in the sentence), and the sentence particles (*=an, =apa, =ašta, =šan, =kan*). These latter words, whose frequency of use increases over the attested life of Hittite at the same time as *=kan* comes to displace all the others, mainly function adverbially (Tjerkstra 1999), but with some verbs they serve to distinguish between imperfective and perfective aspect (e.g., *kuen-*, "to strike, attack," but *=kan . . . kuen-*, "to kill").

The Enclitic Chain

A distinctive characteristic of the languages of the Anatolian family of the second millennium B.C.E. is the presence of a chain of enclitic elements attached to the first word of most sentences. Of course, not all possible constituents of the chain need be present in any particular sentence, but the order in which the categories of these small words appear is invariable: host word + quotative particle + dative and accusative enclitic pronouns + reflexive particle + sentence particles. Example:

ḫaššuš=ma=war=at=šmaš=kan arḫa dāš,

"(He said): 'But the king took it away from them.'"

(SUBJECT + CONJUNCTION + QUOTATIVE PARTICLE + ACCUSATIVE PRONOUN [OBJECT] + DATIVE PRONOUN [INDIRECT OBJECT] + SENTENCE PARTICLE, ADVERB, VERB).

Syntax

The unmarked Hittite sentence follows the order SUBJECT OBJECT VERB, with adverbial elements immediately preceding the verb. Within a phrase, adjectives and genitives normally precede the noun they modify. For example:

nu	*šalliš ḫaššuš*	*utneyaš ḫappiriyuš*	*duddumili*	*kuenta*
Then	the Great King	the cities of the land	secretly	attacked.
CONJUNCTION	SUBJECT	OBJECT	ADVERB	VERB
	{adjective nominative}	{genitive accusative}		

As in any language, word order may be varied for emphasis or to express various special meanings.

In sentences containing a dependent clause, the subordinate clause precedes the main clause. Example: *nu=kan antuḫšaš kuiš parni ēšta n=an ḫaššuš aušta*, "The king saw the person who was in the house," literally "The person who was in the house, the king saw him."

Questions not featuring an interrogative word may in general be distinguished from declarative sentences only from context, but negative rhetorical questions often front the negative (e.g., *natta=(a)n=kan kuenta*, "Didn't he kill him?"; Hoffner 1986:89–91).

Lexicon

Many students of Hittite (e.g., Kammenhuber 1969:266) have remarked on the non-Indo-European origin of much of its vocabulary, but in fact a large proportion of its basic words can be traced back to the stock of the proto-language. The exotic impression made by its lexicon is due to the large number of technical terms for particular areas of life that the Hittites borrowed from initially more culturally advanced groups: from Hattic for architecture (e.g., *daḫanga-*, "shrine"), kingship (e.g., *tabarna-*, "ruler"), and theology (e.g., *purulli-*, "earth"); from Akkadian for writing and bureaucracy (*tuppi-*, "[cuneiform] tablet"); and above all from Hurrian for cult (e.g., *puḫugari-*, "substitute," *zurki-*, "blood [offering]," *ḫuprušḫi-*, "crucible"). During the Empire period, however, Hittite's Anatolian sister Luwian exercised ever greater influence on the official language, leading to the introduction of many Luwian words and even inflectional forms (Melchert 2005), sometimes helpfully identified in the texts as foreign by gloss wedges (*Glossenkeile*).

Conclusion

Further progress in the study of the Hittite (Nesite) language and the other members of the Anatolian family as well as continued research into Hurrian and the peripheral dialects of Akkadian will undoubtedly allow scholars to bring into ever clearer focus our picture of Ḫatti, the earliest literate culture at home in Anatolia.

NOTES

1. This section has been adapted from Beckman (1996).

2. That is, while written in Sumerian or Akkadian or a combination of the two, these words were intended to be read in Hittite. Compare our use of the Latin phrase *et cetera* (etc.) to stand for English "and so on."

3. EA 31 = Götze (1930:no. 1, obv. 1–10). In light of our current knowledge of Hittite, this passage may be translated: "Thus says Amenhotep III, Great King, King of Egypt: Say to Tarhuntaradu, King of the Land of Arzawa: All is well with me. In my lands all is well for me—for my houses, wives, children, noblemen, soldiers, chariotry and . . .

May all be well with you. May all be well in your lands for you—for your houses, children, noblemen, soldiers, chariotry and . . ."

4. Starred forms are those to be expected but not actually attested.

REFERENCES

Alp, Sedat. 1991. *Hethitische Briefe aus Maşat-Höyük*. Ankara: Türk Tarih Kurumu Basımevi.

Beckman, Gary. 1983. Mesopotamians and Mesopotamian Learning at Ḫattuša. *Journal of Cuneiform Studies* 35: 97–114.

———. 1995. Royal Ideology and State Administration in Hittite Anatolia. In *Civilizations of the Ancient Near East*, ed. Jack Sasson, 529–43. New York: Scribner's.

———. 1996. The Hittite Language and its Decipherment. *Bulletin of the Canadian Society for Mesopotamian Studies* 31: 23–30.

Ehelolf, Hans. 1925. *Keilschrifturkunden aus Boghazköi*, vol. 13. Berlin: Vorderasiatische Abteilung der Staatlichen Museen.

Ehringhaus, Horst. 2005. *Götter, Herrscher, Inschriften: Die Felsreliefs der hethitischen Grossreichszeit in der Türkei*. Mainz: Philipp von Zabern.

Forrer, Emil. 1920. Die acht Sprachen der Boghazköi-Inschriften. *Sitzungsberichte der Preussischen Akademie der Wissenschaften* 53: 1029–48.

Friedrich, Johannes, Annelies Kammenhuber, and Inge Hoffman, 1975–. *Hethitisches Wörterbuch*, 2nd ed. Heidelberg: Universitätsverlag Winter.

Goedegebuure, Petra M. 2002/3. The Hittite 3rd Person/Distal Demonstrative *aši* (*uni*, *eni*, etc.). *Die Sprache* 43: 1–32.

———. 2006. A New Proposal for the Reading of the Hittite Numeral '1': *šia-*. In *The Life and Times of Ḫattušili III and Tutḫaliya IV*, ed. Theo van den Hout, 165–88. Leiden: Nederlands Instituut voor het Nabije Oosten.

Götze, Albrecht. 1930. *Verstreute Boghazköi-Texte*. Marburg: Selbstverlag des Herausgebers.

Güterbock, Hans Gustav. 1959. Toward a Definition of the Term "Hittite." *Oriens* 10: 233–39.

Güterbock, Hans G., Harry A. Hoffner, and Theo van den Hout, 1980–. *The Hittite Dictionary of the Oriental Institute of the University of Chicago*. Chicago: Oriental Institute.

Haas, Volkert. 1998. 1906–1912: Hattuscha (Boğazköy): Die Hauptstadt der Hethiter. In *Zwischen Tigris und Nil: 100 Jahre Ausgrabungen der Deutschen Orient-Gesellschaft in Vorderasien und Ägypten*, ed. Gernot Wilhelm, 92–99. Mainz: Philipp von Zabern.

Hawkins, J. D. 1986. Writing in Anatolia: Imported and Indigenous Systems. *World Archaeology* 17: 363–76.

Herodotus. 2007. *The Histories*, ed. Robert B. Strassler. New York: Pantheon Books.

Hoffner, Harry A. 1986. Studies in Hittite Grammar. In *Kaniššuwar: A Tribute to Hans G. Güterbock on His Seventy-Fifth Birthday*, ed. Harry A. Hoffner and Gary M. Beckman, 83–94. Chicago: Oriental Institute.

———. 2004. Ancient Israel's Literary Heritage Compared with Hittite Textual Data. In *The Future of Biblical Archaeology: Reassessing Methodologies and Assumptions*, ed. James K. Hoffmeier and Alan Millard, 176–92. Grand Rapids, Mich.: Eerdmans.

———. 2007. On Higher Numbers in Hittite. *Studi Micenei ed Egeo-Anatolici* 49: 377–85.

Hoffner, Harry A. Jr., and H. Craig Melchert. 2008. *A Grammar of the Hittite Language*. Winona Lake, Ind.: Eisenbrauns.

Hrozný, Bedřich. 1915. Die Lösung des hethitischen Problems. *Mitteilungen der Deutschen Orient-Gesellschaft* 56: 17–50.

———. 1917. *Die Sprache der Hethiter. Ihr Bau und ihre Zugehörigkeit zum indogermanischen Sprachstamm. Ein Entzifferungsversuch*. Leipzig: J. C. Hinrichs.

———. 1931. Le Hittite: Histoire et progrès du déchiffrement des texts. *Archiv Orientalní* 3: 272–95.

Kammenhuber, Annelies. 1969. Hethitisch, Palaisch, Luwisch und Hieroglyphen-luwisch. In *Altkleinasiatische Sprachen*, 119–357. Leiden: Brill.

Kloekhorst, Alwin. 2008. *Etymological Dictionary of the Hittite Inherited Lexicon*. Leiden: Brill.

Knudtzon, J. A. 1902. *Die zwei Arzawa-Briefe: Die ältesten Urkunden in Indo-germanischer Sprache*. Leipzig: J. C. Hinrichs.

Marazzi, Massimiliano. 1994. Ma gli Hittiti scrivevano veramente su "legno." In *Miscellanea di studi linguistici in onore di Walter Belardi*, ed. Palmira Cipriano, Paolo Di Giovine, and Marco Mancini, 131–60. Rome: Il Calamo.

Melchert, H. Craig. 2005. The Problem of Luvian Influence on Hittite. In *Sprachkontakt und Sprachwandel*, ed. Gerhard Meiser and Olav Hackstein, 445–60. Wiesbaden: Ludwig Reichert.

Meyer, Eduard. 1914. *Reich und Kultur der Chetiter*. Berlin: Karl Curtius.

Moran, William. 1992. *The Amarna Letters*. Baltimore, Md.: Johns Hopkins University Press.

Neu, Erich, and Christel Rüster. 1989. *Hethitisches Zeichenlexikon*. Studien zu den Boğazköy-Texten Beiheft 2. Wiesbaden: Harrassowitz.

Puhvel, Jaan. 1984–. *Hittite Etymological Dictionary*. Berlin: Mouton.

Rieken, Elisabeth. 2007. Hethitisch. In *Sprachen des Alten Orients*, ed. Michael Streck, 80–127. Darmstadt: Wissenschaftliche Buchgesellschaft.

Singer, Itamar. 2006. The Hittites and the Bible Revisited. In "*I Will Speak the Riddles of Ancient Times*": *Archaeological and Historical Studies in Honor of Amihai Mazar*, ed. Aren M. Maeir and Pierre de Miroschedji, 723–56. Winona Lake, Ind.: Eisenbrauns.

Sommer, Ferdinand. 1947. *Hethiter und Hethitisch*. Stuttgart: W. Kohlhammer.

Starke, Frank. 1982. Zur Deutung der Arzaua-Briefstelle VBoT 1, 25–27. *Zeitschrift für Assyriologie* 71: 221–31.

Süel, Aygül. 2002. Ortaköy-Šapinuwa. In *Recent Developments in Hittite Archaeology and History: Papers in Memory of Hans G. Güterbock*, ed. K. Aslıhan Yener and Harry A. Hoffner Jr., 157–65. Winona Lake, Ind.: Eisenbrauns.

Tjerkstra, F. A. 1999. *Principles of the Relation between Local Adverb, Verb and Sentence Particle*. Groningen: Styx.

Watkins, Calvert. 2004. Hittite. In *The Cambridge Encyclopedia of the World's Ancient Languages*, ed. Roger D. Woodard, 551–75. Cambridge: Cambridge University Press.

Wilhelm, Gernot. 1997. *Keilschrifttexte aus Gebäude A, Kuşaklı-Sarissa I/1*. Rahden, Westfalen: Verlag Marie Leidorf.

Winckler, Hugo. 1914. *Nach Boghazköi!* Leipzig: J. C. Hinrichs.

Wright, William. 1884. *The Empire of the Hittites*. New York: Scribner and Welford.

CHAPTER 23

LUWIAN AND THE LUWIANS

ILYA YAKUBOVICH

ALTHOUGH the Luwians played at least as important a role as the Hittites in the history of ancient Anatolia, Luwian studies have traditionally been considered a relatively insignificant appendix to Hittitology. A reason for this state of affairs is the structure of Ancient Near Eastern scholarship that traditionally focused on language and language communities associated with well-defined states or religious traditions. Hittitology as a discipline clearly benefited from the fact that the entity called Hittites or Hatti had been known from Hebrew, Egyptian, and Akkadian sources long before the archives of Ḫattuša became available to scholars. By contrast, the Luwians were not known by such a name outside Anatolia. The Hittite Laws contain a handful of references to the country named Luwiya (see Beal, chapter 26 in this volume), which are not accompanied by the geographic identification of this region, while a number of other texts introduce passages that were expected to be uttered *luwili*, "in the Luwian language," even though not all of them are actually recorded in Luwian. This is all of the direct historical information that is available about Luwian and the Luwians.

The situation begins to change with the growing realization among Hittitologists that most of the groups called Hittites by themselves or in foreign traditions were either Luwian speakers or included Luwian language communities (see Bryce, chapter 15, and van den Hout, chapter 41 in this volume). This is now commonly acknowledged in the case of the Neo-Hittite states of the Early Iron Age, whose élites commissioned Luwian monumental inscriptions but apparently did not know any Hittite/Nesite. The study of interference features of New Hittite indicates that in the late fourteenth and the thirteenth centuries B.C.E. the élites of the Hittite Empire, including the king and the members of the royal family, were fully bilingual in

Luwian. Because the progressive language shift from Hittite to Luwian in Ḫattuša cannot be explained through the higher prestige of the Luwian language, one has to assume that the Luwian speakers constituted the bulk of the population in the capital of the Hittite Empire and its surrounding area. A substantial number of Luwian lexical borrowings in Old Hittite suggest that Luwians and Hittites lived side by side already in the Old Kingdom Period. Only in the case of the town of Kaneš/Neša, whose prosopography in the twentieth–eighteenth centuries B.C.E. is reasonably well known from Old Assyrian sources, can one conclude that Hittite speakers formed a majority there (which is expected, given the self designation of the Hittite language as "Nesite"). Summing up, one can no longer claim a priority connection with the Hittite civilization for the language of Neša at the expense of the language of Luwiya.

Luwian Language Communities

The term *luwili* is exclusively used with reference to Luwian utterances cited (with or without translation) in Hittite cuneiform texts (Hawkins 2003:128–29). There is, however, a widespread agreement among modern scholars that Luwian is also the language of all the extensive texts recorded in the Anatolian hieroglyphic script. On the formal side, the ongoing study of Anatolian hieroglyphs has eliminated all the major differences between what was previously known as "Hieroglyphic Hittite" and Luwian (Hawkins 2003:137). On the sociolinguistic side, the same Hittite kings of the thirteenth century B.C.E. were commissioners of monumental hieroglyphic inscriptions and Hittite cuneiform texts with numerous Luwian code-switches (foreign words). It is hard to imagine that in addition to Hittite, they used two distinct Anatolian languages between which we can see no difference.

Whether Luwian is also attested in alphabetic transmission is essentially a terminological question. A number of scholars use the phrase "the Luwian languages" for the group comprising "Cuneiform Luwian," "Hieroglyphic Luwian," Lycian A, Lycian B (Milyan), and now also Carian (see, e.g., Houwink ten Cate 1961 and Morpurgo-Davies 1982/83). On the other hand, Melchert (2003:175–77) introduced the notion of the Luwic family that represents a higher taxonomic unit than the Luwian dialectal continuum and comprises Luwian and its close relatives of the first millennium B.C.E. On the formal side, he argues that the indigenous languages of Lycia, as known from the local inscriptions, represent close relatives of Luwian but not its direct descendants. On the sociolinguistic side, there is no historical/geographic overlap between the language communities associated with the Luwian language in the narrow sense and Lycian or Carian, as attested in the respective written records. In my opinion, the terminological distinction introduced by Melchert is meaningful, and the alphabetic Luwic languages spoken in the western part of Asia Minor in the first millennium B.C.E. remain outside the scope of this section.

Returning to Luwian proper, the dialectological analysis undertaken by Yakubovich (2010a:15–74) is conducive to suggesting a basic stemma reproduced here (figure 23.1). The term *Empire Luwian* is used for a Luwian dialect that was in use in Ḫattuša and its surrounding area in the Empire period. Although all the Bronze Age Luwian texts from Kizzuwatna are recorded in cuneiform and all the Iron Age Luwian texts are hieroglyphic, the Empire Luwian corpus is preserved in a combination of the two writing systems. Therefore, I regard the frequently used terms "Cuneiform Luwian" and "Hieroglyphic Luwian" as misnomers in a dialectological discussion. They should be used only with reference to two different types of corpora, the way one now uses "Syllabic Ugaritic" versus "Alphabetic Ugaritic."

Yakubovich (2010a) also endeavors to account for the propagation of the Luwian language through Anatolia in sociolinguistic terms. The scenario presented there appears to be broadly consistent with the conclusions of other scholars who recently investigated the spread of Luwian by applying different linguistic methods (e.g., Melchert 2005; Rieken 2006; van den Hout 2006; see also Melchert, chapter 31, and van den Hout, chapter 41 in this volume).

Given that the attested Luwian dialects are very close to each other, it is possible to date the common Luwian state to about 2000 B.C.E. This increases the likelihood that the region called Luwiya in the Hittite Laws represents the actual Luwian core area. I equate this region with the central Anatolian plateau to the west of the bend of the Halys River, the Lower Land of later Hittite sources (Yakubovich 2010a:239–48). In the early second millennium B.C.E., part of this territory was controlled by the powerful kingdom of Purušḫanda known from Assyrian and Hittite sources. The conquest of Purušḫanda by Anitta, king of Neša, resulted in the unification of the Hittite and Luwian speaking areas into one polity. When Ḫattuša was refounded as a capital of the new state, the members of both ethnic groups were likely to be among its residents, but Hittites had the upper hand.

The migration beyond the Taurus Range, to the area later known as Kizzuwatna, likewise must have represented a joint venture of Hittite and Luwian population groups. The southeastern expansion of the Hittite Old Kingdom under Ḫattušili I and Muršili I in the late seventeenth century B.C.E. provided an appropriate social context for these migrations. The original population of southeastern Asia Minor was Hurrian at least in part, as evidenced through structural interference between Hurrian and Kizzuwatna Luwian. The name of the kingdom of Kizzuwatna possibly represents a Luwian adaptation of Hittite **kez-udne*, "land on this side (of the

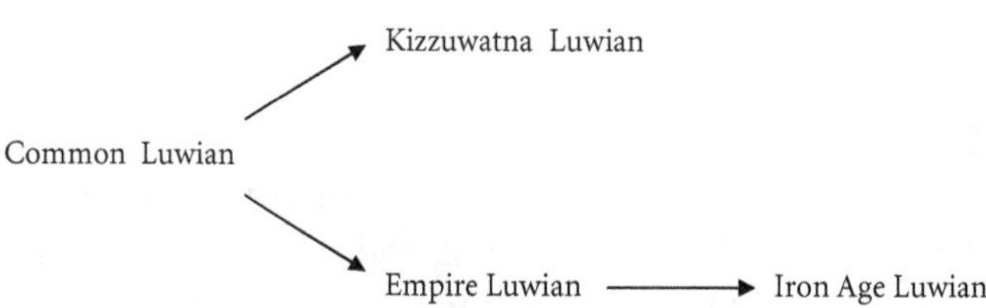

Figure 23.1. Luwian dialectal phyliation.

mountains)," whereas the name of its first king, Išputaḫšu, is definitely Hittite and not Luwian (Yakubovich 2010a:273–74). Nevertheless, the Luwian speakers were probably in the majority in this new kingdom, even though one can register the increase of Hurrian influence in this part of Anatolia after Kizzuwatna became a vassal of the Hurrian state of Mitanni.

The status of the Luwian language in the Hittite kingdom proper changed with the course of time. In the Old Kingdom, it was apparently still associated with a particular geographic area (Luwiya), and the Luwians enjoyed protected status as an ethnic group of the second rank (Yakubovich 2010a:248–60). By the time of the early New Kingdom, we see no more mentions of Luwiya, but references to Luwian commands in instructions for Hittite officials imply that it becomes the main language of the lower classes in Ḫattuša (Yakubovich 2010a:260–72). The distinctive feature of the Empire period is the spread of Hittite–Luwian bilingualism to the higher social orders, indicating an ongoing language shift from Hittite to Empire Luwian (Yakubovich 2010a:303ff., esp. 396–410).

The same shift to Empire Luwian can be reconstructed for the provincial centers of the Hittite Empire. This follows from the fact that after its disintegration, the dialectal descendant of Empire Luwian emerges as the official language of the Neo-Hittite states. This holds even for the former territory of Kizzuwatna, where the Kizzuwatna Luwian dialect has no direct descendant attested in the Iron Age (Yakubovich 2010a:68–74). The gradual shift to Empire Luwian in this region after the annexation of Kizzuwatna to the Hittite Empire in the fourteenth century B.C.E. could be reinforced by the flight of Hittite élites from Ḫattuša in the southeastward direction in the early twelfth century. Another consequence of the abandonment of Ḫattuša was the dispersal of the shrinking Hittite-speaking community and the eventual disappearance of the Hittite (Nesite) language.

The name of the Luwian language in the Early Iron Age is unknown, but the speakers of Iron Age Luwian were apparently called Hittites by their Semitic and Urartian neighbors. The hypothesis that it was also their self-designation appears possible, given that the "Neo-Hittite" states preserved many elements of the Hittite culture, including the Hittite royal names and the Anatolian hieroglyphic script. One should also keep in mind that the designation Hittite need not imply persistent ethnic connotations, because it is derived from the name of Ḫattuša, which was a Hattian foundation, only later to be resettled by the Hittites (Nesites) and Luwians. This constitutes the rationale for maintaining the term "Neo-Hittites" with reference to the Luwian language communities of the first millennium B.C.E.

The proportion of Luwian speakers in Neo-Hittite principalities must have varied from state to state. In some states of Asia Minor proper, they probably constituted the majority, whereas in Syria they were likely to coexist with the Semitic speakers within the same polities. The Semitic principality of Sam'al managed to establish itself right in the middle of the Neo-Hittite area, while both Luwian and Semitic inscriptions from Syria contain examples of mixed pantheons (Yakubovich 2010b). According to one theory, the self-designation of the Armenians, *hay*, goes back to the earlier **hātiyos*, "Hittite." This is conceivable only on the assumption that masses of Proto-Armenians settled in one of the Neo-Hittite states, perhaps Melid (Diakonoff 1984:125–27).

At the same time, Luwian continued to preserve its cultural dominance throughout the Neo-Hittite period. There are two cases when intrusive dynasties of foreign origin shifted to Luwian, at least for purposes of writing (figure 23.2). The Syrian kingdom of Palastina/Walastina has recently emerged as a foundation of the Sea People invaders of uncertain linguistic identity, presumably related to the Biblical Philistines (Hawkins 2009:24). The state of Hiyawa on the Cilician Plain was ruled by the "house of Mopsos," whose founder is prominent in Greek mythology, whereas the Cilicians were known to Herodotus as "sub-Achaeans" (Oettinger 2008). Nevertheless, both polities belonged to the Neo-Hittite cultural sphere, and their rulers left numerous inscriptions in the Anatolian hieroglyphic script.

Figure 23.2. Fragments 3–5 and 6 of the Neo-Hittite royal inscription TELL TAYINAT 1 from the Amuq valley, mentioning King Halparuntiya and a country that has previously been read as Wadasatina (Hawkins 2000:2:366) but now can be read as Walastina (Rieken and Yakubovich 2010). Hawkins (2009) read the name of the same country as Palastina in another hieroglyphic inscription that was recently found in Aleppo. The toponym Walastina/Palastina is no doubt related to the name of the Biblical Philistines and the Peleset mentioned as one of the Sea Peoples in Egyptian sources, but its connection with northern Syria comes as a great surprise. The Black Obelisk of the Assyrian king Šalmaneser III mentions Qalparunda, king of Patina, as one of his tributaries. This is possibly the Assyrian adaptation of Halparuntiya, ninth-century B.C.E. king of Walastina/Palastina (image courtesy of the Oriental Institute, University of Chicago).

The end of the Neo-Hittite civilization came about as a result of the Assyrian expansion in Syria and the Cimmerian depredations in Asia Minor. It spelled the end of Luwian literacy but obviously could not lead to the immediate extinction of the Luwian language, especially in those areas where it had been linguistically dominant. One argument for its maintenance in Cilicia in the Achaemenid period is the Cilician royal title *Συέννεσις*, reflecting Luwian **zuwannassi-*, "of the dog" > "hunter," which Greek authors persistently misunderstood as a personal name of Cilician rulers. This title apparently harkens back to the royal epithet "hunter," attested in the hieroglyphic inscriptions of the last Hittite kings (Simon 2009). In the Hellenistic period, Luwian names are still attested in appreciable quantities in Greek inscriptions coming from Cilicia Aspera (Houwink ten Cate 1961:190–92). This is consistent with the hypothesis that the native transmission of the Luwian language was interrupted only as a result of the gradual Hellenization of the Eastern Mediterranean.

The Luwian Corpus

The present survey is limited to those items that are commonly accepted as Luwian in the narrow sense of the word. For the broad use of the term *Luwian* in the sense of "Luwic," see the preceding section.

The Bronze Age Luwian texts were recorded both in cuneiform and with the help of the Anatolian hieroglyphic script. The Luwian texts in cuneiform transmission are collected in transliteration in Starke's volume (1985). All of them were excavated in Ḫattuša, are preserved on clay tablets, and presumably belong to the Hittite royal archives. Most of them are embedded into a Hittite (Nesite) discourse recorded on the same tablet. Judging by the palaeography of the respective tablets, they appear to have been recorded at various points in time between approximately 1500 and 1200 B.C.E. They are rather coherent with respect to their genres; in the majority of cases we are dealing with religious compositions ranging from prayers to magic incantations. At the same time, they have a wide geographic distribution with respect to the place of their oral composition.

About half of the available cuneiform corpus consists of the Luwian incantations coming from Kizzuwatna in southwestern Asia Minor. The most well-known among them are embedded into the rituals of Zarpiya (CTH 757), Puriyanni (CTH 758), and Kuwatalla/Šilalluḫi (CTH 759–62). These texts are edited in Starke (1985:46–201). Presumably, the original Luwian incantations were embedded into the Hittite text of the ritual without translation to preserve their efficacy. Whether it was done locally or in the Hittite capital is a matter of debate, although I am personally inclined toward the latter suggestion (differently, Miller 2004:256). A typical feature of the Kizzuwatna rituals is the admixture of Hurrian elements, reflecting the cultural symbiosis between Hittites, Luwians, and Hurrians in this part of Anatolia.

The variety of Luwian spoken in the Lower Land, probably to be identified with Luwiya of the Hittite Laws, is likely to be reflected in a short incantation embedded in the Tunnawiya ritual (CTH 409, Starke 1985:43–45). The Luwian forms sprinkled through the texts describing the cult of Ḫuwaššanna (CTH 690–94) and collected by Laroche (1959:175–77) also reflect the dialect of the Lower Land, since the veneration of this female deity was associated with the town of Ḫubišna (classical Kybistra).

More extensive is the Late Bronze Age corpus of Empire Luwian. On one hand, we have a large number of Luwian foreign words in Hittite texts attributed to the kings or reflecting the administration of the Hittite Empire. In many cases, these foreign words are accompanied by special "gloss marks," for which the German term *Glossenkeil* is frequently used. Most Glossenkeil-words spread through Hittite texts failed to find their way into Starke (1985), but Melchert (1993) contains their representative collection. On the other hand, the Empire Luwian corpus includes the extensive hieroglyphic inscriptions of the last Hittite kings, for the philological edition of which one should consult Hawkins (1995).

In some cases it is impossible to decide on historical grounds whether a particular text reflects the variety of Luwian spoken in Ḫattuša or in the Lower Land. This holds for the Hittite rituals preserved in the Old and Middle Scripts and containing alternating Luwian and Palaic passages (CTH 752, Starke 1985:37–42). The same thing can be said about the festival CTH 665, which reflects the Hittite state cult but contains Luwian invocations (Starke 1985:270–94). The ritual practices of the Hittite Old Kingdom apparently drew on the traditions of Luwiya and Pala, but those responsible for the compilation of rituals in the Hittite capital could also rely on their personal knowledge of Luwian. The question, after all, may be moot, since the Luwian dialect of Ḫattuša, shortly after its refoundation by the Hittites, may have been the same as the dialect of the Lower Land.

The westernmost area that can be associated with the preserved Luwian textual passages is the Sakarya River basin. A group of texts devoted to the cultic practices of the town Ištanuwa and containing Luwian poetic passages (CTH 771–72, Starke 1985:294–353) prescribes sacrifices to the River Šahiriya, frequently identified with the Sangarios/Sakarya. The "Songs of Ištanuwa," to be performed at various points between ritual acts, are not known in their entirety. Only the initial lines of the songs, sufficient to recognize them by someone intimately familiar with the local repertoire, are preserved as part of the ritual script. The poetic character of these lines strongly suggests that they are preserved in their original dialect(s). Unfortunately, understanding them is inhibited by the fact that their mundane content apparently has little to do with the rest of the ritual.

Finally, there are Bronze Age Luwian texts that give us confusing historical clues as to their origin. This holds, for example, for the myth about the neglected deity and the accompanying ritual (CTH 764, Starke 1985:236–41). On the other hand, the content of many Luwian fragments is not conducive to hypothesizing about the place from which the respective texts originated. Most of the Luwian magical incantations booked under CTH 765 and 767 belong to this group. This is not surprising, given their folkloric outlook, which suggests that they could simultaneously emerge in various parts of the Luwian-speaking area.

The geographic localization of the Iron Age Luwian texts, which are all recorded in the hieroglyphic script, is easier to accomplish. Given that most of the monumental inscriptions have been found in situ and frequently mention the name and title of the local commissioner, one can normally assume that they reflect the scribal practices of the area of their provenience. The known Neo-Hittite principalities that used Luwian for official purposes include Carchemish, Hama, Gurgum, Kummuh, Masuwari, Melid, Palastina/Walastina, Que/Hiyawa, Tabal, and Tuwana. In geographic terms, this encompasses the area from central Anatolia to central Syria. In chronological terms, the inscriptions that are datable on historical grounds span the period between the fall of the Hittite Empire and approximately 700 B.C.E. Their genres include royal *res gestae*, foundation inscriptions, dedicatory monuments, and boundary stelai. All the Luwian hieroglyphic inscriptions of the Iron Age found and edited before the end of the twentieth century were collected by Hawkins (2000), and their locations are mapped by the same author (2003:142). They are usually named according to the location of their discovery and cited in capital letters (e.g., HAMA 6, BABYLON 2).

In addition to the monumental inscriptions, we have a limited number of Iron Age Luwian texts on lead. The most famous among them are ASSUR letters that are full of angry requests by a group of merchants residing in the Assyrian capital to their business partners (Hawkins 2000:2:533–55), and KULULU lead strips containing formulaic records of commercial transactions (2000:2:503–13). Rare as they are, these texts bear witness to the written use of the Luwian language in the private sphere. It is likely that the small proportion of such texts in the Iron Age Luwian corpus has to do with the chance of preservation and excavation and that more of them will be found in the future.

The legends of several stone seals and clay bullae can be assuredly identified as Luwian. The most famous bulla of this kind belongs to Kuzi-Teššub, prince of Carchemish (Hawkins 2000:2:574–75). By contrast, the majority of Bronze Age hieroglyphic seals and bullae carry legends in an indeterminate language, since the formulaic content of short inscriptions does not allow one to decide whether they are Hittite or Luwian.

Anatolian Hieroglyphs

Anatolian hieroglyphic writing gradually arose out of an indigenous set of commonly used symbols and pictograms during the second millennium B.C.E. The evidence suggests that the Anatolian hieroglyphs were invented in the Hittite–Luwian bilingual environment, and only later came to be specifically associated with Luwian (Yakubovich 2008a). The longer hieroglyphic inscriptions are, however, all written in Luwian, and this provides a justification for treating the Anatolian hieroglyphic script in the present chapter.

As is the case with several archaic writing systems, Anatolian hieroglyphs have three main functions: phonetic signs, logograms, and determinatives (see figure 23.3). Phonetic signs were most commonly deployed for rendering syllables of the structure "consonant + vowel," for example, *pa*, *ti*, *su*. In some cases, different signs were fit for rendering the same syllable: thus, no fewer than seven signs could be used to write *sa*. Logograms were special signs reserved for high-frequency words, which referred to their meaning rather than phonetic structure. Because we do not know the pronunciation of many Luwian words written with logograms, and a number of specialists in Anatolian hieroglyphs happen to be classicists by training, the current convention is to use Latin capitals for writing logograms, for example, DOMINUS, "lord," EDERE, "eat," SUB, "under." Determinatives (or determiners) are frequently the same signs as logograms but do not stand for particular spoken words, being instead appended in writing to clarify the meaning of other words. For example, the logogram TONITRUS, "storm-god," is usually written with the

|wa/i-mu	|á-mi-zi-i	|tá-ti-zi	DEUS-ni-zi-i	|(LITUUS)á-za-ta
wa=mu	ami-nzi	tati-nzi	masani-nzi	aza-nta
And-I.ACC	my-NOM.PL	paternal-NOM.PL	god-NOM.PL	love-3PL.PST

'My paternal gods loved me'

This is an actual quotation from a monumental decree of Halparuntiya, late ninth century B.C.E. ruler of the Neo-Hittite kingdom of Gurgum in southwestern Turkey (MARAŞ 1 § 2, Hawkins 2000:263). In the lines above, individual words recorded in Anatolian hieroglyphs are aligned with their sign-by-sign transliterations, transcriptions, and translations. This example is sufficient to demonstrate the principal structural peculiarities of the Anatolian hieroglyphic script. Thus, the logogram DEUS 'god' is accompanied by the phonetic complement *-ni-zi-i* indicating the plural number. The verb *aza-* 'to love' is preceded by the determinative LITUUS (graphically a crooked staff, symbol of authority in the Ancient Near East), which is otherwise generally placed in front of verbs and nouns related to cognition and perception. The sign¨, marked in transliteration as |, is a word-divider, used with varying degrees of consistency in individual inscriptions. The slanted line above *á* and *tá* represents the modern convention for distinguishing signs with identical or similar phonetic values (for example, *tá* in *tá-ti-zi* is graphically different from *ta* in *á-za-ta*, although the two signs reflect the same syllable /ta/). Note that *n* is systematically omitted in writing in the middle of words before consonants.

Figure 23.3. Sample Luwian sentence in Hieroglyphic transmission

unpronounced determinative DEUS, "god," and the combination of the two signs is rendered in transliteration as (DEUS) TONITRUS.

Anatolian hieroglyphic inscriptions do not have a fixed direction of writing. Usually, a text is divided into horizontal lines, and if a particular line is written right to left, then the next one is written left to right, and vice versa. Philologists refer to this type of writing as boustrophedon, meaning that the text moves along like an ox plowing a field. As a consequence of this practice, the signs in odd and even lines of a text look like mirror images of one another. To make things even more complicated, each line tends to be two or three symbols "thick," and thus individual words are likely to form two-dimensional clusters. A number of Anatolian hieroglyphic signs have cursive shapes, which occasionally creep even into the monumental inscriptions.

Three bilingual inscriptions are to be highlighted in connection with the decipherment of the Anatolian hieroglyphic script. The seal of the western Anatolian king Targašnawa, inscribed in hieroglyphs and in cuneiform, allowed A. H. Sayce to give the correct interpretation of the logograms for king (REX) and land (REGIO) (Sayce 1880). This was the beginning of ancient Anatolian philology. The extensive Luwian and Phoenician bilingual of Karatepe (southeastern Turkey), found in 1947, provided a solid confirmation of many hypothetical readings that Hittitologists had advanced in the 1920s and 1930s. This helped establish the study of Hittite hieroglyphs as a universally accredited philological field. The discovery of short Urartian inscriptions in cuneiform and hieroglyphic transmission on large vessels found at Altıntepe (northeastern Turkey) prompted the reevaluation of phonetic values of several important hieroglyphic signs (Hawkins, Morpurgo-Davies, and Neumann 1974). These "new readings" helped establish a very close genetic relationship between the language of the longer hieroglyphic inscriptions and the Luwian of cuneiform texts.

For a more detailed discussion of the structure of the Anatolian hieroglyphic script, see Hawkins (2003). Laroche (1960), although dated, remains a useful catalogue of the Anatolian hieroglyphic signs. For a more up-to-date discussion of the values of individual signs one should consult Marazzi (1990). At the same time, there remains much space for new interpretations in this area (for a recent discovery, see Rieken 2008).

Structure of Luwian

Luwian and Hittite are two closely related languages, and much that can be said about the structure of Hittite also applies to Luwian. In what follows I dwell on those peculiarities of Luwian that distinguish it from Hittite.

Unlike Hittite, which has preserved the Proto-Anatolian five-vowel system, Luwian reduced its vocalism to the system of three basic vowels: /i/, /a/, and /u/. An archaic feature of Luwian consonantism is the preservation of a threefold contrast between /ts/, /k/, and /kʷ/, which respectively reflect the palatalized velar stop *k^j, plain *k, and labialized *k^w, reconstructed for Proto-Indo-European (Melchert 1987). Most Indo-European languages lack distinct reflexes of either *k^j or *k^w, which provided the main reason for dividing them into the traditional centum and satem groups (in particular, Hittite was classified as a centum language). The comparison between Luwian and Hittite indicates that centum and satem are secondary isoglosses.

Already at the common Luwic stage, one can observe a number of lenitions that have no parallels in Hittite, such as *g > y before front vowel and *g^w > w (Melchert 1994:254–55, 303). The continuation of this tendency can be observed in Bronze Age Luwian, where the laryngeal *h* optionally drops before *u* and *w* (Melchert 2003:182). In Iron Age Luwian, it culminates with the merger of intervocalic **d*, **r*, **l*, and sometimes even **n* into what can be reconstructed as a dental flap [ɾ] (Rieken and Yakubovich 2010). In the earlier literature, a subset of these changes has been described as rhotacism (Morpurgo-Davies 1982/83). Although the conservative hieroglyphic orthography obfuscates the flapping in many cases, it is clear that this change must have profoundly altered the phonological structure of Luwian on the eve of its disappearance from the written record.

The nominal system of Luwian has the same set of grammatical features as does Hittite, except that the Luwian nominal forms do not display formal opposition between ablative and instrumental cases. The detailed discussion of the morphological structure of the Luwian noun can be found in Starke (1990). Probably the most significant discovery of this book is the process labeled "*i*-mutation." Starke describes the mixed declensional paradigm of nouns and adjectives, where *a*-stems and consonantal stems show the unexpected stem-final *i*-vocalism in the nominative/accusative singular and plural of the common gender. Although the earlier investigators of this phenomenon tended to connect the "mutation suffix" with the Indo-European feminine suffix *-ih_2 (Zeilfelder 2001:208–39), a recent study regards the "*i*-mutation" as a result of conflating two cognate but distinct lexemes into a single paradigm. For example, *adduwali-*, "evil (adj.)," and *adduwal*, "evil (noun)," merged into the new adjective *adduwal(i)-* (Rieken 2005/2006).

The Luwic languages have developed a productive class of possessive adjectives, which in Luwian is characterized by the suffix *-assa/i-*. They are sometimes compared with Pre-Hellenic toponyms, such as Knossos or Mt. Parnassos, in an attempt to argue for the prehistoric presence of Anatolians or Luwians in the Aegean area. This argument, however, does not stand close scrutiny, because the majority of the Balkan or Cretan toponyms in *-sso-* cannot be derived from the known Anatolian or Indo-European roots and are likely to reflect a non-Indo-European substrate. The Luwian possessive adjectives, on the other hand, can be derived from the Anatolian extended genitives in **-os(s)o* and **-osyo*, which left no direct reflexes in Hittite but have impeccable cognates in Proto-Indo-European (Yakubovich 2008b). The process that led to their derivation was case attraction in the possessive constructions (e.g., **armazit-assa parn-ati* > **armazit-ass-ati parn-ati*, "from the house of Armaziti," where the ablative ending *-ati* spread from the head noun to its syntactic dependent). The Luwian dialect of Kizzuwatna developed a special marker, -*anz*-, indicating the plurality of the base noun from which a possessive adjective is derived (e.g., *malhass-ass-anz-an* EN-*ya*, "to the patron of the rituals"). This innovation must reflect structural interference with Hurrian (Yakubovich 2010a:45–53).

The Luwian pronominal system is generally similar to that of Hittite, but preserves a number of archaisms. First, it features a system of independent possessive pronouns, whereas Hittite cliticized and subsequently lost them. Second, Luwian preserves a system of reflexive pronominal clitics, which are cognate with the Indo-European dative clitics, while Old Hittite generalized a single reflexive particle =*z*(*a*) (Yakubovich 2010a:162–73, 182–96). Third, the Luwian demonstrative pronouns *za*-, "this," and *apa*-, "that," form archaic ablatives *zin* and *apin* that do not have counterparts elsewhere in Anatolian (Goedegebuure 2007).

An important innovation of the Luwic verbal system is the near-merger of the two verbal classes corresponding to the Hittite -*mi* and -*ḫi* conjugations. In Luwian they are contrasted only in third singular present with the respective endings -*t(t)i* and -*i(a)* (Morpurgo-Davies 1980/81). A remarkable archaic feature of the Luwian verb is the first singular preterit ending -*(h)ha*, which represents a precise match to the first singular ending of the Indo-European perfect (Gk. -*α*, Ved. -*a*). The Hittite cognate of this ending is -*(ḫ)ḫun* (first sg. pret., -*ḫi* conjugation), but it underwent contamination with the matching ending -*un* of the -*mi* conjugation.

In contrast to the Hittite lexicon, which is replete with Luwian loanwords at all stages of its attested development, few Hittite borrowings have been detected thus far in the Luwian lexical stock. To some extent, this may simply reflect the current stage of Luwian lexicography, but at the very least one can say that Luwian had a well-developed political and administrative terminology of its own and did not need to borrow it extensively from the Hittites. There is a limited number of Semitic loanwords in individual Luwian dialects, for example, Kizzuwatna Luwian *halāl(i)*-, "pure," borrowed from West Semitic, or Iron Age Luwian *hazz(iy)ani*-, "mayor," taken from Akkadian. In addition, Luwian features several lexemes borrowed from the local unidentified substrate and showing irregular correspondences with Greek (e.g., Luwian *tuwarsa/i*-, "vineyard," versus Greek *θύρσος*, "*thyrsus*, wand wreathed in ivy").

The most up-to-date grammatical survey of the Luwian language is Melchert (2003). Specifically for the grammar of Luwian texts in hieroglyphic transmission, one should compare Plöchl (2003) and Payne (2010). Melchert (1993) represents a reliable lexicon of Luwian words attested in cuneiform. At the same time, a comprehensive grammar and dictionary of Luwian still remain desiderata.

REFERENCES

Abbreviations

CTH Emmanuel Laroche. 1971. *Catalogue des Textes Hittites*. Paris: Klincksiek.

Secondary Sources

Diakonoff, Igor. 1984. *The Pre-History of the Armenian People*. Trans. L. Jennings. Delmar, N.Y.: Caravan Books.

Goedegebuure, Petra. 2007. The Hieroglyphic Luwian Demonstrative Ablative-Instrumentals *zin* and *apin*. In *VI Congresso Internazionale di Ittitologia, Roma, settembre 5–9, 2005*, ed. Alfonso Archi and Rita Francia. Part 1. *Studi Micenei ed Egeo-Anatolici* 49:319–34.

Hawkins, J. David. 1995. *The Hieroglyphic Inscription of the Sacred Pool Complex at Hattusa (SÜDBURG)*. Studien zu den Boğazköy-Texten, Beiheft 3. Wiesbaden: Harrassowitz.

———. 2000. *Corpus of Hieroglyphic Luwian Inscriptions*. Volume 1, parts 1, 2: Texts; part 3: Plates. Berlin: De Gruyter.

———. 2003. Scripts and Texts. In *The Luwians*, ed. Craig Melchert, 128–69. Handbuch der Orientalistik 1/68. Leiden: Brill.

———. 2009. Cilicia, the Amuq, and Aleppo: New Light in a Dark Age. *Near Eastern Archaeology* 72.4: 164–73.

Hawkins, J. David, Anna Morpurgo-Davies, and Günter Neumann. 1974. Hittite Hieroglyphs and Luwian: New Evidence for the Connection. *Nachrichten der Akademie der Wissenschaften in Göttingen (Philologisch-historische Klasse)* 6: 145–97.

Houwink ten Cate, Philo H. J. 1961. *The Luwian Population Groups of Lycia and Cilicia Aspera during the Hellenistic Period*. Leiden: Brill.

Laroche, Emmanuel. 1959. *Dictionnaire de la langue louvite*. Paris: Adrien-Maisonneuve.

———. 1960. *Les Hiéroglyphes Hittites*. Paris: Centre National de la Recherche Scientifique.

Marazzi, Massimiliano. 1990. *Il geroglifico anatolico: Problemi di analisi e prospettivi di ricerca*. Rome: Università "La Sapienza."

Melchert, H. Craig. 1987. PIE Velars in Luvian. In *Studies in Memory of Warren Cowgill (1929–1985)*, ed. Calvert Watkins, 182–204. Berlin: de Gruyter.

———. 1993. *Cuneiform Luvian Lexicon*. Chapel Hill, N.C.: Author.

———. 1994. *Anatolian Historical Phonology*. Amsterdam: Rodopi.

———. 2003. Language. In *The Luvians*, ed. Craig Melchert, 170–210. Handbuch der Orientalistik 1/68. Leiden: Brill.

———. 2005. The Problem of Luvian Influence on Hittite. In *Sprachkontakt und Sprachwandel. Akten der XI. Fachtagung der Indogermanischen Gesellschaft, September 17–23, 2000, Halle an der Saale*, ed. Gerhard Meiser and Olav Hackstein, 445–59. Wiesbaden: Reichert.

Miller, Jared. 2004. *Studies in the Origins, Development and Interpretation of the Kizzuwatna Rituals*. Studien zu den Boğazköy-Texten 46. Wiesbaden: Harrassowitz.

Morpurgo-Davies, Anna. 1980/81. The Personal Endings of the Hieroglyphic Luvian Verb. *Zeitschrift für vergleichende Sprachforschung* 94: 86–108.

———. 1982/83. Dentals, Rhotacism and Verbal Endings in the Luvian Languages. *Zeitschrift für vergleichende Sprachforschung* 96: 245–70.

Oettinger, Norbert. 2008. The Seer Mopsos (Muksas) as a Historical Figure. In *Hittites, Greeks, and Their Neighbors in Ancient Anatolia*, ed. Billie Jean Collins, Mary Bachvarova, and Ian Rutherford, 64–67. Oxford: Oxbow.

Payne, Annick. 2004. *Hieroglyphic Luwian*. Wiesbaden: Harrassowitz.

Plöchl, Reinhold. 2003. *Einführung ins Hieroglyphen-Luwische*. Dresdner Beiträge zur Hethitologie 8. Dresden: Technische Universität Dresden.

Rieken, Elisabeth. 2005/2006. Neues zum Ursprung der Anatolischen *i*-mutation. *Historische Sprachforschung* 118.1: 48–74.

———. 2006. Zum hethitisch-luwischen Sprachkontact in historischer Zeit. *Altorientalische Forschungen* 33: 271–85.

———. 2008. Die Zeichen <ta>, <tá> und <tà> in den hieroglyphen-luwischen Inschriften der Nachgroßreichszeit. In *VI Congresso Internazionale di Ittitologia, Roma, 5–9 settembre 2005*, ed. Alfonso Archi and Rita Francia. Part II. *Studi Micenei ed Egeo-Anatolici* 50: 637–49.

Rieken, Elisabeth and Ilya Yakubovich. 2010. The New Values of Luvian Signs L 319 and L 172. In *Ipamati kistamati pari tumatimis: Luwian and Hittite Studies presented to J. David Hawkins on the occasion of his 70th birthday*, ed. Itamar Singer, 199–219. Tel Aviv: Institute of Archaeology.

Sayce, Archibald H. 1880. The Bilingual Hittite and Cuneiform Inscription of Tarkondêmos. *Transactions of the Society of Biblical Archaeology* 7: 240–87.

Simon, Zsolt. 2009. Towards an Interpretation of the Hieroglyphic Luwian Pair of Signs *109.*285 and the Phonetic Value of *448. *Kadmos* 47: 20–30.

Starke, Frank. 1985. *Die keilschrift-luwischen Texte in Umschrift*. Studien zu den Boğazköy-Texten 30. Wiesbaden: Harrassowitz.

———. 1990. *Untersuchungen zur Stammbildung des keilschrift-luwischen Nomens*. Studien zu den Boğazköy-Texten 31. Wiesbaden: Harrassowitz.

van den Hout, Theo. 2006. Institutions, Vernaculars, Publics: The Case of Second Millennium Anatolia. In *Margins of Writing, Origins of Cultures*, ed. Seth L. Sanders, 217–56. Chicago: Oriental Institute.

Yakubovich, Ilya. 2008a. Hittite-Luvian Bilingualism and the Origin of Anatolian Hieroglyphs. *Acta Linguistica Petropolitana* 4.1: 9–36.

———. 2008b. The Origin of Luwian Possessive Adjectives. In *Proceedings of the 19th UCLA Indo-European Conference*, ed. Karlene Jones-Bley, Martin E. Huld, Angela della Volpe, and Miriam Robbins Dexter, 193–217. Washington, D.C.: Institute for the Study of Man.

———. 2010a. *Sociolinguistics of the Luvian Language*. Leiden: Brill.

———. 2010b. West Semitic Hod El in Anatolian Hieroglyphic Transmission. In *Pax Hethitica: Studies on the Hittites and their Neighbours in Honour of Itamar Singer*, ed. Yoram Cohen, Amir Gilan, and Jared Miller, 385–98. Wiesbaden: Harrassowitz.

Zeilfelder, Susanne. 2001. *Archaismus und Ausgliederung: Studien zur sprachlichen Stellung des Hethitischen*. Heidelberg: Winter.

CHAPTER 24

URARTIAN AND THE URARTIANS

PAUL ZIMANSKY

WITH a few terminological qualifications, it is easy enough to define the subject of Urartian as a language; the Urartians as a people, however, are another matter. To whom does this designation apply? Urartian texts were produced by a few individuals in a restricted context, and determining the extent of the term's inclusiveness beyond this temporally, spatially, and culturally takes one into the realm of speculation and controversy. The core around which the meanings are layered is the polity of Biainili, known to outsiders as Urartu or Ararat, which dominated eastern Anatolia and adjacent areas in the eighth and seventh centuries B.C.E. This kingdom had a militaristic imperial government and left a distinctive archaeological record, known to us largely from the ruins of fortresses and looted burials. Its ruling dynasty was directly involved in the creation of hundreds of monumental inscriptions in a simplified and quite intelligible cuneiform script, which enable us to identify, classify, and to a certain extent understand the official language we call Urartian.

We do not know the ancient name of this language; no surviving source from antiquity mentions it in the abstract. Nor is it likely that its native speakers called themselves Urartians, although their enemies probably did. In employing these terms, we follow a convention going back to the Assyrians, who originally had a geographical referent in mind when they used the variants Uruaṭri and Uraṭri[1] in the thirteenth century B.C.E. to designate a politically disunified territory in highland eastern Anatolia stretching northwestward from Lake Van. Later, they applied the term *Urartu* to Biainili, a polity that coalesced in eastern Anatolia in the mid-ninth century B.C.E., prospered as the Neo-Assyrian Empire's most persistent rival, and then disappeared, violently and with remarkable thoroughness, a little more than two centuries later. The Bible and Neo-Hittite documents followed the Assyrian lead, the Biblical Ararat simply being a rendering of Urartu transposed by writers who were no longer familiar with the original pronunciation. Only once is the term *Urartu* written out phonetically in Biainili's own inscriptions, and this is in the Akkadian version of a late bilingual text (André-Salvini and Salvini 2002:21). In earlier Akkadian texts, Urartians use the name Nairi for their land, which in Middle Assyrian and early Neo-Assyrian documents appears to refer to a highland area to the south and east of Uruaṭri, closer to Lake Urmia. The kings of Biainili do not provide an ethnic or linguistic designation for their subjects, beyond the literal meaning of Biainili itself, "those of the land of Bia." Because this was an empire put together by military force and importation of captive peoples, the assumption that there was broad ethnic or linguistic uniformity among its subjects is hardly warranted.

After the collapse of both Biainili and the Assyrian Empire, there are scattered cuneiform references to the land of Urašṭu and individuals in some way associated with it. In the absence of an autonomous political entity in the area at this time, the term is probably once again geographical. The Behistun trilingual of the late sixth century B.C.E. uses Urašṭu in the Akkadian version, but replaces it with Armina and Arminiya in the Old Persian and Elamite versions, respectively (King, Thompson, and Budge 1907:1)—the first historical appearance of the term *Armenia* (see Radner, chapter 33 in this volume). If there ever had been a linguistic connotation to Urarṭu/Urašṭu, by this time it must have been a thing of the past.

The most minimal definition of an Urartian would be someone who spoke the language of the royal inscriptions of Biainili. I begin the discussion with linguistic considerations before returning to the question of who should be included among the Urartians.

The Corpus of Urartian Texts

The most substantial Urartian texts are carved into stone in cuneiform characters, sometimes on exposed bedrock, sometimes on worked stones once incorporated in buildings, and sometimes on independent stelai specially erected to display text. It is hard to give meaningful statistics on the number and content size of these, because there are many duplicates, near duplicates, and fragmentary inscriptions. A rough characterization is that there are several hundred texts, most of which consist of a few stock phrases. About sixty extant inscriptions run to twenty or more lines of a few words each, and there are three much longer texts: (1) the annals of Argišti I, carved on the south face of the Van citadel outside a huge, multiroomed rock-cut tomb; (2) the annals of Sarduri II, found on a stele and the walls of a niche on the north side of the Van citadel; and (3) a standard inscription of the seventh-century B.C.E. king Rusa, son of Argišti, of which a complete version was discovered in 1998 (Çilingiroğlu and Salvini 2001:253–70), although parts of variants had long been known from other sites. There are also four bilingual texts, with versions in Neo-Assyrian Akkadian and Urartian. These were all composed by Urartian kings and associated with the buffer state of Muṣaṣir, which lay in the Zagros Mountains west of Lake Urmia, between

Urartu and Assyria (see Radner, chapter 33 in this volume). The best preserved and most important of these is the stele that stood in the Kelishin Pass, with Urartian and Assyrian versions of forty-one and forty-two lines, respectively.

There is also some writing on clay, used for bureaucratic purposes by the Urartians, but in comparison to what comes from Mesopotamian sites, it survives in very modest quantity. Fewer than thirty tablets and tablet fragments have so far been discovered,[2] although there are also short notations in the same style on clay bullae as further testimony to the importance of handwritten cuneiform in the administration of Urartian fortresses. These rare pieces are in a practiced hand and generally well preserved, so it may simply be bad luck that a palace archive containing thousands of them has eluded discovery. Cuneiform was often carved onto the shoulders of large storage vessels to indicate capacity.

Less interesting philologically but accounting for the largest number of inscriptions are hundreds of short notations of possession and dedication inscribed on bronze objects of art. Cuneiform legends were carved on the royal seals and the seals of officials whose personal names are also those common to royalty, but not, significantly, on the seals of other individuals.

Cuneiform was not the only writing employed in Biainili. A hieroglyphic script, which employed characters similar to and in some cases identical with Luwian hieroglyphs, was in general use as well. Most of the examples of this consist of a few symbols scratched onto clay vessels, often with accompanying notations of quantity. They also appear on seals and bronze plaques, and one clay tablet with incised glyphs is known. Although Urartu's hieroglyphs were perhaps more widespread than its cuneiform, they remain largely undeciphered; they may not have constituted a full writing system, and contribute nothing to our understanding of the underlying language.

For many decades, scholarly access to the corpus of Urartian texts was provided by two basic collections, one in German (König 1955–57) and one in Russian (Melikišvili 1960). As more inscriptions were discovered and published in the last decades of the twentieth century, these became obsolete. A new single-volume work in Russian, appearing several years ago (Arutjunjan 2001), updated Melikišvili's work but did not include the important new material from Ayanis. As this chapter was being written, the first three volumes of a long-awaited corpus with Italian translations appeared (Salvini 2008) and promises to be the standard resource for the next generation of Urartian scholars.

Discovery and Early Attempts at Decipherment

Perhaps the best way to introduce Urartian is to follow the footsteps that led to its discovery in the nineteenth century, if only to underscore how long it took scholars to recognize its fundamental difference from the major language families hitherto defined. Classical authors and the Bible had not prepared the world of that time for the rediscovery of a major empire in eastern Anatolia, and before cuneiform was deciphered the Assyrian sources were of course unavailable. Neither Xenophon nor Herodotus had anything to say on the subject of Urartu. Early Armenian historians, who had the physical remains of Biainili's royal tombs and inscriptions before them, followed classical traditions in attributing these to Assyria. Nevertheless, a fair portion of the Urartian corpus was made available to western scholars quite early in the history of Assyriology thanks to the epigraphic mission of a young professor from the University of Giessen, Friedrich Schulz. Dispatched to Persia but prevented from entering that country, he arrived at Van in July 1827 and copied more than forty Urartian cuneiform inscriptions, including the lengthy annals of Argišti I. Schulz was killed before he could return to Europe, but his *mémoire* and text copies were posted to France and published (Schulz 1840) just before the celebrated French and British excavations at the Neo-Assyrian capitals of Nineveh, Khorsabad, and Nimrud got under way.

No analysis of the Urartian language could be undertaken until the cuneiform writing system itself was reasonably well understood. Schulz's copies, exploited by the pioneering genius of Edward Hincks, made a significant contribution to this, thanks to a quirk of Urartian orthography. In the late 1840s, it was clear to those attempting to understand the cuneiform system that some signs represented whole words (logograms), whereas many were pronounced as syllables. A few others, determinatives, were not part of the spoken language at all but were writing devices to indicate the class of an associated word, for example, the name of a land, a personal name, a type of vessel, or an object made of wood. The logograms and determinatives could help someone grasp the general concerns of a text, but only the syllabic signs would provide phonological information for understanding the underlying language. Hincks noted that in the repetitive Urartian texts, which were often nearly duplicates of each other, a small number of signs appeared to be optional; they could either be present or absent. He correctly guessed that these were pure vowels, whereas most of the other signs were vowel and consonant combinations (Hincks 1848). Hincks then turned to the Behistun trilingual, of which the Old Persian passages, written with more or less alphabetic characters, had previously been deciphered thanks to the work of Grotefend and Rawlinson. This provided him with readings for place-names that he could match in the Akkadian version. He was able to discover the correct values of the signs he had identified as vowels in Schulz's copies of Urartian texts and make considerable progress in the understanding of the more common syllabic signs.

Although the cuneiform script of Urartu was essentially the same as that used for the Assyrian and Babylonian dialects of Akkadian in the first millennium B.C.E., it was a good deal more streamlined. Moreover, Urartian monumental texts are very standardized and repetitive. Their simplicity and clarity made Hincks's insights possible, but ultimately the chief value of his work was to provide a toehold for deciphering the full cuneiform script of Akkadian, which was brought close to completion in the 1850s by Hincks, Rawlinson, Oppert, and others.

Understanding the Urartian language, as opposed to its script, was another matter. On this Hincks could make little progress. He did offer one suggestion which, although incorrect, is of some historical interest, both for its misunderstanding of the most fundamental aspect of Urartian grammar and its embrace of an idea whose time came seven decades later with Hittite: he thought he might be dealing with an Indo-European language (Hincks 1848). In short inscriptions, he noted that the name of the actor, invariably the Urartian king, had a case ending marked by the sign read *-še*, and the thing acted on, which he saw as a direct object, usually ended in *-ni*. To a person schooled in Latin and ancient Greek, these look very much like nominative and accusative masculine forms, respectively, if one ignores the vowels, which appear to be very weak in final position in any event. With the materials available to him and the level of linguistic analysis at the time, one can hardly fault Hincks's logic in coming to this conclusion. However, Urartian is not Indo-European and has no accusative case or nominative case as such. Another seventy years were to pass before these case endings were correctly interpreted.

The *-še* did, in fact, mark the agent, or actor, in the sentence, but not in the way a nominative case does. Urartian has what is called an "ergative" structure, which is a very different organizing principle from what one finds in Indo-European or Semitic languages. Ergative languages, of which there are many genetically unrelated examples scattered around the world, lack the formal category of a direct object, and make use of a special marked oblique case to designate the agent in an action. There is a clear distinction in the form and conjugations of transitive and intransitive verbs, and a basic unmarked case is used for what we would consider the subject of an intransitive verb and the object of a transitive one. One can replicate the pattern approximately in English by using the passive voice—"the city was conquered by the king" where the preposition "by" performs the function of identifying the agent given the case ending *-še* in Urartian. The word for city is unmarked and would have exactly the same grammatical form in the intransitive sentence "the city trembled." One hastens to add that this English example is only offered as an analogy; Urartian verbs are not actually passive and there is no active voice in the language with which to contrast a passive.

Without an appreciation of its ergative character, a basic organizing principle which permeates its grammar, it is hard to see how anyone could claim to understand Urartian, but deciphering the cuneiform writing system and work with Neo-Assyrian texts offered scholars of the later nineteenth century a somewhat specious ability to interpret the texts. The simplicity and repetitiveness of Urartian writing, the use of logograms with meanings common to all cuneiform, and the intelligibility of place-names made a rough understanding of what was going on in most of the monumental inscriptions reasonably clear. Archibald Henry Sayce exploited this transparency when he initiated a series of articles in the *Journal of the Royal Asiatic Society* in which all of the known Urartian texts were published and translated, along with a grammar (Sayce 1882). At the time, this was regarded as a breakthrough, with Sayce himself claiming that "the passages and words which still resist translation are but few" (Sayce 1882:387). As late as 1915 a work relating the history of what was still called "Vannic" credited Sayce with solving the mystery of the inscriptions (Rogers 1915:1:270–71). Today we know that Sayce misunderstood even some of the most basic words. His translation of a simple building inscription, "To the children of Khaldis the gracious Menuas son of Ispuinis of Khaldis after this gate had been restored, which was decayed" (Sayce 1882:508–9) would now be read "By the power of Ḫaldi, Minua, son of Išpuini, built these gates of Ḫaldi to perfection."

Understanding how a text says what it does, rather than simple translation, is the real issue with Urartian. In analyzing a grammar so incompletely presented by its own documents, with their nearly exclusive fixation on royal activities narrated in the third person or first person past tense, identification of related languages was of particular importance. We have seen that Hincks erroneously suggested it might be Indo-European, and alternative suggestions were put forward without much rigor throughout the nineteenth century. Sayce, for example, considered a relationship with Georgian, "or with any of the Caucasian languages such as Ude or Abkhas," but admitted he lacked the tools to explore this (Sayce 1882:411). Hurrian, the only close relative of Urartian, did not enter the discussion until the twentieth century.[3]

The discovery and analysis of a substantial body of Hurrian texts at Boğazköy opened the next phase of Urartian decipherment. There were no "eureka!" moments, but rather a gradual progress was effected through incremental contributions by pioneers of Hittitology and Russian scholars familiar with the languages of the Caucasus. A close relationship between Urartian and Hurrian was recognized initially in vocabulary, and therewith a basis for hypothesizing a broader conception of Urartian's grammatical structure was established. The essentially ergative nature of the language was recognized by the 1930s. Although the translations in the major text collections of the 1950s already noted differ from modern ones only in detail, a comprehensive presentation of Urartian grammar in combination with Hurrian was long in coming (Diakonoff 1971). It has been common for philologists to concern themselves with Hurro-Urartian as a single field of academic endeavor, adding to vocabulary and interpretation of grammatical nuance in Urartian as the understanding of Hurrian advances and new texts in both languages are recovered.

Rudiments of Modern Urartian Interpretation

Although no detailed grammar presents Urartian to the full extent that it is currently understood, Gernot Wilhelm's overview (2004, 2008)[4] does a remarkably thorough job of covering the subject in a few pages. A new dictionary and grammatical sketch, not yet published, is promised for the final volume of Salvini's new corpus.

The phonetic values normally read in the cuneiform signs, introduced by the Sumerians and transmitted to the Urartians 2,000 years later through the Akkadian language, are only approximations of Urartian phonemes. In the oldest known text of an Urartian king, repeated on six enormous building blocks at the western foot of the citadel rock at Van, Sarduri I cribbed both the language and script of a Neo-Assyrian royal inscription, changing only the proper names to make it his own. Before the end of the ninth century B.C.E., the next ruler of Biainili, Išpuini, used the same script to write the earliest texts in the Urartian language. The starting point for the sounds of the signs was thus their Neo-Assyrian values, and because there are neither identifiable dialects nor indications of temporal change in the Urartian texts, one assumes that they remained close to those, albeit with allowance for the different phonemes of the two languages.

The inventory of pronounced signs included five for vowels (*a*, *e*, *i*, and two homophonous signs for *u*). The 100 or so syllabic signs with consonantal values were most frequently vowel + consonant (VC), less frequently consonant + vowel (CV), and occasionally consonant + vowel + consonant (CVC). The consonants in question are transliterated as: ‘, b, d, g, k, l, m, n, p, t, k, q, s, ṣ, š, t, ṭ, and z. What sounds did these actually transcribe in Urartian? The values of the sibilants are particularly difficult to pin down, because they also shift among dialects of Akkadian. For example, signs containing the value transliterated as *š* and *s* have reversed pronunciations in Babylonian and Assyrian dialects, and the *š* of Urartian is more likely to have been pronounced as the *s* in "sole" than the *sh* in "shoe." In addition to the voiced and voiceless values familiar to English speakers, there was apparently a phonemically distinct third set of values transliterated by the Semitic emphatics, for example; Wilhelm suggests that they might represent voiceless glottalized or aspirated consonants (Wilhelm 2008:108). Uncertainty on these and other points of phonology inhibits recognition of cognates between Urartian and other languages.

It is also apparent that the Urartians used the syllabary in their own way. Final vowels of words represented by CV signs are apt to be weak or nonexistent. In some cases the sign is seemingly used for a simple consonant (Wilhelm 2008:106). Cases where the vowel is sometimes written as *e* and other times as *i* perhaps indicate reduction to a schwa (/ə/), but elsewhere supplementary vowels are added to make the value of the vowel clear. For example, the Urartians did not use the quite common cuneiform sign for *mi*. In writing the name of the king Minua, they used *me* and followed it with an *i*: ^{m}*Me-i-nu-a*. In analyzing Hurro-Urartian texts, therefore, it is customary to distinguish between transliterations, which are sign-by-sign renderings of the cuneiform into the Latin alphabet, and transcriptions, which analyze the phonology and grammar of the text on a more hypothetical basis and reflect the way the text is thought to have been pronounced and understood.

Urartian nouns begin with a short root, followed by a theme vowel to which various modifiers may be appended, and conclude with endings to indicate case and number. Gender is not marked in Urartian in either nouns or verbs; if there were separate feminine pronouns we would be none the wiser, as only two women are mentioned in the whole Urartian corpus, and in neither instance is a pronoun used for them. Singular and plural are indicated; no dual has been identified. All modern authorities agree on case endings for the absolute, ergative, genitive, dative, directive, and locative, but more obscure cases are variously defined. For example, Wilhelm lists a comitative, directive archaic, and ablative-instrumental contrasting with the simple ablative (Wilhelm 2008:113). Adjectives follow the nouns they modify and agree with them in number and case. When two nouns are linked, an anaphoric particle is used to separate the case endings of the second noun from endings that reiterate the case endings of the first. For example, when Minua, son of Išpuini, is the actor in a transitive sentence, the name of Išpuini also takes an agentive case ending: *Minua=še Išpuini=hi=ni=še* (Minua + agentive Išpuini + patronymic + anaphoric particle + agentive).

Like the noun, the verb also begins with a short root to which modifiers may be suffixed. In a fixed order, short elements are then added to indicate such things as aspect, transitivity (or valence), and mood. The transitive verb concludes with polysynthetic endings reflective of the number and person of the actor and the thing acted upon. For example if a king built a temple, the preterite verb would be *šid=išt=u=bə* (root ["built"] = verbal suffix [maybe some nuance like "up"] = indicator of transitivity or two valences = indicator of third singular subject plus third singular object ["he x-ed it"]). If he built gates, the form would be *šid=išt=u=alə*, the final form indicating third singular agent and third plural object. Intransitive verbs, on the other hand, have simple person/number-indicating endings: *nun=a=də* (root ["came"] = indicator of single valence = first singular), "I came." "He came" would be *nun=a=bə*, and "they came" would be *nun-a-lə*. A few roots may be used both transitively and intransitively, for example, *ušt=a=bə*, "he set out [on campaign]," with *ušt=u=nə*, "he sent it."

Imperatives, jussives (third-person requests), optatives, conditionals, and a few additional nonindicative moods are attested in limited numbers, largely in the curse formulae that sometimes conclude texts. Our understanding of verbal morphology is greatly hampered by the fact that almost all of the documents we have, with the exception of these curse formulae and the relatively rare letters, are framed in the past tense with actors and objects in the first or third person singular indicative. Hurrian suggests various forms, but the Urartian material is neither abundant nor varied enough to hypothesize complete paradigms.

Urartians as People and Polity

How does this language, the official idiom of the state in Biainili, relate to Urartians as a people? At one end of the spectrum is the presumption that Urartian was widely spoken in eastern Anatolia in the late second millennium B.C.E. and that its speakers were the dominant population element within the frontiers of the kingdom of Biainili. In this case, the distribution of Urartian speakers embraces the full range of the term *Urartu* as used by the Assyrians and others in all its variants. At the opposite extreme is the idea that the kingdom of Biainili was a relatively short-lived political and cultural phenomenon, created and maintained by military force, in which the tastes and prejudices of a small ruling élite predominated over an otherwise diverse population. The Urartian language, in this case, might have very little to do with the broader geographical and chronological connotations of the term *Urartu*. Historical reality probably lies somewhere between these two extremes.

Affiliations of the Urartian language with other languages in and around eastern Anatolia have been used to argue for the first position. In particular, the close connection with Hurrian, dialects of which were widely spoken in northern Syria and northern Iraq in the second millennium B.C.E., puts it in this region. The two languages share numerous cognates, for example: *ewri* (Hur.) = *euri* (Ur.), "lord"; *hurati* (Hur.) = *huradi* (Ur.), "soldier"; *pab-* (Hur.) = *bab-* (Ur.), "mountain"; and *ar-* (Hur.) = *ar-* (Ur.), "give" (Gragg 1995:2170; Salvini 1979). Similarities in the phonology and grammatical structure of the two languages are even more significant in establishing a genetic connection than common vocabulary, which can of course be borrowed.

There is now consensus that Hurrian and Urartian are sister languages, although the position that Urartians might be first millennium B.C.E. Hurrian survivors was occasionally put forward in the past. The earliest dialect of Hurrian, seen in the Tišatal royal inscription and reconstructed from various early second millennium B.C.E. sources, shows features that disappeared in later Hurrian but are present in Urartian (Wilhelm 1988:63). In short, "the more we discover or deduce about the earliest stages of Hurrian, the more it looks like Urartian" (Gragg 1995:2170). The Hurrians are often assumed to have intruded into Greater Mesopotamia from the highlands from the third millennium B.C.E. on, although their presence is only documented south of the Taurus. Whereas attempts to link their movements with specific pottery styles, like Kura-Araxes Ware in the third millennium or Khabur Ware in the second millennium B.C.E. are problematic on archaeological grounds, divergence between the two languages is thought to begin in the late third millennium B.C.E. (Gragg 1995:2170) or not much later than 2000 B.C.E. (Wilhelm 2008:105).

That Hurro-Urartian as a whole shared a yet earlier common ancestor with some of the numerous and comparatively obscure languages of the Caucasus is not improbable. Modern Caucasian languages are conventionally divided into southern, (north)western, and (north)eastern families (Smeets 1989:260). Georgian, for example, belongs to the southern family. Diakonoff and Starostin, in the most thorough attempt at finding a linkage yet published, have argued that Hurro-Urartian is a branch of the eastern Caucasian family. This would make it a distant relative of such modern languages as Chechen, Avar, Lak, and Udi (Diakonoff and Starostin 1986). The etymologies, sound correspondences, and comparative morphologies these authors present are quite tentative and viewed with skepticism by many (e.g., Smeets 1989). In any case, a reconstructed parent language dating to the early third millennium B.C.E. at the earliest would do nothing to define the Urartian homeland more precisely.

Alternatively, archaeological and historical evidence for an abrupt emergence of Biainili together with the speed and totality of its disappearance argue for minimizing the number of Urartian speakers. The kingdom of Biainili, to which native inscriptions only indirectly applied the name Urartu toward the end of its history, is associated with cultural characteristics that were imposed from the top down at the end of the ninth century B.C.E. Some, like the writing system and decorative arts, were clearly inspired by Assyria and Greater Mesopotamia generally. The distinctive style of fortress architecture, on the other hand, seems to have been a local invention. Few settlements dating to the centuries prior to the rise of Biainili have been identified in the relevant parts of eastern Anatolia, and almost all Urartian sites are new foundations. The Urartian state religion placed the god Ḫaldi, imported from Muṣaṣir, at the head of a pantheon that included both well-known Hurrian deities, like the storm god Teišeba, and a plethora of local characters, like the mountain god Qilbani. The ruling family itself may have come to Van from the Muṣaṣir area, given the latter's importance in the maintenance of kingship. Urartian literacy was strongly tied to the central government of Biainili, and was probably otherwise quite superficial (Zimansky 2006). In this context, the branch of the Hurro-Urartian family that we know as Urartian may well have arrived in the Van area with the new rulers and have nothing to do with the area that the Assyrians called Uruaṭri in the second millennium B.C.E.

This would help explain why there are so few traces of the language after the collapse of the state. All but a few Urartian sites were abandoned, and only rarely do place-names in Urartian texts carry over into later eras, Erevan from Erebuni being one notable exception. A handful of Hurro-Urartian words appear to have been borrowed by Armenian, but fewer than one would expect if the languages were in close proximity for a long time, and one cannot say whether they came directly through Urartian (Greppin 1991). Fashionable as it once was to see survivors of the great empire in the names of peoples known to the Greeks like the Alarodians and Khaldians (thought to be named for the god Ḫaldi), nothing in what little the classical descriptions tell us of these people shows any continuity with Biainili.

In short, Urartians are not a self-identified people, and language is just one modern alternative used to define them. It may not be the best option when the subject of the discussion is in fact the kingdom of Biainili, its origins, or its fate. Although the official language of Biainili, imperfect though our knowledge of it may be, is certainly at home in eastern Anatolia, a good deal of historical confusion would be obviated if more care were given to the different nuances of geography, polity, and chronology in considering who the Urartians were.

NOTES

1. The ṭ in Urarṭu, Uruaṭri, Uraṭri, and Urašṭu is consistently rendered in cuneiform with the emphatic *tet*, transcribed as a *t* with a dot under it. Although this sound is

phonemically distinct in both Semitic languages and Urartian, a simple *t* is almost universally used in modern scholarship on Urartu unless specifically addressing phonological issues. I follow that practice here.

2. In the summer of 2009, Altan A. Çilingiroğlu discovered five tablet fragments in the citadel at Ayanis in a room that promises to yield more in future excavations. No substantial text was preserved on any of these, but they are further evidence that cuneiform was widely used for nondisplay purposes in Urartu.

3. Robert W. Rogers stated that the discoveries of Belck and Lehmann-Haupt's Armenian expedition of 1898 "may be regarded as the concluding event in the history of the decipherment of the Vannic [i.e., Urartian] inscriptions" (1915:1:272–73) and notes elsewhere in the same work that the language of Mitanni, that is, Hurrian "has thus far not yielded to the numerous efforts made to decipher it" (1915:2:112). He makes no reference to Hurrian in his lengthy discussion of Urartian decipherment, which was regarded as the definitive statement on the eve of World War I and prior to Hrozny's breakthrough on Hittite.

4. Wilhelm's chapter was first published as part of Woodard's full encyclopedia of ancient languages in 2004, and then reprinted, with different pagination, in a smaller volume on the languages of Asia Minor in 2008. In my citations, I use the 2008 publication.

REFERENCES

André-Salvini, Béatrice and Mirjo Salvini. 2002. The Bilingual Stele of Rusa I from Movana (West-Azerbaijan, Iran). *Studi Micenei ed Egeo-Anatolici* 44.1: 5–66.

Arutjunjan, Nikolaj V. 2001. *Korpus urartskich kinoobraznych nadpisej*. Erevan: Izdatel'stvo "gitujun" Nacional'naja Akademija Nauk Respubliki Armenija.

Çilingiroğlu, Altan A. and Mirjo Salvini, eds. 2001. *Ayanis I: Ten Years' Excavations at Rusahinili Eiduru-kai 1989–1998*. Rome: CNR Istituto per gli Studi Micenei ed Egeo-Anatolici.

Diakonoff, I. M. 1971. *Hurrisch und Urartäisch*. Trans. Karl Sdrembek. Münchner Studien zur Sprachwissenschaft, Beiheft 6, Neue Folge, ed. Bernhard Forsmann, Karl Hoffman, and Johanna Narten. Munich: R. Kitzinger.

Diakonoff, I. M., and S. A. Starostin. 1986. *Hurro-Urartian as an Eastern Caucasian Language*. Münchner Studien zur Sprachwissenschaft, Beiheft 12, Neue Folge, ed. Bernhard Forsmann, Karl Hoffman, and Johanna Narten. Munich: R. Kitzinger.

Gragg, Gene. 1995. Less-Understood Languages of Ancient Western Asia. In *Civilizations of the Ancient Near East*, ed. Jack M. Sasson, 2161–79. New York: Scribner's.

Greppin, John A. C. 1991. Some Effects of the Hurro-Urartian People and Their Languages upon the Earliest Armenians. *Journal of the American Oriental Society* 111: 720–30.

Hincks, Edward. 1848. On the Inscriptions at Van. *Journal of the Royal Asiatic Society* 9: 387–449.

King, L. W., R. C. Thompson, and E. A. W. Budge. 1907. *The Sculptures and Inscription of Darius the Great on the Rock of Behistûn*. London: British Museum.

König, Friedrich Wilhelm. 1955–57. *Handbuch der chaldischen Inschriften*. Archiv Für Orientforschung, Beiheft 8. Graz: Selbstverlag Ernst Weidners.

Melikišvili, Georgij A. 1960. *Urartskie klinoobraznye nadpisi*. Moscow: Izdatel'stvo Akademii Nauk SSSR.

Rogers, Robert William. 1915. *A History of Babylonia and Assyria*, 6th ed., 2 vols. New York: Abingdon Press.

Salvini, Mirjo. 1979. Confronti lessicali fra Hurro e Urarteo. In *Florilegium Anatolicum: Mélanges offerts à Emmanuel Laroche*, 305–14. Paris: Éditions E. de Boccard.

———. 2008. *Corpus dei testi urartei*. Documenta Asiana 8. Rome: CNR–Istituto di studi sulle civiltà dell'Egeo e del Vicino Oriente.

Sayce, Archibald H. 1882. The Cuneiform Inscriptions of Van. *Journal of the Royal Asiatic Society* 14: 377–732.

Schulz, Friedrich É. 1840. Mémoire sur le lac Van et ses environs. *Journal Asiatique Ser.* 3, 9: 257–323.

Smeets, Rieks. 1989. On Hurro-Urartian as an Eastern Caucasian Language. *Bibliotheca Orientalis* 46: 259–79.

Wilhelm, Gernot. 1988. Gedanken zur Frühgeschichte der Hurriter und zum hurritisch-urartäischen Sprachvergleich. In *Hurriter und Hurritisch*, ed. Volkert Haas, 43–67. Xenia. Konstanzer Althistorische Vorträge und Forschungen, vol. 21. Konstanz: Universitätsverlag Konstanz.

———. 2004. Urartian. In *The Cambridge Encyclopedia of the World's Ancient Languages*, ed. Roger D. Woodard, 119–37. Cambridge: Cambridge University Press.

———. 2008. Urartian. In *The Ancient Languages of Asia Minor*, ed. Roger D. Woodard, 105–23. Cambridge: Cambridge University Press.

Zimansky, Paul. 2006. Writing, Writers, and Reading in the Kingdom of Van. In *Margins of Writing, Origins of Cultures*, ed. Seth L. Sanders, 257–76. Oriental Institute Seminars no. 2. Chicago: Oriental Institute Press.

CHAPTER 25

PHRYGIAN AND THE PHRYGIANS

LYNN E. ROLLER

The Phrygians appeared in Anatolia during the Early Iron Age, ca. 1200–1000 B.C.E., and retained a distinctive identity there until the end of Classical antiquity. Phrygian settlements can be recognized by the presence of texts in the Phrygian language, architecture and visual arts, and characteristic installations of Phrygian cult practice. The geographical extent of Phrygian territory covers a broad area, including Daskyleion near the Sea of Marmara in northwestern Anatolia, Gordion and Ankara in central Anatolia, and Boğazköy and Kerkenes Dağ east of the Halys River. Taken together, the linguistic and material evidence suggests that Phrygian culture was an influential element in the ethnic mix of populations on the Anatolian plateau.

Origin of the Phrygians

Evidence for the origin of the Phrygians is furnished by Greek literary sources, linguistic analysis, and material culture. Herodotus 7.73 reports that the Phrygians were originally at home in Macedonia, where they were called Briges, and that they changed their name to Phrygians when they migrated into Anatolia. The comment on the name change seems contrived, because the words "Briges" and "Phryges" are essentially the same, but Herodotus's report, corroborated by Xanthos of Lydia (quoted by Strabo 12.8.3, 14.5.29), that the origin of the Phrygian people lay in southeastern Europe, is probably correct. This is demonstrated in part by linguistic evidence. The Phrygian language is a branch of the Indo-European language family that is closely related to Greek and Thracian (Strabo 7.3.2; Neumann 1988). It is notably different from Luwian and Hittite, the principal Bronze Age Anatolian languages, suggesting that the Phrygian language was intrusive into Anatolia, introduced through immigration from northern Greece or the Balkans. There is less consistency in the ancient literary sources on the date of the migration. The *Iliad* describes the Phrygians as allies of the Trojans during the Trojan War (Homer, *Iliad* 2.862, 3.184–88, 16.717–19, 24.545), which would suggest that the Phrygians were established in their Anatolian territory during the Late Bronze Age. Xanthos of Lydia (quoted by Strabo 14.5.29), however, stated that the Phrygian migration into Anatolia took place after the fall of Troy, or, in historical terms, after the end of the Bronze Age. The evidence from material culture at Gordion (see Voigt, chapter 50 in this volume), the only Phrygian site investigated to date with a continuous sequence of habitation levels from the Bronze through Iron Ages, supports both a post-Bronze Age date and the hypothesis of a Balkan homeland. The Gordion Late Bronze Age strata have yielded pottery with close affinities to Late Bronze Age wares of other central Anatolian sites; these are followed by strata containing pottery that is distinctively different in fabric, shape, and decoration, exhibiting parallels with handmade ceramics from Thracian sites in the Balkans (Henrickson 1994:106–8; Sams 1988, 1994:19–22, 126). The combination of linguistic evidence and ceramic parallels strongly suggests an infiltration of population groups from the Balkans during the early first millennium B.C.E.

The nature of the cultural shift occasioned by the arrival of the Phrygians is difficult to assess. At Gordion, significant changes in ceramics and architectural features found in early Iron Age levels appear to signal the arrival of a new people, but there is no evidence for a violent transition between the Late Bronze and Early Iron Age (Voigt 1994:276–78); instead, the material suggests that there may have been several successive waves of new settlers and that the transition lasted over a century or more. The limitation of the evidence to a small area within one single site, Gordion, makes these conclusions tentative (see Voigt, chapter 50 in this volume).

History of Phrygia

The history of the Phrygian people following their establishment in Anatolia is drawn from the material evidence of Phrygian settlements and cult centers coupled with the written documentation of the Phrygians' neighbors, the Assyrians to the east (see Radner, chapter 33 in this volume) and the Greeks to the west (see Harl, chapter 34, and Greaves, chapter 21 in this volume). Written texts in the Phrygian language offer some supplemental information, but no list of Phrygian kings or annalistic tradition that recorded Phrygian history is known. Even the name of the people is uncertain: the word *Phrygian* is Greek and is not attested in any extant Phrygian text.

The earliest evidence for the formation of a complex state in Phrygia comes from Gordion. Iron Age levels at Gordion reveal an abrupt change from simple houses constructed on a frame of wooden posts to substantial stone buildings with carefully worked masonry. Some of the early stone buildings are in the form of a megaron, a two-room rectangular structure with an entrance on the building's short end. This building type is characteristic of the élite quarter in a Phrygian city, extensively attested in subsequent levels at Gordion and also at Kerkenes Dağ. This shift in architecture suggests the instigation of large communal projects involving extensive labor, and its appearance at Gordion signals the emergence of a centralized state where resources are controlled by one individual or a small group of élite individuals. The date of this transition at Gordion should probably be placed in the early ninth century B.C.E. (Voigt and Henrickson 2000; Voigt 2005:28–31). Within a generation or two, an extensive élite quarter in Gordion was constructed, with a monumental gateway, a large central courtyard flanked by several buildings in the megaron plan, and an inner courtyard with additional megara that may have been residences for the ruling class élite. In addition, centralized economic control is implied by multiroom complexes nearby that were devoted to intensive processing of foodstuffs and textiles, probably carried out by servile labor. A destructive fire at the end of the ninth century B.C.E. caused extensive damage to this level of the early Phrygian city, but the fire, probably of accidental origin, did not constitute a major setback in the community, as the élite quarter was soon rebuilt in an even more elaborate architectural complex (Voigt 2007, and see Voigt, chapter 50 in this volume). A major Phrygian center at Daskyleion, near the Sea of Marmara, with evidence of monumental construction, dating from the eighth century B.C.E., offers testimonia that a complex Phrygian community also existed in western Anatolia (Bakır 1995:271–73).

Along with the appearance of monumental architecture are the earliest examples of burial tumuli with rich grave goods, surely burial places of the élite (see Sams, chapter 27, and Voigt, chapter 50 in this volume). Tumulus burials at Gordion first appear during the ninth century B.C.E., and this process accelerates in the eighth century B.C.E. with the construction of larger and more elaborately furnished burial tumuli (Young 1981). Several burial tumuli in the region surrounding Ankara demonstrate that this custom was well established among the Phrygian élite (Caner 1983:13–15; Tuna 2007). The tumuli are noteworthy not only for their size but also for their contents; they contained a rich assortment of fine pottery, bronze vessels, bronze fibulae (ornate dress pins), textiles, decorated bronze-leather belts, and intricate wooden furniture, attesting to a high level of craftsmanship and the wealth of the élite. All tumuli appear to contain the burial of a single individual. Where identifiable, the majority proved to be burials of adult males, but there was at least one burial of a child in Gordion (Tumulus P, Young 1981:9) and one of an adult woman in Ankara (Tumulus II, Caner 1983:15). The construction of the tumulus series continued until the mid-sixth century B.C.E. Taken together, the existence of urban centers with complex plans, monumental architecture, and high quality luxury goods demonstrates the presence of a prosperous and powerful Phrygian society.

It is uncertain whether all Phrygian settlements were part of a single political state, but it seems probable that much of central Anatolia was controlled by a Phrygian monarchy centered at Gordion. Most rulers of this Phrygian kingdom are anonymous, but the name Midas, preserved in Phrygian, Assyrian, Greek, and Latin sources, recurs regularly, suggesting that this individual was an important ruler with a strong international presence. Although Midas could have been a dynastic name borne by several individuals, Classical and Assyrian sources combine to give a vivid picture of one man whose period of rule was ca. 733–677 B.C.E. (Berndt-Ersöz 2008). References to Midas in Greek and Latin texts are often infused with folk tale and legend (Roller 1983), and the occurrences of the name Midas in Phrygian texts, especially the main inscription on the cult monument at Midas City and a stone stele from Tyana (Brixhe and Lejeune 1984:M-01a, T-02) are difficult to date securely. However, an individual named Mita (presumed to be the same as the Phrygian and Greek Midas) is mentioned several times in Assyrian documents from the reign of Sargon II (r. 721–705 B.C.E.), where he is identified as the ruler of the Muški (Berndt-Ersöz 2008:17–21). These documents record the activities of a powerful military figure who was a rival of the Assyrians, first allying himself with several independent Anatolian states, including Que, Tyana, Karkamiš, and Tabal, before being defeated by the Assyrians and becoming their ally (Berndt-Ersöz 2008:34–36; Mellink 1979; Vassileva 2008; see Sams, chapter 27 in this volume).

The Muški are probably to be identified as an Anatolian group in eastern Anatolia under Phrygian political control; thus, Midas was the ruler of both the Phrygians in central Anatolia and the Muški in eastern Anatolia (Mellink 1965, 1991:622–23; Wittke 2004). Assyrian sources make it clear that Midas ruled a powerful kingdom with the resources to rival the contemporary society of Assyria and that a strong Phrygian presence in central and eastern Anatolia continued well into the seventh century B.C.E. The international contacts of the Phrygians are further confirmed by the presence of valuable objects from southeastern Anatolia, north Syria, and Cyprus found in ninth- and eighth-century B.C.E. contexts at Gordion (Young 1962:167–68, 1981:31, 36) and by Phrygian goods at Samos and Delphi (Ebbinghaus 2008; Herodotus 1.14). A marriage alliance between Midas and the daughter of a prominent Greek chieftain from Kyme, a Greek city in northwestern Anatolia (Aristotle frag. 611.37; Pollux, *Onom.* 9.83) offers additional evidence for the international connections of Phrygian rulers. The presence of valuable Phrygian objects, several bearing Phrygian inscriptions, in the burial tumulus of a woman in Lycia, may also be the result of an external marriage alliance (Börker-Klähn 2003; Varinlioğlu 1992).

After the reign of Midas, much less is known about the political status of the Phrygians. During the mid-seventh century B.C.E. the Cimmerians, a nomadic people from the region north of the Black Sea, invaded Anatolia and caused a great deal of damage, including the destruction of Sardis, capital of the Lydian kingdom (Herodotus 1.6, 1.15; Strabo 13.4.8, 14.1.40; Parker 1995; see Sams, chapter 27 in this volume), but their impact on Phrygia is less certain. Strabo 1.3.21 records that a Phrygian king Midas died as a result of a Cimmerian raid; this is likely to be a later Midas, who ruled in the 640s B.C.E., and Greek sources conflated him with the earlier and better known ruler (Berndt-Ersöz 2008:36). However, the series of rich tumulus burials at Gordion continued unbroken through the seventh century B.C.E., and there is little evidence in the Gordion settlement for disruption by the Cimmerians. A more significant change occurred in the late seventh or early sixth century B.C.E., when western Phrygia came under the control of the Lydian kingdom. Herodotus 1.28 records that the Phrygians were subdued by the Lydian king Croesus (ca. 560–546 B.C.E.), although it is likely that much of Phrygia was under Lydian control during the reign of the previous king, Alyattes (ca. 610–560 B.C.E.). Substantial finds of Lydian pottery in Gordion from the later seventh and early sixth century B.C.E., much of it found near the mudbrick fortifications beyond the Gordion citadel mound, offer evidence for an increasing Lydian presence there.

During the later seventh century B.C.E. a new settlement with a strong Phrygian element was established at Kerkenes Dağ, east of the Halys River. This mountaintop site, fortified by a seven-kilometer circuit of walls, provided a strong military presence near a major transportation route extending through central Anatolia. Finds of Phrygian inscriptions, architecture in the Phrygian megaron form, and Phrygian sculpture confirm that the Phrygians formed a key element of the population (Draycott and Summers 2008). The lack of Lydian material suggests that the settlement was not under the control of the Lydian kingdom west of the Halys River. Kerkenes Dağ may be ancient Pteria, an independent city that survived until the 540s B.C.E. when it was captured and demolished by Croesus during his campaigns against the Persian king Cyrus (Herodotus 1.76; Summers 2006; Summers and Summers 2008).

A pivotal event in the history of the Phrygians was the conquest of Anatolia by the Achaemenid Persians. The sack of Sardis by the Persians in the 540s B.C.E. brought the extensive territory of the Lydian kingdom, including Phrygia, under Achaemenian control. This event is reflected in the destruction of the fortress city at Kerkenes Dağ, and is also attested at Gordion, where the mudbrick fortifications were destroyed by military force (see Sams, chapter 27 in this volume). In addition, the occupation levels at Gordion reveal a significant displacement and rebuilding during the later sixth century B.C.E. (Voigt and Young 1999), and the practice of tumulus construction in Gordion ceases, a circumstance that may be connected with the suppression of the élite class in Phrygia (DeVries 2005:53). The Persians divided Phrygia into two administrative units, or satrapies. One, Hellespontine Phrygia, encompassed northwestern Phrygia, with its capital at Daskyleion near the Black Sea. The other, Greater Phrygia, comprised the southern part of Phrygia; its center was at Kelainai (modern Dinar).

The official Persian presence in Hellespontine Phrygia is well demonstrated at Daskyleion. Here a smaller version of the Persian court was constructed, including a residential palace for the satrap, a hunting park, or *paradeisos*, for which the Persians were well known (see Xenophon, *Hellenica* 4.1.15), and a cult sanctuary with a Persian fire altar (Bakır 1995, 1997, 2004, 2006). Fine architecture and sculpture attest that the resources of the Achaemenid satrap made this a prosperous and beautiful city. The population of the city, however, was very mixed; Phrygians continued to be a prominent element, judging from the frequency of inscriptions in the Phrygian language, and there is also evidence for Greek speakers, Lydians, and a Jewish community. The presence of much Greek pottery and Greek workmanship in local sculpture suggests extensive contact with neighboring Greek populations.

Central Phrygia, in contrast, seems to have undergone a period of economic decline, as power and resources were concentrated in the west. At Gordion, much of the fine stone architecture of the eighth-century B.C.E. city had been removed for use in other building projects by the early fourth century B.C.E. (Voigt and Young 1999:236). The city that Alexander found during his visit in 333 B.C.E. was an important regional commercial center but had long since lost its status as an impressive political capital.

Phrygian Language and Texts

The Phrygian language, attested in a variety of written texts, is notable both for its geographical breadth and its longevity. The corpus of Phrygian texts has been collected and classified by region (Brixhe 2002b, 2004; Brixhe and Lejeune 1984; Brixhe and Summers 2006). These are found throughout the full extent of Phrygian settlements, from Bithynia and the site of Daskyleion near the Sea of Marmara in western Anatolia, to the territory east of the Halys River at the sites of Boğazköy, Kerkenes Dağ, and Alaca Höyük. Additional Phrygian texts outside this range are also known, with examples from Tyana (Brixhe and Lejeune 1984:T-01, 02, 03), Lycia (Varinlioğlu 1992), Delphi (Jeffery 1990:39), and Persepolis (Brixhe 2004:118–36). These are likely to be the result of diplomatic treaties, gift exchanges, or personal notations by Phrygians traveling or living abroad.

Phrygian texts fall into two broad chronological groups. The earlier, known as Palaeo-Phrygian, uses an alphabetic script consisting of twenty-six letters; nineteen letters are identical with proto-Greek forms and seven are unique to Phrygian (Brixhe 2007). It is uncertain whether the Phrygians adopted the alphabet from the Greeks, or whether Greek and Phrygian scripts were derived from a common source and developed along parallel lines. The earliest Palaeo-Phrygian inscriptions, found in Tumulus MM at Gordion, are dated to ca. 740 B.C.E.; these consist of proper names incised onto objects found in the tomb (Brixhe, in Young 1981:273–77) and onto the wooden beams used to build the tomb chamber (Liebhart and Brixhe 2009). Palaeo-Phrygian texts continued until the late fourth century B.C.E., when both language and script were superseded by Greek. The latest known Palaeo-Phrygian inscription, a funerary epitaph of the late fourth or early third century B.C.E. from Dokimeion (Brixhe 2004:7–26), is written in the Phrygian language, but uses the

Greek alphabet. Additionally, there is a series of Phrygian inscriptions from the later first through third centuries C.E. known as Neo-Phrygian texts; these use the Phrygian language written in the Greek alphabet.

The subject matter of Palaeo-Phrygian texts is quite varied, and includes religious texts, political documents, and funerary epitaphs on stone, as well as a large number of graffiti on pottery, wood, and metal wares. The most common subject matter of Phrygian stone inscriptions concerns religious texts, including cult dedications and apotropaic formulae. Votive dedications are found on several of the largest cult façades in the Phrygian highlands (Brixhe and Lejeune 1984:M-01a, W-01; Haspels 1971:289–94), and also on monuments from Gordion and Kerkenes Dağ (Brixhe and Lejeune 1984:G-02; Brixhe and Summers 2006:106). Texts that record political documents are less frequent, although three examples found in Tyana in southeastern Anatolia (Brixhe and Lejeune 1984:T-01, 02, 03) may reflect Phrygian diplomatic activities with another Anatolian state in this area. One of these (Brixhe and Lejeune 1984:T-02b) includes the name Midas; this may refer to the late eighth–early seventh century B.C.E. Phrygian ruler already discussed, known from Assyrian sources to have been active in this region.

As already noted, the Phrygian language was part of the Indo-European language family, of the same branch as Greek and Thracian. In a number of key grammar points, such as the case structure of nouns and basic verb forms, Phrygian syntax shows close affinities with Greek. Thus, in many dedicatory texts the name of the dedicator, the object of the dedication, and the verb can be read. There are comparatively few lexical overlaps between Phrygian and Greek, however, and this circumstance means that the language has not been fully deciphered. Most Phrygian texts are very short; many of the pottery graffiti, for example, consist of a single name or just a few letters of a name. Stone inscriptions are sometimes longer, but even these often consist only of a few lines. The longest extant Palaeo-Phrygian text, the late fourth-century B.C.E. epitaph, contains 265 characters, and the second longest, a dedication to Matar Kybeleia found in Bithynia (Brixhe and Lejeune 1984:B-01), contains only 230 characters. All of these factors contribute to the difficulty of interpreting the language.

The inscription above the main cult façade at Midas City (Brixhe and Lejeune 1984:M-01a) helps illustrate the extent of our understanding of Phrygian. The inscription reads *ates arkiaevais akenanogavos midai lavagtaei vanaktei edaes*. (Here I follow the convention, used by Brixhe and Lejeune 1984, of transliterating the Phrygian script into the lowercase Latin alphabet.) The text can be translated "*Ates* (a proper name) *arkiaevais* (patronymic?) *akenanogavos* (title?) dedicated [this] to Midas leader of the people and ruler." Thus we have the subject, Ates, the main verb *edaes*, "he dedicated," which also occurs in other Phrygian texts, and the object of the dedication, Midas, written in the dative case. The dative *Midai* is followed by two nouns, also in the dative, that share a common form with Greek vocabulary; the first, *lavagtaei*, is a compound noun akin to Greek λαός plus ἡγέτης (leader of the people), and the second *vanaktei*, parallels the Greek ἄναξ (lord, ruler). This text demonstrates the close similarity of Phrygian to Greek in grammar, evident in the case endings of nouns and the use of the epsilon augment for the aorist verb, and the overlap in vocabulary. The Phrygian text shows particularly close affinities with the more archaic Greek of the epics, evident in Phrygian use of the digamma (here transliterated as *v*) in the words *lavagtaei* and *vanaktei*, and in the choice of vocabulary, since the words λαός and ἄναξ occur frequently in the *Iliad* and the *Odyssey*, where both use the Greek digamma, but are less common later.

Another example of a Palaeo-Phrygian text, this one from Gordion, offers a similar picture of the Phrygian language. Incised onto a broad flat stone, the text is intertwined around a representation of two footprints (Brixhe and Lejeune 1984:G-02). It reads as follows: (line 1) *agartioi iktes akiokavoi*; (line 2) *iosoporokitis.;* (line 3) *kakoioitovo podaska*[.]. Here again we can recognize the grammatical form and meaning of several words and gather the general sense of the inscription. The first line is likely to begin with a proper name in the dative case, perhaps the object of the dedication; the second line begins with the word *ios*, the relative pronoun equivalent to the Greek ὅς, "whoever"; and the third line contains the words *kakoioi*, probably an optative verb related to the Greek κακόω, "maltreat" or "ruin," and *podas*, a form of the Greek noun πούς, ποδός, "foot"; this latter translation is reinforced by the picture of footprints on the stone. The inscription appears to be a combination of dedication and apotropaic text, which reads approximately: "[Dedication] Whoever sets foot on [this], may he be ruined/cursed." These two examples also illustrate the gaps in our knowledge of the Phrygian language, because both use Phrygian words that do not exhibit close lexical similarities to Greek and remain unknown to us. The brevity of the texts and the formulaic quality of the subject matter also impede more precise understanding.

In addition to more formal inscriptions on stones, there are numerous examples of graffiti incised onto various media. Five bronze bowls from Tumulus MM in Gordion have proper names incised into wax that was added to the rim of the bowl, and eleven silver and bronze objects found in a tumulus in Bayandır bear proper names incised directly onto the metal. Personal names also appear on the wooden beams of Tumulus MM and on wooden furniture in Gordion. Several hundred examples of graffiti scratched on pottery have been found at Daskyleion, Dorylaion, and Gordion, many on ordinary coarse ware fabrics. Most of these are personal names, although some longer texts are known. Although these do not help our understanding of the Phrygian language, they demonstrate that writing was very widespread, suggesting a fairly high rate of literacy among the Phrygian population.

Palaeo-Phrygian texts disappear after the early third century B.C.E. After a gap of more than 300 years, texts written in the Phrygian language but using the Greek alphabet are once again found during the later first through third centuries C.E.; these are known as Neo-Phrygian. One hundred fourteen examples have been published (Brixhe 1993, 1999, 2002a:248). Of these, fifty are monolingual Phrygian texts, sixty-three contain texts in both Greek and Phrygian, and one is ambiguous (Brixhe 1993:292, 2002a:248). All Neo-Phrygian texts are funerary epitaphs, and all but seven consist solely of curses directed toward a potential grave robber. One example (Brixhe and Neumann 1985) preserves the longest known Phrygian text, but most of the other Neo-Phrygian texts are very short. Greek was clearly the more widely understood language in Roman Phrygia, since the Greek precedes the Phrygian text in nearly every example of the sixty-three double-language texts. The Greek-Phrygian epitaphs follow a very standard pattern: the Greek text gives the name or names of the dedicators, their relationship to the deceased and to each other, and often other information about the family, while the Phrygian text is used to express a curse directed at the potential violator of the tomb. A few of the monolingual Phrygian texts record the names and family affiliations of the dedicators in Phrygian, but most contain only the curse formula.

The reason for the renewed use of the Phrygian language during the Roman period is uncertain. One hypothesis posits that Phrygian continued to be spoken by the rural population in central Anatolia even after the written Palaeo-Phrygian language had died out, and the appearance of Neo-Phrygian texts results from increasing affluence in rural areas that enabled stone funerary monuments to be made by a population group that had previously been too poor to afford them (Brixhe 2002a:252–53; Mitchell 1993:I,174). It is also possible that written Phrygian was deliberately revived by a more educated Phrygian population who wished to stress their regional identity and their distance from the dominant Greco-Roman culture.

Phrygian Architecture and Art

Phrygian architecture and art have a distinctive character that contributed greatly to the visual style prevalent in western Anatolia and the Greek cities of Asia Minor. The most characteristic form in Phrygian architecture is the megaron, a long, narrow rectangular building with a single entrance in one short side that leads to two rooms, a smaller front room and a larger room behind it. Although the term *megaron* is borrowed from the architecture of Mycenaean Greece, the Phrygian megaron is a building type with roots in Anatolia that extend back to the third millennium B.C.E. The megaron can be a large structure with internal supports in the main room, attested by examples at Gordion and Kerkenes Dağ; these may have served as a residence or audience hall for the ruling élite. At Gordion, buildings in the megaron plan were also used for utilitarian purposes, such as food preparation and textile production (see Voigt, chapter 50 in this volume).

Phrygian visual arts are characterized by a strong interest in abstract geometric forms, and to a lesser extent in figured art, through representations of human and animal figures. Among the media in which Phrygian craftsmen excelled are pottery, bronze, and wood; objects in precious materials such as ivory and silver are also known. The interest in geometric patterning is apparent in fine pottery, where painted decoration includes a complex repertory of geometric forms (Sams 1994). It is also well attested in the intricate wooden furniture found in Phrygian burial tumuli, in which inlay work forming patterned designs predominates (Simpson

1988; Simpson and Spirydowicz 1999; Simpson 2010). Similar geometric patterns can be observed in a fine mosaic from Gordion (Young 1965:10–11) and were presumably used extensively in textiles (Boehmer 1973; Burke 2005). The complexity of the geometric designs offers evidence of a high level of craftsmanship and aesthetic sensibility, and in some cases may also contain cult symbolism (discussed further below).

Representational art first appears during the ninth century B.C.E. Early examples, such as a series of orthostat reliefs from Early Phrygian Gordion, show extensive influence from Neo-Hittite sculptural relief in both style and subject matter (Sams 1989), but a distinctively Phrygian style soon began to emerge. The lion was a popular subject; lions are found as architectural sculpture in Early Phrygian Gordion (Sams 1989:figs. 1–2; Young 1956:figs. 42–43) and in funerary sculpture in the Phrygian highlands, in reliefs at Arslantaş (figure 25.1) and Yılantaş (Haspels 1971:figs. 131, 141). Comparatively few examples of the human form are known, and these are usually cult objects. The most frequent is the representation of the Phrygian mother goddess (discussed further below); she is shown as a mature female, heavily draped in an elaborate long gown, high headdress, and veil. A series of small youthful male figures, known from Gordion and Boğazköy, probably represents attendants on the mother goddess, since they carry an attribute appropriate to her cult. A sculpture depicting a life-size male figure wearing a long gown, found near the entrance to the palatial complex at Kerkenes Dağ, is also likely to have been part of a cult installation (Draycott and Summers 2008). No examples of sculpture that depicts a narrative, whether legendary or historical, are known. The lack of extensive sculptural monuments may be the result of the dearth of high-quality stone for carving, although the situation may also reflect an ideological choice not to advertise the traditions of the Phrygians through formal public sculpture.

Figure 25.1. Arslantaş, Phrygian grave with relief of lions (photo by author).

The Phrygians also excelled in metal wares, especially bronzes, used for a variety of fine vessels, belts, and fibulae (Ebbinghaus 2008; Young 1981). These exhibit craftsmanship of a very high order and, in the case of fibulae and belts, confirm Phrygian interest in elaborate costume. Some of the bronze motifs, such as animal-headed situlae and cauldron attachments, find parallels in the art of southeastern Anatolia and Assyria. Precious materials were also used; an ivory figurine was found at Gordion (Young 1966:pl. 74), and silver vessels and ivory and silver figurines were recovered from the burial of a Phrygian woman in Lycia (Börker-Klähn 2003:77–84).

During the later sixth and fifth centuries B.C.E. Greek influence becomes a prominent feature of the visual arts in Phrygia. Relief sculptures attached to a Phrygian chamber tomb at Yılantaş include reliefs of hoplite warriors and a Gorgoneion (Haspels 1971:figs. 154–56), both similar to sixth century Greek forms. Similarly, frescoes from a building in Gordion (Mellink 1980) and painted panels from a tomb in Tatarlı (Summerer 2007a, 2007b) display figures drawn in Greek style, although the subject matter and costumes of the figures reflect the traditions of western Asia. These examples indicate that Greek visual style was increasingly integrated into the visual arts of Phrygia during the sixth through fourth centuries B.C.E. This process accelerated toward the end of the fourth century B.C.E. with the conquest of Phrygia by the Macedonians.

Phrygian Cult

Cult practice was a distinctive feature of Phrygian society, one with a continuing legacy in Greek and Roman cult. Yet many features of Phrygian cult practice remain unclear. A few texts in the Phrygian language (largely undeciphered) are found on cult monuments, but most information comes from the physical remains of cult, including images of human and animal cult figures, carved façades, stepped monuments, and idols. Some Phrygian cult places are found in urban settings, whereas others are located in isolated places and may have been centers of pilgrimage. Chronology remains a problem; many cult objects were found reused in later contexts, and monuments that are still standing in the open are often quite worn, making a determination of date difficult. It is likely, though, that most of the major cult monuments were made during the main flourishing period of Phrygian culture, the ninth through early sixth centuries B.C.E.

The Phrygian pantheon probably included a number of deities, both male and female, but only one was consistently represented in anthropomorphic form. This is a female divinity addressed as Matar, meaning "Mother" (Roller 1999:64–115; see Voigt, chapter 50 in this volume). The word *Matar* appears in several Phrygian inscriptions, often with an epithet. One epithet, *Kybeleia*, or "mountain" in the Phrygian language, forms the source of the goddess's Greek name, Cybele. The Phrygian goddess Matar was represented as a mature standing female who wears a long gown and an elaborate high headdress and veil. Most images of the deity are reliefs carved onto stone orthostat blocks or onto rock outcrops that occur in the natural environment. These cult reliefs are widely distributed, with examples known from Boğazköy, Ankara, Gordion, and many in the Phrygian highlands region (Haspels 1971:73–111). The deity can be shown with several attributes, including a drinking cup or bowl, a small round object, perhaps a pomegranate, and a bird of prey. She can also have attendants; the Boğazköy goddess is accompanied by two smaller male figures who play musical instruments, the goddess on the Arslankaya relief in the Phrygian highlands is flanked by two huge lions (figure 25.2), and the deity on a relief from Ankara/Etlik is accompanied by a composite human-animal figure that raises its hands in a gesture of prayer and protection. The goddess is regularly depicted in an architectural frame resembling an open doorway placed in a rectangular building. There are also several reliefs that depict the architectural frame and central doorway niche but have no image of the deity. Among these is the main relief panel at Midas City, the largest Phrygian cult relief (figure 25.3). Here the central niche could have held a portable image of the deity, brought there on the

Figure 25.2. Arslankaya, cult relief depicting goddess flanked by lions (photo by author).

Figure 25.3. Midas City, main façade with cult relief (photo by author).

occasion of special festivals. The reliefs often depict very specific details of the architectural frame, including the timbers that formed the frame of the "building" and a curved akroterion above the roof gable. These are surely features that existed on actual Phrygian buildings: the rectangular building with a central doorway recalls the Phrygian megaron, wooden beams were extensively used in Phrygian architecture, and actual examples of stone akroteria have been found at Gordion. On many of the reliefs, both those with and those lacking an image of the deity, the carved façade was decorated with a rich series of complex patterns that depict mazes built around a series of interlocking cross and square patterns. Examples include several of the most striking reliefs, such as the Midas City façade and the Arslankaya, Büyük Kapıkaya, and Maltaş monuments (Haspels 1971:figs. 8, 189, 183, 157).

The locations of the Matar reliefs offer an indication of the deity's function. Most are found in spaces that marked boundaries controlled by a community. Reliefs are found near city gates (at Boğazköy and Gordion), along roads or other transportation routes (near Ankara and in the Phrygian highlands), and in areas that marked the entrance into a valley with rich tilled land (Arslankaya). Shrines are also found in connection with burial tumuli and chamber tombs (Ankara), implying that the Phrygians created sacred space to mark the boundary between the living and the dead.

The meaning of the architectural frame and geometric designs is uncertain. It is possible that the reliefs imitate the front wall of a temple dedicated to Matar, although to date no examples of temples or other cult buildings within an urban center in Phrygia are known. An alternative interpretation is that the "building" depicted in the Matar reliefs represents a royal residence, and the combination of deity and palatial façade functioned as an advertisement of close contacts between the Phrygian ruler and the deity. This is supported by the close correlation between the geometric patterns found on the façades and very similar patterns on the wooden serving stands from the burial tumuli in Gordion (Simpson 1998; Young 1981:fig. 33, 104). These serving stands, supports for bronze cauldrons that formed part of the banqueting equipment used in the funerals of the Phrygian ruling class, were inlaid with a series of maze patterns composed of interlocking crosses and squares, much like the decorative schema found on the carved façades. The use of the same geometric iconography for the funerary furnishings of Phrygian royalty and for the carved Matar façades is likely to be intentional, emphasizing the connection between goddess and ruler. By depicting this connection in a public context, the façades advertise the goddess Matar as a deity who protects the ruler and, by extension, the Phrygian state. The importance of the ruler in Phrygian cult is further suggested by the life-size statue of a standing male figure found near the main entrance to the city at Kerkenes Dağ. This figure appears to have been a cult monument, perhaps for a heroized ruler or ancestor whose presence protected the city (Draycott and Summers 2008:58–60).

Another common type of Phrygian cult installation is the stepped monument (Berndt-Ersöz 2006:40–49). These can be simply a series of steps, usually three to five, carved into living rock in an outdoor setting. On some monuments the steps are surmounted by a round disc, and in some cases the disc has the simple features of a human being, suggesting that it was a simple idol intended to represent an anthropomorphic deity. Like the Matar reliefs, the stepped monuments, both with and without idols, tend to be located near the walls and gates of settled communities (Midas City, Kerkenes Dağ), along roads or near entrances of valleys and plains with fertile land (many in the Phrygian highlands), or in areas near funerary monuments (Köhnüs valley in the Phrygian highlands). Other stepped monuments are located in remote areas, as if the Phrygians wanted to extend the divine presence beyond the boundaries of the settled community. An example is furnished by Dümrek, a site on a ridge above the Sangarios River about thirty kilometers northwest of Gordion, with roughly a dozen stepped monuments, including one with an idol. Individual idols are also known; a number of small idols were found in domestic contexts in Gordion. Other sacred places include stone hollows and basins, often located near stepped monuments; these may have been sites for offering deposits.

The stepped monuments and idols are rarely inscribed, so we do not know the identity of the deity or deities to whom they were dedicated, although the high frequency of stepped monuments and idols suggests that other deities in addition to the goddess Matar were widely worshiped. Greek sources indicate that the Phrygians worshiped a male deity whom they addressed as "Father," perhaps the masculine counterpart of the mother goddess. In a few cases a group of two idols suggest that a pair of deities, perhaps the father and the mother, was worshiped together.

Examples include a pair of idols on the citadel of Midas City and a relief with two idols near Ankara.

After Phrygia was absorbed into the Achaemenian Persian Empire, construction of new carved façades, reliefs, and stepped monuments became less common, although the older monuments continued in use as places of cult practice. During the Hellenistic period many objects connected with Phrygian cult, especially the images of Matar, become highly Hellenized, but the traditional deities, particularly the Phrygian mother goddess and a Phrygian male deity, often identified with Zeus, continued to be worshiped.

Summary

Although many lacunae remain in our understanding of Phrygian history, culture, and language, the surviving material gives a vivid picture of a dynamic and creative people, one with a profound impact on the history of Anatolia. The Phrygians' migration into central Anatolia was undoubtedly propelled in part by the collapse of the dominant political structures in the eastern Aegean at the end of the Bronze Age. The power gap in Anatolia resulting from the collapse of the Hittite Empire enabled the Phrygians to establish themselves in northwestern and central Anatolia and become a prominent presence in the region. By the ninth century B.C.E. the Phrygians had gained enough political and economic stability to establish a complex state (or states), and by the eighth century B.C.E. they appear to have been the dominant political power in central Anatolia, with sufficient military and diplomatic strength to pose a challenge to the Assyrian Empire. By the end of the seventh century B.C.E. most Phrygian settlements had come under the control of the Lydians, but the Phrygians retained their language and many distinctive cultural features even after the loss of political independence. Phrygian material culture exhibits a high level of skill in many crafts, especially pottery, wood, and metal work. Particularly in the visual arts and in their religious practices, the Phrygians created a distinctive legacy, one with a lasting impact on their Anatolian neighbors and on Greek settlements in Asia Minor.

REFERENCES

Primary Sources

Aristotle. *Fragmenta*. Ed. Valentine Rose. Stuttgart: Teubner 1886, reprinted 1967.

Herodotus. *Histories*, 3rd ed. Oxford Classical Texts, ed. Carl Hude. Oxford: Clarendon Press, 1927.

Homer. *Iliad*, 3rd ed. Oxford Classical Texts, ed. David B. Monro and Thomas W. Allen. Oxford: Clarendon Press, 1920.

Pollux. *Onomasticon*. Ed. E. Bethe. Stuttgart: Teubner, 1967.

Strabo. *Geography*. Trans. Horace Leonard Jones. Loeb Classical Library. London: W. Heinemann, 1917–33.

Xanthos. Lydiaka. In *Die Fragmente der griechischen Historiker* IIIC no. 765, ed. Felix Jacoby. Leiden: Brill, 1958.

Xenophon. *Hellenika*. Oxford Classical Texts, ed. E. C. Marchant. Oxford: Clarendon Press, 1900.

Secondary Sources

Bakır, Tomris. 1995. Archäologische Beobachtungen über die Residenz in Daskyleion. *Pallas* 43: 269–85.

———. 1997. Phryger in Daskyleion. In *Frigi e Frigio. Atti del 1o Simposio Internazionale, Roma, Ottobre 16–17, 1995*, ed. Roberto Gusmani, Mirjo Salvini, and Pietro Vannicelli, 229–38. Rome: Consiglio Nazionale delle Ricerche.

———. 2004. Daskyleion'da Phrygler. In *60 Yaşında Fahri Işık'a Armağan Anadolu'da Doğdu. Festschrift für Fahri Işik zum 60. Geburtstag*, ed. Taner Korkut, 55–67. İstanbul: Ege Yayınları.

———. 2006. Daskyleion. In *Stadtgrabungen und Stadtforschung im westlichen Kleinasien*, ed. W. Radt. *Byzas* 3: 61–71.

Berndt-Ersöz, Susanne. 2006. *Phrygian Rock-Cut Shrines. Structure, Function, and Cult Practice*. Leiden: Brill.

———. 2008. The Chronology and Historical Context of Midas. *Historia* 57: 1–37.

Boehmer, Rainer Michael. 1973. Phrygische Prunkgewänder des 8. Jahrhunderts. *Archäologischer Anzeiger* 2: 149–72.

Börker-Klähn, Jutta. 2003. Tumulus D von Bayındır bei Elmalı als historischer Spiegel. In *Licia e Lidia prima dell'ellenizzazione*, ed. M. Giorgieri, M. Salvini, M.-C. Trémouille, and P. Vannicelli, 69–105. Rome: Consiglio Nazionale delle Ricerche.

Brixhe, Claude. 1993. "Du paléo- au néo-phrygien." *Comptes rendus des séances—Académie des inscriptions et belles lettres*: 323–44.

———. 1999. Prolegomenes au corpus neo-phrygien. *Bulletin de la Société de linguistique de Paris* 94: 285–316.

———. 2002a. Interactions between Greek and Phrygian under the Roman Empire. In *Bilingualism in Ancient Society*, ed. J. N. Adams, Mark Janse, and Simon Swain, 246–66. Oxford: Oxford University Press.

———. 2002b. Corpus des inscriptions paléo-phrygiennes. Supplément I. *Kadmos* 41: 1–102.

———. 2004. Corpus des inscriptions paléo-phrygiennes. Supplément II. *Kadmos* 43: 1–130.

———. 2007. The Phrygians and the Phrygian Language. *Friglerin Gizemli Uygarlığı (The Mysterious Civilization of the Phrygians)*, ed. Hakan Sivas and T. T. Sivas, 148–60. İstanbul: Yapı Kredi Kültür Sanat Yayıncılık Ticaret ve Sanayi A.Ş.

Brixhe, Claude and Michel Lejeune. 1984. *Corpus des inscriptions paléo-phrygiennes*. Paris: Éditions Recherche sur les civilisations.

Brixhe, Claude and Gunther Neumann. 1985. Decouverte du plus long texte néo-phrygien: l'inscription de Gezler Köyü. *Kadmos* 14: 161–84.

Brixhe, Claude and Geoffrey D. Summers. 2006. Les inscriptions phrygiennes de Kerkenes Dağ (Anatolie centrale). *Kadmos* 45: 93–135.

Burke, Brendan. 2005. Textile Production at Gordion and the Phrygian Economy. In *The Archaeology of Midas and the Phrygians: Recent Work at Gordion*, ed. Lisa Kealhofer,

69–81. Philadelphia: University of Pennsylvania Museum of Archaeology and Anthropology.

Caner, Ertuğrul. 1983. *Fibeln in Anatolien I. Prähistorische Bronzefunde Abteilung 14, Band 8*. Munich: C. H. Beck.

DeVries, Keith. 2005. Greek Pottery and Gordion Chronology. In *The Archaeology of Midas and the Phrygians. Recent Work at Gordion*, ed. Lisa Kealhofer, 36–55. Philadelphia: University of Pennsylvania Museum of Archaeology and Anthropology.

Draycott, Catherine M. and Geoffrey D. Summers. 2008. *Kerkenes Special Studies 1. Sculpture and Inscriptions from the Monumental Entrance to the Palatial Complex at Kerkenes Dağ, Turkey*. Oriental Institute Publications 135. Chicago: Oriental Institute Press.

Ebbinghaus, Susanne. 2008. Patterns of Elite Interaction: Animal-Headed Vessels in Anatolia in the Eighth and Seventh Centuries BC. In *Anatolian Interfaces. Hittites, Greeks and Their Neighbours. Proceedings of an International Conference on Cross-Cultural Interaction, September 17–19, 2004, Emory University, Atlanta, GA*, ed. Billie Jean Collins, Mary R. Bachvarova, and Ian C. Rutherford, 181–88. Oxford: Oxbow Books.

Haspels, Caroline Henriette Emilie. 1971. *The Highlands of Phrygia*. Princeton, N.J.: Princeton University Press.

Henrickson, Robert C. 1994. Continuity and Discontinuity in the Ceramic Tradition of Gordion during the Iron Age. In *Anatolian Iron Ages 3. The Proceedings of the Third Anatolian Iron Ages Colloquium Held at Van, August 6–12, 1990*, ed. Altan Çilingiroğlu and David H. French, 95–129. British Institute of Archaeology at Ankara Monograph 16. Ankara: British Institute of Archaeology at Ankara.

Jeffery, Lilian H. 1990. *The Local Scripts of Archaic Greece*, rev. ed. with a supplement by A. W. Johnston. Oxford: Clarendon.

Liebhart, Richard F. and Claude Brixhe. 2009. The Recently Discovered Inscriptions from Tumulus MM at Gordion: A Preliminary Report. *Kadmos* 48: 141–56.

Mellink, Machteld J. 1965. Mita, Mushki and Phrygians. In *Helmuth Theodor Bossert'in Hatırasına Armağan. Anadolu Araştırmaları* 2: 317–25.

———. 1979. Midas in Tyana. In *Florilegium Anatolicum. Mélanges offerts á Emmanuel Laroche*, ed. Ekrem Akurgal and Emmanuel Laroche, 249–57. Paris: De Boccard.

———. 1980. Archaic Wall Paintings from Gordion. In *From Athens to Gordion. Papers of a Memorial Symposium for Rodney S. Young*, ed. Keith DeVries, 91–98. University Museum Papers 1. Philadelphia: University Museum.

———. 1991. The Native Kingdoms of Anatolia. In *The Cambridge Ancient History*, vol. 3, ed. John Boardman, I. E. S. Edwards, E. Sollberger, and N. G. L. Hammond, 619–65. Cambridge: Cambridge University Press.

Mitchell, Stephen. 1993. *Anatolia. Land, Men, and Gods in Asia Minor, vol. 1, The Celts and the Impact of Roman Rule; vol. 2, The Rise of the Church*. Oxford: Clarendon Press.

Neumann, Gunther. 1988. *Phrygisch und Griechisch. Österreichische* Akademie der Wissenschaften, phil.-hist. Klasse, Sitzungsberichte 499. Vienna: Verlag der Österreichischen Akademie der Wissenschaften.

Parker, Viktor. 1995. Bemerkungen zu den Zügen der Kimmerier und der Skythen durch Vorderasien. *Klio* 77: 7–34.

Roller, Lynn E. 1983. The Legend of Midas. *Classical Antiquity* 2: 299–313.

———. 1999. *In Search of God the Mother: The Cult of Anatolian Cybele*. Berkeley: University of California Press.

Sams, G. Kenneth. 1988. The Early Phrygian Period at Gordion: Toward a Cultural Identity. *Source* 7: 9–15.

———. 1989. Sculpted Orthostates at Gordion. In *Anatolia and the Ancient Near East. Studies in Honor of Tahsin Özgüç*, ed. Kutlu Emre, Barthel Hrouda, Machteld Mellink, and Nimet Özgüç, 447–54. Ankara: Türk Tarih Kurumu Basımevi.

———. 1994. *The Gordion Excavations 1950–1973: Final Reports IV. The Early Phrygian Painted Pottery*. University Museum Monograph 79. Philadelphia: University Museum, University of Pennsylvania.

Simpson, Elizabeth. 1988. The Phrygian Artistic Intellect. *Source* 7: 24–42.

———. 1998. Symbols on the Gordion Screens. In *XXXIVème Rencontre Assyriologique Internationale: 6–10 VII 1987 Istanbul: kongreye sunulan bildiriler*, 630–39. Ankara: Türk Tarih Kurumu Basımevi.

———. 2010. *The Gordion Wooden Objects, Vol. 1: The Furniture from Tumulus MM. Culture and History of the Ancient Near East* 32. Leiden: Brill.

Simpson, Elizabeth and Krysia Spirydowicz. 1999. *Gordion Wooden Furniture*. Ankara: Museum of Anatolian Civilizations.

Summerer, Latife. 2007a. From Tatarlı to Munich: The Recovery of a Painted Wooden Tomb Chamber in Phrygia. In *The Achaemenid Impact on Local Populations and Cultures in Anatolia. Papers Presented at the International Workshop, Istanbul May 20–21, 2005*, ed. İnci Delemen, 131–58. İstanbul: Turkish Institute of Archaeology.

———. 2007b. Picturing Persian Victory: The Painted Battle Scene on the Munich Wood. In *Achaemenid Culture and Local Traditions in Anatolia, Southern Caucasus and Iran*, ed. Askold Ivantchik and Vakhtang Licheli, 3–30. Leiden: Brill.

Summers, Geoffrey D. 2006. Phrygian Expansion to the East. Evidence of Cult from Kerkenes Dağ. *Bagdader Mitteilungen* 37: 647–56.

Summers, Geoffrey D. and Françoise Summers. 2008. *Kerkenes News* 10 (2007). METU Press. www.kerkenes.metu.edu.tr.

Tuna, Numan. 2007. Research and Excavations at the Phrygian Necropolis in Ankara. In *Friglerin Gizemli Uygarlığı (The Mysterious Civilization of the Phrygians)*, ed. Hakan Sivas and T. T. Sivas, 99–113. İstanbul: Yapı Kredi Kültür Sanat Yayıncılık Ticaret ve Sanayi A.Ş.

Varinlioğlu, Ender. 1992. The Phrygian Inscriptions from Bayandır. *Kadmos* 31: 10–20.

Vassileva, Maya. 2008. King Midas in Southeastern Anatolia. In *Anatolian Interfaces. Hittites, Greeks and Their Neighbours. Proceedings of an International Conference on Cross-Cultural Interaction, September 17–19, 2004, Emory University, Atlanta, GA*, ed. Billie Jean Collins, Mary R. Bachvarova, and Ian C. Rutherford, 165–71. Oxford: Oxbow Books.

Voigt, Mary M. 1994. Excavations at Gordion 1988–89: The Yassıhoyük Stratigraphic Sequence. In *Anatolian Iron Ages 3. The Proceedings of the third Anatolian Iron Ages Colloquium Held at Van, August 6–12, 1990*, ed. Altan Çilingiroğlu and David H. French, 265–82. British Institute of Archaeology at Ankara Monograph 16. Ankara: British Institute of Archaeology at Ankara.

———. 2005. Old Problems and New Solutions. Recent Excavations at Gordion. In *The Archaeology of Midas and the Phrygians. Recent Work at Gordion*, ed. Lisa Kealhofer, 22–35. Philadelphia: University of Pennsylvania Museum of Archaeology and Anthropology.

———. 2007. The Middle Phrygian Occupation at Gordion. In *Anatolian Iron Ages 6. The Proceedings of the Sixth Anatolian Iron Ages Colloquium Held at Eskişehir, August*

16–20, 2004, ed. Altan Çilingiroğlu and Antonio Sagona, 311–33. Ancient Near Eastern Studies Supplement 20. Leuven: Peeters.

Voigt, Mary M. and Robert C. Henrickson. 2000. Formation of the Phrygian State: The Early Iron Age at Gordion. *Anatolian Studies* 50: 37–54.

Voigt, Mary M. and T. Cuyler Young. 1999. From Phrygian Capital to Achaemenid Entrepot: Middle and Late Phrygian Gordion. *Iranica Antiqua* 34: 191–241.

Wittke, Anne-Maria. 2004. *Mušker und Phryger. Ein Beitrag zur Geschichte Anatoliens vom 12. bis zum 7. Jh. v. Chr. Beihefte zum Tübinger Atlas des Vorderen Orients Reihe B, no. 99*. Wiesbaden: Dr. Ludwig Reichert Verlag.

Young, Rodney S. 1956. The Campaign of 1955 at Gordion: Preliminary Report. *American Journal of Archaeology* 60: 249–66.

———. 1962. The 1961 Campaign at Gordion. *American Journal of Archaeology* 66: 153–68.

———. 1965. Early Mosaics at Gordion. *Expedition* 7: 4–13.

———. 1966. The Gordion Campaign of 1965. *American Journal of Archaeology* 70: 267–78.

———. 1981. (With contributions by Keith DeVries, Ellen L. Kohler, Joanna F. McClellan, Machteld J. Mellink, and G. Kenneth Sams.) *Three Great Early Tumuli. The Gordion Excavations. Final Reports* vol. 1. Philadelphia: University Museum, University of Pennsylvania.

CHAPTER 26

HITTITE ANATOLIA: A POLITICAL HISTORY

RICHARD H. BEAL

The Middle Bronze Age: The Old Assyrian Trading Colonies

Anatolia first comes into the light of history when merchants from Assur in Upper Mesopotamia arrived to trade, incidentally bringing with them facility in writing (see Radner, chapter 33, and Michel 2001 and chapter 13 in this volume). The trade appears to have begun in the reign of Erišum I, after ca. 1974 B.C.E. by the middle chronology.[1] These merchants brought, by donkey caravan, textiles manufactured in Assur or bought elsewhere in Mesopotamia in addition to tin, which was arriving in Assur by another as yet undiscovered trade network stretching eastward, probably to Afghanistan. In return they acquired gold and silver. These merchants found an Anatolia broken up into many small kingdoms, each ruled by a "prince" (or rarely, a "princess") just like the Mesopotamia from which they had come. The major states appear to have been Purušḫanda, Waḫšušana, Kaneš, Ḫattuš, Zalp(uw)a, and Mama. The merchants made their headquarters in the capital of the first state that they reached on the Anatolian plateau after they traversed the passes through the Anti-Taurus Mountains. This capital was known as Kaneš (modern Kültepe near Kayseri; see Kulakoğlu, chapter 47 in this volume, for extensive discussion). They built houses in a walled lower town merchants' quarter (Assyrian *kārum*), which they shared with local merchants, who bore Hattic, Hurrian, Indo-European Hittite, and Luwian names. From their base at Kaneš the merchants' trade network was extended throughout most of Anatolia, with some twenty-one subordinate *kārū* and smaller (*w*)*abrātu* set up in the various towns. The merchants signed treaties with the local rulers in which the princes granted rights of settlement, self government, safe transit, and restitution of any goods stolen, in return for 5 percent import duties and right of first choice of 10 percent of goods. Although there were occasional hostilities between the states, the merchants often had prior warning and were able to work around the problem areas.

This world came crashing down after at least 100 years of trade, in 1837 B.C.E. (by the middle chronology), with the burning of the *kārum* of Kaneš, ending what is known to archaeologists as *Kārum* Level II. The culprit was probably Uḫna of Zalp(uw)a, a state at the mouth of the Maraššanta/Halys/Kızıl Irmak on the Black Sea, who carried off the chief god of Kaneš. Kaneš was eventually rebuilt and ruled by a king named Inar and his son Waršama. These kings were on relatively good terms with Anum-ḫirbe of the powerful kingdom of Mama (in the Maraş-Gaziantep region) and in conflict with Ḫurmeli of Ḫaršamna. Later, Pitḫana, king of Kuššara, took Kaneš by storm at night. He imprisoned the king, but did not harm the city and its inhabitants and moved his capital there. His son Anitta revenged his new kingdom and capital against those who had razed it in 1837 by capturing Ḫuzziya king of Zalp(uw)a and returning the image of Kaneš's god to its home. He then conquered the other states of central Anatolia. He was particularly proud of his conquest of the powerful state of Ḫattuš (modern Boğazköy/Boğazkale) under Piyušti, whose city he destroyed, sowed with weeds, and cursed. The powerful king of Purušḫanda (perhaps modern Acemhüyük, or Üçhöyük near Bolvadin further west; see Barjamovic 2010) agreed to honorable subordination to the new state (KBo 3.22//KUB 26.71//KUB 36.98 (+) 98a (+) 98b, ed. Neu 1974, trans. Hoffner 1997b:182–84). Assyrian merchants resettled the *kārum* and reestablished their network. A man named Zuzu, Great King of Alaḫzina, who was probably ethnically a Hurrian, seems to have taken over Kaneš and other parts of Anatolia from Pitḫana and Anitta's dynasty. At least eighty years after the refounding of the *kārum* the Assyrian merchants stopped coming (ca. 1720 B.C.E.), and our knowledge of the events in Anatolia becomes even murkier.

The Late Bronze Age

The Old Hittite Period

What we see a generation or two later is a kingdom called the Land of Ḫattuš(a) that spoke the language of Kaneš (what we now call Hittite), not the language of Ḫattuš, which they knew to be completely different (what we call Hattic). Kuššara, Pitḫana's original capital, remained an important royal center for this new state. They preserved Pitḫana and Anitta's inscriptions in their archive but never claimed descent from either. Instead, they traced their descent to a certain Ḫuzziya, about whom we know nothing today. The earliest known events detail the conquest again of Zalpa, by a king of Ḫattuša perhaps known by the Hurrian name of PU-Šarruma (ca. 1685–1665 B.C.E.)[2] and his attempts to install a friendly government there (Beal 2003). This king appears to have left his kingdom to his daughter Tawannana and her husband Labarna (ca. 1665–1640 B.C.E.). Labarna extended his kingdom's borders to the seas (Black and Mediterranean) and appointed his sons as governors. The personal names Labarna and Tawannana later became titles of the Hittite kings and queens.

Ḫattušili I (ca. 1640–1610 B.C.E.)

After Labarna's death, a ruinous civil war among contenders for the throne eventually resulted in Tawannana's nephew Ḫattušili I (sometimes calling himself Labarna II) becoming king. This king reestablished order in Anatolia and exerted hegemony over Arzawa, a Luwian-speaking kingdom in the fertile river valleys leading from the plateau down to the Aegean and centered at Apaša (Ephesos) on the Aegean coast (see Bryce, chapter 15 in this volume). However, he had to fight off Hurrian incursions into his heartland. Then he moved southeast into Syria, taking over a number of wealthy established cities, such as Ḫaššu, Ḫaḫḫu, and Uršu, most famously ending what archaeologists know as Level VII at Alalaḫ (modern Tell Atchana) (KBo 10.2, ed. de Martino 2003:21–79; KBo 10.1, ed. Devecchi 2005). The great kingdom of Yamḫad, centered at Aleppo, though much reduced, managed to survive ("he ended its Great Kingship").[3] By ending another's Great Kingship, Ḫattušili could now claim the title Great King for himself; that is, the Hittite kingdom joined the élite group of great powers. As far as we know, this reign marks the reintroduction of writing into Anatolia, this time not using Old Assyrian script but an Old Babylonian script brought back from northern Syria (see van den Hout, chapter 41 in this volume). Ḫattušili's scribes wrote their texts bilingually in Babylonian and in their own native Hittite (Kanešite) language (see Archi 2010). Ḫattušili began the Hittite royal tradition of recording his military conquests. A humorous text of the king mocking his generals' failure to take the city of Uršu (KBo 1.11, ed. Beckman 1995) did not begin a new literary genre dedicated to castigating one's subordinates (though the Hittites did establish several other literary genres). It is probably also this king who issued a collection of legal decisions (KBo 6.2 + KBo 19.1 + KBo 22.62 + KBo 22.61 + KBo 19.1a//KBo 6.3 + KBo 22.63 and many more duplicates, ed. Hoffner 1997a, trans. Hoffner 2000), perhaps another idea he picked up from Mesopotamia.

Muršili I (ca. 1610–1594 B.C.E.)

Ḫattušili's only son, another Ḫuzziya, proved rebellious, as did his sister's son Labarna, so Ḫattušili appointed his daughter's young son Muršili I as his heir. The appointment edict (KUB 1.16 + KUB 40.65, ed. Sommer and Falkenstein 1938, trans. Beckman 2000), in what will become typical of Hittite treaties and edicts, first gives the history of the problem, then the appointment, and finally a bit of fatherly advice. When this boy came of age after a period of regency, he succeeded where his grandfather had failed by conquering Aleppo. Then in the most spectacular feat of

Hittite arms, he swept down the Euphrates, and, perhaps in league with Kassite tribesmen on the middle Euphrates, took and sacked Babylon, ending the dynasty of Ḫammurapi. On his return he appears to have left Babylon's god Marduk in Ḫana with his allies.

Usurpation and Intrigue: Ḫantili I (ca. 1594–1560 B.C.E.), Zidanta I (ca. 1560–1555 B.C.E.), and Ammuna (ca. 1555–1525 B.C.E.)

Muršili I did not long enjoy his victory, for on his return he was assassinated by his sister's husband Ḫantili, who in his apologia wrote that Muršili's sack of Babylon "made the gods sick" (KBo 3.45//KBo 22.7, Hoffner 1975). Ḫantili I had a long and eventful reign, attempting to hold the Syrian provinces of his empire while keeping Hurrian invaders out of his heartland. As Ḫantili was dying, his son-in-law (and onetime co-conspirator) Zidanta murdered Ḫantili's sons and seized the throne. Soon thereafter this dastardly deed was repaid in kind when Zidanta I's own son Ammuna murdered his father and seized the throne. Ammuna's long reign is remembered as a disaster, as the kingdom lost most of its territory, including the extensive and wealthy territories of Arzawa in the west and Adaniya (the Cilician Plain) in the south. The gods were apparently punishing the parricide and what preceded it but passed over the perpetrator, who proceeded to perish peacefully in the palace.

Ḫuzziya II (ca. 1530–1529 B.C.E.) and Telipinu (ca. 1529–1505 B.C.E.)

Ammuna's two sons were not so fortunate and fell in a conspiracy apparently organized by Ammuna's brother Zuru (the Chief of the *MEŠEDI*-guards who were charged with the protection of the king) and his sons, who enthroned Ammuna's bastard son Ḫuzziya II. Telipinu, married to the full sister of the murdered men and fearing for his life, had no option but to take the crown himself. However, breaking with recent precedent, he did not kill Ḫuzziya and the conspirators but rusticated them instead. Despite his generosity, his crown prince and queen were assassinated in a failed coup, and Zuru's three sons killed Ḫuzziya and his brothers, attempting to clear their own way to the throne.

Telipinu then issued an edict, which was prefaced by a historical prologue, describing the domestic tranquility (all imagined) of the good old days of Labarna, Ḫattušili I, and Muršili I, followed by the disasters that occurred once the royal family took to killing each other. The purpose of the edict was to lay out the law of royal succession, which just happened to justify his own claim to the throne. If anyone (even the king) planned or did anything murderous, he was to be tried by an assembly, called the "all" (*panku-*), and if guilty was to be publicly executed, but his family was to be spared and could keep their possessions (KBo 3.1 + KBo 12.5 + KBo 3.68 + KBo 12.7//KUB 11.1 + KBo 19.96 and further duplicates, ed. Hoffmann 1984, trans. van den Hout 1997a). Telipinu also recognized the independence of the former Hittite possession of Adaniya, now known as Kizzuwatna (the Cilician Plain), by making a treaty with its king Išputaḫšu, the first in a long line of treaties that became a defining mark of Hittite foreign policy. Telipinu also attempted to reestablish Hittite control in Syria, but on his return he had to fight his way back through the mountain passes to his capital, and whatever he may have gained in Syria was lost.

Telipinu's Unintended Legacy: Further Assassinations and Disasters

Telipinu was succeeded by one of the rusticated plotters, Taḫurwaili (ca. 1505–1500 B.C.E.), son of Zuru, who ruled long enough to renew treaty relations with Eḫeya of Kizzuwatna. Alluwamna (ca. 1500–1480 B.C.E.), Telipinu's son-in-law, eventually came to the throne, and the deceased Taḫurwaili was condemned never to receive the mortuary offering meals due to dead kings and queens. Alluwamna managed to pass the throne to his crown prince, Ḫantili II (1480–1460 B.C.E.). Although he continued the alliance with Kizzuwatna, making a treaty with its king Paddatiššu (KUB 34.1 + KBo 28.105, trans. Beckman 1995:11–13), his reign was remembered as a disaster; the northern third of the kingdom, including the second holiest city of the realm, Nerik, was lost to the barbarian Kaška people (KUB 25.21 iii, ed. von Schuler 1965:186f.). Judging by their personal names, many of these barbarians were descended from the original Hattic inhabitants of the northern Anatolian plateau.

Ḫantili II was succeeded, apparently peacefully, by Zidanta II (ca. 1460–1440 B.C.E.), son of Ḫantili's (?) brother Ḫaššuili, the Chief of the *MEŠEDI*-guards (Beal 1992:330 with nn. 1259–1261). Zidanta continued the policy of alliance with Kizzuwatna through a treaty with King Pilliya. However, in the reign of Zidanta's successor Ḫuzziya III (ca. 1440–1430 B.C.E.), Pilliya broke away from his Hittite alliance and allied himself with Baratarna of the powerful new Hurrian empire of Mittanni, based at Waššukkani in Upper Mesopotamia. This period again ended in murder as Ḫuzziya III was killed by Muwattalli I (ca. 1430–1425 B.C.E.), his Chief of the *MEŠEDI*-guards, who was likely his younger brother or uncle. Muwattalli gave Ḫuzziya's sons Kantuzili and Ḫimuili high posts in the new administration, apparently in an attempt to conciliate them. The plan backfired when the sons led a rebellion and eventually killed Muwattalli (who joined Taḫurwaili as a forgotten and hungry ghost). Kantuzili may have then become king, or he may have immediately placed his vigorous young son Tudḫaliya II on the throne (Bryce 2005:114f., 421).

Tudḫaliya II (ca. 1425–1395 B.C.E.)

Tudḫaliya II's reign marks a resurgence for the Hittite kingdom. Although his annals (KUB 23.11//23.12, ed. Carruba 2008:31–51) are badly broken, we know something of his attempts to reclaim or acquire territory. His first known campaign was to the west against Arzawa and its allies Šeḫa River Land and Ḫapalla. He subsequently defeated Aššuwa, a name reappearing in the much later Roman province of Asia. The annals give a list of enemies/conquests (?) running from Lukka (Lycia) in the south to Wilušiya (Ilios) and Taruiša (Troy) in the north, indicating the range of his ambition.

As a sidelight to this struggle, a petty potentate named Madduwatta tangled with Attarišiya of Aḫḫiya, and he and his retainers were driven from their land by the latter (KUB 14.1 + KBo 19.38, trans. Beckman 1999:153–60). Aḫḫiya is clearly Achaia, which would mean that Attarišiya was a Mycenaean Greek; whether he bore the same name as Atreus is less clear. Where Attarišiya's capital was located and how much territory he ruled is unknown; all that is clear is that since Madduwatta is an Anatolian name, of the same formation as much later Lydian kings, Attarišiya could project his power into Anatolia.

Then in events that were repeated throughout Hittite history, while Tudḫaliya was busy campaigning against the great power Aššuwa, his kingdom was attacked by the barbarian Kaška. When he returned, the Kaška fled. When he mounted a major campaign northward, the Kaška sensibly tried to stop him in a forest, but Tudḫaliya was able to win a great victory even there.

In the south Tudḫaliya seduced Šunaššura of Kizzuwatna away from Mittanni with a promise of "freedom"; the resulting treaty, although not exactly a parity treaty, is not entirely a subordinating treaty either, resembling more a junior partnership agreement (KBo 1.5 and duplicates, trans. Beckman 1999:17–26). Tudḫaliya's queen Nikal-mati is the first Hittite queen with a Hurrian name; this may be evidence that this agreement was later strengthened with a dynastic marriage. Tudḫaliya and the Mittannian king Šauštatar came to actual blows over Išuwa, the Murat Su river valley east of Hittite lands and north of Mittannian lands, and later Tudḫaliya moved even more actively to reestablish his ancestors' rule in Syria, inflicting a heavy defeat on Mittanni and seizing Aleppo. It is perhaps at this time, when the Hittites were at war with Mittanni, that they signed a "treaty of perpetual friendship" with Mittanni's then enemy Egypt, the so-called Kuruštama treaty.[4]

Arnuwanda I (ca. 1395–1375 B.C.E.)

Because Tudḫaliya and Nikal-mati had only a daughter, Ašmu-nikal, they determined that her husband Arnuwanda, whom they adopted as son, would succeed to the throne, and to make sure of this they made him coregent with Tudḫaliya. Their joint annals describe an account of the conquest of Kizzuwatna (KUB 23.21 obv. 2–11, ed. Carruba 1977:166–67). One could imagine that Tudḫaliya and Arnuwanda were enforcing Nikal-mati's and her heirs' right to Kizzuwatna against other, more distant claimants who preferred independence. A member of the Hittite royal family named Kantuzili was appointed king of this appanage with the title "Priest of Kizzuwatna." Henceforth Hittite kings and perhaps princes as well bore both a traditional "Hittite" name (usually Hattic or Luwian in origin) as king of Ḫattuša and a Hurrian name as ruler of Kizzuwatna (Beal 2002:55–71).

It was on the northern frontier that Arnuwanda had the least success. There are several treaties with the barbarian Kaška (KUB 23.77a + 13.27 + 23.77 + 26.40, KUB 26.19, trans. von Schuler 1965:117–34) in which the Kaška chiefs swear peace and the return of booty. The treaties make clear that these Kaška had reneged on a previous treaty. It is also clear that only some Kaška were willing to sign; they are warned not to pasture their sheep intermingled with the sheep of hostile Kaška, since when the Hittite army attacks the hostile Kaškeans they have no intention of stopping to sort sheep. Even the friendly Kaškeans were not trusted; they may only enter Hittite lands to trade in specifically designated cities. With both military and diplomatic solutions having only indifferent success, Arnuwanda and his queen, Ašmu-nikal, appealed to higher powers. In a prayer they argued that the Kaškeans have sacked the god's temples, scattered temple personnel, and are making no effort to worship the gods. They are blocking or looting attempts to send offerings to the holy city of Nerik. Furthermore the northern lands now held by the Kaška no longer send taxes to help support the gods elsewhere in the kingdom. The royal couple point out that the Hittites know how to treat a deity as one should be treated, whereas the gods themselves are suffering at the hands of the Kaška (KUB 17.21 + KBo 51.16 + 768/v, trans. Singer 2002:40–43). Unfortunately, as far as we know, no direct divine response was forthcoming.

Tudḫaliya III (ca. 1375–1351 B.C.E.)

When Tudḫaliya III sat on the throne of his father, Arnuwanda, disaster loomed. Hittite possessions in Syria were lost to Mittanni, whose peace treaty with Egypt left them free to deal with the Hittites. The situation in the Hittite north grew ever more dire. The archives of a provincial governor and a general who were stationed at Tapigga (modern Maşat Höyük [Özgüç 1982]; and see Mielke, chapter 48 in this volume) on the frontier, one of the most significant collections of Hittite texts discovered outside the capital, shed much light on the situation (Alp 1991a; ed. Alp 1991b; many trans. Hoffner 2009:91–252). Most frighteningly we read: "To the king my lord, thus speaks your servant Tarḫunt-išḫašmiš. The enemy has just now crossed over en-masse in two places. One horde crossed over at the village of Išteruna and another horde crossed over at Zišpa. . . . If your Majesty, my lord, would send some general, the enemy wouldn't bother my land. I have placed long distance scouts on Mt. Ḫapidduin. . . . May the king my lord know" (HKM 46, ed. Alp 1991b:200–203, trans. Hoffner 2009:173–75). The archive ends abruptly when Tapigga was burned to the ground.

Tudḫaliya III signed a treaty with Mariya, king of Azzi-Ḫayaša, which lay in the mountain valleys to the northeast of the Hittites. But when Mariya came to pay his homage to Tudḫaliya, Tudḫaliya spotted him becoming overly intimate with a palace woman and had him executed (Friedrich 1930:128f. iii 53–58 with 134f. iv 41–59; Beckman 1999:32f. §28 with §34–37). The resultant feelings in Azzi-Ḫayaša we can only imagine. A prayer states that the Hittite land was oppressed; there were defeats by the enemy, the population [shrank], there were fewer [servants] of the gods, and many temples ceased to exist (KUB 23.124 i 28–32, ed. Singer 2002:65). A later text recalls a concentric invasion:

> Formerly the Hittite land was laid waste by the enemy. The Kaška came from one direction and made Nenašša the border. Arzawa came in the direction of the Lower Land and also laid waste the Hittite land. It made Tanuwa and Uda the

> border. Arawanna came from a third direction and laid waste all of Kaššiya. Azzi came from a fourth direction, laid waste the Upper Land, and made Šamuḫa the border. Išuwa came from a fifth direction and destroyed Tegarama. Armatana came from a sixth direction, devastated Hittite lands and made Kizzuwatna-city the border. (KBo 6.28 obv. 7–15, ed. Goetze 1940:21f.)

This six-pronged invasion made deep inroads into Hittite territory. Ḫattuša, the capital, itself was burned, and the court apparently was forced to move to Šapinuwa (modern Ortaköy). Tudḫaliya fought on to save the remnant, but it did not appear hopeful. Amenhotep III of Egypt wrote to Tarḫuntaradu of Arzawa (in Hittite) that he had heard that the Land of the Hittites was paralyzed (VBoT 1, ed. Hoffner 2009:273–77).

Fortunately for Tudḫaliya III and the Hittites (and for Hittitologists), Tudḫaliya had a (bastard?) son named Šuppiluliuma. With his father, and by himself in years when his father was too ill to campaign, Šuppiluliuma pushed back the invaders. They fought, among others, Maša (Mysia?) and Karanni of Azzi-Ḫayaša. Each time the Hittite army was on a different front, the Kaška attacked and then had to be pushed back again the following year. Finally, Šuppiluliuma turned toward Arzawa, which seems to have rolled across the whole of the southern Anatolian plateau with its lack of natural defenses. This territory, Hittite since the time of Labarna, was recaptured, and Arzawa was pushed back.

Despite his successes, Šuppiluliuma was not the heir. He and "all of Ḫattuša—the royal princes, lords, captains of country clansmen, captains, [sergeants, infantry] and chariotry—had sworn" to support Tudḫaliya the Younger/the Child, son of King Tudḫaliya. When Tudḫaliya III died, however, Šuppiluliuma was proclaimed king and Tudḫaliya the Younger/the Child was murdered along with his (full) brothers (KUB 19.1 + KUB 14.14 obv. 10–21, trans. Singer 2002:61–62). At the expense of broken oaths and fratricide, the Hittites replaced a child with a proven military hero.

The New Hittite Period ("Empire" Period)

Šuppiluliuma I (ca. 1351–1322 B.C.E.)

In several difficult campaigns Šuppiluliuma defused the threat of Anzapaḫḫaddu of Arzawa. In Mira-Kuwaliya, a large Arzawan tributary, he installed as king a pretender (and new son-in-law), Mašḫuiluwa ("Little Mouse"). Armatana and Išuwa were subdued. Ḫuqqana, the new king of Azzi-Ḫayaša, decided to make peace. Because peace with this important neighbor was essential to Šuppiluliuma's further plans, the peace included the sending of Šuppiluliuma's sister to be Ḫuqqana's bride. Just how important this peace was to the Hittite king can be seen in what the Hittites thought of the people to whom this princess was being sent. Perfectly normal in the treaty provisions was that Ḫuqqana could have no other wife but the Hittite princess, although concubines were acceptable, but then the treaty goes on to insist that although we Hittites know that in barbarian Azzi-Ḫayaša a brother may sleep with his sister, his female cousins, or his wife's sisters, now that Ḫuqqana has become an honorary Hittite he must refrain from incest since that is a capital crime among Hittites (KBo 5.3 + joins and duplicates, ed. Friedrich 1930:103–63, trans. Beckman 1999:26–34).

Šuppiluliuma also sparred with Mittanni over Išuwa. His first efforts were initially unsuccessful, and the Mittannian king Tušratta sent booty taken from the Hittites to his ally in Egypt. Later raids had more success. He began preparing for a showdown with Mittanni. He took in a disgruntled member of the Mittannian royal family named Artatama. To secure an ally on the far side of Mittanni, he agreed to divorce his queen and marry a Kassite Babylonian princess. He also began attempting to lure the small Syrian states back from Mittanni and into a Hittite embrace. Niqmad II of Ugarit (modern Ras Shamra [Yon 2006]) and Šarrupši of Nuḫašše came over. Itur-Addu of Mukiš, Akit-Tešub of Ney, and Addunirari of Nuḫašše and Qatna (modern Mišrife [Du Mesnil du Buisson 1935; Klengel 2000]) formed a pro-Mittannian coalition and attacked Niqmad. Niqmad appealed to Šuppiluliuma. Instead of dropping everything and coming south into Syria, as would no doubt have been expected by all sides, he surprised everyone by marching due east into Išuwa, then crossing the Elâzığ Pass into Alzi/Alše. By handing over a coveted fortress to Antaratli of Alzi he was granted free passage through this tributary state of Mittanni. Suddenly he was plunging south into the heart of Mittanni. Tušratta refused to give battle and hurried eastward, probably hoping that Šuppiluliuma would follow ever deeper into the country. Šuppiluliuma sacked the capital Waššukkani, but instead of pursuing Tušratta, he turned westward to take what he really wanted, namely, Mittanni's Syrian tributaries. The coalition found itself trapped between Ugarit to the west and Šuppiluliuma attacking from the east.

With their overlord, Tušratta, suddenly out of the picture they appealed to his ally Egypt for help, but Egypt, preoccupied with the Amarna revolution, sent no help to speak of. Šuppiluliuma broke up Nuḫašše-Qatna and replaced recalcitrant rulers with those ready to cooperate with the Hittites (Richter 2002:603–18). Aziru of Amurru (Mt. Lebanon) joined Šuppiluliuma (Beckman 1999:36–41) so that he could pick off Mittannian and Egyptian tributary states (such as Sidon and Byblos) for himself, all the while assuring the Egyptians that all of his actions were to help Egypt (Moran 1992 passim). Šuttarna of Qidš (known today incorrectly as Qadeš, Tell Nebi Mend) challenged Šuppiluliuma, lost, was captured, and was then sent off and replaced with his son Aitakama, who of course joined the Hittites against his old allies, while trying to convince the Egyptians that all was not as it obviously was (Moran 1992 no. 189, vs. nos. 53, 54, 140, 151, 174–76, 363).

Šuppiluliuma besieged and took the large strongly fortified Mittannian city of Kargamiš (Carchemish, modern Jerablus [Woolley 1969]), on the west side of the Euphrates after fending off Mittannian and Egyptian counterattacks, and then installed a younger son, Piyašili/Šarri-Kušuḫ, as king of Kargamiš and viceroy over the Hittites' Syrian possessions. Another son, Telipinu, the "Priest of Kizzuwatna" was moved from Kizzuwatna and made king of Aleppo, where he could attend to the all-important Storm God of Aleppo. All the Hittite allies and conquests were tied together by a web of treaties laying out their duties and expectations vis-à-vis their overlords in Ḫattuša and Kargamiš.

During the course of the siege, Šuppiluliuma received a most extraordinary letter from the queen of Egypt, who he thinks is named Daḫamunzu (actually "the Queen"). He thinks that the Egyptians are frightened by his victories over their troops coupled with the recent death of their king and are seeking peace. However, it reads: "My husband has died. I do not have a son. They say you have many sons. If you would give me a son, I would make him my husband. I do not want to pick out a servant of mine and make him my husband. . . . I am afraid" (KBo 5.6 iii 10–15, ed. Güterbock 1956:94, trans. Hoffner 1997c:190). Šuppiluliuma was understandably shocked and said, "Never has such a thing happened to me in my whole life" (KBo 5.6 iii 18–19//KBo 14.9 iii 7–8, ed. Güterbock 1956:95, trans. Hoffner 1997c:190). Was this a joke? He sent his chamberlain Ḫattuša-ziti to Egypt to ascertain the truth. The next spring Ḫattuša-ziti returned with the Egyptian messenger Ḫani. It contained an indignant letter from the queen: "If I had a son would I have written my own and my country's distress to a foreign land?" (KBo 14.12 iii 53–iv 2, ed. Güterbock 1956:96, trans. Hoffner 1997c:190). She repeated her previous offer and said that she would make Šuppiluliuma's son king of Egypt. Šuppiluliuma consulted the archives and found the old so-called Kuruštama treaty of perpetual friendship between his country and Egypt, so he decided to send his son Zannanza to Egypt. But some Egyptians had other plans for the throne and murdered Zannanza on his journey. Whether the deceased king was Ikhnaton or Tutankhamon and the queen Nefertiti or Ankhsenpaaten and the official who ordered the murder Ay or Horemhab has been the subject of much heated debate (Bell 2007; Bryce 2005; Darnell and Manassa 2007; Dodson 2009; Miller 2007; Wilhelm 2009). Šuppiluliuma sent an angry letter to Egypt mocking the Egyptian letter saying that Zannanza had died: "Because a falcon [kills] a single chick [. . .] A falcon does not hunt alone!" (KUB 19.20 + KBo 12.23, ed. van den Hout 1994).[5] Šuppiluliuma could not personally do anything about the situation because he had to attend to the usual problems with the Kaška, now exacerbated by the Kaška uncharacteristically uniting under a king, Piḫḫuniya. However, he sent Crown Prince Arnuwanda to punish Egypt for the murder.

Meanwhile, back in Mittanni the defeated Tušratta was murdered and Šuppiluliuma's protegé Artatama II seized the throne, but since he was an old man, his son Šuttarna III became regent. Tušratta's son Šattiwaza fled to Kassite Karduniyaš (Babylonia), where he was refused refuge. Šuppiluliuma took him in as insurance. If Šuppiluliuma thought that he had solved his Mittannian problem, he was mistaken. Šuttarna III liberally bribed two of his liberated former tributary states, Assyria and Alzi, to support him and moved his capital from wrecked Waššukkanni to Taidi, further from the Hittites and closer to Assyria. Instead of a friend in Waššukkanni, Šuppiluliuma found he had an enemy in Taidi. Šuppiluliuma decided to rely on his insurance. He got Šattiwaza to sign a treaty of equality, more or less, with the Hittites, gave a daughter to him in marriage, and ordered Piyašili, the king of Kargamiš, to install his new brother-in-law as Great King of Mittanni. Piyašili crossed the Euphrates, taking the great cities of Mittanni in succession: Irridi, Harran, and

Waššukkanni. Around the new capital Šuttarna III and his Assyrian allies gave battle. Piyašili must have been successful in installing Šattiwaza because the treaty tablets contain a description of the war (KBo 1.1 and duplicates, trans. Beckman 1999:42–54).

While Šuppiluliuma strove to establish control in Syria, Arnuwanda returned victorious from his punitive victory against the Egyptians. He brought back booty and prisoners, but he also brought back the plague. What specific disease it was is unknown, but it began ravaging the Hittite lands. Soon the great Šuppiluliuma succumbed at the height of his powers. Arnuwanda II (ca. 1322 B.C.E.) became king, but within a year he too was dead. The throne was inherited by the teenaged prince Muršili, who although he had briefly been Arnuwanda II's Chief of the *MEŠEDI*-guards, had no real experience in the government or military.

Muršili II (ca. 1322–1285 B.C.E.)

Muršili II later explained in his Annals (Beal 2000:83–84; Götze 1933:14–23) that when the lands surrounding the Hittites saw the heroic conqueror dead, followed by his experienced general, leaving a boy on the throne, they prepared to undo Šuppiluliuma's victories. Faced with newly invigorated enemies Muršili did not immediately go against the nearest, but spent what remained of his accession year getting the gods to help him. In the first and second years of his reign it was first things first, doing enough damage to the Kaška so that his northern frontier (and the one closest to his capital, Ḫattuša) was stabilized.

With the Kaška quieted, Muršili could turn to bigger but more distant threats. In the west Arzawa under the aging king Uḫḫa-ziti had unsuccessfully tried to oust pro-Hittite Mašḫuiluwa. Now with Arzawa allied with Aḫḫiyawa, the threat was great. After Muršili won a great victory over the Arzawan prince Piyama-Kuruntiya at the border, the Arzawans fled down the river valley; some fled overseas to safety among the Greeks, while others had to be besieged in their fortified cities over into the following year. Manapa-Tarḫunta of Šeḫa-River Land, who had once been installed by Šuppiluliuma, but who had sided with Uḫḫa-ziti and was therefore now in serious difficulties, sent his mother and the elders to beg Muršili for mercy—a ploy that worked. With victory, Muršili signed treaties with Arzawa's constituent pieces, Mašḫuiluwa in Mira-Kuwaliya, Manapa-Tarḫunta in Šeḫa-River Land, and Targašnalli in Ḫapalla, which subordinated them to the Hittite Great King, who promised them aid against outside aggressors, while simultaneously banning fighting between them (trans. Beckman 1999:69–86).

Having settled the situation in the west, the next two years were again spent pushing back the Kaška. In Muršili's seventh year Tette of Nuḫašše in Syria thought he could get a better deal from the Egyptians. Muršili sent a general to aid Piyašili and the loyal Niqmad II of Ugarit in deposing Tette, and to aid DU-Teššub of Amurru in driving back the army of Horemhab, governor of Egypt's Asian territories. Meanwhile, the Kaška had surprisingly managed to unite under a king, Piḫḫuniya. When Muršili demanded back Hittite fugitives whom Piḫḫuniya was harboring, a perennial *casus belli*, Piḫḫuniya threatened to invade Hittite lands before he could be attacked. Muršili, however managed to get to him first, defeated and captured him, and resettled his lands with Hittites.

Refusal to return fugitives next caused a war with Aniya of Azzi-Ḫayaša. Before any dénouement was reached, fate intervened. Piyašili, king of Kargamiš and viceroy of Syria, suddenly died. Several of his Syrian subkings saw fit to secede, led by Aitakama of Qidš and again Nuḫašše. Smelling success, Aniya also attacked in the far northeast. General Nuwanza stopped Aniya, and General Kuruntiya was sent to destroy Nuḫašše and besiege Aitakamma in Qidš. Aitakamma's son, Niqmad, preserved his patrimony by patricide. Muršili then reorganized Syria; he installed Piyašili's son as king of Kargamiš, Telipinu's son Talmi-Šarruma in Aleppo, and replaced Niqmad's son Ar-ḫalbu with another son, Niqmepa, in Ugarit.

In his tenth year, Muršili attacked Azzi-Ḫayaša. After taking a particularly well-fortified town he gave it over to indiscriminate pillage. The other fortresses quickly surrendered and were spared. Ten years after suffering belittling and underestimation by the neighbors, Muršili ordered annals written of his "manly deeds" (KBo 3.4 + KUB 23.125//KBo 16.1 and duplicates, ed. Götze 1933, trans. Beal 2000). These most "historical" of Hittite writings do not simply list events but often give brief explanations of why something was done a particular way. Muršili later expanded this to include his later deeds (ed. Götze 1933) and eventually also produced a multitablet history of his father's "manly deeds" (ed. Güterbock 1956, trans. Hoffner 1997c).

All this is even more remarkable when it is remembered that during this time the Hittites were being killed off by a plague. We know this from a series of prayers in which Muršili attempts to cajole the gods into relenting and lifting the plague (trans. Singer 2002:56–69; Beckman 1997:156–60; see Beal 2000:82f. with n. 3). In the earliest prayers he says that he has been making oracular inquiries concerning the causes of the plague, and so far has gotten no answer, but that he has been busy renovating the temples. He argues that the gods themselves benefit from a strong state and suffer when the state is weak. Later he points out that the plague has been going on for twenty years. He now has found out that the gods are angry because of Šuppiluliuma's murder of his half-brother (?) Tudḫaliya the Younger. However, he argues, everyone involved is long dead, and the rituals to expiate bloodshed have been done and compensation paid, so why continue punishing the innocent? Later more oracular inquiries have found the causes to be that Šuppiluliuma forgot to make sacrifices to the Mala River, which Muršili has now made up, and that Šuppiluliuma broke the old Kuruštama treaty with Egypt by attacking them in retaliation for Zannanza's murder. Muršili tells the gods that he realizes a father's sins will be visited on his son and says he has now confessed and begs for mercy.

Muršili also had a certain amount of drama in his private life. On one of his Azziyan campaigns he suffered some sort of seizure; a magic ritual had to be written to prevent recurrence (ed. Lebrun 1985, with Beckman 1988:143, trans. van den Hout 2004). Because Hittite queens held office until they died, Muršili's stepmother, a Babylonian princess, still reigned. She quarreled with her stepson and his beloved wife Gaššulawiya. Allegedly the queen went well over budget on Šuppiluliuma's mausoleum; she was also buying friends, skimming money from Aštata province, and introducing Babylonian customs. Muršili no doubt needed the money for defense of the realm, but all would probably have been smoothed over, except that in the middle of the quarrel Gaššulawiya got sick and, despite the best medical and magical expertise available, died. The queen was accused of killing her using prayers and witchcraft. The gods, consulted by oracle, upheld the verdict and authorized Muršili to execute her for the crime. He chose instead to demote her from queenship and rusticate her (trans. Singer 2002:70–79).

Muwattalli II (ca. 1285–1269 B.C.E.)

Muršili II was succeeded by his son Muwattalli II, the king portrayed at Sirkeli (Bittel 1976:174f.). From the reign of this king we have a treaty with Alakšandu of Wiluša (i.e., Alexander of Ilios/Troy) (trans. Beckman 1999:87–93). In a surprising move, Muwattalli shifted the capital from the traditional but rather exposed Ḫattuša to the newly built and more centrally located Tarḫuntašša in Rough Cilicia or the adjacent Anatolian Plain to its north. He made his brother Ḫattušili Chief of the *MEŠEDI*-guards, then governor of the whole north, and finally appanage king of Ḫakpiš (Amasya?). The idea presumably was that a king present on the Kaškan frontier could keep a constant eye on the Kaška, while leaving the Great King free to deal with the revived aggressiveness of the Egyptians under Seti I and Ramesses II. Ḫattušili did his job well, pacifying the Kaška, resettling devastated lands and eventually finally retaking the holy city of Nerik. Meanwhile Seti I had attacked the Hittite border states of Qidš and Amurru. When Amurru, now under the control of Aziru's great-grandson Bente-šina, went over to Ramesses, all concerned realized that this would not go unanswered.

In 1275 Muwattalli mustered a huge army, made up of Hittites and contingents from all of the empire's subordinate states in Anatolia and Syria. Mittanni sent troops, and Ḫattušili even brought a contingent of Kaška. When Ramesses, now in his fifth year of reign (1274 B.C.E.), crossed into the territory of the southernmost Hittite subordinate kingdom, Qidš (today incorrectly "Qadesh"), he met two bedouin who told him that the Hittite army was still in the far north of Syria. He immediately took the lead corps (Amon) and rushed ahead of the rest of the army to capture as much Hittite territory as he could before he needed to face the Hittite army. However, the bedouin were Hittite spies. The Hittite army was actually hidden behind the city of Qidš. When the Egyptian second corps (Re) was hurrying by the city, the Hittites attacked and cut it to ribbons and then turned north to attack the now isolated Amon corps. The Hittites, thinking the battle all but over, apparently started plundering the Egyptian camp when they were taken by surprise by a small contingent arriving from the west, perhaps the army of Amurru or perhaps Egyptian marines from their fleet. Ramesses, showing personal bravery to make up for his strategic blunder managed to hack his way out and flee back to his two surviving corps. The Hittites held the field, but were too exhausted to give pursuit until a few days had passed. Meanwhile the primary casus belli, Bente-šina of Amurru, was deposed and handed over to Ḫattušili and replaced by a certain Šapili, and Amurru returned to the Hittite fold. After raiding the Egyptian border district, the Hittites returned to within their original borders. Taking traditional Egyptian territory was never the aim. Ramesses went home and covered Egypt with monuments to his great victory (Kitchen 2000).

Muršili III (ca. 1269–1262 B.C.E.)

On Muwattalli II's death he was succeeded, as intended, by his bastard son Muršili III, who undid his father's work and moved the capital back to Ḫattuša. In the east Mittanni (also now called Ḫanigalbat) under Šattuara I had apparently been trying to please both the Hittites and the Assyrians. When the new king Wasašatta declared himself free from the Assyrians, he begged for Hittite help, but none was sent and his country was conquered by Adad-nirari I (Grayson 1987:136f.). The victorious Assyrian's offer of peace to the Hittites was brusquely rejected (Beckman 1999:146f.).

Perhaps the loss of Mittanni emboldened Muršili's domestic opposition. Worried, he apparently tried to clip the wings of his powerful uncle Ḫattušili. Ḫattušili says that he put up with his nephew for seven years as he lost one territory or position after another until Muršili (to whom he always refers by his Hurrian name, Urḫi-Teššub) tried to take Ḫakpiš and Nerik away from him. With that he rebelled, not by treachery in Muršili's chariot or house but in a manly way—by an open challenge. Discontented Hittites joined with Ḫakpiš's Hittite and Kaškaean army. Since by Hittite belief a petty king cannot defeat a Great King unless his cause is just, it must have been so because Ḫattušili, the experienced general, defeated Muršili in a short civil war. Ḫattušili, rather than killing his royal prisoner and risking the wrath of the gods, sent him into internal exile, but Muršili eventually managed to escape and take refuge in Egypt (ed. Otten 1981, trans. van den Hout 1997b; Beckman 1999:130f.).

Ḫattušili III (ca. 1262–1240 B.C.E.)

Ḫattušili III, as a usurper, had to make as many new friends as possible if he wanted to survive on the throne. He wrote a long text justifying his usurpation, the so-called Apology of Ḫattušili, in which he thanks his patroness, the goddess Šaušga of Šamuḫa, and dedicates considerable spoils to her (KUB 1.1//KBo 3.6 with joins and duplicates, ed. Otten 1981, trans. van den Hout 1997b). Muršili III's younger brother Kuruntiya, who had been raised by Ḫattušili, was bought off by being made king of an appanage kingdom based on his father's capital, Tarḫuntašša (KBo 4.10 + and Bo 86/299, ed. Beckman 1999:107–13). Ḫattušili reinstalled his erstwhile prisoner, Bente-šina, on the throne of Amurru, gave him a daughter as queen and took Bente-šina's daughter as a bride for his son Nerikkaili (Beckman 1999:100–103). He sought to maintain good relations with Kadašman-Turgu and his son Kadašman-Enlil II of Kassite Babylon (Beckman 1999:138–43). Another son of Ḫattušili, Tudḫaliya, the Chief of the *MEŠEDI*-guards, was married to a Kassite Babylonian princess. Ḫattušili was forced to swallow the loss of Mittanni and smooth relations with the Assyrians (Beckman 1999:147–49). He also negotiated a treaty with Ramesses II of Egypt, which was formalized in Ramesses's twenty-first year (1259 B.C.E.) (Beckman 1999:96–100; Wilson 1969a).

Thirteen years later (1246 B.C.E.) this treaty was reinforced when Ramesses demanded and after long negotiations (Beckman 1999; Hoffner 2009:281–90) received a daughter of Ḫattušili to add to his harem. Unlike other powers, the Egyptians found it difficult to accept anyone else as their equal, so they often demanded a foreign woman without being willing to make her the primary wife of the Pharaoh, nor would they reciprocate by sending out a royal daughter. Ḫattušili had to swallow this insult.

Although no annals survive that document in detail the reigns after Muršili II, we know that there was a certain amount of unrest in the interstices between lands controlled by the Hittites and those controlled by Aḫḫiyawa (based at Milawanda [Miletos]), although relations between the two powers seem to have been at least cordial (Hoffner 2009:296–313). Prince Tudḫaliya, the Chief of the *MEŠEDI*-guards, campaigned against the Kaška, which shows that this perennial problem continued to plague Hittite rulers (Alp 1991b:32–35; Riemschneider 1962).

Perhaps during this reign Šattuara II of Mittanni (Ḫanigalbat) tried to free his state from the Assyrian king Šalmaneser I. This time, free from having to worry about the Egyptians, the Hittites sent an army, which by Šalmaneser's own admission fought doggedly and only gave ground grudgingly, but eventually was driven back to Kargamiš (Grayson 1987:183f.). This time Šalmaneser assured the renewed loyalty of the king of Ḫanigalbat by installing his own nephew on the throne (Cancik-Kirschbaum 1996:22, 28). Through it all Ḫattušili was supported by his beloved Kizzuwatnan wife Puduḫepa, who appears beside him in art (at Fıraktin: Bittel 1976:174, 176–77), and whose correspondence with foreign kings and queens shows her to be the most powerful of all Hittite queens.

Tudḫaliya IV (ca. 1240–1210 B.C.E.)

Before Ḫattušili's death, he changed the line of succession so that the throne passed directly to his younger son Tudḫaliya IV, the king portrayed at Yazılıkaya (Bittel 1976:214, 219). The succession of the usurper's younger son was open to all sorts of concerns, and thanks to the combined efforts of the kingdom's best magicians (and presumably Queen Puduḫepa), the succession went smoothly. We have no annals for this king. A long inscription in Luwian hieroglyphs found at Yalburt describes a campaign by Tudḫaliya in Lycia (Hawkins 1995a:66–85a). In the east Tudḫaliya wrote to Šalmaneser recognizing his conquest of "cities of tribute of the gods which the weapon of Šuppiluliuma had won" (KBo 18.24 iv 7–8, ed. Hagenbuchner 1989:241–45). But relations with Assyria soured again after the accession of the Assyrian king Tukulti-Ninurta I, and it may have been Tudḫaliya who lost badly in another attempt to retake Mittanni (KBo 4.14, ed. Stefanini 1965; RS 34.165, ed. Lackenbacher 1991:90–100; see Singer 1985:100–23). In any case Tudḫaliya's treaty with Bente-šina's son (and Tudḫaliya's nephew) Šaušgamuwa of Amurru specifies an economic blockade of Assyria (Beckman 1999:103–7).

On the positive side of the ledger, Tudḫaliya's military conquered the island of Cyprus (Alašiya), which signed a subordination treaty with the king. Judging by the number of surviving texts, Tudḫaliya's primary interest was in cataloguing and then renovating the myriad temples of his kingdom, a royal project no doubt popular with the gods.

Arnuwanda III and Šuppiluliuma II (ca. 1210–1177 B.C.E.)

Tudḫaliya's death brought his crown prince, Arnuwanda III, to the throne, but he apparently died of natural causes soon after succeeding, leaving another perhaps adopted son, Šuppiluliuma II, as king (KUB 26.33 ii 3–13, Bryce 2005:327). It is also clear that at some point Kuruntiya, son of Muwattalli II and king of Tarḫuntašša, made a bid for the Great Kingship and even seems to have held Ḫattuša for a time. Most scholars place this in Tudḫaliya's reign, but it seems just as likely that the old man made his bid in the confused period following the unexpected death of Arnuwanda III, when he could easily claim that the treaty he had sworn with his childhood playmate Tudḫaliya IV had expired. A Luwian hieroglyphic inscription from Boğazköy of Šupppiluliuma II lists a victory over Tarḫuntašša, as well as over many other places from Lycia eastward (Hawkins 1995a). This king also reconquered Cyprus (Alašiya) after fighting three sea battles (KBo 3.38, ed. Güterbock 1967, trans. Hoffner 1997d). Although Šuppiluliuma II had a rather long reign, there are few tablets from Ḫattuša dating to this reign. For this and other reasons, Jürgen Seeher, one of the excavators of Ḫattuša, has suggested that Šuppiluliuma may have moved the capital away from Ḫattuša at some point during his reign (Seeher 2001, 2002:168–70).

During Šuppiluliuma II's reign the problem of seaborne Sardinian and Lycian raiders, a problem that had been around since at least the reign of Pharaoh Amenhotep III, became far worse. It has been suggested that these raiders were set in motion by grain shortages, and that the Hittites could not resist because their land was wracked by famine. Indeed a letter from the Hittite Great King, presumably Šuppiluliuma II, to Ugarit's last king, Ḫammurapi III, repeats a demand for food from his servant Ugarit, dismissing Ḫammurapi's claim that there is no food in his land to send, with the words that "My Majesty myself am perishing" (RS 18.38, RS 18.147, trans. Pardee 2002:94–95, 97). Other undated letters also speak of famine in Ḫatti and the urgent demand for grain shipments from Syria to Hittite ports (RS 20.212, ed. Nougayrol 1968:105–7, trans. Lackenbacher 2002:103f.; Bo 2810, ed. Klengel 1974). Was this sufficient to cause the fall of the Hittite Empire? The Hittites had had famines before. Pharaoh Merneptah sent grain to aid his ally the Hittites, and Ramesses II had sent grain aid to Ḫattušili III at least forty years before. The Assyrian kingdom to the east of the Hittites (heavily dependent on rainfall agriculture, but without a Mediterranean coast) survived with no major political upheaval for another century.

Although Ḫatti may have been suffering famine during her last years, her famine was probably not what brought down the state. In one letter the Hittite Great King orders the regent for the boy king of Ugarit, Ḫammurapi III, to send to Ḫatti for questioning a man who had been captured by the Sicilians (Šikalayau) "who live in ships" (RS 34.129, ed. Malbran-Labat 1991:38–39). In a later letter the king of Ugarit was ordered to fit out and send quickly 150 ships, a huge number. In another, the king of Kargamiš and separately an Alašiyan (Cypriot) official warned Ḫammurapi III that sea raiders were heading his way (RSL 1 and RS 20.18, ed. Nougayrol 1968:83–86, trans. Lackenbacher 2002:102f., 192f.). The king of Ugarit sent warning to the king of Alašiya that seven enemy ships burned the towns and countryside of Ugarit, and that he could not stop them because "all my [. . .] troops are in Hittite-Land and all my ships are in the Luqqa lands (Lycia)" (RS 20.238, ed. Nougayrol 1968:87–9, trans. Lackenbacher 2002:193f.). The Ugaritic general Šipti-Ba'lu wrote to Ḫammurapi: "As for your servant, I am keeping watch with the king in Lawazantiya (in Cilicia). Now the king has just retreated/fled to Sera, where he is sacrificing" (RS 18.40, ed. Pardee 2002:104). Finally a text mentions that the enemy is in Mukiš, the next land north of Ugarit. The king has ordered a garrison commander to send him 2,000 horses, but the commander balks; he writes to the queen, who is presumably in charge in the capital while the king is in the field: "Why has the king, my lord, assigned this (responsibility to furnish) two thousand horses to his servant? You have (thus) placed me in great danger. Why has the king imposed this on me? The enemy has been pressing me, and should I put my wives (and) children at peril before the enemy? . . . The situation they will encounter is a perilous one" (RS 16.402, trans. Pardee 2002:105f.). Another commander writes to his superior: "The Ḫrnk-group has come here and has defeated (our) troops. He has pillaged our town, he has even burned our grain on the threshing floors and destroyed our vineyards. Our town is destroyed. You must know it" (RS 19.11, trans. Pardee 2002:109f.).

Ugarit was soon destroyed at its height. The summer palace suburb of Ras ibn Hani was destroyed and then resettled by people using Mycenaean pottery, people perhaps fleeing the successive destruction of one Mycenaean city after another. Sites in Cilicia are similar. Inland Emar (Meskene on the Euphrates) was destroyed. Pharaoh Ramesses III in his eighth year (1175 B.C.E.) reported that the "Sea Peoples," made up of Sicilians, Sardinians, Etruscans, Daneans (or Adanans), and Philistines, had already destroyed the Hittites, Kizzuwatna, Kargamiš, Arzawa, Alašiya, and Amurru (Wilson 1969b). His reliefs portray the Sea Peoples as a vast migration of warriors accompanied by their families moving by both land and ship (Murnane 1995:708). Ramesses saved Egypt proper from these people in great land and sea battles. Ḫattuša and many other (but not all) sites up on the Anatolia plateau were also destroyed. Perhaps some of this mass of migrating mankind traveled overland, far from ships. But a more likely scenario is that the Hittite Great King was, as we have seen from the letters, attempting to defend his long coast from this mass invasion. However, since he was losing, he was unable to break off and defend his heartland from Kaška incursions, as his predecessors through the ages had repeatedly had to do. The heartland, with its garrisons stripped (as at Ugarit), was overrun by the barbarians. The Hittite language and its cuneiform writing system disappeared from history.

The Early Iron Age (ca. 1180–1000 b.c.e.)

After the downfall of the Hittite Empire ca. 1180 B.C.E., an historical account of events on the Anatolian plateau becomes untenable. For over a century there are no known written records by any people living in Anatolia. Only one text written about them by others is known: the Assyrian king Tiglath-Pileser I (1114–1076 B.C.E.) reports (Grayson 1991:14) that in his first campaign he defeated an army of five kings leading 20,000 Muškians, who for fifty years had been occupying Alše (Alzi), a land just south of the Elâzığ Pass through the Taurus Mountains. Muški is the name the Assyrians later applied to the people known to the Greeks as Phrygians (see Sams, chapter 27 in this volume). This may indicate that proto-Phrygians were already present in Anatolia in the mid-twelfth century B.C.E. (Vassileva 1998; Voigt 1994, 1998; Voigt and Henrickson 2000), and far to the east of their later state. Subsequently in this campaign Tiglath-Pileser subjugated 4,000 Kaška and Uruma, to whom he refers as unsubmissive troops of Ḫatti. That the Kaška, who were previously seen as disorganized but dangerous barbarians in northern Anatolia, are now found with at least 120 chariots this far south and east may well indicate that they were not just a contributor to but a beneficiary of the fall of the Hittite Empire.

For the plateau in this period there is only archaeological evidence. Numerous explanations of early Iron Age occupation on the plateau attempt to piece together the situation in a post-Hittite world (see articles in Çilingiroğlu and Darbyshire 2005; Fischer et al. 2003; Genz 2000, 2004, 2005; Seeher 1998, 2010; Tuna, Aktüre, and Lynch 1998; and see Kealhofer and Grave, chapter 18 in this volume), but no consensus has been reached.

Although the fall of the Hittite state put an end to the Great King Šuppiluliuma II and his line, the cadet dynasty at Kargamiš, descendants of Piyašili and now under Kunzi-Teššub, survived and took for themselves the title Great King (Hawkins 1995b). A junior branch of this line soon established themselves at Malatya. Another dynasty of Hittite Great Kings under Muršili and Ḫartapu was to be found in Tarḫuntašša (Hawkins 1995a:103–7). Hittite culture and the Luwian language survived on the southeastern part of the plateau, where the confederation of Tabal eventually formed (see Yakubovich, chapter 23 in this volume). A Greek named Moksu or Mopsos founded a state on the Cilician Plain called Hiyawa (i.e., Aḫḫiyawa, i.e., Achaia, later written Que by the Assyrians and Hume by the Babylonians), but his descendants had Luwian names and wrote their inscriptions in Luwian hieroglyphs and Phoenician (Çambel 1999; Hawkins 2009; Oettinger 2008; Tekoğlu and Lemaire 2000). There was a migration of Luwians into north Syria, where one of the invading Sea Peoples had initially set up a state stretching at least from Aleppo to

Sheizar. This state, ruled by a certain Taita, king of the Philistines ("Palastin") (Hawkins 2009), was, however, Luwian in culture and writing. Later north Syria broke down into a number of small to medium sized states, with a mixed Luwian and Aramaic culture, some leaving us inscriptions in Luwian hieroglyphs (Çambel 1999; Hawkins 2000) and preserving a semblance of Hittite culture until the inexorable annexation and transportation of the population by the Neo-Assyrian Empire.

Conclusion

Anatolia is a natural geographical unit, but it is also a road for nomadic peoples passing by on the way from the Caucasus or Central Asia to Europe and is vulnerable to periodic turbulence and a general breakdown of law and order, as exemplified by the Roman Third Century Anarchy and the Celali Rebellions of the Ottoman Period. Historically, Anatolia has been ruled by a patchwork of small local states or formed part of some externally based empire. That the Hittites managed to unify a substantial part of Anatolia (more or less) for 500 years in the face of local dynasts, invading tribesmen, competing empires like Arzawa, Egypt, Mittanni, and Assyria must rank as a remarkable achievement.

Like all political entities, the Hittite state suffered its share of weak leaders and succession crises, during which times the state lost territory and people. We may perhaps attribute Hittite long-term success to a number of truly great leaders such as Ḫattušili I, Tudḫaliya II, Šuppiluliuma I, Muršili II, and Muwattalli II, whose military prowess extended the borders of Hittite territory and brought foreign adversaries to their knees. More significant for long-term success, however, were the arts of peace. On the one hand, the Hittites practiced careful record-keeping and administration and issued instructions to their officials to which they had to swear by oath. On the other, the Hittites developed an extremely important tool for diplomacy, the international treaty, by means of which they wove their "brother" empires and their conquered subordinate states into a web of peaceful cooperation and friendship. By extraordinary competence in the arts of peace and war the Hittite state prospered as one of the great powers of the Late Bronze Age.[6]

NOTES

1. Exact dates in second millennium B.C.E. Anatolia are largely dependent on links to events in Mesopotamia and to a lesser extent Egypt, where chronologies are better established. However, the Assyrian king list, after a few minor uncertainties, preserves no figures for lengths of reigns before about 1680 B.C.E. The Babylonian king list presents overlapping

dynasties as successive. Therefore there is a chronological gap between the Middle Assyrian/Babylonian period and the Old Babylonian/Old Assyrian period. Based on astronomical events mentioned in Old Babylonian texts, various modern scholars have postulated different possible date ranges for the older period. The most plausible of these are called "High," "Middle," and "Low." The "High" chronology (fall of Babylon in 1651 B.C.E.), in many ways best fitting the ancients' understanding of their own chronology, is today largely out of favor. The "Low" chronology (fall of Babylon in 1531 B.C.E.), is particularly popular with German scholars. The "Middle" chronology (fall of Babylon in 1595 B.C.E.) accords better with Hittite evidence than the Low and will therefore be followed here. With even the trustworthiness of the astronomic report questioned, all dates are to be taken as suspect and only of some value within their own framework. For discussion see Pruzsinszky (2009). For the chronology and history of the Old Assyrian period see Veenhof (2008).

2. Although the Hittites were very interested in their history, they never dated their texts, nor have any date lists or king lists with the number of regnal years been found. The dates given for Hittite kings between Muršili I and Šuppiluliuma I are only educated guesses based on the average length of a generation. The dates from Šuppiluliuma I on are loosely anchored into the Egyptian chronology, about which a certain scholarly consensus has been reached, whereas the reign of Muršili I is firmly anchored into whichever date for the fall of Babylon one chooses (see note 1). The length of a generation used must be either longer or shorter depending on the time allowed in one's chosen Mesopotamian chronology, between these set points. Using the Middle Chronology, the average Hittite generation between these two kings would be about twenty-two years. This seems rather low; for instance, the English royal family from Ethelwulf in 839 through George V (d. 1936) averaged a bit over 33 years a generation, and the Ottomans had twenty-one generations over 665 years averaging 31 2/3 years per generation. Henige (1974:123–26) found that 66 percent of 737 dynasties worldwide averaged between twenty-five and thirty-four years of reign.

3. Literally: "Formerly the kings of Ḫalpa held a Great-Kingship, but Ḫattušili, Great King, King of Ḫatti, caused the (days of) the kingdom to be full" (KBo 1.6 obv. 11–12, trans. Beckman 1999:94).

4. No longer extant, but it is paraphrased in the Deeds of Šuppiluliluma (KBo 14.12 iv 26–32, ed. Güterbock 1956:98) and mentioned in a plague prayer of Muršili II (KUB 14.8 obv. 13–17, trans. Singer 2002:58).

5. Differently Güterbock and Hoffner P/2 (1995) 145: "A single falcon does not put [an entire army(?)] to flight."

6. For a fuller treatment of Hittite history and culture see Bryce 2005, Gurney 1990, and Klengel 1999.

Abbreviations

Bo, Boğazköy tablet excavated 1906–12, cited by inventory number.

HKM, *Hethitische Keilschrifttafeln aus Maşat-Höyük.* Sedat Alp. Türk Tarih Kurumu Yayınları VI/34. Ankara: Türk Tarih Kurumu Basımevi, 1991.

KBo, Keilscrifttexte aus Boghazköi. 1 (1916)–present. Volumes 1–22 are a subseries of Wissenschaftliche Veröffentlichungen der Deutschen Orient-Gesellschaft. Leipzig and Berlin.

KUB, Keilschrifturkunden aus Boghazköi. I (1921)–LX (1990). Berlin.

RS, Ras Shamra text, cited by inventory number.

VBoT, Verstreute Boghazköi-Texte. Albrecht Götze. Marburg a. d. Lahn: im Selbstverlag des Herausgebers, 1930.

REFERENCES

Alp, Sedat. 1991a. *Hethitische Keilschrifttafeln aus Maşat-Höyük*. Türk Tarih Kurumu Yayınları 6/34. Ankara: Türk Tarih Kurumu Basımevi.

———. 1991b. *Hethitische Briefe aus Maşat-Höyük*. Türk Tarih Kurumu Yayınları 6/35. Ankara: Türk Tarih Kurumu Basımevi.

Archi, Alfonso. 2010. When Did the Hittites Begin to Write in Hittite? In *Pax Hethitica: Studies on the Hittites and their Neighbors in Honour of Itamar Singer*, ed. Yoram Cohen, et al., 37–46. Studien zu den Boğazköy-Texten 51. Wiesbaden: Harrassowitz.

Barjamovic, Gojko. 2010. Sites, Routes and Historical Geography in Central Anatolia. In *ipamati kistamati pari tumatimis: Luwian and Hittite Studies Presented to J. David Hawkins on the Occasion of his 70th Birthday*, ed. Itamar Singer, 10–25. Tel Aviv: Institute of Archaeology—Tel Aviv University.

Beal, Richard. 1992. *The Organisation of the Hittite Military*. Texte der Hethiter 20. Heidelberg: Carl Winter—Universitätsverlag.

———. 2000. The Ten Year Annals of Great King Muršili II of Ḫatti. In *The Context of Scripture* 2, ed. William W. Hallo and K. Lawson Younger, 82–90. Leiden: Brill.

———. 2002. The Hurrian Dynasty and the Double Names of Hittite Kings. In *Anatolia Antica: Studia in Memoria di Fiorella Imparati*, ed. Stefano de Martino and Franca Pecchioli Daddi, 55–71. Eothen 11. Florence: LoGisma.

———. 2003. The Predecessors of Ḫattušili I. In *Hittite Studies in Honor of Harry A. Hoffner Jr.*, ed. Gary Beckman, Richard Beal, and Gregory McMahon, 13–35. Winona Lake, Ind.: Eisenbrauns.

Beckman, Gary. 1988. Review of *Hethitica* 6. *Journal of Near Eastern Studies* 47: 141–43.

———. 1995. The Siege of Uršu text (CTH 7). *Journal of Cuneiform Studies* 47: 23–34.

———. 1997. Plague Prayers of Muršili II. In *The Context of Scripture* 1, ed. William W. Hallo and K. Lawson Younger, 156–60. Leiden: Brill.

———. 1999. *Hittite Diplomatic Texts*, 2nd ed. Writings from the Ancient World 7. Atlanta: Scholars Press.

———. 2000. Bilingual Edict of Ḫattušili I. In *The Context of Scripture* 2, ed. William W. Hallo and K. Lawson Younger, 79–81. Leiden: Brill.

Bell, Lanny. 2007. Conflict and Reconciliation in the Ancient Middle East: The Clash of Egyptian and Hittite Chariots in Syria, and the World's First Peace Treaty between "Superpowers." In *War and Peace in the Ancient World*, ed. Kurt A. Raaflaub, 98–120. Oxford: Blackwell.

Bittel, Kurt. 1976. *Die Hethiter: Die Kunst Anatoliens vom Ende des 3. bis zum Anfang des 1. Jahrtausends vor Christus*. Munich: C. H. Beck.

Bryce, Trevor. 2002. *Life and Society in the Hittite World*. Oxford: Oxford University Press.

———. 2005. *The Kingdom of the Hittites*, 2nd ed. Oxford: Oxford University Press.

Cancik-Kirschbaum, Eva Christiane. 1996. *Die Mittelassyrischen Briefe aus Tall Šeḫ Hamad*. Berichte der Ausgrabung Tall Šeḫ Hamad/Dur-Katlimmu 4/1. Berlin: Dietrich Reimer.

Carruba, Onofrio. 1977. Beiträge zur mittelhethitishen Geschichte. *Studia Micenei ed Egeo-Anatolici* 18: 137–95.

———. 2008. *Annali Etei del Medio Regno*. Studia Mediterranea 18. Pavia: Italian University Press.

Çambel, Halet. 1999. *Corpus of Hieroglyphic Luwian Inscriptions 2: Karatepe-Aslantaş*. Untersuchungen zur indogermanischen Sprach-und Kulturwissenschaft 8.2. Berlin: de Gruyter.

Çilingiroğlu, A. and G. Darbyshire, eds. 2005. *Anatolian Iron Ages 5: Proceedings of the Fifth Anatolian Iron Ages Colloquium Held at Van, 6–10 August 2001*. London: British Institute of Archaeology at Ankara.

Darnell, John Coleman and Colleen Manassa. 2007. *Tutankhamun's Armies: Battle and Conquest During Ancient Egypt's Late Eighteenth Dynasty*. Hoboken, N.J.: Wiley.

de Martino, Stefano. 2003. *Annali e Res Gestae Antico Ittiti*. Studia Mediterranea 12. Pavia: Italian University Press.

Devecchi, Elena. 2005. *Gli Annali di Ḫattušili I nella versione accadica*. Studia Mediterranea 16. Pavia: Italian University Press.

Dodson, Aidan. 2009. *Amarna Sunset: Nefertiti, Tutankhamun, Ay, Horemheb, and the Egyptian Counter-Reformation*. Cairo: American University in Cairo.

Du Mesnil du Buisson, Robert. 1935. *Le Site Archéologique de Mishrife-Qatna*. Paris: De Boccard.

Fischer, Bettina, Hermann Genz, Éric Jean, and Kemalettin Köroğlu, eds. 2003. *Identifying Changes: The Transition from Bronze to Iron Ages in Anatolia and its Neighbouring Regions*. İstanbul: Türk Eskiçağ Bilimleri Enstitüsü.

Friedrich, Johannes. 1930. *Staatsverträge des Ḫatti-Reiches in Hethitischer Sprache 2*. Mitteilungen der Vorderasiatisch-Aegyptischen Gesellschaft 34/1. Leipzig: J. C. Hinrichs.

Genz, Hermann. 2000. Die Eisenzeit in Zentralanatolien im Lichte der keramischen Funde vom Büyükkaya in Boğazköy/Hattuša. *TÜBA-AR* 3: 35–54.

———. 2004. *Büyükkaya I: Die Keramik der Eisenzeit*. Boğazköy-Hattuša 21. Mainz: Verlag Philipp von Zabern.

———. 2005. Thoughts on the Origin of the Iron Age Pottery Traditions in Central Anatolia. In *Anatolian Iron Ages* 5, ed. A. Çilingiroğlu and G. Darbyshire, 75–84. London: British Institute of Archaeology in Ankara.

Goetze, Albrecht. 1940. *Kizzuwatna and the Problem of Hittite Geography*. Yale Oriental Series Researches 22. New Haven: Yale University Press.

Götze, Albrecht. 1933. *Die Annalen von Muršiliš*. Mitteilungen der Vorderasiatisch-Ägyptischen Gesellschaft 38. Leipzig: J. C. Hinrichs.

Grayson, A. Kirk. 1987. *Assyrian Rulers of the Third and Second Millennia BC (to 1115)*. Royal Inscriptions of Mesopotamia: Assyrian Periods 1. Toronto: University of Toronto Press.

———. 1991. *Assyrian Rulers of the Early First Millennium BC 1 (1114–859 BC)*. Royal Inscriptions of Mesopotamia: Assyrian Periods 2. Toronto: University of Toronto Press.

Gurney, O. R. 1990. *The Hittites*. 3rd ed. Harmondsworth: Penguin.

Güterbock, Hans Gustav. 1956. The Deeds of Suppiluliluma as Told by His Son Mursili II. *Journal of Cuneiform Studies* 10: 41–68, 75–98, 107–30.

———. 1967. The Hittite Conquest of Cyprus Reconsidered. *Journal of Near Eastern Studies* 26: 73–81.

Güterbock, Hans Gustav and Harry A. Hoffner. 1995. *The Hittite Dictionary of the University of Chicago*, P/2 Chicago: Oriental Institute.

Hagenbuchner, Albertine. 1989. *Die Korrespondenz der Hethiter* 2. Texte der Hethiter 16. Heidelberg: Carl Winter–Universitätsverlag.

Hawkins, John David. 1995a. *The Hieroglyphic Inscription of the Sacred Pool Complex at Hattusa (SÜDBURG)*. Studien zu den Boğazköy-Texten Beiheft 3. Wiesbaden: Harrassowitz.

———. 1995b. "Great Kings" and "Country Lords" at Malatya and Karkamiš. In *Studio Historiae Ardens: Ancient Near Eastern Studies Presented to Philo H. J. Houwink ten Cate on the Occasion of His 65th Birthday*, ed. Th. P. J. van den Hout and J. de Roos, 73–86. Uitgaven van het Nederlands Historisch-Archaeologisch Instituut te Istanbul 74. Leiden: Nederlands Historisch-Archaeologisch Instituut te Istanbul.

———. 2000. *Corpus of Hieroglyphic Luwian Inscriptions 1: Inscriptions of the Iron Age*. Untersuchungen zur indogermanischen Sprach-und Kulturwissenschaft 8.1. Berlin: de Gruyter.

———. 2009. Cilicia, the Amuq and Aleppo: New Light on a Dark Age. *Near Eastern Archaeology* 72: 164–73.

Henige, David P. 1974. *The Chronology of Oral Tradition: Quest for a Chimera*. Oxford: Clarendon Press.

Hoffmann, Inge. 1984. *Der Erlass Telipinus*. Texte der Hethiter 11. Heidelberg: Carl Winter–Universitätsverlag.

Hoffner, Harry A. 1975. Propaganda and Political Justification in Hittite Historiography. In *Unity and Diversity: Essays in the History, Literature, and Religion of the Ancient Near East*, ed. Hans Goedicke and J. J. M. Roberts, 49–62. Baltimore, Md.: Johns Hopkins University Press.

———. 1997a. *The Laws of the Hittites*. Leiden: Brill.

———. 1997b. Proclamation of Anitta of Kuššar. In *The Context of Scripture 1*, ed. William W. Hallo and K. Lawson Younger, 182–84. Leiden: Brill.

———. 1997c. The Deeds of Šuppiluliuma. In *The Context of Scripture 1*, ed. William W. Hallo and K. Lawson Younger, 185–92. Leiden: Brill.

———. 1997d. The Hittite Conquest of Cyprus: Two Inscriptions of Suppiluliluma II. In *The Context of Scripture 1*, ed. William W. Hallo and K. Lawson Younger, 192–93. Leiden: Brill.

———. 2000. Hittite Laws. In *The Context of Scripture 2*, ed. William W. Hallo and K. Lawson Younger, 106–19. Leiden: Brill.

———. 2009. *Letters from the Hittite Kingdom*. Writings from the Ancient World 15. Atlanta: Society of Biblical Literature.

Kitchen, Kenneth A. 2000. The Battle of Qadesh—The Poem, or Literary Record, and—the "Bulletin Text." In *The Context of Scripture 2*, ed. William W. Hallo and K. Lawson Younger, 32–40. Leiden: Brill.

Klengel, Horst. 1974. "Hungerjahre" in Hatti. *Altorientalische Forschungen* 1: 165–74.

———. 1999. *Geschichte des hethitischen Reiches*. Handbuch der Orientalistik I/34. Leiden: Brill.

———. 2000. Qatna—ein historischer Überblick. *Mitteilungen der Deutschen Orient-Gesellschaft* 132: 239–52.

Lackenbacher, Silvie. 1991. Lettres et Fragments. In *Une bibliothèque au sud de la ville*, ed. Pierre Bordreuil. Ras Shamra-Ougarit 7: 83–104. Paris: Éditions Recherche sur les Civilisations.

———. 2002. *Textes Akkadiens d'Ugarit*. Litteratures ancienne du Proche-Orient 20. Paris: Cerf.

Lebrun, René. 1985. L'aphasie de Mursili II. *Hethitica* 6: 103–37.

Malbran-Labat, Florence. 1991. Lettres. In *Une bibliothèque au sud de la ville*, ed. Pierre Bordreuil. Ras Shamra-Ougarit 7: 27–64. Paris: Éditions Recherche sur les Civilisations.

Michel, Cécile. 2001. *Correspondance des marchands de Kaniš au debut de IIe millenaire avant J.C.* Litteratures ancienne du Proche-Orient 19. Paris: Cerf.

Miller, Jared. 2007. Amarna Age Chronology and the Identity of Nibḫururiya in the Light of a Newly Reconstructed Hittite Text. *Altorientalische Forschungen* 34: 252–93.

Moran, William L. 1992. *The Amarna Letters*. Baltimore: Johns Hopkins University Press.

Murnane, William J. 1995. The History of Ancient Egypt: An Overview. In *Civilizations of the Ancient Near East*, ed. Jack M. Sasson, 2: 691–717. New York: Scribner.

Neu, Erich. 1974. *Der Anitta-Text*. Studien zu den Boğazköy-Texten 18. Wiesbaden: Otto Harrassowitz.

Nougayrol, Jean. 1968. Textes Suméro-accadiens des archives et bibliothèques privées d'Ugarit. *Ugaritica* 5. Mission de Ras Shamra 12: 1–368.

Oettinger, Norbert. 2008. The Seer Mopsos (Muksas) as a Historical Figure. In *Hittites, Greeks and Their Neighbors*, ed. Billie Jean Collins, Mary Bachvarova, and Ian Rutherford, 63–66. Oxford: Oxbow.

Otten, Heinrich. 1981. *Die Apologie Hattusilis III*. Studien zu den Boğazköy-Texten 24. Wiesbaden: Otto Harrassowitz.

Özgüç, Tahsin. 1982. *Maşat Höyük II: A Hittite Center Northeast of Boğazköy*. Türk Tarih Kurumu Yayınları 5/38a. Ankara: Türk Tarih Kurumu Basımevi.

Pardee, Dennis. 2002. Ugaritic Letters. In *The Context of Scripture* 3, ed. William W. Hallo and K. Lawson Younger, 87–116. Leiden: Brill.

Pruzsinszky, Regine. 2009. *Mesopotamian Chronology of the 2nd Millennium B.C.* Denkschriften der Österreichischen Akademie der Wissenschaften 56. Vienna: Österreichische Akademie der Wissenschaften.

Richter, Thomas. 2002. Die "Einjährige Feldzug" Šuppiluliumas I. von Hatti in Syrien nach Textfunden des Jahres 2002 in Mišrife/Qatna. *Ugarit Forschungen* 34: 603–18.

Riemschneider, Kaspar K. 1962. Hethitische Fragmente historischen Inhalts aus der Zeit Hattusilis III. *Journal of Cuneiform Studies* 16: 110–21.

Seeher, Jürgen. 1998. The Early Iron Age Settlement on Büyükkaya, Boğazköy: First Impressions. In *Anatolian Iron Ages 3: The Proceedings of the Third Anatolian Iron Ages Colloquium Held at Van, 6–12 August 1990*, ed. Altan Çilingiroğlu and David H. French, 71–78. Ankara: British Institute of Archaeology at Ankara.

———. 2001. Die Zerstörung der Stadt Ḫattuša. In *Akten des IV. Internationalen Kongresses für Hethitologie, Würzburg, 4–8 Oktober 1990*, ed. Gernot Wilhelm, 623–34. Studien zu den Boğazköy-Texten 45. Wiesbaden: Harrassowitz.

———. 2002. *Hattusha-Guide: A Day in the Hittite Capital*. Istanbul: Ege Yayınları.

———. 2010. After the Empire: Observations on the Early Iron Age in Central Anatolia. In *ipamati kistamati pari tumatimis: Luwian and Hittite Studies Presented to J. David Hawkins on the Occasion of his 70th Birthday*, ed. Itamar Singer, 10–25. Tel Aviv: Institute of Archaeology—Tel Aviv University.

Singer, Itamar. 1985. The Battle of Niḫriya and the End of the Hittite Empire. *Zeitschrift für Assyriologie* 75: 100–123.

———. 2002. *Hittite Prayers*. Writings from the Ancient World 11. Atlanta: Society of Biblical Literature.

Sommer, Ferdinand and Adam Falkenstein. 1938. *Die hethitisch-akkadische Bilingue des Ḫattušili I. (Labarna II)*. Abhandlung der Bayerischen Akademie der Wissenschaften N.F. 16. Munich: Bayerische Akademie der Wissenschaften.

Stefanini, Ruggiero. 1965. KBo IV 14 = VAT 13049. *Atti della Accademia Nazionale dei Lincei* 8/20: 39–79.

Tekoğlu, S. Recai and André Lemaire. 2000. Le bilingue royale louvito-phenicienne de Çineköy. *Comptes rendu de l'Academie des inscriptions et belles-lettres* 2000: 961–1007.

Tuna, Numan, Zeynep Aktüre, and Maggie Lynch, eds. 1998. *Thracians and Phrygians: Problems of Parallelism*. Ankara: METU, Faculty of Architecture Press.

van den Hout, Theo P. J. 1994. Der Falke und das Kücken: der neue Pharaoh und der hethitische Prinz? *Zeitschrift für Assyriologie* 84: 60–88.

———. 1997a. The Proclamation of Telipinu. In *The Context of Scripture 1*, ed. William W. Hallo and K. Lawson Younger, 194–98. Leiden: Brill.

———. 1997b. The Apology of Ḫattušili III. In *The Context of Scripture 1*, ed. William W. Hallo and K. Lawson Younger, 199–204. Leiden: Brill.

———. 2004. Some Thoughts on the Composition Known as Muršili's Aphasia (CTH 486). In *Studia Anatolica et Varia: Mélanges offerts au Professeur René Lebrun*, ed. Michel Mazoyer and Olivier Casabonne, 359–80. Collection Kubaba: Série Antiquité 4. Paris: Kubaba.

Vassileva, Maya. 1998. Thracian-Phrygian Cultural Zone. In *Thracians and Phrygians: Problems of Parallelism*, ed. Numan Tuna, Zeynep Aktüre, and Maggie Lynch, 13–17. Ankara: METU, Faculty of Architecture Press.

Veenhof, Klaas R. 2008. The Old Assyrian Period. In *Mesopotamia: The Old Assyrian Period*, ed. Klaas R. Veenhof and Jesper Eidem, 13–264. Orbis Biblicus and Orientalis 160/5. Fribourg: Academic Press.

Voigt, Mary M. 1994. Excavations at Gordion 1988–89: The Yassıhöyük Stratigraphic Sequence. In *Anatolian Iron Ages 3: The Proceedings of the Third Anatolian Iron Ages Colloquium Held at Van, 6–12 August 1990*, ed. Altan Çilingiroğlu and David H. French, 265–93. Ankara: British Institute of Archaeology at Ankara.

———. 1998. Gordion. In *The Oxford Encyclopedia of Archaeology in the Near East*, ed. Eric M. Meyers, 426–31. Oxford: Oxford University Press.

Voigt, Mary M. and Robert C. Henrickson. 2000. Formation of the Phrygian State: The Early Iron Age at Gordion. *Anatolian Studies* 50: 37–54.

von Schuler, Einar. 1965. *Die Kaškäer*. Berlin: de Gruyter.

Wilhelm, Gernot. 2009. Muršilis II. Konflikt mit Ägypten und Haremhabs Thronbesteigung. *Welt des Orients* 39: 108–16.

Wilson, John A. 1969a. Treaty between the Hittites and Egypt. In *Ancient Near Eastern Texts Relating to the Old Testament*, ed. James B. Pritchard, 199–201. Princeton, N.J.: Princeton University Press.

———. 1969b. The War against the Peoples of the Sea. In *Ancient Near Eastern Texts Relating to the Old Testament*, ed. James B. Pritchard, 262–63. Princeton, N.J.: Princeton University Press.

Woolley, C. Leonard. 1969 [1921]. *Carchemish: Report on the Excavations at Djerablis on Behalf of the British Museum*. London: Trustees of the British Museum.

Yon, Marguerite. 2006. *The City of Ugarit at Tell Ras Shamra*. Winona Lake, Ind.: Eisenbrauns.

CHAPTER 27

ANATOLIA: THE FIRST MILLENNIUM B.C.E. IN HISTORICAL CONTEXT

G. KENNETH SAMS

The End of the Late Bronze Age

The collapse of the Hittite Empire ca. 1200 B.C.E. marked a major turning point for the history of Anatolia. The fall was unquestionably connected at least remotely with other events transpiring in the eastern Mediterranean in the later thirteenth and twelfth centuries B.C.E., including the end of Mycenaean civilization in mainland Greece, the destruction of Troy (VIIa) and Ugarit (Ras Shamra), and the attempted invasion of Egypt on two occasions by the "Sea Peoples" (Sandars 1985; see Beal, chapter 26 in this volume). In central Anatolia and beyond, the prosaic, mass-produced but professional pottery of the Hittite Empire ceases to be made, no doubt because the state organisms that oversaw the production were no longer there (Genz 2003). Similarly, cuneiform script in Hittite (Nesite) and other languages, as known primarily from the Hittite capital at Ḫattuša, is never again attested for Anatolians, with the exception of Urartu in the far east. In many parts of Anatolia, a reversion to subsistence economy in humble settlements, with no powerful polity looking on, seems to have been the rule. The local people involved were Anatolians, that is, those who survived the fall of Hittite and other Late Bronze Age powers. The continuity is seen primarily in the first millennium B.C.E. language groupings across Anatolia. Luwian hieroglyphic script, as had been used in the time of the Empire as a writing system secondary to cuneiform, survives. In central Anatolia, it is found above all in Tabal, an Iron Age land lying generally to the south and southeast of the

Hittite homeland of Ḫatti (Aro 1998; Hawkins 1982:376, 2000:425–28). Further to the southeast, the script and language survived in Cilicia and north Syria, the latter having had in the time of the Empire a Hittite viceroy seated at Carchemish on the Euphrates River (Hawkins 1982:383–84, 2000:73–76; see Beal, chapter 26, and Yakubovich, chapter 23 in this volume). The royal house there in fact seems to have survived the downfall of the Empire as a whole and to have established a branch line in Melid (Arslantepe-Malatya) to the north (Hawkins 1988, 2000:282–86). At the latter site, a member of that line active in the decades around 1100 B.C.E., PUGNUS-Mili by name, shows himself and his gods very much in the style of empire figures, such as those seen at Yazılıkaya near Ḫattuša in the thirteenth century B.C.E. (Akurgal and Hirmer 1962:pls. 103–5). He also refers to himself as "king," using the same hieroglyphic sign found with rulers of the Empire, but he omits the sign that would have made him "Great King," the regular title for his imperial forebears; presumably he did so because of subservience to Carchemish. That title is claimed by four early, post-Empire kings of Carchemish (Hawkins 1988), but by the late tenth century B.C.E. the "Neo-Hittite" rulers of the city have abandoned both the royal title and much of the artistic style of the Empire. Further to the east, the language of Urartu also seems to have survived from the Bronze Age. Although not found in written form until the ninth century B.C.E., Urartian is linguistically so close to Hurrian, a second millennium B.C.E. language of northern Syria and northern Iraq, that the two tongues apparently developed side by side in the course of the second millennium (Zimansky 1995, and chapter 24 in this volume).

Continuity into the First Millennium B.C.E.

The languages of first millennium B.C.E. western Anatolia, including Pisidian, Lycian, Carian, Lydian, and probably Mysian, are, like Hittite (Nesite) and Luwian, members of the so-called Anatolian Group of Indo-European languages (Bryce 2003:93–127; Melchert 1995, and chapter 31 in this volume). The implication is that these tongues survived from the Bronze Age into the Iron along with at least some of their speakers. Place-names also survived. The "Lukka Land" of Hittite imperial texts is surely Lycia (Greek: Lukia), whereas a Bronze Age city there, "Wine Land," is probably none other than the later city of Oenoanda (with the same meaning in a conflation of Greek and Anatolian). Similarly, Hittite Ikkuwaniya becomes Ikonion/Iconium in south central Anatolia (carrying on today as Turkish Konya), and the Bronze Age city of Parḫa survives as Perge in Pamphylia on the southern coast. On the Aegean coast to the west, the names of the renowned later Ionian Greek cities of Ephesus and Miletus mean nothing in the Greek language because they survive as the once Anatolian (and probably Luwian-speaking) centers of Apaša and Millawanda, respectively, as known again from Hittite imperial sources.

Thus the fall of the Hittite Empire did not bring with it anything like a devastating cessation of life in Anatolia. The first millennium B.C.E., rather, surely represents a continuum, albeit one that is not well understood historically or archaeologically. A number of sites report continuity in material culture, primarily pottery, from Bronze to Iron, one such being Boğazköy (Genz 2004a:24–28, 36–50). Despite evidence for continuity, the curtain that eventually rises on early first millennium B.C.E. Anatolia shows a cultural veneer that is considerably different from that of the Bronze Age. The evidence is largely archaeological, supplemented by a variety of written sources. No longer is a great body of internal texts available for gaining a firsthand view of events and activities, since the concept of maintaining records on clay tablets, in any language or script, ceased in Anatolia with the end of the Hittite Empire. However, record-keeping on lead strips in hieroglyphic Luwian is attested (Hawkins 1987, 2000:503–13; see Yakubovich, chapter 23 in this volume). Otherwise, the internal epigraphic evidence consists primarily of inscriptions on stone, pottery, and other materials. Greatly supplementing these local sources are the extensive records of Assyria, particularly those of the Assyrian Empire of the ninth to seventh centuries B.C.E. Already in the thirteenth century, Assyrian rulers were making expeditions into what was to become the kingdom of Urartu in far eastern Anatolia (Zimansky 1995, and see Zimansky, chapter 24, and Radner, chapter 33 in this volume), and from the later twelfth century B.C.E. on they made serious inroads into north Syria (Hawkins 1982:380–82). It was not until the ninth century that an Assyrian king (Šalmaneser III) on expedition "discovered" central Anatolia, namely, the land of Tabal (Hawkins 1982:394, 2000:426–28). In the latter half of the eighth century, rulers of that land, north Syria, and Cilicia were paying tribute to Assyria. By the early seventh century B.C.E., many of the centers of north Syria and Cilicia had become annexed by Assyria, their populations presumably resettled, as was Assyrian practice (Hawkins 1982:424).

As indicated, in the early first millennium B.C.E. peoples of Tabal, Cilicia, and north Syria maintained links with the Late Bronze Age past through language (Luwian) and script (hieroglyphic; see Yakubovich, chapter 23 in this volume). A new component in these regions, however, is West Semitic, as witnessed by a number of Phoenician and Aramaic inscriptions carved in an alphabetic script. The nature of the epigraphic evidence in these areas tends to be site-specific: hieroglyphic Luwian at centers such as Carchemish, Malatya, and Tell Tayinat in the Amuq Plain; Phoenician and Aramaic alphabetic inscriptions at Zincirli-Sam'al in İslahiye, not far from either Carchemish or Tell Tayinat (Hawkins 1982:375–76). The great exception is Azatiwataya-Karatepe in northeastern Cilicia, where public documents in stone were inscribed as bilinguals in both hieroglyphic Luwian and alphabetic Phoenician (Çambel 1999; Hawkins 1982:429–31). The discovery of the inscriptions allowed great strides toward the decipherment of hieroglyphic Luwian. West Semitic speakers had probably moved into the areas sometime soon after the collapse of the Hittite Empire. How they may have mingled with the Luwian-speaking population is unclear and puzzling. A 9th century ruler at Zincirli-Sam'al put up a public inscription in Phoenician, yet his name, Kilamuwa, is Luwian! Luwian personal names survive in southern Anatolia into the Hellenistic period of the later 4th to 1st centuries B.C.E. (Houwink ten Cate 1961).

Newcomers to Anatolia

Although cultural continuity from the Bronze Age into the Iron Age did occur, new elements also came into play. In west central Anatolia, the land of Phrygia emerged in the centuries following the collapse of the Hittite Empire, with its early capital at Gordion (see Voigt, chapter 50 in this volume). For Phrygia and other westerly Anatolian lands of the Iron Age, a new source of testimonial information comes with Greek literature. In the case of Phrygia, for example, Greek sources relate that the Phrygians originally lived in the Balkans, as a people known as the Bryges, and at some point in time migrated to Anatolia (Brixhe 1994a; see Roller, chapter 25 in this volume). The tradition finds both archaeological and linguistic support. The earliest post-Hittite levels at Gordion, dating perhaps as early as the late twelfth century B.C.E., yield handmade pottery with Balkan, more specifically Thracian, affinities, and later elements of Phrygian culture suggest continuing links with southeastern Europe (Sams 1988; see Roller, chapter 25 in this volume). The language of the Phrygians, as known through inscriptions, is Indo-European, but it is not closely related to the Anatolian Group mentioned earlier. Instead, Phrygian seems to belong to an Indo-European subset that includes Greek and the poorly attested Thracian language, as was spoken in southeastern Europe (Brixhe 1994a; see Roller, chapter 25 in this volume). The Phrygians and other west Anatolians find their way into the earliest work of Greek literature. Homer in the *Iliad* (eighth–seventh century B.C.E.) has the Phrygians as allies of Troy in the Trojan War (II.824-77), as also, among other Anatolians, the Lycians, Carians, Mysians, and Lydians (called by him the Maeonians). Hecuba, the wife of King Priam of Troy, was herself a Phrygian from the banks of the Sangarius River, where Gordion is in fact located. Phrygians shared with Greeks an alphabetic writing system derived from West Semitic script but with the addition of vocalization (see Harl, chapter 34 in this volume). It is likely that the two peoples were making the move to literacy somehow in tandem because of certain shared characteristics in the use of Semitic letters (Brixhe 1994b; DeVries 2007:96–97). Phrygian writing is in place by around the middle of the eighth century B.C.E., about the same time the first Greek inscriptions occur. The above-mentioned peoples of western Anatolia who spoke languages belonging to the Anatolian Group of Indo-European came to adopt the same basic alphabetic script, picking it up perhaps from the Greeks or possibly the Phrygians.

Also new to the Anatolian Iron Age scene are the Greeks, who had begun to establish permanent settlements on the Aegean coast by the eleventh century B.C.E.

(Cook 1962:23–35; Kerschner 2006; Harl, chapter 34, and Greaves, chapter 21 in this volume). They had certainly been familiar with the territory earlier, in the Late Bronze Age, by way of commercial and political interests, and perhaps even trading posts, but now they came to stay. In the case of such settlements as Miletus and Ephesus, as implied, the Greeks chose the sites of former Anatolian cities of prominence. By the end of the seventh century B.C.E., Greeks had established themselves at several points along the shores of the Sea of Marmara (Propontis) and the Anatolian coast (plus other coasts) of the Black Sea (Cook 1962:50–59). On the southern coast, the traditions regarding Greek settlement are several and sometimes seemingly contradictory. Phaselis in far western Pamphylia was said to have been founded by Rhodes, and Side, on the Pamphylian–Cilician border, by Cyme in Aeolis. Yet both cities also get caught up in the broader tradition that these parts were settled by a mixed group of wandering Greeks after the Trojan War (Bean 1968:21–24). Be the Trojan War myth or not, the fact remains that Pamphylian Greek is closely related to the Greek of Late Bronze Age Linear B in Greece. The language of Side, Sidetic, appears to belong to the Anatolian Group of Indo-European (Melchert 1995), while Perge, as seen, is with little doubt Hittite Parḫa. Thus any Greeks coming as early as the twelfth century B.C.E. to the area would have found a local Anatolian population already in place. One of the leaders of those wandering Greeks was Mopsus. His name has been equated with Muksas (Luwian)/MPŠ (Phoenician), known from the Karatepe bilingual inscriptions as the eponymous ancestor of the royal house of Adana in Cilicia (Hawkins 1982:430). In the southwest, Lycia had no Greek settlements, even though it did come to be strongly under the influence of Greek artistic culture (Akurgal 1961:122–49).

Assyrians in Anatolia

The Assyrian Empire had two major phases of strength. The first came under Aššurnaṣirpal II (883–859 B.C.E.) and continued under his son, Šalmaneser III (859–824 B.C.E.). Following a period of relative weakness, Assyria saw a resurgence of empire beginning with Tiglatpileser III (744–727 B.C.E.) that lasted at least through the reign of Aššurbanipal (668–627 B.C.E.). Within this span of empire arose and subsided a major Anatolian power to the north, the kingdom of Urartu centered around Lake Van, with its capital at Tušpa. Although the Assyrians made numerous offensive campaigns into Urartu, the land, perhaps because of its rugged, mountainous location, never came under direct Assyrian control (Zimansky 1995; and Radner, chapter 33 in this volume).

Already before the time of the Assyrian Empire, Neo-Hittite dynasties had become established in a number of centers. At Arslantepe, the PUGNUS-Mili cited earlier belonged to a dynasty of at least four rulers active in the later twelfth and early eleventh centuries B.C.E. (Hawkins 1988, 2000:283). In his reliefs at the Lion

Gate (Akurgal and Hirmer 1962:pls. 103–5), he makes libation and sacrifice to a number of deities, including the gods of cities that may well have been under his sway. The Suhis dynasty at Carchemish, the last before submission to Assyria, had at least four rulers spanning from the late tenth into the early ninth century B.C.E. They (especially the last two dynasts, Suhis II and Katuwas) appear to have been responsible for most of the impressive architectural complexes and sculptural programs uncovered there before World War I (Hawkins 1982:383–84, 2000:77–78). Among these is the so-called Long Wall of Sculpture, which documents in script and relief the restoration to Carchemish of the gods of the city (i.e., images) after they had been stolen by an enemy (Hawkins 2000:87–91; Orthmann 1971:500–503; and see Harmanşah, chapter 28 in this volume). It is an odd fact of Carchemish that the rulers' names found on local inscriptions, as in the case of the Suhis dynasty, do not occur in Assyrian sources, while the names of rulers given in Assyrian records are not epigraphically attested on local documents. The latter is the case with the ruler Sangara, who paid tribute to Šalmaneser III beginning in 858, as did a number of other Neo-Hittite rulers (Hawkins 1982:395). At Zincirli, the Kilamuwa mentioned earlier was active around 830 B.C.E. and thus a contemporary of Šalmaneser III. Yet in his Phoenician inscription, set into a wall of his palace, he provides a genealogy for his line that could well take his dynasty back to the late tenth century B.C.E. (Hawkins 1982:397). This is also a reasonable stylistic date for the relief sculptures of the Outer Citadel Gate at Zincirli, which bear several affinities with the sculptures of the Suhis dynasty at Carchemish (Orthmann 1971:538–43).

In 838 B.C.E., when Šalmaneser III became the first Assyrian ruler to penetrate central Anatolia, the king encountered the land of Tabal, where he received submission from at least twenty kings (Hawkins 1982:394). Although details are sparse, the implication is that Tabal had for some time existed as a sophisticated polity with a system (federation?) to coordinate the activities of its some twenty rulers. The archaeology for Tabal in the ninth century B.C.E. and earlier is limited. Pottery from sites such as Kültepe (Özgüç 1971:85–93) and Alişar (von der Osten 1937:350–52) probably goes back to the ninth century B.C.E., especially a distinctive style of painted pottery often characterized by silhouette animals (Sievertsen 2004). At Kültepe the Iron Age levels are badly disturbed by later settlement. A sculpted orthostat from the citadel depicts a falconry god in a style paralleling that of the Suhis dynasty at Carchemish; it and a fragment of a stylistically related griffin orthostat that probably came from the citadel are perhaps the strongest indicators of monumental, that is, state-controlled building in a ninth century (or earlier) context in Tabal (Özgüç 1971:80–83 and pls. XI.1 and XIII.2). Boğazköy, to the northwest of Tabal and seemingly not in its immediate orbit, also has a ceramic sequence that covers the ninth and earlier Iron Age centuries B.C.E. (Genz 2004b; and see Kealhofer and Grave, chapter 18 in this volume).

Further west, in Phrygia and beyond the reach of Šalmaneser's campaign, Gordion in the ninth century B.C.E. was home to an impressive citadel replete with monumental buildings that only a well organized and powerful state could have commanded (Voigt, chapter 50 in this volume). The large-scale construction may have begun already by the end of the 10th century. Most of the structures are of megaron type and, as such, may look back to an architectural tradition of the Late Bronze Age in western Anatolia, as represented at Beycesultan and especially in the Troy VI citadel (Blegen 1963:111–46; Lloyd 1972). Connections with the east and southeast are evident in a series of fragmentary sculpted orthostats that, like the example from Kültepe, show stylistic affinities with those of the Suhis dynasty at Carchemish (Voigt, chapter 50 in this volume). The burial of royalty under colossal mounds of earth or tumuli had already begun in the course of the ninth century B.C.E. Tumulus burial is not attested earlier in Anatolia. The tradition may well have been part of the cultural baggage that Phrygians brought with them from southeastern Europe; it continued for important people in Anatolia into the Roman period. The citadel at Gordion succumbed to a violent fire around 800 B.C.E. The absence of people or weaponry in the extensive level of destruction may imply an accidental conflagration, as does the fact that rebuilding of the citadel began soon after the disaster (Voigt, chapter 50 in this volume). A comparison might be made with the gruesome scene of carnage found at Hasanlu in northwestern Iran after an Urartian sack that took place at just about the same time (Zimansky 1995).

The eighth century saw the resurgence of the Assyrian Empire under Tiglatpileser III. In the decades before his time, however, rulers at Carchemish tell of an interesting episode through the so-called Royal Buttress, which relates in word and picture the establishment of Yariris as regent of the city until the young Kamanis can assume the throne (Akurgal and Hirmer 1962:pls. 119–23, where Yariris is referred to as Araras, an outdated reading; Hawkins 1982:406–7, 2000:78–79, 123–29). Details are dim, but the need was felt to portray and label family members, as though to legitimate the entire line. Again, the names are known only from internal documentation. Kamanis does appear to have eventually become the king. Succeeding him or coming soon after was Pisiris, who paid his first tribute to Tiglatpileser III in 738 B.C.E. Known only through Assyrian records, he was the last king of Carchemish in a series of events that led to the demise of the Neo-Hittite states of Syria. Among the contemporaries of Pisiris was Bar-Rakib of Zincirli/Sam'al, who, as his father before him, was installed on his throne by Tiglatpileser III. Ruling from the late 730s B.C.E. on, Bar-Rakib seems to have been responsible for major building activity at Sam'al, namely, a complex of palaces (*bit hilani*) connected by colonnades (Akurgal and Hirmer 1962:fig. 23). The style of the accompanying sculptures is typical of the time for Neo-Hittite art, showing strong influence from Assyrian work. In a famous relief orthostat from one of his palaces, Bar-Rakib is shown resplendent on a throne, much in the manner of Assyrian kings, with an attendant (scribe?) standing before him (Akurgal and Hirmer 1962:pl. 131). His name is given in a short Aramaic inscription at the top. Pro-Assyrian, Bar-Rakib openly pronounced his subservience to Tiglatpileser III.

Šalmaneser III in the ninth century B.C.E. had merely raided Tabal. Tiglatpileser III brought the land under Assyrian control (Hawkins 1982:412–13). Here, another local ruler of the time, Warpalawas (Assyrian Urballu) of Tuwana is perhaps best known for his rock relief at İvriz, which shows him standing in splendid attire before a much larger figure of the storm god Tarhunzas (Akurgal and Hirmer 1962:pls. 24 and 140; Hawkins 2000:427–28). Warpalawas first paid tribute to Tiglatpileser III in 738 B.C.E.; he was still active in 710 B.C.E., receiving mention in a letter Sargon II sent that year to his governor in Cilicia. The capital of Tuwana appears to have been the mound of Kemerhisar, where excavation has not taken place. Not far to the north, the mountaintop fortress of Göllüdağ may have been connected to Tuwana (Schirmer 1993). Portal lions there in good Assyrianizing style could date to the time of Warpalawas or later (Akurgal and Hirmer 1962:pl. 136).

Phrygians and Lydians

To the west, in Phrygia, still beyond Assyrian reach, the new citadel at Gordion (to replace the old one destroyed by fire) was probably under construction during much of the eighth century B.C.E. Around 740 B.C.E., work crews may have been diverted from the task, on the occasion of the death of a Phrygian king, for the construction of his tumulus, the largest at Gordion (Voigt, chapter 50 in this volume). Traditionally known as the Midas Mound, the tomb was definitely not that of the Midas known to Sargon II later in the century. Nonetheless, the occupant, in his sixties when he died, was possibly the grandfather or even father of Midas. Unlike the Neo-Hittite states, Phrygia has no internal or Assyrian documentation that allows the construction of royal genealogies for this period. When Greek sources mention Midas, he is usually referred to as the son of Gordias.

Midas of Phrygia appears as Mita of Muški in the annals of Sargon II from 718 until 709 B.C.E. (Hawkins 1982:417–22). In one of the earliest references, Sargon accused Pisiris of intrigue with Midas. As a result, Carchemish was taken, its population was dispersed, and the site became the center of an Assyrian province. Other states of the region suffered similar ends at the hands of the Assyrians, to the point that few seem to have survived intact into the seventh century B.C.E. (Hawkins 1982:424).

A notable exception may lie with the site of Karatepe, on the Ceyhan (Classical Pyramus) River in northeastern Cilicia. In the bilingual (hieroglyphic Luwian and alphabetic Phoenician) inscriptions found built into the gateways here we are told that Azatiwatas, a somehow prominent Cilician, founded the city and named it after himself, Azatiwataya (Hawkins 1982:429–31, 2000:45–70). The inscriptions are accompanied by sculpted orthostats that individually show a mix of early and Assyrianizing Neo-Hittite styles, thus complicating the date of the foundation (Akurgal and Hirmer 1962:pls. 142–50; Çambel and Özyar 2003). The suggestion has been made, independently by two scholars, that Azatiwatas be equated with the Cilician ruler Sanduarri, who was put to death by the Assyrian king Esarhaddon in 676 B.C.E. (Hawkins 1979:153–57; Winter 1979). Azatiwatas would thus have been active in the first quarter of the seventh century B.C.E. The date may explain the somewhat debased style of the Assyrianizing sculptures, as though they were the last breath of Neo-Hittite art (Akurgal and Hirmer 1962:pl. 142).

To return to Midas of Phrygia, by 709 B.C.E. he had become an ally of Assyria, after years of intrigue in Tabal and Cilicia, having even annexed cities of the latter (Hawkins 1982:420–21). This Midas was probably the same figure who, according to the Greek historian Herodotus (I.14), was the first non-Greek to offer a dedication to the god Apollo at Delphi in central Greece. Midas may thus have been the first eastern potentate with whom the Greek world came in contact. A Midas was said to have married a Greek princess from the city of Cyme in Aeolis, but more than one Anatolian ruler bore the name (Berndt-Ersöz 2008).

In the last decade of the eighth century B.C.E., a group of migrant raiding people, the Cimmerians, appear in Urartu (Ivanchik 1993). Through a combination of Assyrian and Greek records, we know that they penetrated Anatolia, eventually reaching as far west as Ionia in the seventh century B.C.E. Sargon II dies in battle in 705 B.C.E., probably in Tabal, and perhaps at the hands of a Cimmerian force (Hawkins 1982:422, 2000:427–28). The Cimmerian presence may in part explain why, only a few years earlier, Midas had become a friend of Assyria. The extent of Cimmerian devastation in Anatolia is clearer from the ancient sources than it is from archaeology. One Greek tradition states that Midas died when the Cimmerians invaded his land in the early seventh century B.C.E. In 679 B.C.E., the Assyrian ruler Esarhaddon led an expedition against them in Tabal. His son and successor, Aššurbanipal (668–627 B.C.E.), early in his reign received an appeal from Gyges king of Lydia for support against the Cimmerians. Aid was apparently given, yet in the mid-seventh century B.C.E. Gyges was killed when the Cimmerians took his capital Sardis (Mellink 1991:644–48; see Greenewalt, chapter 52 in this volume). The destruction level has been identified in a sounding (Hanfmann et al. 1966:10–12). It remained for a later king of Lydia, Alyattes (ca. 610–560 B.C.E.), to finally subdue the marauders.

With Gyges and Lydia, as with Midas and Phrygia, we have the benefit of both Assyrian and Greek testimony; the latter are considerably more abundant for Lydia than for Phrygia, with Herodotus being a principal source. Like Midas before him, Gyges made sumptuous offerings to Apollo at Delphi (Herodotus I.14), in this case in gratitude for the Delphic sanction granted him and his line, the Mermnad dynasty. In a bloody coup of around 675 B.C.E., he had killed the last ruler in the previous Heraklid dynasty. Gyges had diplomatic connections not only with Assyria but also with Egypt. He also took or attempted to take Greek cities of neighboring Ionia, setting a precedent for his successors, who take us down to the mid-sixth century B.C.E. and the Persian conquest of Anatolia. The fact that Gyges, instead of a Phrygian king, established diplomatic ties with Assyria may imply a Phrygia weakened by the Cimmerians. Certainly by the early sixth century B.C.E. Lydian hegemony has extended into central Anatolia and Phrygia (see Roller, chapter 25 in this volume). The process may have begun considerably earlier. At Gordion, excavated tumuli of the seventh century B.C.E. are considerably less grand in size and content than those of pre-Cimmerian times. Lydians came to take on the tradition of tumulus burial for important people, perhaps under Phrygian influence. Of three especially large tumuli near Sardis, one surpasses Tumulus MM at Gordion in size; on the strength of Herodotus, it is identified as the tomb of Alyattes (Hanfmann et al. 1983:56–58).

The Assyrian Empire came to an end near the close of the seventh century B.C.E., brought down by a coalition of Babylonians and the Medes, a people centered in western Iran. By this time the kingdom of Urartu had also expired, from unknown causes (Zimansky 1995). Vacuums of power were thus created, and soon filled. Babylon took over much of the territory of the Assyrian Empire south of Anatolia, including Syria and the former Neo-Hittite centers. In Anatolia, the Medes were able to gain control as far west as the region of the Kızıl Irmak (Classical Halys River), that is, what had been the heartland of the Hittite Empire. Although the Medes were geographically verging on Phrygian territory, the defensive interests they primarily aroused were those of the Lydians, by now the controlling force of Anatolia west of the Kızıl Irmak. Under Alyattes of Lydia, war was waged against the Medes, ending in a battle that was halted on May 28, 585 B.C.E., by a solar eclipse; rulers of Babylon and Cilicia helped negotiate the truce (Mellink 1991:649).

Alyattes was no stranger to warfare, having already taken the Greek city of Smyrna around 600 B.C.E. He also fought with other Greek cities and in Caria. Under Alyattes, if not earlier, the Lydians made a profound contribution to economic history through the invention of coinage, initially electrum and then, probably under Croesus, gold and silver (Cahill and Kroll 2005). It was probably also in the reign of Alyattes that the Lydians fortified Sardis with an enormous circuit wall (Greenewalt, Ratté, and Rautman 1994:13–21; Roosevelt 2009:64–65). Alyattes was succeeded around 560 B.C.E. by his son Croesus, who carried on his father's policies against the Greek cities of the Aegean coast. He was also to be the last king of Lydia. Croesus came to be known for his fabulous wealth. He made contributions (presumably significant) to the construction of the enormous temple of Artemis at Ephesus. Following the precedent set by his ancestor Gyges, he courted Delphi with gifts so lavish that only a potentate could have offered them (Herodotus I.50–51). Although the palace complex of these Lydian kings has not survived, large terrace walls of finely cut stone on the acropolis at Sardis no doubt attest to an architectural grandeur fitting for these rulers (Roosevelt 2009:77–80). Some buildings in Sardis at this time were distinguished by having terra cotta tiled roofs and brightly colored revetment plaques that display a variety of abstract and figural designs (Ramage 1978). The architectural concept was Greek in origin.

In central Anatolia, Phrygian cultural life seems not to have diminished under the Lydian hegemony. In fact, if an account by Herodotus (I.35) can be accepted, a Phrygian royal house with names including Midas and Gordias was still in place in the time of Croesus (Berndt-Ersöz 2008:1–2; Mellink 1991:624); the implication may be that Lydia maintained a laissez-faire attitude toward well-behaving central Anatolians. Phrygian expansion (at least the language) to the east is documented by inscriptions on stone and pottery within the bend of the Kızıl Irmak, including one on a stepped altar of generally Phrygian type (Brixhe and Lejeune 1984:223–51; Brixhe and Summers 2006). Elaborate rock-cut building façades in the Phrygian Highlands between Eskişehir and Afyon may in part belong to the sixth century B.C.E., no later than the Lydian hegemony, although the chronology has for long been contested (DeVries 1988; Berndt-Ersöz 2006:89–142). The most famous, the Midas Monument, is so called because a dedicatory inscription bears the name of Midas (which one we do not know) as leader of the people and king (Berndt-Ersöz 2006:72).

At Gordion, still an important center in the time of Alyattes and Croesus, signs of the Lydian connection are rife in the archaeological record. A hoard of electrum coins, no doubt minted at Sardis, shows the spread of the Lydian economic system to central Anatolia (Bellinger 1968; Mellink 1991:649). Similarly, a number of buildings of the rebuilt Phrygian citadel came to bear architectural terra cottas in types and styles generally paralleling those at Sardis, very likely in a transfer of technology from Lydia to inner Anatolia (Glendinning 1996; Mellink 1991:650). Furthermore, much Lydian pottery had made its way to Gordion by the mid-sixth century B.C.E., as part of a much broader pattern of distribution in central and western Anatolia (Gürtekin-Demir 2007). Lydians were also present. An elevated mudbrick fortress (the Küçük Höyük) to the south of the citadel contained such a preponderance of Lydian pottery that it surely housed a Lydian garrison, very likely as an outpost against advances from the east (Mellink 1991:653; R. S. Young 1953).

The Rise of Persia

Around the middle of the sixth century B.C.E., a power shift occurred in Iran, the Medes giving way to their neighbors the Persians under Cyrus the Great, founder of the Persian Empire. In Anatolia, what had been Median territory east of the Kızıl Irmak quickly became Persian, and Anatolians to the west found themselves once again facing an Iranian threat. In the 540s B.C.E., Croesus led his forces against Cyrus in the territory of the Kızıl Irmak. Herodotus (I.76) relates that the Lydian ruler took and enslaved the main city of the region of Pteria. Archaeological candidates for the settlement include Boğazköy (Bossert 2000:166–74) and Kerkenes Dağ (Summers 1997). Thereafter, the Lydian and Persian forces clashed in the same region. The battle was a stalemate, and Croesus returned to Sardis, not realizing that the Persian leader was right behind him. Sardis was taken, and, according to the Greek tradition, Cyrus spared the life of the Lydian monarch (Mellink 1991:651–53). With Lydia secure, the annexation of the Greek cities of the Aegean coast, and also Caria, followed soon thereafter. So too Lycia, which had been outside the reach of Croesus, came under Persian domination with the taking of Xanthus, the leading city of the land, around 540 B.C.E. (Bryce 1986:99–114; Mellink 1991:655–62). Vivid testimony of the fall of Sardis lies in destroyed houses, well furnished, just inside the massive fortification wall; the datable material, primarily pottery, extends no later than the mid-sixth century B.C.E. (Cahill 2002; Greenewalt and Rautman 1998:471–74; Greenewalt, chapter 52 in this volume). At Gordion, the above-mentioned Lydian fortress was destroyed at roughly the same time, again according to datable pottery. Persian involvement seems evident, even though the taking of Gordion is not attested in ancient sources (Mellink 1991:653; R. S. Young 1953).

For over 200 years, Anatolia remained under Persian rule. With relatively few Persian documents available to elucidate the period, we continue to rely most heavily on Greek sources. Local inscriptions, however, can provide colorful details. As elsewhere in the empire, Anatolia was divided into a series of administrative districts or satrapies, each with a governor (satrap) answerable to the royal court in Persia (Mellink 1988:211–16; T. C. Young 1988:87–91; and see Harl, chapter 34 in this volume). Sardis became the capital of the satrapy of Lydia (Roosevelt 2009:26–31), and Dascylium to the north, a Mysian city that had both Lydian and Phrygian connections, was seat to the satrap of Hellespontine Phrygia (Bakır 2001; Bakır-Akbaşoğlu 1997; Mellink 1991:644; Roller, chapter 25 in this volume). A third important satrapal center was at Celaenae (modern Dinar), which became the capital of Greater Phrygia (Roller, chapter 25 in this volume). The Persian Royal Road, as described by Herodotus (V.52–53), extended from Susa to Sardis; it and its branches no doubt followed earlier Anatolian highways (French 1998; Mellink 1988:216–17). The roads would have been busy in all directions, with couriers (as made famous by Herodotus [VIII.98] and the U.S. Postal Service), troops, emissaries, craftsmen, and artisans.

Darius I (522–486 B.C.E.) boasted of using Ionians, Carians, and Lydians (among other peoples of his empire) in the construction of his palace at Susa (Olmstead 1948:168). He was the founder of the Achaemenid dynasty, which remained an unbroken succession of rulers until the death of its last in 330 B.C.E. Persian rule was indeed laissez faire for those who paid tribute, supplied fleets and troops for campaigns, and caused no trouble. The paradigm of a harmonious Persian commonwealth of nations is eloquently set forth in the relief sculptures on the great apadana at Persepolis, begun by Darius I and completed under his son Xerxes I (486–465 B.C.E.) (Wilber 1989). The upsetting of that paradigm, however, could prove disastrous. In 499 B.C.E., Miletus initiated the five-year Ionian Revolt against the empire, beginning with the sacking of Sardis (Roosevelt 2009:28). The uprising was quelled, and in retaliation the Persians destroyed Miletus; what was left of its population was enslaved and deported to Persia (Herodotus VI.19–20), in an action recalling earlier Assyrian practice.

Although the Persians did not force their very different culture on the land, their presence and participation in the life of Anatolia are nonetheless witnessed in a variety of ways. Inscriptions in Aramaic, the diplomatic language of the empire, are found in Cilicia, Phrygia, Lydia, and Lycia (Hanson 1968; Lipiński 1975:146–71; Roosevelt 2009:113, 128). They may occur on stone as grave or boundary markers, or in small format on seals and coins. As though to give official sanction to local activities, multi-lingual inscriptions including Aramaic also occur: with Lydian in Lydia (Roosevelt 2009:155, 200), and with Lycian and Greek in a trilingual document from

Xanthus-Letoon in Lycia (Bryce 1995:1166; Keen 1998:10). In a wise economic move, Cyrus the Great continued to have minted the gold and silver issues of Croesus. Yet by the end of the sixth century B.C.E. they were replaced by coins bearing the image of the Persian king, in the distinctive style of his court (Kraay 1976:30–34); the new money would have been a widely circulated reminder of who the authority now was. A hybrid artistic mode with varying combinations of Anatolian, Greek, and Persian elements (often referred to by the questionable term "Greco-Persian") developed in western Anatolia. It is represented by seals and sealings, coins, wall paintings, and relief sculpture, the last two primarily in connection with the grave (Boardman 2000:150–202). The Persians brought their religion with them (Bivar 2001), and evidence exists, especially in the west, for a degree of cultic interplay among Persians, Greeks, and Anatolians (Hornblower 1994:230; Roosevelt 2009:128).

From the information we have, satraps in Anatolia were normally Iranian. An important exception lay with the Hecatomnid dynasts of Caria, who were granted satrapal status by Artaxerxes II beginning early in the fourth century B.C.E. (Hornblower 1994:209). The most famous of these native satraps was Mausolus (377–353 B.C.E.), who is a good representative of the politicocultural interflux of the time. He forsook the traditional inland capital of his dynasty at Mylasa in favor of the old Greek harbor city of Halicarnassus (birthplace of Herodotus), which he fortified and populated with Carians, and where he built a gleaming palace of brick and marble that was known to the Roman architectural writer Vitruvius (Bean 1971:78–90; Vitruvius II.10). From his new capital, Mausolus controlled a large swath of southwestern Anatolia that extended to Pamphylia and Pisidia and deep into Ionia, if not further north. His domain even included Rhodes and other Greek islands (Hornblower 1994:226–27). Perhaps before his death in 353 B.C.E. Mausolus had a role in the planning of his tomb, even though the credit was given to Artemisia, his sister, wife, and successor. Classed in antiquity as one of the Seven Wonders of the World, the Mausoleum was a massive structure in which Greek architectural elements were applied to an Anatolian type of built tomb, as had already been done on a much smaller scale in Lycia. Greek architects were responsible for the design, and leading Greek sculptors were among those who provided figural embellishment (Bean 1971:81–82; Hornblower 1994:231; Jeppesen 1989, 2002).

Alexander the Great

Before Alexander III of Macedon changed the course of the ancient world, the Spartan king Agesilaus had campaigned against the Persians in western Anatolia. In 395 B.C.E., he took Sardis. Before that, he had led his troops as far inland as Gordion, where he carried out an unsuccessful siege thanks to the prowess of the local Persian commander (Xenophon, *Agesilaus* I.6–38; Oxyrhynchus Historian XXI.6). Agesilaus was cut short in his operations in Anatolia by a recall to Sparta on other business. Some sixty years later, in the spring of 334 B.C.E., Alexander began his conquest of the Persian Empire (Bosworth 1994). He crossed into Anatolia at the Dardanelles and gained a major victory over the Persian forces waiting for him. He then moved in a counterclockwise manner south into Lydia and down to the Aegean coast, east into Lycia and Pamphylia, and north onto the central plateau and Phrygia (see Harl, chapter 34 in this volume). Resistance ran from nil (Sardis) to prolonged siege (Halicarnassus). Like Agesilaus, Alexander came to Gordion, where additional troops joined him. It was also here where, one way or another, he undid the legendary Gordian knot; whoever did so was to become master of Asia. After moving further east into central Anatolia, he turned south to Cilicia to meet, and defeat in 333 B.C.E., the last Persian king, Darius III, near the city of Issus (Kinet Höyük). After Alexander's victories in Anatolia, Asia did indeed lie before him.

When Alexander died in Babylon in 323 B.C.E., his empire extended from Greece to the Indus Valley. Yet it was to be an empire of one man, since he had no effective successor. The remainder of the fourth century B.C.E. saw warrings among his would-be successors, with the result that the one-time empire came by the third century B.C.E. to be divided into a series of kingdoms, several with Macedonian Greek dynasties (Welles 1970:49–95). Anatolia lay open to two such Macedonian monarchies. The Seleucids, based at their new capital of Antioch in northern Syria, controlled much of central and parts of westerly Anatolia; they left their names in such newly founded cities as Stratoniceia and Laodiceia in Caria, and another Antioch in Pisidia. The Ptolemies, ruling from Alexandria in Egypt, were lords over most of the southern and western coasts of Anatolia. In Bithynia and at Pergamon in Aeolis, Anatolians founded monarchies. In the east, dynasts of Iranian stock ruled over what had been the satrapy of Cappadocia, whereas in the former Urartu arose the kingdom of Armenia. Throughout, borders were fluid, and regions and cities were lost and gained as these dynasts fought among themselves. In their bloody disputes, one monarch (Nicomedes of Bithynia) in 278 B.C.E. brought into Anatolia for mercenary purposes the Gauls, a fearsome, wandering group of west Europeans who had long been on an eastward move. Their journey stopped in Anatolia; what had been old Phrygia was to become Galatia.

Far more than political geography changed the face of Anatolia in the aftermath of Alexander. Native Anatolian identities come to be obscured through the process of Hellenization. Even though Anatolians no doubt continued to speak their own tongues, Greek became the primary language for inscriptions, even in what had previously been non-Greek areas; put another way, there were now Greek speakers where Greeks had not earlier been. At places such as Gordion, Greek personal names (sometimes oddly spelled) are incised on pots, and cults of Greek deities are attested. Old ways of drinking and dining disappear in favor of ceramic inventories that echo those of a Greek household (Sams 2005:13–14). With the exception of certain continuing pottery techniques, precious little is left that says Phrygian. It is generally fair to say that Anatolia as we know it before Alexander to a great extent slipped from view in this new and very different world of Hellenistic culture.

REFERENCES

Primary Sources

Herodotus. *The Persian Wars.* Trans. A. D. Godley, 4 vols. Loeb Classical Library. London and Cambridge, Mass.: William Heinemann and Harvard University Press, 1971.

Homer. *Iliad.* Trans. A.T. Murray, revised William F. Wyatt, 2 vols. Loeb Classical Library. Cambridge, Mass. and London: Harvard University Press, 1999.

Oxyrhynchus Historian. *Hellenica Oxyrhynchia.* Ed. and trans. P. R. McKechnie and S. J. Kern. Warminster: Aris and Phillips, 1993.

Vitruvius. *De Architectura.* Trans. Frank Granger, 2 vols. Loeb Classical Library, 1970. Cambridge, Mass. and London: Harvard University Press and William Heinemann.

Xenophon. *Scripta Minora: Agesilaus.* Trans. E. C. Marchant. Loeb Classical Library. Cambridge, Mass. and London: Harvard University Press and William Heinemann, 1962.

Secondary Sources

Akurgal, Ekrem. 1961. *Die Kunst Anatoliens von Homer bis Alexander.* Berlin: de Gruyter.

Akurgal, Ekrem and Max Hirmer. 1962. *The Art of the Hittites.* London: Thames and Hudson.

Aro, Sanna. 1998. *Tabal. Zur Geschichte und materiellen Kultur des zentralanatolischen Hochplateaus von 1200 bis 600 v. Chr.* Helsinki: University of Helsinki dissertation.

Bakır, Tomris. 2001. Die Satrapie in Daskyleion. In *Achaemenid Anatolia. Proceedings of the First International Symposium on Anatolia in the Achaemenid Period, Bandırma 15–18 August 1997*, ed. Tomris Bakır, 169–80. Leiden: Nederlands Instituut voor het Nabije Oosten.

Bakır-Akbaşoğlu, Tomris. 1997. Phryger in Daskyleion. In *Frigi e Frigio. Atti del 1° Simposio Internazionale, Roma, 16–17 Ottobre 1995*, ed. Roberto Gusmani, Mirjo Salvini, and Pietro Vannicelli, 229–38. Rome: Consiglio Nazionale delle Ricerche.

Bean, George E. 1968. *Turkey's Southern Shore. An Archaeological Guide.* London: Ernest Benn.

———. 1971. *Turkey beyond the Maeander.* London: Ernest Benn; New York: Norton.

Bellinger, Alfred R. 1968. Electrum Coins from Gordion. In *Essays in Greek Coinage Presented to Stanley Robinson*, ed. Colin M. Kraay and G. Kenneth Jenkins, 10–15. Oxford: Clarendon.

Berndt-Ersöz, Susanne. 2006. *Phrygian Rock-Cut Shrines: Structure, Function, and Cult Practice.* Culture and History of the Ancient Near East, vol. 25. Leiden: Brill.

———. 2008. The Chronology and Historical Context of Midas. *Historia* 57.1: 1–37.

Bivar, A. D. H. 2001. Magians and Zoroastrians: The Religions of the Iranians in Anatolia. In *Achaemenid Anatolia. Proceedings of the First International Symposium on Anatolia in the Achaemenid Period, Bandırma 15–18 August 1997*, ed. Tomris Bakır, 91–99. Leiden: Nederlands Instituut voor het Nabije Oosten.

Blegen, Carl W. 1963. *Troy and the Trojans.* New York: Praeger.

Boardman, John. 2000. *Persia and the West: An Archaeological Investigation of the Genesis of Achaemenid Art.* London: Thames and Hudson.

Bossert, Eva-Maria. 2000. *Boğazköy-Ḫattuša, Ergebnisse der Ausgrabungen XVIII: Die Keramik phrygischer Zeit von Boğazköy. Funde aus den Grabungskampagnen 1906, 1907, 1911, 1912, 1931–1939 und 1952–1960.* Mainz am Rhein: Verlag Philipp von Zabern.

Bosworth, A. B. 1994. Alexander the Great Part I: The Events of the Reign. In *The Cambridge Ancient History*, 2nd ed., vol. 6: *The Fourth Century B.C.*, ed. D. M. Lewis, John Boardman, Simon Hornblower, and M. Ostwald, 791–845. Cambridge: Cambridge University Press.

Brixhe, Claude. 1994a. Le Phrygien. In *Langues indo-européennes*, ed. Fr. Bader, 165–78. Paris: Centre National de la Recherche Scientifique.

———. 1994b. La saga de l'alphabet et la collaboration des cultures. In *Mélanges François Kerlouégan*, 79–94. Paris: Institut Félix Gaffiot.

Brixhe, Claude and Michel Lejeune. 1984. *Corpus des Inscriptions Paléo-phrygiennes.* Editions Recherche sur les Civilisations, Mémoire no. 45. Paris: Institut Français d'Études Anatoliennes.

Brixhe, Claude and Geoffrey D. Summers. 2006. Les inscriptions Phrygiennes de Kerkenes Dağ (Anatolie Centrale). *Kadmos* 45: 93–135.

Bryce, Trevor R. 1986. *The Lycians I: The Lycians in Literary and Epigraphic Sources.* Copenhagen: Museum Tusculanum Press.

———. 1995. The Lycian Kingdom in Southwest Anatolia. In *Civilizations of the Ancient Near East*, vol. 2, ed. Jack M. Sasson, 1161–72. New York: Scribner's.

———. 2003. History. In *The Luwians*, ed. H. Craig Melchert, 27–127. Handbook of Oriental Studies 68. Leiden: Brill.

Cahill, Nicholas. 2002. Lydian Houses, Domestic Assemblages, and Household Size. In *Across the Anatolian Plateau: Readings in the Archaeology of Ancient Turkey*, ed. David C. Hopkins, 173–85. Annual of the American Schools of Oriental Research, vol. 57. Boston: American Schools of Oriental Research.

Cahill, Nicholas and John H. Kroll. 2005. New Archaic Coin Finds at Sardis. *American Journal of Archaeology* 109: 589–617.

Cook, J. M. 1962. *The Greeks in Ionia and the East.* New York: Praeger.

Çambel, Halet. 1999. *Corpus of Hieroglyphic Inscriptions, Volume II: Karatepe-Aslantaş. The Inscriptions: Facsimile Edition.* Untersuchungen zur indogermanischen Sprach-und Kulturwissenschaft. Neue Folge 8.2. Berlin: de Gruyter.

Çambel, Halet and Aslı Özyar. 2003. *Karatepe-Aslantaş, Azatiwataya: Die Bildwerke.* Mainz am Rhein: Verlag Philipp von Zabern.

DeVries, Keith. 1988. Gordion and Phrygia in the Sixth Century B.C. *Source, Notes in the History of Art* 7.3/4: 51–59.

———. 2007. The Date of the Destruction Level at Gordion: Imports and the Local Sequence. In *Anatolian Iron Ages 6. The Proceedings of the Sixth Anatolian Iron Ages Colloquium held at Eskişehir, 16–20 August 2004*, ed. Altan Çilingiroğlu and Antonio Sagona, 79–101. Ancient Near Eastern Studies, Supplement 20. Leuven: Peeters.

French, David. 1998. Pre- and Early-Roman Roads of Asia Minor: The Persian Royal Road. *Iran* 36: 15–43.

Genz, Hermann. 2003. The Early Iron Age in Central Anatolia. In *Identifying Changes: The Transition from Bronze to Iron Ages in Anatolia and its Neighbouring Regions. Proceedings of the International Workshop, Istanbul, 8–9 November 2003*, ed. Bettina Fischer, Hermann Genz, Éric Jean and Kemalettin Köroğlu, 179–91. İstanbul: Türk Eskiçağ Bilimleri Enstitüsü.

———. 2004a. *Boğazköy-Ḫattuša, Ergebnisse der Ausgrabungen XXI: Büyükkaya I. Die Keramik der Eisenzeit, Funde aus den Grabungskampagnen 1993 bis 1998.* Mainz am Rhein: Verlag Philipp von Zabern.

———. 2004b. Erste Ansätze zu einer Chronologie der frühen Eisenzeit in Zentralanatolien. In *Die Außenwirkung des späthethitischen Kulturraumes: Güteraustausch—Kulturkontakt—Kulturtransfer. Akten der zweiten Forschungstagung des Graduiertenkollegs "Anatolien und seine Nachbarn" der Eberhard-Karls-Universität Tübingen (20. bis 22. November 2003)*, ed. Mirko Novák, Friedhelm Prayon, and Anne-Marie Wittke, 219–36. Alter Orient und Altes Testament, Band 323. Münster: Ugarit-Verlag.

Glendinning, Matthew R. 1996. A Mid-Sixth-Century Tile Roof System at Gordion. *Hesperia* 65: 99–119.

Greenewalt, Crawford H. Jr., Christopher Ratté, and Marcus L. Rautman. 1994. The Sardis Campaigns of 1990 and 1991. *Annual of the American Schools of Oriental Research* 52: 1–36.

Greenewalt, Crawford H. Jr. and Marcus L. Rautman. 1998. The Sardis Campaigns of 1994 and 1995. *American Journal of Archaeology* 102: 469–505.

Gürtekin-Demir, R. Gül. 2007. Provincial Production of Lydian Painted Pottery. In *Anatolian Iron Ages 6. The Proceedings of the Sixth Anatolian Iron Ages Colloquium held at Eskişehir, 16–20 August 2004*, ed. Altan Çilingiroğlu and Antonio Sagona, 47–77. Ancient Near Eastern Studies, Supplement 20. Leuven: Peeters.

Hanfmann, George M. A. et al. 1983. *Sardis from Prehistoric to Roman Times: Results of the Archaeological Exploration of Sardis 1958–1975*. Cambridge, Mass.: Harvard University Press.

Hanfmann, George M. A., G. F. Swift, D. G. Mitten, and Julian Whittlesey. 1966. The Eighth Campaign at Sardis (1965). *Bulletin of the American Schools of Oriental Research* 182: 2–54.

Hanson, Richard S. 1968. Aramaic Funerary and Boundary Inscriptions from Asia Minor. *Bulletin of the American Schools of Oriental Research* 192: 3–11.

Hawkins, J. D. 1979. Some Historical Problems of the Hieroglyphic Luwian Inscriptions. *Anatolian Studies* 29: 153–67.

———. 1982. The Neo-Hittite States in Syria and Anatolia. In *The Cambridge Ancient History*, 2nd ed., vol. 3, part 1: *The Prehistory of the Balkans; and the Middle East and the Aegean World, Tenth to Eighth Centuries B.C.*, ed. John Boardman, I. E. S. Edwards, N. G. L. Hammond, and E. Sollberger, 372–441. Cambridge: Cambridge University Press.

———. 1987. The Kululu Lead Strips, Economic Documents in Hieroglyphic Luwian. *Anatolian Studies* 37: 135–62.

———. 1988. Kuzi-Tešub and the "Great Kings" of Karkamiš. *Anatolian Studies* 38: 99–108.

Hawkins, John David. 2000. *Corpus of Hieroglyphic Luwian Inscriptions, volume 1: Inscriptions of the Iron Age*, three parts. Untersuchungen zur indogermanischen Sprach-und Kulturwissenschaft, 8.1. Berlin: de Gruyter.

Hornblower, Simon. 1994. Asia Minor. In *The Cambridge Ancient History*, 2nd ed., vol. 6: *The Fourth Century B.C.*, ed. D. M. Lewis, John Boardman, Simon Hornblower, and M. Ostwald, 209–33. Cambridge: Cambridge University Press.

Houwink ten Cate, P. H. J. 1961. *The Luwian Population Groups of Lycia and Cilicia Aspera during the Hellenistic Period*. Documenta et Monumenta Orientis Antiqui, vol. 10. Leiden: Brill.

Ivanchik, Askold I. 1993. *Les Cimmériens au Proche-Orient*. Orbis Biblicus et Orientalis 127. Fribourg: Editions Universitaires.

Jeppesen, Kristian. 1989. What Did the Maussolleion Look Like? In *Architecture and Society in Hecatomnid Caria. Proceedings of the Uppsala Symposium 1987*, ed. Tullia Linders and Pontus Hellström, 15–22. BOREAS. Uppsala Studies in Ancient Mediterranean and Near Eastern Civilizations 17. Uppsala: Ekblads.

———. 2002. *The Maussolleion at Halikarnassos, vol. 5: The Superstructure. A Comparative Analysis of the Architectural, Sculptural, and Literary Evidence.* Jutland Archaeological Society Publications 15:5. Moesgaard: Jutland Archaeological Society.

Keen, Antony G. 1998. *Dynastic Lycia: A Political History of the Lycians and their Relations with Foreign Powers c. 545–362 B.C.* Mnemosyne Supplement 178. Leiden: Brill.

Kerschner, Michael. 2006. Die Ionische Wanderung im Lichte neuer archäologischer Forschungen in Ephesos. In *"Troianer sind wir gewesen"—Migrationen in der antiken Welt. Stuttgarter Kolloquium zur Historischen Geographie des Altertums 8, 2000*, ed. Eckart Olshausen and Holger Sonnabend, 364–82. Geographica Historica Band 21. Stuttgart: Franz Steiner Verlag.

Kraay, Colin M. 1976. *Archaic and Classical Greek Coins.* London: Methuen.

Lipiński, Edward. 1975. *Studies in Aramaic Inscriptions and Onomastics I.* Orientalia Louvaniensia Analecta 1. Leuven: Leuven University Press.

Lloyd, Seton. 1972. *Beycesultan* vol. 3, part I: *Late Bronze Age Architecture.* Occasional Papers of the British Institute of Archaeology at Ankara, no. 11. London: British Institute of Archaeology at Ankara.

Melchert, H. Craig. 1995. Indo-European Languages of Anatolia. In *Civilizations of the Ancient Near East*, vol. 4, ed. Jack M. Sasson, John Baines, Gary Beckman, and Karen S. Rubinson, 2151–59. New York: Scribner's.

Mellink, Machteld. 1988. Anatolia. In *The Cambridge Ancient History*, 2nd ed., vol. 4: *Persia, Greece and the Western Mediterranean c. 525 to 479 B.C.*, ed. John Boardman, N. G. L. Hammond, D. M. Lewis, and M. Ostwald, 211–33. Cambridge: Cambridge University Press.

———. 1991. The Native Kingdoms of Anatolia. In *The Cambridge Ancient History*, 2nd ed., vol. 3, part 2: *The Assyrian and Babylonian Empires and Other States of the Near East, from the Eighth to the Sixth Centuries B.C.*, ed. John Boardman, I. E. S. Edwards, E. Sollberger, and N. G. L. Hammond, 619–65. Cambridge: Cambridge University Press.

Olmstead, Arthur T. 1948. *History of the Persian Empire.* Chicago: University of Chicago Press.

Orthmann, Winfried. 1971. *Untersuchungen zur späthethitischen Kunst.* Saarbrücker Beiträge zur Altertumskunde, Band 8. Bonn: Rudolf Habelt.

Özgüç, Tahsin. 1971. *Kültepe and its Vicinity in the Iron Age.* Ankara: Türk Tarih Kurumu Basımevi.

Ramage, Andrew. 1978. *Archaeological Exploration of Sardis, Monograph 5: Lydian Houses and Architectural Terracottas.* Cambridge, Mass.: Harvard University Press.

Roosevelt, Christopher H. 2009. *The Archaeology of Lydia, from Gyges to Alexander.* Cambridge: Cambridge University Press.

Sams, G. Kenneth. 1988. The Early Phrygian Period at Gordion: Toward a Cultural Identity. *Source, Notes in the History of Art* 7.3/4: 9–15.

———. 2005. Gordion: Exploration over a Century. In *The Archaeology of Midas and the Phrygians: Recent Work at Gordion*, ed. Lisa Kealhofer, 10–21. Philadelphia: University of Pennsylvania Museum of Archaeology and Anthropology.

Sandars, N. K. 1985. *The Sea Peoples. Warriors of the Ancient Mediterranean 1250–1150 BC.* London: Thames and Hudson.

Schirmer, Wulf. 1993. Die Bauanlagen auf dem Göllüdağ in Kappadokien. *Architectura* 1993: 121–31.

Sievertsen, Uwe. 2004. Der späthethitische Kulturraum und die eisenzeitliche Keramik Zentralanatoliens. In *Die Außenwirkung des späthethitischen Kulturraumes:*

Güteraustausch—Kulturkontakt—Kulturtransfer. Akten der zweiten Forschungstagung des Graduiertenkollegs "Anatolien und seine Nachbarn" der Eberhard-Karls-Universität Tübingen (20. bis 22. November 2003), ed. Mirko Novák, Friedhelm Prayon, and Anne-Marie Wittke, 237–57. Alter Orient und Altes Testament, Band 323. Münster: Ugarit-Verlag.

Summers, G. D. 1997. The Identification of the Iron Age City on Kerkenes Dağ in Central Anatolia. *Journal of Near Eastern Studies* 56: 81–94.

von der Osten, Hans Henning. 1937. *The Alishar Hüyük, Seasons of 1930–32*, part 2. University of Chicago Oriental Institute Publications vol, 29. Chicago: University of Chicago Press.

Welles, C. Bradford. 1970. *Alexander and the Hellenistic World.* Toronto: Hakkert.

Wilber, Donald N. 1989. *Persepolis: The Archaeology of Parsa, Seat of the Persian Kings.* Princeton, N.J.: Darwin Press.

Winter, Irene J. 1979. On the Problems of Karatepe: The Reliefs and Their Context. *Anatolian Studies* 29: 115–51.

Young, Rodney S. 1953. Making History at Gordion. *Archaeology* 6: 159–66.

Young, T. Cuyler Jr. 1988. The Consolidation of the Empire and its Limits of Growth under Darius and Xerxes. In *The Cambridge Ancient History*, 2nd ed., vol. 4: *Persia, Greece and the Western Mediterranean c. 525 to 479 B.C.*, ed. John Boardman, N. G. L. Hammond, D. M. Lewis, and M. Ostwald, 53–111. Cambridge: Cambridge University Press.

Zimansky, Paul E. 1995. The Kingdom of Urartu in Eastern Anatolia. In *Civilizations of the Ancient Near East*, vol. 2, ed. Jack M. Sasson, John Baines, Gary Beckman, and Karen S. Rubinson, 1135–46. New York: Scribner's.

CHAPTER 28

MONUMENTS AND MEMORY: ARCHITECTURE AND VISUAL CULTURE IN ANCIENT ANATOLIAN HISTORY

ÖMÜR HARMANŞAH

> One could say that, in its world-forming capacity, architecture transforms geological time into human time, which is another way of saying it turns matter into meaning. That is why the sight of ruins is such a reflexive and in some cases an unsettling experience. Ruins in an advanced state of ruination represent, or better they literally embody, the dissolution of meaning into matter. By revealing what human building ultimately is up against—natural or geological time—ruins have a way of recalling us to the very ground of our human worlds, namely the earth, whose foundations are so solid and so reliable that they presumably will outlast any edifices that we build on them.
>
> —Harrison (2003:3)

Tracing a few thousands of years of material culture in a loosely defined region itself constitutes a significant challenge. This is especially true for an area that has always been at the intersection of many networks of interaction in antiquity, being intimately connected to the Near Eastern world on the one hand and the Aegean and Mediterranean maritime spaces on the other. No less significantly, Anatolia also has been a major player in the Black Sea maritime interaction sphere and frequently linked to the Transcaucasian cultures of the steppe (e.g., Sagona, chapter 30; Marro, chapter 12; and Palumbi, chapter 9 in this volume). The variety of its geographical components of river valleys, steppelands, plateaus, and floodplains separated by mountain ranges often present a fragmented cultural landscape that ridicules the ancient historian's desire to narrativize its allegedly wholistic history, which traditionally emphasizes more continuities than ruptures.[1] In this chapter I argue that Anatolia as a region of historical geography is not an unproblematic, naturally given, geographically distinct entity but is a construct of centuries of cultural imagination, academic practice, and nation-state discourse of the modern Turkish Republic in the twentieth century.[2] Today when one refers to "Anatolian archaeology" or "Anatolian civilizations," we more or less assume that Anatolia corresponds to the modern nation-state boundaries of Turkey, although the Anatolian peninsula in that specific configuration was never a (culturally or politically) unified geographical entity in antiquity.[3] Yet in archaeology, such entrenched definitions are rarely questioned and almost always left fuzzy. In this chapter on long-term cultural landscapes of Anatolia, I focus on various episodes of fragmentation and connectivity with adjacent regions through the study of monumental architecture and visual/material culture from prehistory to the end of the Achaemenid period. In a chapter of this length, it is impossible to be exhaustive or comprehensive; therefore I attempt to trace a line of thought around monumentality and social memory, in order to see our paradigms from Anatolian history in a critical long-term perspective.

Monuments and Memory

Buildings and monuments have been mediators of the past with their powerful presence, their representational surfaces, and tectonic masses. Their spectacle-like character often hosts turbulent histories. Stories cling to their stones, which become visible residues of the human lives that shape them. Memories, imaginations, and experiences, collectively shared or individual, give meaning to architectural spaces. In this chapter's epigraph, from his brilliant work *The Dominion of the Dead* (2003), Robert Pogue Harrison describes architecture's own temporality that bridges human time to geological time. Harrison's definition is critical for understanding the operating logic behind monuments.

Monuments gather in themselves the ambitious discursive attempts to stage collective spectacles in the social and political realms. They form foci of collective identities and gather around themselves specific social practices, whether we are speaking of a temple, a monumental vase, a tumulus, a ceremonial complex, a rock relief, or an entire newly founded city (Knapp 2009). Because they are always built as stages for ritual performances and/or commemorative ceremonies, archaeologically monuments can be considered material archives of human practice (Turnbull 2002). Their meanings are never fixed, and their "horizon of meanings" shifts continuously with the historically specific events and cultural practices that take place in them (Alcock 2002:29–30)

Bodies of knowledge ranging from technological (craft) knowledge to remembrances of a shared past are worked into the fabric of monuments; Turnbull referred to monuments as "theaters of knowledge" (2002:127). With the intensive mobilization of rich resources and mass labor force, monument making has always involved elements of a festive undertaking often accompanied with feasting. Speaking of feasting, ritual performance, technological innovation, and monumentality in Anatolian prehistory, the Pre-Pottery Neolithic sites of Göbekli Tepe (9600–8000 B.C.E.) and Nevalı Çori (8600–7900 B.C.E.) in southeastern Turkey present a breathtaking start for this long-term survey.

Located on a flat limestone plateau on the lower slopes of the Taurus Mountains and overlooking the Harran Plain, Göbekli Tepe was a site of social gathering for hunter-forager communities who constructed there a series of stone-built, semi-subterranean, curvilinear and rectangular structures (figure 28.1a; and see Schmidt, chapter 42 in this volume). Locally quarried megalithic T-shaped limestone pillars (some as tall as five meters) carried the roofs of the ritual structures and monumentalized their interiors. The T-shaped pillars were carved in low relief with representations of various animals, especially snakes, boars, foxes, cranes, scorpions, aurochs, gazelles, birds of prey, wild asses, boars, lions/leopards, splayed animals, and other unidentified wild species in various combinations. Peters and Schmidt have recently suggested, based on the human features (hands and arms) on side surfaces of the pillars, that they may have stood for anthropomorphic beings, while the depicted animals articulated and empowered these individuals (figure 28.1b; Peters and Schmidt 2004:208; Schmidt, chapter 42 in this volume). Fragments of anthropomorphic and zoomorphic figurines and architectural sculpture were also found, including ithyphallic figures and various animals. Benches were built alongside the interior walls, and large quantities of faunal deposits of wild species suggest communal feasting. The architectural and iconographic sophistication of the cult buildings and the wealth of the archaeological assemblage, dating to the second half of the tenth millennium B.C.E., have revolutionized our understanding of the Neolithic in the Eastern Mediterranean.

The nearby site of Nevalı Çori, of slightly later occupation in the Pre-Pottery Neolithic B, has similar cult buildings but is rectangular in plan with T-shaped pillars in its Level II (Hauptmann 1999:70–78). Large-scale composite animal-human sculptures were found in secondary deposits. It is important to note that Nevalı Çori's cult buildings are contemporary with a series of residential structures (with substantial stone figurine assemblages), unlike Göbekli Tepe, which is still understood as a solely ceremonial site.

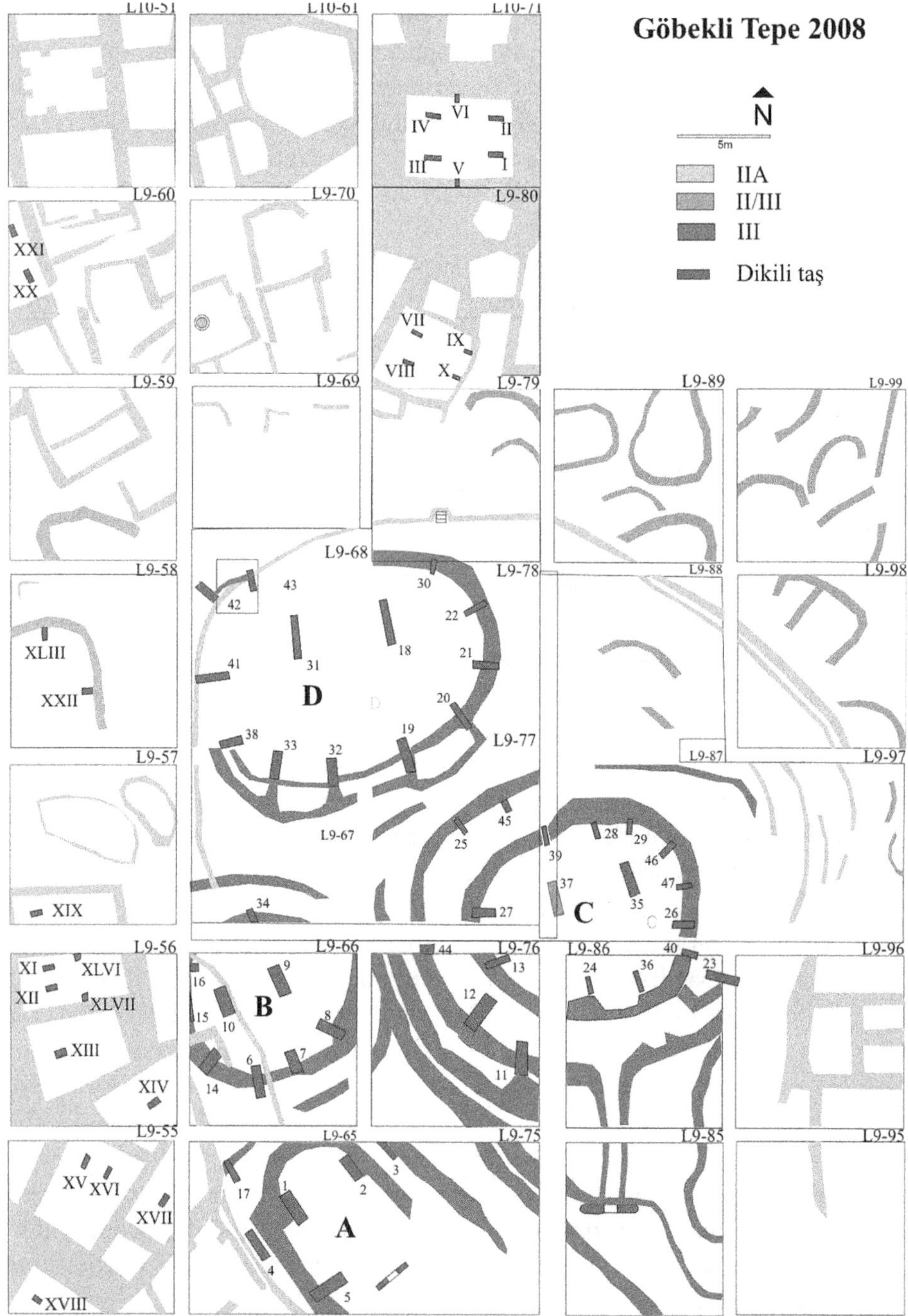

Figure 28.1a. Göbekli Tepe. Plan of excavated structures (Schmidt 2007: fig. 76).

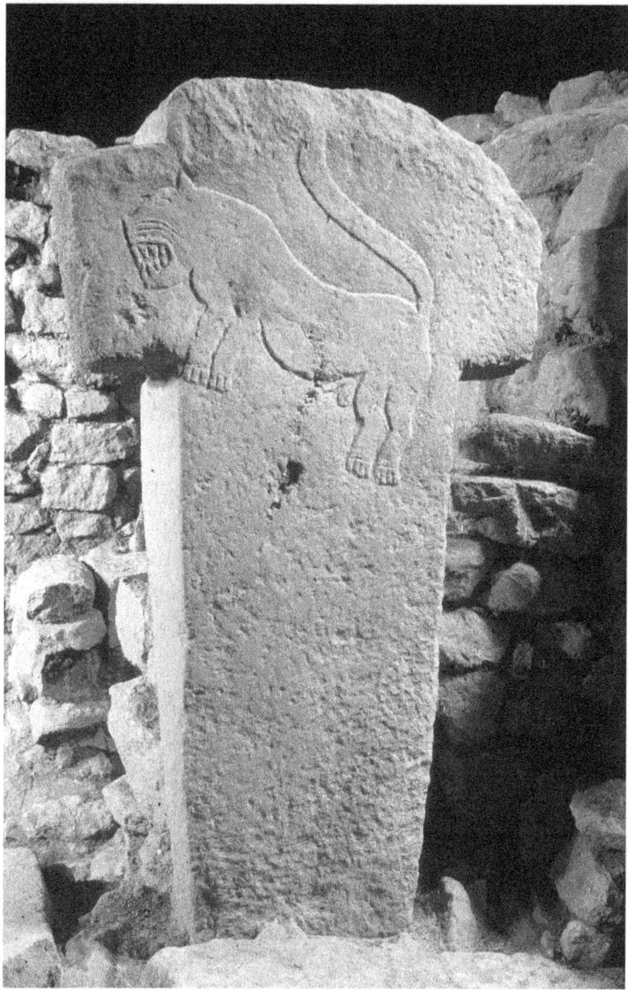

Figure 28.1b. Göbekli Tepe. Pillar with a relief of a roaring lion (Schmidt 2007: fig. 102).

The monumental architecture at Göbekli Tepe and Nevalı Çori presents evidence for a local megalithic technology, reminiscent of the Late Neolithic megalithic structures of Malta in the fifth–third millennia B.C.E. (Turnbull 2002). A massive investment of labor and technological innovation are evident in the construction of cult buildings where feasting and other ritual activities took place, bringing together various hunter-gatherers of the Urfa Plain. The visual culture of representations in relief and sculpture suggests a sophisticated repertoire of animal symbolism and human sexuality, whereas the archaeology of cult buildings provides evidence for a complex set of social events and ritual practices, possibly including "the performance of hunting rituals, initiation and passage rites, spiritual encounters or funeral practices" (Peters and Schmidt 2004) and conceptualization of the supernatural world, perhaps similar to shamanism (Sagona and Zimansky 2009:63).[4] The sequential construction and intensive use and subsequent burial of cult buildings must have maintained the sociosymbolic significance of these powerful places and ancestral history through centuries as they were passed on from generation to generation of semi-sedentary hunter-forager groups.

The houses at the site of Çatalhöyük in the then marshy and wet Konya Plain (south-central Anatolia) contain a very different set of cultic establishments (ca. 7400–6000 B.C.E.) in the context of an Early Ceramic Neolithic settlement where cereals and sheep and goats had already been domesticated (see Hodder, chapter 43 in this volume). Despite their modest domestic contexts, the wall paintings, molded/sculptured reliefs, monumental features such as "benches inset with wild cattle horn cores" (Hodder 2006a:10), and the abundance of animal and human figurines in clay and stone across the site's midden deposits suggest the existence of a rich set of symbolic practices and a complex world of representations. Recently much work has concentrated on the spatial practices and the architectural configuration of the houses (Düring 2001; Hodder and Cessford 2004; Lewis-Williams 2004), and the iconographic complexity of the visual and material culture at Çatalhöyük (Last 1998; Nakamura and Meskell 2009), while pointing to the possibility of the performance of collective events (Hodder 2006b). Most of the houses at the site were loci for art and ritual besides burial and everyday domestic activities. The significant continuities and changes in the animal-based symbolisms from the southeast Anatolian preceramic sites such as Çayönü, Göbekli Tepe, Nevalı Çori, and Çatalhöyük require further scholarly attention. Repeated spatial practices—such as plastering and replastering of walls and floors, burial of family members under various platforms, articulation of figurines, and the long-term architectural continuity of the house layouts especially between Levels VIII–II—provide evidence for specific bodily practices and articulation of social memory among the Neolithic societies.

From Metalsmiths of The Black Sea to State Monuments of Republican Turkey

Looking through a Braudelian lens of the long term in Anatolia, the Late Chalcolithic and the Early Bronze Ages (ca. 4000–2000 B.C.E.) witnessed the formation of the uniquely rural character of the Anatolian landscapes, with its village communities tilling the soil and raising livestock, and patterns of transhumance, especially along the Taurus Mountains. If we are to look for evidence for state formation and urbanization, we would have to turn our attention to eastern and southeastern Anatolia. The process of urbanization in southern Mesopotamia of the Late Uruk period in the fourth millennium B.C.E. seems to have its correlate in the Upper Euphrates region north of the Taurus Mountains, exemplified by the monumental architecture and artifactual evidence for social complexity and early state formation at the site of Arslantepe, Levels VII and VI (ca. 3800–3200 B.C.E.; see Frangipane 2001a, 2001b, and chapter 45 in this volume). Cultural interaction and economic exchange between southern Mesopotamian and east/southeast Anatolian Late Chalcolithic communities has been well documented archaeologically (Rothman 2001). Likewise, southeastern Turkey was part and parcel of the mid–third millennium B.C.E. urbanization in northern Syro-Mesopotamia (the so-called Kranzhügel settlements of the Early Bronze Age II–III periods, ca. 2600–2000 B.C.E.), with impressive sites such as Kazane Höyük, Lidar Höyük, and Titriş Höyük in the Urfa province. Innovations in metal technologies (see Muhly, chapter 39 in this volume), crystallization of urban form, and particular architectural traditions for temples and ceremonial structures as well as regional states with complex administrative systems can be considered the hallmarks of this period.

In this section, I prefer to focus on the Early Bronze Age archaeological evidence in the north central Anatolian plateau, from the vicinity of Çorum and Ankara. Especially in Early Bronze Age II/III burials (2350–2150 B.C.E.), sites such as Alaca Höyük and Horoztepe among others have produced outstanding evidence for innovative metal technologies and highly skilled craft specialization in the production of silver, electrum, and gold. The Alaca Höyük royal tombs assemblage itself is impressive; more than 700 artifacts from 14 "royal" burials have been excavated in the southeast part of the mound, and the stratigraphy and chronological sequence of the burials are very complex.[5] The burial gifts range from personal ornaments, incised weapons, ceramic containers, and metal vessels with repoussé designs, to animal-human figurines and the so-called ritual standards with bulls and stags (Joukowsky 1996:167; Sagona and Zimansky 2009:214). Discovery of comparable Early Bronze Age sites in the vicinity of Alaca Höyük such as Horoztepe, Hasanoğlan, Kalınkaya, Oymaağaç, and Resuloğlu (Özgüç and Akok 1958; Yıldırım and Zimmerman 2006) suggests the existence of an intensive regional development in metallurgical technologies, which are usually linked to the Pontic (circum–Black Sea) interaction zone. The uniqueness of the graves at Alaca Höyük, however, makes it comparable to the Royal Tombs of Ur.

Excavations at the Bronze Age site of Alaca Höyük (Çorum province) in the 1930s was a historically significant project for the history of archaeology in the modern Turkish Republic. The excavation was initiated by the Turkish Historical Society (Türk Tarih Kurumu, formerly Türk Tarihi Tetkik Cemiyeti), founded by Mustafa Kemal Atatürk in 1931 "for the scientific study of Turkish culture and history" (Erimtan 2008:143). Several students were sent to Europe to study archaeology (mainly France, Germany, and Hungary) by Atatürk's own initiative (Özdoğan 1998:118). Under the impact of the political discourse of Anatolianism, the society was established with the flourishing interest in the Hittites of Anatolia as the center of attention for research in constructing a new cultural identity for modernist Turkey and to move away from its Ottoman past (Goode 2007:43–66). As one of the first archaeological excavations of the society (along with Ahlatlıbel, Karalar, and Göllüdağ), Turkish archaeologist Remzi Oğuz Arık started work at Alaca Höyük in 1935 (later joined by Hamit Zübeyr Koşay and Mahmut Akok); they were hugely successful, uncovering the now well-known Early Bronze III royal cemetery that produced an extraordinary wealth of metal artifacts (bronze, silver, gold, electrum, iron, lead, hematite, and sometimes a combination of different metals in one object, including inlays).[6] The unique features of this impressive metal corpus—namely, in the round bull or stag statuettes and openwork ceremonial objects ("ritual standards") combining bulls or stags with geometric designs (figure 28.2)—immediately took over the visual repertoire of the modern Turkish Republic and of course were immediately (albeit anachronistically) associated with the Hittites.[7]

In the mid-1970s, on the main ceremonial artery of Ankara in the neighborhood of Sıhhiye, there rose an enormous monument known as Hitit Güneşi Anıtı (Hittite Sun Monument) during the administration of a left-wing mayor, Vedat Dalokay, and in the midst of political debates and oppositions from parliament. The monument was modeled on one of the ritual standards from the Alaca Höyük royal tombs by sculptor Nusret Suman, greeting all citizens in a very central location in the city. It is significant to see an archaeological artifact such as the Alaca Höyük standard monumentalized in such a way approximately forty years after its excavation, endorsing the historical narrative discourse of Anatolianism that placed Alaca Höyük artifacts in the center of the public sphere and in the realm of social memory. Here, it is important to note that the outstanding circumstances of the excavation of this artifact during the first archaeological project of the Turkish Historical Society must have been effective in its refashioning as a monument that commemorated the deep past of the nation state. President Mustafa Kemal Atatürk was said to have personally inspected Alaca Höyük artifacts in Çankaya immediately after their recovery from the ground. The powerful nature of the craftsmanship of these metal artifacts, the notorious ambiguity of their function, and their hybrid iconography that combined sacred animals with geometries of cosmological symbolism has

Figure 28.2. Alaca Höyük Royal Tomb B. Copper alloy ritual standard. Ankara Museum of Anatolian Civilizations Inv. 18728 (*Art of the First Cities* Catalogue fig. 80).

clearly produced what Alfred Gell would call "the technology of enchantment and the enchantment of technology" (Gell 1992). This seamless interaction between the Early Bronze Age artifacts with the twentieth-century political discourse, ancient metallurgical technologies and ritual practices with contemporary monument making in the modern urban landscape, offers an excellent example of the performative role and agency of archaeological artifacts in the contemporary social world.

Stone Worlds: Cities and Landscapes in The Hittite Empire and The Early Iron Age

As in northwestern Syria and the Middle Euphrates Valley, the early second millennium B.C.E. in the Anatolian highlands marks a period of new urbanization and state formation, the proliferation of cuneiform written documents with the impressive spread of Akkadian literary culture, and increased interregional trade, especially in the circulation of metals (copper, tin, silver, and gold) and textiles (Dercksen 2008). Although the significant urban centers of Upper Mesopotamia at this time period, such as Ebla (Tell Mardikh), Mari (Tell Hariri), Halab/Yamḫad (Aleppo), and Alalakh (Tell Atchana), served as centers of competing regional polities, the Anatolian plateau also saw flourishing urban centers such as Kaneš (Kültepe), Konya Karahöyük, Acemhöyük (Purušḫanda), Beycesultan, and Ḫattuša (Boğazköy) among others, which seem to have heavily relied on mining, processing, and the trade of metals. These urbanized centers flourished as marketplaces, ports of trade (*kārum*) for the Assyrian exchange network that was established throughout the central plateau (Gorny 1989; Kuhrt 1998).

The large circular city of Kaneš in Cappadocia (in the province of Kayseri) of the late twentieth to mid-eighteenth century B.C.E. had impressive palatial complexes, cuneiform archives, several temples, and a city wall. This main mound, built on a natural hill and well fortified, was accompanied with an extramural settlement of Assyrian merchants (*kārum*). The urban plans of Middle Bronze Kültepe present a rather unique configuration, with the large, palatial circular mound and the lower *kārum* settlement adjoining them as an outer lobe, also well fortified. The economic and political (re)integration of the Anatolian highlands with the northern Syro-Mesopotamian region in the early second millennium B.C.E. seems to have led to Anatolia's sustained participation in that cultural *koine* until the end of the Iron Age (see Michel, chapter 13 in this volume). The intensified interregional contacts of the Middle Bronze Age seem to have prepared the geopolitical and economic foundations for the Hittite Empire (Gorny 1995:71) and set the stage for Hittite involvement in north Syria.

The architecture of the Middle Bronze Age cities presents evidence for new building technologies and forms, especially pointing to increased use of worked stone. Particularly in the early second millennium B.C.E., there is a significant regional development in northwestern Syria–southeast Anatolia, including prominent sites such as Ebla, Aleppo, Tilmen Höyük, and Alalakh, which saw the introduction of finely carved plain stone slabs known as orthostats (Harmanşah 2007b). Orthostats (usually basalt or limestone) were used either as socle blocks or thick revetment slabs to serve as a weathering technique on the walls of monumental structures such as city gates, palace complexes, and temples. Prominent examples of such structures with orthostatic walls are the Southwest Gate, Temple D, and western palace at Ebla (Matthiae 1997), the Storm God temple on the Aleppo citadel (Kohlmeyer 2000), the northeast gate building and the palatial complex at Alalakh Level VII (Woolley 1955), and finally the Middle Bronze Age palace complex at Tilmen Höyük (Duru 2003). This newly emerging stone tradition in Middle Bronze Age cities is significant because we are able to follow a powerful tradition of dressed stone masonry and orthostats into the Late Bronze Age and the Early Iron Age uninterrupted. The orthostatic walls of monumental buildings in the Late Bronze Age and more extensively in the Early and Middle Iron Ages were gradually opened to figural relief carving to include cultic and ceremonial imagery and monumental inscriptions. This impressive continuity is attested not only in the architectural technologies but also in the building designs such as the free-standing temples and the so-called three-entrance city gate structures.

Indeed, in the Late Bronze Age at the height of the Hittite Empire, the Anatolian plateau with its variety of microenvironments and diverse cultures saw for the first time the incorporation of many regional material culture traditions under a common supraregional identity that scholars describe today as Hittite. Alongside the political unification of the plateau on an unprecedented scale during the Hittite Empire, scholars point to the emergence of a ubiquitous visual repertoire in monumental art, new architectural forms and building technologies used in urban landscapes, ceramic and other material culture assemblages affiliated with an imperial core, economic administrative technologies such as official sealing practices, and a complex settlement system that benefited from the landscape policies of the Hittite state (Glatz 2009, and chapter 40 in this volume). Although many of these aspects of Hittite Anatolia were built on the foundations of Middle Bronze Age sociopolitical structures and their material world, it is important to highlight some of the extraordinary innovations that were brought to this cultural landscape during the Late Bronze Age. The long-term intimate contacts between the central plateau and the surrounding regions, especially northern Syro-Mesopotamia, the Mediterranean coast (including Kizzuwatna, Tarḫuntašša, Cyprus), and the Aegean coast, as well as the Pontic region, affected the unique hybridity of what one might call the Hittite material cultural assemblage (Genz 2006).

The urban layout of the prominent Hittite cities is not very extensively known archaeologically, with the exception of the capital city Ḫattuša (Boğazköy), which has been explored archaeologically since 1906. Beyond Ḫattuša, one should point out that the regional center of Şapinuwa (Ortaköy), provincial seat of Tapigga (Maşat Höyük), and cult center of Šarišša (Kuşaklı), among others, all located in the "Upper Land," have also contributed to our understanding of Hittite urbanism. As a departure from the earlier extensively occupied mound (*höyük*) settlements of the Chalcolithic, and Early and Middle Bronze Age towns in Anatolia, major Hittite cities are notable with their extraordinary use of difficult, rocky topographies (Schachner 2006a:154–56). This resonates with the much later Iron Age cities of Anatolia, such as Kerkenes Dağ, Göllüdağ, and Van Kalesi/Tušpa. Hittite towns were actually built in a variety of settings, on preexisting mounds, on flat landscapes in the river valleys, and on prominent outcrops. However, Hittites were notable builders of major architectural projects and new urban foundations on a scale that was unattested on the plateau prior to the Late Bronze Age (Glatz 2009:132). The distinct monumental architecture of Hittite cities for the first time offered construction techniques that relied heavily on the use of stone, often in megalithic proportions at city gates, palaces, and temples. New and innovative wall techniques were diverse, from casemate urban fortifications with cyclopean masonry to tightly fitted orthostats lining walls with finely cut socle blocks topped by mudbrick and timber superstructures (Naumann 1971). Highly burnished red wares of the Hittites with ceremonial animal-shaped vessels, massive storage vessels with narrative representations, and libation jugs and bowls can be seen as a significant innovation in the long-term Anatolian ceramic culture.

Ḫattuša was built gradually but innovatively as a spectacular urban landscape of state ceremonies and ritual festivals (Hawkins 1998; Neve 1993; Singer 1998; Seeher 2006) (figure 28.3). The city was constructed in ever-extending urban units around the impressive limestone outcrops of the citadels Büyükkaya and Büyükkale, separated by the Büyükkaya stream. Although the settlement in this area goes back to the Early Bronze Age and involves a *kārum* settlement of the Middle Bronze Age, the Hittite urban renewal program, especially from the sixteenth century B.C.E. onward until its abandonment around 1175 B.C.E., transformed the site into one of the largest fortified cities of the Near East. During the Late Bronze Age, building programs of the Hittite kings endowed Ḫattuša's monumental corpus with several temples, palace complexes, public monuments, sacred ponds, a complex network of fortifications, ceremonial city gates, and streets (see Mielke, chapter 48 in this volume). Büyükkale served as the royal residence and state archives, whereas a massive temple complex, known as Temple 1, stood in the Lower City to the northwest on the plain. It has long been assumed that the Upper City at Ḫattuša, with its many temple complexes and ponds, was the work of a major building program involving a massive southward urban expansion in the thirteenth century B.C.E., in the last century of Hittite occupation of the site. However excavations since 1990 have revealed convincing evidence for the settlement of the Upper City very early on, in the sixteenth and fifteenth centuries B.C.E. (Seeher 2006). The diversity of commemorative monuments and memorials set up in Ḫattuša is hard to survey here; notable are the southern and eastern sacred ponds with the monumental chamber with a royal hieroglyphic Luwian inscription, the rock inscription of Nişantaş by Šuppiluliuma II, Sarıkale rock monument, the stele of Tudḫaliya IV found as spolia in a Byzantine church on the site, and the Bronze Tablet among others.

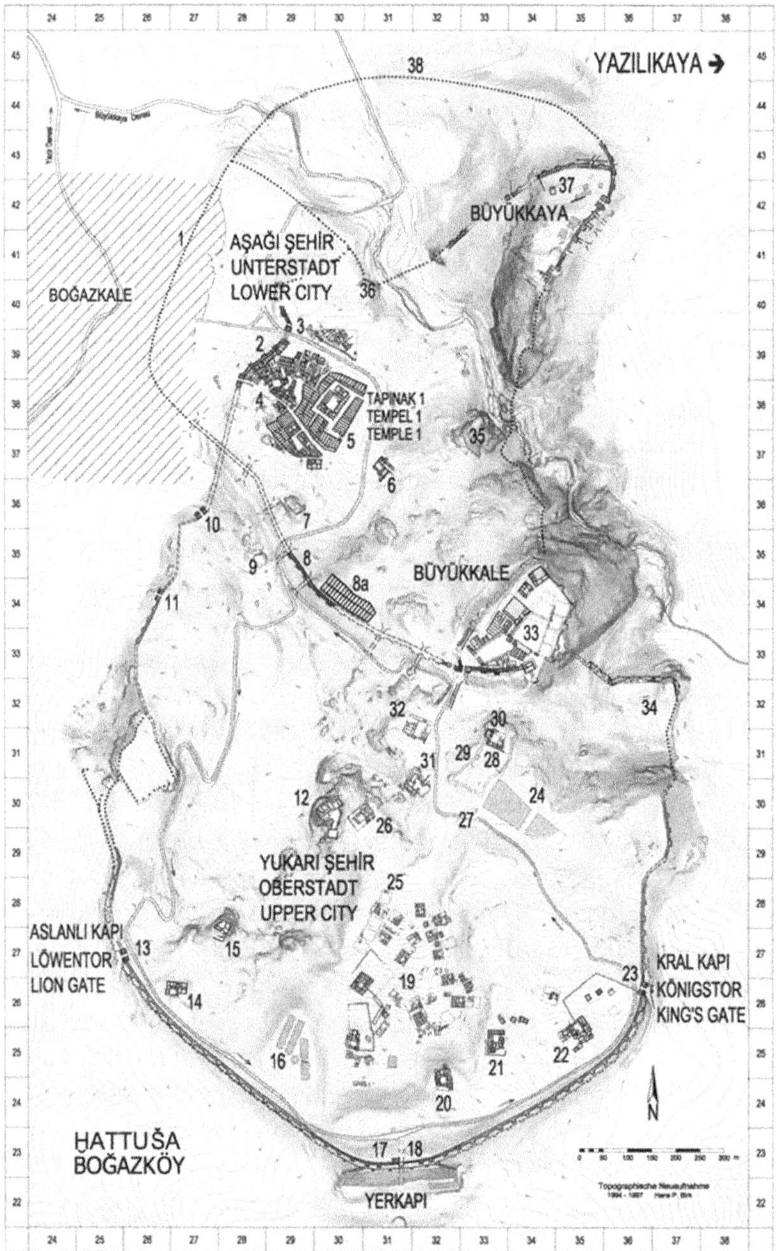

Figure 28.3. Urban plan of Ḫattuša (Boğazköy) (DAI website, http://www.dainst.de/medien/de/hattuscha3k.jpg).

One of the most interesting aspects of Hittite monumental interventions in Anatolian landscapes is the carving of reliefs and inscriptions onto the "living rock" prominently at geologically and culturally significant places, such as springs, river gorges, or mountain passes, and the construction of sacred pool complexes on or near powerful springs (recently grouped under the term "landscape monuments"; see Glatz 2009).

This practice of monument making in both urban and extra-urban contexts took place especially at sites with spectacular settings, but they also took form in impressively diverse ways in their location and character, in a way making it hard to create a typology for them. The rock reliefs and inscriptions in nonurban settings often visually relate to the dramatic mountainous landscapes of southern Anatolia (e.g., the İmamkulu, Hanyeri, Sirkeli, and Fıraktin monuments) and relate to a body of water (Hatip, Sirkeli, Fıraktin, Taşçı, and Yazılıkaya). Sacred pool complexes such as Yalburt and Eflatun Pınar in Konya province were built on top of abundant springs, incorporating commemorative inscriptions and representations of Hittite deities of mountains and springs.

Hittite rock reliefs and spring monuments have been studied from a variety of angles, including comprehensive reviews (Ehringhaus 2005; Kohlmeyer 1982), iconographic analysis of their pictorial representations involving images of the king or members of the royal family and various other cultic representations (Bonatz 2007), the historical reading of their commemorative inscriptions in hieroglyphic Luwian (Hawkins 1992), and their role in the macroscale configuration of Hittite imperial landscapes (Glatz 2009). The most outstanding among these monuments is perhaps the extramural, open-air rock-cut sanctuary of Yazılıkaya, immediately outside the capital Ḫattuša and connected to it with a processional route (Alexander 1986; Bittel 1967; Sagona and Zimansky 2009:276–80). It has been suggested that the multichambered rock sanctuary housed a powerful spring in antiquity and that the cult activity in it dates back to the third millennium B.C.E. (figure 28.4). With the foundation of the

Figure 28.4. **Yazılıkaya, Hittite open-air rock-cut sanctuary near Boğazköy (drawing from Charles Texier, *Asie mineure: description géographique, historique et archéologique des provinces et des villes de la Chersonnèse d'Asie*, 1862).**

Hittite ceremonial capital in its close vicinity, Yazılıkaya seems to have become one of the most important cult places of Anatolian antiquity, possibly associated with the so-called rock-*ḫegur* of Hittite ritual texts, the locus of funerary ceremonies for the Hittite royal family (van den Hout 2002). This is supported by the fact that the route between Ḫattuša and Yazılıkaya seems to have become a burial landscape between the seventeenth and thirteenth centuries B.C.E. The reliefs carved on the walls of the two major chambers of the sanctuary depict processions of the many deities of the empire, perhaps constituting a "divine assembly." The corpus of deities, who were accompanied by epigraphs in hieroglyphic script, make specific references to the Hurrian pantheon, which suggests the incorporation of Hurrian cult practices into the core state religion of the empire. The relief representations of Tudḫaliya IV in the narrow Chamber B have suggested a royal funerary character to this section of the sanctuary. It is quite likely that Ḫattuša and Yazılıkaya were connected with ritual processions during the city's major festivals such as the spring AN.TAḪ.ŠUM or KI.LAM festivals (Bonatz 2007:116).

In urban contexts, one of the most impressive examples of spring monuments is the eastern ponds of Ḫattuša with their hieroglyphic chamber. The stone built chamber was excavated in 1988 on the northwestern corner of the eastern ponds (in the area known as Südburg). On the walls of the chamber, a lengthy hieroglyphic Luwian inscription of the late thirteenth-century B.C.E. king Šuppiluliuma II was found accompanied by the reliefs of the Sun God and the king himself (Hawkins 1995). The inscription commemorates the king's military successes and his foundation of new cities in the lands of Wiyanawanda, Tamina, Maša, Lukka and Ikkuwaniya, and Tarḫuntašša, and ends with a reference to a construction of DEUS.*202 (= DINGIR.KASKAL.KUR), translated by David Hawkins as "Divine Road of the Earth." For the first time, with this inscription, a direct link has been established between the Hittite sacred pool complexes and the Divine Road of the Earth, which was already known from Hittite and Hurrian texts (Gordon 1967). These are considered liminal spaces, entrances to the underworld, places where ritual communication with the dead ancestors could be established.[8]

At Eflatun Pınar (literally, "Spring of Plato"), at the site of an abundant spring near the southeastern shore of Beyşehir Lake, Hittite craftsmen constructed a spectacular pool and a massive cult monument (figure 28.5). The architectural monument of finely dressed trachite masonry houses high-relief representations of mountain and spring deities and composite mythological beings such as bull-men and lion-men and two seated deities supporting winged sun-disk representations (Özyar 2006:130). It has been suggested that the monument may have supported a colossal statue, perhaps similar to the impressive unfinished statue at Fasıllar, a nearby Hittite quarry site (Mellaart 1962). Recent archaeological work at the pool suggests that several other animal and human statues were set around the edges of the pool facing inward (Bachmann and Özenir 2004). We learn from the early twentieth-century antiquarian and archaeologist F. W. Hasluck and his ethnographic account of the Eflatun Pınar monument that the place was associated with Plato, who was conceptualized as a "magician-philosopher-engineer who prevented floods in the area" (Hasluck 1929:363–69; Nixon 2004:433). The sacred pool at Yalburt was built on a high plateau that is rather barren today, with a few seasonal hamlets and villages nearby, but overlooking the broad plain

Figure 28.5. Eflatun Pınar. Hittite sacred pool and spring sanctuary monument near Beyşehir Lake, Konya province (author's photo).

of Ilgın and the basin of Çavuşçu Göl in Konya province. It is the upland pasture or mountain meadow of a series of transhumant communities of the villages down below in the plain. The pool is a monument with one of the lengthiest commemorative Hittite inscriptions in Hieroglyphic Luwian, featuring a detailed account of the military expeditions of Tudḫaliya IV in southwest Anatolia (Hawkins 1992, 1995; Özgüç 1988).

The carving of rock reliefs and inscriptions at springs, mountain peaks, and other geologically significant locations does not cease as a practice with the collapse of the Hittite Empire in the early twelfth century B.C.E. but is taken up by the Assyrians and the Syro-Hittite regional states of the Iron Age. For instance, a series of Hieroglyphic Luwian monuments were found at the sites of Kızıldağ and Karadağ overlooking the southern Konya Plain and Burunkaya further northwest in the area of Ihlara at the heart of the Cappadocian landscape. All three of the monuments make reference to the "Great King Hartapus," who is completely unknown from the late imperial textual corpus. On epigraphic grounds, the monuments are dated to the twelfth century B.C.E., immediately after the disintegration of the Hittite Empire. Likewise, the "Country Lords" of Syro-Hittite Melid/Malizi, which was a regional state established in the Malatya Plain on the west bank of the Upper Euphrates in the early Iron Age, also adopted the commemorative use of Hieroglyphic Luwian inscriptions on stelai (Karahöyük, Izgın, İspekçür, Darende) as well as living rock (Kötükale, Gürün) (see Yakubovich, chapter 23 in this volume, for additional discussion on Luwian-inscribed monuments). Most spectacular in this sense is perhaps the site of İvriz in the land of the Syro-Hittite state of Tabal. At a very abundant spring on the northern foothills of

Figure 28.6. İvriz. Rock relief of Tabalian king Warpalawaš, eighth century B.C.E. (author's photo).

the Taurus Mountains, the eighth-century B.C.E. Tabalian king Warpalawaš had his craftsmen carve his image and inscriptions on the face of living rock, "Kocaburun Kayası" (figure 28.6). He is depicted in veneration of *his* Storm God Tarhunzas, who holds ears of wheat and bunches of grapes and apparently ensures agricultural abundance in the region. Archaeological discovery of other rock carvings and stelai in the vicinity of the rock relief now suggests that the site was a heavily used cultic locus in antiquity from the Iron Age to the Byzantine period (Bier 1976). One could correlate these monuments with the Assyrian practice of the carving of commemorative rock reliefs in the frontiers of their empire in the Iron Age. An impressive example one finds in southeastern Anatolia is the site of the "Source of the Tigris" or "Tigris Tunnel" monuments, which were carved at the mouth of multiple caves where one of the tributaries of the Tigris River, Birklin Çay, emerges. During multiple visits, the Assyrian kings Tiglath-pileser I (1114–1076 B.C.E.) and Šalmaneser III (858–824 B.C.E.) carved "images of kingship" and inscriptions in cuneiform on the rock at this politically contested frontier (Harmanşah 2007a; Schachner 2006b).

Anatolian Iron Ages: A Fragmented Universe

In the margins of former Hittite territories, especially north Syria and southeast Anatolia, following the supraregional collapse of economic networks in the majority of the Near East and eastern Mediterranean, a new process of urbanization marked the early Iron age in the lands of a series of emerging regional states with new ideological affiliations and socioeconomic frameworks (Harmanşah 2005; Mazzoni 1997). Karkamiš on the Euphrates and Melid/Malizi in the Malatya Plain had a special role in the transition of the cultural memory of the Hittite Empire to the Iron Age states. With the new dating at the destruction level at the Phrygian city Gordion/Yassıhöyük, it has become more accepted that the Phrygian state was very much part and parcel of this koine of regional states of northern Mesopotamia (see Sams, chapter 27, and Roller, chapter 25 in this volume). Likewise, the kingdom of Urartu with its core territories in the Lake Van Basin and its western frontiers on the Euphrates was in close contact with the Anatolian and north Mesopotamian states (see Zimansky, chapter 24, and Radner, chapter 33 in this volume). With respect to the history of architecture and monumental art, what is particularly striking in each of these cultural realms is the experimental and innovative use of stone in public buildings, especially in the context of the large-scale building projects of Syro-Hittite, Phrygian, Assyrian, and Urartian kings. The architectural technologies of building with finely dressed stone masonry and lining the monumental walls with thin upright slabs (orthostats) with relief representations were already known from their rare appearance in the Middle and Late Bronze Age cities of northern Syria and Anatolia (such as Ebla, Halab/Yamḫad, Alalakh, Ḫattuša, and Ayn Dara). However, the proliferation of such building programs is a characteristic of the Iron Age contexts, perhaps associated with the more abundant use of iron in the making of stone carving tools. In the politicized urban landscape of early Iron Age cities in Syro-Hittite states and Assyria, the comprehensive pictorial narrative programs of the ruling élite introduced highly animated wall surfaces across the public realm, blending ritual imagery with commemorative inscriptions and ideological narratives of the state. Urban spaces were thus transformed into ceremonial platforms for the spectacles of the state and the construction of social memories.

The most spectacular of these programs is known from the time of the Suhis-Katuwas dynasty at Karkamiš on the Euphrates, dated to the late eleventh and tenth century B.C.E. (Denel 2007). Built on the west bank of the Euphrates at a strategic crossing and at the northern end of the wide and fertile river basin, Karkamiš was the capital city of a regional state and held a pivotal role in the region from the Middle Bronze Age well into the Iron Age. The urban renewal program carried out by the Suhis-Katuwas dynasty at Karkamiš is significant, owing partly to the current availability of archaeological evidence, partly to the complexity of the building operations in this early Iron Age city, and considerably to the wealth of epigraphic material that comes from the site. Woolley's excavations at Karkamiš largely concentrated in a densely urban area immediately south of the citadel mound, the area of the "Great Staircase," "Long Wall of Sculpture," and the "Temple of the Storm God," cumulatively referred to by Woolley as the "Lower Palace Area" (figure 28.7).[9] Stretching from the so-called Water Gate at the southern foot of the citadel by the bank of the Euphrates to the so-called King's Gate, an impressive urban ensemble accommodates a series of monumental structures and an articulate public space, which was defined by monumental terrace walls. More significantly, the entire

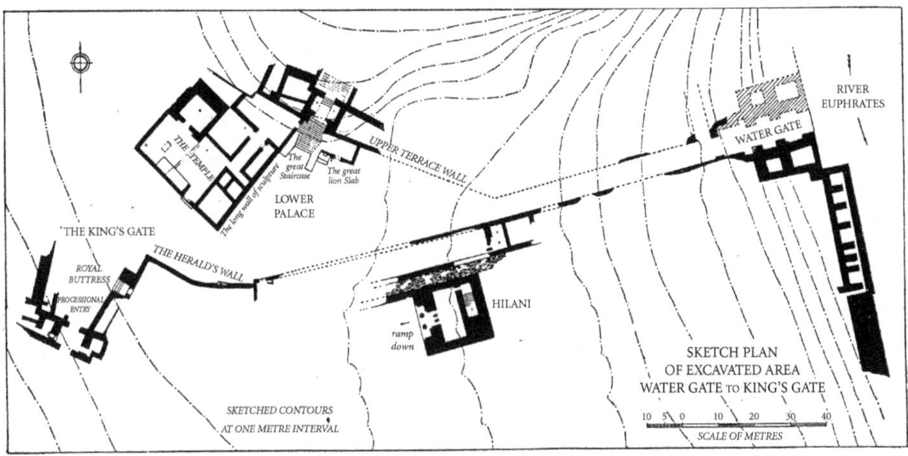

Figure 28.7. Karkamiš, "Lower Palace area" plan (Woolley and Barnett 1952:pl. 41a).

complex was surrounded with basalt and limestone orthostats with relief representations of cultic, mythological, and historical subject matter, as well as monumental Hieroglyphic Luwian inscriptions, apotropaic gate sculptures, and other commemorative monuments. In this way, the urban complex was articulately transformed into a dramatic ceremonial space, where major cultic activities of the city were focused, and precisely in the same spatial realm, political and historical narratives of the imperial élite were communicated to the society.

Similar kinds of commemorative programs mainly concentrating on the city gates are known from Malatya, Arslantepe/Melid, Zincirli/Sam'al, Karatepe/Azatiwataya, and Tell Halaf, which are in a way comparable to the program at Karkamiš, although on less ambitious scales (Aro 2003). Impressive temples with orthostats featuring cultic/ritual representations are known from the newly excavated Weather God temple at the Aleppo citadel as well as the temple at Ayn Dara. The architectural design of monumental "three-entrance" gates at Syro-Hittite cities became extremely ubiquitous with the introduction of orthostatic programs featuring representations of mythological episodes, images of divine ancestors, or particular deities. Palatial structures such as those known from Tell Halaf, Zincirli, and Göllüdağ tend to have columnar façades and monumental staircases that add to their spectacular layout. The double column, *in antis* entrances to such structures are often associated with the so-called *bit hilani*, referred to in Assyrian inscriptions as an exotic building type from Syro-Hittite cities; Assyrians had always been keen on importing this feature to their palace gardens.

At Göllüdağ and Kerkenes Dağ, one sees two fascinating mountaintop urban establishments of the Middle Iron Age. Both of them were clearly built as ceremonial regional capitals that served for only part of the year. There are striking similarities between the two cities in the ambitious monumental structures in the midst of the urban space as well as the extraordinary care given to the planning and construction of residential neighborhoods through the orthogonal allocation of land to families. Kerkenes Dağ has now produced some of the longest monumental inscriptions in Phrygian and is allowing us to rethink the cultural geography of the central Anatolian plateau during the Iron Age.

Urartian cities of the Lake Van Basin present an equally impressive case of urbanization, especially in the eighth and seventh centuries B.C.E. (see Çilingiroğlu, chapter 49; Zimansky, chapter 24; and Roller, chapter 25 in this volume). At the imperially constructed cities such as Tušpa (Van Kalesi), Rusahinili (Van, Toprakkale), Rusahinili Eiduru-kai (Ayanis), Haldiei URU.KUR. Ziuquni (Kef Kalesi), and Sardurihinili (Çavuştepe) among others, spectacular rock outcrops were chosen for the construction of citadels (Sagona and Zimansky 2009:331–35). While giving the impression of military strongholds, the citadels of these cities largely contained sumptuous temple complexes in the form of large economic institutions, and burials for the royal élite (Burney 1998; Çilingiroğlu 2004; Tanyeri-Erdemir 2007). The citadels feature Urartian square planned, stone-built (*susi*?) temples with adjoining multicolumnar courtyards, ingeniously using the topography of the bedrock to monumentalize the cult complexes. Kitchens and massive food storage and processing units have been excavated in a variety of Urartian citadels, whereas other temple storerooms were dedicated to storing dedicatory objects (especially metal) presented to the temple.

In terms of architectural materials and technologies employed in these complexes, Urartians used many innovative schemes, especially involving the embedding and incorporation of monumental walls into the bedrock, high-skilled cut stone masonry in hard volcanic stones such as basalt and andasite, wall paintings, paving of temple interiors with alabaster, and the lining of its walls with intaglio orthostats. Lengthy commemorative inscriptions were carved on living rock stelai or architectural surfaces. The recent excavations and survey work at the mid-seventh century B.C.E. urban foundation at Ayanis, ancient *Rusahinili Eiduru-kai*, located on the eastern coast of Lake Van, has provided much valuable information in the past two decades on Urartian architectural practices and monumental art, whereas the façade of its temple to Haldi provided one of the longest historical inscriptions in Urartian (Çilingiroğlu and Salvini 2001; Çilingiroğlu, chapter 49, and Zimansky, chapter 24 in this volume). The historical circumstances of this late new foundation in Urartian history has incorporated a great deal of experimentation with architectural technologies in monumental structures, especially exemplified in the southern fortification walls and the ceremonial sections of the temple complex (Harmanşah 2009).

It is probably most fitting to conclude this section by speaking of a site that has affected the chronologies of the Iron Ages in Anatolia dramatically and one that brings together the cultural interaction spheres of the Near East and the Aegean worlds: the Phrygian site of Yassıhöyük, long identified as ancient Gordion (Sams 2005; see Voigt, chapter 50 in this volume). The excavations at Yassıhöyük's citadel mound and the tumulus burials of the surrounding landscape as well as the geoarchaeological and survey work in the city's hinterland since 1969 has provided us with a wealth of information on Early and Middle Iron Age building practices in central Anatolia and about what sorts of supraregional interactions existed on the plateau (DeVries 1990). The recent redating of the so-called Destruction Level at Gordion that separates the Early Phrygian and Middle Phrygian building projects to 830–800 B.C.E. has revolutionized the Anatolian chronologies of the Iron Ages and now suggests that the Phrygian capital was in fact intimately connected to Syro-Hittite cities of the early Iron Age (DeVries et al. 2003). Still, the architecture in the complex of monumental megaron structures of the citadel and the material culture suggests that the city was also embedded in the western Anatolian/Aegean world as well. Following a series of experimentations in building form and architectural technologies in the beginning of the early Iron Age (YHSS 7 and 6B), builders at Gordion created a public space with a series of monumental structures in attached rows (TB and CC structures) on a terrace, as well as free-standing megara (such as M3, M4), comprising evidence for food processing, storage, and textile production (Voigt and Henrickson 2000). This impressive complex of industrial and perhaps cultic buildings was destroyed by fire around 830–800 B.C.E. as it was going through yet another dramatic building program. The Phrygian experimentations with stone, and their monumental and ubiquitous use of wood in these buildings, plus the existence of several carved orthostat fragments from the early Iron Age levels, suggest perhaps the foundation of a new capital city at Yassıhöyük and highlight its intimate relationship with the Syro-Hittite cultural realm of the east.

Epilogue: Landscapes of The Dead

From the Early Iron Age warrior stelai of Hakkari to Syro-Hittite funerary stelai and the so-called Greco-Persian stelai of the Achaemenid period in the west from the rock-cut tombs of Urartu, Lycia, and Paphlagonia to the tumuli of Phrygia and Lydia, and to the monumental stone tombs of Sardis, Xanthos, Halicarnassos, Phokaia, and Belevi, Anatolian Iron Age landscapes present us with a spectacular variety of burial practices, funerary architecture, and ancestral monuments as well as a rich iconography of the dead. In the general scheme of things, it is important to see the construction of funerary monuments as a significant practice of place-making and the incorporation or building of landscapes (Harrison 2003). Harrison, whom I have quoted in the beginning of this chapter, writes: "what is a place if not its memory of itself—a site or locale where time turns back upon itself? The grave marks a site in the landscape where time cannot merely pass through, or pass over. Time must now gather around the *sema* and mortalize itself" (Harrison 2003:23).

Urartians are known to have built monumental rock-cut tombs for their kings and other urban élites—such as those found at Tušpa/Van Kalesi, Kayalıdere, and Palu on the Euphrates (Çevik 2000; Köroğlu 2008; Sevin 1994), and this practice should be closely affiliated with their rock-cut commemorative inscriptions and open-air sanctuaries in the form of monumental rabbeted gateways.

In fact, Argišti I's tomb on Van Kalesi was inscribed with a long commemorative inscription of his military expeditions. Many of these tombs have formally planned, multiple chambers with burial niches attached to them, possibly integrating large spaces for funerary ceremonies or feasts (Çilingiroğlu 1997:89). The sculpted and columnar rupestral tombs of Achaemenid Paphlagonia, the mountainous Black Sea region west of the Halys (Kızıl Irmak), are equally fascinating in their place-making qualities and their deliberate use of the living rock. As tombs of the Paphlagonian élite at the time, their iconographic and architectural traditions appear as a politicized hybrid of Anatolian, Persian, and Greek cultural discourses and historically specific sociopolitical affiliations (Johnson 2010). However, the most pervasive and long-term tradition of rock-cut tombs perhaps existed in the mountainous landscapes of Lycia (Keen 1998:182f.). In fact, Lycian funerary architecture from the mid-sixth to early fourth centuries B.C.E. presents a fascinating variety of tombs, including pillar tombs of the urban centers, rupestral house tombs, and sarcophagi across the Lycian landscape at particular burial sites, as well as burial mounds or tumuli. This diversity and richness of monumental tomb building that shaped much of the Lycian landscapes directs attention to the ubiquity of the practice, extending from legendary heroes to urban élites and ordinary households. The Nereid Monument at Xanthos (390–380 B.C.E.) can be seen as one of the most impressive examples of the pillar tombs with its towering mass in the urban landscape topped with an Ionic temple-like structure and its complex narrative relief and sculptural program (figure 28.8). The famous Mausoleum at Halikarnassos in Caria, Belevi Monument near Ephesus, Taş Kule near Phokaia (Eski Foça), and the Pyramid Tomb at Lydian Sardis are other spectacular examples of free-standing tombs that mark the height of Anatolian tomb architecture (Cahill 1988).

Tumulus burials of the Iron Ages demarcate the countryside, especially in Phrygia, Thrace, Paphlagonia, and Lydia, as extra-urban land monuments. Western Anatolian peoples of the Iron Ages often buried their princes, rulers, and prominent élites in stone and timber chambers covered by massive earthen mounds, which then acted as durable components of the steppe landscapes and rolling hills. Tumuli, as visible features of the ancient past, are always vulnerable to extensive looting and yet are the archaeologically best investigated tombs, including Tumulus MM near Yassıhöyük (Young 1981), Beştepeler tumulus in Ankara, the tumulus of Alyattes (Kocamutaf Tepe) in Bintepeler in the territory of Sardis (Roosevelt 2009:144), Karabel and Kızılbel tombs in the Elmalı Plain of Lycia (Mellink 1998), and the Tatarlı tumulus near Afyon (Summerer 2007). The earliest Phrygian tumuli (such as Tumulus MM) had chambers built with massive juniper and pine logs on stone foundations, covered with rubble and earth, and featured sumptuous grave goods. The Lydian tumuli such as that of Alyattes had cut-stone burial chambers roofed with massive limestone slabs, accessed through a forecourt. Persian period tombs such as Kızılbel and Tatarlı present fascinating programs of narrative imagery including representations of battles and feasting (Mellink 1998; Summerer 2007).

Figure 28.8. Nereid Monument (390–380 B.C.E.), Xanthos (British Museum website, http://www.britishmuseum.org/collectionimages/AN00258/AN00258120_001_l.jpg).

Final Remarks

Adolf Loos, one of the prominent architectural theorists of European modernism, identified a tumulus as a primary architectural form: "When we find in the forest a mound, six feet long and three feet wide, raised by a shovel to form a pyramid, we turn serious and something in us says: here someone lies buried. *That is architecture*" (Loos, quoted in Harries 2000:292). In this chapter, I have discussed various episodes in ancient Anatolian history through discussions of how particular urban and non-urban monuments acted as sites of commemoration and enactment of social memory. This panoptic review is painfully fragmentary and incomplete, yet I hope it illustrates the long-term dynamics of cultural affiliations and sociopolitical alignments in its vast and diverse, often fragmented, cultural biography. Telling such a story through monuments and spectacle is unfortunately based on a biased, urban-centric view of the world. However, if we are able to see monuments as sites of creativity and technological innovation, "theaters of knowledge" as well as foci of collective identities that gather around themselves specific social practices, they can tell us much about the social foundations of ideological discourses. The monuments of antiquity stand today in scholarly representations, in museums, and at archaeological sites as testifiers of the rich and heterogeneous nature of Anatolian cultural geographies.

NOTES

I am grateful to the editors of this volume for their continued support and patience. It would have been difficult to assemble this disparate material without their persistent encouragement.

1. Consider for instance the "mother goddess" phenomenon, which is often used by scholars to illustrate the continuity of "Anatolian" material culture from prehistory (Çatalhöyük figurines) to history (Phrygian cult of Matar Kubileya) (e.g., Roller 1999).

2. On the construction of the concept of Anatolia, see now Atakuman (2008), Bilsel (2007), Gür (2006), and Kafadar (2007); in addition see Matthews, chapter 3 in this volume.

3. R. Gorny suggested that Anatolian archaeology has largely been equated with the archaeology of Hittites, which itself flourished with the search for a new nation-state identity for the modern Turkish Republic (Gorny 1989:80). Mellink's memorable (1966) essay on Anatolia archaeology should be noted for its declaration of autonomy of the field from classical and Near Eastern studies.

4. On the "birth" of symbolism and the representational practices in the Pre-Pottery Neolithic, especially the shamanistic aspects of animal symbolism, see Cauvin (2000), Hodder (2006a:185–206), and Peters and Schmidt (2004).

5. For notable discussions of Alaca Höyük Early Bronze Age stratigraphy, see Gürsan-Salzman (1992), Özyar (1999), and Sagona and Zimansky 2009:213–16; see also Steadman, this volume.

6. The site was already known through explorations of Theodor Makridi Bey (İstanbul Archaeological Museum), who uncovered the Late Bronze Age sphinx gate at the site, and later work by a German team. Arık and Koşay were simply resuming the work at the site.

7. Despite the fact that there has never been any evidence for the continuity of the third millennium B.C.E. culture of Alaca Höyük with the Hittites of the second millennium B.C.E., there seems to be a continued tendency to see Alaca Höyük burials and their rich assemblages as the "origin" of Hittite art, although this remains completely unsupported. See, for example, Canby (1989:110–11) and Shaw (2007). This assumption would be comparable to claiming that the material culture of those who were buried in the Royal Tombs of Ur, for example, is contiguous with that of the Old Babylonian kingdom of Isin-Larsa.

8. At the Hittite/Phrygian site of Gavurkalesi, a similar vaulted chamber was found in close association with a rock relief. The chamber is located to the north of the cyclopean structure on top of the settlement and capped with massive monolithic blocks (Lumsden 2002). It is plausible that this chamber at Gavurkalesi served a similar cultic function to the hieroglyphic chamber at Ḫattuša.

9. Woolley and Barnett (1952:157–204). The area of the "Great Staircase," "Long Wall of Sculpture," and the "Temple of the Storm God" was referred to by Woolley as the "Lower Palace area." Across from this complex, the "King's Gate," "Processional Entry," "Royal Buttress," and "Herald's Wall" form yet another building ensemble. Woolley treated the "Hilani" and the "Water Gate" separately. Strikingly, nowhere in the Karkamiš excavation reports does there exist a discussion of the entire complex.

REFERENCES

Alcock, Susan E. 2002. *Archaeologies of the Greek Past: Landscape, Monuments, and Memories*. Cambridge: Cambridge University Press.

Alexander, Robert L. 1986. *The Sculpture and Sculptors of Yazılıkaya*. Newark: University of Delaware Press.

Aro, Sanna. 2003. Art and Architecture. In *The Luwians*, ed. H. Craig Melchert, 281–337. Leiden: Brill.

Atakuman, Çiğdem. 2008. Cradle or Crucible: Anatolia and Archaeology in the Early Years of the Turkish Republic (1923–1938). *Journal of Social Archaeology* 8: 214–35.

Bachmann, Martin and Sırrı Özenir. 2004. Das Quellheiligtum Eflatun Pınar. *Archaeologische Anzeiger* 2004.1: 85–102.

Bier, Lionel. 1976. A Second Hittite Relief at İvriz. *Journal of Near Eastern Studies* 35: 115–26.

Bilsel, S. M. Can. 2007. "Our Anatolia": Organicism and the Making of Humanist Culture in Turkey. In *Muqarnas 24. History and Ideology: Architectural Heritage of the "Lands of Rum,"* ed. Sibel Bozdoğan and Gülru Necipoğlu, 223–41. Leiden: Brill.

Bittel, Kurt. 1967. *Yazılıkaya: Architektur, Felsbilder, Inschriften und Kleinfunde*. Osnabrück: Zeller.

Bonatz, Dominik. 2007. The Divine Image of the King: Religious Representation of Political Power in the Hittite Empire. In *Representations of Political Power: Case Histories from Times of Change and Dissolving Order in the Ancient Near East*, ed. Marlies Heinz and Marian H. Feldman, 111–36. Winona Lake, Ind.: Eisenbrauns.

Burney, Charles. 1998. The Kingdom of Urartu (Van): Investigations in the Archaeology of the Early First Millennium BC within eastern Anatolia (1956–1965). In *Ancient Anatolia: Fifty Years' Work by the British Institute of Archaeology at Ankara*, ed. Roger Matthews, 143–62. London: British Institute of Archaeology at Ankara.

Cahill, Nicholas. 1988. Taş Kule: A Persian-Period Tomb near Phokaia. *American Journal of Archaeology* 92: 481–501.

Canby, Jeanny Vorys. 1989. Hittite Art. *Biblical Archaeologist* 52: 109–29.

Cauvin, Jacques. 2000. *The Birth of the Gods and the Origins of Agriculture*. Trans. Trevor Watkins. Cambridge: Cambridge University Press.

Çevik, Nevzat. 2000. *Urartu Kaya Mezarları ve Ölüm Gömme Gelenekleri*. Ankara: Türk Tarih Kurumu.

Çilingiroğlu, Altan. 1997. *Urarti Krallığı: Tarihi ve Sanatı*. İzmir: Universal A. Ş.

———. 2004. How Was an Urartian fortress Built? In *A View from the Highlands: Studies in Honour of Charles Burney*, ed. Antonio Sagona, 205–32. Leuven: Peeters.

Çilingiroğlu, Altan and Mirjo Salvini, eds. 2001. *Ayanis I: Ten Years' Excavations at Rusahinili Eiduru-kai 1989–1998*. Roma: CNR Istituto per gli Studi Micenei ed Egeo-Anatolici.

Denel, Elif. 2007. Ceremony and Kingship at Carchemish. In *Ancient Near Eastern Art in Context: Studies in Honor of Irene J. Winter by Her Students*, ed. Jack Cheng and Marian H. Feldman, 179–204. Leiden: Brill.

Dercksen, J. G., ed. 2008. *Anatolia and the Jazira during the Old Assyrian Period*. Leiden: Nederlands Instituut voor het Nabije Oosten.

DeVries, Keith. 1990. The Gordion Excavation Seasons of 1969–1973 and Subsequent Research. *American Journal of Archaeology* 94: 371–406.

DeVries, Keith, Peter I. Kuniholm, G. Kenneth Sams, and Mary M. Voigt. 2003. New Dates for Iron Age Gordion. *Antiquity* 77: 296. http://antiquity.ac.uk/ProjGall/devries/devries.html.

Duru, Refik. 2003. *A Forgotten Capital City Tilmen (Story of a 5400 Year Old Settlement in the Islahiye Region-Southeast Anatolia)*. İstanbul: Türsab Kültür Yayınları.

Düring, Bleda. 2001. Social Dimensions in the Architecture of Neolithic Çatalhöyük. *Anatolian Studies* 51: 1–18.

Ehringhaus, Horst. 2005. *Götter, Herrscher, Inschriften: Die Felsreliefs der hethitischen Großreichzeit in der Türkei*. Mainz am Rhein: Verlag Philipp von Zabern.

Erimtan, Can. 2008. Hittites, Ottomans and Turks: Ağaoğlu Ahmed Bey and the Kemalist Construction of Turkish Nationhood in Anatolia. *Anatolian Studies* 58: 141–72.

Frangipane, Marcella. 2001a. Centralization Processes in Greater Mesopotamia: Uruk Expansion as the Climax of Systemic Interactions among Areas of the Greater Mesopotamian Region. In *Uruk Mesopotamia and its Neighbors*, ed. Mitchell S. Rothman, 307–48. Santa Fe, N.M.: School of American Research Press.

———. 2001b. The Transition between Two Opposing Forms of Power at Arslantepe (Malatya) at the Beginning of the 3rd Millennium. *TUBA-AR* 4: 1–24.

Gell, Alfred. 1992. The Technology of Enchantment and the Enchantment of Technology. In *Anthropology, Art and Aesthetics*, ed. Jeremy Coote and Anthony Shelton, 40–63. Oxford: Clarendon Press.

Genz, Hermann. 2006. Imports and Their Methodological Implications for Dating Hittite Material Culture. In *Strukturerung und Datierung in der hethitischen Archäeologie/ Structuring and dating in Hittite archaeology*, ed. Dirk Paul Mielke, Ulf-Dietrich Schoop, and Jürgen Seeher, 185–96. BYZAS 4. İstanbul: Ege Yayınları.

Glatz, Claudia. 2009. Empire as Network: Spheres of Material Interaction in Late Bronze Age Anatolia. *Journal of Anthropological Archaeology* 28: 127–41.

Goode, James F. 2007. *Negotiating for the Past: Archaeology, Nationalism and Diplomacy in the Middle East, 1919–1941*. Austin: University of Texas Press.

Gordon, Edmund I. 1967. The Meaning of the Ideogram ^{d}KASKAL.KUR = "Underground Water-Course" and its Significance for Bronze Age Historical Geography. *Journal of Cuneiform Studies* 21: 70–88.

Gorny, Ronald L. 1989. Environment, Archaeology and History in Hittite Anatolia. *Biblical Archaeologist* 52: 78–96.

———. 1995. Hittite Imperialism and Anti-Imperial Resistance as Viewed from Alişar Höyük. *Bulletin of the American Schools of Oriental Research* 299/300: 65–89.

Gür, Aslı. 2006. Stories in Three Dimensions: Narratives of Nation and the Anatolian Civilizations Museum. In *The Politics of Public Memory in Turkey*, ed. Esra Özyürek, 40–69. Syracuse, N.Y.: Syracuse University Press.

Gürsan-Salzman, Ayşe. 1992. *Alaca Höyük: A Reassessment of the Excavation and Sequence of the Early Bronze Age Settlement*. Ph.D. dissertation. University of Pennsylvania.

Harmanşah, Ömür. 2005. *Spatial Narratives, Commemorative Practices and the Building Project: New Urban Foundations in Upper Syro-Mesopotamia during the Early Iron Age*. Ph.D. dissertation. University of Pennsylvania.

———. 2007a. Source of the Tigris: Event, Place and Performance in the Assyrian Landscapes of the Early Iron Age. *Archaeological Dialogues* 14.2: 179–204.

———. 2007b. Upright Stones and Building Narratives: Formation of a Shared Architectural Practice in the Ancient Near East. In *Ancient Near Eastern Art in Context: Studies in Honor of Irene J. Winter by Her Students*, ed. Jack Cheng and Marian H. Feldman, 69–99. Leiden: Brill.

———. 2009. Stones of Ayanis: New Urban Foundations and the Architectonic Culture in Urartu during the 7th c. BC. In *Bautechnik im Antiken und Vorantiken Kleinasien*.

Internationale Konferenz 13–16 Juni 2007 in Istanbul, ed. Martin Bachmann, 177–97. BYZAS 9. İstanbul: Ege Yayınları.

Harries, Karsten. 2000. *The Ethical Function of Architecture*. Cambridge, Mass.: MIT Press.

Harrison, Robert Pogue. 2003. *The Dominion of the Dead*. Chicago: University of Chicago Press.

Hasluck, Frederick W. 1929. *Christianity and Islam under the Sultans*. Ed. Margaret Hasluck. Oxford: Oxford University Press.

Hauptmann, Harald. 1999. The Urfa Region. In *Neolithic in Turkey: The Cradle of Civilization. New Discoveries*, ed. Mehmet Özdoğan and Nezih Başgelen, 65–86. İstanbul: Arkeoloji ve Sanat Yayınları.

Hawkins, John David. 1992. The Inscriptions of Kızıldağ and the Karadağ in the Light of the Yalburt Inscription. In *Hittite and Other Anatolian and Near Eastern Studies in Honour of Sedat Alp*, ed. Heinrich Otten, Ekrem Akurgal, Hayri Ertem, and Aygül Süel, 259–74. Anadolu Medeniyetlerini Araştırma ve Tanıtma Vakfı Yayınları, Sayı 1. Ankara: Türk Tarih Kurumu Basımevi.

———. 1995. *The Hieroglpyhic Inscription of the Sacred Pool Complex at Hattusa (SÜDBURG)*. Archaeological intro. Peter Neve. Studien zu den Boğazköy-Texten Beiheft 3. Wiesbaden: Harrassowitz Verlag.

———. 1998. Hattusa: Home to the Thousand Gods of Hatti. In *Capital Cities: Urban Planning and Spiritual Dimensions*, ed. Joan G. Westenholz, 65–82. Jerusalem: Bible Lands Museum.

Hodder, Ian. 2006a. *Leopard's Tale: Revealing the Mysteries of Çatalhöyük*. London: Thames and Hudson.

———. 2006b. The Spectacle of Daily Performance at Çatalhöyük. In *Archaeology of Performance: Theaters of Power, Community, and Politics*, ed. Takeshi Inomata and Lawrence S. Coben, 81–102. Lanham, Md.: Altamira Press.

Hodder, Ian and Craig Cessford. 2004. Daily Practice and Social Memory at Çatalhöyük. *American Antiquity* 69.1: 17–40.

Johnson, Peri. 2010. *The Landscapes of Achaemenid Paphlagonia*. Ph.D. dissertation. University of Pennsylvania.

Joukowsky, Martha Sharp. 1996. *Early Turkey: An Introduction to the Archaeology of Anatolia from Prehistory through the Lydian Period*. Dubuque, Iowa: Kendall/Hunt.

Kafadar, Cemal. 2007. A Rome of One's Own: Reflections on Cultural Geography and Identity in the Lands of Rum. In *Muqarnas 24. History and Ideology: Architectural Heritage of the "Lands of Rum,"* ed. Sibel Bozdoğan and Gülru Necipoğlu, 7–25. Leiden: Brill.

Keen, Antony G. 1998. *Dynastic Lycia: A Political History of the Lycians and their Relations with Foreign Powers, C. 545–362 B.C.* Leiden: Brill.

Knapp, Bernard A. 2009. Monumental Architecture, Identity and Memory. In *Proceedings of the Symposium: Bronze Age Architectural Traditions in the East Mediterranean: Diffusion and Diversity (Gasteig, Munich, 7–8 May 2008)*, ed. Emma Blake and A. Bernard Knapp, 47–59. Weilheim: Verein zur Förderung der Aufarbeitung der Hellenischen Geschichte e.V.

Kohlmeyer, Kay. 1982. Felsbilder der hethitischen Großreichszeit. *Acta Praehistorica et Archaeologica* 15: 7–153.

———. 2000. *Der Tempel des Wettergottes von Aleppo*. Münster: Rhema.

Köroğlu, Kemalettin. 2008. Urartu Kaya Mezar Geleneği ve Doğu Anadolu'daki Tek Odalı Kaya Mezarlarının Kökeni. *Arkeoloji ve Sanat* 127: 21–38.

Kuhrt, Amélie. 1998. Old Assyrian Merchants. In *Trade, Traders and the Ancient City*, ed. Helen Parkins and Christopher Smith, 15–29. London: Routledge.

Last, Jonathan. 1998. A Design for Life: Interpreting the Art of Çatalhöyük. *Journal of Material Culture* 3.3: 355–78.

Lewis-Williams, David. 2004. Constructing a Cosmos: Architecture, Power and Domestication at Çatalhöyük. *Journal of Social Archaeology* 4: 28–60.

Lumsden, Stephen. 2002. Gavurkalesi: Investigations at a Hittite Sacred Place. In *Recent Developments in Hittite Archaeology and History: Papers in Memory of Hans G. Güterbock*, ed. K. Aslıhan Yener and Harry A. Hoffner Jr., 111–25. Winona Lake, Ind.: Eisenbrauns.

Matthiae, Paolo. 1997. Ebla and Syria in the Middle Bronze Age. In *The Hyksos: New Historical and Archaeological Perspectives*, ed. Eliezer D. Oren, 379–414. Philadelphia: University of Pennsylvania Museum of Archaeology and Anthropology.

Mazzoni, Stefania. 1997. The Gate and the City: Change and Continuity in Syro-Hittite Urban Ideology. In *Die orientalische Stadt: Kontinuität, Wandel, Bruch*, ed. Gernot Wilhelm, 307–38. Saarbrücken: Saarbrücker Druckerei und Verlag.

Mellaart, James. 1962. The Late Bronze Age Monuments of Eflatun Pinar and Fasillar near Beysehir. *Anatolian Studies* 12: 111–17.

Mellink, Machteld J. 1966. Anatolia: Old and New Perspectives. *Proceedings of the American Philosophical Society* 110.2: 111–29.

———. 1998. *Kızılbel: An Archaic Painted Tomb Chamber in Northern Lycia*. Philadelphia: University of Pennsylvania Museum of Archaeology and Anthropology.

Nakamura, Carolyn and Lynn Meskell. 2009. Articulate Bodies: Forms and Figures at Çatalhöyük. *Journal of Archaeological Method and Theory* 16.3: 205–30.

Naumann, Rudolf. 1971. *Architektur Kleinasiens von ihren Anfängen bis zum Ende der hethitischen Zeit*. Tübingen: E. Wasmuth.

Neve, Peter J. 1993. Hattusha, the City of the Gods and Temples: Results of Excavations in the Upper City. *Proceedings of the British Academy* 80: 105–32.

Nixon, Lucia. 2004. Chronologies of Desire and the Uses of Monuments: Eflatunpınar to Çatalhöyük and Beyond. In *Archaeology, Anthropology and Heritage in the Balkans and Anatolia: The Life and Times of F. W. Hasluck, 1878–1920*, ed. David Shankland, 2:429–52. İstanbul: Isis Press.

Özdoğan, Mehmet. 1998. Ideology and Archaeology in Turkey. In *Archaeology under Fire: Nationalism, Politics and Heritage in the Eastern Mediterranean and the Middle East*, ed. Lynn Meskell, 111–23. London: Routledge.

Özgüç, Tahsin. 1988. *İnandıktepe: Eski Hitit Çağında Önemli Bir Kült Merkezi—An Important Cult Center in the Old Hittite Period*. Ankara: Türk Tarih Kurumu Basımevi.

Özgüç, Tahsin and Mahmut Akok. 1958. *Horoztepe. An Early Bronze Age Settlement and Cemetery*. Ankara: Türk Tarih Kurumu.

Özyar, Aslı. 1999. Reconsidering the "Royal" Tombs of Alacahöyük: Problems of Stratigraphy According to the Topographical Location of the Tombs. *TUBA-AR* 2: 79–85.

———. 2006. A Prospectus of Hittite Art Based on the State of our Knowledge at the Beginning of the 3rd Millennium AD. In *Strukturerung und Datierung in der hethitischen Archäeologie/Structuring and Dating in Hittite Archaeology*, ed. Dirk Paul Mielke, Ulf-Dietrich Schoop, and Jürgen Seeher, 125–48. BYZAS 4. İstanbul: Ege Yayınları.

Peters, Joris and Klaus Schmidt. 2004. Animals in the Symbolic World of Pre-Pottery Neolithic Göbekli Tepe, South-Eastern Turkey: A Preliminary Assessment. *Anthropozoologica* 39.1: 179–218.

Roller, Lynn E. 1999. *In Search of God the Mother: The Cult of Anatolian Cybele*. Berkeley: University of California Press.

Roosevelt, Christopher H. 2009. *The Archaeology of Lydia, from Gyges to Alexander*. Cambridge: Cambridge University Press.

Rothman, Mitchell. 2001. *Uruk Mesopotamia and its Neighbors: Cross-Cultural Interactions in the Era of State Formation*. School of American Research Advanced Seminar series. Santa Fe, N.M.: School of American Research Press.

Sagona, Antonio and Paul Zimansky. 2009. *Ancient Turkey*. London: Routledge.

Sams, G. Kenneth. 2005. Gordion: Exploration over a Century. In *The Archaeology of Midas and the Phrygians*, ed. Lisa Kealhofer, 10–21. Philadelphia: University of Pennsylvania Museum of Archaeology and Anthropology.

Schachner, Andreas. 2006a. Auf welchen Fundamenten? Überlegungen zum Stand der Erforschung der hethitischen Architektur. In *Strukturerung und Datierung in der hethitischen Archäeologie/Structuring and Dating in Hittite Archaeology*, ed. Dirk Paul Mielke, Ulf-Dietrich Schoop, and Jürgen Seeher, 149–65. BYZAS 4. İstanbul: Ege Yayınları.

———. 2006b. An den Ursprung des Tigris schrieb ich meinen Namen—Archäologische Forschungen am Tigris-Tunnel. *Antike Welt* 37: 77–83.

Schmidt, Klaus. 2007. *Göbekli Tepe: En Eski Tapınağı Yapanlar*. İstanbul: Arkeoloji ve Sanat Yayınları.

Seeher, Jürgen. 2006. Chronology in Hattuša: New Approaches to an Old Problem In *Strukturerung und Datierung in der hethitischen Archäeologie/Structuring and Dating in Hittite Archaeology*, ed. Dirk Paul Mielke, Ulf-Dietrich Schoop, and Jürgen Seeher, 197–213. BYZAS 4. İstanbul: Ege Yayınları.

Sevin, Veli. 1994. Three Urartian Rock-Cut Tombs from Palu. *Tel Aviv* 21: 58–67.

Shaw, Wendy. 2007. Rise of the Hittite Sun: A Deconstruction of Western Civilization from the Margin. In *Selective Remembrances: Archaeology in the Construction, Commemoration, and Consecration of National Pasts*, ed. Philip L. Kohl, Mara Kozelsky, and Nachman Ben-Yehuda, 163–88. Chicago: University of Chicago Press.

Singer, Itamar. 1998. A City of Many Temples: Hattuša, Capital of the Hittites. In *Sacred Space: Shrine, City, Land*, ed. Banjamin Z. Kedar and R. J. Zwi Werblowsky, 32–44. New York: New York University Press.

Summerer, Lâtife. 2007. From Tatarlı to Munich: The Recovery of a Painted Wooden Tomb Chamber in Phrygia. In *The Achaemenid Impact on Local Populations and Cultures in Anatolia*, ed. İnci Delemen, 129–56. İstanbul: Turkish Institute of Archaeology.

Tanyeri-Erdemir, Tuğba. 2007. The Temple and the King: Urartian Ritual Spaces and Their Role in Royal Ideology. In *Ancient Near Eastern Art in Context: Studies in Honor of Irene J. Winter by Her Students*, ed. Jack Cheng and Marian H. Feldman, 205–25. Leiden: Brill.

Turnbull, David. 2002. Performance and Narrative, Bodies and Movement in the Construction of Places and Objects, Spaces and Knowledges: The Case of the Maltese Megaliths. *Theory, Culture and Society* 19: 125–43.

van den Hout, Theo. 2002. Tombs and Memorials: The (Divine) Stone House and Hegur Reconsidered. In *Recent Developments in Hittite Archaeology and History: Papers in Memory of Hans G. Güterbock*, ed. K. Aslıhan Yener and Harry A. Hoffner Jr., 73–91. Winona Lake, Ind.: Eisenbrauns.

Voigt, Mary M. and Robert C. Henrickson. 2000. Formation of the Phrygian State: The Early Iron Age at Gordion. *Anatolian Studies* 50: 37–54.

Woolley, C. Leonard. 1955. *Alalakh: An Account of the Excavations at Tell Atchana in the Hatay, 1937–1949*. London: Society of Antiquaries.

Woolley, C. Leonard and R. D. Barnett. 1952. *Carchemish. Report on the Excavations at Djerablis on Behalf of the British Museum. Part III: The Excavations in the Inner Town, and the Hittite Inscriptions*. London: Printed by order of the Trustees.

Yıldırım, Tayfun and Thomas Zimmermann. 2006. News from the Hatti Heartland—The Early Bronze Age Necropoleis of Kalınkaya, Resuloğlu, and Anatolian Metalworking Advances in the Late 3rd Millennium BC. *Antiquity* 80.309. http://www.antiquity.ac.uk/ProjGall/zimmerman.

Young, Rodney S. 1981. *The Gordion Excavations Final Reports Volume I. Three Great Early Tumuli*. Philadelphia: University of Pennsylvania Museum of Anthropology and Archaeology.

PART IV

THEMATIC AND SPECIFIC TOPICS

Intersecting Cultures: Migrations, Invasions, and Travelers

CHAPTER 29

EASTERN THRACE: THE CONTACT ZONE BETWEEN ANATOLIA AND THE BALKANS

MEHMET ÖZDOĞAN

THE interaction between Anatolian cultures and those of the Balkans is one of the most controversial topics in Anatolian prehistory, having been heavily debated for more than half a century. The main reason this subject has given rise to so much debate lies in the fact that the results are consequential for defining the formative history of Europe in general. More significantly, the discussion on the interaction between Anatolian and Balkan cultures is relevant to answering the question of whether the roots of European culture are to be found in the east. Additionally, along with factual matters, the debate has its political concerns. Nevertheless, the diversity between the Near Eastern and southeastern European schools of archaeology, uneven distribution of research in both regions, and lack of research in the contact zone between these regions have all hampered the development of a coherent picture. Still, it would be fair to note that the issues involved have been made to seem more complicated than they actually are. In this respect it is rather significant that the scholars working in Europe have been more concerned with defining the interaction between Anatolian and southeast European cultures than those working in Turkey. In the archaeological literature of Turkey, either descriptive or interpretive references to southeast European cultures are extremely rare (Esin 1979, 1981; French 1967; Kansu 1963; Mellaart 1960) and have been mainly noted in relation to the origin of Hittites and Phrygians. The lack of interest in the events that took place in the western periphery of Anatolia inevitably resulted in a lack of research in the region around the Sea of Marmara, the main contact zone between Anatolia and the Balkans. Thus, until about two decades ago, the discussions remained on a hypothetical level because concrete evidence was lacking. In the past two decades or so, there has been a considerable inflow of data from the northwestern parts of Turkey. This has provided, for the first time, concrete evidence on the interaction between the prehistoric cultures of Anatolia and the Balkans. Even more significantly, it has stimulated an interest among archaeologists working in Anatolia in the prehistory of southeastern Europe. This chapter presents a conspectus on the current state of the field and recent work.

Like the archaeology of the Near East and most of the Aegean, the archaeology of the Anatolian peninsula has gone through several recognizable stages since the early years of research, developing as more information became available (for an overview see Matthews, chapter 3 in this volume). The relative order of the cultural sequence, at least in its basics, had been set almost a century ago, and through time, hundreds of excavations coupled with the availability of new methods of research helped further elaborate the general picture. On the other hand, in southeastern Europe—even in the heartlands of the Balkans where hundreds of archaeological excavations have taken place—the relative sequence is far from being consistent, having no coherency either in the geographic distribution or in the definition of cultural entities. Accordingly, it is not possible to consider the development of archaeology in the Balkans as steady or coherent; on the contrary, it has evolved by fluctuating from one extreme theory to another, having had to go through revolutionary changes with the implementation of radioactive dating. In addition, considering the lack of concrete data from the contact zone between Anatolia and the Balkans, it was evident that the cultural interpretations were more speculative than they were factual.

As noted, the process of thinking about the relation between Near Eastern–Anatolian prehistoric cultures with those of the Balkan–southeast European cultures has gone through a number of contradictory stages. The history of research in the contact zone between Anatolia and the Balkans, as well as various aspects of the changing trends, has been extensively discussed in a number of publications (M. Özdoğan 1997, 2005, 2007, 2008a). Therefore, only major standpoints that have had consequences for our mode of thinking will be noted.

During the earlier years of research, there was a consensus that the beginning of sedentary life, food-producing economies, and the process of urbanization in southeastern Europe, as in western parts of Anatolia and the Aegean, had all been derived from the Near East through colonization. This diffusionist model, as best formulated by Gordon Childe, assumed that Near Eastern communities were able to begin colonizing the west only after attaining a certain cultural level. Thus a chronological baseline of 3400 B.C.E. was set for the beginning of sedentary life in western Anatolia and the Aegean; anything further west was evidently younger. With this view, Troy, in a critical strategic location, was considered to be a bridgehead for the Near Eastern expansion, and the Vinça culture was taken as its offshoot. Childe's diffusionist model (Childe 1951) was soon extended and applied to the point of designating equivalent cultural stages for the Aegean, based on the Near Eastern sequence. In particular, Milojçiç (1960) and Theocharis (1958, 1973) based on their work in Thessaly, designated the initial cultural stage as Aceramic, which was then followed by various Neolithic ceramic cultures. However, because they kept to the short chronology, the assigned duration of the cultural stages was considerably reduced, still sustaining the correlation between Troy and the Vinça culture. One of the consequences of this approach was the rapid increase in the number of prehistoric excavations in the Balkan peninsula, while research in western Turkey came to a standstill. This unequal distribution in research inevitably led to certain biases, which, coupled with political concerns, laid the basis for certain controversies that have continued up to the present.

The implementation of ^{14}C dates almost totally revolutionized the archaeological framework of southeast European prehistory, first by revealing that the previously assumed dates of the Balkan cultures were too recent. ^{14}C dates revealed that prehistoric levels are to be dated up to 3,000 years earlier than previously presumed, consequently invalidating the equation of Troy with Vinça. Revising the dates of the Balkan cultures by several thousand years, while keeping Anatolian dates of sites such as Alişar constant (M. Özdoğan 1996) led to the total collapse of all previous assumptions, including the diffusionist expansion model of Childe. This was soon replaced by an antidiffusionistic model, rejecting all impact originating from Anatolia and the Near East on the formation of European cultures, and, at the same time, propagating an autochthonous model for the emergence of prehistoric cultures in southeastern Europe, best exemplified in the phrase "ex balcanae lux." The antidiffusionistic model, after dominating the academic scene for about thirty years, has now been set aside, giving way to the return of the argument for Anatolian and Near Eastern origins for early European cultures. The commencement of new excavations in the western parts of Turkey, as well as developments in biogenetic studies (Bentley, Chikhi, and Price 2003) and paleolinguistics, has been instrumental in this change in thinking (Harris 2003; Pinhasi 2003; Renfrew 2002; Richards 2003; Richards et al. 2002; Zvelebil 2002, 2005). It is also interesting to note that while research in Turkey gained a new pace, work on the prehistory of the Balkans came to a standstill. At present, various new models have been suggested, ranging from waves of advance to moving frontiers to leapfrog movements to maritime expansion to infiltration to transfer of commodities and/or know how to other modes of expansion (Ammermann and Cavalli-Sforza 1984; Asouti 2007; Efe 2000; Nikolov 2002; Perlès 2005; Richards 2003; Runnels 2003; Sherratt 2004).

An Assessment of the Recent Excavations

Even though the area with which we are concerned covers the northwestern parts of Turkey, mainly eastern Thrace, which constitutes the main contact zone of southeastern Europe with Anatolia, it is necessary to have a supraregional overview to develop an understanding of the role played by this contact zone. There have been a number of recent volumes with extensive coverage on the Neolithic of Greece (Perlès 2001; Runnels 2001), Bulgaria (Bailey 2000; Nikolov 2003), and Turkey (M. Özdoğan and Başgelen 2007; Schoop 2005), as well as on the Bronze Age (Bailey and Panajotov 1995; Erkanal 2008; Nikolova 1996, 1999; Sagona and Zimansky 2009), revealing both detailed descriptions of the recently excavated sites with bibliographic references as well as a general assessment of the evidence, so I will specify and verify their significance instead of repeating this information. As noted previously, there have been no recent excavations in Greece and in the Aegean of prime concern for our understanding of the contact zone; thus, the conventional sequences of Thessaly and Macedonia continue to be the basis of the chronological framework, although more recent details are now available (Reingruber 2008; Wijnen 1982, 1993). Furthermore, the long-standing debate over the presence of an Aceramic period in Thessaly seems to be finally resolved since the presence of pottery sherds has been fully confirmed (Reingruber 2005). Recent work at Makri (Efstratiou 2006) has been more informative on the cultural landscape than on the cultural sequence. Likewise, in Bulgaria, the basic framework is still largely dependent on the Karanovo-Varna-Ezero sequence, with numerous excavations, mostly small scale, elaborating various details. It is worth noting the extensive work carried out at Drama (Lichardus 2000), Koprivets (Boyadzhiev 2006), Kovacevo (Lichardus-Itten et al. 2006), and Yablokovo (Leshtakov 2004, 2007), because they have provided ample evidence on the presence of a monochrome phase predating the painted pottery horizon of Karanovo I. Also worth noting is the work carried out at Derviş Ocak (Leshtakov 1997) that has revealed a Chalcolithic assemblage of the Pre-Cucuteni phase similar to what had been recovered previously in eastern Thrace. Concerning the Bronze Age in Bulgaria, the recovery of a rich Bronze Age cemetery at Dubene (Hristov 2005) is of interest in signifying the interface between the steppe and Anatolian metallurgical complexes. A group of imported Anatolian vessels recovered in a pit at Galabavo (Leshtakov 2002), though a limited assemblage, is worth considering, as it recalls the finds recovered at Kanlıgeçit in Eastern Thrace.

In spite of the stagnancy in prehistoric research in southeastern Europe, there has been an unprecedented increase in the number of excavations covering the entire span of prehistory in Turkey during the past two decades. First, excavations at Ilıpınar in the İznik region, Aşağı Pınar in eastern Thrace, and Ulucak near İzmir have provided the basis for establishing the framework for the sequence from the early Neolithic up to the Middle Chalcolithic period, while also revealing extensive information on critical issues such as site formation, cultural assemblage, and subsistence patterns (see Roodenberg, chapter 44 in this volume). Second, large numbers of other Neolithic excavations, including Hoca Çeşme, Yarımburgaz, Toptepe, and Yenikapı in eastern Thrace; Pendik, Barçın, and Aktopraklık in the eastern Marmara region; and Gürpınar, Yeşilova, Ege Gübre, Çukuriçi Höyük, Araplar, Çine Tepecik, and Heybeli Dedecik in western Anatolia have provided ample data on regional variants of the Neolithic cultures along the contact zone between Anatolia and southeastern Europe. In this respect, it is also worth noting excavations such as Çatal Höyük, Tepecik Çiftlik, Köşk Höyük, and Gelveri further east in central Anatolia, and Bademağacı in the Lake District that have revealed valuable new data from the core area of primary Neolithisation concerning the roots of the westward-moving Neolithic assemblages (see Özbaşaran, chapter 5, and Hodder, chapter 43 in this volume).

Troy still stands as the key site in understanding the Bronze Age cultures of northwestern Turkey. Recently resumed excavations at the site, while upgrading our knowledge through implementation of new technologies, have also drawn a new picture of second millennium B.C.E. state formation (see Jablonka, chapter 32 in this volume). Additionally, a number of recent large-scale excavations in western Anatolia, more specifically at sites such as Beşiktepe, Hacılartepe, Seyitömer, Küllüoba, Bademağacı, Yenibademli, Limantepe, and Baklatepe, have all revealed ample new data on the process of urbanization particular to the western sections of Anatolia and the Aegean (Çevik 2007; M. Özdoğan 2006). Among the later sites of the Bronze Age, the recovery of Minoan and Mycenaean horizons at Miletus, Ephesos, and Panaztepe has revived the discussion on the second millennium B.C.E. historical geography of western Anatolia (Latacz 2002), but at the same time has triggered a new debate on the ethnocultural identity of Troy (Hawkins and Easton 1996; Korfmann 1998; and Bryce, chapter 15 in this volume).

During the past two decades or so, there have also been significant achievements in understanding changes in the natural environment, especially its impact on cultural events (Wagner, Pernicka, and Uerpmann 2003; Yanko-Hombach et al. 2007), the most notable of which have derived from the salvage excavations at Yenikapı within the urban area of İstanbul (Kızıltan 2007). Here, the recovery of Neolithic habitation deposits at 9.5 m below the present level of the Sea of Marmara have, for the first time, provided concrete data on much debated issues, such as the transformation of the Marmara basin from a lacustrine environment to marine conditions. Likewise, due to the excellent preservation of organic material at Yenikapı, it has been possible to recover wooden artifacts, containers as well as plants and trees, thereby drawing an unprecedented picture of the natural habitat (Algan et al. 2007, 2009).

At present there is an overflow of new information from all over western Turkey to such a degree that it is no longer possible to work with the customary generalizations. The recent evidence is forcing the limits of our conventional knowledge, necessitating not only a new setup of the cultural sequence but also the development of new definitions. However, it is evident that for a proper assessment some time is necessary for these new data to sink in.

Cultural Sequence: An Overview

The Neolithic Period

It is now evident that the Neolithic way of life was introduced to the northwest after being fully developed elsewhere. This conclusion brings up two essential questions: were there Mesolithic communities in the region when the Neolithic communities arrived, and if there were, what was the mode of interaction among these two culturally distinct groups? In the present state of our knowledge, the evidence for Mesolithic habitation is mainly confined to the coastal areas, especially along the littoral areas of the Black Sea. A number of Mesolithic sites, known as the Ağaçlı group (Gatsov and Özdoğan 1994), are distinguished by a micro-blade industry akin to the so-called Epi-Gravette complexes of the circum-Pontic region. Besides the coastal strip along the Black Sea, sites of this group have also been recorded, though more sporadically, along the Sea of Marmara and northern Aegean. As no Mesolithic sites have yet been recovered from the inland areas, it seems possible to surmise that the Mesolithic communities were dependent on marine resources, though it should also be noted that the Mesolithic coastlines were much farther away than the present ones due to low sea levels of that time. Here, it is worth noting that both the present Sea of Marmara and the Black Sea, being cut off from the Aegean, were still in lacustrine conditions much lower than open seas.

The time of initial introduction of Neolithic communities in northwestern Turkey is rather difficult to determine with any precision at present, though there are some rather vague indications that the initial dispersal of a Neolithic way of life from the core areas in the east might have begun earlier than previously believed. The presence of the final stages of a Pre-Pottery Neolithic (PPN) stage are indicated by sites such as Çalca and Muslu Çeşme (M. Özdoğan and Gatsov 1998). All of these sites have revealed a lithic assemblage that is notably different from the Mesolithic Ağaçlı industry. Because no pottery has been recovered at those sites, it seems plausible to consider them indicators of the earliest Neolithic expansion taking place prior to the introduction of pottery. Furthermore, the recovery of a naviform core and associated blades at Küçük Çekmece, west of İstanbul (Aydıngün 2009), also seems to support this observation. Nevertheless, it also seems evident that the initial movement of the Neolithic way of life into the northwest was rather thin and sporadic; how far west into the Balkans it reached is, at present, not clear.

There is more reliable evidence on the establishment of Pottery Neolithic communities, which introduced basic components of the Neolithic package, such as village life and architecture, pottery, ground and polished stones, cultivated cereals, and domestic animals (figure 29.1). Actually the presence of this early pottery horizon has been known since the 1950s as the Fikirtepe culture through the excavations at Fikirtepe and Pendik (M. Özdoğan 1983). However, its chronological position within the Early Neolithic (French 1967; Mellaart 1955; M. Özdoğan 1983) to Late

Chalcolithic (Bittel 1970) periods was disputed. Recent work at sites such as Ilıpınar, Barçın, Menteşe and Aktopraklık, all located in the southeastern parts of the Marmara region, have now firmly defined the chronological position of the Fikirtepe culture in the second half of the 7th millennium B.C.E. The earliest available radiocarbon date for the Fikirtepe culture thus far, 6400 cal B.C.E., comes from Menteşe (Roodenberg et al. 2003). Given that Menteşe does not represent the earliest Fikirtepe Phase, it is possible to surmise a date around 6500–6600 B.C.E. for the beginning of this culture. Likewise, excavations such as Bademağacı, Ulucak, and Yeşilova in western Anatolia indicate that the dispersal of the Pottery Neolithic from its core area in central Anatolia had taken place by the beginning of the seventh millennium B.C.E. The latest dates for the Fikirtepe culture are around 5900 B.C.E., indicating that it was of long duration. Through this span of time, the Fikirtepe culture developed gradually, with no indication of a break or a clear distinctive line among its evolutionary stages. The earlier phases of the culture, also known as the

Figure 29.1. Major Neolithic assemblages of eastern Thrace. (a) Early monochrome pottery of the eastern Marmara region from Fikirtepe Classic Phase; bowls and an incised decorated rectangular vessel. (b) Early monochrome pottery of the eastern Marmara region from Hoca Çeşme Phase III–IV; red or black burnished wares. (c) Eastern Thrace pottery of Karanovo I–II stage from Aşağı Pınar layer 6. (d) Eastern Marmara region Yarımburgaz layer 4 pottery assemblage with incised, excised, impressed decoration.

Archaic Fikirtepe stage, are easily recognizable with pottery featuring a monochrome dark brownish to black surface that is highly burnished and consists mainly of hole-mouth profiled jars with heavy flat lugs placed horizontally.

During the next stage, known as Classical Fikirtepe, though most of the early elements continue, there is a gradual increase of red burnished wares with S-curved profiles and incised decoration. Rectangular vessels, the so-called cult tables, are common in both phases. Prestige items are rather rare and confined to bone spoons and belt hooks. The most particular feature of the Fikirtepe group is the lithic industry, mainly consisting of flint with a random usage of obsidian from undetermined sources. The lithic industry is characterized by fine bullet cores and pressure-flaked bladelets along with end, keeled, and round scrapers. Backed blades and geometric microliths are also present in lesser amounts. The lithic assemblage of the Fikirtepe culture differs notably from both the preceding Ağaçlı group, which shows an absence of pressure flaking and bullet cores (Gatsov 2005), and from the later Neolithic cultures, which lack micro-blades and are characterized by large blades (Gatsov 2009).

Assuming that the Fikirtepe culture represents the first wave of endemic movement of Neolithic communities into the contact zone between Anatolia and southeastern Europe, its interaction with local Mesolithic communities is of prime interest. In regions such as southern Marmara, where no Mesolithic sites are known, the earliest Fikirtepe habitation layers reveal the use of mudbrick architecture and buildings with rectangular plans, whereas in the region around İstanbul, where the most intensive sites of the Mesolithic Ağaçlı group existed, Fikirtepe settlements are comprised entirely of round or ovoid huts made of wattle and daub. It is highly significant that while the pottery, bone, and lithic assemblages are identical in both regions, those having rectangular mudbrick architecture are strictly dependent on farming, with very little evidence for hunting, whereas those with round wattle and daub houses have a mixed subsistence pattern, with extensive indications of hunting, fishing, and mollusk collecting along with some domestic animals. Likewise, grinding stones, and other ground and polished stone artifacts, though present, are rather scarce in the latter region. Yet another significant difference is in the burial customs; the former, as recovered at Ilıpınar and Aktopraklık, have extramural cemeteries (Alpaslan-Roodenberg 2008), whereas all the sites around İstanbul, including Fikirtepe and Pendik, have intramural burials below the floors of the huts. It seems possible to surmise that sites along the southern Marmara represent immigrant farmers, bringing with them a new way of life, with those around İstanbul involving the merging of local Mesolithic communities with the newcomers, either by living together or more possibly voluntarily adapting certain aspects of the Neolithic package, resulting in a mixed subsistence pattern but at the same time continuing their main mode of living. How far west into the Balkans the Fikirtepe culture expanded is not clear; the recovery of two sites with a Fikirtepe type of pottery in the Dardanelles indicates that there was at least a westerly expansion along the southern coast of Marmara. In Thrace, only a handful of typical early Fikirtepe sherds are known. Thus it is possible to assume that after encountering the local

Mesolithic communities in the region of the Bosporus, the pace of expansion either stopped or slowed down.

The immediate successor of the Fikirtepe culture is the Yarımburgaz 4 culture, initially recorded at the cave of Yarımburgaz in İstanbul, but now attested at a number of habitation sites, including Ilıpınar, Yenikapı, Demircihöyük, and Aktopraklık. The Yarımburgaz culture, basically covering the same region as Fikirtepe, is easily distinguished by its elaborately decorated vessels depicting complex textile-like designs. Regarding the Yarımburgaz 4 culture, the ongoing excavations at Yenikapı in İstanbul—which have revealed a number of extramural cremation burials, some in pots, others in cremation pits, together with well-preserved wooden artifacts and vessels—are significant. Among the wooden artifacts, a tray, a spear, two bows, and a harpoon-like object are considered the earliest examples of such items. The practice of cremation, the earliest known in Turkey and the Near East, is of interest, as a few cremation burials have also been reported from some contemporary sites in the Balkans (Bacvarov 2004). The Yarımburgaz culture continues more or less in the same region until about 5600 B.C.E., during which time a linear pattern of decoration on ceramics developed.

As has been briefly noted above, the primary introduction of Neolithic elements into Thrace could have taken place as early as the final stages of the Pre-Pottery Neolithic period. It also seems possible that this primary expansion of the Neolithic model continued up to the early stages of the Pottery Neolithic, though this expansion appears to have been very random. However, following this initial stage, there is a clear distinction between the events that took place in the southern and eastern Marmara regions and those occurring in Thrace, indicating a virtual borderline somewhere between sixty and eighty kilometers west of İstanbul. In Thrace, the earliest secure evidence of Neolithic habitation is in the so-called monochrome phase, as recovered at Hoca Çeşme Phase IV dating to 6400 cal B.C.E. and Aşağı Pınar Layer 8. The pottery of this stage is extremely fine, jet black or red colored, lustrously burnished, and is reminiscent of the so-called Dark Faced Monochrome Wares of central Anatolia. The composition of the cultural assemblage is notably different from that of the Fikirtepe and Yarımburgaz cultures. The difference is evident in the types of pottery vessels but more significantly in the lithic assemblage. Sites in Thrace totally lack micro-blades, bullet cores, and the pressure flaking technique. In fact, lithic material is rather scarce, with the only detectable artifacts being large blades. Pottery decoration is also rare and confined to shallow fluting, light incision, and applied motifs. Some of the applied designs are conspicuously similar to those of Köşk Höyük and Tepecik Çiftlik further east in the core area of Neolithisation (see Özbaşaran, chapter 5 in this volume). The settlements are rather small, consisting mainly of round buildings with wooden post structures. At least at Hoca Çeşme, the settlement is encircled by a massive stone wall, reinforced with a palisade.

At present, it is not possible to define the trajectory of the monochrome culture before reaching Thrace, though it clearly signifies an endemic movement. The location of Hoca Çeşme on the Aegean littoral, and the recovery of similar assemblages in the region of İzmir, strongly suggest a maritime route following the Aegean coast.

Further to the west, in Bulgaria, there are at least four sites, Koprivets, Krainitsii, the Polyanitsa plateau, and Yablokovo, where a pre–Karanovo I monochrome phase has been noted (Todorova 2003), implying that this wave of migration extended up to the Danube around 6200 cal B.C.E. if not earlier. However, it is also evident that it was not a dense movement.

To sum up the section on the Neolithisation process, it is evident that it was a much more complex and multifaceted event than considered previously. First, it was not an instantaneous event. On the contrary, it extended through a very long period of time, spanning a millennium, taking place in different waves of expansion, each one with its own trajectory and pace. Second, it is also evident that each wave had its own selection of the Neolithic package. Finally, and probably more significant, is the fact that different modes of Neolithisation such as endemic movement, colonization, acculturation, adaptation, and transfer of technologies and commodities, took place simultaneously. Thus in retrospect, all previous hypotheses on the expansion of the Neolithic way of life, regardless of the controversies, seem to have a measure of legitimacy.

The Transition from the Neolithic to the Early Chalcolithic

The dividing line between the Late Neolithic and Early Chalcolithic that has been set for the Near Eastern cultural sequence has no validity either in western Anatolia or in southeastern Europe, where there is an apparent continuum from the Late Neolithic up to the end of the Early Chalcolithic marked by the extensive presence of painted pottery (see Schoop, chapter 7 in this volume, for extensive discussion on the Chalcolithic in this region). During this period a new, much more intensive endemic movement from central Anatolia to the west took place, filling in the previously uninhabited regions from western Anatolia up to the Danube. From the Lake District in Turkey up to the Danube, over a thousand sites, all using highly burnished painted pottery, seem to have suddenly emerged (M. Özdoğan 2008a). These have been grouped under different cultural names, such as Hacılar, Sesklo, Karanovo I–II, Kremikovci, Gradesnitsa, Starcevo, Körös, and Cris, primarily according to differences in the stylistic composition of the painted decoration in the pottery assemblage. In a general overview, ignoring for the moment the presence of certain differences, they share common elements that are too specific to be considered coincidental. Among these are the extensive presence of steatopygic female figurines, decorated cult tables, anthropomorphic and zoomorphic vessels, stamp seals or the so-called pintaderas, festooned bone objects, bone spoons and spatulas, ear studs, marble or clay bracelets, and other objects. Almost all settlements of this stage display elements of typical farming villages composed of either agglomerated or closely placed massive rectangular structures. In regions closer to the core area, such as western Anatolia, the Aegean, and mainland Greece including Macedonia, the structures in the earliest layers are of mudbrick, occasionally with inner-buttressed walls. It is also worth noting that domed ovens, extensive storage facilities, and especially clay bins are among the markers of this stage.

The rather sudden appearance of so many habitation sites in this extensive geography, and the similarities in their material assemblage, indicate that the movement was rather dense, organized, and rapid. It is also worth noting that farther away from the core region, in the Balkans and in Thrace, some of the typical features become less prominent or stand as remnants of social memory. In this respect, the mudbrick gives way to wooden posts reinforced with wattle and daub, while the ratio and quality of fine painted wares drops, suggesting increased presence of local communities.

What triggered this massive wave of advance is not easy to discern; until recently it was assumed that overexploitation of the habitat by PPNB communities had resulted in an environmental disaster, initiating a massive migratory movement from the core regions (Rollefson and Rollefson 1990). However, there is now growing evidence that this turmoil might have resulted from a climatic event called the "8.2 or the Labrador climatic event," caused by a sudden overflow of the largest glacial lake of Agassiz, which drained catastrophically into the ocean due to the collapse of the Labrador ice barrier. This event, which took place about 6200 B.C.E., had major consequences on the ecological system, lasting for about 300 years. It is also postulated that during this period, the Balkans, Anatolian peninsula, and eastern Mediterranean lived through unstable climatic conditions mainly marked by climatic oscillations, disturbing the hydromorphological conditions, with years of drought broken occasionally by heavy floods, as marked by increased swamps in central Anatolia and extensive colluvial deposits in the Levant. The fact that the time of Neolithic expansion coincides with this climatic event (Alley and Ágústsdóttir 2005; Berger and Guillaine 2008; Roberts and Rosen 2009) is highly suggestive of an environmental impact that triggered mass movement from the core areas to the west. More evidence is needed to discern whether such movement was initiated solely by changing environmental conditions or whether it also involved some sort of a social turbulence.

In Thrace this stage is best represented at Aşağı Pınar in Layers 7 and 6, which reveal identical assemblages to Karanovo I and II, respectively, and indicate close ties between the two regions. At present Hoca Çeşme, where similar cultural layers have been noted in Phases III–II, is the only site of this culture located along the Aegean coast. On the other hand, understanding the relation between Thrace and the eastern Marmara region during this period is rather difficult. Chronologically, the Karanovo I–II horizon is contemporary with the Yarımburgaz 4 culture. However, at Aşağı Pınar, the easternmost known site of this culture, there is no single find reminiscent of the Yarımburgaz culture, nor is there any evidence around the Bosporus for any painted ceramics of Karanovo type. The causes of such a strict borderline are unclear.

The Middle Chalcolithic Period

An overall assessment for the Middle Chalcolithic period suggests that by 5600–5500 cal B.C.E., there is a marked change, both in cultural structures and in the material evidence (also see Schoop, chapter 7, and Düring, chapter 36 in this volume, for discussion), throughout the entire region covered by the previous painted pottery cultures. The last architectural layer of the previous stage is, at most sites, heavily burned, with some sites being deserted. Numerous new settlements appear, even in environmental zones consisting of high plateaus, which were not previously preferred. This suggests an increase in population. By this new stage, with the exception of some large plains such as the Konya Plain and Thessaly, red painted pottery gives way to dark colored, incised, or grooved decorated pottery. The new pottery assemblage (figure 29.2) now comprises more complex forms with tall-necked jars and sharply carinated shapes with heavy handles. Even though in the Balkans a number of local names have been attributed to this new cultural formation, it is more conveniently addressed as the Vinça culture. Where and how this culture originated is one of the most debated problems of Balkan history

Figure 29.2. Middle Chalcolithic pottery assemblage of eastern Thrace. (a) Toptepe assemblage of southern Marmara; pottery recovered in the building of layer 5 at Toptepe, depicting typical features of Toptepe culture with dull burnished micaceous slip, light incised decoration, and carinated forms. (b) Eastern Thrace, Yarımburgaz layer 2–3 assemblage, local white-filled incised wares, together with Toptepe-like vessel. (c) Northern parts of eastern Thrace, pottery assemblage of Aşağı Pınar layers 5–3, depicting a mixture of Karanovo III–IV and Toptepe styles. The anthropomorphic vessel on the right with human figures in relief is from layer 3.

(M. Özdoğan 1993; Srejoviç and Tasiç 1990). Some claim it developed locally in Anatolia and then dispersed to southeastern Europe (Efe 1990), whereas others have argued, to the contrary, for an origin in western Thrace (Nikolov 2004). Yet another theory suggests that it was introduced as an invasion from another region (Mellaart 1960). Nevertheless, it is not presently possible to discern an acceptable solution to this problem.

Regardless, at all three sites in the Marmara region (Aşağı Pınar Layer 5/6, Aktopraklık, and Ilıpınar V) where this transition could be detected, the heavily burned architectural layer of the preceding period, which consisted of rectangular houses, of either mudbrick or wattle and daub, was replaced by a layer with oval hut-like structures containing semi-sunken floors (see Roodenberg, chapter 44 in this volume). Even though this evidence is highly suggestive of an intrusion or invasion by an alien group, the pottery associated with these pit dwellings reflects an amalgamation of the early and late traditions, indicating that at least some of the craftsmen remained in this period. However, by 5350 cal B.C.E., with the completion of the so-called process of Vinçaization, components of the previous culture disappear completely. This period is represented at Aşağı Pınar in Layers 5–2 (Parzinger and Schwarzberg 2005), and at Yarımburgaz 1, and Hoca Çeşme Phase I (Bertram and Karul 2005). At these sites, the cultural profile is almost totally identical with that of the Veselinovo phase of Bulgaria; the steatopygous female figurines of the Neolithic period are now replaced by cylindrically shaped standing figures with small breasts. Throughout this stage, there are a number of distinct, locally developing traditions, among which the Toptepe group, named after the type site on the northern coastline of the Sea of Marmara (M. Özdoğan, Miyake, and Özbaşaran-Dede 1991) and related to the Paradimi group in Greece, seems to have expanded along the northern coastline of the Aegean.

In the later stages of this period, western and central Anatolia and the Balkans, once denominated as the "Balkano-Anatolian Culture Complex" (Garašanin 1997, 2000), seems to have split by the turn of the fifth to the fourth millennium B.C.E., with each area developing independently. Thus, the Sea of Marmara by the end of the Vinça Period becomes a cultural barrier separating southeastern Europe from Anatolia.

Late Chalcolithic Period

The fourth millennium B.C.E. is a period when important developments took place both in the Near East and in southeastern Europe, the former going through a rapid process of urban revolution and state formation, and the latter developing a very complex sophisticated culture known as the Cucuteni-Gumelnitsa group. In northern Bulgaria this epoch is highlighted by the rich cemetery finds of Varna and Durankulak, which now have secure dates extending down to 4200 cal B.C.E. (Pernicka et al. 1997). Although similarities between the Varna culture and that of İkiztepe on the central coastal region of the Black Sea strongly imply close ties between the northern Balkans and central Anatolia, the lack of similar evidence from the western parts of the Anatolian peninsula suggests a maritime connection through the coastal areas of the Black Sea rather than by way of a land route. The cultural formation further to the south of the Cucuteni-Gumelnitsa culture is known as the Karanovo VI–Gumelnitsa-Kocadermen culture in Bulgaria. This corresponds to the period when most of the mounds in Bulgaria increased in height. The only exception to this is the Meriç (Maritsa-Evros) basin near the present political border with Turkey. Nevertheless, Karanovo VI–Gumelnitsa sites are extremely rare in Greece and Turkish Thrace; when they do occur, they are extremely small, with no indication of any complexity. Likewise, the stratigraphic sequence at Aşağı Pınar terminates with the early stages of the Karanovo V period, which is marked by incised-grooved decorated wares of the so-called Maritsa culture.

Pottery typical of early Gumelnitsa type is known in eastern Thrace only from pits at Kanlıgeçit and Toptepe. Furthermore, surface survey of the region also indicates a lack of sites from the Gumelnitsa horizon. On the other hand, a very distinctive pottery, known as the Kocatepe group in eastern Thrace, can be dated to this period. The Kocatepe group primarily consists of cylindrical pot stands with elaborate curvilinear and/or linear motifs (M. Özdoğan 2004:figs. 1-2) reminiscent of the Pre-Cucuteni group of Moldavia. The scarcity of sites containing this distinctive pottery is noteworthy. It has been recorded at only a few sites scattered throughout eastern Thrace, all of which are either small, one-period, flat sites or large deep pits and are best known from Kanlıgeçit, Helvacı Şaban, and Kocatepe (M. Özdoğan 2004). Outside of Turkish Thrace, this pottery is known only from Derviş Ocak in Bulgaria (Leshtakov 1997), which is located in close proximity to the Turkish border with Bulgaria. It is also of significance that during the entire span of the fourth millennium B.C.E., there are no other sites or any material related to the Late Chalcolithic cultures that had emerged on the Anatolian side of the Sea of Marmara. This clearly indicates that the Marmara region became a cultural boundary for the expanding urban cultures of Anatolia during this period. It seems justifiable to consider that in this period Thrace was a buffer zone between two developing cultural centers, Tripolye-Cucuteni in the northern Balkans and the proto-urban Anatolian–Near Eastern center of southwest Asia (M. Özdoğan 2004). In this respect, note also that underwater research in Bulgaria has revealed the presence of at least a dozen submerged Late Chalcolithic and Early Bronze Age sites along the Black Sea coast (Draganov 1995), strongly suggesting that the water exchange through the Bosporus might have been interrupted for some time, probably due to a tectonic event, thus exposing an extensive coastal shelf in the western parts of the Black Sea providing an easy land route between the İkiztepe region and Varna.

The Early Bronze Age

The transition from the Late Chalcolithic to the Early Bronze Age in northwestern Anatolia, as in most parts of the Near East, marks the gradual development of urban centers. On the other hand, what happened in the Balkans is extremely complicated.

It is evident that the flourishing culture of the Gumelnitsa-Cucuteni groups had collapsed somewhere around 3500 B.C.E., possibly due to a massive invasion coming from the Eurasian steppes, putting an end to sedentary life, highly developed metallurgy, and the elaborately decorated pottery of the Gumelnitsa culture. This period of turbulence is known under different names in the Balkans, including Çernovoda, Salcutsa, and others; it is easily recognized by its rather coarse faced pottery. In eastern Thrace, this type of pottery has been recovered from Tilkiburnu (M. Özdoğan 1982), indicating that the impact of this event reached this region. Nevertheless, no indication of intrusive elements can be identified as having come from the south side of the Sea of Marmara.

The development of the Early Bronze Age (EBA) cultures on the Anatolian side is well attested through a number of excavations, with Troy still standing as the key reference site (see Jablonka, chapter 32 in this volume). During the earliest stages, EBA I–II, there are numerous sites using dark burnished handmade pottery throughout northwestern Anatolia. There is a marked change by EBA III, with earlier sites clustering into larger centers. During this stage, fine burnished red slipped wares appear, mainly as prestige vessels and plates, together with occasional use of the potter's wheel. In Thrace, however, sites like those in Anatolia, containing pottery of Troy or of Yortan types, are firmly restricted to the coastal band along the Sea of Marmara. Of these, Menekşe Çatağı is the only one that has been excavated (A. Özdoğan and Işın 2004). Further inland, both the types of sites as well as the pottery assemblages are identical with those in Bulgaria, reflecting local cultures grouped under different names, but conventionally known as the Ezero culture. Throughout the third millennium B.C.E. in Thrace and in most of the Balkans, the cultural process was notably different from that of Anatolia and the Aegean region, being based on animal husbandry (M. Özdoğan 2002). Settlement sites exist, but they are neither intensive nor show any hierarchical organization. The potter's wheel is not introduced until late in the Iron Age. The presence of numerous burial mounds or kurgan-type burials, as well as flint and obsidian arrow points, further supports the presence of steppic elements throughout Thrace during this period (Hristov 2005; Panajotov 1989). However, this does not imply that there was no contact with Anatolia and the Aegean. Some prestige vessels, including the so-called *depas amphikypellon* and metal objects, seem to have been traded. Additionally, the presence of metallic forms and pottery vessels imitating Yortan types, particularly during the Mihalic phase of the Bulgarian Early Bronze Age, exemplifies such contacts.

Presently, Kanlıgeçit (M. Özdoğan 2003; M. Özdoğan and Parzinger 2000; Parzinger and Özdoğan 1996) in eastern Thrace stands as the most unusual, and intriguing, Early Bronze Age site in Thrace (figure 29.3). This site, founded during EBA I and continuing into EBA II as a simple village, was constructed entirely of wattle and daub structures like all other sites in Bulgaria. However, by the beginning of EBA III, at around 2400 cal B.C.E., it had been completely remodeled in the Anatolian fashion with a fortified citadel comprised of mudbrick buildings with stone foundations. Four megara have also been recovered from this site, with the largest one measuring about twenty-six meters long, almost as large as the largest megaron

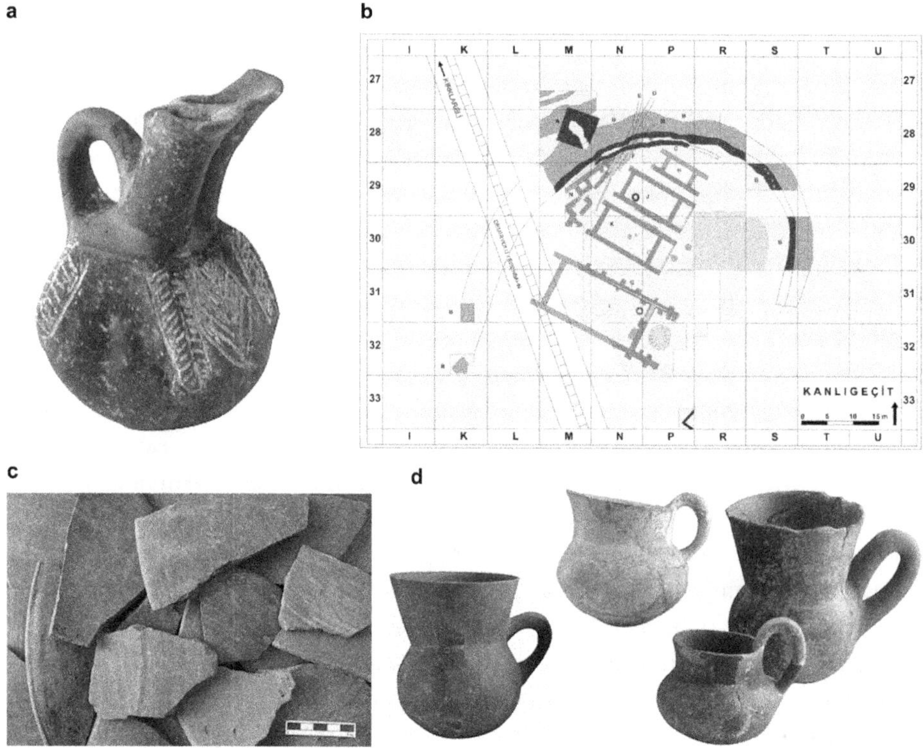

Figure 29.3. Early Bronze Age at Kanlıgeçit. (a). Double-spouted vessel of Yortan type from phase 2, early. (b) Plan of Kanlıgeçit citadel, phase 1–2. (c) Plain or red-slipped wheelmade plates, phase 2. (d) Juglets from phase 2.

in Troy. In addition to a citadel layout based on an Anatolian urban model, about 15 percent of the pottery consists of Anatolian red slipped and/or wheelmade wares in the form of the so-called Trojan plates. What is more striking is the extensive presence of domestic horse bones, which make up almost 15 percent of the total faunal remains (Benecke 2002, 2009). Whether Kanlıgeçit represents a colonial movement of Anatolian EBA cultures or is the reflection of a local élite imitating Anatolian urban centers by bringing in craftsmen is not clear. Nevertheless, it evidently rested on a trade route, which, considering the presence of horses, must be the forerunner of the caravan trade of the early second millennium B.C.E. (Efe 2007). Presumably, the site of Galabovo in western Thrace, which yielded Anatolian and Syrian imports (Leshtakov 2002) must also have been on this route. The Kanlıgeçit citadel was destroyed around 2050 B.C.E., and no further settlement took place anywhere in eastern Thrace in the Early Bronze Age.

The Middle and Late Bronze Age

During the rise of states and empires in Anatolia and in the Aegean, when the Hittites, Mycenaeans (Mountjoy 1997), and their allies were fighting with each other for the procurement of new territories (Niemeier 1998), Thrace remained almost devoid of any settled occupation, strongly suggesting the presence of nomadic tribes. Presumably some of the burial mounds date to this period. Accordingly, there was almost no detectable contact throughout the second millennium B.C.E. between the two sides of the Sea of Marmara. The only find attributable to this period is a metal hoard from Kozmandere, Şarköy (Harmankaya 1995), consisting of 140 metal objects, including a Mycenaean sword and some Anatolian-style bronze axes.

Early Iron Age and Middle Iron Age

By the beginning of the Early Iron Age, Thrace is conventionally considered to be the gateway for migrant groups, including the Phrygians, moving from the Balkans to Anatolia (Tuna, Aktüre, and Lynch 1998; see Sams, chapter 27, and Kealhofer and Grave, chapter 18 this volume). In this regard, the most concrete evidence is the presence of the so-called knobbed ware in layer VIIB2 at Troy (Koppenhöfer 2002), which is identical to the Early Iron Age pottery from the east Balkans and is more conveniently known as the Babadağ or Psenichevo group. Surface survey in Thrace has revealed hundreds of sites, all of which are rather small and hamlet-like, containing this type of pottery, with the easternmost site actually located within the city of İstanbul (Fıratlı 1973). The pottery of this period (figure 29.4), besides occasionally having horn-like projections, is characterized by cord-impressed, incised, and fluted decoration, with most vessels being black burnished. Furthermore, the distribution of these sites, with almost all occurring along river terraces or in low plains, is suggestive of a peaceful environment. It is also noteworthy that this type of pottery, so abundant all over Thrace and Bulgaria, is virtually absent elsewhere in Anatolia. The only exceptions to this are Troy and the small island of Avşa in the Sea of Marmara. Accordingly, it seems that if any group moved from the Balkans to Anatolia, it must have done so prior to the beginning of the Early Iron Age. Besides these small settlements, this period in Thrace is marked by the presence of numerous kurgan-like burial mounds and megalithic monuments (figure 29.4). All of these have been extensively documented for Bulgaria (Fol 1982). In eastern Thrace, excavations at the burial mound of Taşlıcabayır (M. Özdoğan 1987) have revealed the full range of the pottery assemblage. A sacrificial pit was discovered at Menekşe Çatağı (Erim-Özdoğan 2003), and the dolmen-like megalithic monument at Lalapaşa has been excavated (Akman 1999, 2010). These have all revealed pottery of a similar tradition. This culture seems to have continued up to the seventh century B.C.E. without any interference.

The Middle Iron Age sees the formation of Thracian culture. The cord-decorated knobbed ware gave way to coarse surfaced wares. Presently, no settlement sites are known, but numerous tumuli and sanctuaries have been recorded. Of these, the only sanctuary to have been excavated is at Aşağı Pınar (M. Özdoğan 2008b), where numerous sacrificial and votive pits have been discovered within a precinct encircled by a deep ditch. The invasion of the region from Persia seems to have put an end to this phase and to the prehistoric cultures.

Figure 29.4. The Early Iron Age. (a) A megalith from the highlands of Istranca region. (b) Four-spouted ceremonial vessel with cord-impressed decoration from the burial mound at Taşlıcabayır. (c) Vessels from Taşlıcabayır burial mound with cord-impressed, incised, or fluted decoration. (d) A megalith from Lalapaşa-Edirne region.

Conclusion

This chapter presented a conspectus on the prehistory of northwestern Turkey, mainly focusing on the role played by eastern Thrace at the intersection of Anatolia, the Aegean, and the Balkans. Indeed, this chapter could have been composed differently by following alternative trajectories—focusing on problems of stratigraphic sequences, changing technologies, subsistence patterns, or environmental concerns. Rather, the main substance has been to focus on the question of whether Thrace was a bridge or a barrier between the east and the west (French 1986), while acknowledging that there are substantial lacunae in our knowledge on every issue noted herein. Accordingly, what is reported here should not be considered conclusive, but more as general overview. Nevertheless, at least it is clear that the answer was much more complicated than implied by the question.

There are major problems in assessing the evidence from northwestern Turkey and the region known as eastern Thrace, first because it constitutes the buffer zone between distinct cultural entities: Anatolia, the Aegean, Balkan, and Pontic regions. Moreover, it acts as the narrow bottleneck to any sort of supraregional interaction, inevitably merging distinct cultures.

As has been noted, there are many cultural components easily recognizable in areas adjacent to Thrace; once they enter the Thracian region, however, they are altered before transmission to other regions to fit their distinct environmental conditions. Accordingly, tracing the origins of cultural entities in eastern Thrace is much more difficult than elsewhere, and it should also be considered that they are occasionally late or delayed reflections. Thus, it is evident that a narrative covering some 6,000 years in a buffer region is apt to be of a general nature, avoiding details and controversial issues. Thus, note that the actual picture is much more complex and multifaceted than what has been depicted here, and that to every observation, it is possible to find contradicting data; nevertheless, the present evidence allows insight into the position of Thrace in its supraregional framework. To conclude, evidently eastern Thrace, particularly in the process of Neolithisation and urbanization, is peripheral to Anatolia and to the Near East, but at the same time it becomes the core area of the European cultures. In this respect, in evaluating "core" and "periphery," it is necessary to use different criteria depending on the regions under consideration.

NOTE

Our thanks to INSTAP and in particular the Research Funds Commission of the Istanbul University for the support they have provided to our work in eastern Thrace.

REFERENCES

Akman, Murat. 1999. Megalithbauten im türkischen Thrakien. In *Studien zur Megalithik*, ed. Karl W. Beinhauer, Gabriel Cooney, Christian E. Guksch, and Susan Kus, 239–50. Weissbach: Verlag Beier und Beran.

———. 2010. Excavations and Restoration Work at the Lalapaşa Megalithic Monument. *Turkish Academy of Sciences Journal of Cultural Inventory TUBA KED* 8: 167–174.

Algan, Oya, Mustafa Ergin, Şeref Keskin, Erkan Gökaşan, Bedri Alpar, Demet Ongan, and Elmas Kırcı-Elmas 2007. Antik Theodosius Yenikapı Limanı'nın Jeoarkeolojik Önemi: Geç-Holosen Ortam Değişimleri ve İstanbul'un Son 10 bin Yıllık Kültürel Tarihi. In *Gün Işığında: İstanbul'un Sekizbin Yılı. Marmaray, Metro ve Sultanahmet Kazıları*, ed. Zeynep Kızıltan, 242–45. İstanbul: Vehbi Koç Vakfı Yayını.

Algan, Oya, M., Namık Yalçın, Mehmet Özdoğan, İsak Yılmaz, Erol Sarı, Elmas Kırıcı-Elmas, Demet Ongan, Özlem Bulkan-Yeşiladalı, Yücel Yılmaz, and İsmail Karamut.

2009. A Short Note on the Geo-Archeological Significance of the Ancient Theodosius Harbour (İstanbul-Turkey). *Quaternary Research* 72.3: 457–61.

Alley, Richard B. and Anna Maria Ágústsdóttir. 2005. The 8k Event: Cause and Consequences of a Major Holocene Abrupt Climate Dhange. *Quaternary Science Reviews* 24: 1123–49.

Alpaslan-Roodenberg, Songül. 2008. The Neolithic Cemetery. The Anthropological View. In *Life and Death in a Prehistoric Settlement in Northwest Anatolia. The Ilıpınar Excavations, volume 3. With Contributions on Hacılartepe and Menteşe*, ed. Jacob Roodenberg and Songül Alpaslan-Roodenberg, 35–68. Leiden: Nederlands Instituut voor het Nabije Oosten.

Ammerman, Albert J. and Luigi L. Cavalli-Sforza. 1984. *The Neolithic Transition and Genetics of Populations in Europe*. Princeton, N.J.: Princeton University Press.

Asouti, Eleni. 2007. Beyond the Pre-Pottery Neolithic B Interaction Sphere. *Journal of World Prehistory* 20: 1–40.

Aydıngün, Şengül. 2009. Early Neolithic Discoveries at İstanbul. *Antiquity* 83/320: Project Gallery.

Bacvarov, Krum. 2004. The Birth-Giving Pot: Neolithic Jar Burials in Southeast Europe. In *Prehistoric Thrace. Proceedings of the International Symposium in Stara Zagora 30.09–04.10.2003*, ed. Vassil Nikolov, Krum Bacvarov, and Peter Kalchev, 151–60. Sofia: Institute of Archaeology with Museum-BAS.

Bailey, Douglass W. 2000. *Balkan Prehistory*. London: Routledge.

Bailey, Douglass W. and Ivan Panajotov, eds. 1995. *Prehistoric Bulgaria*. Monographs in World Archaeology 22. Madison, Wisc.: Prehistory Press.

Benecke, Norbert. 2002. Die frühbronzezeitlichen Pferde von Kırklareli-Kanlıgeçit, Thrakien, Türkei. *Eurasia Antiqua* 8: 39–59.

———. 2009. On the Beginning of Horse Husbandry in the Southern Balkan Peninsula—The Horses from Kırklareli-Kanlıgeçit (Turkish Thrace). Turkish Academy of Sciences Journal of Archaeology *TÜBA-AR* 12: 13–24.

Bentley, R. Alexander, Lounès Chikhi, and T. Douglas Price. 2003. The Neolithic Transition in Europe: Comparing Broad Scale Genetic and Local Scale Isotopic Evidence. *Antiquity* 77.295: 63–66.

Berger, Jean-François and Jean Guillaine. 2008. The 8200 cal BP Abrupt Environmental Change and the Neolithic Transition: A Mediterranean Perspective. *Quaternary International* 200.1–2: 31–49.

Bertram, Jan-K. and Necmi Karul. 2005. From Anatolia to Europe: The Ceramic Sequence of Hoca Çeşme in Turkish Thrace. In *How Did Farming Reach Europe? Anatolian-European Relations from the Second Half of the 7th through the First Half of the 6th Millennium cal BC. Byzas* 2, ed. Clemens Lichter, 117–29. İstanbul: Ege Yayınları.

Bittel, Kurt. 1970. Bemerkungen über die prähistorische Ansiedlung auf dem Fikirtepe bei Kadıköy (İstanbul). *Istanbuler Mitteilungen* 19/20: 1–19.

Boyadzhiev, Yavor D. 2006. The Role of Absolute Chronology in Clarifying the Neolithisation of the Eastern Half of the Balkan Peninsula. In *Aegean-Marmara-Black Sea. Present State of the Research on the Early Neolithic*, ed. Ivan Gatsov and Heiner Schwarzberg, 7–14. Langenweissbach: Beier and Beran.

Childe, Gordon. 1951. *Man Makes Himself*. New York: Mentor Books.

Çevik, Özlem. 2007. The Emergence of Different Social Systems in Early Bronze Age Anatolia: Urbanisation versus Centralisation. *Anatolian Studies* 57: 131–40.

Draganov, Veselin. 1995. Submerged Coastal Settlements from the Final Eneolithic and the Early Bronze Age in the Sea around Sopozol and the Urdoviza Bay near Kiten. In

Prehistoric Bulgaria, ed. Douglass W. Bailey and Ivan Panajotov, 225–41. Monographs in World Archaeology 22. Madison, Wisc.: Prehistory Press.

Efe, Turan. 1990. An Inland Anatolian Site with Pre-Vinça Elements: Orman Fidanlığı, Eskişehir. *Germania* 68: 67–113.

———. 2000. Recent Investigation in Inland Northwestern Anatolia and its Contribution to Early Balkan-Anatolian Connections. In *Karanovo. Beiträge zum Neolithikum in Südosteuropa,* vol. 3, ed. Stefan Hiller and Vassil Nikolov, 173–83. Wien: Phoibos Verlag.

———. 2007. The Theories of the "Great Caravan Route" between Cilicia and Troy: The Early Bronze Age III Period in Inland Western Anatolia. *Anatolian Studies* 57: 47–64.

Efstratiou, Nikos. 2006. Looking for the Early Prehistory of Greek Thrace: Research Problems, Prospects and First Results. In *Aegean-Marmara-Black Sea. Present State of the Research on the Early Neolithic,* ed. Ivan Gatsov and Heiner Schwarzberg, 69–82. Langenweissbach: Beier and Beran.

Erim-Özdoğan, Aslı. 2003. Kuzeybatı Marmara'da Eski Bir Kıyı Köyü, Menekşe Çatağı. In *From Village to Cities Early Villages in the Near East I,* ed. Mehmet Özdoğan, Harald Hauptmann, and Nezih Başgelen, 217–32. İstanbul: Arkeoloji ve Sanat Yayınları.

Erkanal, Hayat, ed. 2008. *The Aegean in the Neolithic, Chalcolithic and the Early Bronze Age.* Ankara: Ankara Üniversitesi, Sualtı Arkeolojik Araştırma ve Uygulama Merkezi.

Esin, Ufuk. 1979. *İlk Üretimciliğe Geçiş Evresinde Anadolu ve Güneydoğu Avrupa I (G.Ö.10500–7000 Yılları Arası). Doğal Çevre Sorunu.* İstanbul: Edebiyat Fakültesi Basımevi.

———. 1981. *İlk Üretimciliğe Geçiş Evresinde Anadolu ve Güneydoğu Avrupa II (G.Ö.10500–7000 Yılları Arası). Kültürler Sorunu.* İstanbul: Edebiyat Fakültesi Basımevi.

Fıratlı, Nezih. 1973. The First Settlement of Byzantion. *Türkiye Turing ve Otomobil Kurumu Belleteni* 38.317: 21–25.

Fol, Alexander. 1982. *Megalithi Thraciae. Pars II. Thracia Pontica. Monumenta Thraciae Antiquae III.* Sofia: Nauka I Izkustvo.

French, David. 1967. Prehistoric Sites in Northwest Anatolia I. The İznik Area. *Anatolian Studies* 17: 49–100.

———. 1986. Anatolia: Bridge or Barrier? *Türk Tarih Kongresi (Kongreye Sunulan Bildiriler)* 9.1: 117–18.

Garaşanin, Milutin. 1997. Der späte balkanisch-anatolische Komplex. Ein Rückblick nach vier Jahrzehnten. *Starinar* 48: 15–31.

———. 2000. Zum Begriff des Balkanisch-Anatolischen Komplexes des Späten Neolithikums. In *Karanovo. Beiträge zum Neolithikum in Südosteuropa,* vol. 3, ed. Stefan Hiller and Vassil Nikolov, 343–47. Wien: Phoibos Verlag.

Gatsov, Ivan. 2005. Some Observations about Bullet Core Technique during 7th and 6th Millennium BC. In *How Did Farming Reach Europe? Anatolian-European Relations from the Second Half of the 7th through the First Half of the 6th Millennium cal BC. Byzas* 2, ed. Clemens Lichter, 213–20. İstanbul: Ege Yayınları.

———. 2009. *Prehistoric Chipped Stone Assemblages from Eastern Thrace and the South Marmara Region 7th–5th mill. B.C.* BAR International Series 1904. Oxford: BAR International Series.

Gatsov, Ivan and Mehmet Özdoğan. 1994. Some Epi-Palaeolithic Sites from NW Turkey: Ağaçlı, Domalı and Gümüşdere. *Anatolica* 20: 97–120.

Harmankaya, Savaş. 1995. Kozman Deresi Mevkii (Şarköy, Tekirdağ) Maden Buluntuları. In *Halet Çambel İçin Prehistorya Yazıları,* 217–54. İstanbul: Graphis Yayınları.

Harris, David R. 2003. Paradigms and Transitions: Reflections on the Study of the Origins and Spread of Agriculture. In *The Widening Harvest. The Neolithic Transition in Europe: Looking Back, Looking Forward*, ed. Albert Ammerman and Paolo Biagi, 43–58. Boston: Archaeological Institute of America.

Hawkins, J. David and Donald F. Easton. 1996. A Hieroglyphic Seal from Troia. *Studia Troica* 6: 111–18.

Hristov, Martin. 2005. Early Bronze Age Tumulus Cemetery at Dabene, near Karlovo (Preliminary Report). *Archeologia* 46: 127–37.

Kansu, Şevket A. 1963. Marmara Bölgesi ve Trakya'da Prehistorik İskan Tarihi Bakımından Araştırmalar. *Belleten* 27.108: 657–71.

Kızıltan, Zeynep, ed. 2007. *Gün Işığında: İstanbul'un Sekizbin Yılı. Marmaray, Metro ve Sultanahmet Kazıları*. İstanbul: Vehbi Koç Vakfı Yayını.

Koppenhöfer, Dietrich. 2002. Buckelkeramik und Barbarische Ware in Troia: Anmerkungen zur Herkunft. In *Festschrift für Manfred Korfmann. Mauerschau 2*, ed. Rüstem Aslan, Stephan Blum, Gabriele Kastl, Frank Schweizer, and Diane Thumm, 679–704. Remshalden-Grunbach: Verlag Bernhard Albert Greiner.

Korfmann, Manfred. 1998. Stelen vor den Toren Troias: Apaliunas-Apollon in Truisa/Wilusa? In *Light on Top of the Black Hill. Studies Presented to Halet Çambel*, ed. Güven Arsebük, Machteld J. Mellink, and Wulf Schirmer, 471–88. İstanbul: Ege Yayınları.

Latacz, Joachim. 2002. Troia-Wilios-Wilusa: Drei Namen für ein Territorium. In *Festschrift für Manfred Korfmann. Mauerschau 3*, ed. Rüstem Aslan, Stephan Blum, Gabriele Kastl, Frank Schweizer, and Diane Thumm, 1103–21. Remshalden-Grunbach: Verlag Bernhard Albert Greiner.

Leshtakov, Krassimir. 1997. Preliminary Report on the Dervishov Odzhak Rescue Excavations, 1993. In *Maritsa Project I*, ed. Krassimir Leshtakov, 75–146. Sofia: Publishing House "Roads Agency."

———. 2002. Galabovo Pottery and a New Synchronisation for the Bronze Age in Upper Thrace with Anatolia. *Anatolica* 28: 171–211.

———. 2004. Pottery with Incised and Channeled Ornamentation from the Early Neolithic Site at Yabalkovo in the Maritsa River Valley. In *Prehistoric Thrace. Proceedings of the International Symposium in Stara Zagora 30.09–04.10.2003*, ed. Vassil Nikolov, Krum Bacvarov, and Peter Kalchev, 85–93. Sofia: Institute of Archaeology with Museum-BAS. Regional Museum of History-Stara Zagora.

———. 2007. Preliminary Report on the Salvage Archaeological Excavations at the Early Neolithic Site Yabalkovo in the Maritsa Valley: 2002–2005 Field Seasons. *Anatolica* 33: 185–234.

Lichardus, Jan. 2000. *Forschungen in der Mikroregion von Drama (Südostbulgarien). Zusammenfassung der Hauptergebnisse der bulgarisch-deutschen Grabungen in den Jahren 1983–1999*. Bonn: Dr. Rudolf Habelt GMBH.

Lichardus-Itten, Marion, Jean-Paul Demoule, Lilijana Perniceva, Malgorzata Grebska-Kulova, and Ilija Kulov. 2006. Kovaçevo, an Early Neolithic Site in South-West Bulgaria and its Importance for European Neolithisation. In *Aegean-Marmara-Black Sea. Present State of the Research on the Early Neolithic*, ed. Ivan Gatsov and Heiner Schwarzberg, 83–94. Langenweissbach: Beier and Beran.

Mellaart, James. 1955. Some Prehistoric Sites in North-Western Anatolia. *Istanbuler Mitteilungen* 6: 53–72.

———. 1960. Anatolia and the Balkans. *Antiquity* 34: 270–78.

Milojçiç, Vladimir. 1960. Präkeramisches Neolithikum auf der Balkanhalbinsel. *Germania* 38: 320–40.

Mountjoy, Penelope A. 1997. Troia Phase VIf and Phase VIg: The Mycenean Pottery. *Studia Troica* 7: 275–94.

Niemeier, Wolf-Dietrich. 1998. The Myceneans in Western Anatolia and the Origin of the Sea Peoples. In *Mediterranean Peoples in Transition: Thirteenth to Early Tenth Centuries B.C.E.*, ed. Seymour Gitin, Amihai Mazar, and Ephraim Stern, 17–65. Jerusalem: Israel Exploration Society.

Nikolov, Vassil. 2002. Nochmals über die Kontakte zwischen Anatolien und dem Balkan im 6. Jt. v. Chr. In *Festschrift für Manfred Korfmann. Mauerschau* 2, ed. Rüstem Aslan, Stephan Blum, Gabriele Kastl, Frank Schweizer, and Diane Thumm, 673–78. Remshalden-Grunbach: Verlag Bernhard Albert Greiner.

———. 2003. The Neolithic and Chalcolithic Periods in Northern Thrace. *TÜBA-AR* 6: 21–83.

———. 2004. Dynamics of the Cultural Processes in Neolithic Thrace. In *Prehistoric Thrace. Proceedings of the International Symposium in Stara Zagora 30.09–04.10.2003*, ed. Vassil Nikolov, Krum Bacvarov, and Peter Kalchev, 18–25. Sofia: Institute of Archaeology with Museum-BAS.

Nikolova, Lolita, ed. 1996. *Early Bronze Age Settlement Patterns in the Balkans* (CA. *3500–2000 BC., Calibrated Dates*). Reports of Prehistoric Research Projects (vol. 1, nos. 2–4, April–December 1995 [1996]). Sofia: Prehistory Foundation. Agatho Publishers.

———. 1999. *Cultural and Ceramic Sequence and Chronology, The Balkans in Later Prehistory*. BAR International Series 791. Oxford: BAR International Series.

Özdoğan, Aslı and Mehmet A. Işın. 2004. Tekirdağ Menekşe Çatağı, Doğu Çatak Kazısı. *Kazı Sonuçları Toplantısı* 25.2: 421–34.

Özdoğan, Mehmet. 1982. Tilkiburnu, a Late Chalcolithic Site in Eastern Thrace. *Anatolica* 9:1–26.

———. 1983. Pendik: A Neolithic Site of Fikirtepe Culture in the Marmara Region. In *Beiträge zur Altertumskunde Kleinasien, Festschrift für Kurt Bittel*, ed. Rainer M. Boehmer and Harald Hauptmann, 401–11. Mainz: Verlag Philipp von Zabern.

———. 1987. Taşlıcabayır, a Late Bronze Age Burial Mound in Eastern Thrace. *Anatolica* 14: 7–39.

———. 1993. Vinça and Anatolia: A New Look at a Very Old Problem. *Anatolica* 19: 173–93.

———. 1996. Pre-Bronze Age Sequence of Central Anatolia: An Alternative Approach. In *Thomas Beran zu Ehren*, ed. Ursula Magen and Mahmoud Rashad, 185–202. Münster: Ugarit Verlag.

———. 1997. The Beginning of Neolithic Economies in Southeastern Europe: An Anatolian Perspective. *Journal of European Archaeology* 5.2: 1–33.

———. 2002. The Bronze Age in Thrace in Relation to the Emergence of Complex Societies in Anatolia and in the Balkans. In *Anatolian Metal II. der Anschnitt* 15, ed. Ünsal Yalçın, 67–76. Bochum: Bochum Bergbau Museum.

———. 2003. Kanlıgeçit. Une colonie anatolienne de l'âge du Bronze. *Néolithique, découverte d'un berceau anatolien. Dossiers d'Archeologie* 281: 82–86.

———. 2004. The Fourth Millennium in Eastern Thrace: An Archaeological Enigma. In *Zwischen Karpaten und Ägäis. Neolithikum und Ältere Bronzezeit*, ed. Bernard Hänsel and Etela Studeniková, 19–26. Rahden: Verlag Marie Leidorf GmbH.

———. 2005. The Expansion of Neolithic Way of Life. What We Know and What We Do Not Know. In *How Did Farming Reach Europe? Anatolian-European Relations from the Second Half of the 7th through the First Half of the 6th Millennium cal BC. Byzas* 2, ed. Clemens Lichter, 13–27. İstanbul: Ege Yayınları.

———. 2006. Yakın Doğu Kentleri ve Batı Anadolu'da Kentleşme Süreci. In *Cultural Reflections Hayat Erkanal'a Armağan*, ed. Armağan Erkanal-Öktü, 571–77. İstanbul: Homer Kitabevi.

———. 2007. Amidst Mesopotamia-Centric and Euro-Centric Approaches: The Changing Role of the Anatolian Peninsula between the East and the West. *Anatolian Studies* 57: 17–24.

———. 2008a. An Alternative Approach in Tracing Changes in Demographic Composition: The Westward Expansion of the Neolithic Way of Life. In *The Neolithic Demographic Transition and its Consequences*, ed. Jean P. Bocquet-Appel and Ofer Bar Yosef, 139–78. Heidelberg: Springer.

———. 2008b. Kırklareli Aşağı Pınar Kazısında Bulunan Arkaik Döneme Ait Bir Zar. In *Prof. Dr. Haluk Abbasoğlu'na 65. Yaş Armağanı: Euergetes II*, ed. İnci Delemen, Sedef Çokay-Kepçe, Aşkım Özdizbay, and Özgür Turak, 883–89. Antalya: Suna-İnan Kıraç Akdeniz Medeniyetleri Araştırma Enstitüsü.

Özdoğan, Mehmet and Nezih Başgelen, eds. 2007. *Anadolu'da Uygarlığın Doğuşu ve Avrupa'ya Yayılımı. Türkiye'de Neolitik Dönem: Yeni Kazılar, Yeni Bulgular*. İstanbul: Arkeoloji ve Sanat Yayınları.

Özdoğan, Mehmet and Ivan Gatsov. 1998. The Aceramic Neolithic Period in Western Turkey and in the Aegean. *Anatolica* 24: 209–32.

Özdoğan, Mehmet, Yutaka Miyake, and Nilgün Özbaşaran-Dede. 1991. An Interim Report on the Excavations at Yarımburgaz and Toptepe in Eastern Thrace. *Anatolica* 17: 59–121.

Özdoğan, Mehmet and Hermann Parzinger. 2000. Aşağı Pınar and Kanlıgeçit Excavations: Some New Evidence on Early Metallurgy from Eastern Thrace. In *Der Anschnitt 13. Anatolian Metal I*, ed. Ünsal Yalçın, 83–91. Bochum: Bochum Bergbau Museum.

Panajotov, Ivan. 1989. *Pit-Grave Culture in the Bulgarian Lands with Anthropological Study By Jordon Jordanov and Branimira Dimitrova*. Raskopii I Prrecvani 21. Sofia: House of the Bulgarian Academy of Sciences.

Parzinger, Hermann and Mehmet Özdoğan. 1996. Die Ausgrabungen in Kırklareli und ihre Bedeutung für die Kulturbeziehungen zwichen Anatolien und dem Balkan vom Neolithikum bis zur Frühbronzezeit. *Bericht der Römisch-Germanischen Kommission* 76: 5–29.

Parzinger, Hermann and Heiner Schwarzberg, eds. 2005. *Aşağı Pınar II. Die mittel-und spätneolithische Keramik*. Archäologie in Eurasien 18. Studien im Thrakien-Marmara-Raum 2. Mainz: Verlag Philipp von Zabern.

Perlès, Catherine. 2001. *The Early Neolithic in Greece*. Cambridge: Cambridge University Press.

———. 2005. From the Near East to Greece: Let's Reverse the Focus—Cultural Elements that Didn't Transfer. In *How Did Farming Reach Europe? Anatolian-European Relations from the Second Half of the 7th through the First Half of the 6th Millennium cal BC, Byzas 2*, ed. Clemens Lichter, 275–90. İstanbul: Ege Yayınları.

Pernicka, Ernst, F. Begemann, S. Schmitt-Strecker, H. Todorova, and I. Kuleff. 1997. Prehistoric Copper in Bulgaria. Its Composition and Provenience. *Eurasia Antiqua* 3: 41–180.

Pinhasi, Ron A. 2003. New Model for the Spread of the First Farmers in Europe. *Documenta Praehistorica* 30: 1–47.

Reingruber, Agathe. 2005. The Argissa Magoula and the Beginning of the Neolithic in Thessaly. In *How Did Farming Reach Europe? Anatolian-European Relations from the Second Half of the 7th through the First Half of the 6th Millennium cal BC, Byzas 2*, ed. Clemens Lichter, 155–71. İstanbul: Ege Yayınları.

———. 2008. *Die Argissa-Magula. Das Frühe und das Beginnende Mittlere Neolithikum im Lichte Transägäischer Beziehungen*. Bonn: Dr. Rudolf Habelt GMBH.

Renfrew, Colin. 2002. "The Emerging Synthesis": The Archaeogenetics of Farming/ Language Dispersals and Other Spread Zones. In *Examining the Farming/Language Dispersal Hypothesis*, ed. Peter Bellwood and Colin Renfrew, 3–16. Cambridge: McDonald Institute for Archaeological Research.

Richards, Martin. 2003. The Neolithic Transition in Europe: Archaeological Models and Genetic Evidence. *Documenta Praehistorica* 30: 159–67.

Richards, Martin, Vincent Macaulay, and Hans-Jürgen Bandelt. 2002. Analyzing Genetic Data in a Model-Based Framework: Inferences about European Prehistory. In *Examining the Farming/Language Dispersal Hypothesis*, ed. Peter Bellwood and Colin Renfrew, 459–66. Cambridge: McDonald Institute for Archaeological Research.

Roberts, Neil and Arlene Rosen. 2009. Diversity and Complexity in Early Farming Communities of Southwest Asia: New Insights into the Economic and Enviromental Basis of Neolithic Çatalhöyük. *Current Anthropology* 50.3: 393–94.

Rollefson, Gary and Karen Rollefson. 1990. The Impact of Neolithic Subsistence Strategies on the Environment. The Case of Ain Ghazal, Jordan. In *Man's Role in the Shaping of the Eastern Mediterranean Landscape*, ed. Sytze Bottema, 3–14. Rotterdam: Balkema.

Roodenberg, J., A. van As, L. Jacobs, and M. H. Wijnen. 2003. Early Settlement in the Plain of Yenişehir (NW Anatolia). The Basal Occupation Layers at Menteşe. *Anatolica* 29: 17–59.

Runnels, Curtis. 2001. The Stone Age of Greece from the Palaeolithic to the Advent of the Neolithic; Addendum 1995–1999. In *Aegean Prehistory. A Review*, ed. Tracey Cullen, 225–54. Boston: Archaeological Institute of America.

———. 2003. The Origins of the Greek Neolithic: A Personal View. In *The Widening Harvest. The Neolithic Transition in Europe: Looking Back, Looking Forward*, ed. Albert Ammerman and Paolo Biagi, 121–32. Boston: Archaeological Institute of America.

Sagona, Antonio and Paul Zimansky. 2009. *Ancient Turkey*. Oxon: Routledge.

Schoop, Ulf D. 2005. *Das Anatolische Chalkolithikum*. Urgeschichtliche Studien 1. Remshalden: Verlag Bernhard Albert Greiner.

Sherratt, Andrew. 2004. Fractal Farmers: Patterns of Neolithic Origin and Dispersal. In *Explaining Social Change: Studies in Honor of Colin Renfrew*, ed. John Cherry, Chris Scarre, and Stephen Shennan, 53–63. Cambridge: Cambridge University Press.

Srejoviç, Dragoslav and Nikola Tasiç. 1990. *Vinça and its World. International Symposium: The Danubian Region from 6000 to 3000 B.C.* Beograd: Serbian Academy of Sciences and Arts.

Theocharis, Demetrios R. 1958. Ek tis prokeramikis Thessalias. *Thessalika* 1: 70–86.

———. 1973. *Neolithic Greece*. Athena: National Bank of Greece.

Todorova, Henrieta. 2003. Neue Angaben zur Neolithisierung der Balkanhalbinsel. In *Morgenrot der Kulturen. Frühe Etappen der Menschheitsgeschichte in Mittel-und Südosteuropa. Festschrift für Nandor Kalicz*, ed. Erzsébet Jerem and Pál Raczky, 83–88. Budapest: Archaeolingua.

Tuna, Numan, Zeynep Aktüre, and Maggie Lynch, eds. 1998. *Thracians and Phrygians: Problems of Parallelism. Proceedings of an International Symposium on the Archaeology, History and Ancient Languages of Thrace and Phrygia (Ankara, 3–4 June 1995)*. Ankara: METU.

Wagner, Günther A., Ernst Pernicka, and Hans-Peter Uerpmann. 2003. *Troia and the Troad. Scientific Approaches*. Heidelberg: Springer-Verlag.

Wijnen, Marie-Hélène. 1982. *The Early Neolithic I Settlement at Sesklo: An Early Farming Community in Thessaly, Greece*. Leiden: Universitaire Pers Leiden.

———. 1993. Early Ceramics: Local Manufacture versus Widespread Distribution. *Anatolica* 19: 319–27.

Yanko-Hombach, Valentina, Allan S. Gilbert, Nicolae Panin, and Pavel M. Dolukhanov, eds. 2007. *The Black Sea Flood Question. Changes in Coastline, Climate and Human Settlement*. Dordrecht: Springer.

Zvelebil, Marek. 2002. Demography and Dispersal of Early Farming Populations at the Mesolithic-Neolithic Transition: Linguistic and Genetic Implications. In *Examining the Farming/Language Dispersal Hypothesis*, ed. Peter Bellwood and Colin Renfrew, 379–94. Cambridge: McDonald Institute for Archaeological Research.

———. 2005. Looking Back at the Neolithic Transition in Europe. *European Journal of Archaeology* 8.2: 183–90.

CHAPTER 30

ANATOLIA AND THE TRANSCAUCASUS THEMES AND VARIATIONS CA. 6400–1500 B.C.E.

ANTONIO SAGONA

ANATOLIA and the Transcaucasus are connected geographically. One is a peninsula jutting out into the Aegean and Mediterranean, the other an isthmus hemmed in by the Black and Caspian Seas. For the most part, both are jagged landscapes, defined by sweeping mountain chains and plateaus that enabled and constrained cultural development. Here, among the highest peaks of Eurasia, where east–west fracture lines have determined the main avenues of communication, life had its own deep rhythmic forces that affected societies in ways that were different to those in the drier and hotter lowlands and plateaus. Yet despite these environmental interconnections, the shared archaeology between Transcaucasia and eastern Anatolia, where one would expect the strongest pulses of commonality, remains largely fugitive (figure 30.1). Several factors have affected our understanding. The varying intensity of fieldwork on either side of the modern geopolitical border, different national traditions of archaeological research up until perestroika (Kohl 2007:1–22; Smith 2005:229–51), patchy dissemination of information during the Cold War, the many languages of academic discourse, the enduring notion that the Transcaucasus is a geographical borderland, confusing nomenclature that has pandered to nationalist interests (Rubinson 2005; Rubinson and Sagona 2008), and the vexed issue of chronology (Kavtaradze 1981), have all contributed.

The Neolithic and Early Chalcolithic

In studying the broader context of the Anatolian Neolithic, the attention of prehistorians in recent decades has been drawn toward southern and western connections. Comparisons with sites along the Levantine corridor and discussions on the spread of farming into southeastern Europe, for instance, are common. But the interchange with Transcaucasia, an area the Russian botanist Nikolai Vavilov (1952) defined as a center of the earliest cultivated plants, has been neglected.

As the Pre-Pottery Neolithic cultures flourished in Anatolia (ca. 9600–7000 B.C.E.), Mesolithic hunter and forager communities continued to traverse the Transcaucasian landscape for food and raw materials. The impressive monumental public buildings, vibrant art, and distinctive cultic practices of Anatolia, such as those revealed at Nevalı Çori and Göbekli (see Rosenberg and Erim-Özdoğan, chapter 6, and Schmidt, chapter 42 in this volume), are entirely missing in the Caucasus. Absent too are settlements of tightly packed rectilinear houses that are featured in central Anatolia (Sagona and Zimansky 2009:37–81). In Transcaucasia, the first expressions of a built environment are found in western Georgia and date to the second half of the seventh millennium B.C.E., which is where the transition from the Mesolithic to the Pre-Pottery Neolithic is traditionally placed (Kiguradze and Menabde 2004). Timber architecture and single-roomed, wattle and daub structures (known locally as *Patskha*) were erected along the coast of the Black Sea or nestled in the foothills and mountains of this humid landscape. Two subtraditions were defined using lithic technology: Anaseuli communities were situated mostly in the Colchis lowlands and preferred a blade technology based on cone- or bullet-shaped cores; the Paluri, on the other hand, is located in the foothills and is

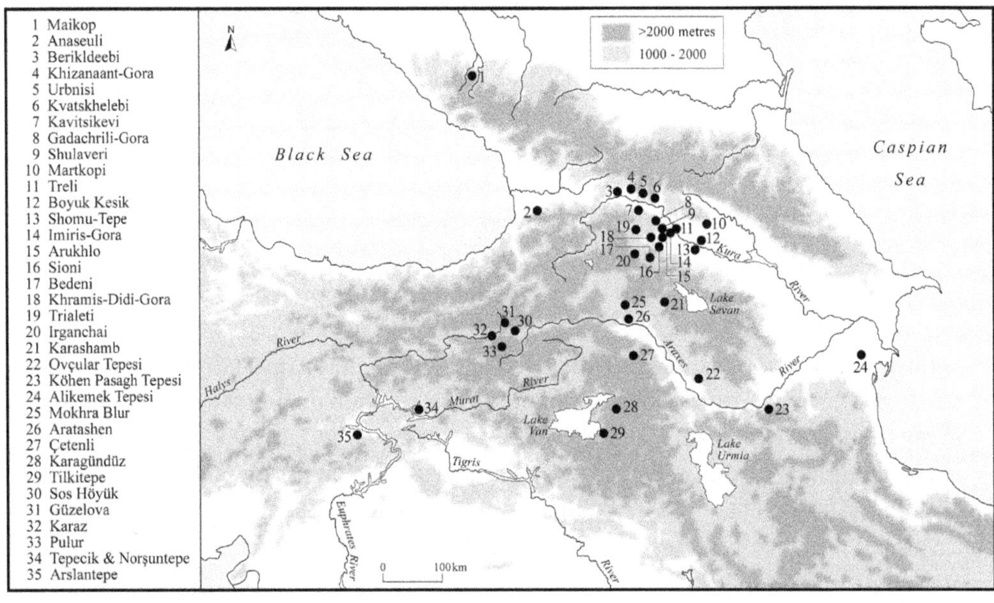

Figure 30.1. Map showing the key sites from the Neolithic through Middle Bronze Age.

distinguished mostly by flakes. One blade type in the Paluri assemblage, however, is noteworthy. Steeply retouched on one side with a hook-like extension, it has often been compared to the "Çayönü blade" (Grigola 1977). Whether the assemblage variability between Anaseuli and Paluri is functional or chronological is unclear. It will be interesting to see, however, whether these subtraditions will turn up along Turkey's eastern Black Sea littoral.

With the introduction of a farming economy, the tempo of cultural change is best observed in the Kura-Araxes interfluve, where some 150 ceramic Neolithic sites (also called "Eneolithic" in some publications such as Munchaev 1982) dot the landscape, from southeast Georgia and the steppes of western Azerbaijan, to the Ararat valley and the region of Nakhichevan. All of them are mound sites, and many are badly eroded or disturbed by modern land use. The majority are less than a hectare in area, though Khramis Didi Gora, in Kvemo Kartli, approaches five hectares (figure 30.1). Other sites of note include Shulaveris Gora, Imiris Gora, Gadachirili Gora, Arukhlo, Alikemek Tepe, Göy Tepe, Aknashen, and Aratashen (Badalyan et al. 2007; Badalyan et al. 2010; Hansen et al. 2006; Hansen et al. 2007; Kiguradze 1986; Kiguradze and Menabde 2004; Lyonnet and Guliyev 2010; Narimanov 1992). Curiously, these farmers did not choose the alluvium of the Iori and Alazani valleys, the most fertile areas in the Transcaucasus, but preferred the light chestnut soils, where dry farming of cereals involves a considerable amount of risk. The general increase in precipitation in the Neolithic no doubt enabled arable farming, but presumably the proximity to stands of wild cereals affected the choice of soils (Connor and Sagona 2007; Lisitsina 1978). Whatever the reason, these sedentary communities in the Kura-Araxes basin appear on the scene with a broad spectrum of crops (emmer, hulled barley, lentil, grass pea, and bitter vetch) and domesticated animals (Hansen et al. 2006).

Munchaev (1982) distinguishes two broad Pottery Neolithic groups based largely on differences in artifact assemblages: one is located in central Transcaucasia (Shulaveri-Shomutepe culture), whereas the other is mostly clustered in southern Transcaucasia (the Nakhichevan-Mil'sk-Mugani group). This division between sites in the Kura and Araxes basins has more or less been supported by recent fieldwork. In Transcaucasia, the Pottery Neolithic (ca. 6400–5000 B.C.E.) began later than in Anatolia, making it roughly contemporary with the Halaf period of Upper Mesopotamia. The settlements comprise compounds of round huts, measuring between 2.5 and 5.0 m in diameter, linked by low walls, which are associated with a series of hearths and smaller storage units that are generally smaller than 2 m in diameter (figure 30.2.1, 30.2.2). Walls had no stone foundations and are built from plano-convex mudbricks set with a mud mortar. At Aratashen bricks are combined with *pisé*, the latter recalling structures further south at Kültepe (Nakhichevan), and northern Iran (Haji Firuz and Dalma Tepe). Structure 22 at Alikemek Tepe Level III, a semi-subterranean circular building about three meters in diameter, is particularly noteworthy. Its lime-plastered interior walls yielded traces of a painted geometric design—circles, lines, dots, and U-shaped motifs—executed in fugitive red ochre (Narimanov 1992:52). Conceptually, these Neolithic settlements from Transcaucasia call to mind the "keyhole plan" of the Middle Halaf, leading some to conjecture a northern origin for the Upper Mesopotamian round house tradition (Dzhavakhishvili 1973; Mellaart 1975:203). That the Neolithic house form is round is significant because the transformation to a rectilinear plan is not simply one of shape and design but involves social behavior and economic structures. More acutely it involves different approaches to risk management. In Neolithic Transcaucasia individuals probably had their own single huts, and their communities preferred to share food and storage, as well as rewards and risks. Not so it seems in Anatolia, where by this time nuclear families were living in houses with a closed plan and private storage facilities.

The relatively small number of sherds found at Neolithic sites in the Transcaucasus suggests that the communities were not readily convinced that baked clay containers had advantages. The nine building levels at Shulaveris Gora yielded a mere seventy-five sherds, whereas at Aratashen only a handful of sherds make a tentative appearance in the earliest levels, IIa–d, increasing in number in Level I, though the total quantity still amounts to only a few hundred sherds (Palumbi 2007). Ceramics have several characteristics; jars with constricted mouths are popular, with bowls and plates practically unknown, and grit (or grog) are added to clay in the early stages, giving way to chaff later on. The earliest vessels have mottled surfaces, whereas later pottery demonstrates more controlled firing and is baked reddish-brown. The impression of a spiral-shaped mat on the bases from Kvemo-Kartli became a hallmark; initially, containers from Kvemo-Kartli were decorated with both incised and relief designs, but relief patterns (especially knobs) dominated, except at Aratashen and Aknashen where pottery is always plain.

Hardly any connections can be established between Shulaveri-Shomutepe pottery and those in neighboring regions, but certain bone tool types have a more widespread distribution. Bone and antler tools are abundant at Shulaveri-Shomutepe sites (figure 30.2.3), but the distribution is by no means homogenous. Antler hoes, for instance, so common at sites in Kvemo-Kartli, are absent from Aratashen (Badalyan et al. 2007). Anatolian connections are seen in the finely carved spoons (figure 30.2.4), which are found across the peninsula to Ilıpınar in the northwest where they are particularly common (Sagona and Zimansky 2009:fig. 4.21). Shaft-hole hammers made from antler bear a resemblance to those at Tilkitepe III, and piercing tools and spatulae are also part of the repertoire from both regions.

Once farming communities were established, Transcaucasia remained virtually closed to Near Eastern influence until the end of the sixth millennium B.C.E. The earliest firm link with surrounding regions is represented by Halaf pottery, fragments of which are mostly recovered from the late Neolithic levels in southern Transcaucasia. Five painted Halaf sherds and an almost complete carinated jar, manufactured from fine, pale brown clay and attributed to Aratashen I, are significant (Palumbi 2007). Similar wares are found in the Van Basin (Tilkitepe) and the Keban region (Tülintepe). Outliers of the late Halaf and subsequent northern Ubaid complex are also found in Nakhichevan, at Kültepe I, whereas in the lower layers at Alikemek Tepesi (figure 30.2.5, 30.2.6), in the Mugan valley of southeastern Azerbaijan, we have imitation forms bearing characteristics motifs—nested

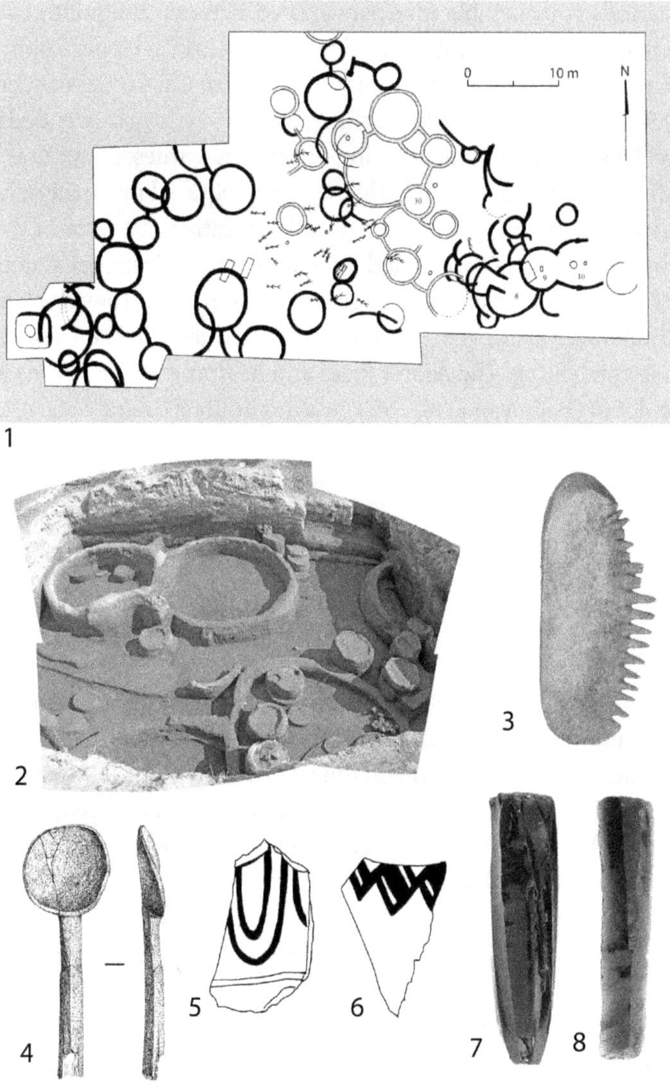

Figure 30.2. Characteristic dwellings and objects from the Transcaucasian Late Neolithic and Early Chalcolithic. 1, 7, 8, Imiris Gora; 2, 4, Aratashen; 3, Khramis Didi Gora; 5, 6, Alikemek Tepesi (images 2 and 4 courtesy of Ruben Badalyan).

triangles, zigzag lines, checkered rectangles, and so on—executed in black, brown, and red paint over a cream or pale brown slip (Chataigner 1995).

How, then, can we account for these earliest sedentary communities in Transcaucasia? The sudden appearance of a farming economy with no apparent antecedents and the use of plano-convex mudbricks to build dense compounds of circular houses are best explained as foreign elements. Whether these were adopted through contact with communities elsewhere, or the result of immigration is by no means clear. External contact becomes apparent in the Transcaucasus in the Late Neolithic and Early Chalcolithic periods. In Anatolia, we have known for some time that during the Halaf and Ubaid periods considerable interplay existed between the polities south of the Taurus Mountains and settlements located along the Turkish Upper Euphrates and its tributaries (Sagona and Zimansky 2009:125–27; and see Castro Gessner, chapter 35 in this volume). The most recent evidence shows that this network extended into southern Caucasus. Upper Mesopotamia during this period witnessed cultural integration in which craft production flourished. This, in turn, required raw materials, especially the much-prized obsidian (figure 30.2.7, 30.2.8), to satisfy the taste of the emerging élite. Long-distance trade networks and a formative organizational system, reflected in the use of seals, were established to cope with the demand. Though by no means as uniform and intensive as the networks that appeared later in the Uruk period, they were nonetheless far-flung. The Ararat Plain and its immediate environs with its rich sources of obsidian (Badalyan et al. 2004) was no doubt a desirable target.

The Late Chalcolithic and Early Bronze Age

In the Late Chalcolithic the dynamics between the Caucasus and Anatolia became more complex and involved several geographical regions: northwestern Caucasus, eastern Transcaucasia, and eastern Anatolia north and south of the Taurus Mountains (see Palumbi, chapter 9 in this volume, for additional discussion of the eastern Anatolian Chalcolithic). Within this zone several major cultural horizons overlapped, reflecting two broad stages of interaction, which must have involved localized population advances as well as the assimilation of foreign ways by indigenous communities. The first involved mainly the Maikop (the north Caucasus), Sioni (the south Caucasus), and Amuq E/F (Chaff-Faced Ware of Syro-Anatolia) traditions, whereas the second is defined by the immense Kura-Araxes horizon.

The degree to which the bearers of these traditions mixed, when they did so, and what prompted the communication are issues that remain pivotal to understanding the dynamics across the highlands during the second half of the fourth millennium B.C.E. As communities settled beyond the limits of the initial Neolithic settlement zone, utilizing new ecological niches, cultural differences became more evident. Despite their different characters, these new groupings were bound together in a number of social and economic networks.

The First Stage

Sioni (ca. 4800/4600–4000 B.C.E.)

The Sioni tradition is distinguished by pottery rather than settlements, which are few in number, rectilinear in plan, and mostly mudbrick in construction. The large building at Berikldeebi V2 and the structures at Leilatepe are the most notable

(Akhundov and Makhmudova 2008; Dzhavakhishivili 1998; Kipiani 1997). Ceramics comprise a somewhat amorphous group of grit-tempered vessels mostly with bulging bodies and straight cylindrical necks (Kiguradze and Sagona 2003). Rims are distinctive (figure 30.3.1). They are notched, impressed, incised, or wavy if viewed from the top. When decorated, containers were scratched with a comb-like tool, or had the occasional knobs and pellets applied to the exterior. Named after the site located in the Marneuli district in southeast Georgia, Sioni pottery has been attested at many sites in eastern Transcaucasia located in the Terek, Kura, and Araxes River basins. Among the most important deposits are the upper layers of Alikemek Tepesi, the lower levels at Berikldeebi, and Aratashen Level 0. Sioni sherds have been collected from the surface of sites in the Ağrı district, especially at Sarıgül and Çetenli (Marro 2008; Marro and Özfırat 2005), and excavated at Kohne Pasgah Tepesi, in the Koda Afarin Valley of northwestern Iran (Maziar 2010).

Here we should flag some recent and very significant discoveries made in western Azerbaijan, at Mentesh Tepe (Lyonnet and Guliyev 2010), which represent a new cultural phase in the fifth millennium B.C.E. Exhibiting a well-developed metallurgy—bone was hardly used to manufacture any tools—Mentesh has yielded a ceramic repertoire that can be distinguished by its type of decoration: painted, combed, and applied. The combed pieces bear affinities with Sioni, but the painted vessels had their design distinctly executed in bitumen. The importance of Mentesh lies in its emerging stratigraphy and radiocarbon dates that place it between the Shulaveri-Shomutepe culture and Leilatepe, yet showing ceramic connections with Sioni and Alikemek Tepesi.

Maikop (ca. 3800–3250 B.C.E.)

Maikop is a cultural horizon known from several hundred burials (*kurgans*) and a dozen or so settlements situated largely in the Kuban valley. The largest, the Oshad kurgan, situated in the town of Maikop, originally rose to a height of eleven meters. Its mortuary chamber was a wooden lined pit paved with stones and roofed with wooden planks. Excavated in the nineteenth century, it and other burials are known both for the wealth of precious objects and the tantalizing links they display with the distant lands further south. Certain items such as beads manufactured from lapis lazuli, carnelian, and turquoise were clearly imports, given that the sources of these semi-precious stones are in the Near East and central Asia. On the other hand, the metalwork—silver goblets, gold and silver bull standards, gold appliqués, beads, and jewelry—are generally attributed to local craftsmen and Near Eastern artistic inspiration (figure 30.3.2). Then there are the less eye-catching objects, namely, chaff-tempered clay vessels that could be easily accommodated into the Amuq E/F and Gawra XII–IX repertoires. These connections have generated considerable debate over chronology, which have placed Maikop between the fourth to the late second millennium B.C.E. Whereas art history favors a late fourth to early third millennium B.C.E. date, roughly contemporary with the Late Uruk Expansion, radiocarbon readings have pushed the beginnings of the Maikop culture to the

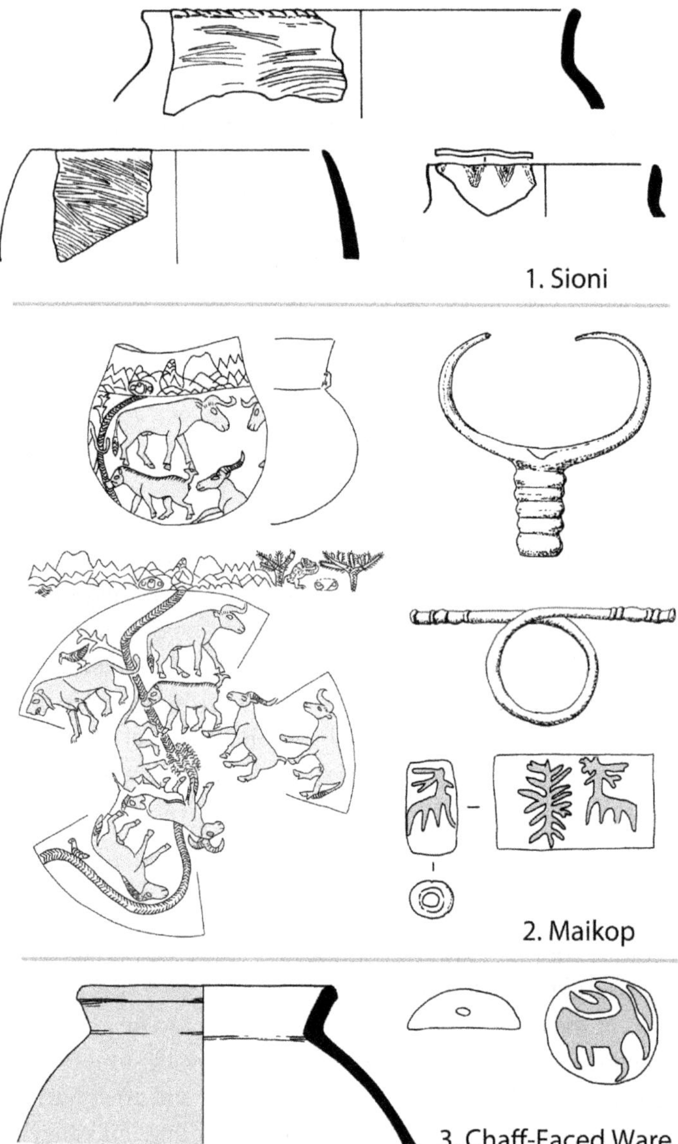

Figure 30.3. Selected objects from the Late Chalcolithic of Caucasia. 1, Pottery from Sioni; 2, Metal object, including a decorated silver bowl, and a cylinder seal from Maikop; 3, Chaff-Faced vessel and stamp seal from Leila Tepe.

beginning of the fourth millennium B.C.E. Somewhere between 3800 and 3250 B.C.E. is probably a reasonable time frame.

Chaff-Faced Ware (4000–3000 B.C.E.)

Chaff-Faced Ware of Amuq E/F, normally associated with northern Syria and Mesopotamia, has recently been identified in the east Anatolian highlands (Marro 2008, and see Marro, chapter 12 in this volume). These discoveries are significant because they provide another link between the regions south of the Taurus and Caucasus, where Chaff-Faced Ware has long been known at sites as far north as Maikop and Berikledeebi (in Shida Kartli), and eastward in Azerbaijan (Akhundov and Makhmudova 2008), sometimes in association with stamp seals (figure 30.3.3).

So how can we explain these fourth millennium B.C.E. connections between the Caucasus and the Syro-Anatolian regions? The emerging view is that they form part of the traffic in metals. Just as obsidian was probably the primary resource exploited in Halaf and early Ubaid periods, the quest for metal ores appears to have fueled this new wave of interconnections (see Muhly, chapter 39 in this volume). Philip Kohl (2007) has made the astute observation that if the origin of the Maikop complex can be dated to the early centuries of the fourth millennium B.C.E., it would coincide with the demise of southeastern Europe as a metallurgical center. The idea is that the center of gravity in metalworking may have shifted from the so-called Carpatho-Balkan Metallurgical Province to the Circumpontic Metallurgical Province (Chernykh 1992; Kohl 2007; Lyonnet 2007). There is certainly merit in this view. In addition to the architecture at Berikledeebi and Leilatepe, southern connections are attested at the settlement of Boyuk Kesik, the kurgans at Soyuq Bulaq in Azerbaijan (Akhundov 2007; Lyonnet and Guliyev 2010), which show a ritual of exposure of the dead, and the pre-Kura-Araxes kurgan at Kavitskhevi (Makharadze 2007). Whether this "pre-Uruk" Mesopotamian incursion into the Caucasus represents colonization (Akhundov 2007; Andreeva 1977), an unlikely scenario, migrant traders (Lyonnet 2007; Marro 2008), or some form of contact remains to be seen. Finally, attention must be drawn to the unfolding work at the extraordinary site of Duzdagi (Nakhchivan). A salt mine of vast proportions, it was first exploited during the second half of the fifth millennium B.C.E., making it one of the earliest such mines in the world (Marro et al. 2010). What exactly the communities did with such quantities of salt is still unclear, though ritual and symbolic usage, in addition to the utilitarian purposes, has been suggested.

The Second Stage

Kura-Araxes

Around 3500 B.C.E., another "phenomenon" expanded swiftly across the highlands. Known as the Kura-Araxes (or Early Transcaucasian), it is a horizon represented by the remains of hundreds of hamlets of agropastoral communities, spread across a vast area that stretched from the Turkish Euphrates to the Caspian Sea (Kohl 2007; Kushnareva 1997; Munchaev 1975; Sagona 1984). Southward it followed the arc of the Taurus and Zagros Mountains, extending down to the Amuq on one side and the Urmia basin through Godin Tepe to the Kangvar Plain on the other (Rothman 2008). A variant of this complex is found in the southern Levant, where it is known as Khirbet Kerak (Greenberg et al. 2006). There are many reference points, but a handful will suffice to illustrate the range. In the Turkish Upper Euphrates the Arslantepe, Norşuntepe, and Pulur (Sakyol) sequences are pivotal in defining the western facies and their interaction with Syro-Mesopotamian regions (Palumbi 2003, and Palumbi, chapter 9 in this volume). Further east, we have Sos Höyük, in the Erzurum province (Sagona and Sagona 2000), accompanied by the less differentiated sequences of Karaz, Pulur, and Güzelova. The Van Basin has the mound of Karagündüz (Kozbe 2004) and several recently discovered sites in the easternmost provinces (Marro and Özfırat 2005). In Nakhichevan, the renewed investigations at Kültepe II with its deep sequence, and at Ovçular Tepesi, an exclusively Late Chalcolithic and Early Bronze Age settlement, will be of great benefit (Bakhchaliyev, Ashurov, and Marro 2009; Bakhchaliyev, Ristvet, and Ashurov 2009). We await the publication of Mokhra Blur in the Ararat Plain, but in the meantime Badalyan and Avetisyan have provided an invaluable survey of material from Mt. Aragats and its environs (Badalyan and Avetisyan 2007). Georgia has a host of well-known sites (Sagona and Abramishvili 2008), though Kvatskhelebi still provides the best evidence for a complete settlement plan (Dzhavakhishvili and Glonti 1962). At the northeastern frontier, we can mention Velikent (Gadzhiev et al. 2000).

The Kura-Araxes expansion has generated considerable debate. Despite the aversion some researchers in the 1970s and 1980s had to the concept of migration, there is no doubt that population movements must explain, at least in part, the rapid spread of this distinctive material culture (Batiuk and Rothman 2007; Rothman 2003; and see Rothman, chapter 37 in this volume). A more recent view is the notion of a Kura-Araxes "package" that gradually crystallized through the active communication between communities across the highlands (Sagona and Zimansky 2009:163–64). It has been argued, for instance, that the red-black color scheme may be an Anatolian concept that moved eastward (Palumbi 2008, and Palumbi, chapter 9 in this volume), whereas certain pottery forms such as the biconical jars, or traits like the silvery, mirror-like burnish, may have emanated from Transcaucasia. The Kura-Araxes horizon spread so quickly that it has fostered the view, based largely on architecture and artifacts, that mobility was a key factor in the lives of these people, who have been portrayed as pastoral nomads. Yet as detailed studies of animal bones emerge, it seems that these communities did not specialize in pastoral production but preferred a diversified agropastoral economy that reflected stability and minimized risk (Howell-Meurs 2001; Piro 2009).

The Kura-Araxes horizon has a number of diagnostic attributes that vary regionally and chronologically, but its most distinctive is pottery. Manufactured by hand and fired to a contrasting red and black color, ceramics are sometimes ornamented with bold motifs, either applied or incised, and occasionally excised. The emergence of this horizon in the second half of the fourth millennium B.C.E. has prompted the provisional term "proto-Kura-Araxes" based on the Sos Höyük repertoire to distinguish it from the later third millennium B.C.E. (Early Bronze Age) repertoire (Kiguradze and Sagona 2003). Essentially, the earliest proto-Kura-Araxes pottery (3400/3300–3000 B.C.E.) is thin-walled, very well burnished, and occasionally ornamented with patterns incised after firing. Jars with tall, swollen necks attached to rounded bodies are typical. Ceramics produced in the first half of the Early Bronze Age, on the other hand, are often biconical in form with thickened walls and rail rims, and they are sometimes decorated with bold, double-spiral, relief patterns.

Houses vary, too, in both mode of construction and plan. They were built of mudbrick, or on a post framework with a daub filling, and even occasionally constructed of stone. Circular structures are more common eastward of Erzurum, whereas single-roomed, free-standing, rectilinear houses are found throughout the culture province. The focus of attention in each house is a central hearth, often with a cloverleaf-shaped center, fixed into the floor. The energy expended in constructing these hearths, which are often decorated with figurative images, and the well-crafted artifacts found within their context suggest that hearths played a central role in domestic religious ritual (Sagona and Sagona 2009). Portable hearths (or andirons) were also used and show a gradual evolution from the twin-horned variety to substantial horseshoe-shaped ones (Sagona and Zimansky 2009:fig. 5.20; Smogorzewska 2004). Other cultural attributes include standardized horned animal figurines molded from clay, well-crafted tools such as tanged projectile points, and a fairly limited range of metalwork (figure 30.4.1).

Interestingly, the large-scale economic transactions that the Late Uruk generated, drawing desirable products across vast areas, did not penetrate Transcaucasia as the earlier networks had. The expansive Kura-Araxes "culture province" was probably the main reason for this.

The Early Barrow Culture

During the second half of the third millennium B.C.E., communities across the highlands began to change their social and ritual behavior. In the archaeological record this transition is best reflected in Transcaucasia by the way communities treated their dead, who were no longer placed, often with few possessions, in flat graves such as simple earthen pits or stone-lined cists. Instead the deceased were now accorded a more elaborate funerary ritual, involving a mound of earth and stone. This complex and prolonged ritual not only suggests that certain members of society (or their families) wished for their legacy to resonate more conspicuously in the afterlife but also reflects changes in symbolic behavior. These new sites are known as barrow, tumulus, kurgan, and even *cromlech*, which are largely synonymous terms that refer to burial under a mound. They can vary in size and internal tomb architecture, depending on the status of the deceased.

The first flush of barrow burials, collectively known as "early kurgan cultures," should be distinguished from the later barrows, which are characterized by their large size and rich panoply (Bertram 2005). The early barrows at Trialeti comprised deep shafts covered with timber planks, whereas those at Martkopi, for instance, had substantial log burial chambers measuring up to 11 × 10 × 2 m superimposed by a mound that rose some 15 m above the ground. At Martkopi, either the dead were cremated or their bones were placed on a wooden platform. The burials were replete with symbols of power—objects of bronze (figure 30.4.2), now the universal medium

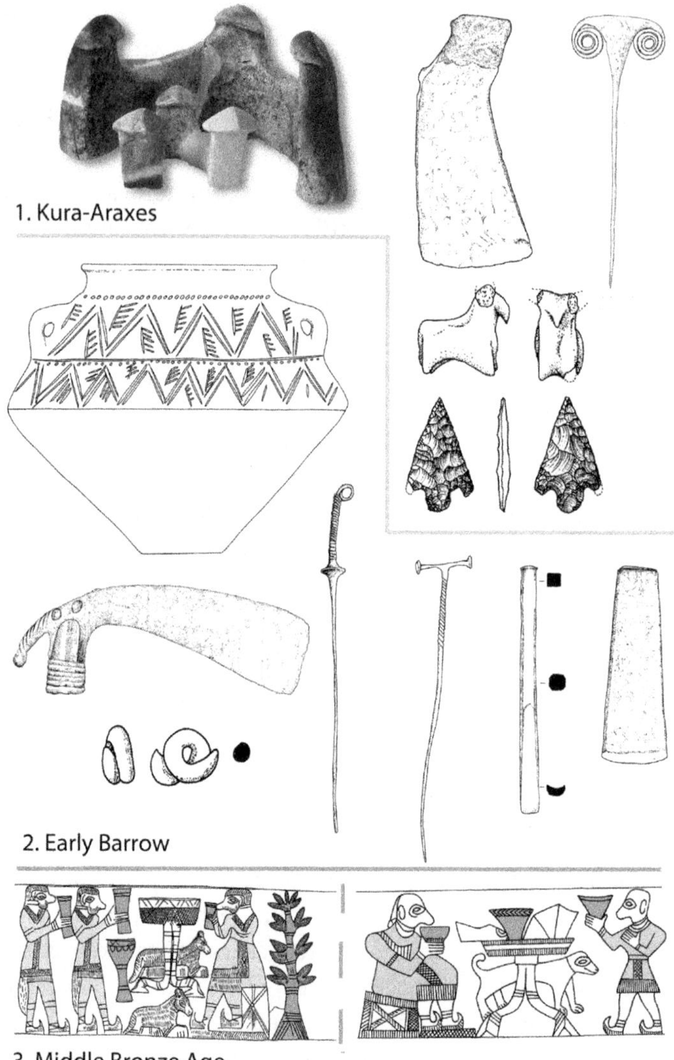

Figure 30.4. Selected objects from the Early and Middle Bronze Ages. 1, Kura-Araxes horizon; 2, the Early Barrow (or kurgan) phase; 3, the Middle Bronze Age, showing details of the Trialeti (left) and Karashamb (right) goblets.

of prestige, gold and silver jewelry, textiles, animal furs, well-finished pottery, and parts of (if not an entire) wheeled vehicle.

In Transcaucasia, this early barrow period has been further divided into three horizons—Martkopi, early Trialeti, and Bedeni—largely distinguished by nuances of pottery forms and decorations. Yet these terms often confuse rather than clarify. Martkopi and early Trialeti ceramics often bear similar traits, such as finely incised ornamentation (figure 30.4.2), which also distinguish late Kura-Araxes pottery (Sagona 2004). Indeed this question of when exactly the Kura-Araxes horizon ended is part of a continuous debate. On the basis of the new burial practices and the apparent invisibility of settlements, many researchers have placed the dividing line between Kura-Araxes and Martkopi in Transcaucasia at around 2500 B.C.E. Accordingly, the end of the Early Bronze Age is ascribed to 2000 B.C.E.

In eastern Anatolia, this transition is not so clear-cut. Evidence from Sos Höyük, in the form of a tight stratigraphy and radiocarbon dates, has challenged the conventional terminus ad quem for the Kura-Araxes horizon. Although no barrows exist at Sos Höyük, two intramural burials clearly belong to the Early Barrow tradition. One was found in the Early Bronze Age III deposits (Period VD) and was comprised of a pit grave two meters deep, which contained the disarticulated and arthritic remains of an elderly man (fifty to sixty years old), who also was buried with modest remains—a black, crudely incised jar and a shell ring. A later burial assigned to the subsequent Middle Bronze Age I (Period IVA) comprised an even deeper shaft—the resting place of a woman, who appears to have been bound at the hands and feet. An incised ceramic vessel of the early Trialeti horizon and a curious Y-shaped object that had been carefully hollowed from the branch of a deer's antler are the most noteworthy gifts. Most important of all, these burials were contemporary with *and* superimposed by Kura-Araxes houses that bear all the usual accoutrements—hearths, benches, and red-black pottery that has been called "Gritty Kura-Araxes." The latest Kura-Araxes architectural level at Sos Höyük has yielded radiocarbon dates well within the second millennium B.C.E. (Sagona 2000), suggesting that the demise of the Kura-Araxes horizon should not be viewed as a uniform occurrence across the highlands.

The north Pontic pit burial tradition is also apparent in central Anatolia, where the Early Bronze Age III "royal burials" at Alaca Höyük recall the earlier Maikop tradition and later Middle Bronze Age barrow burials from Transcaucasia such as Irganchai Barrow 5 and Treli Tomb 43 (Sagona and Zimansky 2009:213–17). The Alaca royal tombs yielded an extraordinary amount of disposable wealth in metals, and, like Maikop before it, its panoply served to express status, authority, and social inequality. The metalwork certainly has connections with the northern regions (Zimmerman 2007), but the tomb architecture and associated ritual are strikingly similar. The tombs at Alaca were rectangular pits roofed with wooden planks. Most had a single interment. The deceased lay in a contracted position surrounded by grave goods, including carts that have since perished except for metal components. Disarticulated animal bones strewn within the tomb and the careful placement of animal skulls and long bones on the wooden roof suggests that feasting must have formed part of the ritual.

We should now turn to a broad theme that embraces not only Anatolia and the Caucasus but also their neighbors, namely, wheel technology and the taming of the horse (Anthony 2007). Both are of fundamental importance in the history of human culture, advancing communications, transport, food production, and warfare. Both belong to the "Secondary Products Revolution," a stretch of time that saw wool being used for fabrics; the milk from cows, ewes, goats and mares being processed as a food component; and the use of traction and plough.

Where and when the first horses were domesticated, bridled, and ridden are contentious issues that draw on a range of information gathered from sites located in the vast steppes north of the Black and Caspian Seas from the Ukraine through Russia to central Asia. Recent evidence suggests that a pastoral people on the Kazakh steppes, bearers of the Botai culture, appear to have been the first to tame and ride horses—around 3500 B.C.E., a millennium earlier than previously thought (Outram et al. 2009). The compelling evidence comes in three categories: osteological (the Botai horses appear to have been more slender than the robust wild horses); marks on the horses' teeth, or "bit wear," which suggests that mouthpieces or bits were inserted for harnessing to control the animals; and carcass fat and fatty acid residues embedded on the inside of pottery containers, which suggests that the horses were eaten and mare's milk was fermented to produce the slightly alcoholic drink called *koumiss.* Until very recently, neither Anatolia nor the Transcaucasus had produced such compelling evidence for the early domestication of the horse. Emerging analysis from Çadır Höyük is changing that. Benjamin Arbuckle has shown the presence of early domesticated horses at Çadır in the early and late fourth millennium B.C.E. (Arbuckle 2009:196–200), effectively placing some of the north central Anatolian evidence comfortably earlier than the bones in Late Chalcolithic deposits at sites in the Turkish Upper Euphrates (Arslantepe, Norşuntepe, Tülintepe, Tepecik, and Değirmentepe) studied in part by Sándor Bökönyi (1987). Both sets of data can be placed within the period of earliest horse domestication, but the presence of wild horses on the central plateau throughout much of the Holocene raises the tantalizing possibility of an independent center of horse domestication in Anatolia.

As the horse was being domesticated, wheeled vehicles were invented. Fitted with four wheels of solid wood, these ponderously heavy wagons were pulled along by oxen. The earliest representations of a wheeled vehicle are found in the pictographic script of the Sumerians dated around 3100 B.C.E.; these vehicles are a modification of earlier sledges with a roofed cabin (Piggott 1983, 1992). At about the same time, images of wagons, incised on pottery, appear in Europe. However, the largest concentration of actual early wagons, solid four-wheeled vehicles pulled by oxen, is found in the steppes, stretching from Bulgaria to southern Russia. Over 250 of these early vehicles have been found in graves under barrows (or kurgans) of the so-called Pit Grave culture, which dates from 3100 to 2500 B.C.E., representing the earliest vehicle burials in prehistory.

The technology of wagons spread fairly quickly. They are found south of the Caucasus at sites like Martkopi, and in the late derivatives of the pit graves in Caucasus at Trialeti, in Georgia, and Lchashen, in Armenia, which date to the middle centuries of the second millennium B.C.E. The importance of these funerary rites is that they reflect a society with a hierarchical structure, which permits members of an élite to demonstrate their status by burials differentiated from others by the ostentatious display of dispensable wealth, including a prestige vehicle. In Anatolia, no actual ox wagons have been found, but the clay wheel model from Arslantepe VIA and clay models of wagons from the late third millennium

B.C.E. sites in the southeast suggest an awareness of the technology on the peninsula, too. The popularity of ox carts declined in the second millennium B.C.E. because of yet another revolution in the history of wheeled vehicles—the invention of the spoked wheel. Pulled by horses, these vehicles were lighter, faster, and more maneuverable.

The Middle Bronze Age

Impressive though these early kurgans are, the wealth of Bronze Age chieftains is most vividly expressed in the later burials, which Boris Kuftin, the first excavator of Trialeti, termed the "Brilliant Stage" of the Trialeti culture (Gogadze 1972; Kuftin 1948). To incorporate comparable material from Armenia, the term "Trialeti-Vanadzor" is often used (Avetisyan and Bobokhyan 2008). Collectively, the dazzling array of objects, both in terms of technical execution and iconography, reveal a fusion of local and foreign influences that reflect growing participation of the southern Caucasus in a far-flung system of exchange that extended to the shores of the eastern Mediterranean during the second millennium B.C.E.

Of the objects found in the wealthy kurgans of this period, two marvelous embossed silver goblets show, more than any other artifacts, a strong artistic connection between Anatolia and Transcaucasia (figure 30.4.3). One comes from Trialeti Kurgan 5, excavated in the 1930s. It consists of two friezes that depict a procession of humans and animals. The other goblet was found in the cemetery at Karashamb, in Armenia, in the late 1980s. Its imagery is more complex and portrayed in four registers. The human figures on both goblets have prominent noses and large eyes, but whereas the Karashamb figures are bald and clean-shaven, those on the Trialeti are bearded and have hairdos. Karen Rubinson has persuasively argued that the combination of certain iconographic details on the two goblets—shoes with turned-up toes (both goblets), figures with one arm flung up and the other down (Karashamb), seated figures (both goblets), furniture with hooved feet (both goblets)—derive directly from the glyptic tradition of the Old Assyrian Colony period, as reflected on the seal impressions from Kültepe Kaneš (Rubinson 2003, 2006). Others have argued that Mesopotamian influence is apparent in the iconography of the Trialeti and Karashamb goblets (Boehmer and Kossack 2000). The central Anatolian connections certainly make sense, and they suggest that the dynamics across the highlands in the early second millennium B.C.E. were east–west, as they were in the Kura-Araxes period, rather than north–south, as they tended to be in the pre-Kura-Araxes period.

The Trialeti culture is largely a central Transcaucasia phenomenon. In southern Transcaucasia, embracing much of Armenia, the Van Basin in eastern Anatolia, and the Urmia basin in northwestern Iran, an altogether different tradition emerged in the second millennium B.C.E. Distinguished by three main assemblages of painted pottery, known rather confusingly as Karmir-Berd (Tazakend), Kizil-Vank, and Van-Urmia, they stand in contrast to the ceramics of the Sevan-Uzerlik horizon, which are black burnished and decorated with punctate designs (Avetisyan and Bobokhyan 2008; Özfırat 2001). All three painted traditions are represented in eastern Anatolia, but the most common is the Van-Urmia. Whereas all painted vessels have a red-brown biscuit, they can be distinguished by their ornamentation, which is confined to the upper part of the vessel. There are many motifs, generally geometric and often empaneled, which are executed in either black paint that is applied directly on the red-brown surface, or as a polychrome (black, brown, and red) design on a thick cream slip. Polychrome vessels are characteristic of the Van-Urmia group.

Conclusion

The five millennia surveyed here have highlighted some broad patterns of cultural interaction. At present, evidence suggests that farming was introduced to the Transcaucasus. It appears fully fledged in the late seventh millennium B.C.E. together with compounds of round houses built for the most part with plano-convex bricks. We cannot ascertain the degree of interplay with surrounding regions, but it does appear that in these formative centuries Transcaucasian communities remained isolated and developed their own distinctive cultural identity. Attitudes changed in the Late Neolithic when Halaf networks made inroads into the mountains of southern Transcaucasia, probably to exploit the rich sources of obsidian. The tempo of communication accelerated during the Late Chalcolithic period. Initially, in the "pre-Uruk" phase, the dynamics were north–south, extending from Syro-Anatolia around the Van Basin all the way to the northern Caucasus to Maikop. This far-flung system was no doubt driven by the search for metals and semi-precious stones to cater to the tastes of the emerging élite. Later, judging by the swift appearance of red and black pottery in the Upper Euphrates in the second half of the fourth millennium B.C.E., the lines of communication shifted along an east–west axis and incorporated the vast expanse of the Anatolian highlands. Sites along the Euphrates and its tributaries became hubs of trade between highland communities and Uruk traders, who saw no more need to venture further into the Transcaucasus than did their predecessors. The introduction of kurgan burials ushered in a new phase of cultural development in the Transcaucasus. The earliest manifestations are detected in Erzurum, but the exuberance of the later Trialeti burials appears to be a local phenomenon, with little evidence that it infiltrated surrounding regions. Art historical connections between the iconography on the silver goblets from Trialeti and Karashamb and seal impressions at Kültepe Kaneš are compelling, to be sure, but we are none the wiser on the nature of that interaction.

REFERENCES

Akhundov, Tufan. 2007. Sites de migrants venus du Proche-Orient en Transcaucasie. In *Les cultures du Caucase (VIe-IIIe millénaires avant notre ère). Leurs relations avec le Proche-Orient*, ed. Bertille Lyonnet, 123–32. Paris: CNRS Éditions.

Akhundov, Tufan I. O. and Bafa A. G. Makhmudova. 2008. *Iuzhnyi Kabkaz v Kavkazsko: Peredneaziatskikh Etnokul'turnykh Protsessakh IV tys. do N.E. 4th Millennium B.C.* Baku: Elm. (In Russian with English summary.)

Andreeva, Marina V. 1977. K voprosu o yuzhnykh svyazakh maikopskoi kul'tury. *Sovetskaiia Arkheologiia* 1: 39–56.

Anthony, David W. 2007. *The Horse, the Wheel and Language: How Bronze-Age Riders from the Eurasian Steppes Shaped the Modern World.* Princeton, N.J.: Princeton University Press.

Arbuckle, Benjamin S. 2009. Chalcolithic Caprines, Dark Age Dairy and Byzantine Beef: A First Look at Animal Exploitation at Middle and Late Holocene Çadir Höyük, North Central Turkey. *Anatolica* 35: 179–224.

Avetisyan, Pavel and Arsen Bobokhyan. 2008. The Pottery Traditions of the Armenian Middle to Late Bronze Age "Transition" in the Context of Bronze and Iron Age Periodization. In *Ceramics in Transitions: Chalcolithic through Iron Ages in the Highlands of the Southern Caucasus and Anatolia*, ed. Karen S. Rubinson and Antonio Sagona, 123–83. Ancient Near Eastern Studies, Supplement 27. Leuven: Peeters.

Badalyan, Ruben and Pavel Avetisyan. 2007. *Bronze and Early Iron Age Archaeological Sites in Armenia, I. Mt Aragats and its Surrounding Region.* British Archaeological Reports, International Series 1697. Oxford: Archaeopress.

Badalyan, Ruben S., Armine A. Harutyunyan, Christine Chataigner, Françoise Le Mort, Jacques Chabot, Jacques Elie Brochier, Adrian Balasescu, Valentin Radu and Roman Hovsepyan. 2010. The Settlement of Aknashen-Khatunarkh, a Neolithic Site in the Ararat Plain (Armenia): Excavation Results 2004–2009. *TÜBA-AR* 13: 185–218.

Badalyan, Ruben, Pierre Lombard, Pavel Avetisyan, Christine Chataigner, Jacques Chabot, Emanuelle Vila, Roman Hovsepyan, George Willcox, and Hugues Pessin. 2007. New Data on the Late Prehistory of the Southern Caucasus: The Excavations at Aratashen (Armenia): Preliminary Report. In *Les cultures du Caucase (VIe–IIIe millénaires avant notre ère). Leurs relations avec le Proche-Orient*, ed. Bertille Lyonnet, 37–61. Paris: CNRS Éditions.

Badalyan, Ruben, Pierre Lombard, Christine Chataigner, and Pavel Avetisyan. 2004. The Neolithic and Chalcolithic Phases in the Ararat Plain (Armenia): The View from Aratashen. In *A View from The Highlands: Archaeological Studies in Honour of Charles Burney*, ed. Antonio Sagona, 399–420. Ancient Near Eastern Studies, Supplement 12. Leuven: Peeters.

Bakhchaliyev, Veli, Safar Ashurov, and Catherine Marro. 2009. The excavations of Ovçular Tepesi (2006–2008): First Results and New Perspectives. In *Azerbaijan—Land between East and West. Transfer of Knowledge and Technology during the "First Globalization" of the VIIth–IVth Millennium BC*, ed. Barbara Helwing, 55–58. (Abstracts of a symposium held in Baku, April 1–3, 2009). Berlin: Deutsches Archäologisches Institut, Eurasien-Abteilung

Bakhchaliyev, Veli, Lauren Ristvet, and Safar Ashurov. 2009. The Chronology of Kura-Araxes Sites: 2006 Excavations at Kültepe II and Maxta I. In *Azerbaijan—Land between East and West. Transfer of Knowledge and Technology during the "First Globalization" of the VIIth–IVth Millennium BC*, ed. Barbara Helwing, 82–84.

(Abstracts of a symposium held in Baku, April 1–3, 2009) Berlin: Deutsches Archäologisches Institut, Eurasien-Abteilung

Batiuk, Stephen and Mitchell Rothman. 2007. Early Transcaucasian Cultures and Their Neighbours: Unravelling Migration, Trade and Assimilation. *Expedition* 49.1: 7–17.

Bertram, Jan-Krzystof. 2005. Probleme der Ostanatolischen/Südkaukasischen Bronzezeit: ca. 2500–1600 v.u.Z. *TÜBA-AR* 8: 61–84.

Boehmer, Rainer M. and Georg Kossack. 2000. Der figürlich verzierte Becher von Karašamb. In *Variatio Delectat. Iran und der Westen. Gedenkschrift für Peter Calmeyer*, ed. Reinhard Dittmann, Barthel Hrouda, Ulrike Löw, Paolo Matthiae, Ruth Mayer-Opificius, and Sabine Thürwächter, 9–71. Alter Orient und Altes Testament, Bd. 272. Münster: Ugarit Verlag.

Bökönyi, Sándor. 1987. Late Chalcolithic Horses in Anatolia. In *Equids in the Ancient World*, ed. Richard H. Meadow and Hans-Peter Uerpmann, 123–31. Beihefte zum Tübinger Atlas des Vorderen Orients. Reihe A, Naturwissenschaften 19/1–2. Wiesbaden: Ludwig Reichert.

Chataigner, Christine. 1995. *La Transcaucasie au Néolithique et au Chalcolithique*. British Archaeological Reports, International Series 624. Oxford: Tempus Reparatum.

Chernykh, Evgenii N. 1992. *Ancient Metallurgy in the USSR*. Cambridge: Cambridge University Press.

Connor, Simon and Antonio Sagona,. 2007. Environment and Society in the Late Prehistory of Southern Georgia, Caucasus. In *Les cultures du Caucase (VI–IIIème millénaires av. notre ère). Leurs relations avec le Proche-Orient*, ed. Bertille Lyonnet, 21–36. Paris: CNRS Éditions.

Dzhavakhishvili, Aleksandr I. 1973. *Stroitelnoye Delo i Arkhitektura Poseleniy Yuzhnogo Kavkaza v. V–III tys. do. n. e.* (In Russian.) Tbilisi: Metsniereba.

———. 1998. Ausgrabungen in Berikldeebi (Shida Kartli). *Georgica* 21: 7–21.

Dzhavakhishvili, Aleksandr I. and Lili I. Glonti. 1962. *Urbnisi I: arkheologicheskie raskopi provedennye v. 1954–1961gg. na selishche Kvatskhelebi (Tvlenia-Kokhi).* (In Georgian with a Russian summary.) Tbilisi: Akademia nauk Gruzinskoi SSR.

Gadzhiev, Magomed, Philip L. Kohl, D. Magomedov, David Stronach, and Sh. Gadzhiev. 2000. Daghestan-American Archaeological Investigations in Daghestan, Russia 1997–99. *Eurasia Antiqua* 6: 47–123.

Gogadze, Elguja M. 1972. *Periodizatsiia i genezis kurgannoi kul'tury Trialeti.* (In Georgian with a Russian summary.) Tbilisi. Metsniereba.

Greenberg, Raphael, Emanuel Eisenberg, Sarit Paz, and Yitzhak Paz. 2006. *Bet Yerah: The Early Bronze Age Mound. Vol. 1. Excavation Reports, 1933–1986.* Israel Antiquities Authority Reports, 30. Jerusalem: Israel Antiquities Authority.

Grigola, Guram. 1977. *Neolit Tsentral'noi Kolkhidy Paluri*. Tbilisi: Metsniereba.

Hansen, Sven, Guram Mirtskhulava, Katrin Bastert-Lamprichs, Norbert Benecke, Ivan Gatsov, and Petranka Nedelcheva. 2006. Aruchlo 2005–2006: Bericht über die Ausgrabungen in einem neolithischen Siedlungshügel. *Archäologische Mitteilungen aus Iran und Turan* 38: 1–34.

Hansen, Sven, Guram Mirtskhulava, Katrin Bastert-Lamprichs, Jochen Görsdorf, Daniel Neumann, Michael Ullrich, Ivan Gatsov, and Petranka Nedelcheva. 2007. Aruchlo 2007: Bericht über die Ausgrabungen in einem neolithischen Siedlungshügel. *Archäologische Mitteilungen aus Iran und Turan* 39: 1–30.

Howell-Meurs, Sarah. 2001. *Early Bronze Age and Iron Age Animal Exploitation in Northeastern Anatolia: The Faunal Remains from Sos Höyük and Büyüktepe Höyük*. British Archaeological Reports, International Series 945. Oxford: Archaeopress.

Kavtaradze, Giorgi L. 1981. *Khronologiia Arkheologicheskikh Kul'tur Gruzii Epokhi Eneolita i Bronzi v Svete Novykh Dannykh.* (In Georgian with Russian and English summaries.) Tbilisi: Metsniereba.

Kiguradze, Tamaz. 1986. *Neolithische Siedlungen von Kvemo-Kartli, Georgien. Materialien zur Allgemeinen und Vergleichenden Archäologie,* 29. Munich: C. H. Beck.

Kiguradze, Tamaz and Medea Menabde. 2004. The Neolithic of Georgia. In *A View from the Highlands: Archaeological Studies in Honour of Charles Burney*, ed. Antonio Sagona, 345–98. Ancient Near Eastern Studies, Supplement 12. Leuven: Peeters.

Kiguradze, Tamaz and Antonio Sagona. 2003. On the Origins of the Kura-Araxes Cultural Complex. In *Archaeology in the Borderlands: Investigations in Caucasia and Beyond,* ed. Adam T. Smith and Karen S. Rubinson, 38–94. Los Angeles: Cotsen Institute Press.

Kipiani, Guram. 1997. Berikldeebi: Galavani da tadzari. *Saqartvelos sakhelmtsipo muzeumis moambe* 42–B: 13–57. (In Georgian).

Kohl, Philip L. 2007. *The Making of Bronze Age Eurasia.* Cambridge: Cambridge University Press.

Kozbe, Gülriz. 2004. Activity Areas and Social Organization within Early Trans-Caucasian Houses at Karagündüz Höyük, Van. In *A View from the Highlands: Archaeological Studies in Honour of Charles Burney*, ed. Antonio Sagona, 35–53. Ancient Near Eastern Studies, Supplement 12. Leuven: Peeters.

Kuftin, Boris A. 1948. *Arkheologicheskie Raskopki 1947 Goda v Tsalkinskom Raione.* Tbilisi: Izv-do Akademii Nauk Gruzinskoi SSR.

Kushnareva, Karina K. 1997. *The Southern Caucasus in Prehistory: Stages of Cultural and Socioeconomic Development from the Eighth to the Second Millennium B.C.* Philadelphia: University of Pennsylvania Museum.

Lisitsina, Gorislava N. 1978. Main Types of Ancient Farming in the Caucasus on the Basis of Palaeo-Ethnobotanical Research. *Berichte der Deutschen Botanischen Gesellschaft* 91: 47–57.

Lyonnet, Bertille. 2007. Introduction. In *Les cultures du Caucase (VIe–IIIe millénaires avant notre ère). Leurs relations avec le Proche-Orient*, ed. Bertille Lyonnet, 11–19. Paris: CNRS Éditions.

Lyonnet, Bertille and Ferhad Guliyev. 2010. Recent discoveries on the Neolithic and Chalcolithic of western Azerbaijan. *TÜBA-AR* 13: 219–28

Makharadze, Zurab. 2007. Nouvelles données sur le Chalcolithique en Géorgie orientale. In *Les cultures du Caucase (VIe–IIIe millénaires avant notre ère). Leurs relations avec le Proche-Orient*, ed. Bertille Lyonnet. 123–32. Paris: CNRS Éditions.

Marro, Catherine. 2008. Late Chalcolithic Cultures in the Anatolian Highlands. In *Ceramics in Transitions: Chalcolithic through Iron Ages in the Highlands of the Southern Caucasus and Anatolia*, ed. Karen S. Rubinson and Antonio Sagona, 9–27. Ancient Near Eastern Studies, Supplement 27. Leuven: Peeters.

Marro, Catherine, V. Bakhshaliyev and S. Sanz, with the collaboration of N. Aliyev. 2010. Archaeological Investigations on the Salt Mine of Duzdagi (Nakhchivan, Azerbaïdjan). *TÜBA-AR* 13: 229–44

Marro, Catherine and Aynur Özfırat. 2005. Pre-Classical Survey in Eastern Turkey, Third Preliminary Report: Doğubeyazit and the Eastern Shore of Lake Van. *Anatolia Antiqua* 12: 319–56.

Maziar, Sepideh. 2010. Excavations At Köhné Pāsgāh Tepesi, the Araxes Valley, Northwest Iran: First Preliminary Report. *Ancient Near Eastern Studies* 47: 165–937.

Mellaart, James. 1975. *The Neolithic of the Near East.* London: Thames and Hudson.

Munchaev, Rauf M. 1975. *Kavkaz na zare bronzovogo veka*. Moscow: Nauka.
———. 1982. Eneolit Kavkaza. In *Eneolit SSR*, ed. Vadim M. Masson and Nikolai Ya. Merpert, 100–64. Moscow: Nauka.
Narimanov, Ideal G. 1992. The Earliest Agricultural Settlements in the Territory of Azerbaidzhan. *Soviet Anthropology and Archaeology* 30.4: 9–66.
Outram, Alan K., Natalie A. Stear, Robin Bendrey, Sandra Olsen, Alexeu Kasparov, Victor Zaibert, Nick Thorpe, and Richard P. Evershed. 2009. The Earliest Horse Harnessing and Milking. *Science* 323.5919: 1332–35.
Özfırat, Aynur. 2001. *Doğu Anadolu Yayla Kültürleri*. İstanbul: Arkeoloji ve Sanat.
Palumbi, Giulio. 2003. Red-Black Pottery: Eastern Anatolia and Transcaucasian Relationships around the Mid-Fourth Millennium BC. *Ancient Near Eastern Studies* 40: 80–134.
———. 2007. A Preliminary Analysis on the Prehistoric Pottery from Aratashen (Armenia). In *Les cultures du Caucase (VIe–IIIe millénaires avant notre ère). Leurs relations avec le Proche-Orient*, ed. Bertille Lyonnet, 63–76. Paris: CNRS Éditions.
———. 2008. Mid-Fourth Millennium Red-Black Burnished Wares from Anatolia: A Cross-Comparison. In *Ceramics in Transitions: Chalcolithic through Iron Ages in the Highlands of the Southern Caucasus and Anatolia*, ed. Karen S. Rubinson and Antonio Sagona, 39–58. Ancient Near Eastern Studies, Supplement 27. Leuven: Peeters.
Piggott, Stuart. 1983. *The Earliest Wheeled Transport: From the Atlantic Coast to the Caspian Sea*. London: Thames and Hudson.
———. 1992. *Wagon, Chariot and Carriage: Symbol and Status in the History of Transport*. London: Thames and Hudson.
Piro, Jennifer. 2009. *Pastoralism in the Early Transcaucasian Culture: The Faunal Remains from Sos Höyük*. Ph.D. dissertation. New York University.
Rothman, Mitchell S. 2003. Ripples in the Stream: Transcaucasia-Anatolian Interaction in the Murat/Euphrates Basin at the Beginning of the Third Millennium BC. In *Archaeology in the Borderlands: Investigations in Caucasia and Beyond*, ed. Adam T. Smith and Karen S. Rubinson, 95–110. Cotsen Institute Monograph 27. Los Angeles: Cotsen Institute of Archaeology, University of California.
———. 2008. Migration and Resettlement: Godin Period IV. In *On the High Road: The History of Godin Tepe, Iran*, ed. Hilary Gopnik and Mitchell S. Rothman, 133–200. Costa Mesa, Calif.: Mazda Publishers.
Rubinson, Karen S. 2003. Silver Vessels and Cylinder Sealings: Precious Reflections of Economic Exchange in the Early Second Millennium BC. In *Archaeology in the Borderlands: Investigations in Caucasia and Beyond*, ed. Adam T. Smith and Karen S. Rubinson, 128–43. Cotsen Institute Monograph 27. Los Angeles: Cotsen Institute of Archaeology, University of California.
———. 2005. Second Millennium B.C. Painted Pottery and Problems of Terminologies. *Archäologische Mitteilungen aus Iran und Turan* 37: 133–38.
———. 2006. Over the Mountains and through the Grass: Visual Information as "Text" for the "Textless." In *Beyond the Steppe and the Sown: Proceedings of the 2002 University of Chicago Conference on Eurasian Archaeology*, ed. David L. Peterson, Laura M. Popova, and Adam T. Smith, 247–63. Colloquia Pontica. Leiden: Brill.
Rubinson, Karen S. and Antonio Sagona. 2008. Introduction: A Question of Nomenclature. In *Ceramics in Transitions: Chalcolithic through Iron Ages in the Highlands of the Southern Caucasus and Anatolia*, ed. Karen S. Rubinson and Antonio Sagona, 1–8. Ancient Near Eastern Studies, Supplement 27. Leuven: Peeters.

Sagona, Antonio G. 1984. *The Caucasian Region in the Early Bronze Age*, vols. 1–3. British Archaeological Reports, International Series 214. Oxford: British Archaeological Reports.

———. 2000. Sos Höyük and the Erzurum Region in Late Prehistory: A Provisional Chronology for Northeastern Anatolian. In *Chronologies des pays du Caucase et de l'euphrate aux IVe–IIIe millénaires*, ed. Catherine Marro and Harald Hauptmann, 329–73. Paris: De Boccard.

———. 2004. Social Boundaries and Ritual Landscapes: The Late Prehistory of Trans-Caucasus. In *A View from the Highlands: Studies in Honour of Charles Burney*, ed. Antonio Sagona, 485–549. Ancient Near Eastern Studies, Supplement 12. Leuven: Peeters.

Sagona, Antonio and Mikheil Abramishvili, eds. 2008. *Archaeology in Southern Caucasus: Perspectives from Georgia*. Ancient Near Eastern Studies, Supplement 19. Leuven: Peeters.

Sagona, Antonio and Claudia Sagona. 2000. Excavations at Sos Höyük, 1998–2000: Fifth Preliminary Report. *Ancient Near Eastern Studies* 37: 56–127.

Sagona, Antonio and Paul Zimansky. 2009. *Ancient Turkey*. London: Routledge.

Sagona, Claudia and Antonio Sagona. 2009. Encounters with the Divine in the Late Prehistoric Period of Eastern Anatolia and Southern Caucasus. In *Studies in Honour of Altan Çilingiroğlu. A Life Dedicated to Urartu on the Shores of the Upper Sea*, ed. Haluk Sağlamtimur, Eşref Abay, Zafer Derin, Aylin Ü. Erdem, Atilla Batmaz, Fulya Dedeoğlu, Mücella Erdalkıran, Mahmut Bilge Baştürk, and Erim Konakçı, 537–63. İstanbul: Arkeoloji ve Sanat.

Smith, Adam T. 2005. Prometheus Unbound: Southern Caucasia in Prehistory. *Journal of World Archaeology* 19: 229–79.

Smogorzewska, Anna. 2004. Andirons and Their Role in Early Trans-Caucasian Culture. *Anatolica* 30: 151–77.

Vavilov, Nikolai I. 1952. *The Origin, Variation, Immunity and Breeding of Cultivated Plants*. Trans. K. S. Chester. Waltham, Mass.: Chronica Botanica.

Zimmerman, Thomas. 2007. Anatolia as a Bridge from North to South? Recent Research in the Hatti Heartland. *Anatolian Studies* 57: 65–75.

CHAPTER 31

INDO-EUROPEANS

H. CRAIG MELCHERT

For more than sixty years after the identification of Hittite as an Indo-European language by Bedřich Hrozný in 1917 (see Beckman, chapter 22 in this volume) it was taken for granted that Indo-European speakers were non-native to Anatolia. They were assumed to have migrated there from somewhere in eastern Europe (following the conventional definition of Europe as stretching to the Urals). Debate centered on three major issues. First, did the migration follow an eastern route through the Caucasus or a western one through the Balkans and across the Black Sea straits? Second, approximately when did this movement take place? Third, what was the nature of this event? The last question is multifaceted, including such issues as (1) was it in the nature of a hostile invasion and conquest or rather of relatively peaceful colonization? and (2) should we envision a mass movement of population or merely small bands of settlers?

The decade of the 1980s brought two radically new and different scenarios. Gamkrelidze and Ivanov (1984) proposed that the dwelling place of the putative Proto-Indo-European (PIE) speech community lay in eastern Anatolia. While Gamkrelidze and Ivanov did retain the prevailing view that the prehistoric stage labeled PIE (alternatively Proto-Indo-Hittite) dated to the fifth or fourth millennium B.C.E., Colin Renfrew (1987) argued not only for a location of the PIE speech community in central Anatolia but also for a much earlier date of approximately 7000 B.C.E. Renfrew based his claim on a presumed association of the movement of the Indo-European languages and the spread of farming into Europe.

There clearly can be no pretense of a true consensus regarding Indo-Europeans in Anatolia. The following summary strives to distinguish what is purely personal opinion from what reflects a majority viewpoint. Important dissenting opinions are also cited, but no claim is made to exhaustiveness in this regard. The present treatment should also be read with the following caveats in mind. First, the notion of "Indo-European(s)" is fundamentally linguistic—hence the references throughout to "Indo-European speakers" or "pre-Luvian speakers." Earlier close linkages of PIE speakers and their descendants with race or ethnicity are now emphatically rejected by all mainstream Indo-Europeanists. A shared language clearly may be an important factor in forging ethnic self-identity, but our knowledge of how inhabitants of second and first millennium B.C.E. Anatolia defined themselves is severely limited (for one recent thoughtful discussion of the problem see Gilan 2008).

A second difficulty is that our evidence for those we conventionally identify as Hittites, Luvians, or Lycians consists largely of written texts, and virtually all of those texts were written by and about limited classes of élites. We have little or no basis for drawing inferences about even the linguistic affinities of other classes of society. A third problem is that we know from modern examples that languages and various cultural practices may spread together, but they may also diffuse independently of each other. Therefore the mere co-occurrence of a certain kind of art or artifact and a Luvian text at the same site does not guarantee that the former may be safely defined as "Luvian." Likewise, archaeological evidence for prehistoric continuity or discontinuity of cultural practices does not per se assure corresponding linguistic maintenance or change.

Nevertheless, we must work with what we have, and in what follows evidence for a particular language being used in a given place at a given time will be taken as a sign of the presence of at least some associated speakers. Furthermore, demonstrable effects of one language on another and the apparent timing of such influence will be used to infer approximate locations of languages and their speakers. We may also with due caution draw some conclusions from the *lack* of evidence for language contact. Finally, few historical linguists believe that the rate of language change can be calculated in absolute terms according to the strong version of what is known as "glottochronology." However, most agree that one can make very rough estimates of the minimal time required to produce significant divergence among related languages.

Indo-Europeans in Anatolia: Autochthonous or Intrusive?

A majority of Indo-Europeanists have not been persuaded by the arguments of either Gamkrelidze and Ivanov or Renfrew for location of the PIE speech community in Anatolia. Among recent general studies of the Hittites MacQueen (1996:26) flatly rejects an Anatolian "homeland" for the Indo-Europeans without argumentation, while Bryce (2005:11–12) and Collins (2007:24) cite this possibility alongside that of in-migration, but remain firmly noncommittal. For a critical assessment of Renfrew's model from an archaeological viewpoint see Anthony (2007:75–81) and Mallory (2009).

A detailed presentation of the linguistic arguments against an Anatolian location for PIE is not possible here, but the main issues are easily summarized. Gamkrelidze and Ivanov present chiefly linguistic evidence as the basis for positing a homeland at the intersection of eastern Anatolia, southern Caucasus, and northern Mesopotamia (most accessible in English in Gamkrelidze and Ivanov 1995:757–79). Their arguments rest on: (1) the presence of significant numbers of Anatolian place-names and river names of Indo-European origin; (2) PIE lexemes for flora and fauna that point distinctly to a southern "homeland" (e.g., "monkey," "ape," "lion," "elephant"); (3) extensive loanwords from Sumerian and Semitic into PIE; (4) extensive loanwords from PIE into South Caucasian (Proto-Kartvelian). The putative etymologies of Anatolian place-names are dubious, and none of the exclusively southern-oriented items of vocabulary are likely to have existed in PIE. There is no compelling basis for a Sumerian or Semitic origin of most of the alleged loanwords. The few that are convincing (such as "ax") are entirely compatible with diffusion by trade that could have reached a PIE speech community even in Europe (see Korfmann 2001 for arguments for extensive long-distance trade already in the third millennium B.C.E.). Gamkrelidze and Ivanov themselves concede (1995:774) that the contact with Proto-Kartvelian may have been with only post-PIE dialect subgroups. Their assumption (1995:794–9 and map on 850–51) of pre-Greek migration into Greece from Anatolia (necessarily *through* the prehistoric forms of the Anatolian Indo-European languages) is also very difficult to reconcile with recognition of a dialect subgroup consisting of Greek, Armenian, and Indo-Iranian.

The chief problem with the thesis of Renfrew (1987) is that we may securely reconstruct for the PIE lexicon words for objects and activities that almost certainly did not exist in 7000 B.C.E. or any time close to that. See Barber (2001) and especially Darden (2001) for detailed arguments for the PIE words for "wool" (as a material suitable for spinning), "yoke," and "hitch-pole." If the Anatolian Indo-European languages have been in situ in Anatolia for five millennia when we first encounter them, as claimed by Renfrew, it is also scarcely credible that there is no evidence for loanwords into Proto-Anatolian from Sumerian, Semitic, or Hattic (or vice versa). Pace Simon (2006:317), the lack of evidence for such contacts cannot be explained due to geographical distance, which is minimal. Nor would the contacts in the fourth and third millennia B.C.E. have been only with proto-languages, since Sumerian dates from at least the fourth millennium B.C.E. and Akkadian from the third millennium B.C.E. The openness of Hittite to lexical loans (though not grammatical influence) once it did come into contact with other languages of the Ancient Near East suggests that there should have likewise been such influence in earlier periods, had opportunity for such contact existed. The weight of current evidence argues for the received view of Indo-European speakers as intrusive to Anatolia.

Time of Entry of Indo-Europeans into Anatolia

It seems prudent to confront this issue in terms of a reverse chronology, starting with the first direct evidence we have for the Anatolian Indo-European languages and working back from there. Our earliest evidence for Hittite and Luvian comes from texts of the Assyrian merchant colonies of the *kārum* period in central Anatolia (nineteenth–eighteenth centuries B.C.E.), chiefly from Kaneš (Kültepe), in the form of both loanwords and personal names. The loanword data have been most recently critically reviewed by Dercksen (2007), who concludes that there is evidence for a considerable number of loanwords from Hittite. These include some with uniquely Hittite formal features such as *išpuruzzinnum* < *išparuzzi-*, "ceiling beam" (or similar) with suffix *-uzzi-* < **-uti-* and *išḫiulum* < *išḫiul-*, "obligation." There are also some assured loanwords from Luvian, such as *kullitannum* < *kullit-* (a small vessel) with specifically Luvian suffix *-it-* and *upatinnum*, "(royal) land-grant" < *ubati-* (on which see Melchert 2004a and Yakubovich 2005). Evidence for Hurrian loanwords is scarce, and that for Hattic uncertain. Dercksen (2007:27) reasonably concludes that Hittite was at this time the dominant local language of Kaneš (thus also Singer 1981:126 and Steiner 1981:164). Both of the loanwords from Luvian just cited may have been transmitted through Hittite, but the presence of Luvian speakers in the area is also beyond doubt.

Personal names from the Old Assyrian "Cappadocian" texts confirm the testimony of the loanwords. Names such as *Šuppiuman-* contain the characteristically Hittite ethnic suffix *-uman-*, whereas others such as *Zida-* and *Ḫutarla-* are based on Luvian appellatives ("man" and "servant," respectively); see among others on these names Carruba (1992) and Tischler (1995).

Direct textual evidence for Hittite, Luvian, and Palaic begins no later than the sixteenth century B.C.E. in the cuneiform archives of Ḫattuša (Boğazköy) and continues there for the first two languages to the end of the thirteenth century B.C.E.[1] Although Hittite is entrenched as our conventional name for the chief administrative language of the kingdom and empire centered on Ḫattuša, its speakers called it *ne/ašili* or *nešumnili*, "in the language of Neša" (i.e., Kaneš). This appellation confirms the evidence of the Assyrian texts already cited that this Indo-European language was originally associated with at least an élite stratum of speakers in Kaneš and that its appearance in Ḫattuša is likely to be relatively late and connected with the choice of Ḫattuša as a capital by the founders of the Hittite dynasty (thus also Singer 1981:129–30).

Later Hittite kings also produced Luvian inscriptions written in a hieroglyphic script invented in Anatolia, those of any length dating to the last two Hittite kings, Tutḫaliya IV and Šuppiluliuma II (see Beal, chapter 26 in this volume). The use of the Anatolian hieroglyphs survived the fall of the Hittite Empire at the end of the thirteenth century B.C.E., and apart from a few inscriptions from the intermediate period, most Luvian texts in hieroglyphs date from the tenth to eighth centuries B.C.E., comprising inscriptions on stone and a few on lead strips, the bulk of them attributable to local rulers from sites in southern Anatolia and northern Syria. There are limited but undeniable differences in the grammar of the language of the ritual texts in Luvian preserved in cuneiform in Ḫattuša and that of the first millennium B.C.E. hieroglyphic texts (see Melchert 2003a:171–72). However, Yakubovich (2010 and chapter 23 in this volume) has now presented extensive arguments that the conventional assumption of "Cuneiform Luvian" and "Hieroglyphic Luvian" dialects is false. In addition to identifying further dialectal features, he makes a compelling case that we should distinguish rather a "Kizzuwatnan Luvian" as the language of the cuneiform ritual texts and an "Empire Luvian," a *koiné* first promoted by the Hittite kings in Ḫattuša that is the source of Luvianisms in Hittite texts of the second millennium B.C.E. and was perpetuated as a prestige medium in the Luvian texts of the first millennium B.C.E.

Yakubovich also thoroughly treats the thorny issue of the status of Hittite and Luvian as spoken languages in Ḫattuša and elsewhere during the period of the Hittite kingdom, but a resolution of this issue is beyond the scope of the present chapter. Of much more relevance for our theme is his demonstration (2010:161–205) that contact with Luvian also caused a major transformation in the Hittite system of reflexive pronouns. It had already been established that Luvian furnished significant numbers of prehistoric loanwords in Hittite (see Starke 1990 and Melchert 2005), but such an influence on the Hittite grammatical system implies much more intensive prehistoric contact between speakers of Hittite and Luvian. This supports the claim of Yakubovich that the core area of Luvian speakers in the prehistoric period was in what the Hittites called "the Lower Land" (the area south of the Tuz Gölü) and that the primary movement of Luvian speakers in the late third millennium B.C.E. was westward, not eastward (contra Bryce 2003:28–35; MacQueen 1996:27–30; Steiner 1981:168). As correctly argued by Yakubovich (2010:140–57), the dearth of Luvian loanwords into Greek and the profile of the few genuine examples also argue against an early significant presence of Luvian speakers in western Anatolia. On the possible but unproven existence of yet another dialect of Luvian, represented in the Istanuvian Songs and localized in the area of the Sangarius (Sakarya) River basin, see Melchert (2003a:174–5) and Yakubovich (2010:22–3).

Our first textual evidence for the western Anatolian languages Lycian, Carian, and Lydian dates only from the second half of the first millennium B.C.E.[2] The size and nature of the respective corpora also limit our understanding of the grammar and lexicon of these languages. These factors severely restrict knowledge of the linguistic situation in the west in the second millennium B.C.E., much less the third. Nevertheless, certain facts allow us to draw some reasonably reliable conclusions. There is widespread agreement that Luvian and Lycian form a well-defined dialect subgroup of Anatolian, based on an impressive number of common innovations (Melchert 2003b:267–69 with refs.), and it is likely that Carian shares many if not most of these features (Adiego 2007:345–47). However, Lycian at least also shows archaisms that preclude its being analyzed as a first millennium B.C.E. form of Luvian (contra Bryce 2003:102 and Starke 1997:468 and 476, n. 108, among others): see Gusmani (1960) and Melchert (2003b:268). Because Luvian as attested in the early second millennium B.C.E. already shows key innovations separating it from Lycian, we may safely conclude that the divergence of Luvian and Lycian must date to at least the late third millennium B.C.E. Similar differences likewise assure that Lydian must have already been distinct from both Lycian and Luvian in the same period, notwithstanding that Lycian and Lydian as attested surely have evolved considerably from the form they had at the turn from the third to the second millennium B.C.E.

The fact that the Assyrian texts from Kaneš from the nineteenth to the eighteenth centuries B.C.E. attest to already distinct Hittite and Luvian, combined with the demonstration by Yakubovich of prehistoric Luvian influence on Hittite grammar, likewise necessarily *after* the two grammatical systems had already significantly diverged, falsifies any notion of a still undifferentiated Anatolian form of Indo-European at the end of the second millennium B.C.E. (contra MacQueen 1996:31). The differences cited between Luvian and the western Anatolian languages reinforce this conclusion. One may safely say that a consensus has therefore developed that divergences among the Anatolian Indo-European languages can have begun no later than ca. 2300 B.C.E. and likely began earlier, arguably as early as the beginning of the third millennium B.C.E. See, among others, Carruba (1995:31), Lehrman (2001:116), Oettinger (2002:52), and Yakubovich (2010:7). This convergence of opinion is all the more significant in that these scholars and others have widely divergent views regarding other aspects of Anatolian and Indo-European linguistic prehistory.

We take it as a given that the spread of Indo-European languages across Asia Minor involved at least some movements of speakers. Since geographic separation of an originally unified speech community typically leads to language differentiation between the respective new communities, the default assumption is that most (if not all) of the early attested divergence among the Anatolian languages is due to the break-up of what we call "Proto-Anatolian," as various groups of speakers scattered into areas of Anatolia. However, the methods of reconstruction that lead us to posit a prehistoric language system like Proto-Anatolian imply only that the attested languages in question underwent some period of common development that differentiates them from the rest of the Indo-European languages. Where this putative common development took place cannot be determined on linguistic grounds. We therefore cannot rule out an alternative scenario by which the isolation that led to Proto-Anatolian took place in, for example, the Balkans, and that the entry of its speakers into Anatolia took place in a series of successive waves (thus Steiner 1990:202–3; see also Darden 2001:220). Even the approximate date of entry of Indo-European speakers into Anatolia thus remains frustratingly indeterminate. However, we may draw one sobering lesson from the preceding discussion. The unavoidable need to assume considerable prehistoric movement *within* Anatolia by various groups speaking pre-Hittite, pre-Luvian, and so forth—and significant contact between them—effectively precludes the use of linguistic evidence to say anything illuminating about the route by which Indo-European speakers entered Asia Minor. Nothing further on this topic is presented here.

Role of the Indo-Europeans in Anatolia

If linguistic evidence gives us only an approximate terminus ante quem for when Indo-European speakers arrived in Anatolia and can tell us next to nothing about how they came, it also follows that it can offer only limited help in defining the nature and circumstances of their in-migration. Therefore, once again it seems useful to focus the following brief discussion on what linguistic facts may be able to contribute regarding the interactions of Indo-European-speaking groups with each other and with speakers of non-Indo-European languages in the prehistoric period immediately preceding our first texts.

For western Anatolia in the older period there is little to say due to the lack of sources. Speculations about "substrate" effects on Luvian and Lycian are no more than that. The notion of a common substrate shared by Greece and western Anatolia based solely on a supposed equation between Greek place-names in *-νθ-* and *-σσ-* and those from Anatolia in *-nd-* and *-ss-* (e.g., Stefanini 2002:794 with refs.) is a very fragile construct. Even if it is true, it tells us next to nothing. Not a single one of the numerous common innovations shared by Luvian and Lycian can be attributed to the influence of a substrate, since we know nothing about the hypothetical source language or languages. Since Carian is indubitably an Indo-European language (see now Adiego 2007:345–47), there is also no evidence for a non-Indo-European Carian substratum (contra Stefanini 2002:795–96).

The case of Hittite and Hattic, where we do know at least something about the latter (see now Soysal 2004), is highly instructive. There are no persuasive examples of Hattic influence on Hittite morphology (the Hittite pronominal genitive ending *-ēl* has developed from inherited material, as per Rieken 2008, and has nothing to do with the Hattic derivational suffix *-il-*). There are any number of possible reasons why Luvian and Lycian may have innovated more in some respects than Hittite, and there is no basis for attributing this fact to substrate influence (pace Puhvel 1990:191–92 and Stefanini 2002:789). The one demonstrable instance of a contact-induced innovation in Luvian is the creation—only in Kizzuwatnan Luvian!—of the form *-aššanza-* to mark plural number of the possessor in the possessive adjective in *-ašša/i-*, shown by Yakubovich (2010:45–53) to be due to Hurrian influence. Although this very phenomenon was quite hard to motivate as an internal change, all the shared innovations of Luvian and Lycian are easily accounted for without any recourse to external forces.

How far the Luvian speech area extended into western Anatolia in the early second millennium B.C.E. remains an open question. While arguing for early forms of Carian and Lydian as having been the spoken languages of that area, Yakubovich (2010:160) concedes that the few scraps of evidence we have do not permit definitive conclusions about narrower linguistic affinities. Nor can we be sure how far the linguistic Indo-Europeanization of western Anatolia had proceeded by that time. Barring a dramatic new discovery, the question of "the language of the Trojans" (more properly, the language of the inhabitants of Wiluša known to the Hittites) will remain unanswerable. It may have been an unknown further western dialect of Indo-European Anatolian or a non-Indo-European language.

Indo-European Anatolian languages do appear to have become dominant in the west during the first millennium B.C.E. By the time of the first attested texts, the societies of Lycia, Caria, and Lydia are under heavy Greek influence. It is almost certain that the cultural exchange went in both directions (see various contributions in Collins, Bachvarova, and Rutherford 2008), but our inability to interpret most of the content of the few longer inscriptions in these languages robs us of the chance to discover more than the dimmest outlines of this activity.

We are in a rather better situation when it comes to central Anatolia in the late third to early second millennium B.C.E., though even here due caution is in order. We can assert that the sum of current linguistic evidence argues decisively against the old idea of a Hittite ruling class overrunning a Hattic population on the central Anatolian plateau. First of all, the supposed substrate influence of Hattic on Hittite has been widely overestimated (most recently, e.g., by Stefanini 2002:789–92). A sober look at the vocabulary of Old Hittite referring to political institutions (see Melchert 2003c:18–21) shows that it reflects a roughly equal mixture of Hattic and Luvian influences. The titles of the Hittite king and queen, *l/tabarna-* and *tawananna-*, are assuredly loanwords from Luvian with an impeccable Indo-European pedigree in terms of the lexical roots, word formation, and phonology (pace Klinger 1996:207–20; Stefanini 2002:791–92; and others); see Melchert (2003c:18–21 with refs. to Carruba and Puhvel). On the other hand, the designation of the crown prince *tuḫkanti-* and the name of the throne dais *ḫalmaššuitt-* are indubitably borrowed from Hattic. In similar fashion *telipuri-*, referring to an administrative district, is from Hattic, while *ubati-*, "(royal) land-grant," is taken from Luvian (Klinger 1996:200). Hittite notions of kingship and the ideal state show a comparable blending of Hattic and Luvian elements (along with some that are probably neither).

The mixed influence of Hattic and Luvian on early Hittite suggests that we should take seriously the Hittites' own designation of their language as belonging to the area of Kaneš and cautiously infer that their "heartland" lay in the upper reaches of the Halys River, in a zone between the Hattians to the north on the central Anatolian plateau and the Luvians to the southwest in the Lower Land, south of the Tuz Gölü. Needless to say, this characterization is meant only to refer to centers of gravity. There is no need or justification to suppose that there were sharp boundaries between the respective speech areas, and the Assyrian texts of the *kārum* period argue in fact for trade, intermarriage, and all kinds of cultural exchange between these (and likely other unidentifiable groups) from whatever time the Indo-European speakers arrived in the area—whenever that may have been.

These results based on linguistic considerations square quite well with those reached by Singer (1981:120–25) on wholly independent grounds. They also support the claim by Yakubovich (2010:239–48) that the Lower Land was the heartland of Luvian speakers in the late third and early second millennium B.C.E. One should note in this connection the strong possibility of a few loanwords from

Hattic into prehistoric Hittite *through* the intermediary of Luvian: the words [É]*arkiw(it)-*, "canopy, awning," and *ḫazziw(it)-*, "rite," show inflectional forms with the Luvian suffix *-it-* (on which see Starke 1990:151–226) but also peculiarities that point to an ultimately Hattic origin (see Weitenberg 1984:239 and 246–47). It is therefore likely that the tentative map offered in Melchert (2003c:9) should be revised by moving the label "Hittite" further to the northeast, while the lower of the two labels "Luwian" should be rotated clockwise about sixty degrees, so that it runs northwest–southeast from just west of the Tuz Gölü. The Hattians naturally may be supposed, as usual, to have been centered on the central Anatolian plateau.

Attempting to infer speaker attitudes from language contact effects is a parlous business. Hostility towards speakers of another language (for whatever reason) does not preclude adoption of loanwords from the latter. Widespread resentment or antipathy toward many aspects of current American culture has hardly slowed the massive worldwide spread of English loanwords, especially in the areas of technology and popular culture. The likely existence of substantial numbers of Hattic loanwords in Hittite for flora, fauna, and the paraphernalia and personnel of religious ritual—our very limited sources for Hattic leave most of these less than strictly proven—does not necessarily exclude the long popular idea of the imposition of an Indo-European ruling class on a native Hattian population referred to above (thus, e.g., still Gurney 1981 [1990]:13). Nevertheless, the nearly seamless blending of Hattian and Luvian elements into the creation of the Hittites' conception of kingship and the ideal state cited above lends support to the arguments of Klinger (1996:16–7 with n. 41, 93, 198 with n. 287; and others) rather for a relatively long and peaceful assimilation of the Indo-European-speaking newcomers with other inhabitants of central Anatolia.

The creation of the Hittite state undoubtedly drew together more strands of influence than just Hattian and Luvian, including imitation of Mesopotamian and Syrian models (thus also Liverani 1988:441). Political conflicts likely arose in terms of competing city states, not from a supposed clash of Indo-European and local Anatolian "values" (against the latter see Liverani 1988:443–44). Forlanini (2007) has argued on nonlinguistic grounds for a three-way power struggle in central Anatolia at the beginning of the second millennium B.C.E. between Purušḫanda, Kaneš, and Ḫattuša. He raises the question (2007:278) as to whether these polities reflected ethnolinguistic divisions between Luvians, Nešites (Hittite-speaking), and Hattians. The answer may be a qualified yes, but we should avoid concluding that the linguistic differences were the *basis* for the conflict. If the rise and fall of dynasties tied to certain cities led to expansion or diminution in the use of various languages (at least in the written record!), the latter was surely an effect of the former. At least, nothing in the available linguistic evidence supports the view that battle lines were drawn along language boundaries (see Steiner 1981:166–70 for an account supposing an actual disconnect between ethnicity and language). As elsewhere, the ascendancy and disappearance of particular languages in ancient Anatolia was due to a combination of nonlinguistic factors, including chance.

Conclusion

The weight of current linguistic evidence supports the traditional view that Indo-European speakers are intrusive to Asia Minor, coming from somewhere in eastern Europe. There is a growing consensus that the differentiation among the Indo-European Anatolian languages begins at least by the mid-second millennium B.C.E. and possibly earlier. It is likely, but not strictly provable, that this differentiation correlates with the entry of the Indo-European speakers into Anatolia and their subsequent dispersal. Nothing definitive can be said about the route by which the Indo-European entry took place.

The very long gap between the approximate time of in-migration and our first textual evidence for western Anatolia precludes any conclusions about the nature of the interaction between the newcomers and any previous inhabitants. Claims of substrate effects on the western Anatolian languages are greatly exaggerated. In any case, our total ignorance of the structure of the putative substrate languages makes it impossible to draw any inferences about the relative social position of the respective sets of speakers. Recent research argues against the notion of Indo-European "invaders" imposing themselves on a Hattian population in central Anatolia and points rather to a gradual assimilation. Conflicts between various city-states may have correlated to some extent with ethnolinguistic differences, but the former, not the latter, were determining.

NOTES

1. For recent overviews of Hittite grammar, see Watkins (2004) and Rieken (2005); for both forms of Luvian, see Melchert (2003a) with modifications by Yakubovich (2010); and for Palaic, see Melchert (2004b).

2. Melchert (2004b) offers short overviews of the grammar of all of these languages. The description of Carian should be supplemented by that of Adiego(2007), while Gérard (2005) furnishes important correctives for Lydian.

REFERENCES

Adiego, Ignacio J. 2007. *The Carian Language*. Leiden: Brill.

Anthony, David W. 2007. *The Horse, the Wheel, and Language: How Bronze-Age Riders from the Eurasian Steppes Shaped the Modern World.* Princeton, N.J.: Princeton University Press.

Barber, Elisabeth. 2001. The Clues in the Clothes: Some Independent Evidence for the Movements of Families. In *Greater Anatolia and the Indo-Hittite Language Family*, ed. Robert Drews, 1–14. Journal of Indo-European Studies Monograph Series 38. Washington, D.C.: Institute for the Study of Man.

Bryce, Trevor. 2003. History. In *The Luwians*, ed. H. Craig Melchert, 27–127. Leiden: Brill.

———. 2005. *The Kingdom of the Hittites*. Oxford: Oxford University Press.

Carruba, Onofrio. 1992. Luwier in Kappadokien. In *La circulation des biens, des personnes et des idées dans le Proche-Orient ancient, XXXVIIIe R.A.I.*, ed. Dominique Charpin and Francis Joannès, 251–57. Paris: Éditions Recherche sur les Civilisations.

———. 1995. L'arrivo dei greci, le migrazioni indoeuropee e il "ritorno" degli Eraclidi. *Athenaeum* 83: 5–44.

Collins, Billie Jean. 2007. *The Hittites and Their World*. Atlanta: Society of Biblical Literature.

Collins, Billie Jean, Mary R. Bachvarova, and Ian C. Rutherford. 2008. *Anatolian Interfaces. Hittites, Greeks and their Neighbors. Proceedings of an International Conference on Cross-Cultural Interaction, 17–19 September 2004, Emory University, Atlanta, GA*. Oxford: Oxbow.

Darden, Bill J. 2001. On the Question of the Anatolian Origin of Indo-Hittite. In *Greater Anatolia and the Indo-Hittite Language Family*, ed. Robert Drews, 184–228. Journal of Indo-European Studies Monograph Series 38. Washington, D.C.: Institute for the Study of Man.

Dercksen, Jan G. 2007. On Anatolian Loanwords in Akkadian Texts from Kültepe. *Zeitschrift für Assyriologie* 97: 26–46.

Forlanini, Massimo. 2007. The Offering List of KBo 4.13 (I 17'-48') to the Local Gods of the Kingdom, Known as "Sacrifice List," and the History of the Formation of the Early Hittite State and its Initial Growing beyond Central Anatolia. *Studi Micenei ed Egeo-Anatolici* 49: 259–80.

Gamkrelidze, Thomas V. and Vyačeslav V. Ivanov. 1984. *Indoevropejskij Jazyk i Indoevropejsky*. Tbilisi: Izdatel'stvo Tbilisskogo Universiteta.

———. 1995. *Indo-European and the Indo-Europeans*. Trans. Johanna Nichols. Berlin: Mouton de Gruyter.

Gérard, Raphaël. 2005. *Phonétique et morphologie de la langue lydienne*. Louvain: Peeters.

Gilan, Amir. 2008. Hittite Ethnicity? Constructions of Identity in Hittite Literature. In *Anatolian Interfaces. Hittites, Greeks and Their Neighbors*, ed. Billie Jean Collins, Mary R. Bachvarova, and Ian R. Rutherford, 107–15. Oxford: Oxbow.

Gurney, Oliver R. 1981 [1990]. *The Hittites*, 2nd ed. Penguin.

Gusmani, Roberto. 1960. Concordanze e discordanze nella flessione nominale del licio e del luvio. *Rendiconti del Istituto Lombardo di Scienze e Lettere. Classe di lettere e scienze morali e storiche* 94: 275–98.

Klinger, Jörg. 1996. *Untersuchungen zur Rekonstruktion der hattischen Kultschicht*. Studien zu den Boğazköy-Texten 37. Wiesbaden: Harrassowitz.

Korfmann, Manfred. 2001. Troia also Drehscheibe des Handels im 2. und 3. vorchristlichen Jahrtausend. In *Troia. Traum und Wirklichkeit*, 355–68. Stuttgart: Theiss.

Lehrman, Alexander. 2001. Reconstructing Proto-Indo-Hittite. In *Greater Anatolia and the Indo-Hittite Language Family*, ed. Robert Drews, 106–30. Journal of Indo-European Studies Monograph Series 38. Washington, D.C.: Institute for the Study of Man.

Liverani, Mario. 1988. *Antico Oriente: Storia, società, economia*. Rome: Laterza.

MacQueen, James G. 1996. *The Hittites and Their Contemporaries in Asia Minor*, rev. ed. London: Thames and Hudson.

Mallory, James P. 2009. The Anatolian Homeland Hypothesis and the Anatolian Neolithic. In *Proceedings of the 20th Annual UCLA Indo-European Conference. Los Angeles. 31 October–November 2, 2008*, ed. Stephanie Jamison, H. Craig Melchert, and Brent Vine, 133–62. Bremen: Hempen.

Melchert, H. Craig. 2003a. Language. In *The Luwians*, ed. H. Craig Melchert, 170–210. Leiden: Brill.

———. 2003b. The Dialectal Position of Lycian and Lydian within Anatolian. In *Licia e Lidia prima dell'Ellenizzazione. Atti del Convegno internazionale Roma, 11–12 ottobre 1999*, ed. Mauro Giorgieri, Mirjo Salvini, Marie-Claude Trémouille, and Pietro Vannicelli, 265–72. Rome: Consiglio Nazionale Delle Ricerche.

———. 2003c. Prehistory. In *The Luwians*, ed. H. Craig Melchert, 8–26. Leiden: Brill.

———. 2004a. A Luwian Dedication. In *Indo-European Perspectives. Studies in Honour of Anna Morpurgo Davies*, ed. John W. Penney, 370–79. Oxford: Oxford University Press.

———. 2004b. Palaic. Lycian. Lydian. Carian. In *The Cambridge Encyclopedia of the World's Ancient Languages*, ed. Roger D. Woodard, 585–613. Cambridge: Cambridge University Press.

———. 2005. The Problem of Luvian Influence on Hittite: When and How Much? In *Sprachkontakt und Sprachwandel. Akten der XI. Fachtagung der indogermanischen Gesellschaft, 17–23 September 2000, Halle an der Saale*, ed. Gerhard Meiser and Olaf Hackstein, 445–60. Wiesbaden: Reichert.

Oettinger, Norbert. 2002. Indogermanische Sprachträger lebten schon im 3. Jahrtausend v. Chr. in Kleinasien. In *Die Hethiter und ihr Reich. Das Volk der 1000 Götter*, 50–55. Stuttgart: Theiss.

Puhvel, Jaan. 1990. Anatolian: Autochthon or Interloper? *Journal of Indo-European Studies* 22: 251–63.

Renfrew, Colin. 1987. *Archaeology and Language: The Puzzle of Indo-European Origins*. London: Cape.

Rieken, Elisabeth. 2005. Hethitisch. In *Sprachen des Alten Orients*, ed. Michael P. Streck, 80–127. Darmstadt: Wissenschaftliche Buchgesellschaft.

———. 2008. The Origin of the *-l* Genitive and the History of the Stems in *-īl-* and *-ūl-* in Hittite. In *Proceedings of the 19th Annual UCLA Indo-European Conference. Los Angeles. 3–4 November 2007*, ed. Karlene Jones-Bley, Martin Huld, Angela Della Volpe, and Miriam Robins Dexter, 239–57. Indo-European Studies Monograph Series 54. Washington, D.C.: Institute for the Study of Man.

Simon, Zsolt. 2006. Review of H. Craig Melchert (ed.), *The Luwians* (Leiden/Boston, 2003). *Acta Antiqua* 46: 313–28.

Singer, Itamar. 1981. Hittites and Hattians in Anatolia at the Beginning of the Second Millennium B.C. *Journal of Indo-European Studies* 9: 119–34.

Soysal, Oğuz. 2004. *Hattischer Wortschatz in hethitischer Textüberlieferung*. Leiden: Brill.

Starke, Frank. 1990. *Untersuchung zur Stammbildung des keilschrift-luwischen Nomens*. Studien zu den Boğazköy-Texten 31. Wiesbaden: Harrassowitz.

———. 1997. Troia im Kontext des historisch-politischen und sprachlichen Umfeldes Kleinasiens im 2. Jahrtausend. *Studia Troica* 7: 448–87.

Stefanini, Ruggiero. 2002. Toward a Diachronic Reconstruction of the Linguistic Map of Ancient Anatolia. In *Anatolica Antiqua. Studi in memoria di Fiorella Imparati*, ed. Stefano de Martino and Franca Pecchioli Daddi, 783–806. Eothen 11. Firenze: LoGisma.

Steiner, Gerd. 1981. The Role of the Hittites in Ancient Anatolia. *Journal of Indo-European Studies* 9: 150–73.

———. 1990. The Immigration of the First Indo-Europeans into Anatolia Reconsidered. *Journal of Indo-European Studies* 18: 185–214.

Tischler, Johann. 1995. Die kappadokischen Texte als älteste Quelle indogermanischen Sprachgutes. In *Atti del II Congresso Internazionale di Hittitologia*, ed. Onofrio

Carruba, Mauro Giorgieri, and Clelia Mora, 359–68. Studia Mediterranea 9. Pavia: Iuculano.

Watkins, Calvert. 2004. Hittite. In *The Cambridge Encyclopedia of the World's Ancient Languages*, ed. Roger Woodard, 551–75. Cambridge: Cambridge University Press.

Weitenberg, Joseph J. S. 1984. *Die hethitischen U-Stämme*. Amsterdam: Rodopi.

Yakubovich, Ilya. 2005. Carian Monument. In *Hṛdāmánasā. Sbornik statej k 70-letiju so dna rozhdenija professora Leonarda Georgijevicha Gerzenberga*, ed. Nikolai N. Kazanskij, 240–51. St. Petersburg: Nauk.

———. 2010. *Sociolinguistics of the Luvian Language*. Brill's Studies in Indo-European Languages and Linguistics vol. 2. Leiden: Brill.

CHAPTER 32

TROY IN REGIONAL AND INTERNATIONAL CONTEXT

PETER JABLONKA

Location and Discovery

The archaeological site of Troy (Turkish Hisarlık, Homer's Ilios, Greek and Roman Ilion/Ilium) in northwestern Turkey occupies a spur on a low ridge five kilometers from the present coastline on the Asiatic side of the Dardanelles (ancient Hellespont). The site overlooks an alluvial plain at the mouth of the rivers Karamenderes Çayı (ancient Scamander) and Dümrek Deresi (ancient Simoeis). Originally, this plain was a wide but shallow bay that has silted up with river sediments over the past 6,000 years (Kayan et al. 2003; Kraft et al. 2003). Early Bronze Age Troy was founded as a coastal settlement. Troy's geographical position between two continents and seas, at the crossing point of land routes from Anatolia to the Balkans and sea routes from the Aegean to the Black Sea, may help explain its prosperity (Höckmann 2003; Korfmann 1986; Wright 1997).

The site consists of a 300 × 200 m wide mound ("citadel") and a surrounding settlement ("lower town") covering the plateau and its slopes to the south and east. It was occupied continuously from ca. 3000 B.C.E. to 600 C.E. Fifteen meters of deposits on the mound contain the ruins of superimposed and frequently enlarged Bronze Age citadels, the sanctuary of Athena Ilias, and other public buildings of Greek and Roman Ilion (see Greaves, chapter 21 in this volume). Although excavations have always concentrated on the citadel mound, parts of classical Ilion and Bronze Age settlement remains have also been discovered in the area of the lower town. The stratigraphic sequence has been subdived into nine major periods, Troy I–IX, called "cities" by the early excavators Schliemann and Dörpfeld. Revised, refined, and radiocarbon dated, this chronology is still valid today (Korfmann and Kromer 1993; Kromer, Korfmann, and Jablonka 2003).

Hisarlık was first noted in 1703 by Franz Kauffer and identified as classical Ilion in 1801 by Edward Daniel Clarke. Coins (Bellinger 1961; Mannsperger 2006) and inscriptions (Frisch 1975) confirm this identification. Charles MacLaren (1822) concluded that according to ancient tradition, Ilion must also be Homer's Troy. Nevertheless, the search for Troy was continued at other sites in the vicinity, influenced by the ancient geographer Strabo, who believed that the Troy of the *Iliad* was not the Ilion of his own time. After first excavations by the British naval officer John Brunton in 1856, Frank Calvert—a British expatriate and amateur scholar living in the region—excavated prehistoric deposits at Hisarlık/Ilion in 1863 and 1865. When Heinrich Schliemann, a retired German merchant considering a second career as scholar and archaeologist, arrived in the Dardanelles in 1868, Calvert pointed the site out to him (Easton 1991; Heuck Allen 1999; Robinson 2007). Schliemann continued excavations from 1870 until his death in 1890 (Easton 2002; Traill 1995). Finding treasures in what looked like the remains of a burned citadel, he mistakenly took this for evidence that the Trojan War had actually taken place at Hisarlık. Later it became clear that his finds belong to the Early Bronze Age, at least 1,000 years older than any possible date for the events related by Homer. Nevertheless, Schliemann's excavations and publications (e.g., Schliemann 1881, 1884) firmly established the site as Homeric Troy in the public mind.

Wilhelm Dörpfeld continued excavations in 1893 and 1894 and subsequently published his own as well as Schliemann's results (Dörpfeld 1902). From 1932 to 1938 Carl W. Blegen and a team from the University of Cincinnati returned to Troy (Blegen 1963; Blegen et al. 1950; Blegen, Caskey, and Rawson 1951, 1953; Blegen, et al. 1958). In 1988, Manfred Korfmann of the University of Tübingen resumed excavations with Charles Brian Rose and an international team. After Korfmann's death in 2005, Ernst Pernicka, also from the University of Tübingen, continued the work at Troy with Peter Jablonka and others (Korfmann 2006; *Studia Troica* 1991–2009).

Apart from the archaeological museums in İstanbul and Çanakkale, the main collections of finds from Troy are in Berlin, Moscow, and St. Petersburg (Antonova, Tolstikov, and Treister 1996; Schmidt 1902; Tolstikow and Trejster 1996). In 1996 the northern Troad was designated a Turkish Historical National Park, and in 1998 Troy was declared a UNESCO World Heritage Site.

The Stratigraphic Levels at Troy

No doubt the attempt to find the setting of the *Iliad* has been the incentive for the large-scale research that has continued at the site for the past 140 years. During this long history of research, however, Troy—its legendary associations aside—has become an important archaeological site in its own right. With its unique, continuous sequence covering the entire Bronze Age and later periods, Troy is certainly among the most prominent sites in Anatolia and the Aegean.

Troy I (ca. 3000–2550 B.C.E.)

Late Neolithic/Chalcolithic (Starting from ca. 6000 B.C.E.; Kumtepe A, 5000–4750 B.C.E.; Kumtepe B, 3300–3000 B.C.E.) sites have been discovered in the vicinity of Troy and on the island of Imbros (Erdoğu 2011; Gabriel 2000; Harmankaya and Erdoğu 2003; see also Özdoğan, chapter 29, Özbaşaran, chapter 5, and Schoop, chapter 7 in this volume). The earliest settlement at Troy from the beginning of the Early Bronze Age was a small village built on terraces above the coast (see figure 32.1). Houses with stone and mudbrick walls were attached to each other. Some were already megaron-type buildings consisting of a large rectangular room with a smaller anteroom. The village was surrounded with stone ramparts that were repeatedly reinforced. Troy I has fourteen known phases (Korfmann 1999:9). Pottery was mostly dark, handmade, often burnished, and sometimes decorated with white encrustation. Although most metal objects were still made from copper, bronze artifacts have been found in Troy I Levels at nearby Beşiktepe (Begemann 2003).

Troy II (ca. 2550–2300 B.C.E.)

Troy II had three successive fortification walls, now consisting of mudbrick walls crowning stone ramparts (see figure 32.1). A monumental gateway was constructed on the southeast side. To the southwest, another gate was approached by a stone-paved ramp. In Middle Troy II five parallel, free-standing megaron buildings, up to forty meters long, possibly used for assemblies, audiences, or religious ceremonies, were erected inside a courtyard at the center of the citadel (Ünlüsoy 2006). Both Middle and Late Troy II ended in a conflagration. Schliemann's "burned city" comprises both of these. We now realize that Blegen's division of the period into eight phases needs adjustment (Easton 2002:307–8). After the first destruction, monumental buildings were replaced by densely clustered blocks of smaller houses during Late Troy II. A similar development can once again be observed in Late Bronze Age Troy VI and VIIa. An area of nine hectares to the south of the citadel was protected by a palisade uncovered during recent excavations (Jablonka 2001, 2006). Houses have been discovered immediately outside the citadel (Sazcı 2005). For the first time, the citadel of Troy II was surrounded by a larger settlement.

Although there was much continuity in pottery shapes and wares throughout Troy I–V, Troy II exhibits several innovations; Wheelmade Plain Ware, notably large quantities of plates, appears in Early Troy II, along with two-handled cups, tankards and goblets (*depas amphikypellon*) during Middle Troy II. The first pots and lids decorated with a face in relief can be dated to Late Troy II. Red-Coated Ware begins in Troy II but continued to be used until Early Troy VI.

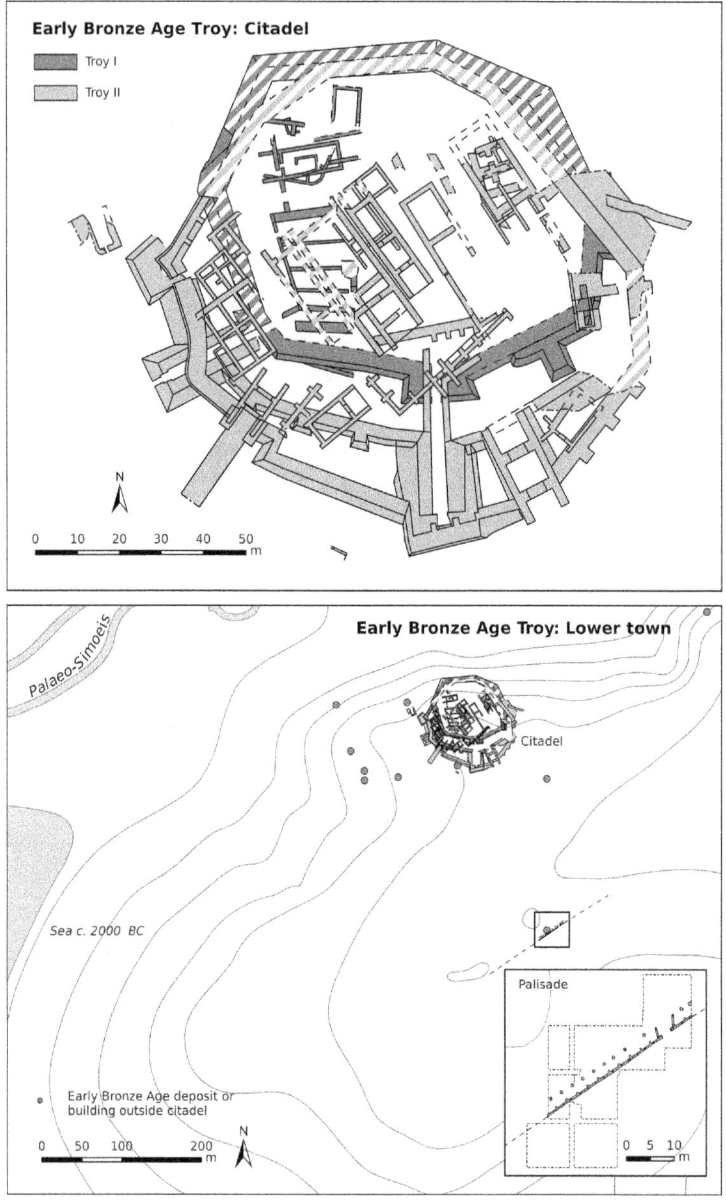

Figure 32.1. Plan of Early Bronze Age Troy. Citadel, lower town area with reconstructed ancient topography (© Peter Jablonka and Troia-Projekt, University of Tübingen).

In the Troy II Levels Schliemann found sixteen hoards, of which treasure A ("Priam's Treasure") is the largest. Their integrity is debated (Easton 1994; Traill 2000). The hoards include thousands of objects made from gold, silver, electrum, bronze, carnelian, and lapis lazuli (Easton 1994; Korfmann 2001a; Sazcı and Treister 2006; Tolstikow and Trejster 1996). Unfinished objects and raw materials are evidence for metalworking on the site (Tolstikow and Trejster 1996:231–34).

Troy III (ca. 2300–2200 B.C.E.), IV (ca. 2200–2000 B.C.E.), and V (ca. 2000–1750 B.C.E.)

The following settlements were seemingly less prosperous, but the impression that Troy III–V were rather modest villages may partly be due to the current state of research (see Blum 2006; Sazcı 2001). Exposing the center of Troy II, Schliemann removed large parts of these levels without sufficient documentation. Blegen ascribed much of what Dörpfeld had called Troy III to a late phase of Troy II. As a result, chronology and interpretation of these periods are still somewhat ambiguous. Similar in style to late Troy II, the area of the citadel in Troy III was covered by densely packed houses with stone and mudbrick walls, but on different alignments. Domed clay ovens appear from Troy IV onward. During Troy III, the ramparts of Troy II may still have been in use. Houses from Troy V have been excavated to the west of the citadel, a clear sign that the settlement was growing again. Pottery from Troy III is almost indistinguishable from that of Troy II. Wheelmade pottery and Red-Coated Ware become more frequent during Troy III–V. Red-Cross bowls are characteristic of Troy V.

Troy VI (ca. 1750–1300 B.C.E.) and VIIa (ca. 1300–1180 B.C.E.)

Troy VI (eight phases) and VIIa (two phases) represent the peak of Troy's prosperity in the Late Bronze Age (see figure 32.2). The citadel by far surpassed its predecessors in size and workmanship. Regrettably, its center was removed when the mound was leveled in the Hellenistic period to make room for the sanctuary of Athena. Still more was dug away, undocumented, by Schliemann.

At the end of the period, the fortification walls (Klinkott 2004) enclosed an area of two hectares. The walls, built of large limestone blocks, with small "sawtooth" offsets every seven to ten meters, were five meters wide, and stood up to ten meters high. Several towers were built against the walls. The fortification walls continued to be used during early Troy VIII and remained partly visible until the Roman period. From the south gate, a paved and drained street led into the citadel. Inside the walls, large, two-storey, free-standing buildings up to thirty-five meters long, with stone walls that resemble the fortification, were built on terraces rising toward the center, exhibiting a variety of layouts: megaron houses, halls with pillars or columns, and irregular floor plans. The massive house walls without ground-floor windows may have served defensive purposes, possibly indicating conflicts among leading families.

Both VI and VIIa were destroyed by unknown causes. There are masses of fallen stones (especially VI), traces of burning (especially VIIa), and some subsidence and other damage in the southeast corner of the citadel, which Blegen attributed to an earthquake at the end of Troy VI. When the citadel was rebuilt in Troy VIIa, some of the buildings inside were reused. Empty spaces were filled with smaller houses. In many rooms, storage vessels (pithoi) were sunk into the ground. This replacement of the almost palace-like buildings of Troy VI almost certainly reflects changes in society. Towers and mudbrick breastworks were added to the citadel walls in Troy

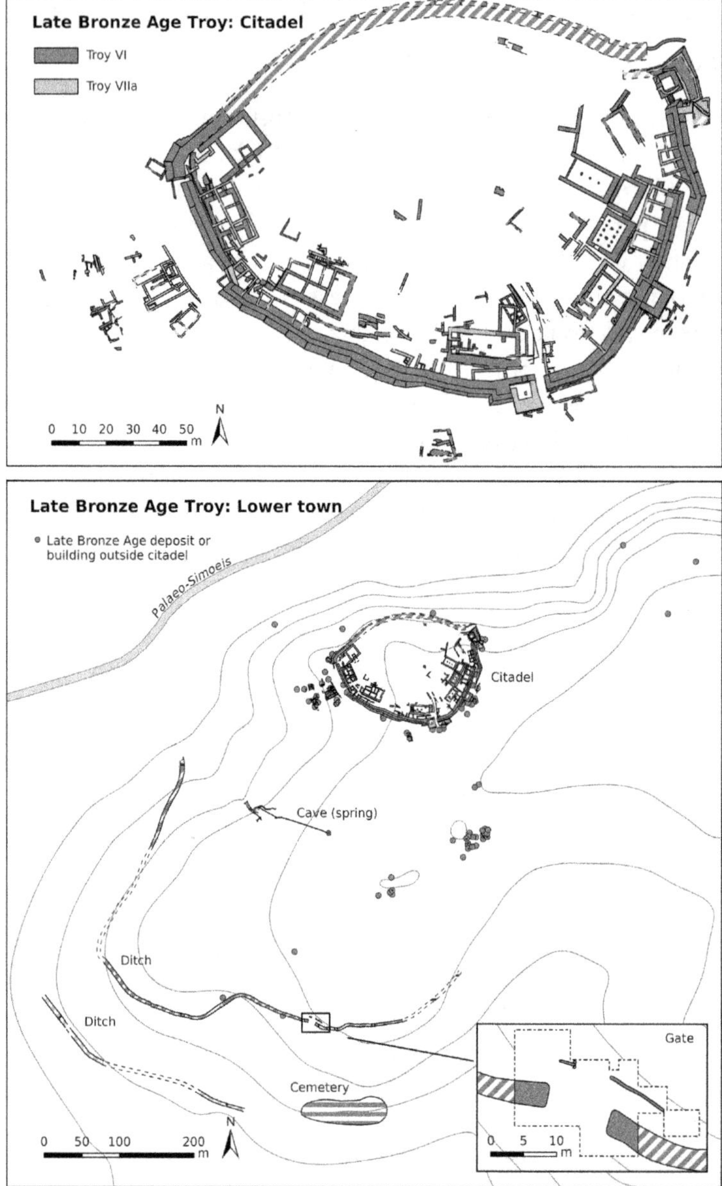

Figure 32.2. Plan of Late Bronze Age Troy. Citadel, lower town with reconstructed ancient topography, rock-cut ditch, and gate (Troy VI) (© Peter Jablonka and Troia-Projekt, University of Tübingen).

VIIa, but at the same time new houses were also built outside (Becks, Rigter, and Hnila 2006).

The Late Bronze Age citadel was surrounded by a larger settlement called the "lower town" (or "lower city") (Becks, Rigter, and Hnila 2006; Jablonka 2006; Jablonka and Rose 2004; Korfmann 1997). Its ill-preserved remains are covered by Hellenistic and Roman Ilion. This larger settlement was surrounded by a rock-cut defensive ditch filled up at the end of Troy VI. A stretch of another rock-cut ditch has been discovered to the south of the first one. This might reflect continuing growth of the settlement during Troy VIIa.

The area inside the first ditch, covering about thirty hectares, was rather densely built up close to the citadel, but some houses have also been found farther away. A systematic surface find collection demonstrated that Late Bronze Age pottery is scattered across a wide area south and east of the citadel (Jablonka 2005). A small cemetery from Late Troy VI, excavated by Blegen, 450 m south of the citadel is situated outside the area protected by a gate bridging the ditch.

Considerable effort was made to secure the settlement's water supply. A system of artificial tunnels and shafts 200 m southwest of the citadel tapping two aquifers was already known to Schliemann but has only recently been excavated. Its beginnings have been dated to the Bronze Age (Frank, Mangini, and Korfmann 2002; Korfmann, Frank, and Mangini 2006). The citadel's northeast bastion was built around a rectangular well accessible through a gate from the "lower town" outside, and there were more wells within the citadel.

Troy VI is not only marked by innovations in architecture. At the beginning of the period, horses were introduced. A gray, wheelmade type of burnished pottery virtually identical with the Middle Helladic Gray Minyan Ware of Greece became predominant (Pavúk 2005). With changing shapes, production of this West Anatolian Gray Ware continued until Troy VIIb. From mid-Troy VI onward, Tan Ware was produced from the same clays using different firing techniques. Mycenaean shapes were imitated in both wares. Although only a small fraction of the pottery was imported, Minoan, Mycenaean, Cypriot, and Levantine pottery occurred throughout Troy VI and VII (Mountjoy 2006; Mountjoy and Mommsen 2006). However, pottery or other finds from Hittite Anatolia are missing.

Troy VIIb (ca. 1180–950 B.C.E.)

During the first phase of VIIb houses were rebuilt inside and outside the citadel, and the citadel walls repaired. In later phases houses outside the citadel had multi-roomed cellars with no doorways. A new building technique—walls using upright stones (orthostats)—was introduced.

At the beginning of the period pottery remains similar to that of Troy VIIa continue, but some handmade wares (Barbarian Ware) begin to appear. Handmade Knobbed Ware ("Buckelkeramik") similar to pottery from southeastern Europe is typical of later phases. Toward the end, Mycenaean imports from Greece are followed by Protogeometric pottery (Catling 1998). Troy VIIb therefore extends into the Iron Age.

Inside a house from the first phase of Troy VIIb a biconvex bronze seal has been found, so far the only evidence of writing at Bronze Age Troy (Hawkins and Easton 1996). The Luwian hieroglyphic inscription gives the names of a woman and a man whose profession is specified as scribe. The seal itself may be earlier than its find context.

Post-Bronze Age Troy

At the end of Troy VIIb there is evidence for some destruction by fire while other houses look as if they have been left intact. Excavations to the south of the citadel indicate that limited activity continued at Troy, maybe connected to a sanctuary (Chabot Aslan 2002). Greeks colonized the area in the eighth century B.C.E. at the latest (Rose 2008). Southwest of the citadel, votive offerings were deposited beginning in the ninth century B.C.E., and in the seventh and sixth centuries B.C.E. Archaic temples were built. During the Classical Period, the city came under the domination of the Persian Empire (see Harl, chapter 34 in this volume). After Alexander's visit in 334 B.C.E., Troy-Ilion became the center of a confederation of cities in the Troad. A theater, a temple of Athena, and other public buildings were erected. The city soon recovered from destruction by Fimbria's troops during the Roman civil war in 85 B.C.E. and flourished once again until the Late Roman period, not least by exploiting its ties with a mythical past. After all, even Roman emperors, especially the Julio-Claudians, believed their ancestors descended from Troy's royal family. After two earthquakes around 500 C.E., occupation came to an end, but there are also Late Byzantine finds and cemeteries.

Troy Between the Aegean and Anatolia

Troy has been regarded as the scene of the Trojan War, a legend told in Homer's *Iliad* and still part of popular culture. Because the same story also lies at the heart of ancient and modern Greek ethnic identity, Troy, although actually a site on the Anatolian mainland, has been considered Aegean and has been excavated by, among others, Carl W. Blegen, a scholar primarily specializing in Mycenaean Greece. But even in the epic, the Trojans were probably not Greeks, and Homer himself might have been born in one of the Ionian Greek cities on the coast of Anatolia.

The link between the Greek epic tradition and the ruins at Hisarlık-Troy is by no means self-evident. Obviously, the stage of the *Iliad* is a place on the Dardanelles, at or near Troy. But in any discussion of the historicity of the Trojan War, the following questions have to be answered: does the Greek epic reflect historical events? If so, where did they take place, and when? Some scholars argue that the epic tales are an amalgamation of traditions, partly mythological, partly containing distant memories of historic events; these derive from several parts of Greece and more than one period, and were collected and transferred to Hisarlık during the Aeolic expansion during the eighth century B.C.E. or not long before (Carpenter 1956; Hertel 2008:194–221). On the other hand, scenes illustrating the sack of a town with attackers arriving by ship have been popular in Minoan and Mycenaean art since the first half of the second millennium B.C.E. (Morris 2007), long before any possible connection with Late Bronze Age Troy.

However, an attempt has been made to reconcile all available sources—archaeology, second millennium B.C.E. written sources, and Greek epic tradition—in one consistent scenario. Given the fragmentary, sometimes ambiguous, nature of the surviving evidence, this is all that can be done. As early as 1923–24, Emil Forrer and Paul Kretschmer noted that some names on cuneiform tablets from the Hittite capital Ḫattuša were similar to names known from the *Iliad*: Wiluša (a country)-(W)ilios, Alakšandu-Alexandros (the Trojan prince Paris's other name), Aḫḫiyawa-Achaioi (Greeks) (Latacz 2004:95f.; and see Bryce, chapter 15 in this volume). Most, but not all, scholars agree that Aḫḫiyawa was Mycenaean Greece or a part of it, Wiluša was a country in northwest Anatolia, and Troy most likely its capital (see Beckman 1999 for an English translation of relevant Hittite sources; Bryce 2006 and chapter 15 in this volume; Latacz 2004; Starke 1997). Remembrance of conflicts between this kingdom of Wiluša and Mycenaean groups during the period of unrest at the end of the second millennium B.C.E. may have survived the fall of Troy, the Hittite Empire, and the Mycenaean palaces. This could have become the core of the story of the Trojan War (Latacz 2004).

Since neither inscriptions confirming the *Iliad* nor definite proof for a violent destruction by invaders from Greece have been discovered at Troy, we will probably never know for certain. However, Heinrich Schliemann could well have found nothing beneath the ruins of Greek and Roman Ilion. But what he and his successors discovered was certainly a Bronze Age regional center. It was always a well-fortified stronghold, and its walls were renewed and enlarged after each of several destructions. Schliemann himself was convinced that the burned citadel of Troy II with its treasures was King Priam's city. In part as a result of Schliemann's own excavations in Greece, it soon became clear that these finds were a millennium older than the civilization of Mycenaean Greece. After excavating the Late Bronze Age citadel, Dörpfeld advocated for Troy VI being Homer's Troy. Blegen argued that the densely packed houses of Troy VIIa with their storage jars showed that the population sought protection behind the citadel walls (Blegen et al. 1958:10–13). However, houses from Troy VIIa have now also been found outside the citadel, and Blegen's interpretation using some burning and a few human bones remains is far from conclusive. But what is Troy's significance beyond Homeric questions? What was its function within the region, and what links did it have with territories beyond?

Troy I was founded as a coastal settlement. Architecture and finds are similar to contemporaneous sites on the shores and islands of the northern Aegean, for example, Poliochni on Lemnos or Thermi on Lesbos (Kouka 2002; Sériadès 1985). Rows of terraced houses with a main room and a porch-like anteroom similar to Troy or nearby Beşiktepe (Korfmann 1988) are not confined to the Aegean but have also been found in inland and southern Anatolia, for example, in Demircihöyük near Eskişehir (Korfmann 1983a) or Bademağacı Höyük north of Antalya (Duru 2004; see Steadman, chapter 10 in this volume, for discussion of these sites). Sloping fortification walls (glacis) with projections (bastions) to the side of a gate as in Late Troy I have been excavated at Limantepe near İzmir (Erkanal 2008).The pottery of Troy I is strongly related to the Babaköy-Yortan group and other sites in western Anatolia. There are only very few imports from Early Helladic/Cycladic II ("Urfirnis" Ware and sauceboats). Finds from the Ezero culture in present-day Bulgaria also bear some resemblance to Troy I and II (see Özdoğan, chapter 29 in this volume). Troy I appears to belong to a distinctively west Anatolian–northeast Aegean–Thracian cultural sphere—already firmly anchored at the intersection of those neighboring regions that continue to be significant throughout its later history.

After several phases of rebuilding and enlargement, what had started as a fortified village had evolved into the monumental citadel of Middle Troy II with a settlement surrounding it. Although the ground plan of the central megaron buildings is similar to that of the earlier terraced houses, the idea of placing one or more monumental halls inside a walled courtyard, which in turn is surrounded by at least one more fortification wall, is new at the site. This plan may go back to Late Neolithic Sesklo and Dimini in Greece. The site of Kanlıgeçit (Özdoğan 2006 and chapter 29 in this volume) in Turkish Thrace looks like a scale model of Troy II. Küllüoba near Eskişehir was another center comparable to and even larger than Troy (Efe 2006). Far away, the layout of the temples in antis in Early Bronze Age cities of Syria resembles the citadel of Troy II. In Halawa A, even details of the courtyard walls are the same (Orthmann 1989:63–84). In the Aegean, places like Lerna, Aegina, or Poliochni served similar functions, even if their architecture looks different.

From Troy II onward, some of the copper and all of the tin used for bronze objects were imported (Pernicka et al. 2003). Raw materials for artifacts from the treasures of Troy II came from regions as far away as Afghanistan and central Asia. Vessels like the two-handled cup (depas amphikypellon), jewelry, and other objects have been found in Bulgaria, Greece, Anatolia, Syria, and Mesopotamia (Tolstikow and Trejster 1996).

During the course of the third millennium B.C.E., cities, states, and writing had already been established in Egypt, Mesopotamia, and Syria. At the periphery, from Anatolia to Greece, secondary centers acted as nodes in a network of exchange and contact with these more developed areas (Korfmann 2001b; Maran 1998; Rahmstorf 2006; Sherratt 1997). Toward the end of the third millennium B.C.E., however, Troy was only one among many places destroyed by a crisis striking the wider region. This may have made room for the subsequent ascent of Minoan Crete.

In Troy IV, domed ovens were introduced. Like the "Red-Cross Bowls" of Troy V (Korfmann 1983b), this seems to be an influence from Anatolia. Similar bowls occurring in the Early Helladic II period at Lerna seem to be an independent phenomenon. At or after the end of Troy V, however, the first Minoan imports appear at Troy and other places in the northeast Aegean (Guzowska 2002).

Some architectural details of Late Bronze Age Troy resemble Mycenaean citadels, such as megaron buildings and "sawtooth" vertical offsets that divide walls into sections. The ground plan of the "Pillar House" is similar to the megaron at Midea. Rectangular towers as well as the concept of a citadel combined with a town or city show influence from Hittite Anatolia. Taken as a whole, however, the layout of the site is without parallels.

The shapes and surface treatment of the gray pottery of Troy VI and VII (Pavúk 2005) have been influenced by Middle Helladic fashions to an extent that it has, like the pottery found in Greece, long been called "Gray Minyan." Although this ware is no longer used after the Middle Helladic Period in Greece, West Anatolian Gray Wares and the Tan Ware made from the same clays continue to be produced until the end of Troy VIIb. Minoan, Mycenaean, and Cypriot, as well as a very few sherds of Levantine, pottery have been found at Troy. On the other hand, West Anatolian Gray Ware has been found as far away as Cyprus and the Levant (Mommsen and Pavúk 2007). Much of the Mycenaean pottery is local imitation, and Mycenaean shapes were locally produced in Gray and Tan Wares. The majority of the pottery is always locally made. No Mycenaean pottery has been found anywhere inside the Dardanelles, whereas Aegean metal types occur in the Black Sea region, and a stone scepter from Romania has been found on the Uluburun shipwreck (Höckmann 2003). Unlike farther south on the west Anatolian coast, where archaeological evidence for a strong Minoan and Mycenaean presence at Miletus, Müsgebi, and other places is supported by Hittite documentary sources (Niemeier 1999; Bryce, chapter 15 in this volume), Mycenaean influence at Troy was limited.

On the other hand, with the exception of the Luwian seal, no Hittite objects have been found at Troy or anywhere west of Eskişehir (Seeher 2005), although west Anatolian Hittite vassal states are known from Hittite documents, and Troy itself may have been the capital of one of them. Exploiting its favorable position at the entrance into the Dardanelles, Late Bronze Age Troy may have served as a gateway between the Mediterranean and the world beyond. Regional centralization processes will also have contributed to its rise.

Toward the end of the Bronze Age, the Knobbed Ware and orthostat architecture of Troy VIIb are both similar to finds from southeastern Europe and along the shores of the Black Sea. This has been thought to reflect the arrival of immigrant population groups, maybe corresponding to "Thracian" invasions of Anatolia remembered in ancient Greek traditions.

Late Bronze Age Troy therefore shows distinctly northwest Anatolian cultural traits. During Troy VI and VIIa, for the second time in its long history, it had several characteristics of a central place, urbanized at least in comparison to its regional setting: monumental architecture, a citadel surrounded by a large settlement, finds that reflect craft specialization, and foreign contacts. Late Bronze Age Troy was as large as medium-sized Hittite cities. On the other hand, several characteristics of Bronze Age civilizations seem to be absent: sculpture or wall paintings, and, with the exception of one seal, writing or other administrative practices. Although this has recently been disputed (see Easton et al. 2002; Hertel and Kolb 2003; Jablonka and Rose 2004; Kolb 2004; Korfmann 1997), it certainly was the center of the surrounding region, most likely the capital of a city state that became a vassal of the Hittite Empire.

Not surprisingly, and in accordance with its geographical position, archaeological Troy represents a regional northwest Anatolian cultural development with strong ties to other parts of Anatolia, the Aegean, and Thrace. To construct "Anatolian," "Aegean," or "Thracian" archaeologies corresponding to present-day political boundaries between Turkey, Greece, and Bulgaria is meaningless. If these divisions exist as academic specializations, it is primarily because, for practical or political reasons, individual scholars have tended to work in only one of those countries.

Conclusion

From the point of few of archaeology, Hisarlık-Troy ranks high among important sites of the Anatolian and Aegean Bronze Age. Both its Early and Late Bronze Age architecture, the treasures as well as ceramics and other finds reflecting long-distance contacts, the size of the site, its layout comprising a fortified stronghold surrounded by a larger, outlying settlement, and its strategic position clearly show that Troy served as the center of the surrounding region.

Unlike central and southeast Anatolia, regions that formed the heartland of the Hittite Empire and are close to literate Syria and Mesopotamia, written sources relating to Bronze Age west Anatolia are few and far between. However, if the hypothesis that Troy was the capital of the Land of Wiluša is correct, at least faint light is thrown on its history.

Persons and places named in Hittite written sources may further connect the site, and Bronze Age history, to similar names in the Greek epic tradition. No doubt Homer's *Iliad* and *Odyssey* are among the most influential texts ever written. For the ancient Greeks, never politically united, their city-states frequently in conflict with each other, being Greek meant to share a common language, tradition, and religion. Homer formed the core of this cultural and ethnic identity. But the story could also be used in many other ways. Political leaders as varied as the Persian king Xerxes, Alexander the Great, Roman emperors, and Sultan Mehmet the Conqueror all visited Troy in memory of the Greek and Trojan heroes. Even the allied landing at the Dardanelles in 1915 was staged as a new Trojan War. The legends have inspired innumerable works of literature, art, music, and—recently—film.

The situation at Troy bears some resemblance to the archaeology in the lands of the Bible. Three complementary strands of evidence pertaining to roughly the same area and period in time draw very different pictures; archaeology and epigraphic sources have been eclipsed by a culturally highly significant and extremely popular text that has undergone a considerable amount of scholarly deconstruction.

This will always leave ample room for a variety of interpretations. But with the discovery of new archaeological evidence and more contemporaneous written sources, our reconstruction of the history that underlies the tradition will become more reliable.

References

Antonova, Irina, Vladimir Tolstikov, and Michail Treister. 1996. *The Gold of Troy: Searching for Homer's Fabled City.* London: Thames and Hudson.

Beckman, Gary. 1999. *Hittite Diplomatic Texts*, 2nd ed. Society of Biblical Literature, Writings from the Ancient World, vol. 7. Atlanta: Scholars Press.

Becks, Ralf, Wendy Rigter, and Pavol Hnila. 2006. Das Terrassenhaus im westlichen Unterstadtviertel von Troia. *Studia Troica* 16: 87–88.

Begemann, Friedrich. 2003. On the Composition and Provenience of Metal Finds from Beşiktepe (Troia). In *Troia and the Troad: Scientific Approaches. Natural Science in Archaeology*, ed. Günther A. Wagner, Ernst Pernicka, and Hans-Peter Uerpmann, 173–201. Berlin: Springer.

Bellinger, Alfred Raymond. 1961. *The Coins*. Troy Supplementary Monograph 2. Princeton: Princeton University Press.

Blegen, Carl W. 1963. *Troy and the Trojans. Ancient Peoples and Places*. London: Thames and Hudson.

Blegen, Carl W., Cedric G. Boulter, John L. Caskey, and Marion Rawson. 1958. *Troy. The Settlements VIIa, VIIb, and VIII. Volume 4*. Princeton, N.J.: Princeton University Press.

Blegen, Carl W., John L. Caskey, and Marion Rawson. 1951. *Troy. The Third, Fourth, and Fifth Settlements. Volume 2*. Princeton, N.J.: Princeton University Press.

———. 1953. *Troy. The Sixth Settlement. Volume 3*. Princeton, N.J.: Princeton University Press.

Blegen, Carl W., John L. Caskey, Marion Rawson, and Jerome Sperling. 1950. *Troy: General Introduction: The First and the Second Settlements*. Volume 1. Princeton, N.J.: Princeton University Press.

Blum, Stephan W. E. 2006. Troia an der Wende von der frühen zur mittleren Bronzezeit: Troia IV und Troia V. In *Troia: Archäologie eines Siedlungshügels und seiner Landschaft*, ed. Manfred O. Korfmann, 145–54. Mainz: Philipp von Zabern.

Bryce, Trevor R. 2006. *The Trojans and Their Neighbours*. London: Routledge.

Catling, Richard. 1998. The Typology of the Protogeometric and Subprotogeometric Pottery from Troia and its Aegean Context. *Studia Troica* 8: 151–88.

Carpenter, Rhys. 1956. *Folk Tale, Fiction and Saga in the Homeric Epics*. Sather Classical Lectures no. 20. Berkeley: University of California Press.

Chabot Aslan, Carolyn. 2002. Ilion before Alexander: Protogeometric, Geometric, and Archaic Pottery from D9. *Studia Troica* 12: 81–129.

Dörpfeld, Wilhelm. 1902. *Troia und Ilion: Ergebnisse der Ausgrabungen in den vorhistorischen und historischen Schichten von Ilion 1870–1894*. Athens: Beck and Barth. Reprint, Osnabrück: Zeller, 1968.

Duru, Refik. 2004. Bademağacı Kazıları 2002 ve 2003 Yılları Çalışma Raporu. *Belleten* 68: 519–60.

Easton, Donald F. 1991. Troy before Schliemann. *Studia Troica* 1: 111–29.

———. 1994. Priam's Gold: The Full Story. *Anatolian Studies* 44: 221–43.

———. 2002. *Schliemann's Excavations at Troia 1870–1873*. Studia Troica Monographien no. 2. Mainz: Philipp von Zabern.

Easton, Donald F., J. David Hawkins, Andrew G. Sherratt, and E. Susan Sherratt. 2002. Troy in Recent Perspective. *Anatolian Studies* 52: 75–109.

Efe, Turan. 2006. Anatolische Wurzeln—Troia und die frühe Bronzezeit im Westen Kleinasiens. In *Troia: Archäologie eines Siedlungshügels und seiner Landschaft*, ed. Manfred O. Korfmann, 15–28. Mainz: Philipp von Zabern.

Erdoğu, Burçin. 2011. A Preliminary Report from the 2009 and 2010. Field Seasons at Uğurlu on the Island of Gökçeada. *Anatolica* 37: 45–65.

Erkanal, Hayat. 2008. Liman Tepe: New Light on Prehistoric Aegean Cultures. In *The Aegean in the Neolithic, Chalcolithic and the Early Bronze Age. Proceedings of the International Symposium Urla-İzmir (Turkey) 1997*, ed. Hayat Erkanal, Harald Haptmann, Vasif Şahoğlu, and Riza Tuncel, 179–90. Ankara: Ankara University Press.

Frank, Norbert, Augusto Mangini, and Manfred Korfmann. 2002. 230TH/U Dating of the Trojan "Water Quarries." *Archaeometry* 44: 305–14.

Frisch, Peter. 1975. *Die Inschriften von Ilion. Inschriften griechischer Städte aus Kleinasien no. 3*. Bonn: Habelt.

Gabriel, Utta. 2000. Mitteilungen zum Stand der Neolithikumforschung in der Umgebung von Troia (Kumtepe 1993–1995; Beşik-Sivritepe 1982–1984, 1987, 1998–1999). *Studia Troica* 10: 233–38.

Guzowska, Marta. 2002. Traces of Minoan Behavioural Patterns in the North-East Aegean. In *Mauerschau: Festschrift für Manfred Korfmann*, ed. Rüstem Aslan, Stephan Blum, Gabriele Kastl, Frank Schweizer, and Diane Thumm, 585–94. Remshalden-Grunbach: Greiner.

Harmankaya, Savaş and Burçin Erdoğu. 2003. The Prehistoric Sites of Gökçeada, Turkey. In *From Villages to Towns. Studies Presented to Ufuk Esin*, ed. Mehmet Özdoğan, Harald Hauptmann, and Nezih Başgelen, 459–79. İstanbul: Arkeoloji ve Sanat.

Hawkins, J. David and Donald F. Easton, 1996. A Hieroglyphic Seal from Troia. *Studia Troica* 6: 111–19.

Hertel, Dieter. 2008. *Das frühe Ilion. Die Besiedlung Troias durch die Griechen 1020-650/25 v. Chr.* Zetemata no. 130. München: C. H. Beck.

Hertel, Dieter and Frank Kolb. 2003. Troy in Clearer Perspective. *Anatolian Studies* 53: 71–88.

Heuck Allen, Susan. 1999. *Finding the Walls of Troy: Frank Calvert and Heinrich Schliemann at Hisarlık*. Berkeley: University of California Press.

Höckmann, Olaf. 2003. Zu früher Seefahrt in den Meerengen. *Studia Troica* 13: 133–60.

Jablonka, Peter. 2001. Eine Stadtmauer aus Holz: Das Bollwerk der Unterstadt von Troia II. In *Troia: Traum und Wirklichkeit. Begleitband zur Ausstellung*, ed. Archäologisches Landesmuseum Baden-Württemberg, 391–94. Stuttgart: Theiss.

———. 2005. Vorbericht zum archäologischen Survey im Stadtgebiet von Troia. *Studia Troica* 15: 27–43.

———. 2006. Leben außerhalb der Burg: Die Unterstadt von Troia. In *Troia: Archäologie eines Siedlungshügels und seiner Landschaft*, ed. Manfred O. Korfmann, 167–80. Mainz: Philipp von Zabern.

Jablonka, Peter and Charles Brian Rose. 2004. Late Bronze Age Troy: A Response to Frank Kolb. *American Journal of Archaeology* 108: 615–30.

Kayan, İlhan, Ertuğ Öner, Levent Uncu, Beycan Hocaoğlu, and Serdar Vardar. 2003. Geoarchaeological Interpretations of the Troian Bay. In *Troia and the Troad: Scientific Approaches*, ed. Günther A. Wagner, Ernst Pernicka, and Hans-Peter Uerpmann, 379–401. Berlin: Springer.

Klinkott, Manfred. 2004. Die Wehrmauern von Troia VI: Bauaufnahme und Auswertung. *Studia Troica* 14: 33–85.

Kolb, Frank. 2004. Troy VI: A Trading Center and Commercial City? *American Journal of Archaeology* 108: 577–613.

Korfmann, Manfred. 1983a. *Architektur, Stratigraphie, und Befunde: Demircihüyük*. Die Ergebnisse der Ausgrabungen 1975–1978, no. 1. Mainz: Philipp von Zabern.

———. 1983b. Red Cross Bowl-Angeblicher Leittyp für Troja V. In *Beiträge zur Altertumskunde Kleinasiens. Festschrift für Kurt Bittel*, ed. Rainer Michael Boehmer and Harald Hauptmann, 291–97. Mainz: Philipp von Zabern.

———. 1986. Troy: Topography and Navigation. In *Troy and the Trojan War: A Symposium Held at Bryn Mawr College, October 1984*, ed. Machteld J. Mellink, 1–16. Bryn Mawr, Pa.: Bryn Mawr College.

———. 1988. Beşik-Tepe. Vorbericht über die Ergebnisse der Grabungen von 1985 und 1986. Grabungen am Beşik-Yassıtepe und im Beşik-Gräberfeld. *Archäologischer Anzeiger* 1988: 391–404.

———. 1997. Troia, an Ancient Anatolian Palatial and Trading Center: Archaeological Evidence for the Period of Troia VI/VII. In *The World of Troy: Homer, Schliemann, and the Treasures of Priam*, ed. Deborah Boedeker, 51–73. Washington, D.C.: Society for the Preservation of the Greek Heritage.

———. 1999. Troia—Ausgrabungen 1998. *Studia Troica* 9: 1–34.

———. 2001a. Der "Schatz A" und seine Fundsituation: Bemerkungen zum historischen und chronologischen Umfeld des "Schatzfundhorizontes" in Troia. In *Beiträge zur vorderasiatischen Archäologie, Winfried Orthmann gewidmet*, ed. Jan-Waalke Meyer, Mirko Novák, and Alexander Pruß, 212–35. Frankfurt: Archäologisches Institut der Universität.

———. 2001b. Troia als Drehscheibe des Handels im 2. und 3. vorchristlichen Jahrtausends: Erkenntnisse zur Troianischen Hochkultur und zur Maritimen Troiakultur. In *Troia: Traum und Wirklichkeit. Begleitband zur Ausstellung*, ed. Archäologisches Landesmuseum Baden-Württemberg et al., 355–68. Stuttgart: Theiss.

———. ed. 2006. *Troia: Archäologie eines Siedlungshügels und seiner Landschaft*. Mainz: Philipp von Zabern.

Korfmann, Manfred, Norbert Frank, and Augusto Mangini. 2006. Eingang in die Unterwelt: Die Höhle von Troia und ihre Datierung. In *Troia: Archäologie eines Siedlungshügels und seiner Landschaft*, ed. Manfred O. Korfmann, 337–42. Mainz: Philipp von Zabern.

Korfmann, Manfred and Bernd Kromer. 1993. Demircihüyük, Beşik-Tepe, Troia: Eine Zwischenbilanz zur Chronologie dreier Orte in Westanatolien. *Studia Troica* 3: 135–72.

Kouka, Ourania. 2002. *Siedlungsorganisation in der Nord-und Ostägäis während der Frühbronzezeit*. Internationale Archäologie, no. 58. Rahden (Westfalen): Marie Leidorf.

Kraft, John C., İlhan Kayan, Helmut Brückner, and George Rapp. 2003. Sedimentary Facies Patterns and the Interpretation of Paleogeographies of Ancient Troia. In *Troia and the Troad: Scientific Approaches*, ed. Günther A. Wagner, Ernst Pernicka, and Hans-Peter Uerpmann, 361–77. Berlin: Springer.

Kromer, Bernd, Manfred Korfmann, and Peter Jablonka. 2003. Heidelberg Radiocarbon Dates for Troia I to VIII and Kumtepe. In *Troia and the Troad: Scientific Approaches*, ed. Günther A. Wagner, Ernst Pernicka, and Hans-Peter Uerpmann, 43–54. Berlin: Springer.

Latacz, Joachim. 2004. *Troy and Homer: Towards a Solution of an Old Mystery.* New York: Oxford University Press.

MacLaren, Charles. 1822. A Dissertation on the Topography of the Plain of Troy, Including an Examination of the Opinions of Demetrius, Chevalier, Dr. Clarke and Major Rendell. Edinburgh.

Mannsperger, Dietrich. 2006. Vom Zahlungsmittel zum Leitartefakt—Münzen und Münzfunde. In *Troia: Archäologie eines Siedlungshügels und seiner Landschaft*, ed. Manfred O. Korfmann, 265–74. Mainz: Philipp von Zabern.

Maran, Josef. 1998. *Kulturwandel auf dem griechischen Festland und den Kykladen im späten 3. Jahrtausend v. Chr. Studien zu den kulturellen Verhältnissen in Südosteuropa und dem zentralen Mittelmeerraum in der späten Kupfer-und frühen Bronzezeit*. Universitätsforschungen zur Prähistorischen Archäologie, no. 53. Bonn: Universität Bonn.

Mommsen, Hans and Peter Pavúk. 2007. Provenience of the Grey and Tan Wares from Troia, Cyprus and the Levant. *Studia Troica* 17: 25–41.

Morris, Sahra P. 2007. Troy between Bronze and Iron Ages: Myth, Cult and Memory in a Sacred Landscape. In *Epos. Reconsidering Greek Epic and Aegean Bronze Age*

Archaeology, ed. Sarah P. Morris, Robert Laffineur, and Emanuele Greco, 59–68. Aegeum no. 28. Liège and Austin: Université de Liège and University of Texas at Austin.

Mountjoy, Penelope A. 2006. Mykenische Keramik in Troia–Ein Überblick. In *Troia: Archäologie eines Siedlungshügels und seiner Landschaft*, ed. Manfred O. Korfmann, 241–52. Mainz: Philipp von Zabern.

Mountjoy, Penelope and Hans Mommsen. 2006. Neutron Activation Analysis of Mycenaean Pottery from Troia (1988–2003 Excavations). *Studia Troica* 16: 97–123.

Niemeier, Wolf-Dietrich. 1999. Mycenaeans and Hittites in War: Western Asia Minor. In *Polemos. Le contexte guerrier en Égée à l'âge du bronze*, ed. Robert Laffineur, 141–55. Aegeum no. 19. Liège and Austin: Université de Liège and University of Texas at Austin.

Orthmann, Winfried, ed. 1989. Halawa 1980–1986. *Vorläufiger Bericht über die 4.–9. Grabungskampagne*. Saarbücker Beiträge zur Altertumskunde no. 52. Bonn: Habelt.

Özdoğan, Mehmet. 2006. Yakın Doğu Kentleri ve Batı Anadolu'da Kentleşme Süreci. In *Cultural Reflections. Studies in Honor of Hayat Erkanal*, ed. Armağan Erkanal-Öktü, 571–78. İstanbul: Homer Kitabevi.

Pavúk, Peter. 2005. Aegeans and Anatolians: A Trojan Perspective. In *Emporia. Aegeans in the Central and Eastern Mediterranean*, ed. Robert Laffineur and Emanuele Greco, 269–79. Aegeum no. 25. Liège and Austin: Université de Liège and University of Texas at Austin.

Pernicka, Ernst, Clemens Eibner, Önder Öztunalı, and Günther A. Wagner. 2003. Early Bronze Age Metallurgy in the North-East Aegean. In *Troia and the Troad: Scientific Approaches*, ed. Günther A. Wagner, Ernst Pernicka, and Hans-Peter Uerpmann, 143–72. Berlin: Springer.

Rahmstorf, Lorenz. 2006. Zur Ausbreitung vorderasiatischer Innovationen in die frühbronzezeitliche Ägäis. *Praehistorische Zeitschrift* 81: 49–96.

Robinson, Marcelle. 2007. *Schliemann's Silent Partner: Frank Calvert (1828–1908). Pioneer, Scholar, and Survivor*. Philadelphia: Xlibris.

Rose, Charles Brian. 2008. Separating Fact from Fiction in the Aiolian Migration. *Hesperia* 77: 399–430.

Sazcı, Göksel. 2001. Gebäude mit vermutlich kultischer Funktion: Das Megaron in Quadrat G6. In *Troia: Traum und Wirklichkeit. Begleitband zur Ausstellung*, ed. Archäologisches Landesmuseum Baden-Württemberg et al., 384–90. Stuttgart: Theiss.

———. 2005. Troia I–III; die Maritime und Troia IV-V, die Anatolische Troia-Kultur: eine Untersuchung der Funde und Befunde im mittleren Schliemanngraben (D07, D08). *Studia Troica* 15: 35–98.

Sazcı, Göksel and Mikhail Treister. 2006. Troias Gold: Die Schätze des dritten Jahrtausends vor Christus. In *Troia: Archäologie eines Siedlungshügels und seiner Landschaft*, ed. Manfred O. Korfmann, 209–18. Mainz: Philipp von Zabern.

Schliemann, Henry (Heinrich). 1881. *Ilios. The City and the Country of the Trojans: The Results of Researches and Discoveries on the Site of Troy and throughout the Troad in the years 1871–1872–1873–1878–1879. Including an Autobiography of the Author*. London: Murray, and New York: Harper.

———. 1884. *Results of the Latest Researches and Discoveries on the Site of Homer's Troy, and the Heroic Tumuli and other Sites made in the year 1882; and a Narrative of a Journey in the Troad in 1881*. London: Murray, and New York: Harper.

Schmidt, Hubert. 1902. *Heinrich Schliemann's Sammlung Trojanischer Altertümer*. Berlin: Reimer.

Seeher, Jürgen. 2005. Überlegungen zur Beziehung zwischen dem hethitischen Kernland und der Westküste Anatoliens im 2. Jahrtausend v. Chr. In *Interpretationsraum Bronzezeit. Bernhard Hänsel von seinen Schülern gewidmet*, ed. Barbara Horejs, Reinhard Jung, Elke Kaiser, and Biba Teržan, 33–44. Universitätsforschungen zur Prähistorischen Archäologie no. 121. Bonn: Habelt.

Sēfériadès, Michel. 1985. *Troie I: Matériaux pour l'étude des sociétés du Nord-Est égéen au début du bronze ancien.* Cahiers (Éditions Recherche sur les civilisations) no. 15. Paris: Éditions Recherche sur les civilisations.

Sherratt, Andrew G. 1997. Troy, Maikop, Altyn Depe: Bronze Age Urbanism and its Periphery. In *Economy and Society in Prehistoric Europe: Changing Perspectives*, ed. Andrew G. Sherratt, 457–70. Edinburgh: Edinburgh University Press.

Starke, Frank. 1997. Troia im Kontext des historisch-politischen Umfeldes Kleinasiens im 2. Jahrtausend. *Studia Troica* 7: 447–88.

Studia Troica. 1991–2009. Vols. 1–18. Mainz: Philipp von Zabern. Vols. 1–15, ed. Manfred Korfmann; vols. 16–18, ed. Peter Jablonka, Ernst Pernicka, and Brian Rose.

Tolstikow, Wladimir P. and Michail J. Trejster. 1996. *Der Schatz aus Troja: Schliemann und der Mythos des Priamos-Goldes: Katalogbuch Ausstellung Puschkin-Museum Moskau 1996/97*. Stuttgart: Belser.

Traill, David A. 1995. *Schliemann of Troy: Treasure and Deceit.* New York: St. Martin's.

———. 2000. *"Priam's Treasure": Clearly a Composite. Anatolian Studies* 50: 17–35.

Ünlüsoy, Sinan. 2006. Vom Reihenhaus zum Megaron—Troia I bis Troia III. In *Troia: Archäologie eines Siedlungshügels und seiner Landschaft*, ed. Manfred O. Korfmann, 133–44. Mainz: Philipp von Zabern.

Wright, James C. 1997. The Place of Troy among the Civilizations of the Bronze Age. In *The World of Troy: Homer, Schliemann, and the Treasures of Priam*, ed. Deborah Boedeker, 33–43. Washington, D.C.: Society for the Preservation of the Greek Heritage.

CHAPTER 33

ASSYRIANS AND URARTIANS

KAREN RADNER

From the mid-ninth century to the seventh century B.C.E., the political landscape of eastern Anatolia was dominated, and indeed shaped, by the relations between two major states: Assyria and Urartu. At that time, the northern Mesopotamian kingdom of Assyria looked back at a documented history spanning a millennium. Its heartland, excellent agricultural land with sufficient rainfalls to support a sizable population, was situated in the triangle between the ancient cities of Assur (modern Qala'at Sherqat), Nineveh (modern Mosul), and Arbela (modern Erbil). In the course of the ninth century B.C.E. Assyria reclaimed those territories in the west which had been lost in the aftermath of the collapse of the Late Bronze Age system and had been controlled by local Aramaean kings for the past two centuries, and the Euphrates was reestablished as Assyria's western border. This phase of intensive military campaigning led the Assyrian army not just into the west but also far into central Anatolia, where a new power came to Assyria's attention. Urartu, to use the Assyrian name for the kingdom, controlled at the time of its greatest extent in the mid-eighth century B.C.E. the area between and around the three lakes of Van (in eastern Turkey), Urmiye (in northwestern Iran), and Sevan (in Armenia), as well as the valley of the Murat Su up to its confluence with the main branch of the Euphrates. These are also the most densely populated regions of Urartu, whereas the mountainous parts of the country, used for pasture farming in the summers, are impossible to inhabit during the winter months.

From the reign of the Urartian king Sarduri, son of Lutibri ("Sarduri I"), a contemporary of the Assyrian king Šalmaneser III (r. 858–824 B.C.E.), perhaps until the end of the kingdom of Urartu (but see Zimansky 1985:78–80), its political capital was the city of Turušpa (also Tušpa: modern Van), situated on the eastern shore of Lake Van. But when Šalmaneser's troops had first come into contact with Urartu, then under the rule of one Arramu, the capital was Arzaškun, an as yet unidentified city. Perhaps it is to be sought west of Lake Urmiye in what may be the original homeland of the Urartian royal house, if its patronage of the god Ḫaldi can indeed be seen in this light (see later discussion). Throughout its long history, Assyria's political centers were located in the Assur-Nineveh-Arbela triangle, but in the relevant period, its capital city was first Kalḫu (modern Nimrud), then Dur-Šarrukin (modern Khorsabad), and finally Nineveh.

This chapter traces the interactions between Assyria and Urartu, military and otherwise, and their impact on the neighboring Anatolian kingdoms, especially the chain of buffer states situated between Assyria's northern and Urartu's southern border.

The Sources

Although archaeological and pictorial evidence is of importance for our subject, the textual sources form the backbone for any study of the relationship between Assyria and Urartu. Relevant texts are numerous but very unevenly distributed; generally speaking, the Assyrian material is not only much more numerous but also far more diverse in nature. Therefore, our reconstructions tend to be biased toward the Assyrian point of view, simply because of the relative scarcity of relevant Urartian materials (see Zimansky, chapter 24 in this volume).

How the Assyrian sources influence, and dominate, our view of Urartu is perhaps most apparent when considering that even the name used for this state today is not a local place-name, and certainly not the name given to the kingdom by its own people, but instead the Assyrian designation; "Urartu" is the conventional Mesopotamian term for Inner Anatolia, well attested already in the Assyrian sources of the late second millennium B.C.E. (Salvini 1967), long before the Iron Age state came into existence. In modern scholarship, "Urartu" is used as the conventional label for this kingdom, but its self-designation was Biainili, a name preserved to the present day as "Van"—designating both the lake in eastern Turkey and the most important settlement on its coast (see Zimansky, chapter 24 in this volume). The name Urartu also lives on in the form of "Ararat," specifying the highest mountain in the region; with an altitude of 5,165 m, this dormant volcano is situated in Turkey's easternmost corner, just 32 km south of the border with Armenia and 16 km west of the border with Iran, in what was ancient Urartu's geographical core region. Today, however, the peak is far better known as the supposed landing place of Noah's ark.

The reconstructed sequence of the Urartian kings, too, which provides the skeleton for all reconstructions of Urartian history, is based primarily on references to them in Assyrian sources (most recently compiled by Fuchs 2011). Only recently the potential of art history has been harnessed for chronological purpose; after Ursula Seidl's (2004:122–24) pioneering analysis, which connected the changing styles of depicting lions on Urartian bronze objects with the inscriptions naming kings engraved on these same objects, these considerations are now taken into account in several new attempts to reconstruct the sequence of Urartian rulers (Kroll 2012;

Roaf 2012; Seidl 2012). However, for the time being, Urartian chronology must be considered with caution and as a work in progress.

The textual sources can be divided into two groups: official inscriptions and archival materials. The relevant official accounts preserved in the royal inscriptions cover the period from the mid-ninth to the seventh century B.C.E. in Assyria (from the reign of Aššurnaṣirpal II to Aššurbanipal) and the period from the late ninth to the seventh century B.C.E. in Urartu (beginning with the reign of Sarduri son of Lutibri [= "Sarduri I"]; figure 33.1), but their availability reflects how active a given ruler was in constructing or renovating temples and palaces (where royal inscriptions were displayed or, in Assyria, also deposited in the building foundations) and in creating monuments (such as statues and stelai) and rock reliefs (see Zimansky, chapter 24 in this volume). Documentation for individual rulers is linked not only to the length of their reign but also to the chances of archaeological recovery. Not all kings commissioned suitable building projects during their lifetime (and as a rule, kings only report their own achievements, never those of their predecessors), and not all buildings or monuments have been discovered. The many recent discoveries of Urartian royal inscriptions in Turkey and Iran are an indication of the intensified research of recent years. Not only is there no complete sequence of *res gestae* of Assyrian and Urartian rulers available, as a rule, but the accounts in royal inscriptions, be they Assyrian (Borger 1956, 1996; Fuchs 1994; Grayson 1991, 1996; Luckenbill 1924; Tadmor 1994) or Urartian (Salvini 2008; figures 33.2, 33.3), only mention the enemy in circumstances that present the commissioner of the inscription in a favorable light, that is, normally as the victor in a military encounter or the recipient of a diplomatic mission.

Figure 33.1. The earliest Urartian inscriptions were written under Sarduri son of Lutibri ("Sarduri I"), a contemporary of the Assyrian king Šalmaneser III (r. 858–824 B.C.E.), using the Neo-Assyrian language and cuneiform script. Stone block of the so-called Fortress of Sarduri at Van Kalesi, inscription edited in Salvini (2008:I 97–99: A 1–1B) (photo by Stephan Kroll).

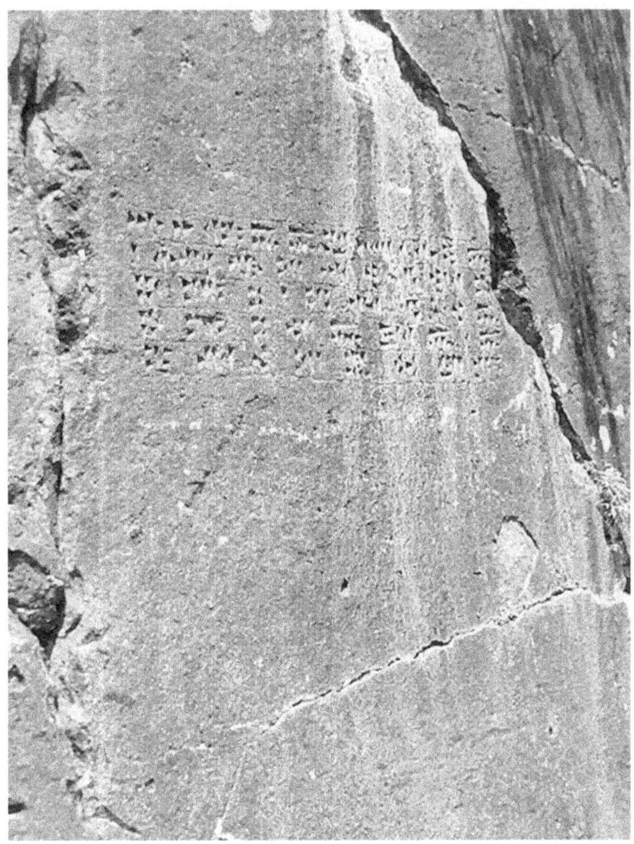

Figure 33.2. Example of an Urartian rock inscription from the vicinity of Marmashen in Armenia. It dates to the reign of Argišti son of Menua (Argišti I, early eighth century B.C.E.) and marks a victory over the local ruler Eriahi: "Thanks to the greatness of the god Ḫaldi, Argišti says: I conquered Eriahi's country, I conquered the city of Irdaniu, (reaching) as far as the country of Išqigulu." Text edition in Salvini (2008:I 350: A 8–10) (photo by Stephan Kroll).

Archival materials, which were not written with the intention of impressing contemporaries and future generations, are far less biased than royal inscriptions but available only for certain periods. The letters from the state correspondence of the Assyrian kings Tiglatpileser III (r. 745–727 B.C.E.) and Sargon II (r. 721–705 B.C.E.) with their top officials, excavated in the Assyrian state archives of Kalḫu (modern Nimrud) and Nineveh (Dietrich 2003; Fuchs and Parpola 2001; Lanfranchi and Parpola 1990; Parpola 1987; Saggs 2001), are by far the most important sources, supplemented by other materials, such as oracle queries (Starr 1990) and the eponym chronicles (Millard 1994). Urartian archival materials are available in very limited numbers and consist of the still poorly understood clay tablets excavated in Bastam in Iran, Karmir Blur in Armenia, and Toprakkale in Turkey (Zimansky 1985:80–83).

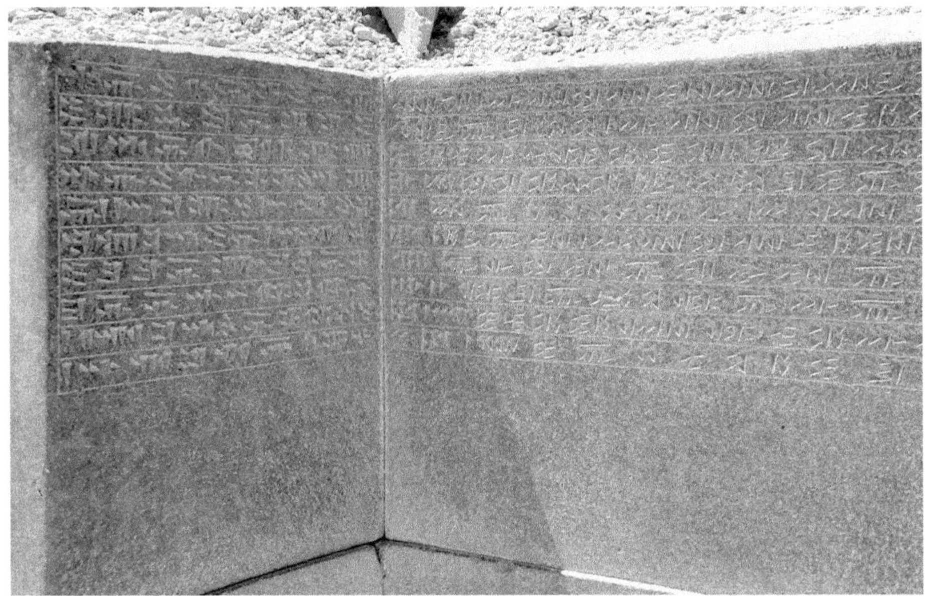

Figure 33.3. Example of an Urartian building inscription that decorates the façade of the temple of the god Irmušini at Çavuştepe (ancient Sardurihinili) in Turkey, built by Sarduri son of Argišti ("Sarduri II," mid-eighth century B.C.E.). Text edition in Salvini (2008:I 442–443: A 9–17) (photo by Stephan Kroll).

Contacts in War and Diplomacy

Since the earliest encounters between Assyrians and Urartians in the mid-ninth century B.C.E., the relationship between the two states was generally hostile and frequently defined by open conflict, which, however, often took the form of a surrogate war. Both countries tried to gain political and commercial control over the kingdoms of northern Syria and the traffic routes providing access to the Mediterranean Sea and western Anatolia. This resulted in a series of military conflicts fought in territories in southeastern Anatolia and northwestern Iran and the successive annexation of these regions by one of the two states. However, until 709 B.C.E., when Assyria annexed the kingdom of Kummuḫḫu (Commagene), they did not even share a common border; while the centers Turušpa and Nineveh were only situated at a distance of about 240 km from each other as the crow flies, they were separated by the soaring peaks of the Taurus main ridge, with altitudes in excess of 3,000 m. The mountain regions between the headwaters of the Tigris and of the Lower Zab housed a string of small kingdoms which were allowed to remain nominally independent (see later discussions).

According to the Assyrian sources, the first contacts between Assyria and Urartu date to the reign of Aššurnaṣirpal II (r. 884–859 B.C.E.) and are the result of Assyrian advances into Anatolia, in the region of the Tigris headwaters (Grayson

1991:A.0.101.2:13 and parallels). Open conflict is first attested in the inscriptions of Šalmaneser III (r. 858–824 B.C.E.), but when recounting his very first campaign in 859 B.C.E. into Urartian territory, ruled by king Arramu (Grayson 1996:A.0.102.2 i 14–25 and parallel), the Assyrian narrative suggests not so much a first encounter but another stage in an ongoing war. It is therefore likely that the open conflict between Assyria and Urartu had already started in the later part of Aššurnaṣirpal's reign, for which we are lacking accounts. It would be a mistake to see in Arramu by default the founder of the Urartian state, for the Assyrian sources suggest nothing of the sort; rather, the accounts create the impression of a firmly established, well-oiled state with an impressive war machinery at its call, which could be seen to imply that Arramu's kingdom was more than a fledgling state at the time. Over the next fifteen years, Arramu and Urartu feature prominently in Šalmaneser's inscriptions, as he raided the country three times (Radner 1998:132–33); Assyria was apparently able to counter the Urartian expansion attempts in the Murat Su region and to the west and south of Lake Urmiye. However, by 830 B.C.E., when the Assyrian army clashed again with the Urartian forces, this time under the command of king Sarduri son of Lutibri, the odds seem to have changed in Urartu's favor (Grayson 1996:A.0.102.14:141–46 and parallel). When an Assyrian army reached the regions west of Lake Urmiye a decade later in 820 B.C.E., they found them to be firmly under Urartian control (Grayson 1996:A.0.103.1 ii 16–30).

For the next four decades, we have no reports on conflicts between Assyria and Urartu; during this time, Assyria was preoccupied with consolidating the gains in territory achieved throughout the ninth century B.C.E., and we may assume a similar situation for Urartu. But between 781 and 774 B.C.E. (Grayson 1996:A.0.104.2010:10–18 and A.0.104.2011; Millard 1994:38–39), Assyria and Urartu found themselves again in a more or less permanent state of war; the theaters of war were again constituted by northwestern Iran (called "Gutium" in the Assyrian inscriptions) and "Ḫatti," that is, the Neo-Hittite successor states on the modern Turkish–Syrian border. While neither side was able to make any territorial gains, we can safely assume that the exploits of the two armies, which lived off the land while on campaign, resulted in severe economic pressure on the local kingdoms, including Carchemish, Marqasu (the region around modern Maraş), and Kummuḫḫu (Commagene).

The following two decades saw Assyria absorbed by internal problems; the Eponym Chronicle mentions a series of epidemics and rebellions as the key events of years during the period, and the Assyrian army was largely occupied at home (Millard 1994:40–43). During that time, Urartu's influence in "Ḫatti" seems to have grown steadily until it reached its pinnacle under Sarduri son of Argišti ("Sarduri II"), who in 754 B.C.E. defeated the Assyrian army in a battle in the kingdom of Arpad in northern Syria (Salvini 2008:I 414, III 253: A 9–1: right side, lines 1–10; Millard 1994:43), striking a hard blow in a region that had formerly accepted the Assyrian king as overlord and arbiter in all border conflicts. Yet only a dozen years later, in 743 B.C.E., just after Tiglatpileser III (r. 744–727 B.C.E.) had taken the Assyrian throne for himself by force, he defeated the Urartian army in a second battle in Arpad and, via Kummuḫḫu (Commagene), where another battle took place, pursued the enemy back to Turušpa (Tadmor 1994:133–35: Summary Inscription 3:15'-26' and parallels). This was the first (and remained the only) time that Assyrian troops had ever reached that Urartian capital. Turušpa, situated on a rock high above Lake Van, proved impregnable, but the siege had high symbolic significance and marked a change in the balance of power, heralding Assyria's supremacy over the Near East. Without Urartian support troops to assist them, the northern Syrian kingdoms of Arpad, Ḫamath, and Unqu were invaded by the Assyrian army in the following years and annexed as provinces (Radner 2006:58–63). Some time after the Urartian campaign, one of Tiglatpileser's officials urged his king to reattempt the capture of Turušpa in order to achieve immortal fame: "When the king, my lord, ascended to Urartu before, the gods Aššur and Šamaš delivered Turušpa into the hands of the king, my lord, and (therefore) the king, my lord, may lead his campaign against Urartu. May they capture Turušpa and may the king, my lord, immortalise his name!" (Saggs 2001:136–37 [NL 45]). Tiglatpileser did not follow this suggestion and seems to have avoided any direct confrontation with Urartu for the remainder of his rule.

In the light of the ongoing Assyrian expansion in the west, the surviving kingdoms in the region, such as Que (Cilicia), are known to have sought Urartu's protection, but these attempts seem to have been unsuccessful, and in some cases, the diplomatic delegations never even reached their destination. Hence, after the annexation of Que as an Assyrian province just prior to or at the very beginning of the reign of Sargon II (r. 721–705 B.C.E.), the province's new Assyrian governor was able to report to his king that "a messenger of Mita of Muški (i.e., Midas the Phrygian) has come to me, bringing me fourteen men of Que whom (their king) Warikas had sent to Urartu as an embassy," to which the king replies: "This is extremely good! My gods Aššur, Šamaš, Bel and Nabû have now taken action, and without a battle or anything, the man of Muški has given us his word and become our ally!" (Parpola 1987:no. 1). But while Urartu was keeping quiet on the western front, it now concentrated its military presence in northwestern Iran and attempted to supplant Assyria as the overlord of its regional vassal kingdoms, such as Mannea (Fuchs 1994:447–50 s. v. Mannaja) and Zikirtu (Fuchs 1994:471). This resulted in a sustained war from 719 to 714 B.C.E., which was again fought neither on Assyrian nor on Urartian territory but instead by proxy in Mannea, Zikurtu, and finally also Muṣaṣir (see later discussion). Though Assyria was able to gain the upper hand in this conflict, this resulted only in a shift of the theater of war back to the Turkish–Syrian border in 709 B.C.E. when Muwatalli, king of Kummuḫḫu (Commagene), had stopped paying tribute to the Assyrians and instead chosen to become an Urartian vassal (Fuchs 1994:413 s. v. Muttallu), after his country had been for at least a century a loyal Assyrian vassal (Radner 2009:232–33). In the light of the Assyrian annexation of the neighboring kingdoms of Carchemish in 717 B.C.E. (Radner 2006:58) and Marqasu in 711 B.C.E. (Radner 2006:61), this may have seemed the only way to preserve his country's independence, but instead it proved its death warrant. Kummuḫḫu was conquered and integrated into Assyria, which for the first time shared a border with Urartu. Because of this sensitive position the new province was not placed under the authority of an ordinary governor but handed over to one of the highest military officials in the Assyrian Empire, the General of the Left (*turtānu šumēlu*) (Radner 2006:48–49), resurrecting a practice employed under Šalmaneser III, who had appointed the highest military commanders over Assyria's border marches, "facing the areas where a major danger was incumbent and a major military activity was necessary" (Liverani 2004:218). During the war of 709 B.C.E., we may assume that Urartu sent at least some troops south of its border with Kummuḫḫu, but the Assyrian sources are silent in this regard. At this time Urartu's northern border, hitherto seemingly out of harm's way, was seriously threatened by the incursions of Cimmerian riders who had entered Anatolia from the Caucasus region, as Assyrian intelligence reports relay to the king (Lanfranchi 1990), and the years of active military conflict between Assyria and Urartu ended. However, to our knowledge, no formal peace treaty was ever concluded.

The significantly changed relations between Assyria and Urartu, which can be observed some time later during the reigns of Esarhaddon (r. 680–669 B.C.E.) and Aššurbanipal (r. 668–627 B.C.E.), can be seen as the direct result of the assassination of Sennacherib (r. 704–681 B.C.E.) and his murderers' escape to Urartu after Esarhaddon's victory in the ensuing succession war (Frahm 1997:18–19). Because the killers were Sennacherib's own sons and Esarhaddon's brothers and therefore had a legitimate claim to the Assyrian throne (patricide or fratricide were not considered an obstacle to an Assyrian prince's claim to the crown), the fact that they found refuge in Urartu would have enabled Assyria's archrival to put considerable pressure on the reigning Assyrian king who could never consider his grasp of the throne absolutely secure as long as Sennacherib's sons were alive. Andreas Fuchs (2012) has argued that this may have resulted in substantial payments to Urartu to ensure that the princes were not allowed to return to Assyria, certainly a compelling hypothesis. It would explain why Esarhaddon and Aššurbanipal were careful not to cross Urartian interests, even when faced with a raid onto their territory as was Aššurbanipal (Borger 1996:37, 222:Prism B § 27), and handed over Urartian fugitives, as did Esarhaddon after annexing the buffer state Šubria in 673 (see later discussion). To assume the existence of such an agreement between Assyria and Urartu would also provide a partial answer to the question of how the numerous Urartian building projects of the seventh century B.C.E. were funded. That Assyrian workers were involved in the construction of the sanctuary of Ayanis on the eastern shore of Lake Van is explicitly stated in the temple inscription (Salvini 2008:I 568, III 341–42: A 12–1: section VI, line 10) and also indicated by the finds of Assyrian pottery in some houses in the residential area, whose occupants' meat consumption (far less beef, more mutton) moreover differed significantly from that of their neighbors (Stone 2012). Craftsmen such as these may have been sent to Urartu as part of the payments to guarantee the royal killers' permanent absence from Assyria and can be connected to the fresh Assyrian impulses detectable in Urartian art at that time (Seidl 2004:207).

Aššurbanipal's careful attitude toward Urartu ended in 652 B.C.E.; this change is illustrated in his inscriptions and also in his Nineveh palace reliefs, which show him treating an Urartian diplomatic delegation with pronounced disrespect, making them witness the humiliation of some Elamite ambassadors who were made to read aloud the letters they had delivered to the Assyrian king for the Urartians to hear, and then executed in the Urartians' presence (Borger 1996:107, 227–28:Prism C §51; Kaelin 1999:26, 28, 30–31: scenes 52, 55, 58, 60, 73–74). The message is clear: Aššurbanipal was no longer willing to make amends with Urartu. Fuchs (2012) sees this change in attitude connected with the death of the royal murderers in Urartu, and I find this a convincing argument. Unlike all his predecessors who were treated as equals, the last Urartian king, another Sarduri, attested in the Assyrian sources is presented as an Assyrian vassal (Borger 1996:71–72, 250:Prism A §86). After this, both the Assyrian and the Urartian sources are silent about their relationship. Although it is certain that when the Assyrian Empire found its end in the wars from 614 B.C.E. onward Urartu was no longer in a position to get involved, be it pro or contra Assyria, the exact circumstances and chronology of Urartu's decline and collapse are obscure (Hellwag 2012).

Cultural Exchange between Assyria and Urartu

So far, we have focused on Assyria's and Urartu's contacts on the battlefield, and while we have touched on the possible impact of Assyrian craftsmen working in Urartu in the seventh century B.C.E., we have not yet dealt with the issue of mutual cultural influence systematically. The ninth and eighth centuries B.C.E. saw a diplomatic ice age between the two states, so that the peaceful transfer of goods and people cannot be expected to have been the norm. However, the sanctuaries of Kumme and Muṣaṣir (see below), where both Urartians and Assyrians worshiped and which enjoyed the patronage of the kings of both states, would have provided an environment where the artifacts of the other, in the form of dedicatory gifts but also merchandise filtering into these cities, would have been accessible. The state letters of Sargon II contain evidence that private trade with Urartu, though strictly forbidden, was nevertheless taking place, using the buffer states as intermediaries (Lanfranchi and Parpola 1990:nos. 100, 103; Parpola 1987:no. 46).

On the other hand, prisoners of war, of whom there must have been many in the course of the numerous wars between the two kingdoms, would have provided another means of cultural exchange, especially in the area of military equipment (see Born and Seidl 1995) and the arts of war. It is likely that the introduction of a cavalry branch in the Assyrian army during the reign of Šalmaneser III was influenced by the encounters with Urartian horseback riders. Most impressively, however, the capture of an Assyrian scribe in the ninth century B.C.E. provided the Urartian kings with the necessary expertise to have their own cuneiform inscriptions fashioned; the earliest inscriptions, of Sarduri son of Lutibri ("Sarduri I"), were written in the Assyrian language and modeled not on the style of Assyrian inscriptions but followed letter writing conventions (Wilhelm 1987), indicating that they were the brainchild of a scribe trained in working with archival materials rather than inscriptions, for which a specialized language was used. While later Urartian inscriptions were composed in the Urartian language (although there are also some Assyrian-Urartian bilinguals: Salvini 2008:I 141–144, III 90–97: A 3–11 [Kelišin stela of Išpuini and Menua], I 497–503, III 295–310: A 10–3 [Movana stela of Rusa I], I 503–505, III 311–315: A 10–4 [Mergeh Karvan stela of Rusa I], I 505–508, III 316–320: A 10–5 [Topzawa stela of Rusa I]), the cuneiform signs retain their Assyrian forms.

Finally, Urartian customs, as observed by the Assyrians when campaigning through the country, may have provided models both for the rise of wine drinking culture in Assyria in the course of the eighth century B.C.E. (Stronach 1995), and the grand irrigation projects of Sargon and Sennacherib to secure water for their capital cities Dur-Šarrukin and Nineveh, respectively (Bagg 2001:314–20). Several Urartian kings, most importantly Menua, son of Išpuini, who ruled over Urartu at the turn of the ninth to the eighth century B.C.E., constructed elaborate irrigation systems (Belli 1997, 1999) to provide water for fields, fruit groves, and the very extensive vineyards of Urartu. The vine is a native plant in the region, and still today Armenia is famous for the quality of its wines. Only religious and cultural reasons prevent eastern Turkey and northwestern Iran presently from competing with products of a similar standard. Ancient Urartu, on the other hand, was not only a wine-producing nation but also a wine-consuming one, as the Assyrian accounts like to stress. According to Sargon II, Urartu housed wine supplies so vast that one could drink wine there as if it were water from a river (Mayer 1983:90–91, Sargon's Eighth Campaign, line 220), and archaeological excavations have confirmed that Urartian fortresses indeed contained huge stocks of wine, stored in enormous clay vessels with a holding capacity of almost 1,000 liters (Payne 2005). Seven of the 70 underground storerooms of the fortress of Teišebaini (modern Karmir-Blur near the Armenian capital Yerevan) were wine cellars, holding a total of 360 such containers, corresponding to about 350,000 liters of wine.

The Buffer States: Šubria, Kumme, and Muṣaṣir

The best documented of the buffer states situated in the mountainous region between Urartu and Assyria are Šubria and Kumme, located in the Taurus Range, and Muṣaṣir, located in the northern Zagros region, all rooted deeply in the ancient Hurrian culture. Though the last kingdom cannot be considered Anatolian, I nevertheless include it in the discussion because of its importance for Urartian kingship and state cult.

The territory of Šubria stretched from the Upper Tigris and its headwaters in the west to the mountains in the north and east, which bordered on Urartu; the western and southern border was the Tigris, shared with the Assyrian provinces of Amedi (Radner 2006:49–51) and Tušḫan (Radner 2006:53). "Šubria" is an Assyrian name (derived from Sumerian Subir and its Akkadian counterpart Šubartu) and denotes simply a "northern country." The Urartians called the kingdom Qulmeri (Diakonoff and Kashkai 1981:69 s. v. Qulmēre) after its capital city, well attested also in Assyrian texts as Kullimeri; this is the most likely candidate for the country's native designation, for which there are no local sources. As the other Šubrian center is Uppummu, which corresponds to the site of Fum near the modern town of Lice (Kessler 1995:57) in the extreme west of the country, Kullimeri should be sought in the east, as the division of Šubria in 673 B.C.E. into a western and eastern Assyrian province (Uppummu and Kullimeri: Radner 2006:63–64) would otherwise make little sense. A likely candidate is the site of Gre Migro (Kessler 1995:57–58) on the eastern bank of the Batman Su, situated some twenty-five kilometers to the north of its confluence with the Tigris.

The kingdom preserved the ancient heritage of its Hurrian tradition into the eighth and seventh centuries B.C.E., and Assyrian sources offer us some detailed information, such as that the members of the royal house all had Hurrian names; a letter from Sargon's correspondence even gives some Hurrian words, with translations (Lanfranchi and Parpola 1990:no. 53). Šubrian scholars, some of whom worked under the patronage of Assyrian kings, specialized in the ancient Hurrian art of augury (Radner 2009:233–34, 237).

A long-standing Assyrian vassal, Šubrian independence ended in 673 B.C.E. when the hitherto trusted ally stood accused of harboring Esarhaddon's enemies, and all efforts of king Ik-Teššub to prove his loyalty were in vain; the situation escalated due to the fact that the murderers of Esarhaddon's father, Sennacherib, were rumored to have found refuge in the area, whose presence endangered Esarhaddon's rule but also any hope of a peaceful succession (see discussion above). Šubria's reputation as a haven for refugees from Assyria and Urartu alike is apparent not only from Esarhaddon's inscriptions (Leichty 2011:85 Esarhaddon 33 iii 28'–34') but also from letters of the Sargon correspondence, which indicate that this was a major problem in the otherwise easy relationship between Assyria and Šubria (Lanfranchi and Parpola 1990:nos. 35, 53–54); people from as far away as the Diyala region fled to Šubria to escape justice and could expect its king to refuse their extradition. This remarkable behavior has to be recognized as a deliberate policy, but what did Šubria stand to gain from such actions, which were directed, after all, against both powerful neighbors in equal measure? Tamás Deszö (2006:37) has argued that Šubria's policy was anchored in a religious tradition and proposed the existence of a refuge sanctuary at Uppummu; a good candidate is the nearby Tigris Grotto, the riverine cave system at Birkleyn (Schachner 2009), a holy precinct with unlimited water and shelter from the powers of nature.

The ancient city of Kumme also housed an important shrine, dedicated to the storm god and well attested since the early second millennium B.C.E. According to the Hittite tradition of the mid-second millennium B.C.E., the storm god of Kumme was the unrivaled ruler of heaven and earth, and he featured in many of the Hurrian myths and rituals preserved on the tablets from the Hittite capital Ḫattuša (Schwemer 2001:456–58), the most prominent being the Song of Ullikummi, which relates the story of the battle between the storm god and the monstrous rock creature Ullikummi, whose programmatic name means "Vanquish (the storm god of) Kumme!" (Hoffner 1990:55–65). In the first millennium B.C.E., Assyrians and Urartians alike frequented this sanctuary.

Kumme was located in the mountainous region on the upper reaches of the Lesser Khabur north of the Turkish–Iraqi border, perhaps at Beytüşşebap (Radner 2012). After Tiglatpileser III's creation of the province of Birtu in 739 B.C.E. (Radner 2006:56–57), Kumme's territory bordered directly on Assyria, while the most convenient route to Urartu led through the land of its eastern neighbor Ukku (modern Hakkari), situated on the Greater Zab (Radner 2012). During the reign of Sargon II, we see Kumme's ruler, the "city lord" Ariye, supplying the Assyrians with manpower, horses, timber, and intelligence on the other states of the region, especially Urartu, with which Kumme continued to entertain close relations, providing also men and information (Lanfranchi and Parpola 1990:nos. 95, 105). But close cooperation with Assyria was ensured by the presence of an ambassador whose letters to Sargon (Lanfranchi and Parpola 1990:nos. 84–100; figure 33.4) describe intelligence gathering and the organization of timber transports to Assyria: most spectacular is a report on an Urartian plan to kidnap several Assyrian governors who stayed in Kumme's territory while their men built a fortress there (Parpola 1987:no. 29).

The collaboration with Assyria was not always easy; Kumme's inhabitants were frequently accused of illicit trading with Urartu, which the Assyrians would not tolerate (see foregoing discussion), and the Assyrian ambassador's presence in Kumme led to a murderous conflict with some local dignitaries (Lanfranchi and Parpola 1990:nos. 106–7). How this particular feud ended is unknown, but when the new king of Urartu questioned the conspicuous absence of messengers from Kumme at his court, the answer from Kumme, according to the information conveyed back to Sargon, was this: "Since we are the slaves of Assyria . . . we cannot put our feet anywhere" (Lanfranchi and Parpola 1990:no. 95). The letter was written sometime after Sargon's desecration of Muṣaṣir and its Ḫaldi temple in 714 B.C.E. (figure 33.5; see following discussion), and Kumme's hesitation to engage with Urartu diplomatically may be the result of the fear which Sargon's attack must have provoked in the rulers of the other buffer states. That even the presence of an ancient and famous temple would not stop the Assyrians must have been most alarming to Kumme. However, at this point our information dries up and to decide whether the Assyrians continued to respect Kumme's autonomy is left to our imagination.

Muṣaṣir, finally, was situated in the area of modern Sidikan in northeastern Iraq, just west of the Zagros main ridge that marked its border with Urartu, while the Greater Zab formed its border with Assyria (Radner 2012). "Muṣaṣir" was the Assyrian name for the city that was locally (and also in Urartu) known under its ancient Hurrian name Ardini, simply meaning "the city." Since the early second millennium B.C.E., it is attested as an important settlement with a major temple, dedicated to the god Ḫaldi, whom the Urartian king Sarduri, son of Lutibri ("Sarduri I"), a contemporary of Šalmaneser III (r. 858–824 B.C.E.), proclaimed the head of Urartu's state pantheon; he and his royal successors erected temples in Ḫaldi's name all over their kingdom. Why Sarduri chose to promote Ḫaldi as the main deity of Urartu remains unclear, but it is perhaps significant that Urartu's first capital, Arzaškun, likely to be the place of origin of the Urartian royal house, was quite probably situated not far from Muṣaṣir, at the eastern side of the Zagros Range. Ḫaldi's importance in Urartian state religion and ideology meant that the kings of Urartu were crowned or at

Figure 33.4. An Assyrian letter by the Assyrian ambassador at Kumme to his king Sargon II (r. 721–705 B.C.E.) providing information on recent events in Urartu. British Museum, 81-2-4, 55, edited in Lanfranchi and Parpola (1990:no. 84) (photo by Greta van Buylaere).

least confirmed in Ḫaldi's temple at Muṣaṣir and that they visited the shrine regularly as part of their cultic duties, together with Urartu's élite (Salvini 1993–97:445; Zimansky 1985:5). Despite this, Muṣaṣir retained its independence and was ruled by its own king, with both Urartu and Assyria respecting its sovereignty.

However, during the reign of Sargon II, Urzana, king of Muṣaṣir, found himself increasingly under pressure to cut his ties to Urartu; a letter from the Assyrian state correspondence paints a vivid picture of the difficulties the ruler faced when the Urartian king and his nobles came for their annual pilgrimage to Ḫaldi's temple, despite Sargon's explicit orders to hinder them from doing so (Lanfranchi and Parpola 1990:no. 147). Sargon later used this as a pretext to justify his plundering of the city and its temple in 714 B.C.E., a deed that was clearly meant to hurt the archenemy

Urartu at its ideological and religious core. It was justified in a publicly read report to the god Aššur (Mayer 1983) and celebrated in Sargon's official royal inscriptions (Fuchs 1994) as well as in the decoration of two of the most important Assyrian buildings of the time. Whereas too few fragments of the multicolored glazed brick reliefs, which decorated the façade of the Aššur temple at Assur (Weidner 1926), remain to allow us to gain a coherent impression of the scenes in question, the stone reliefs from Sargon's palace in Dur-Šarrukin showing the capture of Muṣaṣir and the looting of the temple survived intact until they were excavated in the mid-nineteenth century C.E. Although the reliefs are now lost, the drawings made during the excavations document the depiction of the city and Ḫaldi's shrine which, with its unique roof construction and the façade decorated with shields, spears, and statues (Albenda 1986:pl. 133; Botta and Flandin 1846:pl. 141; figure 33.5), is today perhaps

Figure 33.5. A stone relief from the palace of Sargon II (r. 721–705 B.C.E.) at Dur-Šarrukin, showing the Assyrian conquest and pillaging of the city of Muṣaṣir and the temple of Ḫaldi (drawing from Botta and Flandin 1846:pl. 141).

the most instantly recognizable representation of a building in Assyrian art. Yet despite the invasion, Muṣaṣir seems to have retained its independence; Sargon apparently thought King Urzana's loyalty sufficiently guaranteed by holding his family hostage (Mayer 1983:102–3: Sargon's Eighth Campaign, line 348).

Šubria, Kumme, and Muṣaṣir are not remote backwaters of civilization; they boast continuous human occupation for far longer than the Mesopotamian Plain, and an awareness for the antiquity of their traditions may be indicated by the great respect in which their deities and their sanctuaries were held in the entire Near East. It may not only have been their relatively inaccessible geographical situation but also the respect for their cultural heritage that succeeded in protecting these kingdoms over a long time from their aggressive neighbors Assyria and Urartu.

Conclusion

Our understanding of the relationship between Assyria and Urartu over the course of more than two centuries is heavily influenced by the limitations of the available source material and tends toward an overwhelmingly Assyrian view. To the Assyrian mind, Urartu was on one hand an anti-Assyria, the archenemy and eternal temptation for its vassals, and on the other hand a mirror image, a kind of Assyria in the mountains; inscriptions and archival materials alike attribute Assyrian concepts to Biainili, for example, by superimposing the Assyrian administrative structure onto the other country, referring to provinces and governors and using various specifically Assyrian titles for Urartian officials (see Zimansky 1985:89–94). This tends to promote the idea that the two kingdoms were very much alike, but the fact that climatic conditions and the economic basis of Assyria and Urartu were very different should make it clear that this assumption is implausible. The various states situated in the border region between Assyria and Urartu, too, had their own distinct identities and traditions. Yet despite periods when central governments, especially the Assyrian one, attempted to enforce noncommunication among these different countries, we have seen that there were ample opportunities for the exchange of goods, people, and ideas, which, in the period under study (the ninth to seventh centuries B.C.E.), made the region between the Caucasus, the Black Sea, the Mediterranean Sea, and the Persian Gulf a playground of intersecting cultures.

REFERENCES

Albenda, Pauline. 1986. *The Palace of Sargon, King of Assyria: Monumental Wall Reliefs at Dur-Sharrukin, from Original Drawings Made at the Time of their Discovery in 1843–1844 by Botta and Flandin*. Recherches sur les Civilisations Synthèses 22. Paris: Éditions Recherche sur les Civilisations.

Bagg, Ariel M. 2001. Irrigation in Northern Mesopotamia: Water for the Assyrian Capitals (12th–7th Centuries BC). *Irrigation and Drainage Systems* 14: 301–24.

Belli, Oktay. 1997. *Urartian Irrigation Canals in Eastern Anatolia*. İstanbul: Arkeoloji ve Sanat Yayınları.

———. 1999. Dams, Reservoirs, and Irrigation Canals of the Van Plain in the Period of the Urartian Kingdom. *Anatolian Studies* 49: 11–26.

Borger, Rykle. 1996. *Beiträge zum Inschriftenwerk Assurbanipals: die Prismenklassen A, B, C = K, D, E, F, G, H, J und T sowie andere Inschriften*. Wiesbaden: Harrassowitz.

Born, Hermann and Ursula Seidl. 1995. *Schutzwaffen aus Assyrien und Urartu*. Mainz: Zabern.

Botta, Paul-Émile and Eugène Flandin. 1846. *Monument de Ninive II*. Paris: Imprimerie Nationale.

Deszö, Tamás. 2006. Šubria and the Assyrian Empire. *Acta Antiqua Academiae Scientiarum Hungaricae* 46: 33–38.

Diakonoff, Igor M. and S. M. Kashkai. 1981. *Geographical Names According to Urartian Texts*. Répertoire Géographique des Textes Cunéiformes 9. Wiesbaden: Reichert.

Dietrich, Manfred. 2003. *The Neo-Babylonian Correspondence of Sargon and Sennacherib*. State Archives of Assyria 17. Helsinki: Helsinki University Press.

Frahm, Eckart. 1997. *Einleitung in die Sanherib-Inschriften*. Archiv für Orientforschung Beiheft 26. Wien: Institut für Orientalistik.

Fuchs, Andreas. 1994. *Die Inschriften Sargons II. aus Khorsabad*. Göttingen: Cuvillier.

———. 2012 Urartu in der Zeit. In *Biainili-Urartu: Proceedings of the Symposium Held in Munich 12–14 October 2007*, ed. Stephan Kroll, Claudia Gruber, Ursula Hellwag, Michael Roaf, and Paul Zimansky, 135-161. Acta Iranica 51. Leuven: Peeters.

Fuchs, Andreas and Simo Parpola. 2001. *The Correspondence of Sargon II, Part III*. State Archives of Assyria 15. Helsinki: Helsinki University Press.

Grayson, Albert K. 1991. *Assyrian Rulers of the Early First Millennium BC I (1114–859 BC)*. Royal Inscriptions of Mesopotamia: Assyrian Periods 2. Toronto: Toronto University Press.

———. 1996. *Assyrian Rulers of the Early First Millennium BC II (858–745 BC)*. Royal Inscriptions of Mesopotamia: Assyrian Periods 3. Toronto: Toronto University Press.

Hellwag, Ursula. 2012. Der Niedergang Urartus, In *Biainili-Urartu: Proceedings of the Symposium held in Munich 12–14 October 2007*, ed. Stephan Kroll, Claudia Gruber, Ursula Hellwag, Michael Roaf, and Paul Zimansky, 227–41. Acta Iranica 51. Leuven: Peeters.

Hoffner, Harry A. Jr. 1990. *Hittite Myths*. Atlanta: Scholars Press.

Kaelin, Oskar. 1999. *Ein assyrisches Bildexperiment nach ägyptischem Vorbild: zu Planung und Ausführung der "Schlacht am Ulai."* Alter Orient und Altes Testament 266. Münster: Ugarit-Verlag.

Kessler, Karlheinz. 1995. Šubria, Urartu and Aššur: Topographical Questions around the Tigris Sources. In *Neo-Assyrian Geography*, ed. Mario Liverani. 55–67. Quaderni di geografia storica 5. Rome: Università di Roma La Sapienza.

Kroll, Stephan. 2012. Rusa Erimena in archäologischem Kontext. In *Biainili-Urartu: Proceedings of the Symposium Held in Munich 12–14 October 2007*, ed. Stephan Kroll, Claudia Gruber, Ursula Hellwag, Michael Roaf, and Paul Zimansky, 183–86. Acta Iranica 51. Leuven: Peeters.

Lanfranchi, Giovanni B. 1990. *I Cimmeri: Emergenza delle élites militari iraniche nel Vicino Oriente (VIII–VII sec. a. C.)*. History of the Ancient Near East Studies 2 bis. Padova: Sargon.

Lanfranchi, Giovanni B. and Simo Parpola. 1990. *The Correspondence of Sargon II, Part II*. State Archives of Assyria 5. Helsinki: Helsinki University Press.

Leichty, Erle. 2011. *The Royal Inscriptions of Esarhaddon, King of Assyria (680–669 BC*. The Royal Inscriptions of the Neo-Assyrian Period 4. Winona Lake: Eisenbrauns.

Liverani, Mario. 2004. Assyria in the Ninth Century: Continuity or Change? In *From the Upper Sea to the Lower Sea: Studies on the History of Assyria and Babylonia in Honour of A. K. Grayson*, ed. Grant Frame, 213–26. Leiden: Nederlands Instituut voor het Nabije Oosten.

Luckenbill, Daniel D. 1924. *The Annals of Sennacherib*. Oriental Institute Publications 2. Chicago: University of Chicago Press.

Mayer, Walter. 1983. Sargons Feldzug gegen Urartu—714 v. Chr.: Text und Übersetzung. *Mitteilungen der Deutschen Orient-Gesellschaft* 115: 65–132.

Millard, Alan R. 1994. *The Eponyms of the Assyrian Empire, 910–612 BC*. State Archive of Assyria Studies 2. Helsinki: Neo-Assyrian Text Corpus Project.

Parpola, Simo. 1987. *The Correspondence of Sargon II, Part I*. State Archives of Assyria 1. Helsinki: Helsinki University Press.

Payne, Margaret. 2005. *Urartian Measures of Volume*. Ancient Near Eastern Studies, Supplement 16. Leuven: Peeters.

Radner, Karen. 1998. Arrāmu. In *The Prosopography of the Neo-Assyrian Empire 1/I*, ed. Karen Radner, 132–33. Helsinki: Neo-Assyrian Text Corpus Project.

———. 2006. Provinz. C. Assyrien. *Reallexikon der Assyriologie* 11.1–2: 42–68.

———. 2009. The Assyrian King and His Scholars: The Syro-Anatolian and the Egyptian Schools. In *Of God(s), Trees, Kings, and Scholars: Neo-Assyrian and Related Studies in Honour of Simo Parpola*, ed. Mikko Luukko, Saana Svärd, and Raija Mattila, 221–38. Studia Orientalia 106. Helsinki: Finnish Oriental Society.

———. 2012. Between a Rock and a Hard Place: Musasir, Kumme, Ukku and Šubria: The Buffer States between Assyria and Urartu. In *Biainili-Urartu: Proceedings of the Symposium held in Munich 12–14 October 2007*, ed. Stephan Kroll, Claudia Gruber, Ursula Hellwag, Michael Roaf, and Paul Zimansky, 243–64. Acta Iranica 51. Leuven: Peeters.

Roaf, Michael. 2012. Could Rusa Son of Erimena Have Been King of Urartu during Sargon's Eighth Campaign? In *Biainili-Urartu: Proceedings of the Symposium held in Munich 12–14 October 2007*, ed. Stephan Kroll, Claudia Gruber, Ursula Hellwag, Michael Roaf, and Paul Zimansky, 187–216. Acta Iranica 51. Leuven: Peeters.

Saggs, H. W. F. 2001. *The Nimrud Letters, 1952*. Cuneiform Texts from Nimrud 5. London: British School of Archaeology in Iraq.

Salvini, Mirjo. 1967. *Nairi e Ur(u)atri: contributo alla storia formazione del regno di Urartu*. Incunabula Graeca 16. Rome: Edizioni dell'Ateneo.

———. 1993–97. Muṣaṣir. A. Historisch. *Reallexikon der Assyriologie* 8: 444–46.

———. 2008. *Corpus dei testi urartei: le iscrizioni su pietra e roccia*, vols. 1–3. Documenta Asiana 8. Paris: De Boccard.

Schachner, Andreas, ed. 2009. *Assyriens Könige an einer der Quellen des Tigris: Archäologische Forschungen im Höhlensystem von Bırkleyn und am sogenannten Tigris-Tunnel*. Istanbuler Forschungen 51. Tübingen: Wasmuth.

Schwemer, Daniel. 2001. *Die Wettergottgestalten Mesopotamiens und Nordsyriens im Zeitalter der Keilschriftkulturen: Materialien und Studien nach den keilschriftlichen Quellen*. Wiesbaden: Harrassowitz.

Seidl, Ursula. 2004. *Bronzekunst Urartus*. Mainz: Zabern.

———. 2012. Rusa Son of Erimena, Rusa Son of Argishti and Rusahinili/Toprakkale. In *Biainili-Urartu: Proceedings of the Symposium Held in Munich 12–14 October 2007* ed. Stephan Kroll, Claudia Gruber, Ursula Hellwag, Michael Roaf, and Paul Zimansky, 175–81. Acta Iranica 51. Leuven: Peeters.

Starr, Ivan. 1990. *Queries to the Sungod: Divination and Politics in Sargonid Assyria.* State Archives of Assyria 4. Helsinki: Helsinki University Press.

Stone, Elizabeth. 2012. Social Differentiation within Urartian Settlements. In *Biainili-Urartu: Proceedings of the Symposium Held in Munich 12–14 October 2007*, ed. Stephan Kroll Claudia Gruber, Ursula Hellwag, Michael Roaf, and Paul Zimansky, 89–99. Acta Iranica 51. Leuven: Peeters.

Stronach, David. 1995. The Imagery of the Wine Bowl: Wine in Assyria in the Early First Millennium BC. In *The Origins and Ancient History of Wine*, ed. Patrick E. McGovern, Stuart J. Fleming, and Solomon H. Katz, 175–96. Food and Nutrition in History and Anthropology Series 11. Luxembourg: Gordon and Breach Publishers.

Tadmor, Hayim. 1994. *The Inscriptions of Tiglath-Pileser III King of Assyria.* Jerusalem: Israel Academy of Sciences and Humanities.

Weidner, Ernst F. 1926. Assyrische Emailgemälde vom Achten Feldzuge Sargons II. *Archiv für Orientforschung* 3: 1–6.

Wilhelm, Gernot. 1987. Urartu als Region der Keilschrift-Kultur. In *Das Reich Urartu: ein altorientalischer Staat im 1. Jahrtausend v. Chr.*, ed. V. Haas, 95–116. Xenia: Konstanzer althistorische Vorträge und Forschungen 17. Konstanz: Universitätsverlag Konstanz.

Zimansky, Paul. E. 1985. *Ecology and Empire: The Structure of the Urartian State. Studies in Ancient Oriental Civilization 41.* Chicago: Oriental Institute of the University of Chicago.

CHAPTER 34

THE GREEKS IN ANATOLIA: FROM THE MIGRATIONS TO ALEXANDER THE GREAT

KENNETH W. HARL

Greek Settlements of Asia Minor

The catastrophic collapse of the Late Bronze Age civilization of the Greek mainland seems to have set many Greeks in motion, perhaps fleeing the troubles in their homeland. In the immediate aftermath of this collapse, often referred to as the Dark Age, Greeks settled in strength on the littorals of Asia Minor from the Troad to Pamphylia. Ethnographers and chronographers of the Classical Age constructed aetiological accounts of the migrations of Aeolian, Ionian, and Dorian Greeks. The archaeological record of the destruction of the Mycenaean palaces, and the succeeding "cities of refuge," have been interpreted as bearing out such migrations. This traditional view has been called into question by Jonathan Hall (2000), who has argued that these traditions were invented later as Greeks evolved a distinct identity and rationalized the origins of their institutions. This revisionist view has, in turn, been answered by Margalit Finkelberg (2005), who has reconstructed the linguistic relationship of the Greek dialects based on isoglosses. Her research offers a plausible explanation for the distribution of the dialects in the Late Bronze Age, suggesting that the distribution of Greek dialects in the Archaic Age resulted from migrations of different speakers from their original homes during the Dark Age.

The arrival of the Greeks on the shores of Asia Minor was thus associated by later Classical authors with the downfall of the heroic kingdoms of the Mycenaean age. Scions of great Achaean houses fled overseas; some were credited with a stay in

Athens before taking passage to Ionia. Ionians of the islands and Asia Minor looked to Athens as their mother city (ἡ μητρόπολις). It is impossible to estimate the scale of Greek migrations after the collapse of the Mycenaean kingdoms. As yet, the archaeology of the Archaic settlements of Ionia is in its infancy; the Archaic city of Miletos was destroyed by the Persians in 494 B.C.E., and other cities such as Priene or Knidos were shifted to new locales. The best excavated site, Old Smyrna, reveals a walled city of cramped buildings, possibly home to several thousand residents (see Greaves, chapter 21 in this volume). Ionian settlers intermarried with the Carians among whom they settled, and adapted native cults to Greek counterparts (Herodotus I.171.2–4).

By 900 B.C.E., Greek settlements stretched from the entrances of the Hellespont to the peninsula of Knidos. Aeolian speakers possessed the shores of the Troad, Aeolis, and the island of Lesbos. Many of the communities of the southern Troad or Aeolis were dependent territories (*peraea*) of either Mytilene or Methymna on the island of Lesbos. Ionians settled thickly on the shores from Phocaea to Miletos and on the two great islands Chios and Samos; Dorians settled the shores between the two southern peninsulae of Halicarnassus and Knidos, and the islands of Kos and Rhodes. Of the three major dialect groups, the Ionians possessed the greatest sense of unity based on their religious league, the Panionion, a coalition of the twelve leading cities that shared the rites of Apollo (Herodotus I.148.1–2; see Strabo 8.7.2 and 14.1.20).

Between the ninth and sixth centuries B.C.E., Greeks greatly expanded their settlement of Asia Minor. Two cities, Megara and Miletos, took the lead in colonizing Asia Minor in the Archaic Age (750–480 B.C.E.). These cities lived on commerce, and they quickly found that their growing population could no longer be sustained on limited lands. In the seventh century B.C.E. Megara, a Dorian polis of the Peloponnesus, settled Astacus, Selymbria, and Byzantion on the European shores of the Propontis, Chalcedon on the Asian side of the Bosporus, and, in the sixth century B.C.E., Heraclea Pontica and Mesembria on the Euxine shores of Anatolia and Thrace, respectively.

Miletos stood on a peninsula still surrounded by water on three sides, and jutting into the vast bay of Miletos, today a vast alluvial plain of the Maeander River (for Miletos see also Greaves, chapter 21 in this volume). Across the bay were the cities of Priene, Magnesia, and Mys; to the southeast was Heraclea sub Latmum. Miletos possessed a superb harbor and was the center of a brisk regional trade in the bay. In the late eighth and early seventh centuries B.C.E. Milesians, while drawing settlers from other Ionian cities such as Samos and Phocaea, created the Greek networks of cities in the Black Sea and so opened contact with Phrygia and Urartu. On the Asian shores of the Propontis (Sea of Marmara) Milesians founded Abydos, Parium, and Cyzicus. Along the Euxine shores of Asia Minor, Milesians settled Sinope, Amisos, and Trapezus, opening trade in slaves and raw materials from the northern Anatolian peoples and well-wrought bronze and iron goods from Urartian cities. Milesians colonized the shores of the Tauric Bosporus and the southern Crimea and Taman peninsulae of southern Russia and brought the Greek world into contact with the steppe nomads of southern Russia, the Scythians. By the mid-sixth century B.C.E. Greek cities on the Euxine shores prospered through the export of metals, timber, foodstuffs, and slaves from their hinterlands to the Aegean world.

The Greeks also planted colonies along the southern littoral of Anatolia, as corroborated by ceramics finds in this area (Cook and Blackman 1971; Mitchell and McNicoll 1979). Samians were credited with colonies at Nagidos and Celenderis in Cilicia Tracheia, although these cities never developed far beyond minor ports. Phaselis, a protected harbor on the eastern coast of Lycia, was founded by the Rhodians. With its three harbors, Phaselis prospered and was a member of the Panhellenion at Naucratis in Egypt (Herodotus II.78). On the Pamphylian shores, Greeks settled at prime locales, notably Aspendos, near the mouth of the Eurymedon, and Side (a city composed of at least four distinct ethnic groups in the Archaic Age). These ventures brought East Greeks to Cyprus, the Phoenician ports, and Egypt. Greek Orientalizing ceramics at Al Mina, an emporium at the mouth of the Orontes, and at Ras el-Bassit, likely the Posideion of Herodotus (Herodotus I.91.1; Boardman 1980:62–75; Waldbaum 1997), mark the revival of trade between the Aegean world and the Levant, and ultimately Egypt. By their colonizing and trade, the East Greeks renewed Hellenic contact with the Near East and thus assured the prosperity and cultural flowering of their cities in the Archaic Age.

The Emergence of East Greece

In the Archaic Age (750–480 B.C.E.), Greek settlements on the western shores of Asia Minor emerged as city-states (*poleis*) based on the rule of law as defined by Hesiod and Herodotus (Herodotus VII.103.1–3; Hesiod, *Works and Days* II.201–274). Ionian and Aeolian Greeks, refugees from former Mycenaean kingdoms, had intermingled and intermarried with native Anatolians. By the late eighth century B.C.E., Hellenic cities of East Greece (the Aegean islands and the western shores of Anatolia) were tied by blood, language, and cults to their kin in mainland Greece. From 750 B.C.E., the East Greeks too set themselves aside from other Anatolian peoples, designated barbarians, by a new concept, the polis. The nascent poleis, confined to the fringes of Anatolia, were tiny in comparison to the Phrygian and Lydian kingdoms. However, the polis, a city based on the rule of law determined by the citizens, influenced not only Anatolia but the entire Mediterranean world.

The king (*basileus*) in Homer ruled by consent of his nobles who formed an advisory council (*boule*). They, in turn, referred major decisions to the armed citizens in assembly (*ekklesia*). By 700 B.C.E., aristocrats in many poleis had reduced the kingship to a set of elected offices, and so turned their cities into republics. Improvements in armor and arms, however, undermined aristocratic rule as many more citizens, armed as hoplites or heavy infantry, clamored for more power in the assembly. In the seventh and sixth centuries B.C.E., tyrants in the cities of East Greece, at the head of citizen uprisings, seized power and broke down aristocratic rule. On the eve of the Persian conquest, East Greek poleis enjoyed oligarchic or timocratic constitutions whereby the propertied classes held office and sat on the council but were responsible to a citizenry defined by military service. Political evolution was also fueled by a colonial experience as East Greeks defined themselves by encountering new peoples in the Near East and establishing poleis in the Hellespontine and Euxine lands. The Milesians were in the forefront of this movement, and Miletos decisively shaped the emerging Hellenic civilization of the Archaic Age.

The Greek cities planted on the shores of western Asia Minor prospered as the entrepôts between the Anatolian peoples—Lydians, Carians, and Lycians—and the Aegean world. Foodstuffs, timber, slaves, and finished goods were exported from the Anatolian hinterland to the Hellenic cities, for, just as Plato later noted of the Greeks in the words of Socrates, "we live around the sea like frogs around a pond" (Plato, *Phaedrus* 109B). The landed citizens amassed wealth from their estates and the profits of trade so that they armed themselves first as cavalry and, by the seventh century B.C.E., as hoplites. Great families came to dominate the cities of East Greece, and in the seventh and sixth centuries B.C.E., tyrants, charismatic, aspiring dynasts, seized power. The lyric poet Archilochus first used the word *tyrant* to describe Gyges (ca. 680–644 B.C.E.), the usurper at Sardis; this term of Anatolian origin connoted an alien government to Greeks accustomed to republican rule for generations (Andrewes 1956:20–30; Campbell 1967:2–3, fragment 22). Tyrants in East Greece might have, in part, responded to political conditions common among the cities of western Asia Minor. In Carian and Lycian cities, too, dynasts took power, and Lycian tyrants minted silver coins in their own names in the sixth and fifth centuries B.C.E. (Kraay 1976:239–60).

Miletos emerged as the commercial and cultural center of Greece in the later seventh century B.C.E., surpassing her two leading Ionian competitors, Ephesos and Smyrna. Ephesos owed her fame to the great sanctuary of Artemis, which attracted the patronage of philhellene kings of Lydia, but the city's port did not emerge until the Hellenistic age. Smyrna, at the mouth of the Hermus, suffered from the Cimmerian invasions and wars with Lydian kings. Alyattes (609–560 B.C.E.) sacked Smyrna, and the city was only refounded by Alexander the Great in the fourth century B.C.E.(Strabo XIV.1.137; see *SNGvAulock* 2231, a coin of Philip I [249–244 B.C.E.] with the reverse depicting a dream of Alexander the Great in which the city's two nemeses urge the king to restore the city). The principal rivals to Miletos were the island poleis of Mytilene (on Lesbos), Chios, and Samos. All three cities launched navies comparable to the fleet of Miletos in the Ionian Revolt (499–494 B.C.E.) (Greaves 2002:1–15, fig. 1.1, 1.5, 99–109). Miletos peaked with a population of perhaps 50,000 in the late sixth century B.C.E., but the greater polity of Milesia resembled contemporary Attica as a federation of settlements and sanctuaries on defensible high points on a peninsula jutting into a vast bay (Greaves 2002). The common political center for this federation was probably located somewhere between the Lion Harbor and the settlement atop Kaletepe.

Miletos long offered the finest harbor in East Greece. At the dawn of the Archaic Age, it was the center of a regional trade across the great bay, linking the city to Priene on the southern slopes of Mt. Mycale, Magnesia ad Maeandrum, and Mys on the eastern shores, and to the southeast Heraclea ad Latmum on an arm of the bay that is now Bafa Gölü. Miletos was one of the first Greek cities to mint her own electrum coins (Holloway 1984:5–18; Weidauer 1975). As Milesians sailed to Levantine and Egyptian ports, they clashed with Samos—a rivalry that contributed to the Lelantine War (Thucydides I.15.3; for sources and discussion, see Jeffrey 1976:63–70). The war, a series of clashes between two loose coalitions of commercial states, did not significantly interrupt prosperity in Ionia; the two belligerents, Miletos and Samos, shared in colonizing the northern Aegean, Hellespontine, and Euxine shores, and in opening trade with the Levant and Egypt. Milesians and Samians at Naucratis each built a sanctuary to their tutelary gods, Apollo and Hera, respectively (Herodotus II:178). Chios, Teos, Clazomenae, Phocaea, Mytilene, Rhodes, Knidos, Halicarnassus, and Phaselis founded a common Hellenion to Zeus. For Miletos, prosperity is attested by grave finds, notably the Lion Tomb, excavated in 1906. Preceded by a *dromos* and with flanking guardian lions, the vaulted tomb memorialized members of a leading family in the sixth century B.C.E. in a fashion reminiscent of the royal *tholos* tombs of the Mycenaean Age.

Thus the East Greeks, between the eighth and sixth centuries B.C.E., contributed decisively to the flowering of Archaic Greek civilization by their reception of the alphabet, and of the material culture and aesthetics of the Near East. Finds of ceramics and coins and the pattern of loanwords in Greek testify to the role of Asian Greeks in trade and colonization. At the same time, the East Greeks learned much of their material culture and aesthetics from their Anatolian neighbors and kin.

East Greeks and Philhellene Anatolian Kings

The cities of East Greece prospered during the Archaic age because of the peace and prosperity imposed by the Phrygian kings of Gordion in the ninth and seventh centuries B.C.E., and then the Lydian kings at Sardis, from the mid-seventh to mid-sixth centuries B.C.E. (see Voigt, chapter 50 this volume, for Gordion, and Greenewalt, chapter 52 in this volume, for Sardis). Philhellene kings promoted trade and cultural exchange (see Sams, chapter 27 in this volume). The finds from the great tumulus and citadel of Gordion bear out Phrygian cultural influence on the Greek world (see Voigt, chapter 50 in this volume). The Lydian king Alyattes (ca. 609–560 B.C.E.) imposed order after the Cimmerian invasions. Lydian kings were perceived as philhellenes, offering opportunities for Greeks such as the Athenian nobles Alcaemon and Solon, reported to have visited Sardis. They lavished costly gifts on Greek sanctuaries, too, notably Delphi and Didyma.

Miletos prospered by an alliance with the Lydian kings. Under Lydian protection, Milesians founded their later colonies on the shores of the Hellespontine and Euxine lands, and extended the trade routes that connected the Aegean and Black Sea lands. Abydos on the Asian side of the narrows of the Hellespont was founded by the Milesians with the permission of King Gyges (c. 680–652 B.C.E.). The Milesians, privileged allies of the Lydian king, found it politic to have the blessings of their overlord at Sardis in a venture that could not help but benefit both parties. Likewise, Amisos, at the mouth of the Halys, was founded in 564 B.C.E. as a joint colony of Miletos and Phocaea.

East Greek civilization was tied to, and participated in, the Archaic cultures of Western Anatolia in the Early Iron Age. Scholars have long studied the impact of Anatolian civilizations, notably Phrygia, Lydia, and Urartu, on the nascent Greek civilization, but commerce and aesthetics flowed in the other direction as well, from the Greek world to the kingdoms and cities of Anatolia. Greek cities on Anatolian shores inevitably by trade and blood were tied to their Anatolian neighbors, both near and distant, in a common set of aesthetics and way of life. This fact is becoming clear in a number of artistic styles or influences (Mellink 1988:217–26, 228–32). Greek artists worked at the behest of Phrygian and Lydian kings, and in some fashion East Greek arts (including the Ionian cities and Dorian Rhodes with her colonies) were part of a wider *koine* of Anatolian arts. Court art at Sardis and fragments of wall paintings from Gordion reveal an East Greek inspiration ca. 550–525 B.C.E. Similar paintings have been found at Düver on the frontier of Phrygia and Lycia. These are paintings commissioned by Anatolian lords or possibly even Persian grandees. Likewise, the ceramics show many common themes and techniques, which is expected in a craft art that was produced in massive quantities, often by immigrant artisans. Herodotus reports that King Midas was the first barbarian king to dedicate offerings to Delphi, where he presented a royal throne (Herodotus I.14.3). Gyges, first king of the Mermnad dynasty of Lydia, sent silver bowls to Delphi (Herodotus I.14.1–3). Tripods, expensive table ware, tapestries and carpets, and stamped ingots were among the items in such exchanges; these provided the means whereby artistic motifs were transmitted.

At the same time, philhellene Anatolian kings set a standard of living that was emulated by all the aristocrats of the peninsula, whatever their origin. Phrygian kings constructed vast tumuli on the plains of Gordion. The Phrygian tumulus lacks a dromos and doorway, in contrast to the beehive tombs of Mycenae, and so these Phrygian tumuli were quite distinct. But the monument was quickly associated with royal power. Lydian kings adopted this royal architecture when they fell heir to Anatolia west of the Halys, and so they created their own plain of tumuli at Bin Tepe just east of Sardis. The tumulus was, in turn, adopted as an appropriate burial for any aspiring grandee, so tenaciously that this form of burial persisted down to the Roman imperial age as part of an Anatolian koine of burial practices.

Likewise, clothing, diet, music, construction of homes, and a host of daily objects and manners were shared across the peninsula with the emergence of kingdoms and the establishment of Greek colonies along the shores in the early Iron Age.

These aspects of life welded together the peoples into an Anatolian world, despite many differences, that cut across political boundaries.

Two indications of this common way of life might be sought in the origins and spread of the Phoenician alphabet, and hoplite arms and tactics. It is surmised that the Greeks adopted the alphabet from their Phoenician contemporaries either on the islands of Crete or Rhodes or at a commercial settlement on the northern shores of Syria, ca. 775–750 B.C.E. (Jeffrey 1976:23–28; Powell 1991). However, the Phrygians, Lydians, Carians, Lycians, and native Sidetans are known to have adopted the alphabet as well, along with the adaptation of vowel sounds (essential for all Indo-European languages). They could have acquired the alphabet from the Greeks or directly from the Phoenicians (Masson 1991:666–76). Hoplite arms and tactics, the hallmark of Greek fighting, were also used by the Carians, Lydians, and Lycians, certainly by the time of Xerxes's invasion in 480 B.C.E. In turn, some of these arms, such as the crested helmet, round shield, and thrusting spears, are well attested on Neo-Hittite monuments (Krentz 2002:23–39; Snodgrass 1967:35–47). Greek innovations included improving the shield and disciplining their citizens to fight courageously in dense columns, but they owed some of their equipment and tactics to Anatolians and Urartians.

Greeks were more than merely precocious students. East Greeks, just like their cousins in the homeland, evolved an identity based on political life, the notion of the well-ordered polis governed by laws passed by the citizens. Such an outlook profoundly influenced society, and so the architecture of Greek poleis in the early Archaic Age differed significantly from that of the Mycenaean Age. The palace on the acropolis disappeared; instead, the temples to the gods became the main focus of Greek civic life. The agora, or "gathering zone," served for both the political and commercial life of the citizens, and in time distinct public buildings were devised, such as the *bouleuterion*, *prytaneion*, law courts, and offices of magistrates—all buildings set around the main agora or on a thoroughfare for convenience of access by citizens.

The Greek temple, which was based on the principles of wooden construction, was reinvented as a masonry building on the basis of Greek observation of great shrines in Egypt. In western Anatolia, however, little is known of the appearance of sanctuaries in the Hittite or Early Iron Ages. A wooden frame with solid mudbrick walls and tile roofs was probably the norm. At Assos one of the earliest Doric temples survives, completed ca. 530 B.C.E., with a beautiful setting on the acropolis. Given the ease of identifying their own gods with Hellenic counterparts, Lydians, Carians, Lycians, and Phrygians must have viewed Greek temples as imposing homes of the gods whom they themselves worshiped and thus began emulating Greek religious architecture. Greek temples impressed Anatolian visitors as imposing and dignified. Many Anatolians must have viewed cities such as Miletos, Ephesos, and Colophon as part of the wider cultural milieu of Anatolia even if they were distinctly Greek. Hence, Anatolian kings, notably Midas and the Mermnad kings of Lydia, sent gifts to Delphi; the great shrines of the Artemision and Didyma were also patronized by Lydian kings. At Sardis and Labranda, Greek-style temples were constructed to provide appropriate homes for the Anatolian versions of the

Greek gods. In western Anatolia, well before the conquest of Alexander the Great, cities had acquired Greek-style shrines so that the Greek temple became the preferred residence of many Anatolian gods.

The cultural exchange between Greeks and the peoples of Anatolia was thus never one-sided. Contact was renewed by Greeks with the peoples of the plateau in 750 B.C.E., but by 500 B.C.E. the relationship had shifted. As seafarers, the Greeks rapidly regained their role as merchants in the Archaic Age (lost in the Dark Age), and they added the roles of colonist, tourist, pilgrim, scholar, mercenary, and immigrant. As the Anatolian kingdoms were consolidated and power shifted from Gordion to Sardis, Greeks and their cities along three shores became crucial conduits in long-distance trade and the diffusion of arts, products, and technology. The Anatolian kings came to depend on this relationship. By the time of King Croesus (560–546 B.C.E.), the Lydian capital of Sardis was linked to a number of Greek cities on the shores, and the Lydian upper classes embraced many aspects of Greek life (Boardman 1980:101–18). This relationship persisted between Greek city and Anatolian hinterland thereafter.

The Achievement of East Greek Civilization

Greek cities on the shores of Asia Minor and on the Aegean islands were the nexus of trade and cultural exchange in the early Greek world, so Archaic Greek civilization was to a great extent the product of the Greek cities of Asia Minor. Significant examples of the East Greek contribution to the development of Archaic civilization include the epics of Homer as well as the history of Herodotus.

Homer composed the *Iliad* and *Odyssey* in a distinctive epic form of Greek, a mix of Ionic and Aeolic dialects, that points to the colonial settlements of Asia Minor as the place of origin. Smyrna, on the dialect border, is at least plausible (if not historically provable) as the home of Homer. Homer's epics marked the beginning of Hellenic, and thus arguably Western, literature. They were composed in their current form in the late eighth century B.C.E. The epics reveal the Greeks of the Classical world with their gods and institutions, but as yet they were not designated Hellenes. It is noteworthy that colonial Greeks of Asia cast in definitive form the heroic deeds of their distant forefathers who had warred on the shores of an alien Asia Minor in the thirteenth century B.C.E.

The achievements of East Greek visual arts and material culture rested on contacts with the Anatolian peoples and those of the wider Near East in the Archaic Age. Ionian visitors, merchants, and mercenaries reopened contact with the Levant and Egypt, carrying back innumerable gifts from the Near East, notably the alphabet, iron technology, decorative arts, sculpture, and masonry.

In the late seventh century B.C.E., the Greeks relearned monumental masonry from the Egyptians, but they applied masonry to their native use of post and lintel construction (based on wooden construction) so that the influence of the older tradition can be seen even in the painting of the stone temples, painted as their wooden predecessors had been. Great sanctuaries such as the Artemision, Didyma, and the Heraion on Samos were expanded and transformed. The number of stone temples increased at least threefold in the sixth century B.C.E. as prosperity rose and architects perfected masonry without the later Roman advantages of concrete or the arch. The Doric order, perhaps evolved in the Peloponnesus, was a simple, rustic order; the column rested directly on the platform, and upper decoration was an austere pattern of alternating metopes and trigylphs. The Temple of Athena on the acropolis of Assos, ca. 525 B.C.E., offers the best example of the Doric order in Asia Minor. The temple at Assos was unusual for its incorporation of frieze decorations that characterized the Ionic order. Asian Greeks evolved a more elegant Ionic order, with a more delicate column capital and other decorative elements. By 300 B.C.E. continuous frieze reliefs decorated the upper levels of most Ionic temples in Anatolia. The temple of Athena at Priene offers an early Ionic temple in Asia Minor; the plan and decoration influenced the so-called temple of Artemis at Sardis or the temple of Zeus at Labranda. Lydians, Carians, and Lycians adapted the Greek architectural orders for a variety of buildings other than temples. At the Lycian town of Telmessos (Fethiye) Greek architectural elements were incorporated to decorate the fronts of tombs carved in the cliffs. Xanthos, the leading city in western Lycia, used Greek frieze decorations for pillar tombs, such as the Harpy Tomb (Fedak 1990:66–68). The Ionic tomb known as the Monument of the Nereids at Xanthos, ca. 400 B.C.E. and now reconstructed at the British Museum, masterfully combines Greek and Anatolian architectural elements.

East Greeks erected the first free-standing masonry in Anatolia since the Bronze Age. In addition, Ionian sculptors created the first masterpieces of free-standing sculpture by adapting monumental Egyptian funerary statues. The free standing *kouros* (nude male) and *kore* (draped female) might have been votive offerings by nobles on behalf of deceased family members, as suggested by finds along the sacred way of the Heraion on Samos. Greek advances in painting are virtually undocumented, but recent tomb paintings found near Uşak (Temenothyrai) in Phrygia reveal the subtle, naturalistic styles of this period. Artists commissioned by Iranized Lycian nobles of Elmalı likewise freely mixed Greek and Anatolian elements for commemorative frescoes (Mellink 1971, 1972, 1973, 1974, 1975). East Greek and Anatolian painting was imaginative, naturalistic, and quite unlike the two-dimensional figures on ceramics.

Lyric poets devised new meters in the seventh century B.C.E., and as they expressed their political opinions or personal feelings they set the rhythms and genres of Western poetry. Archilochus of Paros, an illegitimate nobleman turned mercenary, penned lyric poems about his exploits and love, ca. 680 B.C.E., perfecting iambic invective to criticize his faithless love, Neobole (Campbell 1967:1–7). Alcaeus of Mytilene composed lyric diatribes against the tyrant Myrsilus and drinking songs ca. 650–625 B.C.E. (Campbell 1967:52–62). Sappho, an associate of Alcaeus, composed marriage poems and elegiac musings about her students (Campbell 1967:40–51). The lyric poets in verse expressed the individual as sculptors did in stone and tyrants in politics. Parody and spoof characterized many poems, revealing a Hellenic outlook that alternately mocked and exalted the human condition.

Miletos and Ephesos proved to be the homes for the first scientific speculation in the Greek world, as Ionian Greeks learned Babylonian mathematics and astronomy. Thales of Miletos (ca. 640–548 B.C.E.) offered the first cosmology based on the hypothesis of four primary elements (fire, earth, air, and water). Thales was the first to predict a solar eclipse, in 585 B.C.E., as a phenomenon rather than a miracle; he also reasoned by deduction the evolution of life from fossils. His followers Anaximander (611–547 B.C.E.) and Anaximenes (fl. ca. 525–498 B.C.E.) revised Thales's cosmology and developed the analytical language necessary for logical reasoning. Heraclitus of Ephesos, "the weeping philosopher" (fl. ca. 510–470 B.C.E.), proposed a cosmology based on a dynamic equilibrium. Pythagoras of Samos (fl. ca. 532 B.C.E., died ca. 495 B.C.E.) offered a pantheistic vision of cosmology along with a transmigration of souls (for these pre-Socratic philosophers, see Kirk and Raven 1957). Pythagoras made advances in mathematics and music, seen as the basis for the harmony of existence. Ionian thinkers applied their deduction and logical language to the study of human affairs, thereby creating the disciplines of geography and history. Hecataeus of Miletos (fl. ca. 500 B.C.E.) composed a historical geography, and he produced the first map of the world. Herodotus of Halicarnassus (ca. 490–425 B.C.E.) composed the oldest extant history, an inquiry into the cause of the Persian Wars. In so doing he first drew a distinction between Asia and Europe. Herodotus combined traditional storytelling techniques seen in Homeric epic with a historical method based on direct research and logical reasoning. Herodotus, who viewed Athens and Sparta as epitomizing virtues of the polis, could also appreciate the virtues of Persians and other peoples. With Herodotus, Greek historians henceforth assumed a unique perspective of self-criticism and relativist appreciation of other peoples and cultures.

East Greeks under the Achaemenid Kings

The political fortunes of the East Greeks changed with the conquest of the Lydian kingdom by Cyrus of Persia in 546 B.C.E. Ionian, Aeolian, and Dorian cities submitted to Cyrus. The later king Darius I (521–486 B.C.E.) organized Asian Greeks, Carians, Lycians, and Pamphylians into the fourth satrapy and assessed a tribute of 400 talents annually (Herodotus III.88–97). Persian satraps at Sardis ruled as agents of this distant Near Eastern overlord so that the East Greeks became one of many subject peoples rather than the favored allies of philhellene Lydian kings.

Archaeology has revealed that the landed élites of Anatolia quickly adapted Persian manners, dress, and material culture during the second half of the sixth century B.C.E. (Mellink 1988:221–23). The proud Anatolian equestrian élites took service under the Great King. Anatolian grandees came to terms with Persian rule because they shared a common aristocratic ethos. Persian dress, manners, and aesthetics were valued within a generation of the conquest. On the border of southwestern Phrygia and northern Lycia, near the modern town of Elmalı, funerary wall paintings found in tumulus 1 at Karaburun reveal an adaptation of Persian manners and dress by Anatolians depicted in banquet scenes. Tumuli at İkizkepe, near the modern town of Güre (twenty kilometers west of Uşak), have yielded rich finds of wooden furniture, metal ware, and frescoes that reveal a delicate fusion of East Greek, Lydian, and Persian elements by 525 B.C.E. Fragments of frescoes from Gordion point to a similar process. By 500 B.C.E., among the landed classes, a cultural koine emerged in Anatolia with a definite Persian stamp. For the first time, the upper classes of the peninsula saw themselves as part of a wider cultural world. Anatolian cults, too, were recast in Iranian guises, such as the shrines of Artemis Persica at Hypaepa and Hyrcanis in Lydia. The Persian tradition of the worship of Mithras penetrated Pontus, Cappadocia, and Commagene (Balcer 1984:180–89; Goell 1996; Waldmann 1973).

East Greeks in general stood apart from this cultural fusion and remained linked to the Aegean world. Ionians must have resented the fact that they were no longer arbiters of culture for philhellene Anatolian kings, but rather useful, albeit minor, subjects of the Great King at Persepolis who ruled a world empire. East Greeks rose in the Ionian Revolt (499–494 B.C.E.) not so much because Persian rule was oppressive but because it was foreign and remote. East Greeks endured tyrants, imposed by the Persians, to keep order in the cities. Rule by tyrants was a negation of the polis and lawful government. Furthermore, Ionians sensed that they had lost their political and cultural primacy in the Greek world to Athens. From 508/7 B.C.E. on, Athenians defined themselves by their democratic constitution, and their confidence and conduct set them aside as unique among Greeks, either to be emulated or, as in the speech of the Corinthians before the Spartans in 432, to be distrusted (Thucydides I.122–23). Under their democracy, the Athenians gained a spirit that, in Herodotus's words, enabled them "to go from strength to strength" (Herodotus V.78).

Herodotus attributes the outbreak of the Ionian Revolt to the private collusion of two tyrants of Miletos who acted for personal reasons. Yet Aristagoras and Histiaeus operated more as rivals than allies during the revolt. Aristagoras, tyrant of Miletos, was originally encouraged to revolt by his father-in-law, Histiaeus, who was languishing in gilded captivity as King Darius's advisor at Susa. Aristagoras resigned as tyrant of Miletos and was subsequently elected general of the Milesian democracy. He then encouraged the Ionian and Aeolian Greeks to cast out their tyrants. At the conference of Mys, in early 499 B.C.E., the cartographer Hecataeus urged his fellow Ionians to reconsider this course of action, pointing out the vast resources of the Persian Empire. His rational argument fell on deaf ears. In 499 B.C.E. Aristagoras visited Sparta and Athens in search of military assistance. The Spartans refused, but the Athenians sent 20 triremes with marines (400 hoplites and 80 archers)—a major commitment at the time—to their kinsmen in Asia. Eretria on the island of Euboea sent five triremes. In the spring of 498 B.C.E., Aristagoras led out of Ephesos 10,000 men, comprising the Ionian civic levies, Athenians, and Eretrians. He outflanked the Persian forces holding the Karabel Pass, the passageway between the Hermus valley and Ionia, by a bold march up the Cayster valley so that he attacked Sardis from the southeast. The Greeks burst into the marketplace of the city. The Persian satrap Artaphernes held out on the acropolis, but the Greeks torched Sardis in the confused fighting (see Greenewalt, chapter 52 in this volume, for archaeological evidence of these historical events).

Aristagoras and his army retreated to Ephesos. The Athenians and Eretrians thereupon sailed home, but the burning of Sardis signaled rebellion along the western and southern fringes of Persian Anatolia. Aristagoras set out on an Aegean cruise of the Ionian fleets and so incited the Greeks of the Hellespontine regions to join the rebellion. Carians and Lycians revolted. Along the Pamphylian shores, the Greek cities Aspendos and Perge revolted, and Onesilos, younger brother of King Gorgos of Salamis, led the Cypriote Greeks into rebellion. By the spring of 497 B.C.E., King Darius faced rebellions along the shores of his Anatolian satrapies, but the military issue was never in doubt. Persian forces, with the assistance of the Phoenician fleet, landed near Salamis and crushed the Cypriote insurgents. Another Persian army crushed the Carian hoplites in the Maeander valley and then reduced the Lycian cities in a series of sieges that climaxed in the sack of Xanthos (Lycian Arñna). The Ionians managed to defy the Persians somewhat longer. Even so, the Ionian fleet was defeated off the isle of Lade in the Bay of Miletos in 494 B.C.E., due to the superior seamanship and numbers of the Phoenicians and the treachery of the Samians who defected at the crucial point in the battle.

Defeat in 494 B.C.E. proved disastrous for many Ionian cities. Miletos was ruthlessly sacked, and many residents were deported to Central Asia where Alexander the Great (336–323 B.C.E.) found their descendants living in exile a century and a half later. The defeat of the Greek rebels off Lade ended Miletos as a power, and marked the shift of the political, economic, and cultural axis from East Greece to Athens. At the Battle of Lade, the Ionians had mustered 373 triremes, a force manned by well over 70,000 citizen sailors, hoplites, and archers and so comparable in size to the confederate Greek navy that won the Battle of Salamis in 480 B.C.E.[1] At that battle only fourteen years later, the Ionian cities launched only 100 triremes.[2] Even though the Athenians pulled out of the Ionian rebellion, they had to face the wrath of the Great King for supporting their kinsmen. In 490 B.C.E. the Athenians were invaded by Darius and defeated the first Persian invasion at Marathon; a decade later, Athens and Sparta united to repel the invasion of Darius's son Xerxes and then carried the war back to the Ionian shores in 479 B.C.E.

Imperial Athens and the East Greeks

In the spring of 479 B.C.E., the Athenians, Spartans, and their allies annihilated the Persian army in Greece under Mardonius, at Plataea in Boeotia. In early summer of that year the Greek allies sailed to Ionia and destroyed the Persian navy on the beaches beneath the slopes of Mount Mycale. In the course of the battle, the Ionians defected to their kinsmen. The Greek victories at Salamis and Mycale ended Persian naval power, and for the next seventy-five years (480–405 B.C.E.), the triremes of democratic Athens ruled the Euxine, Aegean, and eastern Mediterranean Seas.

The Spartans, reluctant to lead the overseas war against the Great King, withdrew from the naval war, so in 478/7 B.C.E. the Samians, Chians, and Mytileneans turned to Athens and the Athenian general Aristides the Just to organize the Delian League (Plutarch, *Aristides* 23). From the start, the terms of the alliance favored the hegemon Athens and revealed the fears of the East Greeks. Athenian generals commanded expeditions, and *Hellenotamiai* ("stewards of the Greeks"), who were elected by the Athenian assembly, administered league funds at the sanctuary of Apollo on the island of Delos. Aristides assessed dues from those allies who preferred to commute military service by paying silver. Aristides's assessment of 460 talents was far less onerous than what was levied by the Great King, and the allies later cited it as a fair levy when they opposed later tribute increases by Athens.

From 477 to 454 B.C.E., East Greeks served in coalition fleets under Athenian generals, gaining booty and captives (Sealey 1966). Squadrons of East Greek triremes formed a significant part of the Athenian fleets supporting rebellions against Persia. The majority of triremes lost in the expedition to Egypt in 455–454 B.C.E. might well have been allied, including East Greek, rather than Athenian vessels (Meiggs 1972:439–41, 473–76). The Athenians also gradually turned the league into an empire after 465 B.C.E., when Kimon's victory at the Eurymedon River ended hopes of a Persian naval revival. From 465 to 463 B.C.E., Athens mobilized league forces to crush the island polis Thasos over a private dispute concerning title to the mines on the Thracian *peraea*. The Thracians appealed to the Spartans, who failed to respond with aid. However, ensuing events resulted in two changes decisive to the fate of the East Greeks. In 462/1 B.C.E. the radical democrats Ephialtes and Perikles ostracized Kimon and passed democratizing reforms in the Athenian assembly. More significantly, in 460 B.C.E., war erupted between Athens and Sparta.

During this First Peloponnesian War (460–446 B.C.E.) widespread rebellions against the hegemon Athens erupted in Ionia and the Aegean islands in 454–451 B.C.E., and again in 447–445 B.C.E. Perikles emerged as the democratic leader in Athens in 454, when the news of the Athenian military disaster in Egypt sparked the first round of rebellions among Athens's "allies." Perikles stood for the imperial dignity of Athens and therefore insisted on the need to secure the Aegean world. Hence the Athenians crushed rebel cities, imposed democracies and Athenian garrisons and magistrates, and exacted tribute (*phoros*) from wayward league members. Between 449 and 432 B.C.E., Perikles backed laws in the Athenian assembly that ended the freedom and autonomy of the league allies. The tribute was reorganized by the decree of Cleinias in 448/7 B.C.E. (Fornara 1977:107–9, document 98). Another law in 450–446 B.C.E. imposed Athenian weights, measures, and coins throughout the league, so that allied silver coinages were reminted and restruck as Athenian coins (Fornara 1977:102–3, document 97; Martin 1985:196–215).[3] The recoinage not only simplified collection of tribute but also asserted Athenian sovereignty over the allies. Just as important was a provision written into treaties with allies, to send a panoply and cow as gifts to Athena during the Panathenea (Barron 1964; Raubitschek 1966). The earliest instance of this provision is in the regulations of Erythrae in 453 B.C.E.; the provision is intended to be a symbolic acknowledgment of Athens as metropolis (Meiggs and Lewis 1969:89–94, no. 40). The symbolic gifts, sacrificial animals, and dedications of arms were important recognitions of Athens as metropolis, even by non-Ionian cities of the Delian League. They reinforced the power of the oaths sworn at the founding of the Delian League, and they confirmed that Athena Polias, patroness of Athens, had replaced Delian Apollo as the guardian of the league.

Most telling are the oaths recorded in treaty regulations between Athens and an allied city that had rebelled. At Miletos, the Athenians imposed a democracy with popular courts of appeal as well as an *episkopos* ("overseer") and garrison (Fornara 1977:92–93, document 92). The inscription is fragmentary, but the treaty concluded with an oath administered to the Milesians. The oaths recorded on the decrees from Colophon and Chalcis are not consistent with Greek notions of freedom and autonomy (Fornara 1977:106–9, document 99; 110–11, document 103). The Chalcidians must swear to obey and love the Athenian people, and in all cases citizens of an allied city were required to report any would-be rebels. By 431 B.C.E. only Mytilene and Chios remained as free allies in the Delian League with oligarchic constitutions.

The success of the Athenian democracy and civilization in the age of Perikles was paid for by the allies, who quickly came to resent Athens as a tyrant city. The dramatic emergence of Athenian naval power, partially made possible by the forced cooperation of East Greek allies, frightened conservative Spartans. A clique of leading Spartans bent on the destruction of the hated democratic polis pushed for war among the Spartan citizens, who, though hardly friends of Athens, feared even more a long, desultory war that risked Messenian revolt and allied defections. Twice the Spartans felt driven to war with the Athenians, first in the inconclusive First Peloponnesian War (460–446 B.C.E.), and then in the great Peloponnesian War (431–404 B.C.E.). In the first ten years of the second conflict, known as the Archidamian War (431–421 B.C.E.), the Athenians drew on the manpower and resources of their allies. High pay induced many allies to hire themselves into the Athenian fleet and armies. East Greeks, longing for their lost autonomy and freedom, dared not challenge Athens. The swift suppression of the Samian revolt (441–439 B.C.E.) by Perikles had sent a chilling message to allied cities across the Aegean Sea. The Persian satraps at Daskyleion and Sardis, who watched from a respectful distance the clash between Athens and Sparta, offered no assistance to would-be East Greek rebels.

In 428–427 B.C.E., Mytilene revolted, threatening to export rebellion to the Hellespontine and Ionian cities. The Athenians swiftly isolated and reduced Mytilene, and meted out harsh punishment. The Peloponnesian squadron under Alcidas arrived too late to assist Mytilene, but leading citizens at Colophon and Ephesos urged Alcidas to establish a base in Ionia. Alcidas, however, withdrew. The East Greeks dwelling in unwalled cities and without triremes had no choice but to obey Athens. Furthermore, the Athenians had promoted class divisions among the citizens, backing the lower classes against the aristocrats who might have favored the Spartans. In morale and size, Ionian cities, for all their prosperity under the Athenian imperial peace, lacked the will to rebel. The Asian Greeks thus did not stir until news of the defeat of two Athenian expeditions sent against Syracuse in 413 B.C.E. As the Athenians desperately fought to put down rebellions across the Aegean in the final phase of the Peloponnesian War, known as the Ionian War (412–404 B.C.E.), the East Greeks soon found themselves with two ambitious, mutually suspicious, and dangerous allies: Sparta and Persia.

East Greece Between Sparta and Persia

In 412 B.C.E., the Spartans committed to a naval war against Athens, constructing 100 triremes for service in eastern Aegean waters. Sparta courted Chios, Miletos, and lesser Ionian cities, trying to induce them to rebel against Athens. Throughout the naval war in the Aegean and Hellespontine waters from 412 to 405 B.C.E., the Spartans aimed to amass triremes and money at a base in Ionia (either Miletos or Ephesos), enroll East Greek allies, and then sail to the Hellespont to force the Athenians into a decisive naval battle to defend the grain route into the Black Sea. Hence, the East Greek allies were vital for the success of the Peloponnesian fleet.

Simultaneously, the Spartans sought Persian aid. In 412 B.C.E., the Spartans concluded the treaty of Miletos with Tissaphernes, satrap at Sardis. Tissaphernes extended a loan to pay crews of the Peloponnesian fleet operating in Ionian waters. Tissaphernes was late and parsimonious in payment, so the Peloponnesian fleet often could not act for lack of funds. Instead, Tissapherenes aimed to pit Spartans and Athenians against each other in a drawn-out war. The Spartans reluctantly agreed under the treaty that the Great King would have the right to collect tribute from the Ionians, but they insisted that East Greek cities would be free and autonomous. Milesians were outraged over the treaty. Throughout the war many Ionians hoped, for obvious reasons, that Sparta would ultimately oppose reimposition of Persian rule.

In 412 B.C.E. the Peloponnesian fleet based at Miletos failed to achieve decisive results. Chios was won over; oligarches revolted and seized Miletos, Ephesos, and Teos. The Athenian fleet retired to Samos and so contained Spartan strategic movements. In 411 B.C.E. the Athenian Alkibiades returned from exile to command the Athenian fleet at Samos. When the Spartan navarch Mindaros shifted the theater of operations to the Hellespont in hopes of cutting off the Athenian grain supply, Alkibiades and his colleague Thrasybulus won a decisive battle over him at Cyzicus, and Mindaros went down with the entire fleet. Over the next three years, 410–408 B.C.E., Alkibiades and Thrasybulus secured the Hellespontine and northern Aegean waters. The Spartans, assisted by Pharnabazos, satrap of Daskyleion, constructed a new fleet at Antandrus, but the Athenians held the initiative.

In 408 B.C.E., the strategic situation had changed with the arrival at Sardis of Cyrus the Younger, the younger son of Darius II (423–405 B.C.E.). Cyrus, appointed lord (*karanos*) of western Asia Minor, had full authority over policy in the Greek world. He and the Spartan navarch Lysander agreed to cooperate.[4] Their personal alliance assured the final defeat of the Athenian fleet at Aegispotami in 405 B.C.E. Lysander captured the Athenian fleet, cut the grain shipments to Athens from the Euxine lands, and compelled the surrender of Athens in spring 404 B.C.E. Lysander expelled democrats and friends of Athens in the cities of East Greece. He installed Spartan governors, or harmosts, with mercenary garrisons, and personal friends as the governing oligarchies, known as decarchies ("rule of ten") in Ionia and the islands. Lysander, who aspired to leadership of a Spartan empire, was soon forced to retire from public life. The Spartans, however, faced the dilemma of either meeting the terms of the Treaty of Miletos concluded with the Persians, or standing by their oaths to uphold the freedom of the East Greeks.

The Spartans determined to fight for the freedom of the Greeks in Asia Minor. Sparta possessed a navy of over 200 triremes in the Aegean and maintained harmosts and mercenary garrisons in the larger cities of East Greece, notably Miletos, Ephesos, Abydos, Sestos, Cyzicus, Byzantion, and Chalcedon (Rahe 1980). Spartan officials put the cities of East Greece under contribution, assessing supplies, silver, and recruits. Spartans did not maintain a field army in Ionia until 400 B.C.E. because of their alliance with Cyrus the Younger. The strategic situation abruptly changed in September 401 B.C.E. when Cyrus was slain at Cunaxa, in Babylonia, in a bid to seize the Achaemenid throne from his brother Artaxerxes II (405–358 B.C.E.). Cyrus, with the blessings of Sparta, had recruited 13,500 Greek mercenaries who, on the death of their paymaster Cyrus, marched out of the Persian Empire in the famous Retreat of the Ten Thousand, 401–399 B.C.E. (Xenophon, *Anabasis*). Artaxerxes II then declared war on Sparta.

In the spring of 400 B.C.E., the Spartan harmost Thibron arrived at Ephesos with an army of cavalry and hoplites (1,000 *neodameis* [freed helots] and 4,000 Peloponnesian mercenaries). He raised additional forces from the Ionian cities and in 399 B.C.E. hired 6,000 of Cyrus's veterans. Although he commanded the largest Greek army to date in Asia Minor—over 15,000 strong—Thibron achieved only modest results, securing Greek cities between Cyzicus and Ephesos. The Spartan army proved an intolerable burden. Thibron was recalled, tried, and exiled on grounds of mistreatment of the Ionians because he failed to maintain discipline in his mercenary army, which plundered allied communities (Hamilton 1991:87–91; Westlake 1986). Given the costs of warfare and Spartan finances, Thibron clearly had little choice but to allow foraging and plundering if he were to keep his army in the field. The harmost Dercyllidas succeeded to command, but his operations in 398–397 B.C.E. achieved little because the satraps Tissaphernes and Pharnabazos set aside their personal rivalry and cooperated to check the Peloponnesian army from plundering Persian domains.

The Spartans, impatient with the desultory fighting, sent Agesilaus II, the Eurypontid king, to end the war. In spring 396 B.C.E. Agesilaus arrived with reinforcements including 6,000 Peloponnesian mercenaries, 2,000 neodameis, and 30 senior Spartan officers. Peltasts (light infantry) and cavalry are not mentioned, but his force numbered well over 8,000 soldiers (Xenophon, *Hellenica* III.4.2). Aspiring to the role of previous heroic Spartan kings, Agesilaus, just like Alexander the Great later, projected himself as a Homeric hero, styling himself as a new Agamemnon. In 395 B.C.E., Agesilaus shifted the theater of operations away from the familiar battlefields of the Aegean littoral to strike into the heartland of Persian Anatolia. In a brilliant campaign maneuver he inflicted a decisive defeat on the Persian army outside of Sardis. He then retired to Cyme, refitted, and conducted a second campaign, ravaging Mysia and Phrygia and besieging Gordion. The damage to the Persian Period walls and the concealment of a hoard of silver *sigloi* might have resulted from Agesilaus's attack (*Hellenica Oxyrhynchia* 21 [16].6). When Agesilaus failed to capture Gordion, he marched east and crossed the Halys, but he eventually had to withdraw to winter quarters in the Troad.

In the spring of 394 B.C.E., Agesilaus concentrated his army in the Troad for a new invasion of the interior of Asia Minor when he was recalled to Greece due to the outbreak of the Corinthian War. In the winter of 396–395 B.C.E., agents of Artaxerxes II had incited Athens, Thebes, Corinth, and Argos to make common cause against Sparta. For the next decade, the leading Greek states were locked in a desultory struggle, the Corinthian War (395–386 B.C.E.). The military stalemate resulting from this war was ended by negotiations; under the Peace of Antalcidas or King's Peace in 386 B.C.E., the Spartans retained a hegemony over the Greek mainland at the price of handing over the Asian Greek cities to King Artaxerxes II. The Athenians regained their autonomy, freedom, and the right to conclude alliances with other states. The terms of the King's Peace condemned the leading Greek city-states to a series of destructive wars that ended in a Macedonian conquest fifty years later. For East Greece, the same period witnessed a return to peace and prosperity under the Great King.

East Greece under Persian Satraps and Anatolian Dynasts

Under the terms of the King's Peace, the Spartans returned the Asian Greeks to the Great King. With the resultant Persian backing, they were able to make a bid for a lesser hegemony in mainland Greece. For the Ionians, two generations under

Athenian rule had familiarized them with democracy, even if this government had been imposed by the Athenians. The fighting during the Ionian War in 412–406 B.C.E. had been marred by repeated clashes between democrats and oligarchies favored by Sparta. By 386 B.C.E., landed classes dominated the cities of East Greece, and they hardly relished a return to rule by tyrants imposed by Persia. For this reason, in 334 B.C.E. the East Greeks welcomed Alexander the Great because he cast out tyrants and championed democracies.

Yet Persian rule brought peace and order in the fourth century B.C.E. East Greek cities resumed their role as conduits between Aegean and Anatolian worlds. Athenian commercial domination in the fifth century B.C.E. wrought economic and cultural development. It quickened the pace of the diffusion of Hellenizing tastes in western Asia Minor. The Lycians, long in contact with Greeks, cleverly adapted Hellenic architectural elements to their funerary monuments at such cities as Telmessos, Tlos, Xanthos, Myra, and Caunus in the fifth and fourth centuries B.C.E. Lycian dynasts minted local silver coinage inspired by Greek types, and Lycian cities remodeled themselves along Greek civic lines so that towns shared a common political culture with their Greek neighbors.

Foremost were the Hecatomnid dynasts of Caria, who forged a powerful state in southwestern Asia Minor and promoted Hellenic cults, arts, aesthetics, and material culture among the Carians. Mausolos (377–353 B.C.E.), an Anatolian dynast who was invested as satrap by Artaxerxes II (405–358 B.C.E.), united Caria and extended his sway over Lycia and the Dorian Greek cities of southwestern Asia Minor. Mausolos allied with the island poleis Rhodes and Kos and backed their revolt from Athens during the Social War (357–355 B.C.E.). Mausolos made Halicarnassus his capital and commissioned his monumental royal tomb, numbered among the seven wonders of the ancient world. The Hecatomnid court attracted Greek artists, architects, savants, and soldiers, so that Mausolos and his heirs pursued a Hellenizing cultural policy comparable to that of the Argead kings of Macedon. Mausolos and his brother Idrieos (351–344 B.C.E.) rebuilt the national sanctuary of Zeus at Labranda in an Ionic style. The Hecatomnid dynasts of Caria pointed to new directions in Anatolian life, for they forged links as philhellene benefactor and ally with the Greek cities whose wealth and manpower were crucial to running an Anatolian kingdom. Hence, they set a standard for the Macedonian and Anatolian monarchs of the Hellenistic period in their dealings with the Greek cities (Hornblower 1982).

Artaxerxes II and his heirs benefited little from the return of the cities of East Greece to his rule, because after 386 B.C.E. the Great King no longer ruled over his distant satrapies effectively. The Battle of Cunaxa in 401 B.C.E. and the retreat of the Ten Thousand revealed not only the superiority of professional Greek hoplites but also the weakness of the Achaemenid Empire. Persian colonial élites in the western satrapies as well as native dynasts with the title satrap hired Greek mercenaries and defied the Great King in four insurrections, collectively known as the Satraps' Revolt, in 385–383 and 370–362 B.C.E. These insurrections were not nationalist uprisings but rather bids by satraps, backed by Persian colonial élites and Anatolian grandees, to carve out independent states in the Persian west. The satraps Datames of Cappadocia (385–372 B.C.E.) and Orontes of Armenia may even initially have been aiming for the Persian throne. Rebel satraps such as Datames hired Greek mercenaries and minted Greek-style silver coins to pay for their armies and fleets (Moysey 1986:7–29).

By 350 B.C.E., shrewd observers would have predicted that the lands of Anatolia were slipping out of the hands of the Great King. Most could see that Ionian cities were reluctant subjects, but they lacked the resources and will to stage another grand rebellion. Instead, these Greek cities were likely to resume their roles as conduits of Hellenic goods and tastes for new Anatolian kingdoms carved out of the Western satrapies by ambitious colonial Persian élites or native client kings, such as those in Caria or Cilicia. In short, a symbiosis between Hellenic city on the shore and inland Anatolia, similar to that of the seventh and sixth centuries B.C.E., was likely to result from the anticipated dissolution of the Persian Empire. No one could have imagined that a young king, son of a brilliant Macedonian king who turned a Balkan backwater state into the arbiter of the Greek world, would overrun Anatolia after a single battle and then overthrow the Persian Empire in six years of campaigns. Alexander the Great swiftly, unexpectedly, and decisively altered the course of Anatolian civilization, for he alone made Hellenism the dominant cultural force in the peninsula for the next fifteen centuries.

Alexander the Great and the Greeks of Asia Minor

In May 334 B.C.E., Alexander won a decisive victory over the Persian satraps at the river Granicus in northwestern Asia Minor. By successive cavalry attacks, he put to flight the Persian cavalry and surrounded and annihilated the Greek mercenary hoplites who were drawn up behind the main Persian line. In this single battle, Alexander shattered the Persian field army of Asia Minor and slew many of its senior satraps and commanders, so that he encountered no further organized resistance. The victory on the Granicus delivered to Alexander Asia Minor west of the Taurus, and King Darius III was compelled to raise a great army to oppose Alexander at Issus in the next year (Arrian, *Anabasis Alexandri* I–II).

Immediately after his victory on the Granicus, Alexander marched southwest, freeing the Greek cities of the Troad, Aeolis, and Ionia and so depriving the Persian imperial navy of bases in the Aegean. The Greeks of Asia hailed Alexander as their benefactor and savior, and several inscriptions reveal that Alexander treated each city as an autonomous ally. In all the cities, Alexander installed democracies and ended tribute, but as free allies the Ionian and Aeolian cities were expected to offer contributions (*syntaxis*) for the Panhellenic war. The Asian Greek cities were never enrolled in the League of Corinth, the league of Hellenic city-states organized by

Philip II in 337 for the war against Persia. Five cities—Miletos, Teos, Colophon, Abydos, and Lampsacus—struck Macedonian regal coins. At Priene, Alexander lodged at a private residence and ordered repairs to the temple of Athena. Nearby, he ordered the refounding of Smyrna; the citizens created an aetiological legend that in a dream Alexander was inspired by two tutelary Amazons of the city to restore it (Bosworth 1988:55–63; *SNGvAulock* 2231, coin of Philip I). Only at Miletos and Halicarnassus did Greek mercenaries in the employ of Darius III defy Alexander. However, resistance ceased once Alexander defeated Darius III at Issus in 333 B.C.E. Anatolian peoples also hailed Alexander. At Sardis, the Persian satrap surrendered the citadel and treasury, and so Alexander solved both debts and logistics. The Lydians were declared free to live under their own laws, but Asander, a Macedonian officer, was appointed satrap at Sardis. Among the Carians, Alexander again confirmed ancestral privileges, and the Hecatomnid queen Ada adopted Alexander as her son and heir.

The literary sources and inscriptions attest to the ambiguous relationship between the Greek city-states and Alexander the Great. Asian Greeks concluded separate treaties with Alexander so that henceforth their freedom and autonomy were privileges from a Macedonian king. Greek cities were favored by Alexander and the Diadochoi (his successors) so that they became the defining force for the urban civilization of Hellenistic Asia Minor. Asian Greek cities bowed to Alexander's demands for divine orders in 324 B.C.E. and did not dare join the Athenians, Aetolians, and Thessalians in the Lamian War (323–322 B.C.E.) to overthrow Macedonian rule. Instead, the disparity in power compelled the Greek cities of Asia Minor to devise new relationships with Macedonian overlords who styled themselves as Hellenes. Divine honors enabled cities to honor Alexander and later Hellenistic kings within Greek civic traditions. Macedonian kings and Anatolian dynasts thus stood outside the city's rule of law as benefactors and protectors. Furthermore, construction of massive city walls, best seen at Assos or Heraclea ad Latmum, gave a provisional freedom to Greek cities because Macedonian kings waging dynastic wars with expensive mercenary armies were willing to negotiate rather than storm well-fortified cities.

Therefore, despite wars among the Diadochoi who partitioned the empire of Alexander over the years 321–281 B.C.E., Asian Greek cities enjoyed prosperity and a measure of independence. Ionia experienced a renaissance. The cities of Smyrna (refounded by Alexander the Great) and Ephesos (refounded by Lyismachus) emerged as leading commercial and cultural centers of the Aegean world and Asia Minor. Miletos experienced a revival, and from the second century B.C.E. on became a model of the planned city. In the Hellespontine regions, Cyzicus, Chalcedon, and Byzantion emerged as the ports for Attalid Asia, Bithynia, and Thrace. In the lands of the Black Sea, Heraclea, Sinope, Amisos, and Trapezus grew into leading commercial centers linking the Anatolian heartland with the kingdoms of Thrace and the Tauric Chersonesus. In southwestern Asia Minor, Rhodes secured sea lands and ruled over a wide Anatolian Peraea, and along the Pamphylian shores Perge, Aspendos, Side, and the later Attaleia (Antalya) prospered as allies of the great empires.

Simultaneously, Anatolian cities and temple towns transformed themselves into poleis so that the Hellenic city became the primary cultural, political, and religious center of western Anatolia by 200 B.C.E. The cities of Lydia, Caria, Lycia, and Cilicia adopted Greek arts, language, and public institutions. The lesser kings of Asia Minor established Greek-style capitals such as Nicaea, Nicomedia, and Prusa in Bithynia, Cabeira (later Neocaesarea) and Amasia in Pontus, and Mazaca (later Caesarea) in Cappadocia. The royal capitals at Pergamon and Sardis, and Seleucid military colonies, became models of Hellenic cities for towns of inland Anatolia.

Within three generations of Alexander's death, Greek and Hellenized cities of Anatolia had acquired powerful political, religious, and cultural identities, and their ruling classes saw themselves as the heirs of the polis and the achievements of the Classical age. However, Greek cities across Asia Minor were not tied to the destinies of any of the Hellenistic monarchies, so they looked to Rome for protection against the Seleucid king Antiochus III (223–187 B.C.E.), who aspired to unite the peninsula under his rule. They thereby invited Rome into Asia Minor, ending the period of Hellenic and Hellenistic Anatolia, and ushering in the centuries-long Roman era.

NOTES

1. Each trireme carried a crew of 170 men and officers, 20 hoplites, and 4 archers for a total force of 63,410 sailors and officers, 7,460 hoplites, and 1,492 archers.

2. Herodotus VII.89–95 lists a fleet of 1,207 triremes, consisting of 300 Phoenician, 200 Egyptian, 150 Cypriote, 100 Cilician, 30 Pamphylian Greek, 50 Lycian, 30 Asiatic Dorian Greek, 70 Carian, 100 Ionian, 17 from the Cyclades Islands, 60 Aeolian Greek, and 100 Hellespontine Greek triremes. Hence the other subject Greeks, Anatolians, and Cypriotes together comprised nearly 60 percent of Xerxes's total fleet.

3. Electrum and gold coins continued to circulate, and so did certain civic issues of silver coins struck on the Attic weight standard. My thanks to Ute Wartenberg-Kagan, American Numismatic Society, for information from her forthcoming study on electrum coinage.

4. In 408 B.C.E. Darius II had demoted the satrap Tissaphernes, who had to hand over Sardis to Cyrus the Younger. Tissaphernes took up residence at Tralles (Aydın) in the Maeander valley. Tissaphernes was given a satrapy comprising Caria and Lycia, unruly districts without significant Persian military colonies or major cities.

REFERENCES

Abbreviations

SNGvAulock Sylloge Nummorum Graecorum Deutschland. 1957–1968. *Sammlung von Aulock*. Berlin: Deutsches Archäologisches Institut.

Primary Sources

The citations to Arrian, Herodotus, Hesiod, Plato, Strabo, Thucydides, and Xenophon are standard references to the Oxford Classical Texts.

Campbell, D. A. 1967. *Greek Lyric Poetry*. London: Macmillan.
Hellenica Oxyrhynchia. Ed. P. R. McKechnie and S. J. Kern. Warminster: Aris and Phillips, 1988.
Plutarch. Aristides. In *Lives*, vol. 2. Trans. Bernadotte Perrin. Loeb Classical Library 47. Cambridge, Mass.: Harvard University Press, 1914.

Secondary Sources

Andrewes, A. 1956. *The Greek Tyrants*. London: Hutchinson's University Library.
Balcer, Jack Martin. 1984. *Sparda by the Bitter Sea: Imperial Interaction in Western Asia Minor*. Chico, Calif.: Scholars Press.
Barron, John P. 1964. The Religious Propaganda of the Delian League. *Journal of Hellenic Studies* 84: 188–95.
Boardman, John. 1980. *The Greeks Overseas: Their Early Colonies and Trade*, 3rd ed. New York: Thames and Hudson.
Bosworth, A. B. 1988. *Conquest and Empire: the Reign of Alexander the Great*. Cambridge: Cambridge University Press.
Cook, J. M. and D. Blackman. 1971. Greek Archaeology in Western Asia Minor, 1965–1970. *Archaeological Reports* 6(1970–1971): 33–62.
Fedak, Janos. 1990. *Monumental Tombs of the Hellenistic Age: A Study of Selected Tombs from the Pre-Classical to the Early Imperial Era*. Toronto: University of Toronto Press.
Finkelberg, Margalit. 2005. *Greeks and Pre-Greeks: Aegean Prehistory and Greek Heroic Tradition*. Cambridge: Cambridge University Press.
Fornara, Charles W. 1977. *Archaic Times to the End of the Peloponnesian War*. Translated Documents of Greece and Rome 1. Cambridge: Cambridge University Press.
Goell, Theresa B., ed. 1996. *Nemrud Dağı: The Hierothesion of Antiochus I of Commagene: Results of the American Excavations Directed by Theresa B. Goell*, 2 vols. Winona Lake, Ind.: Eisenbrauns.
Greaves, Alan M. 2002. *Miletos: A History*. London: Routledge.
Hall, Jonathan M. 2000. *Ethnic Identity in Greek Antiquity*. Cambridge: Cambridge University Press.
Hamilton, Charles D. 1991. *Agesilaus and the Failure of Spartan Hegemony*. Ithaca, N.Y.: Cornell University Press.
Holloway, R. R. 1984. The Date of the First Greek Coins: Some Arguments from Style and Hoards. *Revue Belge de numismatique* 130: 5–18.
Hornblower, Simon. 1982. *Mausolus*. Oxford: Clarendon Press.
Jeffrey, L. H. 1976. *Archaic Greece: The City-States c. 700–500 B.C.* New York: St. Martin's Press.
Kirk, G. S. and J. E. Raven. 1957. *The Presocratic Philosophers*. Cambridge: Cambridge University Press.
Kraay, Colin M. 1976. *Archaic and Classical Greek Coins*. Berkeley: University of California Press.
Krentz, Peter. 2002. Fighting by the Rules. The Invention of Hoplite Agon. *Hesperia* 71: 23–39.
Martin, Thomas R. 1985. *Coinage and Sovereignty in Classical Greece*. Princeton, N.J.: Princeton University Press.
Masson, O. 1991. Anatolian Languages. In *The Cambridge Ancient History*, vol. 3, part 2, ed. John Boardman, I. E. S. Edwards, E. Sollberger, and N. G. L. Hammond, 666–76. Cambridge: Cambridge University Press.
Meiggs, Russell. 1972. *The Athenian Empire*. Oxford: Clarendon Press.

Meiggs, Russell and David Lewis, eds. 1969. *A Selection of Greek Historical Inscriptions to the End of the Fifth Century B.C.* Oxford: Oxford University Press.

Mellink, Machteld J. 1971. Excavations at Karataş-Semayük and Elmalı, Lycia, 1970. *American Journal of Archaeology* 75: 245–55.

———. 1972. Excavations at Karataş-Semayük and Elmalı, Lycia, 1971. *American Journal of Archaeology* 76: 257–69.

———. 1973. Excavations at Karataş-Semayük and Elmalı, Lycia, 1972. *American Journal of Archaeology* 77: 293–303.

———. 1974. Excavations at Karataş-Semayük and Elmalı, Lycia, 1973. *American Journal of Archaeology* 78: 351–59.

———. 1975. Excavations at Karataş-Semayük and Elmalı, Lycia, 1974. *American Journal of Archaeology* 79: 349–55.

———. 1988. Anatolia. In *The Cambridge Ancient History, vol. 4: Persia, Greece and the Western Mediterranean c. 525 to 479 B.C.*, 2nd ed., ed. John Boardman, N. G. L. Hammond, D. M. Lewis, and M. Ostwald, 211–33. Cambridge: Cambridge University Press.

Mitchell, S. and A. W. McNicoll. 1979. Archaeology in Western and Southern Asia Minor, 1971–1978. *Archaeological Reports* 25(1978–1979): 59–90.

Moysey, Robert A. 1986. The Silver Stater Issues of Pharnabazus and Datames from the Mint of Tarsus in Cilicia. *American Numismatic Society, Museum Notes* 31: 7–61.

Powell, Barry B. 1991. *Homer and the Origin of the Greek Alphabet.* Cambridge: Cambridge University Press.

Rahe, Paul A. 1980. The Military Situation in Western Asia Minor on the Eve of the Battle of Cunaxa. *American Journal of Philology* 101: 79–86.

Raubitschek, A. E. 1966. The Peace Policy of Pericles. *American Journal of Archaeology* 70: 37–42.

Sealey, R. 1966. The Origin of the Delian League. In *Ancient Society and Institutions. Essays Presented to Victor Ehrenberg on His 75th Birthday*, ed. E. Badian, 235–55. Oxford: Blackwell.

Snodgrass, A. M. 1967. *Arms and Armour of the Greeks.* Ithaca, N.Y.: Cornell University Press.

Waldbaum, Jane C. 1997. Greeks in the East or Greeks and the East: Problems of Recognition of Presence. *Bulletin of the American Schools of Oriental Research* 305: 1–17.

Waldmann, Helmut. 1973. *Die kommagenischen Kultreformen unter König Mithradates I. Kallinikos und seinem Sohne Antiochos I.* Leiden: Brill.

Weidauer, Liselotte. 1975. *Probleme der frühen Elektronprägung.* Fribourg: Office du Livre.

Westlake, H. D. 1986. Spartan Intervention in Asia, 400–397 B.C. *Historia* 35: 405–26.

From Pastoralists to Empires: Critical Issues

CHAPTER 35

A BRIEF OVERVIEW OF THE HALAF TRADITION

GABRIELA CASTRO GESSNER

THE Halaf tradition of the ancient Near East spans from approximately 6000 to 5100 cal B.C.E., which largely covers the sixth millennium cal B.C.E. and sits chronologically between the development of agriculture and the rise of urban centers. The name is derived from the eponymous Syrian site of Tell Halaf, where distinctively painted pottery unlike anything found before was first confirmed (von Oppenheim and Schmidt 1943). Since the turn of the twentieth century, when the first Halaf material remains came to light, various interpretations about the economy and social structure of the people living at this time have surfaced. The most recent scholarship suggests that there was not a singular late Neolithic[1] way of life, but a variety of social practices and alliances that were flexible, interconnected, and variable (Akkermans and Schwartz 2003; see also Bernbeck 1994, 1995). The following précis of the Halaf tradition may appear misleading in its portrayal of a coherent "culture," one that is by no means as uniform as it appears or with a firmly delineated set of shared practices. As Akkermans and Schwartz suggest, the Neolithic is characterized by many varied ways of life and "histories localized in space and time" (2003:101). To illustrate some of this variability, discussion on questions of periodization, social organization, and mobility follows the initial summary.

SYNTHETIC OVERVIEW OF THE HALAF TRADITION

The sites that comprise the Halaf tradition cover an arc-shaped region of northern Mesopotamia that extends from the foothills of the Hamrin in eastern central Iraq as far as the Amuq Plain in western Syria and the limits of Cilicia in southeastern

Turkey. The arc is bounded to the north by the Taurus Mountains and to the south by the Syrian Jezirah. Halaf sites in Anatolia tend to be confined to areas south of the Taurus Mountains and the Lake Van region and west of the Zagros foothills (figure 35.1).

Site Location, Size, and Distribution

Halaf sites across the northern Mesopotamian plain are generally close to water sources or wadis and found in areas above the 200/250 mm isohyets, where crops can be grown without the need for irrigation (Algaze, Breuninger, and Knudstad 1994; Lyonnet 2000; McCorriston 1992; Wilkinson and Tucker 1995:40). Our knowledge of the distribution and dimensions of Halaf sites continues to grow. Not all sites are like the typical tells or *höyüks* that dot the Anatolian or Mesopotamian landscape, but rather appear as sherd scatters, such as Boztarla Tarlası in Turkey (Algaze, Breuninger, and Knudstad 1994), or are below surface level, such as Tell Amarna in Syria, buried under meters of sediment (Cruells 2001:143; Tunca and Molist 2004). Based on surveys in Anatolia, Syria, and northern Iraq, however, most sites appear to be less than one or up to three hectares (Algaze, Breuninger, and Knudstad 1994; Lyonnet 2000, Wilkinson and Tucker 1995). Larger sites, according to Lyonnet, tend to appear in the latter part of the Halaf period, and may be up to twenty hectares (Lyonnet 2000:154). Three prominent large sites in Anatolia are Domuztepe (twenty

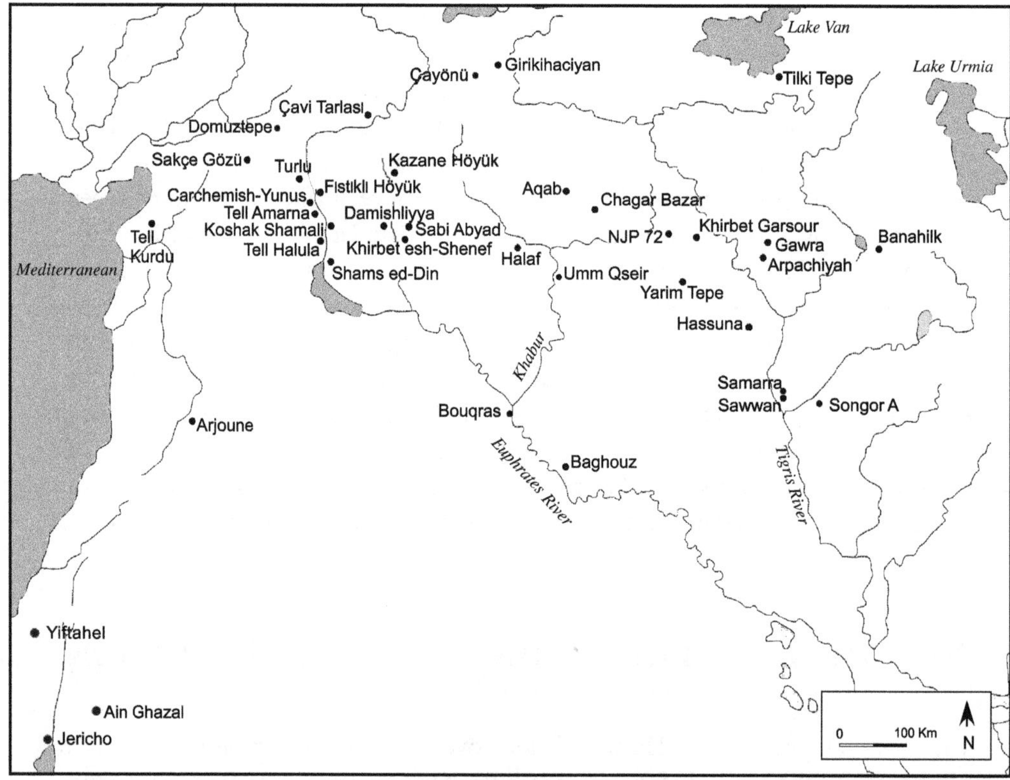

Figure 35.1. Map of Near East with Halaf period sites mentioned in text.

hectares) in the Kahramanmaraş Valley, Kazane Höyük (fifteen to twenty hectares) in the Urfa region, and Takyan (ten hectares) in the Cizre-Silopi Plain (Algaze et al. 1991; Campbell et al. 1999; Wattenmaker and Mısır 1994; respectively). Despite large site sizes, there is growing recognition that people during the Halaf may have resided in multiple locations and occupied different sites during their lifetime; thus, site size is not a good indicator of length of occupation (Bernbeck 2008a, 2008b; see later discussion). Large sites in particular may represent a collection of short, separate, and shifting occupations, rather than single and continuous ones (Akkermans et al. 2006:149–52; Akkermans and Schwartz 2003:120; Bernbeck, Pollock, and Coursey 1999:110). A recent Bayesian approach to radiocarbon dates by Stuart Campbell (2007) appears to confirm that some sites are indeed characterized by short occupation periods, altogether lasting about 100 years (e.g., Fıstıklı Höyük and Sabi Abyad). Larger sites, like Domuztepe, may have had occupation periods of 65 or 100 years with some short abandonment intervals (Campbell 2007).

Subsistence Practices

Evidence for a detailed rendering of subsistence practices is not substantial and is usually generalized from a few sites. Broadly speaking, evidence from many Halaf tradition sites indicates that people consumed grains (wheat, barley, flax), legumes (peas, lentils, chickpeas, vetch), and fruits or other plants, such as pistachios, grapes, and olives (Bernbeck et al. 2003; McCorriston 1992; van Zeist and Waterbolk-van Rooijen 1996; Watson 1983a). Animal bone remains indicate that they also exploited domestic sheep, goats, pigs, and cattle, as well as wild deer, equids (onager), fish, and birds, among other less common species like fox and hare (Akkermans 1993; Bernbeck et al. 2003; Cavallo 2000; Watson 1983a). Notwithstanding the varied menu, there is fluctuation in the exploitation of resources according to different environments. Alain Gaulon (2008) postulates that sites in the wetter areas, usually north (those in Anatolia and northern Syria), commonly had greater proportions of domesticated animal remains and wheat, relative to drier, southerly areas, where wild fauna and barley seem to predominate. This north–south divide remains to be fully explored but adds to other studies that indicate variable use of resources dependent on local environmental conditions and seasons (see Cavallo 2000; McCorriston 1992; Zeder 1994).

Features and Artifacts

Halaf sites show the first occurrence in Mesopotamian prehistory of sites in a wide geographical region with similar architecture, pottery, and small objects, such as seals, figurines, and pendants. The architecture consists of free-standing circular buildings, traditionally, if inappropriately, named *tholoi*, thought to have served for habitation, storage, or mixed use (Akkermans 1993; Tsuneki 1998; Watson 1983a). Tholoi range in size from under three to over five meters in interior diameter and were variably constructed of mudbrick or pisé and sometimes had stone foundations. Another common architectural type in Halaf sites are rectangular, multicellular structures, often closely associated with tholoi, and in some cases annexed to them, serving storage purposes (Pollock forthcoming). Halaf painted designs on pottery typically (but not uniformly) consist of geometric designs, such as cross-hatches, diamonds, and chevrons, and representational, often very stylized motifs in the form of birds, bulls' heads (bucrania), or human figures (figure 35.2). Some of the geometric and abstract designs carry over to stamp seals, which are often incised with such patterns. Figurines may be zoomorphic or carry semblances of people in very stylized ways.

One of the characteristic features of this era is the appearance of intricately painted fine ware pottery, which appears side by side with undecorated and coarsely made vessels. The finely crafted and thin-walled decorated wares of the Halaf tradition are typically considered to have functioned as serving wares, whereas the coarse-tempered and thick-walled coarse wares are thought to have played a role in cooking, storage, and food preparation (Hopwood forthcoming). The relatively quick spread of what appeared to be uniformly styled decorated pottery across a wide geographic region encouraged LeBlanc and Watson to identify this era as the first cultural horizon of the prehistoric Near East (1973:117). This characterization is no longer considered suitable, but there is nevertheless recognition of a relatively quick change in pottery production and consumption from the seventh to the sixth millennium B.C.E. Nieuwenhuyse has suggested that the rapid increase in production of painted fine pottery relative to coarse wares between the seventh and sixth millennia B.C.E. is akin to a "painted pottery revolution" (2007:9). The significance of this sudden increase in painted pottery may speak to changing consumption and social practices that remain subjects of investigation (Campbell 2007).

The number of excavated sites and surveys in the region has increased in recent years, adding to our knowledge and understanding about the people who lived during the Halaf period. Research questions that address social organization and the political economy of the Halaf period remain underexplored. In the remainder of this chapter, after a brief historical overview of the Halaf excavation history, I discuss some of the current issues surrounding the questions of periodization, relations of social organization, and mobility.

Brief Excavation History of the Halaf Period

Halaf painted pottery was first described by John Garstang during the excavation of Sakçe Gözü in Syria (now Turkey) at the beginning of the twentieth century (Garstang 1908). Subsequent work in 1911 and 1927 by Max von Oppenheim at the

Figure 35.2. Examples of Halaf-style painted designs on fine ware vessels from Fıstıklı Höyük. Top: red painted chevrons on exterior side of a tall necked jar. Bottom: red to black stylized bird or bird-like figure on exterior side of a lugged vessel.

Syrian site of Tell Halaf (von Oppenheim and Schmidt 1943) and in 1913 by Sir Leonard Woolley (1934) at the site of Yunus (Carchemish) at the Turko-Syrian border, uncovered colorful decorated pottery and associated undecorated coarse wares, expanding the location of sites with finely crafted and decorated ceramics. During the interwar years, Max Mallowan excavated Tell Arpachiyah in northern Iraq, and the spectacular finds from that site called attention to the far-reaching regional spread of the Halaf tradition as well as to its technological prominence in pottery manufacture (Mallowan and Rose 1935). Arpachiyah, located in the Mosul region, became the type site and the standard against which all other Halaf sites were compared for years to come. Arpachiyah remains an unusual Halaf site, first because it appears to have a long and continuous sequence of Halaf occupation (Early through Late), and second because among its remarkable finds were a burned structure (Burnt House) containing singularly well-crafted painted pottery, jewelry fragments, amulets, figurines, and quantities of stone tools. Mallowan interpreted the burned building and its extraordinary contents as evidence of a craft workshop or a chief's house (Mallowan and Rose 1935:16–17). Mallowan's interpretations influenced subsequent ideas of social and economic organization that in more recent years have been questioned (discussed below).

The advent of World War II delayed systematic archaeological excavation of Halaf tradition sites until the late 1960s. Sites excavated in the postwar years include Banahilk and Yarim Tepe in Iraq, and Girikihaciyan, Tilkitepe, and Tell Turlu in Turkey (Breniquet 1987; Korfmann 1982; Merpert and Munchaev 1993; Watson 1983b; Watson and LeBlanc 1990). Most recent excavations of Halaf sites have resulted from salvage efforts in advance of dam projects on the Euphrates and Tigris Rivers and their tributaries, including sites such as Fıstıklı Höyük, Çavi Tarlası, and Kazane Höyük in Turkey and Tell Amarna, Tell Kosak Shamali, Tell Halula, and Shams ed-Din in Syria, to name a few (Azoury et al. 1980; Bernbeck et al. 2003; Molist 1996; Nishiaki and Matsutani 2001; Tunca and Molist 2004; von Wickede and Herbordt 1988; Wattenmaker and Mısır 1994). The site of Sabi Abyad in the Balikh valley of Syria, excavated since the mid- to late 1980s, has become a key site in recent years because of its continuous occupation sequence from the seventh through the sixth millennium B.C.E. (Akkermans 1989, 1993, 1996). In Turkey, Domuztepe's famous "Death Pit" has added perspectives on ritual practices not evident elsewhere (Campbell et al. 1999; Carter, Campbell, and Gauld 2003), and at Tell Kurdu, the alignment of buildings paralleling streets speaks to apparent urban design unique to that site (Özbal 2006).

Defining and Categorizing the Halaf Tradition

Terminology

The chronological framework that interlaces the Halaf tradition within the overall chronology of the Near East is discussed by Özbal (chapter 8 in this volume). This section is limited to regional and local chronologies for the Halaf tradition. As a caveat to this discussion, it should be recognized that what we consider Halaf is drawn on arbitrary boundaries of similarity and difference; these are based not only on internal ceramic sequences but also the extending or constricting of Halaf boundaries in relation to the earlier Hassuna and Samarra traditions and the later Ubaid. These other ceramic traditions are not elaborated on here; suffice it to say that these are all modern constructs, and any attempt at categorizing and classifying archaeological remains is simply an organizational schema. These labels have remained pervasive in the literature, contributing to a portrayal of these traditions as neat, coherent packages of unique material remains and sustaining a culture-historical approach that has spurred research in particular directions (Bernbeck 2008b; Campbell 2007). I do not expand here on the issues surrounding the use of "the Halaf" as a historical actor (Campbell 2007), but direct readers to Bernbeck's (2008a) excellent discussion on this subject.

Periodization

Because the Halaf tradition has been seen as uniform, the tendency has been to apply a single chronological schema over its entire geographical extent (Campbell 1992:61). The internal phasing of the Halaf tradition is an ongoing discussion among scholars and one that is constantly fine-tuned with absolute dates and pottery sequences from various sites. The entire phasing is based on ceramics from sites in Greater Mesopotamia and to some degree is an arbitrary result of excavation selection and history (Campbell 2007). Scholars working in different areas of northern Mesopotamia and with highly varied samples have contributed by trying to integrate material from new and known sites.

One of the most influential interpretations inherited from Mallowan's research at Arpachiyah is the Early, Middle, and Late (E-M-L) chronological division of the Halaf tradition (Hijjara 1997; Mallowan and Rose 1935; Perkins 1949). This original tripartite model was subsequently modified by Davidson with research from Tell Aqab (Syria), which included a transitional phase at the end identified as Halaf-Ubaid Transitional (HUT) (Davidson 1977). This sequence was modified by Campbell (1992) into Halaf I and II, by adding an earlier phase to the traditional Early phase described by Mallowan, such that Halaf Ia preceded phases Halaf Ib (traditional Early Halaf), Halaf IIa (Middle Halaf), and Halaf IIb (Late Halaf), with the transitional HUT remaining (see also Watkins and Campbell 1987). The most recent modification called for a six-phase sequence by adding transitional phases at the beginning of Campbell's model, so that Pre-Halaf and Proto-Halaf[2] preceded Halaf Ia (Cruells and Nieuwenhuyse 2004; Nieuwenhuyse 2000:156, table 19).

The approaches taken to sort out chronological phases are based on general similarities of pottery shapes, sometimes decorations, and often on the presence or absence of specific items across wide regions. They implicitly share the idea that Halaf sites and pottery shapes follow similar paths of development across northern Mesopotamia. In the past fifteen years or so, there has been an acknowledgment of regional and local distinctions in pottery that need to be taken into account because the Halaf tradition is of long duration and widespread (Akkermans 1993, 1996;

Bernbeck et al. 2003; Pollock et al. 2001). Sites may share general material similarities, but few sites exhibit similar shapes, designs, and quality of pots. The difficulties of building a ceramic sequence with few excavated sites, disparate ceramic material, limited published documentation, and lack of quantitative data are compounded because of a lack of continuity in occupation at most Halaf sites.

Building a Halaf internal chronology may be improved by shifting our approach to consider multisited areas in smaller regions, what Campbell calls "sub-regional chronology" (Campbell 2007). Successful examples of these include the Balikh valley (Akkermans 1993, 1996) and the Rouj basin (Iwasaki and Tsuneki 2003) in Syria, and the Amuq sequence by Braidwood and Braidwood (1960) in Turkey (the location of Tell Kurdu). The finer temporal distinctions that we seek to draw from ceramics, those that are not always possible to capture with radiocarbon dates because of large standards of deviation (although improving with Accelerator Mass Spectrometry carbon dating technology and changing with Bayesian approaches), may work better with sites within close geographical proximity. These local sequences work on interdigitating sites in a valley or basin, building the depth of occupation in a small region. In recent years, the Balikh valley sequence, where the site of Sabi Abyad is located, has served as a temporal framework for sites in western Mesopotamia and those in southeastern Turkey.

Social Relations and Organization

As illustrated herein and by Özbal (chapter 8 in this volume), the painted pottery of the Halaf period played a central role in defining the geographic and chronological extent of this era in northern Mesopotamia. The fine and decorated pottery also influenced earlier perspectives about the economic structure and the potential sociopolitical relations that governed life. Mallowan argued that both the pottery and architecture from Arpachiyah followed a progression toward greater complexity from earlier to later levels. Earlier, naturalistic motifs on vessels progressed into schematic and geometrical designs that spoke of an abstract understanding of nature, and tholoi, with annexes in later levels, illustrated an increase in architectural sophistication. This evolution culminated in the burned structure interpreted as a chief's house or craft workshop (Mallowan and Rose 1935).

Mallowan's suggestions about increasing complexity were very influential in fomenting a view of the Halaf tradition that fit with ideas of evolutionary complexity and hierarchies familiar in the late 1960s. A uniformly styled pottery that endured with little change over time across northern Mesopotamia corresponded with ideas about redistribution that were linked to notions of ranked societies categorized as chiefdoms or tribes (Hijjara 1997; Watson 1983a; Watson and LeBlanc 1990). Thus a recognizable pottery style could only be explained as a result of a stratified society—a society in which craft specialists were the norm or where pottery was produced by "itinerant or localized groups of pottery specialists" (Watson 1983a:241).

The idea of experienced crafters was also supported by the different qualities of pottery found, since some sites had vessels produced with lower levels of expertise than others (LeBlanc and Watson 1973:129). LeBlanc and Watson's stylistic analysis of pottery decorations indicated that designs and affinities were correlated by geographical distance (LeBlanc and Watson 1973:131). In that perspective, sites in a region were likely "chiefly centers" that dominated pottery trade, and overall settlement patterns were "expressive of a center-hinterland . . . settlement hierarchy" (Watson 1983a:241; see also LeBlanc and Watson 1973; Watson and LeBlanc 1990:135–36).

Notions of chiefly centers encouraged studies on clay and ceramics using neutron activation analyses to identify trade networks (Davidson 1977; Davidson and McKerrell 1976, 1980). Clay sources and ceramics analyzed from sites in northern Syria and Iraq (Tell Aqab, Chagar Bazar, Arpachiyah, and Tepe Gawra) confirmed that some pottery produced in large centers was exported or exchanged to smaller ones. Indeed, some of these explanations may be the case for some Halaf sites. Campbell's reexamination of Arpachiyah suggested that the burned structure and its remains, among other evidence, was part of "institutionalized control" at the center of an exchange network that functioned like a "quasi-bureaucracy" (2000:24–25). The site of Domuztepe has not yielded information on socially complex chiefdoms, but its excavators posit that evidence of long-distance trade and unique obsidian artifacts and seals may point to an "emergent complexity" in that region (Campbell et al. 1999; Carter, Campbell, and Gauld 2003:133).

Nonetheless, ideas on social and settlement hierarchies are not evident everywhere. Neutron activation analyses of clay and sherds in other areas, for example, the western Syrian sites of Sabi Abyad and Tell Amarna, did not yield similar results to support ideas about exchange networks (Akkermans and Duistermaat 1997; Clop Garcia, Perez, and Hatert 2004). The question is not whether exchange took place, but whether a hierarchical schema and associated implications of rank are the only explanation. In ethnoarchaeological studies, chiefly or ranked societies are not a precondition for high-quality pottery production (Barnard 2008). A recent comparative study on pottery production between the Halaf sites of Sabi Abyad and Fıstıklı Höyük indicated that people with variable degrees of skill engaged in pottery painting, and not only the very experienced or a designated group of specialists participated. In addition, the contexts in which artists developed their skills in pottery painting differed at each site, suggesting variable approaches to this activity in different places (Castro Gessner 2008, forthcoming). Thus, at least for Halaf sites in the earliest phases, a hierarchical organization with specialists assigned to particular productive tasks is not evident.

Using settlement layout and location of activities for various Halaf sites, Pollock and Castro Gessner (2009) suggest that the community was a basic unit of society. They postulate that productive activities, such as making stone tools, food preparation, and animal processing, tended to occur outdoors and in the shared areas between buildings. The common use of exterior areas was conducive to the engagement of activities within view of other community members, allowing people to share practices and engage in all manner of activities, giving rise to the variable practices at many sites (Castro Gessner 2010). This research has led to the recognition that although Halaf tradition sites share broad similarities in features and artifacts, the practices of producing them differ. Recently Pollock suggested that rather than focusing on the finished products (architecture, vessels, chipped stone), it is necessary to focus on process—the way things were accomplished—to understand degrees of similarity and difference, as well as their role in social organization (Pollock forthcoming).

Mobility

The degrees of Halaf site residents' mobility and sedentism have become topics of current interest for scholars working in this period. The commonly held view of a sedentary population relying primarily on plant and animal domesticates (wheat, barley, sheep, goats) fits not only ideas of surplus trade and settlement hierarchies but also the expectations of progress leading to the first cities. As noted above, however, such perspectives have lost currency in recent interpretations and are not supported by finds that demonstrate a diverse reliance on both domesticate and wild resources. Based on recent research and finds, scholars have posed different kinds of questions that seek to identify the relationships between farmers and herders and their degrees of mobility (Akkermans and Duistermaat 1997; Bernbeck 1997; Bernbeck et al. 2003). The topic of subsistence is intertwined with our knowledge of seasonality and our ideas on mobility and social organization. The examples that follow illustrate perspectives on animal husbandry from Sabi Abyad, seasonal occupation at Umm Qseir, and mobility in multisited communities as a way of life.

Farmers and Herders

The excavators of Sabi Abyad posit an example of symbiotic relationships between farmers and herders with evidence from the Burnt Village of Sabi Abyad during its transitional phase into the Halaf tradition (Akkermans and Verhoeven 1995). A large number of clay sealings were found in two cell-plan buildings. Contrary to traditional interpretations that would assume that the presence of sealings implies administrative monitoring devices, as is common in later periods, Akkermans and Duistermaat (1997) proposed that their presence was not related to exchange and trade networks, but rather represented claims for goods. The clay used to seal containers was of local origin, which meant that the goods sealed were local and not imported (Duistermaat and Schneider 1998). The claims for goods, animals, or services were in the shape of tokens, little clay shapes that fit the small size of the containers found (Akkermans and Duistermaat 1997:29). The seal impressions were created by multiple seals; thus, they assumed that a large portion of the population participated in these agreements. They suggested that the seals and the tokens protected in the containers belonged to the mobile and seasonally absent portion of the population that co-resided with the farmers at Sabi Abyad. The tokens were assumed to be held in trust by the resident cultivators until the return of the herders (Akkermans and Duistermaat 1997:27–30; contra Frangipane 1997; Nissen 1997). For the researchers, a symbiotic relationship among settlers advocated for nonhierarchical arrangements between different segments of the population.

Additional analyses suggested that the cell-plan buildings were used to store items of both the resident and absent populations, and that the sealings were reminders of the goods in possession or services already rendered by the absent population (Verhoeven 1999). Faunal analyses supported these assertions by showing an increased reliance on secondary animal products, suggesting seasonal pastoral movements by some portion of the population (Cavallo 2000:48). In addition, it appealed to the notion of a close association between mobile and settled residents that exchanged animal products or supported each other at times of need (Verhoeven 1999:207–11).

Sabi Abyad's findings indicate that sedentism and mobility are not mutually exclusive practices but may have been negotiated and undertaken in different ways. At other sites such unique evidence is not available, but sites such as Umm Qseir provide evidence of both seasonal and year-round exploitation that supports the possibility of multiple means of subsistence, as well as the notion of residing in multisited communities (Bernbeck 2008a).

Pastoral Encampments

Umm Qseir, unlike other Halaf period sites, lies in a marginal region where crop cultivation is possible only with irrigation. This small site had little evidence of architecture and a high incidence of wild faunal and floral species (Hole and Johnson 1986–87; McCorriston 1992; Zeder 1994). The first excavators interpreted the middens and pits and the preference for wild plants and animals to be suggestive of a short-term, seasonally occupied settlement (Hole and Johnson 1986–87). The botanical remains included wild plants as well as chaff fragments and field weeds that usually accompany the final stages of crop processing (McCorriston 1992). McCorriston's assessment indicated that the population farmed in different locations, taking advantage of water resources wherever possible, and that the inhabitants were likely semi-nomadic pastoralists occupying the site seasonally (1992:325, 330). The faunal remains indicated that although most exploited animals were wild, the culling patterns of pigs, cattle, and caprids pointed to year-round occupation. The presence of pigs in particular would not support a transhumant population (Zeder 1994). Zeder noted, however, that domesticates did not replace wild resources but complemented other dietary strategies. The latter assertions were supported by the second excavation team based on pottery, architecture, and radiocarbon dates (Tsuneki and Miyake 1998). They identified three occupation phases with numerous pits, more than two tholoi, a rectilinear room, and three kilns, all of which were used sequentially and spoke to year-round habitation (Tsuneki and Miyake 1998).

The evidence from Umm Qseir was initially considered an outlier in the context of what was common for the Halaf tradition, in particular because botanical and faunal remains portrayed a complex picture of both seasonal and year-round occupation. It is possible that these remains suggest that in some cases the inhabitants came to the site in spring, and in others, they resided on site year-round. But interval visits are not easy to comprehend when the apparent stability and labor investment in architecture appeal to our ideas of permanency and property. Instead of an either/or situation, it would be more fruitful to conceive of Umm Qseir as part of the larger landscape—a landscape that was inhabited by what Bernbeck calls "multi-sited communities" (2008a). In other words, the communities of the sixth millennium B.C.E. may have indeed subsisted on farming and herding, with special arrangements made between groups for the exchange of food products (e.g., Sabi Abyad), but they could have lived in a broader area, setting up camp in different places, both seasonally and over generations. Untangling these interpretations and choosing seasonal over long-term occupations might not be necessary when they are seen as part of a set of strategies and a way of life.

Multisited Communities

Resource exploitation is just one side of a complex practice, and recognizing that subsistence and mobility are intertwined does not exclude other factors that may have played a role in the residential choices of past inhabitants. Beyond the archaeological challenges associated with identifying repeated instances of short occupations, another aspect includes our willingness to consider nonsedentary options. Reinhard Bernbeck has most recently articulated this by saying that "mobility is thus treated for what it is, an ephemeral, passing way of life, while quotidian sedentary life, just as ephemeral, is functionalized and monumentalized" (2008a:50). He makes the case that we need to see sites as having "biographies" (in the sense of Kopytoff 1986) to extricate the complexities of the multiple practices taking place (Bernbeck 2008a:51).

As an example of a multisited community, Bernbeck uses the site of Fıstıklı Höyük, drawing on stratigraphical evidence among other indicators to reconstruct the biography of the site. The four phases of Halaf occupation at Fıstıklı Höyük are denoted by changes in architectural layout of the hamlet and characterized by the presence and increase of durable structures or features positioned at different places and intervals on the mound. Bernbeck uses subsistence-related finds, such as phytoliths, sickle blades, and calcareous plates (possibly used in food preparation), as well as artifacts such as jetons (mnemonic devices; see Costello 2000), to portray the kinds of activities of the people who came, used, and abandoned the site.

Initially, the site may have been used as a campsite with no durable structures. Subsequently, a small cell-plan structure was built, possibly to store grain. Later, tholoi were erected in close proximity to new and existing cell-plan structures, facilitating storage for each domestic unit. The last phase is characterized by additional buildings and ovens and an increase in the density of wheat and barley husks, jetons, sickle blades, and calcareous plates. The last phase is what Bernbeck calls the "focal site"—the culmination of the phasing in terms of sequential organization (2008a:56). Slowly and over the course of years, tholoi and other structures fell into disuse, but the site could still have been used to store grain or other materials as needed. It may have been used again by a seasonal group that did not leave archaeological traces and subsequently cycled out of the constellation of sites that mobile populations would visit again at later periods.

A constellation of sites in a region that were sequentially organized to serve a variety of purposes is plausible, because early Halaf sites tend to be in the vicinity of fifteen to twenty-five kilometers from each other (Nieuwenhuyse 2000:186, fig. 74). It would not be unmanageable to make several relatively close-by locations "home," depending on times of year, changing river course, family needs, cultigens, culling patterns, or other reasons.

Independent of the types of relationships fostered among and within communities, there is increasing evidence to support the idea that some of the sites are not necessarily those of long-rooted settlers but of mobile communities. There are long-lived settlements occupied continuously with waxing and waning populations, such as Sabi Abyad, and others with short-lived, periodic, and/or seasonal occupations, such as Fıstıklı Höyük or Umm Qseir. In support of arguments about symbiotic relationships between farmers and herders, and of seasonally occupied sites, there is growing evidence that Halaf tradition sites may represent places used by mobile populations as part of a constellation of locales visited in a region. This is in addition to, not to the exclusion of, continuously occupied settlements.

Conclusions

Since its discovery and categorization at the beginning of the twentieth century, the Halaf tradition of the Near East has garnered attention because of its unique circular buildings, stylized small objects, and its intricately decorated pottery. The distinctive finds and features from a few sites were assembled and interpreted as a unified composite that influenced portrayals of the Halaf tradition as coherent and homogenous. The apparent uniformity engendered research and questions whose focus on trade and ranked societies served as explanatory frameworks. This perspective has begun to change in recent years as a result of increased research and variability that speaks to different practices across sites, regions, and time.

Recent research from Halaf sites in Anatolia, such as Domuztepe, Fıstıklı Höyük, and the unique Tell Kurdu, has contributed to the diversity of finds and practices that seem common at this time in the prehistoric past. As Pollock (forthcoming) suggested, there is a need to focus on process and the practices of daily living that involve securing and processing food, the production of tools, and the manufacture of ceramic necessities, as well as looking at the resulting features—areas and buildings used to perform those activities—for their role in delineating a Halaf tradition. As has become clearer in recent years, a single common denominator bound to be applicable to all sites will not be useful; thus, research that identifies degrees of similarity and difference will provide a more nuanced understanding.

NOTES

I kindly thank Sharon Steadman and Greg McMahon for inviting me to contribute to this volume; they were flexible in working with my complicated schedule and were generous with their encouragement.

1. Halaf remains appear to indicate continuity in some ways from earlier Neolithic societies (e.g., Hassuna, Samarra); thus, in this discussion I include the Halaf tradition as part of the late Neolithic, which differs from Özbal's chronological framework (chapter 8 in this volume). This distinction is not unusual and forms part of ongoing discussions about periodization of the prehistoric Near East.

2. Besides their heuristic functions, such labels connote development in a particular direction, which may not necessarily have been evident, as raised by Bernbeck (2008b), and Campbell (2007).

REFERENCES

Akkermans, Peter M. M. G., ed. 1989. *Excavations at Tell Sabi Abyad. Prehistoric Investigations in the Balikh Valley, Northern Syria*. BAR International Series 468. Oxford: BAR International.

———. 1993. *Villages in the Steppe—Late Neolithic Settlement in the Balikh Valley, Northern Syria*. Ann Arbor, Mich.: International Monographs in Prehistory.

———. 1996. *Tell Sabi Abyad. The Late Neolithic Settlement. Vols. 1 and 2*. İstanbul: Nederlands Historisch-Archaeologisch Instituut.

Akkermans, Peter M. M. G., René Cappers, Chiara Cavallo, Olivier Nieuwenhuyse, Bonni Nilhamn, and Iris N. Otte. 2006. Investigating the Early Pottery Neolithic of Northern Syria: New Evidence from Tell Sabi Abyad. *American Journal of Archaeology* 110.1: 123–56.

Akkermans, Peter M. M. G. and Kim Duistermaat. 1997. Of Storage and Nomads. The Sealings from Late Neolithic Sabi Abyad, Syria. *Paléorient* 22.2: 17–44.

Akkermans, Peter M. M. G. and Glenn M. Schwartz. 2003. *The Archaeology of Syria: From Complex Hunter-Gatherers to Early Urban Societies (c. 16,000–300 BC)*. Cambridge World Archaeology. Cambridge: Cambridge University Press.

Akkermans, Peter M. M. G. and Marc Verhoeven. 1995. An Image of Complexity: The Burnt Village at Late Neolithic Sabi Abyad, Syria. *American Journal of Archaeology* 99.1: 5–32.

Algaze, Guillermo, Ray Breuninger, and James Knudstad. 1994. The Tigris-Euphrates Archaeological Reconnaissance Project: Final Report of the Birecik and Carchemish Dam Survey Areas. *Anatolica* 20: 1–96.

Algaze, Guillermo, Ray Breuninger, Chris Lightfoot, and Michael Rosenberg. 1991. The Tigris-Euphrates Archaeological Reconnaissance Project. A Preliminary Report of the 1989–1990 Seasons. *Anatolica* 17: 175–240.

Azoury, Ingrid, Christopher A. Bergman, Carrie E. Gustavson-Gaube, Selma al-Radi, Helga Seeden, and Hans-Peter Uerpmann. 1980. A Stone Village on the Euphrates I–V. Reports from the Halafian Settlement at Shams ed-Din Tannira: AUB Rescue Excavation 1974. *Berytus* 27: 87–126.

Barnard, Hans. 2008. Suggestions for a Chaîne Opératoire of Nomadic Pottery Sherds. In *The Archaeology of Mobility. Old World and New World Nomadism*, ed. Hans Barnard and Willeke Z. Wendrich, 413–39. Cotsen Advanced Seminars 4. Los Angeles: Cotsen Institute of Archaeology.

Bernbeck, Reinhard. 1994. *Die Auflösung der Häuslichen Produktionsweise*. Berlin: Dietrich Reimer Verlag.

———. 1995. Lasting Alliances and Emerging Competition: Economic Development in Early Mesopotamia. *Journal of Anthropological Archaeology* 14: 1–25.

———. 1997. Comments on P. M. M. G. Akkermans and K. Duistermaat's Article "Of Storage and Nomads. The Sealings from Late Neolithic Sabi Abyad, Syria." *Paléorient* 22.2: 33–35.

———. 2008a. An Archaeology of Multi-Sited Communities. In *The Archaeology of Mobility: Old World and New World Nomadism*, ed. Hans Barnard and Willeke Z. Wendrich, 43–77. Cotsen Advanced Seminars 4. Los Angeles: Cotsen Institute of Archaeology.

———. 2008b. Taming Time and Timing the Tamed. In *Proceedings of the 5th International Congress on the Archaeology of the Ancient Near East, Madrid, 3–8 April 2006, vol. 3*, ed. Joaquín M. Córdoba, Miquel Molist, M. Carmen Pérez, Isabel Rubio, and Sergio Martínez, 709–28. Madrid: Centro Superior de Estudios sobre el Oriente Próximo y Egipto.

Bernbeck, Reinhard, Susan Pollock, Susan Allen, Ana Gabriela Castro Gessner, Sarah Kielt Costello, Robert Costello, Melissa Foree, Margarita Y. Gleba, Marie Goodwin, Sarah Lepinski, Carolyn Nakamura, and Sarah Niebuhr. 2003. The Biography of an Early Halaf Village: Fıstıklı Höyük 1999–2000. *Istanbuler Mitteilungen* 53: 9–77.

Bernbeck, Reinhard, Susan Pollock, and Cheryl Coursey.1999. The Halaf Settlement at Kazane Höyük: Preliminary Report on the 1996 and 1997 Seasons. *Anatolica* 25: 109–47.

Braidwood, Robert J. and Linda S. Braidwood. 1960. *Excavations in the Plain of Antioch*. Oriental Institute Publication 61. Chicago: University of Chicago Press.

Breniquet, Catherine. 1987. Note sur les principaux résultats de la fouille de Tell Turlu, 1962. *Paléorient* 13.1: 113–16.

Campbell, Stuart. 1992. Culture, Chronology and Change in the Later Neolithic of North Mesopotamia. Ph.D. dissertation. University of Edinburgh.

———. 2000. The Burnt House at Arpachiyah: A Reexamination. *Bulletin of the American Schools of Oriental Research* 318: 1–40.

———. 2007. Rethinking Halaf Chronologies. *Paléorient* 33.1: 103–36.

Campbell, Stuart, Elizabeth Carter, Elizabeth Healy, Siona Anderson, Amanda Kennedy, and Sarah Whitcher.1999. Emerging Complexity on the Kahramanmaraş Plain, Turkey: The Domuztepe Project, 1995–1997. *American Journal of Archaeology* 103: 1–24.

Carter, Elizabeth, Stuart Campbell, and Suellen Gauld. 2003. Elusive Complexity: New Data from Late Halaf Domuztepe in South Central Turkey. *Paléorient* 29.2: 117–34.

Castro Gessner, A. Gabriela. 2008. The Technology of Learning: Painting Practices of Early Mesopotamian Communities of the 6th Millennium, B.C. Ph.D. dissertation. SUNY Binghamton.

———. 2010. Shared Painting: The Practice of Decorating Late Neolithic Pottery in Northern Mesopotamia. In *Agency and Identity in the Ancient Near East: New Paths Forward*, ed., Sharon R. Steadman and Jennifer C. Ross, 99–116. London: Equinox.

———. Forthcoming. Sequencing Practices, Revealing Traditions: A Case Study on Painters' Brushwork. In *Interpreting the Late Neolithic of Upper Mesopotamia, Conference Proceedings*, ed. Anna Russell, Olivier P. Nieuwenhuyse, Peter M. M. G. Akkermans, and Reinhard Bernbeck. Turnhout, Belgium: Brepols.

Cavallo, Chiara. 2000. *Animals in the Steppe: A Zooarchaeological Analysis of Later Neolithic Tell Sabi Abyad, Syria*. BAR International Series 891. Oxford: BAR International.

Clop Garcia, Xavier, Aureli Alvarez Perez, and Frédéric Hatert. 2004. Characterization Study of Halaf Ceramic Production at Tell Amarna (Euphrates Valley, Syria). In *Tell Amarna (Syrie) I. La Période de Halaf*, ed. Önhan Tunca and Miquel Molist, 201–12. Publications de la Mission Archéologique de l'Université de Liège en Syrie. Leuven: Peeters.

Costello, Sarah Kielt. 2000. Memory Tools in Early Mesopotamia. *Antiquity* 74. 285: 475–76.

Cruells, Walter. 2001. Nuevas Aportaciones a la Cultura Halaf en Siria. In *De la Estepa al Mediterráneo. Actas del 1er Congreso de Arqueología e Historia Antigua del Oriente Próximo. Barcelona, 3–5 de Abril de 2000*, ed. Juan Luis Montero Fenollós, Jordi Vidal Palomino, and Felip Masó Ferrer, 135–57. Monografies Eridu vol. 1. Barcelona: Eridu.

Cruells, Walter and Olivier Nieuwenhuyse. 2004. The Proto-Halaf Period in Syria. New Sites, New Data. *Paléorient* 30.1: 47–68.

Davidson, Thomas E. 1977. Regional Variation within the Halaf Culture. Ph.D. dissertation, University of Edinburgh.

Davidson, Thomas E. and Hugh McKerrell. 1976. Pottery Analysis and Halaf Period Trade in the Khabur Headwaters Region. *Iraq* 38: 45–56.

———. 1980. The Neutron Activation Analysis of Halaf and 'Ubaid Pottery from Tell Arpachiyah and Tepe Gawra. *Iraq* 42: 155–67.

Duistermaat, Kim and Gerwulf Schneider. 1998. Chemical Analyses of Sealing Clays and the Use of Administrative Artefacts at Late Neolithic Tell Sabi Abyad (Syria). *Paléorient* 24.1: 89–106.

Frangipane, Marcella. 1997. Comments on Peter M.M.G. Akkermans and Kim Duistermaat's Article "Of Storage and Nomads. The Sealings from Late Neolithic Sabi Abyad, Syria." *Paléorient* 22.2: 36–38.

Garstang, John. 1908. Excavations at Sakje-Geuzi, in North Syria: Preliminary Report for 1908. *Annals of Archaeology and Anthropology* 1: 97–117.

Gaulon, Alain. 2008. Human Activities and Environment in Halaf Communities as Revealed by Hunting Practices. In *Proceedings of the 4th International Congress of the Archaeology of the Ancient Near East, 29 March–3 April 2004, Freie Universität Berlin*, ed. Hartmut Kühne, Rainer M. Czichon, and Florian J. Kreppner, 77–99. *Volume 1: The*

Reconstruction of the Environment: Natural Resources and Human Interrelations through Time. Wiesbaden: Harrassowitz Verlag.

Hijjara, Ismail. 1997. *The Halaf Period in Northern Mesopotamia*. London: NABU.

Hole, Frank and Gregory A. Johnson. 1986–87. Umm Qseir on the Khabur: Preliminary Report on the 1986 Excavation. *Annales Archéologiques Arabes Syriennes* 36–37: 172–220.

Hopwood, Marie H. Forthcoming. The Fed Community: Food Preparation and the Community at Fıstıklı Höyük. In *Interpreting the Late Neolithic of Upper Mesopotamia*, ed. Anna Russell, Olivier P. Nieuwenhuyse, Peter M. M. G. Akkermans, and Reinhard Bernbeck. Turnhout, Belgium: Brepols.

Iwasaki, Takuya and Akira Tsuneki, eds. 2003. *Archaeology of the Rouj Basin. A Regional Study of the Transition from Village to City in Northwest Syria. 1. Tsukuba*. Tsukuba, Japan: Institute of History and Anthropology, University of Tsukuba.

Kopytoff, Igor. 1986. The Cultural Biography of Things: Commoditization as Process. In *The Social Life of Things: Commodities in Cultural Perspective*, ed. Arjun Appadurai, 64–91. New York: Cambridge University Press.

Korfmann, Manfred. 1982. *Tilkitepe: die ersten Ansätze prähistorischer Forschung in der östlichen Türkei*. Istanbuler Mitteilungen, Beiheft 26. Tübingen: Wasmuth.

LeBlanc, Steven A. and Patty Jo Watson. 1973. A Comparative Statistical Analysis of Painted Pottery from Seven Halafian Sites. *Paléorient* 1: 117–33.

Lyonnet, Bertille, ed. 2000. *Prospection Archéologique Haut-Khabur Occidental. Syrie du N.E.* Bibliothèque Archéologique et Historique, T. 155, vol. 1. Beyrouth: Direction Générale des Relations Culturelles, Scientifiques et Techniques du Ministère des Affaires Étrangères.

Mallowan, Max E. L. and John C. Rose. 1935. Excavations at Tell Arpachiyah, 1933. *Iraq* 2: 1–178.

McCorriston, Joy. 1992. The Halaf Environment and Human Activities in the Khabur Drainage, Syria. *Journal of Field Archaeology* 19.3: 315–33.

Merpert, Nicolai Y. and Rauf M. Munchaev. 1993. Yarim Tepe II: The Halaf Levels. In *Early Stage in the Evolution of Mesopotamian Civilization*, ed. Norman Yoffee and Jeffrey J. Clark, 129–62. Tucson: University of Arizona Press.

Molist, Miquel, ed. 1996. *Tell Halula (Siria). Un Yacimiento Neolítico del Valle Medio del Éufrates. Campañas de 1991 y 1992*. Madrid: Ministerio de Educación y Cultura.

Nieuwenhuyse, Olivier P. 2000. *Halaf settlement in the Khabur headwaters. In Prospection Archéologique Haut-Khabur Occidental. Syrie du N.E.*, ed. Bertille Lyonnet, 151–98. Bibliothèque Archéologique et Historique, T. 155, vol. 1. Beyrouth: Direction Générale des Relations Culturelles, Scientifiques et Techniques du Ministère des Affaires Étrangères.

———. 2007. Plain and Painted Pottery. In *The Rise of Neolithic Ceramic Styles on the Syrian and Northern Mesopotamian Plains*. Turnhout, Belgium: Brepols.

Nishiaki, Yoshihiro and Toshoi Matsutani, eds. 2001. *Tell Kosak Shamali. The Archaeological Investigations on the Upper Euphrates, Syria. 1: Chalcolithic Architecture and the Earlier Prehistoric Remains*. Oxford: Oxbow.

Nissen, Hans. 1997. Comments on Peter M. M. G. Akkermans and Kim Duistermaat's Article "Of Storage and Nomads. The Sealings from Late Neolithic Sabi Abyad, Syria." *Paléorient* 22.2: 39–40.

Özbal, Rana. 2006. Households, Daily Practice, and Cultural Appropriation at Sixth Millennium Tell Kurdu. Ph.D. dissertation. Northwestern University.

Perkins, Ann L. 1949. *The Comparative Archaeology of Early Mesopotamia*. Studies in Ancient Oriental Civilization no. 25. Chicago: University of Chicago Press.

Pollock, Susan. Forthcoming. Subjects and Objects: Defining a Halaf Tradition. In *Interpreting the Late Neolithic of Upper Mesopotamia*, ed. Anna Russell, Olivier P. Nieuwenhuyse, Peter M. M. G. Akkermans, and Reinhard Bernbeck. Turnhout, Belgium: Brepols.

Pollock, Susan, Reinhard Bernbeck, Susan Allen, Ana Gabriela Castro Gessner, Robert Costello, Sarah Kielt Costello, Melissa Foree, Sarah Lepinski, and Sarah Niebuhr. 2001. 1999 Fıstıklı Höyük Kazıları. In *Salvage Project of the Archaeological Heritage of the Ilısu and Carchemish Dam Reservoirs. Activities in 1999*, ed. Numan Tuna, Jean Öztürk and Jale Velibeyoğlu, 1–63. Ankara: TAÇDAM and METU.

Pollock, Susan and Gabriela Castro Gessner. 2009. Engendering Communities: The Contexts of Production and Consumption in Early Mesopotamian Villages. In *Que(e)rying Archaeology. Proceedings of the Thirty-Seventh Annual Chacmool Conference, University of Calgary*, ed. Susan Terendy, Natasha Lyons, and Michelle Janse-Smekal, 240–49. Calgary: Archaeological Association of the University of Calgary.

Tsuneki, Akira. 1998. Tholoi: Their Socio-Economic Aspects. In *Excavations at Tell Umm Qseir in Middle Khabur Valley, North Syria. Report of the 1996 Season*, ed. Akira Tsuneki and Yutaka Miyake, 165–76. Tsukuba, Japan: Institute of History and Anthropology, University of Tsukuba.

Tsuneki, Akira and Yutaka Miyake, eds. 1998. *Excavations at Tell Umm Qseir in Middle Khabur Valley, North Syria. Report of the 1996 Season*. Tsukuba, Japan: Institute of History and Anthropology, University of Tsukuba.

Tunca, Önhan and Miquel Molist, eds. 2004. *Tell Amarna (Syrie) I. La Période de Halaf.* Leuven: Peeters.

van Zeist, Willem and Willemina Waterbolk-van Rooijen. 1996. The Cultivated and Wild Plants. In *Tell Sabi Abyad. The Late Neolithic Settlement*, ed. Peter M. M. G. Akkermans, 2:521–50. İstanbul: Nederlands Historisch-Archaeologisch Instituut.

Verhoeven, Marc. 1999. *An Archaeological Ethnography of a Neolithic Community: Space, Place and Social Relations in the Burnt Village at Tell Sabi Abyad, Syria*. Leiden: Nederlands Historisch-Archaeologisch Instituut.

von Oppenheim, Max and Hubert Schmidt. 1943. *Tell Halaf. Die Prähistorischen Funde*. Berlin: de Gruyter.

von Wickede, Alwo and Suzanne Herbordt. 1988. Çavi Tarlası. Bericht über die Ausgrabungskampagnen 1983–1984. *Istanbuler Mitteilungen* 38: 5–36.

Watkins, Trevor and Stuart Campbell. 1987. The Chronology of the Halaf Culture. In *Chronologies du Proche Orient/Chronologies in the Near East: Relative Chronologies and Absolute Chronology 16,000–4,000 BP*, ed. Olivier Aurenche, Jacques Evin, and Francis Hours, 427–64. BAR International Series 379(ii). Oxford: British Archaeological Reports.

Watson, Patty Jo. 1983a. The Halafian Culture: A Review and Synthesis. In *The Hilly Flanks and Beyond: Essays on the Prehistory of Southwestern Asia Presented to Robert J. Braidwood, 15 November 1982*, ed. T. Cuyler Young, Philip E. L. Smith, and Peder Mortensen, 231–49. Studies in Ancient Oriental Civilization 35. Chicago: Oriental Institute of the University of Chicago.

———. 1983b. The Soundings at Banahilk. In *Prehistoric Archaeology along the Zagros Flanks*, ed. Linda S. Braidwood, Robert J. Braidwood, Bruce Howe, Charles A. Reed, and Patty Jo Watson, 545–613. Oriental Institute Publications 105. Chicago: Oriental Institute of the University of Chicago.

Watson, Patty Jo and Steven A. LeBlanc. 1990. *Girikihaciyan: A Halafian Site in Southeastern Turkey.* Monograph 33. Los Angeles: Institute of Archaeology, University of California.

Wattenmaker, Patricia and Adnan Mısır. 1994. Kazane Höyük—1992. *Kazı Sonuçları Toplantısı* 15: 177–91.
Wilkinson, Tony J. and David J. Tucker. 1995. *Settlement Development in the North Jazira, Iraq: A Study of the Archaeological Landscape.* Warminster: Aris and Phillips.
Woolley, C. Leonard. 1934. The Prehistoric Pottery of Carchemish. *Iraq* 1.1: 146–62.
Zeder, Melinda A. 1994. After the Revolution: Post-Neolithic Subsistence in Northern Mesopotamia. *American Anthropologist* 96.1: 97–126.

CHAPTER 36

MILLENNIA IN THE MIDDLE? RECONSIDERING THE CHALCOLITHIC OF ASIA MINOR

BLEDA S. DÜRING

ONE of the central concerns of archaeological research, from its origins to the present day, is the question of how past societies evolved toward those of the present. Following Childe, this development has been condensed by archaeologists into two key "events": the Neolithic and Urban "revolutions" (Childe 1928, 1936). This "threshold view of the past" has affected research agendas significantly, and it is arguably the case that most scholars working on the prehistory of Asia Minor, and for that matter in archaeology in general, have implicitly adopted a Childean view of the past (Flannery 1994; Trigger 1994).

One consequence of this research paradigm is that the Chalcolithic has often been seen as a tranquil period during which nothing of interest happened. This problem is mitigated to some degree for the Early Chalcolithic, which is often considered an extension of the Neolithic, and the Late Chalcolithic, which is commonly perceived as the initial stage of the subsequent Early Bronze Age, whereas the Middle Chalcolithic in particular has been caught in the middle, one might say.

In this chapter I argue that reducing archaeological analysis to a few key events or sites fundamentally distorts our understanding of the past. The Chalcolithic as an eventless period is above all a projection of our own interpretive frameworks. A consideration of the concept of the "Middle Ages" in European history—undoubtedly a normative phrase coined to designate what was perceived as an insignificant interlude between the Classical period and the Renaissance—can illustrate this. Clearly the Middle Ages were not eventless or insignificant and included, for example, the Christianization of Europe (Brown 2003).

The time span between 5500 and 3000 cal B.C.E. in Asia Minor (referring to the area of Anatolia that rests west of an imaginary line between the modern cities of Iskenderun and Trabzon) is relatively poorly known. This situation can be contrasted with that in the Fertile Crescent and Mesopotamia, where the period between 5400 and 3000 cal B.C.E. is represented by the Ubaid–Uruk sequence, which has been the subject of many systematic investigations (Algaze 1993; Henrickson and Thuessen 1989; Stein 2005; Özbal, chapter 8, and Rothman, chapter 37 in this volume). This difference is, to a large degree, explained by the emergence of increasingly complex societies in the Ubaid and the Uruk periods, culminating in urbanization, writing, states, and the emergence of long-distance trade networks, all of which have fascinated Near Eastern archaeologists.

What happens in contemporary Chalcolithic Asia Minor is much less well understood, but this horizon is commonly perceived as one of small-scale societies lacking complexity, a view that has not really been scrutinized or investigated. Furthermore, the lack of knowledge about Chalcolithic Asia Minor has also created a feedback loop in which few scholars are interested in this period, given that it is difficult to formulate specific research questions and that funding bodies are generally not willing to provide funds toward investigating a gap in cultural historical knowledge.

As things stand, few projects have explicitly aimed to investigate the Middle Chalcolithic in particular. Clear exceptions to this general avoidance of the Middle Chalcolithic are the excavations at Güvercinkayası and Orman Fidanlığı (figure 36.1). On the basis of the Türk Arkeoloji Yerleşmeleri files (http://www.tayproject.org) it seems that the total number of excavated sites with Middle and Late Chalcolithic deposits in Asia Minor is twenty-seven. This compares with 42 for the Neolithic and Early Chalcolithic, and no fewer than 163 for the Early Bronze Age.

In the synthetic literature, the Middle Chalcolithic in particular is poorly represented in contrast to earlier and later periods. Yakar, for example, published both on the Neolithic/Early Chalcolithic, and the Late Chalcolithic/Early Bronze Age, disregarding the Middle Chalcolithic (Yakar 1985, 1991, 1994). In the new synthesis by Sagona and Zimansky, the Middle Chalcolithic of Asia Minor is discussed in a single paragraph (2009:134). Even the major synthesis by Schoop (2005), "das anatolische Chalkolithicum," which is an important resource bringing together a vast amount of data, suffers from this problem. The 3,000-year period of the Chalcolithic is not subdivided, and developments within the Chalcolithic are not considered. In effect, the discussion focuses mainly on the Early Chalcolithic on one hand and the Late Chalcolithic on the other. This absence of a review of the Middle Chalcolithic is understandable, however, given that new evidence on this era has only begun to emerge over the past decade, and Schoop's analysis took place before much of this became available (and see Schoop, chapter 7 in this volume, for extensive discussion).

Characterizing Chalcolithic Asia Minor

In this chapter I focus on aspects other than culture history and the degree to which interregional relations were of importance in Chalcolithic Asia Minor. These aspects are, of course, essential building blocks in any understanding of this period but are treated by others in this volume (Schoop, chapter 7, discusses the Chalcolithic on the plateau; Özdoğan, chapter 29, summarizes the cultural relations between Asia Minor and the Balkans; and Sagona, chapter 30, addresses interaction with Transcaucasia). Instead, I raise the question of what we know about how people lived in Asia Minor between about 5500 and 3000 B.C.E. Thus the focus is on the reconstruction of lifeways rather than chronology and cultural connections. There is no space here to discuss sequences and assemblages at length (but see Düring 2011; Schoop, chapter 7 in this volume), and therefore I focus on selected sites which bring out the key points I want to raise.

One way of beginning this discussion is to evaluate how Chalcolithic Asia Minor has been described in the literature. The following elements appear to dominate this perception (as seen in Gérard 2002:108; Marciniak and Czerniak 2007:126–27; Todd 1980:113, 118). First, settlements are supposed to have been small and strategically located. Second, the Chalcolithic has sometimes been portrayed as the

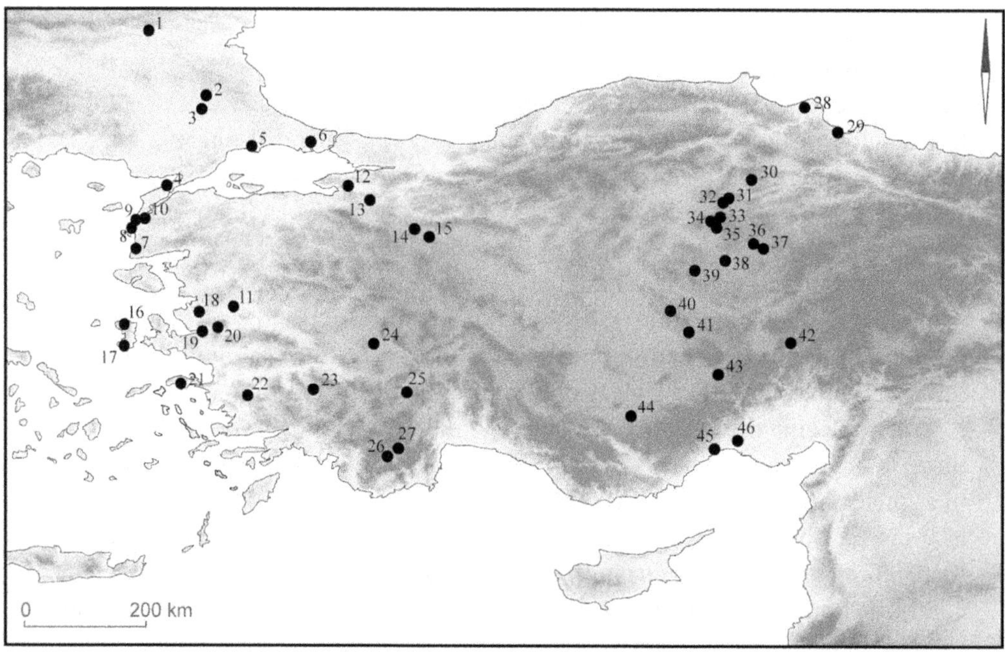

1 Karanovo; 2 Aşağı Pınar; 3 Tilkiburnu; 4 Kilia; 5 Toptepe; 6 Yarımburgaz; 7 Gülpınar; 8 Beşik-Sivritepe; 9 Kumtepe; 10 Alacalıgöl; 11 Kulaksızlar; 12 Ilıpınar; 13 Barcın Höyük; 14 Demircihüyük; 15 Orman Fidanlığı; 16 Ayio Gala; 17 Emporio; 18 Araptepe; 19 Yassıtepe; 20 Ulucak; 21 Tigani; 22 Çine-Tepecik; 23 Aphrodisias-Pekmez; 24 Beycesultan; 25 Kuruçay; 26 Bağbaşı; 27 Kizilbel; 28 İkiztepe; 29 Dundartepe; 30 Kuşsaray; 31 Büyük Göllücek; 32 Alaca Höyük; 33 Büyükkaya; 34 Yarıkkaya; 35 Camlibel Tarlası; 36 Çadır Höyük; 37 Alişar Höyük; 38 Çengeltepe; 39 Hashöyük; 40 Kabakulak; 41 Güvercinkayası; 42 Fıraktın; 43 Köşk Höyük; 44 Canhasan 1; 45 Mersin-Yumuktepe; 46 Tarsus-Gözlükule.

Figure 36.1. Excavated Chalcolithic sites of Asia Minor, ca. 5500–3000 B.C.E.

"real Neolithic": a period in which farming became the cornerstone of the subsistence economy and gathering wild plant resources and hunting animals was no longer of significance. Third, an argument has been put forward that Chalcolithic people more fully exploited natural resources, such as salt and obsidian, presumably for exchange with other groups.

How accurate is this characterization of the Chalcolithic of Asia Minor? Of course it could be argued that the basic premise—that a characterization of the Chalcolithic of Asia Minor is possible in the first place—is mistaken. The two and a half millennia and the size of the geographic area concerned make it plausible that there was considerable diversity in how societies came together in Chalcolithic Asia Minor. Nonetheless, the characteristics put forward provide a useful framework for discussing the Chalcolithic evidence.

Settlements and Subsistence

Although the extant settlement evidence available for Chalcolithic Asia Minor is relatively scant, what there is points to considerable differences between settlements and their subsistence economies. I argue that we can identify at least three distinct types of settlement in Chalcolithic Asia Minor: the first consists of ephemeral settlements, some of which may have been seasonally occupied; the second includes villages and hamlets; and the third encompasses more complex villages, with some evidence for public buildings and defensive structures.

Ephemeral Settlements

"Ephemeral settlements" are defined here as those that have scant architectural remains and occupation horizons, which may be related either to transient occupation of these sites or issues to do with preservation and archaeological research. Ephemeral settlements include a number of sites in the Troad that can be dated to the fifth millennium B.C.E. These consist of Kumtepe Layer 1A, Beşik-Sivritepe, Gülpınar, and Alacalıgöl (Gabriel 2000, 2006; Sperling 1976; Takaoğlu 2006). All these sites in the Troad are relatively shallow, generally not more than seventy centimeters deep, and clear building remains have not been found at any of them. The limited depth of these sites has been linked with wattle and daub building technologies, a way of constructing that would have resulted in less building débris and therefore less substantial deposits (Rosenstock 2005; Seeher 1985:174).

The shallow occupation deposits of the Troadic sites and the fact that researchers have often found it difficult to find architectural remains in them are not exceptional circumstances in Chalcolithic Asia Minor. Similar, for example, is the site of Orman Fidanlığı, where the site deposits do not exceed 150 cm (Efe 1990:67–69, 2001:xvi, 1). Hardly any clear features were found in the Orman Fidanlığı excavations, two exceptions being an apsidal structure with stone walls with an interior measurement of about 2 × 3 m, and a fragmentary oven associated with a surface.

At the Late Chalcolithic site of Bağbaşı in southwestern Anatolia, building remains were likewise poorly preserved, and consequently the only information we have consists of artifacts. A substantial proportion of the ceramics at Bağbaşı, which are comparable to the latest pottery from Late Chalcolithic Beycesultan (Schoop 2005:185), consisted of very large storage vessels with vertical walls and flat bases (Eslick 1992:46), suggesting that storage was important.

Finally, at Canhasan 1, another site to be placed in the Late Chalcolithic, a series of transient buildings constructed with mud were found (French 1998). They were poorly constructed and modified on a more or less constant basis, and as a result no comprehensive plans could be obtained.

How can we interpret these Chalcolithic sites with shallow deposits and ephemeral buildings? At some, it is possible to argue that we are dealing with seasonally occupied settlements, but at others this seems less likely.

The strongest case for seasonal occupation can be made for Level VB at Ilıpınar, dating to ca. 5500–5400 cal B.C.E. (see Roodenberg, chapter 44 in this volume). Here a series of sunken hut structures were uncovered measuring about 2 × 3 m. They were dug about forty centimeters into the mound and covered with plaster. In some cases post holes were found along the perimeters of the huts, hinting at a superstructure that in all probability consisted of a wattle and daub domed roof. A number of the huts had a raised bench along one side. The center of these huts contained various features and containers that took up most of the interior space, including oval domed ovens, grinding installations, plastered baskets, and a multitude of ceramic vessels, some containing large amounts of charred crops (Cappers 2008; Roodenberg 2001:231–35, 2008:78–80). This density of features and objects brings up the question of where people were living in these structures. The excavators interpret the hut structures as seasonally occupied, suggesting that objects found represent a storage situation, with a staple of crops such as emmer, barley, lentil, and chickpea that were kept for sowing purposes later in the year (see Roodenberg, chapter 44 in this volume).

At the sites of Bağbaşı and Canhasan Level 1, we may be dealing with another type of temporary settlement (Eslick 1992; French 1998, 2005). At both sites the buildings appear to be transient in nature, and the ceramic finds show a high proportion of storage vessels. At Canhasan Level 1 buildings were poorly constructed and modified on a more or less constant basis. The loam walls of these structures were narrow, about twenty centimeters wide, and could not have supported a heavy overburden; they were covered with a white plaster on their interior. Various structures with two rooms of considerable dimensions were found, measuring up to 14 × 6 m; these contained benches, large bins, a hearth, and a large vessel set in the floor (French 1998:52–53). Other structures also seem to have been large, poorly constructed, and often containing large bins. Given the characteristics of these buildings, one wonders what purpose they might have served.

Whereas the size of these structures suggests that they might have been used by multiple households, the poor quality of construction and the frequent modification and alteration of buildings hint at episodic occupation of the site. One model that springs to mind is that of pastoral nomads who might have used the site for a short period during their seasonal movements. Ethnographic studies of subrecent pastoralists in the Near East have demonstrated that nomads often construct buildings, ranging from makeshift structures to complete houses, in locations where they reside regularly for extended periods (Böhmer 2004; Cribb 1991). In particular, a well-documented feature of pastoral campsites is the construction of moderate height walls of stone or loam bricks, above which a tent or a temporary roof is raised, thus creating a hybrid building (Cribb 1991:95–96; Saidel 2008). Building remains of campsites from such locations are not unlike those found at Canhasan Level 1 and could explain why the walls were poorly built and structures were often altered. Furthermore, the large storage bins at the site could also have functioned for keeping goods in this location while absent. It can be tentatively suggested that Canhasan Level 1, and possibly also Bağbaşı, are examples of sites used seasonally by pastoral mobile communities otherwise poorly documented in the prehistory of Asia Minor.

A third group of sites with ephemeral settlement remains consists of the Troadic sites already introduced, such as Kumtepe and Beşik-Sivritepe. At these sites marine resources, particularly molluscs, were of great importance; these species were more common in the fifth millennium B.C.E., along with other marine species, than they are at present. In addition people were consuming wild figs, domestic cattle and sheep, and cultivated pulses and some cereals at Kumtepe 1A/A (Boessneck 1986; Özdoğan, Mitake, and Özbaşaran-Dede 1991:76–77; Riehl 1999:27; Riehl and Marinova 2008; Uerpmann 2003). Thus, the food spectrum documented at the Troadic fifth millennium B.C.E. sites is rich and varied and would probably have allowed people to stay put throughout the year. At the site of Toptepe on the northern shore of the Marmara Sea, which also had substantial shell deposits and dates to the end of the sixth millennium B.C.E., a substantial rectangular building was found (Özdoğan, Mitake, and Özbaşaran-Dede 1991); it is not inconceivable that similar buildings might have existed in the Troadic sites that remain to be found.

Villages and Hamlets

A second group of Chalcolithic settlements in Asia Minor can be classed as village settlements probably relying predominantly on farming for their livelihood. Examples of such settlements are Alaca Höyük, Alişar, Beycesultan, Çamlıbel Tarlası, İkiztepe, Kumtepe 1B, Kuruçay 6, and Yarıkkaya. Although the scale of these settlements varies considerably, they are all constituted of rectangular well-built structures, often of considerable size and with multiple rooms.

Yarıkkaya and Çamlıbel Tarlası are two hamlet-type settlements in north central Asia Minor. The Çamlıbel Tarlası settlement has been estimated to have measured about 50 × 50 m. At both sites square rooms measuring about 7 × 5 m were excavated, some of which were free-standing, whereas others shared party walls with adjacent rooms. At Yarıkkaya walls were constructed from stones at the base, with stamped loam in the higher reaches (Hauptmann 1969; Schoop 2008).

At Beycesultan in deep sounding "SX" a long Late Chalcolithic sequence was excavated, consisting of no less than eleven meters of deposits (levels 40–20). Almost all contained architectural remains, suggesting that occupation in this part of the mound was dense and continuous (Lloyd and Mellaart 1962). Most were rooms built of mudbricks and measured about 3 × 4 m.

Undoubtedly the best documented village of Chalcolithic Asia Minor is that of Kuruçay Level 6 (figure 36.2), where a substantial part of the settlement has been excavated, consisting of approximately twenty-three buildings (Duru 1996, 2008). These mostly consisted of single-roomed rectangular buildings, measuring about 4 × 7 m. These buildings were constructed on stone foundations on which rested loam walls with a width of about thirty centimeters.

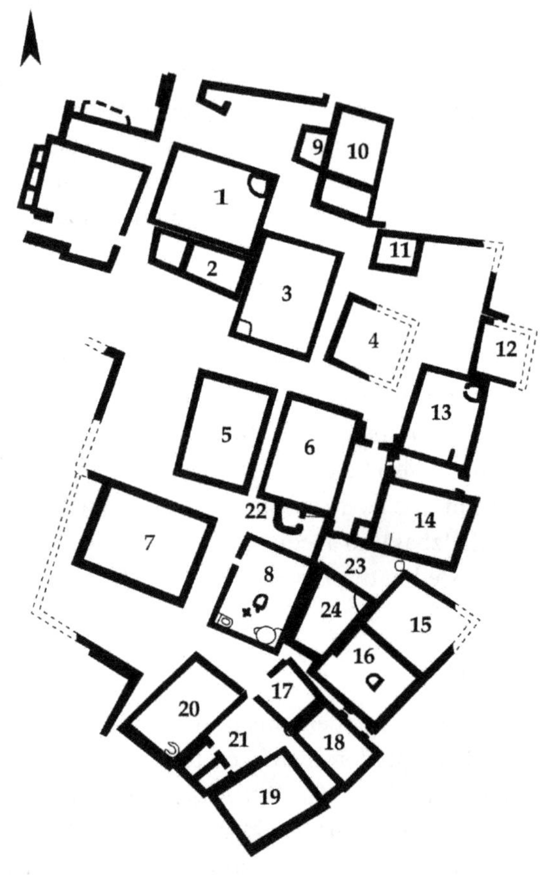

GEC KALKOLİTİK
(GK 6 A2 Yerleşmesi)

KURUÇAY
0 10m

Figure 36.2. Plan of Kuruçay 6A2 (courtesy Refik Duru and Gülsün Umurtak).

Some buildings of Level 6 at Kuruçay were well preserved, with walls standing up to about 1.50 m, and in one instance a door was preserved, complete with the lintel and a section of the wall above. The buildings usually contained a large domed oval oven, which was normally located in one of the corners furthest removed from the entrance. An ovoid central hearth was also common in these buildings, and these usually had a small upstanding pillar at their rear, behind which the central post was placed. Additional features and objects, such as grinding installations, stone grinding vessels, looms, and storage pots, were found in the back of some rooms. Although the well-preserved building 8 was interpreted as a "shrine" by Duru (1996:12), the building and its contents are in no way exceptional apart from the degree of preservation.

According to Duru, Kuruçay 6 was akin to a small urban center. He reconstructs a number of central buildings in the settlement, which included the "shrine" already mentioned, as well as houses for postulated dignitaries, which were surrounded by a series of domestic buildings whose rear walls would have constituted a sawtoothed defense wall, with various small alleys acting as gates. However, this interpretation is a very particular and unconvincing reading of the evidence and requires some manipulation of the data (Schoop 2005:165–6).

Instead, it appears that in all subphases of the Level 6 settlement there are groups of buildings that are spatially associated with the intervening open spaces built up to some degree. This probably means that the settlement at Kuruçay was not inhabited by more or less autonomous households, each occupying a discrete and free-standing building; instead, we are dealing with household clusters of about three to five closely associated households.

For most of the sites in the village category we do not have evidence concerning their subsistence economy. It is plausible, if not demonstrated, that they were used by relatively sedentary populations relying primarily on farming for their subsistence. At Late Chalcolithic Kuruçay, a broad spectrum of cultivated crops has been found, including four kinds of cereals, various pulses, and flax (Nesbit 1996:90). The faunal remains, however, include both domestic and wild animals, the latter encompassing species such as lion, aurochs, deer, bear, wild goat, and wild boar (Deniz 1996:87). At Kumtepe 1B/B, cereals are prominent in the botanical assemblage, in contrast with the earlier fifth millennium B.C.E. levels at the same site, whereas molluscs are less ubiquitous (Riehl 1999; Riehl and Marinova 2008; Uerpmann 2003).

Complex Villages

Finally, there are a number of "complex villages," with some evidence for public buildings and defensive structures. These have been found at Güvercinkayası, Köşk Höyük, Mersin-Yumuktepe 16, and Çadır Höyük. Such settlements have sometimes been interpreted as "proto-urban."

At the sites of Güvercinkayası and Köşk Höyük substantial exposures dating to between about 5200 and 4800 cal B.C.E. have been excavated. Güvercinkayası is placed on top of a steep rock formation, which measured approximately forty by sixty meters (Gülçür 1997; Gülçür and Fırat 2005). Tentatively, on the basis of the available space on the rock outcrop, it can be suggested that no more than forty domestic buildings could have been present at Güvercinkayası, although it is possible that there were additional buildings at the base of the outcrop (figure 36.3).

The houses are more or less standardized in their organization of space and limited in their size range. They are between twenty and thirty square meters in size and consist of a main room with an entrance in the center of one of the short walls. Along the back wall a thin storage room was created by inserting a narrow wall about 1.5 m from the back wall. In this space pots with conical bases were often found embedded in the floor, and silos were encountered. In the main room standard features include an oven located in one of the corners next to the entrance and a hearth placed in the center.

At Köşk Höyük, about sixty kilometers from Güvercinkayası, buildings were found in Level 1 that are nearly identical to those found at Güvercinkayası, with a similar configuration of features (Öztan 2003; Öztan and Faydalı 2003). One building at Köşk Höyük was exceptionally well preserved and appears to have burned twice. In this building an enormous amount of ceramics was found, some of which might have been placed on shelves, as well as grinding stone implements, figurines representing "big females," and bone tools. Moreover, it was possible on the basis of preserved building timbers to estimate that the second building phase occurred fifty-two years after the first (Kuniholm and Newton 2002; Öztan and Faydalı 2003:49).

Figure 36.3. Plan of Güvercinkayası (courtesy Sevil Gülçür).

Although buildings are similar in Köşk Höyük Level 1 and Güvercinkayası, the overall nature of the two settlements differs in significant ways. Whereas at Güvercinkayası we are dealing with a small settlement on top of a rock outcrop that was densely built up, Köşk Höyük is a much more accessible location, and there is much more open space in the settlement. On the basis of the evidence from Güvercinkayası it has been suggested that defense was of key importance in the (Middle) Chalcolithic (Gülçür and Fırat 2005:41). However, the Köşk Höyük settlement location is less convincing as a defensive location and can furthermore be seen as a continuation of an older settlement on the same spot.

Another issue that is presently unclear is the degree to which there were nondomestic or élite buildings present at these sites. At both Köşk Höyük Level 1 and Güvercinkayası buildings have been found that are substantially larger than the normal houses but which appear similar to the domestic buildings in most other respects. In addition, at Güvercinkayası, a double and massive stone wall was found associated with a round tower-like feature. These structures are located in the center of the settlement, and their functions are poorly understood.

The plan of Level 16 at Mersin-Yumuktepe is among the most famous in the prehistory of Asia Minor. The settlement was interpreted as a fortified settlement surrounded by a massive city wall measuring about a meter thick, which was offset at regular distances and had slit windows at regular intervals from which defenders could safely shoot enemies. This wall was complete with a "city gate" flanked by two towers. To the east of the city gate a series of domestic residences was built up against the "city wall," each consisting of a front and a back room. The back rooms were about nine to fifteen square meters and might have served as living rooms of nuclear households; Garstang suggests that they might have been inhabited by soldiers with their families (1953:133).

Recent excavations at Mersin-Yumuktepe have thrown new light on the nature of the Level 16 settlement at the site (Caneva 2004). At some distance south of the city gate, remains were found of a building similar to the "soldiers barracks" found by Garstang, which suggests that if we are dealing with an ovoid citadel, its interior diameter is about thirty-five by forty meters only. Even more revealing is the discovery of a cobble paved road on the slope of the mound, which was bordered by a terrace wall against which were buildings that are similar to the wall-houses found by Garstang. Thus, it appears that we are not dealing with a fortified citadel at all, but a series of terraces, against which terraced buildings were constructed!

To the west of the city gate, a large building was excavated, the extant remains of which include a large hall, measuring about 10 × 4 m, and featuring a number of rooms of substantial size on its eastern side. Garstang interpreted this building as an élite residence. It is equally possible, of course, that this was a communal building of sorts or had a religious function. Garstang further suggested that this building originally had a west wing similar to that in the east. If this reconstruction is accepted, we would be dealing with a large tripartite building of a type that is well known in Ubaid sites across Syro-Mesopotamia (Breniquet 1995:24), which would tie in well with Ubaidian features in the pottery found in the same layer.

Finally, in the Late Chalcolithic levels at Çadır Höyük, dated to about 3600–3100 cal B.C.E., a massive wall with a stone foundation and a mudbrick superstructure of about 1.5 m thick was encountered. This wall had a gateway originally over 2 m wide, also constructed of stone and mudbrick, with gate arms extending about 1.5 m into the settlement and opening into a courtyard. On either side of the gate was a small room of about 2 × 2 m. These rooms are apparently associated with the gateway but are nondomestic. Inside the settlement there was a fairly well-provisioned house, the "burnt house" with a large courtyard and two stories, with an assemblage indicative of craft activities such as stone tool production and textile production and including metal jewelry and lots of pottery in its inventory. Another remarkable building of this phase is the "omphalos building," after a certain style of pottery of which a large concentration was found in the building (Steadman, McMahon, and Ross 2007; Steadman et al. 2008). Although the Late Chalcolithic settlement at Çadır Höyük is unfortunately poorly preserved in many areas, the overall picture that emerges from the excavations is of a complex settlement that included some opulent households, some structures that were nondomestic in nature, such as the omphalos building, and possibly a fortification system.

Exchange Networks in Chalcolithic Asia Minor

Chalcolithic Asia Minor has sometimes been characterized as a period dominated by farming villages, with some exploitation of natural resources such as salt and obsidian, which could be exchanged with other groups for their intrinsic value. Indeed, there is some evidence to support the idea that raw materials were exchanged over considerable distances. This is manifested, for example, in the exchange of obsidian; a site such as Aphrodisias contains obsidian from Cappadocian sources and the Aegean islands of Melos and Giali (Blackman 1986), and a similar situation has been documented at Dedecik-Heybelitepe (Herling et al. 2008).

However, there is also evidence for the exchange of artifacts produced especially for export purposes and produced in labor intensive local industries. The best evidence for this comes from the Middle Chalcolithic site of Kulaksızlar, located in western Asia Minor. At this site, there is evidence for the production of stone vessels and figurines. These were produced from marble, and a large number of blanks, waste by-products, manufacturing rejects, and stone working tools were found here, constituting about 90 percent of the surface assemblage (Takaoğlu 2002:72). The most common artifacts produced at Kulaksızlar are pointed beakers and "Kilia figurines" (figure 36.4). These are stylized humanoid, most likely female, figurines with a long neck, round sloping shoulders, and arms folded upward in front of the chest (Seeher 1992). Whereas the body is flat, the necks are cylindrical, and the heads are much broader than the body and have raised facial features. The beakers

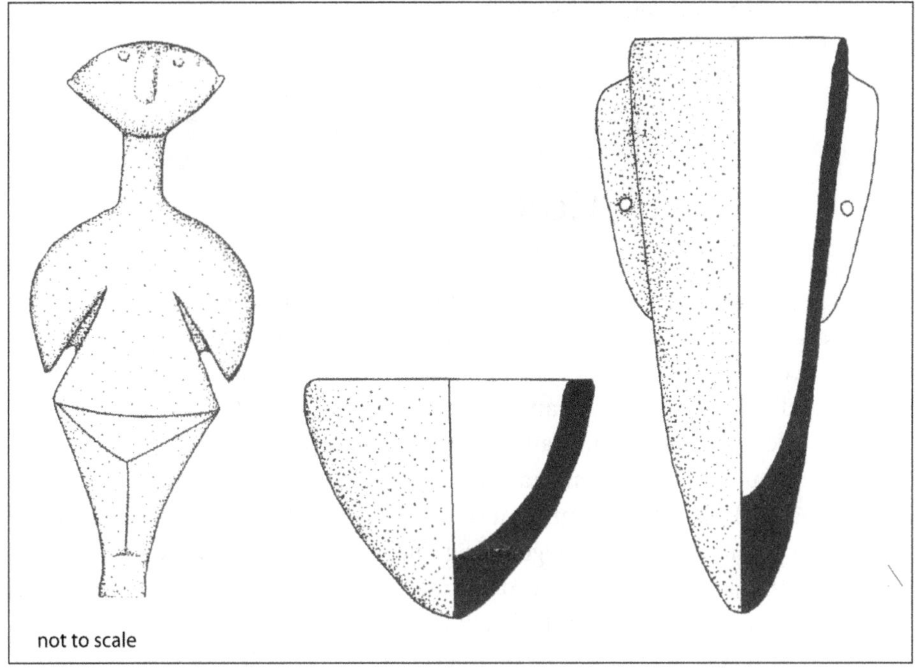

Figure 36.4. Pointed beakers and Kilia figurines produced at Kulaksızlar (courtesy Turan Takaoğlu).

are conical in shape and have two vertical lugs with piercings near the rim. Pointed bowls are also found.

Both the pointed marble beakers and the Kilia figurines have been found over remarkably large areas. Pointed marble beakers similar to those that were produced at Kulaksızlar have also been found at Tigani on Samos, on the islands of Keos and Naxos, at Kumtepe and Beşik-Sivritepe in the Troad, at Demircihöyük in the Eskişehir region, and at Varna in western Bulgaria (Takaoğlu 2002:78–79, 2004:3). Kilia figurines were found across western Anatolia, but not in the Aegean; they were discovered at sites such as Beşik-Yassıtepe, Hanaytepe, and Troy in the Troad and at Yortan, Alaağaç, Selendi, Gavurtepe, Aphrodisias, and Çine-Tepecik in western Anatolia (Seeher 1992; Takaoğlu 2002).

Finally, in the Late Chalcolithic, we see the emergence of sophisticated metal industries, in the form of fan-shaped axes and pins of various sorts, at sites such as Ilıpınar 4, Kuruçay 6, Çadır Höyük, Büyük Güllücek, and İkiztepe. It has been argued that we are dealing with a deliberate alloy of arsenic and copper to create arsenic-bronze artifacts (Begeman, Pernicka, and Schmitt-Strecke 1994; Özbal et al. 2002). The emergence of metallurgy is dealt with in various chapters in this volume (Sagona, chapter 30; Marro, chapter 12; Steadman, chapter 10; and especially Muhly, chapter 39). Here I simply note that although this early metallurgy remains poorly understood in many respects, it is clear that the production of such tools requires considerable expertise and resources, suggesting both that specialization was an important strategy in Late Chalcolithic economies and that these objects were traded with people elsewhere.

Conclusions

I have argued that a threshold perspective on the past, focusing on the Neolithic and urban "revolutions," seriously distorts our understanding of prehistory. It is a mistake to conceive of a period such as the Chalcolithic of Asia Minor, lasting no less than two and a half millennia, as an eventless period.

The Chalcolithic has been mainly envisaged as a period during which settlements were small-scale and often strategically located. It has been argued that people relied almost exclusively on farming, and that the gathering of wild plant resources and hunting of animals was no longer of significance. Finally, it has been postulated that Chalcolithic societies also engaged in some exploitation and exchange of natural resources, such as salt and obsidian, which were intrinsically valuable.

On closer inspection, this idea of a period dominated by small-scale, largely autarchic farming societies does not stand up to scrutiny. Although farming was of significant importance at many Chalcolithic societies in Asia Minor, the idea that wild food resources were no longer important is clearly mistaken. At the Troadic fifth millennium B.C.E. sites people were gathering molluscs and eating wild figs; at Kuruçay a range of wild animals were hunted, including, intriguingly, such species as bovids and goats, which were also kept domestically. Thus, the idea that people were no longer including wild food resources in their subsistence strategies can be discredited.

Instead, it can be argued that in the Chalcolithic people were expanding their economies in multiple and often ingenious ways and were increasingly partners in large exchange networks. Apart from farming, we can document the exploitation of marine resources such as molluscs and fish. The rise of seafaring can be recognized through the distribution of Melos obsidian and the emergence of a cultural horizon in the northern Aegean that included western Asia Minor and the Aegean islands (Takaoğlu 2004). Furthermore, there is some tentative evidence for nomadic pastoralism, as suggested here for the sites of Canhasan Level 1 and Bağbaşı. Finally, we can see the emergence of export driven production of labor-intensive goods such as stone vessels, figurines, and, later, metal artifacts in the Chalcolithic period.

Finally, the idea that Chalcolithic societies in Asia Minor were small-scale and relatively simple is no longer tenable. In the survey of settlements that has been presented here, it has emerged that there is a range of settlement types, some small and ephemeral and perhaps seasonally occupied, others sizable villages relying primarily on farming, such as Kuruçay 6, and yet others including what appear to be monumental nondomestic buildings and possibly also defensive structures, as at Çadır Höyük, Köşk Höyük, Güvercinkayası, and Mersin-Yumuktepe. This diversity clearly demonstrates that societies in Chalcolithic Asia Minor were not uniformly small-scale and simple. Tantalizingly, with the exception of Çadır Höyük, many of these "complex villages" date relatively early in the Chalcolithic, to the late sixth and early fifth millennia B.C.E., suggesting that social complexity did not necessarily increase through time, but may have shifted back and forth during the Chalcolithic.

One idea that could be put forward is that the rise of the exchange-oriented production of labor-intensive goods such as stone vessels, figurines, and metal artifacts, which originally may have been a mechanism for the creation and maintenance of long-distance relationships with other groups, might have facilitated the rise of stratified societies in the subsequent Early Bronze Age. Whether this model has any value can only be discovered by future research into the as yet poorly known Chalcolithic of Asia Minor.

NOTE

This chapter was written as part of a postdoctoral Veni fellowship funded by the Netherlands Organization for Scientific Research and the Faculty of Archaeology at Leiden University. I would also like to thank Sharon Steadman and Gregory McMahon for inviting me to contribute to this volume.

REFERENCES

Algaze, Guillermo. 1993. *The Uruk World System: The Dynamics of Early Mesopotamian Civilization*. Chicago: University of Chicago Press.

Begemann, Friedrich, Ernst Pernicka, and Sigrid Schmitt-Strecke. 1994. Metal Finds from Ilıpınar and the Advent of Arsenic Copper. *Anatolica* 20: 15–36.

Blackman, M. James. 1986. The Provenience of Obsidian Artifacts from Late Chalcolithic Levels at Aphrodisias. In *Prehistoric Aphrodisias I: An Account of the Excavation and Artefact Studies*, ed. M. S. Joukowsky, 279–85. Providence, R.I.: Brown University Press.

Boessneck, Joachim. 1986. Die Weichtieresser vom Beşik-Sivritepe. *Archäologischer Anzeiger* 1986: 329–38.

Böhmer, Harald 2004. *Nomaden in Anatolien: Begegnungen mit einer ausklingenden Kultur*. Ganderkesee: Remhöb Verlag.

Breniquet, Catherine. 1995. La stratigraphie des niveaux prehistoriques de Mersin et l'evolution culturelle en Cilicie. *Anatolia Antiqua* 3: 1–31.

Brown, Peter. 2003. *The Rise of Western Christendom: Triumph and Diversity, A.D. 200–1000*. Malden, Mass.: Blackwell.

Caneva, Isabella. 2004. The Citadel Tradition (5000–4200 BC). In *Mersin-Yumuktepe, A Reppraisal*, ed. Isabella Caneva and Veli Sevin, 57–72. Lecce: Congedo Editore.

Cappers, René. 2008. Plant Remains. In *Life and Death in a Prehistoric Settlement in Northwest Anatolia: The Ilıpınar Excavations III*, ed. Jacob Roodenberg and Söngul Alpaslan-Roodenberg, 117–48. Leiden: Nederlands Instituut voor het Nabije Oosten.

Childe, V.Gordon. 1928. *The Most Ancient East*. London: Routledge and Kegan Paul.

———. 1936. *Man Makes Himself*. London: Routledge.

Cribb, Roger. 1991. *Nomads in Archaeology*. Cambridge: Cambridge University Press.

Deniz, Eşref. 1996. Geç Kalkolitik ve İlk Tunç Çağı Katlarında Bulunan Insan ve Hayvan Kemiklerine Arkeobiyolojik Değerlendirmesi. In *Kuruçay Höyük II: The Late Chalcolithic and Early Bronze Age Settlements*, ed. Refik Duru, 85–88. Ankara: Türk Tarih Kurumu Basımevi.

Duru, Refik. 1996. *Kuruçay Höyük II: The Late Chalcolithic and Early Bronze Age Settlements*. Ankara: Türk Tarih Kurumu Basımevi.

———. 2008. *From 8000 BC to 2000 BC: Six Thousand Years of the Burdur-Antalya Region*. İstanbul: Suna-İnan Kıraç Akdeniz Medeniyetleri Araştırma Enstitüsü.

Düring, Bleda S. 2011. *The Prehistory of Asia Minor: From Complex Hunter-Gatherers to Early Urban Societies, 20.000–2.000 BC*. Cambridge: Cambridge University Press.

Efe, Turan. 1990. An Inland Anatolian Site with Pre-Vinča Elements: Orman Fidanlığı, Eskişehir. A Reexamination of Balkan-Anatolian Connections in the Fifth Millennium B.C. *Germania* 68: 67–113.

———. 2001. *The Salvage Excavations at Orman Fidanlığı: A Chalcolithic Site in Inland Northwestern Anatolia*. İstanbul: TASK.

Eslick, Christine. 1992. *Elmalı-Karataş I: The Neolithic and Chalcolithic Periods, Bağbaşı and other sites*. Bryn Mawr, Pa.: Bryn Mawr Archaeological Monographs.

Flannery, Kent V. 1994. Childe the Evolutionist: A Perspective from Nuclear America. In *The Archaeology of V. Gordon Childe*, ed. David R. Harris, 101–20. Chicago: University of Chicago Press.

French, David. 1998. *Canhasan Sites I, Stratigraphy and Structures*. London: British Institute of Archaeology at Ankara.

———. 2005. *Canhasan I: The Pottery*. London: British Institute at Ankara.

Gabriel, Utta. 2000. Mitteilungen zum Stand der Neolithikumsforschung in der Umgebung von Troia (Kumtepe 1993–1995; Beşik-Sivritepe 1983–1984, 1987, 1998–1999). *Studia Troica* 10: 233–38.

———. 2006. Ein Blick zurück-Das fünfte Jahrtausend vor Christus in der Troas. In *Troia: Archäologie eines Siedlungshügels und seiner Landschaft*, ed. Manfred O. Korfmann, 355–60. Mainz am Rhein: Philipp von Zabern.

Garstang, John. 1953. *Prehistoric Mersin, Yumuk Tepe in Southern Turkey*. Oxford: Clarendon Press.

Gérard, Frédéric. 2002. Transformations and Societies in the Neolithic of Central Anatolia. In *The Neolithic of Central Anatolia: Internal Developments and External Relations during the 9th–6th Millennia cal. BC*, ed. Frédéric Gerard and Laurens Thissen, 105–17. İstanbul: Ege Yayınları.

Gülçür, Sevil. 1997. Güvercinkayası; Eine vorgeschichtliche Felsrückensiedlung in Zentralanatolien. *Anatolica* 23: 85–110.

Gülçür, Sevil and Celine Fırat. 2005. Spatial Analysis of Güvercinkayası: A Middle Chalcolithic Hilltop Settlement in Northwestern Cappadocia: A Preliminary Report. *Anatolia Antiqua* 13: 41–52.

Hauptmann, Harald. 1969. Die Grabungen in der prähistorischen Siedlung auf Yarıkkaya. In *Boğazköy IV, Funde aus den Grabungen 1967 und 1968*, ed. Kurt Bittel, 66–69. Berlin: Gebr. Mann Verlag.

Henrickson, Elizabeth F. and Ingolf Thuesen, eds. 1989. *Upon This Foundation: The 'Ubaid Reconsidered.* Copenhagen: Carsten Niebuhr Institute.

Herling, Lothar, Kirstin Kasper, Clemens Lichter, and Recep Meriç. 2008. Im Westen nichts Neues? Ergebnisse der Grabungen 2003 und 2004 in Dedecik-Heybelitepe. *Istanbuler Mitteilungen* 58: 13–65.

Kuniholm, Peter, and Maryanne Newton. 2002. Radiocarbon and Dendrochronology. In *The Neolithic of Central Anatolia, Internal Developments and External Relations during the 9th–6th Millennia cal. BC*, ed. Frédéric Gerard and Laurens Thissen, 275–77. İstanbul: Ege Yayınları.

Lloyd, Seton and James Mellaart, eds. 1962. *Beycesultan I: The Chalcolithic and Early Bronze Age Levels.* London: British Institute of Archaeology at Ankara.

Marciniak, Arek, and Lech Czerniak. 2007. Social Transformations in the Late Neolithic and the Early Chalcolithic Periods in Central Anatolia. *Anatolian Studies* 57: 115–30.

Nesbit, Mark. 1996. Geç Kalkolik tabakalarında bitkisel kalıntıları hakkında ön raporu. In *Kuruçay Höyük II: The Late Chalcolithic and Early Bronze Age Settlements*, ed. Refik Duru, 89–93. Ankara: Türk Tarih Kurumu Basımevi.

Özbal, Hadi, Necip Pehlivan, Bryan Earl, and Bilge Gedik. 2002. Metallurgy at İkiztepe. In *Anatolian Metal II*, ed. Ünsal Yalçın, 39–48. Bochum: Deutschen Bergbau-Museum.

Özdoğan, Mehmet, Yutake Mitake, and Nilgün Özbaşaran-Dede. 1991. An Interim Report on Excavations at Yarımburgaz and Toptepe in Eastern Thrace. *Anatolica* 17: 59–121.

Öztan, Aliye. 2003. A Neolithic and Chalcolithic Settlement in Anatolia: Köşk Höyük. *Colloquium Anatolicum* 2: 69–86.

Öztan, Aliye, and Erol Faydalı. 2003. An Early Chalcolithic Building from Kösk Höyük. *Belleten* 67/248: 45–75.

Riehl, Simone. 1999. *Bronze Age Environment and Economy in the Troad: The Archaeobotany of Kumtepe and Troy.* Tübingen: Mo Vince Verlag.

Riehl, Simone and Elena Marinova. 2008. Mid-Holocene Vegetation Change in the Troad (W Anatolia): Man-Made or Natural? *Vegetation History and Archaeobotany* 17: 297–312.

Roodenberg, Jacob. 2001. Miscellaneous. In *The Ilıpınar Excavations II*, ed. Jacob Roodenberg and Laurens Thissen, 223–55. İstanbul: Nederlands Historisch Archaeologisch Instituut te Istanbul.

———. 2008. The Inhabitants. In *Life and Death in a Prehistoric Settlement in Northwest Anatolia: The Ilıpınar Excavations III*, ed. Jacob Roodenberg and Söngul Alpaslan-Roodenberg, 69–90. Leiden: Nederlands Instituut voor het Nabije Oosten.

Rosenstock, Eva. 2005. Höyük, Toumba and Mogila, a Settlement Form in Anatolia and the Balkans and its Ecological Determination 6500–5500 cal BC. In *How Did Farming Reach Europe? Anatolian-European Relations from the Second Half of the 7th through the First Half of the 6th Millenium BC*, ed. Clemens Lichter, 221–37. İstanbul: Ege Yayınları.

Sagona, Antonio and Paul Zimansky. 2009. *Ancient Turkey*. London: Routledge.

Saidel, Benjamin A. 2008. The Bedouin Tent: An Ethno-Archaeological Portal to Antiquity or a Modern Construct? In *The Archaeology of Mobility: Old World and New World Nomadism*, ed. Hans Barnard and Willeke Wendrich, 465–86. Los Angeles: Cotsen Institute.

Schoop, Ulf-Dietrich. 2005. *Das anatolische Chalkolithicum*. Remshalden: Albert Greiner Verlag.

———. 2008. Ausgrabungen in Çamlıbel Tarlası 2007. *Archäologischer Anzeiger* 2008: 148–57.

Seeher, Jürgen. 1985. Vorläufiger Bericht über die Keramik des Beşik-Sivritepe. *Archäologischer Anzeiger* 1985: 172–82.

———. 1992. Die kleinasiatischen Marmorstatuetten vom Typ Kiliya. *Archäologischer Anzeiger* 1992: 153–70.

Sperling, Jerome W. 1976. Kum Tepe in the Troad, Trial Excavations, 1934. *Hesperia* 45: 305–64.

Steadman, Sharon R., Gregory McMahon, and Jennifer C. Ross. 2007. The Late Chalcolithic at Çadır Höyük in Central Anatolia. *Journal of Field Archaeology* 32: 515–58.

Steadman, Sharon R, Jennifer C. Ross, Gregory McMahon, and Ronald L. Gorny. 2008. Excavations on the North-Central Plateau: The Chalcolithic and Early Bronze Age Occupation at Çadır Höyük. *Anatolian Studies* 58: 47–86.

Stein, Gil J., ed. 2005. *The Archaeology of Colonial Encounters: Comparative Perspectives.* Santa Fe, N.M.: School of American Research Press.

Takaoğlu, Turan. 2002. Chalcolithic Marble Working at Kulaksızlar in Western Anatolia. *TÜBA-AR* 5: 71–93.

———. 2004. Interactions in the Fifth Millenium BC Eastern Aegean: New Evidence. *Anatolia Antiqua* 12: 1–6.

———. 2006. The Late Neolithic in the Eastern Aegean, Excavations at Gülpınar in the Troad. *Hesperia* 75: 289–315.

Todd, Ian A. 1980. *The Prehistory of Central Anatolia I; The Neolithic Period.* Göteborg: Paul Åström Förlag.

Trigger, Bruce G. 1994. Childe's Relevance to the 1990's. In *The Archaeology of V. Gordon Childe*, ed. David R. Harris, 9–34. Chicago: University of Chicago Press.

Uerpmann, Hans-Peter. 2003. Environmental Aspects of Economic Changes in Troia. In *Troia and the Troad, Scientific Approaches*, ed. Günther A. Wagner, Ernst Pernicka, and Hans-Peter Uerpmann, 251–62. Berlin: Springer.

Yakar, Jak. 1985. *The Later Prehistory of Anatolia, The Late Chalcolithic and Early Bronze Age.* Oxford: British Archaeology Reports International Series.

———. 1991. *Prehistoric Anatolia: The Neolithic Transformation and the Early Chalcolithic Period.* Tel Aviv: Tel Aviv University Press.

———. 1994. *Prehistoric Anatolia, The Neolithic Transformation and the Early Chalcolithic Period.* Tel Aviv: Tel Aviv University Press.

CHAPTER 37

INTERACTION OF URUK AND NORTHERN LATE CHALCOLITHIC SOCIETIES IN ANATOLIA

MITCHELL S. ROTHMAN

Theories of Anatolian–Southern Mesopotamian Interaction

Two themes have dominated the scholarly discussion of Greater Mesopotamia in the fourth millennium B.C.E. One is the origin of complexity, often framed as the origin of the state; the other is the nature of interactions across the region, specifically how exchange relationships affected the evolutionary trajectory of societies in a number of ecologically distinct, geographically separate areas within the Greater Mesopotamian region. That region, in addition to the alluvium of southern Iraq and southwestern Iran, includes southeastern and eastern Turkey as well as western Iran, north Syria, and northern Iraq: that is, areas traversed by the Tigris and Euphrates Rivers and their tributaries.

The first theme found its inspiration in the work of Henry Wright and his students (Johnson 1973; Wright 1977, 1994, 1998; Wright and Johnson 1975; see Rothman 2004). The latter resulted from a theory propounded by Guillermo Algaze, first in his dissertation (1986), then in a series of books and articles (1989, 1993, 2001a, 2001b, 2005, 2008).

The artifactual pattern that underlies Algaze's theory is easy to describe. The societies in the north and east of Greater Mesopotamia shared styles of artifacts, especially pottery, collectively called Late Chalcolithic. In fact, pottery styles vary whether the Late Chalcolithic is southeastern Anatolian–north Syrian or highland eastern Anatolian (figure 37.1a, 37.1b). The alluvial south of Iraq stretching into southwest Iran shared a different style corpus, termed Uruk (figure 37.1c). After approximately 3600 B.C.E., southern Uruk pottery began to appear in an area from the northern steppes into the lower mountain ranges within local Late Chalcolithic sites or in new sites, such as Habuba Kabira and Jebel Aruda, built in previously underpopulated areas of north Syria and northern Iraq. Northern sites with Uruk pottery appeared to be located in a dendritic pattern along one of two major north–south routes following the beds of the Euphrates and Tigris Rivers (figure 37.2). Such a wide distribution of pottery styles had occurred in the preceding Ubaid period. The difference was that the area was more limited, and more important, there was not evidence of such a volume of trade accompanying it. Algaze (2008:95) lists as fourth millennium B.C.E. trade items

> (1) pine used as roofing timber; (2) copper, silver, lead, and gold used as tools, weapons, and jewelry [. . .]; (3) precious stones such as lapis, carnelian, agate, chalcedony, amazonite, amethyst, aragonite, and jasper [. . .]; (4) semi-precious stones such as chlorite, obsidian, rock crystal, quartz, alabaster, gypsum, marble, diorite, serpentine, and bituminous limestone [. . .]; (5) common stones such as basalt, flint, and obsidian [. . .]; (6) bitumen [. . .]; and (7) valuable liquids such as wine.

Some believe that not every variety of sheep produced wool appropriate for spinning into yarn in the fourth millennium B.C.E., and therefore wool also might have been imported into the south (Anthony 2007:60f.). This is especially important as one of the proposed trade goods manufactured in large, specialized workshops in the south was a particularly fine wool cloth (Algaze 1993). Little to none of this imported material was available on the southern alluvial plains. Their source areas were in the surrounding hills and Taurus and Zagros Mountains of modern eastern Turkey or western Iran, possibly the Transcaucasus. For highly valued materials from outside the region like lapis lazuli, only found in Badakshan, Afghanistan, the transport routes passed through these highland areas. In short, the southern city-states were dependent on their neighbors for these goods.

As the cities of the south grew, perhaps as Algaze (2008) now argues because of the production and exchange locally and regionally of finished products, older exchange networks no longer sufficed. Those older networks are usually described as down-the-line exchange, in which people nearest the source extract material, retain some, and then pass some on to nearby settlements. The people at those secondary sites save a percentage of what is now a smaller amount, and then pass some on to their next nearest neighbors. As one goes farther down the line from the source area, ever decreasing amounts of the particular material are found.

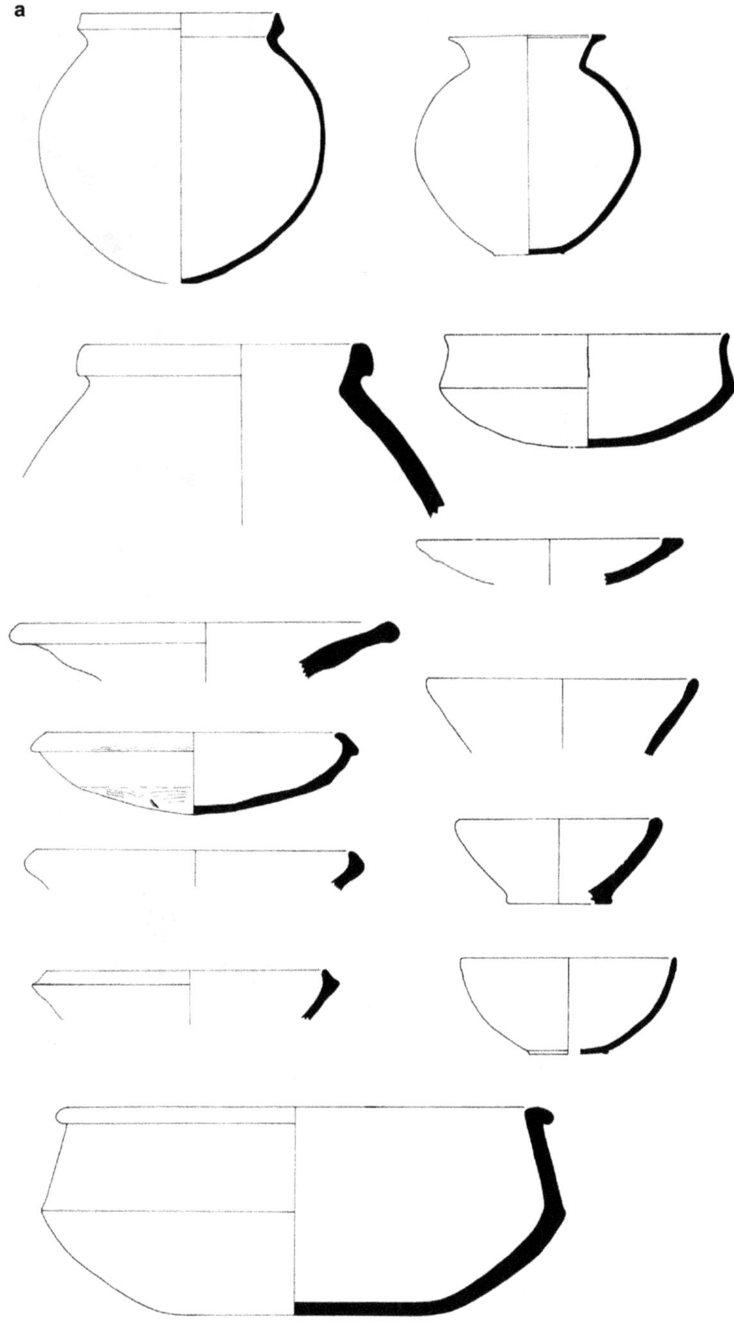

Figure 37.1. (a) Fourth millennium B.C.E. northern Mesopotamian pottery types.

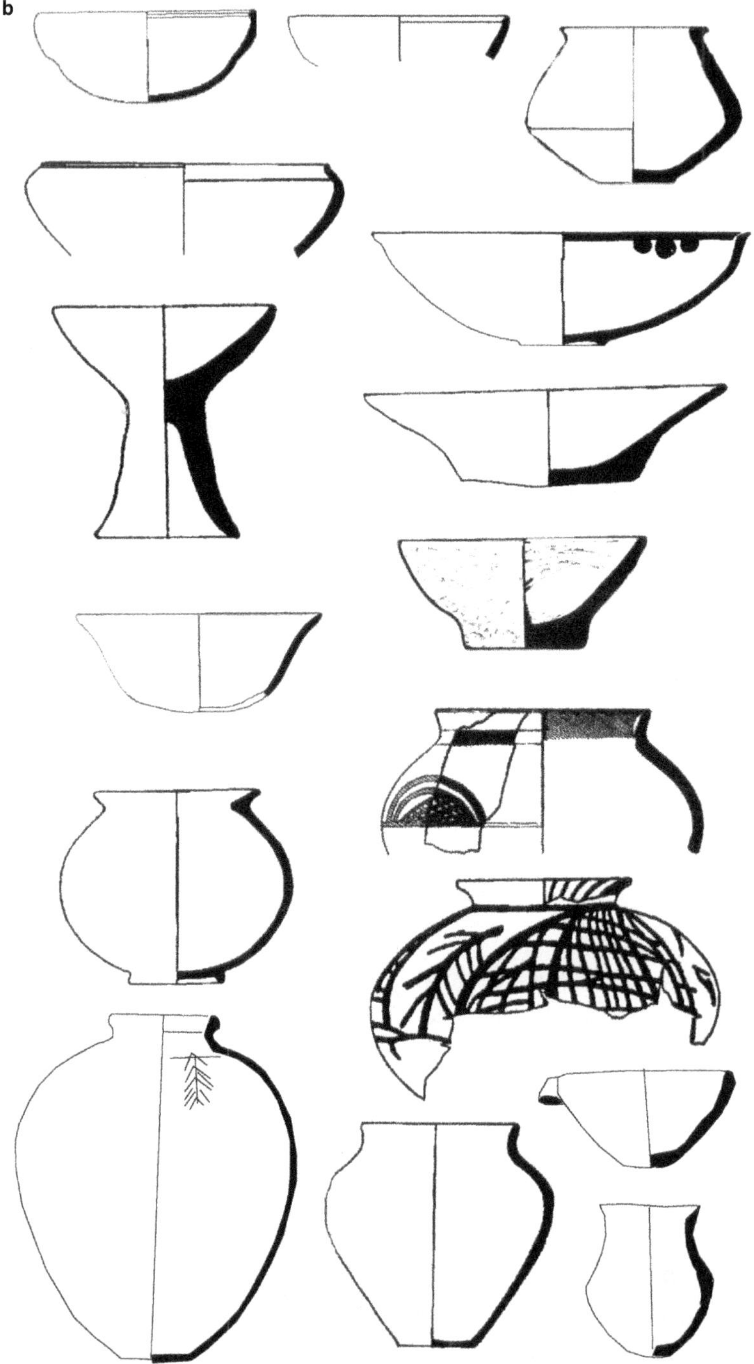

Figure 37.1. (b) Fourth millennium B.C.E. piedmont and highland pottery types.

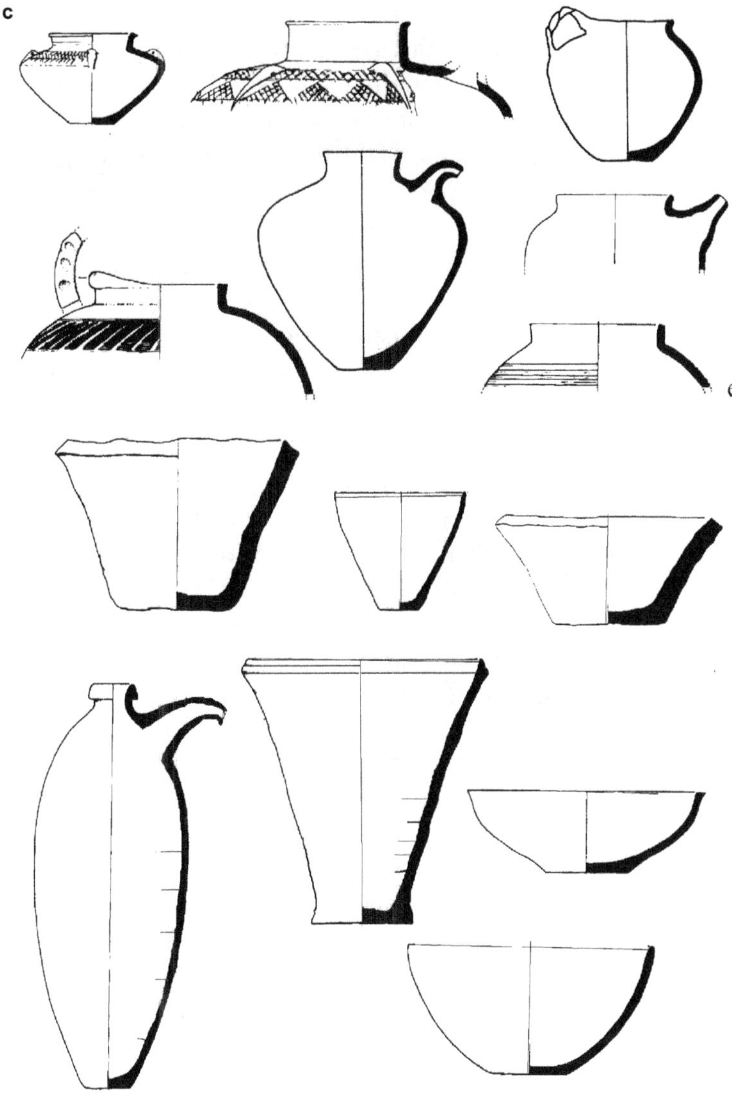

Figure 37.1. (c) Fourth millennium B.C.E. classic Uruk pottery types.

Such down-the-line networks existed in the broader Middle East from Upper Palaeolithic times onward. However, in societies hungry for these resources both as a symbolic representation of new ranks and social arrangements and as materials for production, such essentially haphazard exchange networks would not suffice. Instead, as one part of the new adaptations of the south, they promoted a more formal, controlled trading system, often subsumed under the term "the Uruk Expansion." This system came into being to move the desired raw materials or goods in the desired amounts as directly as possible to their final destination with a minimum of intermediaries. For Algaze—most scholars agree with this point—such an exchange network was more systematic, formal, and controlled (see Wright 1972).

The use of clay sealings on packages stamped or later rolled with a seal bearing the identity of an official who was authorized to open the package at its destination site, supports the idea of a formal, administered system (Rothman 1994). Proof that such control extended from the south into the Anatolian north comes from Hacınebi (see following discussion for greater detail). Its excavator, Gil Stein, believes he found a district of southern traders in residence within the small town. The clay of one of the sealings found in that quarter can be chemically traced back to its source at Susa (Blackman 1999). In short, societies within eastern and southeastern Anatolia played a key role as suppliers in this Uruk Expansion system.

Where the work of Algaze becomes more controversial and where interpretation of materials from Anatolian sites becomes essential is the part of his theory on the political and social consequences of this trading system on the different northern societies involved. He likens the situation to a world system, a concept that Wallerstein (1974) used to describe the trading relations of the Old and New Worlds as capitalism emerged in the sixteenth century C.E. In Algaze's model, southern leaders in various city-states designed and administered this entire system without military force; they created an informal economic empire. For the northern and eastern peripheries, little changed in their economies and polities as a whole, according to Algaze. They were only providing raw materials and simple products. On the other hand, as in any traditional colonial system, the southerners would be

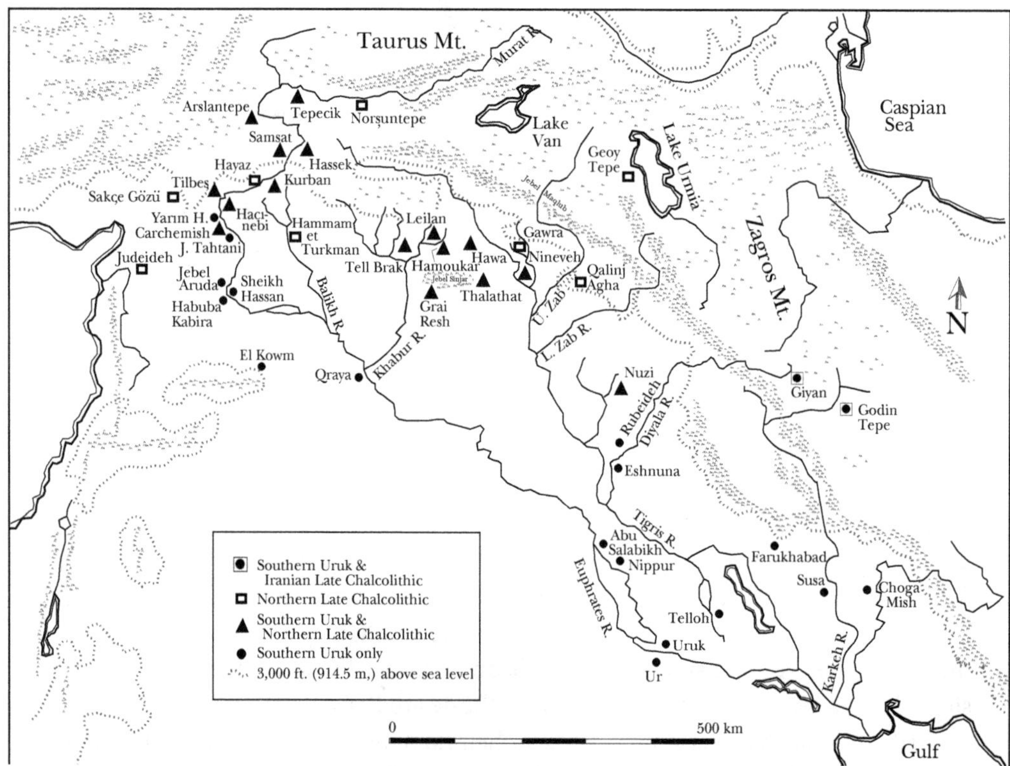

Figure 37.2. Distribution of Greater Mesopotamian fourth millennium B.C.E. sites by cultural affiliation.

converting imported raw materials into products for exchange within the southern core and for export back to the north.

> If, as Jacobs argues, a key cause of development is imports added to capital and labor which produce value-added exports, then southern Mesopotamian societies had a substantial and irrevocable advantage over peripheral polities in that both labor and capital (agricultural and pastoral, and piscatorial surpluses and status-marking exotics) were more easily mobilized and redistributed in the south than elsewhere because of the inherent superiority of southern water-borne transport systems. (Algaze 2001a:214–15)

Certainly, "changes in administrative or generally ranked organization [in an exchange network] are catalyzed only when regulation of long-distance exchange (trade) and production is one of the primary needs served by administrative forms of social organization" (Rothman and Blackman 2003:18). However, does having an advantage necessarily explain what was happening independently in the north?

For Algaze, then, this acquisition of exotic goods was a key both to general economic prosperity and to the development of administrative hierarchy, somewhat like the Mesoamerican site of Teotihuacan, whose place and astounding growth was catalyzed by the production and trade of obsidian blades (Blanton et al. 1993:235). What it produced was unequal development and administrative capability of the core societies, those more politically, socially, and economically sophisticated ones that actually controlled the system (the south), versus those less sophisticated societies on the periphery that are controlled by core states and provide raw materials and a ready market for southern-produced goods.

We have defined a world system as one in which there is an extensive division of labor. As Wallerstein (1974:349) writes, "This division is not merely functional—that is, occupational, but geographical. . . . The peripheries are economies dominated by subsistence agriculture and animal husbandry. The societies of the periphery lack technical skill in craft production and therefore supply the core with raw materials."

In the middle between the core and the peripheral areas, what Wallerstein calls the semi-periphery existed as funnels for trade goods. In Greater Mesopotamia, these would have been the northern Syrian sites, including Habuba Kabira, Jebel Aruda, perhaps Nineveh on the Tigris, and most important of all Tell Brak (Oates and Oates 1997), whose early growth may undermine the claim of no sophistication in the north.

> The semi-periphery is a necessary structural element in a world economy. These areas play a role parallel to that played [. . .] by middle trading groups in an empire. They are collection points of vital skills that are politically unpopular. [. . .] The colonies or emplacements from the core are islands of undiluted core culture stuck in the midst of foreign lands. Locals may adopt some symbolic elements from core cultures, but they do so en masse without adaptation to local customs. (Wallerstein 1974:349)

Algaze emphasizes the importance of the socially signifying "luxury" goods.

> Thus, the ability to acquire, display, and distribute exotic imports becomes crucial to the success of self-aggrandizing leaders in legitimizing their unequal access to resources and power. Those imports become, in short, central to the very reproduction of the social order. More specifically, in the Uruk case the flow of status-validating imports had to be maintained at all costs since an interruption would have led to a loss—no doubt unacceptable—of legitimacy for Uruk urban élites. (Algaze 2001b:59)

The development of the dendritic trading network under the control of centralized leaders in the more powerful city-states therefore met these ideological needs of the state élites to symbolize their new social roles. Because the prevailing images of the gods in LC 1–5 (table 37.1) were as providers from afar (Jacobsen 1976), this also may represent a kind of sanctification (see Drennan 1976 for discussion of religious sanctification as a basis of political authority).

Algaze further proposes that at the end of the fourth millennium B.C.E., this trading system collapsed. Evidence for this is the abandonment of a number of key sites on the dendritic network, a lack of southern pottery styles in the north, and the supposed collapse of northern societies.

Many disagree with one or another element of Algaze's interpretation (for example, Butterlin 2003; Frangipane 2001; Johnson 1988/89; Rothman 1993, 2001b; Schwartz 1988, 2001; Stein 1990, 1999a, 1999b, 2001; Wright 1995). Some of these disagreements highlight the extent of southern reach. For example, Stein (1999a) questions the ability of early city-states to project authority over such a great travel distance; the important factor is not simply distance but the means of transport and the time needed to move between points on the map. For the fourth millennium B.C.E., the Tigris was not easily navigated northward or southward past the area of the later site of Babylon. The Euphrates was more easily navigated southward on rafts and barges for some distance, but travel northward was largely by foot and donkey pack.

For my purposes here, the focus of that disagreement is an analysis of the organization and evolution of societies in southeastern and eastern Anatolia represented by a number of key sites. If one accepts, as most people do, that an Uruk Expansion trading system existed, and furthermore, if one accepts, as Algaze (2008) proposes in his latest work, with which I generally agree, that the south had tremendous structural advantages in this trade, does that necessarily imply that Wallerstein's description of the periphery applies to the Mesopotamian case, in particular to the development of northern and Anatolian societies?

My own predilection is that first, the northern societies were involved in this trade, and it did affect the evolution of these societies, but second, they were already developing, so that the nature of this interaction was not the same in extent or kind as the case of the sixteenth century C.E. and the indigenous societies of the New World and their initial European colonists. Through an analysis of the particular cases from the native point of view of the north, I believe, this position garners support.

Evolution and Interaction with Southern Mesopotamia in Fourth Millennium B.C.E. Anatolia

In focusing on Anatolian sites we must remember that the modern border of Turkey does not represent the ancient landscape (see Ur, chapter 38 in this volume, for specific discussion of Anatolian landscapes in the southeast). Many of the southeasternmost provinces of modern Turkey (Gaziantep, Şanlıurfa, Mardin, and Cizre) are continuations of the north Syrian or northern Iraqi steppe lands. The Hatay is part of the Mediterranean littoral. Malatya with its important site, Arslantepe, and neighboring Elazığ province are within the eastern Turkish Taurus Mountain zone. The area of Siirt province along the east–west branch of the Tigris River north of the Turkish border represents a somewhat different ecological zone from the Upper Euphrates area north of the Syrian–Turkish border to its west. It has more grasslands and a piedmont environment. However, neither in Cizre-Silopi (Algaze 1993:37) nor upstream at Kenan Tepe (Painter 2007; Parker and Dodd 2005) do significant amounts of Uruk-styled artifacts appear. A cultural boundary at the current Turkish–Iraqi border appears odd because the area to its north is a rich source of obsidian, and Uruk Expansion trade affects areas in the Transcaucasus and beyond (Anthony 2007). However, the same sorts of cultural disjuncture between these areas continued for a long period of time.

As a result, I will look at the evolutionary trajectories and the probable role of interaction with the south by zone, primarily the Upper Euphrates area from Carchemish to Samsat, and the highland sites in Malatya and Elazığ. The situation in the northern Tigris has already been mentioned; the Hatay, despite the early survey and excavation work of the Braidwoods on the Amuq Plain (Braidwood and Braidwood 1960) does not yet offer a density of data on the issue at hand (Algaze 1993:93). Table 37.1 sets the relative chronology of the various sites and areas we discuss within the wider region.

The Upper Euphrates Zone

The area of the Upper Euphrates in Turkey is a continuation of the steppes of north Syria. Sites like Habuba Kabira (Strommenger 1980), Jebel Aruda (van Driel 2002; van Driel and van Driel-Murray 1983), Jerablus Tahtani (Bolger and Stephen 1999; Peltenburg et al. 1996), and Shiukh Fawqani (Bachelot and Fales 2005) are really part of this one contiguous area. On the Turkish side of the border, the banks of the river have been surveyed a number of times as part of the salvage for the Keban, Karababa, Birecik, and Carchemish Dam projects (Algaze, Breuninger, and Knudstad 1994; and Özdoğan 1977 are the most complete).

From the late fifth millennium B.C.E. to the beginning of the third, settlement along this stretch changed significantly (figure 37.3). Before the Uruk Expansion

Table 37.1. Modified SAR Chronological Framework

B.C.E.			South		Iran	Syria				Upper Euphrates		Tigris		Southern Mesopotamiaa
3000		IVA									Arslantepe	Mohammad	Nineveh	
	LC5	Eanna		Nippur	Early 17	HabubaKabira	Sheik	Brak		Hassek	VIA Kurban	Arab	(Gut)	Late Uruk
		IVB–V		XV–XVII	Susa	Jebel Aruda	Hassan 4	TW		Höyük	V	Late Uruk	Späturuk	
	late				*Acropole*			11/12					Ninevite	
		Eanna											4	
		VI			Late 18								L: 31–20	
3400	LC 4	Eanna	Abu	Nippur	Susa		Sheikh	Brak		Hacınebi			Norduruk	Late
		VII	Salabikh	XVIII	Early 18		Hassan	TW		B2	Kurban IV		B	Middle
			Uruk		Sharafabad		5–7	13	Leilan				L: 37–31	Uruk
			Mound	hiatus?					IV	Hacınebi	Arslantepe			
3600					Susa	Qraya				B1	VII			
	LC 3	Eanna		Nippur	19–22		Sheikh	Brak				Tepe Gawra	Norduruk	Early
		IX–VIII		XIX–XX			Hassan	TW			Norşuntepe	VIII	A	Middle
							8–10/13	14–17	Leilan		J/K 18/19		L: 45–37	Uruk
3800		Eanna							V			Tepe Gawra		
	late 2	XI–X ?				Hammam and						IX–X	Gawra	
						Turkman				Hacınebi			B	
	LC 2	Eanna				VB		Brak		A		Tepe Gawra	L: 59–45	Early
4000		XII			hiatus?			TW	hiatus?		Norşuntepe	XI/XA		Uruk
	early 2							18–19			J/K 17		Gawra A	
4200						Hammam						Tepe Gawra		
	LC 1	Eanna			Susa	and Turkman					Arslantepe	XIA/B	hiatus?	
		XVI–XIV			Acropolis	VA					VIII	Tepe Gawra		'Ubaid
					23–27	Hammam and			Leilan			XII	L: 60	transitional
	End.					Turkman			late					'Ubaid 4?
	Ubaid					IVD			VIb			XIIA–XIII		

(known as the Contact Period), occupation from Carchemish to Hacınebi was fairly sparse. A few sites existed on the river bank near modern Birecik. South of Birecik toward Carchemish a few more sites, including the hilltop site of Tiladir, were occupied. A number of scholars feel that Carchemish, which became a major river crossing site in Hittite times, was founded in the later fourth millennium B.C.E. (Falsone and Sconzo 2007).

Hacınebi is the site we probably know most about from the early fourth millennium B.C.E., found in Levels A and B1 (Stein 1999a, 1999b, 2001, 2002; Stein and Mısır 1993, 1994a, 1994b, 1996; Stein et al. 1996a, 1996b, 1997, 1998). Aside from agricultural pursuits, the residents of Hacınebi in this pre-Contact Period apparently were already engaged in production of the sorts of metals and lithic remains that later flowed southward. The presence of tuyere blow pipes, smelting pits, and slag "indicates that labor-intensive blowpipe smelting was practiced at the site" (Stein et al. 1998:173). This is not to imply a workshop or centralized production system. Excavators found slag, debitage, and other remains of productive activities in many places (domestic units?) within the site. Nonetheless, signs of some ranking and

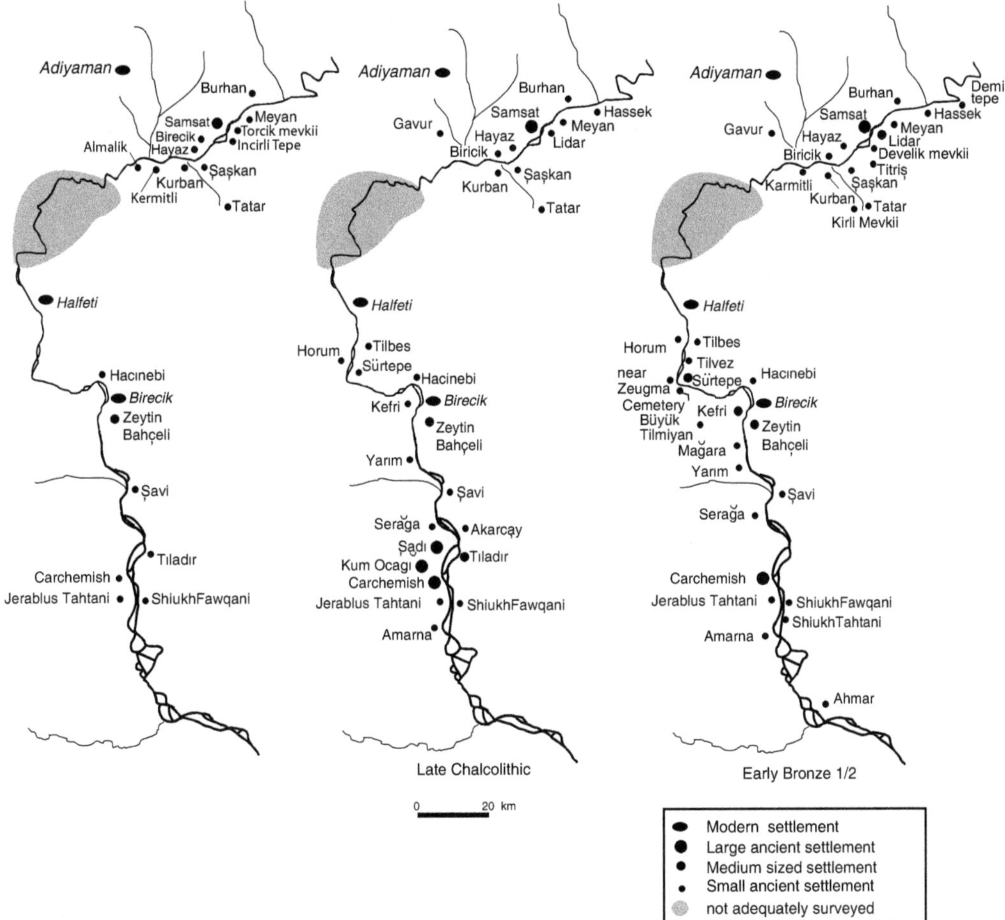

Figure 37.3. Changing Upper Euphrates site distribution during the fourth millennium B.C.E.

control systems existed. Seals and sealings, a technology that had blanketed Mesopotamia since Neolithic times (von Wickede 1990), were present. In addition an enclosure wall and large stone platform suggest the sorts of access to labor that define chiefly societies. The existence of a geographically broad exchange network for fine pottery at the same time in the Iraqi-Syrian Jezirah (Rothman and Blackman 2003) suggests that exchange was important in structuring societies even then. These same pottery styles match those in the highlands of eastern Turkey (especially Norşuntepe; see later discussion; see also Rothman 2002a, 2002b for trade in exotic materials in the pre-Contact Period). The sphere of the exchange was not so much north–south as northeast to northwest in the pre-Contact Period.

Hacınebi in the following B2 phase was characterized by the same basic style repertoire as the previous period. However, concentrated in the northeastern part of the site a full set of southern Uruk pottery was found. In addition excavators uncovered other clearly southern material, such as wall cones that adorned some structures (Stein 2002:151). Other northern sites, such as the southern-inspired Sheikh Hassan have them as well (Boese 1995). Excavators also found southern cruciform stone weights, a conical-headed copper pin, and even clay sickles, never used in the lithics-rich north. In addition, excavators recovered distinctly southern administrative tools like cylinder, as opposed to stamp, seals on hollow clay bullae in this same quarter. One of the most long-lasting ethnic behaviors is food preferences in choice of animal, cuts of meat, and preparation. Bigelow (1999) showed that animal bones from the Uruk quarter reflected typical southern as opposed to northern meat preferences (also more cattle and pig than sheep/goat). Evidence also suggests that each community raised their own food and their own animals.

Overall, the impression one gets from this site is not one of outside control. As Stein (2002:153) writes,

> Perhaps the most telling evidence for the economic autonomy of the two communities at Hacınebi comes from the administrative or record keeping artifacts. The Mesopotamians and Anatolians each had their own culturally specific record keeping systems. [. . .] If the Mesopotamians were being supplied with food, craft goods or other commodities by the local people in a system of asymmetrical exchange, we would expect to find large amounts of Anatolian seals in the Mesopotamian part of the site. [. . .] However, this is *NOT* the case.

This along with an absence of any signs of conflict would not support the idea of southern control, either economically or politically.

The case of Hacınebi raises another problem with the discussion of the Uruk Expansion. What Stein calls a colony is really a trading district within an established town, much like the *kārum* at Kaneš. Schwartz (1988) compares these to Greek trading colonies of a later age. The implication is that the local leaders permitted them to live there. Algaze's colonial, "imperial" model is one in which, more like the British raj in India, the core states have coopted the very administrative core of the local body politic. Stein's argument appears plausible; Algaze's less so. Earlier (Rothman 1993), I raised problems I found apparent in Algaze's theory.

Among other things, I wondered how this could be a peaceful system with no threat of military consequences. Subsequently, some have seen Sheikh Hassan as a barracks town (Boese 1995). Recent excavations at Tell Brak, which its excavators believe was taken over by southern soldiers in the LC 5, Late Uruk, have yielded a suburb with many randomly buried dead (McMahon et al. 2007). They could be the local dead from battle, but more research is necessary. No such evidence appears in Anatolia, however.

Other of the sites south of Birecik yielded remains that imply some southern influence. For example, Tiladir grew to a large size and was covered with Uruk artifactual remains (see Algaze 1993:fig. 13), and Şadi Tepe was blanketed with lithic debitage and Uruk pottery (personal observation). These sites, however, have not been excavated; Tiladir has been bulldozed.

Excavations in the area near modern Adıyaman farther up the Euphrates River have produced much evidence of local development and cross-cultural contact. These sites were in the Karababa Dam reservoir and are now mostly flooded. Samsat, the huge town site that was occupied from Neolithic to Roman times, sits on a major river crossing. The routes to and through the north no doubt defined the dendritic connections that Algaze projects. One of those routes was certainly up (or perhaps more aptly down) the Euphrates. As important was a second route up the Tigris to modern Mosul, ancient Nineveh, where it cut across the Jezirah and Khabur basin past Tell Brak. Later historic (Algaze 1993:fig. 20) and prehistoric routes to Samsat (Rothman and Fuensanta 2003:fig. 4) connect it to the east–west route up the Balikh, not up the Euphrates. The existence of this route is verified by the distribution of Early Bronze Age Karababa painted wares from the Jezirah. This painted pottery is rare south of Adıyaman. Pittman (2001) has been able to trace these routes by analyzing the distribution of fourth millennium B.C.E. seal designs.

Even before the Contact Period, rank and site size analyses indicate that there was a multitiered settlement system with Samsat as its dominating center (Lupton 1996:22–24). Unfortunately, before flooding of the dam reservoir, only limited excavations were conducted at Samsat (e.g., Özgüç 1987). However, two nearby sites, Kurban (Algaze 1990) and sixty kilometers farther north, Hassek Höyük (Behm-Blanke 1985, 1986, 1989, 1992; Behm-Blanke et al. 1981, 1984) relate to our discussion.

Kurban Höyük was excavated in the Karababa Dam reservoir area to look at the developments in this subregion from the earlier prehistoric to the third millennium B.C.E. eras (Marfoe 1990). A particular interest was the sources of historically based trade in a peripheral resource area (Marfoe 1987). Kurban had a pre-Contact level with the typical pottery wares from figure 37.1a. As the fourth millennium B.C.E. continued, more Uruk wares began to appear alongside the Late Chalcolithic ware. Interestingly, all the wares, whether local or Uruk, appear to be made of the same clays and were made using a domestic mode of production (Evins 1989). Wright (in Evins 1989:283) comments that the Uruk pottery styles seem to be converging; Late Chalcolithic "hammer rim bowls" appeared suddenly in the later half of the fourth millennium B.C.E. at Susa. A single tablet-like piece was recovered in mid-fourth millennium B.C.E. Kurban Level IVA, as well as a limited number of stamp seals and sealings (Algaze 1990:fig. 167).

For the Samsat system, the overall structure, however, appears unchanged at the time Uruk wares appear, if perhaps somewhat more integrated (Lupton 1996:53–54). This could be viewed as Uruk influence, but could perhaps also be seen in another way entirely. As I argued for Tepe Gawra Level VIII at the beginning of the Uruk Expansion (Rothman 2002a) and will argue for Arslantepe below, these activities may not be controlled by southerners. Rather, the increased trade may be an opportunity for the already established local leaders to expand their areas of control and build on their already established rank by utilizing a network strategy (Peasnall and Rothman 1999) in which power is acquired by controlling trade relations with groups outside the local system. The center, Samsat in this case, would mediate the trade and be a central place to acquire such foreign goods, or in this case at least use a southern model for local production. This ancient reality belies Wallerstein's idea, already quoted, that the locals in the periphery could not integrate these foreign symbols into their native ideological system. If they could, by that very theory, they are less peripheral and more sophisticated partners in trade.

Seemingly, Hassek Höyük was a counter argument in favor of Algaze's theory. Built during the Contact Period on a bluff above the Euphrates River (see figure 37.4), the site was a small walled settlement, thought to be an Uruk trading station. It has Uruk pottery and glyptics, and wall cones on one building (Behm-Blanke 1986:pl. 2). However, there are problems with this argument as well. Why build your station sixty kilometers north of Samsat, when Samsat was the area's central place? Helwing (1999) points out that not only were there considerable local Late Chalcolithic pottery types—all pottery was locally made—but much of it was a hybrid of north and south forms and techniques. Even the buildings with wall cone design appear to be simple residences. Other tools, like lithic blades, were made in the local Anatolian style. Helwing writes (1999:97), "the assemblage from Hassek Höyük 5a–b can be best interpreted as representing the final outcome of a longer acculturation process."

The creation of a new hybridized pottery style over time at Hassek raises a core question in the interpretation of culture contact. The presence of pottery styles from a foreign source can mean the presence of foreigners, especially when at Hacınebi all other categories of artifacts and especially food preferences can be shown to have existed side by side with local materials. The mere presence of a foreign style, especially after hundreds of years of contact and in a context with local wares and styles, can mean something else entirely (see Özbal, chapter 8 in this volume, for additional discussion on these issues). As I wrote about Tepe Gawra (Rothman 2001b), emulation of foreign styles can have local meanings other than colonization or the presence of foreigners. The Brooklyn dialect began when wealthy New Yorkers copied an affectation of London élites. That élite dialect over time was copied by less wealthy New Yorkers to the point where the Brooklyn dialect became the norm and is often looked down on as working class. Similarly, as Helwing (1999:94) writes, "In order to understand the mechanisms behind that

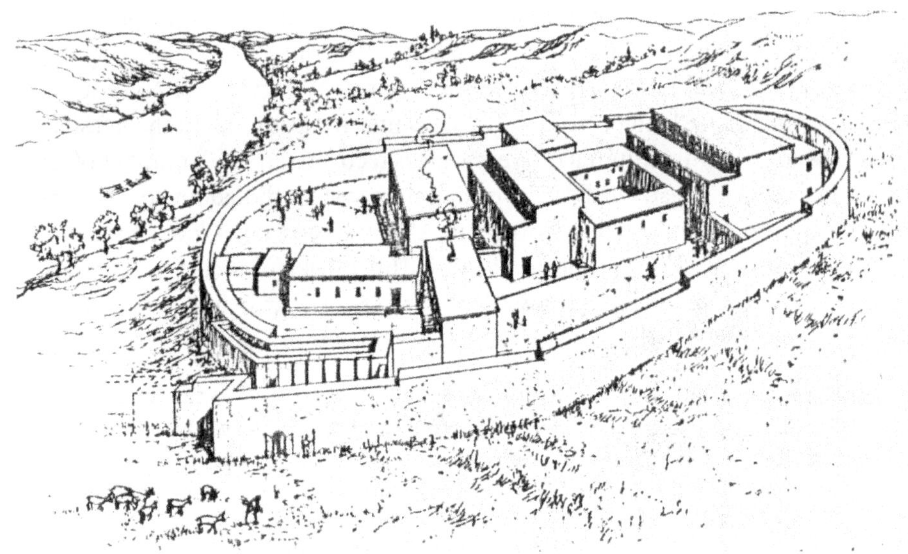

Figure 37.4. Reconstruction of Hassek Höyük fortress.

hybridization process [. . .] each of these continuities would mirror a deliberate decision of the producer which necessarily is based on his personal experience of the world, including his personal group affiliation." We have to be conscious that all these artifactual patterns represent a wide variety of possible native views of their meaning. One single pattern will not apply equally in every place and in every social context. We must see change from the local point of view and local circumstances (Rothman 2001a), a position that runs counter to Wallerstein, in which the unit of evolution is the entire world system.

Highland Eastern Turkey

Another area critical to our understanding of the Uruk influence is in the mountainous zones of Anatolia, which includes the provinces of Malatya and Elazığ. These areas are intermontane areas within the north and south massifs of the Taurus Mountain Range of eastern Turkey. Elazığ sits along the Murat River, which drains into the Euphrates near Arslantepe in Malatya. They are both located in the more optimal agricultural zones in the Taurus, and they sit among the greatest pasturelands of the Near East. The Altınova Plain of Elazığ has the best agricultural land in the more easterly intermontane zone (Yakar 1985:230f.). In Algaze's theory these would be resource extraction areas at the very end of the dendritic exchange networks. They are near a major copper mine at Ergani Maden.

Arslantepe is among the most extensively and carefully excavated sites in eastern Turkey (see Frangipane 1993, 1994, 1997, 2000, 2001, 2007, and chapter 45 in this volume; Frangipane and Palmieri 1983). It sits at the junction of routes from the east, north, south and west, which puts it in a unique position vis-à-vis the Uruk trade system. The site was founded very early in time on a natural bluff. In the pre-Contact Period, a massive temple-palace system was already in place, presumably supported by tribute from local settlers in village sites. A recent survey (Di Nocera 2006) paints a picture of Arslantepe as the primate center for this area. In the latest level, VIA, of the fourth millennium B.C.E., excavators recovered a small number of Uruk pottery forms. The already well-developed sealing system did adopt some cylinder seals, a southern invention, but contrary to Algaze (1993:102), it looks to me like a traditional northern iconography was used. This powerful local system appears to have depended on the acquisition of foodstuffs primarily and secondarily on control of some craft work and trade. As Frangipane (2001:339) writes,

> the public institutions at Arslantepe at the end of the fourth millennium seem to have acquired an enormous amount of power. What was this power based on? I cannot accept the hypothesis that Arslantepe was a secondary state, the result of a powerful outside impetus. [...] In combination, the elements of different cultural origins that one finds at Arslantepe IVA are only superficially related to southern Mesopotamia. [...] This is certainly not to deny the magnitude of the influence of southern groups on the north in the latter half of the fourth millennium. [...] The rarity and particular location of these [Uruk styled] findings clearly indicate that they were either imported materials or made locally on the basis of foreign typological models [...] and may have been elements that circulated at the level of the élites.

As the southerners used foreign and rare objects imported from the north and east as symbols of rank, so apparently did northerners use southern objects or styles.

In the Altınova of Elazığ, a number of sites were excavated. For our purposes the two most important are Norşuntepe (Gülçur 2000; Hauptmann 1972, 1975, 1976, 1982) and Tepecik (Esin 1972, 1975, 1976, 1982). Both of these sites and the earlier Değirmentepe (Esin 1989) produced ample evidence of metal smelting. Norşuntepe, however, had little to no evidence of Uruk artifacts, sharing styles mostly with the Iraqi piedmont sites (figure 37.1b). Tepecik was probably the largest site in the area. Lupton's gravity flow analysis (1996:51–52) suggests little social integration among sites, even those with any Uruk-styled material. These Uruk materials were not found in the center of the site, but only in an isolated structure on the southern slope of the mound. This may have been part of a series of rooms around an open court and surrounded by a wall. Some have referred to this as a trading post. That is certainly possible, but there is not enough known about it to say for certain.

Conclusions

Stating categorically that Algaze's theory is right or wrong ignores both the subtlety and the complexity of the ancient reality. Certainly the southern alluvium and the Anatolian north were aware of one another and in some sort of contact for millennia. I think few would deny that the trading system postulated by Algaze, beginning at about 3600 B.C.E., did exist and had a marked effect across the region. That effect may actually have been more important for the southern city-states than the northern polities. Algaze (2008) makes a strong case in his latest book that the economic and geographic landscape of the south was both primed and pumped by the opportunities presented by the trading system and the import of raw materials to make goods for distribution.

At the same time, the reverse may not be true. Because the trading system and productive and subsequent organizational changes did happen in the south, does that mean that the north was stagnant? In one section of his new book, Algaze (2008:117f.) writes about the "aborted urbanism" of the north as if the goal of northerners was to be urban and "civilized." In short, Wallerstein's World Systems model may be the wrong one for this case. The available evidence certainly argues that most of the societies in the north were not as underdeveloped as the New World societies in Wallerstein's model. The new trading opportunities catalyzed the growth of societies in northern Greater Mesopotamia. As Johnson (1988/89) and Schwartz (1988) have argued, there is no reason to assume that the founding even of the clearly southern sites in north Syria like Habuba Kabira and Jebel Aruda were directed by one city-state. If not, then, why would they be administered by one? It is more opportunistic than centrally planned.

The proof for this may be in the concept of collapse at the end of the fourth millennium B.C.E. The withdrawal of some of the north Syrian sites and the lack of southern pottery as northern polities replaced the older styles with Ninevite V wares in the east and Plain Simple Wares in the west would seem ample proof of a collapse. However, as evidenced by finds in early third millennium B.C.E. southern Mesopotamian sites, such as in the graves from Kish, Ur, and the Diyala (Delougaz 1967; Moorey 1978; Woolley 1955), those same northern-derived goods continued to flow, in regard to metals in ever greater quantities. How would that be possible if the system collapsed? The problem in assuming that the northern societies were too unsophisticated to exert control over their part in the trading system is that one cannot then explain the continuity of trade. New research in the same Upper Euphrates area (Peltenburg 2007; Rothman and Fuensanta 2003) rather implies that the stronger northern leaders took over the trading system, reorganized it, and their polities continued to grow until the emergence of urbanization in the north 300 or 400 years later. This should not be surprising if the residents of Hacınebi, Tepecik, and other places invited traders into their midst. This might be colonial in Stein's sense, but it is not imperialistic. The arrival of Transcaucasian peoples in the "periphery" was also timed to coincide with the activation of trade routes, early at Arslantepe, later at Godin in the Zagros (Rothman 2003).

Furthermore, if we want to understand the strategies of the ancients—that is, if we want to use the concept of agency—we have to follow Vitelli's (1998) suggestion to look up. We have to reconstruct the circumstances as the ancients could have perceived them. Wallerstein's model leads scholars, including Algaze, to frame their hypotheses from the viewpoint of what will come; namely, the Akkadian Empire of the late third millennium B.C.E. (Algaze 1993) or the economy of the early second millennium B.C.E., the Old Babylonian period (Algaze 2008). The ancients were not acting to achieve the results that later occurred. They could only see their actions and plans in terms of what they knew. Therefore, to conflate north Syria, southeastern Turkey, and highland eastern Turkey into one common framework will ultimately not explain local evolution, maybe not even for the south. Each area and each polity probably has somewhat unique circumstances.

Also, we need to consider more subtle alternatives. In some ways, the discussion of Algaze's theory has become like early discussions in the New Archaeology of the 1970s. Everything was either diffusion and migration or local invention, almost always the latter. Of course, all three processes could have and often did happen concomitantly. The same could be said here. In a recent analysis of the Oval at Godin Tepe in Iran (Rothman and Badler 2011), one of the examples Algaze gives of an Uruk emplacement, we concluded that the residents of the Oval were locals, but they were working with a representative of some southern state, who may or may not have been in residence. They marked goods going to the final destination with a southern-styled cylinder seal, whose owner or office would have been recognized at the end point, but used local seals for exchanges within the polity or with close neighbors. Algaze was neither completely right, nor completely wrong.

Last, we need to continue what a number of people have started. We need to explore further the behavioral and ideological correlates of style, so that we can generate more sophisticated interpretations of their meaning, or more realistically, how style was used by the ancients for a variety of purposes.

REFERENCES

Algaze, Guillermo. 1986. *Mesopotamian Expansion and Its Consequences: Informal Empire in the Late Fourth Millennium BC*. Ph.D. dissertation. Oriental Institute, University of Chicago.

———. 1989. The Uruk Expansion: Cross-Cultural Exchange in Early Mesopotamian Civilization. *Current Anthropology* 30: 571–608.

———. 1990. *Town and Country in Southeastern Anatolia. Volume 2: The Stratigraphic Sequence*. Oriental Institute Publications 110. Chicago: Oriental Institute, University of Chicago.

———. 1993. *The Uruk World System*. Chicago: University of Chicago Press.

———. 2001a. Initial Social Complexity in Southwestern Asia: The Mesopotamian Advantage. *Current Anthropology* 43: 199–233.

———. 2001b. The Prehistory of Imperialism: The Case of Uruk Period Mesopotamia. In *Uruk Mesopotamia and its Neighbors: Cross-Cultural Interactions in the Era of State Formation*, ed. Mitchell S. Rothman, 27–84. Santa Fe, N.M.: School of American Research.

———. 2005. The Sumerian Takeoff. Structure and Dynamics 1. http://repositories.cdlib.org/imbs/socdyn/sideas/vol1/issI/art52.

———. 2008. *Ancient Mesopotamia at the Dawn of Civilization*. Chicago: University of Chicago Press.

Algaze, Guillermo, Ray Breuninger, and James Knudstad. 1994. The Tigris-Euphrates Archaeological Reconnaisance Project: Final Report of the Birecik and Carchemish Dam Survey Areas. *Anatolica* 20: 1–96.

Anthony, David. 2007. *The Horse, the Wheel, and Language*. Princeton, N.J.: Princeton University Press.

Bachelot, Luc and Frederick Mario Fales, eds. 2005. *Tell Shiukh Fawqani 1994–1998*. Padova: S.A.R.G.O.N Editrice e libreria.

Behm-Blanke, Manfred. 1985. Die Ausgrabungen auf dem Hassek Höyük im Jahre 1984. *Kazı Sonuçları Toplantısı* 7: 87–102.

———. 1986. Die Ausgrabungen auf dem Hassek Höyük im Jahre 1985. *Kazı Sonuçları Toplantısı* 8: 139–48.

———. 1989. Mosaiksifte am oberen Euphrat-Wandschmuck aus Uruk-Zeit. *Istanbuler Mitteilungen* 39: 73–83.

———. 1992. *Hassek Höyük: Naturwissenschaftliche Untersuchen und Lithische Industrie*. Tübingen: Ernst Wasmuth Verlag.

Behm-Blanke, M., J. Boesneck, A. van der Driesch, M. Roh, and G. Wiegand. 1981. Hassek Höyük: Vorläufiger Bericht über Ausgrabungen den Jahren 1978–1980. *Istanbuler Mitteilungen* 31: 11–94.

Behm-Blanke, Manfred, M. Roh, Norbert Karg, L. Masch, F. Parsche, K. L. Weiner, and Alwo von Wickede. 1984. Hassek Höyük: Vorläufiger Bericht über Ausgrabungen den Jahren 1981–83. *Istanbuler Mitteilungen* 34: 31–150.

Bigelow, Lauren. 1999. Zooarchaeological Investigations of Economic Organization and Ethnicity at Late Chalcolithic Hacınebi: A Preliminary Report. In *The Uruk Expansion: Northern Perspectives from Hacınebi, Hassek Höyük, and Tepe Gawra*, ed. Gil Stein. *Paléorient* 25.1: 83–90.

Blackman, M. James. 1999. Chemical Characterization of Local Anatolian and Uruk Style Sealing Clays from Hacınebi. In *The Uruk Expansion: Northern Perspectives from Hacınebi, Hassek Höyük, and Tepe Gawra*, ed. Gil Stein. *Paléorient* 25.1: 51–56.

Blanton, Richard, Stephen Kowalewski, Gary Feinman, and Laura Finsten. 1993. *Ancient Mesoamerica: A Comparison of Change in Three Regions*, 2nd ed. Cambridge: Cambridge University Press.

Boese, Johannes. 1995. *Ausgrabungen in Tell Sheikh Hassan: Vorläufige Berichte über die Grabungskampagnen 1984–1990 und 1992–1994*. Saarbrücken: Saarbrücker Druckerei und Verlag.

Bolger, Diane and Fiona Stephen. 1999. Scientific Analysis of Uruk Ceramics from Sites of the Syrian and Southeast Anatolian Euphrates: Preliminary Results. In *Archaeology of the Upper Syrian Euphrates, the Tishrin Dam Area, Aula Orientalis-Supplementa* 15, ed. G. del Olmo Lete and J.-L. Montero Fenollòs, 301–10. Barcelona: Editorial Ausa.

Braidwood, Robert and Linda Braidwood. 1960. *Excavations in the Plain of Antioch, the Early Assemblages*. Oriental Institute Publications 61. Chicago: University of Chicago Press.

Butterlin, Pascal. 2003. *Les Temps Proto-Urbains de Mésopotamie*. Paris: CNRS Editions.

Delougaz, Pinhas. 1967. *Private Houses and Graves in the Diyala Region*. Chicago: University of Chicago Press.

Di Nocera, Gian Maria. 2006. Mobility and Stability: Preliminary Observations on Early Bronze Age Settlement Organization. In *Mountains and Valleys: A Symposium on Highland–Lowland Interaction in Bronze Age Settlement Systems of Eastern Anatolia,*

Transcaucasus, and Northwestern Iran, ed. Barbara Helwing and Aynur Özfırat. *Archäologische Mitteilungen aus Iran und Turan* 37: 63–70.
Drennan, Richard. 1976. Religion and Social Evolution in Formative Mesoamerica. In *The Early Mesoamerican Village*, ed. Kent Flannery, 345–63. New York: Academic Press.
Esin, Ufuk. 1972. Tepecik Excavations, 1970. *Keban Project 1970 Activities*. Middle East Technical University 3:149–60. Ankara. Middle East Technical University.
———. 1975. Tepecik 1974. *Anatolian Studies* 25: 46–49.
———. 1976. Tepecik Excavations, 1973. *Keban Project 1973 Activities*. Middle East Technical University 6:97–112. Ankara: Middle East Technical University.
———. 1982. Tepecik Excavations, 1974. *Keban Project 1974–75 Activities*. Middle East Technical University 7:95–118. Ankara: Middle East Technical University.
———. 1989. An Early Trading Center in Eastern Anatolia. In *Anatolia and the Ancient Near East, Studies in Honor of Tahsin Özgüç*, ed. Kutlu Emre, Machteld Mellink, Barthel Hrouda, and Nimet Özgüç, 135–41. Ankara: Türk Tarih Kurumu Basımevi.
Evins, Mary. 1989. The Late Chalcolithic/Uruk Period in the Karababa Basin, Southeastern Turkey. In *Out of the Heartland: The Evolution of Complexity in Peripheral Mesopotamia during the Uruk Period*, ed. Mitchell S. Rothman. *Paléorient* 15.1: 281–82.
Falsone, Gioacchino and Paola Sconzo. 2007. The "Champagne-Cup" Period at Carchemish. In *Euphrates River Settlement: The Carchemish Sector in the Third Millennium BC*, ed. Edgar Peltenburg, 73–93. Oxford: Oxbow Books.
Frangipane, Marcella. 1993. Local Components in the Development of Centralized Societies in Syro-Anatolian Regions. In *Between the Rivers and over the Mountains: Archaeologica Anatolica et Mesopotamica Alba Palmieri Dedicata*, ed. Marcella Frangipane, Harald Hauptmann, Mario Liverani, Paolo Matthiae, and Machteld Mellink, 133–61. Roma: Università di Roma "La Sapienza."
———. 1994. The Record Function of Clay Sealings in Early Administrative Systems as Seen from Arslantepe-Malatya. In *Archives before Writing*, ed. Piera Ferioli, Enrica Fiandra, Gian G. Fissore, and Marcella Frangipane, 125–37. Rome: Scriptorium.
———. 1997. A 4th Millennium Temple/Palace Complex at Arslantepe-Malatya. *Paléorient* 23.1: 45–73.
———. 2000. The Late Chalcolithic/EB I Sequence at Arslantepe. In *Chronologies de Pays du Caucase et de L'Euphrate aux IVe–IIIe Millénaires*, ed. Catherine Marro and Harald Hauptmann, 439–72. Institut Français d'Etudes Anatoliennes d'Istanbul, Varia Anatolica 11. Paris: De Boccard.
———. 2001. Centralization Processes in Greater Mesopotamia: Uruk "Expansion" as the Culmination of an Early System of Intra-Regional Relations. In *Uruk Mesopotamia and its Neighbors: Cross-Cultural Interactions in the Era of State Formation*, ed. Mitchell S. Rothman, 307–48. Santa Fe, N.M.: School of American Research.
———. ed. 2007. *Arslantepe Cretulae: An Early Centralised Administrative System Before Writing*. Rome: Università di Roma "La Sapienza."
Frangipane, Marcella and Alba Palmieri. 1983. A Protourban Centre of the Late Uruk Period. *Origini* 14.2: 287–454.
Gülçur, Sevil. 2000. Norsuntepe: Die Chalkolithische Keramik (Elazığ/Ostanatolien). In *Chronologies de Pays du Caucase et de L'Euphrate aux Ive–IIIe Millénaires*, ed. Catherine Marro and Harald Hauptmann, 375–418. Institut Français d'Etudes Anatoliennes d'Istanbul, Varia Anatolica 11. Paris: De Boccard.
Hauptmann, Harald. 1972. Die Grabungen auf dem Norşun-Tepe, 1970. *Keban Project 1970 Activities*. Middle East Technical University 3: 103–22. Ankara: Middle East Technical University.

———. 1976. Die Grabungen auf dem Norşun-Tepe, 1973. *Keban Project 1973 Activities.* Middle East Technical University 6: 61–78. Ankara: Middle East Technical University.

———. 1982. Die Grabungen auf dem Norşun-Tepe, 1974. *Keban Project 1974–75 Activities.* Middle East Technical University 7: 41–70. Ankara: Middle East Technical University.

Helwing, Barbara. 1999. Cultural Interaction at Hassek Höyük, Turkey: New Evidence from Pottery Analysis. In *The Uruk Expansion: Northern Perspectives from Hacınebi, Hassek Höyük, and Tepe Gawra*, ed. Gil Stein. *Paléorient* 25.1: 91–100.

Jacobsen, Thorkild. 1976. *The Treasures of Darkness.* New Haven, Conn.: Yale University Press.

Johnson, Gregory. 1973. *Local Exchange and State Development in Southwest Iran.* Anthropological Papers of the Museum of Anthropology 51. Ann Arbor: University of Michigan Press.

———. 1988/89. Late Uruk in Greater Mesopotamia: Expansion or Collapse? *Origini* 14: 595–611.

Lupton, Alan. 1996. *Stability and Change: Socio-Political Development in North Mesopotamia and South-East Anatolia 4000–2700.* BAR International Series 627. Oxford: BAR International Series.

Marfoe, Leon. 1987. Cedar Forest to Silver Mountain: Social Change and the Development of Long Distance Trade in Early Near Eastern Societies. In *Centre and Periphery in the Ancient World*, ed. Michael Rowlands, Mogens Larsen, and Kristian Kristiansen, 25–35. Cambridge: Cambridge University Press.

———. 1990. Introduction. In *Town and Country in Southeastern Anatolia. Volume 1*, ed. Guillermo Algaze, 1–20. Oriental Institute Publications 110. Chicago: Oriental Institute of the University of Chicago.

McMahon, Augusta, Joan Oates, Salam al-Quntar, Michael Charles, Carlo Colantoni, Mette-Marie Hald, Philip Karsgaard, Lamya Khalidi, Arkadiusz Soltysiak, Adam Stone, and Jill Weber. 2007. Excavations at Tell Brak 2006–2007. *Iraq* 69: 145–71.

Moorey, Roger. 1978. *Kish Excavations 1923–1933.* London: Clarendon.

Oates, Joan and David Oates. 1997. An Open Gate: Cities of the Fourth Millennium B.C. (Tell Brak 1997). *Cambridge Archaeological Journal* 7: 287–307.

Özdoğan, Mehmet. 1977. *Lower Euphrates Basin Survey.* Ankara: Middle East Technical University.

Özgüç, Nimet. 1987. Samsat Mühürleri. *Belleten* 200: 429–40.

Painter, Catherine. 2007. Kenan Tepe: Exploring a Late Chalcolithic Village of the Upper Tigris. Society of American Archaeology (Austin). http://nes.berkeley.edu/~cpfoster/papers/saa2007_cpainter.pdf.

Parker, Bradley and Lynn Swartz Dodd. 2005. The Upper Tigris Archaeological Research Project: A Preliminary Report from the 2002 Field Season. *Anatolica* 31: 69–110.

Peasnall, Brian and Mitchell S. Rothman. 1999. Societal Evolution of Small, Pre-State Centers and Polities: The Example of Tepe Gawra in Northern Mesopotamia. *Paléorient* 25.1: 101–14.

Peltenburg, Edgar, ed. 2007. *Euphrates River Settlement: The Carchemish Sector in the Third Millennium BC.* Oxford: Oxbow Books.

Peltenburg, Edgar, Diane Bolger, Stuart Campbell, Mary Anne Murray, and Richard Tipping. 1996. Jerablus-Tahtani, Syria, 1995 Preliminary Report. *Levant* 28: 1–25.

Pittman, Holly. 2001. Intra-Regional Relations Reflected through Glyptic Evidence. In *Uruk Mesopotamia and its Neighbors: Cross-Cultural Interactions in the Era of State Formation*, ed. Mitchell S. Rothman, 403–44. Santa Fe, N.M.: School of American Research.

Rothman, Mitchell S. 1993. Another Look at the "Uruk Expansion" from the Tigris Piedmont. In *Between the Rivers and over the Mountains: Archaeologica Anatolica et Mesopotamica Alba Palmieri Dedicata*, ed. Marcella Frangipane, Harald Hauptmann, Mario Liverani, Paulo Matthiae, and Machteld Mellink, 163–77. Rome: Università di Roma "La Sapienza."

———. 1994. Sealings as a Control Mechanism in Prehistory: Tepe Gawra XI, X, and VIII. In *Chiefdoms and Early States in the Near East*, ed. Gil Stein and Mitchell S. Rothman, 103–20. Madison, Wisc.: Prehistory Press.

———. 2001a. The Local and the Regional: Introduction. In *Uruk Mesopotamia and its Neighbors: Cross-Cultural Interactions in the Era of State Formation*, ed. Mitchell S. Rothman, 3–26. Santa Fe, N.M.: School of American Research.

———. 2001b. The Tigris Piedmont and Eastern Jazira in the Fourth Millennium B.C. In *Uruk Mesopotamia and its Neighbors: Cross-Cultural Interactions in the Era of State Formation*, ed. Mitchell S. Rothman, 349–402. Santa Fe, N.M.: School of American Research.

———. 2002a. *Tepe Gawra. The Evolution of a Small, Prehistoric Center in Northern Iraq*. Philadelphia: University of Pennsylvania Museum Publications.

———. 2002b. Tepe Gawra: Chronology and Socio-Economic Change in the Foothills of Northern Iraq in the Era of State Formation. In *Artefacts of Complexity: Tracking the Uruk in the Near East*, ed. J. Nicholas Postgate, 49–77. Wiltshire, U.K.: British School of Archaeology in Iraq.

———. 2003. Ripples in the Stream: Transcaucasia-Anatolian Interaction in the Murat/Euphrates Basin at the Beginning of the Third Millennium B.C. In *Archaeology in the Borderlands: Investigations in Caucasia and Beyond*, ed. Adam Smith and Karen S. Rubinson, 95–110. Los Angeles: Cotsen Institute of Archaeology.

———. 2004. Studying the Development of Complex Society: Mesopotamia in the Late Fifth and Fourth Millennia BC. *Journal of Archaeological Research* 12.1: 75–119.

Rothman, Mitchell S. and Virginia Badler. 2011. Contact and Development in Godin Period VI. In *On the High Road: The History of Godin Tepe, Iran*, ed. Hilary Gopnick and Mitchell S. Rothman, 67–137. Toronto: Royal Ontario Museum/Mazda Press.

Rothman, Mitchell S. and M. James Blackman. 2003. Late Fifth Millennium Exchange Systems in Northern Mesopotamia: Chemical Characterization of Sprig and Impressed Wares. *Al-Rafidan* 26: 1–24.

Rothman, Mitchell S. and Jesús Fuensanta. 2003. The Archaeology of the Early Bronze I and II Periods in Southeastern Turkey and North Syria. In *Köyden Kente Dogu'da İlk Yerleimle*, ed. Mehmet Özdoğan, Harald Hauptmann, and Nezih Başgelen, 583–622. İstanbul: Arkeoloji ve Sanat Yayınları.

Schwartz, Glenn. 1988. Excavations at Karatut Mevkii and Perspectives on the Uruk/Jemdet Nasr Expansion. *Akkadica* 56: 1–41.

———. 2001. Syria and the Uruk Expansion. In *Uruk Mesopotamia and its Neighbors: Cross-Cultural Interactions in the Era of State Formation*, ed. Mitchell S. Rothman, 233–64. Santa Fe, N.M.: School of American Research.

Stein, Gil. 1990. Comment. *Current Anthropology* 31: 66–67.

———. 1999a. *Rethinking World Systems*. Arizona: Arizona University Press.

———. ed. 1999b. The Uruk Expansion: Northern Perspectives from Hacınebi, Hassek Höyük and Gawra. *Paléorient* 25.1: 7–172.

———. 2001. Indigenous Social Complexity at Hacınebi (Turkey) and the Organization of Uruk Colonial Contact. In *Uruk Mesopotamia and its Neighbors: Cross-Cultural Interactions in the Era of State Formation*, ed. Mitchell S. Rothman, 265–306. Santa Fe, N.M.: School of American Research.

———. 2002. The Uruk Expansion in Anatolia: A Mesopotamian Colony and its Indigenous Host Community at Hacınebi, Turkey. In *Artefacts of Complexity: Tracking the Uruk in the Near East*, ed. J. Nicholas Postgate, 149–73. Wiltshire, U.K.: British School of Archaeology in Iraq.

Stein, Gil and Adnan Mısır. 1993. Excavations at Hacınebi Tepe 1992. *Kazı Sonuçları Toplantısı* 15: 131–52.

———. 1994a. Mesopotamian-Anatolian Interaction at Hacınebi: Preliminary Report on the 1992 Excavations. *Anatolica* 20: 145–89.

———. 1994b. Excavations at Hacınebi Tepe 1993. *Kazı Sonuçları Toplantısı* 16: 121–40.

———. 1996. 1994 Excavations at Hacınebi Tepe. *Kazı Sonuçları Toplantısı* 17: 109–28.

Stein, Gil, Christopher Edens, Naomi Miller, Julie Pearce, Hadi Özbal, and Holly Pittman. 1996a. Southeast Anatolia before the Uruk Expansion: Preliminary Report on the 1997 Excavations at Hacınebi. *Anatolica* 22: 85–128.

Stein, Gil, Reinhard Bernbeck, Cheryl Coursey, Augusta McMahon, Naomi Miller, Adnan Mısır, Jeffrey Nicola, Holly Pittman, Susan Pollock, and Henry Wright. 1996b. Uruk Colonies and Anatolian Communities: An Interim Report on the 1992–93 Excavations at Hacınebi, Turkey. *American Journal of Archaeology* 100.2: 205–60.

Stein, Gil, Kenneth Boden, Christopher Edens, Julie Pearce Edens, Augusta McMahon, and Hadi Özbal. 1997. Excavations at Hacınebi 1996 Preliminary Report. *Anatolica* 23: 111–71.

Stein, Gil, Christopher Edens, Julie Pearce, Kenneth Boden, Nicola Laneri, Hadi Özbal, Bryan Earl A. Adriaens, and Holly Pittman. 1998. Southeast Anatolia before the Uruk Expansion: Preliminary Report on the 1997 Excavations at Hacınebi. *Anatolica* 24: 143–93.

Strommenger, Eva. 1980. *Habuba Kabira: Eine Stadt vor 5000 Jahren*. Mainz: Philipp von Zabern.

van Driel, Govert. 2002. Jebel Aruda: Variations on a Late Uruk Domestic Theme. In *Artefacts of Complexity: Tracking the Uruk in the Near East*, ed. J. Nicholas Postgate, 191–206. Wiltshire, U.K.: British School of Archaeology in Iraq.

van Driel, Govert and Carol van Driel-Murray. 1983. Jebel Aruda, the 1982 Season. *Akkadica* 33: 1–26.

Vitelli, Karen. 1998. "Looking up" at Early Eeramics in Greece. In *Pottery and People*, ed. James Skibo and Gary Feinman, 184–98. Salt Lake City: University of Utah Press.

von Wickede, Alwo. 1990. *Prähistorische Stempelglyptik in Vorderasien*. Munich: Profil Verlag.

Wallerstein, Immanuel. 1974. *The Modern World-System I*. New York: Academic Press.

Woolley, Sir Leonard. 1955. *Twelve Years of Digging at Ur*. London: Benn.

Wright, Henry. 1972. A Consideration of Interregional Exchange in Greater Mesopotamia: 4,000–3,000 B.C. In *Social Exchange and Interaction*, ed. Edwin N. Wilmsen, 95–106. Papers of the Museum of Anthropology 46. Ann Arbor: University of Michigan Press.

———. 1977. Toward an Explanation of the Origin of the State. In *Explanation of Prehistoric Change*, ed. James N. Hill, 215–30. Albuquerque: University of New Mexico Press.

———. 1994. Prestate Political Formations. In *Chiefdoms and Early States in the Near East*, ed. Gil Stein and Mitchell S. Rothman, 67–84. Madison, Wisc.: Prehistory Press.

———. 1995. Review of Algaze, Uruk World Systems. *American Anthropologist* 97: 151–52.

———. 1998. Uruk States in Southwestern Iran. In *Archaic States*, ed. Gary Feinman and Joyce Marcus, 173–98. Santa Fe, N.M.: School of American Research.

Wright, Henry and Gregory Johnson. 1975. Population, Exchange and Early State Formation in South Western Iran. *American Anthropologist* 77: 267–91.

Yakar, Jak. 1985. *The Later Prehistory of Anatolia: The Late Chalcolithic and Early Bronze Age*. BAR International Series 268 (i). Oxford: BAR International Series.

CHAPTER 38

ANCIENT LANDSCAPES IN SOUTHEASTERN ANATOLIA

JASON UR

A landscape approach to the archaeological record places past human activities into their geographic context, in relation to each other and to the physical landscape. It emphasizes the relationships between human communities and their landscapes, which include elements of the natural environment but also cultural features, such as settlements, roads, and agricultural systems. The cultural landscape is not limited to products of human modification; mountains, rivers, trees, and other "natural" features are given meaning by humans that conditions further action, whether or not they are physically changed. Such modification, whether through physical alteration, the assignment of meaning, or some combination thereof, separates landscape from environment. By this definition, almost all environments have become landscapes.

Geographic diversity and a long settlement history make southeastern Anatolia an excellent region for archaeological research on ancient landscapes (for the Near East in general, see Wilkinson 2003). Through the millennia, it has hosted agricultural villages, early cities, and great empires, all of which have had meaningful and productive relationships with their landscapes that have left varied traces for archaeological study. This chapter considers the nature of ancient landscapes and their archaeological investigation in southeastern Anatolia, one of the most intensively studied regions in modern Turkey.

Landscapes of Southeastern Anatolia and Their Challenges for Archaeology

The physical landscape of southeastern Anatolia (figure 38.1) originated with tectonic events that produced the Taurus Mountains, which frame this region to the north. Here rise the Tigris and Euphrates Rivers and their major tributaries, which cut their way south and east through the foothills. In the upper reaches, cold temperatures and thin soils limit the human potential to summer pasturing and mineral and ore extraction.

To the south, the rivers drop into the foothill zone, where they occasionally flow into broader alluvial plains such as the Altınova and Aşvan Plains in Elazığ along the Euphrates and Murat Rivers. These low plains are more suitable for cereal cultivation and have been the foci of sedentary settlement since the Neolithic.

The greatest challenge for the recovery of past landscapes in southeastern Anatolia stems from the rapidly changing nature of the modern landscape. Since the early twentieth century C.E., cities and towns have expanded dramatically, and the Turkish Republic has invested heavily in agricultural and infrastructural development to meet their food and energy requirements. These actions have greatly affected the survival of premodern landscape elements. Most obviously, the great hydroelectric dams of the Southeastern Anatolia Project (Güneydoğu Anadolu Projesi, or GAP) have now filled the former river valleys of the Euphrates with lakes, flooding hundreds of recorded sites and landscape features (Shoup 2006).

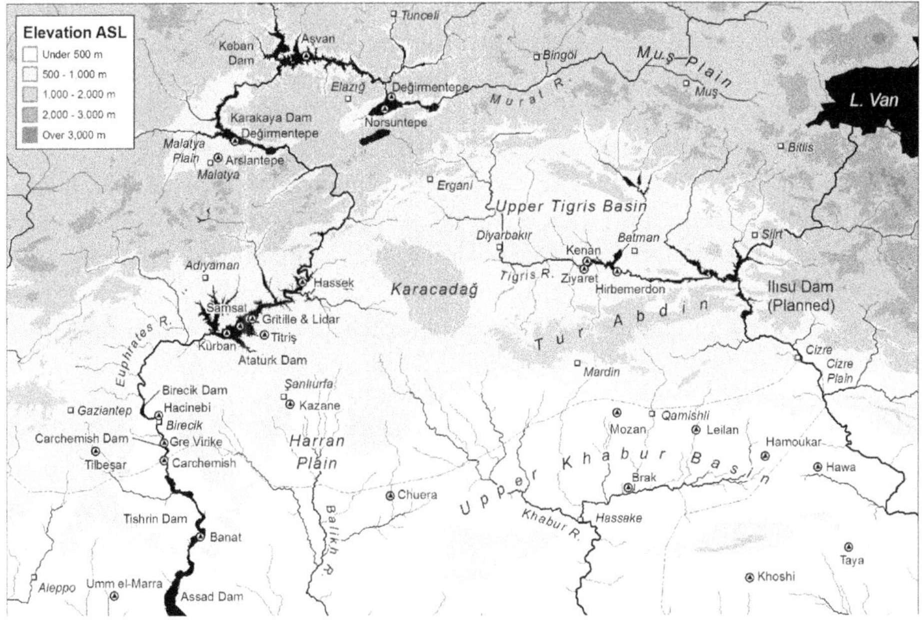

Figure 38.1. Sites, archaeological surveys, and dam zones in southeastern Anatolia.

A greater challenge arises from the secondary impacts: the corresponding expansion of towns and intensification of agriculture on the lands surrounding the dam zones. Population growth, widespread irrigation, and the availability of mechanized agricultural tools have resulted in the furthest extension of cultivation that the region has ever known. As a result, ephemeral landscape elements such as tracks, field systems, campsites, and activity areas have been effaced, and even more durable elements like canals and mounded sites have been partially or completely removed. The challenge is to record what remains of the premodern landscape and develop methods for reconstructing what has already been lost. At the same time, it is important to realize that these destructive processes are hardly unique to the twentieth century C.E. Neolithic landscape elements would have been partially erased by Early Bronze Age (EBA) farmers, their landscapes would have been altered by the actions of Hellenistic settlers, and so forth.

Reconstructions are also hampered by a strong research bias on river valleys, largely out of necessity in advance of dam construction, but the research agendas of archaeologists have coincided with such agendas. The valleys of the Tigris, Euphrates, and their tributaries have indeed been major foci of sedentary settlement, but they represent only one of many geographic zones in southeastern Anatolia. The foothill and montaine areas were the source of the timber, ore, and stone materials that made Anatolia of such importance for indigenous Anatolians and foreign traders and conquerors alike, but they have received little (or in many cases no) archaeological attention. Our landscape data are, therefore, heavily biased toward the settlements and landscapes of sedentary agriculturalists.

Landscape archaeologists often approach their subject matter using the metaphor of the palimpsest, a parchment document that has been written on again and again in such a way that the most recent inscription is the most legible but earlier inscriptions survive in fragmentary form. Cultural landscapes develop in an analogous process of construction, natural and cultural dismantlement, and further modification, so that what exists at a given moment is a highly complex product (Crang 1998:22–23; Wilkinson 2003:7). The attrition of past landscape elements is not a random process, however; landscape destruction is often patterned in ways that can be misleading for archaeological interpretation of earlier landscapes if taphonomic processes are not properly appreciated (Williamson 1998). In the case of southeastern Anatolia, the nearly continuous use of lowland plains and river valleys for agriculture since the Neolithic has left prehistoric and Bronze Age mounded sites standing as islands, with little or no evidence for contemporary off-site activity. Furthermore, the pastoral nomadic campsites in the river valleys in winter (Turkish *kışlak*) have been removed altogether. A naïve assessment might assume that pastoral nomads had avoided or been excluded from this zone (Alizadeh and Ur 2007).

The development of the landscape approach has been further hampered by the strong chronodisciplinary boundaries that characterize Near Eastern archaeology. Specialists in prehistory, the Bronze and Iron Ages, the Classical Periods, and the Late Antique/Islamic eras publish in different journals, attend different conferences, and are often housed in different academic departments, with infrequent interactions. Landscapes, however, preserve the impacts of human communities in all of these periods, none of which can be understood without a knowledge of antecedent conditions and succeeding development. The disinterest of most archaeologists in the Classical, Medieval, and Ottoman Periods in southeastern Anatolia is unfortunate, not just because these are the latest and therefore best-preserved elements of the landscape palimpsest, but also because they transformed the surviving record of Bronze and Iron Age landscapes. Imagine a future archaeologist who is interested in the Iron Age but professes no interest in the Republican period of the twentieth century C.E. His reconstruction of the Middle Bronze Age (MBA) landscape will be unaware of the sites inundated by the late twentieth-century dam and irrigation projects. It is unlikely that anyone would fail to account for the archaeological impacts of these major infrastructure projects, but what about earlier archaeological ones? The region was intensively cultivated and heavily irrigated in the sixteenth century (Göyünç and Hütteroth 1997), and we know that the Assyrians and Urartians were capable of major landscape transformations as well (Belli 1999; Ur 2005). Without appreciating these "late" landscapes, our interpretations of earlier ones will be flawed at best.

Thus landscape archaeology in southeastern Anatolia finds itself in a difficult position. The geographic emphases have been on the regions of highest landscape damage and the chronological emphases on the earliest phases, the broader landscapes of which are least likely to survive. Basic groundwork has been undertaken, especially in the realm of settlement pattern studies, but the task now falls on the more widespread adoption of a diachronic approach and the investigation of the full diversity of geographic regions in order for a more holistic picture of southeastern Anatolian landscapes to emerge.

Elements of Anatolian Landscapes

The most visible landscape elements are the foci of traditional archaeological research: habitation sites. They take a variety of forms in southeastern Anatolia. Most prominent are high mounds (Turkish *höyük*, Kurdish *tepe* or *gir*, Arabic *tell*), the products of centuries or millennia of continuous or recurrent settlement at a single location (Rosen 1986; Wilkinson 2003:100–10). Mounded sites cover a range of scales, from massive high mounds to smaller village sites of five to ten meters in height and covering 1 hectare or less; the latter are far more common. Mounding results from the steady accumulation of collapsed mudbrick architecture and household débris in a single place. Elsewhere in the Near East, mounded sites were occupied from the fourth into the early second millennium B.C.E., but settlement on mounded sites in southeastern Anatolia continued into the Iron Age and beyond (Wilkinson, Ur, and Casana 2004).

Mounds are only a small subset of all types of habitation sites. The folded nature of the bedrock in the Taurus foothills and regions to the south provided caves that have been inhabited since the Palaeolithic period. A particular expansion of cave dwellings came in the Medieval period, as exemplified by the urban landscape of Hasankeyf on the Tigris (Sinclair 1989:230–39). They continue to be a significant element of the modern landscape for nomadic and village-based pastoralists, who shelter animals in them.

The climate and topography of eastern Anatolia are well suited for vertical transhumance, wherein humans and their animals move seasonally from a high altitude in the summer to a lower altitude in winter. Despite their historical and economic importance, the physical remains of pastoral nomads have proven difficult to document archaeologically. Occasionally, an ephemeral layer might be interpreted as a seasonal campsite, for example, at Ziyaret Tepe on the Tigris (Matney et al. 2007:25–29), but systematic attempts at campsite identification and excavation are rare. The supposed archaeological invisibility of campsites stems from the preponderant archaeological focus on the most disturbed parts of the landscape palimpsest, the river valleys and terraces. In fact, campsites do survive and can be identified in other, less disturbed zones (see later discussion).

Recorded sites have been analyzed primarily through the methods of settlement pattern analysis, in which sites of distinct ceramically defined time periods are mapped and compared to the distributions of sites of other periods (e.g., Algaze, Breuniger, and Knudstad 1994). Of particular importance is the scale and spatial distribution of sites. For example, a pattern of a few very large sites significantly bigger than their neighbors suggests an urban settlement system (e.g., around Titriş Höyük; Algaze et al. 1992, 2001), whereas an even distribution of small sites suggests either village subsistence or deliberate agricultural colonization (e.g., Parker 2001). An absence of ceramics of a given time period is interpreted as a phase of abandonment.

These former loci of seasonal or permanent habitation that we call "sites" represent a small but highly visible fraction of the cultural landscape. The traces of various types of past activities are to be found beyond the boundaries of habitation sites (reviewed in Wilkinson 2003:44–70). Such "off-site" or landscape features can be difficult to identify and date. Most site-focused surveys have not recorded them systematically, if at all, generally on the assumption that they date to late periods and therefore are not of interest.

The most durable features tend to be connected to past economic activities. Agriculture was (and is) a central aspect of daily life, especially in lowland river valleys. Most of the physical elements of the agricultural economy (e.g., stone and earthen field boundaries, irrigation channels, threshing and winnowing surfaces, etc.) are easily removed or recycled and therefore survive only rarely. In response, landscape archaeologists have developed indirect methods of documenting agricultural activities. For example, some settlement sites are surrounded by zones of small and abraded potsherds that resulted from manuring (Wilkinson 1982, 1989). These scatters were settlement-derived débris, organic and otherwise, that was dumped onto the fields to introduce nutrients and raise yields. Such techniques were employed at the time of maximum urbanization in the mid-late EBA and again in the Hellenistic to late Roman periods around Kurban Höyük and Titriş Höyük, but especially in the earlier phase on the Mesopotamian plains further to the south (Wilkinson 1994). The geochemical signature of manuring can also be identified but is more difficult to interpret because of various postdepositional processes (Wilkinson 1990:73–78).

Rainfall in southeastern Anatolia is seasonal and prone to interannual variation; artificial irrigation of crops supplements rainfall, increases yields, and reduces the risk of a poor or failed crop. Physical remains of irrigation systems are poorly documented, although it is quite likely that such systems were in existence from an early date. In adjacent parts of northern Iraq and northeastern Syria, large irrigation systems were functioning at least as early as the Neo-Assyrian period (Bagg 2000; Ergenzinger et al. 1988; Ur 2005). The best evidence for such large-scale irrigation in eastern Anatolia comes from the Van region, where canals, dams, aqueducts, and associated monumental inscriptions can be attributed to the kings of Urartu (Belli 1999; Zimansky 1985:66–70). Many of these features, including the fifty-one-kilometer-long Menua canal, are still in use today. These monumental systems were all state-planned projects; smaller village-level systems surely existed in the past, as they do at present, but have not been documented archaeologically.

Southeastern Anatolia was a major crossroads, and the physical traces of past movement survive in two forms. Roads are constructed features that can be very elaborate (graded and elevated paved surfaces), simple (clearance of loose stones to either side of a surface), or somewhere in between (French 1981:19–22). Tracks or paths are nonconstructed features that take their form, often a shallow linear depression, through continuous traversal by humans, animals, and vehicles. With a few exceptions (e.g., Sevin 1988), movement took place on tracks. Such movement was well preserved on the northern plains of Mesopotamia in the form of over 6,000 km of hollow ways (Ur 2003, 2009; Wilkinson 1993), where they are associated primarily with sites of the mid- to late EBA and, to a lesser extent, with sites of the Late Antique–Early Islamic period. Landscape traces are far less common further north and west, where only fragments of roads dating to the Roman period and later survive (Comfort and Ergeç 2001; French 1981; Wilkinson 1990). In the case of Roman roads, milestones can indicate former routes (French 1988).

Movement can also be reconstructed in the absence of the tracks and roads themselves. The locations of settlement sites are often assumed to have been termini (Comfort and Ergeç 2001; Lebeau 2000), although this method assumes no social or political barriers to movement between them. For historical periods, itineraries and other texts often list sequential towns and cities along routes; if these places can be located on the ground, a reasonable reconstruction of past communication routes is possible (Marro 2004). This method is particularly common in research on the Old Assyrian caravan trade between Aššur and Kaneš (Forlanini 2004, 2006; Joannès 1996) and campaigns and communications on the northern edge of the Neo-Assyrian Empire (Radner 2006, and see chapter 33 in this volume). For later periods, the Peutinger Map is often used to reconstruct routes along the Roman–Persian frontier (Dillemann 1962:133–38; Oates 2005:76–80; Poidebard 1934). These late routes are frequently used as models for earlier corridors of movement; for example, Algaze's reconstruction of trade routes during the Uruk Expansion of the mid- to late fourth millennium B.C.E. begins with Classical period roads (Algaze 2005:42–53).

The mineral richness of Anatolia is particularly well known through historical sources going back to the Akkadian kings of the third millennium B.C.E. However, empirical evidence for premodern mines is rare, mostly because sources have continued to be exploited, often into the modern period, obliterating the earliest traces in the process. Exceptions include the central Anatolian mine at Kestel and the Bolkardağ region of southern Turkey, where tin and other ores were extracted as early as the EBA (Yener and Özbal 1987; Yener et al. 1989). Earlier, obsidian from Anatolian sources was traded widely throughout the Near East (Cauvin et al. 1998). Again, empirical evidence for specific extraction areas is rare, but provenience studies have demonstrated the intensity and geography of exploitation and exchange. For example, obsidian from the Bingöl source near Lake Van was moved directly to a site near Hamoukar called Khirbat al-Fakhar, where extensive evidence for blade production covers 300 ha (Khalidi, Gratuze, and Boucetta 2009; Ur 2010:96–98). From this center, finished products were distributed to other nearby contemporary sites, such as Tell Brak, and presumably points further south (Khalidi, Gratuze, and Boucetta 2009:890–91).

Resource extraction was not only for trade; stone, clay, and timber, for example, were standard household construction materials at all times prior to the twentieth-century age of concrete. At the EBA city of Titriş Höyük, Guillermo Algaze, Jennifer Pournelle and colleagues identified a limestone quarry one kilometer north of the city, from which the stones for building foundations had been mined (Algaze et al. 2001:50–54). Their calculations of the total foundation stones in the construction of the site could be matched closely to the volume of the quarry, and the estimated rate of deforestation on account of the roof timber requirement coincided well with increased soil erosion and reduction in perennial surface water (Pournelle in Algaze et al. 2001:58–66).

Symbolic landscape elements can be more difficult to interpret than economic elements. The Hittites, Urartians, and Assyrians carved rock inscriptions and images of kings and gods at significant points in the landscape (Bachmann 1927; Harmanşah 2007; Schachner 2009; Zimansky 1985). These reliefs materialized the cosmic significance of a particular place, or made a statement, sometimes more aspirational than real, about political control. Features that we might interpret as elements of economic infrastructure also made up the symbolic landscape. The mastery over the natural hydrology represented by Menua's canals, and the city walls of Amida (Diyarbakır) and Tušḫan (Ziyaret Tepe), would have impressed on the local inhabitants the power of their creators. In most cases, aspects of meaning imposed on Anatolian landscapes will be lost to us in the absence of written inscriptions, and indeed landscapes such as mountains and streams can be meaningful without any human modification (Bradley 2000). In other cases, ritually significant places might be marked by elaborate burials, such as at Nemrut Dağı, or enigmatic built features, such as the EBA cultic platform at Gre Virike on the Euphrates (Ökse 2007).

Tools, Methods, and Research

The most common methodological tool in investigating Anatolian landscapes has been site-focused field survey, which has a long tradition in the Near East going back to the surveys of Braidwood (1937) on the Amuq Plain. The earliest research was valuable but nonsystematic and perhaps better termed reconnaissance (e.g., Burney 1958; Russell 1980). The quantity and intensity of survey work expanded with the planning for the GAP dams. The first surveys targeted the Aşvan and Altınova Plains behind the Keban Dam on the Euphrates River (METU Faculty of Architecture 1967; Whallon 1979). These surveys were concerned primarily with documentation of standing architecture and prehistoric mounds, but they also resulted in methodological innovations for surface collection involving sampling (Whallon 1983).

The subsequent Karakaya and Karababa (now Atatürk) Dams received similar extensive survey for architecture (Serdaroğlu 1977) and prehistoric mounds (Özdoğan 1977). The Karababa zone, however, was subjected to several intensive surveys covering subregions (Blaylock, French, and Summers 1990) or the hinterlands of excavated sites including Gritille (Stein 1998), Lidar Höyük (Gerber 1996), Kurban Höyük (Wilkinson 1990), and Titriş Höyük (Algaze et al. 1992, 2001). The zones behind smaller dams at Zeugma/Belkis and between Birecik and Carchemish were also surveyed (Algaze, Breuniger, and Knudstad 1994; Comfort, Abadie-Reynal, and Ergeç 2000; Comfort and Ergeç 2001), as was the upper Batman River (Rosenberg and Togul 1991). Future dam zones on the Tigris have also now been surveyed, such as the Ilısu Dam zone, which includes stretches of its Batman, Bohtan, and Garzan tributaries. Algaze's initial surveys (1989; Algaze et al. 1991) have been complemented by period-specific follow-up projects, discussed further shortly.

Unlike the case in northeastern Syria (see Wilkinson 2000), the larger alluvial plains of southeastern Anatolia have not received as much attention from archaeological surveys. The exceptions are the Urfa/Harran Plain (Creekmore 2008; Yardımcı 2004), the Malatya Plain (Di Nocera 2008), and the Cizre/Silopi Plain (Algaze 1989; Algaze et al. 1991; Kozbe 2008; Parker 2001).

In most of these surveys, sites are identified by vehicular transects, preexisting maps, and information from local residents. Sites are most frequently collected by subdividing their surfaces into discrete zones to collect surface artifacts separately (e.g., Wilkinson 1990:68). In some cases, the surfaces of sites have been sampled in smaller units, generally 10 × 10 m, using various systematic (Whallon 1979, 1983) and probabilistic (Redman and Watson 1970) methods. More recently, low-density artifact scatters have been recognized using walking transects and by plotting individual surface artifacts (Ur and Hammer 2009).

Archaeologists have been unable to access aerial photographs of southeastern Anatolia, but recent survey projects have made extensive use of satellite imagery. For example, the declassified intelligence satellite photographs of the U.S. CORONA program have been used to examine Roman roads and sites along the Euphrates (Kennedy 1998), sites and landscape features on the Harran Plain (Creekmore 2008), and the hinterland of Titriş Höyük (Algaze et al. 2001). Others have used low-resolution Landsat imagery (Zimansky 1985), more recent Soviet imagery (Comfort, Abadie-Reynal, and Ergeç 2000; Di Nocera 2008) or high-resolution Ikonos imagery (Ur and Hammer 2009).

The cumulative result of these surveys is an emerging picture of settlement and landscape development throughout the Holocene. Here I focus briefly on the major results for southeastern Turkey between the Late Chalcolithic and Iron Age (see also Algaze 1999; Wilkinson 2000).

Algaze's surveys of the Tigris and Euphrates Valleys (1989, Algaze, Breuniger, and Knudstad 1994; Algaze et al. 1991) were an important component of his analysis of the Uruk Expansion event of the mid- to late fourth millennium B.C.E., in which aspects of southern Mesopotamian material culture appeared throughout the Near East (see Rothman, chapter 37 in this volume). On the basis of southern versus indigenous artifacts and architecture, he proposed a variety of settlement configurations ranging from full colonization to small enclaves within indigenous settlements, interpreted within a world systems framework (Algaze 2005). Algaze's conclusions have inspired a range of critical studies, most prominently the excavations at Hacınebi Tepe, where southern and indigenous communities lived together (Stein 1999).

More recent survey work has focused on relations with the Caucasus region (e.g., Lyonnet 2007). Surveys and excavations have demonstrated that the chaff-tempered ceramics typical of the indigenous sites of northern Mesopotamia (i.e., Amuq F; see Özbal, chapter 8, and Sagona, chapter 30 in this volume) are to be found far into Armenia, Georgia, and Azerbaijan (e.g., Akhundov 2007). The sites occur in both highland and lowland areas and might represent an expansion of both northern Mesopotamian pastoralists and agriculturalists into the region (Marro 2007b).

Following the collapse of the Uruk system, in the early EBA, settlements were uniformly small agricultural settlements in the wider parts of the river valleys and across the alluvial plains, and in fewer numbers than in the fourth millennium B.C.E. On the Euphrates, many of these sites were fortified, suggesting intense boundary competition among small polities (Peltenburg 2007:13–15).

Southeastern Anatolia also experienced the sudden urbanization that characterized northern Mesopotamia in the middle of the third millennium B.C.E. (Stein 2004; Ur 2010; Wilkinson 1994). Sites expanded in size in the Euphrates River Valley, but the greatest urban expansions occurred in sites in broad alluvial plains adjacent to the valleys: Tilbeşar (56 ha; Kepinski 2007:155), Titriş Höyük (43 ha; Algaze et al. 2001:56–57), and Kazane Höyük (100 ha; Creekmore 2008; Wattenmaker 1994). Around Titriş, a four-tier settlement hierarchy could be identified, with Titriş at the pinnacle, down to fourth-tier sites of under one hectare, which had a dramatic impact on its surrounding landscape (figure 38.2; Algaze et al. 2001:56–57; Algaze and Pournelle 2003). At present, the Upper Tigris basin appears to have been

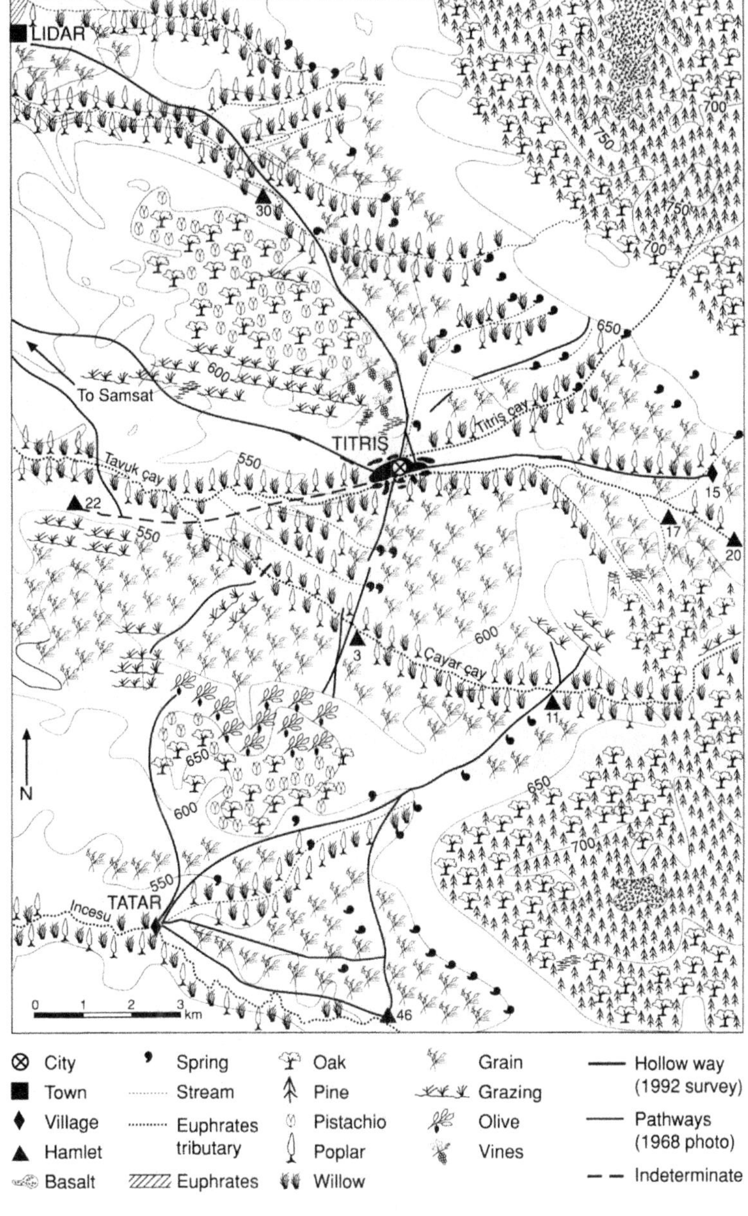

Figure 38.2. Settlement hierarchy and landscape reconstruction around Titriş Höyük (Algaze et al. 2001:fig. 26).

overlooked by this urban expansion (Algaze et al. 1991:181; Özfırat 2006); the largest settlement was Pir Hüseyin (about nineteen hectares; Peasnall and Algaze 2010), although further survey may alter this picture. Even more strangely, the Cizre Plain was depopulated at this time (Algaze et al. 1991:196; Kozbe 2008), despite its proximity to some of the most urbanized areas of the northern Mesopotamian Plains (Ur 2010:150-157; Wilkinson 1994). Furthermore, mid- to late EBA settlements in southeastern Anatolia apparently did not produce the extensive network of tracks and field systems that characterize the Syrian plains (Ur 2003; Wilkinson 1989, 1993), even in similar alluvial environments. This absence, however, may be a result of greater landscape transformations within Turkey and predominantly site-focused survey methodologies.

Settlement landscapes of southeastern Anatolia appear to have escaped the environmental "crisis" proposed for the Near East in ca. 2200 B.C.E. (see, most recently, Staubwasser and Weiss 2006 with earlier literature). In the Euphrates Valley, there is considerable continuity of settlement and material culture from the late EBA to the MBA (Marro 2007a). Titriş Höyük, Tilbeşar, and other sites in the Karababa basin went through transitions that often involved a reduction in scale, but most continued to be settled to the end of the millennium (Abay 2007; Algaze et al. 2001; Algaze 1999:553–54; Algaze and Pournelle 2003; Kepinski 2007). In the Upper Tigris region, a distinctive late third millennium B.C.E. dark rimmed orange bowl form is common on the surfaces of surveyed sites (Özfırat 2006; Ökse, chapter 11 in this volume), suggesting strong continuity into the end of the millennium there as well.

At the northern fringes of southeastern Anatolia, sites of the Early Transcaucasian (ETC) or Kura-Araxes culture (actually a heterogeneous group of cultures with general similarities in ceramics) emerged in the mid-fourth millennium B.C.E. and expanded into the third millennium B.C.E. (see, most recently, Kohl 2007:86–102; Rothman 2003; Marro, chapter 12, and Sagona, chapter 30 in this volume). The communities using this material culture appear to have dislodged or replaced the communities using northern Mesopotamian ceramics in the Caucasus (Marro 2007b). Although frequent in the Karakaya and Keban Dam regions, the distinctive ETC ceramics are very uncommon in the lower plains and river valleys of southeastern Anatolia.

In most regions, the MBA (Laneri and Schwartz, chapter 14 in this volume) saw an expansion in numbers of sites, although at a reduced level of urban agglomeration. The Cizre Plain was densely resettled (Kozbe 2008), mirroring settlement trends in the Upper Khabur basin (Ristvet 2008). Settlement expanded in the Malatya Plain as well (Di Nocera 2008). MBA sites are common throughout the Upper Tigris region, where they occur as small villages on mounded sites (Özfırat 2006).

For much of southeastern Anatolia, the Late Bronze Age (LBA) is a time of low site density, but settlements expanded dramatically in the Iron Age, particularly in the context of the Assyrian Empire (reviewed in Wilkinson et al. 2005). Site numbers expanded in the Cizre Plain and the Tigris Valley near Batman, including the appearance of an urban center at Ziyaret Tepe (Algaze et al. 1991:197–98; see Matney, chapter 19 in this volume). These sites were characterized by ceramics identical to those found on sites in the Assyrian core area, but occurred alongside sites with an indigenous ceramic tradition (Parker 2001, 2003), making the region an excellent case study in frontier dynamics (Parker 2006).

The Upper Tigris Valley: A Case Study

Until the late 1980s, the Upper Tigris Valley (figure 38.3) was almost completely unknown archaeologically. Since then, it has been subjected to a range of landscape approaches, resulting in an emerging picture of settlement and landscape in the Holocene. An initial survey begun by Algaze and colleagues in 1988 in advance of the construction of the dam at Ilısu recovered sites from the Palaeolithic to the Medieval period (Algaze 1989; Algaze et al. 1991). Emphasis was on the future reservoir zone, and collection was done mostly on the larger mounded sites. Surveys targeting habitation sites of specific periods followed, including the Palaeolithic (Taşkıran and Kartal 2004), Neolithic (Tekin 2009), Bronze Age (Ay 2001), and the

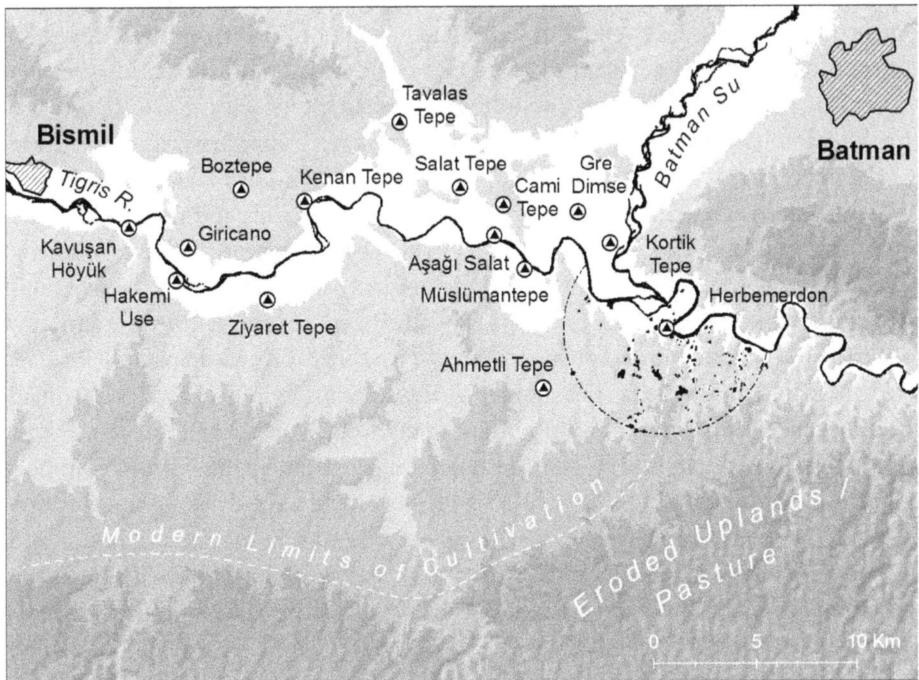

Figure 38.3. Sites and landscapes of the Upper Tigris region, with the Hirbemerdon Tepe Survey area indicated.

Classical period (Barın, Akın, and Şahin 2004). Site-focused extensive surveys of the western (Köroğlu 1998; Özfırat 2006) and northern (Peasnall 2004) parts of the basin have also been carried out. Two studies have examined the changing geomorphology of the river valley (Doğan 2005; Kuzucuoğlu 2002). Most of these studies have been focused on the remains of sedentary agriculturalists in the river valleys or adjacent terraces and have employed low intensity field methods, most often out of necessity.

For these reasons, a new survey in the region around the MBA site of Hirbemerdon was initiated in 2007 (Laneri et al. 2008:200–204; Ur and Hammer 2009).[1] In an effort to examine the landscape elements that have been overlooked by previous projects, it is an intensive survey involving pedestrian transects in a small study region (forty-eight square kilometers), and it considers not only the terraces adjacent to the Tigris but also the upland areas further away from the river where agriculture would have been less productive or impossible. The region is perfectly suited for such an undertaking, as it is located at the point where the Tigris Valley narrows to flow between steep cliffs. The eastern third of the survey region is characterized by deep valleys with thin soils.

Traditional Near Eastern survey methods have effectively identified mounded Bronze and Iron Age sites (Wilkinson, Ur, and Casana 2004), a conclusion confirmed by the intensive survey around Hirbemerdon, where all such sites had already been identified by Algaze's survey (Algaze et al. 1991). To see what might have been missed by such methods, survey team members walked linear transects at twenty-five-meter intervals across fallow fields. Individual artifacts were flagged and recorded with a GPS-enabled handheld computer. These methods revealed flat areas of settlement adjacent to mounded settlements and isolated low-density scatters of lithics and pottery, including several scatters within a kilometer of Hirbemerdon itself (figure 38.4). None of these sites were apparent without walking over them, nor could they be identified from CORONA or Ikonos satellite imagery.

The eastern eroded landscape revealed a diversity of sites and features that are overlooked by extensive survey methods or do not survive on the river terraces. Palaeolithic caves and lithic scatters were abundant, and pastoral nomadic campsites could also be identified. Some of the latter were recent, within the last two centuries, when the region has been the winter pasture for Kurdish groups (Beşikçi, cited in Cribb 1991:185–211; Erhan 1992; Hütteroth 1959), but others were much older. Because they were often little more than circular or linear rock alignments without associated material culture, dating them is extremely difficult—a common problem in landscape archaeology. Also difficult to date were dwellings cut directly into the rock walls of the valleys, with elaborate interior niches, windows, and benches (see also Barın, Akın, and Şahin 2004). These dwellings have been heavily reused for animal shelters in recent centuries, but probably date back to the Medieval period on the basis of analogy with Hasankeyf (Sinclair 1989:230–39), or earlier.

Because the eastern upland areas have limited agricultural potential, they have been left largely untouched and therefore preserve a wide array of off-site features, most related to the pastoral economy. Isolated dry stone corrals were found adjacent

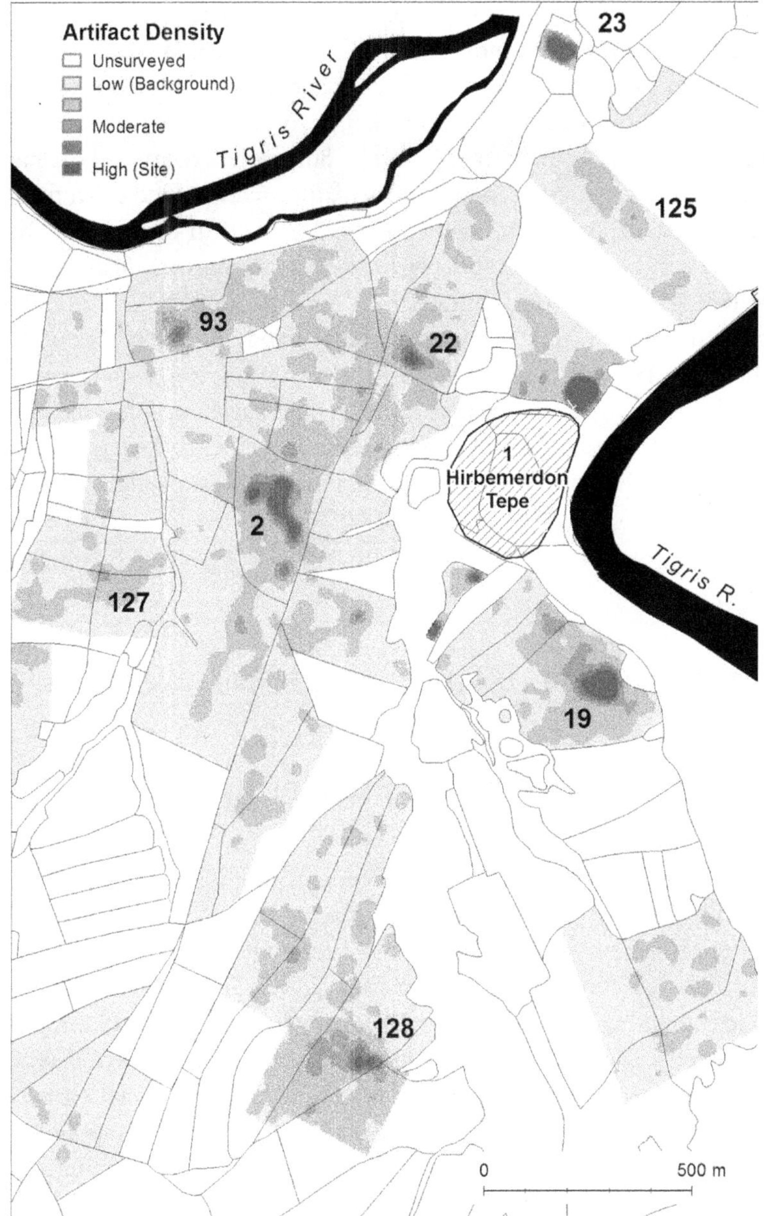

Figure 38.4. Modern fields and low-density surface scatter sites on the agricultural lands around Hirbemerdon Tepe.

to small areas of pasture. Small stone and earth constructions were placed across natural drainages to capture runoff. These features were intended to water animals during the winter months. Greater investment went into the construction of cisterns, subterranean holding tanks carved into the bedrock that collect surface runoff. The larger features have capacities in excess of ten cubic meters. Aside from these economic features, some aspects of symbolic landscapes survive in the form of fields of stone cairns, generally no more than two meters in diameter and less than a meter high. They occur most commonly in groups of fewer than ten, but two vast fields of almost 200 features have been mapped. Without associated material culture, these landscape features pose challenges for dating.

In three seasons, the Hirbemerdon Tepe Survey has recovered 131 habitation sites, campsites, caves, cisterns, dams, terraces, flint scatters, and cairn fields where previous low-intensity surveys had recovered a handful of mounds. Intensive methods on a variety of terrain types will produce more sites and features representing a greater variety of past activities. This is not an argument for the replacement of extensive methods with the intensive methodology of the Hirbemerdon Tepe Survey, however. High intensity comes with a corresponding reduction in the area investigated. Research questions that can only be answered at the macroregional level will require the broad spatial coverage that only extensive survey can provide. Nonetheless, intensive surveys serve as a check on what gets overlooked with extensive methodologies.

Conclusions: Present and Future Landscape Archaeology in Southeastern Turkey

Southeastern Anatolia's diversity of environments and long history of settlement make it an ideal region for a landscape approach to the human past. Shifting constellations of settlement, in response to environmental, social, and political factors, have been revealed through decades of field survey and have provided a broad geographic frame that complements the spatially limited results of excavation. At present, particularly vivid trends in settlement and land use have been demonstrated for the Late Chalcolithic Uruk Expansion, the mid- to late third millennium B.C.E. phase of urban growth, and the Iron Age/Neo-Assyrian period, to name a few examples. The results of the initial extensive surveys are being tested and expanded by more intensive projects, and previously underinvestigated regions are now under study, especially by Turkish teams (see publications in recent volumes of the *Araştırma Sonuçları Toplantısı* series).

The increased adoption of landscape approaches by foreign and Turkish archaeologists is encouraging, but it may not match the rate at which the archaeological landscape is being destroyed, most obviously by dam construction, but on a wider scale by the expansion and intensification of agriculture, especially where water-intensive cash crops like cotton are planted. It is ironic that just as landscape archaeology has become accepted as complementary to excavation, rather than merely a means to locate sites for excavation, its subject matter is under threat from the modern world as never before. Pressures for development will not abate in the coming decades, so we can only hope that the current enthusiasm for the landscape approach will continue to grow.

NOTES

1. Survey fieldwork around Hirbemerdon Tepe was encouraged and supported by the Hirbemerdon Tepe excavation team, especially director Nicola Laneri, co-director Mark Schwartz, and Stefano Valentini. I am also grateful to the Turkish Ministry of Culture and the Diyarbakır Museum, especially Nilüfer Babacan and Nevin Soyukaya, for permission to undertake this work. This manuscript was improved by comments from Emily Hammer.

REFERENCES

Abay, Eşref. 2007. Southeastern Anatolia after the Early Bronze Age: Collapse or Continuity? A Case Study from the Karababa Dam Area. In *Sociétés humaines et changement climatique à la fin du troisième millénaire: une crise a-t-elle eu lieu en haute Mésopotamie?*, ed. Catherine Kuzucuoğlu and Catherine Marro, 403–13. Varia Anatolica 19. İstanbul: Institut Français d'études anatoliennes Georges-Dumézil.

Akhundov, Tufan. 2007. Sites de migration venus du Proche-Orient en Transcaucasie. In *Les cultures du Caucase (VIe–IIIe millénaires avant notre ère): Leur relations avec le Proche-Orient*, ed. Bertille Lyonnet, 95–121. Paris: Éditions Recherche sur les Civilisations.

Algaze, Guillermo. 1989. A New Frontier: First Results of the Tigris-Euphrates Archaeological Reconnaissance Project, 1988. *Journal of Near Eastern Studies* 48: 241–81.

———. 1999. Trends in the Archaeological Development of the Upper Euphrates Basin of Southeastern Anatolia during the Late Chalcolithic and Early Bronze Ages. In *Archaeology of the Upper Syrian Euphrates: The Tishrin Dam Area*, ed. Gregorio del Olmo Lete and Juan-Luis Montero Fenollós, 535–72. Barcelona: Editorial Ausa.

———. 2005. *The Uruk World System: The Dynamics of Expansion of Early Mesopotamian Civilization*, 2nd ed.: University of Chicago Press.

Algaze, Guillermo, Ray Breuniger, and James Knudstad. 1994. The Tigris-Euphrates Archaeological Reconnaissance Project. Final Report on the Birecik and Carchemish Dam Survey Areas. *Anatolica* 20: 1–97.

Algaze, Guillermo, Ray Breuninger, Chris Lightfoot, and Michael Rosenberg. 1991. The Tigris-Euphrates Archaeological Reconnaissance Project: A Preliminary Report of the 1989–1990 Seasons. *Anatolica* 17: 175–240.

Algaze, Guillermo, Gulay Dinckan, Britt Hartenberger, Timothy Matney, Jennifer Pournelle, Lynn Rainville, Steven Rosen, Eric Rupley, Duncan Schlee, and Regis Vallet. 2001. Research at Titriş Höyük in Southeastern Turkey: The 1999 Season. *Anatolica* 27: 23–106.

Algaze, Guillermo, Adnan Mısır, Tony Wilkinson, Elizabeth Carter, and Ronald Gorny. 1992. Şanliurfa Museum/University of California Excavations and Surveys at Titriş Höyük, 1991: A Preliminary Report. *Anatolica* 18: 33–49.

Algaze, Guillermo and Jennifer Pournelle. 2003. Climatic Change, Environmental Change, and Social Change at Early Bronze Age Titriş Höyük. In *From Village to Towns: Studies Presented to Ufuk Esin*, ed. Mehmet Özdoğan, Harald Hauptmann, and Nezih Başgelen, 103–28. İstanbul: Arkeoloji ve Sanat.

Alizadeh, Karim and Jason A. Ur. 2007. Formation and Destruction of Pastoral and Irrigation Landscapes on the Mughan Steppe, North-Western Iran. *Antiquity* 81: 148–60.

Ay, Eyyüp. 2001. Upper Tigris Valley Survey: 1999 Season. In *Salvage Project of the Archaeological Heritage of the Ilısu and Carchemish Dam Reservoirs, Activities in 1999*, ed. Numan Tuna, Jean Öztürk, and Jâle Velibeyoğlu, 715–28. Ankara: Middle East Technical University.

Bachmann, W. 1927. *Felsreliefs in Assyrien: Bawian, Maltai und Gundük*. 52. Wissenschaftliche Veröffentlichung der Deutschen Orient-Gesellschaft. Leipzig: J.C. Hinrichs'sche Buchhandlung.

Bagg, Ariel M. 2000. *Assyrische Wasserbauten*. Baghdader Forschungen Band 24. Mainz am Rhein: Philipp von Zabern.

Barın, Gürol, Enver Akın, and Feridun Suha Şahin. 2004. Ilısu Klâsik Yüzey Araştırmaları 2002. *Araştırma Sonuçları Toplantısı* 21.1: 127–38.

Belli, Oktay. 1999. Dams, Reservoirs and Irrigation Channels of the Van Plain in the Period of the Urartian Kingdom. *Anatolian Studies* 49: 11–26.

Blaylock, Stuart R., David H. French, and Geoffrey D. Summers. 1990. The Adıyaman Survey: an Interim Report. *Anatolian Studies* 40: 81–135.

Bradley, Richard. 2000. *An Archaeology of Natural Places*. London: Routledge.

Braidwood, Robert J. 1937. *Mounds in the Plain of Antioch: An Archeological Survey*. Oriental Institute Publications 48. Chicago: University of Chicago Press.

Burney, Charles A. 1958. East Anatolia in the Chalcolithic and Early Bronze Age. *Anatolian Studies* 8: 157–209.

Cauvin, Marie-Clare, Alain Gourgaud, Bernard Gratuze, Nicholas Arnaud, Gerard Poupeau, Jean-Louis Poidevin, and Christine Chataigner, eds. 1998. *L'obsidienne au Proche et Moyen Orient: Du volcan à l'outil*. BAR International Series 738. Oxford: Archaeopress.

Comfort, Anthony, Catherine Abadie-Reynal, and Rifat Ergeç. 2000. Crossing the Euphrates in Antiquity: Zeugma Seen from Space. *Anatolian Studies* 51: 99–126.

Comfort, Anthony and Rifat Ergeç. 2001. Following the Euphrates in Antiquity: North-South Routes around Zeugma. *Anatolian Studies* 51: 19–49.

Crang, Mike. 1998. *Cultural Geography*. London: Routledge.

Creekmore, Andrew. 2008. Kazane Höyük and Urban Life Histories in Third Millennium Upper Mesopotamia. Ph.D. dissertation. Northwestern University.

Cribb, Roger. 1991. *Nomads in Archaeology*. Cambridge: Cambridge University Press.

Dillemann, Louis. 1962. *Haute Mesopotamie orientale et pays adjacents: Contribution á la géographie historique de la région, du Ve s. avant l'ère chrétienne au VIe s. de cette ère*. Bibliotheque archéologique et historique tome 72. Paris: Paul Geuthner.

Di Nocera, Gian Maria. 2008. Settlements, Population and Landscape on the Upper Euphrates between V and II Millennium BC: Results of the Archaeological Survey Project 2003–2005 in the Malatya Plain. In *Proceedings of the 5th International Congress on the Archaeology of the Ancient Near East*, vol. 1, ed. Joaquin M. Córdoba, Miguel Molist, M. Carmen Pérez, Isabel Rubio, and Sergio Martínez, 633–46. Madrid: Universidad Autónoma.

Doğan, Uğur. 2005. Holocene Fluvial Development of the Upper Tigris Valley (Southeastern Turkey) as Documented by Archaeological Data. *Quaternary International* 129: 75–86.

Ergenzinger, Peter J., Wolfgang Frey, Hartmut Kühne, and Harald Kurschner. 1988. The Reconstruction of Environment, Irrigation and Development of Settlement in the Habur in North-East Syria. In *Conceptual Issues in Environmental Archaeology*, ed. John Bintliff, Donald A. Davidson, and Eric Grant, 108–28. Edinburgh: Edinburgh University Press.

Erhan, Selahattin. 1992. *Identity Formation and Political Organization among Anatolian Nomads: The Beritanlı Case*. Ph.D. dissertation. University of Texas at Austin.

Forlanini, Massimo. 2004. Dall'Alto Habur alle montagne dell' Anatolia nel II millennio A.C., Note sulla Geografia storica di una regione poco conosciuta. In *Nomades et sédentaires dans le Proche-Orient ancien*, Amurru 3, ed. Christophe Nicolle, 405–26. Paris: Éditions Recherche sur les Civilisations.

———. 2006. Étapes et itinéraires entre Assur et l'Anatolie des marchands paléo-assyriens: nouveaux documents et nouveaux problèmes. *Kaskal* 3: 147–75.

French, David H. 1981. *Roman Roads and Milestones of Asia Minor, Fasc. 1: The Pilgrim's Road*. BAR International Series 105. Oxford: British Archaeological Reports.

———. 1988. *Roman Roads and Milestones of Asia Minor, Fasc. 2: An Interim Catalogue of Milestones*. BAR International Series 392. Oxford: British Archaeological Reports.

Gerber, Christoph. 1996. Die Umgebung des Lidar Höyük von hellenistischer bis frühislamischer Zeit: Interpretation der Ergebnisse einer Gelandebegehung. In *Continuity and Change in Northern Mesopotamia from the Hellenistic to the Early Islamic Period*, ed. Karin Bartl and Stefan R. Hauser, 303–32. Berliner Beiträge zumVorderen Orient 17. Berlin: Dietrich Reimer.

Göyünç, Nejat and Wolf-Dieter Hütteroth. 1997. *Land an der Grenze: Osmanliche Verwaltung im heutigen türkisch-syrisch-irakischen Grenzgebiet im 16. Jahrhundert*. İstanbul: Eren.

Harmanşah, Ömür. 2007. "Source of the Tigris." Event, Place and Performance in the Assyrian Landscapes of the Early Iron Age. *Archaeological Dialogues* 14: 179–204.

Hütteroth, Wolf-Dieter. 1959. *Bergnomaden und Yaylabauern im mittleren kurdischen Taurus*. Marburger Geographische Schriften 11. Marburg: Geographischen Institutes der Universität Marburg.

Joannès, Francis. 1996. Routes et voies de communication dans les archives de Mari. In *Amurru 1: Mari, Ébla et les Hourrites*, ed. Jean-Marie Durand, 323–61. Paris: Éditions Recherche sur les Civilisations.

Kennedy, David. 1998. Declassified Satellite Photographs and Archaeology in the Middle East: Case Studies from Turkey. *Antiquity* 72: 553–61.

Kepinski, Christine. 2007. Dynamics, Diagnostic Criteria and Settlement Patterns in the Carchemish Area during the Early Bronze Period. In *Euphrates River Valley Settlement: The Carchemish Sector in the Third Millennium BC*, ed. Edgar Peltenburg, 152–63. Levant Supplementary Series 5. Oxford: Oxbow.

Khalidi, Lamya, Bernard Gratuze, and Sophie Boucetta. 2009. Provenience of Obsidian Excavated from Late Chalcolithic Levels at the Sites of Tell Hamoukar and Tell Brak, Syria. *Archaeometry* 51: 879–93.

Kohl, Philip L. 2007. *The Making of Bronze Age Eurasia*. Cambridge: Cambridge University Press.

Kozbe, Gülriz. 2008. A New Archaeological Survey Project in the South Eastern Anatolia: Report of the Cizre and Silopi Region. In *Proceedings of the 5th International Congress on the Archaeology of the Ancient Near East*,vol. 2, ed. Joaquin M. Córdoba, Miguel Molist, M. Carmen Pérez, Isabel Rubio, and Sergio Martínez, 322–40. Madrid: Universidad Autónoma.

Köroğlu, Kemalettin. 1998. *Üçtepe I*. Ankara: Türk Tarih Kurumu Yayınları.

Kuzucuoğlu, Catherine. 2002. Preliminary Observation on the Tigris Valley Terraces between Bismil and Batman. In *Salvage Project of the Archaeological Heritage of the Ilısu and Carchemish Dam Reservoirs: Activities in 2000*, ed. Numan Tuna and Jale Velibeyoğlu, 766–71. Ankara: Middle Eastern Technical University.

Laneri, Nicola, Mark Schwartz, Jason A. Ur, Stefano Valentini, Anacleto D'Agostino, Rémi Berthon, and Mette Marie Hald. 2008. The Hirbemerdon Tepe Archaeological Project 2006–2007: A Preliminary Report on the Middle Bronze Age "Architectural Complex" and the Survey of the Site Catchment Area. *Anatolica* 34: 177–240.

Lebeau, Marc. 2000. Les voies de communication en Haute Mésopotamie au IIIe millénaire avant notre ère. In *La Djéziré et l'Euphrate syriens de la protohistoire à la fin du IIe millénaire av. J.-C.: tendances dans l'interprétation historique des données nouvelles*, ed. Olivier Rouault and Markus Wäfler, 157–62. Subartu 7. Turnhout: Brepols.

Lyonnet, Bertille, ed. 2007. *Les cultures du Caucase (VIe–IIIe millénaires avant notre ère): Leur relations avec le Proche-Orient*. Paris: Éditions Recherche sur les Civilisations.

Marro, Catherine. 2004. Upper Mesopotamia and the Caucasus: An Essay on the Evolution of Routes and Road Networks from the Old Assyrian Kingdom to the Ottoman Empire. In *A View from the Highlands: Archaeological Studies in Honour of Charles Burney*, ed. Antonio G. Sagona, 91–120. Ancient Near Eastern Studies Supplement 12. Herent: Peeters.

———. 2007a. Continuity and Change in the Birecik Valley at the End of the Third Millennium B.C.: The Archaeological Evidence from Horum Höyük. In *Sociétés humaines et changement climatique à la fin du troisième millénaire: une crise a-t-elle eu lieu en haute Mésopotamie?*, ed. Catherine Kuzucuoğlu and Catherine Marro, 383–401. Varia Anatolica 19. İstanbul: Institut Français d'études anatoliennes Georges-Dumézil.

———. 2007b. Upper-Mesopotamia and Transcaucasia in the Late Chalcolithic Period (4000–3500 BC). In *Les cultures du Caucase (VIe–IIIe millénaires avant notre ère): Leur relations avec le Proche-Orient*, ed. Bertille Lyonnet, 77–94. Paris: Éditions Recherche sur les Civilisations.

Matney, Timothy, Lynn Rainville, Kemalettin Köroğlu, Azer Keskin, Tasha Vorderstrasse, Nursen Özkul Fındık, and Ann Donkin. 2007. Report on Excavation at Ziyaret Tepe, 2006 Season. *Anatolica* 33:23–74.

METU Faculty of Architecture. 1967. *Doomed by the Dam: A Survey of the Monuments Threatened by the Creation of the Keban Dam Flood Area*. Ankara: Middle Eastern Technical University.

Oates, David. 2005. *Studies in the Ancient History of Northern Iraq*. Cambridge: British School of Archaeology in Iraq.

Ökse, A. Tuba. 2007. A "High" Terrace at Gre Virike to the North of Carchemish: Power of Local Rulers as Founders? In *Euphrates River Valley Settlement: The Carchemish Sector in the Third Millennium BC*, ed. Edgar Peltenburg, 94–104. Levant Supplementary Series 5. Oxford: Oxbow Books.

Özdoğan, Mehmet. 1977. *Aşağı Fırat Havzası 1977 Yüzey Araştırmaları*. Orta Doğu Teknik Üniversitesi Aşağı Fırat Projesi yayınları, Seri 1, no. 2. İstanbul: Orta Doğu Teknik Üniversitesi Keban ve Aşağı Fırat Havzası Projeleri Müdürlüğü.

Özfırat, Aynur. 2006. *Üçtepe II: Tunç Çağları (13.–10. Yapı Katları)*. İstanbul: Ege Yayınları.

Parker, Bradley J. 2001. *The Mechanics of Empire: The Northern Frontier of Assyria as a Case Study in Imperial Dynamics*. Helsinki: Neo-Assyrian Text Corpus Project.

———. 2003. Archaeological Manifestations of Empire: Assyria's Imprint on Southeastern Anatolia. *American Journal of Archaeology* 107: 525–57.

———. 2006. Toward an Understanding of Borderland Processes. *American Antiquity* 71: 77–100.

Peasnall, Brian. 2004. 2002 Diyarbakır Small Streams Archaeological Survey. *Araştırma Sonuçları Toplantısı* 21.2: 29–44. Ankara: T.C. Kültür ve Turizm Bakanlığı Yayınları.

Peasnall, Brian and Guillermo Algaze. 2010. The Survey of Pir Hüseyin, 2004. *Anatolica* 36: 165–195.

Peltenburg, Edgar. 2007. New Perspectives on the Carchemish Sector of the Middle Euphrates River Valley in the 3rd Millennium BC. In *Euphrates River Valley Settlement: The Carchemish Sector in the Third Millennium BC*, ed. Edgar Peltenburg, 3-24. Levant Supplementary Series 5. Oxford: Oxbow.

Poidebard, Anton. 1934. *La trace de Rome dans le désert de Syrie*. Bibliothéque Archéologique et Historique 18. Paris: Librairie Orientaliste Paul Geuthner.

Radner, Karen. 2006. How to Reach the Upper Tigris: The Route through the Tūr ʿAbdīn. *State Archives of Assyria Bulletin* 15: 273–305.

Redman, Charles L. and Patty Jo Watson. 1970. Systematic, Intensive Surface Collection. *American Antiquity* 35: 279–91.

Ristvet, Lauren. 2008. Legal and Archaeological Territories of the Second Millennium BC in Northern Mesopotamia. *Antiquity* 82: 585–99.

Rosen, Arlene Miller. 1986. *Cities of Clay: The Geoarchaeology of Tells.*: University of Chicago Press.

Rosenberg, Michael and Hakan Togul. 1991. The Batman River Archaeological Site Survey, 1990. *Anatolica* 17: 241–54.

Rothman, Mitchell. 2003. Ripples in the Stream: Transcaucasia-Anatolian Interactions in the Murat/Euphrates Basin at the Beginning of the Third Millennium BC. In *Archaeology in the Borderlands: Investigations in Caucasia and Beyond*, ed. Adam T. Smith and Karen S. Rubinson, 94–109. Los Angeles: Cotsen Institute of Archaeology.

Russell, Henry F. 1980. *Pre-Classical Pottery of Eastern Anatolia, Based on a Survey by Charles Burney of Sites along the Euphrates and around Lake Van*. BAR International Series 85. Oxford: British Archaeological Reports.

Schachner, A. 2009. *Assyriens Könige an einer der Quellen des Tigris*. Istanbuler Forschungen Band 51. Tübingen: Ernst Wasmuth.

Serdaroğlu, Ümit. 1977. *Aşağı Fırat Havzasında Araştırmalar, 1975*. O.D.T.Ü. Aşağı Fırat Projesi Yayınları Seri 1, no. 1. Ankara: O.D.T.Ü. Aşağı Fırat Projesi.

Sevin, Veli. 1988. The Oldest Highway: Between the Regions of Van and Elazığ in Eastern Anatolia. *Antiquity* 62: 547–51.

Shoup, Daniel. 2006. Can Archaeology Build a Dam? Sites and Politics in Turkey's Southeast Anatolia Project. *Journal of Mediterranean Archaeology* 19: 231–58.

Sinclair, T.A. 1989. *Eastern Turkey: An Architectural and Archaeological Survey*, vol. 3. London: Pindar Press.

Staubwasser, Michael and Harvey Weiss. 2006. Holocene Climate and Cultural Evolution in Late Prehistoric-Early Historic West Asia. *Quaternary Research* 66: 372–87.

Stein, Gil J. 1998. Medieval Regional Settlement Organization in the Gritille Hinterlands. In *The Archaeology of the Frontier in the Medieval Near East: Excavations at Gritille, Turkey*, ed. Scott Redford, 253–68. Philadelphia: University Museum Publications.

———. 1999. *Rethinking World-Systems: Diasporas, Colonies, and Interaction in Uruk Mesopotamia*. Tucson: University of Arizona Press.

———. 2004. Structural Parameters and Sociocultural Factors in the Economic Organization of North Mesopotamian Urbanism in the Third Millennium BC. In *Archaeological*

Perspectives on Political Economies, ed. Gary M. Feinman and Linda M. Nicholas, 61–78. Salt Lake City: University of Utah Press.

Taşkıran, Harun and Metin Kartal. 2004. 2001 Palaeolithic Survey in the Ilısu Dam Region. In *Salvage Project of the Archaeological Heritage of the Ilısu and Carchemish Dam Reservoirs: Activities in 2001*, ed. Numan Tuna, Jean Greenhalgh, and Jale Velibeyoğlu, 725–37. Ankara: Middle East Technical University.

Tekin, Halil. 2009. Ilısu Projesi Seramikli Neolitik Yerleşmeleri Yüzey Araştırması, 2007. *Araştırma Sonuçları Toplantısı* 26.1: 279–87.

Ur, Jason A. 2003. CORONA Satellite Photography and Ancient Road Networks: A Northern Mesopotamian Case Study. *Antiquity* 77: 102–15.

———. 2005. Sennacherib's Northern Assyrian Canals: New Insights from Satellite Imagery and Aerial Photography. *Iraq* 67: 317–45.

———. 2009. Emergent Landscapes of Movement in Early Bronze Age Northern Mesopotamia. In *Landscapes of Movement: Paths, Trails, and Roads in Anthropological Perspective*, ed. James E. Snead, Clark Erickson, and W. Andrew Darling, 180–203. Philadelphia: University of Pennsylvania Museum Press.

———. 2010. Cycles of Civilization in Northern Mesopotamia, 4400–2000 BC. *Journal of Archaeological Research* 18: 387–431.

———. 2010. *Urbanism and Cultural Landscapes in Northeastern Syria: The Tell Hamoukar Survey, 1999–2001*. Oriental Institute Publications 137. Chicago: University of Chicago Oriental Institute.

Ur, Jason A. and Emily L. Hammer. 2009. Pastoral Nomads of the Second and Third Millennia AD on the Upper Tigris River, Turkey: Archaeological Evidence from the Hirbemerdon Tepe Survey. *Journal of Field Archaeology* 34: 37–56.

Wattenmaker, Patricia. 1994. Kazane Höyük 1992. *Kazı Sonuçları Toplantısı* 17: 177–92.

Whallon, Robert. 1979. *An Archaeological Survey of the Keban Reservoir Area of East-Central Turkey*. Memoirs of the Museum of Anthropology, University of Michigan 11. Ann Arbor: University of Michigan Press.

———. 1983. Methods of Controlled Surface Collection in Archaeological Survey. In *Archaeological Survey in the Mediterranean Area*, ed. Donald R. Keller and David W. Rupp, 73–83. BAR International Series 155. Oxford: British Archaeological Reports.

Wilkinson, Tony J. 1982. The Definition of Ancient Manured Zones by Means of Extensive Sherd-Sampling Techniques. *Journal of Field Archaeology* 9: 323–33.

———. 1989. Extensive Sherd Scatters and Land-Use Intensity: Some Recent Results. *Journal of Field Archaeology* 16: 31–46.

———. 1990. *Town and Country in Southeastern Anatolia, vol. 1: Settlement and Land Use at Kurban Höyük and Other Sites in the Lower Karababa Basin*. Oriental Institute Publications 109. Chicago: Oriental Institute.

———. 1993. Linear Hollows in the Jazira, Upper Mesopotamia. *Antiquity* 67: 548–62.

———. 1994. The Structure and Dynamics of Dry-Farming States in Upper Mesopotamia. *Current Anthropology* 35: 483–520.

———. 2000. Regional Approaches to Mesopotamian Archaeology: The Contribution of Archaeological Surveys. *Journal of Archaeological Research* 8: 219–67.

———. 2003. *Archaeological Landscapes of the Near East*. Tucson: University of Arizona Press.

Wilkinson, Tony J., Jason A. Ur, and Jesse Casana. 2004. From Nucleation to Dispersal: Trends in Settlement Pattern in the Northern Fertile Crescent. In *Side-by-Side Survey: Comparative Regional Studies in the Mediterranean World*, ed. John Cherry and Susan Alcock, 198–205. Oxford: Oxbow Books.

Wilkinson, Tony J., Eleanor Wilkinson, Jason A. Ur, and Mark Altaweel. 2005. Landscape and Settlement in the Neo-Assyrian Empire. *Bulletin of the American Schools of Oriental Research* 340: 23–56.

Williamson, Tom. 1998. Questions of Preservation and Destruction. In *The Archaeology of Landscape: Studies Presented to Christopher Taylor*, ed. Paul Everson and Tom Williamson, 1–24. Manchester: Manchester University Press.

Yardımcı, Nurettin. 2004. *Harran Ovası Yüzey Araştırması /Archaeological Survey in the Harran Plain*. İstanbul: A. Grafik ve Matbaacılık San.

Yener, K. Aslıhan and Hadi Özbal. 1987. Tin in the Turkish Taurus Mountains: The Bolkardağ Mining District. *Antiquity* 61: 220–26.

Yener, K. Aslıhan, Hadi Özbal, Ergun Kaptan, A. Necip Pehlivan, and Martha Goodway. 1989. Kestel: An Early Bronze Age Source of Tin Ore in the Taurus Mountains, Turkey. *Science* 244: 200–203.

Zimansky, Paul E. 1985. *Ecology and Empire: The Structure of the Urartian State*. Studies in Ancient Oriental Civilization 41. Chicago: Oriental Institute.

CHAPTER 39

METALS AND METALLURGY

JAMES D. MUHLY

In a popular account of ancient Anatolian metallurgy, Aslıhan Yener presents the following summation: "The most striking feature of this metallurgical tradition is its precociousness. From the earliest occurrence of metal objects in the aceramic Neolithic (eighth millennium B.C.E.) through the discovery of iron metallurgy, this innovative characteristic never altered" (Yener 2000a:36). The present discussion should make clear the soundness of this evaluation. Several important surveys documenting these developments have appeared in recent years. Yener herself is the author of a very important synthesis of the early development of metallurgical technology in Anatolia, a study of special value because of its comprehensive discussions of material published in Turkish (Yener 2000b). This monograph takes for granted the existence of tin deposits in the Taurus Mountains (see later discussion). Andreas Müller-Karpe has presented a very detailed, well-illustrated (with drawings) presentation of metalworking in Anatolia, from the Aceramic Neolithic to the Early Iron Age (Çayönü to Toprakkale), with emphasis on production paraphernalia (Müller-Karpe 1994). His dating of early metallurgical sites has, however, raised considerable discussion (see Pernicka 1997). A brief but very usable survey of Anatolian metallurgy, from earliest times down to 500 B.C.E., has been published by Yener, Geçkinli, and Özbal (1996). Ünsal Yalçın has also recently published an up-to-date general survey with excellent illustrations (Yalçın 2008).

Metal and Metallurgical Studies

Anatolia is a land blessed with abundant natural resources, including a wealth of mineral deposits and abundant forests, the two elements necessary for a major metal industry. Recent calculations provide the following figures: 415 major copper-rich zones, more than 136 complex lead-zinc-copper ore deposits, and almost 200 silver-lead deposits, as well as numerous deposits of gold, zinc, antimony, arsenic, and iron (Yener, Geçkinli, and Özbal 1996:375). The copper deposits of Anatolia have been studied in great detail in a comprehensive field survey organized by the Max-Planck Institut für Kernphysik in Heidelberg, Germany (for a detailed summary of the results see Wagner et al. 2003). Those deposits with evidence for ancient exploitation have been catalogued in a separate study (Wagner and Öztunalı 2000). The mines at Murgul (TG 211) and Kozlu (TG 275) provide the best evidence for Chalcolithic mining activity (Wagner and Öztunalı 2000:46–47, 49–50).

The geological evidence for Anatolian deposits of gold and silver has now been presented in a detailed survey article with an excellent distribution map (Bayburtoğlu and Yıldırım 2008:44, map, fig. 1). The most famous silver mines are those at Nakhlak, where exploitation can be documented at least as early as the fourth millennium B.C.E. (Stöllner and Weisgerber 2004). The famous gold of the Pactolus River has been studied by the team working at the ancient Lydian capital of Sardis (Ramage and Craddock 2000; see also Geçkinli 2008), but the theory that Pactolus gold was a source for the gold vessels and jewelry found in the Royal Cemetery of Ur, ca. 2500 B.C.E. (Whitmore and Young 1973; Young 1972), can no longer be accepted (Meeks and Tite 1980; Ogden 1977). The iron ore deposits of Anatolia have been studied within the context of the Hittite iron industry (Muhly et al. 1985) and also as potential sources of raw material for the Assyrian iron industry (Maxwell-Hyslop 1974).

Anatolia as a source of tin, especially in the third millennium B.C.E., is still a matter of considerable controversy (see discussion for and against the existence of tin from the Taurus Mountains in Muhly 1993; Yener and Vandiver 1993; Yener, Vandiver, and Willies 1993; also Yener 2000b:71–123, 2008; and see Steadman, chapter 10 in this volume). Much of the discussion has gone on within the context of the beginnings of bronze metallurgy in the third millennium B.C.E. (Muhly 1985; Pare 2000). The possibility that the Taurus Mountains could have supplied the tin for this extensive bronze production has been discounted (Pernicka 1998:143; Yalçın 2003:535). Transcaucasian sources seem to be more probable, on the basis of present evidence (Parzinger 2002; Weisgerber and Cierny 2002), but the matter is still far from settled (Weisgerber and Cierny 2002:185). It is important to remember that the main reason the Assyrians sent quantities of tin and Babylonian textiles to Anatolia was to obtain gold and silver from the local Anatolian princes. This certainly implies an absence of tin resources in Anatolia as well as Anatolian access to quantities of gold and silver (Dercksen 2005:17).

The study of ancient metal technology, the series of processes from ore to artifact, has undergone dramatic changes in recent decades. In the past scholars tended to study only the end product, the artifact itself, concentrating almost entirely on artifact typology. The culmination of such research is represented by the series *Prähistorische Bronzefunde*. Starting in 1969, under the direction of Hermann

Müller-Karpe, this project has now published dozens of detailed volumes. Almost every volume deals with the regional distribution of a particular type of artifact, with a very detailed catalogue and excellent drawings. Anatolia is, unfortunately, very poorly served by this massive research project, the exceptions being the volumes on *Die Äxte und Beile des 2. Jahrtausends in Zentralanatolien* (Erkanal 1977) and *Fibeln in Anatolien I* (Caner 1983).

In recent years research interests have moved away from typology to sources of raw materials and methods of fabrication. Initial emphasis was on the composition of relevant artifacts: were they made of unalloyed copper, arsenical copper, bronze, or leaded bronze? Implicit in this work was the hope that a study of elemental analyses would provide insights into the sources of the raw materials themselves, especially the copper. As part of the great SAM Project (Studien zu den Anfängen der Metallurgie), established by S. Junghans and E. Sangmeister, some 22,000 copper and copper-based artifacts from the Bronze Age world were analyzed (for an evaluation of this project see Muhly 2008:36–39). Those from Anatolia were studied by Ufuk Esin in a volume that remains the basic corpus of spectrographic metal analyses of copper and copper-based artifacts from Anatolia (Esin 1969). Conclusions regarding metal types and sources of copper based on these analyses soon became matters of great controversy (for summary see Muhly 1973:339–42).

Although many new analytical techniques have been introduced in recent years, the basic problem remains the same. Elemental analysis provides excellent evidence for the types of copper alloys in use; it cannot provide reliable evidence for determining the provenience of raw materials. In 1982 it was proposed that the geological technique of lead isotope analysis could be used to study the trace amounts of lead present in all copper ore deposits (Gale and Stos-Gale 1982). The distribution of the four stable isotopes of lead in objects of ancient copper was not affected by any human manipulation of that metal, thus making provenience study based on lead isotope evidence far more reliable than earlier work based on elemental composition (Gale and Stos-Gale 2000; Stos-Gale 1989). Lead isotope analysis has been used to study the copper and bronze artifacts from Troy II, from the palace and the "royal" tomb at Arslantepe, and the hoard from Tülintepe (Pernicka 1998; Yalçın and Gönül Yalçın 2008). The lead isotope technique is best known from its use in the study of Late Bronze Age (LBA) copper oxhide ingots, especially those from the Cape Gelidonya and Uluburun shipwrecks (Hauptmann, Maddin, and Prange 2002; Stos 2009:166–73).

The initial reaction to this new method for studying the provenience of metals was little short of euphoric. As so often in scholarly debates, the pendulum soon swung in the opposite direction. Can we identify Anatolian copper, Cypriot copper, Transcaucasian copper? Does lead isotope analysis provide the key to unlock all the problems involved in the study of the LBA metals trade? For a judicious summary of where we stand, see M. S. Tite (1996). For a more critical evaluation of the problem, see A. M. Pollard (2009).

Earliest Anatolian Metals and Metallurgy: The Neolithic and Chalcolithic

In a recent review of Aegean archaeometallurgy, published in 2008, I noted "a shift in the nature of archaeometallurgical research in the Aegean, a movement away from the emphasis upon the composition of finished artifacts to more basic issues of mining, smelting and production" (Muhly 2008:41). The same holds true for Anatolia, but this is best seen within a review of the ongoing archaeological evidence. Evaluation of that evidence has been transformed in recent years by two fundamental developments: (1) the remarkable discoveries of new sites with important metallurgical remains, and (2) the introduction of calibrated radiocarbon dates suggesting radical revisions in traditional archaeological chronology.

One factor has remained constant. However much the absolute dates have changed, the beginnings of metal use in Anatolia are still best documented at the site of Çayönü Tepesi (and for the cultural background of this site, and for Aceramic and Early Neolithic Anatolia, see the remarkable publication Vor 12.000 Jahren in Anatolien. Die ältesten Monumente der Menschheit 2007; for basic analytical work on metal artifacts from Çayönü see Maddin, Muhly, and Stech 1999; Muhly 1989). All calibrated radiocarbon dates for sites in what is designated as Upper Mesopotamia, comprising southeastern Turkey, north Syria, and north Iraq, covering the period eleventh–sixth millennia B.C.E., have been compiled, as of December 2006, in an Internet document by Bischoff, Reingruber, and Thissen (2006). This includes, for example, twenty-nine dates from Çayönü and twenty dates from Nevalı Çori; for general survey of Mesopotamian and Anatolian metal finds, see Schoop 1995. Ünsal Yalçın (2000b, 2003) has presented a five-stage sequence for the development of early metallurgy in Anatolia, from ca. 8200 to ca. 2800 B.C.E. (see Yalçın 2003:529, table 1). One must first distinguish between finds of malachite as a semi-precious stone, for use as decoration, and malachite to be used as a source of copper. Prior to the development of smelting technology, ca. 5000 B.C.E. (Yalçın 2000a), all copper finds represent the use of native copper. Very early finds of malachite, from Pre-Pottery Neolithic (PPN) A levels at Hallan Çemi and Çayönü (Yalçın 2000b:19, table 1), have nothing to do with copper metallurgy, just as early finds of hematite have nothing to do with iron metallurgy. The earliest known copper finds from Çayönü, consisting of 113 copper beads, come from PPN B levels at the site and are now dated to ca. 8200–7500 B.C.E. (Yalçın 2000b:19, table 2). Slightly later, ca. 7800–7600 B.C.E., are the forty-five copper beads from Aşıklı Höyük in which lumps of native copper were heated and then hammered to form a strip of metal that was then rolled to form a bead (Yalçın and Pernicka 1999; for excavation and series of ^{14}C dates see Esin 1999).

Similar finds, in much smaller quantities, are known from sites such as Nevalı Çori, Çatal Höyük, and Hacılar (Yalçın 2000b:19, table 2). All represent Yalçın's

Phase II in the development of Anatolian metallurgy, the Anfangsphase, ca. 8200–7300 B.C.E. (Yalçın 2003:529, table 1), that is, the use of native copper. Hammering, hot working, and annealing were being employed, but no smelting or casting. Contrary to earlier reports, the macehead from House 3, Level 2b at Can Hasan, now dated to ca. 6000 B.C.E., was still made of native copper that had been hammered and annealed (Yalçın 1998). The Can Hasan macehead can thus be seen as representing the final phase of Yalçın's Phase II, involving the first production of a substantial metal artifact, prior to the development of Phase III, the Entwicklungs phase of extractive metallurgy, a period that can properly be called Early Chalcolithic (Yalçın 2003:531).

The early part of Phase III is best documented by the finds from Mersin Level XVI, now dated ca. 5000–4900 B.C.E. (Yalçın 2000a), which, in Mesopotamian terms, represents the height of Ubaid influence at the site (Caneva 2000:70–71). This influence continued throughout the fifth millennium B.C.E., and the typology of metal artifacts remained constant during this period (Mersin XVI–XIIB). In 1969 Ufuk Esin published spectrographic analyses of 53 objects from Mersin. Most of these were from later periods, the Middle and Late Bronze Ages, and the dating of many objects has been revised on the basis of new excavations conducted by Isabella Caneva (2000). A new study of forty-one samples from Mersin encountered all the same problems, but seemed to indicate the use of unalloyed copper and arsenical copper even in the LBA, with very little use of tin (Kuruçayırlı and Özbal 2005b:55, 58; table of analyses in Kuruçayırlı and Özbal 2005a:190, table 5). Yalçın dealt with nine early copper objects from Mersin, two pins probably from Mersin XXI, and five pins and two chisels from Mersin XVI (Yalçın 2000a:114, table 3). The objects were basically made of unalloyed copper, but with trace element impurities and metal structures that indicated the use of copper smelted from its ores and then cast.

From Late Ubaid levels at sites in southeastern Anatolia, excavated as part of the Keban Dam salvage project, we now have a series of important metallurgical sites. The unfortunate aspect of this work is that although we have an excellent series of preliminary reports, in Turkish, German, and English, not one of these sites has received a final excavation report. What this means is that general outlines are clear, but details of excavation contexts remain unpublished. In basic terms these sites seem to cover a late fifth to early fourth millennium B.C.E. chronological horizon. The most significant of these sites seems to be that at Değirmentepe, especially the area of Building I excavated by Esin from 1978 to 1986 and then flooded by the Karakaya Dam in 1987. The most important metallurgical remains come from Level 7 of this building, dated to what can be called Regional Ubaid (Ubaid 3; Amuq E and F); preliminary reports can be found in *Kazı Sonuçları Toplantısı* V (1984, 71–79), VI (1985, 11–29), VII (1986, 55–85), VIII (1987, 95–137), IX (1988, 79–125); a synthesis is available in Yener 2000b:33–44. As at all related sites, this building had schematic red and black wall decoration on white plaster, monumental hearths, and altar tables, all within structures that have been identified as temples (Esin 1983:180–81).

The problem with this identification is that metallurgical slag and structures identified as copper smelting furnaces were found in almost every part of the building, even in the central room I (Yener 2000b:34, 36). It is hard to believe that copper ore was being smelted within the confines of a temple precinct, but Yener claims that over 30 percent of the site of Değirmentepe was directly involved in the production, storage, or distribution of copper and other related materials (Yener 2000b:13). Değirmentepe, it is claimed, was a special purpose site devoted to metallurgy (Yener 2000b:41). Complete furnaces were supposedly excavated at Değirmentepe (Yener, Geçkinli, and Özbal 1996:337), but no details or plans have ever been published, and the entire site is now under water. Analytical evidence, from this and related sites, indicates that, by ca. 4000 B.C.E., arsenical copper had become the dominant alloy in use (Özbal 1986).

We are in a somewhat better position to describe metallurgical activities at the site of Norşuntepe, the largest site in the Altınova valley, excavated for six seasons (1968–74) by Harald Hauptmann, as part of the Keban Salvage Project (summary in Yener 2000b:57–61). Again there are only preliminary reports (Gladiß and Hauptmann 1974; H. Hauptmann 1969–70, 1976, 1982), but better illustrated and with more detail than was the case at Değirmentepe. At Norşuntepe we have a large central building with traces of black and red wall painting (level 9, rooms 8 and 9), representing a regional Ubaid culture clearly contemporary with Değirmentepe. A number of Chalcolithic furnaces were excavated, but the best preserved example, a natural-draft domed furnace of keyhole shape, came from Early Bronze Age (EBA) I levels at the site, along with pits full of casting ladles, crucibles, and copper slag (H. Hauptmann 1982:Pl. 18, no.4 and Pl. 31: excellent drawing of furnace). Next to the furnace were found two-piece molds for casting shaft-hole axes and even the ceramic cores used in forming the shaft hole itself (H. Hauptmann 1982:57 and Pl. 26, nos. 9 and 10). Norşuntepe clearly functioned as a major Chalcolithic metallurgical site (H. Hauptmann 1982:61).

Important analytical work has been done on metal finds from the sites of Tepecik and Tülintepe (Özbal 1983), including an important study of the hoard from Tülintepe (Yalçın and Gönül Yalçın 2008), with lead isotope analysis of objects from the hoard. Esin gave an excellent account of early work at Tepecik back in 1975, in which she summarized the relative status of the sites in the Altınova valley: Değirmentepe, a small riparian village, Tepecik, a town, and Norşuntepe, a city (Esin 1975:47). It is most unfortunate that we still lack a final publication of any one of these very important Keban Salvage Project sites, which, in addition to their importance for early metallurgical developments, preserve some of the earliest evidence for wall painting in the ancient world.

One of the outstanding features at all of these sites is the appearance at the end of the fifth millennium B.C.E. of the distinctive Transcaucasian pottery known as Khirbet Kerak or Karaz ware. The metallurgical implications of this ceramic intrusion can best be seen at the site of Arslantepe. The metal finds here consist of two important bodies of material: the palace hoard from Level VIA, from a context that can be described as Late Chalcolithic or Late Uruk (3300–3000 B.C.E.), and the finds from the "royal" tomb dating to the very beginning of EB I (level VII B1, ca. 3000–2900 B.C.E.). Both bodies of material have been discussed in extensive detail in recent years (summary in Yener 2000b:48–57; analytical work in Hauptmann et al. 2002). The twenty-two metal artifacts found in the mudbrick collapse of Building III consist of nine short swords (very unusual at this early date), twelve spearheads, and a quadruple spiral plaque. Atomic absorption analyses of these artifacts present a confused picture, as it is difficult to compare the 1988 analyses (Caneva and Palmieri 1988) with those published in 2002 (Hauptmann et al. 2002:table 5). The new analyses, of four spearheads and three swords, document the use of an arsenical copper, averaging 3.89 percent arsenic. This puts Arslantepe VIA in agreement with contemporary Keban sites, documenting the importance of arsenical copper during the Late Chalcolithic–EB I transitional period.

During the time of the "royal" tomb there seem to have been three different types of metal in circulation (Hauptmann et al. 2002:49, 52):

1. the arsenical copper alloy, present in objects from the palace hoard;
2. a copper-arsenic-nickel alloy, found already in limited amounts in the palace hoard but now much more predominant and derived from different ores than those used for the arsenical copper alloy; and
3. a copper-silver alloy, found in twenty-eight examples from the royal tomb, but present already in the remarkable quadruple spiral pendant from the palace hoard, with 64 percent silver and 16 percent copper, whereas the pieces from the royal tomb have roughly equal amounts of copper and silver. As such they all represent remarkable hypoeutectic alloys, as the eutectic composition of such an alloy is 28 percent copper, 72 percent silver.

All this is evidence for the remarkable complexity of the archaeology of eastern Anatolia during this Late Chalcolithic–EB I transitional period (see Frangipane, chapter 45; Palumbi, chapter 9; Marro, chapter 12; and Sagona, chapter 30 in this volume). The copper-arsenic-nickel alloy must be the result of the introduction of new sources of copper from Transcaucasia, associated with the introduction of Khirbet Kerak/Karaz pottery, but this alloy must also have some connection with the contemporary appearance of a similar alloy during the Late Chalcolithic of southern Palestine, best documented in the hoard from Nahal Mishmar (Tadmor et al. 1995). Analytical work on objects from the Nahal Mishmar hoard, as well as contemporary finds from the site of Shiqmim (Golden, Levy, and Hauptmann 2001), indicates that although the unalloyed copper artifacts from these sites seem to be made of copper imported as ore from Faynan (on the other side of the Jordan River) and were manufactured locally, the complex, ritual artifacts, made of the copper-arsenic-nickel alloy, represent a technology that cannot be documented in the southern Levant or anywhere else (A. Hauptmann 2007:291–301). There must be some common center of metallurgical technology for southeastern Anatolia and for the southern Levant that at present we can locate only somewhere in Transcaucasia. It is difficult to understand the context of the Royal Tomb at Arslantepe, as it seems to have been created in isolation, with no other contemporary material in the area (Frangipane et al. 2001:121).

To the southeast, however, in the vicinity of Birecik, a huge EB I cemetery has been excavated (Sertok and Ergeç 1999). The 312 tombs excavated to date contained a large number of "bronze" weapons and spearheads, similar to those from Arslantepe (Frangipane et al. 2001:122–23). Northeast of Birecik is the site of Hassek Höyük, where metal analyses have demonstrated very clearly the dominance of arsenical copper at ca. 3000 B.C.E. Chemical analyses of seventy-five metal artifacts from Hassek Höyük have shown that fifty-two were made of arsenical copper, averaging 1.9 percent arsenic, whereas only one of these objects had more than 1.0 percent tin (Schmitt-Strecker, Begemann, and Pernicka 1992). Hassek Höyük was also part of the arsenical copper tradition associated with the Ninevite V culture of north Syria and north Mesopotamia (Behm-Blancke 2003; Muhly and Stech 2003).

The copper-silver objects from the royal tomb at Arslantepe represent a remarkable technology, in which the copper-rich part of the alloy was selectively oxidized, producing a copper scale that was removed during the hammering and annealing necessary to produce the finished artifact. The result was an alloy with a bright silvery surface (Hauptmann et al. 2002:52). Such objects, appearing to be of silver but with significant copper content, are known from all over the ancient world at the end of the fourth millennium B.C.E., from Croatia (Balen and Mihelić 2007) and the tumulus of Mala Gruda on the Adriatic coast of Montenegro (Maran 2007:8–9; Primas 1988, 1996). This copper-silver alloy was also being used in Early Minoan I Crete, ca. 3000 B.C.E., as we know from a series of six "silver" daggers, of which three, from the site of Koumasa, have been analyzed. They have 27.0 percent, 18.7 percent, and 10 percent copper (Stos-Gale 1985:366, and 372, table 1; Vasilakis 2008:82–83 and figs. 21–26).

The use of these copper-silver alloys suggests a shortage of silver, which for Anatolia is quite surprising given the country's extensive silver deposits, as well as the archaeological evidence for the early use of silver. The earliest silver object from Anatolia has long been thought to be the small silver ring from level XXXIV at Beycesultan, dated to the late fifth millennium B.C.E. (Stronach 1962:282). This dating, however, has now been lowered by ca. 1,000 years, putting this hoard, the silver ring, and the objects of arsenical copper in the late fourth millennium B.C.E. (Mellink 1967:3–9). As such, this silver ring is actually contemporary with the silver inlays on some of the short swords from the palace hoard at Arslantepe (Frangipane 2004:72–73, nos. 59–62). Some of the most remarkable silver from this period comes from the poorly published objects excavated at the Late Chalcolithic Keban site of Korucutepe (Brandt 1978). The cemetery at this site included the burial of a young woman whose grave contained a silver band, four small silver rings, a crescent-shaped gorget of silver, and two lozenge-shaped beads of sheet silver. Most remarkable was a bracelet made of thin silver threads (diameter approximately four millimeters) woven together to form the bracelet. This object is, to my knowledge, totally without precedent (see also van Loon 1973). What is most surprising about this early Anatolian silver is that it does not seem to represent the exploitation of local sources. Such is the conclusion derived from analytical study of the silver from the palace hoard at Arslantepe, the only silver from this period subjected to scientific analysis (Hauptmann et al. 2002:68–69).

Due to the lack of final publication, the extent of Late Chalcolithic–EB I metallurgy in eastern Anatolia has been greatly underestimated. A recent investigation of the storerooms of the Elazığ museum identified a total of some 4,700 unpublished metal artifacts dating to this period, demonstrating "the urgent need of scientific investigations on this subject" (Yalçın and Gönül Yalçın 2009:132, n. 3). What remains to be discovered has been made clear by the results of just one such study, that on the small hoard of metal objects from Tülintepe, discovered by chance in 1966. Examination of this small hoard, consisting of a short sword and five spearheads, using the scanning electron microscope, revealed that all objects had been completely covered with tin (Yalçın and Gönül Yalçın 2009:128). This is all the more remarkable given that the objects from this hoard were made of arsenical copper, containing no more than 0.016 percent tin (Yalçın and Gönül Yalçın 2009:137, table 3).

This highly unexpected situation suggests that Late Chalcolithic metalworkers thought of tin as a metal to be used for coating the surface of a copper artifact, presumably to imitate the appearance of silver, before they thought of adding tin to molten copper to produce bronze. There is, however, one other artifact from Tülintepe, a roll-headed pin also thought to be Late Chalcolithic, that has 5.27 percent tin. If the dating is correct this would be "probably the earliest tin bronze in the whole Near East" (Yalçın and Gönül Yalçın 2009:129). If this pin really is Late Chalcolithic, contemporary with the arsenical copper objects in the hoard, this suggests that in the late fourth millennium B.C.E., the metalworkers of eastern Anatolia were experimenting with how to make use of tin, a new metal they were learning how to utilize.

Bronze Age Metals and Metallurgy

The transition from Late Chalcolithic to the beginning of the Early Bronze Age, ca. 3000 B.C.E., marks a geographical transition as well. The main focus of metallurgical development in Anatolia now shifts from the eastern part of the country to central and western Anatolia. The most important early developments seem to be concentrated in the western part of the country, especially the northwest. This shift also marks a change in the foreign influences affecting Anatolian metallurgy. A strong Aegean orientation replaces the Mesopotamian traditions of the past. This can be seen in the relations between metalwork from Troy I–III and that from related sites in the north Aegean, especially Poliochni (Lemnos) and Thermi (Lesbos), as well as metalwork from new excavations carried out under the direction of Hayat Erkanal, especially from the site of Bakla Tepe (excellent summaries by Ourania Kouka 2008, 2009a). A great deal of analytical work, including lead isotope analysis, has been carried out on many of the finds from these sites (Pernicka 1998).

Although the various "treasures" (actually hoards) excavated by Schliemann at Troy have always taken pride of place in any discussion of this period, I argue that metallurgically the most important development was the introduction of tin and the development of bronze metallurgy. I further confine the use of the term *bronze* to the alloy of copper and tin; the alloy of copper and arsenic should be called arsenical copper; thus the expression "tin-bronze" is redundant. The source of this tin remains the great enigma. Lead isotope analysis has actually compounded the mystery, for the early examples of bronze, from Troy IIg, Poliochni "yellow," and Kastri, are made from a copper-tin alloy with trace element lead of Precambrian geological date. Such ore deposits do not exist in the Aegean or in Anatolia, but are found in Central Asia (Gale 2008). In other words, the beginnings of bronze metallurgy, in northwestern Anatolia and the north Aegean, seems to be associated with the exploitation of a copper ore (for tin contains no lead) from parts of the world now also being seen as potential sources for the tin itself (Muhly and Pernicka 1992). Anatolian copper, on the other hand, seems to have been exported to Cyprus, where it was used to fashion the copper-based artifacts of the contemporary Philia Culture (Webb et al. 2006).

This is not the place to deal with all the problems involved in assigning an absolute date to material from Troy II and related sites. Suffice to say that from a metallurgical perspective, all of these EB II sites can be placed in the middle (extending into the third quarter) of the third millennium B.C.E. Earlier and later dates are simply no longer acceptable (Kouka 2009b). This is the period often called the "Age of Gold," when bronze metallurgy, gold jewelry, and semi-precious stones such as carnelian and lapis lazuli came into use over a broad geographical expanse, from southern Mesopotamia to the Aegean and beyond (Rahmstorf 2006). Yener (2000b:67) speaks of this period as representing "a renaissance of industrial metallurgy in the ancient Near East," but it really represents something entirely new, not any sort of a "revival" or "rebirth." Within this historical context we must now evaluate the metal finds from such central Anatolian sites as Alaca Höyük and İkiztepe.

The renewed excavations at Troy, carried out under the direction of Manfred Korfmann (1988–2003), have made it possible to confirm the EB II date for the various hoards of metalwork uncovered by Schliemann (Korfmann 2003; Sazcı and Korfmann 2000). In the case of Alaca Höyük we have only the excavations of H. Z. Koşay (1936–39), and the date of the metalwork found in these Royal Tombs has long been debated. Still the subject of serious debate is not only the date but also the meaning of the elaborate "standards" and "sun disks" that have made this site so famous. The first serious study of the metalwork was published by Mellink (1956). Like most scholarship published in the 1950s, 1960s, and 1970s, Mellink put great emphasis on parallels with the metalwork from the famous Caucasian site of Maikop. This is no longer possible, as calibrated radiocarbon dates now put Maikop at ca. 3600–3300 B.C.E., contemporary with Uruk IVa in southern Mesopotamia (Anthony 2007:289). Attempts have been made to connect the Alaca Höyük paraphernalia with Caucasian wagons (Mansfeld 2001; Orthmann 1967) or with the worship of the "great goddess" (Korfmann 1986; Özyar 2000), all without much success (Zimmermann 2008b). More convincing is the connection with the Hattian population of EBA Anatolia, known mainly from later copies of texts written in the Hattic language. This implies an EB III date for Alaca and a connection with a number of other sites, including İkiztepe and Horoztepe, as well as that from very recent excavations at Bekaroğlu and Kalınkaya, making up what has been called the Central Black Sea Cultural Region (İpek and Zimmermann 2007:50, fig. 1; Yıldırım and Zimmermann 2006; Zimmermann 2007a). Metallurgically, the most important consideration here is the emphasis on local production. The elaborate "standards" and "sun disks" were locally made, presumably by Hattian metalworkers (Zimmermann 2008b:516–17).

Within the context of Alaca Höyük must also be considered the two metal hoards from Eskiyapar (Özgüç and Temizer 1993:613–28), including the earliest example, from Anatolia, of a silver quadruple spiral bead, an artifact with an extensive archaeological literature (Huot, Pardo, and Rouguelle 1980). There is a surprising quantity of silver from EB II–III Anatolia, including many silver vessels, as well as those of gold (Toker and Öztürk 1992), and silver used in inlay work. The six silver ingots from "Treasure" A at Troy are very well known (Renfrew 1972:408–9; Schliemann 1881:470–72, nos. 787–92). Less well known are the sixteen large and small silver ingots from EB II Mahmatlar (Koşay and Akok 1950). Analyses of two of the ingots from Mahmatlar and two from Troy showed surprisingly high levels of zinc, as much as 13 percent (Yener 2000b:68; Yener, Geçkinli, and Özbal 1996:380). Such levels of zinc in silver are hard to explain. Six of the sixteen ingots from Mahmatlar have been studied by lead isotope analysis, indicating that the silver probably came from the Aladağ outlier of the Taurus Mountains (Yener et al. 1991:573). This would not be surprising, as the Taurus have long been identified with the "Silver Mountains" mentioned in the inscriptions of Sargon of Akkad (Frayne 1993:28–29; Yener 1983; for the Taurus as a source of silver in Greco-Roman times see Cary 1932). Seven pieces of silver from the Trojan "treasures" are also said to have been made of silver from the central Taurus (Yener et al. 1991:558–59). During the uncertain conditions following the collapse of the Akkadian Empire (ca. 2200 B.C.E.) there seems to have been considerable hoarding of silver, in southern Mesopotamia, northern Syria, and even into Anatolia (Matthews 1994).

The silver finds from Karataş-Semayük, where ^{14}C dates indicate that the earliest tombs go back to ca. 3000 B.C.E. (Stech and Pigott 1986:51) include a pin with a head in the shape of a wild boar (Bingöl 1999:197, no. 219). This extensive use of silver continues into the early second millennium B.C.E. The 1992 excavations at Acemhöyük produced a pot containing 211 silver artifacts (Öztan 1992). Of all the sites making up the Black Sea complex the most extensively excavated is that of İkiztepe, under investigation since 1974 (for extensive bibliography and recent evaluation, see Zimmermann 2008a). There has also been much confusion regarding the date of the metal finds from this site (for summary by the current excavator, Önder Bilgi, see Bilgi 2001). What has traditionally been called EB III is now considered to be transitional Late Chalcolithic–EB I. This is especially true of the so-called ring idols made of gold (Zimmermann 2007b). The typical copper alloy at İkiztepe was arsenical copper, often with quite high levels of arsenic (Yener, Geçkinli, and Özbal 1996:378). Much of the metalwork from İkiztepe can be compared with that from Ilıpınar, on the Sea of Marmara, another transitional Late Chalcolithic–EB I site with early use of arsenical copper (Begemann, Pernicka, and Schmitt-Strecker 1994).

From EB III Cilicia, there are two important groups of metal artifacts. The first consists of a hoard of seventy-seven metal artifacts found by a shepherd in a pithos burial in 1889. This hoard was published by Bittel (1940). The typology of the artifacts, including daggers, spearheads, axes, and seals, is typical for the period. What is of special importance is the strong presence of bronze. Ten of the artifacts were analyzed by means of wet chemistry. Five proved to be made of bronze, averaging 9.1 percent tin (Kuruçayırlı and Özbal 2005a:181). This certainly demonstrates the use of bronze in Cilicia during the EB III period. The second important body of metal finds is that from the excavations of Hetty Goldman (1956) at Tarsus-Gözlükule. The metal objects were all excavated during the seasons 1936–38. Goldman published a total of 512 metal objects, from EB II through Roman times. Recent work in the storerooms of the museum has discovered an additional 215 metal finds (Kuruçayırlı and Özbal 2005a:180). In 1969, Esin published a total of seventy spectrographic analyses from Tarsus. The most recent study of this material provides a total of eighty-seven Tarsus analyses (Kuruçayırlı and Özbal 2005a:187–91, table 4). Most of these are of artifacts of post-EB date. Twelve are said to be of EB II date; twenty of EB III. Arsenical copper is the dominant alloy. There is one EB II bronze artifact, a toggle pin with 5.4 percent tin, and several low-tin EB III bronzes.

Metallurgical developments at EB II–III Tarsus are not impressive. The area seems to have been something of a backwater and has always been a puzzle. The most recent study of metallurgy at Tarsus makes the following observations:

> Surprisingly, although Tarsus probably controlled the argentiferous galena deposits of the Bolkar Mountains and regulated the silver trade to the south, no silver objects were recovered from the excavations. (Kuruçayırlı and Özbal 2005a:180)
>
> Utilization of tin in the production of bronze during the EB and MB periods both at Tarsus and neighboring settlements are rather limited, yet Tarsus must have played an active role in the trade of Kestel tin to the south. (Kuruçayırlı and Özbal 2005a:194)

It is, however, very unlikely that Tarsus played any role in a trade in silver or tin. Trade in Kestel tin is unlikely to begin with, and in general, trade between southeastern Anatolia and Syro-Mesopotamia followed major river courses and had nothing to do with Tarsus. Recent research by Yener, as part of her Amuq survey and her new excavations at Alalakh, has emphasized the importance of the Orontes River, now shown to have been navigable at least as far north as Alalakh.

Conclusion

Space considerations prevent the extension of this chapter into the second millennium B.C.E. Given the detailed exposition of the metallurgy of this period already presented by A. Müller-Karpe (1994), I thought it best to concentrate on the periods that have been the subject of most recent fieldwork in Turkey and have witnessed many of the most exciting archaeological discoveries. Although Hittite texts present a wealth of evidence relevant to metal technology (Siegelová 2005), the artifacts themselves indicate that no significant metallurgical developments took place during the period (ca. 1700–1200 B.C.E.) when the Hittite Empire was one of the dominant powers in the ancient world. The only exception to this might be the Hittite role in the development of iron metallurgy. Hittite Anatolia seems to have remained outside the expansive development of the international trade in metals that is the most distinctive characteristic of this period. With the wealth of mineral resources available locally, the Hittites saw no need to go abroad in search of new supplies of basic raw materials. The unanswered question for Middle and Late Bronze Age metallurgy in Anatolia, Cyprus, and the Aegean still remains the source(s) of tin.

REFERENCES

Anthony, David W. 2007. *The Horse, the Wheel, and Language: How Bronze Age Riders from the Eurasian Steppes shaped the Modern World.* Princeton, N.J.: Princeton University Press.

Balen, Jacqueline and Sanjin Mihelić. 2007. Silver Axes from Stari Jankovci and the Problem of Finds of Precious Metals during the Early Bronze Age in Continental Croatia. In *Between the Aegean and Baltic Seas: Prehistory across Borders*, ed. Ioanna Galanaki, Helena Tomas, Yannis Galanakis, and Robert Laffineur, 105–11. Aegaeum 27. Liège: Université de Liège.

Bayburtoğlu, Bülent and Selahattin Yıldırım. 2008. Gold and Silver in Anatolia. In *Anatolian Metal IV*, ed. Ünsal Yalçın, 43–53. Bochum: Deutsches Bergbau-Museum.

Begemann, Friedrich, Ernst Pernicka, and Sigfrid Schmitt-Strecker. 1994. Metal Finds from Ilıpınar and the Advent of Arsenical Copper. *Anatolica* 20: 203–19.

Behm-Blancke, Manfred Robert. 2003. Northern Frontiers: Early Ninevite 5 Contacts with Southeastern Anatolia. In *The Origins of North Mesopotamian Civilization: Ninevite 5 Chronology, Economy, Society*, ed. Elena Rova and Harvey Weiss, 481–92. Subartu 9. Turnhout: Brepols.

Bilgi, Önder. 2001. *Protohistoric Age. Metallurgists of the Central Black Sea Region: A New Perspective on the Question of the Indo-Europeans' Original Homeland.* İstanbul: TASK Vakfı.

Bingöl, F. R. Işik. 1999. *Ancient Jewellery*. Ankara: Museum of Ancient Civilizations.

Bischoff, Damien, Agathe Reingruber, and Laurens Thissen. 2006. Upper Mesopotamia (SE Turkey, N. Syria and N. Iraq) 14C databases: 11th–6th millennia cal BC. In *Central Anatolian Neolithic e-Workshop*, ed. Frédéric Gérard and Laurens Thissen. (Available on Internet).

Bittel, Kurt. 1940. Der Depotfund von Soloi-Pompeiopolis. *Zeitschrift für Assyriologie* 46: 183–205.

Brandt, Roelof W. 1978. The Cemetery. In *Korucutepe. Final Report on the Excavations of the Universities of Chicago, California (Los Angeles) and Amsterdam in the Keban Reservoir, Eastern Anatolia 1968–1970, vol. 2*, ed. Maurits N. van Loon, 61–62. Amsterdam: North-Holland.

Caner, Ertuğrul. 1983. *Fibeln in Anatolien I. Prähistorische Bronzefunde XIV/8.* Munich: C. H. Beck Verlag.

Caneva, Claudio and Alberto M. Palmieri. 1988. Metalwork at Arslantepe in Late Chalcolithic and Early Bronze I: The Evidence from Metal Analyses. In *Perspectives on Protourbanization in Eastern Anatolia: Arslantepe (Malatya). An Interim Report on 1975–1983 Campaigns*, ed. Marcella Frangipane, and Alba Palmieri, 637–54. Origini XII/2.

Caneva, Isabella. 2000. Early Metallurgy in Cilicia: A Review from Mersin. In *Anatolian Metal I*, ed. Ünsal Yalçın, 69–74. Bochum: Deutsches Bergbau-Museum.

Cary, Max. 1932. The Sources of Silver for the Greek World. In *Mélanges Gustave Glotz*, 133–42. Paris: Presses Université de France.

Dercksen, Jan Gerrit. 2005. Metals According to Documents from Kültepe-Kanish Dating to the Old Assyrian Colony Period. In *Anatolian Metal III*, ed. Ünsal Yalçın 17–34. Bochum: Deutsches Bergbau-Museum.

Erkanal, Hayat. 1977. *Die Äxte und Beile des 2. Jahrtausends in Zentralanatolien*. Prähistorische Bronzefunde IX/8. Munich: C. H. Beck Verlag.

Esin, Ufuk. 1969. *Kuantatif Spektral Analiz Yardımıyla Anadolu'da başlangıcından Asur Kolonileri Çağına kadar Bakır ve Tunç Madenciliği I*. İstanbul: İstanbul University.

———. 1975. Tepecik, 1974. *Anatolian Studies* 25: 46–49.

———. 1983. Zur Datierung der vorgeschichtlichen Schichten von Degirmentepe bei Malatya in der östlichen Türkei. In *Beiträge zur Altertumskunde Kleinasiens: Festschrift für Kurt Bittel*, ed. Rainer M. Boehmer and Harald Hauptmann, 175–90. Mainz: Von Zabern.

———. 1999. Copper Objects from the Pre-Pottery Neolithic Site of Aşlık (Kızılkaya Village, Province of Aksaray, Turkey). In *The Beginnings of Metallurgy*, ed. Andreas Hauptmann, Ernst Pernicka, Thilo Rehren, and Ünsal Yalçın, 23–30. Bochum: Deutsches Bergbau-Museum.

Frangipane, Marcella, ed. 2004. *Alle origini del potere. Arslantepe, la collina dei leoni*. Milan: Mondadori Electa.

Frangipane, Marcella, Gian Maria Di Nocera, Andreas Hauptmann, Paola Morbidelli, Alberto Palmieri, Laura Sadori, Michael Schultz, and Tyede Schmidt-Schultz. 2001. New Symbols of a New Power in a "Royal" Tomb from 3000 BC Arslantepe, Malatya (Turkey). *Paléorient* 27: 105–39.

Frayne, Donald. 1993. *RIM Early Periods, Vol. 2: Sargonic and Gutian Periods (2334–2113 BC)*. Toronto: University of Toronto Press.

Gale, Noel. 2008. Metal Sources for Early Bronze Age Troy and the Aegean. In *The Aegean in the Neolithic, Chalcolithic and the Early Bronze Age*, ed. Hayat Erkanal, Harald Hauptmann, Vasıf Şahoğlu, and Riza Tuncel, 203–22. Ankara: Ankara University.

Gale, Noel H. and Zofia A. Stos-Gale. 1982. Bronze Age Copper Sources in the Mediterranean: A New Approach. *Science* 216: 11–19.

———. 2000. Lead Isotope Analyses Applied to Provenience Studies. In *Modern Analytical Methods in Art and Archaeology*, ed. Enrico Ciliberto and Giuseppe Spoto, 503–84. New York: Wiley.

Geçkinli, E. Emel. 2008. On the Pactolus Alluvial Gold of Sardis, Turkey. In *Ancient Mining in Turkey and the Eastern Mediterranean*, ed. Ünsal Yalçın, Hadi Özbal, and A. G. Paşamehmetoğlu, 119–38. Ankara: Atılım University.

Gladiß, Almut von and Harald Hauptmann. 1974. Norşuntepe. *Antike Welt* 5.2: 9–19.

Golden, Jonathan, Thomas E. Levy, and Andreas Hauptmann. 2001. Recent Discoveries Concerning Chalcolithic Metallurgy at Shiqmim, Israel. *Journal of Archaeological Science* 28: 951–63.

Goldman, Hetty. 1956. *Excavations at Gözlükule, Tarsus, II*. Princeton, N.J.: Princeton University Press.

Hauptmann, Andreas. 2007. *The Archaeometallurgy of Copper: Evidence from Faynan, Jordan*. Berlin: Springer Verlag.

Hauptmann, Andreas, Robert Maddin, and Michael Prange. 2002. On the Structure and Composition of Copper and Tin Ingots Excavated from the Shipwreck of Uluburun. *Bulletin of the American Schools of Oriental Research* 328: 1–30.

Hauptmann, Andreas, Sigfrid Schmitt-Strecker, Friedrich Begemann, and Alberto Palmieri. 2002. Chemical Composition and Lead Isotopy of Metal Objects from the "Royal" Tomb and Other Related Finds at Arslantepe, Eastern Anatolia. *Paléorient* 28: 43–69.

Hauptmann, Harald. 1969–70. Norşun-Tepe. Historische Geographie und Ergebnisse der Grabungen 1968/69. *Istanbuler Mitteilungen* 19–20: 21–78.

———. 1976. Die Entwicklung der frühbronzezeitlichen Siedlung auf dem Norşuntepe in Ostanatolien. *Archäologisches Korrespondenzblatt* 6.1: 9–20.

———. 1982. Die Grabungen auf dem Norşuntepe, 1974. In *Keban Project 1971 Activities* I.7: 41–70. Ankara: Middle Eastern Technical University.

Huot, J. L., V. Pardo, and A. Rougeulle. 1980. A propos de la perle L.76.5 de Larsa: Les perles à quatre spirales. *Iraq* 42: 120–29.

İpek, Önder and Thomas Zimmermann. 2007. Another Glimpse at "Hattian" Metalwork? A Group of Bronze Age Metal Items from Bekaroğlu Köyü, District of Çorum, Turkey. *Anatolia Antiqua* 15: 49–58.

Korfmann, Manfred. 1986. Die "grosse Göttin" in Alaca Höyük. *IX. Türk Tarih Kongresi* (Ankara 1981) 1: 153–63.

———. 2003. *Troia in Light of New Research*. Trier: Universität Trier.

Koşay, Hamit Z. and M. Akok. 1950. Amasya Mahmatlar Köyü Definesi. *Belleten* 14: 481–85.

Kouka, Ourania. 2008. Diaspora, Presence or Interaction? The Cyclades and the Greek Mainland from the Final Neolithic to Early Bronze II. In *Horizon: A Colloquium on the Prehistory of the Cyclades*, ed. Neil J Brodie, Jennifer Doole, Giorgos Gavalas, and Colin Renfrew, 311–19. Cambridge: Cambridge University Press.

———. 2009a. Cross-Cultural Links and Elite Identities: The Eastern Aegean/Western Anatolia and Cyprus from the Early Third Millennium through the Early Second Millennium BC. In *Cyprus and the East Aegean: Intercultural Contacts from 3000 to 500 BC*, ed. Vassos Karageorghis and Ourania Kouka, 31–47. Nicosia: Leventis Foundation.

———. 2009b. Third Millennium BC Aegean Chronology: Old and New Data from the Perspective of the Third Millennium AD. In *Tree-Rings, Kings, and Old World Archaeology and Environment: Papers Presented in Honor of Peter Ian Kuniholm*, ed. Sturt W. Manning and Mary Jaye Bruce, 133–49. Oxford: Oxbow Books.

Kuruçayırlı, Emre and Hadi Özbal. 2005a. New Metal Analysis from Tarsus-Gözlükule. In *Field Seasons 2001–2003 of the Tarsus-Gözlükule Interdisciplinary Research Project*, ed. Aslı Özyar, 177–95. Ankara: Efe Yayınları.

———. 2005b. New Metal Analysis from Tarsus-Gözlükule. In *Anatolian Metal III*, ed. Ünsal Yalçın, 49–61. Bochum: Deutsches Bergbau-Museum.

Maddin, Robert, James D. Muhly, and Tamara Stech. 1999. Early Metallurgy at Çayönü. In *The Beginnings of Metallurgy*, ed. Andreas Hauptmann, Ernst Pernicka, Thilo Rehren, and Ünsal Yalçın, 37–44. Bochum: Deutsches Bergbau-Museum.

Mansfeld, Günther. 2001. Die 'Königsgräber' von Alaca Höyük und ihre Beziehungen nach Kaukasien. *Archäologische Mitteilungen aus Iran und Turan* 33: 19–61.

Maran, Joseph. 2007. Seaborne Contacts between the Aegean, the Balkans and the Central Mediterranean in the 3rd Millennium BC: The Unfolding of the Mediterranean World. In *Between the Aegean and Baltic Seas: Prehistory across Borders*, ed. I. Galanaki and Robert Laffineur, 3–21. Aegaeum 27. Liège: Université de Liège.

Matthews, Roger. 1994. Imperial Catastrophe or Local Incident? An Akkadian Hoard from Tell Brak, Syria. *Cambridge Archaeology Journal* 4: 290–316.

Maxwell-Hyslop, K. Rachael. 1974. Assyrian Sources of Iron. *Iraq* 36: 139–54.

Meeks, Nigel D and Mike S. Tite. 1980. The Analysis of Platinum-Group Element Inclusions in Gold Antiquities. *Journal of Archaeological Science* 7: 267–75.

Mellink, Machteld J. 1956. The Royal Tombs at Alaca Hüyük and the Aegean World. In *The Aegean and the Near East. Studies Presented to Hetty Goldman*, ed. Saul S. Weinberg, 39–58. New York: Augustin.

———. 1967. Beycesultan: A Bronze Age Site in Southwestern Turkey. *Bibliotheca Orientalis* 24: 3–9.

Muhly, James D. 1973. *Copper and Tin. The Distribution of Mineral Resources and the Nature of the Metals Trade in the Bronze Age.* Transactions of the Connecticut Academy of Arts and Sciences 43. New Haven, Conn.: Archon Books.

———. 1985. Sources of Tin and the Beginnings of Bronze Metallurgy. *American Journal of Archaeology* 89: 275–91.

———. 1989. Çayönü Tepesi and the Beginnings of Metallurgy in the Old World. In *Archäometallurgie der Alten Welt*, ed. Andreas Hauptmann, Ernst Pernicka, and Günther A. Wagner, 1–11. Bochum: Deutsches Bergbau-Museum.

———. 1993. Early Bronze Age Tin and the Taurus. *American Journal of Archaeology* 97: 239–54.

———. 2008. An Introduction to Minoan Archaeometallurgy. In *Aegean Metallurgy in the Bronze Age*, ed. Iris Tzachili, 35–41. Rethymnon: University of Crete.

Muhly, James D., Robert Maddin, Tamara Stech, and Engin Özgen. 1985. Iron in Anatolia and the Nature of the Hittite Iron Industry. *Anatolian Studies* 35: 67–84.

Muhly, James D. and Ernst Pernicka. 1992. Early Trojan Metallurgy and Metals Trade. In *Heinrich Schliemann. Grundlagen und Ergebnisse moderner Archäologie 100 Jahre nach Schliemanns Tod*, ed. Joachim Herrmann, 309–18. Berlin: Akademie Verlag.

Muhly, James D. and Tamara Stech. 2003. The Metallurgy of Ninevite 5. In *The Origins of North Mesopotamian Civilization: Ninevite 5 Chronology, Economy, Society*, ed. Elena Rova and Harvey Weiss, 417–28. Subartu 9. Turnhout: Brepols.

Müller-Karpe, Andreas. 1994. *Altanatolisches Metallhandwerk*. Offa-Bücher, Band 75. Neumünster: Wachholtz Verlag.

Ogden, Jack M. 1977. Platinum Group Metal Inclusions in Ancient Gold Artifacts. *Journal of the Historical Metallurgy Society* 11: 53–72.

Orthmann, Winfried. 1967. Zu den "Standarten" aus Alaca Hüyük. *Istanbuler Mitteilungen* 17: 34–54.

Özbal, Hadi. 1983. Tepecik ve Tülintepe Metal. Filiz ve Cüruf Analizleri Sonuçları. *Arkeometri Ünitesı Bilimsel Toplantısı Bildirileri* 3: 203–18.

———. 1986. Değirmentepe Metal. *Cüruf ve Filiz Analizleri. Arkeometri Ünitesi Bilimsel Toplantısı Bildirileri* 6: 101–13.

Özgüç, Tahsin and Raci Temizer. 1993. The Eskiyapar Treasure. In *Anatolia and its Neighbours: Studies in Honor of Nimet Özgüç*, ed. Machteld J. Mellink, Edith Porada, and Tahsin Özgüç, 613–28. Ankara: Turkish Historical Society.

Öztan, Aliye. 1992. 1991 Yılı Acemhöyük Kazıları. *Kazı Sonuçları Toplantısı* 14: 245–55.

Özyar, Aslı. 2000. Noch einmal zu den Standartenaufsätzen aus Alacahöyük. In *Anatolian Metal I*, ed. Ünsal Yalçın, 101–12. Bochum: Deutsches Bergbau-Museum.

Pare, Christopher. 2000. Bronze and the Bronze Age. In *Metals Make the World Go Round: The Supply and Circulation of Metals in Bronze Age Europe*, ed. C. F. E. Pare, 1–38. Oxford: Oxbow Books.

Parzinger, Hermann. 2002. Das Zinn in der Bronzezeit Eurasiens. In *Anatolian Metal II*, ed. Ünsal Yançın, 159–77. Bochum: Deutsches Bergbau-Museum.

Pernicka, Ernst. 1997. Review of Müller-Karpe 1994. In *Prähistorische Zeitschrift* 72: 251–56.

———. 1998. Die Ausbreitung der Zinnbronze im 3. Jahrtausend. In *Man and Environment in the European Bronze Age*, ed. Bernard Hänsel, 135–47. Kiel: Oetker-Voges Verlag.

Pollard, A. Mark. 2009. What a Long, Strange Trip It's Been: Lead Isotopes and Archaeology. In *From Mine to Microscope: Advances in the Study of Ancient Technology*, ed. Andrew J. Shortland, Ian C. Freestone, and Thilo Rehren, 181–89. Oxford: Oxbow Books.

Primas, Margaret. 1988. Waffen aus Edelmetall. *Jahrbuch des Römisch-germanischen Zentralmuseums Mainz* 35: 161–85.

———. 1996. *Velika Gruda I. Hügelgräber des frühen 3. Jahrtausends v. Chr. im Adriagebeit—Velika Gruda, Mala Gruda und ihre Kontext. Universitätsforschung zur Prähistorischen Archäologie,* 32. Bonn: Habelt.

Rahmstorf, Lorenz. 2006. Zur Ausbreitung vorderasiatischer Innovationen in die frühbronzezeitliche Ägäis. *Prähistorische Zeitschrift* 81: 49–96.

Ramage, Andrew and Paul Craddock, eds. 2000. *King Croesus' Gold: Excavations at Sardis and the History of Gold Refining*. Cambridge, Mass.: Harvard University Press.

Renfrew, Colin. 1972. *The Emergence of Civilization. The Cyclades in the Third Millennium BC*. London: Methuen.

Sazcı, Göksel and Manfred Korfmann. 2000. Metallfunde des 3. Jahrtausends v.u.Z. aus Troia—Eine Studie in Verbindung mit den Ergebnissen der neuen Ausgrabungen. In *Anatolian Metal I*, ed. Ünsal Yalçın, 93–100. Bochum: Deutsches Bergbau-Museum.

Schliemann, Heinrich. 1881. *Ilios. Stadt und Land der Trojaner. Forschungen in der Troas und besonders auf der Baustelle von Troja*. Munich: F. A. Brockhaus.

Schmitt-Strecker, Sigfrid, Friedrich Begemann, and Ernst Pernicka. 1992. Chemische Zusammensetzung und Bleiisotopenverhältnisse der Metallfunde vom Hassek Höyük. *Istanbuler Forschungen* 38: 108–23.

Schoop, Ulf-Dietrich. 1995. *Die Geburt des Hephaistos. Technologie und Kulturgeschichte neolithischer Metallverwendung im Vorderer Orient*. Espelkamp: Verlag Marie L. Leidorf.

Sertok, Kemal and Rifat Ergeç. 1999. A New Early Bronze Age Cemetery: Excavations near Birecik Dam, Southeastern Turkey. Preliminary Report (1997–98). *Anatolica* 25: 87–107.

Siegelová, Jana. 2005. Metalle in hethitischen Texten. In *Anatolian Metal III*, ed. Ünsal Yalçın, 35–40. Bochum: Deutsches Bergbau-Museum.

Stech, Tamara and Vincent C. Pigott. 1986. The Metals Trade in South-West Asia in the Third Millennium BC. *Iraq* 48: 39–64.

Stos, Zofia A. 2009. Across the Wine Dark Seas . . . Sailor Tinkers and Royal Cargoes in the Late Bronze Age Eastern Mediterranean. In *From Mine to Microscope: Advances in the Study of Ancient Technology*, ed. Andrew J. Shortland, Ian C. Freestone, and Thilo-Rehren, 163–80. Oxford: Oxbow Books.

Stos-Gale, Zofia. 1985. Lead and Silver Sources for Bronze Age Crete. In *Proceedings of the 5th International Cretological Congress*, vol. 1, 365–72. Heraklion: Institute for Cretan Studies.

Stos-Gale, Zofia A. 1989. Lead Isotope Studies of Metals and the Metal Trade in the Bronze Age Mediterranean. In *Scientific Analysis in Archaeology and its Interpretation*, ed. Julian Henderson, 274–301. Oxford: Oxford University Committee for Archaeology Monographs.

Stöllner, Thomas and Gerd Weisgerber. 2004. Die Blei-/Silbergruben von Nakhlak und ihre Bedeutung im Altertum. *Der Anschnitt* 56.2–3: 76–97.

Stronach, David. 1962. Metal Objects. In *Beycesultan, vol. I: The Chalcolithic and Early Bronze Age Levels*, ed. Seton Lloyd and James Mellaart, 280–92. London: British Institute of Archaeology at Ankara.

Tadmor, Miriam, D. Kedem, Frederich Begemann, Andreas Hauptmann, Ernst Pernicka, and Sigrid Schmitt-Strecker. 1995. The Nahal Mishmar Hoard from the Judean Desert: Technology, Composition, and Provenience. *Atiqot* 27: 95–148.

Tite, Michael S. 1996. In Defence of Lead Isotope Analysis. *Antiquity* 70: 959–62.

Toker, Ayşe and Jean Öztürk. 1992. *Metal Vessels*. Ankara: Museum of Anatolian Civilizations.

van Loon, Maurits. 1973. The Excavations at Korucutepe, Turkey, 1968–1970: Preliminary Report, Part I: Architecture and General Finds. *Journal of Near Eastern Studies* 32: 357–423.

Vasilakis, Adonis. 2008. Silver Metalworking in Prehistoric Crete. An Historical Survey. In *Aegean Metallurgy in the Bronze Age*, ed. Iris Tzachili, 75–85. Rethymnon: University of Crete.

Vor 12.000 Jahren in Anatolien: Die ältesten Monumente der Menschheit. 2007. Karlsruhe: Badisches Landesmuseum.

Wagner, Günther A. and Önder Öztunalı. 2000. Prehistoric Copper Sources in Turkey. In *Anatolian Metal I*, ed. Ünsal Yalçın, 31–67. Bochum: Deutsches Bergbau-Museum.

Wagner, Güther A., Imtrud Wagner, Önder Öztunalı, Sigrid Schmitt-Strecker, and Friedrich Begemann. 2003. Archäometallurgischer Bericht über Feldforschung in Anatolien und bleiisotopische Studien an Erzen und Schlacken. In *Man and Mining: Studies in Honour of Gerd Weisgerber*, ed. Thomas Stöllner, Gabriele Körlin, Gero Steffens, and Jan Cierny, 475–94. Bochum: Deutsches Bergbau-Museum.

Webb, Jennifer, David Frankel, Zofia A. Stos, and Noel Gale. 2006. Early Bronze Age Metal Trade in the Eastern Mediterranean. New Compositional and Lead Isotope Evidence from Cyprus. *Oxford Journal of Archaeology* 25: 261–88.

Weisgerber, Gerd and Jan Cierny. 2002. Tin for Ancient Anatolia? In *Anatolian Metal II*, ed. Ünsal Yalçın, 179–86. Bochum: Deutsches Bergbau-Museum.

Whitmore, Florence E. and William J. Young. 1973. Application of the Laser Microprobe and Electron Microprobe in the Analysis of Platiniridium Inclusions in Gold. In *Application of Science in Examination of Works of Art*, ed. William J. Young, 88–95. Boston: Museum of Fine Arts.

Yalçın, Ünsal. 1998. Der Keulenkopf von Can Hasan (TR). Naturwissenschaftliche Untersuchung und neue interpretation. In *Metallurgica Antique In Honour of Hans-Gert Bachmann and Robert Maddin*, ed. Thilo Rehren, Andreas Hauptmann, and James D. Muhly, 279–89. Bochum: Deutsches Bergbau-Museum.

———. 2000a. Frühchalcolitische Metallfunde von Mersin-Yumuktepe: Beginn der extraktiven Metallurgie? *TÜBA-AR* 3: 109–28.

———. 2000b. Anfänge der Metallverwendung in Anatolien. In *Anatolian Metal I*, ed. Ünsal Yalçın, 17–30. Bochum: Deutsches Bergbau-Museum.

———. 2003. Metallurgie in Anatolien. In *Man and Mining: Studies in Honour of Gerd Weisgerber on the Occasion of His 65th Birthday*, ed. Thomas Stöllner, Gabriele Körlin, Gero Steffens, and Jan Cierny, 527–36. Bochum: Deutsches Bergbau-Museum.

———. 2008. Ancient Metallurgy in Anatolia. In *Ancient Mining in Turkey and the Eastern Mediterranean*, ed. Ünsal Yalçın, Hadi Özbal, and A. Günhan Paşamehmetoğlu, 15–40. Ankara: Atılım University.

Yalçın, Ünsal and H. Gönül Yalçın. 2008. Der Hortfund von Tülintepe, Ostanatolien. In *Anatolian Metal IV*, ed. Ünsal Yalçın, 101–23. Bochum: Deutsches Bergbau-Museum.

———. 2009. Evidence for Early Use of Tin at Tülintepe in Eastern Anatolia. *TÜBA-AR* 12: 123–41.

Yalçın, Ünsal and Ernst Pernicka. 1999. Frühneolithische Metallurgie von Aşlıkı Höyük. In *The Beginnings of Metallurgy*, ed. Andreas Hauptmann, Ernst Pernicka, Thilo Rehren, and Ünsal Yalçın, 45–54. Bochum: Deutsches Bergbau-Museum.

Yener, K. Aslıhan. 1983. The Production, Exchange and Utilization of Silver and Lead Metals in Ancient Anatolia. *Anatolica* 10: 1–15.

———. 2000a. Swords, Armor, and Figurines: A Metalliferous View from the Central Taurus. In *Across the Anatolian Plateau. Readings in the Archaeology of Ancient Turkey*, ed. Donald C. Hopkins, 35–42. Annual of the American Schools of Oriental Research 57. Boston: American Schools of Oriental Research.

———. 2000b. *The Domestication of Metals: The Rise of Complex Metal Industries in Anatolia*. Leiden: Brill.

———. 2008. Revisiting Kestel Mine and Göltepe: The Dynamics of Local Provisioning of Tin during the Early Bronze Age. In *Ancient Mining in Turkey and the Eastern Mediterranean*, ed. Ünsal Yalçın, Hadi Özbal, and A. Günhan Paşamehmetoğlu, 57–64. Ankara: Atılım University.

Yener, K. Aslıhan, Emel Geçkinli, and Hadi Özbal. 1996. A Brief Survey of Anatolian Metallurgy prior to 500 BC. In *Archaeometry 1994: Proceedings of the 29th International Symposium on Archaeometry*, ed. Ş. Demirci, A. M. Özer, and G. D. Summers, 375–91. Ankara: Tübitak.

Yener, K. Aslıhan, E. V. Sayre, E. C. Joel, H. Özbal, I. L. Barnes, and R. H. Brill. 1991. Stable Lead Isotope Studies of Central Taurus Ore Sources and Related Artifacts from Eastern Mediterranean Chalcolithic and Bronze Age Sites. *Journal of Archaeological Science* 18: 541–77.

Yener, K. Aslıhan and Pamela B. Vandiver. 1993. Tin Processing at Göltepe, an Early Bronze Age Site in Anatolia. *American Journal of Archaeology* 97: 207–38.

Yener, K. Aslıhan, Pamela B. Vandiver, and Lynn Willies. 1993. Reply to J.D. Muhly, "Early Bronze Age Tin and the Taurus." *American Journal of Archaeology* 97: 255–64.

Yıldırım, Tayfun and Thomas Zimmermann. 2006. News from the Hatti Heartland—The Early Bronze Age Necropoleis of Kalınkaya, Resuloğlu, and Anatolian Metalworking Advances in the Late 3rd Millennium BC. *Antiquity Project Gallery* 80.309: 1–5.

Young, William J. 1972. The Fabulous Gold of the Pactolus Valley. *Bulletin, Boston Museum of Fine Arts* 70: 5–13.

Zimmermann, Thomas. 2007a. Kalınkaya-Toptaştepe, eine chalkolithisch-frühbronzezeitliche Siedlung mit Nekropole im nördlichen Zentralanatolien: Die Grabfunde der Kampagnen von 1971 und 1973. *Istanbuler Mitteilungen* 57: 7–26.

———. 2007b. Anatolia and the Balkans, Once Again—Ring-Shaped Idols from Western Asia and a Critical Reassessment of Some "Early Bronze Age" Items from Ikiztepe, Turkey. *Oxford Journal of Archaeology* 26: 25–33.

———. 2008a. Kultureller Austausch im südosteuropäisch-türkischen Schwarzmeergebiet vom 5. bis zum 3. Jahrtausend v. Chr.—Annäherungen an ein chronologisches und forschungsgeschichtliches Dilemma. *Regensburger Beiträge zur Prähistorischen Archäologie* 20: 461–79.

———. 2008b. Symbols of Salvation? Function, Semantics and Social Context of Early Bronze Age Ritual Equipment from Central Anatolia. *Anodos* 6–7 (2006–2007): 509–20.

CHAPTER 40

THE HITTITE STATE AND EMPIRE FROM ARCHAEOLOGICAL EVIDENCE

CLAUDIA GLATZ

In their recent textbook on Anatolian archaeology, Sagona and Zimansky (2009:266) state that "the archaeology of the Hittites in the Late Bronze Age is an archaeology of imperialism." The impressive material remains of the Hittite Empire (figure 40.1) in the shape of its central Anatolian cities, in particular the capital at Boğazköy-Ḫattuša, are well known and have been described and analyzed many times (for recent overviews see Kunst- und Ausstellungshalle der Bundesrepublik Deutschland GmbH 2002; Genz and Mielke 2011). However, despite over a century of excavation efforts and over a decade of encouragement (Gorny 1995; Steadman and Gorny 1995), an archaeology of the Hittite state and empire, that is, the exploration of its internal structures and dominance relationships through material evidence, is still in its infancy. The most pervasive explanation for the dearth of archaeological studies of this kind in Anatolia and the Near East in general (e.g., Adams 1979; Matthews 2003:127–28; Postgate 1992, 1994) is the ready availability of documentary sources (see van den Hout, chapter 41 in this volume) and their preferred utilization in the study of early states and empires. Just as the outline of Hittite historical development seemed, until recently (see later discussion) firmly established, Hittite political organization was apparent enough from the textual record:

> The Hittite system is known better than any other due to the discovery of the extensive royal archives in Ḫattusa. It was basically simple; the domination of

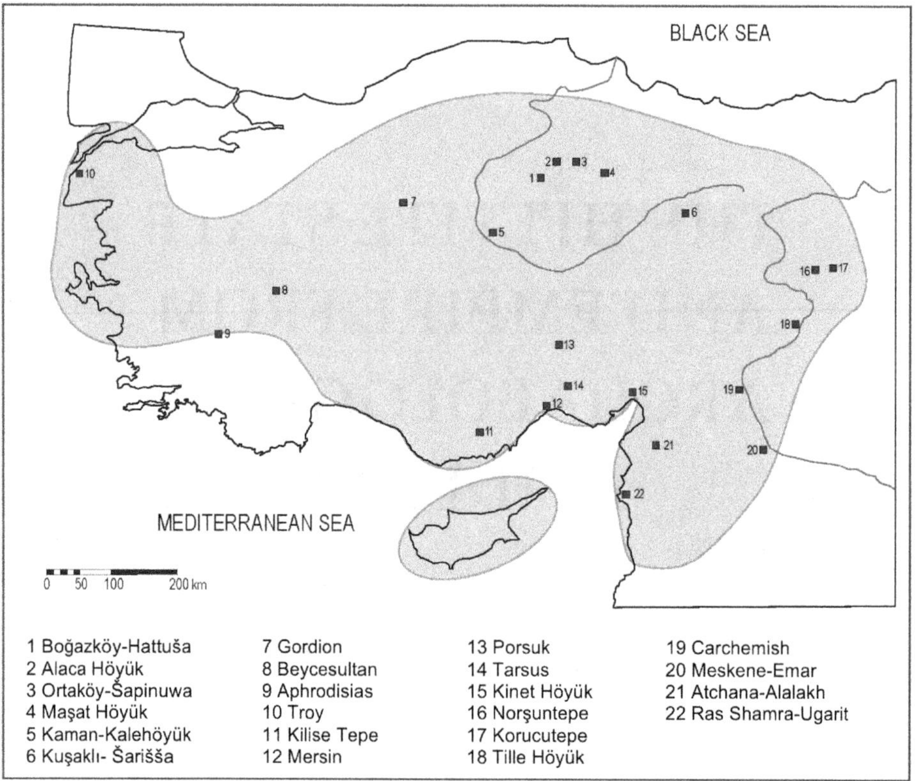

Figure 40.1. Map of the Hittite Empire at its maximum extent as suggested by the textual sources (fourteenth and thirteenth century B.C.E.) and major sites mentioned in the text.

> the Great King was based on sworn treaties with vassals and clients of varying status, all of them referred to as "Kings." They had to acknowledge a number of duties towards the Great King, both of a military and economic nature, and they could not have independent diplomatic contacts with other kings. This amounts to an intricate system of indirect rule which covered all of the Hittite area. (Larsen 1979:83)

Although vital for an understanding of the overall structure of dominance relations in specific areas, the perspective provided by the textual-historical sources clearly cannot be taken a priori as representative of the totality of Hittite imperial organization and modes of engagement. This becomes especially apparent when we take into account the biases affecting the written record. They include the geographically highly restricted nature of substantive text finds to a small number of central Anatolian sites (Boğazköy-Ḫattuša, Maşat-Tapikka, Ortaköy-Šapinuwa, and Kuşaklı-Šariššа; see Seeher, chapter 16, and Mielke, chapter 48 in this volume), and the Syrian principalities under Hittite hegemony (Ras Shamra-Ugarit, Atchana-Alalakh, and Meskene-Emar). Hittite documentary sources, moreover, are heavily skewed toward cultic texts, political-diplomatic correspondence, and historiographic accounts with little detailed information on economic organization and day-to-day imperial administration. On one hand, this leaves large parts of potentially Hittite-controlled Anatolia with no textual voice of their own. On the other hand, it presents us with a two-tiered imperial interaction model—diplomacy and warfare—that leaves open a whole array of key questions of how imperial policies were implemented in practice, their synchronic and diachronic range of variation, and their implications for the social and economic organization and cultural identities of subordinate and surrounding societies. Despite these shortcomings, the over-reliance on the textual record in tandem with a perception that political structure and particularly indirect or hegemonic rule are somehow hard to detect in the archaeological record (Postgate 1994:1–3; Smith and Montiel 2001 for a general discussion) has relegated archaeological research to the back row of Hittite studies.

Yet material culture as the expression and medium of relationships ranging from cultural contact to domination, negotiation, and resistance is the most abundant class of evidence available for the analysis of the Hittite state and empire. In addition to its overwhelming abundance, archaeological data offer the possibility of asking new questions about Hittite imperialism and the impact its life cycle had on different subject populations, or to rephrase old queries to fit the possibilities and restrictions of the archaeological record (sensu Adams 1979).

This is not to challenge the importance of the textual-historical information available—far from it. But to develop a successful integrated methodology, a better balance has to be struck between the two sources of evidence with respect to the attribution of interpretive weight. This requires a more critical examination of the circumstances under which we may interlock the medium- to long-term patterns of the material record with the events of textual history. One of the biggest obstacles for the development of a successful archaeology of the Hittite state and empire has been a flawed methodology in which historical questions determine archaeological research agendas and simultaneously provide their principle interpretive framework (Gorny 2002; Mielke, Schoop, and Seeher 2006a:1–3). Van Loon's (1980:275) discussion of the fortification walls at Korucutepe exemplifies this unnecessarily bleak outlook on the potential of archaeological research: "what historical events the archaeological remains are to be correlated with is better left for the historians to decide."

However, things are changing. Over the past years, archaeologists have become more emphatic in their call for a methodological separation of textual-historical agendas and archaeological data at primary levels of investigation. As part of this paradigm shift, previously firmly established "common knowledge" about Hittite Anatolia is in the process of critical reassessment. First results carry wide-ranging implications for our understanding of settlement developments and their timeframe at the Hittite capital and other central Anatolian sites (papers in Fischer et al. 2003; Mielke, Schoop, and Seeher 2006b). The most prominent example of this development is the redating of the construction of the upper city at Boğazköy-Ḫattuša from the last decades of the Hittite Empire in the thirteenth century B.C.E. (e.g., Neve 1999:146) to sometime in the 15th century B.C.E. (Mielke, Schoop, and Seeher 2006b; Seeher 2008, and see chapter 16 in this volume), thus dramatically lengthening the existence of the southern extension of the Hittite capital city.

Another site which has been redated convincingly is İnandıktepe Level IV. Mielke (2006) was able to show, through a careful comparison of the ceramic repertoires of İnandıktepe and Kuşaklı-Šariššа, and with a series of dendrochrology dates for the latter site, that İnandıktepe IV is also likely to date to the last quarter of the sixteenth century B.C.E. rather than the previously advocated earliest phase of the Hittite Old Kingdom (Özgüç 1988:107–10; Wilhelm 2005 for a redating of the land-grant document found at the site). The establishment of a relative ceramic chronology, based on frequency seriation techniques from independently dated contexts at Boğazköy-Ḫattuša (Schoop 2006, 2008; for earlier quantitative studies see Müller-Karpe 1988; Parzinger and Sanz 1992) and a similar effort at Kaman-Kalehöyük (Katsuno 2004, 2006) are currently under way and will prove an invaluable advance in the archaeological study of 2nd millennium B.C.E. central Anatolia and beyond. Regarding the end of the Hittite state and empire, Seeher (2001) demonstrated that the flamboyant doomsday scenarios of the fall of the Hittite capital envisaged by past commentators determinedly ignored clear archaeological evidence for an abandonment of the city by the royal court and a resulting dilapidation of the official structures rather than for a simultaneous destruction by a large-scale enemy attack.

This new wave in Late Bronze Age Anatolian archaeology has brought with it a great promise of advance in the discipline. The critical reexamination of the evidence on which past interpretations are based is a crucial first step in this process, but there is also the danger of focusing too intensely on questions of archaeological data quality, formation processes, and the biases inherent in specific finds contexts. These concerns form, without a doubt, a vital part of all good archaeological practice, as only a critical awareness of the biases inherent in our data allows for meaningful hypothesis building, testing and interpretation to take place. However, these issues ought not to detract our attention entirely from the questions we are really interested in exploring: past human behavior, in this case Hittite political relationships and development. Otherwise this important paradigm shift risks perpetuating the problems of earlier text-focused approaches, namely, that the numerous archaeological projects conducted in central and surrounding regions of the Hittite Empire have had comparatively little *actual* impact on common interpretations of the functioning of this military and political enterprise and the economic, social, and cultural relationships created by its expansion. Speed, or rather the lack thereof, in the dissemination of research results is partly to blame, but for the most part it is a lack of research vision and suitable large-scale interpretive frameworks that would allow the findings of the archaeological record more vigorously to contribute to, as well as challenge, existing ways of thinking about the Hittite state in its center and in subordinated territories.

Agricultural production is only one example of how archaeological evidence can illuminate in great detail aspects of the Hittite political economy that are mentioned in the textual sources, but with relatively little specific information. Agricultural overproduction and large-scale storage of surplus are well-known aspects of the political economies of early states and empires for a number of intertwined reasons ranging from redistribution and the buffering of bad harvests to forming one aspect of the materialization of élites' ideologies.

From the textual sources we know that cereals formed a major component of an otherwise varied central Anatolian diet (Hoffner 1974) and therefore of agricultural production. Land was taxed through its produce (Hoffner 1997), which was collected, stored, and redirected to the central authority or redistributed locally as seeds for the coming year either by regional palaces (É.GAL) (Siegelová 2001:196), or lower level administrative entities such as the *BĒL MADGALTI* (border official) (e.g., Alp 1991), or AGRIG officials and their sealhouses (Singer 1984). The latter were responsible in particular for the forwarding of agricultural produce to the capital for cult activities. Hittite festivals were numerous, and two were specifically dedicated to the opening and sealing of grain storage containers (Hazenboos 2003:168–69).

The excavation of several large-scale Late Bronze Age grain silos at Boğazköy-Ḫattuša (Seeher 2000), Kaman-Kalehöyük (Omura 2001:11–27, 2002:6–19), and Kuşaklı-Šarišša (Mielke 2001) has opened up the possibility of exploring not only questions associated directly with Late Bronze Age agricultural practices—the types of crops planted, storage techniques, pests affecting harvest, and preservation—but also provides several strands of investigation through which key aspects of the political economy, demography, and spatial organization may be explored. Population size, or available labor power, is one of the key variables affecting imperial development. The approximate figures calculated by Mielke (2001:241; Seeher 2000) for the number of persons that could be fed per year by the provisions stored at the above sites, and the estimated agricultural space required to produce the storable quantities, shed light on the demographic realities of early empires. The population estimates from the silo complexes, combined with considerations of transport logistics (e.g., Lattimore 1962:477–79; Mann 1986:10, 137–40), more detailed assessments of soil quality and crop yield, integrated with the results of regional settlement studies, could contribute immensely to our understanding of the workings of the Hittite state far beyond a generalized confirmation of what is mentioned about grain and its storage in the textual record (e.g., Bryce 2002:77).

Recent archaeobotanical research underscores the potential of the archaeological record to explore dominance relationships and questions of political economy from both the perspective of the central institutions as well as from that of the population affected by its policies. Tentative archaeological evidence for agricultural taxation comes from grain deposits found in two monumental structures at Kuşaklı-Šarišša. According to Pasternak (1998:163–64), the diversity and generally poor quality of cereals—small grain size and frequent admixture of weeds—routinely recovered from Temple 1 and Building C in Level 2 are likely the remnants of taxation payments (*Abgabewirtschaft*). The hypothesis is that fields whose produce is intended for taxation payments are less well tended than others. That small grain size and weeds in the Kuşaklı-Šarišša finds are not the result of ignorance or inadequate agricultural techniques is demonstrated by a contemporary find of high quality emmer in Building C, which is thought to represent temple provisions. We are thus dealing with a possible form of rural resistance to state control, which is often restricted to small-scale insubordination, disobedience, and delay tactics rather than outright defiance (Scott 1990). Similar strategies, but at a wholly different sociopolitical level, are evident in the delay tactics of the kingdom of Ugarit, which are documented in its correspondence with the Hittite court (Glatz, in press). One example is the delaying of much-needed grain shipments to Anatolia toward the very end of the Late Bronze Age (RS 20.212, lines 5–26; Nougayrol 1968:105).

Another problem, one of archaeology's own making, in the development of an archaeology of the Hittite state and empire is the concentration of much past and present research on a small number of key sites, in particular the capital city, Boğazköy-Ḫattuša. Excavation at Boğazköy-Ḫattuša, as Sagona and Zimansky (2009:259) have put it, "presents a kind of anchor for Hittite archaeology," and rightly so since our understanding of "Hittite" material culture is almost exclusively defined on the basis of the Boğazköy material. Although vital in this respect, this focus on the capital is also proving to be somewhat of a weight around the neck of Anatolian and Hittite studies. Completed or ongoing work at central Anatolian sites such as Maşat Höyük, Ortaköy-Šapinuwa, Kaman-Kalehöyük, Kuşaklı-Šarišša, Kayalıpınar, Gordion, and Beycesultan in the west; Kilise Tepe, Mersin, Tarsus, Kinet Höyük, and Atchana-Alalakh in the south; as well as the east Anatolian sites excavated in the wake of the Euphrates dam constructions all help in contextualizing this unique site. The geographical gaps, however, remain vast, and cross-regional syntheses are rare.

The question of what constitutes "Hittite" material culture and how its appearance in incorporated regions relates directly or indirectly to political power, is another well-known but largely disregarded problem. The first question to be asked in this context has to be "by what criteria do we decide to classify something as Hittite?" (Gorny 2002:2). It seems to warrant a rather obvious answer and has perhaps for this reason not received the attention it requires, but it is important both in a spatial context: "Where is the dividing line between Hittite and Anatolian?" (Gorny 2002:2) and from a chronological perspective (Schoop 2003:172): when do we start/stop calling something Hittite? (See also Gorny 2002:2; Güterbock 1957; Mellink 1956:51–57.) Clarity in terminology is, therefore, crucial. I follow Mellink (1956) in arguing that the term "Hittite" is an entirely unsuitable label for material culture. This is particularly true for cultural traditions and settlements in areas outside the central Anatolian plateau, where the term acquires, explicitly or implicitly, the notion of a conquering and, in one way or another, "civilizing" process. In this way, it obscures the likely diverse spectrum of mechanisms and motivations for the transmission, adoption, and transformation of cultural attributes. I prefer to use "north-central Anatolian" (NCA), because it is a more appropriate, value-free label for the material culture tradition of the geographical and cultural heartland of the Hittite polity. Artifacts produced outside this cultural and political core region but stylistically comparable or identical to those in this central region are referred to as "north-central Anatolian-style" (NCA-style). In this way we avoid an a priori ethnic, linguistic, or cultural labeling of producers and consumers as well as of the mechanisms, motivations, and directions of cultural flows.

Toward an Archaeology of the Hittite Empire

A successful archaeology of the Hittite state and empire requires a broader perspective than that traditionally adopted for Late Bronze Age Anatolia with respect to both the types of archaeological data investigated and the geographical scope of investigation (see Sinopoli 1994). It also necessitates a more rigorous theorization of the concept of empire and the nature and materiality of dominance relationships.

Empire is here conceptualized as both a relationship and a process that underlie recurring episodes of individual and collective interaction on a multitude of sociopolitical and cultural levels, what Mann (1986:1) described as "multiple overlapping and intersecting socio-spatial networks." Material culture is formed by, expresses, and mediates all the relationships that constitute these networks of interaction. This is a dynamic model; as a relationship, empire is always in the making and subject to continuous processes of reestablishment, renegotiation, and redefinition. To understand the time depth and processes necessary for the establishment of different networks of interaction and their subsequent maintenance and transformation, this approach requires a diachronic perspective. This involves the consideration of pre- and different stages of postconquest regional situations, rather than the more conventional anachronistic portrayals of empire that use spatial extent at the apex of political power and the entirety of material remains of the central polity in peripheral regions (see also Schreiber 2005).

An archaeology of imperial relationships is the investigation of overlapping spatial and temporal patterns of material categories that are diagnostic of interregional interaction. Through the superimposition of the spatial and chronological patterns of change and continuity in selected aspects of the archaeological record we can begin to gain an understanding of the different cultural, political, economic, and ideological relationships that existed between a politically and militarily central region and its surrounding societies. To define interregional modes of engagement we require, first, archaeological evidence indicative of interaction between the cultural and political heartland and surrounding regions. Next, we have to identify transformations in local sociopolitical, cultural, or economic strategies and organization that can be associated with imperial interference or local responses to it. Ideally the selected material categories should represent spheres of interaction and transformations at different sociopolitical and cultural levels, but in practice they are determined to a large degree by the types of data that can be consistently gathered across a large geographical region.

In the case of Late Bronze Age Anatolia, four archaeological data categories seem particularly suited for such an analysis. They include, at approximately ascending sociopolitical scales of interaction, (1) regional ceramic traditions and the degree of NCA cultural influence they display, (2) regional settlement systems and the changes in sociopolitical organization that may be related to Hittite control or its absence,

(3) the distribution of NCA administrative technology and practice as an indicator of direct administrative contact with the Hittite imperial élite, and (4) the spatial patterns and political origins of Late Bronze Age landscape monuments as signs of territorial competition and the projection of political hegemony. This approach provides a more nuanced and bottom-up perspective on the continuum of strategies of domination as well as local responses to them. It also allows us to compare the type and intensity of interregional interaction specified in the textual sources with those represented, or absent, in the archaeological record (for a more extensive discussion, see Glatz 2009).

Pottery and Politics

The development of locally manufactured, monochrome NCA-style pottery in different parts of Asia Minor has been at the center of recent discussions of the Hittite Empire (papers in Fischer et al. 2003; Jean, Dinçol, and Durugönül 2001; Mielke, Schoop, and Seeher 2006b). Explanations based on generalized economic, administrative, and political strategies of domination have been favored by past commentators, but the appearance of NCA ceramic elements in surrounding regions is thought by most to reflect, at one level or another, the political circumstances of the time as evidenced by the textual sources (Burney 1980:165; Garstang 1953:141–42; Gates 2001:141, 2006:308; Goldman 1956:350; Gunter 1991:105, 2006:360–61; Henrickson 1993, 1994, 2002:123; Jean 2006:328–30; Korbel 1985; Macqueen 1986:105; Müller 2005; Müller-Karpe 2002:257; Postgate 2005, 2007; Symington 2001). Little actual comparative work, however, has been conducted on the ceramic assemblages in question (Gunter 2006 for an overview of western Anatolia; Glatz 2007, 2009).

The primary questions are, thus, just how homogenous Late Bronze Age regional ceramic assemblages actually were, the timeframe of NCA stylistic introductions, and their proportion in local assemblages. They are considered here with respect to formal and technical traits in the published ceramic assemblages from Porsuk (Dupré 1983), Gordion (Gunter 1991), Beycesultan (Mellaart and Murray 1995), Aphrodisias (Joukowsky 1986), Tarsus (Goldman 1956), Korucutepe (Griffin 1980), Norşuntepe (Korbel 1985), and Tille Höyük (Summers 1993) in comparison to the repertoire of the Hittite capital city, Boğazköy-Ḫattuša (Fischer 1963; Müller-Karpe 1988; Parzinger and Sanz 1992). To establish a general measure of similarity between the eight regional assemblages and Boğazköy-Ḫattuša, the comparative analysis includes the entire formal spectrum from each site. The question of imperial influence, however, requires cultural traits that both originated on the NCA plateau and are chronologically restricted to the Late Bronze Age, ideally its second half. Cultural continuity from the Middle Bronze Age to the Late Bronze Age and simple vessel forms with parallels in other contemporary pottery traditions severely restrict the range of diagnostic types. They include so-called plates with stepped rim profiles, which are an NCA invention of the LBA (Fischer 1963:103; Schoop 2006:231). Multipurpose shallow bowls with inverted (*Schwapprandschalen*) and everted rims are known also from neighboring ceramic traditions and are therefore not ideally suited to identify NCA cultural influence. They are, however, restricted to the Late Bronze Age in the NCA tradition and provide at least a chronological framework for comparison. The same applies to coarsely produced miniature bowls and juglets with string-cut bases, whose functions have been related to cult activities and communal drinking.

Sites outside the NCA cultural sphere have been shown to display a "truncated repertoire" of NCA vessel types (Gates 2001:138; Goldman 1956:203–5; Gunter 2006:353, 359; Henrickson 2002:129). A comprehensive typological comparison confirms that Late Bronze Age ceramic assemblages across Anatolia do not feature the full formal spectrum known from the Hittite capital. The truncated repertoires at these sites, however, neither overlap completely, as would be expected of an imperial service, nor are all the shapes that have counterparts at Boğazköy-Ḫattuša restricted to the Late Bronze Age. The regional, spatial, and chronological patterns of NCA influence are much more complex than what might be expected of a straightforward imposition of an empire-wide standard of pottery production.

Plates with stepped rim profiles, for instance, appear in varying quantities at six of the eight sites. They seem to be relatively common in LBA levels at Porsuk (11 examples listed in the pottery report) and Korucutepe (107), whereas more moderate numbers are known from Gordion (5), Norşuntepe (5), Beycesultan (3), and Tarsus (2). No plates were found at Aphrodisias and Tille Höyük. The timing of their appearance at the six sites is also not identical, nor are their patterns of continuity and discontinuity during the second part of the Late Bronze Age. The earliest occurrence of plates with stepped rim profiles is reported from Korucutepe in the Late Bronze Age I (ca. 1600–1400 B.C.E.), for which they constitute a type fossil. At Gordion and Tarsus, plates were found for the first time in the Late Bronze Age II (ca. 1400–1200 B.C.E.). This seems also to be the case at Norşuntepe, whereas Beycesultan I is likely to date to the Early Iron Age (Mellaart and Murray 1995:96).

Bowls with inverting rims are present at seven of the eight sites. None are published for Aphrodisias. Small numbers of predecessors are known from Middle Bronze Age Gordion and Korucutepe, while inverted rim bowls are most prominent in the second part of the Late Bronze Age at Tarsus and at Late Bronze Age/Early Iron Age Beycesultan. Bowls with everted rims are proportionally dominant in the final phases of the Late Bronze Age at Boğazköy-Ḫattuša (Müller-Karpe 1988; Parzinger and Sanz 1992). They are absent at Porsuk, Aphrodisias, and Tille Höyük. At Gordion, Beycesultan, and Korucutepe, everted rims are found in all Late Bronze Age levels, as well as Early Iron Age contexts. They concentrate in the early part of the Late Bronze Age at Korucutepe and in the second half at Gordion.

Miniature bowls are found at six of the eight sites, with Aphrodisias and Porsuk forming the exceptions. Single occurrences of such bowls are reported from Gordion, Beycesultan, and Tille Höyük; seventeen are known from Tarsus, twenty from Korucutepe, and two from Norşuntepe. Except for Korucutepe, where they appear in the first half of the Late Bronze Age, they concentrate in the second half of the Late Bronze Age at all other sites. More distinctive are miniature juglets, of which one example was found at Korucutepe and Norşuntepe, respectively, while altogether thirteen are published from Tarsus.

There seem to be at least four different processes of cultural influence and adoption active with respect to the ceramic record (figure 40.2). We find that the core region of NCA-style ceramic production extended to the northwest and southeast fringes of the central Anatolian plateau (Gordion and Porsuk), whereas regions to the south and east began at different points in time to select formal elements to incorporate into local traditions. Korucutepe in the second half of the Late Bronze Age shows a large proportion of formal similarities with the NCA repertoire, but this is carried by a single type of simple shallow bowl, found also in a number of other contemporary pottery traditions. NCA cultural influence, furthermore, is already strong in the first half of the Late Bronze Age, which predates the textually attested imperial incorporation of the Altınova in the 14th century B.C.E. In contrast, the repertoires of Tarsus and Norşuntepe show a number of similarities with the central plateau while displaying equally strong local characteristics. The spectrum of NCA-style types and their timeframes of introduction, however, differ at the two sites. Fewer connections still can be detected in the repertoires of Beycesultan and Tille Höyük, which lie at the western and southeastern fringes of NCA ceramic influence. The diversity of special purpose vessels and high investment in surface finishes at Beycesultan also hints at a rather different social investment in ceramic production and consumption than on the central plateau. At Tille Höyük a clear cultural shift seems to have taken place during the Late Bronze Age. Diagnostic NCA types, however, are absent from the Tille Höyük repertoire. Western Anatolia,

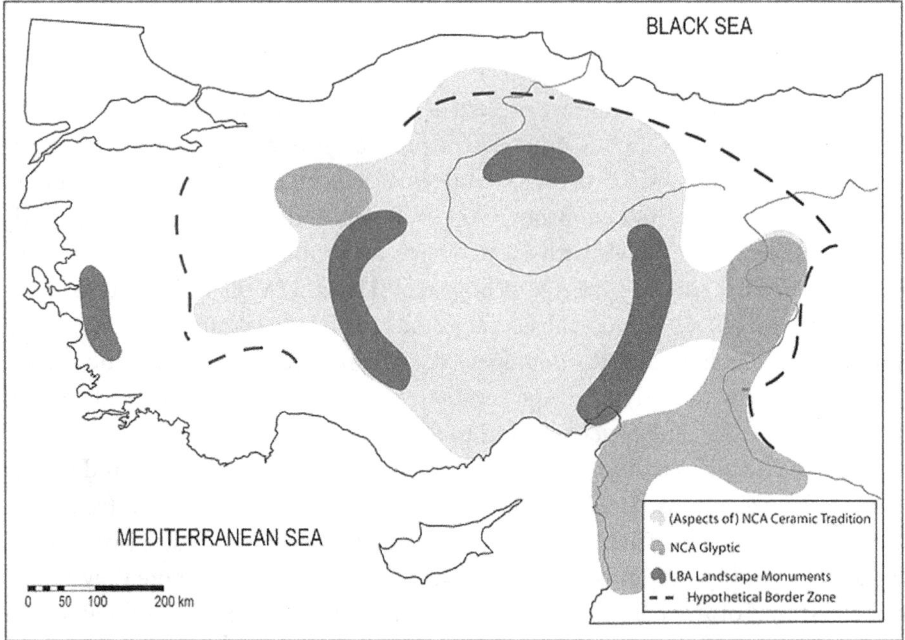

Figure 40.2. Overlapping networks of interregional interaction in LBA Anatolia and north Syria.

as represented by Aphrodisias, was largely untouched by this ceramic phenomenon, a picture we find perpetuated in most of the following data categories.

Spatial Signatures of Empire

Archaeological field survey has seen a dramatic surge in Turkey and neighboring regions over the past decades. A growing but essentially disarticulate corpus of regional settlement data is available in various stages of publication and is begging for interregional analysis. Looking beyond the biases affecting survey data and the problems specific to cross-regional analyses (divergent data quality and quantity, chronological compatibility), a comparative approach to settlement patterns is particularly fruitful in the investigation of spatially extensive phenomena such as urbanization, state formation, and imperial incorporation (e.g., Adams 1981; Alcock 1993; Cherry and Davis 2001; Wilkinson 2000; Wilkinson et al. 2005). This is based on the hypothesis that the location, organization, and distribution of settlements depend not only on physical and environmental conditions but that they are equally conditioned by historical and sociopolitical circumstances (e.g., Roberts 1996:29). In this way, diachronic developments in settlement systems can be seen as expressions of regional sociopolitical and economic organization and as sensitive indicators of continuity and change within these domains, including processes related to political integration (Alcock 1993:3–6; de Montmollin 1989).

Combining the results of around sixty survey projects, diachronic fluctuations in settlement numbers, rates of continuity/discontinuity in settlement location, and changes in regional hierarchical organization and site-size distributions were observed. Long-term trends include a cross-regional drop in site numbers after the Early Bronze Age (1,552 sites) to less than half in the Middle Bronze Age (612) and a slight increase in identified Late Bronze Age sites (647). In the Iron Age (IA) (1,055), site numbers rise again to almost double that of the previous phase. It would appear that a less densely settled landscape was the demographic background against which second millennium B.C.E. state formations and imperial expansions occurred.

Survey evidence is available in sufficient detail in some regions to allow a more fine-grained but still preliminary characterization of settlement trends indicative of the nature of local-imperial inter-relations. These include among others a process of territorial integration in key central regions and an intensive model of hegemonic control as a possibility in southern and eastern Anatolia (figure 40.3).

During the Late Bronze Age, powerful Middle Bronze Age centers such as Karahöyük-Konya (thirty-nine hectares) and Acemhöyük (forty-four hectares) on the southern plateau, and Alişar Höyük (fourteen hectares) further north, appear to have been replaced at the top of regional settlement hierarchies by old secondary centers or newly established sites of lower spatial extent. The sites that appear to be taking over regional control during the Late Bronze Age tend to range between ten and twenty hectares in size, which compares well with the dimensions of excavated settlements such as the cult center of Kuşaklı-Šarišša (18.2 hectares—intramural) and the district center of Maşat-Tapikka (about eight hectares). Settlements larger

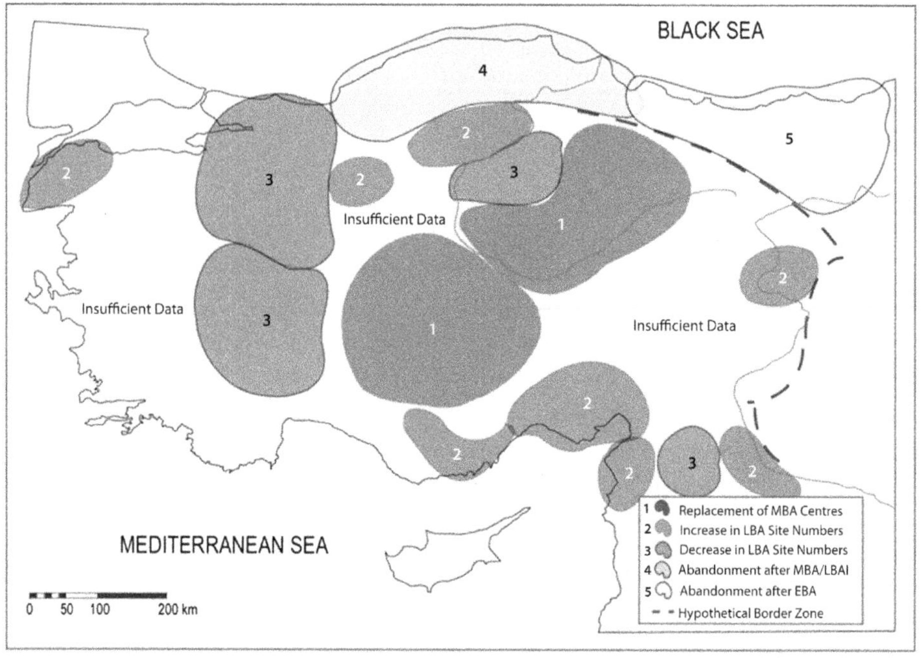

Figure 40.3. Regional settlement trends during the Late Bronze Age.

than twenty hectares seem to represent highest-order regional centers in the Late Bronze Age. One of these, Kayalıpınar in Sivas province, may be Šamuḫa, the capital of the Upper Land (Müller-Karpe 2000:364), the largest administrative unit in the Hittite core region. In addition to Boğazköy-Ḫattuša and a debatable Troy, only five Late Bronze Age settlements seemingly exceeded the twenty-hectare threshold. Interestingly, the habitation areas at Boğazköy-Ḫattuša, despite recent efforts to unearth further living quarters (e.g., Seeher 2003), cover also only about thirty hectares (Mora 1977:236), the equivalent of a large regional center. A question for future research is thus whether settlements between 20–30 hectares in size define the carrying capacity of average Anatolian landscapes under prevailing economic conditions and agricultural practices (see previous discussion).

The replacement of larger established power bases with new and smaller settlements must have served not only the practical aspects of the exertion of intensive control, but also sent a strong symbolic message of the shift of power from a local to a spatially more extensive polity (see also Branting 1996 for the Alişar region). From the data currently available, it appears that this transformation had a different pace on the eastern and the southern plateau. Much more research is needed to confirm or contradict this hypothesis, but perhaps we are looking at two temporally overlapping but not entirely congruent sequences in what appears to be the expansion of intensive territorial control. This particular spatial signature seems to be restricted to the central Anatolian plateau. Patterns observed in southern and southeastern parts of Anatolia point to a less intensive mode of domination and degree of spatial transformation.

Hypothetical elements of the spatial signatures of hegemonic control include the continuation of traditional power bases. Variations may be expected in the vulnerability or capabilities for self-defense of these central settlements (Gorny 1995; Smith 2003:210; Van De Mieroop 1997:48–48, 73). From a regional perspective, increases in site numbers in the lower echelons of settlement hierarchies may be expected as responses to economic pressures as well as improved security situations.

During the Late Bronze Age, site numbers rise in the Altınova against a background of relative stability in settlement location (Whallon 1979). New settlements were established primarily in the lower levels of the settlement hierarchy. The number of small sites increased by about 37 percent, and that of medium-sized sites by about 60 percent. A similar trend of continuity of central places and a general increase in site numbers seems to have occurred in parts of Rough Cilicia and Cilicia, although the evidence is not as reliable (French 1965; Seton-Williams 1954). In concert with other types of evidence such as the distribution of NCA administrative implements and practices, and the locations of landscape monuments discussed below, it would seem that the settlement trends in southern and southeastern Anatolia represent the spatial aspects of an intermediate form of external control, which may be called "intensive hegemony."

The Administrative Sphere of Interaction

Although the use of seals was not restricted to the ruling élite in Late Bronze Age Anatolia, primarily state-related find contexts as well as the titles and professions of seal owners inscribed onto them in Luwian hieroglyphs (see Yakubovich, chapter 23 in this volume), do suggest a principal association of this material category with the Hittite élite in charge of imperial administration. NCA administrative implements and evidence for their use may be indicative of a number of events and practices, including the exchange of correspondence, the management of a peripheral polity by imperial officials, and the local adoption of imperial administrative routines and cultural styles. Seal finds could be taken to imply the physical presence of imperial administrative personnel at a site. Object and owner, however, are alienable, as are official allegiance and personal interest, the nuances of which must be kept in mind, as they are difficult to identify in the available material. More commonly found than seals are seal impressions on bullae, sealings, and cuneiform tablets, which may either represent the use of NCA practices in local contexts, or the receipt of documents or goods from sources linked to the imperial administration (see van den Hout, chapter 41 in this volume). Changes in local administrative and sealing practices to accommodate elements of the NCA tradition may be indicative of political and cultural ties. The quantities of texts and glyptic finds in a particular location as well as the professions represented provide us with additional clues about the social level and intensity of this interaction and about the nature of the political relationship.

A clear geographical pattern emerges from the distribution of contextually documented NCA and NCA-style administrative technology outside the central

Anatolian plateau, which is excluded from this analysis (figure 40.2). The vast majority of fourteenth and thirteenth century B.C.E. NCA (-style) glyptic and tablet finds concentrate in four main find-spots located to the south and southeast of the Hittite core region: Tarsus, Korucutepe, Ras Shamra-Ugarit, and Meskene-Emar.

The distribution pattern, quantity, and type of glyptic evidence and text finds at these four sites would suggest the operation of at least three different modes of interregional administrative interaction—one Anatolian and two north Syrian—involving geographically as well as hierarchically distinct segments of the imperial authority. At Tarsus and Korucutepe contact with the Hittite center is attested by the local use of NCA-style administrative technology during the second half of the LBA, but also stretching back into the previous period in the case of Tarsus. At both sites potential parallels can be found between persons represented on local seal impressions and at the imperial capital. Some of these carried central or local royal titles or fulfilled official functions. The majority of glyptic finds at these two sites are sealed bullae, administrative devices attached to writing tablets or containers, which are documented in large quantities at Boğazköy-Ḫattuša and suggest similarities in administrative practices.

This contrasts with the two main find-spots in Syria, which yielded little evidence for the use of clay bullae in administrative procedures. Beyond that the two sites share little in common with respect to their administrative relationships with the Hittite Empire. Ugarit appears to have been under highest-level political control and was interfered with in exceptional circumstances, whereas Emar was more directly administered by the Hittite authorities at Carchemish. Two scribal schools operated in parallel at Emar (Beyer 2001). One adhered to traditional Syrian tablet formats and glyptic styles, while the other represents an amalgamation of Anatolian and Syrian styles. The Hittite viceroy at Carchemish and his officials are mentioned in the Emar texts. They were involved in local legal decisions and witnessed contracts. A Hittite administrator, "the overseer of the land," was in charge of the land of Aštata (Beckman 1995:28). With the exception of Muršili II, the main dynastic line of Ḫattuša is not represented in this way at Emar. By contrast, Ugarit's leadership communicated directly with the imperial court at Boğazköy-Ḫattuša, and numerous treaties, edicts, and letters attest to the rather more frequent interference of the Hittite great king in local affairs. Hittite royal and official seals are attested on a number of tablets relating to political and legal matters, but local scribal tradition and administration practices show no signs of NCA influences (Genz 2006; Neu 1995:124–25).

Projected Hegemony and Territorial Competition

Landscape monuments such as rock reliefs, dams, and pool sanctuaries outside settlement contexts provide another perspective on high level imperial–local relationships, albeit one of competition rather than cooperation (see Harmanşah, chapter 28 in this volume).

Traditionally, Late Bronze Age landscape monuments have tended to be treated as a diverse yet coherent category of art historical and philological interest. A consensus of strong stylistic homogeneity has emerged in the literature as well as the explicit or implicit connection of these monuments with the Hittite imperial venture (Akurgal 1964:103; Bittel 1976:191; Börker-Klähn 1982; Ehringhaus 2005; Emre 2002:233; Kohlmeyer 1983:103). Such an identification is arguably correct in a small number of cases where Luwian hieroglyphic inscriptions name Hittite great kings (Sirkeli 1, Fıraktin, Yazılıkaya, Yalburt, and Karakuyu) or related officials (Taşçı A). Owing to a series of recent discoveries of new monuments and success in deciphering old inscriptions (Dinçol 1998; Ehringhaus 1995, 2005:100–101; Hawkins 1998; Herbordt 2001; Peschlow-Bindokat 2001), the majority of known Late Bronze Age landscape monuments can now be attributed to either local kings (Karabel, Hatip), princes (İmamkulu, Hanyeri, Hamite, Akpınar, Suratkaya, and possibly Malkaya), or persons of official rank (Taşçı A). Links to the Hittite imperial administration can be established for the authors of some of these monuments through textual or glyptic syncretisms (Hawkins 2005; Herbordt 2005). These sometimes contingent connections with the Hittite center, however, are not straightforward confirmations of the assertion of imperial power in these areas.

The rock reliefs of Kurunta and Tudḫaliya IV most vividly attest to the use of landscape monuments in the negotiation of dynastic and territorial supremacy. The problematic relationship between Kurunta, king of Tarḫuntašša in Rough Cilicia, and his cousin, the Hittite great king, is detailed in cuneiform sources as well as hieroglyphic Luwian inscriptions (Hawkins 1995). Among all Hittite great kings, Tudḫaliya IV in particular appears to have invested in representational monuments at Boğazköy-Ḫattuša, the nearby Yazılıkaya, and on the fringes of the central Anatolian plateau (see Beal, chapter 26 in this volume). As Ehringhaus (2005:119) pointed out, Tudḫaliya IV seems to have been under pressure to underwrite the legitimacy of his rule in this way. By the same token, it can be argued that all monumental representations in peripheral regions are born out of similar pressures of or aspirations to legitimation. In other words, rock reliefs and inscriptions, besides their more immediate functions of water storage and/or cult, can be interpreted as projections of power and claims over territories via their boundaries and access routes rather than as manifestations of achieved centralized control.

This hypothesis gains further support when the striking geographical distribution of landscape monuments is considered (figure 40.2). Monuments of Hittite great kings outside the capital and its immediate surroundings are located on the western and eastern fringes of the central Anatolian plateau either directly on important communication routes or in locations generally associated with passages to other parts of Anatolia. A temporal component, indicative of changing interests and concerns in the projection of imperial power, may also be tentatively proposed. It seems that earlier generations of great kings concentrated ideological strategies, at least in the form of landscape monuments, in the southeast and along routes that allowed Hittite access to the natural and mercantile resources of southeast Anatolia and northern Syria. In the reign of Tudḫaliya IV, although the Karakuyu inscription attests to his concern also with this eastern area, identifiable imperial stone carvings for the first time appear on the southwest edges of the plateau.

It would thus appear that landscape monuments directly associated with Hittite rulership were concerned with the framing or guarding of an interior rather than the subjugation of an exterior (also Seeher 2005:42). This interior corresponds with the region undergoing major reorganization in what can be interpreted as the spatial implementation of territorial control as well as the extended core region of NCA ceramic production.

Conclusion: Hittite Imperial Relationships and Processes

The evidence for the selective adoption of NCA ceramic traditions in neighboring regions, changes and continuity in local settlement systems, the direction and intensity of Hittite administrative efforts, and the dialogue of territorial hegemony carried out via landscape monuments show that empire, rather than a monolithic entity, is best conceptualized as a complex web of interactions. Imperial–local relationships were less clear cut and in favor of all-encompassing central control than one might infer from the Hittite documents. Instead, we gain

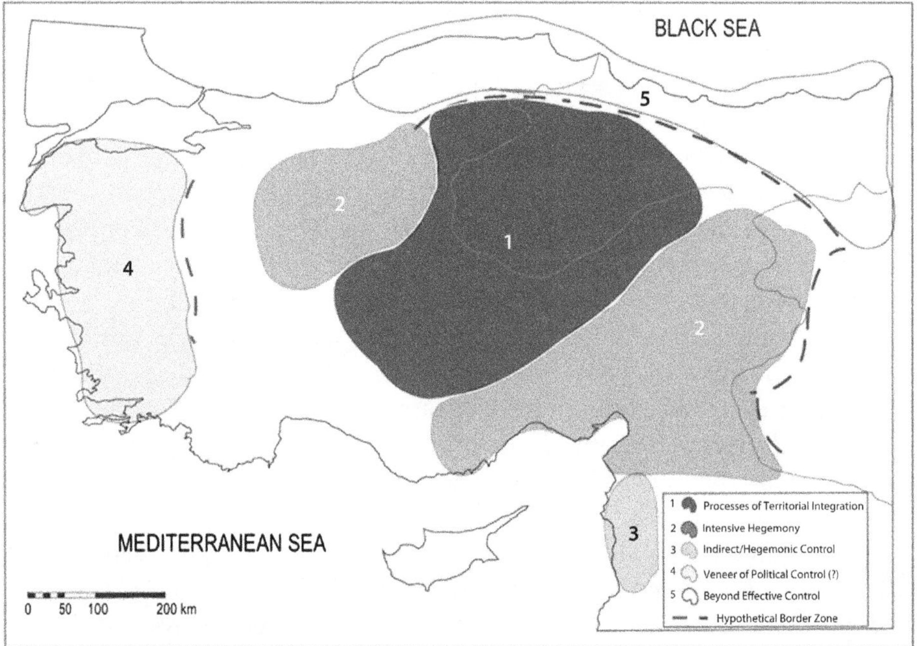

Figure 40.4. Reconstruction of dominance relationships in the Hittite Empire.

the impression of an ongoing process or negotiation of empire that is carried out on a range of different cultural, political, and social levels and that is neither complete nor uncontested in its closest periphery and throughout its existence. Here we observe a sphere of increasingly materially manifested direct imperial control on the central Anatolian plateau (figure 40.4). Close relationships, on multiple cultural and political levels, with southern and southeastern Anatolia and along the Syrian Euphrates point toward a level of control somewhere between territorial and hegemonic rule, which may be called "intensive hegemony." A more hands-off "ideal" type of hegemonic control may be postulated for the case of Ugarit, whose cultural tastes as well as administrative practices retain a fiercely independent character. A veneer of political control can be inferred from the textual sources for western Anatolia, with little or no tangible material signs of Hittite government or, with the exception of monumental display, of cultural interaction. Finally, the archaeological record of northern and northeastern Anatolia suggests the absence of effective Hittite control over these regions.

REFERENCES

Adams, Robert. 1979. Common Concerns but Different Standpoints: A Commentary. In *Power and Propaganda. A Symposium on Ancient Empires*, ed. Mogens T. Larsen, 393–404. Mesopotamia 7. Copenhagen: Akademisk Forlag.

———. 1981. *Heartlands of Cities: Surveys of Ancient Settlement and Land Use on the Central Floodplain of the Euphrates*. Chicago: University of Chicago Press.

Akurgal, Ekrem. 1964. Die Kunst der Hethiter. In *Neuere Hethiterforschung. Historia*, ed. Gerold Walser. Zeitschrift für Alte Geschichte, Einzelschriften 7. Wiesbaden: Steiner.

Alcock, Susan E. 1993. *Graecia Capta. The Landscapes of Roman Greece*. Cambridge: Cambridge University Press.

Alp, Sedat. 1991. *Hethitische Briefe aus Maşat Höyük*. Ankara: Türk Tarih Kurumu Basımevi.

Beckman, Gary. 1995. Hittite Provincial Administration in Anatolia and Syria: The View from Maşat and Emar. In *Atti del II Congresso Internazionale di Hittitologia*, ed. Onofrio Carruba, Mauro Giorgieri, and Clelia Mora, 19–37. Studia Mediterranea 9. Pavia: Iuculano.

Beyer, Dominique. 2001. *Emar IV: les sceaux: mission archéologique de Meskéné-Emar, recherches au pays d'Aštata*. Fribourg: Editions Universitaires Fribourg.

Bittel, Kurt. 1976. *Die Hethiter. Die Kunst Anatoliens vom Ende des 3. bis zum Anfang des 1. Jahrtausends vor Christus*. München: Beck.

Börker-Klähn, Jutta. 1982. *Altvorderasiatische Bildstelen und vergleichbare Felsreliefs*. Band I–II. Baghdader Forschungen 4. Mainz: von Zabern.

Branting, Scott A. 1996. The Alişar Regional Survey 1993–1994: A Preliminary Report. *Anatolica* 12: 146–55.

Bryce, Trevor. 2002. *Life and Society in the Hittite World*. Oxford: Oxford University Press.

Burney, Charles. 1980. Aspects of the Excavations in the Altınova, Elâzığ. *Anatolian Studies* 30: 157–67.

Cherry, John F. and Jack L. Davis. 2001. "Under the Sceptre of Agamemnon": The View from the Hinterlands of Mycenae. In *Urbanism in the Aegean Bronze Age*, ed. Keith Branigan, 141–59. Sheffield Studies in Aegean Archaeology 4. Sheffield: Centre for Aegean Archaeology, University of Sheffield.

de Montmollin, Olivier. 1989. *The Archaeology of Political Structure. Settlement Analysis in a Classical Maya Polity*. Cambridge: Cambridge University Press.

Dinçol, Ali M. 1998. Die Entdeckung des Felsmonuments in Hatip und ihre Auswirkungen über [*sic*.] die historischen und geographischen Fragen des Hethiterreichs. *TÜBA-AR* 1: 27–35.

Dupré, Sylvestre. 1983. *Porsuk I: La céramique de l'Age du Bronze et de l'Age du Fer*. Paris: Éditions Recherche sur les Civilisations.

Ehringhaus, Horst. 1995. Hethitische Felsreliefs der Großreichszeit entdeckt. *Antike Welt* 1: 66.

———. 2005. *Götter, Herrscher, Inschriften: Die Felsreliefs der hethitischen Großreichszeit in der Türkei*. Mainz: von Zabern.

Emre, Kutlu. 2002. Felsreliefs, Stelen, Orthostaden. Großplastiken als monumentale Form staatlicher und religiöser Repräsentation. In *Die Hethiter und ihr Reich. Das Volk der 1000 Götter*, ed. Kunst- und Ausstellungshalle der Bundesrepublik Deutschland GmbH, 218–33. Stuttgart: Theiss.

Fischer, Bettina, Hermann Genz, Éric Jean, and Kemalettin Köroğlu, eds. 2003. *Identifying Changes: The Transition from the Bronze to the Iron Ages in Anatolia and its Neighbouring Regions. Proceedings of the International Workshop, Istanbul, 8–9 November 2002*. İstanbul: Türk Eskiçağ Bilimleri Enstitüsü.

Fischer, Franz. 1963. *Die hethitische Keramik von Boğazköy*. Berlin: Gebr. Mann.

French, David H. 1965. Prehistoric Sites in the Göksu Valley. *Anatolian Studies* 15: 177–201.

Garstang, John. 1953. *Prehistoric Mersin, Yümük Tepe in Southern Turkey*. Oxford: Clarendon Press.

Gates, Marie-Henriette. 2001. Potmarks at Kinet Höyük and the Hittite Ceramic Industry. In *La Cilicie: Espaces et pouvoirs locaux (2e millénaire av. J.-C.–4e siècle ap. J.-C.). Actes de la table ronde internationale d'Istanbul, 2–5 novembre 1999*, ed. Éric Jean, Ali M. Dinçol, and Serra Durugönül, 137–57. Paris: De Boccard.

———. 2006. Dating the Hittite Levels at Kinet Höyük: A Revised Chronology. In *Strukturierung und Datierung der hethitischen Archäologie: Voraussetzungen-Probleme-Neue Ansätze. Internationaler Workshop Istanbul, 26–27 November 2004*, ed. Dirk P. Mielke, Ulf-Dietrich Schoop, and Jürgen Seeher, 293–309. BYZAS 4. İstanbul: Ege Yayınları.

Genz, Hermann. 2006. Hethitische Präsenz im spätbronzezeitlichen Syrien: Die archäologische Evidenz. *Baghdader Mitteilungen* 37: 499–509.

Genz, Hermann and Dirk Paul Mielke, eds. 2011. *Insights into Hittite History and Archaeology*. Leuven: Peeters.

Glatz, Claudia. 2007. *Contact, Interaction, Control—The Archaeology of Interregional Relations in Late Bronze Age Anatolia*. Ph.D. dissertation. University College London.

———. 2009. Empire as Network: Spheres of Material Interaction in Late Bronze Age Anatolia. *Journal of Anthropological Archaeology* 28: 127–41.

———. In press. Negotiating Empire—A Comparative Investigation into the Responses to Hittite Imperialism by the Vassal State of Ugarit and the Kaska Peoples of the Pontic Region. In *Empires and Complexity: On the Crossroads of Archaeology, History and Anthropology*, ed. Gregory Areshian. Los Angeles: Cotsen Institute of Archaeology.

Goldman, Hetty. 1956. *Excavations at Gözlü Kule, Tarsus II. From the Neolithic through the Bronze Age*. Princeton, N.J.: Princeton University Press.

Gorny, Ronald L. 1995. Hittite Imperialism and Anti-Imperial Resistance as Viewed from Alişar Höyük. *Bulletin of the American Schools of Oriental Research* 299/300: 65–89.

———. 2002. Anatolian Archaeology: An Overview. *In Across the Anatolian Plateau: Readings in the Archaeology of Ancient Turkey*, ed. David C. Hopkins, 1–4. Annual of the American Schools of Oriental Research, vol. 57. Boston: American Schools of Oriental Research.

Griffin, Elisabeth. 1980. Chapter 1: The Middle and Late Bronze Age Pottery. In *Korucutepe 3. Final Report on the Excavations of the Universities of Chicago, California (Los Angeles) and Amsterdam in the Keban Reservoir. Eastern Anatolia 1968–1970*, ed. Maurits N. van Loon, 3–109. Amsterdam: North-Holland.

Gunter, Ann. 1991. *The Bronze Age. Gordion Excavations Final Reports III*. Philadelphia: University Museum.

———. 2006. Issues in Hittite Ceramic Production: A View from the Western Frontier. In *Strukturierung und Datierung der hethitischen Archäologie: Voraussetzungen–Probleme–Neue Ansätze. Internationaler Workshop Istanbul, 26–27 November 2004*, ed. Dirk P. Mielke, Ulf-Dietrich Schoop, and Jürgen Seeher, 349–63. BYZAS 4. İstanbul: Ege Yayınları.

Güterbock, Hans G. 1957. Toward a Definition of the Term Hittite. *Oriens* 10: 233–39.

Hawkins, J. David. 1995. *The Hieroglyphic Inscription of the Sacred Pool Complex at Hattusa (SÜDBURG)*. Studien zu den Boğazköy-Texten Beiheft 3. Wiesbaden: Harrassowitz.

———. 1998. Tarkasnawa King of Mira, Tarkondemos, Boğazköy Sealings and Karabel. *Anatolian Studies* 48: 1–31.

———. 2005. Commentaries on the Readings. In *Die Prinzen- und Beamtensiegel der hethitischen Großreichszeit auf Tonbullen aus dem Nişantepe-Archiv in Hattusa*, ed. Suzanne Herbordt, 248–313. Boğazköy-Hattuša 19. Mainz: von Zabern.

Hazenboos, Joost. 2003. *The Organization of the Anatolian Local Cults during the Thirteenth Century B.C. An Appraisal of the Hittite Cult Inventories*. Leiden: Brill, Styx.

Henrickson, Robert C. 1993. Politics, Economics and Ceramic Continuity at Gordion in the Late Second and First Millennia B.C. In *Social and Cultural Contexts of New Ceramic Technologies*, ed. W. D. Kingery, 89–176. Westville: American Ceramic Society.

———. 1994. Continuity and Discontinuity in the Ceramic Tradition at Gordion during the Iron Age. In *Iron Ages 3. Proceedings of the Third International Anatolian Iron Age Symposium in Van, Turkey 6–11 August 1990*, ed. David H. French and Altan Çilingiroğlu, 95–129. Monograph 16. London: British Institute of Archaeology at Ankara.

———. 2002. Hittite Pottery and Potters: The View from Late Bronze Age Gordion. In *Across the Anatolian Plateau. Readings in the Archaeology of Ancient Turkey*, ed. David C. Hopkins, 123–31. Annual of the American Schools of Oriental Research, vol. 57. Boston: American Schools of Oriental Research.

Herbordt, Suzanne. 2001. Lesung der Inschrift eines hethitischen Großprinzen aus dem Latmos. *Archäologischer Anzeiger* 2001: 367–78.

———. 2005. *Die Prinzen- und Beamtensiegel der hethitischen Großreichszeit auf Tonbullen aus dem Nişantepe-Archiv in Hattuša*. Boğazköy-Hattuša 19. Mainz: von Zabern.

Hoffner, Harry A. 1974. *Alimenta Hethaeorum. Food Production in Hittite Asia Minor*. American Oriental Series 55. New Haven, Conn.: American Oriental Society.

———. 1997. *The Laws of the Hittites. A Critical Edition*. Leiden: Brill.

Jean, Éric. 2006. The Hittites at Mersin-Yumuktepe: Old Problems and New Directions. In *Strukturierung und Datierung der hethitischen Archäologie: Voraussetzungen–Probleme–Neue Ansätze. Internationaler Workshop Istanbul, 26–27 November 2004*, ed. Dirk P. Mielke, Ulf-Dietrich Schoop, and Jürgen Seeher, 311–32. BYZAS 4. İstanbul: Ege Yayınları.

Jean, Éric, Ali M. Dinçol, and Serra Durugönül, eds. 2001. *La Cilicie: espaces et pouvoirs locaux (2e millénaire av. J.-C.–4e siècle ap. J.-C.). Actes de la table ronde internationale d'Istanbul, 2–5 novembre 1999*. Paris: De Boccard.

Joukowsky, Martha. 1986. *Prehistoric Aphrodisias. An Account of the Excavations and Artifact Studies*. Vols. 1–2. Court-St-Étienne: Oleffe.

Katsuno, Tadashi. 2004. Beobachtungen zur Keramikentwicklung der Schicht III von Kaman-Kalehöyük. *Anatolian Archaeological Studies* 13: 95–106.

———. 2006. Zur Keramik des 2. Jahrtausends v. Chr. von Kaman-Kalehöyük. Ein Beitrag zur Kenntnis der Keramikentwicklung von der "Übergangsperiode" zwischen der Frühen und Mittleren Bronzezeit bis in die Spätbronzezeit. In *Strukturierung und Datierung der hethitischen Archäologie: Voraussetzungen–Probleme–Neue Ansätze. Internationaler Workshop Istanbul, 26–27 November 2004*, ed. Dirk P. Mielke, Ulf-Dietrich Schoop, and Jürgen Seeher, 277–86. BYZAS 4. İstanbul: Ege Yayınları.

Kohlmeyer, Kay. 1983. Felsbilder der hethitischen Großreichszeit. *Acta Praehistorica et Archaeologica* 15: 7–135.

Korbel, Günther. 1985. *Die spätbronzezeitliche Keramik von Norşuntepe*. Hannover: Institut für Bauen und Planen in Entwicklungsländern.

Kunst-und Ausstellungshalle der Bundesrepublik Deutschland GmbH, ed. 2002. *Die Hethiter und ihr Reich. Das Volk der 1000 Götter*. Stuttgart: Theiss.

Larsen, Mogens.T. 1979. The Tradition of Empire in Mesopotamia. In *Power and Propaganda. A Symposium on Ancient Empires*, ed. Mogens T. Larsen, 75–103. Mesopotamia 7. Copenhagen: Akademisk Vorlag.

Lattimore, Owen. 1962 *Studies in Frontier History. Collected Papers 1928–1958*. London: Oxford University Press.

Macqueen, James G. 1986. *The Hittites and Their Contemporaries in Asia Minor*. London: Thames and Hudson.

Mann, Michael. 1986. *The Sources of Social Power. A History of Power from the Beginning to A.D. 1760*. Vol. 1. Cambridge: Cambridge University Press.

Matthews, Roger. 2003. *The Archaeology of Mesopotamia. Theories and Approaches*. London: Routledge.

Mellaart, James and Ann Murray. 1995. *Beycesultan III, Part II: Late Bronze Age and Phrygian Pottery and Middle and Late Bronze Age Small Objects*. London: British Institute of Archaeology at Ankara.

Mellink, Machteld J. 1956. *A Hittite Cemetery at Gordion*. Philadelphia: University Museum, University of Pennsylvania.

Mielke, Dirk P. 2001. Die Grabungen an der Südspitze. In A. Müller-Karpe, Untersuchungen in Kuşaklı 2000. *Mitteilungen der Deutschen Orient-Gesellschaft* 133: 237–43.

———. 2006. İnandıktepe und Sarissa. Ein Beitrag zur Datierung althethitischer Fundkomplexe. In *Strukturierung und Datierung der hethitischen Archäologie: Voraussetzungen–Probleme–Neue Ansätze. Internationaler Workshop Istanbul, 26–27 November 2004*, ed. Dirk P. Mielke, Ulf-Dietrich Schoop, and Jürgen Seeher, 251–76. BYZAS 4. İstanbul: Ege Yayınları.

Mielke, Dirk P., Ulf-Dietrich Schoop, and Jürgen Seeher. 2006a. Zu diesem Workshop. In *Strukturierung und Datierung der hethitischen Archäologie: Voraussetzungen–Probleme–Neue*

Ansätze. Internationaler Workshop Istanbul, 26–27 November 2004, ed. Dirk P. Mielke, Ulf-Dietrich Schoop, and Jürgen Seeher, 1–3. BYZAS 4. İstanbul: Ege Yayınları.

———, eds. 2006b. *Strukturierung und Datierung der hethitischen Archäologie: Voraussetzungen–Probleme–Neue Ansätze. Internationaler Workshop Istanbul, 26–27 November 2004*. BYZAS 4. İstanbul: Ege Yayınları.

Mora, Clelia. 1977. Saggio per uno studio sulla populazione urbana nell'Anatolica antica. *Studi Micenei ed Egeo-Anatolici* 18: 227–41.

Müller, Uwe. 2005. Norşun Tepe and Lidar Höyük. Two examples for cultural change during the Early Iron Age. In *Anatolian Iron Ages 5. Proceedings of the Fifth Anatolian Iron Ages Colloquium Held at Van, 6–10 August 2001*, ed. Altan Çilingiroğlu and Gareth Darbyshire, 107–14. British Institute of Archaeology at Ankara Monograph 31. London: British Institute of Archaeology at Ankara.

Müller-Karpe, Andreas. 1988. *Hethitische Töpferei der Oberstadt von Hattuša. Ein Beitrag zur Kenntnis spät-großzeitlicher Keramik und Töpferbetriebe unter Zugrundelegung der Grabungsergebnisse von 1978–82 in Boğazköy*. Marburg: Hitzeroth.

———. 2000. Kayalıpınar in Ostkappadokien: Ein neuer hethitischer Tontafelfundplatz. *Mitteilungen der Deutschen Orient-Gesellschaft* 132: 355–65.

———. 2002. Die Keramik des mittleren und jüngeren hethitischen Reiches. Die Entwicklung der anatolischen Keramik—ihre Formen und Funktionen. In *Die Hethiter und ihr Reich: Das Volk der 1000 Götter*, ed. Kunst- und Ausstellungshalle der Bundesrepublik Deutschland GmbH, 256–63. Stuttgart: Theiss.

Neu, Erich. 1995. Hethiter und Hethitisch in Ugarit. In *Ugarit: Ein ostmediterranes Kulturzentrum im Alten Orient. Ergebnisse und Perspektiven der Forschung*, ed. Manfried Dietrich and Oswald Loretz, 115–29. Band 1. Ugarit und seine altorientalische Umwelt. Münster: Ugarit-Verlag.

Neve, Peter. 1999. *Die Oberstadt von Hattuša. Die Bauwerke. I Das Zentrale Tempelviertel*. Boğazköy-Hattuša 16. Berlin: Gebr. Mann.

Nougayrol, Jean. 1968. Textes suméro-accadiens des archives et bibliothèques privées d'Ugarit. In *Ugaritica V*, ed. Jean Nougayrol, Emmanuel Laroche, Charles Virolleaud, and Claude F. Schaeffer, 1–446. Paris: Imprimerie Nationale/Geuthner.

Omura, Sachihiro. 2001. Preliminary Report on the 15th Excavation Season at Kaman-Kalehöyük (2000). *Anatolian Archaeological Studies* 10: 1–35.

———. 2002. Preliminary Report on the 16th Excavation Season at Kaman-Kalehöyük (2001). *Anatolian Archaeological Studies* 11: 1–43.

Özgüç, Tahsin. 1988. *İnandıktepe. An Important Cult Centre in the Old Hittite Period*. Ankara: Türk Tarih Kurumu.

Parzinger, Hermann and Rosa Sanz. 1992. *Die Oberstadt Keramik von Hattuša. Hethitische Keramik aus dem Zentralen Tempelviertel*. Berlin: Gebr. Mann.

Pasternak, Rainer. 1998. Übersicht über die Ergebnisse der archaeobotanischen Arbeiten in Kuşaklı 1994–1997 und ein Interpretationsansatz zu den Befunden. In A. Müller-Karpe, Untersuchungen in Kuşaklı 1997. *Mitteilungen der Deutschen Orient-Gesellschaft* 130: 160–70.

Peschlow-Bindokat, Anneliese. 2001. Eine hethitische *Großprinzeninschrift* aus dem Latmos. Vorläufiger Bericht. *Archäologischer Anzeiger* 2001: 363–67.

Postgate, J. Nicholas. 1992. The Land of Assur and the Yoke of Assur. *World Archaeology* 23.3: 247–63.

———. 1994. In Search of the First Empires. *Bulletin of the American Schools of Oriental Research* 293: 1–13.

———. 2005. Identifying the End of the Hittite Empire. Problems of Reuniting History and Archaeology at Kilise Tepe. *Bilkent University: Department of Archaeology and History of Art Newsletter* 4: 26–30.

———. 2007. The Ceramics of Centralisation and Dissolution: A Case Study from Rough Cilicia. *Anatolian Studies* 57: 141–50.

Roberts, Brian K. 1996. *Landscapes of Settlement: Prehistory to the Present*. London: Routledge.

Sagona, Antonio and Paul Zimansky. 2009. *Ancient Turkey*. London: Routledge.

Schoop, Ulf-Dietrich. 2003. Pottery Traditions of the Later Hittite Empire: Problems of Definition. In *Identifying Changes: The Transition from the Bronze to the Iron Ages in Anatolia and its Neighbouring Regions. Proceedings of the International Workshop Istanbul, 8–9 November 2002*, ed. Bettina Fischer, Hermann Genz, Éric Jean, and Kemalettin Köroğlu, 176–78. İstanbul: Türk Eskiçağ Bilimleri Enstitüsü.

———. 2006. Dating the Hittites with Statistics. Ten Pottery Assemblages from Boğazköy-Hattuša. In *Strukturierung und Datierung der hethitischen Archäologie: Voraussetzungen–Probleme–Neue Ansätze. Internationaler Workshop Istanbul, 26–27 November 2004*, ed. Dirk P. Mielke, Ulf-Dietrich Schoop, and Jürgen Seeher, 215–39. BYZAS 4. İstanbul: Ege Yayınları.

———. 2008. Wo steht die Archäologie in der Erforschung der Hethitischen Kultur? Schritte zu einem Paradigmenwechsel. In *Hattuša-Boğazköy. Das Hethiterreich im Spannungsfeld des Alten Orients. 6. Internationales Colloquium der Deutschen Orient-Gesellschaft 22–24 März 2006, Würzburg*, ed. Gernot Wilhelm, 35–60. Wiesbaden: Harrassowitz.

Schreiber, Katharina J. 2005. Imperial Agendas and Local Agency: Wari Colonial Strategies. In *The Archaeology of Colonial Encounters: Comparative Perspectives*, ed. Gil J. Stein, 237–62. Oxford: Currey.

Scott, James C. 1990. *Domination and the Arts of Resistance: Hidden Transcripts*. New Haven, Conn.: Yale University Press.

Seeher, Jürgen. 2000. Getreidelagerung in unterirdischen *Großspeichern*: Zur Methode und ihrer Anwendung im 2. Jahrtausend v. Chr. am Beispiel der Befunde in Hattuša. *Studi Micenei ed Egeo-Anatolici* 42.2: 261–301.

———. 2001. Die Zerstörung von Hattuša. In *Akten des IV. Internationalen Kongresses für Hethitologie, Würzburg, 4–8 Oktober 1999*, ed. Gernot Wilhelm, 623–34. Studien zu den Boğazköy-Texten 45. Wiesbaden: Harrassowitz.

———. 2003. Die Ausgrabungen in Boğazköy-Hattuša 2002. *Archäologischer Anzeiger* 2003.1: 1–14.

———. 2005. Überlegungen zur Beziehung zwischen dem hethitischen Kernreich und der Westküste Anatoliens im 2. Jahrtausend v. Chr. In *Interpretationsraum Bronzezeit, Bernhard Hänsel von seinen Schülern gewidmet*, ed. Barbara Horejs, Reinhard Jung, Elke Kaiser, and Biba Terzan, 33–44. Bonn: Habelt.

———. 2008. Abschied von Gewusstem. Die Ausgrabungen in Hattuša am Beginn des 21. Jahrhunderts. In *Hattuša-Boğazköy. Das Hethiterreich im Spannungsfeld des Alten Orients. 6. Internationales Colloquium der Deutschen Orient-Gesellschaft 22–24 März 2006, Würzburg*, ed. Gernot Wilhelm, 1–13. Wiesbaden: Harrassowitz.

Seton-Williams, M. Veronica. 1954. Cilician Survey. *Anatolian Studies* 4: 121–74.

Siegelová, Jana. 2001. Der Regionalpalast in der Verwaltung des hethitischen Staates. *Altorientalische Forschungen* 28.2: 193–208.

Singer, Itamar. 1984. The AGRIG in the Hittite Texts. *Anatolian Studies* 34: 97–127.

Sinopoli, Carla M. 1994. The Archaeology of Empires. *Annual Review of Anthropology* 23: 159–80.

Smith, Adam. T. 2003. *The Political Landscape. Constellations of Authority in Early Complex Polities.* Berkeley: University of California Press.

Smith, Michael and Lisa Montiel. 2001. The Archaeological Study of Empires and Imperialism in Pre-Hispanic Central Mexico. *Journal of Anthropological Archaeology* 20: 245–84.

Steadman, Sharon R. and Ronald L. Gorny. 1995. Introduction: The Archaeology of Empire in Ancient Anatolia. *Bulletin of the American Schools of Oriental Research* 299–300: 1.

Summers, Geoffrey D. 1993. *Tille Höyük 4. The Late Bronze and Iron Age Transition.* Monograph Series no. 15. London: British Institute of Archaeology at Ankara.

Symington, Dorit. 2001. Hittites at Kilisetepe. In *La Cilicie: Espaces et pouvoirs locaux (2e millénaire av. J.-C.–4e siècle ap. J.-C.). Actes de la table ronde internationale d'Istanbul, 2–5 novembre 1999*, ed. Éric Jean, Ali M. Dinçol, and Serra Durugönül, 167–84. Paris: De Boccard.

Van De Mieroop, Marc. 1997. *The Ancient Mesopotamian City.* Oxford: Oxford University Press.

van Loon, Maurits N. 1980. Conclusion. In *Korucutepe 3. Final Report on the Excavations of the Universities of Chicago, California (Los Angeles) and Amsterdam in the Keban Reservoir, Eastern Anatolia 1968–1970*, ed. Maurits N. van Loon, 271–77. Amsterdam: North-Holland.

Whallon, Robert. 1979. *An Archaeological Survey of the Keban Reservoir Area of East-Central Turkey.* Memoirs of the Museum of Anthropology, University of Michigan no. 11. Ann Arbor: University of Michigan Press.

Wilhelm, Gernot. 2005. Zur Datierung der älteren hethitischen Landschenkungsurkunden. *Altorientalische Forschungen* 32.2: 272–79.

Wilkinson, Tony J. 2000. Regional Approaches to Mesopotamian Archaeology: The Contribution of Archaeological Surveys. *Journal of Archaeological Research* 8: 219–67.

Wilkinson, Tony J., Eleanor Barbanes Wilkinson, Jason Ur, and Mark Altaweel. 2005. Landscape and Settlement in the Neo-Assyrian Empire. *Bulletin of the American Schools of Oriental Research* 340: 23–56.

CHAPTER 41

THE HITTITE EMPIRE FROM TEXTUAL EVIDENCE

THEO VAN DEN HOUT

A History of Writing in Hittite Anatolia

Writing in Anatolia made its first known appearance in the form of the Old Assyrian cuneiform script. It was introduced by the merchants coming from Assyria around 2000 B.C.E., who established a trading network that lasted well into the thirties of the eighteenth century B.C.E. Especially the tablet collections found at Kaneš (also Neša, Turkish Kültepe), the center of this network, record the business and personal lives of these foreign traders and their interactions with the local Anatolian population (see Kulakoğlu, chapter 47, and Michel, chapter 13 in this volume). Most tablets were found in the so-called *kārum*, the trading area located in the lower city of Kaneš, and they come from two distinct levels; according to the most recent insights (Veenhof 2003) Level II dates to ca. 1950–1836 B.C.E. and Level Ib between ca. 1800 and 1730 B.C.E. Trade in Level II was very intensive, judging by the number of documents preserved: over 20,000 tablets generally dating to the last three generations of the Assyrians living in the *kārum*. The Level Ib settlement, on the other hand, thus far has yielded only some 200–300 documents, while the subsequent Level Ia shows no sign of foreign presence at all.

The Old Assyrian cuneiform used in these records is written on ruled tablets with a characteristic right slant (figure 41.1). The script is simple, with a basic syllabary of about 100 signs that could easily be mastered by the merchants themselves

Figure 41.1. Old Assyrian tablet OIP 27 n. 59 (A2531, 9 × 6.5 cm) (photo courtesy Oriental Institute, University of Chicago).

or their administrators. There are relatively few instances where local Anatolians seem to have used the script (Dercksen 2007), and in the Level Ib palace a spearhead was found with the inscription "Palace of Anitta, Great Prince." In all cases, however, the Assyrian language was used, and there is no evidence that an attempt was ever made to use Old Assyrian cuneiform to write Hittite. Therefore, the fact that the local Anatolian population never seems to have adopted it systematically for internal purposes and that—when the traders gave up their network—the script disappeared as suddenly from Anatolia as it had come, points to a lack of interest and perceived need. The local government surely must have had its own system of administration, but writing in the sense of a codified system of visible symbols recording language (Coulmas 2003:1) is by no means necessary for a detailed accounting over a longer period. As shown by the sealings and their symbols found at places like Arslantepe (Frangipane 2007) and Konya-Karahöyük (Alp 1994), detailed bookkeeping is very possible without a writing system.

When Level Ib at Kaneš came to an end toward the last quarter of the eighteenth century B.C.E., writing practices in Anatolia seem to have come to a halt temporarily. The subsequent Level Ia seems not to have contained any evidence of writing, and almost a century passed before a script emerged again. The new writing system seems to have coincided with the beginnings of Ḫattuša as the Hittite capital around the middle of the seventeenth century B.C.E. This was also cuneiform, but of a completely different type (figure 41.2), and it became the preferred medium of the Hittite kingdom and empire until it disintegrated around 1200 B.C.E.

How and when exactly the cuneiform script that we call Hittite developed is unknown. It is traditionally held that this type of cuneiform was brought in during the reign of Ḫattušili I (ca. 1650 B.C.E. according to the middle chronology) (Rüster and Neu 1989), and this remains the most attractive scenario. The Hittite cuneiform variant finds its closest parallel in the script used at Alalaḫ in northern Syria, and the reigns of Ḫattušili and his successor Muršili I (ca. 1600 B.C.E.) with their Syrian campaigns provide both the time and the place. According to his Annals, Ḫattušili captured and destroyed Alalaḫ in his second year (Beckman 2006:220), and Muršili finished his grandfather's work by taking the city of Aleppo. It is easily conceivable that along with the rich booty, some Syrian scribes were brought back to Ḫattuša. We even have tangible evidence that Ḫattušili employed such scribes: a letter written in the name of a Hittite king to be identified as Ḫattušili and addressed to a local Syrian ruler has been preserved (Salvini 1994). It is written in Akkadian and in the Syrian cuneiform, for which he must have had recourse to scribes from that area. That the letter was in Akkadian rather than Hittite is to be expected since it is a piece of diplomatic correspondence and thus uses the lingua franca of the time. Several internal compositions, however, among them the Annals just mentioned, have to be ascribed to these first two Hittite kings and exist in both an Akkadian and a Hittite version. Of others we have either an Akkadian or a Hittite version only. Some of the Akkadian texts are written in the Syrian script variant (Klinger 1998), whereas other Akkadian examples and all Hittite compositions show the Hittite cuneiform. The idea is therefore that after the introduction of the Syrian cuneiform, scribes in the Hittite capital immediately started to write in both languages, employing two cuneiform variants.

This view is not without its problems. First, it is quite atypical for a society that adopts a script from another society with a different language to begin composing its texts immediately in its own language. The process of training a first native generation in the new technique and of adapting the foreign script to the local tongue easily takes a generation or two (Klinger 1998:374; van den Hout 2009b:88–94). Because it has been assumed that Hittite was written already in Ḫattušili I's time, this would push the introduction of the new script back to a period before him, for which we have no records at all. Second, the distribution of internal records in Akkadian and Hittite seems random, and this problem is compounded by one of text dating: most compositions that go back to Ḫattušili, Muršili, and some of their early successors are preserved in late thirteenth-century B.C.E. copies only. Among these we find the Akkadian versions. Those, on the other hand, that we consider "old" or "contemporary" float in a time frame of over 200 years (ca. 1650–1400 B.C.E.) and cannot be dated with any precision. This is the group to which the monolingual Hittite texts belong.

Figure 41.2. Hittite fragment VBoT 30 (A6004); (a) obverse; (b) reverse (photo courtesy Oriental Institute, University of Chicago).

A possible solution to this confusing picture seems to offer itself when we restrict ourselves to those texts in the Hittite cuneiform that *can* be dated with certainty, that is, records for which we can be sure that they were issued when composed and where the chance of later copies is virtually absent (van den Hout 2009a:29–33, 2009b:90–92). These are, for instance, texts that bear the sealing of a Hittite king and that can as a consequence be ascribed to a specific reign. Such "true and legally authentic originals" are not attested before the late sixteenth century B.C.E. and are all written in Akkadian. A more likely scenario therefore for the reintroduction of the cuneiform script after the demise of the Old Assyrian variant and for the development from the Syrian into the typically Hittite variant could be sketched as follows. After the introduction of scribes from Syria in the reign(s) of Ḫattušili I (and Muršili I), there was not much writing going on other than for diplomatic and limited internal purposes. To the latter belonged royal commissions of inscriptions to be displayed publicly and perhaps also certain compositions that may have been considered didactic. Given the scarcity of texts from before ca. 1500 B.C.E. and the fact that they are written in the Syrian ductus, the volume of writing activity was probably low but perhaps just enough to sustain the development that resulted during the course of the sixteenth century B.C.E. in the variant that we call Hittite.

Pivotal in the change toward the Hittite ductus and responsible for an increased scribal output may have been Telipinu, king towards the end of the sixteenth century B.C.E. With him starts a whole series of charters or land donation records, he was the first known Hittite king to conclude an international treaty, and he is the author of an edict regulating royal succession, transforming the revenue system, and formulating some unrelated law paragraphs (see Beal, chapter 26 in this volume). It is even possible, although hard to prove, that the Hittite law collection was for the first time written down during his reign (Hoffner 1995:214) or shortly thereafter. The Hittite kingdom slipped into a period of relative decline after him, but we have, for all his successors up to the later fifteenth century B.C.E., an ongoing series of charters preserved as well as some new treaties. The charters are framed in an Akkadian formula with Hittite technical terms inserted. The use of this formula may well have become the standard for these texts, but it seems likely that during that same fifteenth century B.C.E. Hittite started to be used as a written language. The use of Akkadian for internal purposes came to an end with the rule of Tudḫaliya I at the close of this century. From his reign onward, Akkadian was no longer used for this, and Hittite became the official language of all state administration in the widest sense of the word.

Around this same time, that is, around 1400 B.C.E., a new script surfaces in the Hittite kingdom. It seems to have been based on an indigenous iconic repertoire and possibly grew out of a set of symbols that may have served local administrative systems in non-literate societies going as far back as the Assyrian Colony period (Yakubovich 2008). By 1400 B.C.E. it had probably developed a full syllabary of a highly pictographic ("hieroglyphic") nature. Although always considered to have originated among speakers of Luwian and therefore called Luwian hieroglyphs (see Yakubovich, chapter 23 in this volume), a good case has been made (Yakubovich 2008) that the script received its impetus from the Hittite ruling class. Anatolian hieroglyphs may therefore be a more neutral name. Their oldest use was to write names and titles on seals, which is likely to go back to early administrative-economic origins. The first attestation of their use for publicly displayed inscriptions dates to shortly after 1300 B.C.E. (Muwatalli II). As far as the often highly logographic nature of these early hieroglyphic inscriptions allows a judgment, they are invariably written in Luwian and not Hittite. A clear dichotomy thus existed: Hittite was the official language of the Hittite state for all its internal records written in cuneiform, but as soon as the ruling class felt the need to address a larger audience, be it through seals or propagandistic inscriptions, they used the Luwian language in the Anatolian hieroglyphs. A gradual demographic shift toward an ever-increasing Luwian-speaking population along with an awareness that these hieroglyphs were an original Anatolian creation as opposed to the imported cuneiform may have prompted this choice (Melchert 2005, and chapter 31 in this volume; Rieken 2006; van den Hout 2007a). Moreover, this script is easier to master than the highly abstract cuneiform and more accessible to the population at large because the iconic inventory used by the script must have reflected daily life in Anatolia. Maintaining Hittite for internal purposes, on the other hand, might well have had ideological reasons for an ever more isolated ruling class that tried to hold out against the Luwian "masses."

Luwian linguistic influence on Hittite can be traced back to the earliest Hittite compositions. It becomes ever more apparent until the many so-called glosses, that is, Luwian words interspersed in thirteenth-century B.C.E. Hittite texts and very often marked explicitly by the ancient scribes as foreign words, force us to assume a largely Luwian-speaking population and ruling class, with an administrative staff that was fluent in both languages. This "popularity" of Luwian at the expense of Hittite may finally explain why at the end of the Hittite Empire the Hittite language and its cuneiform script became extinct. Luwian, on the other hand, along with its hieroglyphs, survived well into the Iron Age.

Writing as a craft was the domain of a group of scribes employed by the state. Although they regularly "signed" the tablets they wrote ("Hand of PN") they remain otherwise largely anonymous. They belonged to the class of craftsmen along with priests, singers and musicians, bakers, beer brewers, cooks and waiters, spearmen, gate keepers, water carriers, bird breeders, and potters. A Hittite text (KBo 19.28) listing a total of 205 employees of the "workshop/house of craftsmen" (Sum. É.GIŠ.KIN.TI) mentions 19 scribes on clay and 33 "wood scribes." The latter distinction is usually taken to refer to the material on which they wrote. Wooden tablets were the wax covered diptychs just like the one preserved in the shipwreck found off the coast of Lycia (Marazzi 2000). The wooden writing boards may be supposed to have been used for the more ephemeral texts because of the diminished durability and their greater risk for being tampered with. They were also much lighter than clay tablets and therefore easier to transport. Whether lead was ever used as a writing surface, like the lead strips that survive from the Iron Age, remains unknown (see Yakubovich, chapter 23 in this volume).

Although wood scribes may have been more administrative than anything else, clay scribes were responsible for the bulk of the empire's records. Special (foreign?) experts were probably used for the Akkadian and Hurrian language texts. In the case of Akkadian, this is evident because of the apparent familiarity with the language (as opposed to the often poor knowledge displayed by the regular Hittite scribes) and the sometimes non-Hittite cuneiform in which these texts are written. Many officials belonging to the upper echelons of Hittite society added the designation "scribe" to their titles, especially on their seals, but this is in all likelihood an indication of their (probably mostly passive) literacy and does not imply that they were responsible for the tablets that have come down to us (van den Hout 2007b). It does, however, point to a relatively widespread literacy in those circles.

A History of Writings from Hittite Anatolia

Writings from Hittite Anatolia are understood here as the entire written legacy of the Hittite kingdom and empire, that is, all the preserved inscribed material left behind by the ruling class of the Hittite state, their officials, and staff. This legacy encompasses not only the clay tablets written in cuneiform but also the rock inscriptions in Hieroglyphic Luwian and the thousands of seal impressions and sometimes original seals, both bearing names and titles mostly in the Anatolian hieroglyphs but also sometimes in cuneiform. To this corpus one can add graffiti on objects and rock surfaces as well as the so-called pottery marks.

The total corpus of cuneiform clay tablets and fragments now numbers around 30,000. The overwhelming majority of them come from Boğazköy, the site of the former capital Ḫattuša, but since the early 1970s several sites in the periphery of the capital have started to yield texts as well. The more such provincial sites are unearthed, the clearer it becomes how centralized the Hittite state was. No Anatolian site has brought to light records that were not connected to the state administration. Often the compositions have close parallels to ones that we know from Ḫattuša. Table 41.1 gives a list of all genres that constitute the corpus (the CTH numbers refer to Laroche 1971, a classification of all texts into genres. This is still maintained online: see http://www.hethport.uni-wuerzburg.de/hetkonk).

Table 41.1 shows a basic distinction between long-term (A) and short-term (B) records. Most of the long-term records were stored for sometimes several centuries in the tablet collections because of their general or potential usefulness. As such they were often kept updated, and the royal chancery often made sure to have more than one copy in one place. This does not mean that for every single composition in these genres we have more than one version or duplicate, but the trend is unmistakable and for most compositions multiple copies do exist. This means that there was

Table 41.1. Overview of Hittite Text Genres

A: Texts with Duplicates	B. "Unica"
Historiography, treaties, edicts (CTH 1–147, 211–16)	Letters (CTH 151–210)
	Land deeds (CTH 221–25)
	Administrative texts: • Palace and temple administration (CTH 231–50) • Cult inventories (CTH 501–30) • Tablet inventories (CTH 276–82) • Labels (CTH 283)
Instructions and loyalty oaths (CTH 251–75)	
Laws (CTH 291–92)	Court depositions (CTH 293–97)
Oracle theory (CTH 531–60)	Oracle practice (CTH 561–82)
Hymns and prayers (CTH 371–89)	Vows (CTH 583–90)
Festival scenarios (CTH 591–721)	
Ritual scenarios (CTH 390–500)	
Mythology (Anatolian and non-Anatolian) (CTH 321–70)	
Hattic, Palaic, Luwian, Hurrian compositions (CTH 725–91)	
Sumerian and Akkadian compositions (CTH 310–16, 792–819)	
Hippological texts (CTH 284–87)	
Lexical lists (CTH 299–309)	

a constant copying activity resulting in often multiple copies of a single composition. Of the first series of the Hittite Laws, for instance, there existed at least six but probably many more copies (Friedrich 1971:5–9), whereas the composition known as the Hittite Royal Funerary Ritual is extant in at least three or four (van den Hout 1994:57). One can easily imagine how the law collection was regularly consulted, and how the series containing the Funerary Ritual was pulled from the shelf whenever a king or queen had died and the ritual needed to be performed. For similar reasons, treaties and edicts, instructions and loyalty oaths addressing various professional groups in Hittite society, ritual and cultic festival scenarios, hymns, prayers, and the Anatolian myths that were acted out (Bryce 2002:211–29) as part of certain rituals were kept and copied for future use and consultation. Apart from their primary function as legal instruments, the treaties and edicts were also for the Hittites themselves an important historical source as well as an efficient point of departure whenever new documents of this type had to be drawn up. For this reason too, perhaps, historiography was stored and kept. This is the most elusive of genres under the A group in table 41.1 in terms of its *Sitz im Leben*, goal, and audience. It has also sometimes been praised for its lack of all too obvious propaganda in comparison to, for instance, Mesopotamian historiography, as well as for its—at times—relatively sophisticated narrative style. There is room for reflection as well as for the achievements of others than the king. Although they can be seen as accounting to the gods for whom kings administered the land, the texts sometimes contain hints at a worldly public as well. How their dissemination took place, however, remains largely in the realm of speculation.

It is likewise difficult to assign a function to the more "literary" genres of the foreign, that is, Akkadian, Hurrian, and Sumerian compositions, to the so-called lexical lists or vocabularies, and also to some of the rituals. It has been convincingly shown that several rituals as recorded bear little relation to reality in the sense that they were useless as scenarios for real-life proceedings. These texts may well have been deliberately collected out of some academic interest (Christiansen 2006), and as such they come closest to our modern notion of a library. The same may be true of the Hittite versions of foreign myths like the Gilgameš Epic. Based on parallels with Mesopotamia, these texts are often assigned a role in the scribal curriculum, but evidence for this is completely lacking. It cannot be excluded either that these were (also?) used for entertainment purposes at the royal court.

Most of the genres under group B in table 41.1 can be characterized as administrative and of only short-term importance. It is no coincidence that with a single well-defined exception, all texts belonging to this group date to the last period of the Hittite Empire. They have survived only by virtue of the fact that they had not yet been recycled when the ruling class decided to give up the capital Ḫattuša and move elsewhere. As in every administration there was an ongoing appraisal of records, deciding which could be discarded and which should be stored for some time to come. Incoming correspondence was only kept as long as it was necessary and relevant for the administration. Although most of it was destroyed relatively soon, a very small percentage of letters was stored for the long term (de Martino 2005). Outgoing correspondence was likewise sometimes filed for future consultation, and some letters were copied and bundled into dossiers. Similarly, court depositions, oracle reports, and vows are almost exclusively late thirteenth-century B.C.E. documents whose destruction was preempted by the decision to abandon the capital. Again, the occasional old manuscript among these genres is to be explained either through strategic considerations or as simple administrative oversight.

The palace and temple administration under group B mostly deals with the Hittite system of taxes and the redistribution of goods. Taxes were presumably levied on a yearly basis and consisted of metals and textiles on one hand and food products and livestock on the other. On a more incidental basis tributes may have been demanded for special occasions such as the accession ceremony of a new king. Practically all preserved records concern metals, textiles, and further luxury items. Perishable materials such as food products may have been recorded to some extent on the more ephemeral wooden writing boards.

The real exception under group B are the charters or land deeds. These form a special group in many respects: shape, language, date, and storage. They record the bestowing of extensive land and properties by the king on members of the royal dynasty. The tablets are thick and pillow-shaped, with a royal seal in the middle, and in all probability clay bullae were attached to them by means of strings embedded in the clay core of the tablet with the seals of the witnesses impressed on them.

The language is Akkadian, composed according to a strict formula, and regularly Hittite technical terms are inserted into the text. They were not kept with the other records of groups A or B but stored separately along with other documents or objects that were or had been sealed with clay bullae. The charters were unique documents as far as the tablet collections of the capital were concerned. It is possible and maybe even likely that the beneficiary kept a sealed copy "in the form of original" as well. This may be the explanation for two such charters found outside Ḫattuša in İnandık and Tarsus. Finally, there is the chronological anomaly: unlike all other texts in group B, these original land deeds were stored and kept for hundreds of years. The oldest ones date to the reign of Telipinu of the late sixteenth century B.C.E. but were found as an integral part of the tablet collections of the late thirteenth-century B.C.E. residence that was given up by the Hittite ruling class.

Since the early 1970s, several provincial centers in the periphery of the capital have come to light (see Mielke, chapter 48 in this volume and figure 48.1 therein). Without exception, all attest to the tight grip the rulers at Ḫattuša exercised on the country. Script, language, formulas, and genres are all the ones already known from the capital. Many tablets even originated from there or find close parallels with the texts of Ḫattuša.

Apart from the cuneiform sources that were used for all internal records, the Anatolian hieroglyphs increasingly appeared as the preferred medium for reaching a larger audience. In keeping with this, a new genre of historiography arose. The historiographic inscriptions in Luwian that start appearing in the latter half of the thirteenth century B.C.E. by their very nature of being publicly displayed were much less balanced than the Hittite annalistic prose in cuneiform of, for instance, Muršili II in the last quarter of the fourteenth century B.C.E. The new texts are very much centered around the royal person, highly formulaic, and show none of the sophistication of the cuneiform Hittite annals. This shift in medium and dissemination may thus explain why annals like those of Muršili are not attested for the last kings of the Hittite Empire (Bolatti Guzzo and Marazzi 2004:155–58).

By far the largest corpus of hieroglyphic writing is the seals, mostly preserved impressed on bullae (Dinçol and Dinçol 2008; Güterbock 1940, 1942; Herbordt 2005; Mora 1987, 1990; and see Seeher, chapter 18 in this volume). They were probably the prerogative of the upper class and were a legal instrument to seal objects to guarantee their genuineness and inviolability. Impressed on tablets or attached to them, they lent authority and validity. At several places in the capital collections of bullae were found, sometimes in connection with the land deeds, but not always. These find complexes show how they were kept in chronological order. Chronologically, these bullae are complementary to the deeds; the last known land deed dates to Arnuwanda I at the beginning of the fourteenth century B.C.E., and the earliest datable bullae start with Šuppiluliuma I from around 1350 B.C.E. and continue until the very end. A still unsolved question is what these thousands of bullae were attached to and what their function was. Because of the ephemeral character of the wooden writing boards, it seems unlikely that they were attached to new charters that were from this point written on wooden writing boards (Marazzi 2000). If so, why did this change occur and why did they not keep the bullae that were once attached to the older clay ones? Or was the genre of land deeds discontinued, and are the bullae the vestiges of a completely different administrative process? The fact is, whatever their function, they were as integral a part of the state administration as the cuneiform records.

Of course, the total number of approximately 30,000 tablets and fragments does not represent 30,000 records to which one could add the thousands of bullae. Many of the fragments join each other as pieces of once complete documents, and many may still be recognized as joining others in the future. Yet it is highly likely that at any one time in the heyday of the Hittite Empire the tablet collections in the capital managed at least several thousands of records of various kinds. There is ample evidence in these written sources of efficient record management. Regularly older tablets are referred to, and they were used to create new ones. It is clear that such older tablets could be retrieved at will and without much difficulty. We can discern several places of primary tablet storage in Ḫattuša, three of which clearly stand out. They are the storerooms 10, 11, and 12 immediately east of the Great Temple 1, the House on the Slope further southeast toward the acropolis Büyükkale, and Building A on Büyükkale itself. Although with few exceptions fragments of all genres have been found at all three locations, there are obvious differences in the numbers in which these genres are represented in each of them. These differences allow us to sketch a more or less coherent picture of how the three locales functioned in relation to each other (van den Hout 2008).

As might be expected from their location in the Lower City, within easy walking distance from two city gates in the west where one can imagine most regular daily travel in and out of the city took place, the storerooms and the House on the Slope dealt with current administration. Their layout alone clearly shows the function of the storerooms, and the House on the Slope lies at the end of a street that led directly to one of the two gates. The tablet collection found in and near the storerooms contained practically all bookkeeping-type records that kept track of incoming goods, their redistribution, and their return as finished objects. At the same time, however, the storerooms collections also contained texts of practically all genres from groups A and B, as did the House on the Slope, except for bookkeeping records, which seem completely absent from this location. A striking feature of the House on the Slope is that texts mentioning the last known Hittite king, Šuppiluliuma II, were found exclusively there, whereas his father, Tudḫaliya IV, is well represented among the storeroom documents. In keeping with this is the observation that the House on the Slope shows the largest number of texts written in the most recent type of Hittite cuneiform. This suggests that this building housed the foremost political and diplomatic current affairs office or even chancery, whereas the storerooms concentrated on daily economic transactions and served as a first place to store documents that were no longer active. It is possible that a final appraisal of what was to be recycled and what was to be filed away indefinitely was taken there. Those that were to be kept were ultimately moved to Building A on the acropolis. Over 40 percent of the records stored there stem from before 1350 B.C.E., and it also contains the lowest percentage of fragments showing the latest type of Hittite cuneiform dating to the very end of the thirteenth century B.C.E. This suggests that Building A was used as a record center where all records were filed that were no longer active but still deemed important enough to be kept for future reference (van den Hout 2008).

Conclusion

The Hittite written legacy is unique in the ancient Near East in that it allows us to sketch the development of a major power over the course of its almost 500 years of history from a state of basic illiteracy through incipient literacy to a booming administrative apparatus that has earned it the reputation of a true bureaucracy. It was a state with two scripts: the cuneiform used for its inner administrative workings in the widest sense of the word with the Hittite language as its official medium, and the Anatolian hieroglyphs for the state's face to the outside. In the case of longer inscriptions, Luwian was here the preferred medium.

The record management system at Ḫattuša illustrates the ruling class's historical awareness, which also clearly emerges from the texts themselves. The smaller corpora unearthed in peripheral sites in the Anatolian heartland attest to the tight grip the central power held over its provinces. Yet in the end the ruling class for whom holding on to the Hittite language must have been part of an ideology was unable to resist the ever-growing pressure that may have come from the Luwian-speaking population groups. When the empire broke down, Hittite and the cuneiform script disappeared, and Luwian with its hieroglyphs survived into the Iron Age. The hieroglyphic script finally fell victim to the onslaught of the Neo-Assyrian Empire. The last hieroglyphic sources date to shortly after 700 B.C.E., and with them the Luwian language vanished.

REFERENCES

Alp, Sedat. 1994. *Zylinder- und Stempelsiegel aus Karahöyük bei Konya*. Ankara: Türk Tarih Kurumu Basımevi.

Beckman, Gary. 2006. Annals of Ḫattušili I. In *The Ancient Near East. Historical Sources in Translation* Mark Chavalas, 219–22. Malden, Mass.: Blackwell.

Bolatti Guzzo, Natalia and Massimiliano Marazzi. 2004. Storiografia hittita e geroglifico anatolico: per una revisione di KBo 12.38. In *Šarnikzel: Hethitologische Studien zum Gedenken an Emil Orgetorix Forrer (10.02.1894–10.01.1986)*, ed. Detlev Groddek and Sylvester Rössle, 155–85. Dresden: Verlag der TU Dresden.

Bryce, Trevor R. 2002. *Life and Society in the Hittite World*. Oxford: Oxford University Press.

Christiansen, Birgit. 2006. *Die Ritualtraditon der Ambazzi. Eine philologische Bearbeitung und entstehungsgeschichtliche Analyse der Ritualtexte CTH 391, CTH 429 und CTH 463*. Wiesbaden: Harrassowitz.

Coulmas, Florian. 2003. *Writing Systems. An Introduction to Their Linguistic Analysis*. Cambridge: Cambridge University Press.

de Martino, Stefano. 2005. Hittite Letters from the Time of Tuthaliya I/II, Arnuwanda I and Tuthaliya III. *Altorientalische Forschungen* 32: 291–321.

Dercksen, Jan Gerrit. 2007. On Anatolian Loanwords in Akkadian Texts from Kültepe. *Zeitschrift für Assyriologie* 97: 26–46.

Dinçol, Ali and Belkıs Dinçol. 2008. *Die Prinzen- und Beamtensiegel aus der Oberstadt von Boğazköy-Ḫattuša vom 16. Jahrhundert bis zum Ende der Grossreichszeit*. Mainz am Rhein: Philipp von Zabern.

Frangipane, Marcella, ed. 2007. *Arslantepe Cretulae. An Early Centralised Administrative System Before Writing*. Roma: Edizioni CIRAAS.

Friedrich, Johannes. 1971. *Die hethitischen Gesetze*. Leiden: Brill.

Güterbock, Hans Gustav. 1940. *Siegel aus Boğazköy. Erster Teil: Die Königssiegel der Grabungen bis 1938* (= Archiv für Orientforschung, Beiheft 5). Berlin: Im Selbstverlage des Herausgebers. Reprint, Osnabrück: Biblio-Verlag, 1967.

———. 1942. *Siegel aus Boğazköy. Zweiter Teil: Die Königssiegel von 1939 und die übrigen Hieroglyphensiegel* (= Archiv für Orientforschung, Beiheft 7). Berlin: Im Selbstverlage des Herausgebers. Reprint, Osnabrück: Biblio-Verlag, 1967.

Herbordt, Suzanne. 2005. *Die Prinzen- und Beamtensiegel der hethitischen Grossreichszeit auf Tonbullen aus dem Nişantepe-Archiv in Hattusa*. Mainz am Rhein: Philipp von Zabern.

Hoffner, Harry A. Jr. 1995. Hittite Laws. In *Law Collections from Mesopotamia and Asia Minor*, ed. Martha T. Roth, 213–47. Atlanta: Society of Biblical Literature.

Klinger, Jörg. 1998. "Wer lehrte die Hethiter das Schreiben?" Zur Paläographie früher Texte in akkadischer Sprache aus Boğazköy: Skizze einiger Überlegungen und vorläufiger Egebnisse. In *Acts of the IIIrd International Congress of Hittitology*, ed. Sedat Alp and Aygül Süel, 365–75. Ankara: n.p.

Laroche, Emmanuel 1971. *Catalogue des textes hittites*. Paris: Klincksieck.

Marazzi, Massimiliano. 2000. Sigilli e tavolette di legno: le fonti letterarie e le testimonianze sfragistiche nell'Anatolia hittita. In *Administrative Documents in the Aegean and Their Near Eastern Counterparts*, ed. Massimo Perna, 79–98. Roma: Ministero per i beni e le attività culturali, ufficio centrale per i beni archivistici.

Melchert, H. Craig. 2005. The Problem of Luvian Influence on Hittite. In *Sprachkontakt und Sprachwandel*, ed. Gerhard Meiser and Olav Hackstein, 445–60. Wiesbaden: Ludwig Reichert Verlag.

Mora, Clelia. 1987. *La glittica anatolica del II millennio a.c.: Classificazione tipologica. I. I sigilli a iscrizione geroglifica*. 2 vols. Pavia: Gianni Iuculano Editore.

———1990. *La glittica anatolica del II millennio a.c.: Classificazione tipologica. I. I sigilli a iscrizione geroglifica. Primo supplemento*. Pavia: Gianni Iuculano Editore.

Rieken, Elisabeth. 2006. Zum hethitisch-luwischen Sprachkontakt in historischer Zeit. *Altorientalische Forschungen* 33: 271–85.

Rüster, Christel and Erich Neu. 1989. *Hethitisches Zeichenlexikon. Inventar und Interpretation der Keilschriftzeichen aus den Boğazköy-Texten*. Wiesbaden: Harrassowitz.

Salvini, Mirjo. 1994. Una lettera di Hattušili I relativa alla spedizione contro Hahhum. *Studi Micenei ed Egeo-Anatolici* 34: 61–80 with Tav. I–IV.

van den Hout, Theo. 1994. Death as a Privilege. The Hittite Royal Funerary Ritual. In *Hidden Futures. Death and Immortality in Ancient Egypt, Anatolia, the Classical, Biblical and Arabic-Islamic World*, ed. J. M. Bremer, T. P. J. van den Hout, and R. Peters, 37–75. Amsterdam: Amsterdam University Press.

———. 2007a. Institutions, Vernaculars, Publics: The Case of Second Millennium Anatolia. In *Margins of Writing, Origins of Cultures*, ed. Seth L. Sanders, 221–62. Chicago: Oriental Institute.

———. 2007b. Seals and Sealing Practices in Hatti-Land: Remarks à Propos the Seal Impressions from the *Westbau* in Hattuša. *Journal of the American Oriental Society* 127: 339–48.

———. 2008. A Classified Past: Classification of Knowledge in the Hittite Empire. In *Proceedings of the 51st Rencontre Assyriologique Internationale. Held at the Oriental Institute of the University of Chicago, 18–22 July 2005*, ed. Robert D. Biggs, Jennie Myers, and Martha T. Roth, 211–19. Chicago: Oriental Institute.

———. 2009a. A Century of Hittite Text Dating and the Origins of the Hittite Cuneiform Script. *Incontri Linguistici* 32: 11–35.

———. 2009b. Reflections on the Origins and Development of the Hittite Tablet Collections in Hattuša and Their Consequences for the Rise of Hittite Literacy. In *Central-North Anatolia in the Hittite Period. New Perspectives in Light of Recent Research*, ed. Franca Pecchioli Daddi, Giulia Torri, and Carlo Corti, 71–96. Studia Asiana 5. Roma: Herder.

Veenhof, Klaas R. 2003. *The Old Assyrian List of Year Eponyms from Karum Kanish and its Chronological Implications*. Ankara: Türk Tarih Kurumu.

Yakubovich, Ilya. 2008. Hittite-Luvian Bilingualism and the Development of Anatolian Hieroglyphs. *Acta Linguistica Petropolitana* 4: 9–36.

PART V

KEY SITES

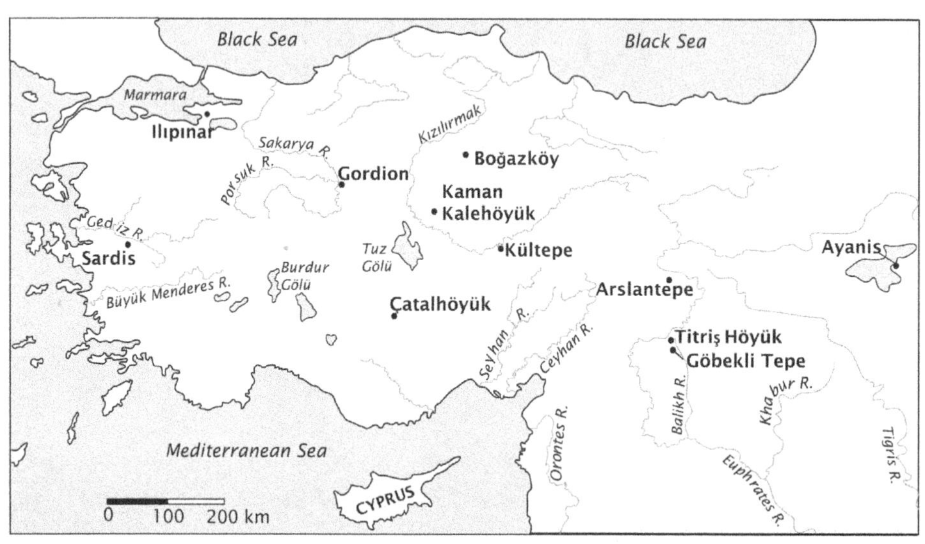

Map of sites discussed in the Key Site section.

CHAPTER 42

GÖBEKLİ TEPE: A NEOLITHIC SITE IN SOUTHEASTERN ANATOLIA

KLAUS SCHMIDT

Fifteen kilometers northeast of the town of Şanlıurfa in southeastern Turkey and 2.5 km east of the village of Örencik (formerly known as Karaharabe), Göbekli Tepe has been known since 1963 as an Aceramic Neolithic site, but its importance was not recognized by the early explorers (Benedict 1980). Since 1995 the German Archaeological Institute has been carrying out archaeological research at the site in cooperation with the Museum of Şanlıurfa (Schmidt 1995, 2006, 2009a, 2009b).

At a height of 785 m asl, the mound of Göbekli Tepe rests at the highest elevation of the Germuş Range northeast of Şanlıurfa (figure 42.1). It stands above the Harran Plain, which spreads out to the south. Springs are accessible in the plains that surround the mountain on the north, east, and south, but there is no access to water in the immediate vicinity of the site. Though only partially excavated, it has become increasingly obvious that the findings from Göbekli Tepe may contribute significantly to our understanding of the transition from a subsistence pattern based exclusively on hunting and foraging at the end of the Pleistocene to the appearance of agriculture and animal husbandry in the course of the early Holocene.

Figure 42.1. The artificial mound of Göbekli Tepe from the air (2004) (photo by Orhan Durgut, DAI).

Material Culture and Subsistence

The people of Göbekli Tepe were still hunter-foragers. Animal husbandry was not practiced there, according to the results of the osteological investigations done by Angela von den Driesch and Joris Peters (Peters and Schmidt 2004; von den Driesch and Peters 1999, 2001), and the botanical studies by Reinder Neef (2003). The small finds from the site corroborate these results. Göbekli Tepe and its material culture are part of the world of the Pre-Pottery Neolithic (PPN) of the Near East, a period name deriving from Kathleen Kenyon's work at Jericho in the 1950s. Bidirectional cores, often of the typical naviform shape, were used extensively at Göbekli Tepe. The range of artifacts includes arrowheads, burins, endscrapers and scrapers, and notched and denticulated tools. Byblos, Nemrik, and Helwan points are distinctive types (Schmidt 2007:107, fig. 3). Obsidian was used only for a very few tools; 99.9 percent of the industry is based on homogenous dark-colored flint of high quality.

In contrast to the common flint artifacts, tools made of bone or antler are very rare. The typical metapodial awls known from many prehistoric sites are almost completely missing. There are some fragments of spatula and hook-shaped bone artifacts and a few fragments of polished needles with incised holes and round sections.

The ground stone industry seems to be very standardized. Heavy oval-shaped mortars made of basalt are very common. Cylindrical and conical pestles were made from basalt as well. Large and heavy containers made of limestone also are quite frequent. The common occurrence of limestone slabs covered with groups of small cup marks have often been interpreted as game boards; however, their function is as obscure as the equally interesting large and heavy rings made of limestone with diameters between one-half and one meter (Schmidt 2006:fig. 23).

Spacer beads with two or more drillings, known from contexts at Çayönü and Nevalı Çori, are a common object of jewelry at Göbekli Tepe. Several fragments of thin-walled decorated stone vessels from Göbekli Tepe (Schmidt 2007:107, fig. 4) belong to the Hallan Çemi type (Rosenberg 1999; and see Rosenberg and Erim-Özdoğan, chapter 6 in this volume). Geometric and figurative motifs are incised in the outer face of the cups and bowls. Complete vessels of this group have recently been discovered at Körtik Tepe (Özkaya and San 2007). Other sites with comparable findings are Çayönü, Nevalı Çori, Jerf el Ahmar, Tell Abr, and Tell Qaramell. All these sites date to the PPNA/Early PPNB, in the second half of the tenth and the ninth millennium cal B.C.E. All of these can be described as settled hunter-gatherer settlement sites, with a spatial division of residential and specialized workshop areas and a growing importance given to *Sondergebäude* used for communal and ritual purposes, including open courtyards as communal space (Cauvin 1997; Hauptmann 1993, 1999; Özdoğan and Özdoğan 1998; Rosenberg et al. 1995; Schmidt 2006; Stordeur 2000; and see Rosenberg and Erim-Özdoğan, chapter 6 in this volume).

Göbekli Tepe is of similar date, but it is very different in comparison with these sites. It is unique not only in its location on top of a hill and in its monumental architecture but also its diverse set of objects of art, ranging from small stone figurines through sculptures and statues of animals to decorated megaliths, all of which set it apart. Göbekli Tepe is not a settlement; it is a mountain sanctuary.

Stratigraphic Excavations and Architecture

The excavations at Göbekli Tepe have been focused on the southern slope of the mound (figure 42.2). There is a post-Neolithic Layer I that consists of accumulations resulting from natural erosion and sedimentation processes due to

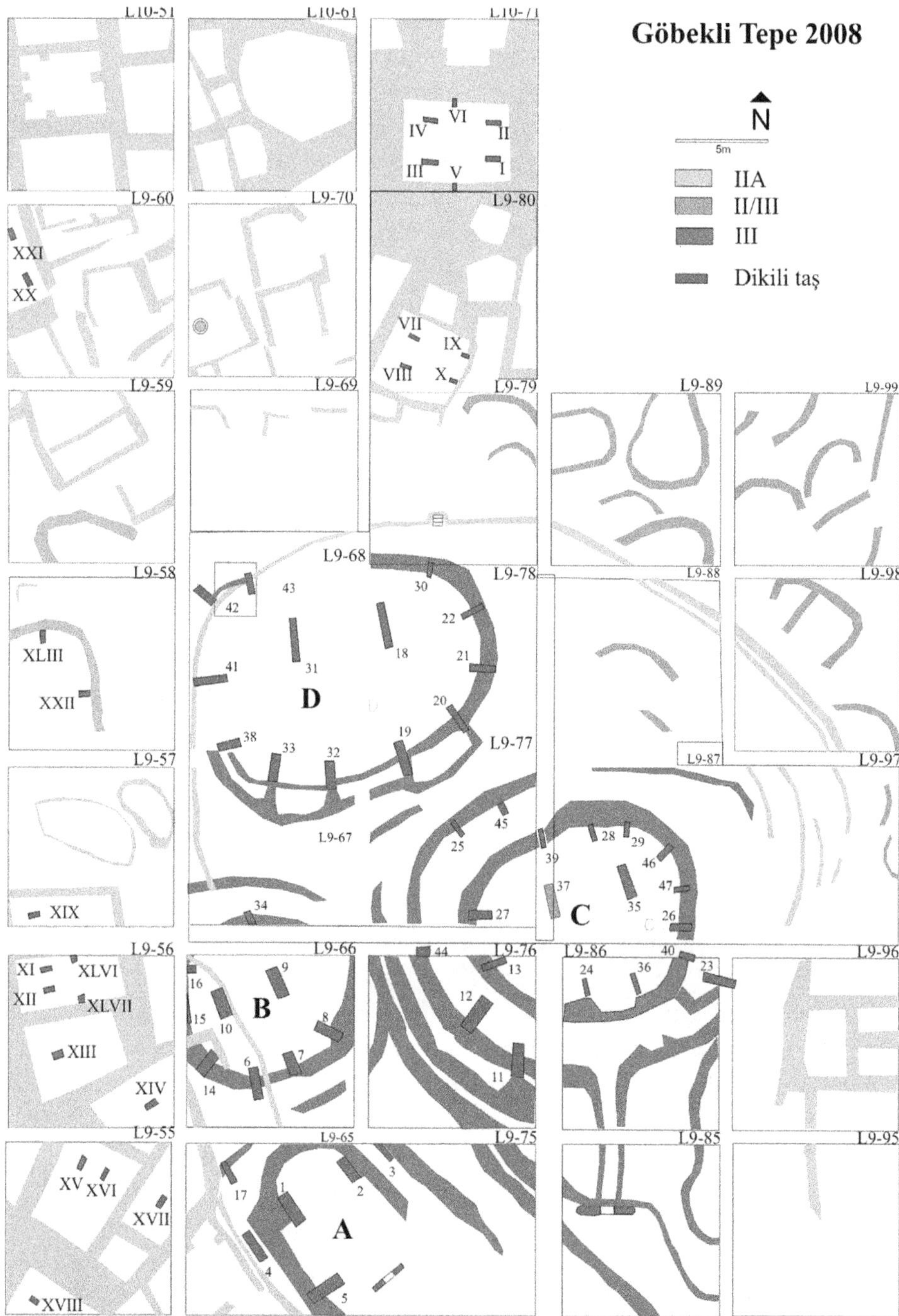

Figure 42.2. Schematic map of the main excavation area at the southern slope (graphic by DAI).

agricultural practices in medieval and modern times. Layer II is Early–Middle PPNB and is restricted to the upper zone of the hill; it contains buildings consisting of several rectangular rooms with terrazzo floors. Layer III dates to the

PPNA/Early PPNB. It consists of megalithic enclosures with diameters from ten to thirty meters, which were excavated in the center of a large depression on the southern slope. These structures are overlain by the buildings of layer II, as each of the megalithic enclosures had been backfilled soon after its erection to cover it completely. A volume of at least 300 m^3 has been estimated for the filling of one enclosure.

A geomagnetic survey, including ground penetrating radar, substantiated the prediction, based on the archaeological surface investigations, that the megalithic enclosures were not restricted to a specific part of the mound but existed all over the site. More than ten large enclosures were located on the geophysical map. As there are several areas at the surface of the mound without clear contours in the map—areas where further enclosures could exist—it seems very probable that at least twenty enclosures in total existed inside the Göbekli Tepe mound.

The most characteristic feature of the buildings of both Layers II and III are the T-shaped monolithic pillars, a type that was first discovered at the Early–Middle PPNB settlement of Nevalı Çori (Hauptmann 1993, 1999; see Harmanşah, chapter 28 in this volume, for discussion on the role of monuments in Anatolian prehistory). Of interest is the fact that on the shaft of some of the pillars a pair of arms and hands are depicted in bas-relief. The arms and hands are without doubt those of humans. Thus, it is clear that the pillars are much more than architectural elements. They are three-dimensional sculptures, representing stylized humans, the horizontal part being the head, the vertical shaft being the body and legs. This highly stylized expression of a human body was intentionally chosen, rather than being due to any inability of the craftsmen to represent humans naturalistically. There must have been certain reasons not to depict the eyes, the nose, the mouth, or the breast, vagina, or penis, if sex were to be indicated. To "modern eyes," the T-shaped beings belong to another sphere of reality, and it seems very probable that a similar meaning was intended by the Stone Age people.

On several pillars there are two parallel stripes in bas-relief on the stomach. They end always just above the fingers, if arms and hands have been depicted. In some way the stripes remind one of a garment such as a stole. Regarding the question of their meaning it is most probable that the stole of the Göbekli Tepe pillars represents a specific kind of dress, presumably worn not by everybody but only by a certain group of people.

The pillars are not only megalithic, they are monolithic. Like a menhir, they were made from one single stone, and it seems that the monolithic nature of the pillars was very important. Whereas in Layer II the height of the pillars measures only an average of 1.5 m, we observe a height of up to 5.5 m and a weight of up to fifteen tons in the older Layer III. The transport of such colossi took an enormous effort. For a calculation of how many people may have been involved in such a project, an ethnographical example from the beginning of the twentieth century may be helpful. A report details an event in 1914 on the island of Nias in Indonesia, during which a soul-menhir of the king of Bawomataluo, weighing nearly ten tons, was dragged into place by 525 men (Bakker 1999:153, fig. 6). It seems very probable that like the event on Nias, major feasts provided the reason for the gathering of so many people at Stone Age Göbekli Tepe as well.

Through 2009 four monumental enclosures with forty-seven pillars have been discovered in situ. Up to twelve pillars are arranged purposefully in a circle or an oval to delineate the enclosures. The pillars are interconnected by walls and stone benches. In the central part of each circle, there is a pair of pillars. As a rule these central pillars are much larger than the surrounding ones and of a superior quality; for example, their surface is extremely well prepared, and they are always decorated with figurations.

The origin of the raw material of the megaliths is no surprise; the surrounding limestone plateaus served as a quarry in Neolithic times. Many cavities cut into the living rock can be explained as the places used for the extraction of large megalithic stones from the natural limestone beds (Schmidt 2009a:figs. 14–17). Some quarries can be easily recognized as the place for the extraction of T-shaped pillars. An unfinished example in the quarry on the northern plateau has a length of nearly seven meters and an estimated weight of nearly fifty tons (Schmidt 2006:fig. 33).

The megalithic enclosures and the pillars have been numbered according to the order of their discovery. Enclosure A had been recognized already in 1996. Despite the fact that it was discovered first, it is only partially excavated, as it had been partially destroyed in ancient times. Fortunately the central pillars—1 and 2—survived. On pillar 1 there are a stole and five snakes in bas-relief on the stomach (Schmidt 2006:fig. 44). The right face of the shaft is not yet visible. On the left face there is—again in bas-relief—a so far unique motif. Based on the triangular form of its endings, the object depicted seems to represent a "tapestry" of interwoven snakes, a sort of "net" made up of seventeen animals (Schmidt 2006:fig. 45). Below that object there is a quadruped, most probably a ram.

On pillar 2 there are the bas-reliefs of a bull, a fox, and a crane (Schmidt 2006:fig. 46). A stole is not depicted on the front of the pillar shaft, but on its back side there is one with a bukranium on top of the stole (Peters and Schmidt 2004:fig. 12). Because the motif of the stole is quite frequent and usually placed on the stomach of the pillar, it is very obvious that the stole on pillar 2 is in the wrong place. It will be proved by other observations in the forthcoming discussion that the reuse and replacement of pillars seems to have been a common phenomenon. Pillar 2 is the first clear example of such a replacement. Of the remaining pillars of Enclosure A (nos. 3–5, 17) it is only on pillar 5 that the relief of a snake is thus far visible (Schmidt 2006:fig. 47).

Pillars 9 and 10 are the central pillars of Enclosure B. The floor of the enclosure is a terrazzo floor, and in front of the eastern pillar 9 a stone bowl had been set into the floor (Schmidt 2007:108, fig. 6). On the shaft of each of the central pillars a male fox is depicted. Below the fox on pillar 10 is a graffito of a boar, tracked by three dogs (Schmidt 2000:23, fig. 10a–b). Around the circumference of the pillars (nos. 6–8, 14–16, 34) quite a few reliefs are thus far visible, including a fox (Schmidt 2006:fig. 53), an animal looking like a four-footed reptile (Schmidt 2006:fig. 54), and two snakes. The position of the "reptile" and the snakes at the rear of pillars 6 and 14 can again be regarded as evidence for the replacement of these pillars. Another observation seems to be noteworthy: none of the pillars wear a stole in Enclosure B.

The natural bedrock was used as the floor in Enclosure C (figure 42.3). It had been carefully smoothed, and two pedestals had been cut out of the rock for the central pillars. The upper parts of these pillars had been destroyed in ancient times, but both shafts were found in situ, each set in a rectangular hollow in the middle of the pedestal. Both pillars wear a stole. On the inner face of the shaft of the western pillar 37 is the relief of a fox. Opposite to it on the eastern pillar 35, there is the relief of a bull. The height of pillar 35 was reconstructed using laser scanning of the fragments found nearby, which could be joined virtually to the pillar's shaft. The original height was five meters above the pedestal.

Enclosure C consists of two concentric circles of walls with inserted pillars (nos. 11–13, 24–29, 39, 40, 44–47). Several of the pillars bear bas-reliefs. The motifs are dominated by wild boars and ducks (Schmidt 2006:fig. 59). On pillar 40 engraved hands can be observed at the stomach. Two foxes and several abstract symbols are also depicted. It is interesting to note that snakes, the most frequent motif at Göbekli Tepe, are completely absent within the reliefs of the pillars of Enclosure C.

One of the most astonishing discoveries at Göbekli Tepe was a high relief of a predator on the stomach of pillar 27, directly above a boar in bas-relief (figure 42.4). Pillar and animal had been made from one stone, a masterpiece of ancient stone masonry. It became obvious that several of the sculptures discovered in the débris fill of the enclosures originally had been similar high reliefs, attached to pillars;

Figure 42.3. Enclosure C seen from the air (2009) (photo by Klaus Schmidt, DAI).

these sculptures had been intentionally smashed down for unknown reasons during the PPN Period.

Enclosure D was found north of B and C. It is the largest structure and preserved in excellent condition. As at Enclosure C, the floor is made of natural bedrock, which again had been carefully smoothed. Again, each of the central pillars—numbers 18 and 31—was set in a hollow in the middle of a pedestal, which had been cut out of the rock. Both pillars have a height of 5.5 m and are still in situ. At the southern face of the eastern pedestal there is a surprise: directly above the floor there are the reliefs of several ducks, depicted in a movement from east to west.

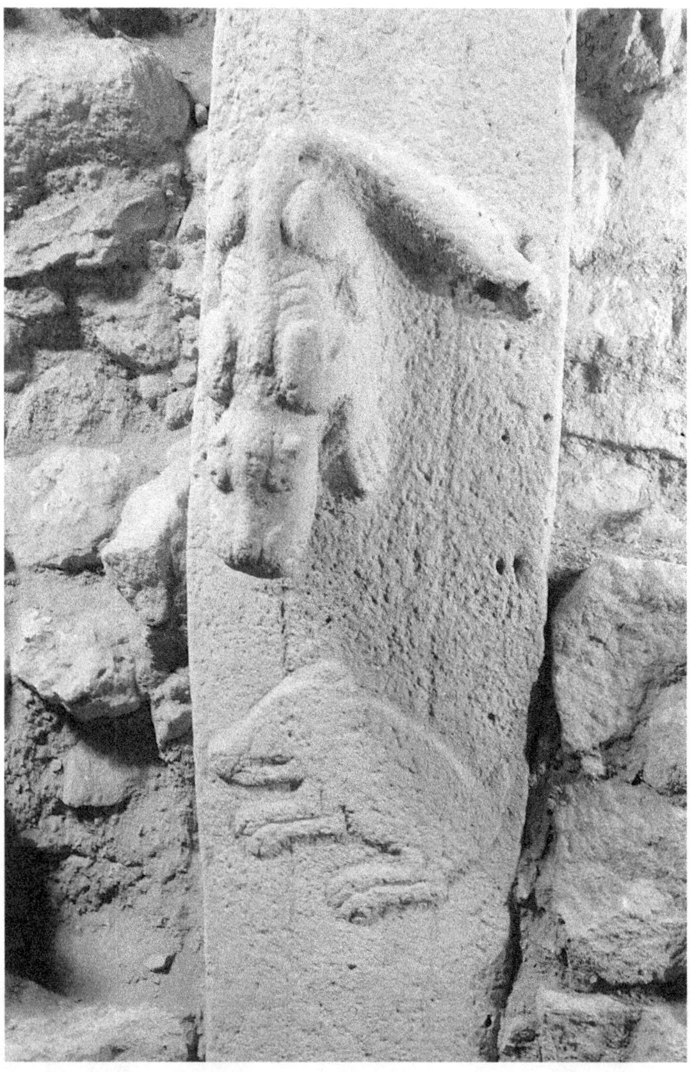

Figure 42.4. High relief of a predator and bas-relief of a wild boar on pillar 27 in Enclosure C (photo by Dieter Johannes, DAI).

On both pillars a stole, arms, and hands had been depicted, but only on the eastern pillar 18 does the pillar being hold a fox in its right elbow. It wears a necklace with ornaments in the shape of an H-shaped symbol, a circle, and a crescent. The western pillar 31 also wears a necklace, in this case in the shape of a bukranium. Both pillars portray beings wearing a belt and a loincloth made of animal skin, probably that of a fox, covering the genital region. On both belts there are U-shaped buckles visible, but only the belt of pillar 18 is decorated with H- and C-shaped motifs.

On the other pillars (nos. 19–22, 30, 32–33, 38, 41–43) depictions of foxes and snakes are most common, but there is a wide range of different figurations, which include such diverse fauna as aurochs, gazelle, wild ass, crane, duck and vulture, spider, scorpion, and insect. On pillar 43 there is a very rich combination of different motifs (figure 42.5), including a vulture, an ibis and snakes, a scorpion, and a headless, ithyphallic person, as well as many other motifs.

Interpretations of Göbekli Tepe

Because it can be safely assumed that the pillars represent anthropomorphic beings, one of the most relevant questions concerns the meaning of the combination of the anthropomorphic carvings and the various motifs depicted on the pillars. Preliminarily it can be concluded that animals played an important role in the spiritual world of the PPN community at Göbekli Tepe. Since the site's inhabitants relied on hunting for their protein supply, one possible explanation for these figurations might be the performance of hunting rituals; however, a comparison between the faunal assemblage attested at the site and the iconography does not support that idea (Peters and Schmidt 2004; Peters et al. 2005; von den Driesch and Peters 2001). Mammalian bone fragments form the bulk of the material, but remains of ungulates predominate, constituting over 90 percent of the total sample. This is also the case in other PPN archaeofaunas collected in the Upper Euphrates basin (Helmer, Gourichon, and Stordeur 2004; Peters et al. 1999).

Did the animals serve as guards to protect the stone beings? With respect to the mammals, with one exception only male individuals are displayed on the pillars. One explanation may center not on their biological sex but rather that the depiction of strong and aggressive (male) animals was the intended message. This scenario could apply well to taxa such as carnivores or snakes and eventually also to wild boar and aurochs, but wild sheep, gazelle, wild ass, or crane would be difficult to fit into this concept. Thus, although each enclosure features animal figures that look threatening, we doubt whether the role of animals within the symbolic world of the PPN can be reduced to this simple level of apotropaica. It is important to note that not only are animals depicted on the pillars, but also a complex system of symbols (Morenz and Schmidt 2009).

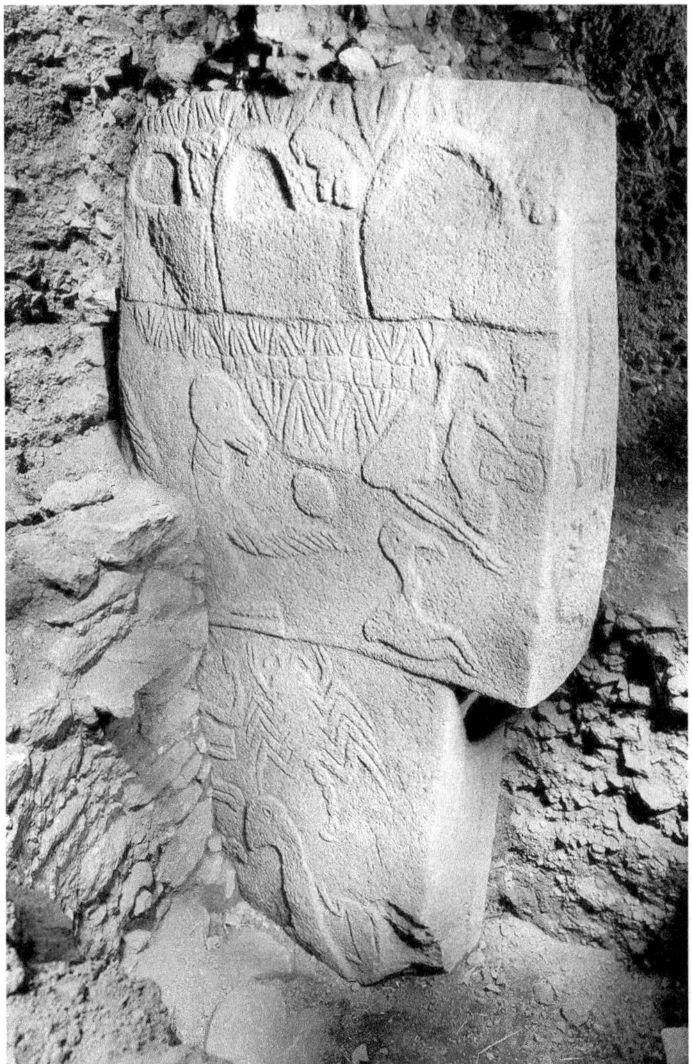

Figure 42.5. Pillar 43 in Enclosure D (photo by Berthold Steinhilber).

In addition to the animals and symbols depicted in bas-relief, there is the group of three-dimensional sculptures and high reliefs, which seems to offer somewhat different symbolism. There are two main species depicted, a wild boar and a predator, reminiscent respectively of the Erymanthian boar and the Kerberos of Greek mythology by their appearance (Schmidt 2009c). It thus seems probable that there is a slight difference in the meaning of both groups. The sculptures and high reliefs seem to be mainly apotropaic in their function. The animals and symbols depicted in bas-relief are meant to transmit mythic narrations. However, it is difficult to investigate the entire inventory of images in a specific enclosure. First, most of the pillars are not completely visible due either to the stage of excavation, or because walls and benches, often constructed and placed after the erection of the pillars, cover parts of their shafts and the reliefs. Second, there is the reuse of pillars. We cannot be sure if the position of a pillar is the original one, if the pillar has been replaced but the reliefs are still the original ones, or if new stone furnishing and a new "layer" of images greet our modern eyes. Because of that we will try to evaluate some of the motifs individually rather than the complete *Bildprogramm* (symbolic ensemble) of the enclosures—a task that will be important for the future when the excavations have finished and we can be sure how many motifs exist in the enclosures.

At Göbekli Tepe, snakes are the most commonly depicted figures. They appear either isolated or in small groups of four or five individuals. The reliefs are mainly located on the stomach of the pillars. Only in two cases do we find snakes on the back side of a pillar, both in Enclosure B, but it is very probable that these pillars have been repositioned. With few exceptions, the snakes are moving downward. In three cases there are more than ten snakes depicted together. The net-like object made of interwoven snakes on pillar 1 has been mentioned. On pillar 33 there are two bundles of snakes. All the snakes depicted are thick, short animals with large, flattened triangular heads. Several highly venomous species are known to occur in the Urfa region, including the Levantine viper (*Vipera lebetina*), and it may be these that are depicted.

The importance of the snake is repeated in the iconography of the PPN sites of Upper Mesopotamia, where the snake motif is widespread. This is illustrated by findings from Hallan Çemi, where snakes carved out of bone have been found (Rosenberg 1999:fig. 11), or by artifacts depicting snakes found at PPNA sites like Körtik Tepe (Özkaya and San 2007), Jerf el Ahmar (Stordeur and Willcox 2009), and Tell Qaramel (Mazurowski 2009; Mazurowski et al. 2009), or at the Early–Middle PPNB settlement of Nevalı Çori, where a limestone sculpture of a life-size human head crowned with a snake was found inside a wall of a ritual building when the building was completely removed for re-erection in the museum in Şanlıurfa in advance of the rising water of the Atatürk Dam lake (Hauptmann 1993, 1999). Quite obviously this snake from Nevalı Çori is an anticipation of the Uraeus snake of the Old Egyptian pharaohs.

Looking further west to central Anatolia, at Çatalhöyük snakes are completely absent from the wall paintings, although there exists a handle of a flint knife made of bone and carved in the shape of a snake (Mellaart 2003:126, resim 88). The blades for such tools are bifacially pressure flaked, and it is obvious that the knives are not made for daily use. Again, the snake motif seems to be connected with the threatening aspect of this animal and its apotropaic meaning.

Interestingly, depictions of snakes at Göbekli Tepe are completely absent at the pillars in Enclosure C. They seem to be replaced by the wild boar, which is depicted a number of times in bas-relief. The partially very naturalistic representations show a male individual signaling its readiness to attack, its mouth opened to display its impressive fangs (Schmidt 2006:fig. 59). The omnipresence of wild boars in bas-relief in Enclosure C is notable in that of the ten sculptures (or fragments of sculptures) hitherto found depicting a wild boar, nine have been discovered in Enclosure C (e.g., Schmidt 2006:fig. 60); the tenth is from Enclosure A (Schmidt 1999:11, bo. A15 pl. 3.1–2).

The fox is another common motif at Göbekli Tepe. It is depicted either singly or in combination with other species, for example, aurochs and a crane on pillar 2 (Schmidt 2006:fig. 46), aurochs and a snake on pillar 20 (Schmidt 2006:fig. 83), or a boar and three birds on pillar 38 (Schmidt 2006:fig. 87). Its presence on the central pillars P9 and P10 in Enclosure B and on the western central pillar of Enclosure C denotes its importance. In Enclosure D it is the anthropomorphic pillar itself, the eastern central pillar (pillar 18), which holds a fox in the right elbow, and both central pillars are wearing loincloths probably of fox skin. The relatively high frequency of fox remains in the archaeofauna at Göbekli Tepe compared to other carnivores and in most of the PPNA/Early PPNB faunal assemblages (Helmer 1994; Helmer et al. 1998; Peters et al. 1999) underscores the significance of this taxon in the spiritual world of the PPN in Upper Mesopotamia. The presence of the fox at the Cypriot Neolithic site of Shillourokambos (Vigne 2000) may perhaps relate to the role this animal already played in the symbolic world on the mainland prior to the colonization of Cyprus by PPN human groups.

It is interesting to note that the fox, like the wild boar, is nearly absent in the cave art of the Upper Palaeolithic. But there was something special about the fox in that period, too: fox teeth are in the first assemblage of raw materials from which animal teeth pendants were made in the Upper Palaeolithic sites of Europe. One would expect that the teeth of bear or wolf would be the first choice for pendants, but the fox is the winner in that respect. Although we can only guess at the role *Vulpes* played in the PPN Near Eastern symbolic world, it is a fact that in the mythology of post-Neolithic cultures of the ancient Near East, the fox is rarely present, and its role is that of the trickster as in European fairy tales. In contrast to other species, for example, the bull, lion, or dog (Black and Green 1992), the fox was not associated with a certain deity in the post-Neolithic, especially in Sumerian, Akkadian, Babylonian, or Assyrian mythology.

A Complex Prewriting System of Symbols

Finds with images of symbolic value are not restricted to the reliefs on the monumental T-shaped pillars. Similar motifs appear in many of the PPN sites of Upper Mesopotamia en miniature, for example, on the stone vessels at Hallan Çemi, which have already been mentioned as a characteristic feature of the material culture of the PPN in the north. There are other groups of artifacts that feature figurative decoration. Shaft straighteners often have incised decorations of animals and various symbols. Several examples from Jerf el Ahmar and Tell Qaramel bear rich combinations of motifs showing groups of animals like snakes and scorpions, quadrupeds, and birds.

Very similar motifs and symbols were incised into the so-called plaquettes of Jerf el Ahmar type. In contrast to the shaft straighteners, which have been grooved deeply as a defining functional attribute, the plaquettes (often little more than coin size) show no indication of an obvious use for any specific function. They probably were produced just for the purpose of bearing the symbols incised on them. Their general presentation is very like the clay tablets of the cuneiform texts of the ancient Near East invented several thousand years later in the Sumerian period. These plaquettes have been discovered in significant numbers at Tell Qaramel, Tel Abr, and Jerf el Ahmar; only one example has been found so far at Göbekli Tepe. From Körtik Tepe there are several plaquettes with animals in bas-relief, animals which seem to depict the chrysalis state of an insect (Özkaya and San 2007:2:24 fig. 19). There may be some connection between this and the spider and insect motifs known from some pillars at Göbekli Tepe. These images offer a new symbolic world, a symbolic language, which had commonalities among the residents of the PPN sites in Upper Mesopotamia.

Buttons, made of greenish stone like the plaquettes, are another interesting type within the small finds category (Schmidt 2005:32–33, fig. 6). Their shape is similar to stamp seals of the Hittite period; the "handle" has an oblique perforation at its end. Outside Göbekli Tepe such buttons are known only from Nevalı Çori, where there are only a few examples. At other sites this distinctive form has not been found. It seems appropriate to call these artifacts the Göbekli Tepe button type. They were owned by people living mainly at Göbekli Tepe and not commonly found in the surrounding settlement sites. A similar situation may be the case for small pendants whose shape reminds one of a cucumber (Schmidt 2000:33, fig. 14.d). They form another type characteristic for the inventory of Göbekli Tepe and again seem to be rare at other sites. All these groups of artifacts seem to be part of a system of symbols, existing not only on the pillars and plaquettes with their two-dimensional reliefs and engravings but also as a system that includes objects like garments and ornaments. On the other hand, bracelets known from several other PPN sites are very rare at Göbekli Tepe, and clay figurines are completely missing. The absence of clay figurines at Göbekli Tepe is especially remarkable as that group usually is very common in the early Neolithic settlements of the Near East.

However, figurines made of limestone exist at Göbekli Tepe in some numbers. A small figurine of a vulture (Schmidt 2007:114, fig. 23) seems to be the miniature version of a large sculpture known from Nevalı Çori (Hauptmann 1999:2:48 fig. 15). A head of a lion again very closely resembles an example from Nevalı Çori (Hauptmann 1999:50, fig. 20), both in the motif and in its miniature size. Large-scale sculptures of the same type have been found at Göbekli Tepe. It becomes quite clear that the small figurines made of limestone often repeat the repertoire of the large sculpture, which we know so far from Nevalı Çori and Göbekli Tepe. The inventory of the early Neolithic large-scale statues is completed by a more than life-size human head found at Göbekli Tepe (Schmidt 2006:fig. 28) and an isolated statue discovered in Şanlıurfa (Bucak and Schmidt 2003), which probably came from the context of a PPN site in the center of Şanlıurfa itself, now nearly completely lost due to the expansion of the modern town.

Conclusion

To conclude, the most characteristic feature of the monuments of Göbekli Tepe are the monumental T-shaped pillars. They are arranged in round or oval enclosures, always with a pair of free-standing pillars in the center. It is highly probable that the T-shaped pillars are meant to represent anthropomorphic beings. The fact that mainly animals have been depicted on them underscores this assumption. Sometimes they are accompanied by symbols and/or pictograms. How should the images be interpreted? We have excluded the possibility that the animal motifs represent favorite game species. We recognized that the meaning of two-dimensional bas-reliefs and the engravings en miniature seems to be a little different from the meaning of the three-dimensional sculptures. These seem to have mainly an apotropaic function, the species functioning as guardians. The other group most probably represents a symbolic system which illustrates mythic narrations.

The overall shape of the pillars is very standardized, and an indication of their sex is always lacking. Except for a graffito on a stone slab (Schmidt 2006:fig. 104) no female representation has so far been found at Göbekli Tepe. The Magna Mater, whose presence—following the *opinio communis*—actually should be expected in such an important ritual site as Göbekli Tepe, remains completely invisible. However, the central pillars of Enclosure D, with their height of 5.5 m, show monumental and unquestionably important beings wearing belts and loincloths. Belts seem to indicate male persons, as seen in the group of clay figurines from Nevalı Çori where belts are restricted to the male examples (Morsch 2002:148). It is not clear what kind of beings the T-shaped monoliths personify, but their faceless impersonality makes it probable that they represented mythical ancestors or even theomorphic beings from another world.

No doubt the amount of time, energy, craftsmanship, and manpower necessary for the construction and maintenance of this site is indicative of a complex, hierarchical social organization and a division of labor involving large numbers of people. Feasting was presumably the immediate reason for the gathering of hundreds of individuals at the site. Seen from this perspective, the emergence of food production in the course of the PPN may represent the outcome of a series of innovations and adjustments to the subsistence patterns to meet and secure the energy demands of these large sedentary communities. A major driving force behind the process of plant and animal domestication may have been provided by the spiritual concepts of these PPN peoples, in particular the investment of effort by generations of PPNA groups in the materialization of their complex immaterial world.

REFERENCES

Bakker, Jan Albert. 1999. Dutch Megalithic Tombs, with a Glance at Those of North-West Germany. In *The Megalithic Phenomenon. Recent Research and Ethnoarchaeological Approaches*, ed. Karl W. Beinhauer, Gabriel Cooney, Christian E. Guksch, and Susan Kus, 145–62. Beiträge zur Ur-und Frühgeschichte Mitteleuropas 21. Weißbach: Beier and Beran.

Benedict, Peter. 1980. Survey Work in Southeastern Anatolia. In *Prehistoric Research in Southeastern Anatolia*, ed. Halet Çambel and Robert J. Braidwood, 150–91. İstanbul: University of Istanbul, Faculty of Letters Press.

Black, Jeremy and Anthony Green. 1992. *Gods, Demons and Symbols of Ancient Mesopotamia. An Illustrated Dictionary.* London: British Museum Press.

Bucak, Eyüp and Klaus Schmidt. 2003. Dünyanın en Eski Heykeli. *Atlas. Aylık coğrafya ve keşif dergisi Sayı* 127: 36–40.

Cauvin, Jacques. 1997. *Naissance des Divinités, Naissance de l'agriculture. La Revolution des Symboles au Néolithique.* Paris: CNRS Éditions.

Hauptmann, Harald. 1993. Ein Kultgebäude in Nevalı Çori. In *Between the Rivers and over the Mountains. Archaeologica Anatolica et Mesopotamica Alba Palmieri Dedicata*, ed. Marcella Frangipane, Harald Hauptmann, Mario Liverani, Paolo Matthiae, and Machteld Mellink, 37–69. Rome: Università di Roma "La Sapienza."

———. 1999. Frühneolithische Steingebäude in Südwestasien. In *The Megalithic Phenomenon. Recent Research and Ethnoarchaeological Approaches*, ed. Karl W. Beinhauer, Gabriel Cooney, Christian E. Guksch, and Susan Kus, 227–38. Beiträge zur Ur-und Frühgeschichte Mitteleuropas 21. Weißbach: Beier & Beran.

Helmer, Daniel. 1994. La domestication des animaux d'embouche dans le Levant Nord (Syrie du Nord et Sinjar), du milieu du 9e millénaire BP à la fin du 7e millénaire BP. Nouvelles données d'après les fouilles récentes. *Anthropozoologica* 20: 41–54.

Helmer, Daniel, Lionel Gourichon, and Danielle Stordeur. 2004. A l'aube de la domestication animale. Imaginaire et symbolisme animal dans les premières sociétés néolithiques du nord du Proche-Orient. *Anthropozoologica* 39.1: 143–63.

Helmer, Daniel, Valérie Roitel, Maria Saña Segui, and George Willcox. 1998. Interprétations environnementales des données archéozoologiques et archéobotaniques en Syrie du nord de 16000 BP à 7000 BP, et les débuts de la domestication des plantes et des animaux. In *Espace naturel, espace habité en Syrie du Nord (10e–2e millénaires av. J.-C.* ed. Michel Fortin and Olivier Aurenche, 9–33. Bulletin 33. Travaux de la Maison de l'Orient 2. Quebec: Canadian Society for Mesopotamian Studies.

Mazurowski, Ryszard F. 2009. Tell Qaramel. General Remarks about the Site and Excavations. In *Documents d'archeologie Syrienne*, ed. Ryszard F. Mazurowski and Youseffa Kanjou, 59–74. Damascus: DGAM.

Mazurowski, Ryszard F., Danuta J. Michczynska, Anna Pazdur, and Natalia Piotrowska. 2009. Chronology of the Early Pre-Pottery Neolithic Settlement Tell Qaramel, Northern Syria, in the Light of Radiocarbon Cating. *Radiocarbon* 51: 771–81.

Mellaart, James. 2003. *Çatalhöyük. Anadolu'da bir neolitik kent.* İstanbul: Yapı Kredi Yayınları.

Morenz, Ludwig D. and Klaus Schmidt. 2009. Große Reliefpfeiler und kleine Zeichentäfelchen. Ein frühneolithisches Zeichensystem in Obermesopotamien. In *Non-Textual Marking Systems, Writing and Pseudo Script from Prehistory to Modern*

Times, ed. Petra Andrássy, Julia Budka, and Frank Kammerzell, 13–31. Lingua Aegyptia-Studia monographica 8. Göttingen: Seminar für Ägyptologie und Koptologie.

Morsch, Michael. 2002. Magic Figurines? Some Remarks about the Clay Objects of Nevali Cori. In *Magic Practices and Ritual in the Near Eastern Neolithic*, ed. Hans Georg Gebel and Bo Dahl Hermansen, 145–58. Studies in Early Near Eastern Production, Subsistence, and Environment 8. Berlin: Ex Oriente.

Neef, Reinder. 2003. Overlooking the Steppe-Forest. A Preliminary Report on the Botanical Remains from Early Neolithic Göbekli Tepe (Southeastern Turkey). *Neo-Lithics. A Newsletter of Southwest Asian Lithics Research* 2/3: 13–16.

Özdoğan, Mehmet and Aslıhan Özdoğan. 1998. Buildings of Cult and the Cult of Buildings. In *Light on Top of the Black Hill. Studies Presented to Halet Çambel*, ed. Güven Arsebük, Machteld J. Mellink, and Wulf Schirmer, 581–601. İstanbul: Ege Yayınları.

Özkaya, Vecihi and Oya San. 2007. Bulgular Işığında Kültürel Doku Üzerine İlk Gözlemler. In *Anadolu'da Uygarlığın Doğuşu ve Avrupa'ya Yayılımı. Türkiye'de Neolitik Dönem: Yeni Kazılar, Yeni Bulgular*, ed. Mehmet Özdoğan and Nezih Başgelen, 21–36. İstanbul: Arkeoloji ve Sanat Yayınları.

Peters, Joris, Daniel Helmer, Angela von den Driesch, and Maria Saña Segui. 1999. Early Animal Husbandry in the Northern Levant. *Paléorient* 25.2: 27–48.

Peters, Joris and Klaus Schmidt. 2004. Animals in the Symbolic World of Pre-Pottery Neolithic Göbekli Tepe, South-Eastern Turkey: A Preliminary Assessment. *Anthropozoologica* 39: 179–218.

Peters, Joris, Angela von den Driesch, Nadja Pöllath, and Klaus Schmidt. 2005. Birds and the Megalithic Art of Pre-Pottery Neolithic Göbekli Tepe, Southeast Turkey. In *Feathers, Grit and Symbolism. Birds and Humans in the Ancient Old and New Worlds, Proceedings of the 5th Meeting of the ICAZ Bird Working Group in Munich 2004. Documenta Archaebiologiae 3*, ed. Gisela Gruppe and Joris Peters, 223–34. Rahden/Westfalen: Marie Leidorf.

Rosenberg, Michael. 1999. Hallan Çemi. In *Neolithic in Turkey. The Cradle of Civilization*, ed. Mehmet Özdoğan and Nezih Başgelen, 25–33. İstanbul: Arkeoloji ve Sanat Yayınları.

Rosenberg, Michael, R. Mark Nesbitt, Richard W. Redding, and Thomass F. Strasser. 1995. Hallan Çemi Tepesi: Some Preliminary Observations Concerning Early Neolihic Subsistence Behaviours in Eastern Anatolia. *Anatolica* 21: 1–12.

Schmidt, Klaus. 1995. Investigations in the Upper Mesopotamian Early Neolithic: Göbekli Tepe and Gürcütepe. *Neo-Lithics. A Newsletter of Southwest Asian Lithics Research* 2.95: 9–10.

———. 1999. Frühe Tier-und Menschenbilder vom Göbekli Tepe. *Istanbuler Mitteilungen* 49: 5–21.

———. 2000. "Zuerst kam der Tempel, dann die Stadt." Vorläufiger Bericht zu den Grabungen am Göbekli Tepe und am Gürcütepe 1995–1999. *Istanbuler Mitteilungen* 50: 5–41.

———. 2005. "Die Stadt" der Steinzeit. In *Wege zur Stadt—Entwicklung und Formen urbanen Lebens in der alten Welt*, ed. Harry Falk, 25–38. Vergleichende Studien zu Antike und Orient 2. Bremen: Hempen.

———. 2006. *Sie bauten die ersten Tempel. Das rätselhafte Heiligtum der Steinzeitjäger.* München: C. H. Beck.

———. 2007. Göbekli Tepe. In *Anadolu'da Uygarlığın Doğusu ve Avrupa'ya Yayılımı. Türkiye'de Neolitik Dönem: Yeni Kazılar, Yeni Bulgular*, ed. Mehmet Özdoğan and Nezih Başgelen, 115–29. İstanbul: Arkeoloji ve Sanat Yayınları.

———. 2009a. Göbekli Tepe. Eine Beschreibung der wichtigsten Befunde erstellt nach den Arbeiten der Grabungsteams der Jahre 1995–2007. *In Erste Tempel—frühe Siedlungen. 12000 Jahre Kunst und Kultur. Ausgrabungen und Forschungen zwischen Donau und Euphrat*, ed. ArchaeNova e.V., 187–223. Oldenburg: Isensee.

———. 2009b. Von den ersten Dörfern zu frühurbanen Strukturen. In *Grundlagen der globalen Welt. Vom Beginn bis 1200 v. Chr.*, ed. Albrecht Jockenhövel, 128–44. WBG-Weltgeschichte in sechs Bänden, herausgegeben von Walter Demel, et al., Band 1. Darmstadt: Wissenschaftliche Buchgemeinschaft.

———. 2009c. Göbekli Tepe—eine apokalyptische Bilderwelt aus der Steinzeit. *Antike Welt. Zeitschrift für Archäologie und Kulturgeschichte* 4: 45–52.

Stordeur, Danielle. 2000. Jerf el Ahmar et l'émergence de Néolithique au Proche Orient. In *Premiers Paysans du Monde. Naissance des Agricultures*, ed. Jean Guilaine, 33–60. Paris: Éditions Errance.

Stordeur, Danielle and George Willcox. 2009. Indices de culture et d'utilisation des céréales à Jerf el Ahmar. In *De Méditerranée et d'ailleurs . . . Mélanges offerts à Jean Guilaine*, ed. collective, 693–710. Toulouse: Archives d'Écologie Préhistorique.

Vigne, Jean-Denis. 2000. Les débuts néolithiques de l'élevage des ongulés au Proche Orient et en Méditerranée: acquis récents et questions. In *Premiers Paysans du Monde. Naissances des Agricultures*, ed. Jean Guilaine, 143–68. Paris: Éditions Errance.

von den Driesch, Angela and Joris Peters. 1999. Vorläufiger Bericht über archäozoologische Untersuchungen am Göbekli Tepe und am Gürcütepe bei Urfa, Türkei. *Istanbuler Mitteilungen des Deutschen Archäologischen Instituts* 49: 23–39.

———. 2001. Früheste Haustierhaltung in der Südosttürkei. In *Lux orientis. Archäologie zwischen Asien und Europa. Festschrift für Harald Hauptmann zum 65. Geburtstag*, ed. Rainer Michael Boehmer and Joseph Maran, 113–20. Rahden/Westfalen: Marie Leidorf.

CHAPTER 43

ÇATALHÖYÜK: A PREHISTORIC SETTLEMENT ON THE KONYA PLAIN

IAN HODDER

History of Research

Çatalhöyük was first excavated by James Mellaart between 1961 and 1965. His excavations were mainly confined to the southwest corner of the Neolithic East Mound (the pitted area around "South" in figure 43.1), although two small trenches were also dug on the Chalcolithic West Mound. Initially the importance of the site was recognized by its large size (Çatalhöyük East is 13.5 ha and 21 m high) and complex art at an early date, and by its location outside the supposed "cradle" of civilization in the Middle East.

Since 1993, an international project made up of multiple teams has been working at the site.[1] There are presently six excavation teams working at Çatalhöyük—three from Turkey (from İstanbul University led by Mihriban Özbaşaran, from Selçuk University in Konya led by Ahmet Tırpan and Asuman Baldıran, and from Thrace University in Edirne led by Burçin Erdoğu), one from Poland (led by Arek Marciniak and Lech Czerniak), one from the United States (led by Peter Biehl at SUNY Buffalo), and the main U.K.–U.S. team based in London and Stanford. In the past there have also been a Greek team from Thessaloniki led by Kostas Kotsakis as well as other U.S. and U.K. teams (the Berkeley Archaeologists at Çatalhöyük [BACH] led by Ruth Tringham and Mirjana Stevanović, and a U.K. team led by Jonathan Last and Catriona Gibson). There are also teams dealing with related themes, such as regional survey and palaeo-environmental reconstruction.

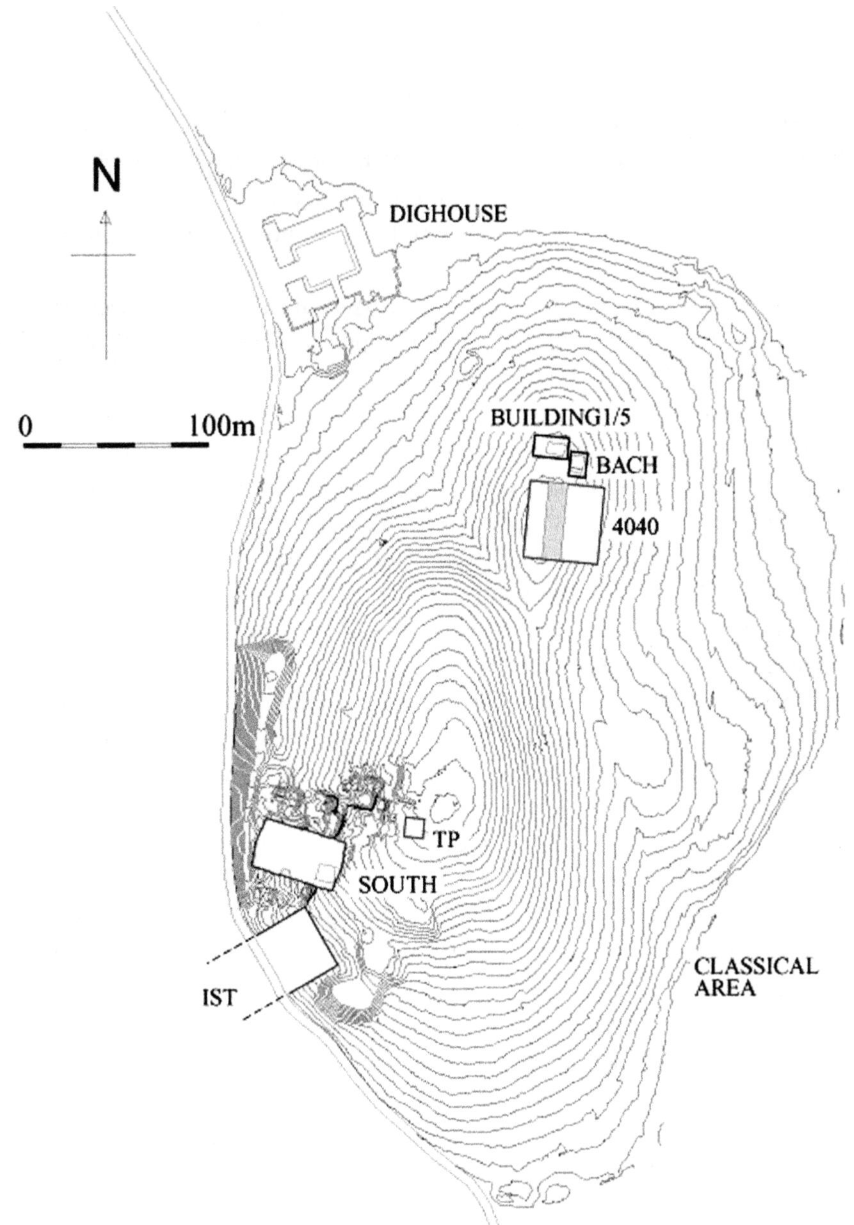

Figure 43.1. The excavation areas on the East Mound at Çatalhöyük.

Çatalhöyük in Context

Much has changed in our knowledge of the Neolithic in Anatolia since the 1960s. In some ways, Çatalhöyük is no longer so exceptional. It is late in the Neolithic sequence, occurring at the end of the Aceramic Neolithic and continuing through the Ceramic Neolithic and into the Chalcolithic (the East Mound dates from 7400 to 6200/6000 cal B.C.E., and the ensuing West Mound has dates in the early sixth millennium B.C.E.). Earlier major sites have been excavated in central Turkey at, for example, Aşıklı Höyük (Esin and Harmankaya 1999), and locally in the Konya Plain earlier precursors of Çatalhöyük have been excavated at Pınarbaşı and Boncuklu (Baird 2007). In southeast Anatolia, elaborate and large sites with complex art that date to periods even earlier than Çatalhöyük have been discovered at, for example, Göbekli and Jerf el Ahmar (Schmidt 2006, and see Schmidt, chapter 42 in this volume; Stordeur et al. 2000).

But there are ways in which Çatalhöyük remains distinctive. The sheer amount of the art—its concentration in so many houses at one site—remains particular. Indeed, the main mystery of Çatalhöyük remains the question of why all this art and symbolism, this flowering of imagery, should occur in this place at this time. One factor concerns the depositional processes. Through much of its sequence, Çatalhöyük provides a richly textured record of the minutiae of daily life. Rather than making hard lime floors that could be used over decades (as in many aceramic sites in Anatolia and the Middle East), at Çatalhöyük the floors were mostly made of a lime-rich clay plaster that remained soft and in need of continual resurfacing. Thus, on an annual or even monthly basis, floors and wall plasters were resurfaced with extremely thin layers. Within ten centimeters of floor or wall deposit it is possible to find up to 450 layers of replasterings. These provide a detailed record of daily life inside buildings. Middens, too, are finely layered, so that individual dumps of refuse from the hearth can be identified.

On abandonment of a house, paintings were covered over, and ovens and other internal features were sometimes carefully filled with earth. The upper walls were demolished and the lower half of the house often carefully filled in with fairly clean soil. In these ways the lower parts of the house were well protected and preserved. A new house was constructed using the lower halves of the walls of an earlier house as a base for new walls. Gradually the twenty-one-meter-high mound was built up as house was constructed on house. Together with the soil conditions that led to good survival of carbonized plants, animal and human bone, and so on these depositional processes resulted in a remarkably well-preserved site with much detailed information covering long periods of time. Çatalhöyük is exceedingly difficult to excavate because of its complexity; however, the rewards in terms of detailed information are high.

Mellaart's large-scale work established the importance of the site (Mellaart 1967). He demonstrated the extraordinary density of buildings on the site, with houses built up against each other so that movement around the settlement could only be across the roofs of houses. Entrance into houses was through the same hole in the roof through which the smoke from hearths and ovens escaped.

One of the most remarkable aspects of Mellaart's findings was the size of the Neolithic East Mound. Population estimates vary between 3,500 and 8,000 for any one phase of occupation (Cessford 2005). There is little evidence so far of internal specialization or differentiation of functions. There are houses, animal pens, and areas of refuse at Çatalhöyük, but as yet, despite extensive survey work, no evidence of public buildings, industrial areas (except lime burning off at the edge of the site), cemeteries (burial occurs within houses), ceremonial centers, and so on.

Figure 43.2. Agglomerated houses and possible "street" beneath a shelter in the 4040 Area of Çatalhöyük.

On the whole, the recent field research at Çatalhöyük has corroborated the findings of Mellaart (Hodder 1996, 2000, 2005a, 2005b, 2005c, 2006, 2007). The work in recent seasons has found much evidence of occupation, even in the most elaborate buildings identified by Mellaart as shrines. We have termed all buildings at the site domestic houses, although we recognize differences in the internal elaboration of houses (see the discussion of history houses below).

One indication of large-scale divisions of the Neolithic East Mound is a large dip or trough across the middle, dividing it into two hills. Although we have not yet been able to identify any clear stylistic or cultural differences between the two parts of the mound at contemporary phases, the mound does seem to have developed in two halves (a small, low, and late third prominence has also been provisionally identified in the eastern part of the East Mound [Hodder 1996]).

As well as these moiety-like divisions of the settlement, large-scale groupings of houses have been identified. In the upper levels of the site Mellaart found some evidence of "streets" winding between houses. In recent research we have also begun to find alleyways or boundaries between "sectors" of the mound, each sector containing ten to fifty houses (figure 43.2). There are smaller groupings of houses that seem to have both social and economic implications. Small groups of perhaps three to six houses often seem to be linked in that they use a common main house (perhaps corresponding to Mellaart's shrines and dubbed "history houses" by the current team) for burial. There is also some evidence of small-scale specialization of obsidian reduction and figurine manufacture or use in these history houses.

In the north part of the site, excavation areas include the 4040, the BACH Building 3, and Buildings 1 and 5. Most of the deposits so far excavated in this part of the site date from Level VII and above. In the south part of the mound, the main excavation areas are the South Area, the TP (Team Poznan) Area, and the IST (İstanbul) Area. The sequence in the South Area covers all levels at the site except for the uppermost levels (III, II, I, 0), which occur in the TP Area.

The use of Space Inside Buildings

Much economic, social, and ritual life was organized at the house level at Çatalhöyük. The houses through most of the sequence (the houses become multiroomed complexes in the upper levels and in the West Mound) consist of a main room (e.g., figure 43.3) with one to three side rooms that are used for storage and food preparation. The main rooms have walls that are more frequently replastered and normally contain the entrance ladder or stairs on the south wall, with the oven and hearth beneath the ladder. The northern floors in the main room tend to be higher, whiter, and cleaner, with more frequent replasterings. Paintings, sculptures, installations, and burials occur above and beneath these northern platforms on the whole. (However, neonate and child burials sometimes occur near the ovens and hearths in the south parts of the main rooms.)

What did it mean to "live" in these houses? How much time did people spend in them, and what was it like? It is often said that the houses were dark inside. But an experimental house built at the site by Mira Stevanović has shown that during the day so much light comes in from the ladder entry that the main rooms are quite bright. The white plastered walls were frequently renewed and often burnished, so they reflect light well. Even the side rooms receive some reflected light so that one's eyes get used to the relative dark in them and activities can be carried out there. We know that people knapped obsidian near the ladder entries in the main rooms and that they stored obsidian in caches in the same location. Indeed, the location of the obsidian caches and the nearby working of obsidian may be related to the need for a light source.

The rooms were probably smoky. This is clear from the layers of soot that are found on the plaster walls. The frequent (annual, seasonal, and monthly—Matthews 2005) replastering of the walls may have been necessary to maintain the light reflection in the main rooms. Several individuals buried beneath the floors of houses who had carbon residues on their ribs (Andrews, Molleson, and Boz 2005) are older people, and most old people had these residues. The carbon on the ribs has been interpreted in terms of the layers of soot identified on the plaster walls and the lack of architectural evidence for good air draughts in the houses—and in terms of the need to spend time in the houses over the harsh winters. The evidence can be interpreted in terms of the build-up of residues from an indoor life, for both men and

Figure 43.3. Building 77 was heavily burned during abandonment. Two pedestals with wild bull horns are set around a burial platform in the northeast corner of the main room.

women. Certainly by their later years people spent a good amount of time indoors. On the other hand, some young people and children are buried in houses in significant locations, including special neonate foundation deposits by doors and burial by hearths. So both the old and the young, as we might expect, have an especially close relationship with the house.

As people lived their lives, they spent part of it, especially when young and old and especially in the winter, closely tied to the house. This immersing in the house provided an opportunity for socialization. How was the house organized internally so as to socialize the inhabitants into social roles? Was the house used to create routines and structures in the "town" as a whole?

It has long been recognized (Mellaart 1967) that there was much repetition in the use of space inside houses. Matthews (2005) has shown that the main room in Building 5 had over 450 fine white silty clay plasters on the walls, whereas adjacent rooms were only plastered three to four times with orange and brown silt loam plasters. Other repeated patterns are well known. The floors of the main rooms are usually divided into platforms, or areas of different height, and the higher of these have a white plaster. The different floor areas are often demarcated by raised edges. These differences may also relate to floor covering—the white floors may have been more thickly covered so that no residues got through onto floors. In Building 1 phytolith evidence suggests different types of matting on the different platforms (Cessford 2007; Rosen 2005). There is also a link to burial.

The main burial platforms seem to be those with white laid plaster floors. Few burials occur beneath occupation floors (the "dirtier" floors with ash and small artifacts near ovens and hearths), although neonates may be buried here. Burials never contain pottery.

There is a tendency for different categories of people to be buried under different platforms. For example, in Building 1 there are more young people buried beneath the northwest platform and more older individuals under the central-east platform (Cessford 2007). The distribution of "art" and symbolism in the house also respects spatial divisions. Painting and sculpture are rarely found in the southern area of the house, and cattle heads with horns (bucrania) are most common on east and west walls. Vulture paintings only occur on north and east walls (Russell and Meece 2005). Burial is most common beneath platforms against the north and east walls, and since the vulture paintings also show headless corpses, a spatial and conceptual link between vultures and death is suggested.

It seems that the house at Çatalhöyük takes over many of the roles that were earlier associated with the community at large. Burial is less strongly associated with the house in earlier sites in Anatolia and the Middle East. Some burial occurs between buildings or in special buildings as at Çayönü. But at Çatalhöyük burial rarely occurs outside the house (see Roodenberg, chapter 44 in this volume, for further discussion of Neolithic burial patterns in western Anatolia). Symbolism and ritual are also taken from public buildings (at Aşıklı Höyük, Çayönü, Göbekli Tepe, and elsewhere) and centered in the house at Çatalhöyük. Food preparation and many productive activities that earlier had often taken place in public, open areas, become concentrated in the Çatalhöyük house.

The house was an important location for socialization into roles and behaviors at Çatalhöyük. But in the process, it can be argued that the house unit grew at the expense of the community at large. In the upper levels at the site there is some evidence of economic change and of some fragmentation of strong community-wide rules. House units came to act more independently, and the early cohesiveness of society began to be eroded (Düring 2001; see later discussion).

The Construction of Social Memories

As noted by Woodburn (1980), immediate return hunter-gatherer societies live in the present and have very little relationship with the past. By the time of the delayed return systems of the Neolithic, people lived in a material world embedded in the past (see Özbaşaran, chapter 5 in this volume, for additional discussion of the Neolithic plateau). The deep stratigraphy at Çatalhöyük, as house was built upon house, allows temporal processes to be examined in some detail (figure 43.4).

It was in the house that there was greatest concern to control the transmission of memory. Some houses were lived in for 50–100 years and then abandoned, the

Figure 43.4. Overall view of the excavations in the South Area at Çatalhöyük.

abandoned lot being used for refuse deposition (e.g., Building 2). Other buildings were replaced in the same location, using the same layout of walls over four to six rebuilds—and on average each rebuild has been shown to last around 70–100 years. We have found empirically (see also Düring 2006) that some of these long-lived building sequences have more burials beneath their floors. Although some houses have no burials, and the average number of burials in a house is five to eight, Building 1 had sixty-two humans buried beneath the platforms, including parts of bodies interred as secondary burials—perhaps initially buried in other or earlier buildings. As noted, we have come to call "history houses" those with numerous burials, more elaboration, and with evidence of multiple rebuilds in the same location.

There is much evidence of spatial continuity in these history houses, so that histories were established in the repetitive use of space. There are also examples of the repetition of painting and relief sculpture from phase to phase and level to level within buildings. Sometimes these seem too specific to be accidental products of site-wide preferences. For example, pairs of relief leopards are found in five buildings (Russell and Meece 2005), but in two cases, "shrine" 44 in Levels VI and VII, they occur immediately above each other and are both in a distinctive style. This seems like a clear case of commemorative memory.

The "history" that was accumulated in these houses seems to have included human remains. This accumulation is seen in the concentration of primary and secondary burials beneath the house floors, and it is also seen in the retrieval and reuse of body parts. In recent work, Başak Boz has identified teeth taken from a skeleton in one house in the 65-56-44-10 sequence (the numbers referring to a sequence of four buildings rebuilt on top of each other in the same place in the South Area of the site, the lowest is Building 65 and the topmost is Building 10) and placed in the jaw of an individual in a later building in the sequence. In Building 49 the limbs and scapulae had been carefully removed from an otherwise complete and well-articulated skeleton. But it was mainly skulls that were kept and passed down. In a small number of instances, we have discovered skulls removed from those buried beneath house floors. The skulls seem to have been kept and then placed at the base of house posts, added to burials, or in abandonment deposits. In one case, the skull had been plastered to represent the flesh of the face. These individual skull depositions have been found in a number of different types of houses. But the bodies from which they have been removed seem all to occur in history houses (although the sample remains small—only 7 clear examples in over 150 skeletons studied by the current project). It seems possible that heads (and perhaps other body parts) were removed from individuals in history houses and placed in other houses. In these ways, alliances with history houses could be built through the circulation of the dead.

The construction of "histories" in place, in the repetition of houses and the passing down of human skulls, emerged early and was a long-term component of Neolithic societies in the Middle East (Hodder 2007). Others have made similar arguments in relation to the circulation and deposition of human skulls (e.g., Kuijt 2008). The role of the house in the construction and maintenance of memory at Çatalhöyük is also seen in the circulation of other types of heads. Wild animal heads were also circulated. In Building 2, there is evidence of removal of something large from the west wall of the main room, possibly linked to a wild cattle horn found on the floor (Farid 2007). Mellaart (1967) records a frequent pattern of the destruction of the west walls of main rooms to remove sculpture. The heads and feet/hands of the relief figures with upraised arms (probably depicting bears) have always been removed before the infilling of buildings. In Building 1 there is clear evidence that a pit was dug down to retrieve sculpture (perhaps a plastered cattle skull?) from the west wall after the building had been abandoned and filled in and after intermediary phases of occupation and infilling.

Figurines are often found with the heads missing (Meskell et al. 2008). This pattern could easily be the result of normal breakage processes, since the neck is often the weakest part of a figurine. But in several examples, there is evidence of detachable heads, as have been found at Höyücek. In some cases at Çatalhöyük there is evidence of special deposition of broken heads as in a hearth in Building 17 (Hodder 2006). However, in most cases clay and stone figurines at Çatalhöyük were deposited with refuse in middens—there is very little specially structured deposition (Meskell et al. 2008).

One of the most impressive images in some of the art scenes at Çatalhöyük is the wild bull, and a clue to the interpretation of such paintings is the discovery that wild bulls are used preferentially in feasting (Russell and Martin 2005). This claim is based on the association between the bones of male cattle (all of which are wild through most of the sequence at Çatalhöyük) and concentrations of large numbers of relatively complete large animal bones, often in contexts such as house foundations, house abandonment, or discard between house walls. There is no evidence as yet that such feasting deposits concentrate in the history houses, but on the other hand the elaboration of the history houses is often expressed in the presence of wild bull horns set in pedestals (e.g., figure 43.3) or otherwise displayed in houses.

Figure 43.5. Face pot found in midden contexts in the 4040 Area.

The association between bull and human heads is shown in the pot in figure 43.5, discovered fragmented in a midden in the 4040 Area (see figure 43.1) in a level probably equating to Mellaart's Level VI. The pot shows a human head with empty eyes—a motif seen also on the plastered skull. The face is repeated on both ends of the pot, and on both sides are cattle horns and head. The two types of head most commonly passed down to create histories are brought together on the same pot.

It should be emphasized that the degree of differentiation between history and nonhistory houses is slight. In one nonhistory house, eleven bull horns were stacked above a bucranium (Building 52, see Twiss et al. 2008). There is some slight evidence that history houses had less storage and less side room space than other houses, suggesting perhaps that other houses participated in the provision of functions for the history houses, but the differences are not marked. Study of microvariation in teeth has suggested that membership of history houses was not based on genetic affinity (Pilloud, personal communication). In many house societies (Carsten and Hugh Jones 1995; Joyce and Gillespie 2000; Lévi-Strauss 1982), membership of the house is based on residence and the passing down of heirlooms rather than on kinship. Çatalhöyük was a largely egalitarian society cross-cut by a variety of different forms of social affiliation, but with slight differentiation based on membership of history houses on the basis of residence and the passing down of skulls and other objects.

Change Through Time

However, the history house system declines in the upper levels of the site. The focus on elaborately plastered houses with bucrania, reliefs, and paintings occurs mainly in the early levels (from Level XII to V). There is a decline in the occurrence of actual bull horns and other wild animal part installations in the upper levels of the site. Although some bucrania continue, these are often made of plaster rather than real horns. There is much faunal evidence that hunting of wild cattle declined in the upper levels of the site—there may have been fewer wild bulls present in the landscape by this time. In contrast to the plain pottery found in the early part of the sequence (pottery is introduced by Level XII), small symbolic bull heads are found from Level V as handles on pottery. Paintings showing the teasing and baiting of wild animals, including bulls occur from Level V onward, and these have a clear narrative component. There seems to be a shift in ritual from the presencing of wild animals to their representation.

The greater discursive component of religious life in the upper levels of the site is also seen in the emergence after Level V of stamp seals. These may have been used to stamp human or animal skin, and they use a distinct array of codified signs (Türkcan 2005). These signs are abstract, but some refer to hands and perhaps to navels, and there are a few examples that indicate a leopard and a bear.

In the lower levels of the site, as noted, obsidian is found in hoards or caches below the floors. In the upper levels of the site, these hoards cease. Pottery gradually becomes more diverse and more decorated from Level V onward until by the time of Çatalhöyük West (Chalcolithic, from 6000 B.C.E.) it is heavily decorated with complex designs. By the time of the West Mound, too, burial in houses of adults largely ends. It is presumed that burial occurs off-site and perhaps in cemeteries. Excavations in the uppermost levels of the East Mound by a team from Poznan, Poland (TP in figure 43.1), have uncovered changing burial rituals, including collective burial in a decorated "tomb," and associations of animal and human bones (not found in earlier levels). The rituals involved in the abandoning of houses also change. Now frequently houses are burned (from level VI onward on the Neolithic East Mound) before being reused.

How can we account for these changes? A simple contributing impulse would have been the "hunting out" of wild cattle that we seem to see in the upper part of the site. By the time of the West Mound, domesticated cattle are in use. It is likely that other wild animals (leopards, boar, etc.) were less present in the landscape than before and were thus less available for celebrating important feasts and for presencing powerful animal spirits. At the same time, in the upper part of the site centralizing tendencies are increasingly present in the increasingly complex and specialized pottery and obsidian production, and in the emergence of large houses based on integrated and more intensive production of domesticated plants and animals. After Level III there is evidence from age distributions for the secondary exploitation of sheep. This economic transformation seems to have been associated with an overall change in the layout of the town and the organization of houses. After Level VI/V, some parts of the site are abandoned and other parts are settled—the town becomes more dispersed and fragmented. Streets occur, and street-level entrances into houses appear. Houses become much larger, and on the West Mound they become two-storey. They are rebuilt more frequently (Düring 2006). After Level III on the Neolithic East Mound, houses become larger and more multiroomed. They have a large main room with central hearth. This trend continues onto the West Mound, where the main rooms are surrounded by multiple smaller rooms.

All this could have come about as wild bulls were hunted out from the landscape, thus undermining a social system based on the building of history houses founded on the killing and feasting of those bulls. There may also have been an internal process whereby houses (history or otherwise) were able to build up resources based on domestic animal and cereal production so that they could become more independent of an elaborate residence-ritual system. But it is undoubtedly the case that external factors may have been involved. Through much of the occupation of the Neolithic East Mound, it was located in a wetland environment, but toward the end of the East Mound's occupation, cores in the surrounding alluvial deposits show a weakly developed buried soil, dated to 5800–6200 B.C.E., marking the end of alluvial deposition and flooding and the establishment of a stable ground surface around the site (Roberts and Rosen 2009). The end of occupation on the East Mound also coincided with a major perturbation in global climate (Alley and Ágústsdóttir 2005; Clare et al. 2008; and see Özdoğan, chapter 29 in this volume). This climatic event prompted drought conditions over much of Africa and Asia (Gasse 2000) around 6200 B.C.E. (Thomas et al. 2007), the same time as the flooding phase ended and dry conditions began at Çatalhöyük. Clare et al. (2008) and Roberts and Rosen (2009) have argued that this phase of drying may be associated with the changes observed at the end of the East Mound and the relocation to the West Mound.

Ceramics and Other Material Culture

The earliest levels at the site are aceramic, and the first pottery appears in Level XII. The pottery at this early stage is organic-tempered and thick-walled with open bowls the main form. From Level VII onward the pottery is mineral-tempered, thin-walled, with open and close-mouthed jars being the main forms. These cooking pots were burnished but never incised or decorated in other ways. From Level V onward, and particularly from Level III onward there is a greater variety of forms and fabrics, including miniature vessels and vessels with incised decoration. Some painted decoration also begins to appear in the uppermost levels, and red on cream painted pottery predominates on the Chalcolithic West Mound. Other material culture includes a wide range of worked bone, mainly points but also belt fastenings, fish hooks, and finger rings. In the upper levels there are clay stamps with incised geometric decoration. There is a rich groundstone industry, both for grinding plant material and ochres, and for small axes and maces. The lithic assemblage is predominantly obsidian, and the main sources are in Cappodocia, with the specific sources changing through time. There is a wide range of lithic production processes, some taking place on site, but with the finer production of bifacial points often taking place off site.

Conclusions

There is limited evidence for specialized and differentiated economic, political, and social functions at Çatalhöyük. Rather the effect of a "town" (a large agglomeration of people living packed against each other) is produced by the repetition of social behavior within houses. Daily acts were heavily routinized and reconfirmed the social order. People were brought up within daily routines through which they learned the roles and rules of society. In addition, these rules and conventions were set within an elaborate symbolic system that centered around wild animals and the ancestors buried beneath the floors. So it may be the case that two of the most distinctive aspects of Çatalhöyük were related. The relative lack of hierarchy and public ceremonial might be related to the elaborate symbolism in the house. Perhaps the social rules of society were learned and enforced within the house, and they were all the more powerful and meaningful because they were set within the performance of rituals embedded within myth and sanctioned by the ancestors. Rather than investing in centralized rituals, the people at Çatalhöyük invested in dispersed domestic cults and regulations of the body in the process of socialization. This alternative form of power produced what is in effect a very large village.

As people wished to gain access to the rights and resources of the "house" they needed to become part of the construction of its memories. They needed to be physically associated with its fabric, its burials, its symbolism, its history. We have little notion of how the site as a whole grew. My hypothesis for the moment is that houses clustered around history houses (those with many burials and a long period of reuse). Physical and spatial propinquity to these history houses ensured access to rights and resources. As the group of houses grew, expanded, and fissioned, living near these ancestral homes remained significant. The end result was a dense packing of houses as people used up every available nook and cranny in order to be located close to the ancestral home and participate in the transmission of its physical rights. Co-presence and co-history here equated with collective membership.

Through time, however, changes were encountered, partly human-produced and partly climate-related. Toward the upper levels in the site and the later part of the seventh millennium B.C.E., there was an economic shift to more intensive use of domesticated plants and animals and decreased reliance on wild animals. Rather than being central to a web of ritual and social relationships, houses came to be centers of production and consumption. The history house system began to break down, and houses became larger, multiroom, and multistorey. Settlement dispersed at Çatalhöyük, and over the whole alluvial fan. Neolithic Çatalhöyük East stood alone on the Çarşamba Fan, but sixth millennium B.C.E. Çatalhöyük West is one of fifteen similar small- to medium-sized Early Chalcolithic sites recorded on or near the fan (Baird 2005).

NOTE

1. The project works under the auspices of the British Institute of Archaeology at Ankara, with a permit from the Turkish Ministry of Culture and Tourism. The main sponsors are Yapı Kredi Bankası, Boeing, and the Templeton Foundation. Our long-term sponsors are Shell, Merko, and Thames Water. Our main institutional partners are Selçuk University, Stanford University, University College London, Poznan University, İstanbul University, Trakya University (Edirne), and SUNY Buffalo.

REFERENCES

Alley, Richard B. and Anna Maria Ágústsdóttir. 2005. The 8k Event: Cause and Consequences of a Major Holocene Abrupt Climate Change. *Quaternary Science Reviews* 24: 1123–49.

Andrews, Peter, Theya Molleson, and Başak Boz. 2005. The Human Burials at Çatalhöyük. In *Inhabiting Çatalhöyük: Reports from the 1995–1999 Seasons*, ed. Ian Hodder, 263–80, 469–89. McDonald Institute Monographs 38. Cambridge: McDonald Institute for Archaeological Research.

Baird, Douglas. 2005. The History of Settlement and Social Landscapes in the Early Holocene in the Çatalhöyük Area. In *Çatalhöyük Perspectives: Themes from the 1995–99 Seasons*, ed. Ian Hodder, 55–74. McDonald Institute Monographs 40. Cambridge: McDonald Institute for Archaeological Research.

——. 2007. The Boncuklu Project: The Origins of Sedentism, Cultivation and Herding in Central Anatolia. *Anatolian Archaeology* 13: 14–18.

Carsten, Janet and Stephen Hugh-Jones, eds. 1995. *About the House: Levi-Strauss and Beyond*. Cambridge: Cambridge University Press.

Cessford, Craig. 2005. Estimating the Neolithic Population of Çatalhöyük. In *Inhabiting Çatalhöyük: Reports from the 1995–1999 Seasons*, ed. Ian Hodder, 323–26. McDonald Institute Monographs 38. Cambridge: McDonald Institute for Archaeological Research.

——. 2007. Neolithic Excavations in the North Area, East Mound, Çatalhöyük 1995–98. In *Excavating Çatalhöyük: South, North, and KOPAL Area Reports from the 1995–1999 Seasons*, ed. Ian Hodder, 345–549. McDonald Institute Monographs 37. Cambridge: McDonald Institute for Archaeological Research.

Clare, Lee, Eelco J. Rohling, Bernhard Weninger, and Johanna Hilpert. 2008. Warfare in Late Neolithic/Early Chalcolithic Pisidia, Southwestern Turkey. Climate Induced Social Unrest in the late 7th Millennium cal BC. *Documenta Praehistorica* 35: 65–91.

Düring, Bleda. 2001. Social Dimensions in the Architecture of Neolithic Çatalhöyük. *Anatolian Studies* 51: 1–18.

———. 2006. *Constructing Communities: Clustered Neighbourhood Settlements of the Central Anatolian Neolithic, ca. 8500—5500 Cal. BC.* Leiden: Nederlands Instituut voor het Nabije Oosten.

Esin, Ufuk and Savaş Harmankaya. 1999. Aşıklı. In *Neolithic in Turkey, the Cradle of Civilization*, ed. Mehmet Özdoğan and Nezih Başgelen, 115–32. İstanbul: Arkeoloji ve Sanat Yayınları.

Farid, Shahina. 2007. Neolithic Excavations in the South Area, East Mound, Çatalhöyük 1995–99. In *Excavating Çatalhöyük: South, North, and KOPAL Area Reports from the 1995–1999 Seasons*, ed. Ian Hodder, 41–342. McDonald Institute Monographs 37. Cambridge: McDonald Institute for Archaeological Research.

Gasse, F. 2000. Hydrological Changes in the African Tropics since the Last Glacial Maximum. *Quaternary Science Reviews* 19: 189–211.

Hodder, Ian, ed. 1996. *On the Surface: Çatalhöyük 1993–95*. McDonald Institute Monographs 22. Cambridge: McDonald Institute for Archaeological Research.

———. ed. 2000. *Towards Reflexive Method in Archaeology: The Example of Çatalhöyük*. McDonald Institute Monographs 28. Cambridge: McDonald Institute for Archaeological Research.

———. ed. 2005a. *Inhabiting Çatalhöyük: Reports from the 1995–1999 Seasons*. McDonald Institute Monographs 38. Cambridge: McDonald Institute for Archaeological Research.

———. ed. 2005b. *Changing Materialities at Çatalhöyük: Reports from the 1995–1999 Seasons*. McDonald Institute Monographs 39. Cambridge: McDonald Institute for Archaeological Research.

———. ed. 2005c. *Çatalhöyük Perspectives: Themes from the 1995–99 Seasons*. McDonald Institute Monographs 40. Cambridge: McDonald Institute for Archaeological Research.

———. 2006. *Çatalhöyük. The Leopard's Tale*. London: Thames and Hudson.

———. ed. 2007. *Excavating Çatalhöyük: South, North, and KOPAL Reports from the 1995–1999 Seasons*. McDonald Institute Monographs 37. Cambridge: McDonald Institute for Archaeological Research.

Joyce, Rosemary A. and Susan D. Gillespie, eds. 2000. *Beyond Kinship. Social and Material Reproduction in House Societies*. Philadelphia: University of Pennsylvania Press.

Kuijt, Ian. 2008. The Regeneration of Life: Neolithic Structures of Symbolic Remembering and Forgetting. *Current Anthropology* 49: 171–97.

Lévi-Strauss, Claude. 1982. *The Way of the Masks*. Seattle: University of Washington Press.

Matthews, Wendy. 2005. Micromorphological and Microstratigraphic Traces of Uses and Concepts of Space. In *Inhabiting Çatalhöyük: Reports from the 1995–1999 Seasons*, ed. Ian Hodder, 355–98. McDonald Institute Monographs 38. Cambridge: McDonald Institute for Archaeological Research.

Mellaart, James. 1967. *Çatal Hüyük: A Neolithic Town in Anatolia*. London: Thames and Hudson.

Meskell, Lynn M., Carolyn Nakamura, Rachel King, and Shahina Farid. 2008. Figured Lifeworlds and Depositional Practices at Çatalhöyük. *Cambridge Archaeological Journal* 18.2: 139–61.

Roberts, Neil and Rosen, Arlene. 2009. Diversity and Complexity in Early Farming Communities of Southwest Asia: New Insights into the Economic and Environmental Basis of Neolithic Çatalhöyük. *Current Anthropology* 50.3: 393–402.

Rosen, Arlene M. 2005. Phytolith Indicators of Plant and Land Use at Çatalhöyük. In *Inhabiting Çatalhöyük: Reports from the 1995–1999 Seasons*, ed. I. Hodder, 203–12. McDonald Institute Monographs 38. Cambridge: McDonald Institute for Archaeological Research.

Russell, Nerissa and Louise Martin. 2005. The Çatalhöyük Mammal Remains. In *Inhabiting Çatalhöyük: Reports from the 1995–1999 Seasons*, ed. Ian Hodder, 33–98. McDonald Institute Monographs 38. Cambridge: McDonald Institute for Archaeological Research.

Russell, Nerissa and Stephanie Meece. 2005. Animal Representations and Animal Remains at Çatalhöyük. In *Çatalhöyük Perspectives: Themes from the 1995–99 Seasons*, ed. Ian Hodder, 209–30. McDonald Institute Monographs 40. Cambridge: McDonald Institute for Archaeological Research.

Schmidt, Klaus. 2006. *Sie bauten die ersten Tempel: das rätselhafte Heiligtum der Steinzeitjäger: die archäologische Entdeckung am Göbekli Tepe*. Munich: Beck.

Stordeur, Danielle, Michel Brenet, Gerard der Aprahamian, and Jean-Claude Roux. 2000. Les bâtiments communautaires de Jerf el Ahmar et Mureybet Horizon PPNA (Syrie). *Paléorient* 26: 29–44.

Thomas, Elizabeth R., Eric W. Wolff, Robert Mulvaney, Jorgan P. Steffensen, S. J. Johnsen, Carol Arrowsmith, James W. C. White, Bruce Vaughn, and Trevor Popp. 2007. The 8.2 ka Event from Greenland Ice Cores. *Quaternary Science Reviews* 26: 70–81.

Türkcan, Ali Umut. 2005. Some Remarks on Çatalhöyük Stamp Seals. In *Changing Materialities at Çatalhöyük: Reports from the 1995–1999 Seasons*, ed. Ian Hodder, 175–86. McDonald Institute Monographs 39. Cambridge: McDonald Institute for Archaeological Research.

Twiss, Katheryn C., Amy Bogaard, Duru Bogdan, Tristan Carter, Michael P. Charles, Shahina Farid, Nerissa Russell, Mirjana Stevanović, E. Nurcan Yalman, and Lisa Yeomans. 2008. Arson or Accident? The Burning of a Neolithic House at Çatalhöyük. *Journal of Field Archaeology* 33: 41–57.

Woodburn, James. 1980. Hunters and Gatherers Today and Reconstruction of the Past. In *Soviet and Western Anthropology*, ed. Ernest Gellner, 95–117. London: Duckworth.

CHAPTER 44

ILIPINAR: A NEOLITHIC SETTLEMENT IN THE EASTERN MARMARA REGION

JACOB ROODENBERG

History of Research and Environmental Context

Against the background of early farming migration throughout Anatolia, the regions surrounding the Sea of Marmara constitute an attractive landscape for settlement. In particular the well-watered lowlands of the eastern part of this region, with a marginal Mediterranean climate exposed to winds from the Black Sea, escape the torrid summer heat and benefit from mild, rainy winters (today's annual precipitation around İznik Lake is 800 mm). The contrast with the Anatolian plateau with a mean altitude of 1,000 m is striking. Aside from ecological niches such as the Burdur Lake district (Duru 2008) and the Konya Plain (Hodder 2007), among others, early farming on the plateau with its continental climate of extreme cold and heat and low precipitation (300–400 mm/year) was carried out in less favorable conditions. Therefore, as recent research has revealed, it is not accidental that farming communities at certain points in time seem to concentrate in the coastal zones of the Aegean, the Sea of Marmara, and adjacent hinterlands. By means of a long-standing multidisciplinary research project comprising excavations at Ilıpınar, Menteşe, and Barcın, teams from the İstanbul-based Netherlands

Institute in Turkey (NIT) and its main office NINO-Leiden, have begun to expose deposits that explain the ways of early settlement development in that region.

The investigations at Ilıpınar and Menteşe lasted from 1987 until 2002 and were inspired by the expectation that the lowlands east of the Sea of Marmara would reveal clues for the spread of Neolithic farmers in search of new land suitable for animal husbandry and cultivation. Although prehistoric settlement was attested intermittently along the coastline of the Marmara Sea (see Özdoğan, chapter 29 in this volume), the eastern shore and its hinterland with their ecological advantages had remained unexplored until this project.

The geographical setting of both settlements is comparable: Ilıpınar in the İznik Lake basin and Menteşe in the Plain of Yenişehir, an ancient lake basin, separated from the former by a 600-m-high mountain ridge (Roodenberg et al. 2003). This is also true for Barcın, a site located five kilometers east of Menteşe and of roughly the same date (Roodenberg et al. 2008).

These villages, which were founded around 6400 cal B.C.E. (Menteşe, Barcın) and 6000 cal B.C.E. (Ilıpınar), shared identical environmental conditions. The villages lay in alluvial plains at a short distance from the lakes but relied on nearby springs for their fresh water supply. The plains and slopes of the surrounding mountains were covered with deciduous forest including most commonly oak, with smaller quantities of hazel and beech (Bottema and Woldring 1995).

This chapter deals in particular with Ilıpınar, which was investigated at length. This is due to the fact that Menteşe was mainly explored by using soundings during a few short campaigns and because the excavations at Barcın are still in their preliminary stages.[1]

Ilıpınar's environment was advantageous for an economy based on crop cultivation and stock breeding. Founded at the start of the sixth millennium B.C.E. as a settlement with a handful of houses centered around a spring, it gradually expanded into a village covering one hectare until it was deserted 500 years later. Afterward the mound was used as a burial ground in the second quarter of the fourth millennium B.C.E. (Late Chalcolithic), the second quarter of the third millennium B.C.E. (Early Bronze Age), and in the sixth–seventh centuries C.E. (Early Byzantine). Moreover there were traces of ephemeral habitation during these intervals. The total occupation deposit measured more than seven meters, the total surface nearly three hectares.

Village Economy

The first settlers arrived at the spring as full-fledged farmers with cattle, sheep, goats, pigs, and a large variety of domesticated food plants. The proportions of the different domestic species in the fauna seem to reflect the human impact on the local environment. At the beginning sheep were the principal animal exploited by the farmers, but soon the numbers of goat and pig increased in response to the woodland environment. Then halfway into the life of the village, cattle and again sheep took advantage of open areas that had been created for plant cultivation around the settlement (Buitenhuis 2008:210). Boar, deer, and to a lesser extent auroch were the main wild sources of animal protein, but with a slight exception during the initial habitation phase, hunting was of minor importance for the diet.

Although the retrieval of plant seeds depends strongly on preservation conditions and archaeological context, a clear tendency was observed at Ilıpınar; during the second half of the village's lifetime the economy shows a spectacular increase in crop cultivation. The cultivated plants include cereals such as barley, predominant during the early sixth millennium B.C.E., einkorn, emmer, and a short-sized grain, the latter two more frequent during the next couple of centuries. In addition to cereals, a variety of pulses such as lentil and bitter vetch were utilized, and flax was probably also grown (Cappers 2008:127). The collection of edible wild plants—pear, hazel, grape, and fig—was of minor influence on the diet, a trend already seen in the spare usage of wild animals. As will be shown, the economy had a strong impact on village development (see Özbaşaran, chapter 5 in this volume, for additional discussion on the intersection between environment and settlement in the Neolithic).

Architecture and Settlement

The First Period: The Postwall Building Village (Phases X–VII)

Data relative to the first occupation period were collected in a 400 square-meter excavation trench northeast of the spring, the so-called Big Square (figure 44.1). The initial village was built between the spring and a ditch curving from northwest to south. Given the fact that the village lay on an alluvial fan, this ditch has been interpreted as belonging to a natural drainage system discharging into the spring basin (Roodenberg 2008a:2). Soon after the initial habitation stage, this ditch silted up and was built on by the expanding village. Houses—the majority of the excavated buildings are thought to have been dwellings—consisted of two construction types: those built with heavy outer walls constructed with mud slabs (a variety of *pisé*), and others with walls made of wooden posts set in ditches that were interlinked with ropes and lathing constituting a matrix for a mud coating. The house plans, which were on average thirty square meters in size, consisted of a single room including accommodations for storage, fire making, food preparation, and space for resting.

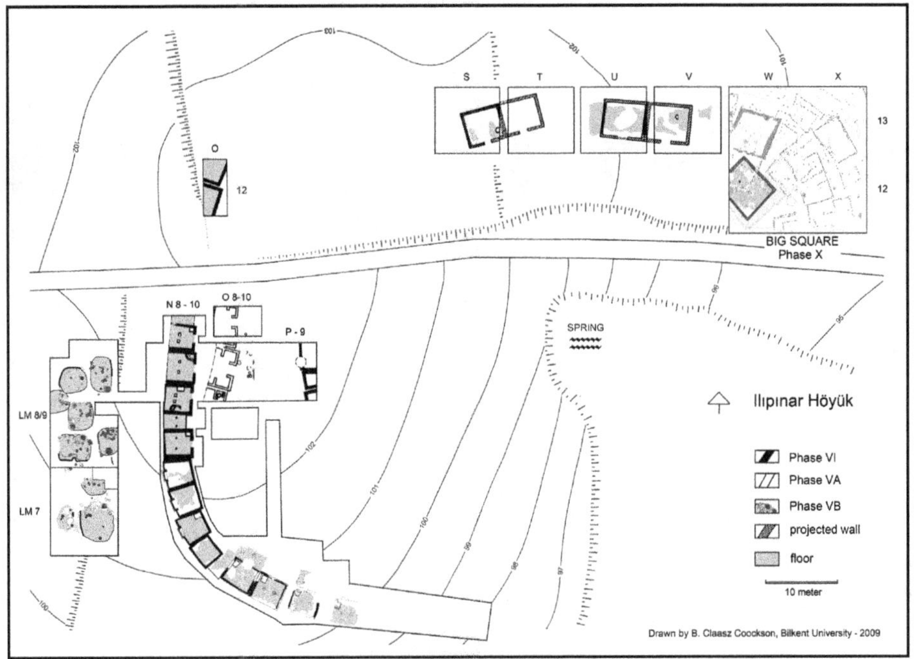

Figure 44.1. Overview of the building plans from the different early village phases. The Big Square shows the top level of Phase X.

After the initial habitation stage the construction of wooden postwall houses prevailed. In the Big Square the contours of dozens of such house plans, marked by rows of postholes, came to light. Evidence suggests that these houses were rebuilt on the same spot up to five times; from this we deduce that land parcels remained in the same family for generations, while the rapid reconstruction of these buildings—approximately one per generation—was due to the perishable nature of the construction materials. Houses were set in a radial pattern with the spring as its focal point, each surrounded by an open space.

The framework of the house walls consisted of upright posts with a diameter of eight to ten centimeters, spaced at intervals of ten to fifteen centimeters, and set in forty-to-seventy-centimeter-deep trenches. Ropes and thin laths fixed, respectively, between and along these posts served as an inner framework for the mud coating applied on both wall sides. Floors were made of stamped mud or laid with wooden boards. Central posts carried the heaviest weight of the roof, which was probably of a relatively light saddle-shape construction, covered with reeds (figure 44.2).

Judging from the huge quantities of faunal remains, the community's subsistence in the first centuries of the sixth millennium B.C.E. depended strongly on animal exploitation. Courtyard surfaces were littered with butchering waste, whereas rare indoor storage facilities containing plant seeds suggest that crop cultivation was at a rather low level. That picture would be reversed in the second period starting around 5700 cal B.C.E.

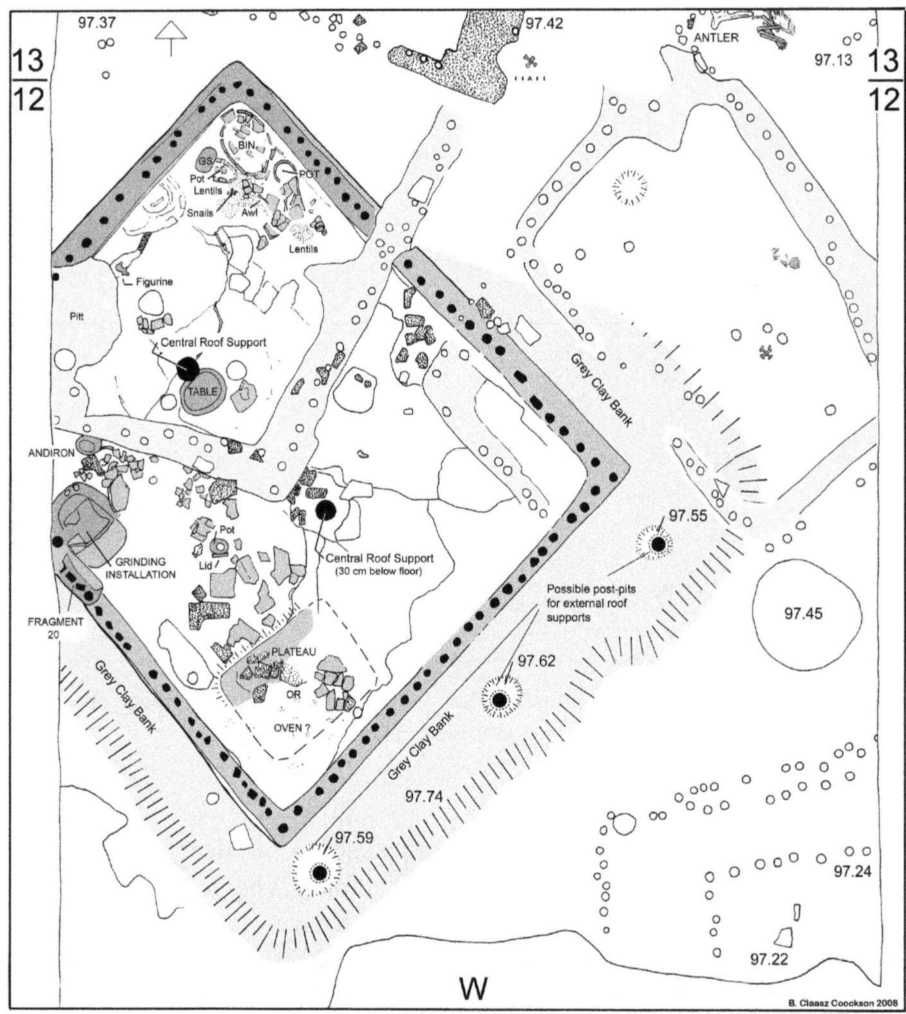

Figure 44.2. Burned house from the top level of Phase X.

The Second Period: The Mudbrick Building Village (Phases VI–VA)

The second period is marked by the introduction of mudbrick architecture. This had far-reaching consequences. Mudbrick architecture, not to be confused with the technique of mud slab building in the initial stage, which can best be considered a variety of pisé construction, resulted in a different method of house construction and village layout. For unknown reasons ground plans grew smaller, but buildings were provided with an upper storey. As a result, the total floor space remained equivalent with that of single-storey dwellings of the previous period. The buildings were equipped for storing, processing large quantities of harvest products, and food preparation. Ground and upper floors had a range of storage facilities such as built-in bins, mud-coated baskets, and pottery vessels sufficient to hold an estimated 1,000 liters of plant seeds, which would approximate the yearly consumption of an average family (Roodenberg 2008b:77). Moreover there were grinding slabs of basalt and granite mounted on mudbrick footings, and andirons probably used as footings for keeping perishable goods off the floors. Almost all ground floors—and sometimes also the second floor—had large square ovens with walls made of upright mudbricks. Their tray-like roofs were designed to dry or roast grain kernels when the ovens were heated. Compared to the first settlement period, storage capacity of the second period had grown considerably, indicating an expansion of crop cultivation. This means that large areas had been deforested and brought under cultivation. After harvest these fields were grazed by herds of cattle and sheep, illustrated by the increase of these species in the faunal record (Buitenhuis 2008:210).

The excavations revealed buildings that were aligned in a nearly semicircular row and made up the west and southwest edge of the village of Phase VI (figure 44.1). After fourteen units were excavated the investigations stopped, but there is little doubt that the boundary had originally encircled the entire agglomeration. These units were structurally identical and similarly equipped. The square mudbrick wall foundation was provided with an opening at the front side to ventilate the space under the floor (Claasz Coockson 2008:157). This floor was made with round and split wood and covered with a thick layer of smeared mud, the whole construction carried by cross-beams sealed in the walls. In the central axis two posts resting on logs in the subsoil ran through the ground floor and upper floor straight up to support the ridge-pole of the roof. The upper storey's floor was constructed the same way as the ground floor and carried a panoply of baskets, vessels, and grinding stones (figure 44.3). Débris found on top of this inventory indicates that the roof was made of a light construction and possibly saddle-shaped, because this form would easily have adapted to the alignment of these buildings. The alignment was purposefully created as a boundary, originally enclosing the village grounds. The whole structure had been destroyed by a conflagration, leaving complete inventories that were sealed by collapsed floors and walls. The buildings had their entrance at the village side via raised platforms, which were constructed in the same way as the suspended house floors and which included fireplaces and kitchen utensils. At a few spots the alignment of buildings was interrupted by narrow lanes that were secondarily blocked and made into sheds. Not much is known from the central village plan, because the central sector of the mound was greatly eroded as a result of successive construction and burial activities and by recent cultivation. The few house remains investigated there demonstrated, however, that these were of the same type and function as the boundary buildings and therefore can also be considered family houses.

Inside the curve of the boundary buildings, a large area marked by a thick deposit of animal dung indicated that the livestock were penned inside the settlement (Roodenberg 2001:241). This phenomenon would explain the purpose of the boundary structure, that is, offering nightly shelter for the herds of cattle and sheep, the increasing importance of which has already been mentioned. Moreover, because

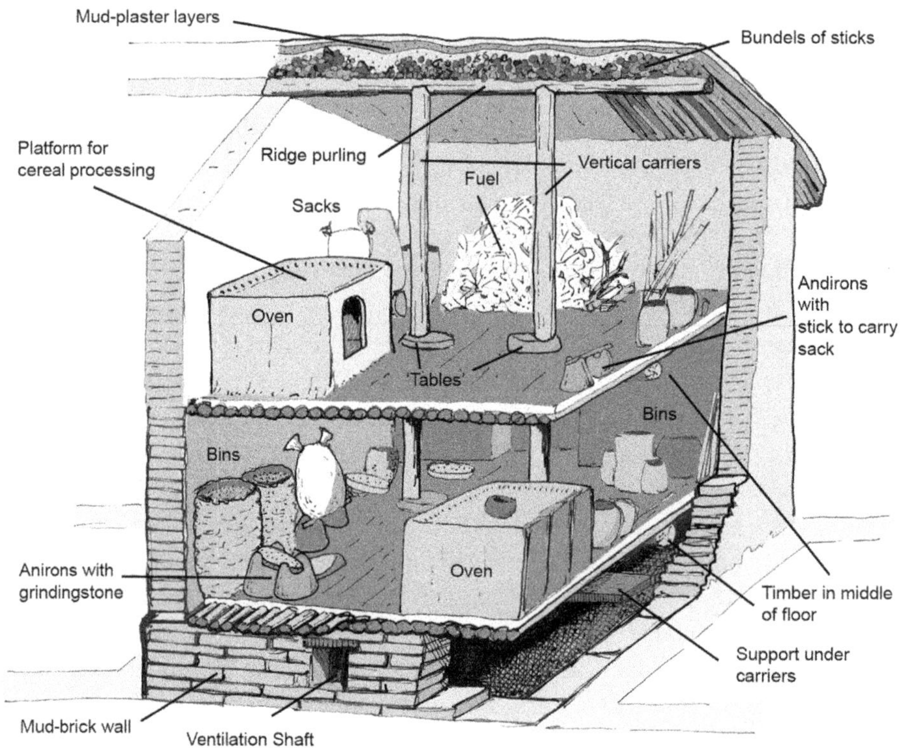

Figure 44.3. Reconstruction of a standard boundary building of Phase VI.

an increased reliance on dairy production occurred in the Marmara region (Evershed et al. 2008:530), this enclosure may have also been used for milking the animals. The picture that emerges is a village economy that was largely based on a combination of successful crop cultivation and cattle and sheep breeding (figure 44.4a, b). Other settlements such as Aktopraklık, which is sixty kilometers southwest of Ilıpınar, and Aşağıpınar in Turkish Thrace provide examples of curvilinear alignment showing similarities with the boundary buildings (N. Karul and M. Özdoğan personal communication). This suggests that the reason for this particular layout was to facilitate meeting the need for penning and milking the livestock.

On the burned ruins of the boundary new buildings arose: single-storey dwellings with larger ground plans that were subdivided into various spaces. This village (Phase VA), of which the contours remain unknown, also fell victim to a fire, but this time the village was not rebuilt.

The Final Stage: Seasonal Occupation (Phase VB)

The destruction by fire of Phase VA, around 5500 B.C.E., was the final blow to the settlement, which meant an end to 500 years of continuous occupation. However, Phase VA was followed by a short period of intermittent occupation characterized

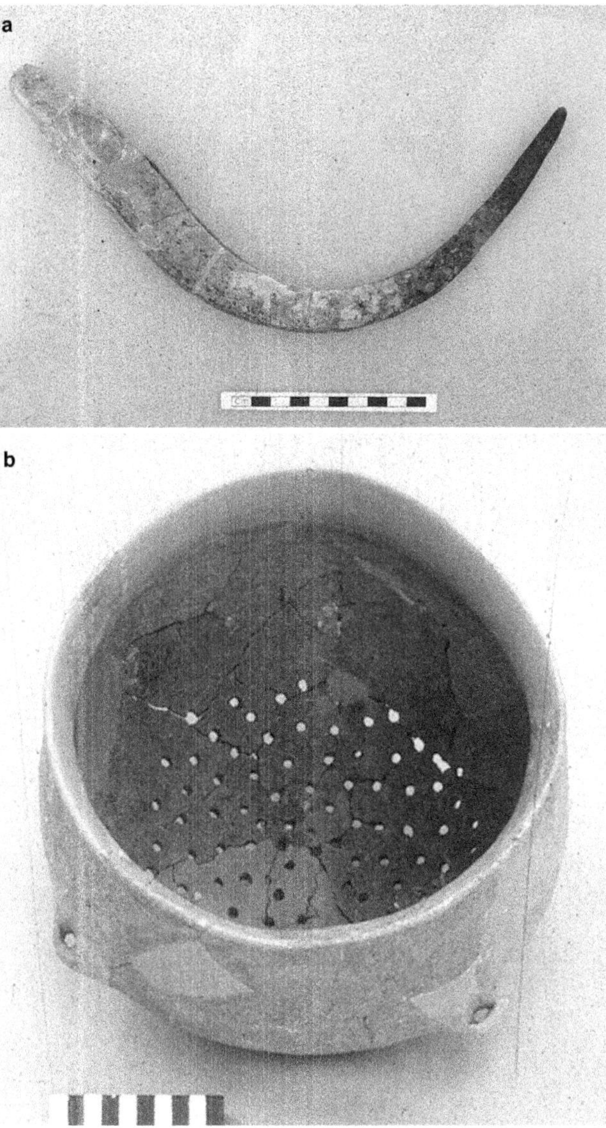

Figure 44.4. (a) Horn sickle handle without flint sickle elements. The missing flints were fixed in a slot at the inner side of the handle (Phase VA). (b) Strainer pot possibly used for making cheese (Phase VI).

by basic shelters built on the mound's west flank. These were huts dug into the ground or erected on the slope with superstructures made of wattle and daub and sometimes provided with benches (figure 44.5). Their inventories comprised ovens and grinding installations, baskets, and pottery vessels, many of the latter filled with charred plant seeds. Both the utensils and the plant species suggest a certain continuation of the daily farming practice, although the huts were unsuitable for year-round dwelling because of the extreme humidity during the long cold season. Botanical analysis revealed that the contents of the vessels were

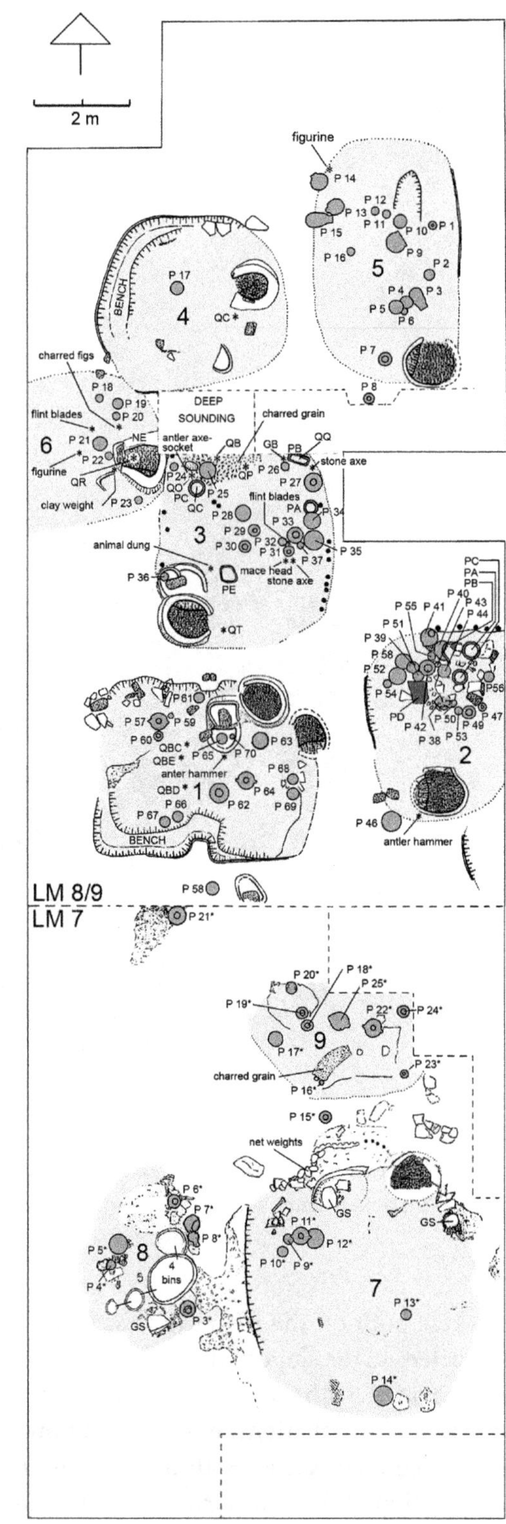

Figure 44.5. Plan of huts and courtyards built on the west flank of the mound (Phase VB).

almost pure crop seed. Wild plant seeds had apparently been sorted out from this assemblage with the purpose of using the remaining crop seed for sowing (Cappers 2008:131). It was therefore concluded that these shelters had served as garden-houses. It seems that although the population of the last village had resettled somewhere in the neighborhood, the huts served as temporary shelters for those who were charged with the tillage of the fields. During Phase VB a new kind of pottery—vases with tall necks and open bowls, both with rippled surfaces—joined the large storage vessels that were part of the previous pottery assemblage (Thissen 2008:91ff.).

Discussion

From Ilıpınar's foundation until its final abandonment, some elements of its material culture underwent gradual shifts, which are exemplified by the pottery assemblage (Thissen 2001, 2008). Ground stone, bone, and antler industries were subject to little alteration, and most tool types persisted unchanged over the centuries. In particular architecture is a category where thorough changes took place, as we have already observed. We have not been able to unravel the functional difference (if there was one) between the postwall buildings and the mud slab buildings that occurred simultaneously during the initial occupation phase, but the former subsequently replaced the latter. Both types had ground plans of comparable sizes and occasionally floors laid with wooden boards. Also enigmatic is the advent of mudbrick building halfway through the settlement's lifetime ca. 5700 cal B.C.E. Long before its application in the eastern Marmara region, the molded and sun-dried mudbrick was a well-employed building material in southeast and central Anatolia. Because it is recommended for dry climates and less for the rainy lowlands of northwest Anatolia and eastern Thrace, this shift in construction mode may have been triggered by climatic change. Even a minor fluctuation in temperature and related rainfall could have influenced the way people built their houses, but unfortunately such slight oscillations are not perceptible in palaeo-environmental studies (Bottema and Woldring 1995). The simultaneous occurrence of mudbrick architecture at Menteşe would have strengthened the climatic shift argument, but the general use of this type of building mode could not be substantiated because of the limited excavations at that site. Consequently, this explanation remains hypothetical.

Perhaps another explanation may be more credible. At Aktopraklık and in contemporaneous settlements on the Aegean coast, for example, at Ulucak, the same sequence of building methods can be observed: a shift from postwall and/or *pisé* construction to mudbrick building (Derin 2005:85; Karul and Özeren 2007:20). As at Ilıpınar this probably happened at a time of expansion when sophisticated construction methods were required to meet the demand for better housing and a more adequate village plan. This demand could be met by mass production of standard building elements, namely, mudbricks, made possible by a greater availability of manpower.

The People

In the deepest layers of Ilıpınar's Big Square numerous human skeletons were exhumed. These belonged to the community of the first settlers (Phases X and IX), who were accustomed to burying their dead in the backyard of their houses; as a rule, they buried infants near the houses and adults at some distance. Together with the twenty individuals buried at Menteşe (Alpaslan Roodenberg 2001:7) the forty-eight from Ilıpınar constitute a valuable sample of the early sedentary population of west Anatolia. They were inhumed separately in single graves and are considered primary burials since the bones were still articulated when excavated.

The life expectancy of adults, who were primarily females, was almost equal for both sexes—between twenty-three and forty-three years; the average stature of females and males was 155 and 169 cm, respectively. Child mortality was high, especially the death rate of newborn babies (Alpaslan Roodenberg 2006:48). The contracted position was common practice for adults and children, who were found in oval grave pits. Some were laid in a strongly flexed position, from which we conclude that they were tightly wrapped up before rigor mortis occurred.

At Ilıpınar, there was a tendency to bury adult males and females on their right sides in a south–north orientation. Adult graves were between sixty and ninety centimeters deep, and in a few cases had wooden boards placed at the base of the grave, suggesting that the dead had been laid to rest on some sort of bier (figure 44.6). Funeral gifts such as pottery vessels or personal belongings including necklaces of stone beads and pendants occasionally accompanied the deceased.

Among the prehistoric villagers osteoarthritis and anemia were common diseases. Osteoarthritis was a general health problem, a disorder caused by hard labor and increasing age. At Ilıpınar this illness struck both sexes almost equally, whereas at Menteşe males especially suffered from it. Anemia, caused by iron deficiency, was particularly frequent among the children and adult females from Ilıpınar. It could be expected that a diet principally based on cereals may lead to iron deficiency, but there are indications that this was not the reason. In particular, the first settlers turned out to have consumed a diet in which meat was an important component. Moreover, the spring-fed marshy surroundings of the village make malaria a plausible cause of this illness since it would explain the high death rate of infants (Alpaslan Roodenberg 2008:49).

The people from both settlements constituted no exception to the bad dental health that is characteristic of prehistoric populations. Dental caries occurred from early childhood to old ages. In some cases caries were associated with severe abscess cavities. Food preparation methods play a role in the frequency of caries and dental attrition. Due to coarse food and abrasive residual from grinding tools, teeth showed strong wear, as could be expected. In addition, quite a few women (nearly half of the females of Ilıpınar and one from basal Menteşe) had grooves (sulci) at the back of their front teeth, which were probably the effect of holding fibers in their mouths during the process of weaving, twining, or basket making (Alpaslan Roodenberg

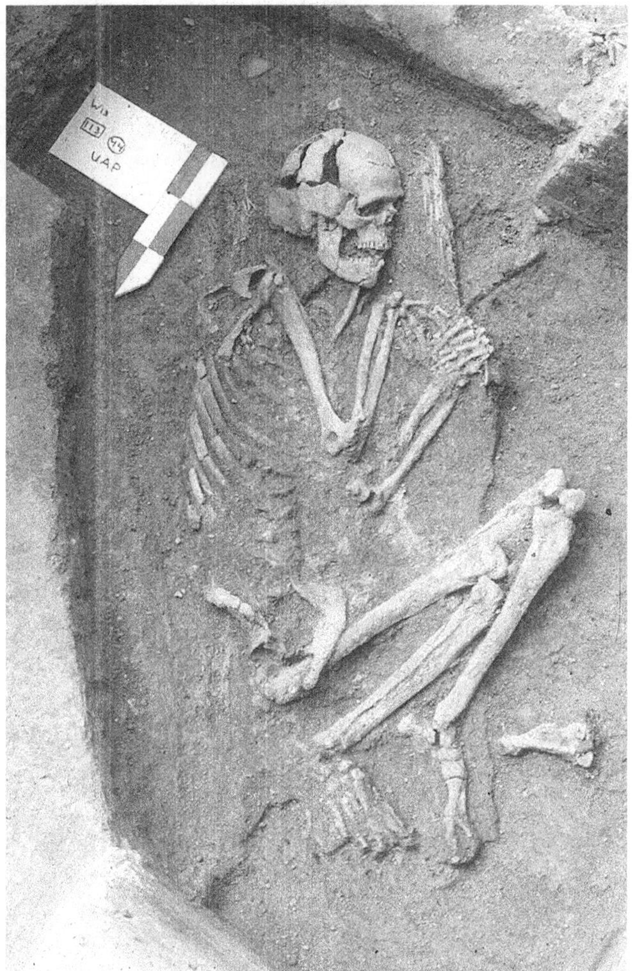

Figure 44.6. A male individual aged above forty buried on a wooden board (Phase X).

2008:44). These grooves were never found on male teeth, indicating that this activity was a women's job. Women with bad dental health and skeletal disorders were presumably physically unable to do such work, and therefore these grooves were not observed on individuals of this category. A few cases of arthritic changes were noticed. Among them a middle-aged female from Ilıpınar was apparently struck with a severe joint disease, causing her to be buried at the end of her life in a half-sitting position (Alpaslan Roodenberg 2008:42).

As already mentioned, the early inhabitants of Ilıpınar buried their dead in the backyard, but after the first 150 years this custom seems to have come to an abrupt end. It is true that in the phase following the initial occupation (Phase VIII) the village ground became rapidly built over, reducing the surface of open areas. Yet it is striking that no single burial was found in the successive occupation layers spanning 350 years until the village was finally deserted. Interestingly, Phase VIII can be linked to occupation levels at Yenikapı—a newly excavated contemporaneous settlement in Istanbul—on the basis of similarities in the pottery ranges from both sites. One large open bowl type from Yenikapı which was well represented at Yarımburgaz 4 (Özdoğan 1989:204) was used as a container for human cremation remains (personal observation); this type of bowl also occurs in Ilıpınar Phase VIII (Thissen 2001:139). Therefore, the question arises as to whether the sudden disappearance of burials from Phase VIII on could suggest the introduction of cremation in Ilıpınar as well.

In the framework of early farming development research, the Marmara region is often referred to as a zone of transition between Anatolia and the eastern Balkans (see Özdoğan, chapter 29 in this volume). As far as mortuary practices are concerned, the adherence to one or the other is not unequivocal. The relatively limited information we possess from the Balkans reveals that inhumation occurred below house floors as well as in open spaces (Bačvarov 2000:138). In contrast to the Balkans, burying members of the community in the houses where they probably had lived (as at Çatal Höyük [Farid 2007:291ff.; and see Hodder, chapter 43 in this volume]) or in specially arranged buildings (as at Çayönü [Erim-Özdoğan 2007:71; and see Rosenberg and Erim-Özdoğan, chapter 6 in this volume]) were often observed common practices in central Anatolia and further southeast.

Remarkable is the frequency of burial discoveries in Anatolian settlements of the seventh and sixth millennia B.C.E., which contrasts with the poor records of the early Neolithic period in the Balkans. In this respect, the Anatolian tradition is fully represented in the eastern Marmara region, of which a recently discovered burial ground with dozens of graves at Aktopraklık near Bursa constitutes a new example (Karul 2007).

The Ceramic Assemblages and Material Culture

The pottery of sixth millennium B.C.E. ılıpınar is handmade and displays a steady transformation during the 600 years of occupation (Thissen 2001, 2008). After an initial use of chaff-tempered clay for globular pots and bowls, often with oval mouths (Phase X), grit-tempered pots with S-shape profiles and plain rim restricted bowls become dominant until Phase VI. Particular to this period are handles, triangular or crescent-shaped, horizontally fixed to the pots. Tones are gray to dark brown, and surfaces were burnished. During Phases VIII–VII nail impressions and incised geometric patterns served as surface decoration. With the introduction of mudbrick architecture (Phase VI) vessels change in shape and decoration; squat pots, often with simple excised grooves on the shoulders, constitute an important component of the well-preserved inventories of the boundary buildings; other types include carinated open bowls or dishes, also with groove ornaments.

The end of the Neolithic–Early Chalcolithic occupation, characterized by semi-permanent dwellings (Phase VB), demonstrates a new kind of pottery added to the large storage vessels manufactured in the tradition of the preceding period: pots with pumpkin-like bodies surmounted by tall necks. These pots, in tones from brown to anthracite, have shiny and rippled surfaces resulting from intensive burnishing.

Interregional Links

As a result of two decades of archaeological investigations an outline emerges from the beginnings of sedentarization in the lowland areas east of the Sea of Marmara. The features are still roughly sketched and many questions remain unanswered, but excavations have demonstrated that halfway through the seventh millennium B.C.E. this region was already being exploited by farmers who were in search of new land. These pioneers introduced a fully developed farming economy and settled near springs, water courses, and lake shores. Their subsistence was a mixed one of animal breeding and crop cultivation, with emphasis on one or the other component depending on local circumstances. The aforementioned study by Evershed et al. (2008) on the residue of lipids in pottery point in particular to the Marmara region, where milking played a dominant role. Simultaneously, the occurrence of grooves in the front teeth of women from Ilıpınar and Menteşe are clues for spinning and weaving of wool (and flax)[2] as part of the home industry. These secondary products of husbandry prove that animals were no longer kept solely for their meat supply but also served to reinforce the community's well-being.

The early occupation horizons from Ilıpınar and Menteşe, and also from Barcın, are assumed to be part of a larger socioeconomic context to which belong settlements along the north coast of the Marmara Sea, namely, Pendik, Fikirtepe, and also Yenikapı in Istanbul. This so-called Fikirtepe culture comprises a number of material traits which are best recognized in the domestic inventories, including pottery, and bone and stone tools; with the exception of Ilıpınar, Fikirtepe residential patterns and burial treatment remain insufficiently explored. The different subsistence components varied from village to village and apparently depended on the potentials offered by the local environment, as is illustrated by the coastal site of Fikirtepe where the diet consisted of a significant amount of seafood (Boessneck and von den Driesch 1979). Coastal settlements west of İstanbul and in Turkish Thrace adhere to a different cultural province where not only the pottery but also the flint industry show a more pronounced Balkanic identity (Gatsov 2008:243) which is embodied by the Karanovo culture (see Özdoğan, chapter 29 in this volume, for further discussion).

However, in farming communities of this supraregion that encloses various areas of west Anatolia such as the Aegean coast, the northern and eastern Marmara region,[3] and on a more general level also Turkish Thrace, a number of common characteristics are recognizable: (1) an accomplished exploitation of all major food plants and animals, the latter also for their secondary products, coupled with an insignificant role of hunting; (2) an elaborated bone industry next to an impoverished—compared to central and eastern Anatolia—chipped stone industry where arrowheads are quasi-absent; and (3) construction methods and village layout.

This specific Neolithic model seems to have developed in the lower regions of western Anatolia, where climatic conditions more suitable for an intensive form of agriculture than those on the plateau dominated. The genesis of this model is not yet clarified, but its nature is distinct in various aspects from the east and central Anatolian clusters of farming communities, where a sophisticated chipped flint and obsidian industry, and a comprehensive tool range of projectile points (arrows and spearheads), allowed for regular hunting based strategies (Todd 1976:82 ff.). The latter stage of Neolithisation, roughly coinciding with the aceramic Neolithic of the second half of the ninth and the eighth millennia B.C.E., was based on a more incipient and experimental level of food production when hunting and foraging were indispensable for supplemental nourishment (Özdoğan 2005:16).

The west Anatolian Neolithic was exported to the European continent, possibly initially to Thessaly where the oldest settlements are dated to the second half of the seventh millennium B.C.E. (Thissen 2005:33). It is often assumed that the donor region for the Neolithisation of mainland Greece was the Aegean coast, where a growing number of settlements is being investigated that were founded halfway through the seventh millennium B.C.E., with some even earlier. On the other hand, the Marmara region, inhabited by contemporary farming communities and with a closely comparable cultural identity, certainly influenced early farming developments in the adjacent European zone.[4] At least during the later centuries (from 5700 B.C.E. on), Ilıpınar shared elements in its material culture, such as standing female figurines and specific pottery styles, with the eastern Balkans. As for innovation in architecture, western Anatolia with Ilıpınar as the best example was a zone where experiments took place with different construction materials and methods. Here the postwall or timber building had its origin before it followed its way along the Danube valley to the plains of northwest Europe.

Conclusion

The foregoing account outlined the beginning and development of agricultural settlement in the lowlands east of the Sea of Marmara by means of investigations at Ilıpınar and two contemporary sites. Sedentary life, based on factual evidence, can be traced from the mid-seventh millennium B.C.E. onward and continues without interruption until half way through the sixth millennium B.C.E. The material culture was subject both to gradual shifts (pottery assemblage) and drastic changes (architecture), but a long series of radiocarbon dates allows us to conclude that there was no discontinuity in the five to six centuries of initial occupation at Ilıpınar. In this respect it is best to avoid the term "Early Chalcolithic" for the first half of the sixth millennium B.C.E. This denomination is not only an empty shell because copper as a medium for the manufacture of objects was then quasi nonexistent, but more important, the centuries following the start of the sixth millennium B.C.E. do not differ from the preceding (Late) Neolithic in a sociocultural and economic sense (Sagona and Zimansky 2009:124).

This period of developed farming communities came to an end around 5500–5400 B.C.E.—an event that was not limited to the eastern Marmara region but apparently spread throughout Anatolia. At Ilıpınar this desertion was marked by a short stage of seasonal occupation and was linked with the appearance of a new pottery type—a dark burnished ware characterized by rippled surfaces in shapes of tall-necked vases and open bowls that are well known as a roughly contemporary occurrence with different parts of the Balkans. Whether the sudden appearance of this pottery was somehow linked to the abandonment of Neolithic–Early Chalcolithic settlements in various zones of the peninsula is an issue that remains beyond the scope of this chapter.

NOTES

1. Since 2007 Barcın has been excavated by Fokke Gerritsen, director of the NIT, and his team.
2. Flax was cultivated at Ilıpınar (Cappers 2008:128). Pieces of woven fabric were found in Phase X.
3. On the basis of pottery typology, a few sites in the Eskişehir-Kütahya region show affinities with the Marmara group (Efe 2000:172). Lack of data on settlement structure and economy make further comparison difficult.
4. There is growing evidence of Neolithisation in (north)eastern Bulgaria starting in the second half of the seventh millennium B.C.E., which was possibly established through links with Turkish Thrace and the Marmara region.

REFERENCES

Alpaslan Roodenberg, Songül. 2001. Newly Found Human Remains from Menteşe in the Yenişehir Plain: The Season of 2000. *Anatolica* 27: 1–14.

———. 2006. Death in Neolithic Ilıpınar. In *Aegean-Marmara-Black Sea: Present State of the Research on the Early Neolithic*, ed. Ivan Gatsov and Heiner Schwarzberg, 47–57. Langenweisbach: Beier and Beran.

———. 2008. The Neolithic Cemetery. The Anthropological View. In *Life and Death in a Prehistoric Settlement in Northwest Anatolia. The Ilıpınar Excavations, vol.* 3, ed. Jacob Roodenberg and Songül Alpaslan Roodenberg, 35–68. Pihans 110. Leiden: Netherlands Institute for the Near East.

Bačvarov, Krum. 2000. The Karanovo Neolithic Mortuary Practices in Their Balkan and Anatolian Context. In *Karanovo. Beiträge zum Neolithikum in Südosteuropa*, vol. 3, ed. Stefan Hiller und Vassil Nikolov, 137–40. Wien: Phoibos Verlag.

Boessneck, Joachim A. and Angela von den Driesch. 1979. *Die Tierknochenfunde aus der neolithischen Siedlung auf den Fikirtepe bei Kadikoy am Marmarameer*. München: Institut für Palaeoanatomie, Domestikationsforschung und Geschichte der Tiermedizin der Universität München.

Bottema, Sytze and H. Woldring. 1995. The Prehistoric Environment of the Lake İznik Area; A Palynological Study. In *The Ilıpınar Excavations I. Five Seasons of Fieldwork in NW Anatolia, 1987–91*, ed. Jacob Roodenberg, 8–16. Pihans 72. Leiden: Netherlands Institute for the Near East.

Buitenhuis, Hijlke. 2008. Faunal Remains from the Late Neolithic and Early Chalcolithic Levels. In *Life and Death in a Prehistoric Settlement in Northwest Anatolia. The Ilıpınar Excavations, vol. 3*, ed. Jacob Roodenberg and Songül Alpaslan Roodenberg, 105–26. Pihans 110. Leiden: Netherlands Institute for the Near East.

Cappers, René. 2008. Plant Remains from the Late Neolithic and Early Chalcolithic Levels. In *Life and Death in a Prehistoric Settlement in Northwest Anatolia. The Ilıpınar Excavations, vol. 3*, ed. Jacob Roodenberg and Songül Alpaslan Roodenberg, 117–48. Pihans 110. Leiden: Netherlands Institute for the Near East.

Claasz Coockson, Ben. 2008. The Houses from Ilıpınar X and VI Compared. In *Life and Death in a Prehistoric Settlement in Northwest Anatolia. The Ilıpınar Excavations, vol. 3*, ed. Jacob Roodenberg and Songül Alpaslan Roodenberg, 149–204. Pihans 110. Leiden: Netherlands Institute for the Near East.

Derin, Zafer. 2005. The Neolithic Architecture of Ulucak Höyük. In *How Did Farming Reach Europe? Anatolian-European Relations from the Second Half of the 7th through the First Half of the 6th Millennium cal BC*. ed. Clemens Lichter, 85–94. BYZAS 2. İstanbul: Ege Yayınları.

Duru, Refik. 2008. *From 8000 B.C.E. to 2000 B.C.E. Six Thousand Years of the Burdur-Antalya Region*. Antalya: Suna-İnan Kıraç Akdeniz Medeniyetleri Araştırma Enstitüsü.

Efe, Turan. 2000. Recent Investigations in Inland Northwestern Anatolia and its Contribution to Early Balkan-Anatolian Connections. In *Karanovo. Beiträge zum Neolithikum in Südosteuropa*, vol. 3, ed. Stefan Hiller and Vassil Nikolov, 171–83. Wien: Phoibos Verlag.

Erim Özdoğan, Aslı. 2007. Çayönü. In *Türkiye'de Neolitik Dönem*, ed. Mehmet Özdoğan and Nezih Başgelen, 57–98. İstanbul: Arkeoloji ve Sanat Yayınları.

Evershed, Richard P., Sebastian Payne, Andrew G. Sherratt, Mark S. Copley, Jennifer Coolidge, Duska Urem-Kotsu, Kostas Kotsakis, Mehmet Özdoğan, Aslı E. Özdoğan, Olivier Nieuwenhuyse, Peter M.M.G. Akkermans, Douglass Bailey, Radian-Romus Andeescu, Stuart Campbell, Shahina Farid, Ian Hodder, Nurcan Yalman, Mihriban Özbaşaran, Erhan Bıçakcı, Yossef Garfinkel, Thomas Levy, and Margie M. Burton. 2008. Earliest Date for Milk Use in the Near East and Southeastern Europe Linked to Cattle Herding. *Nature* 455.7212: 528–31.

Farid, Shahina. 2007. Level VII. In *Excavating Çatalhöyük. South, North and KOPAL Area Reports from the 1995–99 Seasons*, ed. Ian Hodder, 283–330. Çatalhöyük Research Project vol. 3. BIAA Monograph no. 37. Cambridge: McDonald Institute for Archaeological Research.

Gatsov, Ivan. 2008. Chipped Stone Assemblages from Ilıpınar. Part I: A Techno-Typological study. In *Life and Death in a Prehistoric Settlement in Northwest Anatolia. The Ilıpınar Excavations, vol. 3*, ed. Jacob Roodenberg and Songül Alpaslan Roodenberg, 227–67. Pihans 110. Leiden: Netherlands Institute for the Near East.

Hodder, Ian. 2007. *Excavating Çatalhöyük. South, North and KOPAL Area reports from the 1995–99 seasons*. Çatalhöyük Research Project vol. 3. BIAA Monograph no. 37. Cambridge: McDonald Institute for Archaeological Research.

Karul, Necmi and Öcal Özeren. 2007. Aktopraklık Höyüğü 2006 Yılı Kazı Sonuçları. *Haberler* 23: 19–20.

Özdoğan, Mehmet. 1989. Neolithic Cultures of Northwestern Turkey. A General Appraisal of the Evidence and Some Considerations. In *Neolithic of Southeastern Europe and its Near Eastern Connections*, ed. Sándor Bököny, 201–15. Budapest: Varia Archaeologica Hungarica II.

———. 2005. The Expansion of the Neolithic Way of Life: What We Know and What We Do Not Know. In *How Did Farming Reach Europe? Anatolian-European Relations from the Second Half of the 7th through the First Half of the 6th Millennium cal BC. Byzas* 2, ed. Clemens Lichter, 13–27. İstanbul: Ege Yayınları.

Roodenberg, Jacob. 2001. Miscellaneous. In *The Ilıpınar Excavations II*, ed. J. J. Roodenberg and L. C. Thissen, 223–256. Pihans 93. Leiden: Netherlands Instute for the Near East.

———. 2008a. Stratigraphy and Architecture. The Basal Occupation Levels (Phases X and IX). In *Life and Death in a Prehistoric Settlement in Northwest Anatolia. The Ilıpınar Excavations, vol.* 3, ed. Jacob Roodenberg and Songül Alpaslan Roodenberg, 1–34. Pihans 110. Leiden: Netherlands Institute for the Near East.

———. 2008b. The Inhabitants. In *Life and Death in a Prehistoric Settlement in Northwest Anatolia. The Ilıpınar Excavations, vol.* 3, ed. Jacob Roodenberg and Songül Alpaslan Roodenberg, 69–90. Pihans 110. Leiden: Netherlands Institute for the Near East.

Roodenberg, Jacob, Abram van As, Lou Jacobs, and Marie-Hélène Wijnen. 2003. Early Settlement in the Plain of Yenişehir (NW Anatolia). The Basal Occupation Layers at Menteşe. *Anatolica* 29: 17–59.

Roodenberg, Jacob, Abrahm van As and Songül Alpaslan-Roodenberg, 2008. Barcın Hüyük in the Plain of Yenişehir (2005–2006). A Preliminary Note on the Fieldwork, Pottery and Human Remains of the Prehistoric Levels. *Anatolica* 34: 53–66.

Sagona, Antonio and Paul Zimansky. 2009. *Ancient Turkey*. London: Routledge.

Thissen, Laurens C. 2001. The Pottery of Ilıpınar, Phases X to VA. In *The Ilıpınar Excavations II*, ed. Jacob Roodenberg and Laurens C. Thissen, 3–154. Pihans 60. Leiden: Netherlands Institute for the Near East.

———. 2005. Coming to Grips with the Aegean in Prehistory: An Outline of the Temporal Framework, 10,000–5500 cal. B.C.E. In *How Did Farming Reach Europe? Anatolian-European Relations from the Second Half of the 7th through the First Half of the 6th Millennium cal BC. Byzas* 2, ed. Clemens Lichter, 29–40. İstanbul: Ege Yayınları.

———. 2008. The Pottery of Phase VB. In *Life and Death in a Prehistoric Settlement in Northwest Anatolia. The Ilıpınar Excavations, vol.* 3, ed. Jacob Roodenberg and Songül Alpaslan Roodenberg, 91–116. Pihans 110. Leiden: Netherlands Institute for the Near East.

Todd, Ian A. 1976. *Çatal Hüyük in Perspective*. Menlo Park, Calif.: Cummings.

CHAPTER 45

ARSLANTEPE-MALATYA: A PREHISTORIC AND EARLY HISTORIC CENTER IN EASTERN ANATOLIA

MARCELLA FRANGIPANE

Arslantepe is a tell about 4.5 hectares in extension and 30 meters high, at the heart of the fertile Malatya Plain, some 12 kilometers from the right bank of the Euphrates, and surrounded by mountains, which, in the past, were covered by forests (Bökönyi 1993; Sadori, Susanna, and Balossi Restelli 2008) (figure 45.1). The long sequence of the site covers several millennia, from at least the sixth millennium cal B.C.E. until the final destruction of the Neo-Hittite town—Malitiya according to Hittite sources, Melid, Meliddu, or Meliteya in Neo-Assyrian and Urartian sources (Hawkins 1993)—by Sargon II of Assyria in 712 B.C.E. There may also have been a short period of occupation in the Neo-Assyrian age, immediately after the conquest, evidenced by the discovery of three fragments of Sargonid clay cylinders (Castellino 1975; Delaporte 1939; Frame 2004, 2009) and some architectural ruins. The remains of an imposing building, excavated by Delaporte (1940:pl. XI) and recently reexcavated by an Italian team, appeared to overlap the Neo-Hittite buildings on the western side of the Lions Gate and might be dated to the Neo-Assyrian period (Liverani 2009). The site was reoccupied in the late Roman age after a period of abandonment and subsequently used as a cemetery in the Byzantine/Medieval period.

Although small in comparison with Syro-Mesopotamian sites, Arslantepe is nevertheless the largest in the Malatya Plain and was always the dominant center in its region. Its long history, which has been largely brought to light over more than

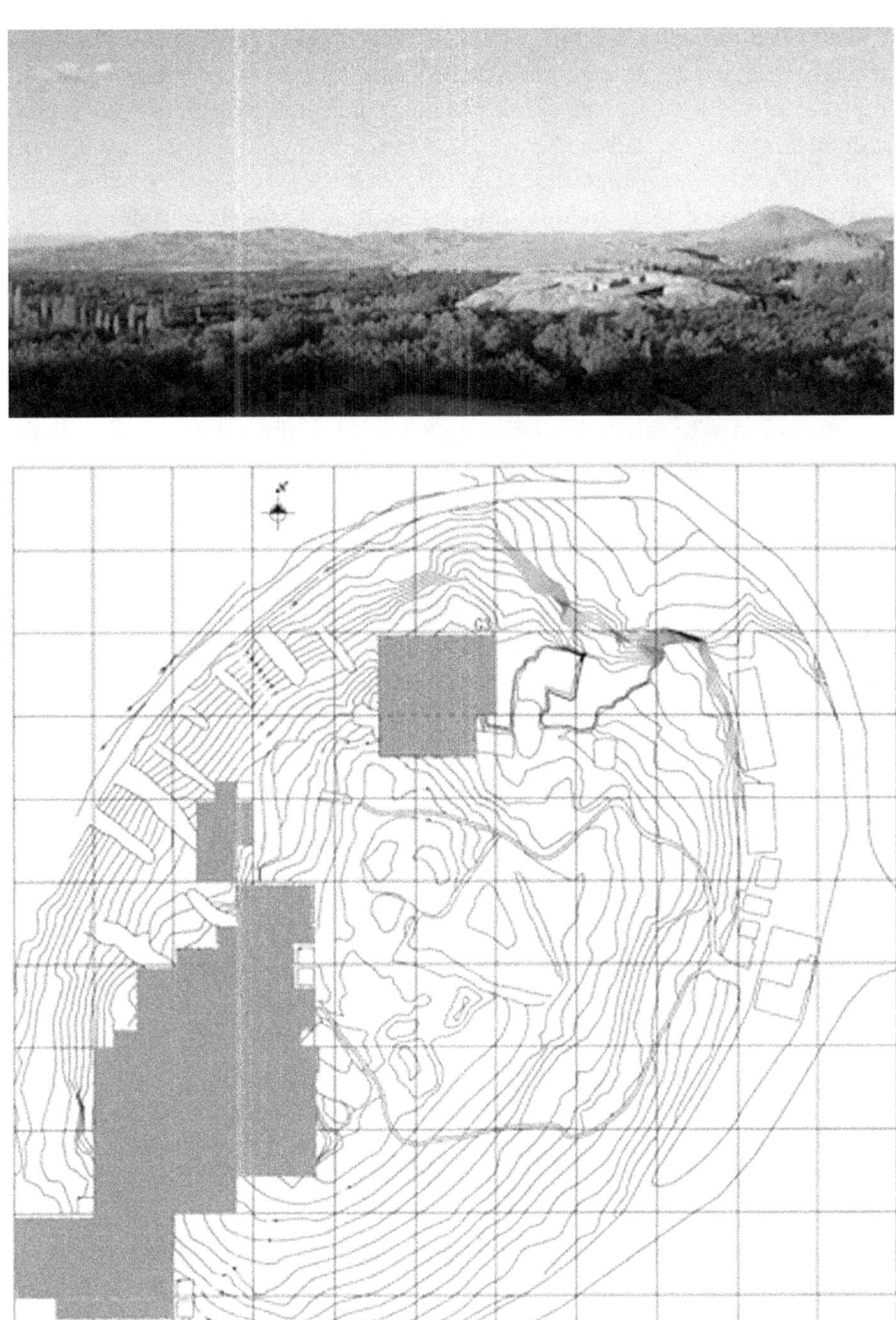

Figure 45.1. The mound of Arslantepe and the excavated areas.

forty-five years of excavations by the Italian Archaeological Mission of the Sapienza University of Rome, very clearly reflects the history of the whole area as well as the complex events that marked its developments and changing relations with various and different civilizations of the Near East. In the earliest phases of its history, in the Chalcolithic period, Arslantepe had close links with the Syro-Mesopotamian world with which it shared many cultural features, structural models, and development trajectories. But in the early centuries of the third millennium B.C.E., far-reaching changes took place in the site which halted the development of the Mesopotamian-type centralized system and reoriented Arslantepe's external relations toward eastern Anatolia and Transcaucasia (see Sagona, chapter 30; Palumbi, chapter 9; Marro, chapter 12; and Khatchadourian, chapter 20 in this volume). A further radical change occurred in the second millennium B.C.E., when the site interacted with the rising Hittite civilization, which exerted a strong influence on it. Relations with central Anatolia had already been established in the late phases of the Late Chalcolithic, even though they are still ill-defined and unclear. But it was with the Late Bronze I and, more evidently, Late Bronze II that the expanding Hittite state, which expanded as far as the banks of the Euphrates, imposed its cultural and political domination over the populations in the Malatya region, heralding another important stage in the history of Arslantepe (Frangipane 1993c; Hawkins 1993:35).

History of Research

Excavations began in the 1930s, conducted by a French mission headed by Delaporte. By investigating the upper part of the mound, Delaporte unearthed the remains of remarkable Iron Age buildings, among which are the so-called Neo-Assyrian palace (end of eighth–beginning of seventh century B.C.E.) and the well-known Lions Gate (ninth–eighth centuries B.C.E.) (Delaporte 1939, 1940). The gate was flanked on either side by lion statues carved from stone blocks with high relief bodies and round heads, which probably gave the name to the site (Arslan Tepe, namely, "Lion Hill"); its walls were lined with stone slabs decorated with bas-reliefs, whose iconography and style were typical of the Neo-Hittite kingdoms' art (Delaporte 1940). Inside the gate was a great royal statue that had been felled and probably intentionally concealed.[1] World War II put an end to the work of the Delaporte expedition, and after a short and rather fruitless resumption of excavations in 1949–51 by C. Schaeffer, the French activity at the site came to an end.

In 1961 a new Italian archaeological project began at Arslantepe, originally under P. Meriggi and S. Puglisi and soon after under the latter alone (Puglisi and Meriggi 1964), which is still operating at the site and has since become one of the major archaeological projects of La Sapienza University of Rome. After Puglisi, the excavations were taken over by Alba Palmieri and continue under the present author's direction. The Italian mission started investigating the same northeast zone where the French had previously worked, identifying the stratigraphic sequence along the northern edge of the mound. There, a number of building levels dating back to the first and second millennia B.C.E.—Neo-Hittite (Iron Age), Imperial Hittite (Late Bronze II), and Early Hittite (Late Bronze I) periods (Palmieri 1978; Pecorella 1975)—have been brought to light above insubstantial Early Bronze layers with scanty architectural remains and a series of seven building levels with domestic structures from the Late Chalcolithic 3–4,[2] built on virgin soil (Palmieri 1978:315–30). The sequence ended with the remains of a late Roman occupation (Equini Schneider 1970).

In the past thirty-five years research has focused on the prehistoric and protohistoric levels of Arslantepe, by operating in the W and SW zones of the mound, where the earliest settlements made up the original nucleus of the tell. There, a long and detailed sequence of Late Chalcolithic, Early Bronze, and Middle Bronze levels, from the end of the fifth to the beginning of the second millennium cal B.C.E., has been investigated over vast areas (Frangipane 1993b, 1993c, 1996; Frangipane and Palmieri 1983; Palmieri 1973, 1981), supported by about 100 ^{14}C dates (Di Nocera 2000a, 2000b).

Only recently, in 2008, were excavations in the northeast zone resumed using modern research methodologies. These are intended to investigate the important phases in the late history of the site, between the Hittite "conquest" of the region, the subsequent dismantling of the imperial system, and the formation of the Neo-Hittite kingdom of Malatya (Liverani 2009).

The Late Chalcolithic Period at Arslantepe

Recent Research in Post-Ubaid Phases: Arslantepe Period VIII

Though the presence of Halaf and Ubaid sherds found out of context in a recently opened excavation area on the lower western slope of the mound indicates that Arslantepe was certainly occupied as early as the sixth millennium B.C.E., the earliest excavated evidence so far well documented dates back to the end of the fifth millennium B.C.E.: Arslantepe Period VIII/Late Chalcolithic 1–2 (4300–3900 cal B.C.E.). This period is represented by three superimposed building levels, which comprise domestic structures full of equipment for cooking food (numerous ovens, some very large, inside and outside the dwellings). The pottery recovered in these levels belongs to a local repertoire connected with areas of southeastern Turkey west of the Euphrates, for example, Oylum Höyük (Özgen et al. 1999). Nevertheless, in general terms, the assemblage forms part of a wider typically post-Ubaid ceramic horizon that links the various areas of Upper Mesopotamia and eastern Anatolia in the initial phase of the Late Chalcolithic (LC 1–2) (Balossi Restelli 2008).

The Background to Centralization. The Emergence of the Élites and the Ideological-Religious Component: Arslantepe Period VII

In Period VII (Late Chalcolithic 3–4, 3800–3400 cal B.C.E.), the settlement, which has been investigated over wide areas, seems to have grown to cover the whole surface of the present mound and is characterized by a clear differentiation between functionally and symbolically diverse areas.

On the northeastern edge of the site, the excavations conducted in the 1960s and 1970s brought to light common mudbrick houses of rather small dimensions consisting of one to three rooms, in one case with a geometric painting on a house wall that featured alternating black and white triangles (Palmieri 1978). Once again, numerous ovens were found, mainly outside the dwellings, and burials underneath the floors or close to the houses with simple and poorly differentiated grave goods were also present. Adults were buried in a flexed position lying on one side, often with shell and bead ornaments; in only one instance was the body accompanied by a stone stamp seal, while in another case the body was resting on two large cooking pots and had a set of two bowls and one beaker at its feet (Frangipane 2007; Palmieri 1978). Small children and infants were buried in pots underneath the floors of the houses, continuing an older and very widespread tradition that was also documented in Arslantepe Period VIII.

In the higher part of the western area of the mound, toward the center of the settlement and on the top of the ancient hill, more recent excavations have conversely brought to light imposing large buildings with mudbrick walls over 1–1.20 m thick, covered with white plaster and often displaying paintings on the walls, belonging to several successive levels. The main and earlier construction phase so far excavated in this area consisted of a fairly monumental building with a large hall which, before being reused and subdivided into four smaller rooms, had wall paintings and four white-plastered mudbrick columns lining the walls (Frangipane 1993a) (figure 45.2). Though the paintings were part of a well-rooted tradition in the Upper Euphrates area, beginning at least in the late Ubaid period,[3] the monumental character of this building, its ground plan, its topographic location, and the material unearthed there suggest that like the superimposed buildings in the same zone, it was a residence for the élites.

Close by these residences, immediately south-southwest of them and near the western edge of the mound, excavations recently revealed a large and monumental tripartite ceremonial building (Temple C), which was isolated and built on a low platform made of huge stone slabs and mud layers (Frangipane 2000a, 2002, 2003). Whereas the tripartite floor plan, which was used only in this building at Arslantepe, and the presence of multiple recessed niches decorating the short sides of the

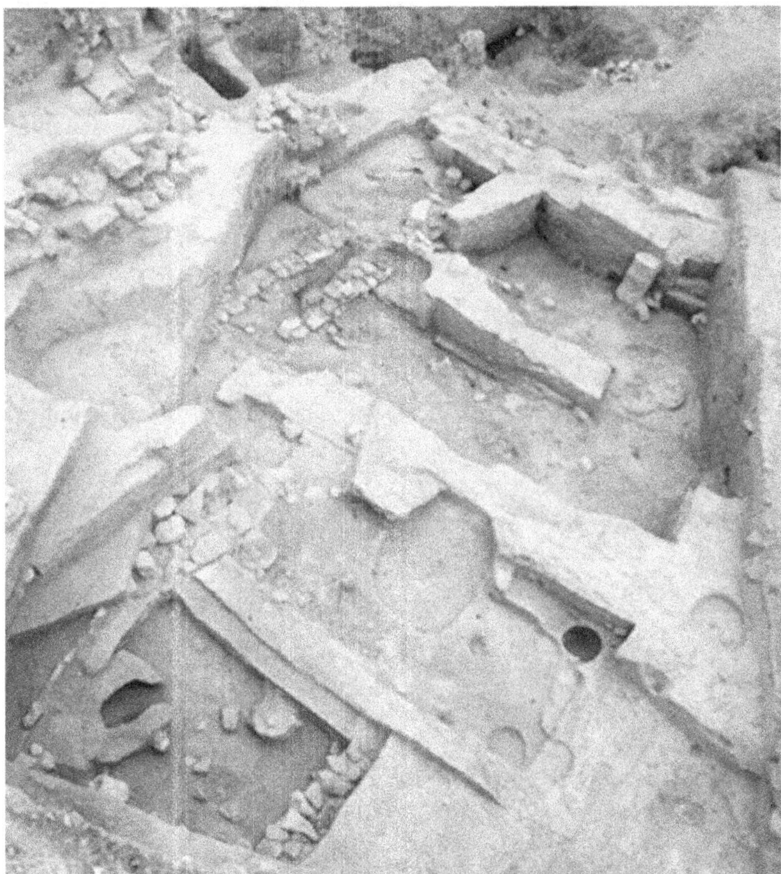

Figure 45.2. Arslantepe, Period VII (Late Chalcolithic 3–4). Élite residence (the so-called column building) on the upper part of the mound.

central room, are reminiscent of Mesopotamian architecture, there are also features of local, or at all events northern, traditions, such as the wall paintings in the northern niches of the main room and a particular construction technique using wooden beams laid horizontally under the floor, also attested at Tell Brak in Level 20 (LC 2) (Oates et al. 2007) (figure 45.3). This building belonged to the final construction phase of Period VII and was linked at the back to a set of long rooms with thick walls, perhaps for storing or manufacturing craft products.[4] The large central room of Temple C, measuring 18 × 7.20 m, contained a low and wide platform in a central position, where meals must have been distributed in a ritual context, as evidenced from the presence of a large number of mass-produced bowls (both flint-scraped and wheel-turned) found scattered on the floor. In the eastern side rooms (on the western side the rooms were almost entirely destroyed) huge quantities of mass-produced bowls were found piled up and overturned, partly still in situ, some of which had probably fallen from an upper storey; it appears they were ready to be used. In the southeastern room, there were also numerous *cretulae*[5] bearing seal impressions that were grouped roughly together and had probably fallen from an upper storey. The presence of cretulae and bowls in large quantities suggests that redistribution practices were performed in this ceremonial environment in connection with an initial process of centralizing goods and labor, which developed fully at Arslantepe at the end of the fourth millennium B.C.E.

Although the pottery from Period VII reflected the general trend toward mass production, evidenced by the use of chaff pastes, lack of decoration, and poor firing observed in the whole Late Chalcolithic Upper Mesopotamian environment, the shapes and the ceramic repertoire revealed a local cultural horizon typical of the Malatya Plain, linking both the VII and VIII periods with the regions to the west of the Euphrates and the ʿAmuq (Frangipane 1993a). Manufacture mainly featured the slow wheel and is similar for all types of pots, which seem to have been mass-produced by the same workshops. Potter's marks appeared, and may be interpreted as signs for recognizing the single potter's or workshop's products, which were then taken to common areas for drying or firing (Frangipane 1993a; Palmieri 1985; Trufelli 1994).

Centralization at the End of the Fourth Millennium B.C.E.: The Period VI A "Palace" Complex

Economic and political centralization reached its climax in the next period, VI A (Late Chalcolithic 5/Late Uruk, 3350–3000 B.C.E.). Temple C was abandoned, and to the south of it, along the southwestern slope of the mound, a huge and quite imposing architectural complex was built, made up of agglutinated monumental buildings standing on several terraces and linked by corridors and courtyards, where various public functions (religious/ceremonial, administrative, storage, reception) were performed (Frangipane 1997, 2004, 2010 Frangipane and Palmieri 1983) (figures 45.4 and 45.5). In the complex, there were two temples (A and B),

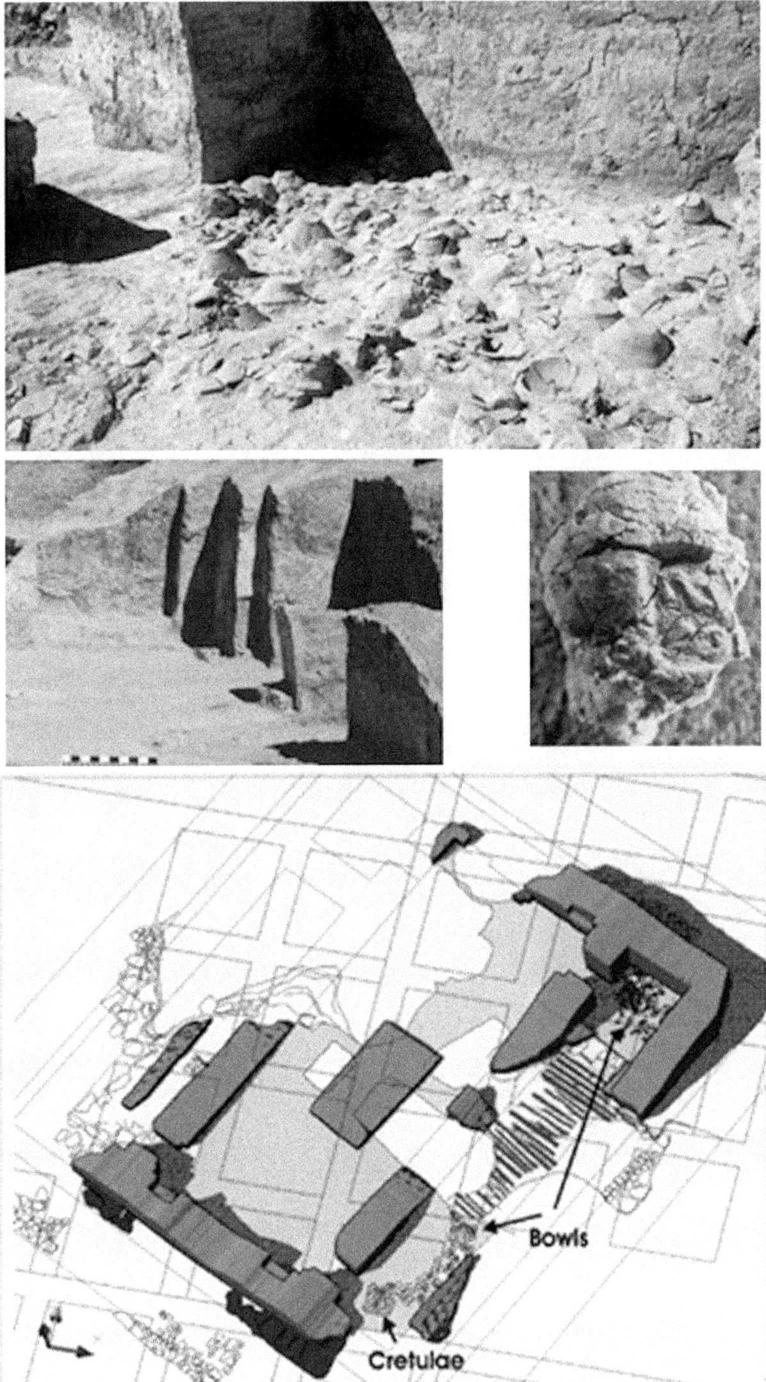

Figure 45.3. Arslantepe, Period VII (LC4). The ceremonial building (Temple C) with materials in situ. Top: bowls upside down on the floor of the northern side room; center left: niches on the northeastern corner of the large central room; center right: cretula from the southern side room; bottom: isometric plan of the building.

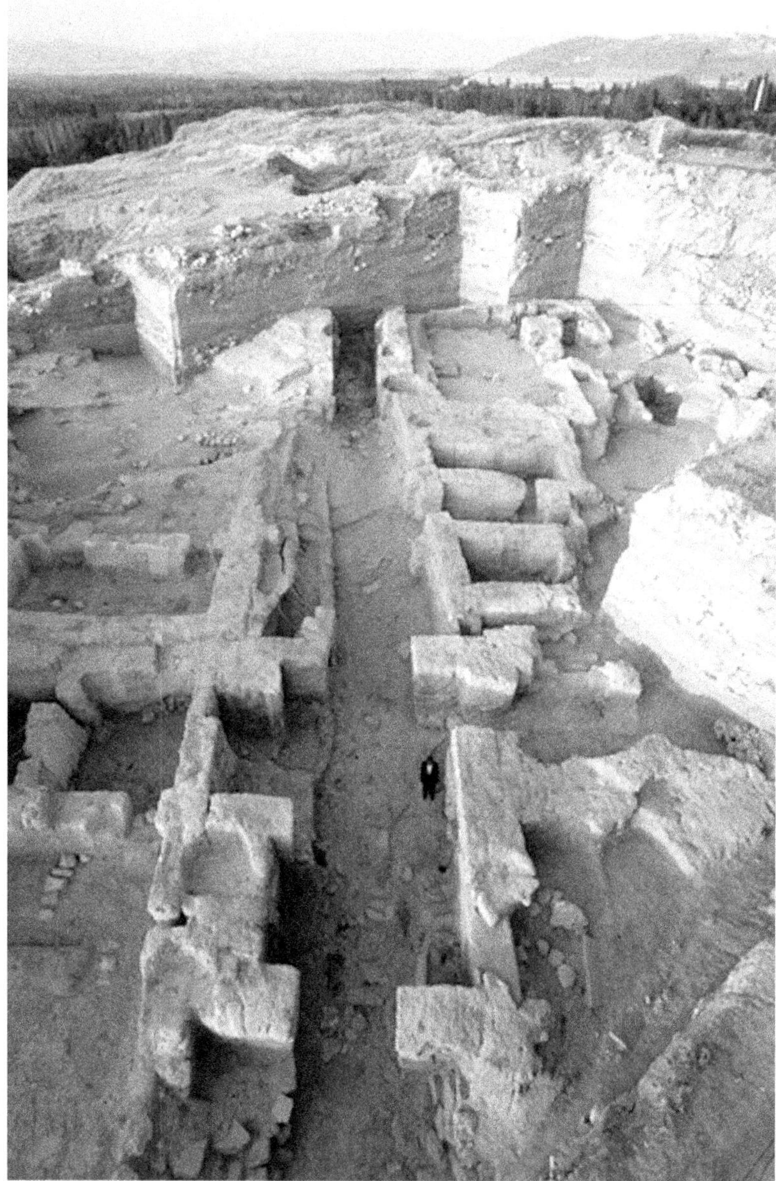

Figure 45.4. Arslantepe, Period VI A (Late Chalcolithic 5). The 4th millennium "palatial" complex.

whose importance was emphasized by the fact that they were built on the higher parts of the terraces. However, the religious aspect, though still important, seems to have decreased somewhat. This is demonstrated by the reduced size of the temples, which were much smaller than the older Temple C and only bipartite, as well as from the activities performed there, which seem to have been restricted to a limited number of persons. The main cult room had only a single entrance, restricting usage

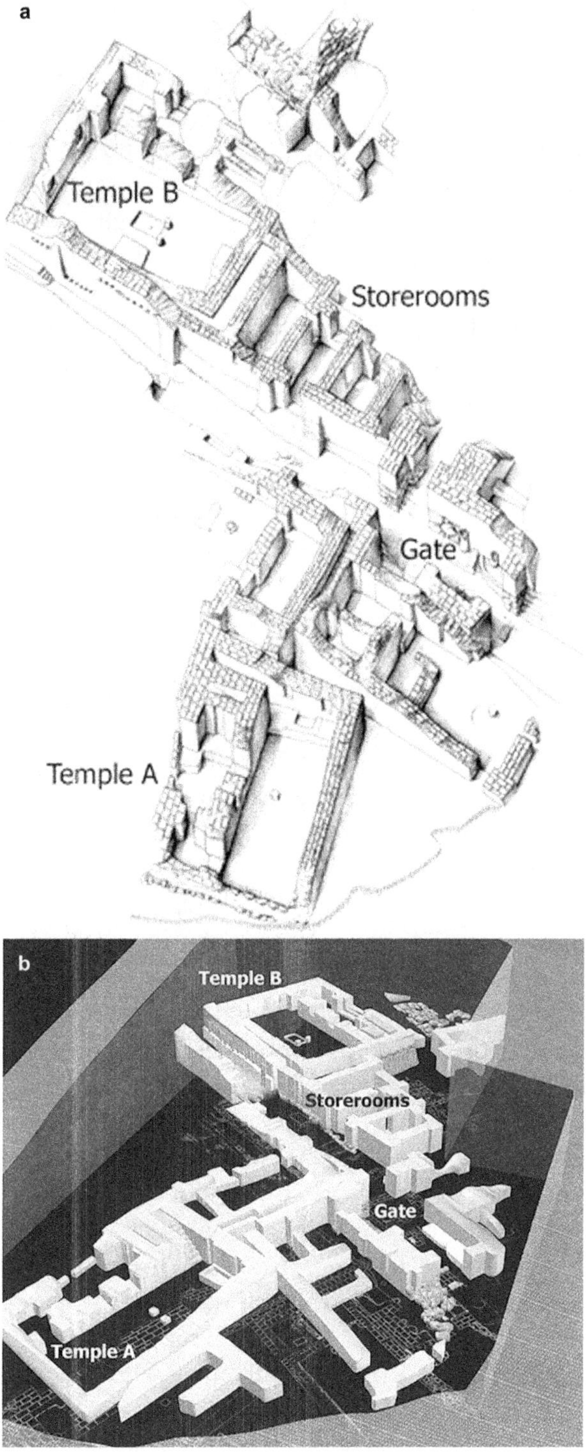

Figure 45.5. (a) Arslantepe, Period VI A (LC5). (b) Isometric views of the fourth millennium B.C.E. "Palace." (The 3D CAD drawing is by Corrado Alvaro.)

perhaps only to temple personnel; communication with the public most likely took place through two windows opening to the central side room. There was probably a less substantial redistribution of food from these two smaller temples as well. The Arslantepe VI A architectural complex on the whole therefore appears, rather than a single large temple complex, as perhaps the earliest known example of a public "palace-like" aggregation.[6]

The religious and power ideology merged with a complex administrative organization for the control of goods, particularly food, evidenced by stores containing dozens of large and medium-sized pots (pithoi and jars), together with a number of spouted bottles and small jars, indicating that different types of foods were stored there (D'Anna 2010). In the only storeroom complex so far brought to light there is an interesting and pronounced difference in the function of the two rooms mainly used for this purpose (the central room was more a passageway leading to the two others, in which goods were probably sorted). The larger northern room was full of large pots and was the main goods storage site; the smaller southern room contained only 3 pithoi, 2 large jars, and a few cooking pots, but there were hundreds of wheelmade mass-produced bowls, probably used for the distribution of meals or food rations, and 130 cretulae bearing seal impressions (Frangipane and Palmieri 1988–89; Frangipane et al. 2007). Some of the cretulae had fallen to the floor from the containers to which they had been attached, while others were piled up in a corner of the room, probably temporarily set aside; some more had probably fallen from a collapsed upper storey (Frangipane 1994; Frangipane et al. 2007).

In this southern room, which was perhaps supplied from the northern room, the stored foodstuffs were probably redistributed in the form of meals for the workers employed by the central élites (Frangipane 1994; Palmieri 1989).[7] The movement of goods was now controlled in an administrated and "secularized" form, independently of any of the religious or ceremonial practices that had characterized the earliest archaic forms of redistribution. Thousands of cretulae were found in the palace complex, some 2,200 still bearing the seal impression and the clear imprint of the sealed objects, with the impressions of over 200 different seals (Frangipane et al. 2007). The vast majority of these cretulae had been discarded in ordered groups in specific dumping places inside the palace, after being temporarily set aside and subsequently accounted (Ferioli and Fiandra 1983, 1994; Frangipane et al. 2007). The studies conducted on this vast amount of well-contextualized materials show that at Arslantepe there existed a highly sophisticated administrative system and hierarchically organized class of officials, who, through the sealing operations and the documentary value assigned to the cretulae, perfectly managed and temporarily recorded the economic transactions even in the absence of writing.

A significant role was also attributed to the wall paintings, which, in this case, were not only wall decorations but figurative motifs and actual scenes painted on the sides of doors and along the main corridor, sending ideologically important and highly meaningful messages to everyone entering the palace (figure 45.6). The best preserved of these paintings are two almost identical stylized anthropomorphic figures associated with powerfully symbolic elements on both sides of what had originally been the

Figure 45.6. Arslantepe, Period VI A (LC5). Wall paintings in the palatial complex.

door (subsequently walled in) leading from the access corridor to the internal courtyard of the palace, passing through the central room in the stores (Frangipane 1992). Even more complex and interesting is the depiction of a scene with a sort of cart (or plough?) drawn by two oxen and driven by a coachman, which seems to be moving in the direction leading out of the building, painted on the eastern wall of the inner corridor (Frangipane 2002, 2004).

The pottery was mostly wheelmade, fine, well fired, and pale in color, and was now strongly influenced by the Mesopotamian models of the Uruk culture, though retaining typically local features (Frangipane 1993b, 1997, 2002; Frangipane and Palmieri 1983). Mass production was restricted to conical wheelmade bowls, which were now mass-produced on the fast wheel. However, in addition to the wheelmade wares derived from the Syro-Mesopotamian Uruk world, a variety of other production styles characterized the Period VI A pottery. A type of handmade Red-Black Ware, which had appeared at the end of Period VII, now became established at Arslantepe; its shapes, aesthetic taste, and manufacturing techniques demonstrate connections with contemporary central Anatolian wares. Moreover, there is a clear-cut difference between all these pottery classes and the kitchenware, which appeared to have been handmade and produced in a nonspecialized environment.

The discovery of a group of arsenical copper weapons (nine swords, some decorated with silver inlay, and twelve spearheads) with a quadruple spiral plaque in a room in one of the buildings (III) together with an interesting arsenical copper door socket at the corner of a monumental entrance to another building, and various objects made of sophisticated alloys, demonstrate the high technological standards attained in metallurgy and, for the first time, the use of the sword (Frangipane and Palmieri 1983; Frangipane and A. M. Palmieri 1994–95; A. M. Palmieri, Sertok, and Chernykh 1993; A. M. Palmieri et al. 1999; Hauptmann et al. 2002; and see Muhly, chapter 39 in this volume).

In this period, Arslantepe probably had a major role as an intermediary center in the vast network of interregional relations involving the Syro-Mesopotamian communities and those living in the mountain areas of central-eastern and northeastern Anatolia (see Rothman, chapter 37 in this volume), while at all times retaining its marked autonomy. The development of a powerful system of centralized political and economic control[8] on a site that never actually became "urban" in any real sense of the term shows that whereas Arslantepe played an important and active part in the state formation process in connection with the Mesopotamian world, it also followed its own specific, and different, development pattern, which was less well entrenched than those of the highly urbanized environments (Frangipane 2009).

The Early Bronze Age

Crisis and Instability at the Beginning of the Third Millennium: Period VI B

A radical crisis overwhelmed the central institutions at the beginning of the third millennium B.C.E., leading to the collapse of the Mesopotamian-type centralized system, and changing the course of Arslantepe's history forever. Around 3000 B.C.E. a devastating fire completely destroyed the palace, putting an end to the early state organization of the Late Chalcolithic society. Relations with the southern areas and with Syro-Iraqi Jezirah were weakened, although close links remained for a short time (during Early Bronze I) with the rest of the Upper and Middle Euphrates Valley; at the same time relations were strengthened with the northeastern Anatolian and Transcaucasian world (Frangipane and Palumbi 2007; and see Sagona, chapter 30; Marro, chapter 12; and Palumbi, chapter 9 in this volume).

Two phases have been recognized at Arslantepe in Early Bronze I (3000–2800 cal B.C.E., Period VI B), providing evidence of instability, and probably conflicts, that are clearly shown by a complex sequence of events that occurred on the site for one or two centuries following the collapse of the palace system (Frangipane 2000b, 2004; Frangipane and Palmieri 1983).

In the first phase of the Early Bronze I period (VI B1) the areas previously occupied by the public and élite buildings were abandoned; seasonal settlements were built on their ruins probably by groups of transhumant pastoralists who may have previously been moving around the region, joining it to a vast system of relations with the eastern Anatolian and Transcaucasian world, with which they shared customs and cultural features (Frangipane, Di Nocera, and Palumbi 2005). They lived in subquadrangular huts with wattle and daub walls coated with mud, separated by wide open areas, often with rows of postholes that may have been post fences used for stabling livestock. The pottery used by these groups was exclusively handmade, red-black in color, and burnished. It was made using identical firing techniques and according to identical aesthetic standards (black was always used on the most visible surfaces of the pots[9]) to those of Late Chalcolithic Red-Black Ware, but new shapes were adopted that were reminiscent of the repertoire belonging to the Transcaucasian culture (Palumbi 2003, 2008, and see Palumbi, chapter 9 in this volume).

In the second phase of the Early Bronze I (period VI B2) there was a revival of the mudbrick construction traditions and the wheelmade light-colored pottery of Uruk origin. This shows both a continuation of the earlier typological features, such as the LC-derived necked jars with reserved slip decoration, and the appearance of a number of new shapes which produced a general change in the repertoire on the whole (Frangipane 2000b). A few odd fragments of these ceramics have also been found in the VI B1 hut levels, showing that in other areas of the site, or in the plain, the sedentary population had always continued to pursue their traditional way of life and had maintained their customs. Further evidence of the coexistence of the two groups and the two cultural horizons is the continuing presence, in the Period VI B2 pottery range, of the Red-Black Ware belonging to the Transcaucasian tradition, though with a restricted selection of shapes. To sum up, the VI B2 pottery horizon as a whole possessed both the Uruk-derived cultural features of the Middle and Upper Euphrates Valley and the new elements introduced into the northern areas of the Upper Euphrates from Transcaucasian and related cultures (Frangipane 1998).

In this period, new forms of power also seem to have been reestablished, perhaps readapting and regenerating in a new way the power of the former élites or as a result of the introduction of a new political system and new leadership. On the top of the mound a stout four-meter-thick mudbrick fortification wall, built on stone foundations with internal buttresses, surrounded the upper part of the settlement, whose features are yet to be identified, thereby separating it from the rest of the village like a kind of acropolis (Frangipane 2007). The village settled along the slope of the mound, outside the great wall, was comprised of small mudbrick dwellings (with one to three rooms), in which domestic activities clearly took place (Alvaro et al. 2008); floors were covered with many kilos of charred grains (mostly barley, but also wheat and pulses), which had probably fallen from upper floors, where the harvest had been stored before the fire destroyed the village. There were courtyards and open areas for activities performed in common, such as slaughtering livestock or working metals (smelting) (Palmieri et al. 1999; Palmieri and Morbidelli 2003).

It was probably to the beginning of this period that the so-called Royal Tomb (T1) belonged (figure 45.7): this is an imposing stone cist built at the bottom of a large irregular five-meter-wide pit, located on the edge of the village, outside the fortification wall. It contained an adult lying in a flexed position on its right side accompanied by a very rich assortment of grave goods, including vessels, personal ornaments made of cornelian, rock crystal, silver, and gold, together with a hoard of metal objects placed behind its back, comprising weapons, tools, and ornaments made of arsenical copper, copper-silver alloy, silver, and gold (Frangipane et al. 2001; Hauptmann et al. 2002; A. M. Palmieri, Hauptmann, and Hess 1998; and see Muhly, chapter 39 in this volume). On the top of the cist were the bodies of four adolescents, who had probably been sacrificed: two of them, a girl and probably a boy, lay on the top of the tombstone, wearing copper pins and a diadem and hair spirals made of copper-silver alloy, similar to the items found among the grave goods buried with the "lord" in the cist, which may indicate kinship or some other kind of close linkage with him. Two other individuals, again very young and both female, were found outside the area of the cist, in the zone of the foot of the dead lord, with no burial goods, and may have been servants.

The presence of this extraordinary burial, dated to 3000–2900 B.C.E., and the large fortification wall on the top of the mound, together with the disappearance of cult areas, cretulae, and mass-produced bowls, may indicate that a new type of power had been installed, focusing more on defense and on the political and military role of the chiefs rather than on their capacity to centralize resources and labor, as had been the case in the fourth millennium B.C.E. (Frangipane 2001).

New Developments in Early Bronze II and III: Periods VI C and VI D

Following the fire that also destroyed the Period VI B2 settlement, a new and more radical fracture occurred, marked by a temporary abandonment of the site before it slowly reemerged with wholly new cultural and political features. Between 2750 and 2500 B.C.E. (Early Bronze II, Arslantepe Period VI C) the site was first reoccupied by nomadic groups that perhaps settled there on a seasonal basis, leaving light structures behind, as in the earlier Period VI B1. This time, however, they built a few

Figure 45.7. Arslantepe, Period VI B (Early Bronze I). The "Royal Tomb."

scattered slightly sunken circular huts paved with mud and even rarer round well-plastered semi-subterranean houses, together with tiny pole structures, which may have been awnings or wooden roofs, and rubbish pits. It was only in a second phase in this period that a large terraced multiroomed building was erected on the upper part of the tell. It seems to be a sort of cluster of large quadrangular rooms fitted with new types of domestic equipment, such as mortars sunk into the floors, horse-shoe-shaped hearths, and articulated ovens with high cooking platforms and basins for ashes (Conti and Persiani 1993). This large isolated building, which also showed evidence of conservation and processing of agricultural products (Sadori, Susanna, and Persiani 2006), may have housed an extended family or kinship group. All around this building, nomadic people continued to use the site, perhaps seasonally.

All the pottery was handmade, and comprised two main classes of production. A black or dark burnished ware originated from the red-black pottery belonging to the Transcaucasian tradition but this time using new shapes with new typological traits, such as large-mouthed jars with thickened square rims (the so-called rail-rim). The second class was a light buff ware, painted with red or brown linear geometric motifs in a very distinctive local style (Gelincik ware) (Conti and Persiani 1993; Palmieri 1967).

The shape of the houses, the domestic equipment, and pottery all show a radical cultural change in a period characterized by the fragmentation of groups and pronounced provincialism (see also Ökse, chapter 11 in this volume, on regionalization in the southeast). Arslantepe may have remained as a benchmark site in the narrow territory of the Malatya Plain, but it no longer dominated it. From that moment onward the history of the site and of the region was completely separated from the history of the Syro-Mesopotamian areas and that of the southernmost region of the Middle/Upper Euphrates Valley; it now began to gravitate toward the eastern Anatolian world.

During the Early Bronze III (Period VI D, 2500–2000 B.C.E.), settlement gradually spread to occupy the slope of the mound with increasing planning and density, and provision was made for roads, channels, courtyards, and craft workshops (Conti and Persiani 1993; Frangipane 2001b, 2004:145–55; Palmieri 1973). At the beginning of this period the groups with semi-subterranean round houses continued to frequent the site, mainly settling in free spaces or on the ruins of abandoned houses, but they gradually disappeared as the densely built-up settlement expanded to cover the whole of the mound. The Early Bronze III settlements slightly changed across time as the houses and the quarters were continually refurbished and rebuilt, but there were no more massive widespread episodes of destruction. Arslantepe once again became the largest and most important center in the Malatya Plain, even though there is no clear evidence of any new political centralization. Indeed, the evidence suggests that the organization was based on small autonomous centers, increasing in number in the plain and on the surrounding hills (Di Nocera 2005, 2008). This new organization was perhaps connected with new defense requirements, now affecting the whole of the settlement, shown by the construction of a huge fortification wall, with a stout semicircular bastion, on the edge of the mound (Frangipane 1993b:90–92, 2004:146–49).

The pottery, which was still handmade, very closely followed the tradition of the previous period, keeping the two main classes, black burnished and painted, and developing a number of typological traits, which became well characterized and fully established in this period. A much more dense, complex, and standardized style of painting emerged, closely related to similar items produced in the province of Elazığ, which may have been the work of specialized craftsmen who distributed their products throughout the whole area. The discovery of a metallurgist workshop with numerous moulds confirms that the craftsmanship was highly specialized.

From Middle Bronze to the Iron Age (Periods V–III): New Developments Under the Hittite "Domination" and the End of Arslantepe

Most of the evidence from the Middle Bronze Age (period V A, 2000–1750 B.C.E.) has been found in the southwestern area of the mound, exhibiting very close continuity in terms of the architecture and material culture with the Early Bronze III settlements, on which they were directly superimposed. The buildings were seriously damaged because of their closeness to the top of the mound and due to later terracing operations. The architecture was therefore limited to only a few structures preserved in good condition, among which was one dwelling comprising a single large square room with an imposing central horseshoe-shaped double hearth and the remains of what was probably a weaving loom, suggested by the discovery of dozens of clay loom weights piled up in the NW corner of this room (Di Nocera 1998; Frangipane et al. 2009; Palmieri 1973). The pottery also indicates partial continuity with the previous period, even though new classes of wheelmade ware now appeared, some of which indicate that contacts had been resumed, albeit sporadically, with the Syro-Mesopotamian world (Di Nocera 1998, 2001).

The political breakup that is thought to have occurred in the territory of Malatya and Elazığ in the second half of the third millennium B.C.E. may have created favorable conditions for the cultural and, later, political domination by the eastward-expanding Hittite state during the second millennium B.C.E. The effects of this influence may already have begun to be felt in the Early Kingdom Period, judging from the fact that in the Late Bronze I (Period V B, 1750–1600 B.C.E.), a town gate was built in the Arslantepe earthen wall defense system, flanked by two bipartite quadrangular towers, which was highly reminiscent of similar central Anatolian gates, such as those at Alişar or Boğazköy (Palmieri 1978). The entrance to the town now pointed in a north-northeast direction, namely toward the Euphrates, in contrast to protohistoric times; this fortification system arrangement remained unchanged throughout the imperial Hittite and Neo-Hittite periods, although there was a slight shift of the gates westward. Although the gate of the "imperial" period (Late Bronze II, Period IV, 1400–1200 B.C.E.) had a different ground plan—of "tenaille" type—it also appears to be wholly central Anatolian in style. There was also a gallery with a "false vault" belonging to this phase, which has evident parallels with the Alişar and Alaca posterns, and may have been a tunnel leading to a water source (Pecorella 1975).

The Hittite citadel, which was mainly located in the north-northeast area of the mound, was probably destroyed after the collapse of the empire. A new fortification wall with town gate was built and once more destroyed by a big fire between the end of the second and the very beginning of the first millennia B.C.E. This destruction was followed by a phase in which the town was at least partially abandoned and then occasionally frequented for a while by small nonurbanized groups living among the ruins of the ancient structures.[10]

With the foundation of the new Neo-Hittite kingdom of Malatya (Iron Age, Period III), Arslantepe was once again to flourish as the capital of this kingdom with the construction of new imposing buildings, among which were a large pillared hall (Liverani 2009) and the famous Lions Gate. The settlement increasingly took the form of a small citadel, a seat of political and administrative power, while the existence of a lower town is still unknown at the present state of research.

Even though the remains of minor occupation dating back to the late Roman and Byzantine age have been uncovered (Equini Schneider 1970), the destruction of the Neo-Hittite town by Sargon II of Assyria in 712 B.C.E. put an end to Arslantepe's prosperity and centrality.

NOTES

1. These finds are exhibited today in the Museum of Anatolian Civilizations in Ankara. All the excavated materials since 1969 have been deposited in the Malatya Museum.

2. We are using here the Late Chalcolithic chronology recently proposed in a Santa Fe workshop (Rothman 2001:5–9).

3. Wall paintings are attested, besides at Arslantepe, in the late Ubaid period at Değirmentepe in the Malatya Plain (Esin 1983) and in the Late Chalcolithic at Norşuntepe, Elazığ (H. Hauptmann 1976:pl.42, 3).

4. Fragments of semi-precious stones and ochre, probably manufacturing residues, and numerous never-used obsidian arrowheads have been found in these rooms. The ground plan of these structures is reminiscent of similar buildings from Hacınebi LC3 (Stein et al. 1998:figs. 3, 9).

5. The term *cretulae* has been proposed as a universal term for clay sealings (Frangipane et al. 2007).

6. This does not mean it was the king's residence but a public space where public functions of different kinds were performed, probably in the name of a king or paramount chief.

7. It is interesting to note that a group of domestic vine seeds have been found here (Belisario, Follieri, and Sadori 1994).

8. A remarkable change has been also observed in the animal breeding pattern, which became caprine- and particularly sheep-oriented (Bartosiewicz 1998. 2010; Bökönyi 1983).

9. Black is always seen on the inner surface of bowls and outer surface of jars.

10. These levels are presently under investigation.

REFERENCES

Alvaro, Corrado, Cristina Lemorini, Giulio Palumbi, and Paola Piccione. 2008. From the Analysis of the Archaeological Context to the Life of a Community. "Ethnographic" Remarks on the Arslantepe VIB2 Village. In *Proceedings of the 5th International Congress on the Archaeology of the Ancient Near East*, ed. Joaquín M. Cordoba, Miguel Molist, M. Carmen Perez, Isabel Rubio, and Sergio Martinez, 127–36. Madrid: Universidad Autonoma de Madrid Ediciones.

Balossi Restelli, Francesca. 2008. Post-Ubaid Occupation on the Upper Euphrates: Late Chalcolithic 1–2 at Arslantepe (Malatya, Turkey). In *Proceedings of the 4th International Congress on the Archaeology of the Ancient Near East*, ed. Hartmut Kühne, Rainer M. Czichon, and Florian Janoscha Kreppner, 21–32. Wiesbaden: Harrassowitz Verlag.

Bartosiewicz, László. 1998. Interim Report on the Bronze Age Animal Bones from Arslantepe (Malatya, Anatolia). In *Archaeozoology of the Near East III*, ed. Hijlke Buitenhuis, László Bartosiewicz, and Alice Choyke, 221–32. Gröningen: ARC Publications.

———. 2010. Herding in Period VI A. Development and Changes from Period VII. In *Economic Centralisation in Formative States. The Archaeological Reconstruction of the Economic System in 4th Millennium Arslantepe*, ed. Marcella Frangipane, 119-48. Studi di Preistoria Orientale (SPO) 3. Rome: Università di Roma La Sapienza.

Belisario, M. Vittoria, Maria Follieri, and Laura Sadori. 1994. Nuovi dati archeobotanici sulla coltivazione di Vitis Vinifera L. ad Arslantepe (Malatya, Turchia). In *Drinking in Ancient Societies. History and Culture of Drinks in the Ancient Near East*, ed. Lucio Milano, 77–91. Padova: Sargon.

Bökönyi, Sándor. 1983. Late Chalcolithic and Early Bronze I Animal Remains from Arslantepe (Malatya), Turkey: A Preliminary Report. *Origini* 12.2: 581–97.

———. 1993. Hunting in Arslantepe, Anatolia. In *Between the Rivers and Over the Mountains. Archaeologica Anatolica et Mesopotamica Alba Palmieri Dedicata*, ed. Marcella Frangipane, Harald Hauptmann, Mario Liverani, Paolo Matthiae, and Machteld Mellink, 341–59. Rome: Università di Roma "La Sapienza."

Castellino, Giorgio R. 1975. Il Frammento degli Annali di Sargon II. In *Malatya—III. Rapporto Preliminare delle Campagne 1963–1968*, ed. Paolo Emilio Pecorella, 69–73. Orientis Antiqui Collectio 12. Rome: Centro per le Antichità e la Storia dell'Arte de Vicino Oriente.

Conti, Anna Maria and Carlo Persiani. 1993. When Worlds Collide. Cultural Developments in Eastern Anatolia in the Early Bronze Age. In *Between the Rivers and over the Mountains. Archaeologica Anatolica et Mesopotamica Alba Palmieri Dedicata*, ed. Marcella Frangipane, Harald Hauptmann, Mario Liverani, Paolo Matthiae, and Machteld Mellink, 361–413. Rome: Università di Roma "La Sapienza."

D'Anna, Maria Bianca. 2010. The Ceramic Containers of Period VI A. Food Control at the time of Centralisation. In *Economic Centralisation in Formative States. The Archaeological Reconstruction of the Economic System in 4th Millennium Arslantepe*, ed. Marcella Frangipane, 167-91. Studi di Preistoria Orientale (SPO) 3. Rome: Università di Roma La Sapienza.

Delaporte, Louis. 1939. La troisième campagne de fouilles à Malatya. *Revue Hittite et Asianique* 5.34: 43–56.

———. 1940. *Arslantepe. La Porte des Lions*. Paris: De Boccard.

Di Nocera, Gian Maria. 1998. *Die Siedlung der Mittelbronzezeit von Arslantepe. Arslantepe vol. 8*. Rome: Università di Roma "La Sapienza."

———. 2000a. Radiocarbon Datings from Arslantepe and Norşuntepe: The Fourth–Third Millennium Absolute Chronology in the Upper Euphrates and Transcaucasian Region. In *Chronologies des pays du Caucase et de l'Euphrate aux IVe et IIIe millénaires*, ed. Catherine Marro and Harald Hauptmann, 73–93. Varia Anatolica 11. Paris: De Boccard.

———. 2000b. C–14 Datings at Arslantepe and Bronze Age Chronology in the Upper and Middle Euphrates. In *Proceedings of the First International Congress on the Archaeology of the Ancient Near East*, ed. Paolo Matthiae, Alessandra Enea, Luca Peyronel, and Frances Pinnock, 333–48. Rome: Università degli Studi di Roma "La Sapienza."

———. 2001. Arslantepe und die Befestigungsanlage vom Beginn des zweiten Jahrtausends v.Chr. am oberen Euphrat. In *Lux Orientis: Archäologie zwischen Asien und Europa; Festchrift für Harald Hauptmann*, ed. Rainer M. Boehmer and Joseph Maran, 85–96. Heidelberg: Rahden/Westf.

———. 2005. Mobility and Stability: Preliminary Observations on the Early Bronze Age Settlement Organisation in the Malatya Plain. *Archäologische Mitteilungen aus Iran und Turan* 37: 3–69.

———. 2008. Settlements, Population and Landscape on the Upper Euphrates between V and II Millennium B.C. Results of the Archaeological Survey Project 2003–2005 in the Malatya Plain. In *Proceedings of the 5th International Congress on the Archaeology of the Ancient Near East*, ed. Joaquín M. Cordoba, Miguel Molist, M. Carmen Perez, Isabel Rubio, and Sergio Martinez, 633–46. Madrid: Universidad Autonoma de Madrid Ediciones.

Equini Schneider, Eugenia. 1970. *Malatya—II*. Orientis Antiqui Collectio 10. Roma: Centro per le Antichità e la Storia dell'Arte de Vicino Oriente.

Esin, Ufuk. 1983. Zur Datierung der vorgeschichtlichen Schichten von Degirmentepe bei Malatya in der Östlichen Türkei. In *Beiträge zur Altertumskunde Kleinasiens, Festschrift für Kurt Bittel*, ed. Rainer M. Boehmer and Harald Hauptmann, 175–90. Mainz: Philipp von Zabern.

Ferioli, Piera and Enrica Fiandra. 1983. Clay-Sealings from Arslantepe VIA: Administration and Bureaucracy. *Origini* 12.2: 455–509.

———. 1994. Archival Techniques and Methods at Arslantepe. In *Archives before Writing*, ed. Piera Ferioli, Enrica Fiandra, Gian G. Fissore, and Marcella Frangipane, 149–61. Roma: Ministero per i Beni Culturali e Ambientali, Ufficio Centrale per i Beni Archivistici.

Frame, Grant. 2004. Cilindro con iscrizione di Sargon II. In *Alle Origini del Potere. Arslantepe, la Collina dei Leoni*, ed. Marcella Frangipane, 175–77. Milan: Mondadori/Electa.

———. 2009. A "New" Cylinder Inscription of Sargon II of Assyria from Melid. In *Of God(s), Trees, Kings, and Scholars. Neo-Assyrian and Related Studies in Honour of Simo*

Parpola, ed. Mikko Luukko, Saana Svärd, and Raija Mattila, 65–82. Studia Orientalia 106. Helsinki: Finnish Oriental Society.

Frangipane, Marcella. 1992. Dipinti murali in un edificio palaziale di Arslantepe-Malatya: aspetti ideologici nelle prime forme di centralizzazione economica. *Studi Micenei ed Egeo-Anatolici* 30: 143–54.

———. 1993a. Local Components in the Development of Centralized Societies in Syro-Anatolian Regions. In *Between the Rivers and over the Mountains. Archaeologica Anatolica et Mesopotamica Alba Palmieri Dedicata*, ed. Marcella Frangipane, Harald Hauptmann, Mario Liverani, Paolo Matthiae, and Machteld Mellink, 133–61. Roma: Università di Roma "La Sapienza."

———. 1993b. Arslantepe-Melid-Malatya. In *Arslantepe, Hierapolis, Iasos, Kyme. Scavi Archeologici Italiani in Turchia*, ed. Fede Berti, 31–103. Venezia: Marsilio.

———. 1993c. Melid/Malatya. *Reallexikon der Assyriologie und vorderasiatische Archäologie* 8/1.2: 42–52.

———. 1994. The Record Function of Clay-Sealings in Early Administrative Systems as Seen from Arslantepe-Malatya. In *Archives before Writing* ed. Piera Ferioli, Enrica Fiandra, Gian G. Fissore, and Marcella Frangipane, 125–36. Rome: Ministero per i Beni Culturali e Ambientali, Ufficio Centrale per i Beni Archivistici.

———. 1996. Arslantepe. In *The Oxford Encyclopedia of Archaeology in the Near East*, vol. 1, ed. Eric M. Meyers, 212–15. Oxford: Oxford University Press.

———. 1997. A 4th Millennium Temple/Palace Complex at Arslantepe-Malatya. North-South Relations and the Formation of Early State Societies in the Northern Regions of Greater Mesopotamia. *Paléorient* 23.1: 45–73.

———. 1998. Changes in Upper Mesopotamian/Anatolian Relations at the Beginning of 3rd Millennium BC. *Subartu* 4.1: 195–218.

———. 2000a. Origini ed evoluzione del sistema centralizzato ad Arslantepe: dal "Tempio" al "Palazzo" nel IV millennio a.C. *Revista sobre Oriente Próximo y Egypto en la Antigüedad* 3: 53–78.

———. 2000b. The Late Chalcolithic/EB I Sequence at Arslantepe. Chronological and Cultural Remarks from a Frontier Site. In *Chronologies des pays du Caucase et de l'Euphrate aux IVe et IIIe millénaires*, ed. Catherine Marro and Harald Hauptmann, 439–71. Varia Anatolica 11. Paris: De Boccard.

———. 2001. The Transition between Two Opposing Forms of Power at Arslantepe (Malatya) at the Beginning of the 3rd Millennium. *TÜBA-AR* 4: 1–24.

———. 2002. "Non-Uruk" Developments and Uruk-Linked Features on the Northern Borders of Greater Mesopotamia. In *Artefacts of Complexity. Tracking the Uruk in the Near East*, ed. Stuart Campbell and Nicholas Postgate, 123–48. Warminster: Aris and Phillips.

———. 2003. Developments in Fourth Millennium Public Architecture in the Malatya Plain: From Simple Tripartite to Complex and Bipartite Pattern. In *From Villages to Cities, Studies Presented to Ufuk Esin*, ed. Mehmet Özdoğan, Harald Hauptmann, and Nezih Başgelen, 147–69. İstanbul: Arkeoloji ve Sanat Yayınları.

———. ed. 2004. *Alle Origini del Potere. Arslantepe, la Collina dei Leoni*. Milano: Mondadori/Electa.

———. 2007. The Arslantepe "Royal Tomb": New Funerary Customs and Political Changes in the Upper Euphrates Valley at the Beginning of the Third Millennium BC. *Scienze dell'Antichità* 14: 45–70.

———. 2009. Non-Urban Hierarchical Patterns of Territorial and Political Organisation in Northern Regions of Greater Mesopotamia: Tepe Gawra and Arslantepe. In *A propos de Tepe Gawra, le monde proto-urbain de Mésopotamie*, ed. Pascal Butterlin, 133–46. Subartu 23. Brussels: Editions Brepols.

———. ed. 2010. *Economic Centralisation in Formative States. The Archaeological Reconstruction of the Economic System in 4th Millennium Arslantepe*, Studi di Preistoria Orientale (SPO) 3. Rome: Università di Roma La Sapienza.

Frangipane, Marcella, Eva Andersson, Romina Laurito, Susan Möller-Wiering, Marie-Louise Nosch, Antoinette Rast Eicher, Agnese Wisti Lassen. 2009. Arslantepe, Malatya (Turkey): Textiles, Tools and Imprints of Fabrics from the Fourth to the Second Millennium B.C.E. *Paléorient* 35.1: 5-29.

Frangipane, Marcella, Gian Maria Di Nocera, Andreas Hauptmann, Paola Morbidelli, Alberto Palmieri, Laura Sadori, Michael Schultz, and Tyede Schmidt-Schultz. 2001. New Symbols of a New Power in a "Royal" Tomb from 3000 BC Arslantepe, Malatya (Turkey). *Paléorient* 2.2: 105–39.

Frangipane, Marcella, Gian Maria Di Nocera, and Giulio Palumbi. 2005. L'interazione tra due universi socio-culturali nella piana di Malatya (Turchia) tra IV e III millennio: dati archeologici e riconoscimento di identità. *Origini* 27: 123–70.

Frangipane, Marcella (ed.), Piera Ferioli, Enrica Fiandra, Romina Laurito, and Holly Pittman. 2007. *Arslantepe Cretulae. An Early Centralised Administrative System Before Writing*. Arslantepe vol. 5. Rome: Università di Roma "La Sapienza."

Frangipane, Marcella and Alba Palmieri, eds. 1983. Perspectives on Protourbanization in Eastern Anatolia: Arslantepe (Malatya). An Interim Report on the 1975–1983 Campaigns. *Origini* 12.2: 287–668.

———. 1988–89. Aspects of Centralization in the Late Uruk Period in the Mesopotamian Periphery. *Origini* 14: 539–60.

Frangipane, Marcella and Alberto M. Palmieri. 1994–95. Un modello di ricostruzione dello sviluppo della metallurgia antica: Il sito di Arslantepe. *Scienze dell'Antichità* 8–9: 59–77.

Frangipane, Marcella and Giulio Palumbi. 2007. Red-Black Ware, Pastoralism, Trade, and Anatolian-Transcaucasian Interactions in the 4th–3rd Millennium BC. In *Les Cultures du Caucase (VIe–IIIe millénaires avant notre ère). Leurs relations avec le Proche-Orient*, ed. Bertille Lyonnet, 233–55. Paris: CNRS Editions.

Hauptmann, Andreas, Sigrid Schmitt-Strecker, Friedrich Begemann, and Alberto M. Palmieri. 2002. Chemical Composition and Lead Isotopy of Metal Objects from the "Royal" Tomb and Other Related finds at Arslantepe, Eastern Anatolia. *Paléorient* 28.2: 43–69.

Hauptmann, Harald. 1976. Die Grabungen auf dem Norsun-Tepe, 1973. *Keban Project 1973 Activities*, 61–78. METU Series 1, no. 6. Ankara: Middle East Technical University.

Hawkins, J.D. 1993. Melid (Malatya, Arslan-Tepe). A. Historisch. *Reallexikon der Assyriologie und Vorderasiatischen Archäologie* 8.1–2: 35–41.

Liverani, Mario. 2009. Il salone a pilastri della Melid neo-hittita. *Scienze dell'Antichità* 15: 649-75.

Oates Joan, Augusta McMahon, Philip Karsgaard, Salam Al Quntar, and Jason Ur. 2007. Early Mesopotamian Urbanism: A New View from the North. *Antiquity* 81: 585–600.

Özgen, Engin, Barbara Helwing, Olivier Nieuwenhuyse, and R. Spoor. 1999. Oylum Höyük 1997–98. Die Spätchalkolithische Siedlung auf der Westterrasse. *Anatolia Antiqua* 7: 19–67.

Palmieri, Alba. 1967. Insediamento del Bronzo Antico a Gelinciktepe (Malatya). *Origini* 1: 117–93.

———. 1973. Scavi nell'area sud-occidentale di Arslantepe. Ritrovamento di una struttura templare dell'Antica Età del Bronzo. *Origini* 7: 55–228.

———. 1978. Scavi ad Arslantepe (Malatya). Quaderni de "La Ricerca Scientifica" 100, *Consiglio Nazionale delle Ricerche* 100: 311–52.

———. 1981. Excavations at Arslantepe (Malatya). *Anatolian Studies* 31: 101–19.

———. 1985. Eastern Anatolia and Early Mesopotamian Urbanization: Remarks on Changing Relations. In *Studi di Paletnologia in Onore di S.M. Puglisi*, ed. Mario Liverani, Alba Palmieri, and Renato Peroni, 191–213. Rome: Università di Roma "La Sapienza."

———. 1989. Storage and Distribution at Arslantepe-Malatya in the Late Uruk Period. In *Anatolia and the Ancient Near East. Studies in Honor of Tahsin Özgüç*, ed. Kutlu Emre, Barthel Hrouda, Machteld Mellink, and Nimet Özgüç, 419–30. Ankara: Türk Tarih Kurumu Basımevi.

Palmieri, Alberto M., Marcella Frangipane, Andreas Hauptmann, and Kersten Hess. 1999. Early Metallurgy at Arslantepe during the Late Chalcolithic and the Early Bronze Age IA–IB Periods. In *Proceedings of the International Conference "The Beginning of Metallurgy,"* ed. Andreas Hauptmann, Ernst Pernicka, Thilo Rehren, and Ünsal Yalçın, 141–48. Bochum: Deutschen Bergbau-Museum.

Palmieri, Alberto M., Andreas Hauptmann, and Kersten Hess. 1998. Les objets en métal du tombeau monumental d'Arslantepe de 3000 Av. J.-C. (Malatya, Turquie). *Revue d'Archeometrie* 22: 39–43.

Palmieri, Alberto M. and Paola Morbidelli. 2003. Archaeometric Study on Crucibles from Arslantepe, Turkey (IV–II mill. BC). In *Ceramic in Society. Proceedings of the 6th European Meeting on Ancient Ceramics*, ed. Simonpietro Di Pierro, Vincent Serneels, and Mario Maggetti, 231–43. Fribourg: University of Fribourg.

Palmieri, Alberto M., Kemal Sertok, and Evgenij Chernykh. 1993. From Arslantepe Metalwork to Arsenical Copper Technology in Eastern Anatolia. In *Between the Rivers and over the Mountains. Archaeologica Anatolica et Mesopotamica Alba Palmieri Dedicata*, ed. Marcella Frangipane, Harald Hauptmann, Mario Liverani, Paolo Matthiae, and Machteld Mellink, 573–99. Rome: Università di Roma "La Sapienza."

Palumbi, Giulio. 2003. Red-Black Pottery: Eastern Anatolian and Transcaucasian Relationships around the Mid-Fourth Millennium BC. *Ancient Near Eastern Studies* 40: 80–134.

———. 2008. *The Red and Black. Social and Cultural Interaction between the Upper Euphrates and Southern Caucasus Communities in the Fourth and Third Millennium BC*. Studi di Preistoria Orientale (SPO) 2. Rome: Università di Roma "La Sapienza."

Pecorella, Paolo Emilio. 1975. *Malatya—III*. Orientis Antiqui Collectio 12. Rome: Centro per le Antichità e la Storia dell'Arte de Vicino Oriente.

Puglisi, Salvatore M. and Piero Meriggi. 1964. *Malatya I*. Orientis Antiqui Collectio 3. Rome: Centro per le Antichità e la Storia dell'Arte de Vicino Oriente.

Rothman, Mitchell S., ed. 2001. *Uruk Mesopotamia and Its Neighbors*. Santa Fe, N.M.: School of American Research Press.

Sadori, Laura, Francesca Susanna, and Francesca Balossi Restelli. 2008. Collapsed Beams and Wooden Remains from a 3200 BC Temple and Palace at Arslantepe (Malatya, Turkey). In *Charcoals from the Past, Cultural and Palaeoenvironmental Implications*, ed. Girolamo Fiorentino and Donatella Magri, 103–16. British Archaeological Reports, International Series 1807. Oxford: Archaeopress.

Sadori, Laura, Francesca Susanna, and Carlo Persiani. 2006. Archaeobotanical Data and Crop Storage Evidence from an Early Bronze Age 2 Burnt House at Arslantepe (Malatya, Turkey). *Vegetation History and Archaeobotany* 15: 205–15.

Stein, Gil, Christopher Edens, Julie Pearce Edens, Kenneth Boden, Nicola Laneri, Hadi Özbal, Bryan Earl, A. Mieke Adriaens, and Holly Pittman. 1998. Southeast Anatolia before the Uruk Expansion: Preliminary Report on the 1997 Excavations at Hacınebi, Turkey. *Anatolica* 24: 143–93.

Trufelli, Franca. 1994. Standardization, Mass Production and Potter's Marks in the Late Chalcolithic Pottery of Arslantepe (Malatya). *Origini* 18: 245–89.

CHAPTER 46

TITRIŞ HÖYÜK: THE NATURE AND CONTEXT OF THIRD MILLENNIUM B.C.E. URBANISM IN THE UPPER EUPHRATES BASIN

GUILLERMO ALGAZE AND
TIMOTHY MATNEY

Research and Excavation Background

In the second half of the third millennium B.C.E., the high rolling plains straddling the borders of present-day southeastern Turkey south of the Taurus, northern Syria, and northern Iraq (hereafter Syro-Mesopotamia) became the focal point for one of the earliest processes of urban agglomeration in the world. This resulted in the emergence of numerous competing indigenous Early Bronze Age (EBA) polities throughout the area, each centered at a fortified center of considerable size and surrounded by a corona of dependent towns and villages.

Research at these various EBA centers has yielded valuable insights about the causal factors contributing to their emergence (Weiss 1983, 1990; Wilkinson 1994) and about the nature of the agricultural infrastructure based on the extensive exploitation of rain-fed cereals (Wilkinson et al. 2007) that made them possible.

Moreover, the discovery of palace archives, first at Ebla and now at Beydar, helps us better understand the political structure of these capitals, the degree of regional economic control they exercised, and the extent of their commercial contacts with contemporary polities elsewhere (Arcari 1988; Astour 1988; Lebeau and Suleiman 2003; Matthiae 2003; Pettinato 1991).

Hugely informative as these individual archives are, the tablets are written only from the narrow point of view of what royal scribes considered worthy of recording, principally palace-dominated economic, political, and ritual activities. The problem is compounded by the fact that save for a few notable exceptions (e.g., Tells Beydar and Bderi, see Pfälzner 2003), existing excavations have generally focused on core institutions at the center of such sites and have not fully explored more habitation neighborhoods within the ancient cities and extramural activity areas.

Seeking to tackle these important conceptual gaps in our understanding of the Bronze Age cities that emerged in Syro-Mesopotamia during the third millennium B.C.E., an archaeological excavation and survey project was initiated in 1991 at the site of Titriş Höyük in southeastern Turkey. Titriş was a modest medium-sized EBA urban center that flourished in the Upper Euphrates basin of southeastern Turkey during the second half of the third millennium B.C.E. Today, it adjoins and, on its eastern edge, lies partially under the modern village of Bahçeli, which is situated some forty-five kilometers north of the modern Turkish city of Şanlıurfa. At its apogee, EBA Titriş controlled a natural route leading from the Upper Mesopotamian plains east of the Euphrates to the Gaziantep area west of the river via the historical Upper Euphrates fording area centered at the great ancient site of Samsat.

Titriş Höyük

Titriş is situated some fourteen kilometers due east of Samsat within a small agricultural plain flanked by barren limestone hills that is watered by the Tavuk Çay, a minor spring-fed perennial tributary of the Euphrates. Although only about fifty square kilometers in extent, this plain represents the area nearest to the Samsat ford possessing an agricultural catchment large enough to support an urban settlement in antiquity, given the prevailing constraints of rain-fed cereal agriculture that characterize the Syro-Mesopotamian plains (Wilkinson 1994:fig. 6).

Between 1991 and 1999, the site of Titriş and the immediately surrounding corridor area were the focus of eight seasons of excavations and survey by a team of American, Turkish, and European researchers (Algaze et al. 1992, 1995, 1996, 2001; Algaze and Mısır 1993, 1994; Honça and Algaze 1998; Matney and Algaze 1995; Matney, Algaze, and Pittman 1997; Matney, Algaze, and Rosen 1999). The site was selected for excavation because earlier surveys conducted by Tony Wilkinson in the 1980s suggested that EBA deposits were readily accessible over large portions of the ancient settlement with little effort (Wilkinson 1990).

Accordingly, we expected that Titriş would be an ideal location at which to document both the overall layout of an ancient Syro-Mesopotamian EBA city and the nature of its domestic neighborhoods away from core urban institutions on the citadel. To a significant degree, our results justified this approach. Over the course of eight field seasons, the project traced the evolution of the site throughout the third millennium B.C.E., as the settlement abruptly grew from a small village of seemingly modest size of Early EBA date (ca. 3100(?)–2600 B.C.E.) into a sprawling urban center with substantial architecture at its core surrounded by modest extramural habitation and specialized production areas in the Middle EBA (ca. 2600/2500–2400/2300 B.C.E.), and as it later evolved into a compact and carefully planned city crammed with houses cowering behind a massive city wall in the Late EBA (ca. 2400/2300–2100 B.C.E.) (see Rupley in Algaze et al. 2001:47–50, figs. 19–20 for the absolute chronology underlying this periodization). In so doing, the project (1) conducted an intensive site survey of the corridor surrounding the city, (2) mapped the city's surface in its entirety and about 50 percent of its subsurface remains, (3) uncovered some 750 m² of the Middle EBA city and about 3,000 m² of the succeeding Late EBA settlement, and (4) assessed the ecological impact that building activities within the city had on its immediate environs.

Site Morphology and Occupational Sequence

At its apogee in the middle and late third millennium B.C.E. (see later discussion), Titriş consisted of a citadel surrounded by a compact and much more extensive lower city (figure 46.1). The settlement grew at the juncture of the Tavuk Çay, noted earlier, and the Titriş Çay, a now dry and deeply incised seasonal stream that carried water year-round in the EBA (see later discussion). Only its eastern end was open to the surrounding plain and, at least by the Late EBA, that end was defended, as will be discussed, by a massive fortification wall.

High Mound

The core of the city was a citadel 22 m in height and 3.2 ha in extent situated on a Pleistocene terrace overlooking the floodplain of the Tavuk Çay. The earliest remains identified in the High Mound are contemporary with the main periods of occupation of the city in the Mid–Late EBA (Carter and Gorny in Algaze et al. 1992), but the High Mound continued to be in use in later periods as well, minimally including the early second millennium B.C.E. (Kurban III), and the Iron, Classical (Hellenistic/Late Roman), and Medieval ages; those latter periods account for the bulk of the observed stratification.

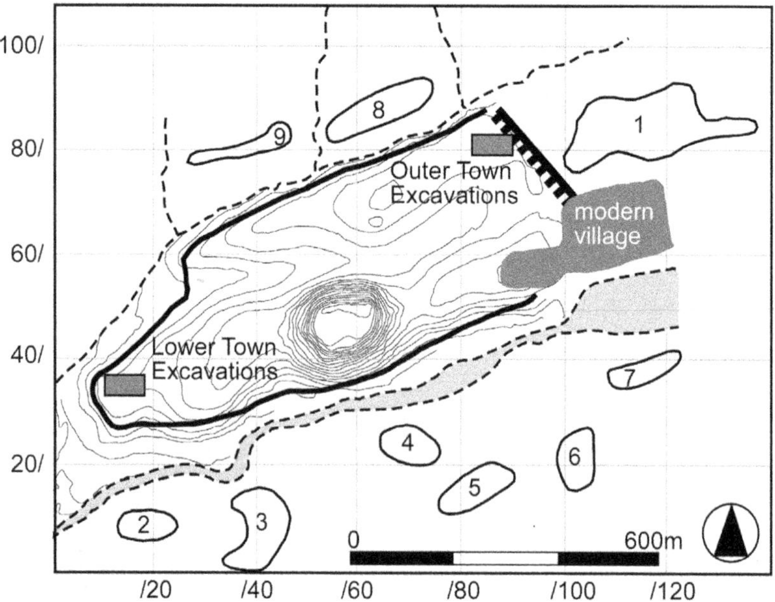

Figure 46.1. Topographic plan of Titriş Höyük showing the limits of the site, the location of the Late EBA fortification wall, and the primary excavated areas. The Middle EBA suburbs are numbered 1–9.

Lower City

The High Mound was surrounded by a much more extensive lower city, comprising just under thirty-five hectares of contiguous occupation. This lower city can be further subdivided into two distinct gross morphological areas: a "Lower Town" (approximately fourteen hectares), which sits on the same Pleistocene ridge on which the citadel was built and extended directly to the west and east of it, and an "Outer Town" (about sixteen hectares), which was emplaced over a second Pleistocene ridge that runs directly north of and parallel to the preceding.

The Lower Town, in turn, is subdivisible into two discrete sectors located due east and west of the High Mound. Both sectors overlook the Tavuk Çay floodplain and have direct access to it. The portion of the Lower Town that extended directly east of the citadel is now almost completely overlain by the modern village of Bahçeli, and much of its surface has been disturbed by modern construction activities. Accordingly, the subsurface structure of this portion of the settlement was not mapped. However, examination of numerous cuts and pits excavated by modern villagers in this sector of the city suggests the presence of extended Iron and Classical Age occupations overlying earlier Mid–Late EBA deposits.

In turn, the portion of the Lower Town extending due west of the citadel comprises an area eight hectares in extent. About a third of this extent, near the base of the High Mound, appears to have been the locus of a Medieval occupation (Algaze et al. 1992). However, farther away from the citadel, EBA remains were situated just under the surface, and three separate excavation areas were opened. These exposures (discussed below) indicate that the western lobe of the Lower Town was first occupied in the Early EBA, but the bulk of its deposition is of Middle and Late EBA date.

Directly north of the High Mound and adjoining the Lower Town was a further sector of the ancient city, which we arbitrarily labeled the "Outer Town." This sector extended up to the edge of the Titriş Çay and measures some sixteen hectares in extent. It dates entirely to the Middle and Late EBA and is undisturbed by modern occupations, save for a handful of pre-Islamic pit graves cut into its highest point (Honça and Algaze 1998). Three separate excavation areas were opened across the Outer Town. The bulk of architectural remains uncovered in those exposures date to the Late EBA, and it is clear that the full extent of the area was occupied at that time.

Suburbs

Surveys in the immediate vicinity of the site allowed us to identify nine noncontiguous areas with seemingly shallow occupational deposits that lined the banks of promontories overlooking the small tributaries immediately adjacent to the city. Only one of those areas (Suburb 1, discussed below) was excavated.

Titriş and its Hinterland in the Early EBA

The earliest remains uncovered at Titriş date to the Early EBA. Those remains were only uncovered in a deep sounding in Trench 40–34 in the western lobe of the Lower Town. Early EBA levels are stratified directly above virgin soil, at about four and a half meters below the modern surface (Rupley in Algaze et al. 2001). As comparable levels are absent everywhere else where virgin soil was reached across the Lower Town and the Outer Town, we must presume that Titriş was but a village at the time. If so, Titriş was one among a handful of villages that surveys show characterized the relatively undifferentiated landscape of the Upper Euphrates area in the environs of Samsat in the first half of the third millennium B.C.E. (Algaze et al. 2001:fig. 24, top, left).

Titriş and its Hinterland in the Middle EBA

The Titriş corridor was abruptly transformed in the earliest phase of the Middle EBA, sometime around 2600/2500 B.C.E., when the village developed into a small urban center. Surface ceramics show that the city grew to about thirty-two hectares at this time. All of the "suburb" areas that surrounded the city were also occupied in the Middle EBA, making for a further eleven hectares of occupation (i.e., forty-three hectares) (figure 46.1). At least one external cemetery area is known for the Middle EBA city (situated in a promontory some 400 m west of the site).

Because Middle EBA levels across the Lower and Outer Town sectors of Titriş tend to be relatively deeply buried under Late EBA structures, exposures of Middle EBA date within the EBA city thus far have been relatively modest. Remains of the period were reached in three distinct operations, making for a total exposed area of 365 m² (265 m² in the eastern end of the Outer Town and 100 m² in the Lower Town). Due east of the city proper, an additional area of 400 m² of Middle EBA remains has also been exposed in the largest of the suburbs surrounding the site.

Presuming that these limited and widely separated exposures can be considered representative, striking differences can be observed in both the type and scale of architecture and the use of space between the main occupation at Titriş proper and its surrounding suburb areas during the Middle EBA.

The structures discovered thus far in the Outer and Lower Towns of Titriş are difficult to characterize because only small portions of the buildings in question were contained within our trenches. However, they clearly represent compounds of massive size that extend well beyond the confines of each of the exposed areas. One fragmentary Middle EBA structure, partially uncovered in the Outer Town (Trenches 80–81, 81–81, 82–81) in 1991–92 almost certainly represents a public building because of its massive walls and associated foundation deposit consisting of an articulated but decapitated dog (Algaze and Mısır 1994), possibly placed as part of an apotropaic ritual. Another compound (Trench 40–34), recovered in the Lower Town in 1994 and 1998–99 (Rupley in Algaze et al. 2001:fig. 18), is more likely to represent élite housing because of its well-built and frequently replastered hearth areas.

In contrast, only modest and flimsily constructed structures, including both domestic quarters and specialized activity areas, were uncovered in the contemporary Middle EBA suburbs. This is attested in the largest of those suburbs, Suburb 1, located due east of the site, which was explored in 1998–99. The exposed area was devoted to the mass production of Canaanean blades, possibly for regional consumption, as evidenced by thousands of discarded cores and associated debitage (Rosen in Algaze et al. 2000; Rosen and Hartenberger in Algaze et al. 2001:fig. 14; Hartenberger 2003; Hartenberger, Rosen, and Matney 2000).

However fragmentary these data from three widely separated points across the kilometer-long site may be, they clearly suggest that a substantial amount of spatial differentiation and specialization existed within Middle EBA Titriş. Extrapolating from such data, the main occupation at the site proper appears to have consisted mostly of élite housing and public structures, whereas economically specialized but impoverished inhabitants of the city appear to have been relegated to a corona of dependent suburbs surrounding the main settlement.

Rural settlement in the corridor surrounding Titriş at this time is equally sharply stratified. Our regional surveys indicate that Middle EBA Titriş was the pinnacle of a four-tier settlement hierarchy within its catchment. Although significantly smaller than many contemporary capitals in the Balikh and Upper Khabur areas (Wilkinson 1994), at forty-three hectares in extent, Titriş was nearly four times larger than the contemporary second-tier sites in its immediate vicinity and eight times as large as third-tier sites in its environs. Additionally, Titriş was surrounded by a corona of dependent village or hamlet-sized occupations in its vicinity, forming a fourth tier of settlement in the environs of the city (Algaze et al. 2001:fig. 24, top right).

Titriş and its Hinterland in the Late EBA

The onset of the Late EBA in the Titriş area is characterized by a thorough reorganization of human settlement, both within the site and within its immediate hinterland (and see Ökse, chapter 11 in this volume, for discussion of the larger region). Starting with the latter, our surveys indicate that although the total number of dependent villages surrounding Titriş in the Late EBA is identical to the Middle EBA number, the location of sites in the city's catchment varies considerably. All villages and hamlets south of Titriş were abandoned at the end of the Middle EBA, and an equal number of sites were founded north of the settlement in the Late EBA (Algaze et al. 2001:fig. 24, bottom, left). Also abandoned at the end of the Middle EBA were all of the suburbs that had surrounded Titriş. By the Late EBA, therefore, Titriş had contracted from an estimated occupied area of forty-three to a more compact settlement of about thirty-three hectares (figure 46.1).

The reasons for this contraction are unknown, but the shift of regional settlement away from the areas directly south of the site suggest, possibly, the start of hostilities between Titriş and Tatar Höyük, a twelve-hectare site some ten kilometers southwest of Titriş (Algaze et al. 2001). Interestingly, the incidence of violent trauma substantially increases at this time in the skeletal remains found at the site, as compared to the Middle EBA (Erdal 2010).

Be that as it may, the changes within the Titriş hinterland in the Late EBA were accompanied by a thorough internal reorganization of the settlement itself, which can be described as a massive and well-planned urban renewal program (Matney 2002; Matney and Algaze 1995). Evidence for this program is provided by a combination of extensive horizontal exposures in the Outer and Lower Town sectors and an equally extensive program of mapping the subsurface remains of substantial parts of the site by means of magnetic gradiometry. We now turn to a discussion of these efforts.

Subsurface Mapping

During the 1993–95 seasons, a program of subsurface survey by means of magnetic field gradiometry was undertaken at Titriş under the direction of Lewis Somers of GeoScan Research USA (figure 46.2). This effort focused on those portions of the settlement that were relatively undisturbed by modern and Medieval activities and where Late EBA remains could be found immediately under the surface, as indicated both by early exposures and surface ceramics. This included almost the full extent of the Outer Mound and about half of the western lobe of the Lower Town, amounting to about 16.5 ha or about half of the full extent of the site in the Late EBA. Because the Late EBA was the last period of occupation in the surveyed portions of the site, there can be no doubt that the bulk of the materials visible in the subsurface mapping reflect the structure of the city as it existed at that time, and this is confirmed by overlaps between the excavated and the mapped remains where the full extent and plan of the former can be directly and coherently extrapolated by means of the latter, as may be observed in figure 46.2.

Subsurface mapping was made easier by the fact that the limestone used in the Late EBA wall foundations, containing little or no iron, contrasted well against the

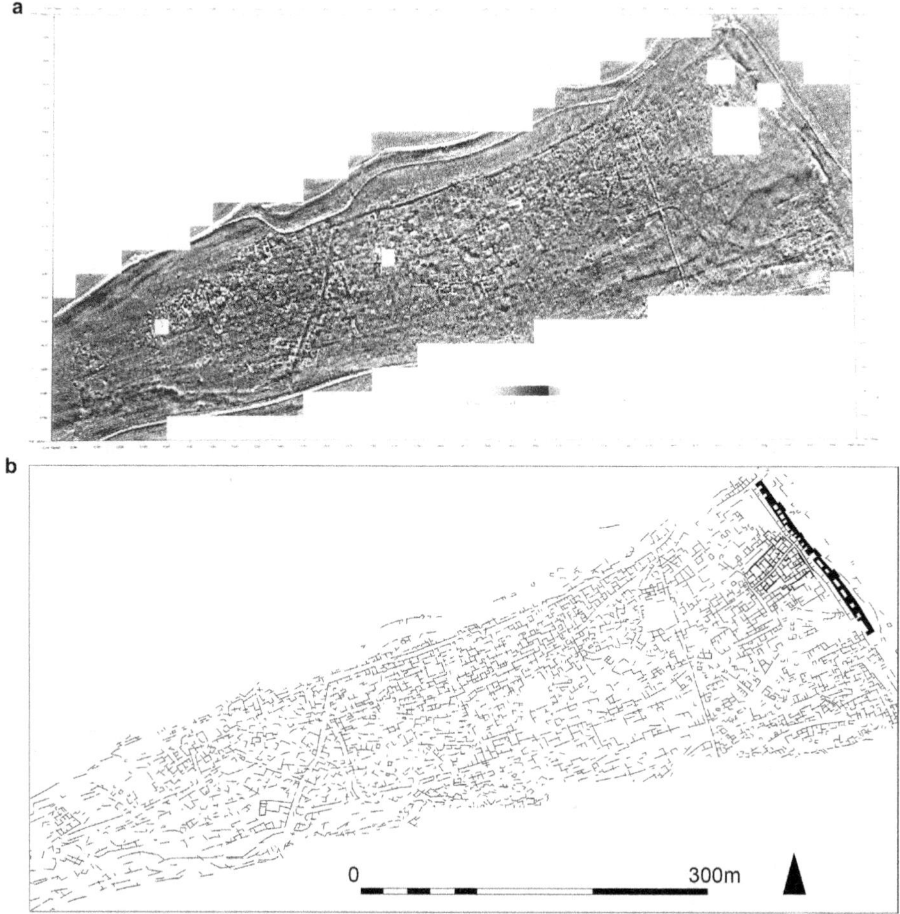

Figure 46.2. (a) Gradiometry plan of the Outer Town. (b) Interpretation of the city plan based on the processed magnetometry data. The city fortification wall can be seen at the eastern edge of the surveyed area (courtesy of Dr. Yoko Nishimura).

iron-rich soils derived from the mudbrick collapse that filled the rooms, and against the surrounding streets, which often contained thick layers of highly magnetic broken pottery.

The geophysical maps were used to select areas for extensive horizontal exposures in the later seasons of work at the site, as discussed below. More important, however, the geophysical maps allow us to extrapolate results from our excavations of Late EBA remains (3,000 m², or just under 1 percent of the Late EBA settlement) to better understand the much wider contemporary areas of the ancient city. At least within the areas mapped, the urban housing stock of the Late EBA city is continuous, showing no open spaces within all of the Outer Town and within the surveyed portions of the western lobe of the Lower Town. Interestingly, the maps show no obvious restrictions to internal movement within the city's neighborhoods, which appear well articulated by long-running streets. In fact, as recently noted by Yoko Nishimura (2008), Late EBA housing stock is always oriented to the nearby streets, and house plans, although standardized across the site, were adapted to fit within sometimes irregular plots defined by street intersections.

Although the gradiometry maps allow us to better understand the overall structure of the ancient settlement, details about the nature of Late EBA housing at Titriş are best discerned from the relatively extensive horizontal exposures that were practicable in two broadly separated areas situated almost at opposite ends of the ancient city (figures 46.3 and 46.4).

Late EBA Housing

Our most extensive exposure of Late EBA houses at Titriş took place in a large contiguous area of 1,600 m² in the northeastern portion of the Outer Town. Over the course of five seasons of excavations, all or part of seven domestic residences were brought to light here (figure 46.3). The architecture consisted of unmasoned limestone wall foundations with a mudbrick superstructure. The floors of the houses were primarily beaten earth, although some roughly cobbled spaces mark the location of open courtyards within the houses.

Most houses had a similar array of permanent features: bread ovens, plastered circular basins, hearths, and large basalt grinding stones (Nishimura 2008). Additionally, most of the exposed houses contained at least one well-built subterranean stone cist burial, which were generally constructed at the same time as the houses themselves (discussed later). Houses varied in size from fewer than ten rooms to more than twenty, and in nearly all cases comprised a central courtyard and an array of surrounding rooms.

The exposed Outer Town houses abutted the city's fortification wall, which was partially uncovered in the northeastern corner of the excavated area. On its external face, the fortification wall led to a moat or glacis built of sloping layers of densely packed clay, earth, and crushed limestone. Although not fully excavated, the width of this defensive feature was traced for at least fourteen meters, and it was found to slope three meters within that distance (Algaze and Mısır 1993:157). Towering over

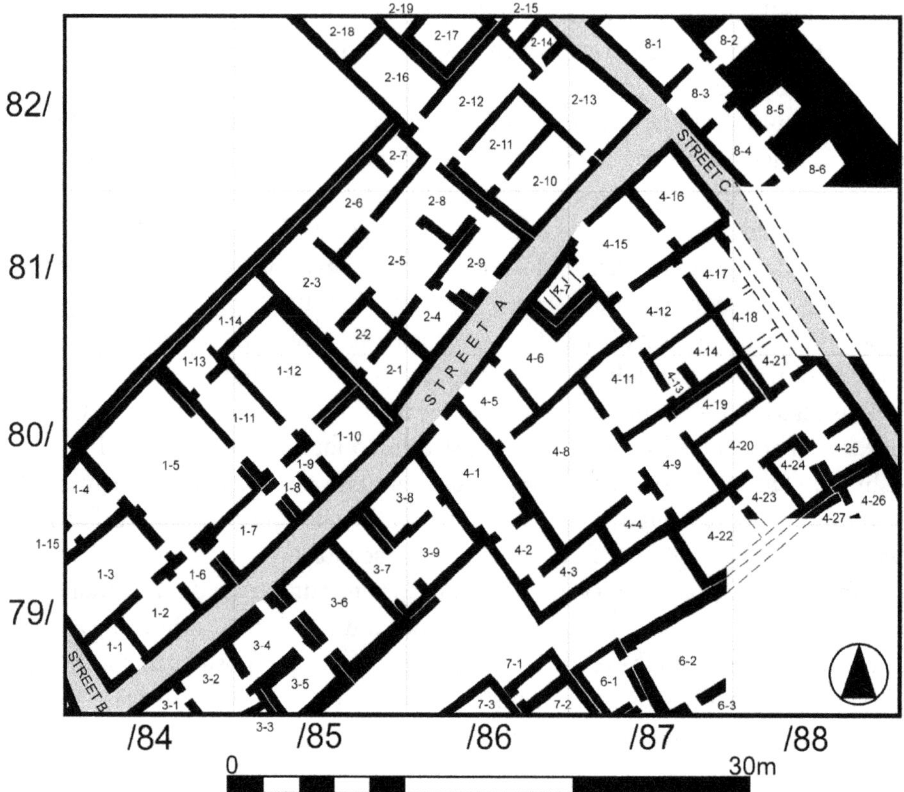

Figure 46.3. Plan of the excavated Outer Town architecture.

the moat/glacis, the fortification wall was nearly six m in width and was inset with small rooms, which appear to be of a domestic nature. The wall can be traced in the gradiometry map for a distance of approximately 150 m along the eastern flank of the Late EBA city (figures 46.1–2).

In 1996, in order to better sample the variability of Late EBA architecture at Titriş, a new exposure of about 1,000 m^2 was opened in the western end of the Lower Town, some 900 m away from the Outer Town exposures just described (figure 46.4). Again, we recovered domestic residences centered around large courtyards erected alongside streets, almost identical in plan and layout to those in the Outer Town. The complete plan of one house (building 5) and parts of seven other domestic units were exposed. These structures had a similar array of domestic installations to those in the Outer Town.

Late EBA City Planning

One of the most significant discoveries revealed by our exposures of Late EBA houses at Titriş was the substantial evidence for city planning at that time (Matney 2002; Matney and Algaze 1995). This is particularly clear in the Outer Town where

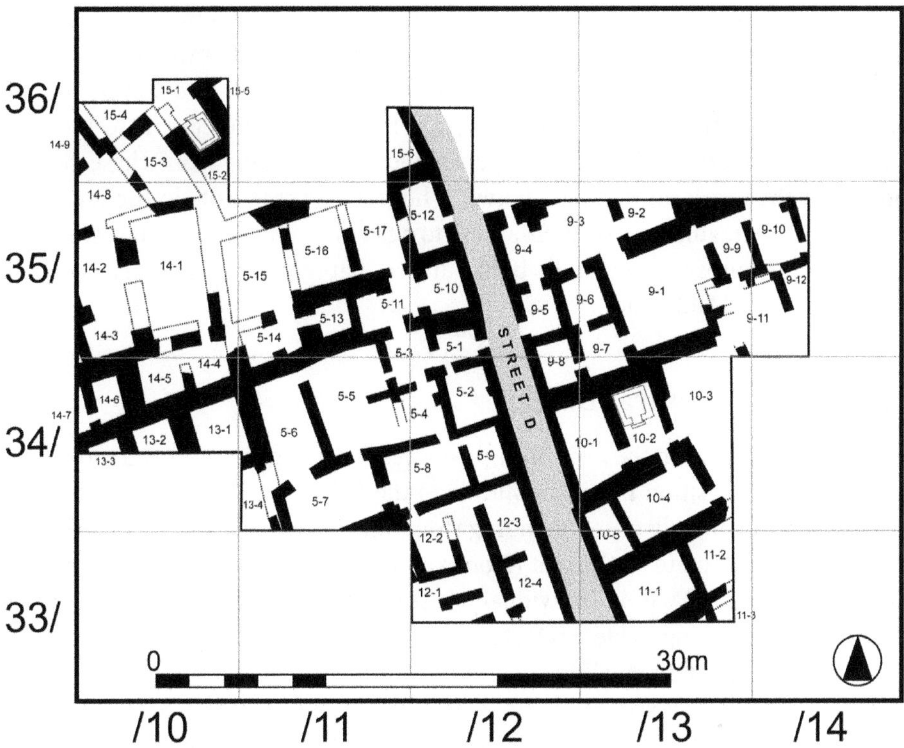

Figure 46.4. Plan of the excavated Lower Town architecture.

the exposed houses abut the nearby city wall in a manner suggesting that both were erected as part of a single coherent construction effort. Further evidence for careful planning and collective site-wide efforts is provided by the fact that houses often appear to have been built to fit irregular plots of land demarcated by street intersections. From this it may be deduced that the long-running streets were laid first and the houses built later. A test pit across one of the streets in the Late EBA exposure in the Lower Town confirms this; the wall foundations of the nearby house had been partially cut into the edge of the street, clearly indicating the sequence of construction: streets before houses.

Another indication of neighborhood-wide planning in the Late EBA is provided by the fact that at least in the Outer Town, houses along a street shared both a common terracing wall and subfloor drainage systems. Moreover in both of our broad Late EBA exposures, it can be seen that wall alignments often continued across different houses, and alignments even between houses at opposite sides of a single street are not uncommon (Matney 2002; Matney and Algaze 1995; Nishimura 2008).

Additionally, the houses appear to have been erected within standardized plots, suggesting that the urban landscape in the Late EBA city was deliberately parceled into predetermined sizes prior to development. Likewise, houses in different and widely distributed areas of the site show a remarkable degree of similarity in plan, as may be observed in figures 46.3 and 46.4, suggesting at a minimum the existence of a coherent urban template, and possibly that the Outer and Lower Town sectors of the settlement were developed in tandem as part of a massive and deliberate reorganization of the city's inner landscape at the onset of the Late EBA. Interestingly, a preliminary analysis of the palaeobotanical remains from these houses shows that the regularities in plan between households at the site in the Late EBA are matched by regularities in their access to agricultural products, suggesting not only that the houses were centrally built but also that they may have been centrally supplied as well (Hald 2009).

Late EBA Intramural Burial

An important change in the relationship between the living and the dead took place at Titriş at the transition from the Middle to the Late EBA. Whereas Middle EBA burials consisted mainly of self-standing stone-lined cists clustered in a segregated area outside of the main settlement (Honça and Algaze 1998), Late EBA cist burials were instead situated within individual houses inside the main settlement (Laneri 2007). Although comparable EBA stone-lined cist tombs have wide distribution across Syro-Mesopotamian (Yilmaz 2006), the Titriş cist tombs are unique in that they represent the clearest example we possess thus far from any EBA Syro-Anatolian urban site for built burials *directly* associated with specific private dwellings, although interestingly, such interments have a long history of use in third millennium B.C.E. southern Mesopotamia, where they have been identified at a variety of sites (minimally at Kish, Fara, Abu Salabikh, Tell Asmar, and Khafajah; for references, see Algaze 1983–84; Laneri 2007:n. 126). In any event, at Titriş, intramural house tombs were placed beneath the floors of rooms or courtyards and were frequently reopened and reused; with, in some cases, as many as seven or eight individuals interred sequentially within a single (family) crypt (figure 46.5). In addition to bronze pins and, more rarely, weapons, associated grave goods commonly included multiple ceramic cups, bowls, and jars of types often found within the houses and, less commonly, pedestaled painted vases and imported vessels, such as Syrian bottles and two-handled *depas* cups (e.g., Laneri 2007:figs. 5–6), which are largely restricted to funerary contexts at Titriş.

Titriş: Ceramics and EBA Relative Chronology

The relative chronology of third millennium B.C.E. deposits at Titriş and sites in its immediate hinterland outlined in the preceding sections is largely based (with modifications) on the published ceramic sequence from the site of Kurban Höyük

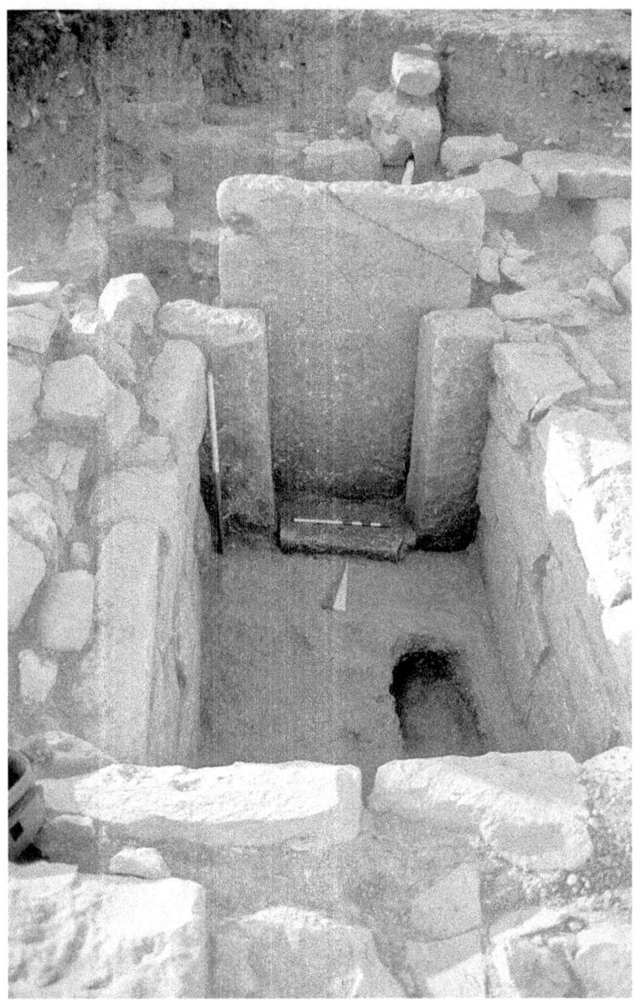

Figure 46.5. Excavated Late EBA cist burial. Note that an unusual child burial has been cut into the floor of the main burial chamber itself.

(Algaze 1990), situated some twenty-five kilometers due west of Titriş. The Early EBA assemblage identified in the basal layers of the 40–34 sounding at Titriş is wholly equivalent to that of Period V at Kurban, and is recognized most readily by the presence of highly fired, greenish, *cyma recta*-style goblets and diagonally reserved slip ware (see Ökse, chapter 11 in this volume, for further discussion on this and other EBA wares). In turn, the Middle and Late EBA assemblages at Titriş can be broadly equated with the Period IV sequence at Kurban.

Although there is substantial continuity of some types and wares between the Middle and Late EBA assemblages at Titriş, there are also some noteworthy differences that can be observed even before the final statistics of ceramic work at the site are tabulated. At the level of ware frequency, for instance, we find that Metallic, Horizontally Reserve Slipped, and Karababa Painted Wares (Algaze 1990), which are particularly common in Middle EBA groups, diminish to statistically insignificant amounts by the Late EBA. By the same token, some wares are only common in the latter phase and are not present in the Middle EBA, for example, a variant of Karababa Painted Ware that uses deep incisions to delineate and separate painted panels (e.g., Matney and Algaze 1995:fig. 16, center right). Particularly sensitive for chronological differentiation are the small cups and the cooking pots of the two assemblages. Whereas Middle EBA cups are invariably conical and outflaring (type as Algaze 1990:pl. 53 M–V; Algaze et al. 2001:fig. 21:1 F–I), the vast majority of Late EBA cups are barrel-shaped and have inturned walls (e.g., Matney and Algaze 1995:fig. 8B) that recall, at least in outline if not in proportions, the Hama goblets of EB IV Syrian sites. Middle EBA cooking pots, similarly, are easily distinguished from their Late EBA counterparts. Both have triangular ledge lugs, but those of the earlier phase are commonly highly burnished and have outflaring rims (type as Algaze 1990:pl. 93 A–M), whereas those of the later phase are usually only crudely burnished and have sharply inturning upper walls, approaching a hole-mouth shape (type as Algaze 1990:pl. 135 A–F).

Titriş: Environmental Context

The relative frequency of tree crops and wood charcoal in our palaeobotanical samples, both in Middle and Late EBA levels, leaves little doubt that the Titriş area was significantly more forested at the time of the site's apogee than at present (Schlee in Algaze et al. 1995:32). This conclusion is both reinforced and expanded by the results of geological test trenches opened across the two streams immediately bordering the site by Arlene Miller-Rosen and Paul Goldberg (Algaze et al. 1995). From the sedimentary record in these trenches, it can be deduced not only that Titriş was delimited by streams on three sides throughout the Mid–Late EBA, but also that there was an actively aggrading floodplain with alluvial deposition in the Holocene terrace surrounding the city at the time, which accordingly would have been characterized by fertile moist soils providing high yields for both cereal and horticultural products.

The uppermost layers of the sedimentological sequence just discussed indicate that strong flooding and, later, stream incision marked the end of the Mid–Late EBA alluvial phase. These changes could have resulted from either human factors, such as the stripping of vegetation for construction, fuel, or agriculture (Miller-Rosen in Algaze et al. 1995; Pournelle in Algaze et al. 2001), or environmental factors, such as an erratic rainfall pattern characterized by periods of drought punctuated by heavy storms (Weiss et al. 1993).

Although these possibilities are not mutually exclusive, our research has produced persuasive (though circumstantial) evidence pointing to the city's massive redevelopment program of the Late EBA as the most likely explanation for most of the observed changes at the very end of the third millennium B.C.E., as we explain next.

The Impact of the City on its Hinterland

In 1999, members of the Titriş project used available excavation and subsurface mapping data from Titriş to calculate the resources required to effect the Late EBA urban renewal program attested at Titriş and used the resulting calculations to extrapolate the potential impact of that program on the city's immediate hinterland. As these analyses have been discussed in full in an earlier report (Pournelle in Algaze et al. 2001), only a brief summary is provided here, focusing on the environmental impact of the extraction of limestone and timber from the Titriş hinterland during the Late EBA.

Limestone

Extrapolating from the density and type of construction in our Late EBA exposures, Pournelle estimated that over the full extent of the site, the Late EBA urban renewal program at Titriş would have required the quarrying, dressing, and transport of about 46,000 m^3, or 92,400 metric tons, of limestone. The quarry from which the stone was obtained was situated in hills about a kilometer due north of the ancient city (Algaze et al. 2001:fig. 28, top). The impact of such a massive stone quarrying operation is not difficult to imagine: accelerated erosion in the headwaters of the Titriş Çay, which was situated immediately downslope from the quarry, transforming that tributary from a perennial source of water with an easily exploited floodplain into a deeply incised silted-up channel prone to episodic and destructive flooding.

Wood and Timber

The amounts of timber needed for the city were equally impressive. Presuming that most structures had a second storey and presuming a roofing beam spacing consonant with modern ethnographic parallels for mudbrick architecture in the area, Pournelle estimated that 317,670 m^3 of timber would have been required to roof the built area of Late EBA Titriş. This represents nearly a million linear meters of roofing timber—an estimate that does not include the no doubt considerable amount of wood used as fuel at the site (Pournelle in Algaze et al. 2001).

It is possible to estimate the impact that procuring this large amount of wood must have had on the site's immediate hinterland. On the basis of satellite imagery,

Pournelle calculated the total available area where timber could be obtained within the Titriş corridor at 6,795 ha, and basing her analysis on the existing data for the density of wood resources in forested areas in present-day Turkey (38 m^3 per hectare) and data for the sustainable yields in those forests (1.65 m^3 per ha/year), she suggests that 11,212 m^3 per annum could have been harvested annually by the Late EBA inhabitants of the city without degrading forest cover. Thus, the estimated 317,670 m^3 of timber needed for roofing the architecture of the city could have been obtained with no significant detriment to the surrounding environment over twenty-eight years. However, this estimate does not include the undoubtedly much more considerable use of available wood for fuel, which no doubt dwarfed roofing needs. Presuming an arbitrary, and no doubt quite conservative two-to-one ratio between ongoing use of wood for fuel and its one time use for roofing, eighty-four years of sustainable exploitation would have been needed to rebuild the city in the Late EBA without significant environmental degradation of its hinterland.

It is likely, however, that the well-coordinated building program brought to light by our research was carried out within a much shorter period of time than this, perhaps within a generation (thirty years) or so. Such a tempo of extraction would have resulted in a net loss of over 20,000 m^3 of wood from the forest cover surrounding the city per year of the Late EBA construction program. Over the thirty-year life of the Late EBA reconstruction program, this annual deficit would have led to the almost total deforestation of the Titriş hinterland.

Conclusions

At the time of its foundation as an urban center in the Middle EBA, Titriş Höyük possessed the combined advantages of locally available timber, multiple perennial water sources and associated year-round cultivable floodplains suited to garden crops, and broad, rain-fed arable tracts suited to grain cultivation. Additionally, the site was surrounded by gentle limestone hills well suited to viticulture and livestock grazing. However, this benign framework provided a necessary but not sufficient condition for the development of the site. The sufficient condition, in our opinion, was the city's location along the road to the Samsat ford, which made it a natural arbiter of a portion of long distance east–west trade across the northern fringes of "Greater Mesopotamia" in the third millennium—a fact attested by the number and variety of imports found in excavated mortuary and domestic contexts across the city (Matney and Algaze 1995).

As local resource extraction intensified, largely as a result of the massive Late EBA urban redevelopment of the site, timber cutting, limestone quarrying, and, possibly, grazing combined to strip the protective cover from the slopes directly above the city, degrading many of the selective advantages that surely played a part in the rise of Titriş in the first place.

Additionally, there is good evidence for conflict at this time, such as the abandonment of the undefended suburbs surrounding the city, the erection of the city's fortifications, and the creation of a gruesome mortuary monument displaying the severed crania of nineteen individuals, mostly young males, at the intersection of two major streets in the Outer Town (Laneri 2007:255–56, fig. 7; Erdal 2010; Matney et al. 2010), and it is not illogical to imagine that if local, such conflict may have been exacerbated by the anthropogenic degradation of the city's hinterland. Under these conditions, the city's inhabitants were unable to withstand or circumvent the local effects of the climatic deterioration that affected large portions of the Ancient Near East in the last quarter of the third millennium B.C.E. (Weiss et al. 1993), resulting in the effective collapse of Titriş as an urban center at the end of the third millennium and the dispersal of much of its population into the surrounding hinterland (Algaze et al. 2001:fig. 24, bottom, right).

REFERENCES

Algaze, Guillermo. 1983–84. Private Houses and Graves at Ingharra: A Reconsideration. *Mesopotamia* 18/19: 135–94.

———. 1990. The Ceramic Sequence and Small Finds. In *Town and Country in Southeastern Anatolia II. The Stratigraphic Sequence at Kurban Höyük*, ed. Guillermo Algaze, 211–398. Oriental Institute Publications 110. Chicago: Oriental Institute of The University of Chicago.

Algaze, Guillermo, Gülay Dinckan, Britt Hartenberg, Timothy Matney, Jennifer Pournelle, Lynn Rainville, Steven Rosen, Eric Rupley, Duncan Schlee, and François Vallet. 2001. Research at Titriş Höyük, Southeastern Turkey: The 1999 Season. *Anatolica* 27: 23–106.

Algaze, Guillermo, Paul Goldberg, Deirdre Honça, Timothy Matney, Adnan Mısır, Arlene M. Rosen, Duncan Schlee, and Lewis Somers. 1995. Titriş Höyük, a Small Urban Center in SE Anatolia: The 1994 Season. *Anatolica* 21: 13–64.

Algaze, Guillermo, John Kelly, Timothy Matney, and Duncan Schlee. 1996. Late EBA Urban Structure at Titriş Höyük, Southeastern Turkey: The 1995 Season. *Anatolica* 22: 129–43.

Algaze, Guillermo, Timothy Matney, Steve A. Rosen, and Dilek Erdal, 2000. Excavations at Titris Höyük, Şanlıurfa Province: Preliminary Report for the 1998 season. *Kazı Sonuçları Toplantısı* 21: 145–56.

Algaze, Guillermo and Adnan Mısır. 1993. Excavations at Titriş Höyük: A Small Mid-Late Third Millennium Urban Center in Southeastern Anatolia, 1992. *Kazı Sonuçları Toplantisı* 15: 153–70.

———. 1994. Titriş Höyük, an EBA Urban Center in SE Anatolia, 1993. *Kazı Sonuçları Toplantisı* 16: 107–20.

Algaze, Guillermo, Adnan Mısır, Tony Wilkinson, Elizabeth Carter, and Ronald Gorny. 1992. Şanlıurfa Museum/University of California Excavations and Surveys at Titriş Höyük, 1991. *Anatolica* 18: 33–60.

Arcari, Elena. 1988. The Administrative Organization of the City of Ebla. In *Wirtschaft und Gesellschaft von Ebla*, ed. Harald Hauptmann and Hartmut Waetzoldt, 125–29. Heidelberg: Orient Verlag.

Astour, Michael C. 1988. The Geographical and Political Structure of the Ebla Empire. In *Wirtschaft und Gesellschaft von Ebla*, ed. Harald Hauptmann and Hartmut Waetzoldt, 139–58. Heidelberg: Orient Verlag.

Erdal, Ömur D. 2010. A Possible Massacre at Early Bronze Age Titriş Höyük, Anatolia. *International Journal of Osteoarchaeology*. DOI: 10.1002/oa.1177

Hald, Mette Marie. 2009. Distribution of Crops at Late Early Bronze Age Titriş Höyük, SE Anatolia: Towards a Model for the Identification of Centrally Organised Food Distribution. *Vegetation History and Archaeobotany*. DOI 10.1007/s00334-009-0223-9.

Hartenberger, Britt. 2003. *A Study of Craft Specialization and the Organization of Chipped Stone Production at Early Bronze Age Titriş Höyük, Southeastern Turkey*. Ph.D. dissertation. Department of Archaeology, Boston University.

Hartenberger, Britt, Steven Rosen, and Timothy Matney. 2000. The Early Bronze Age Blade Workshop at Titriş Höyük: Lithic Specialization in an Urban Context. *Near Eastern Archaeology* 63.1: 51–58.

Honça, Deirdre and Guillermo Algaze. 1998. Preliminary Report on the Human Skeletal Remains at Titriş Höyük: 1991–1996. *Anatolica* 24: 101–41.

Laneri, Nicola. 2007. Burial Practices at Titriş Höyük, Turkey: An Interpretation. *Journal of Near Eastern Studies* 66: 241–66.

Lebeau, Marc and Antoine Suleiman. 2003. *Tell Beydar, the 1995–1999 Seasons of Excavations*. Turnhout: Brepols.

Matney, Timothy. 2002. Urban Planning and the Archaeology of Society at EBA Titriş Höyük. In *Across the Anatolian Plateau: Readings in the Archaeology of Ancient Turkey*, ed. David C. Hopkins, 19–34. Boston: American Schools of Oriental Research.

Matney, Timothy and Guillermo Algaze. 1995. Urban Development at Mid-Late Early Bronze Age Titriş Höyük in Southeastern Anatolia. *Bulletin of the American Schools of Oriental Research* 299/300: 33–52.

Matney, Timothy, Guillermo Algaze, and Holly Pittman. 1997. Excavations at Titriş Höyük, Southeastern Turkey: A Preliminary Report of the 1996 Season. *Anatolica* 23: 61–84.

Matney, Timothy, Guillermo Algaze, and Steven Rosen. 1999. Early Bronze Age Urban Structure at Titriş Höyük: The 1998 Season. *Anatolica* 25: 185–201.

Matney, Timothy, Guillermo Algaze, Matt C. Dulik, Ömur D. Erdal, Yilmaz S. Erdal, Ömer Gokcumen, Joseph Lorenz, and Hattice Mergen. 2010. Understanding Early Bronze Age Social Structure Through Mortuary Remains: A Pilot aDNA Study from Titriş Höyük, Southeastern Turkey. *International Journal of Osteoarchaeology*. DOI: 10.1002/oa.1213

Matthiae, Paolo. 2003. Ebla and the Early Urbanization of Syria. In *The Art of the First Cities*, ed. Joan Aruz, 165–68. New York: Metropolitan Museum of Art.

Nishimura, Yoko. 2008. *North Mesopotamian Urban Space: A Reconstruction of Household Activities and City Layout at Titriş Höyük in the Third Millennium B.C.* Ph.D. dissertation. Institute of Archaeology, UCLA.

Pettinato, Giovanni. 1991. *Ebla: A New Look at History*. Baltimore, Md.: Johns Hopkins University Press.

Pfälzner, Peter. 2003. *Haus und Haushalt. Wohnformen des Dritten Jt. V.Chr. in Nordmesopotamien*. Mainz: Philipp von Zabern.

Weiss, Harvey. 1983. Excavations at Tell Leilan and the Origins of North Mesopotamian Cities in the Third Millennium B.C. *Paléorient* 9: 39–52.

———. 1990. Tell Leilan 1989: New Data for Mid Third Millennium Urbanization and State Formation. *Mitteilungen der Deutschen Orient-Gesellschaft* 122: 193–218.

Weiss, Harvey, Marie-Agnes Courty, Wendy Wetterstrom, François Guichard, Louise Senior, Richard Meadow, and Anne Curnow. 1993. The Genesis and Collapse of Third Millennium North Mesopotamian Civilization. *Science* 261: 995–1004.

Wilkinson Tony J. 1990. *Town and Country in Southeastern Anatolia, vol. I: Settlement and Land Use at Kurban Höyük and Other Sites in the Lower Karababa Basin.* Chicago: Oriental Institute.

———. 1994. The Structure and Dynamics of Dry Farming States in Upper Mesopotamia. *Current Anthropology* 35: 483–520.

Wilkinson, Tony J., John H. Christiansen, Jason Ur, Magnus Widell, and Mark Altaweel. 2007. Urbanization within a Dynamic Environment: Modeling Bronze Age Communities in Upper Mesopotamia. *American Anthropologist* 109: 52–69.

Yilmaz, Derya. 2006. Burial Customs of the Chamber Tombs in Southeast Anatolia during the Early Bronze Age. *Anadolu/Anatolia* 31: 71–90.

CHAPTER 47

KÜLTEPE-KANEŠ: A SECOND MILLENNIUM B.C.E. TRADING CENTER ON THE CENTRAL PLATEAU

FİKRİ KULAKOĞLU

KÜLTEPE is at the center of the plain formed at the foot of Erciyes Dağı, the highest mountain in the Central Anatolian plateau. The Kızıl Irmak, the longest river in Anatolia, flows from its source in Sivas through the mountainous region north of Kültepe and into the core of the Hittite region. The plain where Kültepe was built is enriched by the alluvial fill of the Sarımsaklı stream, which joins the Karasu to the north of the Kayseri Plain and flows into the Kızıl Irmak. The plain of Kayseri is twenty-five kilometers wide at its maximum; once marshland, it is the most fertile plain in the region, which is mainly steppe land (figure 47.1).

Kültepe is on the ancient trade route connecting central Anatolia to Malatya, a center that always had close links to Mesopotamian cultures (T. Özgüç 1950). Central Anatolia was also accessible from the Mediterrannean through passes in the Taurus Mountains, such as Yahyalı-Develi, Zamantı-Gezbeli-Sirkeli, or Tufanbeyli-Ceyhan, which led to Kültepe; the passes were narrow but convenient in the proper seasons and were also used during the Hittite Empire period.

Figure 47.1. Aerial view of the Kültepe Mound and the *kārum* from the south.

History of Research

Kültepe is one the largest mounds in Anatolia, but also one of the most damaged, primarily by researchers who were unacquainted with scientific excavation methods and techniques; E. Chantre in 1893–94, H. Winckler in 1906, and B. Hrozný in 1925 undertook excavations for the sole purpose of finding tablets and antique objects (T. Özgüç 1999). In addition to these unscientific activities, the local villagers dug into the mound down to the Early Bronze Age strata to remove soil for gardens, building houses, and other residental endeavors; as a result almost a third of the mound is too disturbed for modern scientific investigation.

Scientific excavations started in 1948 under the auspices of the Turkish Historical Association, directed by Tahsin Özgüç and his spouse, Nimet Özgüç, from the Faculty of Languages, History, and Geography of the University of Ankara (T. Özgüç 1950, 1959, 1971, 1986a, 1999, 2003; Özgüç and Özgüç 1953); this team carried out excavations until 2005. Following this, excavation continued with the current expedition directed by Kutlu Emre and by the present author.

Kültepe is formed of two parts. The circular mound is 550 m in diameter and 20 m higher than the surrounding alluvial plain. Because of the fortifications encircling the mound, it is higher at the edges than at the relatively hollow middle. The Lower City surrounds the mound from the north, east, and south in the approximate shape of a crescent. The waters of Engir Lake extend to the west, a larger lake in antiquity but marshland at present.

The Mound

Mound Levels	Periodization	Major Architecture/Discoveries
Level 18	Early Bronze Age I	
Levels 17–14	Early Bronze Age II	Close relations with Mesopotamia and North Syria and Cilicia; imported pottery from Upper Euphrates
Levels 13–11	Early Bronze Age III	Close relations with Mesopotamia, north Syria, and western Anatolia; appearance of monumental buildings
Levels 10–6	Kingdom of Kaneš in Assyrian Colony Period	Palaces, temples, and an official storage building
Levels 5–4	Iron Age	Late Hittite relief orthostats
Level 3	Hellenistic	City wall
Levels 2–1	Roman	

Intermittent excavations on the mound from 1955 to 2010 reached the earliest phase of the Early Bronze Age I, establishing eighteen cultural levels in all. Due to the depth of the deposits, only Level 18 dates to the Early Bronze I period. Levels 17–14 are dated to Early Bronze Age II. The Early Bronze Age III at Kültepe immediately precedes the Assyrian Colony period, when close links with Mesopotamia and northern Syria were established. During Levels 13–11, Kültepe was enriched with monumental buildings. The close relations between the plateau and northern Mesopotamia are documented with imported pottery, cylinder seals, and metal objects revealed in the excavations. The examples of jewelry at Kültepe that are foreign to central Anatolia are similar to the finds from the Ur III royal tombs. The Early Dynastic and Akkadian Period materials and styles were brought from southern Mesopotamia and northern Syria during this period. The presence of Akkadian and Post-Akkadian cylinder seals at Kültepe, and foreign pottery with origins in the south and southeast, prove the continous nature of the relationships between Kültepe and Mesopotamia (T. Özgüç 1986b, 1999).

Alabaster statuettes of gods and goddesses, peculiar to the Early Bronze II and III period, were discovered in the inner sancta of temples and in the graves. The indigenous characteristics of plastic art in Kültepe are represented by the disc-shaped alabaster idols with long necks and by the enthroned naked alabaster goddesses that hold their breasts. The alabaster gods and goddesses and the lion figures in high relief are more naturalistic in style compared to the metal figures from the north (T. Özgüç 1999).

Even though contacts were established with culturally developed societies where writing was known, Anatolia had not yet developed or borrowed a writing system. The earliest information from this period is in the legendary "King of Battle/ šar tamḫari" texts on the deeds of King Sargon of Akkad and his grandson Narām-Sīn, from the version in the Hittite language written 800 years after the death of Sargon: "'The King of Battle' made war on the city of Purušḫattum (Acemhöyük) because of the complaints of merchants," and in later years, "Narām-Sīn (2260–2223 B.C.E.) defeated the coalition of 17 kings, among them Pampa the King of Ḫatti and Zippani the King of Kaneš." (Veenhof and Eidem 2008)

A text relating a story about King Sargon of Akkad, written in the Old Assyrian dialect and in the style of the period, was discovered in building level II of the *kārum* in the archive of an Assyrian merchant, dated 400 years after Sargon. The Assyrian merchant who lived in Kaneš kept this important text in his house, apparently in memory of the heroic story of the legendary king (Günbattı 1997). However late or legendary these accounts are, the preserved documents prove that in the reign of these two Akkadian kings, relationships had been established between Anatolia and their domains in northern Syria and Mesopotamia.

In the Assyrian Colony period Kültepe was the center of the kingdom of Kaneš (Garelli 1963; Larsen 1967; Veenhof 1972; and see Michel, chapter 13 in this volume). Building levels 10–6 revealed on the mound represent this period. In spite of the earlier damage caused by unscientific probes and by local villagers, the excavations performed by the expedition directed by T. Özgüç obtained essential information on the earliest known kings of Kaneš/Neša, on the palaces where they lived and administered state affairs and which also functioned as caravanserais, on the temples they built, on the technical characteristics of the buildings, their dimensions, outlays, dates, and even on their owners. Three separate palaces have been revealed in Building Levels 7–8 of Kaneš. Each palace has an individual plan.

There are two palaces in Level 8, the first on the southern terrace of the mound (figure 47.2). This structure corresponds to squares CV-CXV/85–93 and is nearly ninety meters long. The building was to a great extent destroyed in later periods; the southern end could not be excavated because the Roman-Hellenistic fortified city wall corresponding to square CXV/91 was built on it. The palace is composed of a long corridor partly overlaid with wooden planks and partly with large, flat stones, leading to a courtyard with wings on each side. Service rooms, storerooms, and living rooms were revealed in the ground floor of the palace; the upper floor was probably reserved for reception rooms and the royal residence. On the ground floor, the benches along the walls of the rooms with the big fireplaces, the storage jars for grain, and the pitchers in the smaller rooms are indications that the building had a commercial function as well. The contents of the building had been removed before the fire, and very little was left in the rooms except for provision jars and some pottery. Most notable in the fire débris was the discovery of two tablets, a scorched cylinder seal, and a bulla bearing a cylinder seal impression. Most of the pottery is typical of Level II of the *kārum* of Kaneš (see later discussion); as in Level II, the grain storage jars in this building are decorated with paint in the Alişar III style.

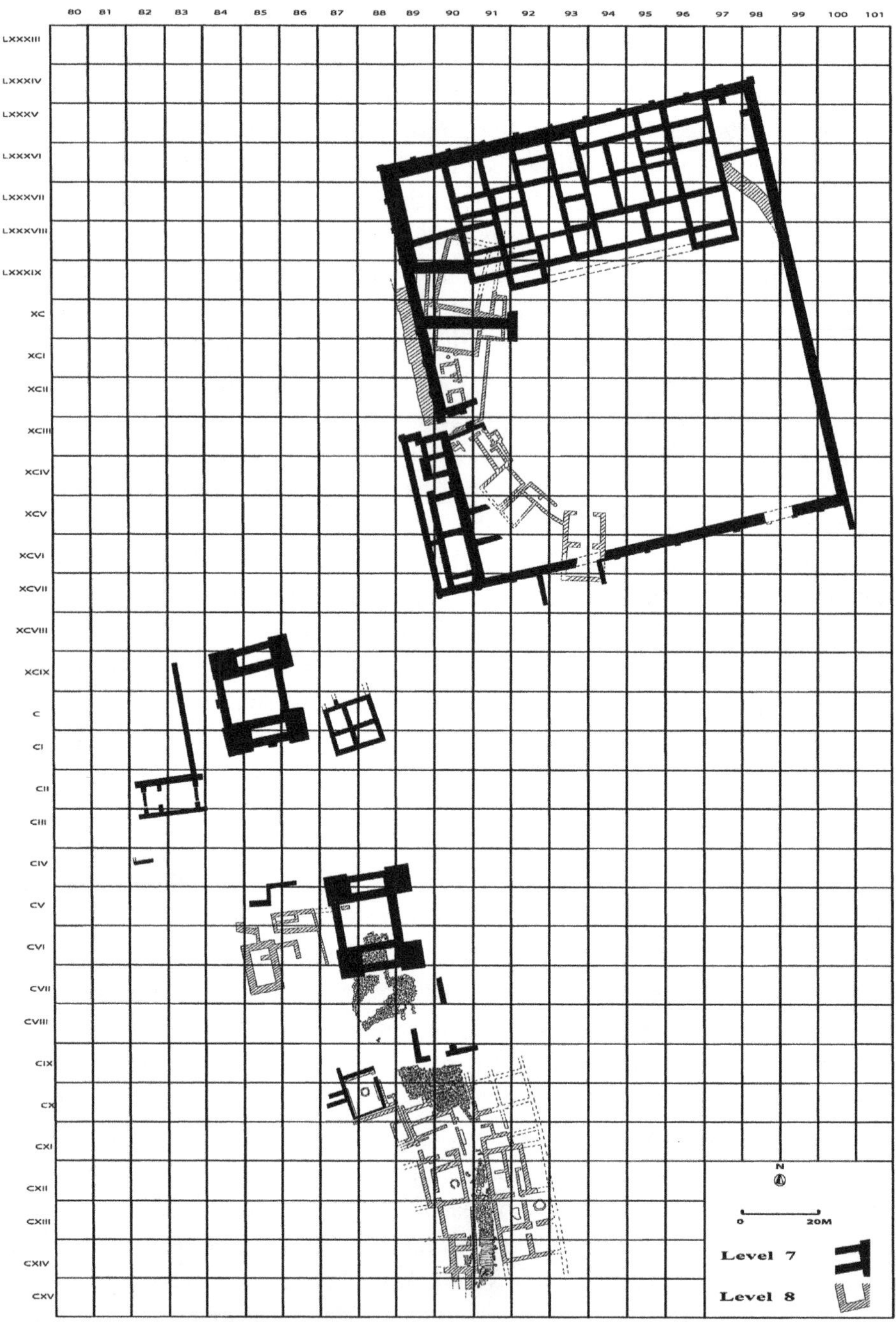

Figure 47.2. The general plan of the Old Assyrian Trading Colony period monumental buildings at Kültepe-Kaneš.

The "Old Palace" is the second administrative building in level 8 of the mound (figure 47.2: LXXXVIII–XCVI/88–94). It is located at the center of the citadel, in an eighty-meter-long excavated area, under the walls and fortifications of the later

Building Level 7 palace, "The Palace of Waršama." The mudbrick walls were well preserved, and the stone foundations to a lesser extent. The eastern walls of the palace were demolished during the 1925 excavation. As the plan indicates, the western walls of the rooms were cut off to build the later fortifications. Unlike the later palace built above it, the Old Palace is not formed of a single structure but consists of at least three buildings. The entrance to the complex was probably from the south.

Some of the rooms were built at different times, constructed next to others as annexes; others were built close together but on separate foundations. In the northern part of the palace where the large hall stood, there were service units as annexes to the south, with furnaces, ovens, firepots, and floors paved with stone to guard against the damp; alternatively, it is possible that a small separate building was built next to the main structure. This manner of building is very much in accordance with the old Anatolian building tradition. The monochrome and polychrome pottery found on the floors of rooms are undifferentiated from pottery in *Kārum* Level II. In spite of extensive structural damage, this palace has contributed to our understanding of the history of Neša. The Old Palace and its surrounding four-meter-wide fortification wall built in saw tooth technique were not restored and inhabited after the fire; they were abandoned and a new palace and city wall were subsequently built on their remains.

Very few small objects were found in the Old Palace; the contents were possibly removed before the fire or more probably plundered by the newcomers. In various parts of the structure and in related débris some tablets and envelopes with cylinder seal impressions were found, mostly in fragments. There were no tableware, metal items, cult objects, bullae, or other works of art. Some undamaged vases, kitchen utensils, bronze swords, and written documents were preserved accidentally.

The Building Level 7 palace is known as "The Palace of Waršama" in archaeological literature (figure 47.2: LXXXIV–LXXXVII/88–98). The citadel wall, which also functioned as the enclosure wall for the palace, is 120 × 110 m long, and its foundation is 2.5–4 m thick. There are buttresses at intervals of seven meters to the north, west, and south. The eastern buttresses were destroyed and lost in antiquity. The fortification walls were built simultaneously with the palace, and they were burned and abandoned with it. The palace appears to have been built with a specific plan and constructed on the remains of the Old Palace, in agreement with the topography of the mound; its prime significance is the architectural plan, which is the earliest example of its kind in Anatolia. The system consists of rooms arranged around a central courtyard and is the predecessor of Hittite palaces and temples. In the limited areas that escaped damage in 1925, excavations revealed that the rooms may have been connected to the courtyard by means of corridors. The building materials were stone, mudbricks, wood, and mud. Wooden poles were set up between the foundation stones at regular intervals. The fire that destroyed the palace burned more intensely because of the extensive use of wood.

The palace has forty-two rooms in the north section. The stone foundations are level with the floors, where mudbrick wall construction begins. The palace had two floors, judging from the thick mudbrick walls, the numerous wooden poles and pillars, the condition of the fire débris filling the rooms, and the stairwells. The main door of the palace is to the west. The entrance is controlled with two reciprocal stone towers and two rooms. The plan of the entrance is similar to the ones at Alişar and is the prototype for Boğazköy's main doors. Below the walls to the south of the entrance there is a postern, more than two meters high, the earliest example in Anatolia. The letter written by King Anum-Ḫirbi of Mama to King Waršama of Kaneš was discovered under the débris around the northern wall of the portal, on the floor near the northern base of the wall (Balkan 1957).

The excavations to the east of the citadel indicate that on the eastern and central parts of the citadel, the palace was constructed over the remains of buildings dated to the Early Bronze Age. The eastern wall faces of these Early Bronze buildings on the mound were battered, paved, and fortified with flat stones. The monochrome pottery found in these architectural features was identical to Early Bronze Age III pottery discovered in various other sections of Kültepe, offering a building date for these earlier structures.

The small objects found in the Palace of Waršama, in particular the pottery, the stamp seals, and the bullae with stamp seal impressions, were burned and destroyed together with the palace, and some of the pottery was reduced to slag. The finer ware of the palace, metal items, cult objects, works of art, and the archive were either removed before the fire or collected by the newcomers.

In the Assyrian Colony period the palaces of Kaneš had an important additional function. The palaces were also great economic centers where foreign merchants brought their merchandise for safe storage, similar to a caravanserai, and where procedures for commercial taxes were instituted. In this system, the wide courtyards and the numerous storerooms must have been functionally important.

Besides the palaces, two large buildings on the mound, forty meters apart, are remarkable because of their structural plans, both of which have been completely revealed (figure 47.2: XCVIII–CI/84–86 and CIV–CVII/87–89). Both are about 27 × 22 m in size, with large, turret-shaped projections on four corners of both buildings. On the northern and southern faces, between the inner and outer walls, each has a small rectangular room 3 × 10 m in size, with earthen floors. No objects were found on the floors in these rooms. The small rooms in the turrets were filled in with stone rubble of all sizes. There were tablets and a few examples of pottery on the floor of the halls, contemporary with Level Ib of the *kārum* in form and technique. The buildings had been abandoned after a great fire, the common fate of all the monumental buildings on the mound. These two buildings were probably sacred temples, even though there were no statues of deities or altars remaining. It is well known that King Anitta (the first Hittite king) wrote about the temples he built in Neša; the structures were most likely two of the temples mentioned in the Anitta text (Hoffner 1997:183).

The rectangular building corresponding to squares CII–CIII/82–83 is contemporaneous with the temples; one of its rooms functioned as a storeroom for unworked obsidian, and the so-called Anitta dagger (an elaborate spearhead) was discovered on the floor of this building. The rectangular structure, 7.5 m wide and 18 m long, had four sections. The northern and southern walls each extend to the east and west, forming antehalls at the front and at the back of the building, thereby giving the appearance of a megaron. The spearhead with the Anitta inscription was discovered on the floor of the large room in CII/83. The eastern side of the smaller room contained pieces of unworked obsidian in various sizes, weighing three tons in total.

Building Levels 4–5 represent the Late Hittite period. At this time, Kültepe was the center of one of the kingdoms under the dominion of the Great Land of Tabal. It continued as a strong political unit during the tenth to eighth centuries B.C.E. At about the end of the eighth century B.C.E. Kültepe was captured and destroyed by the Assyrians, at which time the hieroglyphic stelai, the statues, and the relief orthostats were shattered.

The last two ages on the mound are the Hellenistic period, represented by one building level (3), and the Roman period, with two building levels (2–1). The city walls built in the Hellenistic and Roman periods are under the steep sides of the mound. The walls were built over Assyrian Trade Colony period structures, indicating the reduced size of the city in the Hellenistic–Roman age. At this time, a sizable part of the Lower City functioned as a necropolis. Even though some objects of Achaemenid origin were found in the vicinity of Kültepe, no building level in the citadel is associated with the Achaemenids. The mound was abandoned in the late Roman period and remained in ruins during the Byzantine, Seljuk, and Ottoman ages (T. Özgüç 1999).

The *Kārum* of Kaneš

Mound Levels	Periodization	Cultural Horizons
Kārum Level IV *Kārum* Level III	Late third–early second millennium B.C.E.	ca. 2050/2000–1920 B.C.E.; the first appearance of wheelmade Hittite pottery
Kārum Level II	ca. 1950–1836 B.C.E.	Assyrian merchants arrived and established the trading system in Anatolia
Interval	ca. 1836–1833 B.C.E.	
Kārum Level Ib	ca. 1833–1719(?) B.C.E.	The city of Kaneš resettled after a short duration and lasted until the reign of King Samsuiluna of Babylon
Kārum Level Ia	ca. 1719–1685 (?) B.C.E.	

The Lower City is a part of Kültepe that was inhabited for only about 250 years. "Kaneš Harbor," the *kārum* Kaneš, the center of the Old Assyrian Trade Colony in Anatolia, is located in the Lower City. According to data available at present, the

Lower City is about two kilometers in diameter and encircles Kültepe mound from the north, east, and south in the shape of a crescent. The west of the mound is marshland. The excavations (which have continued to the present) in the Lower City have revealed four habitation levels, the latest one in two phases. The earliest settlement is Level IV, built on virgin soil. In the small, mudbrick buildings, the earliest examples of wheelmade Hittite pottery were present in smaller numbers along with the handmade monochrome and polychrome pottery. In Level III, on the other hand, the amount of wheelmade pottery exceeds the handmade, polychrome variety. The excavators have dated the two building levels from the end of the third millennium B.C.E. to the beginning of Level II of the *kārum*. No written documents were found in the settlements corresponding to Levels IV and III (Emre 1989).

Building Levels IV and III are succeeded by Level II, when the Assyrian merchants arrived and settled here for commercial activity, leaving behind them thousands of documents in cuneiform writing. According to the earliest *līmu* name attested in these written sources, discovered in 2001, the beginning of trade is dated to 1927 B.C.E. (Günbattı 2008). Kaneš suffered a great disaster of fire in approximately 1836 B.C.E., corresponding to the reign of King Narām-Sīn of Assur, but was inhabited again a few years later. It was resettled as Building Level Ib, but this period eventually came to an end a short time after 1719 B.C.E. (Günbattı 2008; Veenhof 2003). The *kārum* of Kaneš was in complete decline during Level Ia.

The foreign merchants who came to Kaneš settled on the mound and in the Lower City, which was inhabited by native Anatolians. The *Kārum* II city is composed of quarters, separated by squares and streets usually paved with stone and wide enough for carts to pass through easily. Streets had drainage channels for wastewater, which were paved over with stone slabs. The pavement stones on both sides of the roads served as walkways for the pedestrians and also helped protect the houses from external damage. The discarded pottery sherds on the streets helped stabilize the muddy paths.

The written documents inform us that the *kārum* was a fortified city protected with strong city walls, in both building levels (see Michel, chapter 13 in this volume). Inside these walls the quarters are formed of buildings built very close together, side by side and back to back. Some houses were enlarged with extensions built later, which gave them irregular appearances. The houses are usually in blocks, formed of six to eight residences, built together back to back. The Assyrian merchants either bought existing buildings or had new ones built and lived in these quarters together with the native population. The technique of construction and the materials used for the houses are in the traditional Anatolian style. The houses are built very close together according to indigenous building techniques, on stone foundations with the mudbrick walls supported with wooden timbers; they have two to six rooms and usually two stories. Most Level II buildings have two sections: the living rooms–pantry, and the archive and storage rooms. The walls were plastered and were usually whitewashed more than once. The long and narrow rooms in some houses are paved with stones. The floors are stamped earth.

The merchant houses have, through continuous excavation, been entirely revealed, complete with contents. In these buildings, the residential parts of the houses are set apart from the comparatively small, locked-up, and sealed archive rooms, and the storage rooms where merchandise was kept to be marketed. The tablets in the archive rooms were arranged on wooden shelves, or stored neatly in pots or wooden chests, or wrapped in matting and placed in sacks, and were classified according to content. The inhabitants of the *Kārum* II city apparently barely escaped from the conflagration that destroyed it, abandoning the tablets and other fireproof objects for later discovery by our excavations. As the fire broke out, many merchants had no chance to send their letters, which were already in their respective envelopes, while some letters they had received remained unopened.

Metal and textiles were of primary importance in this colonial center; in the excavated workshops, both production and retail activities took place (Dercksen 1996). The metal workshops are in various parts of the settlement. The architectural structure of workshops is not different from other houses, but they have large and sturdy furnaces and the floors are paved with stone. They are identifiable by the stone molds, melting pots, blow-pipes, and bellows they contained, which were much more numerous than a household would normally possess. The people who worked there were mainly indigenous Anatolians. However, they also produced imported forms that were foreign to Anatolia. Judging from the abundant spindle whorls found in houses, the women possibly wove textiles for their husbands, as they did in Assur.

In the *kārum*, in all building levels, the dead were buried in graves under the floors of the houses, either in cist graves or sarcophagi. The form and orientation of graves are not differentiated in the two cities (i.e., *Kārum* Levels II and Ib). Although tomb robbery was already occurring at this time, the still plentiful remaining burial gifts were rich and varied. The dead were buried with their weapons and personal ornaments; they were sent off to the afterworld with pottery or metal vessels for their needs, and even with their capital funds to do business in afterlife, accompanied with depictions of deities according to their religious beliefs.

The Ceramic Assemblage

Kaneš was one of the most distinguished centers of pottery production in the ancient Near East because of its high output and richly varied forms and techniques (Emre 1963, 1989). In this period, Anatolian pottery was at its highest level in the richness and variety of forms and ornamentation. There is no differentiation between the utensils in native households and the households of Assyrian merchants, since all were made in accordance with native traditions.

Much of the *Kārum* Levels IV–III ceramic assemblage has a great deal in common with the style known as Alişar III, based on the assemblage excavated at

Alişar Höyük. Cream slipped and painted in red or black, the Alişar III pottery is peculiar to the Kayseri region, which includes Kültepe; although it appears in Levels IV and III it continued to be used in Level II, though in lesser numbers.

The fast potter's wheel that was used was highly effective in the production technique and in the variation of forms characterizing the Assyrian Colony period pottery. In their form and technique, the majority of pottery imitates metal vessels used in Anatolia from the beginning of the last quarter of the third millennium B.C.E., which testifies to the potters' technical competence and contributes to the variety of forms found. Many different forms of pottery appeared for the first time in Level II; some continued into Level Ib, while others disappeared completely. In addition, new forms appeared in Level Ib, and some of these continued to be used in later periods. The rich and varied *kārum* assemblage is not observed in the later Old Hittite Kingdom, or in the Hittite Empire periods. Discoveries at other central Anatolian sites indicate that some main forms from the Assyrian Colony period continued to be used in the following ages as well (Emre 1963).

The pottery made with the fast potter's wheel is typical to Kaneš with respect to the paste, the slipping and polishing, the techniques of ornamentation, and the variety of forms. Two thirds of the larger vessels are slipped in red, brown, cream, dark gray, buff, and black. The fine paste is mixed with sand. Apart from kitchenware with coarse paste, vessels are always highly burnished. The majority of the pottery is monochrome; there are very few examples of painted pottery, and the painting tradition did not survive long beyond Level Ib.

The jars and the big pots of grain were neatly stored in the storerooms. The houses contained abundant examples of varied pottery types used for tableware. The amount of pottery found in some houses was much more than a family would normally need. Judging from their pristine condition, such pottery was apparently merchandise stored for the market. Some pottery vessels were not suitable for daily use. These are peculiar to Kaneš and do not have parallels in the ancient Near East. They were used for religious rituals or were placed in graves as burial gifts.

In the *kārum* of Kaneš much of the pottery from Levels II and Ib is decorated with animal figures. Most vessels have spouts in the shape of a bull's or ram's head. Similarly, most vessels have animal-shaped handles. The fantastic ornamentation in the form of antelopes, bulls, lions, and birds that were set within the vessel or on the orifice rim are unique to Kültepe (T. Özgüç 2003).

The animal figures in relief depicting the bull, the lion, and the bird, attached to the body of the vessel in appliqué technique, were also later used in the Old Hittite Kingdom, which followed the Assyrian Colony period. The continuation of pottery styles into the "Old Hittite Kingdom Period" beginning with the reign of Ḫattušili, shows closest similarities to the late phase pottery of the Assyrian Trade Colony period (Kulakoğlu 1996). The origins of the terracotta cult objects from the Old Hittite Kingdom period, described as "relief vases," are also linked to Kültepe.

The animal- and bird-shaped terracotta drinking cups are the first examples of zoomorphic vessels made of precious metals, called *BIBRU*, "rhyton," in Akkadian, which were used in religious ceremonies according to Hittite sources. Though the drinking cups found at Kültepe are terracotta, the *BIBRU* mentioned in Hittite texts are made of precious metals! These drinking cups may take the form of a lion, bull, ox, antelope, rabbit, dog, boar, eagle, partridge, or snail; they occur in four main groups. One group depicts animal figures standing or lying on their folded legs; animal heads, especially eagle, form another group. The perched or flying eagles form subgroups in this category. A third group consists of drinking cups that are boat-shaped, with the spout usually formed as the head of a ram or a water buffalo. The legs of the animal are sometimes depicted beneath the boat. The boatmen figurines are at the sides, holding the oars; their bodies below the waist are within the boat. The boat-shaped vessels represent the ritualistic river journey that the deity inside the shrine made during a festival as described in Sumerian literature. In an international center such as Kaneš it was important to enact rituals from the Sumerian-Akkadian tradition. The fourth group of cult vessels are boot-shaped. They are monochrome, brightly polished, or decorated with geometrical designs; the majority are peculiar to Kültepe. They were usually discovered in the archive rooms (T. Özgüç 2003).

The anthropomorphic vessels and the vessels in the form of human heads and ornamented with human head reliefs were likely not used for mundane purposes. The anthropomorphic vases with or without horns were most probably designated as cult objects. As with the lead figurines (see later discussion), the indigenous gods and goddesses were also portrayed in groups on the clay vases, which probably were used for their cult ceremonies.

Besides native pottery, there were examples of imported vessels as well. The origin of such pottery was usually northern Syria, and they became even more varied in building Level Ib. Because they appear in levels dated with the help of written documents, they can be synchronized with their places of origin (Emre 1994, 1995, 1999).

Other Material Culture

The statuettes of gods and goddesses discovered in Level Ib, following the destruction of Level II, are made of bronze, faience, lead, gold with ivory, and clay (T. Özgüç 2003). The statuettes of the principal goddess, depicted naked and in the act of offering her breasts in her hands, are made of ivory, faience, and bronze. The ivory statuette of the enthroned naked goddess who holds her breasts in her hands was discovered in a Level Ib grave (figure 47.3). This is the prototype of the statuettes of goddesses which were made of bronze and gold during the Hittite Empire period; it is one of the earliest examples depicting the characteristic physiognomic attributes of Hittite art.

The lead figurines and stone molds used to cast and duplicate them depict the principal goddess, or the goddess grouped with her children and with mythological creatures; they attest that the pantheon of this period was composed of distinct deities, differentiated by their individual insignia (Emre 1971). The lead figurines and their stone molds is the second largest group of figural finds at Kültepe, following the seals and seal impressions. The small figurines were destined for religious use and are known to have been widely distributed in the Near East. As with the seal impressions, the figurines represent various gods and goddesses, different divine families, and mythological creatures (Hirsch 1972). It is possible to distinguish the divine beings through their symbols and attributes, but written documents do not provide information on their identities. Most probably they were the "tutelary gods" of the households.

During the Assyrian Trade Colony period the lead figurines depicting gods, goddesses, and divine families began to display a distinct physical appearance, with a large nose, full face, large ears, and a slightly smiling expression on the face.

Figure 47.3. Ivory statuette of the nude goddess of level Ib.

This physiognomic mode of representation continued until the end of the Hittite Empire period.

The most exciting find from the *kārum* of Kaneš excavation campaign of 2006 is an oval-shaped thin gold folio with the depiction of a deity (Kulakoğlu 2008). The figure stands on a lion; his head and lower body are in profile while his upper body is depicted frontally. In his right hand he holds a shaft-hole ax, resting on his right shoulder; in his left hand he holds the hind legs of a smaller lion figure. Like the lead figurines, this item was a depiction of a god that was kept in a private household. The tablets from the Assyrian Trade Colony period show that people possessed their own personal figurines of the deities. It is worth noting that this item, which displays entirely Hittite stylistic features, was found in Building Layer Ib of the *kārum*. This deity, the earliest example of depictions rendered in the Hittite artistic style, provides further evidence that Hittite art originated in Kültepe (figure 47.4).

The jewelry made of precious stones and metals, the bronze vessels, and the weapons were mostly discovered in graves (T. Özgüç 1986a). The workshops in Levels Ib and II, which were excavated completely, also contained stone moulds for casting all kinds of metal objects. The weapons, figurines, and pottery imported from northern Syria and Mesopotamia define the international character of this great trading center. Most of the metal objects are made of copper, bronze, silver, gold, electrum, and lead. Copper and bronze vessels, weapons, belt buckles, spools,

Figure 47.4. Gold folio with the depiction of a deity found in *Kārum* Ib.

cymbals, pins, zoomorphic and anthropomorphic figurines, and rings with various functions constitute an important collection. The cuneiform documents refer to metal objects weighing nearly 100 kg in total, mostly vessels, which were part of the inventory of a merchant's house. The vessels were formed by using forging and casting techniques, whereas riveting and soldering were used for joining the handles and the other details.

The metal objects left as burial gifts in the tombs of the *kārum* of Kaneš are mainly weapons. Stone molds for casting these weapons were also found in the workshops of Levels II and Ib. Most weapons that were not common in Anatolia were imports from northern Syria and Mesopotamia or were locally manufactured by using the imported examples as models (T. Özgüç 1986a).

Texts And Seals

Seals

Among the most significant archaeological materials found at Kültepe are the cylinder seals imported to Anatolia from both Mesopotamia and Syria, and the seal impressions (N. Özgüç 1965, 1968). The clay envelopes for the tablets, and the "bullae," are impressed with cylinder seals in Level II, whereas in Level Ib it may be either cylinder or stamp seals (N. Özgüç 2001, 2006). Beginning from Level Ib the tablets and envelopes were both sealed; toward the end of this period, however, only the tablets were sealed. Usually there are inscriptions and seal impressions on the face of the lumps of clay attached to the portable or nonportable items required to be protected, and to the merchandise, tablets, or personal possessions that were being transported. The cosmopolitan nature of Kültepe's population led to the development of at least four distinct styles in glyptic art. The cylinder seal impressions discovered in Kültepe are mainly in the Old Assyrian style; the most typical example discovered in Kültepe is the seal of King Sargon of Assur (figure 47.5). The style is differentiated by the sharp body contours of the figures, the forked hands, the schematic faces, and the cross-hatchings that fill in the garments and body details. The main subject matter of Old Assyrian seals, made in the Ur III dynastic tradition, are scenes of worship. In Level Ib there were fewer seals in the Old Assyrian style, reflecting the general course of trade relations, but this earlier tradition continued to some extent in seals carved under its influence. Other variations are the so-called Provincial Old Babylonian style, in which early Babylonian motifs were worked under the influence of the Old Assyrian style, and another tradition where the extremely stylized figures are indicated with angular lines. The typical Old Babylonian style with origins in southern Mesopotamia is notable for its fine workmanship, typified by figures with rounded contours and skillfully used registers, where the worship scenes are again the principal theme.

Figure 47.5. Seal impression of Sargon, king of Assur.

The style of a third group of seals from Level II appears to be peculiar to Kaneš and is designated "Syrian-Cappadocian" or "Syrian-Colony"; the most notable features on these seals are the garments of the worshipers wearing caps with narrow edges and overcoats with rounded skirts. These seals appear in three subgroups. The first subgroup is linked to the Ur III dynastic style; these seals are very well modeled and offer the most extensive repertoire. The second subgroup is linear and comprises Syrian elements influenced by the Old Assyrian style. In the third group of seals, which are probably the source of the "Common Style" of the Mitannian period, drilling techniques were used to work the head and shoulders of the figures. The seals of Syrian origin, found in Level Ib, belong to the Syrian seals group contemporary with King Ḫammurabi of the Old Babylonian dynasty. The deities being worshiped generally wear Old Babylonian garments.

The fourth group is a new style in Level II and is represented by homogenous and highly developed stamp seals unique to Kültepe, called the "Native-Anatolian" group. They are highly individualized, varied in their style and worked in very fine detail; the scenes depicted portray ceremonies, hunting and battle scenes, and processions of deities standing on their sacred animals. All free spaces have been filled with motifs and symbols. The Native-Anatolian style evolved to its highest level at Kültepe and became the source of later Hittite glyptic art.

In the Level Ib Period, in contrast to Level II, the tablets also bore seal impressions. The first group of Level Ib seals in Anatolian style remained true to Level II style, but a second group represents the initial examples of the Hittite stamp seals that became common in later Hittite periods. The stamp seals depict scenes of worship, deities, hybrid creatures, heraldic eagles, animals, and astral motifs. A limited part of Assyrian style seals continue the Level II tradition, whereas others are influenced by the Old Babylonian style. This characteristic, that is, the multiple use of styles, is a sign of the weakening political relations with Assur. Furthermore, Level II Old Babylonian style seals were kept into Level Ib times, with the depictions modified for reuse. Some seals in the Syrian style continued to be used in the Ib level, and elements of Classical Syrian styles and Egyptianizing techniques also appeared (T. Özgüç 2003).

Tablets

So far, the excavations at Kültepe have brought to light a total of 23,500 tablets, of which 23,000 tablets are from Level II and 500 from Level Ib (see Michel, chapter 13 in this volume for detailed information). A very substantial portion of these finds were from the excavations in the *kārum* area (Bilgiç 1964). The tablets discovered at Kültepe are primarily significant because they represent the beginning of written history in Anatolia. Here at Kültepe Anatolians learned how to read and write for the first time. As a result of Anatolian relations with Mesopotomia and northern Syria, which we learn of through the information gained from these tablets, the people of central Anatolia perfected the skills of establishing and administering a state, and learned about legal systems and bureaucracy. Though no written documents have so far been discovered, and the architectural remains are poor, finds from Level Ia point to the birth of Hittite culture in this period. In particular, data derived from the graves of Level Ia indicate that there was a fairly short interval between the end of the settlement in this level and the establishment of the Old Hittite Kingdom period (Kulakoğlu 1996).

Conclusion

After the end of the Level Ia settlement, the *kārum* area was not inhabited for a long time. In the Iron Age, the signs of habitation we find on the mound do not appear in the Lower City. Judging from the metal coins and the pottery found in the excavations, during the Late Roman period the Lower City was partly used by farming communities, while a portion of it served as a necropolis.

Material cultural remains from the period of the Hittite Empire, one of the three Near Eastern superpowers during the second half of the second millennium B.C.E., have not been discovered at Kültepe. Some coins and pottery finds from the Seljuk and Ottoman periods provide signs of habitation at that time on lands that were part of the city of Kaneš. The regional designation “Karye-i Kınış” from the seventeenth century C.E. judicial registers of Kayseri reflects a memory of the most ancient name of Kaneš, reminding us of the legacy of this most important cultural center of the Middle Bronze Age.

REFERENCES

Balkan, Kemal. 1957. *Letter of King Anum-Hirbi of Mama to King Warshama of Kanish*. Türk Tarih Kurumu Yayınlarından VII.31a. Ankara: Türk Tarih Kurumu Basımevi.

Bilgiç, Emin. 1964. Three Tablets from the City Mound of Kültepe. *Anadolu/Anatolia* 8: 145–63.

Dercksen, Jan-Gerrit. 1996. *The Old Assyrian Copper Trade in Anatolia*. İstanbul: Nederlands Historisch-Archaeologisch Institut te Istanbul.

Emre, Kutlu. 1963. The Pottery of the Assyrian Colony Period According to the Building Levels of the Kaniš Karum. *Anadolu/Anatolia* 7: 87–99.

———. 1971. *Anadolu Kurşun Figürinleri ve Taş Kalıpları/Anatolian Lead Figurines and Their Stone Moulds*. Türk Tarih Kurumu Yayınlarından VI.14. Ankara: Türk Tarih Kurumu Basımevi.

———. 1989. Pottery of Levels III und IV at the Karum of Kanesh. Tahsin Özgüç'e Armağan. In *Anatolia and the Ancient Near East. Studies in Honor of Tahsin Özgüç*, ed. Kutlu Emre, Barthel Hrouda, Machteld Mellink, and Nimet Özgüç, 111–28. Ankara: Türk Tarih Kurumu.

———. 1994. A Type of Syrian Pottery from Kültepe/Kaniš. In *Beiträge zur Altorientalischen Archäologie und Altertumskunde. Festschrift für Barthel Hrouda zum 65. Geburtstag*, ed. Peter Calmeyer, Karl Hecker, Liane Jakob-Rost, and C. B. F. Walker, 91–96. Wiesbaden: Otto Harrassowitz.

———. 1995. Pilgrim-Flask from Level I of the Karum of Kanish. *Bulletin of the Middle Eastern Culture Center in Japan* 6: 175–200.

———. 1999. Syrian Bottles from the Karum of Kanish. *Bulletin of the Middle Eastern Culture Center in Japan* 11: 39–50.

Garelli, Paul. 1963. *Les assyriens en Cappadoce*. Paris: Adrien Maisonneuve.

Günbattı, Cahit. 1997. Kültepe'den Akadlı Sargon'a Ait Bir Tablet. *Archivum Anatolicum* 3: 131–55.

———. 2008. An Eponym List (KEL G) from Kültepe. *Altorientalische Forschungen* 35.1: 103–32.

Hirsch, Hans. 1972. *Untersuchungen zur altassyrischen Religion*. *Archiv für Orientforschung*. Beiheft 13/14.

Hoffner, Harry A. Jr. 1997. Proclamation of Anitta of Kuššar. In *The Context of Scripture*, vol. 1, ed. William W. Hallo and K. Lawson Younger Jr., 182–84. Leiden: Brill.

Kulakoğlu, Fikri. 1996. Ferzant-Type Bowls from Kültepe. *Bulletin of the Middle Eastern Culture Center in Japan* 9: 69–86.

———. 2008. A Hittite God from Kültepe. In *Old Assyrian Studies in Memory of Paul Garelli*, ed. Cécile Michel, 13–19. Old Assyrian Archives Studies, vol. 4. Leiden: Nederlands Instituut voor het Nabije Oosten.

Larsen, Mogens T. 1967. *Old Assyrian Caravan Procedures*. İstanbul: Nederlands Historisch-Archaeologisch Institut te Istanbul.

Özgüç, Nimet. 1965. *Kültepe Mühür Baskılarında Anadolu Grubu/The Anatolian Group of Cylinder Seal Impressions from Kültepe*. Türk Tarih Kurumu Yayınlarından V.22. Ankara: Türk Tarih Kurumu Basımevi.

———. 1968. *Kaniš Karumu Ib Katı Mühürleri ve Mühür Baskıları/Seal and Seal Impressions of Level Ib from Karum Kaniš*. Türk Tarih Kurumu Yayınlarından V.25. Ankara: Türk Tarih Kurumu Basımevi.

———. 2001. *Kültepe-Kaniš Mühürlü ve Yazıtlı Kil Bullalar/Sealed and Inscribed Clay Bullae.* Türk Tarih Kurumu Yayınlarından V.48. Ankara: Türk Tarih Kurumu Basımevi.

———. 2006. *Kültepe-Kaniš/Neša, Yerli Peruwa ve Ašur-ımittī'nin oğlu Assur'lu Tüccar Uşur-ša-Ištar'ın Arşivlerine ait Kil Zarfların Mühür Baskıları/Seal Impressions on the Clay Envelopes from the Archives of the Native Peruwa and Uşur-ša-Ištar son of Ašur-ımittī the Assyrian.* Türk Tarih Kurumu Yayınlarından V.50. Ankara: Türk Tarih Kurumu Basımevi.

Özgüç, Nimet and Tahsin Özgüç. 1953. *Kültepe Kazısı 1949/Ausgrabungen in Kültepe 1949.* Türk Tarih Kurumu Yayınlarından V.12. Ankara: Türk Tarih Kurumu Basımevi.

Özgüç, Tahsin. 1950. *Kültepe Kazısı 1948/Ausgrabungen in Kültepe 1948.* Türk Tarih Kurumu Yayınlarından V.10. Ankara: Türk Tarih Kurumu Basımevi.

———. 1959. *Kültepe-Kaniş. Assur Ticaret Kolonilerinin Merkezinde Yapılan Yeni Araştırmalar/New Researches at the Center of the Assyrian Trade Colonies.* Türk Tarih Kurumu Yayınlarından V.19. Ankara: Türk Tarih Kurumu Basımevi.

———. 1971. *Demir Devrinde Kültepe ve Civarı/Kültepe and its Vicinity in the Iron Age.* Türk Tarih Kurumu Yayınlarından V.29. Ankara: Türk Tarih Kurumu Basımevi.

———. 1986a. *Kültepe-Kaniş II. Eski Yakındoğu'nun Ticaret Merkezinde Yeni Araştırmalar/ New Researches at the Trading Center of the Ancient Near East.* Türk Tarih Kurumu Yayınlarından V.41. Ankara: Türk Tarih Kurumu Basımevi.

———. 1986b. New Observations on the Relationship of Kültepe with Southeast Anatolia and North Syria during the Third Millennium BC. In *Ancient Anatolia, Aspects of Changes and Cultural Development, Essays in Honor of Machteld J. Mellink,* ed. Jeanny Vorys Canby, Edith Porada, Brunilde Sismondo Ridgway, and Tamara Stech, 31–47. Wisconsin: University of Wisconsin Press.

———. 1999. *Kültepe-Kaniš/Neša Sarayları ve Mabedleri/The Palaces and Temples of Kültepe Kaniš/Neša.* Türk Tarih Kurumu Yayınlarından V.46. Ankara: Türk Tarih Kurumu Basımevi.

———. 2003. *Kültepe/Kaniş-Neša. The Earliest International Trade Center of the Ancient World and the Oldest Hittite Capital Town.* İstanbul: MAS Matbaacılık.

Veenhof, Klaas R. 1972. *Aspects of Old-Assyrian Trade and its Terminology.* Leiden: Brill.

———. 2003. *The Old Assyrian List of Year Eponyms from Karum Kanish and its Chronological Implications.* Türk Tarih Kurumu Yayınlarından VI.64. Ankara: Türk Tarih Kurumu Basımevi.

Veenhof, Klaas R. and Jesper Eidem. 2008. Mesopotamia. The Old Assyrian Period. Annäherungen 5. *Orbis Biblicus et Orientalis* 160.5. Academic Press Fribourg. Vandenhoeck & Ruprecht Göttingen.

CHAPTER 48

KEY SITES OF THE HITTITE EMPIRE

DIRK PAUL MIELKE

Archaeological and historical sources allow us to reconstruct a highly developed and organized system of settlements for the Hittite period (Mielke 2011; Schachner 2009b; and see Glatz, chapter 40 in this volume). It is therefore astounding that so few archaeological sites can be characterized as key sites for Hittite research. This state of affairs is partially attributable to the fact that settlement areas have only been exposed extensively in a small number of excavations. Furthermore, significant findings often have been insufficiently published. In this respect documents, in the form of clay tablets, are of particular importance, as they provide concrete historical insights. However, such tablets have only been discovered at a few locations (van den Hout 2011:fig. 5, and see van den Hout, chapter 41 in this volume). For these reasons, the field of Hittite archaeology has been largely dominated to date by the excavations at Boğazköy-Ḫattuša. Due to space constraints, only a small selection of key sites is presented in the following discussion (figure 48.1). Nevertheless, because of their varied significance, they illuminate the diversity of Hittite settlements. For a survey of additional important excavation sites, the reader should consult the overview by Genz and Mielke (2011) as well as Seeher's contribution to this volume (chapter 16).

The Capital: Boğazköy-Ḫattuša

The impressive ruins of Boğazköy (Çorum province) drew the attention of numerous travelers to the Near East as early as the nineteenth century (figure 48.2), yet English and German archaeologists initially struggled in vain to obtain a license

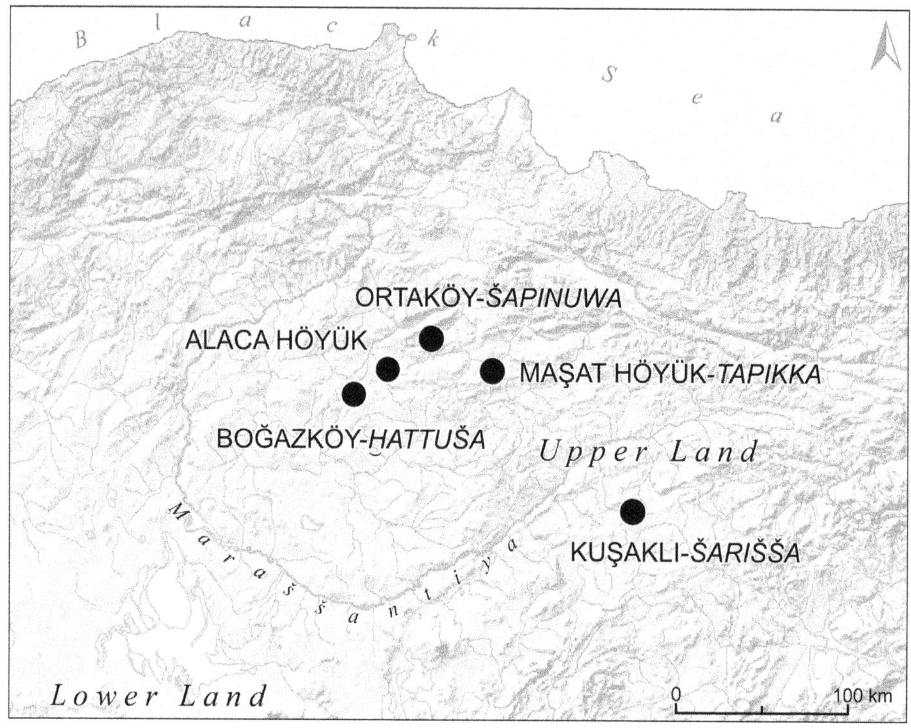

Figure 48.1. Map of Hittite key sites in central Anatolia.

for excavating this most promising site (Alaura 2006). Ultimately it was a Frenchman, Ernst Chantre, who made the first test excavations at Boğazköy in 1893–94. Not until the excavations led by Hugo Winckler and Theodor Makridi Bey in 1906–7 and 1911–12 were the ruins identified on the basis of textual finds as Ḫattuša, the capital city of the Hittites. These early excavations were directed primarily toward the discovery of clay tablets, but Heinrich Kohl and Otto Puchstein excavated the ruins in parallel and undertook an initial comprehensive survey of the architectural remains and topography, which remains valuable for research to this day (Puchstein 1912). The excavations organized between 1931 and 1939 by the German Archaeological Institute and the German Oriental Society, under the direction of Kurt Bittel, were then able to expand on this earlier work. These excavations, which focused on the royal citadel of Büyükkale, were able to place both the temporal depth and the material basis of Hittite culture on a solid foundation for the very first time.

Interrupted by World War II, research at Boğazköy resumed once again in 1952 under the direction of Kurt Bittel (until 1977) (Bittel 1970, 1983). From 1952 to the present, excavation work has continued at Boğazköy without interruption. The work on Büyükkale lasted until 1966. Since then, research has concentrated on the lower city, but unfortunately has not led to any comprehensive publications. Under the new director of excavations, Peter Neve (1978–93), the focus of work shifted to the upper city and its numerous temples (Neve 1996). His successor, Jürgen Seeher (1994–2005), then brought the economic life of the city to the attention of scientific

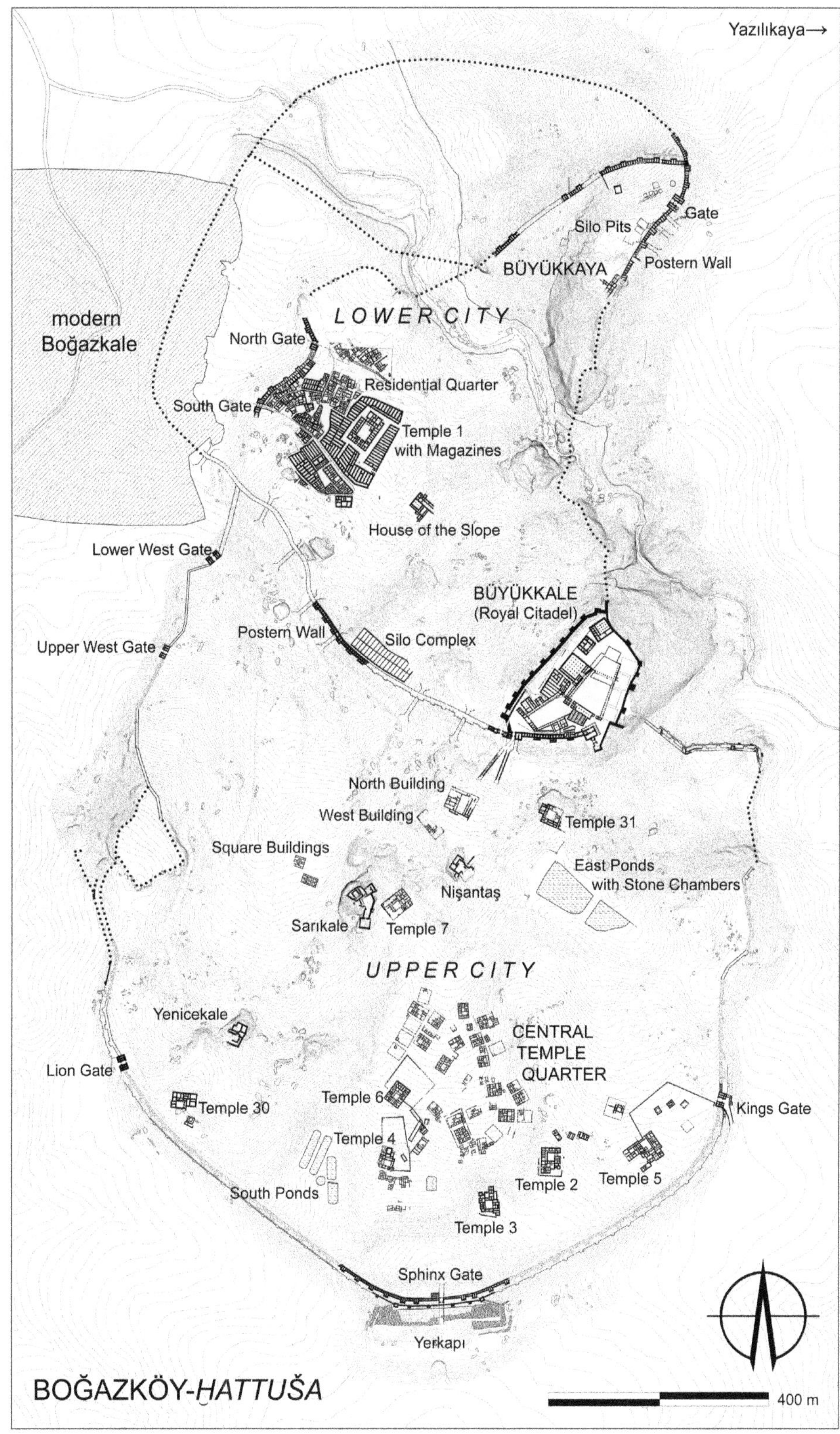

Figure 48.2. Plan of the capital Boğazköy-Ḫattuša (Boğazköy expedition).

research through excavations on Büyükkaya and in the upper city (Seeher 2000). In addition, a new comprehensive topographic survey (Seeher 1999) was completed, and, in a major archaeological experiment, a portion of the city wall was reconstructed (Seeher 2007). The work he initiated in the western upper city has been continued more recently under Andreas Schachner, the most recent director of excavations (since 2006), and expanded through new research in the lower city. In addition to innumerable archaeological finds, about 30,000 clay tablets or fragments thereof have been unearthed in Boğazköy to date. These fragments have formed the basis for a discipline in its own right—Hittitology—and continue to lead to numerous new insights (van den Hout 2011).

The more than 100 years of research undertaken at Boğazköy have brought forth an immense wealth of publications, only the most significant of which can be cited here. Preliminary reports on the excavations were initially published in the *Mitteilungen der Deutschen Orient-Gesellschaft* (35, 1907; 70–106, 1932–74), and have regularly appeared since 1979 in the journal *Archäologischer Anzeiger*. Individual findings from archaeological work were published in the series *Boğazköy* (I–VI, 1935–84), and its sequel, *Boğazköy-Berichte* (7–8, 2004–6). In addition, the final publication series, *Boğazköy-Hattuša: Ergebnisse der Ausgrabungen* (I–XXII, 1952–2008) is of great importance. The directors of excavations have published periodic summary papers about the current state of excavation work (Bittel 1970, 1983; Neve 1996; Seeher 2006e; Schachner forthcoming). Special publication series were founded for the numerous cuneiform texts, including *Keilschrifturkunden aus Boğazköy* (KUB I–LX, 1921–90), *Keilschrifttexte aus Boğazköi* (KBo 1–60, 1916–2009), and *Studien zu den Boğazköy-Texten* (StBoT 1–48, 1965–2006).

The settlement of Boğazköy is situated at the end of the long Budaközü valley that opens to the northeast. This valley was settled as early as the Chalcolithic period (see Schoop, chapter 7 in this volume). In the vicinity of the ruins of the Hittite city, archaeological evidence indicates continuous habitation since the early Bronze Age. The city is first mentioned in historical records with the name Ḫattuš during the *kārum* period (see Michel, chapter 13 in this volume). This settlement was largely destroyed, and an Old Hittite text even records its execration (Neu 1974:13, l. 48), yet after a brief hiatus, resettlement took place under the name Ḫattuša.

In the following 470 years (1650–1180 B.C.E.), Ḫattuša, as the capital of the Hittite Empire, was one of the most important cities of the ancient Near East. The site of Boğazköy also provides important remains for the Iron Age period (see Kealhofer and Grave, chapter 18 in this volume). The remains of the Hittite city stretches out over a surface area of 180 ha. The area enclosed by the city fortifications rises from the north to the south, and its topography is sharply divided by mountain ridges, rocky crags, plateaus, and basins. The distinctive rocky crag of Büyükkale is located halfway up the eastern edge of the city and was the site of the so-called Royal Citadel. The postern wall that runs toward the west from this point divides the city area into an upper and lower city. Because the fortifications of the upper city are symmetrically aligned with the gigantic passageway complex of Yerkapı (Neve 2001), it was long believed that this area of the city was a later expansion.

Newer studies have shown, however, that the lands of the upper city already belonged to the municipal area at the time of the Old Hittite Kingdom (Schachner 2009b; Seeher 2006a, 2006b, 2008). The fortifications of Ḫattuša remain to be fully studied, but it is clear, especially in the lower city, that there were numerous intermediary walls that divided off individual districts (Neve 2004). A number of typical Hittite gate structures, with a passageway between two massive gate towers, guarded access to the city at a number of different places (Puchstein 1912; Seeher 2006e). A few of them were decorated with relief sculptures, such as the famous Lion Gate or the King's Gate in the upper city. Some of the walls, such as the postern wall mentioned previously and those of Büyükkaya, additionally featured underground vaulted passageways, whose exact function—as a failsafe during sieges or for the daily passage of people and animals—has not yet been sufficiently clarified (Miglus 2005).

Excavations in different districts over the years have generated a complex chronological framework (see the summary in Mielke 2006a:14–18), and it has proven problematic to link the sequence of layers with the historical record (Klinger 2006; Seeher 2008). Only in the past few years, thanks especially to the introduction of scientific dating methods, has it been possible to establish a discrete and independent chronological framework, which has made it clear that historical events and archaeological developments seldom occur synchronously (Schoop and Seeher 2006).

The heart of the city was the so-called royal citadel on the rocky crag of Büyükkale (Bittel 1983:87–132; Neve 1982; Seeher 2002b). This was the palace area of the Hittite kings, which developed into a complex series of structures over the course of time. Most of the exposed ruins come from the last period of utilization, the time of the Late Kingdom (thirteenth century B.C.E.). At this time, Büyükkale was equipped with its own fortifications and encompassed an area of about 32,000 m^2. The central feature of this palace complex was an array of courtyards, around which were grouped a number of different rooms and buildings with colonnades. The courtyards were connected by gateways.

The lower city was dominated by the Great Temple 1, which was located in a spacious storehouse district (Neve 1969, 1995/1996). This complex, which originates from the period of the Great Kingdom, exemplifies through architecture the important position of temples in the Hittite economic system. Toward the south of the temple, there was a second area of storehouses, along with what seem to have been artisan workshops. Between the temple complex and the city wall lay a narrowly cropped area with simpler residential houses. New investigations in the lower city have brought new insights about the complex history of the fortifications in this area, as was the case in the excavations at Büyükkaya (Neve 1994:294–312; Seeher 1995:600–604). During the late Empire period (thirteenth century B.C.E.), a series of large silos were dug into these mountain ridges, designed for the long-term storage of grain (Seeher 2000). An older, immense granary from the sixteenth century B.C.E., still entirely filled with carbonified remains, was also discovered at the postern wall (Seeher 2006c).

The urban layout of the upper city was of a different character (Neve 1996). To date, thirty temples built in this area since the end of the Old Hittite period have been unearthed (Seeher 2006a, 2006b, 2008). Most of them are located in the so-called central temple quarter (Neve 1999), while the largest temples (temples 2, 3, 5, 30, and 31) were built at other prominent locations in the upper city. In addition, on a few striking cliff formations in this portion of the city, there are small, self-contained building complexes that may have also been connected to religious activities (Seeher 2006e; van den Hout 2002). The precise function of these so-called rock castles of Sarıkale, Yenicekale, and Nişantaş remains obscure. Newer investigations in the upper city have additionally revealed the existence of several large pond structures that provided water to the city (Neve 1996:63–80; Seeher 1998:216–17, 2001:341–61, 2002a:59–70) and also had a religious function, as revealed by the two stone chambers in the wall of the eastern pond (Neve 1996:67–80). In the upper city, buildings with an official character have also been found. The most prominent of these is known as the West Building, which has been the source of the largest inter-related set of clay bullae bearing an official seal ever discovered (Herbordt 2005; Neve 1996:52–58). The North Building, which is similarly located at Büyükkale, may have been the site of the royal stables (Mielke 2011:171). The function of the "square buildings" that were unearthed during new excavations in the western upper city, however, remains unclear (Schachner 2008:121–29; Seeher 2004:59–66, 2006d:171–78). The upper city also underwent significant changes over the course of its history, which encompasses many centuries. Thus, many of the temples were no longer functioning during the period of the late Hittite Empire. During this time, pottery workshops and small, simple houses had made themselves at home in amongst the ruins of the temples (Neve 1999).

Despite 100 years of research, many areas of the Hittite capital still remain unknown. Through the more intensive application of geophysical prospection methods (see excavation reports in *Archäologische Anzeiger* from 1998 onward) and thanks to a new micro-survey (Schachner 2007, 2008, 2009a), these knowledge gaps will be closed little by little. The surrounding countryside is also being subjected to greater scrutiny. A survey of the local area has already been completed and has led to new discoveries about the city's ties with the surrounding environment (Czichon 1997, 1998, 1999). New geophysical prospections in this surrounding area indicate the existence of reservoir dams and artificial ponds outside of the city wall (Schachner 2008:142–46). The much earlier discovery of the rock sanctuary of Yazılıkaya, located about a kilometer northeast of the city, already afforded some understanding of such environmental ties (Bittel, Naumann, and Otto 1941; Bittel et al. 1975). The pictorial representations of a procession of gods found there, which largely originates from the thirteenth century B.C.E., are among the most impressive legacies of Hittite culture.

Knowledge about the material culture of the Hittites, derived from long-term excavations, has made the excavations at Boğazköy the standard for all other Hittite discovery sites with regard to the typology of ceramics or temples. Only in recent years has Boğazköy's "monopoly" of the field been broken by new research at other Hittite settlements. Without any doubt, however, the ruins of Boğazköy-Ḫattuša are among the most significant archaeological sites anywhere in the world, and for this reason, they have been included on the World Heritage List since 1987 (see http://whc.unesco.org/en/list/377).

THE ROYAL RESIDENCE: ORTAKÖY-ŠAPINUWA

The excavations at Ortaköy (Çorum province) are among the new investigations that have shown that remarkable surprises can still be anticipated in Hittite studies (figure 48.3a). In 1990, Aygül and Mustafa Süel began their work at Ortaköy, which has continued to this day. Aside from regular but brief reports on the excavations in the *Kazı Sonuçları Toplantısı* (14, 1993; 17–21, 1996–2000; 23, 2002; 25–27, 2004–5; 29, 2007), several general overviews have appeared in print (A. Süel 1992, 1998b, 2002, 2009; M. Süel 1998, 2008a, 2008b); however, many important questions regarding the site remain unresolved. It is, as yet, difficult to understand the site's history from the excavation record and get a coherent picture of the urban layout. Nevertheless, Ortaköy is of extraordinary importance in Hittite studies. With more than 3,500 clay tablet fragments, this site has brought forth the largest quantity of cuneiform texts found anywhere in Hittite Anatolia outside of Boğazköy (A. Süel 1997, 1998a, 2002:163–65, 2005).

The location of the city on a level plain, which is only interrupted in the north and west by deeply cut creek valleys, is itself quite unusual. No comprehensive topographic plan has been published yet that would allow a more precise assessment of the location of the city or the connections between its individual buildings. Presently, the only sources of information helpful in this regard are published aerial photographs (M. Süel 2008b) and publicly accessible satellite images. The excavations currently stretch over an area of about 400 m. Although some fragments of fortifications have indeed been excavated, especially in the area of Building A, it remains unclear whether they surrounded the entire city or only a palace district. The excavators' suggestion that the dimensions of the city encompass nine square kilometers (A. Süel 2002:165) is as yet unsupportable, especially given that no evidence has been presented for such an exorbitant size.

According to evidence from the clay tablets, the ruins of the city unearthed thus far seem to date to the Middle Kingdom and the early Hittite Empire (fifteenth to the fourteenth century B.C.E.). There appear to have been at least two distinct phases of construction. Dendro-datable wood remains are available from several buildings (A and B), but the samples are problematic and there is also no contextual information known about them, making them of little value for resolving questions of chronology (Mielke 2006b:89). The city was apparently destroyed in the fourteenth century B.C.E. and was never rebuilt.

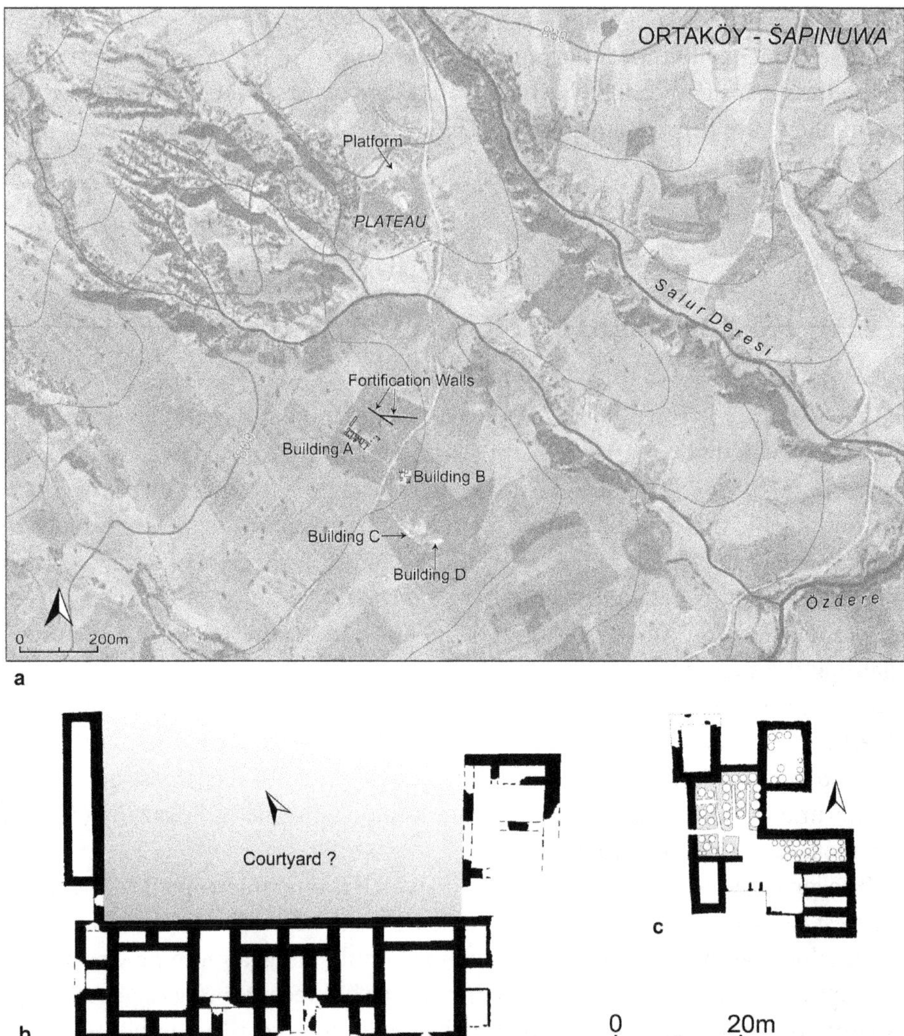

Figure 48.3. (a) Sketch of the residence city Ortaköy-Šapinuwa, according to satellite images (author). (b) Ground plan of Building A of Ortaköy-Šapinuwa (after A. Süel 2002:fig. 4, modified by the author). (c) Ground plan of Building B of Ortaköy-Šapinuwa (after M. Süel 2001:681, modified by the author).

The excavations have concentrated until now on individual buildings, which have been named in alphabetical sequence. Only an incomplete plan for Building A (figure 48.3b) has been published, but it shows the characteristics of a palace (Mielke 2011:165–66; A. Süel 2002:158–62 with fig. 4; M. Süel 2008b:13–21). The southwestern front—the longest unearthed—stretches almost eighty meters and shows a symmetrically structured wing consisting of different groups of chambers with recesses on their exterior side. It is unclear whether the structure contained a courtyard. Newer investigations have shown that the building was surrounded by pavement stones and had a ramp-like entrance. Although much remains unclear about this building, we are clearly dealing with an imposing and significant edifice, which originally contained additional rooms on a second storey.

Building B (figure 48.3c), which is located about 100 m east of Building A, appears to be a storehouse with an irregular floor plan and a surface area of about 1,250 m² (A. Süel 2002:162–63; M. Süel 2001, 2008b:22–27). The structure was full of numerous pithoi and large jars. Many of the storage vessels were placed on recessed clay pedestals that were arranged in rows or at right angles. About 120 m south of this unusual storehouse, the small Building C was unearthed, which has been interpreted as a religious structure (M. Süel 2008b:28–32). The most recently uncovered Building D is located about 260 m southeast of Building A (M. Süel 2008b:33–35). Its dimensions are about 20 × 20 m with a surface area of about 600 m². The remarkable thing about this structure is its entrance, which is furnished with an ornate orthostat. The orthostat depicts the lower half of a figure that probably represents a king as warrior with a bow and spear (M. Süel 2005).

Since 2000 there have also been excavations on a plateau that is situated about 500 m north of Building A, which is divided from the first excavation area by a deeply cut creek valley (M. Süel 2008a, 2008b:36–61). Aside from a number of different architectural ruins, storage pits and a great multilevel platform were discovered. It is thought that the platform was used for religious activities. It is questionable whether this plateau still belonged to the actual urban area.

Thanks to clay tablet evidence, the Hittite settlement of Ortaköy can be identified as Šapinuwa, an important city already known from the Boğazköy texts. The archaeologists who excavated it consider Šapinuwa the second capital of the Hittite kingdom or perhaps a royal residence. Since the excavations and the research regarding the texts have only been partially reported, they have generated a number of questions as yet unanswered. We must therefore await future publications to evaluate the interpretations advanced by the excavators. However, on the basis of its important artifacts and ruins, it is certain that the settlement of Ortaköy-Šapinuwa will achieve a special status among Hittite cities.

The Cult City: Alaca Höyük

The small settlement mound of Alaca Höyük (Çorum province) is located only twenty-five kilometers northeast of Boğazköy, known since W. J. Hamilton visited in 1836 (figure 48.4a). The first major archaeological work was undertaken by Theodor Makridi Bey in 1907, but it was not until the excavations by Hâmit Zübeyr Koşay, Remzi Oğuz Arık, and Mahmut Akok between 1935 and 1983 that large areas were opened up. These excavations led to numerous discoveries, including rich Hittite layers and the renowned Early Bronze Age burials (see Steadman, chapter 10 in this volume). In 1997 a new excavation project was launched by Aykut Çınaroğlu.

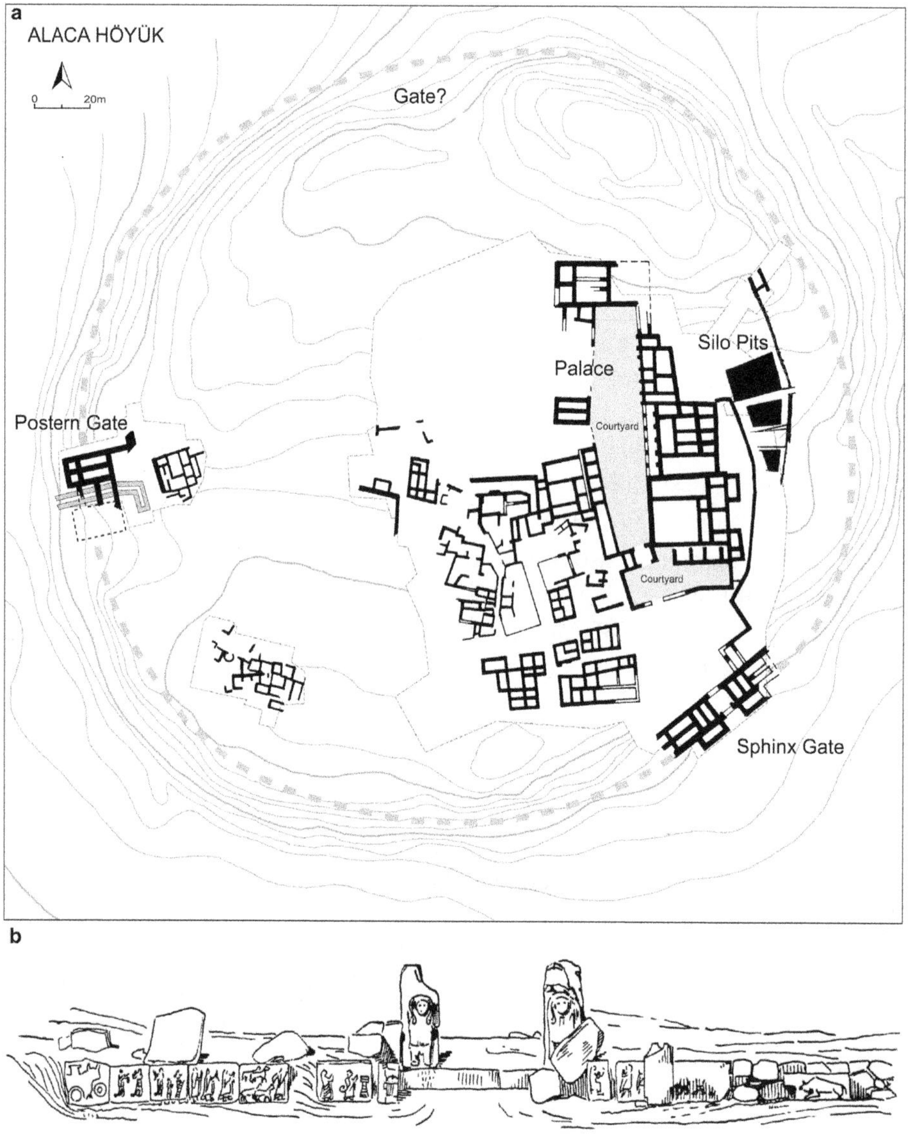

a

b

Figure 48.4. (a) Plan of the cult city Alaca Höyük (after Koşay and Akok 1973:taf. 85 and Çınaroğlu and Genç 2007:fig. 1, newly created by the author). (b) Sketch of the Sphinx Gate of Alaca Höyük (after Naumann 1971:fig. 65).

A number of monographs have been published about the earlier excavations (Arık 1937; Koşay 1938, 1951; Koşay and Akok 1966, 1973), yet these older monographs provide an incomplete picture of the archaeological work conducted, as a great deal of important information remains to be reported. For example, the excavators only established a very rough chronological classification of the layers (Koşay and Akok 1973:57–60 with pl. XCIII), which was subsequently reevaluated in 1993 by Tahsin Özgüç (1993:473–75; for more details see Mielke 2006a:18–19). Results from the new excavations have appeared in issues of *Kazı Sonuçları Toplantısı* (21, 2000; 23–30, 2001–8). A general overview of Alaca Höyük with further bibliographic references is also provided by Özgüç (2002a).

The approximately fifteen meters high and almost round höyük of Alaca had a long history of continuous settlement layers, encompassing all phases of the Hittite epoch. Because of the informational gaps in older publications, it is often difficult to relate archaeological artifacts to the structural findings, thus reducing the significance of Alaca Höyük for resolving questions of chronology. Thus, the architectural remains themselves lend Alaca Höyük its significance. In this connection, attention must be drawn to the detailed architectural reconstructions made by Akok in the older publications.

The mound, which is about 250 m in diameter on average, was surrounded by a city fortification, of which only the two gates on the western and southeastern sides have been partly excavated. A third gate is also likely to exist on the northern side. The city was very small, with an area of only five hectares. The remarkable Sphinx Gate was exposed at a very early date (Koşay and Akok 1966:123–24; Makridy 1908; Naumann 1971:285), and on its exterior side, it exhibits a unique orthostat frieze with figural representations (Bittel 1976:figs. 209–27). The scenes show various activities in a religious festival and display the royal couple among the principal actors (figure 48.4b). Comparable representations have only been found on Hittite artifacts, like relief pottery or metal vessels. It is probable that the Sphinx Gate served as the principal entrance to Alaca Höyük, both on account of the uniqueness of its representations as well as its location in the immediate proximity of the palace area. The second gate, located on the western side, has only been partially excavated and was named after a postern that runs beneath the gateway (Koşay and Akok 1966:124–25). This is a special feature of Hittite gates (Miglus 2005). The dating of the fortifications remains problematic. They were assigned to Layer II of the second cultural layer, which encompasses the entire Middle and Late Bronze Age. It is generally accepted that this layer dates from the time of the Great Hittite Empire, and thus from the second half of the fourteenth and the thirteenth century B.C.E., but a closer approximation has not been possible.

The so-called Temple Palace of Alaca Höyük (Koşay and Akok 1966:121–28; Naumann 1971:401–4), which, with its 3,600 m^2 area, occupies almost the entire eastern half of the city, also belongs to Layer II. However, doubts remain whether all the assigned architectural remains were originally part of one palace complex. The unfortunate appellation was assigned by the excavators due to evidence of cult activities in the northwest portion of the building (Koşay and Akok 1966:126). This evidence should not have led to the functional characterization of the entire building, however. The building complex actually has all the hallmarks of a palace and is one of very few palace ruins excavated over such a large area (Mielke 2011:165). A central courtyard that unifies an agglomeration of variously grouped rooms (often featuring colonnades) is the distinguishing feature of Hittite palace complexes. A visitor arriving at the palace of Alaca Höyük first steps into a vestibule before going through a double-gated structure to enter into the actual elongated courtyard.

The central area on the eastern side is dominated by a colonnade, which provides access to the group of rooms that lies behind it, which clearly represented an important area. Numerous additional rooms are located around the courtyard, whose function remains indeterminate. The silo structures discovered in the new excavations on the eastern side of the palace complex are a testament to its administrative and redistributive functions (Çınaroğlu and Genç 2003:280–81, 2007:527), an interpretation which is also corroborated by written sources. The palace complex of Alaca Höyük probably had a Middle Hittite precursor in the earlier Layer III, but it has only been exposed in small sections (Naumann 1971:403–4 with fig. 537).

Of the remaining architectural ruins at Alaca Höyük—which probably represent additional official buildings or simple residential houses—there is little additional information available. Newer investigations have led to the discovery of a nearby reservoir dam, whose specific relation to the city still remains a question (Çelik 2008; Çınaroğlu and Genç 2003, 2004, 2005, 2007:529).

The impressive Hittite architectural ruins of Alaca Höyük have often been identified with the cult cities of Arinna (Erkut 1992) and Zippalanda (Popko 2000) mentioned in Hittite texts, but there have been no clay tablets or other sources discovered at the site itself to confirm this association. Nevertheless, the unique Sphinx Gate and palace, which is large in relation to the small size of the city, do suggest a special status for Alaca Höyük, so the designation of "cult city" would seem to be justified.

The Province Center: Kuşakli-Šariššа

Thanks to an interdisciplinary approach and good archaeological conditions, the excavation at the site of Kuşaklı near Başören/Altınyayla (Sivas province) has transformed the face of Hittite archaeology inside the space of only a few years (figure 48.5). Between 1992 and 2004, Andreas Müller-Karpe headed the excavations at Kuşaklı. The excavation reports were published in the *Mitteilungen der Deutschen Orient-Gesellschaft* (127–34, 1995–2002; 136, 2004; 138, 2006). A dedicated publication series with final reports (*Kuşaklı-Sarissa* 1–5, 1997–2010) and comprehensive summaries (Müller-Karpe 2002a, 2002b) make the research findings readily accessible.

The geophysical field survey that was undertaken at the site remains unique in its scale and comprehensiveness. Both the city and surrounding area were assessed in a survey that still stands as a model for the successful application of geophysical prospection methods. Optimal geologic conditions made it possible to recognize almost all urban structures, and the entire city fortifications could be reconstructed without putting a spade into the ground. The fortifications at the site consist of four gates at the ends of the two principal axes of the city and a "Kastenmauer" defensive wall. The city wall sits on its own raised rampart, which encircles a central acropolis-like hill whose sides slope steeply to the wall. In total, the fortifications encompass

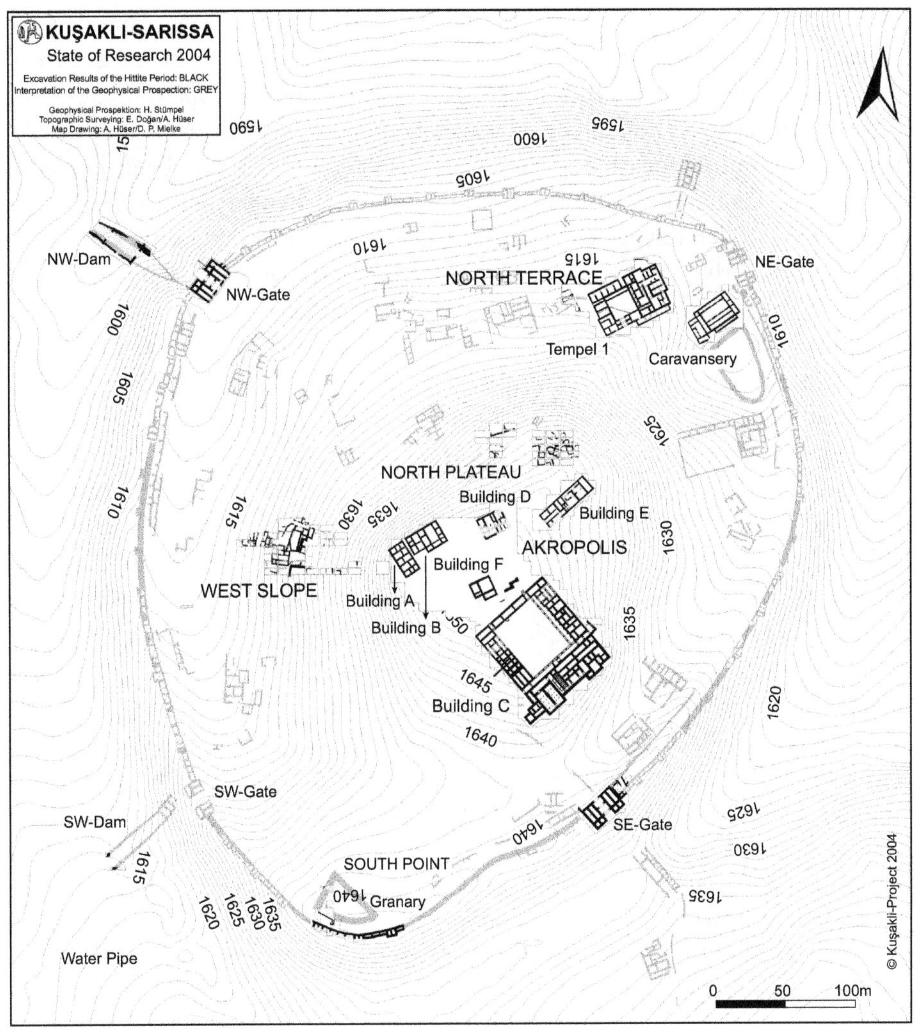

Figure 48.5. Plan of the provincial center Kuşaklı-Šariššа (Kuşaklı expedition).

an area of eighteen hectares. The city is embedded at the base of a long mountain range. Over the course of twelve excavation seasons, the acropolis was substantially exposed and excavated at various locations both inside and outside the city walls. Research has shown that the settlement was newly founded in the last quarter of the sixteenth century B.C.E. based on the dendrochronological investigation of numerous carbonized wooden remains (see the summary of Mielke 2006c:266–69). The city subsequently went on to experience an active history of repopulation and change that lasted until the end of the Hittite period (Müller-Karpe 2004:108–11). Some 100 years later parts of the former Late Bronze Age town were occupied by a small Middle Iron Age settlement.

One of the most significant buildings dating from the Hittite foundation period is the structure known as Building C on the acropolis, which is likely to represent a temple of the local weather god (Müller-Karpe 1999/2000, 2000). This massive structure is the largest temple from the entire Hittite period to be excavated to date. A second temple, also of large proportions, has been completely excavated on the north terrace (Müller-Karpe 1995:9–21, 1996). Not far from this second temple, near the northeast portal, a larger stable complex has been exposed. This building is of great significance for the understanding of Hittite vernacular architecture (Müller-Karpe 2007). During these excavations, a number of buildings from this early period were also discovered on the western slope, including some with an official character, and others that might be described as simple residential dwellings (Mielke 2006a:3–6). Among the four entryways previously mentioned, two gates, the Northwest and the Southeast Gates, have been almost completely excavated (Mielke 2004). Because of their good state of preservation, the architectural remains have yielded important new insights regarding Hittite city gates in general, as well as about the wood and mudbrick architecture of Hittite buildings (Mielke 2009). In addition, there are two structures first made visible by means of geophysical prospection that should be mentioned, as they demonstrate the evolved level of urbanization in the city. One structure is the large, half-underground silo complex at the southern cusp of Kuşaklı, which could hold more than 700 tons of cereal grains (Mielke 2001:237–41). The second structure is a large dam unearthed outside the city walls at the Northwest Gate. Its function was to collect water that flowed down from the surrounding mountains (Hüser 2007). The geophysical prospection has indicated the existence of more of these structures around the city wall, but these were investigated only with small trenches (Hüser 2007). The study of the nearby and more distant surroundings has additionally led to the discovery of a sanctuary located in the mountains above the city, with an artificial pond and a temple structure (Müller-Karpe 1999:79–91). Research that has been conducted beyond the actual city walls has made it clear that the city's construction apparently occurred against the backdrop of a deliberate reshaping of the landscape.

In the fourteenth century B.C.E., the city was completely destroyed in the course of violent conflicts. The traces of this catastrophe are visible in virtually all of the older buildings. However, there was another later phase of rebuilding and settlement that lasted until the end of the thirteenth century B.C.E. A series of smaller new structures of an official character was built on the acropolis (Arnhold 2009; Müller-Karpe 1999/2000). In one of these, Building A, a substantial archive of clay tablets was found (Wilhelm 1997). On the western slope, new residential buildings were built atop the old architectural remains (Mielke 2006a:3–6), while near the abandoned silo on the south summit, a pottery workshop was found (Mielke 2001:241–43). Within the city, there must have been ruins that remained exposed that were not cleared or overbuilt, such as those of the massive Building C. The remains suggest that the city gates, as well as the entire fortifications of the city, were no longer functional but were used as dwellings. The city was then apparently abandoned little by little toward the end of the thirteenth century B.C.E. In this connection, several buildings on the acropolis show signs of fire damage.

The excavations generated numerous new insights regarding Hittite cities. The clay tablet fragments discovered during the course of the excavations were essential in this regard, as they allowed the ruins to speak for themselves. Thus, the ancient name of the city—Šarišša—could be identified for the first time. This, in turn, allowed connections to be established to other ancient Hittite texts, which identify Šarišša as a provincial center in the so-called Upper Land (Siegelová 2001; Wilhelm 1997). Elsewhere mention is also made of the *ḫuwaši* shrine discovered in the mountains, which was apparently of special significance, as the Great King traveled from Ḫattuša to visit it during a spring festival (Wilhelm 1997). The excavations in Kuşaklı have acquired a key position in Hittite archaeology not only on account of these important historical and cultural discoveries but also primarily because of the unusually good conditions of the findings and, as a result, the high reliability of their scientific dating (Mielke 2006b, 2006c; Müller-Karpe 2003).

The Border City: Maşat Höyük-Tapikka

The mound of Maşat Höyük (figure 48.6) is located on a fertile plain about twenty kilometers south of Zile (Tokat province) near the contemporary village of Yalınyazı. It consists of a steep rock massif elevated about thirty meters above the plain, which slopes away more gently only on the southeastern side. Spurred by the discovery of a Hittite clay tablet (Güterbock 1944), initial investigations took place there in 1945, but it was not until the later excavations conducted between 1973 and 1984 under the direction of Tahsin Özgüç that Maşat Höyük was transformed into an important site of discovery in Hittite research. This was the first time outside Boğazköy that a large number of clay tablets had been uncovered in central Anatolia (see Beal, chapter 26 in this volume). Although findings from the excavations were presented in two monographs (Özgüç 1978, 1982) and in several surveys (Özgüç 1980, 2002b), detailed information on some discoveries is still lacking. The presentation of the clay tablet finds (Alp 1980, 1991a, 1991b) led to several important additional publications (e.g., Beckman 1995; Klinger 1995; van den Hout 2007).

The settlement area at Maşat Höyük is not very large. Its greatest dimension is only about 225 × 450 m, and it consists of a "citadel" on the rock massif and a "lower city" stretched out over the southern slope. The most significant remains originate from the Hittite period, but other settlement phases from the Early Bronze Age, *kārum* period (Hittite Layer V), and Iron Age have also been identified. The four Hittite building layers cover the entire time period from the Old Hittite Kingdom (sixteenth century B.C.E.) to the end of the Great Empire era (end of the thirteenth/beginning of the twelfth century B.C.E.). All layers show traces of major fires, which are interpreted as evidence of violent destruction. To date, no fortifications have been found, yet it can be assumed that the settlements from different periods were originally surrounded by a wall (Özgüç 1982:89). From the Old Hittite Layer IV

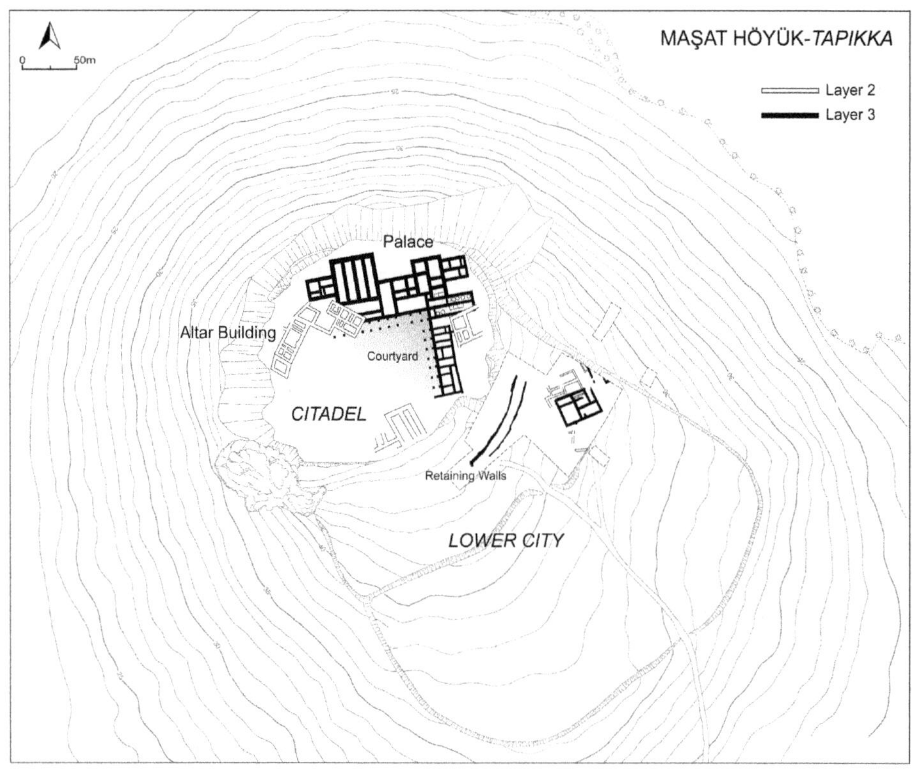

Figure 48.6. Plan of the border city Maşat Höyük. Building remains of layers III and II (after Özgüç 1982:plan 3 and 4, newly created by the author).

there are only a few ruins remaining in the lower city, which do not allow for a more detailed description (Özgüç 1982:85–89).

The most important building complex at Maşat Höyük is associated with the Middle Hittite period Layer III (fifteenth to the first half of the fourteenth century B.C.E.). Without doubt, we are dealing with a palace that occupied essentially the entire cliff top of the "citadel" (Özgüç 1978:11–17, 1982:73–83). The building complex could not be fully excavated because of subsequent redevelopment, destruction, and erosion, but one can nevertheless recognize all the typical elements of a palace (Mielke 2011:165). The groups of rooms contained on the northern and eastern sides are organized into elongated wings, which are oriented toward a courtyard by colonnades. The excavated portions cover an area of about 3,300 m^2, but there were comparable groups of rooms on the western and southern sides of the courtyard, such that the original area may have been twice as large. From the inventory one can determine the functions of the different areas; in addition to archival rooms, the complex contained storage chambers with large embedded pithoi and silo bins. Based on the conditions at the site, however, the rooms of the archive must have been located in an upper storey. The clay tablets discovered at the site not only revealed the Hittite name for Maşat Höyük—Tapikka—but also showed that the settlement served as the base for a border commander (*BĒL MADGALTI*). From the texts it has been possible to gain valuable insights concerning the positioning of a Hittite border post in relation to the enemy territory of Kaška. The palace complex was set off from the lower city by retaining walls. The excavations in the lower city have uncovered a few architectural remains from this layer, but they have been only fleetingly described in print (Özgüç 1982:85–89).

In the succeeding early Hittite Empire Layer II (fourteenth century B.C.E.), the city was completely rebuilt. The western part of the citadel was henceforth dominated by a large "altar building" (Özgüç 1982:80–83), in which both clay tablets and imperial seal impressions have been found. In the lower city as well, rebuilding took place (Özgüç 1982:85–89). As is the case with the preceding Layer III, this layer bears evidence of a major fire catastrophe.

In the final Hittite Layer I, which is generally dated to the New Kingdom Period (thirteenth century B.C.E.), no additional large buildings were constructed (Özgüç 1982:73–83). Clay tablets and seal impressions have also been found from this settlement period. Of particular significance is the discovery of some Late Helladic IIIA2/IIIB Mycenaean vessels in a smaller building on the acropolis (Genz 2011:309; Özgüç 1978:66, 1982:102–3), whose precise location cannot be determined from the documentation. Dendrochronological data from this building are also available, but they are unfortunately not usable for the precise dating of the artifacts or structural remains (Mielke 2006b:84–87).

Without a doubt, Maşat Höyük ranks among the most important Hittite archaeological sites. Existing publications contain some deficiencies with respect to the categorization of artifacts and architectural remains, and the limited selection of finds and brief architectural descriptions also leave many questions unanswered, yet the textual and archaeological discoveries still provide us with significant insights into a border city 150 km distant from the Hittite capital.

Conclusion

Despite its brevity, this overview of key sites sheds light on both the characteristic features and diversity of Hittite urban forms. In classifying Hittite settlements, archaeologists have generally used the contrasting terms "höyük" to indicate older settlements and "mountain city" to describe newer foundations. However, these terms—which actually refer to topographic circumstances—are in no way appropriate for characterizing the complex system of Hittite settlements (Mielke 2011:153–54). Analytical approaches employed by modern urban geography that conceive of cities as a reflection of social and political structures—thus paying tribute to the human forces that shape them—are much more appropriate than these outmoded concepts. Indeed, the adoption of new analytical approaches should make it possible to survey in a fitting manner the general characteristics of Hittite cities as well as questions pertaining to settlement politics and hierarchies.

Such a survey would require a thorough reassessment of the existing archaeological and philological record, an effort that has only been undertaken on a limited basis to date on account of the fragmented nature of archaeological sources (Mielke 2011). Clearly, a categorization solely based on topography is inadequate, as Hittite urban structures are strongly influenced by administrative and religious factors—this is true, however, of cities from many different cultures and times. More specifically, Hittite urban structures should be characterized in terms of the architectural and conceptual design of their temples, palaces, fortifications, storage installations, and so on, and the social organization behind that. The special characteristics of these Hittite urban forms are Anatolian in origin and in many instances have their roots in the preceding *kārum* period. The social and organizational forms that defined Hittite settlements were not perpetuated into the subsequent Iron Age, as the collapse of the Hittite state led to a new social and political order. Only the Hittite successor states in southeastern Anatolia and northern Syria display remnants of Hittite urban forms, yet these remnants are subsumed into structures with their own unique characteristics (see Matney, chapter 19 in this volume).

REFERENCES

Alaura, Silvia. 2006. *"Nach Boghaskoi!" Zur Vorgeschichte der Ausgrabungen in Boğazköy-Ḫattuša und zu den archäologischen Forschungen bis zum Ersten Weltkrieg*. 13. Sendschrift der Deutschen Orient-Gesellschaft. Berlin: Deutschen Orient-Gesellschaft.

Alp, Sedat. 1980. Die hethitischen Tontafelentdeckungen auf dem Maşat-Höyük. Vorläufiger Bericht. *Belleten* 44: 25–59.

———. 1991a. *Maşat-Höyük'te Bulunan Çivi Yazılı Hitit Tabletleri. Hethitische Keilschrifttafeln aus Maşat-Höyük*. Ankara: Türk Tarih Kurumu.

———. 1991b. *Hethitische Briefe aus Maşat-Höyük*. Ankara: Türk Tarih Kurumu.

Arık, Remzi Oğuz. 1937. *Les fouilles d'Alaca Höyük, entreprises par la Société d'Histoire Turque. Rapport preliminaire sur les travaux en 1935*. Ankara: Türk Tarih Kurumu.

Arnhold, Simone. 2009. *Das hethitische Gebäude E auf der Akropolis von Kuşaklı*. Kuşaklı-Sarissa 4. Rahden/Westfalen: Leidorf.

Beckman, Gary M. 1995. Hittite Provincial Administration in Anatolia and Syria. The View from Maşat and Emar. In *Atti del II Congresso Internazionale di Hittitologia. Pavia 28 giugno-2 luglio 1993*, ed. Onofrio Carruba, Mauro Giorgieri, and Clelia Mora, 19–37. Studia Mediterranea 9. Pavia: Gianni Iuculano Editore.

Bittel, Kurt. 1970. *Hattusha. Capital of the Hittites*. New York: Oxford University Press.

———. 1976. *Die Hethiter. Die Kunst Anatoliens vom Ende des 3. bis zum Anfang des 1. Jahrtausends vor Christus*. Universum der Kunst. München: Beck.

———. 1983. *Hattuscha. Hauptstadt der Hethiter. Geschichte und Kultur einer altorientalischen Großmacht*. Köln: DuMont (updated German version of Bittel 1970).

Bittel, Kurt, Joachim Boessneck, Bernhard Damm, Hans Gustav Güterbock, Harald Hauptmann, Rudolf Naumann, and Wulf Schirmer. 1975. *Das hethitische Felsheiligtum Yazılıkaya*. Boğazköy-Ḫattuša 9. Berlin: Gebr. Mann.

Bittel, Kurt, Rudolf Naumann, and Heinz Otto. 1941. *Yazılıkaya. Architektur, Felsbilder, Inschriften und Kleinfunde*. Wissenschaftlicher Veröffentlichungen der Deutschen Orient-Gesellschaft 61. Leipzig: Hinrichs.

Czichon, Rainer M. 1997. Studien zur Regionalgeschichte von Ḫattuša-Boğazköy 1996. *Mitteilungen der Deutschen Orient-Gesellschaft* 129: 89–102.

———. 1998. Studien zur Regionalgeschichte von Ḫattuša-Boğazköy 1997. *Mitteilungen der Deutschen Orient-Gesellschaft* 130: 83–92.

———. 1999. Studien zur Regionalgeschichte von Ḫattuša-Boğazköy 1998. *Mitteilungen der Deutschen Orient-Gesellschaft* 131: 47–56.

Çelik, Duygu. 2008. Alaca Höyük Hitit Barajı. In *Aykut Çınaroğlu'na Armağan. Studies in Honour of Aykut Çınaroğlu*, ed. Elif Genç and Duygu Çelik, 87–104. Ankara: Kitap Kağıdı.

Çınaroğlu, Aykut and Elif Genç. 2003. Alaca Höyük ve Alaca Höyük Hitit Barajı Kazıları, 2002. *Kazı Sonuçları Toplantısı* 25.1: 278–88.

———. 2004. 2003 Yılı Alaca Höyük ve Alaca Höyük Hitit Barajı Kazıları. *Kazı Sonuçları Toplantısı* 26.1: 265–76.

———. 2005. 2004 Yılı Alaca Höyük ve Alaca Höyük Hitit Barajı Kazıları. *Kazı Sonuçları Toplantısı* 27.1: 1–6.

———. 2007. 2006 yılı Alaca Höyük Kazıları. *Kazı Sonuçları Toplantısı* 29.2: 525–36.

Erkut, Sedat. 1992. Hitit Çağının Önemli Kült Kenti Arinna'nın Yeri. In *Hittite and Other Anatolian and Near Eastern Studies in Honor of Sedat Alp*, ed. Heinrich Otten, Hayri Ertem, Ekrem Akurgal, and Aygül Süel, 159–65. Ankara: Türk Tarih Kurumu.

Genz, Hermann. 2011. Foreign Contacts of the Hittites. In *Insights into Hittite History and Archaeology*, ed. Hermann Genz and Dirk Paul Mielke, 301–31. Colloquia Antiqua 2. Leuven: Peeters.

Genz, Hermann and Dirk Paul Mielke. 2011. Hittite Research: A Short Overview. In *Insights into Hittite History and Archaeology*, ed. Hermann Genz and Dirk Paul Mielke, 1–30. Colloquia Antiqua 2. Leuven: Peeters.

Güterbock, Hans Gustav. 1944. Zile Yakınında Maşat'tan Gelme Bir Eti Mektubu. Ein hethitischer Brief aus Maşat bei Zile. *Ankara Üniversitesi Dil ve Tarih-Coğrafya Fakültesi Dergisi* 2: 389–405.

Herbordt, Suzanne. 2005. *Die Prinzen- und Beamtensiegel der hethitischen Grossreichszeit auf Tonbullen aus dem Nişantepe-Archiv in Ḫattuša*. Boğazköy-Ḫattuša 19. Mainz: Philipp von Zabern.

Hüser, Andreas. 2007. *Hethitische Anlagen zur Wasserversorgung und Entsorgung*. Kuşaklı-Sarissa 3. Rahden: Leidorf.

Klinger, Jörg. 1995. Das Corpus der Maşat-Briefe und seine Beziehungen zu den Texten aus Ḫattuša. *Zeitschrift für Assyriologie und vorderasiatische Archäologie* 85: 74–108.

———. 2006. Der Beitrag der Textfunde zur Archäologiegeschichte der hethitischen Hauptstadt. In *Strukturierung und Datierung in der hethitischen Archäologie. Voraussetzungen-Probleme-Neue Ansätze. Structuring and Dating in Hittite Archaeology. Requirements-Problems-New Approaches. Internationaler Workshop, Istanbul, November 26–27, 2004*, ed. Dirk Paul Mielke, Ulf-Dietrich Schoop, and Jürgen Seeher, 5–17. BYZAS 4. İstanbul: Ege Yayınları.

Koşay, Hâmit Zübeyr. 1938. *Türk Tarih Kurumu tarafından yapılan Alaca Höyük hafriyatı 1936 çalışmalara ve keşiflere ait ilk rapor. I. Bericht über die Arbeiten und Ergebnisse der Ausgrabungen des Türk. Geschichtsvereins bei Alaca Höyük*. Ankara: Türk Tarih Kurumu.

———. 1951. *Türk Tarih Kurumu tarafindan yapılan Alaca Höyük kazısı. 1937–1939'daki çalişmalara ve keşiflere ait ilk rapor. Les fouilles d'Alaca Höyük entreprises par la Société d'Histoire Turque. Rapport preliminaire sur les travaux en 1937–1939*. Ankara: Türk Tarih Kurumu.

Koşay, Hâmit Zübeyr and Mahmut Akok. 1966. *Alaca Höyük Kazısı. 1940–1948'deki Çalışmalara ve Keşiflere Ait İlk Rapor. Ausgrabungen von Alaca Höyük. Vorbericht über die Forschungen und Entdeckungen von 1940–48*. Ankara: Türk Tarih Kurumu.

———. 1973. *Alaca Höyük Kazısı. 1963–1967 Çalışmaları ve Keşiflere Ait İlk Rapor. Alaca Höyük Excavations. Preliminary Report on Research and Discoveries 1963–1967*. Ankara: Türk Tarih Kurumu.

Makridy, Theodor. 1908. La porte des sphinx à Euyuk. Fouilles du Musée Impérial Ottoman. *Mitteilungen der Vorderasiatischen Gesellschaft* 13: 1–29.

Mielke, Dirk Paul. 2001. Die Grabungen an der Südspitze. In A. Müller-Karpe, Untersuchungen in Kuşaklı 2000. *Mitteilungen der Deutschen Orientgesellschaft* 133: 237–43.

———. 2004. Die Stadttore von Kuşaklı-Sarissa. *Alter Orient Aktuell* 5: 23–27.

———. 2006a. *Die Keramik vom Westhang*. Kuşaklı-Sarissa 2. Rhaden: Leidorf.

———. 2006b. Dendrochronologie und hethitische Archäologie–Einige kritische Anmerkungen. In *Strukturierung und Datierung in der hethitischen Archäologie. Voraussetzungen-Probleme-Neue Ansätze. Structuring and Dating in Hittite Archaeology. Requirements-Problems-New Approaches. Internationaler Workshop, Istanbul, November 26–27, 2004*, ed. Dirk Paul Mielke, Ulf-Dietrich Schoop and Jürgen Seeher, 77–94. BYZAS 4. İstanbul: Ege Yayınları.

———. 2006c. İnandıktepe und Sarissa—Ein Beitrag zur Datierung althethitischer Fundkomplexe. In *Strukturierung und Datierung in der hethitischen Archäologie. Voraussetzungen-Probleme-Neue Ansätze. Structuring and Dating in Hittite Archaeology. Requirements-Problems-New Approaches. Internationaler Workshop, Istanbul, November 26–27, 2004*, ed. Dirk Paul Mielke, Ulf-Dietrich Schoop and Jürgen Seeher, 251–76. BYZAS 4. İstanbul: Ege Yayınları.

———. 2009. Alte Paradigmen und neue Erkenntnisse zur hethitischen Holz-Lehmziegel-Architektur. In *Bautechnik im antiken und vorantiken Kleinasien. Internationale Konferenz 13-16 Juni 2007 in Istanbul*, ed. Martin Bachmann, 81–106. BYZAS 9. İstanbul: Ege Yayınları.

———. 2011. Hittite Cities: Looking for a Concept. In *Insights into Hittite History and Archaeology*, ed. Hermann Genz and Dirk Paul Mielke, 153–94. Colloquia Antiqua 2. Leuven: Peeters.

Miglus, Peter A. 2005. *s.v. Poterne. Reallexikon der Assyriologie und Vorderasiatischen Archäologie* 10: 605–8. Berlin: de Gruyter.

Müller-Karpe, Andreas. 1995. Untersuchungen in Kuşaklı 2000. *Mitteilungen der Deutschen Orient-Gesellschaft* 127: 225–50.

———. 1996. Kuşaklı. Ausgrabungen in einer hethitischen Stadt. *Antike Welt* 4: 350–12.

———. 1999. Untersuchungen in Kuşaklı 1998. *Mitteilungen der Deutschen Orient-Gesellschaft* 131: 57–131.

———. 1999/2000. Die Akropolis der hethitischen Stadt Kuşaklı-Sarissa. *Nürnberger Blätter zur Archäologie* 16: 91–110.

———. 2000. Ein Großbau in der hethitischen Stadtruine Kuşaklı. Tempel des Wettergottes von Sarissa? *Alter Orient Aktuell* 1: 19–22.

———. 2002a. Kuşaklı-Sarissa. Kultort im Oberen Land. In *Die Hethiter und ihr Reich. Das Volk der 1000 Götter*, ed. Kunst- und Ausstellungshalle der Bundesrepublik Deutschland, 176–89. Bonn: Theiss.

———. 2002b. Kuşaklı-Sarissa: A Hittite Town in the "Upper Land." In *Recent Developments in Hittite Archaeology and History. Papers in Memory of Hans G. Güterbock*, ed. K. Aslıhan Yener and Harry A. Hoffner Jr., 145–55. Winona Lake, Ind.: Eisenbrauns.

———. 2003. Remarks on Central Anatolian Chronology of the Middle Hittite Period. In *The Synchronisation of Civilisations in the Eastern Mediterranean in the Second Millennium B.C., II. Proceedings of the SCIEM 2000-EuroConference, Haindorf, 2nd of May–7th of May 2001*, ed. Manfred Bietak and Hermann Hunger, 383–94. Contributions to the Chronology of the Eastern Mediterranean 4. Vienna: Österreichische Akademie der Wissenschaften.

———. 2004. Untersuchungen in Kuşaklı 2002. *Mitteilungen der Deutschen Orient-Gesellschaft* 136: 103–35.

———. 2007. Die sogenannte "Karawanserei" von Kuşaklı-Sarissa. In *Von der Prospektion zur Rekonstruktion. In Geophysik und Ausgrabung. Einsatz und Auswertung zerstörungsfreier Prospektion in der Archäologie*, ed. Martin Posselt, Benno Zickgraf and Claus Dobiat, 111–19. Rahden: Leidorf.

Naumann, Rudolf. 1971. *Architektur Kleinasiens von ihren Anfängen bis zum Ende der hethitischen Zeit*, 2nd ed. Tübingen: Wasmuth.

Neu, Erich. 1974. *Der Anitta-Text.* Studien zu den Boğazköy-Texten 18. Wiesbaden: Harrassowitz.

Neve, Peter. 1969. Der große Tempel und die Magazine. In *Boğazköy IV, 9–19. Funde aus den Grabungen 1967 und 1968*. Berlin: Gebr. Mann.

———. 1982. *Büyükkale. Die Bauwerke. Grabungen 1954–1966*. Boğazköy-Ḫattuša 12. Berlin: Gebr. Mann.

———. 1994. Die Ausgrabungen in Boğazköy-Ḫattuša 1993. *Archäologischer Anzeiger* 1994.3: 289–325.

———. 1995/1996. Der große Tempel (Tempel 1) in Boğazköy-Ḫattuša. *Nürnberger Blätter zur Archäologie* 12: 41–62.

———. 1996. *Ḫattuša. Stadt der Götter und Tempel. Neue Ausgrabungen in der Hauptstadt der Hethiter*. Mainz: Philipp von Zabern.

———. 1999. *Die Oberstadt von Ḫattuša. Die Bauwerke. I. Das zentrale Tempelviertel.* Boğazköy-Ḫattuša 16. Berlin: Gebr. Mann.

———. 2001. *Die Oberstadt von Ḫattuša. Die Bauwerke. II. Die Bastion des Sphinxtores und die Tempelviertel am Königs-und Löwentor*. Boğazköy-Ḫattuša 17. Mainz: Philipp von Zabern.

———. 2004. Die hethitischen Stadtmauern von Ḫattuša: Eine Bestandsaufnahme. *Architectura* 34: 169–82.

Özgüç, Tahsin. 1978. *Maşat Höyük Kazıları ve Çevresindeki Araştırmaları. Excavations at Maşat Höyük and Investigations in its Vicinity*. Ankara: Türk Tarih Kurumu.

———. 1980. Excavations at the Hittite Site, Maşat Höyük: Palace, Archives, Mycenaean Pottery. *American Journal of Archaeology* 84: 305–9.

———. 1982. *Maşat Höyük II. Boğazköy'ün Kuzeydoğusunda bir Hitit Merkezi. A Hittite Centre northeast of Boğazköy*. Ankara: Türk Tarih Kurumu.

———. 1993. Studies on Hittite Relief Vases, Seals, Figurines and Rock-Carvings. In *Aspects of Art and Iconography: Anatolia and its Neighbors. Studies in Honor of Nimet Özgüç*, ed. Machteld Mellink, Edith Porada, and Tahsin Özgüç, 427–99. Ankara: Türk Tarih Kurumu.

———. 2002a. Alacahöyük. Ein Kultort im Kerngebiet des Reiches. In *Die Hethiter und ihr Reich. Das Volk der 1000 Götter*, ed. Kunst- und Ausstellungshalle der Bundesrepublik Deutschland, 172–75. Bonn: Theiss.

———. 2002b. *Maşathöyük. In Die Hethiter und ihr Reich. Das Volk der 1000 Götter*, ed. Kunst- und Ausstellungshalle der Bundesrepublik Deutschland, 168–71. Bonn: Theiss.

Popko, Maciej. 2000. Zippalanda and Ankuwa Once More. *Journal of the American Oriental Society* 120.3: 445–48.

Puchstein, Otto. 1912. *Boghasköi. Die Bauwerke.* WVDOG 19. Leipzig: Hinrichs.

Schachner, Andreas. 2007. Die Ausgrabungen in Boğazköy-Ḫattuša 2006. *Archäologischer Anzeiger* 2007.1: 67–93.

———. 2008. Die Ausgrabungen in Boğazköy-Ḫattuša 2007. *Archäologischer Anzeiger* 2008.1: 113–61.

———. 2009a. Die Ausgrabungen in Boğazköy-Ḫattuša 2008. *Archäologischer Anzeiger* 2009.1: 21–72.

———. 2009b. Das 16. Jahrhundert v. Chr.–eine Zeitenwende im hethitischen Zentralanatolien. *Istanbuler Mitteilungen* 59: 9–34.

———. Forthcoming. *Hattuša—auf den Spuren des sagenhaften Großreichs der Hethiter.* München: Beck.

Schoop, Ulf-Dietrich and Jürgen Seeher. 2006. Absolute Chronologie in Boğazköy-Hattusa: Das Potential der Radiokarbondaten. In *Strukturierung und Datierung in der hethitischen Archäologie. Voraussetzungen-Probleme-Neue Ansätze. Structuring and Dating in Hittite Archaeology. Requirements-Problems-New Approaches. Internationaler Workshop, Istanbul, November 26–27, 2004*, ed. Dirk Paul Mielke, Ulf-Dietrich Schoop, and Jürgen Seeher, 53–76. BYZAS 4. İstanbul: Ege Yayınları.

Seeher, Jürgen. 1995. Die Ausgrabungen in Boğazköy-Ḫattuša 1994. *Archäologischer Anzeiger* 1995.4: 597–625.

———. 1998. Die Ausgrabungen in Boğazköy-Ḫattuša 1997. *Archäologischer Anzeiger* 1998.2: 215–41.

———. 1999. Die Ausgrabungen in Boğazköy-Ḫattuša 1998 und ein neuer topographischer Plan des Stadtgeländes. *Archäologischer Anzeiger* 1999: 317–44.

———. 2000. Getreidelagerung in unterirdischen Großspeichern: zur Methode und ihrer Anwendung im 2. Jahrtausend v. Chr. am Beispiel der Befunde in Ḫattuša. *Studi Micenei ed Egeo-Anatolici* 42.2: 261–301.

———. 2001. Die Ausgrabungen in Boğazköy-Ḫattuša 2000. *Archäologischer Anzeiger* 2001.2: 333–62.

———. 2002a. Die Ausgrabungen in Boğazköy-Ḫattuša 2001. *Archäologischer Anzeiger* 2002.1: 59–78.

———. 2002b. Großkönigliche Residenz–Mittelpunkt staatlichen Lebens. Die Palastanlage in der hethitischen Hauptstadt. In *Die Hethiter und ihr Reich. Das Volk der 1000 Götter*, ed. Kunst- und Ausstellungshalle der Bundesrepublik Deutschland, 94–99. Bonn: Theiss.

———. 2004. Die Ausgrabungen in Boğazköy-Ḫattuša 2003. *Archäologischer Anzeiger* 2004.1: 59–76.

———. 2006a. Chronology in Ḫattuša: New Approaches to an Old Problem. In *Strukturierung und Datierung in der hethitischen Archäologie. Voraussetzungen-Probleme-Neue Ansätze. Structuring and Dating in Hittite Archaeology. Requirements-Problems-New Approaches. Internationaler Workshop, Istanbul, November 26–27, 2004*, ed. Dirk Paul Mielke, Ulf-Dietrich Schoop, and Jürgen Seeher, 197–214. BYZAS 4. İstanbul: Ege Yayınları.

———. 2006b. Ḫattuša-Tuthalija-Stadt? Argumente für eine Revision der Chronologie der hethitischen Hauptstadt. In *The Life and Times of Hattusili III and Tuthaliya IV. Proceedings of a Symposium Held in Honour of J. de Roos, December 12–13, 2003, Leiden*, ed. Theo P. J. van den Hout, 131–46. PIHANS 103. Leiden: Netherlands Institute for the Near East.

———. 2006c. Die Grabungen am mittleren Büyükkale-Nordwesthang 1998–2000. In *Ergebnisse der Grabungen an den Ostteichen und am mittleren Büyükkale-Nordwesthang in den Jahren 1996–2000*, ed. Jürgen Seeher, 43–84. Boğazköy-Berichte 8. Mainz: Philipp von Zabern.

———. 2006d. Die Ausgrabungen in Boğazköy-Ḫattuša 2005. *Archäologischer Anzeiger* 2006.1: 171–78.

———. 2006e. *Hattusha Guide. A Day in the Hittite Capital*, 3rd ed. İstanbul: Ege Yayınları.

———. 2007. *A Mudbrick City Wall at Hattuša. Diary of a Reconstruction.* İstanbul: Ege Yayınları.

———. 2008. Abschied von Gewußtem. Die Ausgrabungen in Ḫattuša am Beginn des 21. Jahrhunderts. In *Ḫattuša-Boğazköy. Das Hethiterreich im Spannungsfeld des Alten Orients. 6. Internationales Colloquium der Deutschen Orient-Gesellschaft, 22.-24. März 2006, Würzburg*, ed. Gernot Wilhelm, 1–13. Wiesbaden: Harrassowitz.

Siegelová, Jana. 2001. Der Regionalpalast in der Verwaltung des hethitischen Staates. *Altorientalische Forschungen* 28.2: 193–208.

Süel, Aygül. 1992. Ortaköy: Eine hethitische Stadt mit hethitischen und hurritischen Tontafelentdeckungen. In *Hittite and Other Anatolian and Near Eastern Studies in Honor of Sedat Alp*, ed. Heinrich Otten, Hayri Ertem, Ekrem Akurgal, and Aygül Süel, 487–92. Ankara: Türk Tarih Kurumu.

———. 1997. Ortaköy-Šapinuwa Arşivleri. *1996 Yılı Anadolu Medeniyetleri Müzesi Konferansları* 1997: 93–99.

———. 1998a. Ortaköy-Šapinuwa Tabletlerinin Tarihlendirilmesi. In *III. Uluslararası Hititoloji Kongresi Bildirileri, Çorum 16–22 Eylül 1996. Acts of the IIIrd International Congress of Hittitology, Çorum, September 16–22, 1996*, ed. Sedat Alp and Aygül Süel, 551–58. Ankara.

———. 1998b. Ortaköy-Şapinuwa: Bir Hitit Merkezi. *Türkiye Bilimler Akademisi Arkeoloji Dergisi* 1: 37–61.

———. 2002. Ortaköy-Šapinuwa. In *Recent Developments in Hittite Archaeology and History. Papers in Memory of Hans G. Güterbock*, ed. K. Aslıhan Yener and Harry A. Hoffner Jr., 157–65. Winona Lake, Ind.: Eisenbrauns.

———. 2005. Ortaköy tabletlerinde geçen bazı yeni coğrafya isimleri. In *V. Uluslararası Hititoloji Kongresi Bildirileri. Acts of the Vth International Congress of Hittitology Corum, September 02–08, 2002*, ed. Aygül Süel, 679–85. Ankara.

———. 2009. Another Capital City of Hittite State: Šapinuwa in Central-North Anatolia in the Hittite Period. New Perspectives in Light of Recent Research. In *Acts of the International Conference held at the University of Florence (February 7–9, 2007)*, ed. Franca Pecchioli Daddi, Gulia Torri, and Carlo Corti, 193–206. Rome: Herder.

Süel, Mustafa. 1998. Ortaköy-Šapinuwa Hitit Şehri. In *III. Uluslararası Hititoloji Kongresi Bildirileri, Çorum 16–22 Eylül 1996. Acts of the IIIrd International Congress of Hittitology, Çorum, September 16–22, 1996*, ed. Sedat Alp and Aygül Süel, 559–72. Ankara.

———. 2001. Ortaköy–Şapinuwa "B" Binası. In *Akten des IV. Internationalen Kongresses für Hethitologie Würzburg, 4.-8. Oktober 1999*, ed. Gernot Wilhelm, 679–84. Wiesbaden: Harrassowitz.

———. 2005. Ortaköy-Şapinuva "D" Yapısı Hitit Dini Mimarisinde Değişik bir Yorum. In *V. Uluslararası Hititoloji Kongresi Bildirileri. Acts of the Vth International Congress of Hittitology Corum, September 02–08, 2002*, ed. Aygül Süel, 687–700. Ankara.

———. 2008a. Ortaköy/Šapinuwa Antik Kenti, Ağilönü Bölgesinde Yeni Çalışmalar. In *VI Congresso Internazionale di Ittitologia, Roma, 5–9 settembre 2005, Parte II*, ed. Alfonso Archi and Rita Francia, 721–27. *Studi Micenei ed Egeo-Anatolici* 50. Rome.

———. 2008b. *Ortaköy Şapinuva. Bir Hittit Başkenti.* Ankara: Uyum Ajans.

van den Hout, Theo P.J. 2002. Tombs and Memorials: The (Divine) Stone-House and *ḫegur* Reconsidered. In *Recent Developments in Hittite Archaeology and History, Papers in Memory of Hans G. Güterbock*, ed. K. Aslıhan Yener and Harry A. Hoffner Jr., 73–91. Winona Lake, Ind.: Eisenbrauns.

———. 2007. Some Observations on the Tablet Collection from Maşat Höyük. In *VI Congresso Internazionale di Ittitologia, Roma, 5–9 settembre 2005, Parte I*, ed. Alfonso Archi and Rita Francia, 387–98. *Studi Micenei ed Egeo-Anatolici* 49. Rome.

———. 2011. The Written Legacy of the Hittites. In *Insights into Hittite History and Archaeology*, ed. Hermann Genz and Dirk Paul Mielke, 47–84. Colloquia Antiqua 2. Leuven: Peeters.

Wilhelm, Gernot. 1997. *Keilschrifttexte aus Gebäude A*. Kuşaklı-Sarissa 1. Rahden: Leidorf.

CHAPTER 49

AYANİS: AN IRON AGE SITE IN THE EAST

ALTAN ÇİLİNGİROĞLU

THE Ayanis fortress lies thirty-five kilometers north of the modern town of Van and near the village of Agartı, on the eastern shore of Lake Van (Çilingiroğlu 2007a, 2007b, 2008b; Çilingiroğlu and Kozbe 1994; Çilingiroğlu and Salvini 1997). The fortress was originally built on a rocky hill 150 × 400 m in size; the lower town lies below, covering an area of at least eighty hectares (figures 49.1, 49.2). The fortress offers two occupational levels, the earlier dating to the Iron Age II Period and the later to the Medieval, ca. tenth to eleventh centuries C.E.

HISTORY OF RESEARCH

Ayanis excavations have been under way since 1989, when exploration of the fortress commenced (Çilingiroğlu 1991, 1993, 1994a, 1996; Çilingiroğlu and Salvini 1995, 1997; Derin and Çilingiroğlu 2000). The lower town excavations have been ongoing since 1997 (Stone and Zimansky 2001, 2003, 2004).

My first visit to Ayanis was in 1969, while working at Çavuştepe as an archaeology student together with the late Professor Afif Erzen. This visit allowed me to formulate my future plans to excavate at Ayanis. The early years of the excavation were difficult in terms of facilities—we were camping in a garden with no running water or electricity. However, the results of the excavations at the fortress have justified our commitment, yielding a number of very important architectural results together with countless bronze, gold, and iron artifacts (e.g. Çilingiroğlu 2005).

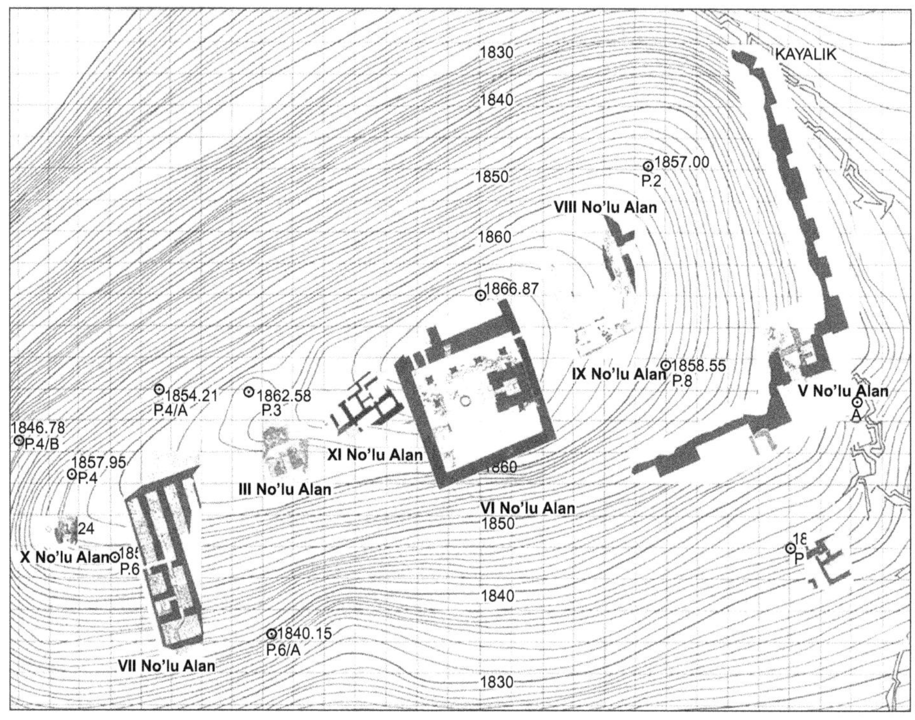

Figure 49.1. Plan of Ayanis.

Figure 49.2. View of Ayanis.

It was a great help and support for us to be joined by a team consisting of Elizabeth Stone and Paul Zimansky and their students from the United States beginning in 1996. The Ayanis excavation is not simply an archaeological excavation but is also a school, teaching archaeology for students all over the world, including the United States, Germany, France, Iran, Italy, Holland, England, Australia, Poland, Iraq, and Norway, and also teaching cooperation and friendship.

Excavations

Since 1989 excavations have been undertaken in five different sectors within the Ayanis fortress (Çilingiroğlu 1991, 1993, 1994b, 1996; Çilingiroğlu and Sağlamtimur 1997). Citadel walls surrounding the fort were excavated on the east and south, and the monumental gate structure was uncovered at the southeastern corner. A cuneiform inscription in front of the monumental gate says that the fortress was built by Rusa II, son of Argišti, and that its name was "Rusahinili in front of Mound Eiduru" (Çilingiroğlu and Salvini 1999; and see Zimansky, chapter 24, and Radner, chapter 33 in this volume). The inscription also tells us that the fortress (E-GAL) and the structures within the fortress (E-BARA) were built by Rusa II. One and a half lines were left blank in the inscription, presumably meant to be inscribed later with the name of a structure not yet completed. This structure is most probably the "East Pillared Hall" uncovered in the eastern section of the fortress.

The E-BARA structure mentioned in the inscription must be the "temple area," which is located at the highest point of the fortress and has been under investigation since the beginning of the excavations. The square-shaped core temple found within this area in 1987 must belong to the E-BARA complex. The cuneiform inscription on the front side of the temple, composed of eighty-six lines, not only is the longest Urartian temple inscription ever discovered but also carries great importance by giving us historical, social, and religious information about the reign of Rusa II. Hundreds of sacrifice weapons, dedicated to the god Ḫaldi as vows, and other finds discovered in the temple area and temple storage rooms also provide us with information on Urartian art and religious traditions. Information about the temple area, where excavations were completed in 2005, and related issues will not be included in this study as all of these were presented in detail previously (Çilingiroğlu and Salvini 2001).

Another area of the fortress, under excavation for some years, is the section called the "West Storage Rooms." On each side (north and south) of a monumental wall located in the western part of the fortress and extending in an east–west direction is a structure at least two stories high. A total of nine rectangular-shaped rooms have been uncovered in the basement of this structure, which was built using the monumental wall as its main support. To date, these rooms, where a total of 236 monumental jars and hundreds of storage pots were uncovered, have revealed data providing us with valuable information on the economic structure of the fortress. Although these structures and the finds discovered within them were mentioned in detail in the 2001 Ayanis publication (Çilingiroğlu and Salvini 2001), finds and architectural remains uncovered in recent years will be summarized here as well.

The monumental structure referred to as the "East Pillared Hall" is probably the building whose name was left out of the cuneiform inscription because its construction had not yet been completed. This structure, thought to be associated with the temple complex, is a place where priests and priestessess lived, and its basement levels were used to store thousands of earthenware dishes and bowls of different forms. This structure must be the *aši̮ḫusi* building mentioned on a bulla found in the Ayanis Fortress. According to the inscription on the bulla, the year when this building was built gave its name to a year; the building was thus named and so was the year: "the year when the ašiḫusi building was constructed."

The "domestic sections," under excavation since 2005, start immediately to the west of a mudbrick wall surrounding the temple area. In general mostly monumental structures such as temples and pillared halls have been excavated in Urartian fortress excavations as a means of obtaining data and reaching conclusions on Urartian art. The data derived from discoveries of material culture and architecture related to people from lower social classes serving the élite class residing within the fortress will enable us to assess Urartian art and culture from a different point of view. Data obtained from the domestic sections in Ayanis revealed that the fortress contained not only personal belongings of the élites but also many different items used during daily chores.

Domestic Sections

The excavation section labeled Area no. XI at the Ayanis excavations includes grids E 23 and E 22. Archaeological excavations carried out outside the thick mudbrick wall located west of the temple area and surrounding the room confirmed the presence of sections with no direct connection to the temple area. During the 2005–2008 seasons, nine rooms were excavated that constituted parts of the building located at this spot (figures 49.3, 49.4). Some of the square and rectangular sections were connected to one another by means of doors and openings, but the doors and the openings between other sections have not been found yet. Two rectangular rooms built adjacent to the south wall but which had no connection to domestic sections had totally different functions.

One of the fully excavated rooms is Room 1. This 4.60 × 4.60 m square room was found in a fairly well-preserved condition, and its four mudbrick walls have survived until today. The section opens to Room 3 from the east through a niche door and to Room 2 through another door. There is a platform of 0.50 × 0.80 m at the northeast corner of the room. The room, which did not contain much in the way of pottery and small finds, was probably used as a passageway.

North of Room 1 lies Room 2, which is connected to Rooms 4 and 5 through a passageway. Containing a huge collection of finds, Room 2 showed evidence of having experienced a great fire. Large wooden beams, which probably constituted

Figure 49.3. Area XI: Domestic section, east of Temple Area.

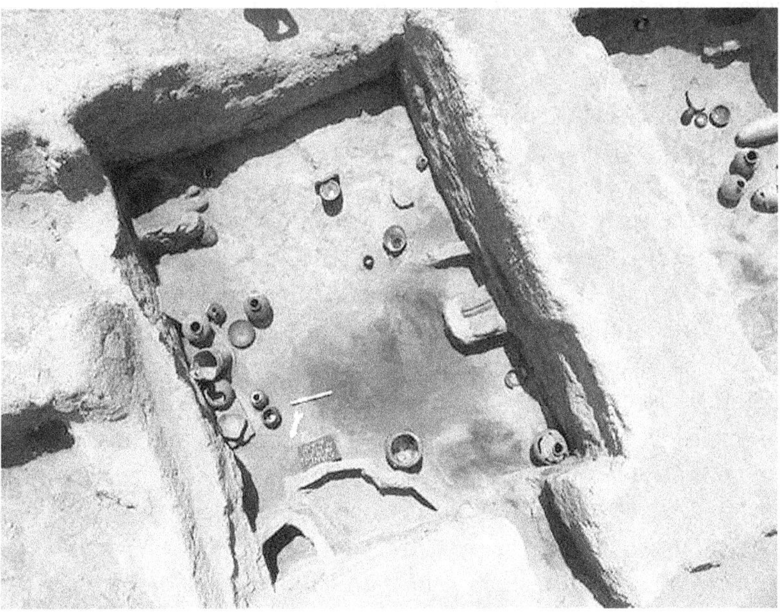

Figure 49.4. Area XI: Domestic section, in situ pots in kitchen.

the floor material of the upper floor, were found within the room. A large number of small jars were uncovered inside a stone bench attached to the north wall of the room, and the area at the northeast corner was surrounded by a mudbrick elevation. It was also found that the stone bench was covered with a piece of cloth. Other important finds included all the pot sherds found on the floor of the room as well as a woven basket containing millet. Two swords made of bronze and iron are the first specimens of their type uncovered in the Ayanis Fortress. The close resemblance between the iron sword and the one worn by the god Teišeba as depicted on a bas-relief in Adilcevaz immediately attracts the eye and cannot be overlooked. A round bone object with an artistic rendering of an "animal-style" horse figure was found next to the sword; it must have been decoration for the pommel of the sword. Swords as well as hammers and pieces of furniture made of small tree branches and small blue stones used to decorate the furniture were found scattered around the room and probably fell from the upper floor, which had collapsed. The pottery, the storage jars unearthed, and the basket recovered in situ, clearly reveal the domestic function of Room 2. The bowls placed on the stone bench as well as the pottery of various shapes heaped in a corner indicate that the room was a small storage area for everyday use.

Rooms 4 and 5, which are attached to Room 2 on the west, are entered through openings measuring one meter in width. Remains of mudbrick walls making up the rooms were preserved up to a height of two meters. As seen in other places at the site (such as the temple and East Storage Rooms), the walls were whitewashed. Data obtained show that whitewashing had been repeated four times. Three earthenware jars containing millet were recovered next to the walls of Room 4.

Room 5, with dimensions of 3.10 × 2.56 m, has a stairwell leading upward from south to north (2.10 × 1.03 m). The great quantities of burned beams have led us to believe that the stairwell leading up to the upper floor of the building was constructed of wood. Inside the almost square room, three storage jars, a huge shallow cauldron, and a vessel-shaped yeast bowl with a mouth length of 1.10 m and a height of 0.8 m were uncovered attached to the south and the west walls. A mixture of barley and wheat, each in great quantities, was found in the vessel. Analyses of the specimens recovered have revealed that this bowl was used for brewing beer. The lower parts of the jars were buried in the ground, supported by stones at the bottom. Placed just north of the bowl is a rectangular platform made of mudbricks measuring 2.56 m in length and 1.10 m in width. The height of the platform is 0.40 m above ground; it was built with two rows of 0.37 × 0.37 m mudbricks. The grinding stone associated with this complex was recovered from this mudbrick platform.

Room 6 is located to the north of Room 2. Sufficient data are not available on this structure. As yet its northeast corner remains unexcavated, though the room has the appearance of a gallery at present. The excavated section of the room covers an area of 4.85 × 1.30 m. The north wall located in the north of the room has been preserved up to a height of 2.50 m. Excavations to be carried out in future years are expected to shed more light on this area.

People living or working in any Urartian fortress surely needed domestic buildings and other areas around religious structures. The fact that administrators, soldiers, and servants in addition to clergymen lived in a fortress required domestic areas to accommodate these people. In other words, fortresses did not consist only of splendid temples and halls, storage areas of monumental size, and prestigious royal belongings. It was inevitable that some domestic sections in parts of the fortresses as well as some domestic finds within these areas would eventually be unearthed. Structures excavated west of the temple area within the Ayanis Fortress fall into this category. Data obtained from these rooms present information on daily life, an aspect of Urartian culture that has not previously been excavated or investigated in detail.

Data obtained were limited to the ground floor of the nine structures excavated thus far. It is believed that the building complex is likely to cover a much larger area, with new rooms expected to be uncovered in years to come. Discovery of a stairwell as well as some small artifacts likely to have fallen onto the floor have led us to believe that the building had a second floor as well. Swords, pieces of furniture, and ornamental elements obtained in Room 2 were not expected in a section where domestic materials were found.

It is noteworthy that an organic relationship existed among the rooms unearthed. There were openings instead of doors, and the sites were small and had various sizes. The pottery in Rooms 2, 4, and 5 consisted of storage pots containing remnants of cereals such as millet, barley, and wheat. Small earthenware jars were uncovered inside the elevated (1.5 m radius) platform. This is also true for the stone bench attached to the northern wall of the room. A wide and shallow basket with a diameter of 75 cm, and woven with thick reeds and thin branches, was also used for daily storage; it was filled with millet. Earthenware jars, cauldrons, and troughs for storage make up the finds in Room 5. These storage vessels contained different kinds of cereals. It is probable that a low platform uncovered in the area was used for various kinds of food preparation. The combined material culture from these collective rooms suggests that they were used for storage and service purposes. Other finds supporting this hypothesis include grinding stones uncovered in Rooms 2 and 5. Evidence indicates that these rooms were not used for long-term storage but for storing goods for daily needs. In addition, there is a sufficient number of long-term storage rooms in the area located on the western part of the fortress. Further excavation will probably reveal the residences of the inhabitants who used these storage rooms.

Domestic sections have no connection with the rooms uncovered in the south in 2008 (Rooms 10 and 11). The dimensions of Room 10 were 3.15 × 9.30 m. However, the dimensions of Room 11 are not known at this time because the excavation has not been completed yet. Great quantities of red polished Urartian vessels as well as a bronze oil lamp were discovered on the floor of Room 10. A total of thirty-five gold rosettes discovered along the north wall of the room appear to be wall decorations. Pins attached to the back of the rosettes were used to mount them on the walls. A limestone basin as well as numerous wooden remains of furniture and eye-shaped mosaics unearthed on the floor in the northwest corner of the room indicate the presence of a piece of furniture at this spot. A five-centimeter hole bored through the middle of the basin was used to let the water out. An Egyptian blue sample in flat rectangular shape, a very rare find outside of Egypt, was found in a room of the domestic section; it is quite important to have discovered material of a synthetic nature in Urartu. Further research is ongoing and will soon be published.

One of the most significant finds unearthed in Room 10 is the solid gold ornamented and inscribed handle of a fly-whisk. Remnants of wood were found inside the handle, which had a length of 20.6 cm and a diameter of 1.35 cm. The inscription on the gold artifact is extremely important and belongs to the second named woman in Urartu, after Tariri, whose name we had previously known. The inscription reveals that the artifact belongs to Queen Kakuli, who must be King Rusa II's wife. The artifact is important in that it mentions the name of an Urartian queen for the first time. It is clear that Rooms 10 and 11 were not reserved for domestic use. It is most likely that these rooms were places where some important activities for the royal family took place. Final results related to these rooms will come to light in excavations to be carried out in future years.

West Storage Rooms

The section called "West Storage Rooms" contains some of the most important structures used for storage purposes in the Ayanis Fortress (figures 49.5, 49.6). New excavations being conducted in this area for many years now show that storage rooms extend into the westernmost part of the fortress. Excavations in Area VII reported on in the excavation publications (Çilingiroğlu 2006a, 2006b, 2007c, 2008a) have provided valuable information on the nature of Urartian and post-Urartian cultural layers as well as the cultural layers of the fortress. The Urartian soverignty in the Ayanis Fortress came to an end between 653 and 650 B.C.E., and the fortress was not used by the Urartians again. Excavations carried out in different sectors have confirmed that the fortress was reconstructed in the Middle Ages (tenth and eleventh centuries C.E.). However, whether there was another cultural period belonging to the Medians, Achaemenids, or Persians

Figure 49.5. Area VII, Urartian mudbrick wall under medieval stone walls.

Figure 49.6. Area VII, Urartian pithoi in storage room.

in the period between Urartu and the Middle Ages is a matter of controversy among our colleagues. Excavations carried out in the Western Storage Rooms are particularly significant in that they bring to light almost conclusive archaeological data.

A rectangular structure with a stone foundation dating back to the Middle Ages was excavated west of Area VII. In this area were discovered stone foundations as deep as one meter and three floors of different buildings belonging to different periods of the Middle Ages. The floors of these buildings can be clearly seen along with associated stone walls and pillar footings. Storage jars and bowls dating to the Middle Ages were uncovered in sections belonging to different periods in history. It was eventually established that the stone walls belonging to the Middle Ages were built on top of a 2.65-m-wide mudbrick wall that certainly belonged to the Urartian period. Recovery of earthenware jars belonging to the Middle Ages, resting in situ on an Urartian sun-dried brick wall, is quite noteworthy. These archeological data indicate that the fortress had not been used for settlement after the Urartian period until the Middle Ages. Another piece of evidence belonging to this period came from the temple area. Urartian mudbricks at the southwest corner of the temple wall were destroyed by the medieval inhabitants down to the stone foundations, but the stone foundations were preserved. No archeological data dated between the Urartian period and the Middle Ages were found in any sector excavated within the fortress.

A second wall extending along the northwest–southeast axis was discovered at a depth of −9.45 m at the corner of the section. Apparently the two walls constituted a new magazine (Magazine 10). This magazine was excavated in the I14 a + b + c + d squares. After the medieval deposit was removed, the Urartu layer was reached at a depth of −9.31 m. Excavations revealed that this area experienced a fire event at this depth in the Urartu level. As excavations proceeded into deeper levels, fairly large burned beams were recovered in this fire layer at a depth of –9.54 m, demonstrating that the fire caused significant damage.

An Urartian floor was found at –10.09 m in the northern section of the site. In addition to bronze bowls on the ground (figure 49.7), jars and pots, which could not be fully preserved, were also uncovered. Moreover, ceramic and bone finds were scattered on the floor. Bronze bowls were found at the northwest corner, while the other ceramics were uncovered in front of the north cross-section and immediately south and west of the east wall at the northeast corner. The floor in question was sloped toward the south, the highest level at –10.09 m and the lowest at –10.84 m. This floor was laid on a foundation of bedrock which was itself sloped; the floor was plastered in an effort to create level ground. Magazine 10 constitutes the western border of the West Storage Area. Its width is 3.20 m, just like the ones unearthed during previous excavation seasons. Future excavations to be carried out will probably reveal pithoi, expected in a storage area such as this.

East Pillared Room

A new pillared structure uncovered in the east area of the gate that provides entrance to the temple area from the east must be connected to the temple complex. New remains built adjacent to the rooms found during the early years of the Ayanis excavations and referred to as the "East Storage Rooms" in publications were unearthed. Five pillars (2.56 × 2.56 m) extending in the north–south direction verified the

Figure 49.7. A fluted bronze bowl from a storage room in Area VII, west of the fortress.

presence of a structure whose roof was supported by pillars. Future excavations will almost certainly uncover more pillars. Although this structure's connection with the temple area is not exactly known at this time, this connection must be through the gallery extending adjacent to the east side of the temple. It became clear that the area where great quantities of jars and pottery were unearthed (Area VIII) was the basement of this structure. Early excavations focusing on this structure have elsewhere been described in detail (Çilingiroğlu and Salvini 2001:74–75).

Although its architectural plan has not yet been exactly determined, the structure is a pillared hall built on a clearing east of the temple area. Given the distance of 3.80 m between the pillars, dimensions of the pillared hall must be 36.0 × 30.0 m. The basement of the structure, with similar plan and dimensions to the pillars in the temple complex, was used as a storage area. Large jars and bowls of different forms were uncovered in the storage rooms. Excavations carried out in recent years showed that the structure contained hundreds of bowls in rooms found at a depth of four meters under the ground level. A hundred wheelbarrow loads of pot sherds and whole pottery were uncovered from a 2.5 × 10.0 m excavated area. Work is in progress on the pots, whose records and drawings have not yet been completed. Excavations to be carried out in years to come will surely increase the quantity of these artifacts. There were neither any units of measurement printed on large and small jars recovered in the East Pillared Hall nor bullae tied to their open tops. This is completely different from the West Storage Rooms. Just like the artifacts stored in the temple storage rooms, those stored in the East Pillared Hall were probably kept out of the distribution system within and outside the fortress. Despite the presence of such a great quantity and variety of pottery in the storage rooms, it is interesting to note that some pots unearthed in domestic sections were used after being repaired by boring holes. Based on information found on a seal impression recovered in the fortress, it is possible that the East Pillared Hall is in fact an ašiḫusi building. Although the true meaning of the ašiḫusi building is not exactly known, it is believed to refer to a whole building that includes storage rooms. The name of the previously mentioned ašiḫusi building would have probably been carved in the blank sixth and seventh lines of the Ayanis gate inscription. However, the turn of historical events that followed made this impossible even after the building was completed.

The Ceramics

The excavations at Ayanis have yielded significant quantities of ceramics from good archaeological context (Çilingiroğlu and Salvini 2001; Derin 1999). Apart from different sectors of Ayanis, a 2.5 × 6.0 m trench in Area IX (East Storage Rooms) has yielded more than 60,000 sherds. This number will rise in the coming season when we continue further excavation in the same trench. A great amount of red polished and buff slipped pots and sherds were excavated in Area XI. Due to the variety of ceramic types excavated at Ayanis over the years, our understanding of the Urartian ceramic assemblage has evolved.

The forms of pottery unearthed at Ayanis fortress consist of bowls, jars, pitchers, plates, and pithoi. There is no painted decoration in the Urartian pottery tradition. Different ware categories have been identified at Ayanis, such as Urartian red polished ware, coarse ware, grit-tempered buff slipped ware, and grit-tempered brown slipped ware.

The term "Urartian red polished ware" represents a specialized ceramic that is distinctive in color, surface treatment, and firing and is often seen as the hallmark of the Urartian pottery corpus, making up 30 percent (this figure may change in the coming years) of the total Urartian ceramic assemblage from the Ayanis fortress. Nearly all specimens of the red polished ware are wheelmade with the exception of a couple of large vessels. Coarse ware vessels were found in every section of the fortress. These are distinguished by their coarse, gritty, and sometimes porous paste ranging in color from brown and reddish-brown to black and gray.

The sherds and complete vessels of grit tempered buff slipped ware can be distinguished by their well-fired dense paste, usually buff but sometimes brown or light brown in color. The slip is always present and shows little variety in color or form and is similar in color to the paste.

Grit tempered brown slipped ware makes the largest component within the Urartian ceramic assemblage. A majority of the examples have a dense paste ranging in color among several brown tones, but some sherds have a black or gray paste.

Conclusion

The Fortress of Ayanis was the last fortress built by Rusa II in 673/72 B.C.E., and after its destruction there was no Urartian occupation. It is archaeologically clear that King Rusa II and his queen, Kakuli, used to live here for some part of the year. Great numbers of artifacts such as bronze shields, arrowheads, spearheads, helmets, quivers, cauldrons, swords, every kind of pot, domestic artifacts, gold rosettes, gold figurines, and a temple with the longest extant temple inscription have contributed greatly to our understanding of Urartian art and history. We are certain that future excavations at Ayanis will provide further knowledge for scholars dealing with eastern Anatolian archaeology in the first millennium B.C.E.

References

Çilingiroğlu, Altan. 1991. Van-Ayanis (Agartı) Kalesi Kazıları. *Kazı Sonuçları Toplantısı* 12: 201–7.

——. 1993. Van-Ayanis (Agartı) Kalesi Kazıları, 1990–1991. *Kazı Sonuçları Toplantısı* 14: 431–39.

——. 1994a. Excavations at the Fortress of Ayanis. In *Anatolian Iron Ages 3. The Proceeedings of the Third Anatolian Iron Ages Colloquium Held at Van, August 6–12,*

1990, ed. Altan Çilingiroğlu and David H. French, 41–47. London: British Institute of Archaeology at Ankara.
———. 1994b. Decorated Stone Vessels from the Urartian Fortress of Ayanis. *Tel Aviv* 21.1: 68–76.
———. 1996. Van-Ayanis Kalesi Kazıları, 1993–1994. *Kazı Sonuçları Toplantısı* 17: 363–77.
———. 2005. Bronze Arrowheads of Ayanis (Rusahinili Eiduru-kai): Indicate Ethnic Identity? Metal III Symposium. *Der Anschnitt. Zeitschrift für Kunst und Kultur im Bergbau, Beiheft* 18: 63–66.
———. 2006a. An Urartian Fortress in Front of Mound Eiduru: Ayanis. *Aramazd* I: 135–42.
———. 2006b. Ayanis Kalesi'nde Bulunan Demir Bir Sadak ve Bazı Görüşler. In *Hayat Erkanal'a Armağan: Kültürlerin Yansıması/Studies in Honor of Hayat Erkanal: Cultural Reflctions*, ed. Armağan Erkanal-Öktü, 237–40. İstanbul: Homer Kitabevi.
———. 2007a. Ayanis Tapınak Alanında Bir Ocak ve Bereketlilik Kültü İle İlişkisi. In *Refik Duru'ya Armağan/Studies in Honour of Refik Duru*, ed. Gülsün Umurtak, Şevket Dönmez, and Aslıhan Yurtseven, 265–69. İstanbul: Ege Yayınları.
———. 2007b. Properties of the Urartian Temple at Ayanis. In *Anatolian Iron Ages 6: The Proceedings of the Sixth Anatolian Iron Ages Colloquium Held at Eskişehir, August 16–20, 2004*, ed. Altan Çilingiroğlu and Antonio Sagona, 41–46. Leuven: Peeters.
———. 2007c. *Urartu Kültürü ve Ayanis Kazıları*. Ankara: TÜBA.
———. 2008a. Ayanis Kalesi Depo Odaları İle İlgili Bazı Öneriler. In *Muhibbe Darga Armağanı/Studies in Honor of Muhibbe Darga*, ed. Taner Tarhan, Aksel Tibet, and Erkan Konyar, 187–96. İstanbul: Sadberk Hanım Museum Publications.
———. 2008b. Ayanis Kalesi'ndeki Evsel Mekânlar. In *Doğudan Yükselen Işık: Arkeoloji Yazıları*, ed. Birol Can and Mehmet Işıklı, 37–43. İstanbul: Atatürk University.
Çilingiroğlu, Altan and Gülriz Kozbe. 1994. Van-Ayanis Kalesi Kazısı, 1992. *Kazı Sonuçları Toplantısı* 15: 445–56.
Çilingiroğlu, Altan and Haluk Sağlamtimur. 1997. Van-Ayanis Kalesi Kazıları, 1995. *Kazı Sonuçları Toplantısı* 18: 363–77.
Çilingiroğlu, Altan and Mirjo Salvini. 1995. Rusahinili in Front of Mount Eiduru: The Urartian Fortress of Ayanis (7th. century B.C.). *Studi Micenei ed Egeo-Anatolici* 35: 111–24.
———. 1997. The 1997 Excavation Campaign at the Urartian Fortress of Ayanis. *Studi Micenei ed Egeo-Anatolici* 39: 287–89.
———. 1999. When Was the Castle of Ayanis Built and What Is the Meaning of the Word "Suri"? In *Anatolian Iron Ages 4, Proceedings of the Fourth Anatolian Iron Ages Colloquium Held at Mersin, 19–23. May 1997*, ed. Altan Çilingiroğlu and Roger J. Matthews. *Anatolian Studies* 49: 55–60.
———. 2001. *Ayanis I. Ten Years' Excavations at Rusaḫinili Eiduru-Kai 1989–1998*. Documenta Asiana 6. Rome: CNR, Istituto per gli Studi Micenei ed Egeo-Anatolici.
Derin, Zafer. 1999. Potters' Marks of Ayanis Citadel, Van. In *Anatolian Iron Ages 4, Proceedings of the Fourth Anatolian Iron Ages Colloquium held at Mersin, 19–23 May 1997*, ed. Altan Çilingiroğlu and Roger J. Matthews. *Anatolian Studies* 49: 81–100.
Derin, Zafer and Altan Çilingiroğlu. 2000. Ayanis Kalesi Kazıları-1998. *Kazı Sonuçları Toplantısı* 21: 397–408.
Stone, Elizabeth C. and Paul Zimansky. 2001. Survey and Excavations in the Outer Town, 1997–1998. In *Ayanis I: Ten Years' Excavations at Rusaḫinili Eiduru-kai, 1989–1998*, ed. Altan Çilingiroğlu and Mirjo Salvini, 355–75. Documenta Asiana 6. Rome: Istituto per gli Studi Micenei ed Egeo-Anatolici.

———. 2003. The Urartian Transformation in the Outer Town of Ayanis. In *Archaeology in the Borderlands: Investigations in the Cauacasus and Beyond*, ed. Adam Smith and Karen S. Rubinson, 213–28. Los Angeles: Cotsen Institute.

———. 2004. City Planning at Ayanis. In *A View from the Highlands: Trans-Caucasus, Eastern Anatolia and Northwestern Iran. Studies in Honor of C. A. Burney*, ed. Antonio Sagona, 233–43. Leuven: Peeters.

CHAPTER 50

GORDION: THE CHANGING POLITICAL AND ECONOMIC ROLES OF A FIRST MILLENNIUM B.C.E. CITY

MARY M. VOIGT

NEAR the juncture of the Porsuk and Sakarya Rivers in west-central Turkey lies a large, flat-topped mound called Yassıhöyük (39°39' N, 32°00' E). The size and form of the mound, typical of important long-term settlements in this region, plus the presence of conical burial mounds on nearby slopes, suggest a place of some importance to any archaeologist. In 1893 Alfred Körte visited the site, hoping to find ancient Gordion, capital of the Phrygian kingdom of the first millennium B.C.E. (Körte 1897). Convinced that Yassıhöyük was the best match for descriptions left by ancient historians, Körte returned to the site in 1900 with his brother Gustav to carry out excavations on the mound and five of the surrounding tumuli (Körte and Körte 1904; Sams 2005:10). Today an identification of Yassıhöyük as Gordion is supported by excavated remains of appropriate scale and date and by associated inscriptions in the Phrygian language. The site has not, however, yielded inscribed material attesting the place-name Gordion, and the name of its most famous king, Midas, occurs only as a graffito on a potsherd (Brixhe and Lejeune 1984:137). In fact, with the exception of a few references to well-known historical figures and pivotal events, most of our information about Gordion and the Phrygians comes from archaeology rather than texts (Rose and Darbyshire forthcoming).

Site Description

Initially, the archaeological exploration of Gordion as a settlement focused on Yassıhöyük ("flat-topped mound" in Turkish), and on the fortifications adjacent to its south. Today, surface survey, geophysical prospection, and limited excavation have established that Gordion is composed of three distinct topographic units (figure 50.1). At the center of the site is Yassıhöyük, which covers an area of 13 hectares at its base, and rises about 16.5 m above plain level; more than 4 more meters of archaeological deposit lie beneath the modern land surface, so that the mound consists of over 20 m of occupation débris. Excavated deposits date from the Early Bronze Age to Medieval times, but it is possible that earlier periods lie beneath the water table. Heavily fortified during much of its history, this central area is referred to here as the Citadel Mound (formerly the "City Mound"). Bordering the Citadel Mound to the north and south are walled Lower Town areas, each sector anchored by a fortress (the Küçükhöyük to the south and Kuş Tepe to the north); the residential area enclosed within these walls is estimated at fifty-one hectares (Sams 2009). To the northwest of the Citadel lies a large Outer Town partially or completely enclosed by an earth rampart. Even further west are subterranean chambers, cut into conglomerate beds, that are today empty, but were probably Phrygian rock-cut tombs. The total settlement area during the period when Gordion reached its maximum size (eighth century B.C.E.) is approximately one square kilometer.

Geomorphological research conducted by Ben Marsh has clarified the relationship of Gordion to the Sakarya and its river bed in antiquity (Marsh 1999, 2005, forthcoming). A study of the area within about ten kilometers of Gordion has shown that serious disruption of the landscape began at the start of the Early Bronze Age, ca. 3000 B.C.E. Material eroded from the surrounding hillsides was deposited on the Sakarya floodplain to a depth between three and five meters, so that land surfaces associated with the occupation of the site are deeply buried. Coring and an examination of river banks and other modern cuts through the plain, along with a limited number of radiocarbon dates, were used to reconstruct the history of the river. Among the most significant findings for an understanding of settlement form are recent changes in the river's course. Today, the Sakarya flows to the west of the Citadel Mound, separating it from the Outer Town and part of the northern Lower Town, but from the mid-Holocene until post-Medieval times the river flowed along the eastern edge of the settlement. Recent geomorphological prospection clearly shows the recent meandering course of the Sakarya cutting through the northern Lower Town, confirming Marsh's interpretation based on geomorphological observations.

Scattered along the ridgetops and slopes surrounding Gordion are over 200 burial mounds or tumuli, of which 44 have been archaeologically investigated (Kohler 1995; Liebhart et al. 2009; Temizsoy 1992, 1993, 1994; Young 1981). The greatest number lies to the northeast of the settlement, where linear distributions suggest that they lined ancient roads. The mounds vary considerably in size; the largest

Figure 50.1. Air view of the Citadel Mound and the southern part of the Lower Town in June 1989 showing Young excavations (eastern half of mound) and Mellink excavations (lower right corner). (Photo by J. Wilson and Eleanor Myers, courtesy the Gordion Project.)

(Tumulus MM) is about 53 m in height with a diameter of nearly 300 m, whereas some of the smaller mounds have been so reduced by erosion and plowing (not to mention robber trenches) that they are barely visible. The excavated tombs range in date from the ninth to first century B.C.E., with the preferred location for construction of the tumuli changing through time (Liebhart et al. 2009).

History of Archaeological Research at Gordion

Alfred and Gustav Körte placed three trenches on the Citadel Mound and excavated five tumuli. Far more extensive in scope and duration was the research carried out by the University of Pennsylvania Museum's Gordion Project directed by Rodney S. Young.

Young excavated for sixteen seasons between 1950 and 1973, working closely with Machteld Mellink and G. Roger Edwards in the early years (DeVries 1990; Edwards 1959; Young 1950, 1951, 1953, 1955, 1956, 1957, 1958, 1960, 1962a, 1964, 1966, 1968). On the eastern half of the Citadel Mound, Young focused his interests on the Phrygians, and dug relatively rapidly down through later occupations to expose a burned settlement destroyed by fire ca. 800 B.C.E. (figure 50.2). Large soundings on the western half of the Citadel were excavated in 1950 but were abandoned after that season because they exposed deep and relatively well-preserved Roman and Medieval deposits.[1] Young's team also explored the fortification system for the southern part of the Lower Town (Mellink 1958, 1959) and excavated thirty-one burial mounds (Kohler 1995; Young 1981). To document early Iron Age and Bronze Age occupations, Young and Mellink dug below the Early Phrygian Destruction Level; the deepest sounding was stopped when ground water filled the trench (Gunter 1991).

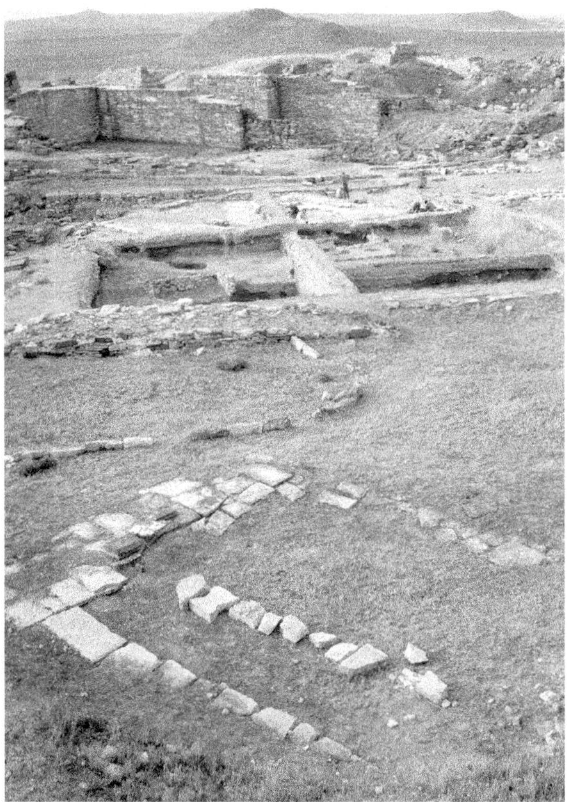

Figure 50.2. The Gate Complex of the Early Phrygian/YHSS 6A palace quarter is visible at the top of this photo. Immediately in front of this massive structure are the remains of the earlier, YHSS 6B, PAP structure, which had been demolished down to its foundations. The foundations of a second 6B structure are visible in the foreground.

This phase of fieldwork ended with Young's accidental death in 1974. From 1974 to 1988, Keith DeVries served as project director, leading a research team engaged in the analysis of material excavated by Young and his colleagues.

In 1988 a new cycle of excavation and regional surface survey began, directed by Mary M. Voigt in cooperation with Gordion Project Director G. Kenneth Sams.[2] The initial goals of Voigt's research were to record a detailed stratigraphic record for occupation on the Citadel Mound. This was accomplished through two soundings, one extending down from the Early Phrygian Destruction Level surface (the Lower Trench Sounding), and the second from the present mound surface to the Destruction Level (the Upper Trench Sounding) (figure 50.3). Related goals were the recovery of information on the economy of the settlement, including subsistence systems and manufacturing activities, and the documentation of domestic architecture and features such as hearths, bins, and pits. The result of this research was a well-defined stratigraphic sequence (YHSS) for periods extending from the Late Bronze Age/YHSS 10 to Medieval/YHSS 1 times, with large associated samples of ceramics, animal bone, and plant remains (table 50.1; see Henrickson 1991, 1993, 1994, 1995, 2005; Miller 1999, 2010; Miller, Zeder, and Arter 2009; Voigt 1994; Voigt and Henrickson 2000b). Beginning in 1993, attention shifted to an exploration of the western half of the Citadel Mound (in cooperation with T. Cuyler Young Jr.) and the Lower and

Figure 50.3. General view of the Terrace Buildings with a 1989 stratigraphic section cut from the modern mound surface down to the floor of Terrace Building 2A. In the section, the burned fill and leveling of TB2A (YHSS 6A Destruction Level) is at the base with the massive fill level of Middle Phrygian/YHSS 5 and rubble foundations for a YHSS 5 wall above.

Table 50.1. The Yassıhöyük Stratigraphic Sequence (YHSS)

YHSS Phase	Period Name	Approximate Dates
0	Modern	1920s
1	Medieval	10–15th century C.E.
2	Roman	1st century B.C.E.–4th century C.E.
3A	Later Hellenistic	260?–100 B.C.E.
3B	Early Hellenistic	333–?260 B.C.E.
4	Late Phrygian	540s–333 B.C.E.
5	Middle Phrygian	After 800–540s B.C.E.
6A–B	Early Phrygian	900–800 B.C.E.
7	Early Iron Age	1100–900 B.C.E.
9–8	Late Bronze Age	1400–1200 B.C.E.
10	Middle Bronze Age	1600–1400 B.C.E.

Notes: Although the period names are those originally employed by Rodney Young and his colleagues, the material assigned to each phase sometimes differs due to increased stratigraphic precision. This is especially true for the Middle and Late Phrygian periods. The absolute dates for each period also differ from those used before 1988, reflecting a larger sample and more detailed studies of the material from some periods, as well as new radiocarbon and dendrochronological dates.

Outer Towns. The primary goals were to document periods that were not well represented in the 1988–89 soundings and to examine variation in material culture and subsistence between areas within the city. This research greatly enhanced our picture of the Middle Phrygian/YHSS 5 through Medieval/YHSS 1 phases (Voigt 2003; Voigt et al. 1997; Voigt and Young 1999). Excavation that was specifically focused on the Roman/YHSS 2 occupation was carried out on the western area of the Citadel Mound by Andrew Goldman between 1997 and 2005 (Bennett and Goldman 2009; Goldman 2007; Sams, Burke, and Goldman 2007). The history of the settlement along the southern edge of the Citadel was investigated by Brendan Burke between 2001 and 2006 (Burke forthcoming; Sams and Burke 2008; Sams, Burke, and Goldman 2007).

Surface survey in the area surrounding the site was carried out informally by members of the Gordion team during the Young years, but the first formal examination of land surfaces began in 1987 when William Sumner walked around the site and biked and drove around the region. Sumner's observations at Gordion showed that there was occupation débris over a broad area to the north and west of the Citadel, and an intensive walking survey of this area carried out in 1992 by Andrew Goldman and Keith Dickey resulted in the definition of a broad area of settlement within the Outer Town. In 2007–10 geophysical prospection under the direction of Brian Rose provided a better definition of the walled Lower Town to the south of the Citadel and confirmed the presence of a similar area to the north that had been suspected based on massive stone walls in the Sakarya River bed (Sams 2009; Brian Rose personal communication).

Building on an extensive regional survey conducted by Sumner in 1987 and 1988, Lisa Kealhofer carried out an intensive sampling strategy for the investigation of sites and land surfaces from 1996 to 2002 (the Gordion Regional Survey, GRS).

Incorporating information on ancient environments collected by Tony Wilkinson, Arlene Rosen, and Ben Marsh, the GRS provides information on past settlement patterns and land use that can be used to document agricultural and economic changes and their relationship to major shifts in political and social organization (Kealhofer 2005; Marsh 2005). Detailed information on modern land use and subsistence systems collected by Ayşe Gürsan-Salzmann (2005), coupled with excavated plant and animal remains from Gordion, will aid in the final interpretation of data collected by the GRS.

The Archaeological Sequence

The earliest known settlement in the Gordion region is a single site that dates to the Chalcolithic found by the GRS (Kealhofer 2005). Early Bronze (EB) Age sites (ca. 2500–2000 B.C.E.) are more numerous, and these small settlements tend to be located near springs in the foothills east of Gordion (Kealhofer 2005). This period is also documented by excavated remains (Gunter 1991). A single cist grave found below an Iron Age tumulus near Gordion can be dated to EB I. Deep soundings on the Citadel Mound document a late third millennium B.C.E. (EB IIIA–B) occupation similar to that from the nearby Polatlı Mound. The Gordion settlement consisted of small mud-walled houses that may have been surrounded by an embankment and fortification wall. The final EB level, which had been burned, produced a large sample of ceramics, with an estimated total of approximately 1,100 vessels. Pottery from these levels was handmade and includes both burnished red-slipped and painted wares; red-slipped pottery occurs in a variety of shapes (pitchers, bowls, dippers, jars), but painted pottery was rare and occurred in a limited range of shapes (cups, small bowls, jars).

During the first half of the second millennium B.C.E. or Middle Bronze Age there is a great increase in the number of sites documented by surface survey, and settlement moves down onto the alluvial plain (Kealhofer 2005). Kealhofer suggests that this shift in location may reflect the appearance or increased importance of irrigation in the Gordion region. Unfortunately, the Middle Bronze Age is poorly documented by excavation. The ceramic sample is limited to poorly preserved sherds from the Citadel Mound soundings excavated by Mellink and Young, supplemented by a small number of complete vessels from extramural cemeteries excavated by Mellink (Gunter 1991; Mellink 1956; see also Voigt 1994). The Middle Bronze Age pottery is wheelmade and has a gritty fabric that is fired to buff and orange; surfaces are frequently red-slipped and polished. Common forms are bowls with incurved rims, carinated bowls, pitchers with beak spouts, teapots, and pithoi, the latter used as burial containers in extramural cemeteries. Pottery as well as seals and sealings provides evidence of contact with Hittite sites to the east (Dusinberre 2005; Gunter 1991).

During the Late Bronze Age (LBA) the number of sites in the Gordion region "drops off substantially" as smaller towns and villages are abandoned (Kealhofer 2005:147). Whether this drop represents a decline in population or a consolidation into a smaller number of larger sites has not yet been determined. From Gordion we have a broad range of excavated materials from the Young-Mellink deep soundings, and from the 1988–89 Lower Trench Sounding, where this period has been designated as YHSS phases 8–9 (Gunter 1991; Voigt 1994). The only complete architectural unit is dated near the end of the Late Bronze Age and consists of a house with associated storage pits (Voigt 1994). The house was constructed by cutting a rectangular "cellar" more than a meter deep and lining the walls with large stones; the floor of the cellar was very soft and apparently served as the foundation for a wooden superstructure that had some kind of wooden structure or porch on one end. The pits were cylindrical with a flat bottom and nearly vertical sides; layers of phytoliths in the pit bottoms indicate that they were initially used for grain, but they were eventually filled with domestic trash. The LBA pottery is simple and standardized, suggesting that it was mass-produced by specialist potters (Henrickson 1993, 1994, 1995; Henrickson and Blackman 1996), an inference supported by the presence of potters' marks (Gunter 1991). Vessels are consistently fired to buff or light orange with a plain surface; rare decorative elements are limited to red slip or painted bands, burnished lines, and impressions from stamp seals (Dusinberre 2005; Henrickson 1994, 1995). Common vessel forms include round-bottomed bowls, tall narrow jars with pointed bases, and globular cooking pots (Henrickson 1994; Henrickson and Voigt 1998). Rare but distinctive are zoomorphic vessels, the best-preserved of these perhaps an import (Henrickson 1995). Manufacturing techniques vary, depending on vessel size; smaller vessels are thrown on the wheel, while larger vessels employed several hand-forming techniques (molding, coiling) and were then finished on a wheel or tournette (Henrickson 1994).

Although the archaeological sample for Late Bronze Age/YHSS 9–8 Gordion is limited, it permits some inferences about economic and political organization. We cannot estimate the size of the settlement, but mass production of ceramics points to an economy based on specialization and exchange (Henrickson 1993, 1994, 1995). Both ceramic and glyptic evidence suggests that it was part of a small polity in contact with the Hittites and affiliated with them to some degree; the Gordion LBA ceramics replicate forms found at Hittite Empire settlements, and production sequences are similar if not identical at Gordion and Ḫattuša (Henrickson 1995). Stamp seals and sealings are also similar to those found at Imperial Hittite sites, as were sealing practices (Dusinberre 2005). Finally, a sealing found impressed into a vessel rim that seems to be locally made bears a personal name in Hittite hieroglyphics, suggesting the presence of a local élite (Henrickson 1995).

Built directly above the latest Bronze Age/YHSS 8 deposits in the 1988–89 Lower Trench Sounding was an architectural complex assigned to the Early Iron Age or YHSS 7 (Voigt 1994). At the start of this period (YHSS 7B, late second millennium B.C.E.) small houses were built, set in rectilinear pits that were thirty to fifty centimeters deep. These pits were lined with mud, or where the pit had cut through soft deposits, stone slabs. Around the edge of the house pits, walls of reeds or other lightweight material were covered with mud, the latter presumably derived from soils excavated to create the initial pit. Characteristic domestic features include a horseshoe-shaped oven and bins built of vertical stone slabs plastered inside and out with mud. Contemporary pits were bell-shaped, with wide bottoms and narrow mouths. Found on the floors of these houses and in the storage pits were complete and restorable ceramic vessels that are different in nearly every attribute from those of the Late Bronze Age. The Early Iron Age pottery is handmade, fired at low temperatures, and highly variable in form and decoration—all attributes of a household ceramic industry (Henrickson 1994; Voigt and Henrickson 2000a). Architecture, artifacts, and a preliminary assessment of household subsistence economy suggest a relatively small and isolated community. This inference is supported by the very small number of sites of this period that have been identified by surface survey, but the YHSS 7 ceramics are fragile and might not survive as well as the hard-fired wares of preceding and subsequent periods. It is also possible that most of the settlements at this time were ephemeral—campsites used by nomadic pastoralists.

The archaeological sequence represented by YHSS 8 and 7B can be used to address a question raised by historians: what was the relationship between the migration of Phrygian speakers from Thrace into Anatolia and the fall of the Hittite Empire? Gordion provides no evidence for a significant hiatus in settlement between the Late Bronze Age/YHSS 8 and Early Iron Age/YHSS 7B occupations; nevertheless, there are changes in virtually every aspect of material culture between these periods, from house form and construction to the way that people dug their storage pits and made their pots. Thus the archaeological remains suggest that the Late Bronze Age/Hittite-affiliated population moved out of the area or at least away from Gordion, and that a new group occupied the site near the beginning of the second millennium B.C.E. Based on admittedly vague similarities between the Early Iron Age handmade pottery at Gordion and roughly contemporary pottery from Thrace and Troy VIIb 2–3, it is reasonable to identify the archaeological remains of this period with the immigration of Phrygian speakers into central Anatolia (see Roller, chapter 25, and Kealhofer and Grave, chapter 18 in this volume; Henrickson 1994; Sams 1988, 1994b; Voigt and Henrickson 2000b).

Midway through the Early Iron Age sequence in the Lower Trench Sounding, the Burnt Reed House (BRH) was built, marking the start of YHSS 7A. The BRH differs in orientation, construction methods, and contents from the houses that immediately preceded it (i.e., 7B) and those that followed (later in 7A). Like the other Early Iron Age houses, the BRH consists of a single large room set in a shallow pit, but in this case far more wood was used in construction (Voigt 1994). A narrow shelf was cut around the edges of the pit, and small timbers were set into this shelf at regular intervals; bundles of reeds were placed between the timbers to form the wall matrix, and the interior surface of the building (floor and walls) was then covered with a layer of mud plaster, which preserved reed and post impressions when the structure burned. A line of postholes running parallel to the east wall of the structure served to divide the house into two spaces. Along the north wall of the

BRH was a platform with a double bin, and in the northwest corner was an oven found with a pottery tray resting across the top opening; a constriction in the oven interior may mark the boundary between the firing chamber and a chimney (Henrickson and Voigt 1998). On the floor of this building lay a wooden tray, along with the remains of baskets of wheat, barley, and bitter vetch (Miller 2010). Also preserved in situ were pots that were broken and sometimes partially vitrified; the vessels are wheelmade or wheel-finished, and fired to light colors. Vessel forms include one-handled cups, a pedestal-based goblet, a hemispherical bowl decorated with grooves, globular pots with lugs on the shoulders, and jars with ledge rims (Henrickson 1994; Voigt and Henrickson 2000a, 2000b). Houses built after the destruction of the BRH (i.e., later in YHSS 7A) mark a return to construction techniques and orientation found at the start of YHSS 7B, but both houses and associated refuse pits contain pots made in the Early Iron Age buff tradition as well as the older Early handmade tradition (Henrickson and Voigt 1998; Voigt and Henrickson 2000a, 2000b).

With such a limited sample it is difficult to interpret this sequence, but given differences in technology and typology, the Early Iron Age buff ware that appears in YHSS 7A represents something new within the Gordion sequence and cannot be derived from the YHSS 7B Early Iron Age handmade ceramic tradition. The Early Iron Age buff pottery is made from Sakarya River clays and was probably produced by potters who were part-time specialists (Henrickson and Voigt 1998). The style of domestic architecture represented by the people who built and lived in the BRH is an anomaly in the archaeological record at Gordion, but the potters producing Early Iron Age buff continued to work in the area and exchanged their products with the people living at Gordion during later YHSS 7A. Although Early Iron Age handmade pottery continues to be made and used by people living in the latest 7A houses (people who, we have argued, are ethnic Phrygians), the Early Iron Age buff craft tradition becomes dominant in succeeding periods, developing into what we know as Early Phrygian pottery during YHSS 6B (Robert Henrickson personal communication; for the development of Early Phrygian pottery, see Sams 1994b).

Near the start of the first millennium B.C.E., Gordion's growing political power is reflected in a new and ambitious building program: above the Early Iron Age/YHSS 7A houses in the Lower Trench Sounding were hard-packed surfaces that represent the beginning of the Early Phrygian Period or YHSS 6B (Voigt 1994). Layers of stone chips separated by clean clay fills document the construction of buildings with stone foundations around an open area or court. The only excavated structures dated to the beginning of 6B are a gate building and massive fortification wall excavated by Rodney Young (Sams 1994b; see also DeVries 1990; Young 1966). Much better documented is the final phase of Early Phrygian/YHSS 6B, dated ca. 900 B.C.E. (Voigt and Henrickson 2000b). By this time the early gate building had been modified and served as a side entrance to the site. A new gate building constructed of red, white, and gray stone (the Polychrome Gate House) now led through the early fortification wall. Once through the gatehouse, visitors to the Citadel would have walked north across a stone paving made of red and white blocks laid in a checkerboard pattern and into a court with a packed earth surface. This earth court was bordered by at least four rectangular buildings constructed of soft white stone ("poros") and wood (figure 50.2). The best preserved building of Late YHSS 6B (the PAP Structure) had a megaron plan and a stone paved floor; it was probably built up against the fortification wall and was surrounded on the other three sides by a pebble-paved walkway that seems to have been roofed. Poros blocks and other architectural fragments recovered from the foundations of YHSS 6A Megaron 9 were probably derived from the PAP when it was torn down at the end of Phase YHSS 6B (Sams 1994a; Young 1964). Some of these blocks suggest that the PAP had a pitched roof, perhaps topped with an akroterion (Sams 1994a).

A series of carved stone slabs or orthostat sculptures in a style related to Syro-Hittite reliefs found at sites such as Carchemish and Zincirli had been associated with the formal architecture of 6B by Kenneth Sams (1989), who suggested that these sculptures were originally placed in the Polychrome Gate House. This inference is now supported by recovery of a small sculpted fragment in débris associated with the construction of the PAP building.[3] Placing the orthostats securely within YHSS 6B is important for two reasons. First, these sculptures show that the earliest representatives of a Phrygian élite looked to established states in the east for ways of making statements of power. Second, this stylistic comparison provides a rough date for late YHSS 6B in the late tenth–early ninth century B.C.E., which accords well with radiocarbon determinations from earlier (YHSS 7A) and later (YHSS 6A) deposits at Gordion (Rose and Darbyshire forthcoming).

The ceramics recovered from YHSS 6B deposits established what has come to be regarded as the Early Phrygian ceramic style. Pots are wheelmade, often fired to gray, and are usually burnished (Sams 1994b). Light-colored fabrics are rare, and vessels with dark-colored painted designs are even less common. Vessel forms include carinated bowls, trefoil jugs, and ledge-rim jars.

Although the scale of the architecture and adoption of images and styles associated with eastern states suggest a strongly hierarchical social and political system at Gordion during YHSS 6B, we cannot be very specific about its form. The ceramics associated with this relatively short period are not sufficiently distinct to permit a segregation of surface collections into early and late Early Phrygian/YHSS 6 occupations (i.e., 6B and 6A), so we cannot use settlement patterns to document changes in population size and organization for the surrounding region. What we can say is that YHSS 6B represents the beginning of a process that culminates in a state-level polity, probably in the latter years of YHSS 6A (see later discussion).

With the exception of the fortification walls and the Polychrome Gate House, the initial Early Phrygian/YHSS 6B structures were demolished as part of a rebuilding of the élite quarter during the early ninth century. It is this second Early Phrygian architectural phase (YHSS 6A) that was preserved by fire around 800 B.C.E. (DeVries et al. 2003, Rose and Darbyshire forthcoming),[4] and that became the focus of Rodney Young's research. By the late ninth century B.C.E., the Early Phrygian city had grown, so Gordion may have extended over most of the area now lying beneath Yassıhöyük. There were now two distinct zones within the city: the walled élite quarter to the east, and a low area to the west that was presumably occupied by ordinary people. Although only two square meters of the western, non-élite zone has been excavated, the élite quarter has been exposed over an area of more than two hectares (figure 50.4; Sams 1995; Voigt 2002).

During YHSS 6A the fortification system was remodeled. Initially a large court was built to the southeast of the Polychrome Gate House; somewhat later, a second court was built to the north, so that the walls of the two courts formed a massive gateway (Young 1962b).[5] Inside the Polychrome Gate House, the élite quarter had three functionally differentiated zones that were physically separated by walls and changes in level: a palace complex divided into two courts, two long service buildings elevated above the level of the courts, and an area to the north that lies unexcavated beneath later buildings.[6] The stone-paved Outer Court of the palace complex was bordered to both east and west by large megara built of stone or mud-brick with timber elements, and gabled (?) roofs made of reeds covered with clay.

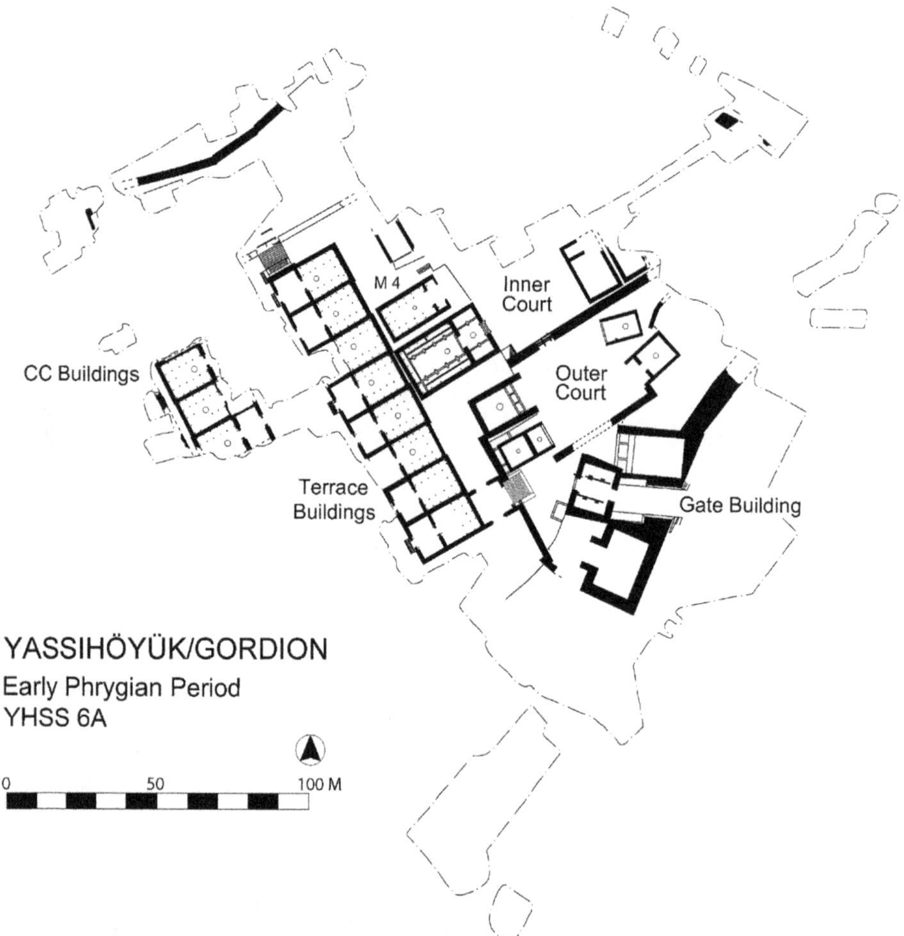

Figure 50.4. The Early Phrygian Level or YHSS 6A before the initiation of a major remodeling project underway at the time of the 800 B.C.E.fire.

Because the Outer Court buildings were largely empty at the time of the catastrophic fire that ended YHSS 6A, there is little direct evidence of building function, but from their location we might surmise that they housed reception and storage areas, and it has been suggested that one of these buildings may have been a temple. The most elaborate structure (Megaron 2) had a multicolored pebble mosaic floor set in geometric motifs (Young 1965); incised on the soft stone walls of this building were many graffiti, showing gable-roofed buildings, birds, animals, and (occasionally) people (Roller 2009). While the purpose of these "doodle stones" remains obscure, hawk and lion graffiti can be linked to *Matar*, the primary goddess of the Phrygians (see Roller, chapter 25 in this volume). Stylistically, the doodles have ties to Syro-Hittite orthostats which date to the first half of the ninth century (Roller 2008, 2009), a date that fits well with other evidence for the earliest YHSS 6A structures.

A thick wall separated the Outer Court from an Inner Court that was again bordered by megara. The largest of these was Megaron 3, which consisted of a small anteroom or vestibule and a large interior room or hall, each with a large round hearth. The hall was two stories high, and wooden beam beds and vertical supports suggested to Rodney Young (1962b) that it had a balcony running around three sides. Megaron 3 contained large quantities of smashed and charred artifacts, including metal and ceramic storage and serving vessels, foodstuffs, carved wooden furniture, ivory inlays, textiles, and iron tools (DeVries 1980). Either this building or the adjacent and newly built Megaron 4 (which was disturbed after the fire and so presumed to have contained things worth salvaging) served as the royal residence at the time of the fire.

To the west of the Early Phrygian/YHSS 6A palace complex was a high terrace with two long service buildings facing each other across a broad street: the Terrace Building to the east, and the Clay Cut Building to the west. Each of these structures is divided into a series of megaron units consisting of a large inner room and a smaller anteroom. These buildings often contained ovens in the anteroom, and most had rows of grinding stones set on mud platforms in the inner rooms; their function as cooking and storage areas is also indicated by charred grain and other seeds and masses of pottery (DeVries 1980). Other evidence for domestic production includes spindle whorls, loom weights, and partially woven textile fragments (Burke 2005). DeVries estimated the number of people working in these rooms at around 300, probably women and perhaps slaves in the service of the ruler and his court. Two of the terrace buildings (TB1 and 2) were unusual in that they lacked cooking facilities and contained valuable items such as imported ivory horse trappings, bronze vessels and animal figurines, and gold and electrum jewelry. It seems possible that these were the treasuries of the Phrygian kings.

These kings, their names unknown, began to construct massive funerary monuments or tumuli around the middle of the ninth century B.C.E. (see Sams, chapter 27 in this volume). The largest of these, Tumulus W, is also the earliest of the excavated tumuli based on artifact styles (Rose and Darbyshire forthcoming; Young 1981). This tomb established a construction pattern for élite burials that continued during Middle Phrygian times. A wooden chamber was covered with logs and rubble and then encased in a clay mound that in the case of W reached a height of 22 m with a base 150 m across. Although the tomb chamber of W had collapsed, the artifacts recovered included many bronze vessels, fibulae, and a belt; textiles, and wooden objects; and both painted and plain pottery. A deep petaled bronze bowl was compared by Young (1981) to an Assyrian example dated to the late ninth century B.C.E., providing an approximate date, as well as a suggestion that the Phrygians had retained and even expanded their earlier contacts with north Syria and Mesopotamia.

Near the end of the ninth century B.C.E., the Phrygians began a new construction project (DeVries 1990; Voigt forthcoming). The Polychrome Gate House was demolished in preparation for a new fortification system. To the west of the gate, a stairway that had led up to the terrace with service buildings was blocked, and the Phrygians began to lay a deep layer of fill that is best preserved immediately to the southeast of Megaron 1. In this fill they set rubble foundations for a new structure (Proto-Building C). This project was truncated by the 800 B.C.E. fire, but it was soon resumed as part of the Middle Phrygian/YHSS 5 rebuilding program.

What kind of political and economic system was in place at Gordion at the time of the fire? We cannot determine the extent to which food and other organic resources flowed into the city, but several lines of evidence based on inorganic materials suggest that Gordion was a powerful regional polity collecting tax and/or tribute. A study of the provenience of the clay used for a large sample of ceramics from the YHSS 6B Destruction Level (i.e., the Palace Quarter) indicates that there is an unusually high percentage of imports occurring in a wide range of shapes and styles. Grave et al. (2009) suggest that these vessels were part of élite food practices that emphasized the inflow of goods from a wide geographical region. Distinctive metal imports from north Syria certainly show contact and perhaps an exchange of gifts between Phrygian and north Syrian leaders. Finally, the construction of massive tumuli and the initiation of a late ninth-century B.C.E. building project that would have raised and transformed the palace quarter show an impressive command over people's time and labor.

The Middle Phrygian/YHSS 5 rebuilding began almost immediately after the 800 B.C.E. fire and affected all three topographic zones of the site. Above the eastern élite quarter, a three-to-five-meter-thick layer of fill was laid, supporting new stone buildings that had rubble foundations and ashlar walls (figure 50.5a; Voigt 1994, 2007). The fill is sometimes clean clay dredged from the surrounding plain, but sometimes this fill contained Bronze Age pottery, indicating the leveling of earlier sites in the search for construction materials. In plan, the élite quarter of the Middle Phrygian/YHSS 5 Eastern Mound replicates key elements of the Early Phrygian/YHSS 6A settlement lying directly below. There are, however, differences in construction methods and in the plan of individual structures, especially the gate complex (figure 50.5b). Most of the Middle Phrygian/YHSS 5 buildings had been robbed down to their foundations, so we have little in situ evidence for material culture from buildings within the Phrygian capital, especially for the eighth century

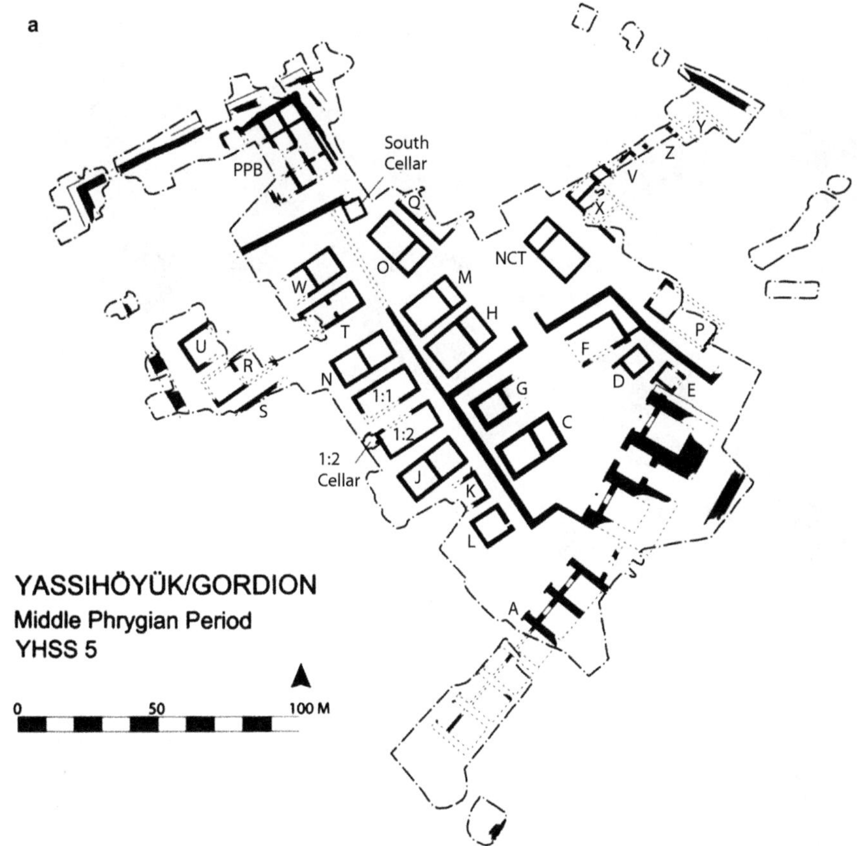

Figure 50.5. (a) Plan of the main excavation area (Eastern Mound) during Middle Phrygian/YHSS 5 times. The wall that borders the street that ran between Eastern and Western Mounds is clearly shown to the left. (b) The Middle Phrygian/YHSS 5 settlement was badly preserved due to systematic wall robbing during Late Phrygian/YHSS 5 and later times. At the bottom of the photo are structures (including a drain) that had been under construction at the time of the YHSS 6A fire (the Unfinished Project). To the left, set in the YHSS 5 fill layer as it was put down, are the rubble foundations and ashlar walls of Building C1. To the right of Building C1 are massive foundations cut into the clay, supporting the walls of Building C2.

B.C.E. An exception is a dump recovered from a semi-subterranean stone structure, the South Cellar. Discarded within its walls were fine Black-Burnished pots that imitated metal forms, ceramic imports from Greece dating to the last quarter of the eighth century B.C.E., bronze belt fragments and fibulae, and a bone image paralleled at Ephesus and Bayındır Tumulus (DeVries 2005, 2008; Rose and Darbyshire forthcoming).

To the west, five to six meters of clay fill was laid to form a new mound with a surface at approximately the same height as the élite quarter. Between the old Eastern and new Western Mounds was a broad, paved avenue that led north and south

Figure 50.5. (*Continued*)

into the fortified Lower Town. There is no excavated evidence for walls around the YHSS 5 Western Mound, but without some kind of protection its clay sides would have soon eroded. Along the northern edge of the Western Mound, formal buildings with deep rubble foundations were built (Voigt 2007); these were demolished by later pitting so that their function is unknown. To the south were substantial houses that produced fine pottery with graffiti, suggesting the presence of minor officials or merchants.

The southern part of the Lower Town is relatively well documented as a result of excavation as well as geophysical prospection (figure 50.6). Stone and mud buildings built in the eighth century B.C.E. (Voigt and Young 1999) were protected by a 3.5-m-thick fortification wall with square towers set at regular intervals; the walls were anchored by a mudbrick fortress, the Küçükhöyük. The eastern edge of the southern Lower Town and the Eastern Citadel Mound were protected by the Sakarya, and geophysical prospection suggests the location of a bridge across the river, leading into the Lower Town (Brian Rose personal communication; Sams 2009). The Lower Town area to the north is smaller than that to the south, and has only recently been documented by surface remains and geophysical evidence (Sams 2009). Heavy stone walls which today form rapids in the Sakarya River bed lead toward a small mound (Kuş Tepe), which seems to be a small fortress mirroring the Küçükhöyük. Without excavation we cannot be certain of the date of this part of the site, but symmetry with the Southern Lower Town suggests a similar construction date, that is, within the Middle Phrygian/YHSS 5 Period. On the slopes to the north and west of the Citadel Mound and the Northern Lower Town lay an Outer Town where houses may have been interspersed with gardens or small fields. Only one YHSS 5 house has been excavated (Sams and Voigt 1995), but

Figure 50.6. Excavation in the southern part of Gordion's Lower Town exposed houses dating to the Middle/YHSS 5 and Late/YHSS 4 periods. Foundations of Middle Phrygian houses had a mudbrick superstructure, and Late Phrygian pithouses vary significantly in size; one of the larger examples is in the foreground.

surface remains suggest a much broader occupied area. A massive earthworks discovered by geomorphologist Ben Marsh appears to enclose much or all of the occupied area, but its date has not been determined through excavation. The number of people living in the Gordion region also expanded during Middle Phrygian/YHSS 5 times, and settlement forms included good-sized towns as well as small villages (Kealhofer 2005).

The ruling élite of Middle Phrygian/YHSS 5 Gordion included its greatest kings, Gordias and Midas. These rulers are known only from scattered references in texts written by people in adjacent regions, but their power is well documented by the archaeological record (see Sams, chapter 27 in this volume). The Middle Phrygian kings were able to mobilize a substantial labor force to re-create and enhance a citadel that was both product and symbol of their right to collect tribute or taxes. The wealth and craftsmanship of the Phrygians at this time is well documented by their tombs, especially Tumuli MM and P which were well preserved. MM (figure 50.7), the largest of the Phrygian tumuli, has a wooden tomb chamber with a gabled roof that was built of sawn planks; the planks were then surrounded by huge logs and encased first in stone and then in clay (Liebhart and Johnson 2005; Young 1981). Tumulus MM was originally interpreted as the tomb of Midas, who died no earlier than 709 B.C.E.; however, dendrochronological dates for the log tomb chamber indicate that the tomb was built around 740 B.C.E., suggesting that an earlier ruler was

Figure 50.7. Tumulus MM, built around 740 B.C.E., dominates the valley of the Sakarya near Gordion. The modern village and excavation house are visible to the left of MM. (Photo taken in 1975, used courtesy Peter Kuniholm.)

interred there—perhaps Midas's father (Liebhart and Johnson 2005; Rose and Darbyshire forthcoming)

Finds from within the tomb chambers of MM and the slightly earlier P provide ample evidence of Phrygian crafts. They include beautiful inlaid wooden furniture, bronze and brass vessels, bronze fibulae and belts, and pottery (Simpson forthcoming; Simpson and Spirydowicz 1999; Young 1981). Each tomb also has its own unique finds. From P, the burial place of a child, came small, quirky bronze and wooden animals, presumably toys, as well as pottery with painted animal panels that is paralleled on the YHSS 5 citadel mounds. Tumulus MM has nondescript pottery but provides the earliest secure evidence for writing; names written with the Phrygian alphabet were found inscribed on wax panels applied to bronze bowls and on a roof beam laid above the tomb chamber (Sams 2009; Young 1981).

During the seventh century B.C.E. the power of the Phrygian dynasty declined, and by the early sixth century B.C.E., Middle Phrygian Gordion was under strong Lydian influence, if not actually incorporated into the kingdom of Alyattes and Croesus (see Sams, chapter 27 in this volume). YHSS 5 ended when the Persians took the city at some point in the 540s B.C.E., an event documented archaeologically by the destruction of the Küçükhöyük fortress. Under the Persians, Gordion was reduced in importance as a political center, but its role as an economic center continued or was perhaps enhanced by the unification of Anatolia within the Persian Empire (Voigt and Young 1999). One source of prosperity during Late Phrygian/YHSS 4 seems to be manufacturing, with evidence for the production of stone, bone, ivory, and metal artifacts. The items received in exchange for such goods included glass (Jones 2005), Attic and Lydian fine pottery, and Greek wines (Voigt et al. 1997). Gordion under the Achaemenids was in fact a fascinating place: juxtaposed with elements of indigenous Phrygian material culture were new Iranian ceramic forms and horse harness elements, a building decorated with reused painted tiles in Lydian style (the Mosaic Building; Glendinning 2005), and a room decorated with polychrome murals painted in Greek style (the Painted House; Mellink 1980). No archaeological remains testify to the visit of Alexander the Great in 334/3 B.C.E., but with the fall of the Persian Empire Gordion's importance and prosperity declined.

Conclusion

Gordion is best known as the capital of the Phrygians, an early first millennium B.C.E. city that was the capital of a state that stretched over much of central Anatolia in the second quarter of the first millennium B.C.E. and was sufficiently powerful to engage in diplomatic fencing with the king of Assyria. Excavations carried out by Young and his team documented a burned and thus well-preserved series of buildings that served as the palace quarter for Phrygian kings who included Midas and his father, Gordias. Enormous heaps of clay preserved wooden tombs that were explored by Young, and the Körte brothers provided more evidence for the material culture of élite individuals.

Recent research at Gordion has focused on daily life and evidence for change in economy and political organization through time. Two strategies were used to provide basic information on subsistence and manufacturing systems, population distribution, land use, and environment: the collection of plant and animal remains and manufacturing débris through excavation, and regional survey to collect information on past settlement and environments (Kealhofer 2005). Permanent settlement in the area surrounding Gordion took place relatively late in comparison to regions to the west and south, with no known Neolithic sites and only one possible Chalcolithic site. During the Early Bronze Age, a period of increased rainfall, groups of farmers and herders move into the Gordion area, settling close to permanent water sources, especially a line of springs located on low hillsides. Despite increasingly unstable environmental conditions (vegetation degradation, erosion) that took place after ca. 4,000 years ago, the number and size of sites steadily increases until the Late Bronze Age, when many sites were abandoned, probably a result of political and economic structures resulting from interaction with the Hittite Empire as documented by excavated ceramics and glyptic evidence. With the Hittite collapse, there is a decrease in the size of the sedentary population within the Gordion region. Gordion itself may have been abandoned for a brief time, but was soon reoccupied by a group of people whose material culture is very different from that of the

Bronze Age. Sites are apparently small and few in number, and tend to represent new locations rather than a resettlement of older mounded sites (Kealhofer 2005). This break in the location of settlements supports an argument for a population replacement that is based on discontinuities in virtually every aspect of material culture in the excavated settlement at Gordion, a discontinuity that most likely reflects the arrival of Phrygian speakers from the west.

At the start of the ninth century B.C.E. the first formal, nondomestic stone buildings are constructed at Gordion, ornamented with sculptures that reflect themes associated with Neo-Hittite states to the east. Over the next 200 years the power of the Phrygian leaders grew as reflected by the amount of labor that they were able to expend on their capital and tombs, and by regional population growth and the development of a settlement hierarchy. Although they were apparently literate, the Phrygian kings did not leave us records of their strength and accomplishments, but documentary sources extending from Greece to Assyria indicate that by the eighth century B.C.E. they dominated central Anatolia, a pattern reflected in the expansion of Phrygian ceramic technology and ceramic styles (see Kealhofer and Grave, chapter 18 in this volume). The economic base for this expansion is not obvious. Gordion is located in a region that today requires irrigation for reliable crop production, leading Naomi Miller (2010) to describe the environment as "harsh" for farmers relying on the traditional Near Eastern domesticates. Subsistence strategies that include a significant dependence on herding have provided some stability and balance in recent times (Gürsan-Salzmann 2005), and Miller, Zeder, and Arter's (2009) analysis of floral and faunal remains from the Late Bronze Age through Roman times indicates that there was indeed an emphasis on pastoral production during most of the first millennium B.C.E. The exception is the Middle Phrygian Period, when the archaeobiological data indicate a greater dependence on agriculture. The increased importance of plant crops in the archaeological record for Gordion can be explained in several ways. For example, with an ample supply of free or slave labor, the Phrygian kings could have constructed large-scale irrigation systems to provide a reliable water supply for cereal crops, and their control over other regions with better soils and more reliable rainfall could have supplied crops as tribute. There may also be an environmental component that spurred Phrygian economic and political success. Miller (2010) has pointed out that climatic data indicate a greater amount of moisture within a broad geographical area that includes Anatolia during the ninth century B.C.E. Such a climatic amelioration would have facilitated (but not caused) the Phrygian prosperity indicated by building programs and foreign contacts during this period.

Nevertheless, if we focus on agricultural potential, the location of Gordion as a long-term capital for a prosperous state remains an enigma. A more promising explanatory factor is Gordion's location at the juncture of major routes of trade and transport, a characteristic that was emphasized by Greek and Roman historians. During Early and Middle Phrygian times the strategic location of the site would have enhanced its political and economic role, but the real test of the importance of this factor is not documented for this period as well as it is for Late Phrygian times when the city retained its size and prosperity despite the fact that it was ruled by and paid tribute to the Persian Empire. Excavation has provided abundant evidence for manufacturing activities, ranging from iron working to the production of antler horse trappings and bone furniture ornaments. That these items were not strictly for local use is demonstrated by a sudden increase in imports. For example, Robert Henrickson estimates that around 2 percent of the fine wares during this period were imported from Greece. Thus it may be that Alexander's long journey from the south coast of Anatolia to Gordion was inspired by legend and a desire to fulfill a prophecy, but the knot that he cut was perhaps metaphorical, and by taking Gordion he assured himself of control over a strategic point that allowed his progression to dominance over all of Asia.

NOTES

1. The Roman settlement, for which we have now defined four distinct phases of occupation, was confined to the western part of Yassıhöyük. The Medieval (Selçuk) settlement extends over much of the eastern area, but was not present in the areas initially excavated by Young.

2. Excavation and survey at Gordion since 1988 has been supported by grants from the National Endowment for the Humanities, the National Science Foundation, the Social Science and Humanities Research Council of Canada, the National Geographic Society, the Royal Ontario Museum, the Kress Foundation, the IBM Foundation, and the Tanberg Trust, by grants to individual project members, and by gifts from generous private donors. All modern archaeological research at Gordion (1950–) has been sponsored and supported by the University of Pennsylvania Museum; the College of William and Mary has been a co-sponsor since 1991, and the Royal Ontario Museum co-sponsored work carried out between 1994 and 2002.

3. The fact that the relatively complete orthostats published by Sams were recovered from the foundations of Middle Phrygian/YHSS 5 buildings makes sense, since the Polychrome Gate House was torn down late in Phase 6A, at the start of the building project that became YHSS 5 (the Unfinished Project, see later discussion). Note that Roller's statement that the orthostats were reused as paving is incorrect (Roller 2008).

4. The redating of the Early Phrygian/YHSS 6A Destruction Level has been the subject of some controversy (Muscarella 2003, 2008a, 2008b), but most scholars have accepted a date of ca. 800 B.C.E. based on a large suite of entirely consistent radiocarbon dates run on short-lived samples. The new dating is supported by stylistic comparisons of Early and Middle Phrygian artifacts with materials from other sites made by Keith DeVries and G. Kenneth Sams (DeVries 2005, 2007, 2008; Rose and Darbyshire forthcoming). For a summary of major changes in the chronology of Iron Age Gordion and the arguments that supported each of the proposed chronological sequences see Voigt (2009).

5. A revision of our thinking about the gate structure and its history is now under way, stimulated by ideas put forth by Richard Liebhart (personal communication).

6. Another partition wall separated the Inner Court from the area to the north. Here lies the so-called Phrygian-Persian Building, a structure made up of small rectangular

rooms. This structure contained material dated to Middle Phrygian/YHSS 5 times, and there is no evidence that it was constructed before YHSS 5 as had been thought.

REFERENCES

Bennett, Julian and Andrew L. Goldman. 2009. Report on the Roman Military Presence at Gordion, Galatia. In *Limes XX, XXth International Congress of Roman Frontier Studies*, ed. A. Morillo, N. Hanel, and E. Martin, 1605–16. Madrid: Ediciones Polifemo.

Brixhe, Claude and Michel LeJeune. 1984. *Corpus des inscriptions paléo-phrygiennes*. Recherche sur les civilizations, Memoire, 45. Paris: Èd. Recherche sur les Civilisations.

Burke, Brendan. 2005. Textile Production at Gordion and the Phrygian Economy. In *The Archaeology of Midas and the Phrygians: Recent Work at Gordion*, ed. Lisa Kealhofer, 69–81. Philadelphia: University of Pennsylvania Museum of Archaeology and Anthropology.

———. Forthcoming. The Rebuilt Citadel at Gordion. In *The Archaeology of Phrygian Gordion*, ed. C. Brian Rose. Philadelphia: University of Pennsylvania Museum of Anthropology and Archaeology.

DeVries, Keith. 1980. Greeks and Phrygians in the Early Iron Age. In *From Athens to Gordion: The Papers of a Memorial Symposium for Rodney S. Young*, ed. Keith DeVries, 33–49. University Museum Papers 1. Philadelphia: University Museum of the University of Pennsylvania.

———. 1990. The Gordion Excavation Seasons of 1969–1973 and Subsequent Research. *American Journal of Archaeology* 94: 371–406.

———. 2005. Greek Pottery and Gordion Chronology. In *The Archaeology of Midas and the Phrygians: Recent Work at Gordion*, ed. Lisa Kealhofer, 36–55. Philadelphia: University of Pennsylvania Museum of Archaeology and Anthropology.

———. 2007. The Date of the Destruction Level at Gordion: Imports and the Local Sequence. In *Anatolian Iron Ages 6: The Proceedings of the Sixth Anatolian Iron Ages Colloquium Held at Eskisehir, August 16–20, 2004*, ed. Altan Çilingiroğlu and Antonio Sagona, 79–101. Ancient Near Eastern Studies Supplement Series 20. Leuven: Peeters.

———. 2008. The Age of Midas at Gordion and Beyond. *Ancient Near Eastern Studies* 45: 30–64.

DeVries, Keith, Peter I. Kuniholm, G. Kenneth Sams, and Mary M. Voigt. 2003. New Dates for Iron Age Gordion. *Antiquity* 77.296. http://www.antiquity.ac.uk/projgall/devries296.

Dusinberre, Elspeth R. M. 2005. *Gordion Seals and Sealings: Individuals and Society*. Gordion Special Studies 3. University Museum Monograph 124. Philadelphia: University of Pennsylvania Museum of Archaeology and Anthropology.

Edwards, G. Roger. 1959. Gordion Campaign of 1958: Preliminary Report. *American Journal of Archaeology* 63: 263–68.

Glendenning, Matt. 2005. A Decorated Roof at Gordion: What Tiles Are Revealing about the Phrygian Past. In *The Archaeology of Midas and the Phrygians: Recent Work at Gordion*, ed. Lisa Kealhofer, 82–100. Philadelphia: University of Pennsylvania Museum of Archaeology and Anthropology.

Goldman, Andrew. 2007. From Phrygian Capital to Rural Fort—New Evidence for the Roman Military at Gordion, Turkey. *Expedition* 49: 6–12.

Grave, Peter, Lisa Kealhofer, Ben Marsh, G. Kenneth Sams, Mary Voigt, and Keith DeVries. 2009. Ceramic Production and Provenience at Gordion, Central Anatolia. *Journal of Archaeological Science* 36: 2162–2176.

Gunter, Ann C. 1991. *The Bronze Age*. Gordion Excavations: Final Reports 3. University Museum Monograph 73. Philadelphia: University Museum of the University of Pennsylvania.

Gürsan-Salzmann, Ayşe. 2005. Ethnographic Lessons for Past Agro-Pastoral Systems in the Sakarya-Porsuk Valleys. In *The Archaeology of Midas and the Phrygians: Recent Work at Gordion*, ed. Lisa Kealhofer, 172–89. Philadelphia: University of Pennsylvania Museum of Archaeology and Anthropology.

Henrickson, Robert C. 1991. Wheelmade or Wheel-Finished? Interpretation of "Wheelmarks" on Pottery. In *Material Issues in Art and Archaeology II*, ed. Pamela B. Vandiver, James R. Druzik, and George Wheeler, 523–41. Pittsburgh: Materials Research Society.

———. 1993. Politics, Economics and Ceramic Continuity at Gordion in the Late Second and First Millennia B.C. In *The Social and Cultural Contexts of New Ceramic Technologies*, ed. W. D. Kingery, 89–176. Westerville, Ohio: American Ceramic Society.

———. 1994. Continuity and Discontinuity in the Ceramic Tradition at Gordion during the Iron Age. In *Anatolian Iron Ages 3: The Proceedings of the Third Anatolian Iron Ages Colloquium Held at Van, 6–12 August, 1990*, ed. Altan Çilingiroğlu and David H. French, 95–129. British Institute of Archaeology at Ankara Monograph 16. Ankara: British Institute of Archaeology.

———. 1995. Hittite Potters and Pottery: The View from Late Bronze Age Gordion. *Biblical Archaeology* 58.2: 82–90.

———. 2005. The Local Potter's Craft at Phrygian Gordion. In *The Archaeology of Midas and the Phrygians: Recent Work at Gordion*, ed. Lisa Kealhofer, 124–35. Philadelphia: University of Pennsylvania Museum of Archaeology and Anthropology.

Henrickson, Robert C. and M. James Blackman. 1996. Large Scale Production of Pottery at Gordion: A Comparison of the Late Bronze and Early Phrygian Industries. *Paléorient* 22.1: 67–88.

Henrickson, Robert C. and Mary M. Voigt. 1998. The Early Iron Age at Gordion: The Evidence from the Yassıhöyük Stratigraphic Sequence. In *Thracians and Phrygians: Problems of Parallelism*, ed. Numan Tuna, Zeynep Aktüre, and Maggie Lynch, 79–107. Ankara: METU Faculty of Architecture Press.

Jones, Janet. 2005. Glass Vessels from Gordion: Trade and Influence along the Royal Road. In *The Archaeology of Midas and the Phrygians: Recent Work at Gordion*, ed. Lisa Kealhofer, 101–16. Philadelphia: University of Pennsylvania Museum of Archaeology and Anthropology.

Kealhofer, Lisa. 2005. The Gordion Regional Survey: Settlement and Land Use. In *The Archaeology of Midas and the Phrygians: Recent Work at Gordion*, ed. Lisa Kealhofer, 137–48. Philadelphia: University of Pennsylvania Museum of Archaeology and Anthropology.

Kohler, Ellen. 1995. *The Lesser Phrygian Tumuli, Part 1: The Inhumations*. Gordion Excavation Reports, vol. 2. University Museum Monograph 88. Philadelphia: University Museum of the University of Pennsylvania.

Körte, Alfred. 1897. Kleinasiatische Studien II. Gordion und der Zug des Manlius gegen die Galater. *Mitteilungen des Deutschen Archäologischen Instituts, Athenische Abteilung* 22: 1–51.

Körte, Gustav and Alfred Körte. 1904. *Gordion: Ergebnisse der Ausgrabung im Jahre 1900*. Jahrbuch des Deutschen Archäologischen Instituts, Supplement 5. Berlin: G. Reimer.

Liebhart, Richard, Gareth Darbyshire, Evin Erder, and Ben Marsh. 2009. A Fresh Look at the Tumuli of Gordion. Paper delivered at Tumulistanbul 2009, İstanbul, June 2009.

Liebhart, Richard F. and Jessica S. Johnson. 2005. Support and Conserve: Conservation and Environmental Monitoring of the Tomb Chamber of Tumulus MM. In *The Archaeology of Midas and the Phrygians: Recent Work at Gordion*, ed. Lisa Kealhofer, 191–203. Philadelphia: University of Pennsylvania Museum of Archaeology and Anthropology.

Marsh, Ben. 1999. Alluvial Burial of Gordion, an Iron Age City in Anatolia. *Journal of Field Archaeology* 26.2: 163–75.

———. 2005. Physical Geography, Land Use, and Human Impact at Gordion. In *The Archaeology of Midas and the Phrygians: Recent Work at Gordion*, ed. Lisa Kealhofer, 161–71. Philadelphia: University of Pennsylvania Museum of Archaeology and Anthropology.

———. Forthcoming. Reading Early Gordion History in the Sediment Record. In *The Archaeology of Phrygian Gordion*, ed. C. Brian Rose. Philadelphia: University of Pennsylvania Museum of Archaeology and Anthropology.

Mellink, Machteld J. 1956. *A Hittite Cemetery at Gordion*. Philadelphia: University Museum.

———. 1958. Küçük Hüyük 1958. Report Labeled "to RSY." Manuscript in the Gordion Archives, University of Pennsylvania Museum of Archaeology and Anthropology.

———. 1959. The City of Midas. *Scientific American* July: 100–109.

———. 1980. Archaic Wall Paintings from Gordion. In *From Athens to Gordion: The Papers of a Memorial Symposium for Rodney Young*, ed. Keith DeVries, 91–98. University Museum Papers 1. Philadelphia: University Museum of the University of Pennsylvania.

Miller, Naomi. 1999. Seeds, Charcoal and Archaeological Contexts: Interpreting Ancient Environment and Patterns of Land Use. *TÜBA-AR* 2: 15–27.

———. 2010. *Botanical Aspects of Environment and Economy at Gordion, Turkey*. Gordion Excavation Special Studies 5, Museum Monograph 131. Philadelphia: University of Pennsylvania Museum of Archaeology and Anthropology.

Miller, Naomi F., Melinda A. Zeder, and Susan R. Arter. 2009. From Food and Fuel to Farms and Flocks: The Integration of Plant and Animal Remains in the Study of the Agropastoral Economy at Gordion, Turkey. *Current Anthropology* 50.6: 915–24.

Muscarella, Oscar White. 2003. The Date of the Destruction of the Early Phrygian Period at Gordion. *Ancient West and East* 2.2: 225–52.

———. 2008a. Again Gordion's Early Phrygian Destruction Date: ca. 700 +/– B.C. In *Aykut Çınaroğlu'na Armağan—Studies in Honor of Aykut Çınaroğlu*, ed. Elif Genç and Duygu Çelik, 175–87. Ankara: Yapı Kredi Bankası.

———. 2008b. Review of *Anatolian Iron Ages 6: The Proceedings of the Sixth Anatolian Iron Ages Colloquium held at Eskişehir, August 16–20, 2004*, ed. Altan Çilingiroğlu and Antonio Sagona. *Bulletin of the Asia Institute* 18: 167–79.

Roller, Lynn. 2008. Early Phrygian Sculpture: Refining the Chronology. *Ancient Near Eastern Studies* 45: 188–201.

———. 2009. *The Incised Drawings from Early Phrygian Gordion*. Gordion Special Studies 4. University Museum Monograph 130. Philadelphia: University of Pennsylvania Museum of Archaeology and Anthropology.

Rose, C. Brian and Gareth Darbyshire, eds. Forthcoming. *The Chronology of Iron Age Gordion*. Philadelphia: University of Pennsylvania Museum of Archaeology and Anthropology.

Sams, G. Kenneth. 1988. The Early Phrygian Period at Gordion: Toward a Cultural Identity. *Source* 7.3–4: 9–15.

———. 1989. Sculpted Orthostates at Gordion. In *Anatolia and the Ancient Near East: Studies in Honor of Tahsin Özgüç*, ed. Kutlu Emre, Barthel Hrouda, Machteld Mellink, and Nimet Özgüç, 447–54. Ankara: Türk Tarih Kurumu Basımevi.

———. 1994a. Aspects of Early Phrygian Architecture at Gordion. In *Anatolian Iron Ages 3: The Proceedings of the Third Anatolian Iron Ages Colloquium Held at Van, August 6–12, 1990*, ed. Altan Çilingiroğlu and David H. French, 211–20. British Institute of Archaeology at Ankara Monograph 16. Ankara: British Institute of Archaeology at Ankara.

———. 1994b. *The Early Phrygian Pottery. The Gordion Excavations, 1950–1973: Final Reports IV (2 vols.)*. University Museum Monograph 79. Philadelphia: University Museum.

———. 1995. Midas of Gordion and the Anatolian Kingdom of Phrygia. In *Civilizations of the Ancient Near East*, ed. Jack Sasson, 1147–59. New York: Scribner's.

———. 2005. Gordion: Exploration over a Century. In *The Archaeology of Midas and the Phrygians: Recent Work at Gordion*, ed. Lisa Kealhofer, 10–21. Philadelphia: University of Pennsylvania Museum of Archaeology and Anthropology.

———. 2009. Gordion, 2007. 30. *Kazı Sonuçları Toplantısı* 3: 139–50.

Sams, G. Kenneth and R. Brendan Burke. 2008. Gordion, 2006. 29. *Kazı Sonuçları Toplantısı* 2: 329–42.

Sams, G. Kenneth, R. Brendan Burke, and Andrew L. Goldman. 2007. Gordion, 2005. 28. *Kazı Sonuçları Toplantısı* 2: 365–86.

Sams, G. Kenneth and Mary M. Voigt. 1995. Gordion Archaeological Activities, 1993. 16. *Kazı Sonuçları Toplantısı* 1: 369–92.

Simpson, Elizabeth. Forthcoming. *The Gordion Wooden Objects, Vol. 1: The Furniture from Tumulus MM*. Culture and History of the Ancient Near East no. 32. Leiden: Brill.

Simpson, Elizabeth and Krysia Spirydowicz. 1999. *Gordion: Ahşap Eserler/Wooden Furniture*. Ankara: Museum of Anatolian Civilizations.

Temizsoy, İlhan. 1992. Ankara Anadolu Medeniyetleri Müzesi Ankara—Polatlı İlçesi Beylik Köprü Köyü. *Anadolu Medeniyetleri Müzesi* 1991 Yıllığı: 3–28.

———. 1993. Mamaderesi Tümülüsü Kazısı Küçük Buluntular. *Anadolu Medeniyetleri Müzesi* 1992 Yıllığı: 110–37.

———. 1994. Mamaderesi Tümülüsü Kazısı Küçük Buluntular II. *Anadolu Medeniyetleri Müzesi* 1993 Yıllığı: 5–33.

Voigt, Mary M. 1994. Excavations at Gordion 1988–89: The Yassihöyük Stratigraphic Sequence. In *Anatolian Iron Ages 3: The Proceedings of the Third Anatolian Iron Ages Colloquium Held at Van, August 6–12, 1990*, ed. Altan Çilingiroğlu and David H. French, 265–93. British Institute of Archaeology at Ankara Monograph 16. Ankara: British Institute of Archaeology at Ankara.

———. 2002. Gordion: Rise and Fall of an Iron Age Capital. In *Across the Anatolian Plateau: Readings on the Archaeology of Ancient Turkey*, ed. David C. Hopkins, 187–96. Annual of the American Schools of Oriental Research vol. 57. Boston: American Schools of Oriental Research.

———. 2003. Celts at Gordion: The Late Hellenistic Settlement. *Expedition* 45.1: 14–19.

———. 2007. The Middle Phrygian Occupation at Gordion. In *Anatolian Iron Ages 6: The Proceedings of the Sixth Anatolian Iron Ages Colloquium Held at Eskişehir, August 16–20, 2004*, ed. Altan Çilingiroğlu and Antonio Sagona, 311–34. Ancient Near Eastern Studies Supplement Series 20. Leuven: Peeters.

———. 2009. The Chronology of Phrygian Gordion. In *Tree-Rings, Kings, and Old World Archaeology and Environment: Papers Presented in Honor of Peter Ian Kuniholm*, ed. Sturt W. Manning and Mary Jaye Bruce, 319–27. Oxford: Oxbow Books.

———. Forthcoming. The Unfinished Project of the Gordion Early Phrygian Destruction Level. In *The Archaeology of Phrygian Gordion*, ed. C. Brian Rose. Philadelphia: University of Pennsylvania Museum of Archaeology and Anthropology.
Voigt, Mary M., Keith DeVries, Robert C. Henrickson, Mark Lawall, Ben Marsh, Ayşe Gürsan, and T. Cuyler Young Jr. 1997. Fieldwork at Gordion: 1993–1995. *Anatolica* 23: 1–59.
Voigt, Mary M. and Robert C. Henrickson. 2000a. The Early Iron Age at Gordion: The Evidence from the Yassıhöyük Stratigraphic Sequence. In *The Sea Peoples*, ed. Eliezer D. Oren, 327–60. University Museum Monograph 108. Philadelphia: University of Pennsylvania Museum of Archaeology and Anthropology.
———. 2000b. Formation of the Phrygian State: The Early Iron Age at Gordion. *Anatolian Studies* 50: 37–54.
Voigt, Mary M. and T. Cuyler Young Jr. 1999. From Phrygian Capital to Achaemenid Entrepot: Middle and Late Phrygian Gordion. *Iranica Antiqua* 34: 192–240.
Young, Rodney S. 1950. Excavations at Yassihüyük-Gordion 1950. *Archaeology* 3: 196–201.
———. 1951. Gordion–1950. *University Museum Bulletin* 16.1: 3–20.
———. 1953. Progress at Gordion, 1951–1952. *University Museum Bulletin* 17.4: 2–39.
———. 1955. Gordion Preliminary Report, 1953. *American Journal of Archaeology* 59: 1–18.
———. 1956. The Campaign of 1955 at Gordion: Preliminary Report. *American Journal of Archaeology* 60: 249–66.
———. 1957. Gordion 1956: Preliminary Report. *American Journal of Archaeology* 61: 319–31.
———. 1958. The Gordion Campaign of 1957. *American Journal of Archaeology* 62: 139–54.
———. 1960. The Gordion Campaign of 1959: Preliminary Report. *American Journal of Archaeology* 64: 227–43.
———. 1962a. The 1961 Campaign at Gordion. *American Journal of Archaeology* 66: 153–68.
———. 1962b. Gordion: Phrygian Construction and Architecture II. *Expedition* 4.4: 2–12.
———. 1964. The 1963 Campaign at Gordion. *American Journal of Archaeology* 68: 279–92.
———. 1965. Early Mosaics at Gordion. *Expedition* 7.3: 4–13.
———. 1966. The Gordion Campaign of 1965. *American Journal of Archaeology* 70: 267–78.
———. 1968. The Gordion Campaign of 1967. *American Journal of Archaeology* 72: 231–42.
———. 1981. *Three Great Early Tumuli*. Gordion Excavation Reports vol. 1. University Museum Monograph 43. Philadelphia: University Museum of the University of Pennsylvania.

CHAPTER 51

THE STRATIGRAPHY OF KAMAN-KALEHÖYÜK IN CENTRAL ANATOLIA

SACHIHIRO OMURA

Kaman-Kalehöyük is situated 3 km directly east of the city of Kaman in Kırşehir province, approximately 100 km southeast of Ankara. It is circular, with a diameter of 280 m. The shape of the *höyük* is trapezoidal and approximately 16 m in height. As the cross-section diagrams of the mound reveal, the northern side of the höyük is slightly higher in elevation, and the top of the mound gradually slopes to the south. This can be detected in the topographical map, which shows a gentle slope from the northern to the southern side of the flat top of the höyük. The vicinity of Kaman-Kalehöyük is under cultivation, planted mostly with wheat. National Highway 60, which connects Ankara and Kırşehir, passes by the north side of the höyük, and at the mound's southern base an older route known variously as Göç Yolu (migration route) or Kervan Yolu (caravan route) runs on an east–west axis. Before the construction of the new national highway, the Göç Yolu was the route the villagers used to travel to Kaman and Kırşehir. Two small streams flow south to north about 30 m from the foot of both the eastern and the western slopes of Kaman-Kalehöyük, joining at a spring 150 m to the mound's northeast. The village of Çağırkan lies approximately 1.5 km to the south of Kaman-Kalehöyük. The Baran Mountain Range rises behind Çağırkan from the northwest to the southeast, cutting a line through the central Anatolian plateau.

In 1985, the Middle Eastern Culture Center in Japan engaged in a preliminary archaeological excavation at this site (Mikami and Omura 1991a; see annual site reports in the *Anatolian Archaeological Studies* and the *Kazı Sonuçları Toplantısı* series, Omura 1989, 1991–2009). In 1986, full-scale excavations began, which continue to the present. There are currently three trenches at the site: the North Trench, the South Trench, and the City-Wall Trench (figure 51.1).

The excavations at Kaman-Kalehöyük have two goals. The first is to establish a stratigraphy of the North Trench (figure 51.2). The second is to gain an understanding of the settlement patterns corresponding to the Ottoman Period in the South Trench and the Iron Age in the North Trench.

Between 1986 and 2009, four main strata have been identified in the North Trench: Stratum I, the Ottoman Period, fifteenth to seventeenth centuries C.E.; Stratum II, the Iron Age, twelfth to fourth centuries B.C.E.; Stratum III, Middle–Late Bronze Ages, twentieth to twelfth centuries B.C.E.; and Stratum IV, the Early Bronze Age, twenty-third to twentieth centuries B.C.E. This chapter mainly reports on architectural discoveries. A discussion of Iron Age ceramic assemblages can be found in Kealhofer and Grave, chapter 18 in this volume.

Kaman-Kalehöyük: Stratigraphy

According to the artifactual evidence and the architectural remains from each stratum, the main levels are further subdivided into Stratum Ia and Ib; Stratum IIa, IIc, and IId; Stratum IIIa—Hittite Empire period, IIIb—Old Hittite period,

Figure 51.1. Kaman-Kalehöyük from the air.

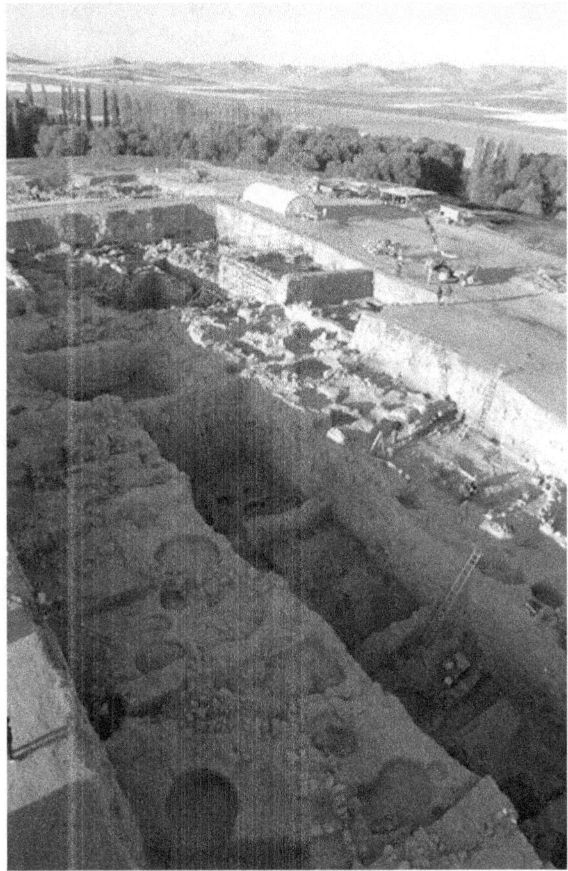

Figure 51.2. View of the North Trench.

and IIIc—Assyrian Colony period; Stratum IVa—Intermediate Period, and Stratum IVb— Early Bronze Age.

Architectural Remains of Stratum I

During the excavation seasons of 1986–2009, architectural remains of Stratum I have been discovered in almost all sectors of the North and South Trenches. All of the architectural remains of the first building level of Stratum I were located a mere ten to twenty centimeters below the surface level (figure 51.3). Five building levels were identified in Stratum I. The stratigraphy of Stratum I at Kaman-Kalehöyük is as follows:

- Stratum Ia 1–3: Ottoman Period,
- Stratum Ib 4–5: Byzantine Period.

In an assessment of all the architectural remains of Stratum I, the possibility arises that a number of architectural complexes consisting of four to five rooms may exist throughout the entire Kaman-Kalehöyük site. There is not much difference in

Figure 51.3. Kaman-Kalehöyük Stratum I.

architectural remains between the two periods; rather, the differences were in ceramic remains. A number of Chinese porcelain sherds of the Ming Dynasty were collected in the deposit of Stratum Ia; however, there were scarcely any in Stratum Ib. On the contrary, Byzantine pottery sherds were identified in Stratum Ib (Omura 1996b; Vroom 2006).

Furthermore, although pottery sherds of Chinese porcelain, bronze objects, iron objects, personal ornaments, pipes, and coins have been unearthed from every building level discovered in Stratum I, they are extremely few when compared to the number of such artifacts unearthed from Strata II and III. When this fact is considered together with the complete absence of signs of fire damage in all building levels of Stratum I, and the excellent preservation of architectural remains, the obvious supposition is that the residents left the area in peace, taking their possessions with them.

Based on the architectural remains that have been discovered to date, as well as the presence of the Chinese porcelain, there is sufficient evidence to conclude that Stratum Ia 1–3 of Kaman-Kalehöyük was a major community in Kaman in the sixteenth and seventeenth centuries C.E. (Mikami and Omura 1991b), whereas Stratum Ib 4–5 preserves remains of the fifteenth century C.E.

Architectural Remains and Artifacts of Stratum II Iron Age

Architectural remains of the Stratum II Iron Age periods date from the twelfth to fourth centuries B.C.E. (Newton and Kuniholm 2001; Omori and Nakamura 2006, 2007) and have been exposed almost entirely throughout both the North Trench and the South Trench. What follows is an account of the main architectural remains in the North Trench and the South Trench, from the upper strata down. (For comments on the Iron Age ceramics of Kaman-Kalehöyük, see Kealhofer and Grave, chapter 18 in this volume.) As stated earlier, the Iron Age at Kaman-Kalehöyük is divided into Stratum IIa, IIc, and IId. The stratigraphy of the Iron Age at Kaman-Kalehöyük is as follows:

- Stratum IIa 1–2: Hellenistic period (Alexander the Great and after),
- Stratum IIa 3–5: Late Iron Age (Lydian, Achaemenid),
- Stratum IIa 6–IIc 1: Middle Iron Age (Phrygian rule),
- Stratum IIc 2–3: Middle Iron Age (Alişar IV culture),
- Stratum IId 1–3: Early Iron Age (Dark Age).

Some of the distinguishing architectural remains of Stratum IIa 3–5, Stratum IIa 6–IIc 1, and Stratum IId 1–3 are worth noting in some detail in the following sections.

Architectural Remains of Megaron-Shaped Buildings and Corridors in Stratum IIa 3–5

One very interesting development was the discovery of a megaron-style structure (figure 51.4) (Omura 1998a, 1998b) discovered in the excavation seasons of 1995–1998. These architectural remains, consisting of two rooms and belonging to Stratum IIa 3–5, were excavated in the middle of the mound. This structure was 19 m long and 6.6 m wide, and includes several important details.

After removing the stone wall foundations of the megaron-shaped architectural remains, traces of pillars were found under all of the walls, encircled by medium-sized stones. The pillar foundation's bottom consisted of a set of stones with a flat stone located in the center. These probably once held wooden pillars as part of the megaron structure. As can be seen from the fact that these traces of pillars were found immediately beneath the floor area, the megaron-shaped structures were likely rebuilt several times.

Corridor or walkway-type structures were identified alongside the megaron-shaped structure in the same level of the North Trench. These were wide pavements composed of roughly placed large stones covered with tamped soil and fist-sized stones. The width of these walkway structures is about two meters.

The stones inside the structures were very roughly laid, suggesting that the smaller stones were simply packed in after the placing of the large stones on both sides of the corridor structures. From the manner in which the stones of the structures were laid, however, it is not clear that it would have been used as a corridor. The majority of stones seem to have simply been thrown into the trench. Similar corridor-style structures were also identified in the South Trench, oriented northwest–southeast or northeast–southwest. The direction of these structures in the South Trench was the same as in the North Trench. The corridor structure in the South Trench had been constructed several times in the same place. Tamped soil

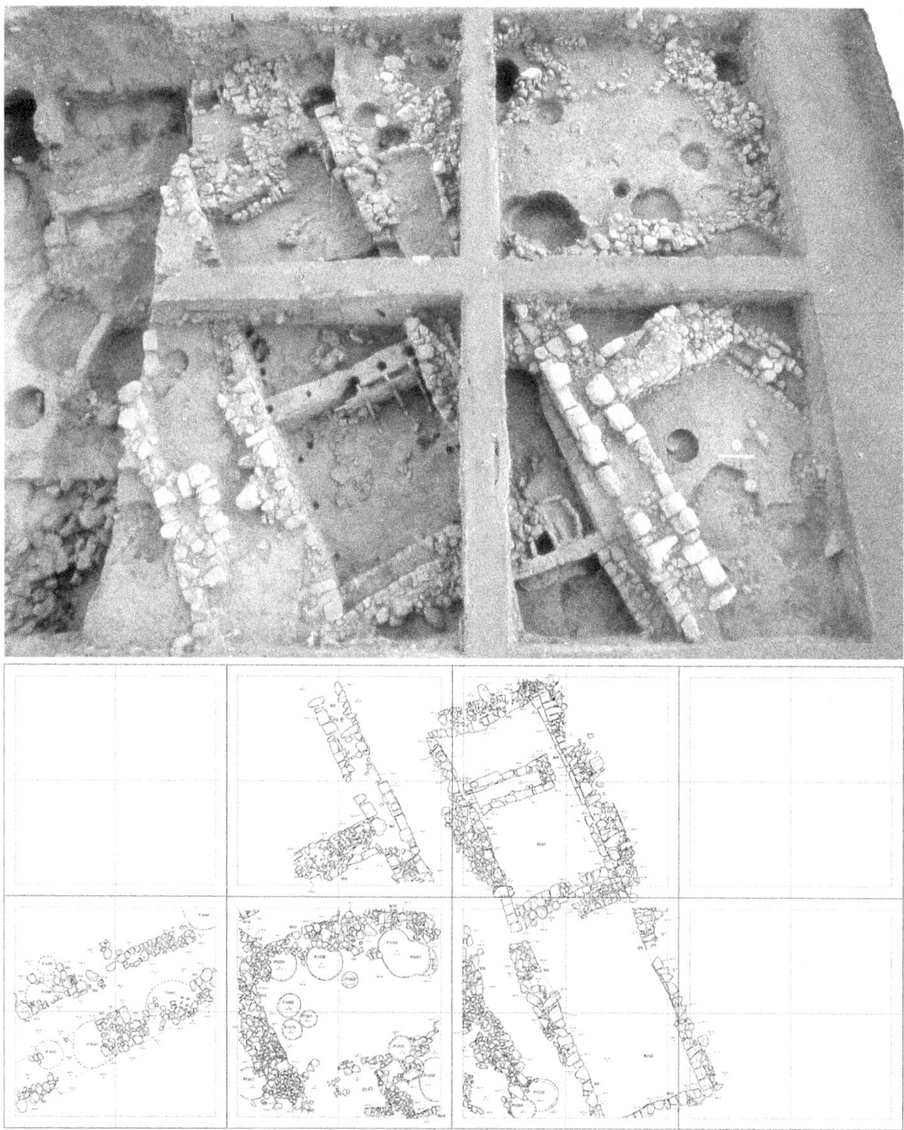

Figure 51.4. Photo and plan of the megaron-style structure in Stratum IIa.

and fist-sized stones created an interior paved floor in the South Trench corridor. The floor of tamped soil was apparently used as a passageway. After removing this corridor structure, another structure constructed with rather large stones oriented northeast–southeast was uncovered.

The megaron-shaped architectural remains and the corridor structures were not parts of ordinary houses. The megaron-shaped structure in particular suggests a ceremonial purpose. The construction of the corridors was not robust, which could imply that each corridor was used only for a short time. One hypothesis is that these corridors might have been constructed whenever a ceremony was performed in the megaron-shaped structures.

Architectural Remains of Stratum IIc 1

There are two architectural types in the architectural remains of Stratum IIc (Omura 2001a, 2001b, 2002a, 2002b). One is a half-basement type; in the other type, the interior floor and exterior living areas are on the same level. The half-basement type of structure was unearthed in Stratum IIc 1. The most distinguishing feature was that the majority of structures were one-roomed. Though one-room structures have been discovered in Stratum IIc 1, they cover an average area of 25–30 m^2. The architectural remains of this type of structure were identified in the North and South Trenches.

There is one more special feature in the half-basement style. Most of the walls of this type were made of a single row of stones. Pebbles were packed behind the single walls. During the course of the wall excavation, a bench-like feature made of sun-dried mudbricks was attached to the walls. The same feature was found in other architectural remains of Stratum IId 1. The function of these bench features was not determined; they might have been used as a facility on which to place vessels or other objects. These half-basement structures of Stratum IIc 1 were apparently not used as living areas, based on the lack of domestic materials within them. Rather, they were more likely used for storage.

Architectural Remains of Stratum IId 1–3

After removing all the architectural remains of Stratum IIc, the structures of Stratum IId were identified in the North and South Trenches. In the structures unearthed in Stratum IId, there are two types. One is the half-basement style as was seen in Stratum IIc 1. The other consists of rooms with floors and wall foundations that extend just a bit below the exterior living space. The interior floor of the half-basement rooms is one-half to one meter lower than that of the exterior living area. The walls are built by the random piling of stones, but larger stones are used in the lowest layer of the foundation and at the corners. Some of the corners of the stone walls were curved rather than square.

All the architectural remains of Stratum IId showed signs of heavy fire damage, and the past existence of pillars that once stood in the pillar holes could be ascertained by the carbonized remains in the holes. Based on the ^{14}C results, Stratum IId dates to the eleventh to ninth centuries B.C.E., or the so-called Dark Age.

In Stratum IId, some painted ceramics with a pattern of wavy lines, as well as handmade pottery, were unearthed. Similar handmade pottery with incised decoration has also been identified at Gordion and Troy. Painted ceramics similar to those at Kaman-Kalehöyük have also been unearthed at Porsuk and Kilisetepe. During general survey, similar pottery sherds were collected at the sites in the area to the south of Kaman-Kalehöyük, namely, in Aksaray, Nevşehir, and Niğde provinces.

Architectural Remains of Stratum III: Middle to Late Bronze Ages

The Stratum III periods include the Middle Bronze to Late Bronze Ages, ranging from the twentieth to twelfth centuries B.C.E. (Omura 2001a, 2001b, 2002a, 2002b, 2003a, 2003b, 2004, 2005, 2009). The main work on architectural remains of Stratum III has been undertaken in the North Trench. Based on small finds and architectural remains, the stratigraphy of the Middle and Late Bronze Ages at Kaman-Kalehöyük is as follows:

- Stratum IIIa: Hittite Empire period,
- Stratum IIIb: Old Hittite period,
- Stratum IIIc: Assyrian Colony period.

The North Trench architectural remains of Stratum III were primarily discovered in the 1989–2007 seasons. Architectural remains such as those identified in the North Trench have not been discovered in any clearly identifiable form in the South Trench. The most remarkable architectural remains in Stratum III were unearthed in Strata IIIb and IIIc. The architectural remains of Stratum IIIa, the Hittite Empire period, were found in poorly preserved condition.

Round Structures of Stratum IIIb Old Hittite

Stratum IIIb has remains that date from the seventeenth to fifteenth centuries B.C.E. One of the main architectural forms is known as Round Structure 1, 15 m in diameter with the wall preserved to a height of 5 m, identified in sectors I, II, and XXIII almost in the middle of the mound. Moreover, four other round structures were unearthed to the west of Round Structure 1. The five round structures have clearly cut into the architectural remains of the Assyrian Colony period, identified in 1994 and 1995 (Omura 1996b). In other words, they belong to a time subsequent to the Assyrian Colony period.

The walls of Round Structure 1 (figure 51.5) are constructed of stones of medium size (about 20 × 20 cm) and are slanted toward the floor, but the pressure of soil has forced parts of the walls into a convex bulge. The floor was paved with stones. Inside the round structure were stones believed to have fallen from the wall. The wall probably stood approximately 5 m high, according to the amount of tumbled stones in the round structure. Beside the stones, there was ash and other material discarded in the round structure after its abandonment. In this round structure, a number of bullae were discovered (Omura 2002a, 2002b; Sanada et al. 2002). Careful examination of the stratigraphy revealed that the bullae had been thrown into the round structure after it had been abandoned. The stones fallen from the wall provided clear stratigraphy of this, and the bullae, inscribed with hieroglyphic signs, were found in a stratum mixed with ash, situated above these fallen stones. Under the fallen stones, the number of bullae decreased dramatically. Some of the bullae are dated to the beginning of the fourteenth century B.C.E. (figure 51.6)—the center of this bulla shows three hieroglyphs: CERVUS$_3$-ti-wi(ya) (Yoshida 2006).

Round Structure 2 is situated to the west of the first round structure. The structure measures approximately 10 m in diameter, and it rests 3 m deep. This was dug into the ground like a pit, without constructed walls. Careful examination of the floor revealed six postholes. The postholes were rather large: 0.3–0.5 m in diameter and approximately 0.5–0.7 m deep. Stones were set in the bottom and sides of these postholes; the remnants of decayed timbers were likely the remains of the wooden uprights used to support the upper structure of Round Structure 2. In the fill deposit of collapsed material above the floor of Round Structure 2, bullae with hieroglyphic signs were collected.

Round Structure 3 was identified to the south area of Round Structure 2. Its diameter is about 7.5 m, and it is 1 m deep. Round Structure 3 was cut into Round Structure 2, demonstrating that Round Structure 3 was newer than Round Structure 2. A large quantity of burned wheat was collected on the floor of Round Structure 3, suggesting that it may have been used as a grain storage building (Omura 2001a, 2001b, 2002a, 2002b); it is possible that all the round structures were similarly used.

Figure 51.5. Photos and plan of Round Structure 1.

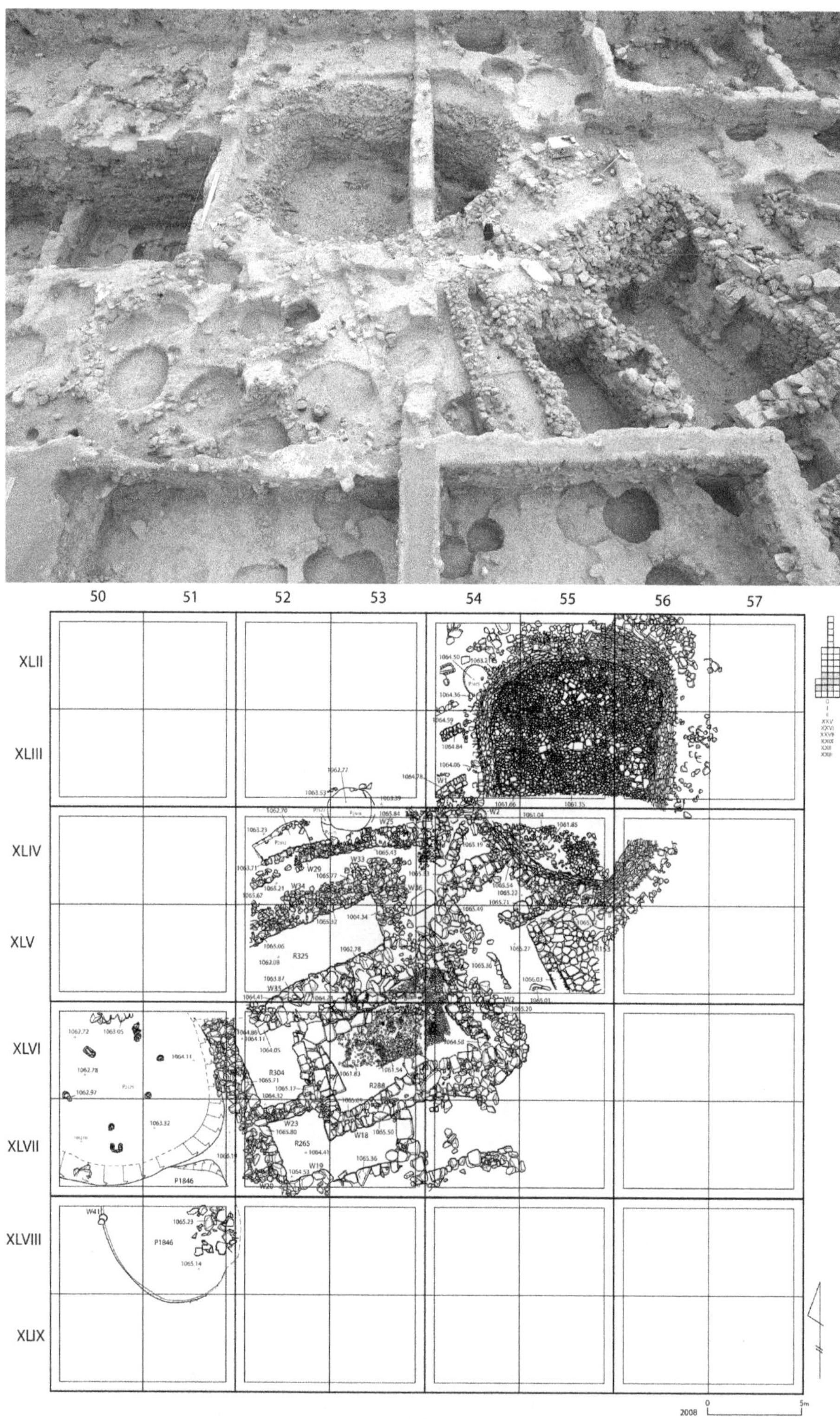

Figure 51.5. (*Continued*)

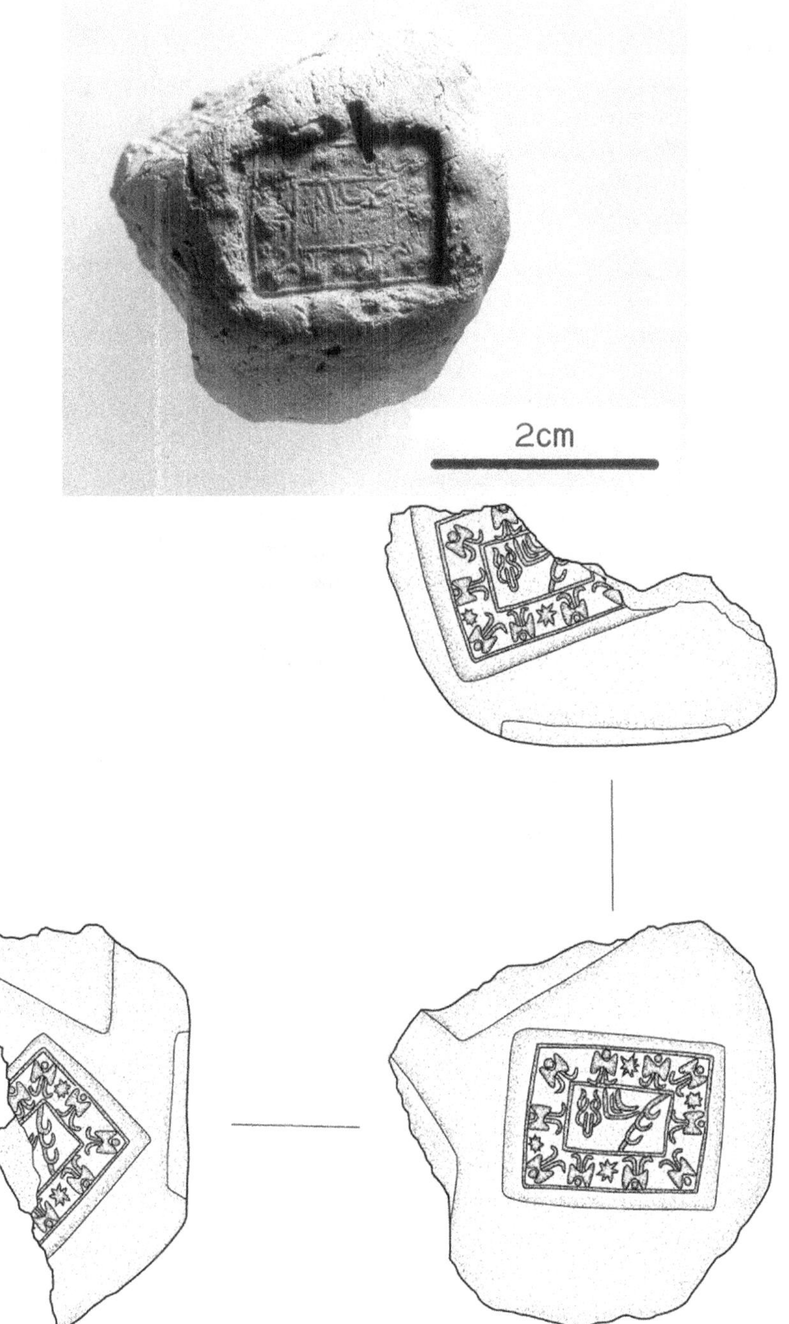

Figure 51.6. Bullae inscribed with hieroglyphic.

Large Architectural Remains of Stratum IIIb

Large architectural remains of Stratum IIIb between Round Structure 1 and Round Structures 2–5 were not found; however, the foundations of a significant structure discovered in this stratum were constructed using stones (Omura 2006, 2007). This architectural complex consisted of five rooms; one had a basement under the first floor, and earthenware sherds were spread all over the floor of the basement. On the floor, large fragments of jars were discovered. There is a high possibility that the basement was used for storage. Another basement constructed of stones connected to the north of the main building was identified; the walls of this structure are approximately 3 m high. This room was also burned by severe fire. The deposits of this room on the floor consisted of burned mudbricks and timber. It is supposed that they fell down from the roof and the walls. There were no artifacts except the earthenware sherds in Stratum IIIb.

The lack of artifactual evidence impeded a compelling interpretation of the architectural remains' function. It is very clear that there was a very strong relationship between the large architectural structure and the Round Structures and that they were constructed nearly at the same time.

Based on the scale of the site, several hundred people may have lived at Kaman-Kalehöyük. The wheat that was apparently stored in the five round structures was far more than was necessary for Kaman-Kalehöyük's population at that time. This suggests that the quantity of the wheat in the Round Structures was meant not only for the people at Kaman-Kalehöyük but also may have served people in other settlements. This implies that during the Stratum IIIb settlement there is a high possibility that Kaman-Kalehöyük was a regional distribution center.

Burned Architectural Remains of the Stratum IIIc Assyrian Colonial Period

During the excavations of the Round Structures and the large architectural complex, burned architectural remains dating to the Assyrian Colony period were identified near the large architectural complex in Stratum IIIb (figure 51.7) (Omura 2008, 2009).

After removing some of the stone walls of Stratum IIIb, the burned layer was unearthed, and in carefully surveying the burned soil, a sun-dried brick wall, approximately 0.8 m wide, was identified. Nine rooms of the Assyrian Colony period were completely unearthed. The walls of the structures were made of sun-dried brick. On the inner side of some walls a bench-like facility, about half a meter wide, was identified; this feature was probably used for the placement of vessels and other objects. Some of the walls had a thick coat of plaster.

All the architectural structures in Stratum IIIc were burned by a severe fire. Portions of carbonized beams, thought to have fallen from the ceiling, were identified on the floors of several rooms. After removing the carbonized beams, a lightly tamped earthen floor was uncovered. The carbonized matter forms two layers over the floor of the room.

Excavation of the first layer revealed three human skeletons, two of which were children and one an adult in R (Room) 150. Beneath the skeletons of the two children and the adult was another layer of carbonized remains. Underlying the carbonized matter beneath the three skeletons were twenty-three additional human skeletons; all of these were men.

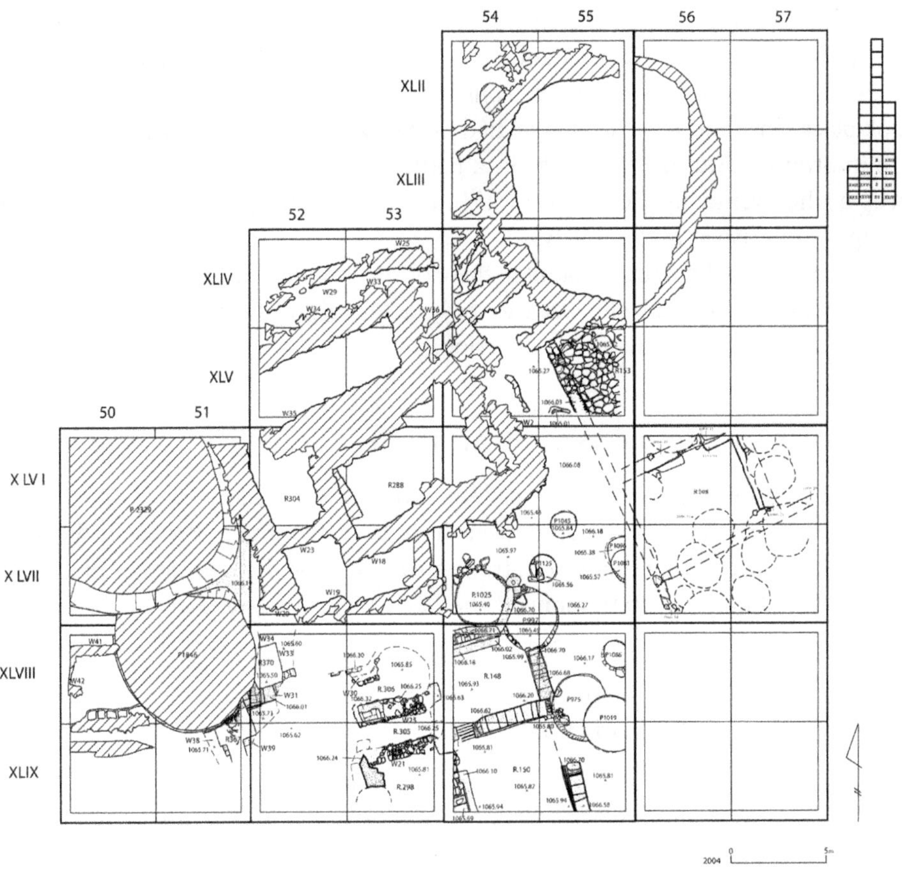

Figure 51.7. Plan of burned architectural remains dating to the Assyrian Colonial period.

The major discovery in this stratum was surely the human skeletons in the burned architectural remains (Hunt 2006, 2007). As already mentioned, all of the skeletons are heavily damaged, testifying to the intensity of the blaze. All the architectural remains of the Stratum IIIc Assyrian Colony period were rather broken by the pits and the construction of the Round Structures in Stratum IIIb. In particular, some of the small rooms in the nine-room complex were destroyed by the building of Round Structures 3–4. The floor of the smallest room in the nine-room complex was scorched and preserved in good condition. A very interesting discovery was a feature that looked like a window in the wall. An even more striking discovery was that of yet more human skeletons in the small room, which measured 1.7 m × 2.5 m. They were also damaged by severe fire. The human bones appear to represent eleven human skeletons. Some of these human skeletons were articulated. Most of them appeared to be infants aged two to three years.

As stated earlier, human skeletons were identified in other rooms; moreover, a large number of human skeletons were also unearthed in the courtyard (Hunt 2006, 2007). Most of these skeletons found in the courtyard are in poor condition, having been severely damaged by fire. Copper alloy daggers, swords, and spearheads (Akanuma 2004, 2007; Omura 2007) were discovered near the human skeleton. A spearhead was found embedded in one of the skeletons. This suggests that a battle took place here, and that the people died in the battle and the fire. The cause of the fire in Stratum IIIc might have been a battle between two groups: one group of people who eventually died by fire within the architectural remains and the other group who perished in the courtyard.

According to the artifacts found in these burned rooms, the Stratum IIIc architectural complex destroyed by fire dates to the middle of the eighteenth century B.C.E., in the latter part of the Assyrian Colony period.

Architectural Remains of Stratum IV: Early Bronze Age

Excavations in the Early Bronze Age levels were conducted in Sectors III and IV in the North Trench. Six building levels have been identified. Based on the artifacts and architectural remains of Stratum IV, it can be divided into Stratum IVa and Stratum IVb. The stratigraphy of the Early Bronze Age at Kaman-Kalehöyük is as follows:

- Stratum IVa 1–4: Intermediate Period,
- Stratum IVb 5–6: Early Bronze Age.

All of the architectural remains from the first building level to the sixth building level in Stratum IV were damaged heavily by fire. A large quantity of burned wooden beams and sun-dried mudbricks were unearthed on the floor. The foundations of the architectural remains were built of stones. The walls consisted of a single row or two rows of stones. Some sun-dried bricks were identified in the stone walls. The lightly tamped earthen floors were discovered in all six building levels.

Approximately half of the ceramics unearthed in Stratum IVa are handmade and half are wheelmade, whereas most of the ceramics found in Stratum IVb are handmade. In addition, wheelmade earthenwares were also present in the Stratum IIIc Assyrian Colony period. There is a great possibility that Stratum IVa represents a transitional period between the Early and Middle Bronze Ages.

Conclusion

During the past 25 years, four strata have been identified in the North Trench. There were several problems in the sequencing of the strata. The first problem concerns the relationship between Stratum Ia and Stratum Ib. Though many Chinese ceramic fragments and pipes were identified in Stratum Ia, there were none at all in Stratum Ib. As stated earlier, Byzantine pottery sherds also were found in Stratum Ia. This suggests that the culture of Stratum Ia was influenced by Byzantine culture. Future work will focus on the boundary line between the two cultures at Kaman-Kalehöyük. In addition, we have to take up the stratigraphy of the Iron Age, especially the cultures of Strata IIc and IId. With regard to painted pottery from Strata IIc and IId, there are many similarities; the main differences are in the stylized deer found in Stratum IIc but not in Stratum IId. We suppose that the painted pottery of Stratum IId was not produced in the Kaman region, since all the shapes of the ceramics in Stratum IId are well developed. These ceramics were found in the earliest building level of Stratum IId. We did not find similar ceramics in Stratum IIIa of the Late Bronze Age at Kaman-Kalehöyük. This implies that the pottery of Stratum IId did not originate in the Kaman-Kalehöyük region. As mentioned, there is a high probability that the ceramics of Stratum IId were carried into the Kaman-Kalehöyük region from a different area, probably south Anatolia. This scenario presents very important research issues regarding the culture of the Early Iron Age in central Anatolia.

Another problem concerns the function of the large architecture remains and the round structures of Stratum IIIa and IIIb, especially the main buildings between the round structures. In 2003 and 2004, a large quantity of grain was found on the floors of Round Structures 2 and 3, strongly suggesting that these round structures must have been for grain storage. It is proposed that grain stored in the round structures was gathered from Kaman-Kalehöyük and its outskirts and that Kaman-Kalehöyük served as the area's grain storage and administration center. The large architectural remains between the round structures therefore may well have functioned as a collecting agency.

We also continue to consider carefully possible explanations of the function of the architectural remains of the Stratum IIIc Assyrian Colony period, which suffered a severe fire. In this level the typical cylinder seals, bullae, stamp seals, and tablets belonging to the Old Assyrian Colony period, particularly to Level Ib of the Kültepe *kārum*, were unearthed (see Michel, chapter 13, and Kulakoğlu, chapter 47 in this volume). However, the function of the building is not clear. Currently nine rooms have been unearthed in the architectural remains; additional rooms belonging to the architectural remains will probably be unearthed in the unexcavated area in the future. Normally the houses of Stratum IIIc consisted of three to four rooms. In that respect, it is very clear that the architectural remains were not used as a private house but rather as a public building. Based on the objects discovered therein, particularly the tablets from Stratum IIIc, it is supposed that these architectural remains destroyed by a severe fire might be one of the small trading centers of Assyrian merchants.

Finally, in Stratum IVa, we identified two types of pottery. One is handmade and the other is wheelmade. The latter almost certainly belonged to the Assyrian Colony period; similar types have been identified in Levels Ib and II of the Kültepe *kārum*. This implies that already in Stratum IVa Kaman-Kalehöyük was under the cultural influence of Assyrian merchants.

REFERENCES

Akanuma, Hideo. 2004. Archaeometallurgical Analysis of Iron and Copper Objects from the Stratum IIIb to Stratum IIa at Kaman-Kalehöyük in 2001: Correlation between Composition and Archaeological Levels. *Anatolian Archaeological Studies* vol. 13. *Kaman-Kalehöyük* 13: 163–74.

——. 2007. Analysis of Iron and Copper Production Activity in the Central Anatolia during the Assyrian Colony Period. *Anatolian Archaeological Studies* vol. 16. *Kaman-Kalehöyük* 16: 125–39.

Hunt, Veronica. 2006. Preliminary Report on Human Material Excavated at Kaman-Kalehöyük 1989, 1991, 2004 and in August 2005. *Anatolian Archaeological Studies* vol. 15. *Kaman-Kalehöyük* 15: 111–20.

——. 2007. Preliminary Report on Human Remains Analysed in 2006. *Anatolian Archaeological Studies* vol. 16. *Kaman-Kalehöyük* 16: 141–50.

Mikami, Tsuguo and Sachihiro Omura. 1991a. General Survey of Kaman-Kalehöyük in Turkey (1985). *Bulletin of the Middle Eastern Culture Center in Japan* 4: 62–86.

——. 1991b. A Preliminary Report on the First Excavation at Kaman-Kalehöyük in Turkey. *Bulletin of the Middle Eastern Culture Center in Japan* 4: 87–130.

Newton, Maryanne and Peter Ian Kuniholm. 2001. Dendrochronological Investigations at Kaman-Kalehöyük: Dating Early Iron Age Level IId. *Anatolian Archaeological Studies vol. 10. Kaman-Kalehöyük* 10: 125–27.

Omori, Takayuki and Toshio Nakamura. 2006. Radiocarbon Dating of Archaeological Materials Excavated at Kaman-Kalehöyük: Initial Report. *Anatolian Archaeological Studies* vol. 15. *Kaman-Kalehöyük* 15: 263–68.

——. 2007. Radiocarbon Dating of Archaeological Materials Excavated at Kaman Kalehöyük: Second Report. *Anatolian Archaeological Studies* vol. 16. *Kaman-Kalehöyük* 16: 111–23.

Omura, Sachihiro. 1989. 1987 yılı Kaman-Kalehöyük Kazıları. X. *Kazı Sonuçları Toplantısı* I: 353–68.

——. 1991. 1989 Yılı Kaman-Kalehöyük Kazıları. *Kazı Sonuçları Toplantısı* 12.1: 427–42.

——. 1992. 1990 Yılı Kaman-Kalehöyük Kazıları. *Kazı Sonuçları Toplantısı* 13.1: 319–36.

——. 1993. 1991 Yılı Kaman-Kalehöyük Kazıları. *Kazı Sonuçları Toplantısı* 14.1: 307–25.

——. 1994. 1992 Yılı Kaman-Kalehöyük Kazıları. XV. *Kazı Sonuçları Toplantısı* 15. 1: 273–92.

——. 1995. 1993 Yılı Kaman-Kalehöyük Kazıları. *Kazı Sonuçları Toplantısı* 16.1: 313–30.

——. 1996a. 1994 Yılı Kaman-Kalehöyük Kazıları. *Kazı Sonuçları Toplantısı* 17.1: 189–207.

——. 1996b. A preliminary Report on the Tenth Excavation at Kaman-Kalehöyük (1995). *Anatolian Archaeological Studies* vol. 5. *Kaman-Kalehöyük* 5: 1–69 (in Japanese).

——. 1997. 1995 Yılı Kaman-Kalehöyük Kazıları. *Kazı Sonuçları Toplantısı* 18.1: 201–12.

——. 1998a. 1996 Yılı Kaman-Kalehöyük Kazıları. *Kazı Sonuçları Toplantısı* 19.1: 311–22.

——. 1998b. A Preliminary Report on the Twelfth Excavation at Kaman-Kalehöyük (1997). *Anatolian Archaeological Studies* vol. 7. *Kaman-Kalehöyük* 7: 1–84 (in Japanese).

——. 1999. A Preliminary Report on the Thirteenth Excavation at Kaman-Kalehöyük (1998). *Anatolian Archaeological Studies* Vol. 8. *Kaman-Kalehöyük* 8: 1–78 (in Japanese).

——. 2000a. 1998 Yılı Kaman-Kalehöyük Kazıları. *Kazı Sonuçları Toplantısı* 21.1: 217–28.

——. 2000b. Preliminary Report on the 14th Excavation at Kaman-Kalehöyük (1999). *Anatolian Archaeological Studies* Vol. 9. *Kaman-Kalehöyük* 9: 1–36.

———. 2001a. 1999 Yılı Kaman-Kalehöyük Kazıları. *Kazı Sonuçları Toplantısı* 22.1: 327–36.

———. 2001b. Preliminary Report on the 15th Excavation at Kaman-Kalehöyük (2000). *Anatolian Archaeological Studies* Vol. 10. *Kaman-Kalehöyük* 10: 1–35.

———. 2002a. 2000 Yılı Kaman-Kalehöyük Kazıları. *Kazı Sonuçları Toplantısı* 23.1: 389–96.

———. 2002b. Preliminary Report on the 16th Excavation at Kaman-Kalehöyük (2001). *Anatolian Archaeological Studies* vol. 11. *Kaman-Kalehöyük* 11: 1–43.

———. 2003a. 2001 Yılı Kaman-Kalehöyük Kazıları. *Kazı Sonuçları Toplantısı* 14.1: 11–16.

———. 2003b. Preliminary Report on the 17th Excavation at Kaman-Kalehöyük (2002). *Anatolian Archaeological Studies* vol. 12. *Kaman-Kalehöyük* 12: 1–35.

———. 2004. Preliminary Report on the 18th Excavation at Kaman-Kalehöyük (2003). *Anatolian Archaeological Studies* vol. 13. *Kaman-Kalehöyük* 13: 1–35.

———. 2005. Preliminary Report on the 19th Excavation at Kaman-Kalehöyük (2004). *Anatolian Archaeological Studies* vol. 14. *Kaman-Kalehöyük* 14: 1–54.

———. 2006. Preliminary Report on the 20th Excavation at Kaman-Kalehöyük (2005). *Anatolian Archaeological Studies* vol. 15. *Kaman-Kalehöyük* 15: 1–61.

———. 2007. Preliminary Report on the 21st Excavation at Kaman-Kalehöyük (2006). *Anatolian Archaeological Studies* vol. 16. *Kaman-Kalehöyük* 16: 1–43.

———. 2008. 2003–2006 Yılları Kaman-Kalehöyük Kazıları. *Kazı Sonuçları Toplantısı* 29.3: 1–16.

———. 2009. 2007 Yılı Kaman-Kalehöyük Kazıları. *Kazı Sonuçları Toplantısı* 30.3: 197–205.

Sanada, Takashi, Masako Omura, Daisuke Yoshida, and Izumi Nakai. 2002. Characterization of Bullae Excavated from Kaman-Kalehöyük Based on Chemical Composition of Clay Determined by X-ray Fluorescence Analysis. *Anatolian Archaeological Studies* vol. 11. *Kaman-Kalehöyük* 11: 181–89.

Vroom, Joanita. 2006. Some Byzantine Pottery Finds from Kaman-Kalehöyük at First Observation. *Anatolian Archaeological Studies* vol. 15. *Kaman-Kalehöyük* 15: 163–69.

Yoshida, Daisuke. 2006. "Mittelhethitische" Siegelfunde von Kaman-Kalehöyük. *Anatolian Archaeological Studies* vol. 16. *Kaman-Kalehöyük* 15: 151–62.

CHAPTER 52

SARDIS: A FIRST MILLENNIUM B.C.E. CAPITAL IN WESTERN ANATOLIA

CRAWFORD H. GREENEWALT JR.

SARDIS (at modern Sart) is located about 90 km (60 miles) east of the Aegean coast at Smyrna (modern İzmir); it rests on the south side of the valley and plain of the Hermus River (modern Gediz Çayı), where that plain meets the foothills of Mt. Tmolus (modern Boz Dağı) (figure 52.1). One foothill, high (300 m) and steep-sided, was the physical nucleus of settlement: a citadel or acropolis. Flanking the acropolis were two perennial mountain streams, the westerly one called Pactolus (modern Sart Çayı). Ancient settlement existed on the north slopes of the acropolis and extended into the plain, mainly between the two streams (figures 52.1, 52.2). Outside settlement limits, especially in the two stream valleys, were cemeteries (the best known today being those flanking the Pactolus stream). In its ancient heyday, Sardis controlled the river plain immediately to the north (known as the Sardiane). On the north side of the plain, a low limestone ridge was the site of an élite tumulus cemetery (modern Bin Tepe), and just beyond it, further to the north, lies a large lake, the Gygaean Lake or Lake Koloe (modern Marmara Gölü) (figure 52.1).

Environment probably played a role in the emergence and continuity of settlement. Some environmental features would have fulfilled basic requirements; the acropolis was both a refuge (in recorded history never taken by direct assault) and a stronghold, the Pactolus stream a dependable source of fresh water. Other features would have become assets after settlement was established: the river plain a resource

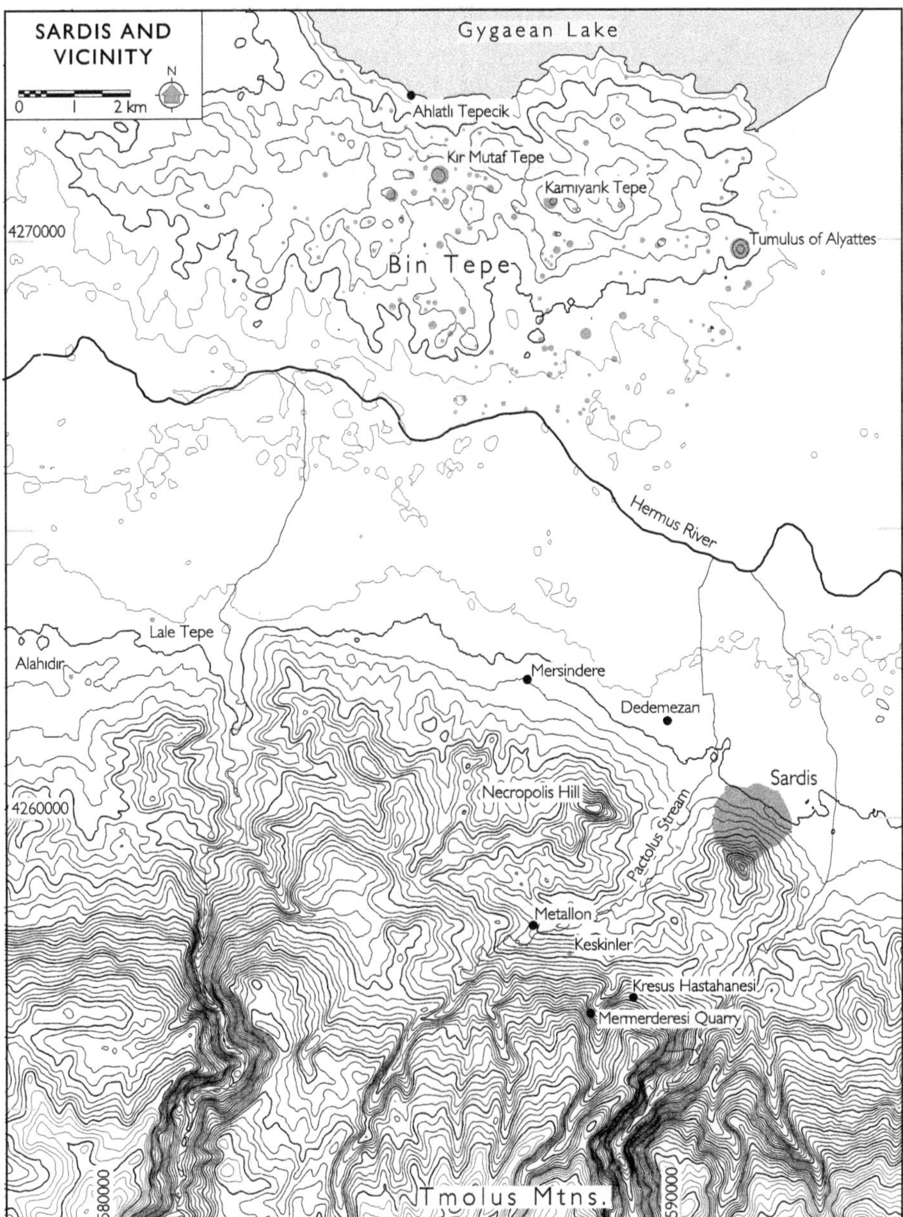

Figure 52.1. Sardis and vicinity. The Hermus River plain is in the center of the map; the lower north slopes of the Mt. Tmolus range in the lower part. The south part of the Gygaean Lake appears at the top; below it are indicated major tumuli of the cemetery at Bin Tepe; the tumulus of Alyattes (figure 52.6) is toward the right. Shaded at lower right is the intramural core of Sardis and the summit of its acropolis. The Pactolus stream is to the left of the city core.

for large-scale agriculture and a corridor for communication between inland Anatolia and the Aegean, Tmolus for timber, fuel, and summer pasturage in its highland valleys, the Pactolus and other mountain streams on the north side of Tmolus for alluvial gold.

Settlement at Sardis has existed for three and a half millennia, from ca. 1500 B.C.E. to the present (Greenewalt 2006; Hanfmann 1983); it may have existed even earlier, in the third millennium B.C.E. (perhaps even before that). During its long existence, the settlement hosted many cultures: western Anatolian, Lydian, Persian, Greek, Roman, Byzantine, Turkish. Contemporaneous cultures typically merged (e.g., Anatolian and Greek, Byzantine and Turkish), and earlier cultural traditions affected later ones (Hanfmann 1975). In the first half of the first millennium B.C.E., Sardis was the capital of an independent state created by the Lydians, a western Anatolian people who inhabited valleys of the Hermus, Kayster, and Maeander Rivers and adjacent highlands and mountains and who had distinctive cultural traditions; the Lydian language, an Anatolian sub-branch of Indo-European, is known from a relatively small number of alphabetic texts (Gusmani 1964, 1980; Melchert 2010). The nature and extent of settlement has fluctuated between the extremes of a

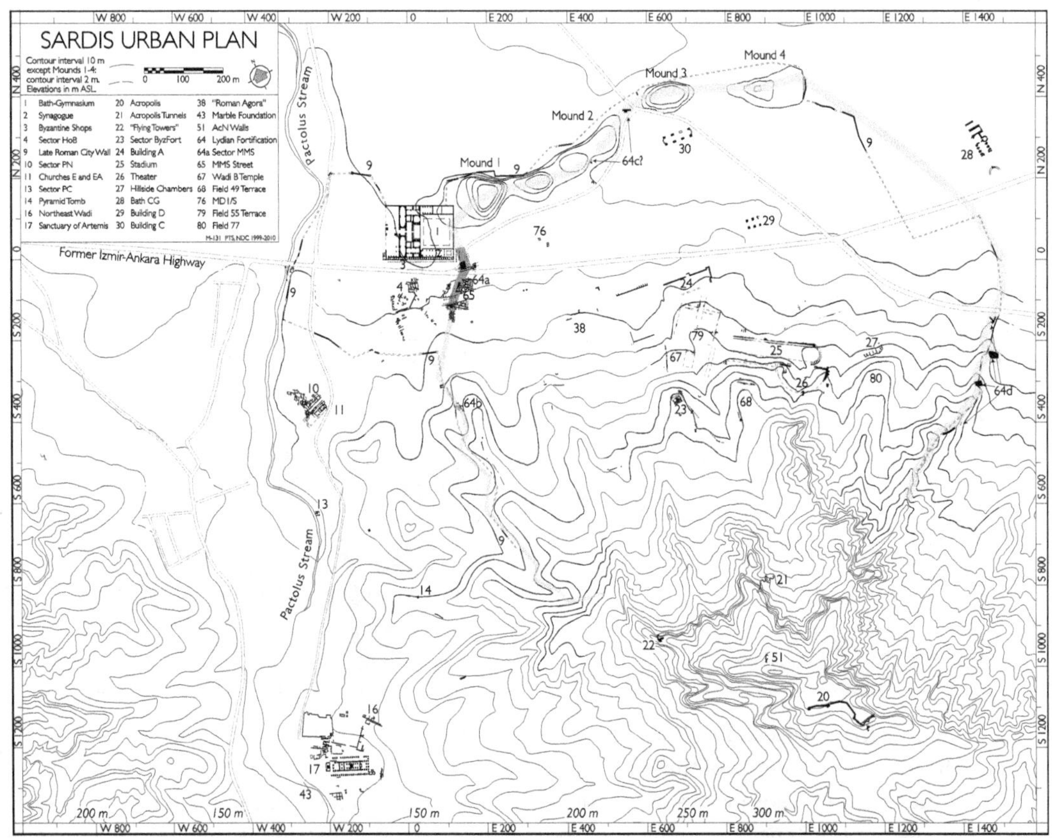

Figure 52.2. Sardis, site plan. The acropolis is at lower right. The Lydian city core defenses are marked by a broad gray line; the segment with the gate shown in figure 52.3 is at no. 64a. Terracing shown in figure 52.4 is at nos. 23 and 68. Lydian installations for refining precious metal are at no. 10. The temple of Artemis in figure 52.6 is at no. 17. Lydian houses are located at nos. 4, 64a, 65, and 26 (under the theater). The Hellenistic and Roman theater is at no. 26. The plan also shows many Roman, Late Roman, and Byzantine architectural features.

large prosperous city and a modest hamlet or group of hamlets, sometimes coexisting with transhumant populations. For more than a millennium, from the seventh century B.C.E. to the seventh century C.E., Sardis was a large city of major political and cultural importance, occupying at maximum extent an estimated 200 ha of land (including an intramural core of 108 ha in the mid-sixth century B.C.E., 127.6 ha in the fourth century C.E., an acropolis summit of perhaps 5 ha, and extramural zones possibly totaling 100 ha) (figure 52.2).

Stratigraphy And Occupation Deposits

Stratigraphy at Sardis varies, with respect to major as well as minor occupation phases, in different parts of the large, topographically complex site. In the archaeological record to date, Late Bronze and Early Iron Age occupation strata are known only from very small spaces in an extramural region; strata of the Persian era are insubstantial; monumental architecture of the Hellenistic era, apart from the temple of Artemis, is absent, and no graves earlier than the sixth century B.C.E. have been identified in Sardis cemeteries (although a few earlier graves have been located in zones of later occupation). Chronological demarcations are provided by a destruction stratum of the eighth century B.C.E. in an extramural zone and another of the mid-sixth century B.C.E., identifiable with the Persian capture of Sardis in the 540s B.C.E., in intramural zones (Cahill and Kroll 2005; Cahill 2010b; Greenewalt 1992); but none so far have been securely identified with the historical events of the Cimmerian capture in the seventh century, Ionian destruction in 499, and destruction by Antiochus III in 215–213 B.C.E. (Rotroff and Oliver 2003:11–15).

Beginnings Through Iron Age Sardis (ca. 700 B.C.E.)

Sardis is not mentioned in the *Iliad* (although the Hermus River, Mt. Tmolus, and the Gygaean Lake are: *Iliad* 2:864–66; 20.381–92), which may have led Strabo to suppose that its foundation postdated the Trojan War (13.4.5/625). Strabo reported the tradition of an early name, Hyde, for the city or its acropolis (13.4.5–6/625–26). The site name has also not been identified in Hittite texts. The name Sardis (in one of its variant forms) is first attested in Greek literature (Sappho frr. 96, 98; perhaps Alcaeus fr. 105e). The root of the Lydian name was *ʹsfar-*(*ʹsfard-*? *ʹsfari-*?); the Akkadian, Hebrew, and Persian names, respectively, *Sapardu*, *Sepharad*, and *Sparda*. In Greek and Latin, the plural form Sardeis and Sardes is common. The root of the name, Sart, has survived for the settlement that exists at the site today.

According to Herodotus (1.7) Lydia was ruled for more than 500 years in the later second and early first millennia B.C.E. by the Atyad and Heracleid Dynasties; the latter founded by Herakles and the Lydian queen Omphale or her serving lady. A Lydian origin for the Etruscans, associated with Lydian migration to Italy in the reign of Atys (Herodotus 1.94), was alleged and disputed in antiquity (Beekes 2003; Briquel 1991); inundation of Lydian lands by tephra from the explosion of Thera/ Santorini in the second millennium B.C.E., however, could have created famine conditions of the kind that reportedly prompted migration (Sullivan 1988, 1990). Lydia has been identified with the Šeḫa River Land of Hittite texts; rulers of this region in the fourteenth and thirteenth centuries B.C.E. were vassals of the Hittite king, and one reportedly was in communication with the king of Aḫḫiyawa (i.e., a Mycenaean Greek state? [Hawkins 1998; see Beal, chapter 26, and Bryce, chapter 15 in this volume]). A few Neolithic and Early Bronze Age artifacts (stone celt and mace head, and some pottery) recovered out of context in the city site might or might not attest to settlement during those eras, but Early Bronze Age cemeteries exited seven miles away, on the south shores of the Gygaean Lake, close to an élite cemetery of the Lydian and Persian eras (Greenewalt 2010b; Roosevelt 2010). Occupation in the Late Bronze and Early Iron Ages at Sardis is attested by pottery in a continuous sequence of occupation strata, exposed in one part of the site. The earliest pottery in that sequence has broad affinities with Mycenaean shapes and decoration. A few pottery items recovered elsewhere in the site and out of context have shapes and burnished surfaces of Hittite tradition. As yet, no architectural remains in Bronze Age contexts are known.

Lydian Sardis, Seventh And Sixth Centuries B.C.E.

With the last Lydian dynasty of the Mermnadai and its kings Gyges, Ardys, Sadyattes, Alyattes, and Croesus, who ruled in patrilineal succession between ca. 680 and the 540s B.C.E., Lydian history and culture and Sardis topography emerge from the shadows of earlier eras (Greenewalt 1995, 2006, 2010b; Cahill 2010a). Those rulers created an empire in western Anatolia (its eastern limit defined by the River Halys, modern Kızıl Irmak; Herodotus 1.6, 72) and made the Lydian state an international power. International events reported in ancient sources include the following. Gyges attacked Smyrna and Miletus, took Colophon (Herodotus 1.15) controlled the Troad (Strabo 13.1.22/590), fought against Cimmerian nomadic invaders, sought aid against them from Assyria, and sent military aid to Egypt (Akkadian texts of Aššurbanipal; Cogan and Tadmor 1977). Ardys took Priene, attacked Miletus, and suffered raids by nomadic invaders, the Cimmerians, who took Sardis "all but the Acropolis" (Herodotus 1.15). Alyattes took Smyrna, attacked

Miletus, invaded Clazomenae, drove the Cimmerians from Asia, received Scythian refugees in Lydia, warred against the Medes, and accepted peace terms (which involved a dynastic marriage) (Herodotus 1.28, 69–70, 73–91; Huxley 1997-8) brokered by the kings of Cilicia and Babylon (Herodotus 1.16–22, 73–74; Summers 1999). Croesus made tributary Ionian and Aeolian Greek states (notably Ephesus), held in subjugation all Anatolian peoples west of the Halys River except for Cilicians and Lycians, made an alliance with Sparta, and went to war with the Persians, who defeated his forces in battle, captured Sardis, ended his rule, and made Lydian lands part of their empire (Herodotus 1.28, 69–70, 73–91).

Major resources of precious metal that Mermnad dynasts controlled were proverbial already in the reign of Gyges (Archilochus fr. 19) and are directly related to Lydian territorial expansion and to the beginnings of coin money in electrum, gold, and silver, which Lydians were either the first or among the first to issue, presumably at Sardis (Xenophanes ap. Pollux 9.3; Herodotus 1.94; Cahill and Kroll 2005; Kroll 2010). Spectacular testimonials to those resources, which survived the Lydian kingdom by several centuries, were the fabulous offerings of precious metal, as well as architecture and works of art, which Gyges, Alyattes, and Croesus dedicated at Greek sanctuaries (notably Delphi, Ephesus, Didyma, and Assesos; Herodotus 1.14, 25, 50–51, 92; Pausanias 10.16.1–2; Buxton 2002; Kalaitzoglu 2008). The best-known source of Lydian gold is the Pactolus stream at Sardis (Herodotus 1.93; Strabo 13.4.5/625–26; other primary sources in Pedley 1972), but other mountain streams on the north side of Mt. Tmolus also contain alluvial gold, and gold deposits elsewhere were reportedly controlled or accessible to Lydian kings (at Astyra in the Troad and between Atarneus and Pergamon in Mysia; Strabo 13.1.23/591, 14.5.28/680). Silver may have been a resource of Lydia (Herodotus 5.49; How and Wells 1928:20).

By the end of Croesus's reign, Sardis was a city of monumental architecture that included: a fortification wall twenty meters thick (figure 52.3) that enclosed a lower city area of about 108 hectares; terraces of white ashlar masonry that regularized natural slopes and contours of the acropolis (figures 52.4, 52.5; Ratté 2011); probably the triple-wall defenses of the acropolis—if they are not Persian—that later impressed Alexander the Great (Arrian, *Anabasis Alexandri* 1.17.5; Lucian, *Charon* 9); three huge tumuli at Bin Tepe—the largest more than 350 m in diameter (figure 52.6)—that were visible from afar and heralded the city to those approaching it (Roosevelt 2009).

Of urban organization and major buildings and building, notably within the city core, little is known. A large extramural zone that accommodated residential, commercial, and industrial quarters extended west and northwest of the city core (at least as far as the Pactolus stream). Cemeteries included rock-cut chamber tombs, small tumuli, and cist and sarcophagus burials (best known from the Pactolus valley; Butler 1922; Baughan 2010). A palace of Croesus, substantially built of mudbrick, reportedly was still standing in the time of Christ, when it was being used as a *gerousia* (Vitruvius 2.8.9–10; Pliny, *Historia Naturalis* 35.49.172). An important sanctuary of Cybele that was burned in ca. 498 B.C.E. probably antedated

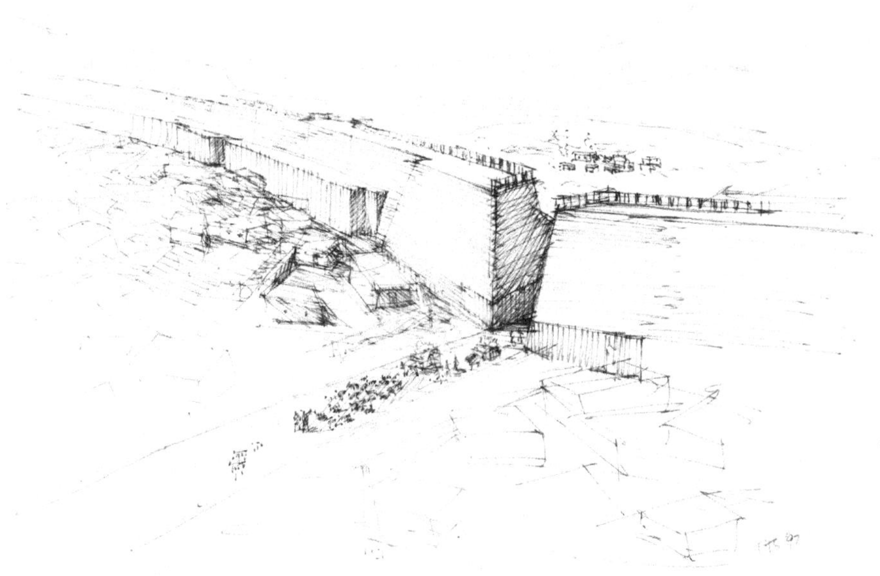

Figure 52.3. Lydian defenses of Sardis: reconstruction, showing a segment on the west side of the city, with one of the city gates; view looking west, from the inner city toward extramural parts. The wall is supplemented on its farther side (and not visible in this view) by an earthwork glacis more than thirty meters thick at the base, and probably a ditch.

the Persian conquest; it may have been located near the site of the Late Roman synagogue, in which Archaic marble votive sculpture appropriate for a mother goddess (and building parts from a Classical or Hellenistic *metroon*) had been reused as building material (Hanfmann and Ramage 1978). In another part of the site, a relatively simple altar may be identified with Cybele (because of a pottery fragment inscribed *kuvav* [that was found nearby and because it contained four small stone statues of lions, Cybele's favored animal]); it may have been a thank offering for success in gold refining (Ramage and Craddock 2000; see later discussion). Beginnings of an extramural sanctuary of Artemis in the Pactolus valley may be attested by marble sculpture (statues of two lions and a raptor; perhaps a huge lion head) and a few fragments of architectural ornament in an Archaic style. A sanctuary or temple of Apollo is alleged by Ctesias (*Persica* F9.5; see Herrmann 1996). Folk religion is attested in extramural (to date) parts of the city by buried offerings in the form of dinner services; each service consisting of pottery cooking pot containing an immature canid skeleton, dish, pitcher, cup, and iron knife (Greenewalt 1978; Greenewalt 2010d: 239–46 and references). Houses of the seventh and sixth century B.C.E. have been excavated in different parts of the city site (intramural and extramural, the latter not far west of the city wall and near the west bank of the Pactolus

Figure 52.4. Lydian terrace walls on lower north slopes of the acropolis, restored; view looking south. (The terraces are at nos. 23 and 68 in figure 52.2.)

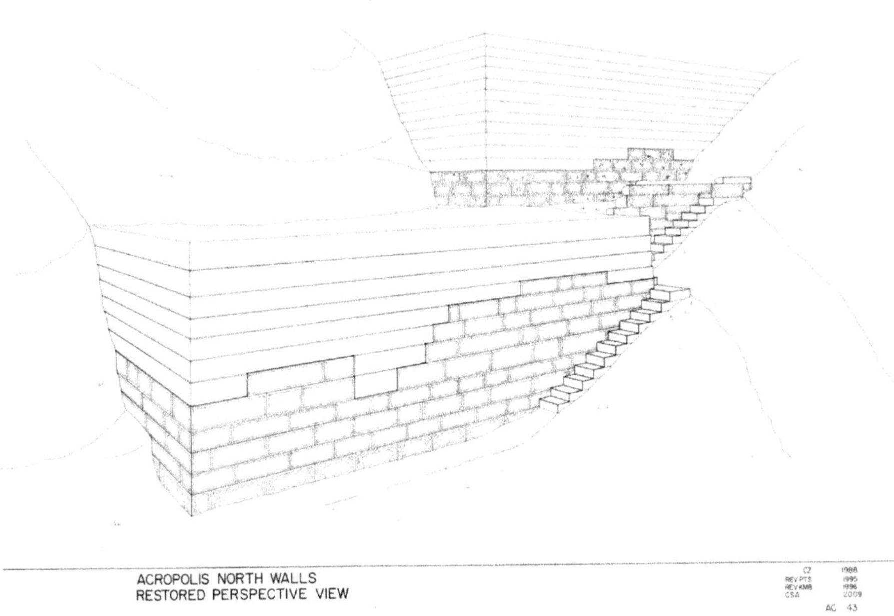

Figure 52.5. Lydian terrace wall, upper parts and staircase restored, near the summit of the acropolis; view looking southeast. (These walls are marked near the summit of the acropolis in figure 52.3.)

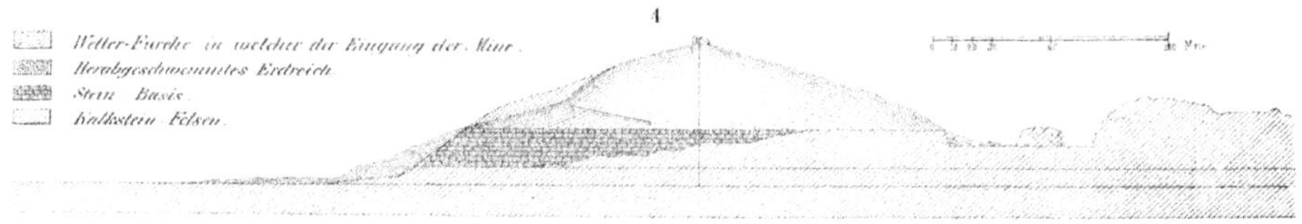

Figure 52.6. The tumulus at Bin Tepe identified as the Tomb of Alyattes. Elevation, showing on its south side the eighteen-meter-high crepis wall identified by excavator L. Spiegelthal. The tumulus has a base diameter of 355 m. (Reproduced from von Olfers 1859:pl. II.)

stream); noteworthy for well-preserved contents are intramural houses located near the western gate and on the site of the later theater, which were destroyed and soon thereafter buried under destruction débris in the middle of the sixth century B.C.E., probably when Sardis was captured by the Persians. Houses were multiroom and included courtyards. Their walls were built of fieldstone and mudbrick, their roofs commonly of clay and straw (as Herodotus 5.101 reported for houses at Sardis in the beginning of the fifth century B.C.E.), although roof tiles—of Corinthian, "Sicilian," and composite pan- and cover-tile systems—as well as decorated sima and geison tiles were used in Lydian Sardis, and probably for affluent houses as well as public buildings. Because no complete house has been excavated, overall size and form are unknown. The only functionally identifiable rooms are for food preparation (Cahill 2004; Cahill, 2010a); for the Persian destruction of houses, see Cahill 2010b; Cahill and Kroll 2005; Greenewalt 1992). Separation of gold and silver from alluvial gold was accomplished in an extramural environment of simple installations near the Pactolus stream; there cementation, smelting, and cupellation processes were used to separate gold from electrum and recover metallic silver from silver chlorides that had been created in the cementation process (Ramage and Craddock 2000; Craddock, Cowell, and Guerra 2005). (That metallurgical activity may be related to the production of coins; but there is no evidence for nearby location of the mint.) Pleasure gardens at Sardis are reported in the context of relaxed Lydian morals (Clearchus ap. Athenaeus 12.515e–516a, 540f; see Herodotus 7.8.ß3).

Persian Sardis, ca. 547–334 B.C.E.

The capture of Sardis by the Persians, under Cyrus the Great, in the 540s B.C.E. (following the Persian defeat of Lydian forces in the field) ended the reign of Croesus, the Lydian Empire, and Lydian independence. Under Persian rule Sardis was the capital of a province (both called Sparda in Persian texts) that included Lydia and, at various times, other parts of western Anatolia; the region was regularly ruled by a viceroy called a satrap. The city remained internationally important even after the Lydian defeat (see also Harl, chapter 34, and Sams, chapter 27 in this volume); at the west frontier of the Persian Empire, it was on a major communications route, the "Royal Road" (Herodotus 5.52–54; 8.98). Two of its satraps were brothers of the king: Artaphernes, brother of Darius I, and Cyrus the Younger, brother of Artaxerxes II, and two reigning kings sojourned there: Darius I, in 512 B.C.E., and Xerxes in 480 B.C.E. Destruction by Greek raiders of the sanctuary or temple (*hieron*) of Cybele in ca. 498 B.C.E. was a pretext for Persian invasion of continental Greece (Herodotus 5.102; 7.8.ß3).

Sardis played a major role in Persian–Greek relations. Its satraps—notably Tissaphernes, Tiribazos, and Autophradates—were intimately involved in Persian policy toward Greek states and in Athenian and Spartan politics. Important Greek leaders visited or spent time at Sardis, including the Spartan commanders Lysander and Kallikratidas, and the Athenian Alcibiades. The "Ten Thousand" Greek mercenaries who marched with Cyrus the Younger to Mesopotamia, and whose successful retreat through Persian territory opened Greeks' eyes to the weakness of Persia, in 401 B.C.E., mustered for their expedition with Cyrus at Sardis (Xenophon, *Expeditio Cyri* 1.2.1–5). The Spartan king Agesilaus raided the city, in 395 B.C.E. (Xenophon, *Hellenica* 3.4.21–25). The Athenian admiral Konon was briefly imprisoned at Sardis, in 392 B.C.E. (Xenophon, *Hellenica* 4.8.16). Terms of the "King's Peace" of Artaxerxes II, or "Peace of Antalcidas," probably were announced to delegates of Greek states at Sardis, in 386 B.C.E. (Xenophon, *Hellenica* 5.1.30–31).

The historical record of Persian Sardis is brilliant, the archaeological record shadowy, the shadows due partly to scarcity of material evidence, partly to chronological ambiguity in late Lydian and early Persian eras. Lydian culture continued to flourish under Persian rule, and a local élite class evidently prospered. Many, possibly most, of the smaller tumuli that predominate in the tumulus cemetery at Bin Tepe (the total number of tumuli is slightly more than one hundred) date from the Persian era, and contemporaneous chamber tombs in the upper Pactolus valley contained handsome jewelry and silver and silver-gilt plate. Although direct evidence for ethnic identity of those burials is lacking, the Lydian character of graves and many grave goods suggests that they are more likely to have been for Lydians, who had accepted Persian cultural ideas, than for Persians "gone native." The riches of Pythios, a Lydian who offered to help finance Xerxes's campaign in Greece (Herodotus 7.27–29), represents an extreme example of Lydian affluence under Persian rule. Persian culture—itself a poorly understood hybrid, which included Lydian elements—may have had limited impact on Sardis. In the archaeological record, architecture and artifacts of later Lydian and Persian eras often are indistinguishable, and demonstrably Persian cultural material is uncommon; it includes sumptuary arts (jewelry and plate), Aramaic script (attested on one gravestone of Sardis, where it follows a text with the same content in Lydian; no. 1 in the Lydian corpus; see no. 41), and one kind of ceramic vessel, the Achaemenid bowl (Dusinberre 1999, 2003). The last, however, is common in ordinary habitation contexts at Sardis and is evidence for the adoption of Persian ideas in middle-class Sardis society. A monumental altar (?) of stepped pyramidal form, ca. 500 B.C.E. (figure 52.7), may be the

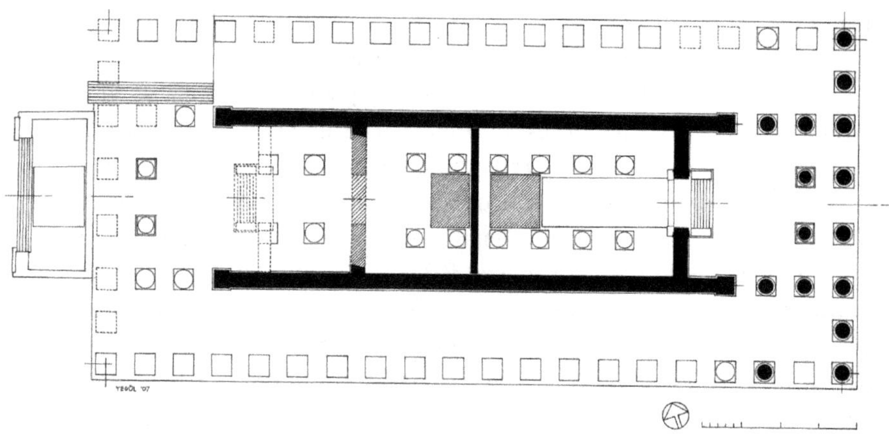

Figure 52.7. Altar and temple of Artemis, plan of surviving features (at no. 17 in figure 52.2). Both altar (far left) and temple had several construction phases, major features of which are combined in this plan. The square core of the altar was built during Persian rule. The Hellenistic temple faced west and had a single cella and deep porch (the cross-wall is shown hatched), both of which contained interior columns; a peripteral colonnade probably was intended but never begun. Alterations in Roman times resulted in two back-to-back cellas of equal length, with two short porches of equal depth (the west cross-wall is shown in outline). A peripteral colonnade was begun but never completed.

earliest structure in situ of the Artemis sanctuary in the Pactolus valley. A sanctuary of Zeus near or within that sanctuary may be implied by a text recording the dedication of a statue to Zeus by a high Persian administrative official during the reign of Artaxerxes (Briant 2002; Herrmann 1996; Robert 1975). Invocation of Artemis of Koloe on a grave stele inscribed in the time of King Artaxerxes suggests that Artemis's sanctuary by the Gygaean Lake/Lake Koloe (Strabo 13.4.5/626) was in existence. Persian domination at Sardis may have been dramatized in material culture through creative art forms that leave little or no trace in the archaeological record and receive only brief citation in ancient literature: for example, luxury textiles (pile carpets, cloth of gold, transparent, flesh-colored garments) and textile dyes (blue, red), which are cited in Greek sources of the Persian era (Greenewalt and Majewski 1980), and landscape architecture—the *paradeisoi*, orchards, and hunting parks of Tissaphernes and Cyrus the Younger at Sardis (Diodorus 14.80.2; Xenophon, *Oeconomicus* 4.20–24). To appreciate the powerful cultural statement that those art forms can make, one need only consider the monumental, richly colored tents of Ottoman armies and the vernacular gardens of Isfahan, Versailles, and Shugborough.

Hellenistic Sardis

Sardis passed quietly out of the Persian Empire in 334 B.C.E., when it was surrendered by the Persian commander of the acropolis and leading citizens—the satrap having been killed at Granikos—to Alexander the Great, who restored "to Sardians and Lydians the old customs/laws (*nomoi*) of the Lydians" and gave them their freedom (Arrian, *Anabasis Alexandri* 1.17.3–4). For nearly 200 years after Alexander's death in 323 B.C.E., Sardis was part of the kingdoms of Hellenistic dynasts: of Antigonus Monophthalmos and Lysimachus for about twenty years each (321–281 B.C.E.), of Seleucids, from Seleucus I through Antiochus III, for a century (281–180 B.C.E.), and of Attalids for half a century (180–133 B.C.E.). It was coveted, at least partly because of its acropolis, "the strongest place in the world" (Polybius 8.20.12; Lucian, *De Mercede Conductis* 13). The city was besieged twice, by Seleucus I, in 281 B.C.E., and by Antiochus III—attacking his rebellious uncle Achaios—in 215–213 B.C.E. (neither succeeded in taking the acropolis by assault; Polyaenus 4.9.4; Polybius 7.15–18; 8.15–21). Alexander the Great's only full sister, Cleopatra, lived at Sardis for more than a decade, after her brother's death, and was murdered there (at the orders of Antigonus Monophthalmos; Diodorus 20.37.3–6); the Seleucid king Antiochus I and his wife Stratonike (daugher of Demetrius Poliorcetes) spent time there in 276/75 B.C.E., and she died there in 254 B.C.E. (Akkadian texts in Austin 2006, no. 163; Kugler 1922, no. 4). Jews from Palestine probably were settled at Sardis—as they were in other parts of western Anatolia—by Antiochos III, in the late third century B.C.E. (Josephus, *Antiquitates Judaicae* 12.147–53). With the creation of the Roman province of Asia in 129 B.C.E., Sardis came under the control of Rome.

In the Hellenistic era, Sardis was a Greek city in important respects. Greek is the language of formal inscriptions on stone (except for some grave epitaphs and dedicatory texts in Lydian), and city government featured a council (*boule*) and assembly (*ekklesia*). Major public buildings of Greek form included a prytaneion, gymnasion (both cited in inscriptions), theater and hippodrome (Polybius 7.17–18), and temples: a *metroon* (attested by inscribed anta blocks; Gauthier 1989) and the huge temple of Artemis, featured in an extramural sanctuary of Artemis in the Pactolus valley (Butler 1925; Yegül 2010). The latter temple (figure 52.7) received a dedication from Stratonike, daughter of Demetrius Poliorcetes, in the form of a marble sphere (perhaps a substitution for the original dedication; Buckler and Robinson 1932).

Later History

Sardis remained a large and prosperous city through Roman and Late Roman times. Decline began in the seventh century C.E., reaching its nadir in the eighteenth and nineteenth centuries (when settlement consisted of one or two hamlets, each with only a few houses). Revival came in the twentieth century (Foss 1976; Hanfmann 1983).

Pottery at Sardis and Lydian Material Culture

Pottery predominates in the archaeological record of artifacts at Sardis, as elsewhere, and provides a valuable index of popular taste. Both Anatolian and Aegean Greek ceramic traditions appear in pottery of the later second and early first millennia B.C.E.; they are more explicitly definable in the shapes and decorative systems of local pottery of the later seventh and sixth centuries, and distinctive varieties and combinations of those shapes and decorative systems may reasonably be identified as Lydian. Common Lydian shapes include table amphora, column crater, skyphos crater, lebes, pyxis, one-handled mug, skyphos, "Ionian cup," stemmed dish, lekythos, lydion, and ring askos; column crater and skyphos are especially common, and evidently are derived from Corinthian shapes. Lydian decorative systems include Anatolian bichrome and black on red, Phrygian bucchero, and East Greek orientalizing. Uniquely Lydian are the lydion (powder or salve container) shape and streaky-glaze and marbled glaze decorative systems, the last derived from multiple-brush motifs of bichrome. Narrative imagery is rare in Lydian painted pottery as it is uncommon in East Greek (Greenewalt 2010c). Imported pottery included Corinthian (Late Geometric through Late Corinthian), Attic (black-figure, red-figure, black-glaze), and Lakonian (II and black-figure) wares from Greece (Schaeffer, Ramage, and Greenewalt 1997), probably bucchero from Phrygia.

In the second half of the sixth century B.C.E., following the Persian conquest, and continuing into the fifth century, many traditional Lydian shapes and decorative systems continued, and the Achaemenid bowl became common in local ceramic repertory (Dusinberre 1999, 2003). In later Classical and Hellenistic eras, Greek shapes and decorative conventions (e.g., echinus bowls, fish plates, lagynoi, unguentaria, West Slope pottery, mold-made relief bowls, black-glazed, Pergamene appliqué, and lead-glazed wares) are conspicuous in the record.

The strong Greek element in Lydian pottery design and decoration and in pottery imports of the Lydian era also occurs in the design and style of architectural ornament, stone sculpture, and architectural terracottas of that era at Sardis, and in the Lydian alphabetic script (Gusmani 1975; Hanfmann and Ramage 1978; Ramage 1978; Ratté 1994), showing that the Hellenophile attitude of Lydian kings that is attested in Greek sources also was a feature of popular culture at Sardis. Lydian expertise in stone masonry, notably exhibited in the huge limestone ceiling beams and beautifully jointed and smoothed marble wall blocks of the tomb chamber in the tumulus identified with King Alyattes (died ca. 560 B.C.E.) at Bin Tepe (figure 52.6), may reflect cultural interchange with both Greece and the Near East (Ratté 1993, 2011). At the other end of the scale, the exquisite glyptic art of seals and jewelry recovered at Sardis may have been a special craft of the city in Lydian and Persian eras (Curtis 1925; Meriçboyu 2010; Dusinberre 2010). Aspects of Lydian and Lydo-Persian culture that impressed the Greeks have left little or no significant trace in the archaeological record: music, fine textiles and textile dyes (if they were not exclusively products of the Persian era; see foregoing discussion), cosmetics (an unguent called *brenthium*; a salve or powder called *bakkaris*, evidently made from a plant of the same name), and horsemanship. Cosmetics are attested by their containers, notably the *lydion*, perhaps meant for bakkaris (Greenewalt 2010e). Horse bridle ornaments decorated in a nomadic animal style might reflect the impact on Lydian horsemanship of Cimmerians and Scythians, who were present at Sardis in the seventh and early sixth centuries B.C.E. (Herodotus 1.15–16, 73–74; Ivantchik 2001; Greenewalt 2010a).

History of Research at Sardis

If Roman "robbers'" tunnels in the tumuli at Bin Tepe partly reflect antiquarian concerns of the Second Sophistic, archaeology at Sardis began in antiquity. Otherwise, the beginnings of scholarly research may be associated with Cyriac of Ancona's visit in 1444 (when he copied the texts of inscriptions on stone, recorded columns of the temple of Artemis, and panned for gold in the Pactolus stream; Cyriac of Ancona 2003). The first reported excavation purely driven by intellectual curiosity was conducted in 1750 by the Robert Wood expedition (around column no. 16 in the temple of Artemis). Short-term excavation in the nineteenth and early twentieth centuries focused on specific monuments: tumuli at Bin Tepe, including one identified as the tomb of Alyattes, between 1854 and 1882, by Prussian Consul L. Spiegelthal and British Consul G. Dennis, the temple of Artemis in 1882 by Dennis and in 1904 by G. Mendel on behalf of the Imperial Ottoman Museums in Constantinople (Greenewalt et al. 2003; Greenewalt 2010b). Sustained excavations were conducted in 1910–14 and in 1922 by the American Society for the Exploration of Sardis, founded by H. C. Butler (primarily in the temple and sanctuary of Artemis and in cemeteries of the Pactolus valley), and from 1958 to the present by the Archaeological Exploration of Sardis, sponsored by Harvard and Cornell Universities and founded by G. M. A. Hanfmann (in many parts of the site, including the acropolis and cemeteries).

REFERENCES

Primary/Ancient Sources

Ancient sources for Sardis in Greek and Roman literature and Near Eastern texts are collected in Pedley (1972). Some of the many important epigraphic texts are collected in Buckler and Robinson (1932). Greek and Roman sources cited in the text of this chapter include the following.

Alcaeus. In *Greek Lyric, Volume 1: Sappho and Alcaeus*, ed. David A. Campbell. Loeb Classical Library 142. Cambridge, Mass.: Harvard University Press, 1982.

Archilochus. In *Greek Iambic Poetry*, ed. Douglas E. Gerber. Loeb Classical Library 259. Cambridge, Mass.: Harvard University Press, 1999.

Arrian. *Flavii Arriani Anabasis Alexandri*, ed. A. G. Roos. Leipzig: Teubner, 2002.

Athenaeus. *Deipnosophistae*, ed. Georg Kaibel. Leipzig: Teubner, 1890.

Ctesias. *Persica*. In *Ctésias de Cnide: La Perse, L'Inde, Autres Fragments*, ed. Dominique Lenfant. Collection Budé. Paris: Les Belles Lettres, 2004.

Diodorus Siculus. *Bibliotheca Historica*, ed. Friedrich Vogel. Leipzig: Teubner, 1893.

Herodotus. *Historia*, ed. Carolus Hude. Oxford: Oxford University Press, 1908.

Homer. *Iliad*, ed. D. B. Monro and Thomas W. Allen. Oxford: Oxford University Press, 1920.

Josephus. *Antiquitates Judaicae*, ed. Ralph Marcus. Loeb Classical Library. Cambridge, Mass.: Harvard University Press, 1943.

Lucian. *Contemplantes* [*Charon*], ed. Matthew David MacLeod. Oxford Classical Texts. Oxford: Oxford University Press, 1974.

Pliny. *Historia Naturalis*, ed. Karl Mayhoff. Leipzig: Teubner, 2002.

Polyaenus. *Strategica*, ed. Peter Krentz and Everett L. Wheeler. Chicago: Ares, 1994.

Polybius. *Historiae*, ed. Theodor Buettner-Wobst. Leipzig: Teubner, 1889.

Sappho. In *Greek Lyric, Volume 1: Sappho and Alcaeus*, ed. David A. Campbell. Loeb Classical Library 142. Cambridge, Mass.: Harvard University Press, 1982.

Vitruvius. *De Architectura*, vol. 1, trans. Frank S. Granger. Loeb Classical Library 251. Cambridge, Mass.: Harvard University Press, 1931.

Xenophon. *Expeditio Cyri [Anabasis]*, ed. E. C. Marchant. Oxford: Oxford University Press, 1904.

———. *Historia Graeca [Hellenica]*, ed. E. C. Marchant. Oxford: Oxford University Press, 1900.

———. *Oeconomicus*, ed. E. C. Marchant. Oxford: Oxford University Press, 1921.

Secondary Sources

Austin, Michel M. 2006. *The Hellenistic World from Alexander to the Roman Conquest*, 2nd ed. Cambridge: Cambridge University Press.

Baughan, Elizabeth. 2010. Lidya Gömü Gelenekleri/Lydian Burial Customs. In *Lidyalılar ve Dünyaları/The Lydians and Their World*, ed. Nicholas D. Cahill, 273-304. İstanbul: Yapı Kredi Yayınları.

Beekes, Robert S. P. 2003. *The Origin of the Etruscans*. Amsterdam: Koninklijke Nederlandse Akademie van Wetenschappen.

Briant, Pierre. 2002. *From Cyrus to Alexander. A History of the Persian Empire*. Winona Lake, Ind.: Eisenbrauns.

Briquel, Dominique. 1991. L'Origine lydienne des Étrusques. *Histoire de la doctrine dans l'Antiquité*. Collection de l'École Française de Rome, 1939. Rome: École Française de Rome.

Buckler, William H. and David M. Robinson. 1932. *Greek and Latin Inscriptions, Part I. Sardis*, 8. Leiden: Brill.

Butler, Howard C. 1922. *Sardis I. The Excavations, Part I. 1910–1914*. Leiden: Brill.

———. 1925. *Sardis II. Architecture, Part I. The Temple of Artemis*. Leiden: Brill.

Buxton, Angela H. 2002. *Lydian Royal Dedications in Greek Sanctuaries*. Ph.D. dissertation. University of California at Berkeley.

Cahill, Nicholas D. 2004. Household Industry in Greece and Anatolia. In *Ancient Greek Houses and Households. Chronological, Regional, and Social Diversity*, ed. Bradley A. Ault and Lisa C. Nevett, 54–66. Philadelphia: University of Pennsylvania Press.

———. ed. 2010. *Lidyalılar ve Dünyaları /The Lydians and Their World*. İstanbul: Yapı Kredi Yayınları.

———. 2010a. Sardeis Şehri/The City of Sardis. In *Lidyalılar ve Dünyaları/The Lydians and Their World*, ed. Nicholas D. Cahill, 74-105. İstanbul: Yapı Kredi Yayınları.

———. 2010b. Sardeis'te Pers Tahribi/The Persian Sack of Sardis. In *Lidyalılar ve Dünyaları/ The Lydians and Their World*, ed. Nicholas D. Cahill, 339-61. İstanbul: Yapı Kredi Yayınları.

Cahill, Nicholas D. and John H. Kroll. 2005. New Archaic Coin Finds at Sardis. *American Journal of Archaeology* 109: 589–617.

Cogan, Mordechai and Hayim Tadmor. 1977. Gyges and Ashurbanipal. A Study in Literary Transmission. *Orientalia* 46: 65–85.

Craddock, Paul T., Michael R. Cowell, and Maria F. Guerra. 2005. Controlling the Composition of Gold and the Invention of Gold Refining in Lydian Anatolia. In *Anatolian Metal*, III, ed. Ünsal Yalçın, 67-77. Der Auschnitt Beiheft 18. Bochum: Deutsches Bergbau-Museum.

Curtis, C. Densmore. 1925. *Sardis XIII. Jewelry and Gold Work Part I, 1910–1914*. Rome: Sindacato Italiano Arti Grafiche.

Cyriac of Ancona. 2003. *Later Travels*, ed. and trans. Edward W. Bodnar. I Tatti Renaissance Library 10. Cambridge, Mass.: Harvard University Press.

Dusinberre, Elspeth R. M. 1999. Satrapal Sardis: Achaemenid Bowls in an Achaemenid Capital. *American Journal of Archaeology* 103: 73–102.

———. 2003. *Aspects of Empire in Achaemenid Sardis*. Cambridge: Cambridge University Press.

———. 2010. Sardeis'ten Lidya-Pers Mühürleri/Lydo-Persian Seals from Sardis. In *Lidyalılar ve Dünyaları/The Lydians and Their World*, ed. Nicholas D. Cahill, 177-90. İstanbul: Yapı Kredi Yayınları.

Foss, C. 1976. *Byzantine and Turkish Sardis*. Archaeological Exploration of Sardis, Monograph 4. Cambridge, Mass.: Harvard University Press.

Gauthier, Philippe. 1989. *Archaeological Exploration of Sardis. Nouvelles Inscriptions de Sardes II*. Centre de Recherche d'Histoire et de Philologie de la IVe Section de l'École Pratique des Hautes Études, 3. Hautes Études du Monde Gréco-Romain, 15. Geneva: Droz.

Greenewalt, Crawford H. Jr. 1978. *Ritual Dinners in Early Historic Sardis*. University of California Publications, Classical Studies, 17. Berkeley: University of California Press.

———. 1992. When a Mighty Empire Was Destroyed: The Common Man at the Fall of Sardis, ca. 546 B.C. *Proceedings of the American Philosophical Society* 136: 247–71.

———. 1995. Croesus of Sardis and the Lydian Kingdom of Anatolia. In *Civilizations of the Ancient Near East,* 2, ed. Jack M. Sasson, 1173–83. New York: Scribner's.

———. 2006. Sardis. In *Stadtgrabungen und Stadtforschung im westlichen Kleinasien—Geplantes und Erreichte; Internationales Symposion 6./7. August 2004 in Bergama (Türkei)*, ed. Wolfgang Radt, 359–72. Byzas 4. İstanbul: Ege Yayınları.

Greenewalt, Crawford H., Jr. 2010a. Atçılık/Horsemanship. In *Lidyalılar ve Dünyaları/The Lydians and Their World,* ed. Nicholas D. Cahill, 217-223. İstanbul: Yapı Kredi Yayınları.

———. 2010b. Giriş/Introduction. In *Lidyalılar ve Dünyaları/The Lydians and Their World,* ed. Nicholas D. Cahill, 6-36. İstanbul: Yapı Kredi Yayınları.

———. 2010c. Lidya'da Çömlekçilik/Lydian Pottery. In *Lidyalılar ve Dünyaları/The Lydians and Their World,* ed. Nicholas D. Cahill, 106-24. İstanbul: Yapı Kredi Yayınları.

———. 2010d. Lidya Tanrıları/The Gods of Lydia. In *Lidyalılar ve Dünyaları/The Lydians and Their World,* ed. Nicholas D. Cahill, 233-46. İstanbul: Yapı Kredi Yayınları.

———. 2010e. Lidya Kozmetiği/Lydian Cosmetics. In *Lidyalılar ve Dünyaları/The Lydians and Their World,* ed. Nicholas D. Cahill, 201-16. İstanbul: Yapı Kredi Yayınları.

Greenewalt, Crawford H. Jr., Nicholas D. Cahill, Philip T. Stinson, and Fikret K. Yegül. 2003. *The City of Sardis. Approaches in Graphic Recording.* Cambridge, Mass.: Archaeological Exploration of Sardis.

Greenewalt, Crawford H. Jr. and Lawrence Majewski. 1980. Lydian Textiles. In *From Athens to Gordion: The Papers of a Memorial Symposium for Rodney S. Young,* ed. Keith DeVries, 133–47. University Museum Papers, 1. Philadelphia: University Museum.

Gusmani, Roberto. 1964. *Lydisches Wörterbuch mit grammatischer Skizze und Inschriftensammlung.* Heidelberg: Carl Winter Verlag.

———. 1975. Neue Epichorische Schriftzeugnisse aus Sardis (1958–1971). *Sardis Monograph* 3. Cambridge, Mass.: Harvard University Press.

———. 1980. *Lydisches Wörterbuch mit grammatischer Skizze und Inschriftensammlung, Ergänzungsband.* Heidelberg: Carl Winter Verlag.

Hanfmann, George M.A. 1975. *From Croesus to Constantine. The Cities of Western Asia Minor and Their Arts in Greek and Roman Times.* Jerome Lectures, 10. Ann Arbor: University of Michigan Press.

———. 1983. *Sardis from Prehistoric to Roman Times. Results of the Archeological Exploration of Sardis 1958–1975.* Cambridge, Mass.: Harvard University Press.

Hanfmann, George M.A. and Nancy H. Ramage. 1978. Sculpture from Sardis. *The Finds through 1975.* Sardis Report 2. Cambridge, Mass.: Harvard University Press.

Hawkins, John D. 1998. Tarkasnawa King of Mira, "Tarkondemos," Bogazköy Sealings and Karabel. *Anatolian Studies* 48: 1–31.

Herrmann, Peter 1996. Mystenvereine in Sardeis. *Chiron* 26: 315–48.

How, Walter W. and Joseph Wells. 1928. *A Commentary on Herodotus with Introduction and Appendixes,* II. Oxford: Clarendon.

Huxley, George L. 1997-8. A Lydo-Median Treaty in Herodotos (1.74.3-4), *Deltio Kentrou Mikrasiatikon Spoudon* 12: 9–11.

Ivantchik, Askold I. 2001. *Kimmerier und Skythen. Kulturhistorische und chronologische Probleme der Archäologie der osteuropäischen Steppen und Kaukasiens in vor-und frühskythischer Zeit.* Steppenvölker Eurasiens, 2. Berlin: German Archaeological Institute.

Kalaitzoglou, Georg. 2008. *Assesos: Ein geschlossener Befund sudionischer Keramik aus dem Heiligtum der Athen a Assesia.* Milesische Forschungen 6. Mainz: Philipp von Zabern.

Kroll, John H. 2010. Sardeis Sikkeleri/The Coins of Sardis. In *Lidyalılar ve Dünyaları/The Lydians and Their World*, ed. Nicholas D. Cahill, 142-56. İstanbul: Yapı Kredi Yayınları.

Kugler, Franz X. 1922. *Von Moses bis Paulus. Forschungen zur Geschichte Israels nach biblischen und profangeschichtlichen insbesondere neuen Keilinschriftlichen Quellen.* Münster: Aschendorffsche Verlagsbuchhandlung.

Melchert, H. Craig. 2010. Lidya Dili ve Yazıtları/Lydian Language and Inscriptions. In *Lidyalılar ve Dünyaları/The Lydians and Their World*, ed. Nicholas D. Cahill, 266-72. İstanbul: Yapı Kredi Yayınları.

Meriçboyu, Yıldız A. 2010. Lidya Dönemi Takıları. In *Lidyalılar ve Dünyaları/The Lydians and Their World*, ed. Nicholas D. Cahill, 157-76. İstanbul: Yapı Kredi Yayınları.

Pedley, John G. 1972. *Ancient Literary Sources on Sardis*. Sardis Monograph 2. Cambridge, Mass.: Harvard University Press.

Ramage, Andrew. 1978. *Lydian Houses and Architectural Terracottas*. Sardis Monograph 5. Cambridge, Mass.: Harvard University Press.

Ramage, Andrew and Paul Craddock. 2000. *King Croesus' Gold. Excavations at Sardis and the History of Gold Refining*. Sardis Monograph 11. Cambridge, Mass.: Archaeological Exploration of Sardis.

Ratté, Christopher. 1993. Lydian Contributions to Archaic East Greek Architecture. In *Les Grands Ateliers d'Architecture dans le Monde Egeen du VIe Siècle av. J.-C. Actes du colloque d'Istanbul, 23–25 mai 1991*, ed. Jacques des Courtils and Jean-Charles Moretti, 1–12. İstanbul: Institut Français d'Études Anatoliennes d'Istanbul.

———. 1994. Archaic Architectural Terracottas from Sector ByzFort at Sardis. *Hesperia* 63: 361–90.

———. 2011. *Lydian Architecture: Ashlar Masonry Structures of Sardis*. Sardis Report 5. Cambridge, Mass.: Archaeological Exploration of Sardis.

Robert, Louis. 1975. Une Nouvelle Inscription de Sardes: Règlement de l'autorité perse relatif à un culte de Zeus. *Comptes Rendus des séances de l'Académie des inscriptions et belles-lettres*: 306–30.

Roosevelt, Christopher H. 2009. *The Archaeology of Lydia, from Gyges to Alexander*. Cambridge: Cambridge University Press.

———. 2010. Lidyalılardan Önce Lidya/Lydia Before the Lydians. In *Lidyalılar ve Dünyaları/The Lydians and Their World*, ed. Nicholas D. Cahill, 37-73. İstanbul: Yapı Kredi Yayınları.

Rotroff, Susan I., and Andrew Oliver, Jr. 2003. *The Hellenistic Pottery from Sardis: The Finds through 1994*. Sardis Monograph 4. Cambridge Mass.: Archaeological Exploration of Sardis.

Schaeffer, Judith S., Nancy H. Ramage, and Crawford H. Greenewalt Jr. 1997. *The Corinthian, Attic, and Lakonian Pottery from Sardis*. Sardis Monograph 10. Cambridge, Mass.: Harvard University Press.

Sullivan, Donald G. 1988. The Discovery of Santorini Tephra in Western Turkey. *Nature* 333: 552–54.

———. 1990. Minoan Tephra in Lake Sediments in Western Turkey: Dating the Eruption and Assessing the Atmospheric Dispersal of the Ash. In *Thera and the Aegean World 3, volume 3. Chronology*, ed. D. A. Hardy with A. C. Renfrew, 114–18. London: Thera Foundation.

Summers, Geoffrey D. 1999. Medes, Lydians, the "Battle of the Eclipse" and the Historicity of Herodotus, http://www.kerkenes.metu.edu.tr/kerk1//12propub/wwwpaper/eclbygds/index.html

von Olfers, J. F. M. 1859. Über die Lydischen Königsgräber bei Sardes und den Grabhügel des Alyattes. *Abhandlungen der Königlichen Akademie der Wissenschaften zu Berlin: Aus dem Jahre* 1958: 539–56.

Yegül, Fikret K. 2010. Sardeis Artemis Tapınağı/The Temple of Artemis at Sardis. In *Lidyalılar ve Dünyaları/The Lydians and Their World*, ed. Nicholas D. Cahill, 362-88. İstanbul: Yapı Kredi Yayınları.

Index

Page references followed by *fig* indicate illustrated figures, maps, or photographs.

CPSIA information can be obtained
at www.ICGtesting.com
Printed in the USA
BVHW052222270221
600938BV00002B/3